GENERAL MOTORS | CAVALIER / CIMARRON / FIRENZA / SKYHAWK / SUNBIRD
1982-92 REPAIR MANUAL

CHILTON'S

Loewith
Hoxter

reeman, S.A.E.
Conti, Jr. □ W. Calvin Settle, Jr., S.A.E.
drea
ffney □ Ken Grabowski, A.S.E., S.A.E.
Grady □ Richard J. Rivele, S.A.E.
Smith □ Jim Taylor
o
perio
Tortorici, A.S.E., S.A.E.

TON BOOK COMPANY

DIVERSIFIED PUBLISHING COMPANIES,
APITAL CITIES/ABC, INC.

n USA
Book Company
adnor, PA 19089

ISBN 0-8019-8269-3
Library of Congress Catalog Card No. 91-058863
2345678901   2109876543

Contents

Contents

SAFETY NOTICE

Proper service and repair procedures are vital to the safe, reliable operation of all motor vehicles, as well as the personal safety of those performing repairs. This manual outlines procedures for servicing and repairing vehicles using safe, effective methods. The procedures contain many NOTES, CAUTIONS and WARNINGS which should be followed along with standard safety procedures to eliminate the possibility of personal injury or improper service which could damage the vehicle or compromise its safety.

It is important to note that the repair procedures and techniques, tools and parts for servicing motor vehicles, as well as the skill and experience of the individual performing the work vary widely. It is not possible to anticipate all of the conceivable ways or conditions under which vehicles may be serviced, or to provide cautions as to all of the possible hazards that may result. Standard and accepted safety precautions and equipment should be used when handling toxic or flammable fluids, and safety goggles or other protection should be used during cutting, grinding, chiseling, prying, or any other process that can cause material removal or projectiles.

Some procedures require the use of tools specially designed for a specific purpose. Before substituting another tool or procedure, you must be completely satisfied that neither your personal safety, nor the performance of the vehicle will be endangered.

Although information in this manual is based on industry sources and is complete as possible at the time of publication, the possibility exists that some car manufacturers made later changes which could not be included here. While striving for total accuracy, Chilton Book Company cannot assume responsibility for any errors, changes or omissions that may occur in the compilation of this data.

PART NUMBERS

Part numbers listed in this reference are not recommendations by Chilton for any product by brand name. They are references that can be used with interchange manuals and aftermarket supplier catalogs to locate each brand supplier's discrete part number.

SPECIAL TOOLS

Special tools are recommended by the vehicle manufacturer to perform their specific job. Use has been kept to a minimum, but where absolutely necessary, they are referred to in the text by the part number of the tool manufacturer. These tools can be purchased, under the appropriate part number, from your General Motors dealer or regional distributor, or an equivalent tool can be purchased locally from a tool supplier or parts outlet. Before substituting any tool for the one recommended, read the SAFETY NOTICE at the top of this page.

ACKNOWLEDGMENTS

The Chilton Book Company expresses appreciation to General Motors Corp., Detroit, Michigan for their generous assistance.

1

GENERAL INFORMATION AND MAINTENANCE

HOW TO USE THIS BOOK

Chilton's Total Car Care for the Chevrolet Cavalier, Buick Skyhawk, Cadillac Cimarron, Pontiac 2000 and Sunbird, and the Oldsmobile Firenza is intended to help you learn more about the inner workings of your vehicle and save you money on its upkeep and operation.

The first two sections will be the most used, since they contain maintenance and tune-up information and procedures. Studies have shown that a properly tuned and maintained car can get at least 10% better gas mileage than an out-of-tune car. The other sections deal with the more complex systems of your car. Operating systems from engine through brakes are covered to the extent that the do-it-yourselfer becomes mechanically involved. It will give you detailed instructions to help you change your own brake pads and shoes, replace spark plugs, and do many more jobs that will save you money, give you personal satisfaction, and help you avoid expensive problems.

A secondary purpose of this book is a reference for owners who want to understand their car and/or their mechanics better. In this case, no tools at all are required.

Before removing any bolts, read through the entire procedure. This will give you the overall view of what tools and supplies will be required. There is nothing more frustrating than having to walk to the bus stop on Monday morning because you were short one bolt on Sunday afternoon. So read ahead and plan ahead. Each operation should be approached logically and all procedures thoroughly understood before attempting any work.

All sections contain adjustments, maintenance, removal and installation procedures, and repair or overhaul procedures. When repair is not considered practical, we tell you how to remove the part and then how to install the new or rebuilt replacement. In this way, you at least save the labor costs.

Two basic mechanic's rules should be mentioned here. One, whenever the left side of

the car or engine is referred to, it is meant to specify the driver's side of the car. Conversely, the right side of the car means the passenger's side. Secondly, most screws and bolts are removed by turning counterclockwise, and tightened by turning clockwise.

Safety is always the most important rule. Constantly be aware of the dangers involved in working on an automobile and take the proper precautions. See the section in Servicing Your Vehicle Safely and the SAFETY NOTICE on the acknowledgment page.

Pay attention to the instructions provided. There are 3 common mistakes in mechanical work:

1. Incorrect order of assembly, disassembly or adjustment. When taking something apart or putting it together, doing things in the wrong order usually justs cost you extra time; however, it CAN break something. Read the entire procedure before beginning disassembly. Do everything in the order in which the instructions say you should do it, even if you can't immediately see a reason for it. When you're taking apart something that is very intricate (for example, a carburetor), you might want to draw a picture of how it looks when assembled at one point in order to make sure you get everything back in its proper position. (We will supply exploded view whenever possible). When making adjustments, especially tune-up adjustments, do them in order; often, one adjustment affects another, and you cannot expect even satisfactory results unless each adjustment is made only when it cannot be changed by any order.

2. Overtorquing (or undertorquing). While it is more common for over-torquing to cause damage, undertorquing can cause a fastener to vibrate loose causing serious damage. Especially when dealing with aluminum parts, pay attention to torque specifications and utilize a torque wrench in assembly. If a torque figure is not available, remember that if you are using the right tool to do the job, you will probably not have to strain yourself to get a fastener tight

enough. The pitch of most threads is so slight that the tension you put on the wrench will be multiplied many, many times in actual force on what you are tightening. A good example of how critical torque is can be seen in the case of spark plug installation, especially where you are putting the plug into an aluminum cylinder head. Too little torque can fail to crush the gasket, causing leakage of combustion gases and consequent overheating of the plug and engine parts. Too much torque can damage the threads, or distort the plug which changes the spark gap.

There are many commercial products available for ensuring that fasteners won't come loose, even if they are not torqued just right (a very common brand is Loctite®). If you're worried about getting something together tight enough to hold, but loose enough to avoid mechanical damage during assembly, one of these products might offer substantial insurance. Read the label on the package and make sure the products is compatible with the materials, fluids, etc. involved before choosing one.

3. Crossthreading. This occurs when a part such as a bolt is screwed into a nut or casting at the wrong angle and forced. Cross threading is more likely to occur if access is difficult. It helps to clean and lubricate fasteners, and to start threading with the part to be installed going straight in. Then, start the bolt, spark plug, etc. with your fingers. If you encounter resistance, unscrew the part and start over again at a different angle until it can be inserted and turned several turns without much effort. Keep in mind that many parts, especially spark plugs, used tapered threads so that gentle turning will automatically bring the part you're treading to the proper angle if you don't force it or resist a change in angle. Don't put a wrench on the part until its's been turned a couple of turns by hand. If you suddenly encounter resistance, and the part has not seated fully, don't force it. Pull it back out and make sure it's clean and threading properly.

Always take your time and be patient; once you have some experience, working on your car will become an enjoyable hobby.

TOOLS AND EQUIPMENT

♦ SEE FIG. 1

Naturally, without the proper tools and equipment it is impossible to properly service

you vehicle. It would be impossible to catalog each tool that you would need to perform each or any operation in this book. It would also be

unwise for the amateur to rush out and buy an expensive set of tool on the theory that he may need on or more of them at sometime.

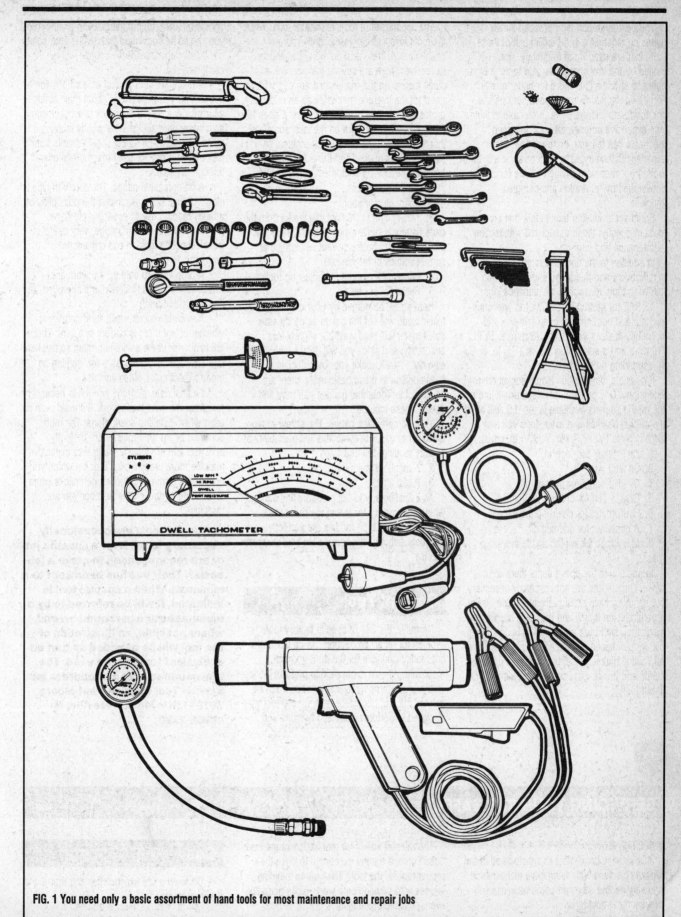

FIG. 1 You need only a basic assortment of hand tools for most maintenance and repair jobs

The best approach is to proceed slowly gathering together a good quality set of those tools that are used most frequently. Don't be misled by the low cost of bargain tools. It is far better to spend a little more for better quality. Forged wrenches, 6- or 12-point sockets and fine tooth ratchets are by far preferable to their less expensive counterparts. As any good mechanic can tell you, there are few worse experiences than trying to work on a car with bad tools. Your monetary savings will be far outweighed by frustration and mangled knuckles.

Begin accumulating those tools that are used most frequently; those associated with routine maintenance and tune-up.

In addition to the normal assortment of screwdrivers and pliers you should have the following tools for routine maintenance jobs:

1. SAE (or Metric) or SAE/Metric wrenches-sockets and combination open end-box end wrenches in sizes from 1/8 in. (3 mm) to 3/4 in. (19 mm) and a spark plug socket (13/16 in. or 5/8 in. depending on plug type).

If possible, buy various length socket drive extensions. One break in this department is that the metric sockets available in the U.S. will all fit the ratchet handles and extensions you may already have (1/4 in., 3/8 in., and 1/2 in. drive).

2. Jackstands for support.
3. Oil filter wrench.
4. Oil filler spout for pouring oil.
5. Grease gun for chassis lubrication.
6. Hydrometer for checking the battery.
7. A container for draining oil.
8. Many rags for wiping up the inevitable mess.

In addition to the above items there are several others that are not absolutely necessary, but handy to have around. these include oil dry, a transmission funnel and the usual supply of lubricants, antifreeze and fluids, although these can be purchased as needed. This is a basic list for routine maintenance, but only your personal needs and desire can accurately determine you list of tools.

The second list of tools is for tune-ups. While the tools involved here are slightly more sophisticated, they need not be outrageously expensive. There are several inexpensive tach/dwell meters on the market that are every bit as good for the average mechanic as an expensive professional model. Just be sure that it goes to a least 1,200-1,500 rpm on the tach scale and that it works on 4, 6, 8 cylinder engines. (A special tach is needed for diesel engines). A basic list of tune-up equipment could include:

1. Tach/dwell meter.
2. Spark plug wrench.
3. Timing light (a DC light that works from the car's battery is best, although an AC light that plugs into 110V house current will suffice at some sacrifice in brightness).
4. Wire spark plug gauge/adjusting tools.
5. Set of feeler blades.

Here again, be guided by your own needs. A feeler blade will set the points as easily as a dwell meter will read well, but slightly less accurately. And since you will need a tachometer anyway. . . well, make your own decision.

In addition to these basic tools, there are several other tools and gauges you may find useful. These include:

1. A compression gauge. The screw-in type is slower to use, but eliminates the possibility of a faulty reading due to escaping pressure.
2. A manifold vacuum gauge.
3. A test light.

As a final note, you will probably find a torque wrench necessary for all but the most basic work. The beam type models are perfectly adequate, although the newer click type are more precise.

Special Tools

Normally, the use of special factory tools is avoided for repair procedures, since these are not readily available for the do-it-yourself mechanic. When it is possible to preform the job with more commonly available tools, it will be pointed out, but occasionally, a special tool was designed to perform a specific function and

should be used. Before substituting another tool, you should be convinced that neither your safety nor the performance of the vehicle will be compromised.

• A hydraulic floor jack of at least 1 1/2 ton capacity. If you are serious about maintaining your own car, then a floor jack is as necessary as a spark plug socket. The greatly increased utility, strength, and safety of a hydraulic floor jack makes it pay for itself many times over through the years.

• A compression gauge. The screw-in type is slower to use but it eliminates the possibility of a faulty reading due to escaping pressure.

• A manifold vacuum gauge, very useful in troubleshooting ignition and emissions problems.

• A drop light, to light up the work area (make sure yours is Underwriter's approved, and has a shielded bulb).

• A volt/ohm meter, used for determining whether or not there is current in a wire. These are handy for use if a wire is broken somewhere and are especially necessary for working on today's electronics-laden vehicles.

As a final note, a torque wrench is necessary for all but the most basic work. It should even be used when installing spark plugs. The more common beam-type models are perfectly adequate and are usually much less expensive than the more precise click type on which you pre-set the torque and the wrench clicks when that setting arrives on the fastener you are torquing).

➡ **Special tools are occasionally necessary to perform a specific job or are recommended to make a job easier. Their use has been kept to a minimum. When a special tool is indicated, it will be referred to by a manufacturer's part number. and, where possible, an illustration of the tool will be provided so that an equivalent tool may be used. The tool manufacturer and address is: Service Tool Division Kent-Moore 29784 Little Mack Roseville, MI 48066-2298**

SERVICING YOUR CAR SAFELY

◆ SEE FIG. 2

It is virtually impossible to anticipate all of the hazards involved with automotive maintenance and service, but care and common sense will prevent most accidents.

The rules of safety for mechanics range from "don't smoke around gasoline," to "use the proper tool for the job." The trick to avoiding injuries is to develop safe work habits and take every possible precaution.

Dos

• Do keep a fire extinguisher and first aid kit within easy reach.

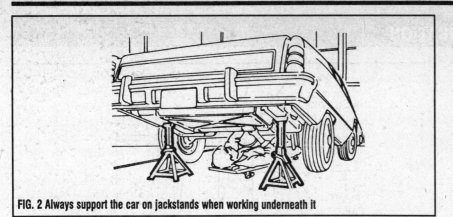

FIG. 2 Always support the car on jackstands when working underneath it

• Do wear safety glasses or goggles when cutting, drilling, grinding or prying, even if you have 20-20 vision. If you wear glasses for the sake of vision, they should be made of hardened glass that can serve also as safety glasses, or wear safety goggles over your regular glasses.

• Do shield your eyes whenever you work around the battery. Batteries contain sulphuric acid. In case of contact with the eyes or skin, flush the area with water or a mixture of water and baking soda and get medical attention immediately.

• Do use safety stands for any undercar service. Jacks are for raising vehicles; safety stands are for making sure the vehicle stays raised until you want it to come down. Whenever the car is raised, block the wheels remaining on the ground and set the parking brake.

• Do use adequate ventilation when working with any chemicals or hazardous materials. Like carbon monoxide, the asbestos dust resulting from brake lining wear can be poisonous in sufficient quantities.

• Do disconnect the negative battery cable when working on the electrical system. The secondary ignition system can contain up to 40,000 volts.

• Do follow manufacturer's directions whenever working with potentially hazardous materials. Both brake fluid and antifreeze are poisonous if taken internally.

• Do properly maintain your tools. Loose hammerheads, mushroomed punches and chisels, frayed or poorly grounded electrical cords, excessively worn screwdrivers, spread wrenches (open end), cracked sockets, slipping ratchets, or faulty droplight sockets can cause accidents.

• Likewise, keep your tools clean; a greasy wrench can slip off a bolt head, ruining the bolt and often ruining your knuckles in the process.

• Do use the proper size and type of tool for the job being done.

• Do when possible, pull on a wrench handle rather than push on it, and adjust you stance to prevent a fall.

• Do be sure that adjustable wrenches are tightly closed on the nut or bolt and pulled so that the face is on the side of the fixed jaw.

• Do select a wrench or socket that fits the nut or bolt. The wrench or socket should sit straight, not cocked.

• Do strike squarely with a hammer; avoid glancing blows.

• Do set the parking brake and block the drive wheels if the work requires the engine running.

Don'ts

• Don't run the engine in a garage or anywhere else without proper ventilation-EVER! Carbon monoxide is poisonous; it takes a long time to leave the human body and you can build up a deadly supply of it in your system by simply breathing in a little every day. You may not realize you are slowly poisoning yourself. Always use power vents, windows, fans or open the garage doors.

• Don't work around moving parts while wearing a necktie or other loose clothing. Short sleeves are much safer than long, loose sleeves; hard-toed shoes with neoprene soles protect your toes and give a better grip on slippery surfaces. Jewelry such as watches, fancy belt buckles, beads or body adornment of any kind is not safe working around a car. Long hair should be tied back under a hat or cap.

• Don't use pockets for toolboxes. A fall or bump can drive a screwdriver deep into your body. Even a wiping cloth hanging from the back pocket can wrap around a spinning shaft or fan.

• Don't smoke when working around gasoline, cleaning solvent or other flammable material.

• Don't smoke when working around the battery. When the battery is being charged, it gives off explosive hydrogen gas.

• Don't use gasoline to wash your hands; there are excellent soaps available. Gasoline may contain lead, and lead can enter the body through a cut, accumulating in the body until you are very ill. Gasoline also remove all the natural oils from the skin so that bone dry hands will such up oil and grease.

• Don't service the air conditioning system unless you are equipped with the necessary tools and training. The refrigerant, R-12, is extremely cold when compressed, and when released into the air will instantly freeze any surface it contacts, including your eyes. Although the refrigerant is normally non-toxic, R-12 becomes a deadly poisonous gas in the presence of an open flame. One good whiff of the vapors from burning refrigerant can be fatal.

• Don't use screwdrivers for anything other than driving screws! A screwdriver used as an prying tool can snap when you least expect it, causing injuries. At the very least, you'll ruin a good screwdriver.

• Don't use a bumper jack (that little ratchet, scissors, or pantograph jack supplied with the car) for anything other than chaining a flat! These jacks are only intended for emergency use out on the road; they are NOT designed as a maintenance tool. If you are serious about maintaining your car yourself, invest in a hydraulic floor jack of a least 1$\frac{1}{2}$ ton capacity, and at least two sturdy jackstands.

SERIAL NUMBER IDENTIFICATION

▶ SEE FIGS. 3-20

Vehicle

The vehicle identification number is a seventeen place sequence stamped on a plate attached to the left front of the instrument panel, visible through the windshield.

Body

The body style identification plate is located on the front bar, just behind the right headlamp.

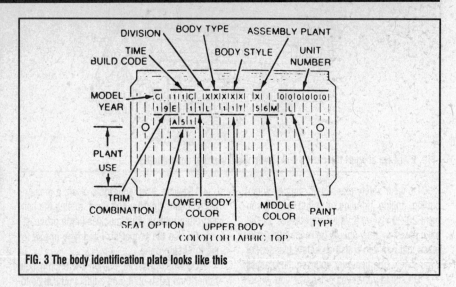

FIG. 3 The body identification plate looks like this

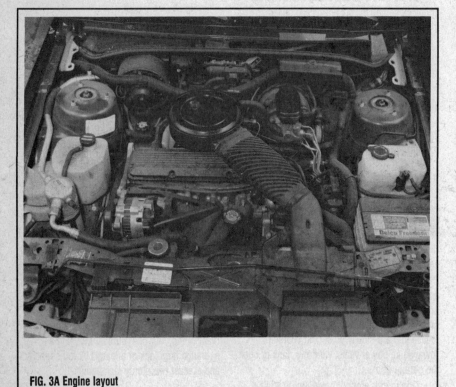

FIG. 3A Engine layout

Engine

The engine VIN code is stamped on a pad at various locations on the cylinder block.

Transaxle

The manual transaxle identification number is stamped on a pad on the forward side of the transaxle case, between the upper and middle transaxle-to-engine mounting bolts. The automatic transaxle identification number is stamped on the oil flange pad to the right of the oil dipstick, at the rear of the transaxle. The automatic transaxle model code tag is on top of the case, next to the shift lever.

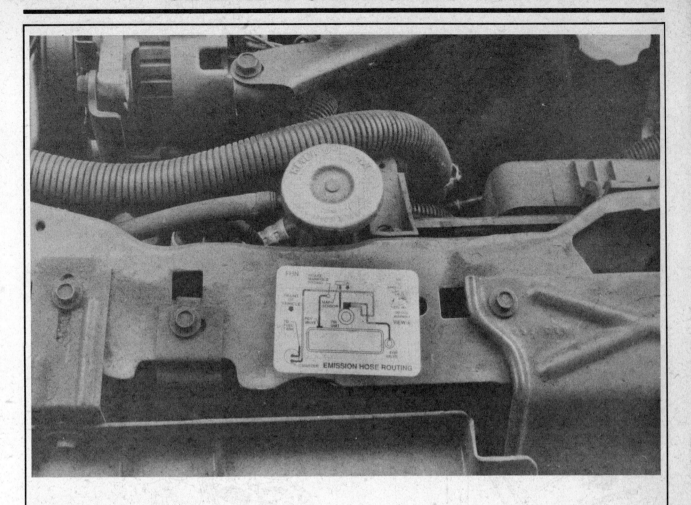

FIG. 3B Emission hose routing label

FIG. 3C Vehicle identification number

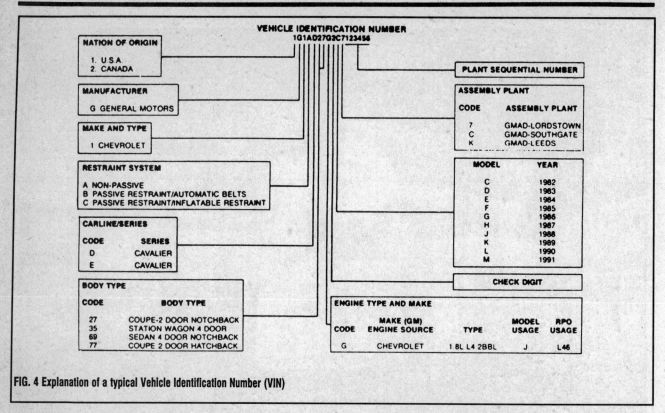

VEHICLE IDENTIFICATION NUMBER

1G1AD27G2C7123456

NATION OF ORIGIN

1. U.S.A.
2. CANADA

MANUFACTURER

G GENERAL MOTORS

MAKE AND TYPE

1 CHEVROLET

RESTRAINT SYSTEM

A NON-PASSIVE
B PASSIVE RESTRAINT/AUTOMATIC BELTS
C PASSIVE RESTRAINT/INFLATABLE RESTRAINT

CARLINE/SERIES

CODE	SERIES
D	CAVALIER
E	CAVALIER

BODY TYPE

CODE	BODY TYPE
27	COUPE-2 DOOR NOTCHBACK
35	STATION WAGON 4 DOOR
69	SEDAN 4 DOOR NOTCHBACK
77	COUPE 2 DOOR HATCHBACK

PLANT SEQUENTIAL NUMBER

ASSEMBLY PLANT

CODE	ASSEMBLY PLANT
7	GMAD-LORDSTOWN
C	GMAD-SOUTHGATE
K	GMAD-LEEDS

MODEL	YEAR
C	1982
D	1983
E	1984
F	1985
G	1986
H	1987
J	1988
K	1989
L	1990
M	1991

CHECK DIGIT

ENGINE TYPE AND MAKE

CODE	MAKE (GM) ENGINE SOURCE	TYPE	MODEL USAGE	RPO USAGE
G	CHEVROLET	1 8L L4 2BBL	J	L46

FIG. 4 Explanation of a typical Vehicle Identification Number (VIN)

FIG. 5 The VIN plate is visible through the windshield

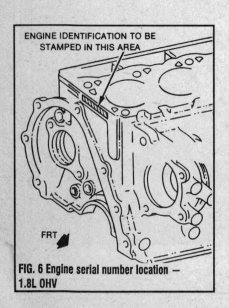

ENGINE IDENTIFICATION TO BE STAMPED IN THIS AREA

FRT

FIG. 6 Engine serial number location — 1.8L OHV

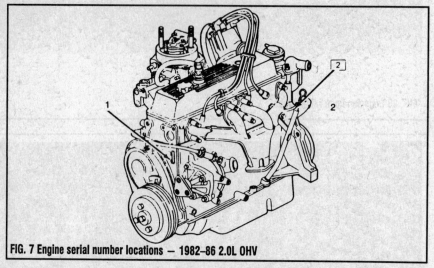

FIG. 7 Engine serial number locations — 1982–86 2.0L OHV

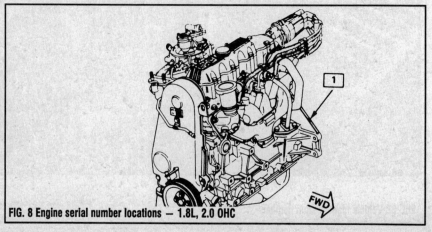

FWD

FIG. 8 Engine serial number locations — 1.8L, 2.0 OHC

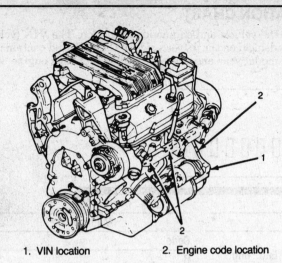

1. VIN location
2. Engine code location

FIG. 9 Engine serial number locations — 1985–87 2.8L V6

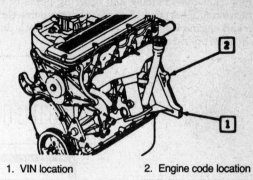

1. VIN location
2. Engine code location

FIG. 10 Engine serial number locations — 1987 — 92 2.0L and 2.2L OHV

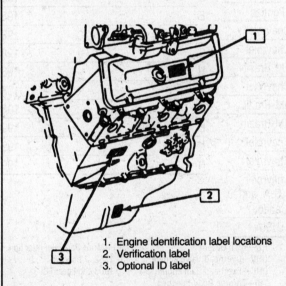

1. Engine identification label locations
2. Verification label
3. Optional ID label

FIG. 11 Engine label locations — 1988–92 2.8L and 3.1L V6

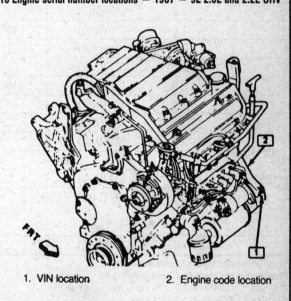

1. VIN location
2. Engine code location

FIG. 12 Engine serial number locations — 1988–92 2.8L and 3.1L V6

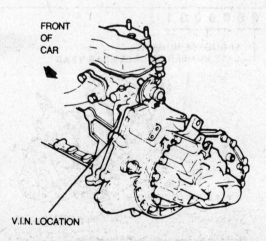

FRONT OF CAR

V.I.N. LOCATION

FIG. 13 Manual transaxle serial number locations — 1982–86 76mm (Muncie) 4 speed

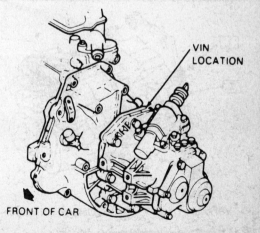

VIN LOCATION

FRONT OF CAR

FIG. 14 Manual transaxle serial number locations — 1983–87 76mm (Isuzu) 5 speed

VEHICLE IDENTIFICATION CHART

It is important for servicing and ordering parts to be certain of the vehicle and engine identification. The VIN (vehicle identification number) is a 17 digit number visible through the windshield on the driver's side of the dash and contains the vehicle and engine identification codes. The tenth digit indicates model year and the eighth digit indicates engine code. It can be interpreted as follows:

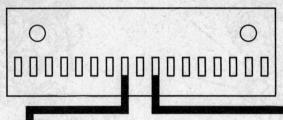

Engine Code						Model Year	
Code	**Liters**	**Cu. In. (cc)**	**Cyl.**	**Fuel Sys.**	**Eng. Mfg.**	**Code**	**Year**
G (1982)	1.8	110 (OHV)	4	2 bbl	Chevrolet	B	1981
0	1.8	110 (OHC)	4	TBI	Pontiac	C	1982
J	1.8	110 (OHC)	4	MFI Turbo	Pontiac	D	1983
B	2.0	121 (OHV)	4	①	Chevrolet	E	1984
P	2.0	121 (OHV)	4	TBI	Chevrolet	F	1985
M	2.0	121 (OHC)	4	MFI Turbo	GM-Brazil	G	1986
1	2.0	121 (OHV)	4	TBI HO	Chevrolet	H	1987
K	2.0	121 (OHC)	4	TBI	GM-Brazil	J	1988
H	2.0	121 (OHC)	4	MFI	GM-Brazil	K	1989
W	2.8	173	V6	MFI	Chevrolet	L	1990
G (1990–91)	2.2	134 (OHV)	4	TBI	Chevrolet	M	1991
T	3.1	192 (OHV)	V6	MFI	Chevrolet (U.S.A. and Canada)	N	1992
4	2.2	134 (OHV)	4	MFI	U.S.A.		

The seventeen digit Vehicle Identification Number can be used to determine engine identification and model year. The tenth digit indicates model year, and the fourth digit indicates engine code.

NOTE: Some 1983–85 Canadian models with the 2.0 Liter engine use a 2 bbl carburetor

HO—High Output
OHV—Overhead Valve engine
OHC—Overhead Cam engine
TBI—Throttle Body Injection

MFI—Multi-Port Fuel Injection
① 1982: 2 bbl carb.
  1983 and later: TBI

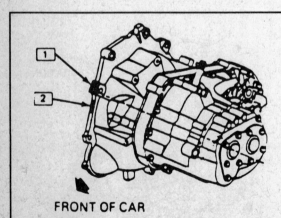

1. VIN location   2. Optional VIN location

FIG. 15 Manual transaxle serial number locations — 1987 (Getrag) 5 speed

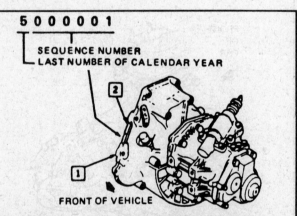

1. VIN location   2. Optional VIN location

FIG. 16 Manual transaxle serial number locations — 1988–92 Code MK7/MT2 (Isuzu) 5 speed

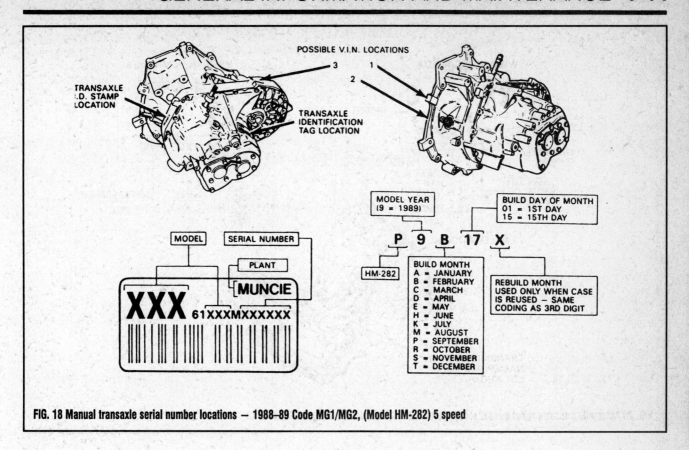

FIG. 18 Manual transaxle serial number locations — 1988–89 Code MG1/MG2, (Model HM-282) 5 speed

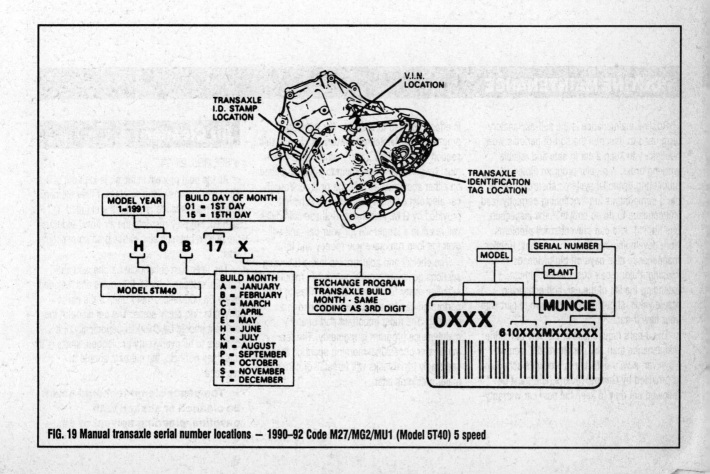

FIG. 19 Manual transaxle serial number locations — 1990–92 Code M27/MG2/MU1 (Model 5T40) 5 speed

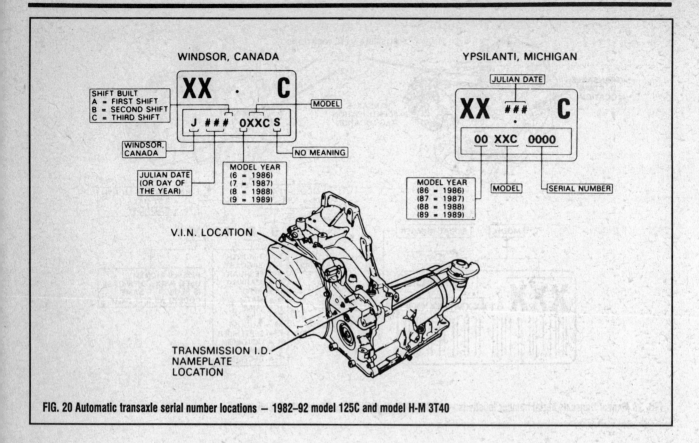

FIG. 20 Automatic transaxle serial number locations — 1982–92 model 125C and model H-M 3T40

ROUTINE MAINTENANCE

Routine maintenance is the self-explanatory term used to describe the sort of periodic work necessary to keep a car in safe and reliable working order. A regular program aimed at monitoring essential systems ensures that the car's components are functioning correctly (and will continue to do so until the next inspection, one hopes), and can prevent small problems from developing into major headaches. Routine maintenance also pays off big dividends in keeping major repair costs at a minimum, extending the life of the car, and enhancing resale value, should you ever desire to part with your new J-car.

The J-cars require less in the way of routine maintenance than any cars in recent memory. However, a very definite maintenance schedule is provided by General Motors, and must be followed not only to keep the new car warranty

in effect, but also to keep the car working properly. The Maintenance Intervals chart in this section outlines the routine maintenance which must be performed according to intervals based on either accumulated mileage or time. Your J-car also came with a maintenance schedule provided by G.M. Adherence to these schedules will result in a longer life for your car, and will, over the long run, save you money and time.

The checks and adjustments in the following sections generally require only a few minutes of attention every few weeks; the services to be performed can be easily accomplished in a morning. The most important part of any maintenance program is regularity. The few minutes or occasional morning spent on these seemingly trivial tasks will forestall or eliminate major problems later.

Air Cleaner

♦ SEE FIGS. 21-24

All the dust present in the air is kept out of the engine by means of the air cleaner filter element. Proper maintenance is vital, as a clogged element not only restricts the air-flow, and thus the power, but may also cause premature engine wear.

The filter element should be checked and cleaned at least every 15,000 miles and replaced every 50,000 miles; more often if the car is driven in dry, dusty areas. The condition of the element should be checked periodically; if it appears to be overly dirty or clogged, shake it, if this does not help, the element should be replaced.

➡ **The paper element should never be cleaned or soaked with gasoline, cleaning solvent or oil.**

CLEANING OR REPLACING THE FILTER ELEMENT

On most engines the air cleaner is located in the center of the engine compartment, directly over the carburetor or throttle body. On some 1987 and later 4-cyl. engines the air cleaner is more conveniently located toward the front of the engine compartment with an air duct connected to the throttle body.

1. Unscrew the wing nut on top of the air cleaner and then lift off the housing lid.

2. Lift out the filter element and shake the dirt out of it. If it remains clogged, replace it with a new one.

3. Before reinstalling the filter element, wipe out the housing with a damp cloth. Check the lid gasket to ensure that it has a tight seal.

4. Position the filter element, replace the lid and tighten the wing nut.

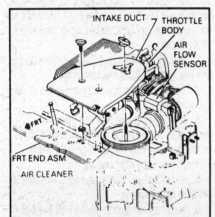

FIG. 21 The part of the air cleaner assembly, containing the air filter element, is off to one side of the engine compartment on 1987–89 2.0L OHV engines

FIG. 21A Removing the air cleaner assembly lid

FIG. 21B Replacing the air filter

FIG. 21C Replacing the air filter

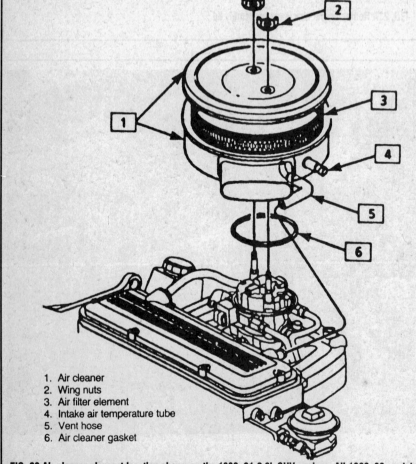

1. Air cleaner
2. Wing nuts
3. Air filter element
4. Intake air temperature tube
5. Vent hose
6. Air cleaner gasket

FIG. 22 Air cleaner element location shown on the 1990–91 2.2L OHV engines. All 1983–86 models equipped with the 2.0L engine use a similar design

Fuel Filter

REPLACEMENT

Carbureted Engines

▶ SEE FIG. 23

✳ CAUTION

Never smoke when working around gasoline! Avoid all sources of sparks or ignition. Gasoline vapors are EXTREMELY volatile!

All models have a fuel filter located within the carburetor body. The fuel filter has a check valve to prevent fuel spillage in the event of an accident. When the filter is replaced, make sure the new one is of the same type. All filters are of the paper element type. Replace the filter every 15,000 miles.

1. Place a few absorbent rags underneath the fuel line where it joins the carburetor.
2. Disconnect the fuel line connection at the fuel inlet nut.
3. Unscrew the fuel inlet nut from the carburetor. As the nut is removed, the filter will be pushed part way out by spring pressure.
4. Remove the filter and spring.
5. Install the new spring and filter. The hole in the filter faces the nut.
6. Install a new gasket on the inlet nut and install the nut into the carburetor. Tighten securely.
7. Install the fuel line. Tighten the connector to 18 ft. lbs. (24 Nm.) while holding the inlet nut with a wrench.
8. Start the engine and check for leaks.

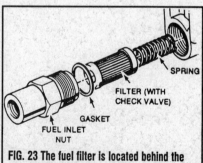

FIG. 23 The fuel filter is located behind the large inlet nut on the carburetor

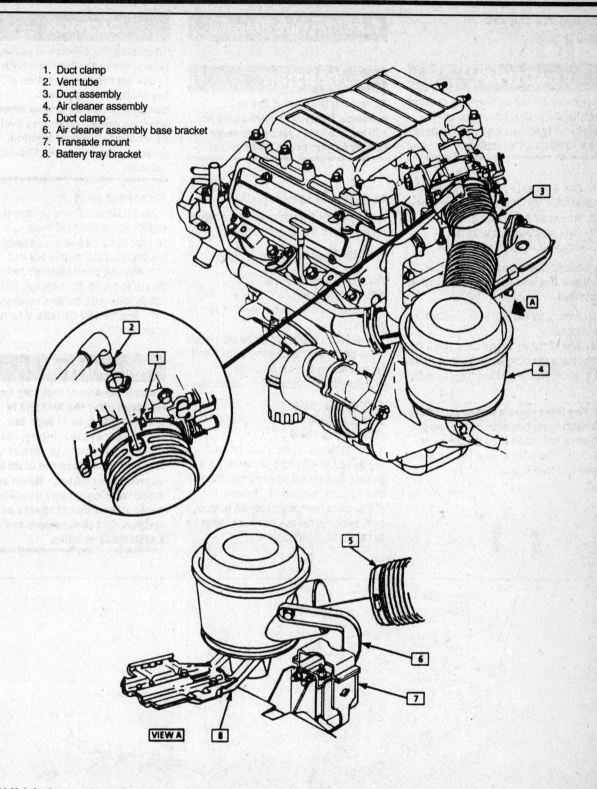

1. Duct clamp
2. Vent tube
3. Duct assembly
4. Air cleaner assembly
5. Duct clamp
6. Air cleaner assembly base bracket
7. Transaxle mount
8. Battery tray bracket

VIEW A

FIG. 24 Air induction assembly on the 3.1L engine. The air cleaner assembly containing the filter element is off to one side

Fuel Injected Engines

▶ SEE FIG. 25

✳ CAUTION

Never smoke when working around gasoline! Avoid all sources of sparks or ignition. Gasoline vapors are EXTREMELY volatile!

An inline filter can be found in the fuel feed line attached to the rear crossmember of the vehicle.
1. Release the fuel system pressure.
2. Place absorbent rags under the connections and disconnect the fuel lines.

➡ **Always use a back-up wrench anytime the fuel filter is removed or installed.**

3. Remove the fuel filter from the retainer or mounting bolt.
4. When installing, always use a good O-ring at the coupling locations and torque the fittings at 22 ft. lbs. Start the engine and check for leaks.

➡ **The filter has an arrow (fuel flow direction) on the side of the case, be sure to install it correctly in the system, the with arrow facing away from the fuel tank.**

Fuel Pressure Release

✳ CAUTION

To reduce the risk of fire or personal injury, it is necessary to relieve the fuel system pressure before servicing the fuel system.

Carbureted Engines

To release the fuel pressure on the carbureted system, remove and replace the fuel tank cap.

Throttle Body Injection (TBI)

1983-91 1.8L and 2.0L (OHC)
1983-84 2.0L (OHV)

1. Remove the fuel pump fuse from the fuse block.
2. Crank the engine. The engine will run until it runs out of fuel. Crank the engine again for 3 seconds making sure it is out of fuel.
3. Turn the ignition off and replace the fuse.

1985-86 2.0L (OHV)
1989 2.0L (OHV)
1990–91 2.2L (OHV)

The TBI injection systems used on these engines contain a constant bleed feature in the pressure regulator that relieves pressure any time the engine is turned off. Therefore, no special relieve procedure is required, however, a small amount of fuel may be released when the fuel line is disconnected.

✳ CAUTION

To reduce the chance of personal injury, cover the fuel line with cloth to collect the fuel and then place the cloth in an approved container. Never smoke when working around gasoline! Avoid all sources of sparks or ignition. Gasoline vapors are EXTREMELY volatile!

1987-88 2.0L (OHV)

The TBI Model 700 used on these engines contains no constant bleed feature to relieve pressure as the 1985-86 models therefore, the following procedure must be followed:
1. Place the transmission selector in Park (Neutral on manual transmissions), set the parking brake and block the drive wheels.
2. Disconnect the fuel pump at the rear body connector.

✳ CAUTION

A small amount of fuel may be released after the fuel line is disconnected. To reduce the chance of personal injury, cover the fuel line with cloth to collect the fuel and then place the cloth in an approved container. Never smoke when working around gasoline! Avoid all sources of sparks or ignition. Gasoline vapors are EXTREMELY volatile!

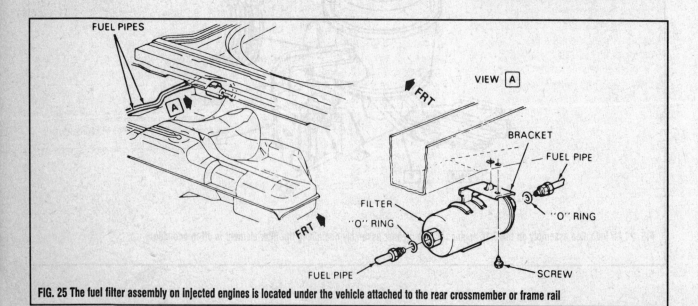

FIG. 25 The fuel filter assembly on injected engines is located under the vehicle attached to the rear crossmember or frame rail

FIG. 25A Replacing the fuel filter (EFI)

3. Start the engine and allow it to run a few seconds until it stops for lack of fuel.

4. Engage the starter for three seconds to dissipate fuel pressure in the lines. The fuel connections are now safe for servicing.

5. When pressure is relieved and servicing is complete, reconnect the fuel pump at the rear body connector.

Port Fuel Injection (PFI)

2.0L VIN CODE M (OHC)
2.8L, 3.lL V6

1. Connect a J-34730-1 fuel gage or equivalent to the fuel pressure valve. Wrap a shop towel around the fitting while connecting the gage to avoid spillage.

2. Install a bleed hose into an approved container and open the valve to bleed the system pressure.

✳ CAUTION

Never smoke when working around gasoline! Avoid all sources of sparks or ignition. Gasoline vapors are EXTREMELY volatile!

1992 2.2L VIN CODE 4 (OHV)
1992 2.0L VIN CODE H (OHC)

1. Loosen fuel filter cap to relieve tank pressure (do not tighten at this time).

2. Raise the vehicle.

3. Disconnect fuel pump electrical connector.

4. Lower the vehicle.

5. Start engine and run until fuel supply remaining in fuel pipes is consumed. Engage starter for 3 seconds to assure relief of any remaining pressure.

6. Raise vehicle.

7. Connect fuel pump electrical connector.

8. Lower vehicle.

9. Disconnect negative battery cable. Perform the necessary service work.

PCV Valve

REMOVAL & INSTALLATION

▶ SEE FIGS. 26-32

The Positive Crankcase Ventilation (PCV) valve regulates crankcase ventilation during

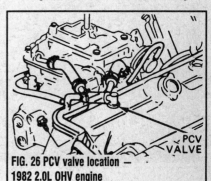

FIG. 26 PCV valve location — 1982 2.0L OHV engine

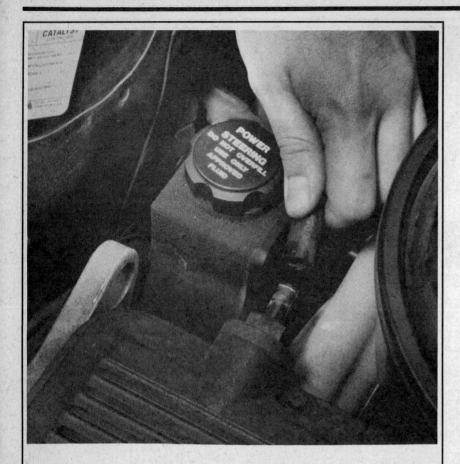

FIG. 26A Removing the PCV valve hose

FIG. 26B Removing the PCV valve assembly

various engine running conditions. At high vacuum (idle speed and partial load range) it will open slightly and at low vacuum (full throttle) it will open fully. This causes vapors to be drawn from the crankcase by engine vacuum and then sucked into the combustion chamber where they are dissipated.

The PCV valve must be replaced every 30,000 miles. Details on the PCV system, including system tests, are given in Section 4.

The valve is located in a rubber grommet in the valve cover, connected to the air cleaner housing by a large diameter rubber hose. To replace the valve:

1. Pull the valve (with the hose attached) from the rubber grommet in the valve cover.
2. Remove the valve from the hose.
3. Install a new valve into the hose.
4. Press the valve back into the rubber grommet in the valve cover.

PCV Filter

Some models have a PCV filter, located in the air cleaner housing. This filter must be replaced at every 50,000 miles, or sooner, upon inspection.

1. Remove the air cleaner housing lid.
2. Slide back the filter retaining clip and remove the old filter.
3. Install the new filter, replace the retaining clip and replace the housing lid.

Evaporative Emissions System

Check the evaporative emission control system every 15,000 miles. Check the fuel vapor lines and the vacuum hoses for proper connections and correct routing, as well as condition. Replace clogged, damaged or deteriorated parts as necessary.

For more details on the evaporative emissions system, please refer to Section 4.

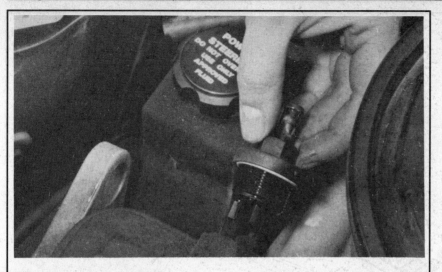

FIG. 26C Replacing the PCV valve

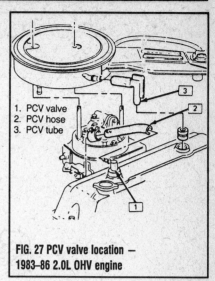

1. PCV valve
2. PCV hose
3. PCV tube

FIG. 27 PCV valve location —
1983–86 2.0L OHV engine

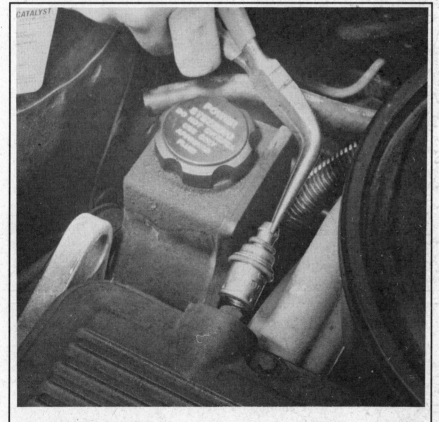

FIG. 26D Replacing the PCV valve

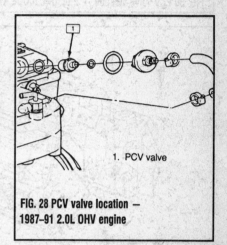

1. PCV valve

FIG. 28 PCV valve location —
1987–91 2.0L OHV engine

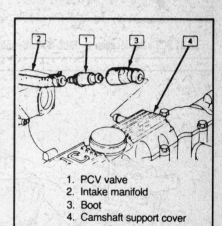

1. PCV valve
2. Intake manifold
3. Boot
4. Camshaft support cover

FIG. 29 PCV valve location —
2.0L OHC (CODE M) engine

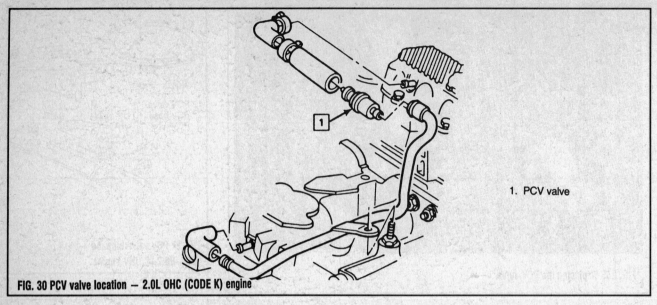

FIG. 30 PCV valve location — 2.0L OHC (CODE K) engine

1. PCV valve

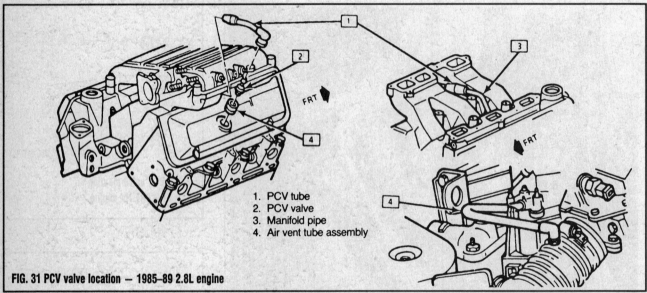

1. PCV tube
2. PCV valve
3. Manifold pipe
4. Air vent tube assembly

FIG. 31 PCV valve location — 1985–89 2.8L engine

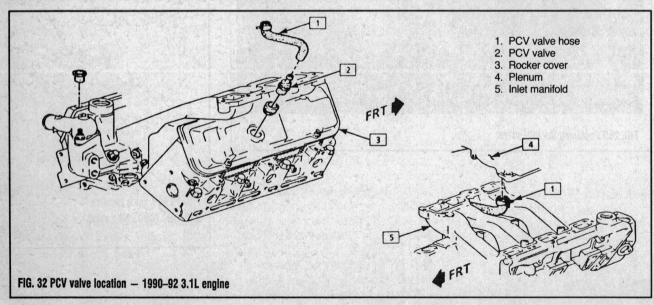

1. PCV valve hose
2. PCV valve
3. Rocker cover
4. Plenum
5. Inlet manifold

FIG. 32 PCV valve location — 1990–92 3.1L engine

1	HOSE	**4**	SEALS - (O-RINGS)
2	INSTALL HOSE SO THAT ARROW IS POINTING TOWARD COVER	**5**	CRANKCASE VENT VALVE (PCV)
3	COVER - TORQUE TO 10 N·m (89 lb. ft.)	**6**	PUSH AIR INTAKE DUCT (NOT SHOWN) ON TO FITTING UNTIL FULLY SEATED

FIG. 32A PCV system — 1992 2.2L (CODE 4) engine

Battery

GENERAL MAINTENANCE

♦ SEE FIGS. 33-36

The J-cars have a maintenance free battery as standard equipment, eliminating the need for fluid level checks and the possibility of specific gravity tests. On top of the battery is a built-in temperature compensated hydrometer. When observing the hydrometer, make sure that the battery has a clean top. A light may be required in some poorly lit areas. Although claimed to be maintenance free, the battery does require some attention.

Once a year, the battery terminals and the cable clamps should be cleaned. Remove the side terminal bolts and the cables and the battery terminals with a wire brush until all corrosion, grease, etc. is removed and the metal is shiny. It is especially important to clean the inside of the clamp thoroughly, since a small deposit of foreign material or oxidation there will prevent a sound electrical connection and inhibit either starting or charging. Special tools are available for cleaning the side terminal clamps and terminals.

Before installing the cables, loosen the battery hold-down clamp, remove the battery, and check the battery tray. Clear it of any debris and check it for soundness. Rust should be wire brushed away, and the metal given a coat of anti-rust paint. Replace the battery and tighten the hold-down clamp securely, but be careful not to overtighten, which will crack the battery case.

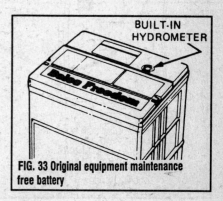

FIG. 33 Original equipment maintenance free battery

After the clamps and terminals are clean, reinstall the cables, negative cables last. Give the clamps and terminals a thin external coat of grease after installation, to retard corrosion.

Check the cables at the same time that the terminals are cleaned. If the cable insulation is

JUMP STARTING A DEAD BATTERY

The chemical reaction in a battery produces explosive hydrogen gas. This is the safe way to jump start a dead battery, reducing the chances of an accidental spark that could cause an explosion.

Jump Starting Precautions

1. Be sure both batteries are of the same voltage.
2. Be sure both batteries are of the same polarity (have the same grounded terminal).
3. Be sure the vehicles are not touching.
4. Be sure the vent cap holes are not obstructed.
5. Do not smoke or allow sparks around the battery.
6. In cold weather, check for frozen electrolyte in the battery. Do not jump start a frozen battery.
7. Do not allow electrolyte on your skin or clothing.
8. Be sure the electrolyte is not frozen.

CAUTION: Make certin that the ignition key, in the vehicle with the dead battery, is in the OFF position. Connecting cables to vehicles with on-board computers will result in computer destruction if the key is not in the OFF position.

Jump Starting Procedure

1. Determine voltages of the two batteries; they must be the same.
2. Bring the starting vehicle close (they must not touch) so that the batteries can be reached easily.
3. Turn off all accessories and both engines. Put both vehicles in Neutral or Park and set the handbrake.
4. Cover the cell caps with a rag—do not cover terminals.
5. If the terminals on the run-down battery are heavily corroded, clean them.
6. Identify the positive and negative posts on both batteries and connect the cables in the order shown.
7. Start the engine of the starting vehicle and run it at fast idle. Try to start the car with the dead battery. Crank it for no more than 10 seconds at a time and let it cool for 20 seconds in between tries.
8. If it doesn't start in 3 tries, there is something else wrong.
9. Disconnect the cables in the reverse order.
10. Replace the cell covers and dispose of the rags.

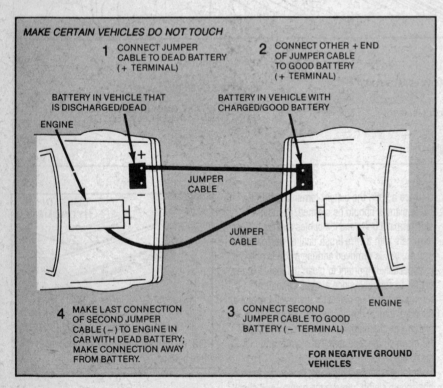

MAKE CERTAIN VEHICLES DO NOT TOUCH

1 CONNECT JUMPER CABLE TO DEAD BATTERY (+ TERMINAL)

2 CONNECT OTHER + END OF JUMPER CABLE TO GOOD BATTERY (+ TERMINAL)

BATTERY IN VEHICLE THAT IS DISCHARGED/DEAD

BATTERY IN VEHICLE WITH CHARGED/GOOD BATTERY

ENGINE

JUMPER CABLE

JUMPER CABLE

ENGINE

4 MAKE LAST CONNECTION OF SECOND JUMPER CABLE (−) TO ENGINE IN CAR WITH DEAD BATTERY; MAKE CONNECTION AWAY FROM BATTERY.

3 CONNECT SECOND JUMPER CABLE TO GOOD BATTERY (− TERMINAL)

FOR NEGATIVE GROUND VEHICLES

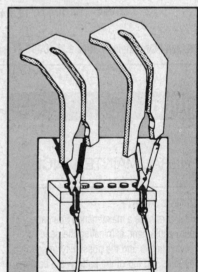

Side terminal batteries occasionally pose a problem when connecting jumper cables. There frequently isn't enough room to clamp the cables without touching sheet metal. Side terminal adaptors are available to alleviate this problem and should be removed after use

cracked or broken, or if the ends are frayed, the cable should be replaced with a new cable of the same length and gauge.

❈ CAUTION

Keep flame or sparks away from the battery; it gives off explosive hydrogen gas. Battery electrolyte contains sulphuric acid. If you should get any on your skin or in your eyes, flush the affected areas with plenty of clear water; if it lands in your eyes, get medical help immediately.

REPLACEMENT

Refer to the necessary Removal and Installation service procedures in Section 3.

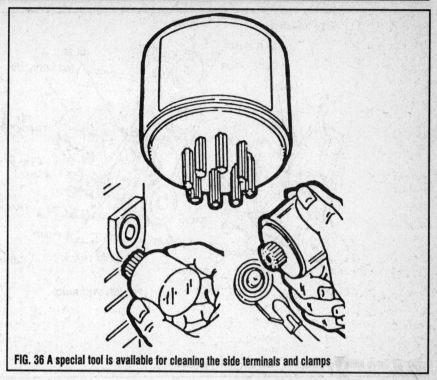

FIG. 36 A special tool is available for cleaning the side terminals and clamps

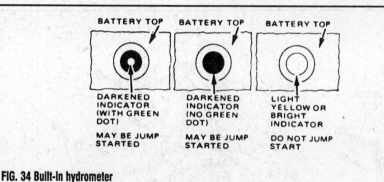

FIG. 34 Built-in hydrometer

ESTIMATED TEMPERATURE	MINIMUM VOLTAGE
70° F. (21° C.)	9.6
50° F. (10° C.)	9.4
30° F. (0° C.)	9.1
15° F. (−10° C.)	8.8
0° F. (−18° C.)	8.5
0° F. (BELOW: −18° C.)	8.0

FIG. 35 Battery temperature VS. voltage drop

Standard Drive Belts

BELT TENSION

◆ SEE FIGS. 37-38

Every 12 months or 15,000 miles, check the water pump, alternator, power steering pump (if so equipped), and air conditioning compressor (if so equipped) drive belts for proper tension. Also look for signs of wear, fraying, separation, glazing and so on, and replace the belts as required.

Belt tension should be checked with a gauge made for the purpose. If a gauge is not available, tension can be checked with moderate thumb pressure applied to the belt at its longest span midway between pulleys. If the belt has a free span less than twelve inches, it should deflect approximately $1/8$-$1/4$ in. If the span is longer than twelve inches, deflection can range between $1/8$-$3/8$ in.

1. Loosen the driven accessory's pivot and adjustment bolts. The pivot bolts are the bolts that enable the accessory to move in the either direction for adjustment. The adjustment bolts are the bolts in the slotted brackets.

2. Move the accessory toward or away from the engine until the tension is correct. You can use a wooden hammer handle or a broomstick as a lever, but do not use anything metallic.

3. Tighten the bolts and recheck the tension. If new belts have been installed, run the engine for a few minutes, then recheck and readjust as necessary.

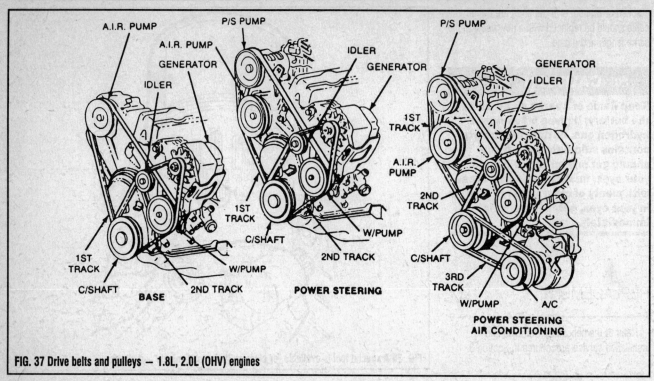

FIG. 37 Drive belts and pulleys — 1.8L, 2.0L (OHV) engines

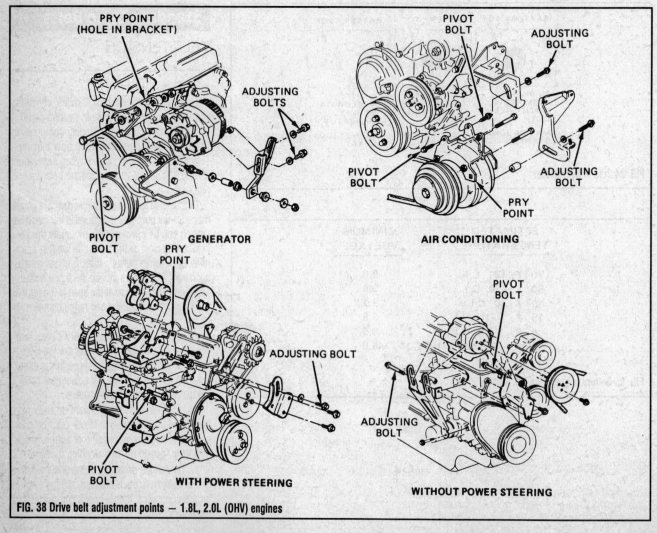

FIG. 38 Drive belt adjustment points — 1.8L, 2.0L (OHV) engines

HOW TO SPOT WORN V-BELTS

V–Belts are vital to efficient engine operation—they drive the fan, water pump and other accessories. They require little maintenance (occasional tightening) but they will not last forever. Slipping or failure of the V–belt will lead to overheating. If your V–belt looks like any of these, it should be replaced.

Cracking or Weathering

This belt has deep cracks, which cause it to flex. Too much flexing leads to heat build–up and premature failure. These cracks can be caused by using the belt on a pulley that is too small. Notched belts are available for small diameter pulleys.

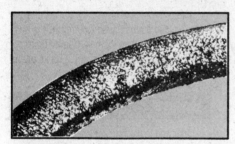

Softening (Grease and Oil)

Oil and grease on a belt can cause the belt's rubber compounds to soften and separate from the reinforcing cords that hold the belt together. The belt will first slip, then finally fail altogether.

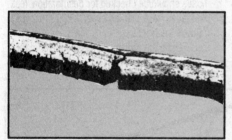

Glazing

Glazing is caused by a belt that is slipping. A slipping belt can cause a run-down battery, erratic power steering, overheating or poor accessory performance. The more the belt slips, the more glazing will be built up on the surface of the belt. The more the belt is glazed, the more it will slip. If the glazing is light, tighten the belt.

Worn Cover

The cover of this belt is worn off and is peeling away. The reinforcing cords will begin to wear and the belt will shortly break. When the belt cover wears in spots or has a rough jagged appearance, check the pulley grooves for roughness.

Separation

This belt is on the verge of breaking and leaving you stranded. The layers of the belt are separating and the reinforcing cords are exposed. It's just a matter of time before it breaks completely.

It is better to have belts too loose than too tight, because overtight belts will lead to bearing failure, particularly in the water pump and alternator. However, loose belts place an extremely high impact load on the driven component due to the whipping action of the belt.

Serpentine Belts

♦ SEE FIGS. 39-43

Models equipped with the V6 engine and most 1987 and later engines use a single (serpentine belt) to drive all engine accessories. The serpentine belt driven accessories are rigidly mounted with belt tension maintained by a spring loaded tensioner assembly. The belt tensioner has the ability to control belt tension over a fairly broad range of belt lengths. However, there are limits to the tensioner's ability to compensate for varying lengths of belts. Poor tension control and/or damage to the tensioner could result with the tensioner operating outside of its range.

INSPECTION

1. If fraying of the belt is noticed, check to make sure both the belt and the tensioner assembly are properly aligned and that the belt edges are not in contact with the flanges of the tensioner pulley.

2. If, while adjusting belt tension, tensioner runs out of travel, the belt is stretched beyond adjustment and should be replaced.

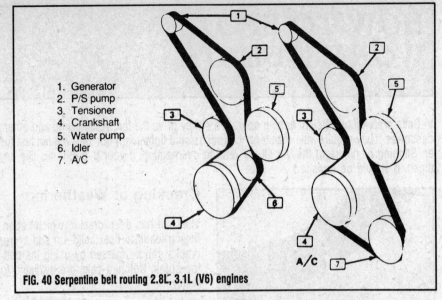

1. Generator
2. P/S pump
3. Tensioner
4. Crankshaft
5. Water pump
6. Idler
7. A/C

FIG. 40 Serpentine belt routing 2.8L, 3.1L (V6) engines

3. If a whining is heard around the tensioner or idler assemblies, check for possible bearing failure.

➡ **Routine inspection of the belt may reveal cracks in the belt ribs. These cracks will not impair belt performance and therefore should not be considered a problem requiring belt replacement. However, the belt should be replaced if belt slip occurs or if sections of the belt ribs are missing.**

REPLACEMENT

To replace the belt push (rotate) the the belt tensioner and remove the belt. Use a 15mm socket on the 4-cyl. engines and a 3/4 in. open end wrench on the V6 engines.

Hoses

Upper and lower radiator hoses and all heater hoses should be checked for deterioration, leaks and loose hose clamps every 15,000 miles. To remove the hoses:

1. Drain the radiator as detailed later in this section.

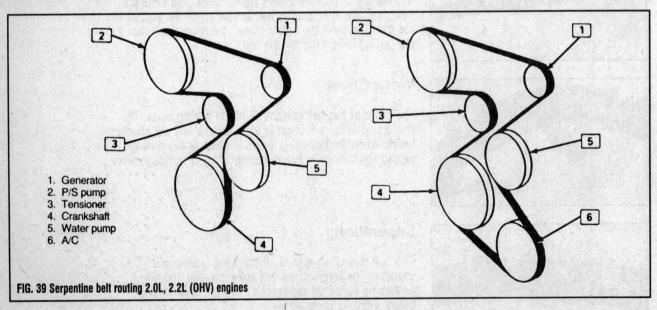

1. Generator
2. P/S pump
3. Tensioner
4. Crankshaft
5. Water pump
6. A/C

FIG. 39 Serpentine belt routing 2.0L, 2.2L (OHV) engines

HOW TO SPOT BAD HOSES

Both the upper and lower radiator hoses are called upon to perform difficult jobs in an inhospitable environment. They are subject to nearly 18 psi at under hood temperatures often over 280°F, and must circulate nearly 7500 gallons of coolant an hour — 3 good reasons to have good hoses.

Swollen Hose

A good test for any hose is to feel it for soft or spongy spots. Frequently these will appear as swollen areas of the hose. The most likely cause is oil soaking. This hose could burst at any time, when hot or under pressure.

Cracked Hose

Cracked hoses can usually be seen but feel the hoses to be sure they have not hardened; a prime cause of cracking. This hose has cracked down to the reinforcing cords and could split at any of the cracks.

Frayed Hose End (Due to Weak Clamp)

Weakened clamps frequently are the cause of hose and cooling system failure. The connection between the pipe and hose has deteriorated enough to allow coolant to escape when the engine is hot.

Debris In Cooling System

Debris, rust and scale in the cooling system can cause the inside of a hose to weaken. This can usually be felt on the outside of the hose as soft or thinner areas.

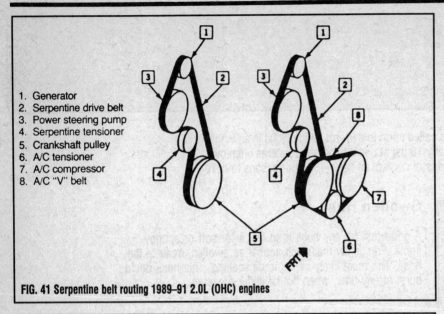

1. Generator
2. Serpentine drive belt
3. Power steering pump
4. Serpentine tensioner
5. Crankshaft pulley
6. A/C tensioner
7. A/C compressor
8. A/C "V" belt

FIG. 41 Serpentine belt routing 1989–91 2.0L (OHC) engines

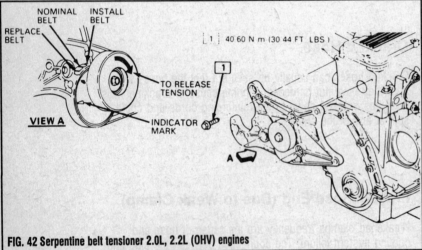

FIG. 42 Serpentine belt tensioner 2.0L, 2.2L (OHV) engines

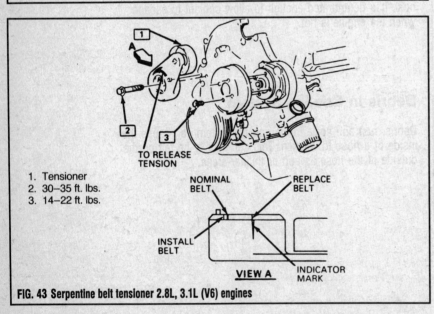

1. Tensioner
2. 30–35 ft. lbs.
3. 14–22 ft. lbs.

FIG. 43 Serpentine belt tensioner 2.8L, 3.1L (V6) engines

2. Loosen the hose clamps at each end of the hose to be removed.

3. Working the hose back and forth, slide it off its connection and then install the new hose.

➡ **If the hose Is stuck, use a suitable razor cutting tool or knife, and carefully slit the hose enough to split it open along the connecting neck.**

4. Position the hose clamps at least 1/4 in. from the end of the new hose and tighten them.

➡ **Always make sure that the hose clamps are beyond the bead and placed in the center of the clamping surface before tightening them.**

Air Conditioning

GENERAL SERVICING PROCEDURES

The most important aspect of air conditioning service is the maintenance of a pure and adequate charge of refrigerant in the system. A refrigeration system cannot function properly if a significant percentage of the charge is lost. Leaks are common because the severe vibration encountered in an automobile can easily cause a sufficient cracking or loosening of the air conditioning fittings; as a result, the extreme operating pressures of the system force refrigerant out.

The problem can be understood by considering what happens to the system as it is operated with a continuous leak. Because the expansion valve regulates the flow of refrigerant to the evaporator, the level of refrigerant there is fairly constant. The receiver/drier stores any excess of refrigerant, and so a loss will first appear there as a reduction in the level of liquid. As this level nears the bottom of the vessel, some refrigerant vapor bubbles will begin to appear in the stream of liquid supplied to the expansion valve. This vapor decreases the capacity of the expansion valve very little as the valve opens to compensate for its presence. As the quantity of liquid in the condenser decreases, the operating pressure will drop there and throughout the high side of the system. As the R-12 continues to be expelled, the pressure available to force the liquid through the expansion valve will continue to decrease, and, eventually, the valve's orifice will prove to be too much of a restriction for adequate flow even with the needle fully withdrawn.

At this point, low side pressure will start to drop, and severe reduction in cooling capacity, marked by freeze-up of the evaporator coil, will result. Eventually, the operating pressure of the evaporator will be lower than the pressure of the atmosphere surrounding it, and air will be drawn into the system wherever there are leaks in the low side.

Because all atmospheric air contains at least some moisture, water will enter the system and mix with the R-12 and the oil. Trace amounts of moisture will cause sludging of the oil, and corrosion of the system. Saturation and clogging of the filter/drier, and freezing of the expansion valve orifice will eventually result. As air fills the system to a greater and greater extent, it will interfere more and more with the normal flows of refrigerant and heat.

From this description, it should be obvious that much of the repairman's time will be spent detecting leaks, repairing them, and then restoring the purity and quantity of the refrigerant charge. A list of general precautions that should be observed while doing this follows:

1. Keep all tools as clean and dry as possible.
2. Thoroughly purge the service gauges and hoses of air and moisture before connecting them to the system. Keep them capped when not in use.
3. Thoroughly clean any refrigerant fitting before disconnecting it, in order to minimize the entrance of dirt into the system.
4. Plan any operation that requires opening the system beforehand, in order to minimize the length of time it will be exposed to open air. Cap or seal the open ends to minimize the entrance of foreign material.
5. When adding oil, pour it through an extremely clean and dry tube or funnel. Keep the oil capped whenever possible. Do not use oil that has not been kept tightly sealed.
6. Use only refrigerant 12. Purchase refrigerant intended for use in only automatic air conditioning systems. Avoid the use of refrigerant 12 that may be packaged for another use, such as cleaning, or powering a horn, as it is impure.
7. Completely evacuate any system that has been opened to replace a component, or that has leaked sufficiently to draw in moisture and air. This requires evacuating air and moisture with a good vacuum pump for at least one hour. If a system has been open for a considerable length of time it may be advisable to evacuate the system for up to 12 hours (overnight).
8. Use a wrench on both halves of a fitting that is to be disconnected, so as to avoid placing torque on any of the refrigerant lines.
9. When overhauling a compressor, pour some of the oil into a clean glass and inspect it. If there is evidence of dirt or metal particles, or

both, flush all refrigerant components with clean refrigerant before evacuating and recharging the system. In addition, if metal particles are present, the compressor should be replaced.

10. Schrader valves may leak only when under full operating pressure. Therefore, if leakage is suspected but cannot be located, operate the system with a full charge of refrigerant and look for leaks from all Schrader valves. Replace any faulty valves.

Additional Preventive Maintenance Checks

ANTIFREEZE

In order to prevent heater core freeze-up during A/C operation, it is necessary to maintain permanent type antifreeze protection of +15°F, or lower. A reading of –15°F is ideal since this protection also supplies sufficient corrosion inhibitors for the protection of the engine cooling system.

➡ **The same antifreeze should not be used longer than the manufacturer specifies.**

RADIATOR CAP

For efficient operation of an air conditioned car's cooling system, the radiator cap should have a holding pressure which meets manufacturer's specifications. A cap which fails to hold these pressures should be replaced.

CONDENSER

Any obstruction of or damage to the condenser configuration will restrict the air flow which is essential to its efficient operation. It is therefore a good rule to keep this unit clean and in proper physical shape.

➡ **Bug screens are regarded as obstructions.**

CONDENSATION DRAIN TUBE

This single molded drain tube expels the condensation, which accumulates on the bottom of the evaporator housing, into the engine compartment. If this tube is obstructed, the air conditioning performance can be restricted and condensation buildup can spill over onto the vehicle's floor.

SAFETY PRECAUTIONS

Because of the importance of the necessary safety precautions that must be exercised when working with air conditioning systems and R-12 refrigerant, a recap of the safety precautions are outlined.

1. Avoid contact with a charged refrigeration

system, even when working on another part of the air conditioning system or vehicle. If a heavy tool comes into contact with a section of copper tubing or a heat exchanger, it can easily cause the relatively soft material to rupture.

2. When it is necessary to apply force to a fitting which contains refrigerant, as when checking that all system couplings are securely tightened, use a wrench on both parts of the fitting involved, if possible. This will avoid putting torque on refrigerant tubing. (It is advisable, when possible, to use tube or line wrenches when tightening these flare nut fittings.)

3. Do not attempt to discharge the system by merely loosening a fitting, or removing the service valve caps and cracking these valves. Precise control is possible only when using the service gauges. Place a rag under the open end of the center charging hose while discharging the system to catch any drops of liquid that might escape. Wear protective gloves when connecting or disconnecting service gauge hoses.

4. Discharge the system only in a well ventilated area, as high concentrations of the gas can exclude oxygen and act as an anesthetic. When leak testing or soldering, this is particularly important, as toxic gas is formed when R-12 contacts any flame.

➡ **All refrigerant should be discharged in a Enviromental Protection Agency (E.P.A.) approved container.**

5. Never start a system without first verifying that both service valves are back-seated, if equipped, and that all fittings throughout the system are snugly connected.

6. Avoid applying heat to any refrigerant line or storage vessel. Charging may be aided by using water heated to less than 125° to warm the refrigerant container. Never allow a refrigerant storage container to sit out in the sun, or near any other source of heat, such as a radiator.

7. Always wear goggles when working on a system to protect the eyes. If refrigerant contacts the eyes, it is advisable in all cases to see a physician as soon as possible.

8. Frostbite from liquid refrigerant should be treated by first gradually warming the area with cool water, and then gently applying petroleum jelly. A physician should be consulted.

9. Always keep refrigerant drum fittings capped when not in use. Avoid sudden shock to the drum, which might occur from dropping it, or from banging a heavy tool against it. Never carry a drum in the passenger compartment of a car.

10. Always completely discharge the system before painting the vehicle (if the paint is to be baked on), or before welding anywhere near refrigerant lines.

Air Conditioning Tools and Gauges

Test Gauges

♦ SEE FIG. 44

Most of the service work performed in air conditioning requires the use of a set of two gauges, one for the high (head) pressure side of the system, the other for the low (suction) side.

The low side gauge records both pressure and vacuum. Vacuum readings are calibrated from 0 to 30 inches and the pressure graduations read from 0 to no less than 60 psi.

The high side gauge measures pressure from 0 to at least 600 psi.

Both gauges are threaded into a manifold that contains two hand shut-off valves. Proper manipulation of these valves and the use of the attached test hoses allow the user to perform the following services:

1. Test high and low side pressures.
2. Remove air, moisture, and contaminated refrigerant.
3. Purge the system (of refrigerant).
4. Charge the system (with refrigerant).

The manifold valves are designed so they have no direct effect on gauge readings, but serve only to provide for, or cut off, flow of refrigerant through the manifold. During all testing and hook-up operations, the valves are kept in a closed position to avoid disturbing the refrigeration system. The valves are opened only to purge the system of refrigerant or to charge it.

When purging the system, the center hose is uncapped at the lower end, and both valves are cracked open slightly. This allows refrigerant pressure to force the entire contents of the system out through the center hose. During charging, the valve on the high side of the manifold is closed, and the valve on the low side is cracked open. Under these conditions, the low pressure in the evaporator will draw refrigerant from the relatively warm refrigerant storage container into the system.

Service Valves

For the user to diagnose an air conditioning system he or she must gain "entrance" to the system in order to observe the pressures. There are two types of terminals for this purpose, the hand shut off type and the familiar Schrader valve.

The Schrader valve is similar to a tire valve stem and the process of connecting the test hoses is the same as threading a hand pump outlet hose to a bicycle tire. As the test hose is threaded to the service port the valve core is

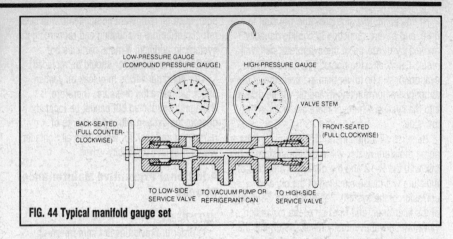

FIG. 44 Typical manifold gauge set

depressed, allowing the refrigerant to enter the test hose outlet. Removal of the test hose automatically closes the system.

Extreme caution must be observed when removing test hoses from the Schrader valves as some refrigerant will normally escape, usually under high pressure. (Observe safety precautions.)

Some systems have hand shut-off valves (the stem can be rotated with a special ratcheting box wrench) that can be positioned in the following three ways:

1. FRONT SEATED — Rotated to full clockwise position.

a. Refrigerant will not flow to compressor, but will reach test gauge port. COMPRESSOR WILL BE DAMAGED IF SYSTEM IS TURNED ON IN THIS POSITION.

b. The compressor is now isolated and ready for service. However, care must be exercised when removing service valves from the compressor as a residue of refrigerant may still be present within the compressor. Therefore, remove service valves slowly observing all safety precautions.

2. BACK SEATED — Rotated to full counter clockwise position. Normal position for system while in operation. Refrigerant flows to compressor but not to test gauge.

3. MID-POSITION (CRACKED) — Refrigerant flows to entire system. Gauge port (with hose connected) open for testing.

USING THE MANIFOLD GAUGES

The following are step-by-step procedures to guide the user to correct gauge usage.

1. WEAR GOGGLES OR FACE SHIELD DURING ALL TESTING OPERATIONS. BACKSEAT HAND SHUT-OFF TYPE SERVICE VALVES.

2. Remove caps from high and low side service ports. Make sure both gauge valves are closed.

3. Connect low side test hose to service valve that leads to the evaporator (located between the evaporator outlet and the compressor).

4. Attach high side test hose to service valve that leads to the condenser.

5. Mid-position hand shutoff type service valves.

6. Start engine and allow for warm-up. All testing and charging of the system should be done after engine and system have reached normal operation temperatures (except when using certain charging stations).

7. Adjust air conditioner controls to maximum cold.

8. Observe gauge readings.

When the gauges are not being used it is a good idea to:

a. Keep both hand valves in the closed position.

b. Attach both ends of the high and low service hoses to the manifold, if extra outlets are present on the manifold, or plug them if not. Also, keep the center charging hose attached to an empty refrigerant can. This extra precaution will reduce the possibility of moisture entering the gauges. If air and moisture have gotten into the gauges, purge the hoses by supplying refrigerant under pressure to the center hose with both gauge valves open and all openings unplugged.

SYSTEM CHECKS

♦ SEE FIGS. 45-47

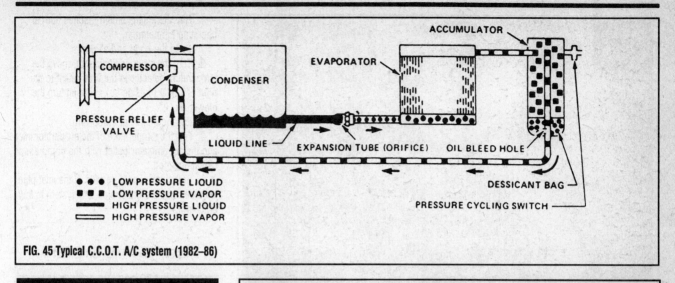

FIG. 45 Typical C.C.O.T. A/C system (1982–86)

LOW PRESSURE LIQUID
LOW PRESSURE VAPOR
HIGH PRESSURE LIQUID
HIGH PRESSURE VAPOR

※ CAUTION

Do not attempt to charge or discharge the refrigerant system unless you are thoroughly familiar with its operation and the hazards involved. The compressed refrigerant used in the air conditioning system expands and evaporates (boils) into the atmosphere at a temperature of –21.7°F (–29.8°C) or less. This will freeze any surface that it comes in contact with, including your eyes. In addition, the refrigerant decomposes into a poisonous gas in the presence of flame.

Most models through 1986 and all 2.0L turbo engine equipped models, utilize a CCOT refrigerant system. The (CCOT) Cycling Clutch Orfice Tube refrigeration system is designed to cycle the compressor on and off to maintain desired cooling and to prevent evaporator freeze.

Most models after 1986, except those equipped with the 2.0L turbo engines, use a Variable Displacement Orfice Tube (VDOT) refrigerant system which employs the constant run V–5 compressor. The V–5 is a variable displacement compressor that can match the automotive air conditioning demand under all conditions without cycling.

➡ **If your car is equipped with an aftermarket air conditioner, the following system checks may not apply. Contact the manufacturer of the unit for instructions on system checks.**

The air conditioning system on all cars does not include a sight glass.

FIG. 45A A/C low side service port

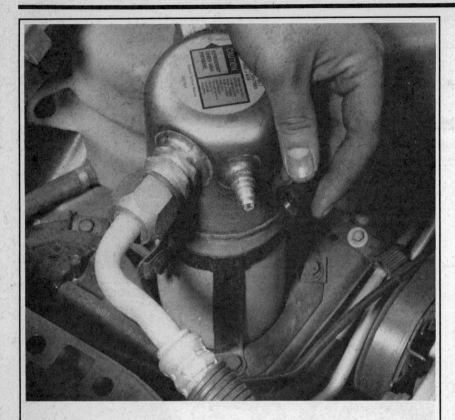

FIG. 45B A/C low side service port

1. Run the engine until it reaches normal operating temperature.

2. Open the hood and all doors.

3. Turn the air conditioning on, move the temperature selector to the first detent to the right of COLD (outside air) and then turn the blower on HI.

4. Idle the engine at 1,000 rpm.

5. Feel the temperature of the evaporator inlet and the accumulator outlet with the compressor clutch engaged.

6. Both lines should be cold. If the inlet pipe is colder than the outlet pipe, the system is low on charge.

CHARGING THE SYSTEM

✳✳ CAUTION

Never attempt to charge the system by opening the high pressure gauge control while the compressor is operating. The compressor accumulating pressure can burst the refrigerant container, causing sever personal injuries.

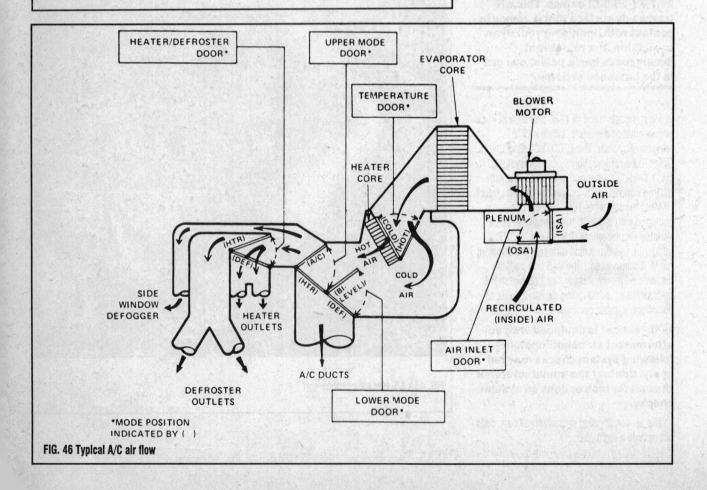

FIG. 46 Typical A/C air flow

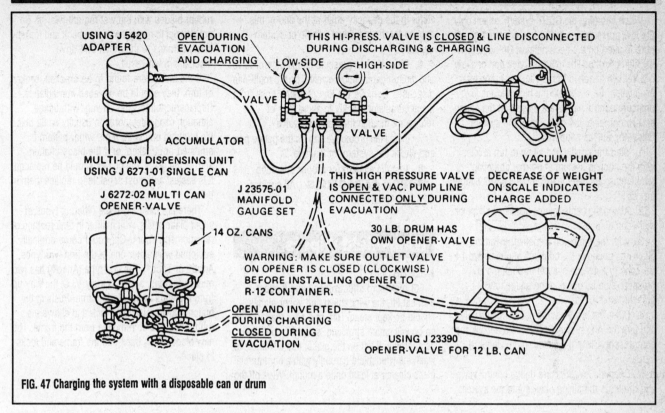

FIG. 47 Charging the system with a disposable can or drum

VACUUM VALVE LOGIC		MODE LEVER POSITION						
PORT	CONNECTION	OFF	MAX	NORM	BI-LEVEL	VENT	HEAT	DEFROST
1	INPUT	3, 5	2, 3, 4	3, 4	3	3, 4	3, 5	5
2	OSA RECIRC	VENT	VAC	VENT	VENT	VENT	VENT	VENT
3	DEFROST	VAC	VAC	VAC	VAC	VAC	VAC	VENT
4	A/C MODE	VENT	VAC	VAC	VENT	VAC	VENT	VENT
5	HEAT MODE	VAC	VENT	VENT	VENT	VENT	VAC	VAC

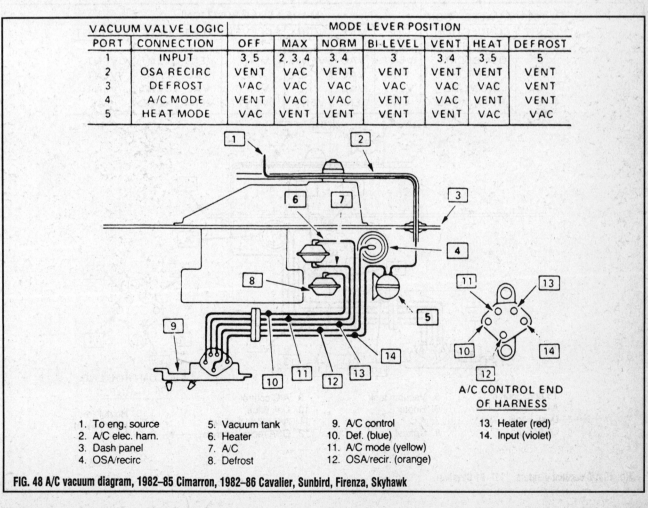

1. To eng. source
2. A/C elec. harn.
3. Dash panel
4. OSA/recirc
5. Vacuum tank
6. Heater
7. A/C
8. Defrost
9. A/C control
10. Def. (blue)
11. A/C mode (yellow)
12. OSA/recir. (orange)
13. Heater (red)
14. Input (violet)

FIG. 48 A/C vacuum diagram, 1982–85 Cimarron, 1982–86 Cavalier, Sunbird, Firenza, Skyhawk

When charging the CCOT system, attach only the low pressure line to the low pressure gauge port, located on the accumulator. Do not attach the high pressure line to any service port or allow it to remain attached to the vacuum pump after evacuation. Be sure both the high and the low pressure control valves are closed on the gauge set. To complete the charging of the system, follow the outline supplied.

1. Start the engine and allow to run at idle, with the cooling system at normal operating temperature and set the A/C mode control button on "OFF".

2. Attach the center gauge hose to a single or multi-can dispenser.

3. With the multi-can dispenser inverted, allow one pound or the contents of one or two 14 oz. cans to enter the system through the low pressure side by opening the gauge low pressure control valve.

4. Close the low pressure gauge control valve and turn the A/C system to NORM to engage the compressor. Place the blower motor in its HI mode.

5. Open the low pressure gauge control valve and draw the remaining charge into the system.

Refer to the capacity chart at the end of this section for the individual vehicle or system capacity.

6. Close the low pressure gauge control valve and the refrigerant source valve, on the multi-can dispenser. Remove the low pressure hose from the accumulator quickly to avoid loss of refrigerant through the Schrader valve.

7. Install the protective cap on the gauge port and check the system for leakage.

8. Test the system for proper operation.

FREON CAPACITIES All engines: 2.25 lbs. (1.02 kg).

Windshield Wipers

♦ SEE FIG. 52

For maximum effectiveness and longest element lift, the windshield and wiper blades should be kept clean. Dirt, tree sap, road tar and so on will cause streaking, smearing and blade deterioration if left on the glass. It is advisable to wash the windshield carefully with a commercial glass cleaner at least once a month. Wipe off the rubber blades with the wet rag afterwards. Do not attempt to move the wipers back and forth by hand; damage to the motor and drive mechanism will result.

If the blades are found to be cracked, broken or torn, they should be replaced immediately. Replacement intervals will vary with usage, although ozone deterioration usually limits blade life to about one year. If the wiper pattern is smeared or streaked, or if the blade chatters across the glass, the blades should be replaced. It is easiest and most sensible to replace them in pairs.

There are basically three different types of wiper blade refills, which differ in their method of replacement. Your J-Car could come originally equipped with either one of the first two types, Anco® or Trico®. The first type (Anco®) has two release buttons, approximately 1/3 of the way up from the ends of the blade frame. Pushing the buttons down releases a lock and allows the rubber blade to be removed from the frame. The new blade slides back into the frame and locks in place.

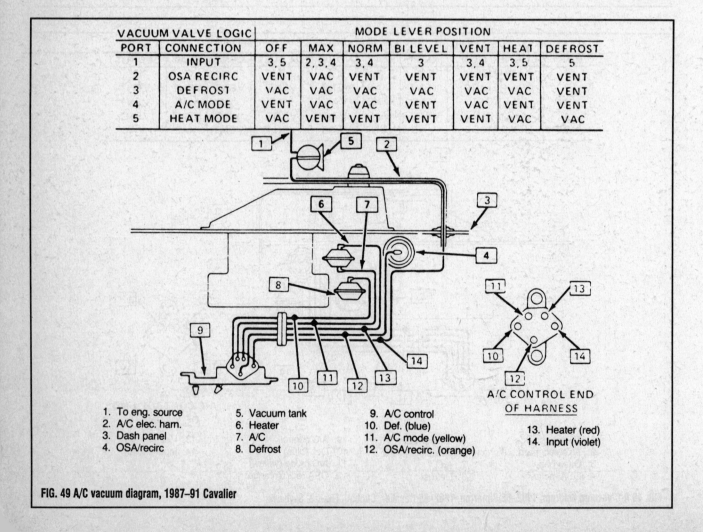

VACUUM VALVE LOGIC		MODE LEVER POSITION						
PORT	CONNECTION	OFF	MAX	NORM	BI LEVEL	VENT	HEAT	DEFROST
1	INPUT	3,5	2,3,4	3,4	3	3,4	3,5	5
2	OSA RECIRC	VENT	VAC	VENT	VENT	VENT	VENT	VENT
3	DEFROST	VAC	VAC	VAC	VAC	VAC	VAC	VENT
4	A/C MODE	VENT	VAC	VAC	VENT	VAC	VENT	VENT
5	HEAT MODE	VAC	VENT	VENT	VENT	VENT	VAC	VAC

A/C CONTROL END OF HARNESS

1. To eng. source
2. A/C elec. harn.
3. Dash panel
4. OSA/recirc
5. Vacuum tank
6. Heater
7. A/C
8. Defrost
9. A/C control
10. Def. (blue)
11. A/C mode (yellow)
12. OSA/recirc. (orange)
13. Heater (red)
14. Input (violet)

FIG. 49 A/C vacuum diagram, 1987–91 Cavalier

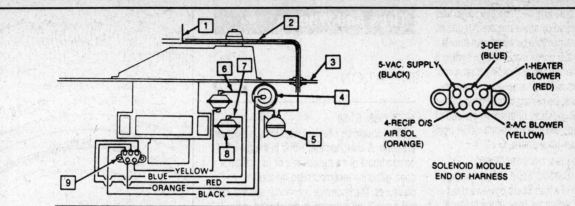

VACUUM VALVE LOGIC		MODE LEVER POSITION						
PORT	CONNECTION	OFF	MAX	NORM	BI-LEVEL	VENT	HEAT	DEFROST
1	INPUT	3,5	2,3,4	3,4	3	3,4	3,5	5
2	OSA RECIRC	VENT	VAC	VENT	VENT	VENT	VENT	VENT
3	DEFROST	VAC	VAC	VAC	VAC	VAC	VAC	VENT
4	A/C MODE	VENT	VAC	VAC	VENT	VAC	VENT	VENT
5	HEAT MODE	VAC	VENT	VENT	VENT	VENT	VAC	VAC

1. To eng. source
2. A/C elec. harn.
3. Dash panel
4. OSA/recirc valve
5. Vacuum tank
6. Heater valve
7. A/C valve
8. Defrost valve
9. Vacuum connector

FIG. 50 A/C vacuum diagram, 1986–88 Cimarron

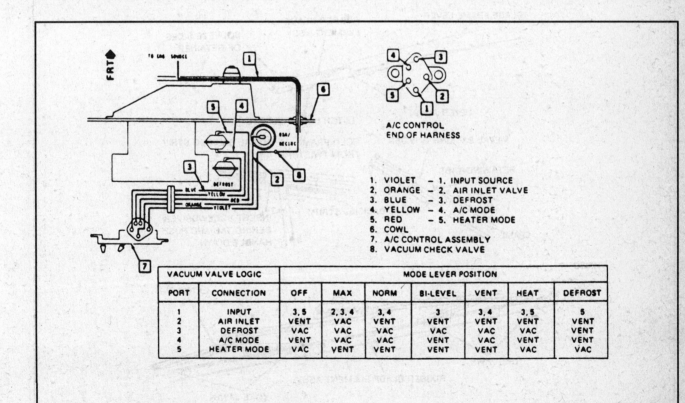

VACUUM VALVE LOGIC		MODE LEVER POSITION						
PORT	CONNECTION	OFF	MAX	NORM	BI-LEVEL	VENT	HEAT	DEFROST
1	INPUT	3,5	2,3,4	3,4	3	3,4	3,5	5
2	AIR INLET	VENT	VAC	VENT	VENT	VENT	VENT	VENT
3	DEFROST	VAC	VAC	VAC	VAC	VAC	VAC	VENT
4	A/C MODE	VENT	VAC	VAC	VENT	VAC	VENT	VENT
5	HEATER MODE	VAC	VENT	VENT	VENT	VENT	VAC	VAC

FIG. 51 A/C vacuum diagram, 1987–91, Sunbird, Firenza, Skyhawk

The second type (Trico®), has two metal tabs which are unlocked by squeezing them together. The rubber blade can then be withdrawn from the frame jaws. A new one is installed by inserting it into the front frame jaws and sliding it rearward to engage the remaining frame jaws. There are usually four jaws; be certain when installing that the refill is engaged in all of them. At the end of its travel, the tabs will lock into place on the front jaws of the wiper blade frame.

The third type is a refill made from polycarbonate. The refill has a simple locking device at one end which flexes downward out of the groove into which the jaws of the holder fit, allowing easy release. By sliding the new refill through all the jaws and pushing through the slight resistance when it reaches the end of its travel, the refill will lock into position.

Regardless of the type of refill used, make sure that all the frame jaws are engaged as the refill is pushed into place and locked. The metal blade holder and frame will scratch the glass if allowed to touch it.

Tires and Wheels

INFLATION

▶ SEE FIGS. 53-58

Tires should be checked weekly for proper air pressure. A chart, located either in the glove compartment or on the driver's or passenger's door, gives the recommended inflation pressures. Maximum fuel economy and tire life will result if the pressure is maintained at the highest figure given on the chart. Pressures should be checked before driving since pressure can increase as much as six pounds per square inch (psi) due to heat buildup. It is a good idea to have you own accurate pressure gauge, because not all gauges on service station air pumps can be trusted. When checking pressures, do not neglect the spare tire. Note that some spare tires require pressures considerably higher than those used in the other tires.

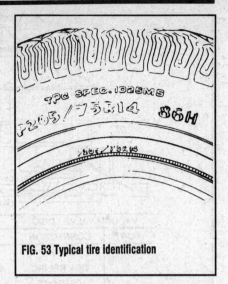

FIG. 53 Typical tire identification

While you are about the task of checking air pressure, inspect the tire treads for cuts, bruises and other damage. Check the air valves to be sure that they are tight. Replace any missing valve caps.

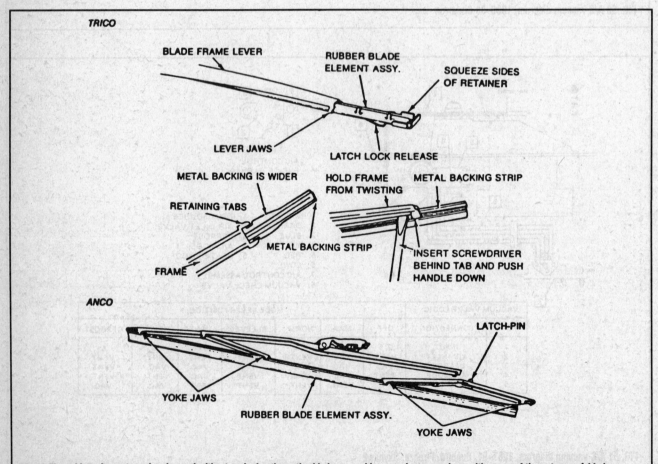

FIG. 52 The rubber element can be changed without replacing the entire blade assembly; your J-car may have either one of these types of blades

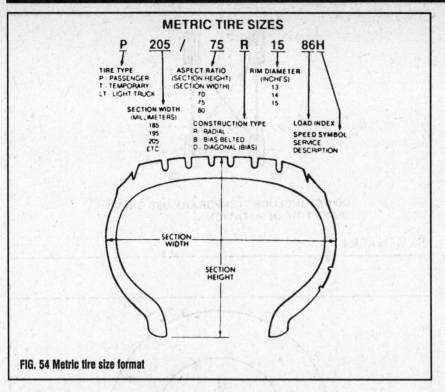

METRIC TIRE SIZES

P   205 / 75   R   15   86H

TIRE TYPE
P - PASSENGER
T - TEMPORARY
LT - LIGHT TRUCK

ASPECT RATIO
(SECTION HEIGHT)
(SECTION WIDTH)
70
75
80

RIM DIAMETER
(INCHES)
13
14
15

SECTION WIDTH
(MILLIMETERS)
185
195
205
ETC

CONSTRUCTION TYPE
R - RADIAL
B - BIAS BELTED
D - DIAGONAL (BIAS)

LOAD INDEX

SPEED SYMBOL
SERVICE
DESCRIPTION

SECTION WIDTH

SECTION HEIGHT

FIG. 54 Metric tire size format

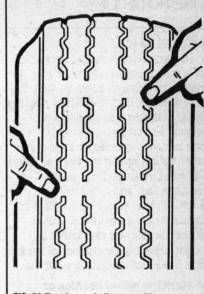

FIG. 56 Tread wear indicators will appear as brands across the tread when the tire is due for replacement

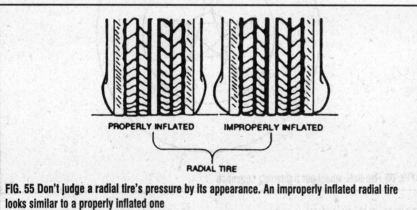

PROPERLY INFLATED   IMPROPERLY INFLATED

RADIAL TIRE

FIG. 55 Don't judge a radial tire's pressure by its appearance. An improperly inflated radial tire looks similar to a properly inflated one

FIG. 57 You can use a penny for tread wear checks; if the top of Lincoln's head is visible in two adjacent grooves, the tire should be replaced

Check the tires for uneven wear that might indicate the need for front end alignment or tire rotation. Tires should be replaced when a tread wear indicator appears as a solid band across the tread.

TIRE DESIGN

When buying new tires, give some thought to the following points, especially if you are considering a switch to larger tires or a different profile series:

1. All four tires must be of the same construction type. This rule cannot be violated, Radial, bias, and bias-belted tires must not be mixed.

2. The wheels should be the correct width for the tire. Tire dealers have charts of tire and rim compatibility. A mis-match will cause sloppy handling and rapid tire wear. The tread width should match the rim width (inside bead to inside bead) within an inch. For radial tires, the rim should be 80% or less of the tire (not tread) width.

3. The height (mounted diameter) of the new tires can change speedometer accuracy, engine speed at a given road speed, fuel mileage, acceleration, and ground clearance. Tire manufacturers furnish full measurement specifications.

4. The spare tire should be usable, at least for short distance and low speed operation, with the new tires.

5. There shouldn't be any body interference when loaded, on bumps, or in turns.

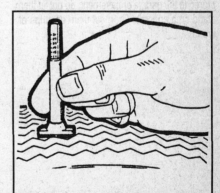

FIG. 58 Inexpensive gauges are also available for measurement of tread wear

TIRE ROTATION

◆ SEE FIGS. 59-60

Tire rotation is recommended every 6,000 miles or so, to obtain maximum tire wear. The pattern shown does not include the "temporary use only" spare. Due to their design, radial tires tend to wear faster in the shoulder area particualrly in front positions. Radial tires in non-drive locations may develop an irregular wear pattern that can increase tire noise if not rotated. This makes regular rotation especially necessary. Snow tires sometimes have directional arrows molded into the side of the carcass; the arrow shows the direction of rotation. They will wear very rapidly if the rotation is reversed. Studded tires will lose their studs if their rotational direction is reversed.

➡ **Mark the wheel position or direction or rotation on radial tires or studded snow tires before removing them.**

❋ CAUTION

Tighten the lug nuts to 100 ft. lbs., in the pattern indicated. Avoid overtightening the lug nuts to prevent damage to the brake disc or drum. Alloy wheels can also be cracked by overtightening. Use of a torque wrench is highly recommended.

STORAGE

Store the tires at the proper inflation pressure if they are mounted on wheels. Keep them in a cool dry place, laid on their sides. If the tires are stored in the garage or basement, do not let them stand on a concrete floor; set them on strips of wood.

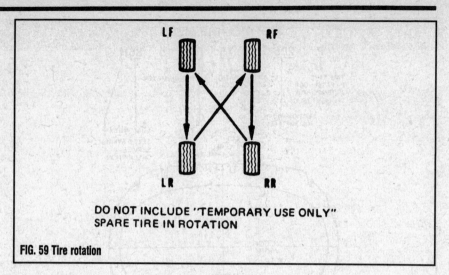

DO NOT INCLUDE "TEMPORARY USE ONLY" SPARE TIRE IN ROTATION

FIG. 59 Tire rotation

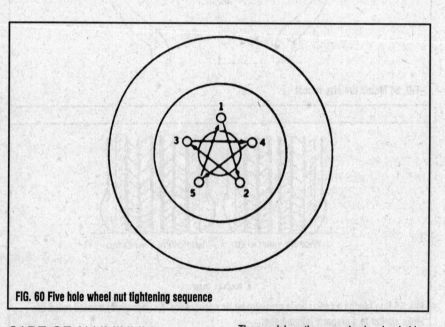

FIG. 60 Five hole wheel nut tightening sequence

CARE OF ALUMINUM WHEELS

Normal appearance maintenance of aluminum wheels includes frequent washing and waxing. However, you must be careful to avoid the use of abrasive cleaners. Failure to heed this warning will cause the protective coating to be damaged.

The special coating may also be abraded by repeated washing of the car in an automatic car wash using certain types of brushes. Once the finish abrades, it will provide less protection; then, even normal exposure to either caustic cleaners or road salt will cause the process to continue. If the wheel reaches this point it will require refinishing.

FLUIDS AND LUBRICANTS

Fuel and Engine Oil Recommendations

Oil

▶ SEE FIG. 61

The SAE (Society of Automotive Engineers) grade number indicates the viscosity of the engine oil, and thus its ability to lubricate at a given temperature. The lower the SAE grade number, the lighter the oil; the lower the viscosity, the easier it is to crank the engine in cold weather.

The API (American Petroleum Institute) designation indicates the classification of engine oil for use under given operating conditions. Only oils designated for use Service SG should be used. Oils of the SG type perform a variety of functions inside the engine in addition to the basic function as a lubricant. Through a balanced system of metallic detergents and polymeric dispersants, the oil prevents the formation of high and low temperature deposits, and also keeps sludge and dirt particles in suspension. Acids, particularly sulfuric acid, as well as other by products of combustion, are neutralized. Both the SAE grade number and the API designation can be found on the top of the oil can.

➡ **Non-detergent or straight mineral oils must never be used. Oil viscosities should be chosen from those oils recommended for the lowest anticipated temperatures during the oil change interval.**

Multi-viscosity oils offer the important advantage of being adaptable to temperature extremes. They allow easy starting at low temperatures, yet give good protection at high speeds and engine temperatures. This is a decided advantage in changeable climates or in long distance touring.

Fuel

All G.M. J-cars must use unleaded fuel. The use of leaded fuel will plug the catalyst rendering it inoperative, and will increase the exhaust back pressure to the point where engine output will be severely reduced. The minimum octane for all engines is 91 RON. All unleaded fuels sold in the U.S. are required to meet this minimum octane rating.

Use of a fuel too low in octane (a measurement of anti-knock quality) will result in spark knock. Since many factors affect operating efficiency, such as altitude, terrain, and air temperature and humidity, knocking may result even though the recommended fuel is being used. If persistent knocking occurs, it may be necessary to switch to a slightly higher grade of unleaded gasoline. Continuous or heavy

knocking may result in serious engine damage, for which the manufacturer is not responsible.

➡ **Your car's engine fuel requirement can change with time, due to carbon buildup, which changes the compression ratio. If your car's engine knocks, pings, or runs on, switch to a higher grade of fuel, if possible, and check the ignition timing. Sometimes changing brands of gasoline will cure the problem.**

Engine

OIL LEVEL CHECK

The engine oil level should be checked at every fuel stop, or once a week, whichever occurs more regularly. The best time to check is when the engine is warm, although checking immediately after the engine has been shut off will result in an inaccurate reading, since it takes a few minutes for all of the oil to drain back down into the crankcase. If the engine is cold, the engine should not be run before the level is checked. The oil level is checked by means of a dipstick, located at the front of the engine compartment:

1. If the engine is warm, it should be allowed to sit for a few minutes after being shut off to allow the oil to drain down into the oil pan. The car should be parked on a level surface.

2. Pull the dipstick out from its holder, wipe it clean with a rag, and reinsert it firmly. Be sure it is pushed all the way home, or the reading you're about to take will be incorrect.

3. Pull the dipstick again and hold it horizontally to prevent the oil from running. The dipstick is marked with Add and Full lines. The oil level should be above the Add line.

4. Reinstall the dipstick.

If oil is needed, it is added through the capped opening in the cylinder head cover. One quart of oil will raise the level from Add to Full. Only oils labeled SF should be used; select a viscosity that will be compatible with the temperatures expected until the next drain interval. See the Oil and Fuel Recommendations section later in this section if you are not sure what type of oil to use. Check the oil level again after any additions. Be

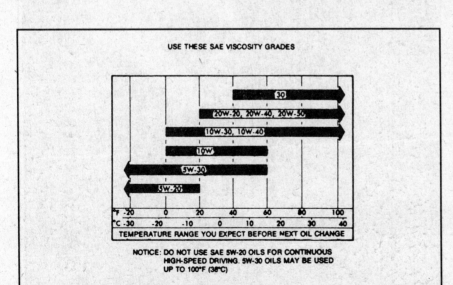

USE THESE SAE VISCOSITY GRADES

NOTICE: DO NOT USE SAE 5W-20 OILS FOR CONTINUOUS HIGH-SPEED DRIVING. 5W-30 OILS MAY BE USED UP TO 100°F (38°C)

FIG. 61 Oil viscosity chart; multi-viscosity oils offer greater temperature latitude

careful not to overfill, which will lead to leakage and seal damage.

OIL AND FILTER CHANGE

▶ SEE FIGS. 62-64

✳✳ CAUTION

The EPA warns that prolonged contact with used engine oil may cause a number of skin disorders, including cancer! You should make every effort to minimize your exposure to used engine oil. Protective gloves should be worn when changing the oil. Wash your hands and any other exposed skin areas as soon as possible after exposure to used engine oil. Soap and water, or waterless hand cleaner should be used.

If you purchased your J-car new, the engine oil and filter should be changed at the first 7,500 miles or 12 months (whichever comes first), and every 7,500 miles or 12 months thereafter. You should make it a practice to change the oil filter at every oil change; otherwise, a approximately a pint of dirty oil remains in the engine every other time the oil is changed. The change interval should be halved when the car is driven under severe conditions, such as in extremely dusty weather, or when the car is used for trailer towing, prolonged high speed driving, or repeated short trips in freezing weather.

1. Drive the car until the engine is at normal operating temperature. A run to the parts store for oil and a filter should accomplish this. If the engine is not hot when the oil is changed, most of the acids and contaminants will remain inside the engine.

2. Shut off the engine, and slide a pan of at least 6 quarts capacity under the oil pan.

➡ **Six quart plastic drain pan/ containers are available, which can be capped, and taken later to a recycling station to dispose of the dirty oil. Do not pour on the ground.**

3. Remove the drain plug from the engine oil pan, after wiping the plug area clean. The drain plug is the bolt inserted at an angle into the lowest point of the oil pan.

4. The oil from the engine will be HOT. It will probably not be possible to hold onto the drain plug. You may have to let it fall into the pan and

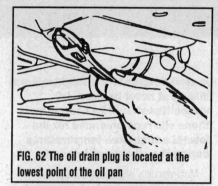

FIG. 62 The oil drain plug is located at the lowest point of the oil pan

FIG. 62A Engine oil fill cap

fish it out later. Allow all the oil to drain completely. This will take a few minutes.

5. Wipe off the drain plug, removing any traces of metal particles. Pay particular attention to the threads. Replace it, and tighten it snugly.

6. The oil filter is at the back of the engine. It is impossible to reach from above, and almost as inaccessible from below, because of the location of the fender skirt. It may be easiest to remove the right front wheel and reach through the fender opening to get at the four cylinder oil filter. Use an oil filter strap wrench, or a wrench that fits like a cap over the oil filter, along with a rachet wrench, to loosen the oil filter; these are available at auto parts stores. Place the drain pan on the ground, under the filter. Unscrew and discard the old filter. It will be VERY HOT, so be careful.

7. If the oil filter is on so tightly that it collapses under pressure from the wrench, drive a long punch or a nail through it, across the diameter and as close to the base as possible, and use this as a lever to unscrew it. Make sure you are turning it counterclockwise.

8. Clean off the oil filter mounting surface with a rag. Apply a thin film of clean engine oil to the filter gasket.

9. Screw the filter on by hand until the gasket makes contact. Then tighten it by hand an additional $1/2$-$3/4$ turn. Do not overtighten.

10. Remove the filler cap on the rocker (valve) cover, after wiping the area clean.

FIG. 62B Engine oil dipstick

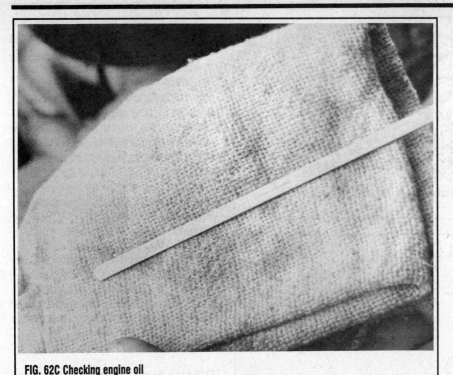

FIG. 62C Checking engine oil

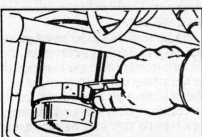

FIG. 63 Use an oil filter strap wrench to remove the oil filter; install the new filter by hand

FIG. 64 Apply a thin film of clean oil to the new gasket to prevent it from tearing upon installation

11. Add the correct number of quarts of oil specified in the Capacities chart. If you don't have an oil can spout, you will need a funnel. Be certain you do not overfill the engine, which can cause serious damage. Replace the cap.

12. Check the oil level on the dipstick. It is normal for the level to be a bit above the full mark. Start the engine and allow it to idle for a few minutes.

> ❊❊ **CAUTION**
>
> **Do not run the engine above idle speed until it has built up oil pressure, indicated when the oil light goes out.**

Check around the filter and drain plug for any leaks.

13. Shut off the engine, allow the oil to drain for a minute, and check the oil level.

After completing this job, you will have several quarts of filthy oil to dispose of. If you didn't use a drain pan/container as noted earlier, the best thing to do with it is to funnel it into old plastic milk or detergent containers. Then, you can pour it into the recycling container at a gas station or service center.

Manual Transaxle

FLUID RECOMMENDATION AND LEVEL CHECK

▶ SEE FIGS. 65-66

The fluid level in the manual transaxle should be checked every 12 months or 7,500 miles, whichever comes first.

1. Park the car on a level surface. The transaxle should be cool to the touch. If it is hot, check the level later, when it has cooled.

2. Remove the dipstick from the left side of the transaxle.

3. If lubricant is needed, add it through the filler tube until the level is correct. All 4-speeds use DEXRON®II transmission fluid. All 5-speeds through 1986 use 5W-30 engine oil. All 5-speeds from 1988–92 use GM part number 12345349 transaxle oil. When the level is correct, reinstall the dipstick firmly.

DRAIN AND REFILL

The fluid in the manual transaxle normally does not require changing, however you may want to change it if the car is used under severe conditions.

1. The fluid should be hot before it is drained. If the car is driven until the engine is at normal operating temperature, the fluid should be hot enough.

2. Remove the filler plug (or dipstick) from the left side of the transaxle to provide a vent.

3. The drain plug is located on the bottom of the transaxle case. Place a pan under the drain plug and remove it.

> ❊❊ **CAUTION**
>
> **The fluid will be HOT. Push up against the threads as you unscrew the plug to prevent leakage.**

4. Allow the fluid to drain completely. Check the condition of the plug gasket and replace it if necessary. Clean off the plug and replace, tightening it until snug.

5. Fill the transaxle with fluid through the fill or dipstick tube. You will need the aid of a long neck funnel or a funnel and a hose to pour through.

6. Use the dipstick to gauge the level of the fluid.

7. Replace the filler plug or dipstick and dispose of the old fluid in the same manner as you would old engine oil.

Take a drive in the car, stop on a level surface, and check the oil level.

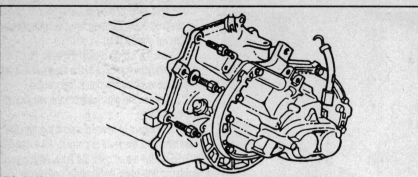

FIG. 65 Most models use a dipstick and tube like this to check the level of the manual transaxle lubricant

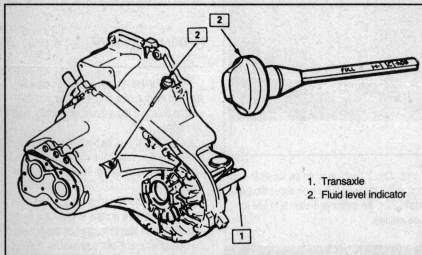

1. Transaxle
2. Fluid level indicator

FIG. 66 Some earlier models use a dipstick and plug such as this to check the level of the manual transaxle lubricant

3. With the engine still running, remove the dipstick, wipe it clean, then reinsert it, pushing it fully home.

4. Pull the dipstick again and, holding it horizontally, read the fluid level.

5. Cautiously feel the end of the dipstick to determine the temperature. Note that on the J-cars the cool and warm level dimples are above the hot level area. If the fluid level is not in the correct area, more will have to be added.

6. Fluid is added through the dipstick tube. You will probably need the aid of a spout or a long-necked funnel. Be sure that whatever you pour through is perfectly clean and dry. Use an automatic transmission fluid marked DEXRON®II. Add fluid slowly, and in small amounts, checking the level frequently between additions. Do not overfill, which will cause foaming, fluid loss, slippage, and possible transaxle damage. It takes only one pint to raise the level from Add to Full when the transaxle is hot.

DRAIN AND REFILL

♦ SEE FIGS. 68-72

The fluid should be changed according to the schedule in the Maintenance Intervals chart. If the car is normally used in severe service, such as stop and start driving, trailer towing, or the like, the interval should be halved. If the car is driven under especially nasty conditions, such as in heavy city traffic where the temperature

Automatic Transaxle

FLUID RECOMMENDATION AND LEVEL CHECK

♦ SEE FIG. 67

The fluid level in the automatic transaxle should be checked every 12 months or 7,500 miles, whichever comes first. The transaxle has a dipstick for fluid level checks.

1. Drive the car until it is at normal operating temperature. The level should not be checked immediately after the car has been driven for a long time at high speed, or in city traffic in hot weather; in those cases, the transaxle should be given a half hour to cool down.

2. Stop the car, apply the parking brake, then shift slowly through all gear positions, ending in Park. Let the engine idle for about five minutes with the selector in Park. The car should be on a level surface.

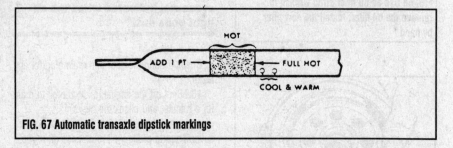

FIG. 67 Automatic transaxle dipstick markings

FIG. 68 Loosen the pan bolts and allow one corner of the pan to tilt slightly to drain the fluid

FIG. 68A Automatic transaxle dipstick

normally reaches 90°F, or in very hilly or mountainous areas, or in police, taxi, or delivery service, the fluid should be changed every 15,000 miles (24,000 km.).

The fluid must be hot before it is drained; a 20 minute drive should accomplish this.

1. There is no drain plug; the fluid pan must be removed. Place a drain pan underneath the transaxle pan and remove the pan attaching bolts at the front and sides of the pan.

2. Loosen the rear pan attaching bolts approximately four turns each.

3. Very carefully pry the pan loose. You can use a small prybar for this if you work CAREFULLY. Do not distort the pan flange, or score the mating surface of the transaxle case. You'll be very sorry later if you do. As the pan is pried loose, all of the fluid is going to come pouring out.

4. Remove the remaining bolts and remove the pan and gasket. Throw away the gasket.

5. Clean the pan with solvent and allow it to air dry. If you use a rag to wipe out the pan, you risk leaving bits of lint behind, which will clog the small hydraulic passages in the transaxle.

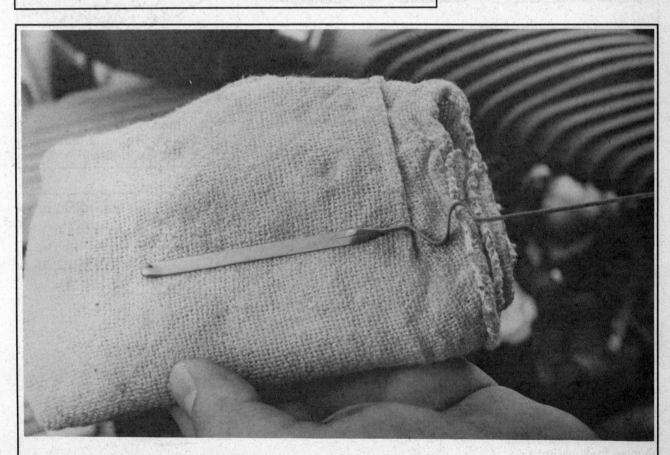

FIG. 68B Checking the automatic transaxle fluid level

FIG. 68C Adding automatic transaxle fluid

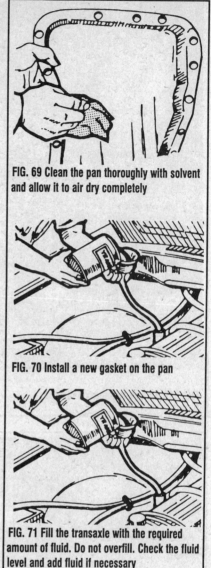

FIG. 69 Clean the pan thoroughly with solvent and allow it to air dry completely

FIG. 70 Install a new gasket on the pan

FIG. 71 Fill the transaxle with the required amount of fluid. Do not overfill. Check the fluid level and add fluid if necessary

6. Remove and discard the filter and the O-ring seal.

7. Install a new filter and O-ring, locating the filter against the dipstick stop.

8. Install a new gasket on the pan and install the pan. Tighten the bolts evenly and in rotation to 8 ft. lbs. (11 Nm.). Do not overtighten.

9. Add approximately 4 qts. (3.8 L) of DEXRON®II automatic transmission fluid to the transaxle through the dipstick tube. You will need a long necked funnel, or a funnel and tube to do this.

10. With the transaxle in Park, put on the parking brake, block the front wheels, start the engine and let it idle. DO NOT RACE THE ENGINE. DO NOT MOVE THE LEVER THROUGH ITS RANGES.

11. With the lever in Park, check the fluid level. If it's OK, take the car out for a short drive, park on a level surface, and check the level again, as outlined earlier in this section. Add more fluid if necessary. Be careful not to overfill, which will cause foaming and fluid loss.

➡ **If the drained fluid is discolored (brown or black), thick, or smells burnt, serious transmission troubles, probably due to** **overheating, should be suspected. Your car's transaxle should be inspected by a reliable transmission specialist to determine the problem.**

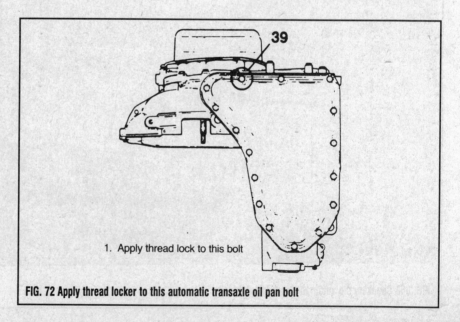

39

1. Apply thread lock to this bolt

FIG. 72 Apply thread locker to this automatic transaxle oil pan bolt

Cooling System

FLUID RECOMMENDATION AND LEVEL CHECK

◗ SEE FIG. 73

❈❈ CAUTION

Never remove the radiator cap under any conditions while the engine is running! Failure to follow these instructions could result in damage to the cooling system or engine and/or personal injury. To avoid having scalding hot coolant or steam blow out of the radiator, use extreme care when removing the radiator cap from a hot radiator. Wait until the engine has cooled, then wrap a thick cloth around the radiator cap and turn it slowly to the first stop. Step back while the pressure is released from the cooling system. When you are sure the pressure has been released, press down on the radiator cap (still have the cloth in position) turn and remove the radiator cap.

Dealing with the cooling system can be dangerous matter unless the proper precautions are observed. It is best to check the coolant level in the radiator when the engine is cold. The cooling system has, as one of its components, a coolant recovery tank. If the coolant level is at or near the FULL COLD line (engine cold) or the FULL HOT line (engine hot), the level is satisfactory. Always be certain that the filler caps on both the radiator and the recovery tank are closed tightly.

In the event that the coolant level must be checked when the engine is hot on engines without a coolant recovery tank, place a thick rag over the radiator cap and slowly turn the cap counterclockwise until it reaches the first detent. Allow all hot steam to escape. This will allow the pressure in the system to drop gradually, preventing an explosion of hot coolant. When the hissing noise stops, remove the cap the rest of the way.

If the coolant level is found to be low, add a

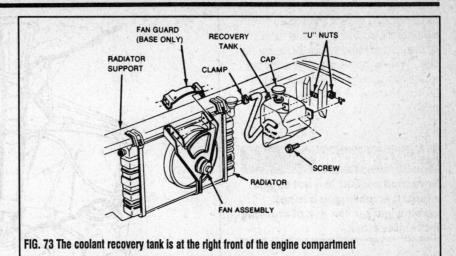

FIG. 73 The coolant recovery tank is at the right front of the engine compartment

FIG. 73A Engine coolant recovery tank

50/50 mixture of ethylene glycol-based antifreeze and clean water. On older models, coolant must be added through the radiator filler neck. On newer models with the recovery tank, coolant may be added either through the filler neck on the radiator or directly into the recovery tank.

> ### ❈ CAUTION
>
> **Never add coolant to a hot engine unless it is running. If it is not running you run the risk of cracking the engine block.**

If the coolant level is chronically low or rusty, refer to Cooling System Troubleshooting Chart at the end of this section.

At least once every 2 years, the engine cooling system should be inspected, flushed, and refilled with fresh coolant. If the coolant is left in the system too long, it loses its ability to prevent rust and corrosion. If the coolant has too much water, it won't protect against freezing.

The pressure cap should be looked at for signs of age or deterioration. Fan belt and other drive belts should be inspected and adjusted to the proper tension. (See checking belt tension).

Hose clamps should be tightened, and soft or cracked hoses replaced. Damp spots, or accumulations of rust or dye near hoses, water pump or other areas, indicate possible leakage, which must be corrected before filling the system with fresh coolant.

CHECK THE RADIATOR CAP

While you are checking the coolant level, check the radiator cap for a worn or cracked gasket. It the cap doesn't seal properly, fluid will be lost and the engine will overheat.

Worn caps should be replaced with a new one.

CLEAN RADIATOR OF DEBRIS

▶ SEE FIGS. 74-76

Periodically clean any debris — leaves, paper, insects, etc. — from the radiator fins. Pick the large pieces off by hand. The smaller pieces can be washed away with water pressure from a hose.

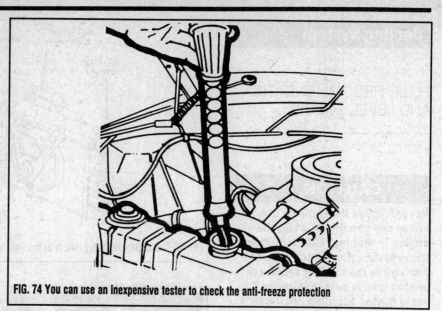

FIG. 74 You can use an inexpensive tester to check the anti-freeze protection

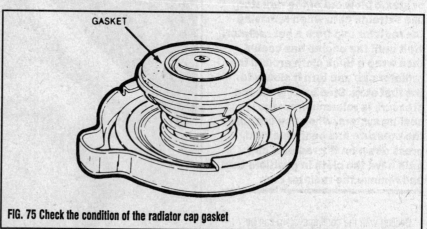

FIG. 75 Check the condition of the radiator cap gasket

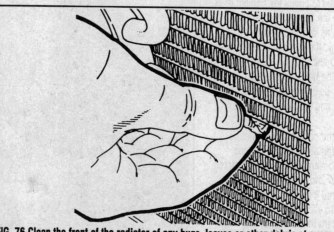

FIG. 76 Clean the front of the radiator of any bugs, leaves or other debris at every yearly coolant change

Carefully straighten any bent radiator fins with a pair of needle nose pliers. Be careful — the fins are very soft. Don't wiggle the fins back and forth too much. Straighten them once and try not to move them again.

DRAIN AND REFILL

Completely draining and refilling the cooling system every two years at least will remove accumulated rust, scale and other deposits. Coolant in late model cars is a 50/50 mixture of ethylene glycol and water for year round use. Use a good quality antifreeze with water pump lubricants, rust inhibitors and other corrosion inhibitors along with acid neutralizers.

1. Drain the existing antifreeze and coolant. Open the radiator and engine drain petcocks, or disconnect the bottom radiator hose, at the radiator outlet.

✳✳ CAUTION

When draining the coolant, keep in mind that cats and dogs are attracted by the ethylene glycol antifreeze, and are quite likely to drink any that is left in an uncovered container or in puddles on the ground. This will prove fatal in sufficient quantity. Always drain the coolant into a sealable container. Coolant should be reused unless it is contaminated or several years old.

2. Close the petcock or reconnect the lower hose and fill the system with water.
3. Add a can of quality radiator flush.
4. Idle the engine until the upper radiator hose gets hot.
5. Drain the system again.
6. Repeat this process until the drained water is clear and free of scale.
7. Close all petcocks and connect all the hoses.
8. If equipped with a coolant recovery system, flush the reservoir with water and leave empty.
9. Determine the capacity of your coolant system (see capacities specifications). Add a 50/50 mix of quality antifreeze (ethylene glycol) and water to provide the desired protection.
10. Run the engine to operating temperature.
11. Stop the engine and check the coolant level.
12. Check the level of protection with an antifreeze tester, replace the cap and check for leaks.

Master Cylinder

FLUID RECOMMENDATION AND LEVEL CHECK

◆ SEE FIGS. 77-79

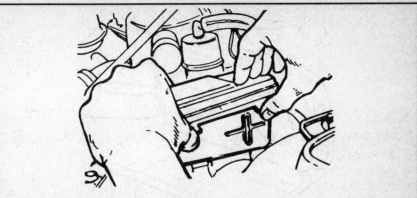

FIG. 77 Use thumb pressure to remove the brake master cylinder cover on models through 1987

FIG. 77A Master cylinder fluid level check

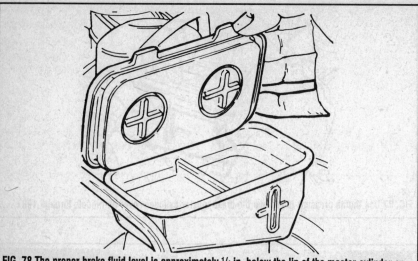

FIG. 78 The proper brake fluid level is approximately ¼ in. below the lip of the master cylinder on models through 1987

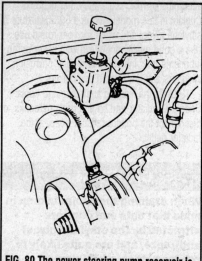

FIG. 80 The power steering pump reservoir is located at the back of the engine compartment

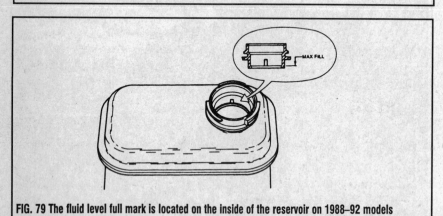

FIG. 79 The fluid level full mark is located on the inside of the reservoir on 1988–92 models

Once a month, the fluid level in the brake master cylinder should be checked.

1. Park the car on a level surface.

2. Clean off the master cylinder cover before removal.

3. The early models without a filler cap the cover simply snaps onto the master cylinder body. Use your thumbs to press up on the two tabs on the side of the cover to unsnap it. Remove the cover or cap, being careful not to drop or tear the rubber diaphragm underneath. Be careful also not to drip any brake fluid on painted surfaces; the stuff eats paint.

➡ **Brake fluid absorbs moisture from the air, which reduces effectiveness, and will corrode brake parts once in the system. Never leave the master cylinder or the brake fluid container uncovered for any longer than necessary.**

4. The fluid level should be about ¼ in. below the lip of the master cylinder well on early models or the full mark on the inside on later models.

5. If fluid addition is necessary, use only extra heavy duty disc brake fluid meeting DOT 3 specifications. The fluid should be reasonably fresh because brake fluid deteriorates with age.

6. Replace the cover or cap, making sure that the diaphragm is correctly seated.

If the brake fluid level is constantly low, the system should be checked for leaks. However, it is normal for the fluid level to fall gradually as the disc brake pads wear; expect the fluid level to drop not more than ⅛ in. for every 10,000 miles of wear.

Steering Gear

The rack and pinion steering gear used on the J-cars is a sealed unit; no fluid level checks or additions are ever necessary.

Power Steering Pump

♦ SEE FIG. 80

The power steering hydraulic fluid reservoir is

attached to the firewall at the back of the engine compartment. It is a translucent plastic container with fluid level markings on the outside. Check the fluid level every 12 months or 7,500 miles, whichever comes first. If the level is low, add power steering fluid until it is correct. Be careful not to overfill as this will cause fluid loss and seal damage.

Windshield Washer Fluid

Check the fluid level in the windshield washer tank at every oil level check. The fluid can be mixed in a 50% solution with water, if desired, as long as temperatures remain above freezing. Below freezing, the fluid should be used full strength. Never add engine coolant antifreeze to the washer fluid, because it will damage the car's paint.

Chassis Greasing

♦ SEE FIG. 81

There are only two areas which require regular chassis greasing: the front suspension components and the steering linkage. These parts should be greased every 12 months or 7,500 miles (12,000 Km.) with an EP grease meeting G.M. specification 6031M.

If you choose to do this job yourself, you will need to purchase a hand operated grease gun, if you do not own one already, and a long flexible extension hose to reach the various grease fittings. You will also need a cartridge of the appropriate grease.

Press the fitting on the grease gun hose onto the grease fitting on the suspension or steering linkage component. Pump a few shots of grease into the fitting, until the rubber boot on the joint begins to expand, indicating that the joint is full. Remove the gun from the fitting. Be careful not to overfill the joints, which will rupture the rubber boots, allowing the entry of dirt. You can keep the grease fittings clean by covering them with a small square of tin foil.

➡ **This is a good opportunity, while under the vehicle, to check for any tears or holes in the axle CV-joint boots, which may cause loss of or contamination of the axle grease. Damaged boots must be replaced as soon as possible or joint failure could result.**

Chassis Lubrication

Every 12 months or 7,500 miles (12,000 km.), the various linkages and hinges on the

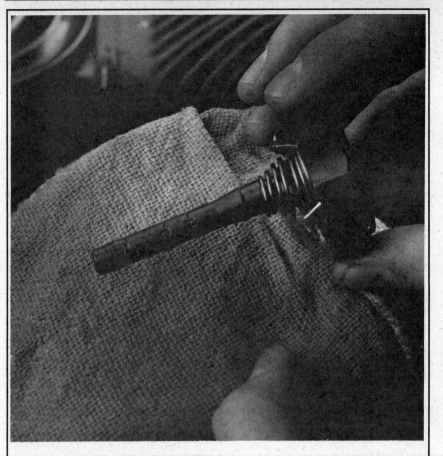

FIG. 80A Power steering fluid level check

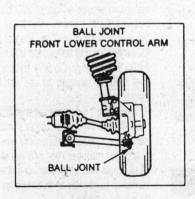
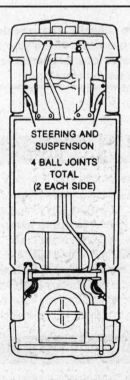
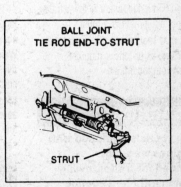

STEERING AND SUSPENSION

4 BALL JOINTS TOTAL (2 EACH SIDE)

BALL JOINT FRONT LOWER CONTROL ARM

BALL JOINT

BALL JOINT TIE ROD END-TO-STRUT

STRUT

FIG. 81 Lubrication points

chassis and body should be lubricated, as follows:

TRANSAXLE SHIFT LINKAGE

Lubricate the manual transaxle shift linkage contact points with the EP grease used for chassis greasing, which should meet G.M. specification 6031M. The automatic transaxle linkage should be lubricated with clean engine oil.

HOOD LATCH AND HINGES

Clean the latch surfaces and apply clean engine oil to the latch pilot bolts and the spring anchor. Use the engine oil to lubricate the hood hinges as well. Use a chassis grease to lubricate all the pivot points in the latch release mechanism.

DOOR HINGES

The gas tank filler door, car door, and rear hatch or trunk lid hinges should be wiped clean and lubricated with clean engine oil. Silicone spray also works well on these parts, but must be applied more often. Use engine oil to lubricate the trunk or hatch lock mechanism and the lock bolt and striker. The door lock cylinders can be lubricated easily with a shot of silicone spray or one of the may dry penetrating lubricants commercially available.

PARKING BRAKE LINKAGE

Use chassis grease on the parking brake cable where it contacts the guides, links, levers, and pulleys. The grease should be a water resistant one for durability under the car.

ACCELERATOR LINKAGE

Lubricate the carburetor stud, carburetor lever, and the accelerator pedal lever at the support inside the car with clean engine oil.

Throttle Body Mounting Torque

Check torque of mounting bolts and or nuts of the throttle body assembly. Refer to Section 5 for specifications.

TRAILER TOWING

General Recommendations

Your car was primarily designed to carry passengers and cargo. It is important to remember that towing a trailer will place additional loads on your vehicle's engine, drive train, steering, braking and other systems. However, if you find it necessary to tow a trailer, using the proper equipment is a must.

Local laws may require specific equipment such as trailer brakes or fender mounted mirrors. Check your local laws.

❄ WARNING

Some early models equipped with the V6 engines were not recommended for trailer towing because of insufficient cooling system capacity. These vehicles could overheat. Check your owners manual or local GM dealer for any trailer towing warnings.

Trailer Weight

The weight of the trailer is the most important factor. A good weight-to-horsepower ratio is about 35:1, 35 lbs. of GCW (Gross Combined Weight) for every horsepower your engine develops. Multiply the engine's rated horsepower by 35 and subtract the weight of the car passengers and luggage. The result is the approximate ideal maximum weight you should tow, although a a numerically higher axle ratio can help compensate for heavier weight.

Hitch Weight

Figure the hitch weight to select a proper hitch. Hitch weight is usually 9-11% of the trailer gross weight and should be measured with the trailer loaded. Hitches fall into three types: those that mount on the frame and rear bumper or the bolt-on or weld-on distribution type used for larger trailers. Axle mounted or clamp-on bumper hitches should never be used.

Check the gross weight rating of your trailer. Tongue weight is usually figured as 10% of gross trailer weight. Therefore, a trailer with a maximum gross weight of 2,000 lb. will have a maximum tongue weight of 200 lb. Class I trailers fall into this category. Class II trailers are those with a gross weight rating of 2,000-3,500 lb., while Class III trailers fall into the 3,500-6,000 lb. category. Class IV trailers are those over 6,000 lb. and are for use with fifth wheel trucks, only.

When you've determined the hitch that you'll need, follow the manufacturer's installation instructions, exactly, especially when it comes to fastener torques. The hitch will subjected to a lot of stress and good hitches come with hardened bolts. Never substitute an inferior bolt for a hardened bolt.

Cooling

ENGINE

One of the most common, if not THE most common, problems associated with trailer towing is engine overheating.

If you have a standard cooling system, without an expansion tank, you'll definitely need to get an aftermarket expansion tank kit, preferably one with at least a 2 quart capacity. These kits are easily installed on the radiator's overflow hose, and come with a pressure cap designed for expansion tanks.

Another helpful accessory is a Flex Fan. These fan are large diameter units are designed to provide more airflow at low speeds, with blades that have deeply cupped surfaces. The blades then flex, or flatten out, at high speed, when less cooling air is needed. These fans are far lighter in weight than stock fans, requiring less horsepower to drive them. Also, they are far quieter than stock fans.

If you do decide to replace your stock fan with a flex fan, note that if your car has a fan clutch, a spacer between the flex fan and water pump hub will be needed.

Aftermarket engine oil coolers are helpful for prolonging engine oil life and reducing overall engine temperatures. Both of these factors increase engine life.

While not absolutely necessary in towing Class I and some Class II trailers, they are recommended for heavier Class II and all Class III towing.

Engine oil cooler systems consist of an adapter, screwed on in place of the oil filter, a remote filter mounting and a multi-tube, finned heat exchanger, which is mounted in front of the radiator or air conditioning condenser.

TRANSMISSION

An automatic transmission is usually recommended for trailer towing. Modern automatics have proven reliable and, of course, easy to operate, in trailer towing.

The increased load of a trailer, however, causes an increase in the temperature of the automatic transmission fluid. Heat is the worst enemy of an automatic transmission. As the temperature of the fluid increases, the life of the fluid decreases.

It is essential, therefore, that you install an automatic transmission cooler.

The cooler, which consists of a multi-tube, finned heat exchanger, is usually installed in front of the radiator or air conditioning compressor, and hooked inline with the transmission cooler tank inlet line. Follow the cooler manufacturer's installation instructions.

Select a cooler of at least adequate capacity, based upon the combined gross weights of the car and trailer.

Cooler manufacturers recommend that you use an aftermarket cooler in addition to, and not instead of, the present cooling tank in your radiator. If you do want to use it in place of the radiator cooling tank, get a cooler at least two sizes larger than normally necessary.

➡ **A transmission cooler can, sometimes, cause slow or harsh shifting in the transmission during cold weather, until the fluid has a chance to come up to normal operating temperature. Some coolers can be purchased with or retrofitted with a temperature bypass valve which will allow fluid flow through the cooler only when the fluid has reached operating temperature, or above.**

Handling A Trailer

Towing a trailer with ease and safety requires a certain amount of experience. It's a good idea to learn the feel of a trailer by practicing turning, stopping and backing in an open area such as an empty parking lot.

PUSHING AND TOWING

◆ SEE FIG. 82

The J-cars may not be pushed or towed to start, because doing so may cause the catalytic converter to explode. If the battery is weak, the engine may be jump started, using the procedure outlined in the following section.

Your J-car may be towed on all four wheels at speeds less than 35 mph (60 km/h) for distances up to 50 miles (80 km). The driveline and steering must be normally operable. If either one is damaged, the car may not be flat-towed. If the car is flat-towed (on all four wheels), the steering must be unlocked, the transaxle shifted to Neutral, and the parking brake released. Towing attachment must be made to the main structural members of the chassis, not to the bumpers or sheetmetal.

The car may be towed on its rear wheels by a

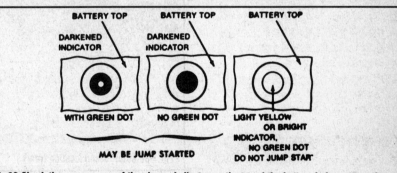

FIG. 82 Check the appearance of the charge indicator on the top of the battery before attempting a jump start; if its not green or dark, do not jump start the car

wrecker; make sure that safety chains are used. J-cars with manual transaxles may be towed on their front wheels, for short distances and at low speeds. Be sure the transaxle is in Neutral. Cars with automatic transaxles should not be towed on their front wheels; transaxle damage may result. If it is impossible to tow the car on its rear wheels, place the front wheels on a dolly.

JACKING AND HOISTING

◀ SEE FIG. 83

The J-cars are supplied with a scissors jack for changing tires. This jack engages in notches behind the front wheel and forward of the rear wheel under the rocker flange. This jack is satisfactory for its intended purpose; it is not meant to support the car while you go crawling around underneath it. Never crawl under the car when it is supported by only the scissors jack.

The car may also be jacked at the rear axle between the spring seats, or at the front end at the engine cradle crossbar or lower control arm. The car must never be lifted by the rear lower control arms.

The car can be raised on a four point hoist which contacts the chassis at points just behind the front wheels and just ahead of the rear wheels, as shown in the accompanying diagram. Be certain that the lift pads do not contact the catalytic converter.

It is imperative that strict safety precautions be observed both while raising the car and in the subsequent support after the car is raised. If a jack is used to raise the car, the transaxle should be shifted to Park (automatic) or First (manual), the parking brake should be set, and the opposite wheel should be blocked. Jacking should only be attempted on a hard level surface.

FIG. 83A Safety stand location (front)

FIG. 83B Safety stand location (rear)

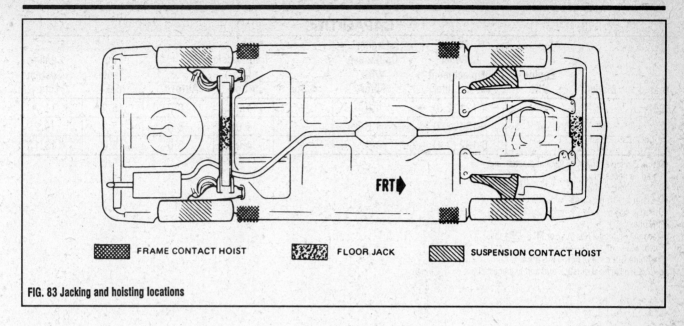

FRAME CONTACT HOIST   FLOOR JACK   SUSPENSION CONTACT HOIST

FIG. 83 Jacking and hoisting locations

CAPACITIES

Year	Model	Engine VIN	No. Cylinder Displacement cu. in. (liter)	Engine Crankcase With Filter	Transmission (pts.) 4-Spd	5-Spd	Auto. ⑥	Fuel Tank (gal.)	Cooling System (qts.)
1982	All	G	4-110 (1.8)	4.0	5.9	—	10.5	14	8.0
	All	B	4-121 (2.0)	4.0	5.9	—	10.5	14	8.3
1983	All	O, J	4-110 (1.8)	①	—	5.0	10.5	14	7.9
	All	P	4-121 (2.0)	4.0	5.9	—	10.5	14	8.3
1984	All	O, J	4-110 (1.8)	①	—	5.0	10.5	14	7.9
	All	P	4-121 (2.0)	4.0	5.9	—	10.5	14	8.3
1985	All	O, J	4-110 (1.8)	①	—	5.0	10.5	14	7.9
	All	P	4-121 (2.0)	4.0	5.9	—	10.5	14	8.3
	All	W	6-173 (2.8)	4.0	6.0	—	8.0	14③	12.4
1986	All	O, J	4-110 (1.8)	①	5.9	5.3	8.0	14	7.9
	All	P	4-121 (2.0)	4.0	5.9	—	8.0	14	8.3
	All	W	6-173 (2.8)	4.0	6.0	—	8.0	14	12.4
1987	All	M, 1, K	4-121 (2.0)	4.0	6.0	④	8.0	13.6	8.8
	All	W	6-173 (2.8)	4.0	5.36	—	8.0	14③	11.4
1988	All	M, 1, K	4-121 (2.0)	4.0⑦	—	⑤	8.0	13.6	9.7⑥
	All	W	6-173 (2.8)	4.0⑦	—	⑤	8.0	13.6	11.0
1989	All	M, 1, K	4-121 (2.0)	4.0⑦	—	4.0	8.0	13.6	9.7⑥
	All	W	6-173 (2.8)	4.0⑦	—	4.0	8.0	13.6	11.0
1990	All	M, K	4-121 (2.0)	4.0⑦	—	4.0	8.0	13.6	8.5
	All	G	4-134 (2.2)	4.0⑦	—	4.0	8.0	13.6	8.5
	All	T	6-192 (3.1)	4.0⑦	—	4.0	8.0	13.6	11.0
1991	All	K	4-121 (2.0)	4.0⑦	—	4.0	8.0	13.6	11.7
	All	G	4-134 (2.2)	4.0⑦	—	4.0	8.0	13.6	11.7
	All	T	6-192 (3.1)	4.0⑦	—	4.0	8.0	13.6	14.2

CAPACITIES

Year	Model	Engine VIN	No. Cylinder Displacement cu. in. (liter)	Engine Crankcase With Filter	Transmission (pts.)			Fuel Tank (gal.)	Cooling System (qts.)
					4-Spd	5-Spd	Auto. ⑥		
1992	All	H	4-121 (2.0)	4.0⑦	—	4.0	8.0	15.2	11.7
	All	4	4-134 (2.2)	4.0⑦	—	4.0	8.0	15.2	9.2
	All	T	6-192 (3.1)	4.0⑦	—	4.0	8.0	15.2	13.1

① Add 3 quarts, check oil level at dipstick and
   add as necessary
② Cimarron 8.0 pints
③ Cimarron 16.0 gallons
④ Isuzu: 5.3
   Muncie: 4.1
⑤ Transaxle Model No. MK7 or MT2—5.4 pts.,
   No. MG1 and MG2—4.0 pts.
⑥ Engine VIN code M or K—8.5 qts.
⑦ Check oil level at dipstick and add as necessary

MAINTENANCE INTERVALS CHART

Intervals are for number of months or thousands of miles, whichever comes first.

Maintenance	Service Intervals
Air cleaner (Replace)	30,000 mi. (48,000 km.)
PCV filter element (Replace)	50,000 mi. (48,000 km.)
PCV valve (Replace)	30,000 mi. (48,000 km.)
Power steering (Check)	12 mo./7,500 mi. (12,000 km.)
Belt tension (Adjust)	12 mo./15,000 mi. (24,000 km.)
Engine oil and filter (Change)	12 mo./7,500 mi. (12,000 km.)
Fuel filter (Change)	15,000 mi. (24,000 km.)
Manual transaxle Check Change	12 mo./7,500 mi. (12,000 km.) 100,000 mi (160,000 km.)
Automatic transaxle Check Change	12 mo./7,500 mi. (12,000 km.) 100,000 mi (160,000 km.)
Engine coolant Check Change	Weekly 24 mo./30,000 mi. (24,000 km.)
Chassis lubrication	12 mo./7,500 mi. (12,000 km.)
Rotate tires	7,500 (12,000 km.)
Brake fluid (Check)	12 mo./7,500 mi. (12,000 km.)
Spark plugs and wires, ignition timing, idle speed	30,000 mi. (48,000 km.)
Torque throttle body mounting bolts	6,000 mi. (10,000 km.)

NOTE: Heavy-duty operation (trailer towing, prolonged idling, severe stop and start driving) should be accompanied by a 50% increase in maintenance. Cut the interval in half for these conditions.

Troubleshooting Basic Air Conditioning Problems

Problem	Cause	Solution
There's little or no air coming from the vents (and you're sure it's on)	• The A/C fuse is blown • Broken or loose wires or connections • The on/off switch is defective	• Check and/or replace fuse • Check and/or repair connections • Replace switch
The air coming from the vents is not cool enough	• Windows and air vent wings open • The compressor belt is slipping • Heater is on • Condenser is clogged with debris • Refrigerant has escaped through a leak in the system • Receiver/drier is plugged	• Close windows and vent wings • Tighten or replace compressor belt • Shut heater off • Clean the condenser • Check system • Service system
The air has an odor	• Vacuum system is disrupted • Odor producing substances on the evaporator case • Condensation has collected in the bottom of the evaporator housing	• Have the system checked/repaired • Clean the evaporator case • Clean the evaporator housing drains
System is noisy or vibrating	• Compressor belt or mountings loose • Air in the system	• Tighten or replace belt; tighten mounting bolts • Have the system serviced

Sight glass condition
  Constant bubbles, foam or oil streaks
  Clear sight glass, but no cold air
  Clear sight glass, but air is cold
  Clouded with milky fluid
	
	• Undercharged system
	
	• No refrigerant at all
	• System is OK
	• Receiver drier is leaking dessicant
		
		• Charge the system
		
		• Check and charge the system
		
		• Have system checked

Large difference in temperature of lines	• System undercharged	• Charge and leak test the system
Compressor noise	• Broken valves • Overcharged • Incorrect oil level • Piston slap • Broken rings • Drive belt pulley bolts are loose	• Replace the valve plate • Discharge, evacuate and install the correct charge • Isolate the compressor and check the oil level. Correct as necessary. • Replace the compressor • Replace the compressor • Tighten with the correct torque specification
Excessive vibration	• Incorrect belt tension • Clutch loose • Overcharged • Pulley is misaligned	• Adjust the belt tension • Tighten the clutch • Discharge, evacuate and install the correct charge • Align the pulley
Condensation dripping in the passenger compartment	• Drain hose plugged or improperly positioned • Insulation removed or improperly installed	• Clean the drain hose and check for proper installation • Replace the insulation on the expansion valve and hoses

Troubleshooting Basic Air Conditioning Problems (cont.)

Problem	Cause	Solution
Frozen evaporator coil	• Faulty thermostat • Thermostat capillary tube improperly installed • Thermostat not adjusted properly	• Replace the thermostat • Install the capillary tube correctly • Adjust the thermostat
Low side low—high side low	• System refrigerant is low • Expansion valve is restricted	• Evacuate, leak test and charge the system • Replace the expansion valve
Low side high—high side low	• Internal leak in the compressor—worn	• Remove the compressor cylinder head and inspect the compressor. Replace the valve plate assembly if necessary. If the compressor pistons, rings or
Low side high—high side low (cont.)	 • Cylinder head gasket is leaking • Expansion valve is defective • Drive belt slipping	cylinders are excessively worn or scored replace the compressor • Install a replacement cylinder head gasket • Replace the expansion valve • Adjust the belt tension
Low side high—high side high	• Condenser fins obstructed • Air in the system • Expansion valve is defective • Loose or worn fan belts	• Clean the condenser fins • Evacuate, leak test and charge the system • Replace the expansion valve • Adjust or replace the belts as necessary
Low side low—high side high	• Expansion valve is defective • Restriction in the refrigerant hose	• Replace the expansion valve • Check the hose for kinks—replace if necessary
Low side low—high side high	• Restriction in the receiver/drier • Restriction in the condenser	• Replace the receiver/drier • Replace the condenser
Low side and high normal (inadequate cooling)	• Air in the system • Moisture in the system	• Evacuate, leak test and charge the system • Evacuate, leak test and charge the system

Troubleshooting Basic Wheel Problems

Problem	Cause	Solution
The car's front end vibrates at high speed	• The wheels are out of balance • Wheels are out of alignment	• Have wheels balanced • Have wheel alignment checked/adjusted
Car pulls to either side	• Wheels are out of alignment • Unequal tire pressure • Different size tires or wheels	• Have wheel alignment checked/adjusted • Check/adjust tire pressure • Change tires or wheels to same size
The car's wheel(s) wobbles	• Loose wheel lug nuts • Wheels out of balance • Damaged wheel • Wheels are out of alignment • Worn or damaged ball joint • Excessive play in the steering linkage (usually due to worn parts) • Defective shock absorber	• Tighten wheel lug nuts • Have tires balanced • Raise car and spin the wheel. If the wheel is bent, it should be replaced • Have wheel alignment checked/adjusted • Check ball joints • Check steering linkage • Check shock absorbers
Tires wear unevenly or prematurely	• Incorrect wheel size • Wheels are out of balance • Wheels are out of alignment	• Check if wheel and tire size are compatible • Have wheels balanced • Have wheel alignment checked/adjusted

Troubleshooting Basic Tire Problems

Problem	Cause	Solution
The car's front end vibrates at high speeds and the steering wheel shakes	• Wheels out of balance • Front end needs aligning	• Have wheels balanced • Have front end alignment checked
The car pulls to one side while cruising	• Unequal tire pressure (car will usually pull to the low side) • Mismatched tires • Front end needs aligning	• Check/adjust tire pressure • Be sure tires are of the same type and size • Have front end alignment checked
Abnormal, excessive or uneven tire wear See ''How to Read Tire Wear''	• Infrequent tire rotation • Improper tire pressure • Sudden stops/starts or high speed on curves	• Rotate tires more frequently to equalize wear • Check/adjust pressure • Correct driving habits
Tire squeals	• Improper tire pressure • Front end needs aligning	• Check/adjust tire pressure • Have front end alignment checked

Tire Size Comparison Chart

"60 Series"	"70 Series"	"78 Series"	1965–77	"60 Series"	"70 Series"	"80 Series"
"Letter" sizes			Inch Sizes	Metric-inch Sizes		
		Y78-12	5.50-12, 5.60-12 6.00-12	165/60-12	165/70-12	155-12
		W78-13	5.20-13	165/60-13	145/70-13	135-13
		Y78-13	5.60-13	175/60-13	155/70-13	145-13
			6.15-13	185/60-13	165/70-13	155-13, P155/80-13
A60-13	A70-13	A78-13	6.40-13	195/60-13	175/70-13	165-13
B60-13	B70-13	B78-13	6.70-13	205/60-13	185/70-13	175-13
			6.90-13			
C60-13	C70-13	C78-13	7.00-13	215/60-13	195/70-13	185-13
D60-13	D70-13	D78-13	7.25-13			
E60-13	E70-13	E78-13	7.75-13			195-13
			5.20-14	165/60-14	145/70-14	135-14
			5.60-14	175/60-14	155/70-14	145-14
			5.90-14			
A60-14	A70-14	A78-14	6.15-14	185/60-14	165/70-14	155-14
	B70-14	B78-14	6.45-14	195/60-14	175/70-14	165-14
	C70-14	C78-14	6.95-14	205/60-14	185/70-14	175-14
D60-14	D70-14	D78-14				
E60-14	E70-14	E78-14	7.35-14	215/60-14	195/70-14	185-14
F60-14	F70-14	F78-14, F83-14	7.75-14	225/60-14	200/70-14	195-14
G60-14	G70-14	G77-14, G78-14	8.25-14	235/60-14	205/70-14	205-14
H60-14	H70-14	H78-14	8.55-14	245/60-14	215/70-14	215-14
J60-14	J70-14	J78-14	8.85-14	255/60-14	225/70-14	225-14
L60-14	L70-14		9.15-14	265/60-14	235/70-14	
	A70-15	A78-15	5.60-15	185/60-15	165/70-15	155-15
B60-15	B70-15	B78-15	6.35-15	195/60-15	175/70-15	165-15
C60-15	C70-15	C78-15	6.85-15	205/60-15	185/70-15	175-15
	D70-15	D78-15				
E60-15	E70-15	E78-15	7.35-15	215/60-15	195/70-15	185-15
F60-15	F70-15	F78-15	7.75-15	225/60-15	205/70-15	195-15
G60-15	G70-15	G78-15	8.15-15/8.25-15	235/60-15	215/70-15	205-15
H60-15	H70-15	H78-15	8.45-15/8.55-15	245/60-15	225/70-15	215-15
J60-15	J70-15	J78-15	8.85-15/8.90-15	255/60-15	235/70-15	225-15
	K70-15		9.00-15	265/60-15	245/70-15	230-15
L60-15	L70-15	L78-15, L84-15	9.15-15			235-15
	M70-15	M78-15				255-15
		N78-15				

NOTE: Every size tire is not listed and many size comaprisons are approximate, based on load ratings. Wider tires than those supplied new with the vehicle should always be checked for clearance

2

ENGINE PERFORMANCE AND TUNE-UP

TUNE-UP SPECIFICATIONS

Year	VIN	No. Cylinder Displacement cu. in. (liter)	Spark Plugs Gap (in.)	Ignition Timing (deg.) MT	Ignition Timing (deg.) AT	Compression Pressure (psi)	Fuel Pump (psi)	Idle Speed (rpm) MT	Idle Speed (rpm) AT	Valve Clearance In.	Valve Clearance Ex.
1982	G	4-110 (1.8)	0.045①	12B	12B	NA	4.5–6.0	②	②	Hyd.	Hyd.
	B	4-122 (2.0)	②	②	②	NA	4.5–6.0	②	②	Hyd.	Hyd.
1983	0	4-110 (1.8)	0.060	8	8B	NA	9–13	②	②	Hyd.	Hyd.
	J	4-110 (1.8)	0.035	②	②	NA	30–40	②	②	Hyd.	Hyd.
	P	4-121 (2.0)	0.035	②	②	NA	12	②	②	Hyd.	Hyd.
	B	4-121 (2.0)	0.035	—	12B	NA	12	②	②	Hyd.	Hyd.
1984	0	4-110 (1.8)	0.060	8	8B	NA	9–13	②	②	Hyd.	Hyd.
	J	4-110 (1.8)	0.035	②	②	NA	30–40	②	②	Hyd.	Hyd.
	P	4-121 (2.0)	0.035	②	②	NA	12	②	②	Hyd.	Hyd.
1985	0	4-110 (1.8)	0.060	8	8B	NA	9–13	②	②	Hyd.	Hyd.
	J	4-110 (1.8)	0.035	②	②	NA	30–40	②	②	Hyd.	Hyd.
	P	4-121 (2.0)	0.035	②	②	NA	12	②	②	Hyd.	Hyd.
	W	6-173 (2.8)	0.045	②	②	NA	40.5–47	②	②	Hyd.	Hyd.
1986	0	4-110 (1.8)	0.060	8	8B	NA	9–13	②	②	Hyd.	Hyd.
	J	4-110 (1.8)	0.035	②	②	NA	30–40	②	②	Hyd.	Hyd.
	P	4-121 (2.0)	0.035	②	②	NA	12	②	②	Hyd.	Hyd.
	W	6-173 (2.8)	0.045	②	②	NA	40.5–47	②	②	Hyd.	Hyd.
1987	M	4-121 (2.0)	0.060	②	②	NA	35–38	②	②	Hyd.	Hyd.
	1	4-121 (2.0)	0.035	②	②	NA	10–12	②	②	Hyd.	Hyd.
	K	4-121 (2.0)	0.060	②	②	NA	10	②	②	Hyd.	Hyd.
	W	6-173 (2.8)	0.045	②	②	NA	40.5–47	②	②	Hyd.	Hyd.
1988	M	4-121 (2.0)	0.035	②	②	NA	35–38	②	②	Hyd.	Hyd.
	1	4-121 (2.0)	0.035	②	②	NA	9–13	②	②	Hyd.	Hyd.
	K	4-121 (2.0)	0.060	②	②	NA	9–13	②	②	Hyd.	Hyd.
	W	6-173 (2.8)	0.045	②	②	NA	40.5–47	②	②	Hyd.	Hyd.
1989	M	4-121 (2.0)	0.035	②	②	NA	35–38	②	②	Hyd.	Hyd.
	1	4-121 (2.0)	0.035	②	②	NA	9–13	②	②	Hyd.	Hyd.
	K	4-121 (2.0)	0.060	②	②	NA	9–13	②	②	Hyd.	Hyd.
	W	6-173 (2.8)	0.045	②	②	NA	40.5–47	②	②	Hyd.	Hyd.
1990	K	4-121 (2.0)	0.045	②	②	NA	9–13	②	②	Hyd.	Hyd.
	M	4-121 (2.0)	0.035	②	②	NA	35–38	②	②	Hyd.	Ex.
	G	4-134 (2.2)	0.035	②	②	NA	9–13	②	②	Hyd.	Hyd.
	T	6-192 (3.1)	0.045	②	②	NA	40.5–47	②	②	Hyd.	Hyd.
1991	K	4-121 (2.0)	0.045	②	②	NA	9–13	②	②	Hyd.	Hyd.
	G	4-134 (2.2)	0.035	②	②	NA	9–13	②	②	Hyd.	Hyd.
	T	6-192 (3.1)	0.045	②	②	NA	40.5–47	②	②	Hyd.	Hyd.
1992	H	4-121 (2.0)	0.045	②	②	NA	41–47	②	②	Hyd.	Hyd.
	4	4-134 (2.2)	0.045	②	②	NA	40.5–47	②	②	Hyd.	Hyd.
	T	6-192 (3.1)	0.045	②	②	NA	40.5–47	②	②	Hyd.	Hyd.

NOTE: The underhood specifications sticker often reflects tune-up specification changes in production. Sticker figures must be used if they disagree with those in this chart.

Part numbers in this chart are not recommendations by Chilton for any product by brand name

B—Before top dead center

NA—Not available

① Certain models may use 0.035 in. gap. See underhood specifications sticker to be sure

② See underhood specifications sticker

TUNE-UP PROCEDURES

In order to extract the full measure of performance and economy from your car's engine it is essential that it be properly tuned at regular intervals. Although the tune-up intervals have been stretched to limits which would have been thought impossible a few years ago, periodic maintenance is still required. A regularly scheduled tune-up will keep your car's engine running smoothly and will prevent the annoying minor breakdowns and poor performance associated with an untuned engine.

A complete tune-up should be performed at the interval specified in the Maintenance Intervals chart in Section 1. This interval should be halved if the car is operated under severe conditions, such as trailer towing, prolonged idling, continual stop-and-start driving, or if starting and running problems are noticed. It is assumed that the routine maintenance described in the first section has been kept up, as this will have a decided effect on the results of a tune-up. All of the applicable steps should be followed in order, as the result is a cumulative one.

If the specifications on the tune-up label in the engine compartment of your vehicle disagree with the Tune-Up Specifications chart in this section, the figures on the sticker must be used. The label often reflects changes made during the production run.

Spark Plugs

♦ SEE FIGS. 1-6

Spark plugs ignite the air and fuel mixture in the cylinder as the piston reaches the top of the compression stroke. The controlled explosion that results forces the piston down, turning the crankshaft and the rest of the drive train.

The average life of a spark plug in your vehicle is 30,000 miles. Part of the reason for this extraordinarily long life is the exclusive use of unleaded fuel, which reduces the amount of deposits within the combustion chamber and on the spark plug electrodes themselves, compared with the deposits left by the leaded gasoline used in the past. An additional contribution to long life is made by the HEI (High Energy Ignition) System, which fires the spark plugs with over 35,000 volts of electricity. The high voltage serves to keep the electrodes clear, and because it is a cleaner blast of electricity than that produced by conventional breaker-points ignitions, the electrodes suffer less pitting and wear.

Nevertheless, the life of a spark plug is dependent on a number of factors, including the

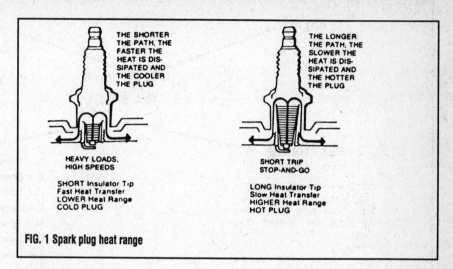

FIG. 1 Spark plug heat range

mechanical condition of the engine, driving conditions, and the driver's habits.

When you remove the plugs, check the condition of the electrodes; they are a good indicator of the internal state of the engine. Since the spark plug wires should be checked every 15,000 miles, the spark plugs can be removed and examined at the same time. This will allow you to keep an eye on the mechanical status of the engine.

A small deposit of light tan or rust-red material on a spark plug that has been used for any period of time is to be considered normal. Any other color, or abnormal amounts of wear or deposits, indicates that there is something amiss in the engine.

The gap between the center electrode and the side or ground electrode can be expected to increase not more than 0.001 in. every 1,000 miles under normal conditions.

When a spark plug is functioning normally or, more accurately, when the plug is installed in an engine that is functioning properly, the plugs can be taken out, cleaned, regapped, and reinstalled in the engine without doing the engine any harm.

When, and if, a plug fouls and begins to misfire, you will have to investigate, correct the cause of the fouling, and either clean or replace the plug.

There are several reasons why a spark plug will foul and you can learn which is at fault by just looking at the plug. A few of the most common reasons for plug fouling, and a description of the fouled plug's appearance, are shown in the Color Insert section.

Spark plugs suitable for use in your car's engine are offered in a number of different heat ranges. The amount of heat which the plug absorbs is determined by the length of the lower insulator. The longer the insulator, the hotter the plug will operate; the shorter the insulator, the cooler it will operate. A spark plug that absorbs (or retains) little heat and remains too cool will accumulate deposits of oil and carbon, because it is not hot enough to burn them off. This leads to fouling and consequent misfiring. A spark plug that absorbs too much heat will have no deposits, but the electrodes will burn away quickly and, in some cases, pre-ignition may result. Pre-ignition occurs when the spark plug tips get so hot that they ignite the fuel/mixture before the actual spark fires. This premature ignition will usually cause a pinging sound under conditions of low speed and heavy load. In severe cases, the heat may become high enough to start the fuel/air mixture burning throughout the combustion chamber rather than just to the front of the plug. In this case, the resultant explosion (detonation) will be strong enough to damage pistons, rings, and valves.

In most cases the factory recommended heat range is correct; it is chosen to perform well under a wide range of operating conditions. However, if most of your driving is long distance, high speed travel, you may want to install a spark plug one step colder than standard. If most of your driving is of the short trip variety, when the engine may not always reach operating temperature, a hotter plug may help burn off the deposits normally accumulated under those conditions.

REMOVAL

1. Number the wires with pieces of adhesive tape so that you won't cross them when you replace them.

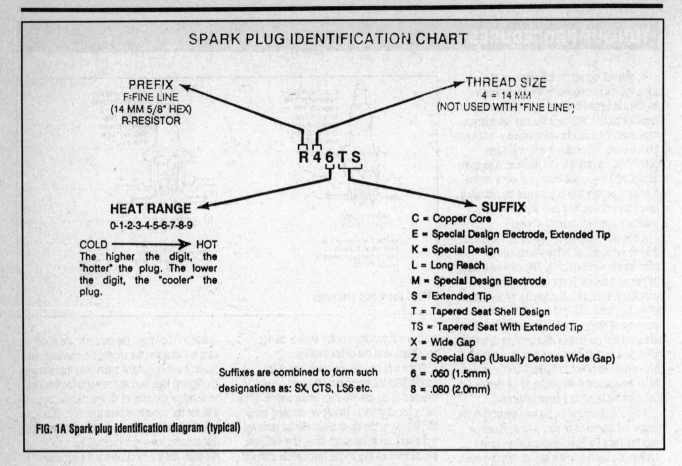

SPARK PLUG IDENTIFICATION CHART

PREFIX
F=FINE LINE
(14 MM 5/8" HEX)
R-RESISTOR

THREAD SIZE
4 = 14 MM
(NOT USED WITH "FINE LINE")

R 4 6 T S

HEAT RANGE
0-1-2-3-4-5-6-7-8-9

COLD ──────→ HOT
The higher the digit, the "hotter" the plug. The lower the digit, the "cooler" the plug.

SUFFIX
C = Copper Core
E = Special Design Electrode, Extended Tip
K = Special Design
L = Long Reach
M = Special Design Electrode
S = Extended Tip
T = Tapered Seat Shell Design
TS = Tapered Seat With Extended Tip
X = Wide Gap
Z = Special Gap (Usually Denotes Wide Gap)
6 = .060 (1.5mm)
8 = .080 (2.0mm)

Suffixes are combined to form such designations as: SX, CTS, LS6 etc.

FIG. 1A Spark plug identification diagram (typical)

2. The spark plug boots have large grips to aid in removal. Grasp the wire by the rubber boot and twist the boot 1/2 turn in either direction to break the tight seal between the boot and the plug. Then twist and pull on the boot to remove the wire from the spark plug. DO NOT PULL ON THE SPARK PLUG WIRE ITSELF OR YOU WILL DAMAGE THE CARBON CORD CONDUCTOR.

3. Use a 5/8 in. spark plug socket to loosen all of the plugs about two turns. A universal joint installed at the socket end of the extension will ease the process.

If removal of the plugs is difficult, apply a few drops of penetrating oil or silicone spray to the area around the base of the plug, and allow it a few minutes to work.

4. If compressed air is available, apply it to the area around the spark plug holes. Otherwise, use a rag or a brush to clean the area. Be careful not to allow any foreign material to drop into the spark plug holes.

5. Remove the plugs by unscrewing them the rest of the way.

INSPECTION

Check the plugs for deposits and wear. If they are not going to be replaced, clean the plugs thoroughly. Remember that any kind of deposit will decrease the efficiency of the plug. Plugs can be cleaned on a spark plug cleaning machine, which can sometimes be found in service stations, or you can do an acceptable job of cleaning with a stiff brush. If the plugs are cleaned, the electrodes must be filed flat. use an ignition points file, not an emery board or the like, which will leave deposits. The electrodes must be filed perfectly flat with sharp edges; rounded edges reduce the spark plug voltage by as much as 50%.

Check spark plug gap before installation. The ground electrode (the L-shaped one connected to the body of the plug) must be parallel to the center electrode and the specified size wire gauge (see Tune-Up Specifications) should pass through the gap with a slight drag. Always check the gap on new plugs, too; they are not always set correctly at the factory. Do not use a flat feeler gauge when measuring the gap, because the reading will be inaccurate. Wire gapping tools usually have a bending tool attached. Use that to adjust the side electrode until the proper distance is obtained. Absolutely never bend the center electrode. Also, be careful not to bend the side electrode too far or too often; it may weaken and break off within the engine, requiring removal of the cylinder head to retrieve it.

INSTALLATION

1. Lubricate the threads of the spark plugs with a drop of oil or a shot of silicone spray. ALWAYS INSTALL THE SPARK PLUGS AND TIGHTEN THEM HAND TIGHT FIRST. Take care not to cross-thread them.

2. Tighten the spark plugs with the socket. Do not apply the same amount of force you would use for a bolt; just snug them in. These spark plugs do nut use gaskets, and over-tightening will make future removal difficult. If a torque wrench is available, tighten to 7-15 ft. lbs.

➡ **While over-tightening the spark plug is to be avoided, under-tightening is just as bad. If combustion gases leak past the threads, the spark plug will overheat and rapid electrode wear will result.**

3. Install the wires on their respective plugs. Make sure the wires are firmly connected. You will be able to feel them click into place.

FIG. 2 Twist and pull on the rubber boot to remove the spark plug wires; never pull on the wire itself.

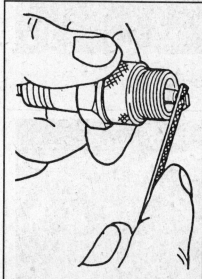

FIG. 3 Plugs that are in good condition can be filed and reused

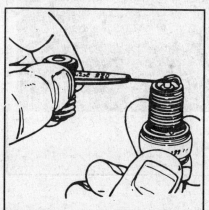

FIG. 4 Always use a wire gauge to check the electrode gap

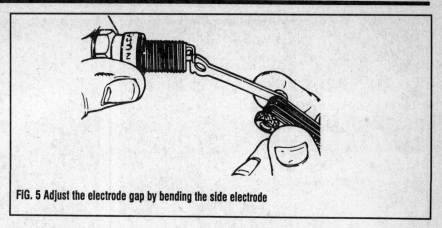

FIG. 5 Adjust the electrode gap by bending the side electrode

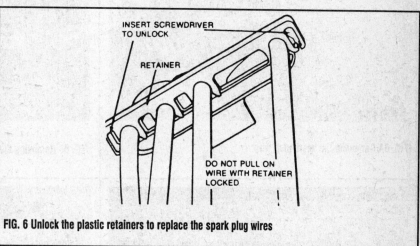

INSERT SCREWDRIVER TO UNLOCK

RETAINER

DO NOT PULL ON WIRE WITH RETAINER LOCKED

FIG. 6 Unlock the plastic retainers to replace the spark plug wires

CHECKING AND REPLACING SPARK PLUG WIRES

Every 15,000 miles, inspect the spark plug wires for burns, cuts, or breaks in the insulation. Check the boots and the nipples on the distributor cap. Replace any damaged wiring.

Every 45,000 miles or so, the resistance of the wires should be checked with an ohmmeter. Wires with excessive resistance will cause misfiring, and may make the engine difficult to start in damp weather. Generally, the useful life of the cables is 45,000-60,000 miles.

To check resistance, remove the distributor cap, leaving the wires in place. Connect one lead of an ohmmeter to an electrode within the cap; connect the other lead to the corresponding spark plug terminal (remove it from the spark plug for this test). Replace any wire which shows a resistance over 30,000Ω. The following chart gives resistance values as a function of

length. Generally speaking, however, resistance should not be considered the outer limit of acceptability.

- 0-15 in.: 3,000-10,000Ω
- 15-25 in.: 4,000-15,000Ω
- 25-35 in.: 6,000-20,000Ω
- Over 35 in.: 25,000Ω

It should be remembered that resistance is also a function of length; the longer the wire, the greater the resistance. Thus, if the wires on your car are longer than the factory originals, resistance will be higher, quite possible outside these limits.

WHEN INSTALLING NEW WIRES, REPLACE THEM ONE AT A TIME TO AVOID MIXUPS. START BY REPLACING THE LONGEST ONE FIRST.

Install the boot firmly over the spark plug. Route the wire over the same path as the original. Insert the nipple firmly onto the tower on the distributor cap, then install the cap cover and latches to secure the wires.

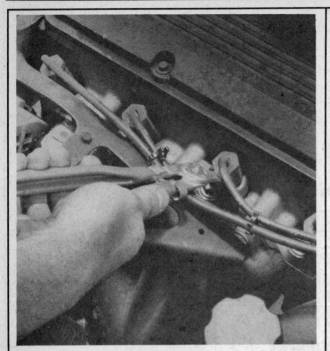

FIG. 6A Removing the spark plug wire

FIG. 6B Removing the spark plug wire

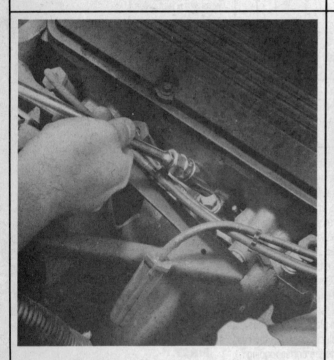

FIG. 6C Removing the spark plug

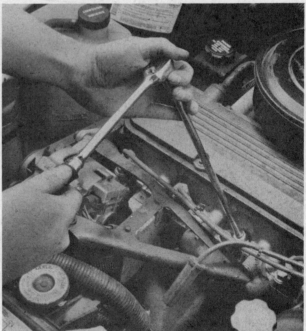

FIG. 6D Removing the spark plug

FIG. 6E Removing the spark plug

FIG. 6F Removing the spark plug

FIRING ORDERS

♦ SEE FIGS. 7-11

To avoid confusion, replace the spark plug wires one at a time.

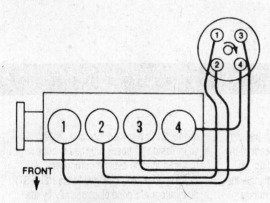

FIG. 7 1.8L, 110 cu. in. (VIN CODE G), 1982
2.0L, 122 cu. in. (VIN CODE B & P), 1983–86
4 cylinder, overhead valve engine
Firing order: 1–3–4–2
Distributor rotation: clockwise

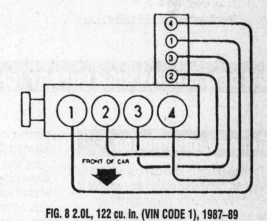

FIG. 8 2.0L, 122 cu. in. (VIN CODE 1), 1987–89
2.2L, 134 cu. in. (VIN CODE G and 4), 1990–92
4 cylinder, overhead valve engine
Firing order: 1–3–4–2
Distributorless

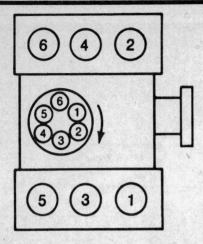

FIG. 9 2.8L, 173 cu. in. (VIN CODE W) 1985–86
V6 overhead valve engine
Firing order: 1–2–3–4–5–6
Distributor rotation: clockwise

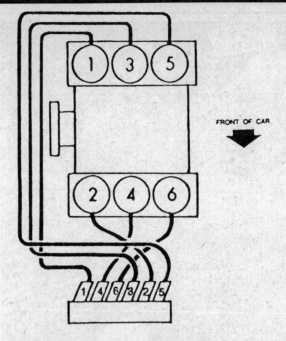

FIG. 10 2.8L, 173 cu. in. (VIN CODE W) 1987–89
3.1L, 192 cu. in. (VIN CODE T) 1990–92
V6 overhead valve engine
Firing order: 1–2–3–4–5–6
Distributorless

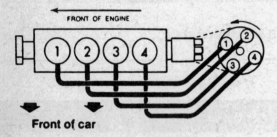

FIG. 11 1.8L, 110 cu. in. (VIN CODE O & J), 1983–86
2.0L, 122 cu. in. (VIN CODE M & K), 1987–91
4 cylinder, overhead cam engine
Firing order: 1–3–4–2
Distributor rotation: counterclockwise

GM DELCO-REMY HIGH ENERGY IGNITION (HEI)

General Information

The High Energy Ignition distributor is used on all engines. The ignition coil is either mounted to the top of the distributor cap or is externally mounted on the engine, having a secondary circuit high tension wire connecting the coil to the distributor cap and interconnecting primary wiring as part of the engine harness.

The High Energy Ignition distributor is equipped to aid in spark timing changes, necessary for Emissions, Economy and performance. This system is called the Electronic Spark Timing Control (EST). The HEI distributors use a magnetic pick-up assembly, located inside the distributor containing a permanent magnet, a pole piece with internal teeth and a pick-up coil. When the teeth of the rotating timer core and pole piece align, an induced voltage in the pick-up coil signals the electronic module to open the coil primary circuit. As the primary current decreases, a high voltage is induced in the secondary windings of the ignition coil, directing a spark through the rotor and high voltage leads to fire the spark plugs. The dwell period is automatically controlled by the electronic module and is increased with increasing engine rpm. The HEI System features a longer spark duration which is instrumental in firing lean and EGR (Exhaust Gas Recirculation) diluted fuel/air mixtures. The condenser (capacitor) located within the HEI distributor is provided for noise (static) suppression purposes only and is not a regularly replaced ignition system component.

All spark timing changes in the HEI (EST) distributors are done electronically by the Electronic Control Module (ECM), which monitors information from the various engine sensors, computes the desired spark timing and signals the distributor to change the timing accordingly. With this distributor, no vacuum or centrifugal advances are used.

Electronic Ignition/Fuel Injection System Application Chart

Manufacturer	Year	Model	Engine cu. in. (liter)	VIN	Electronic Ignition System	Fuel Injection System
Buick	1982–86	Skyhawk	110 (1.8)	O	HEI/EST	TBI
			110 (1.8)	J	HEI/EST	MPI-Turbo
			122 (2.0)	P	HEI/EST	TBI
	1987–89	Skyhawk	122 (2.0)	K	HEI/EST	TBI
			122 (2.0)	M	HEI/EST	MPI
			122 (2.0) HO	1	HEI/EST	TBI
Cadillac	1982–85	Cimarron	122 (2.0)	P	HEI/EST	TBI
	1986	Cimarron	122 (2.0)	P	HEI/EST	TBI
			173 (2.8)	W	HEI/EST	MPI
	1987–88	Cimarron	173 (2.8)	W	HEI/EST	MPI
Chevrolet	1982–86	Cavalier	122 (2.0)	P	HEI/EST	TBI
	1985–86	Cavalier	173 (2.8)	W	HEI/EST	MPI
	1987–89	Cavalier	122 (2.0)	1	DIS	TBI
			173 (2.8)	W	DIS	MPI
	1990–91	Cavalier	134 (2.2)	G	DIS	TBI
			192 (3.1)	T	DIS	MPI
Oldsmobile	1982–86	Firenza	110 (1.8)	O	HEI/EST	TBI
			122 (2.0)	P	HEI/EST	TBI
	1986–87	Firenza	173 (2.8)	W	HEI/EST	MPI
	1987–88	Firenza	122 (2.0)	K	HEI/EST	TBI
			122 (2.0) HO	1	HEI/EST	TBI
Pontiac	1982–84	2000, Sunbird	110 (1.8)	O	HEI/EST	MPI-Turbo
			110 (1.8)	J	HEI/EST	TBI
			122 (2.0)	P	HEI/EST	TBI
	1985–86	Sunbird	110 (1.8)		HEI/EST	MPI-Turbo
			110 (1.)		HEI/EST	TBI
	1987–91	Sunbird				MPI-Turbo

HEI SYSTEM PRECAUTIONS

Before going on to troubleshooting, it might be a good idea to take note of the following precautions:

Timing Light Use

Inductive pick-up timing lights are the best kind of use with HEI. Timing light which connect between the spark plug and the spark plug wire occasionally (not always) give false readings.

Spark Plug Wires

The plug wires used with HEI systems are of a different construction than conventional wires. When replacing them, make sure you get the correct wires, since conventional wires won't carry the voltage. Also, handle them carefully to avoid cracking or splitting them and never pierce them.

Tachometer Use

Not all tachometers will operate or indicate correctly when used on a HEI system. While some tachometers may give a reading, this does not necessarily mean the reading is correct. In addition, some tachometers hook up differently from others. If you can't figure out whether or not your tachometer will work on your car, check with the tachometer manufacturer. Dwell readings, or course, have no significance at all.

HEI System Testers

Instruments designed specifically for testing HEI systems are available from several tool manufacturers. Some of these will even test the module itself.

Troshooting

➡ An accu
step to prob step to pro
For several of nosis is the first
HEI spark teste and repair.
has a spring clip steps, a
ground. Use of this which
recommended, as th
control of the high ene
and less chance of being
If a tachometer is connect
TACH terminal on the distri
disconnect it before proceedi
with this test.

SECONDARY CIRCUIT

Testing

SECONDARY SPARK

1. Check for spark at the spark plugs by attaching the HEI spark tester, tool ST 125, to one of the plug wires, grounding the HEI spark tester on the engine and cranking the starter.

2. If no spark occurs on one wire, check a second. If spark is present, the HEI system is good.

3. Check fuel system, plug wires, and spark plugs.

4. If no spark occurs from EST distributor, disconnect the 4 terminal EST connector and recheck for spark. If spark is present, EST system service check should be performed.

➡ **Before making any circuit checks with test meters, be sure that all primary circuit connectors are properly installed and that spark plug cables are secure at the distributor and at the plugs.**

Distributor Component Testing

DISTRIBUTOR WITH SEPARATE COIL TYPE ONE

◆ SEE FIG. 12

➡ **This type distributor has no vacuum or centrifugal advance mechanism and has the pick-up coil mounted above the module.**

This distributor is used with the EST system.

Testing

IGNITION COIL
◆ SEE FIG. 13

1. Disconnect the primary wiring connectors and secondary coil wire from the ignition coil.

2. Using an ohmmeter on the high scale, connect one lead to a grounding screw and the second lead to one of the primary coil terminals.

3. The reading should be infinite. If not, replace the ignition coil.

4. Using the low scale, place the ohmmeter leads on both the primary coil terminals.

5. The reading should be very low or zero. If not, replace the ignition coil.

6. Using the high scale, place one ohmmeter lead on the high tension output terminal and the other lead on a primary coil terminal.

7. The reading should NOT be infinite. If it is, replace the ignition coil.

Testing

PICK-UP COIL
◆ SEE FIG. 14

1. Remove the rotor and pick-up coil leads from the module.

2. Using an ohmmeter, attach one lead to the distributor base and the second lead to one of the pick-up coil terminals of the connector.

3. The reading should be infinite at all times.

4. Position both leads of the ohmmeter to the pick-up terminal ends of the connector.

5. The reading should be a steady value between 500-1500Ω.

6. If not within the specification value, the pick-up coil is defective.

➡ **While testing, flex the leads to determine if wire breaks are present under the wiring insulation.**

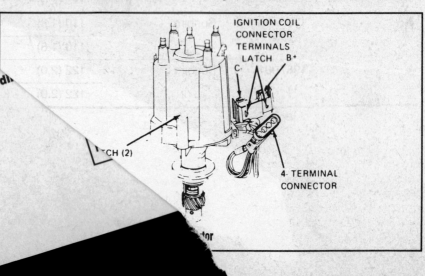

IGNITION COIL CONNECTOR TERMINALS LATCH B+

C

CH (2)

4- TERMINAL CONNECTOR

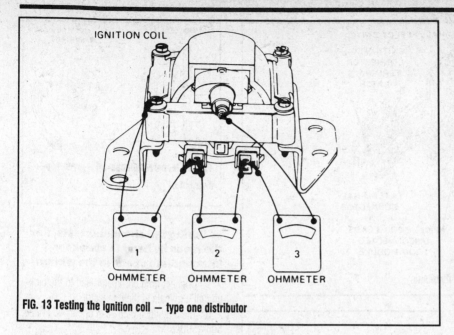

FIG. 13 Testing the ignition coil — type one distributor

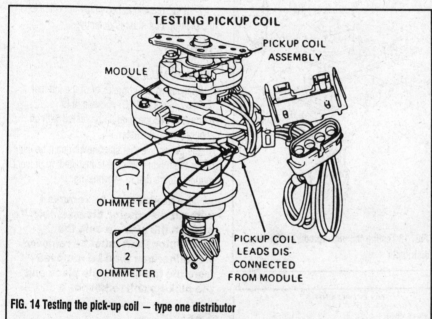

FIG. 14 Testing the pick-up coil — type one distributor

IGNITION MODULE

Because of the complexity of the internal circuitry of the HEI/EST module, it is recommended the module be tested with an accurate module tester.

It is imperative that silicone lubricant be used under the module when it is installed, to prevent module failure due to overheating.

➡ **The module and the Hall Effect switch (if used) can be removed from the distributor without disassembly. To remove up coil, the distributor be removed to expo retaining ring (C-w the pick-up coil in**

HALL EFFECT SWITCH

The Hall Effect Switch, in the HEI distributor is to sense engi information

switch connectors from the

a 12 volt battery and voltmeter to the switch. Note and follow the polarity markings.

3. With a knife blade inserted straight down and against the magnet, the voltmeter should read within 0.5 volts of battery voltage. If not, the switch is defective.

4. Without the knife blade inserted against the magnet, the voltmeter should read less than 0.5 volts. If not, the switch is defective.

DISTRIBUTOR WITH SEPARATE COIL TYPE TWO

◆ SEE FIG. 16

➡ **This type distributor has no vacuum or centrifugal advance mechanisms and the module has two outside terminal connections for the wiring harness. This distributor is used with the EST system.**

Testing

IGNITION COIL

◆ SEE FIG. 17

1. Using an ohmmeter set on the high scale, place one lead on a ground of the ignition coil.

2. Place the second lead into one of the rearward terminals of the ignition coil primary connector.

3. The ohmmeter scale should read infinite. If not, replace the ignition coil.

4. Using the low scale, place the ohmmeter leads into each of the outer terminals of the coil connector.

5. The reading should be or very low. If not, replace the igniti place one ohmmeter terminal and the

6. Using the rearward terminal of the lead on th connector.
secor ding should not be infinite. If so, e ignition coil.

sting

PICK-UP COIL

◆ SEE FIGS. 18–20

1. Remove the rotor and pick-up leads from the module.

2. Using an ohmmeter, connect one of the leads to the distributor base.

3. Connect the second lead to one of the pick-up coil lead terminals

4. The reading should be infinite. If not, the pick-up coil is defective.

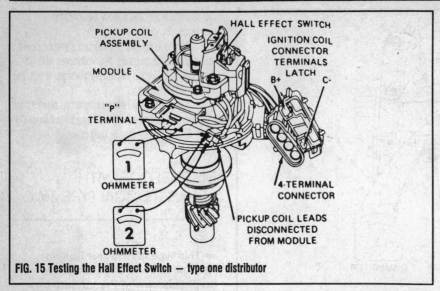

FIG. 15 Testing the Hall Effect Switch — type one distributor

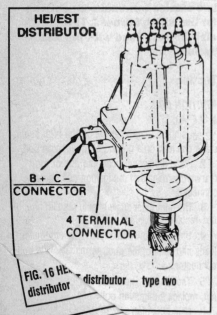

FIG. 16 HEI ... distributor — type two distributor

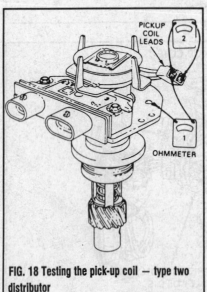

FIG. 18 Testing the pick-up coil — type two distributor

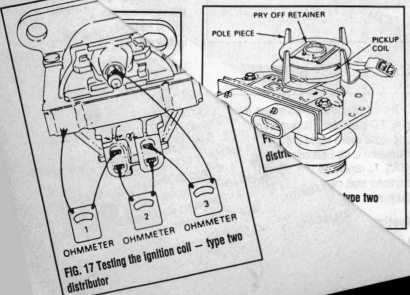

FIG. 17 Testing the ignition coil — type two distributor

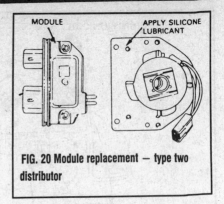

FIG. 20 Module replacement — type two distributor

➡ **During the ohmmeter tests, flex the leads by hand to check for intermediate opens in the wiring.**

5. Connect both ohmmeter lead to the pick-up coil terminals at the connector.

6. The reading should be of one steady value, 500-1500Ω.

7. If the reading is not within specifications, the pick-up coil must is defective.

Testing

IGNITION MODULE

Because of the complexity of the internal circuitry of the HEI/EST module, it is recommended the module be tested with an accurate module tester.

It is imperative that silicone lubricant be used under the module when it is installed, to prevent module failure due to overheating.

➡ **The module can be removed without distributor disassembly. To remove the pick-up coil, the distributor shaft must be removed. A retainer can then be removed from the top of the pole piece and the pick-up coil removed.**

DISTRIBUTOR WITH SEPARATE COIL TYPE THREE W/TANG DRIVE

◆ SEE FIG. 21

➡ **This distributor is used with the EST system. The unit is mounted horizontally to the valve cover housing and is driven by the camshaft, through a tang on the distributor shaft.**

Electronic Ignition/Fuel Injection System Application Chart

Manufacturer	Year	Model	Engine cu. in. (liter)	VIN	Electronic Ignition System	Fuel Injection System
Buick	1982–86	Skyhawk	110 (1.8)	O	HEI/EST	TBI
			110 (1.8)	J	HEI/EST	MPI-Turbo
			122 (2.0)	P	HEI/EST	TBI
	1987–89	Skyhawk	122 (2.0)	K	HEI/EST	TBI
			122 (2.0)	M	HEI/EST	MPI
			122 (2.0) HO	1	HEI/EST	TBI
Cadillac	1982–85	Cimarron	122 (2.0)	P	HEI/EST	TBI
	1986	Cimarron	122 (2.0)	P	HEI/EST	TBI
			173 (2.8)	W	HEI/EST	MPI
	1987–88	Cimarron	173 (2.8)	W	HEI/EST	MPI
Chevrolet	1982–86	Cavalier	122 (2.0)	P	HEI/EST	TBI
	1985–86	Cavalier	173 (2.8)	W	HEI/EST	MPI
	1987–89	Cavalier	122 (2.0)	1	DIS	TBI
			173 (2.8)	W	DIS	MPI
	1990–91	Cavalier	134 (2.2)	G	DIS	TBI
			192 (3.1)	T	DIS	MPI
Oldsmobile	1982–86	Firenza	110 (1.8)	O	HEI/EST	TBI
			122 (2.0)	P	HEI/EST	TBI
	1986–87	Firenza	173 (2.8)	W	HEI/EST	MPI
	1987–88	Firenza	122 (2.0)	K	HEI/EST	TBI
			122 (2.0) HO	1	HEI/EST	TBI
Pontiac	1982–84	2000, Sunbird	110 (1.8)	O	HEI/EST	TBI
			110 (1.8)	J	HEI/EST	MPI-Turbo
			122 (2.0)	P	HEI/EST	TBI
	1985–86	Sunbird	110 (1.8)	O	HEI/EST	TBI
			110 (1.8)	J	HEI/EST	MPI-Turbo
	1987–91	Sunbird	122 (2.0)	K	HEI/EST	TBI
			122 (2.0)	M	HEI/EST	MPI-Turbo

HEI SYSTEM PRECAUTIONS

Before going on to troubleshooting, it might be a good idea to take note of the following precautions:

Timing Light Use

Inductive pick-up timing lights are the best kind of use with HEI. Timing light which connect between the spark plug and the spark plug wire occasionally (not always) give false readings.

Spark Plug Wires

The plug wires used with HEI systems are of a different construction than conventional wires. When replacing them, make sure you get the correct wires, since conventional wires won't carry the voltage. Also, handle them carefully to avoid cracking or splitting them and never pierce them.

Tachometer Use

Not all tachometers will operate or indicate correctly when used on a HEI system. While some tachometers may give a reading, this does not necessarily mean the reading is correct. In addition, some tachometers hook up differently from others. If you can't figure out whether or not your tachometer will work on your car, check with the tachometer manufacturer. Dwell readings, or course, have no significance at all.

HEI System Testers

Instruments designed specifically for testing HEI systems are available from several tool manufacturers. Some of these will even test the module itself.

Troubleshooting

➡ **An accurate diagnosis is the first step to problem solution and repair. For several of the following steps, a HEI spark tester, tool ST 125, which has a spring clip to attach it to ground. Use of this tool is recommended, as there is more control of the high energy spark and less chance of being shocked. If a tachometer is connected to the TACH terminal on the distributor, disconnect it before proceeding with this test.**

SECONDARY CIRCUIT

Testing

SECONDARY SPARK

1. Check for spark at the spark plugs by attaching the HEI spark tester, tool ST 125, to one of the plug wires, grounding the HEI spark tester on the engine and cranking the starter.

2. If no spark occurs on one wire, check a second. If spark is present, the HEI system is good.

3. Check fuel system, plug wires, and spark plugs.

4. If no spark occurs from EST distributor, disconnect the 4 terminal EST connector and recheck for spark. If spark is present, EST system service check should be performed.

➡ **Before making any circuit checks with test meters, be sure that all primary circuit connectors are properly installed and that spark plug cables are secure at the distributor and at the plugs.**

Distributor Component Testing

DISTRIBUTOR WITH SEPARATE COIL TYPE ONE

♦ SEE FIG. 12

➡ **This type distributor has no vacuum or centrifugal advance mechanism and has the pick-up coil mounted above the module.**

This distributor is used with the EST system.

Testing

IGNITION COIL

♦ SEE FIG. 13

1. Disconnect the primary wiring connectors and secondary coil wire from the ignition coil.

2. Using an ohmmeter on the high scale, connect one lead to a grounding screw and the second lead to one of the primary coil terminals.

3. The reading should be infinite. If not, replace the ignition coil.

4. Using the low scale, place the ohmmeter leads on both the primary coil terminals.

5. The reading should be very low or zero. If not, replace the ignition coil.

6. Using the high scale, place one ohmmeter lead on the high tension output terminal and the other lead on a primary coil terminal.

7. The reading should NOT be infinite. If it is, replace the ignition coil.

Testing

PICK-UP COIL

♦ SEE FIG. 14

1. Remove the rotor and pick-up coil leads from the module.

2. Using an ohmmeter, attach one lead to the distributor base and the second lead to one of the pick-up coil terminals of the connector.

3. The reading should be infinite at all times.

4. Position both leads of the ohmmeter to the pick-up terminal ends of the connector.

5. The reading should be a steady value between 500-1500Ω.

6. If not within the specification value, the pick-up coil is defective.

➡ **While testing, flex the leads to determine if wire breaks are present under the wiring insulation.**

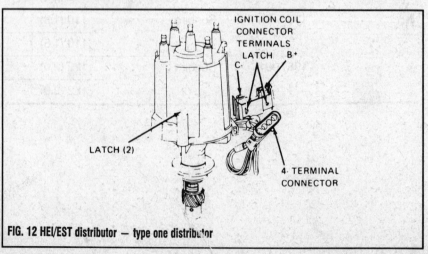

FIG. 12 HEI/EST distributor — type one distributor

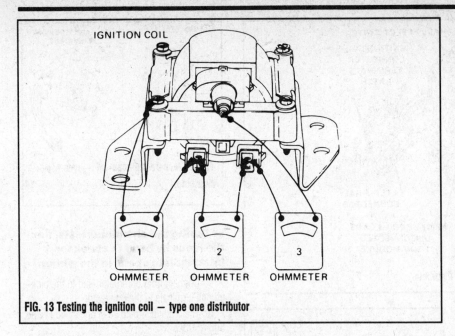

FIG. 13 Testing the ignition coil — type one distributor

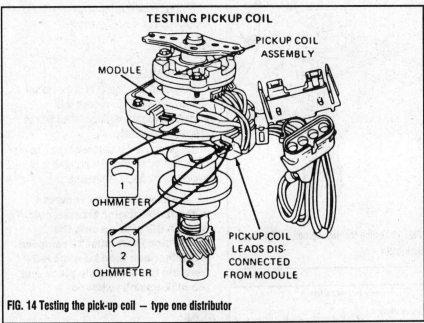

FIG. 14 Testing the pick-up coil — type one distributor

IGNITION MODULE

Because of the complexity of the internal circuitry of the HEI/EST module, it is recommended the module be tested with an accurate module tester.

It is imperative that silicone lubricant be used under the module when it is installed, to prevent module failure due to overheating.

➡ **The module and the Hall Effect switch (if used) can be removed from the distributor without disassembly. To remove the pick-up coil, the distributor shaft must be removed to expose a waved retaining ring (C-washer) holding the pick-up coil in place.**

HALL EFFECT SWITCH

The Hall Effect Switch, when used, is installed in the HEI distributor. The purpose of the switch is to sense engine speed and send the information to the Electronic Control Module (ECM). To remove the Hall Effect Switch, the distributor shaft must be removed from the distributor.

Testing

◆ SEE FIG. 15

1. Remove the switch connectors from the switch.
2. Connect a 12 volt battery and voltmeter to the switch. Note and follow the polarity markings.
3. With a knife blade inserted straight down and against the magnet, the voltmeter should read within 0.5 volts of battery voltage. If not, the switch is defective.
4. Without the knife blade inserted against the magnet, the voltmeter should read less than 0.5 volts. If not, the switch is defective.

DISTRIBUTOR WITH SEPARATE COIL TYPE TWO

◆ SEE FIG. 16

➡ **This type distributor has no vacuum or centrifugal advance mechanisms and the module has two outside terminal connections for the wiring harness. This distributor is used with the EST system.**

Testing

IGNITION COIL

◆ SEE FIG. 17

1. Using an ohmmeter set on the high scale, place one lead on a ground of the ignition coil.
2. Place the second lead into one of the rearward terminals of the ignition coil primary connector.
3. The ohmmeter scale should read infinite. If not, replace the ignition coil.
4. Using the low scale, place the ohmmeter leads into each of the outer terminals of the coil connector.
5. The reading should be zero or very low. If not, replace the ignition coil.
6. Using the high scale, place one ohmmeter lead on the coil secondary terminal and the second lead into the rearward terminal of the ignition coil primary connector.
7. The reading should not be infinite. If so, replace the ignition coil.

Testing

PICK-UP COIL

◆ SEE FIGS. 18-20

1. Remove the rotor and pick-up leads from the module.
2. Using an ohmmeter, connect one of the leads to the distributor base.
3. Connect the second lead to one of the pick-up coil lead terminals
4. The reading should be infinite. If not, the pick-up coil is defective.

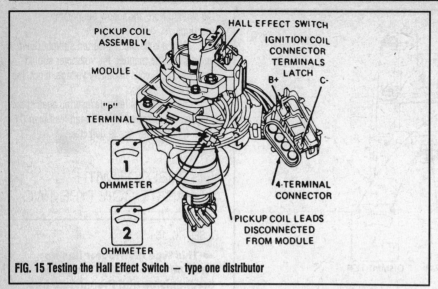

FIG. 15 Testing the Hall Effect Switch — type one distributor

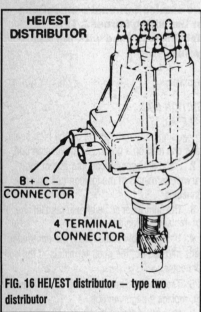

FIG. 16 HEI/EST distributor — type two distributor

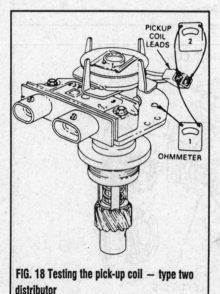

FIG. 18 Testing the pick-up coil — type two distributor

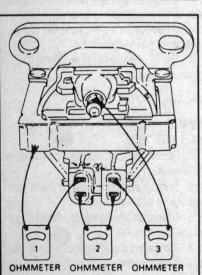

FIG. 17 Testing the ignition coil — type two distributor

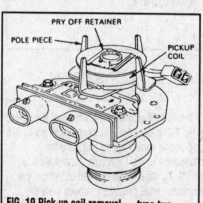

FIG. 19 Pick-up coil removal — type two distributor

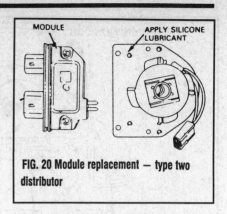

FIG. 20 Module replacement — type two distributor

➡ **During the ohmmeter tests, flex the leads by hand to check for intermediate opens in the wiring.**

5. Connect both ohmmeter lead to the pick-up coil terminals at the connector.

6. The reading should be of one steady value, 500-1500Ω.

7. If the reading is not within specifications, the pick-up coil must is defective.

Testing

IGNITION MODULE

Because of the complexity of the internal circuitry of the HEI/EST module, it is recommended the module be tested with an accurate module tester.

It is imperative that silicone lubricant be used under the module when it is installed, to prevent module failure due to overheating.

➡ **The module can be removed without distributor disassembly. To remove the pick-up coil, the distributor shaft must be removed. A retainer can then be removed from the top of the pole piece and the pick-up coil removed.**

DISTRIBUTOR WITH SEPARATE COIL TYPE THREE W/TANG DRIVE

◆ SEE FIG. 21

➡ **This distributor is used with the EST system. The unit is mounted horizontally to the valve cover housing and is driven by the camshaft, through a tang on the distributor shaft.**

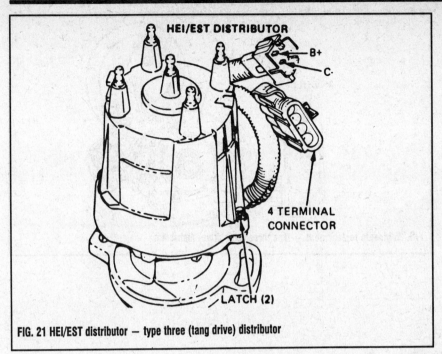

FIG. 21 HEI/EST distributor — type three (tang drive) distributor

Testing

IGNITION COIL

▶ SEE FIG. 22

1. Using an ohmmeter set on the high scale, place one lead on a ground of the ignition coil.

2. Place the second lead into one of the rearward terminals of the ignition coil primary connector.

3. The ohmmeter scale should read infinite. If not, replace the ignition coil.

4. Using the low scale, place the ohmmeter leads into each of the outer terminals of the coil connector.

5. The reading should be zero or very low. If not, replace the ignition coil.

6. Using the high scale, place one ohmmeter lead on the coil secondary terminal and the second lead into the rearward terminal of the ignition coil primary connector.

7. The reading should not be infinite. If so, replace the ignition coil.

Testing

PICK-UP COIL

▶ SEE FIGS. 23-25

1. Remove the rotor and pick-up leads from the module.

2. Using an ohmmeter, connect one of the leads to the distributor base.

3. Connect the second lead to one of the pick-up coil lead terminals

4. The reading should be infinite. If not, the pick-up coil is defective.

➡ **During the ohmmeter tests, flex the leads by hand to check for intermediate opens in the wiring.**

5. Connect both ohmmeter lead to the pick-up coil terminals at the connector.

6. The reading should be of one steady value, 500-1500Ω.

7. If the reading is not within specifications, the pick-up coil must is defective.

Testing

IGNITION MODULE

Because of the complexity of the internal circuitry of the HEI/EST module, it is recommended the module be tested with an accurate module tester.

It is imperative that silicone lubricant be used under the module when it is installed, to prevent module failure due to overheating.

➡ **The module can be removed without distributor disassembly. The distributor shaft and C-clip must be removed before the pick-up coil can be removed. Before removing the roll pin from the distributor tang drive to shaft, a spring must first be removed.**

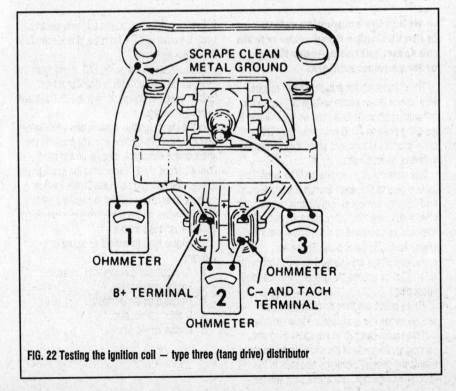

FIG. 22 Testing the ignition coil — type three (tang drive) distributor

FIG. 23 Testing the pick-up coil — type three (tang drive) distributor

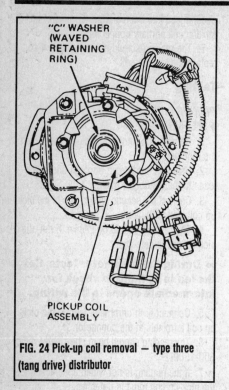

FIG. 24 Pick-up coil removal — type three (tang drive) distributor

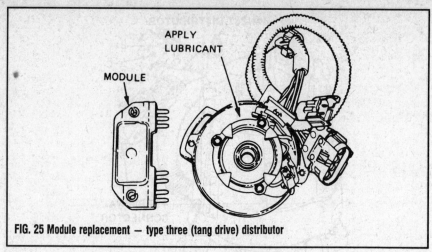

FIG. 25 Module replacement — type three (tang drive) distributor

GENERAL MOTORS DIRECT IGNITION SYSTEM (DIS) ELECTRONIC SPARK TIMING (EST)

General Information

The Direct Ignition System (DIS) is used on the 1987–92 2.0L (VIN 1), 2.2L (VIN G and 4) and all V6 engines.

The Direct Ignition System (DIS) does not use the conventional distributor and ignition coil. The system consists of ignition module, crankshaft sensor or combination sensor, along with the related connecting wires and Electronic Spark Timing (EST) portion of the Electronic Control Module (ECM).

The DIS system uses a "waste spark" method of spark distribution. Companion cylinders are paired and the spark occurs simultaneously in the cylinder with the piston coming up on the compression stroke and in the companion cylinder with the piston coming up on the exhaust stroke.

Example of firing order and companion cylinders:

- 1-2-3-4-5-6; 1/4, 2/5, 3/6
- 1-6-5-4-3-2; 1/4, 6/3, 5/2
- 1-3-4-2; 1/4, 2/3

➡ **Notice the companion cylinders in the V6 engine firing order remain the same, but the cylinder firing order sequence differs.**

The cylinder on the exhaust stroke requires very little of the available voltage to arc, so the remaining high voltage is used by the cylinder in the firing position (TDC compression). This same process is repeated when the companion cylinders reverse roles.

It is possible in an engine no-load condition, for one plug to fire, even though the spark plug lead from the same coil is disconnected from the other spark plug. The disconnected spark plug lead acts as one plate of a capacitor, with the engine being the other plate. These two capacitors plates are charged as a current surge (spark) jumps across the gap of the connected spark plug.

These plates are then discharged as the secondary energy is dissipated in an oscillating current across the gap of the spark plug still connected. Because of the direction of current flow in the primary windings and thus in the secondary windings, one spark plug will fire from the center electrode to the side electrode, while the other will fire from the side electrode to the center electrode.

These systems utilize the EST signal from the ECM, as do the convention distributor type ignition systems equipped with the EST system to control timing.

In the Direct Ignition system and while under 400 rpm, the DIS ignition module controls the spark timing through a module timing mode. Over 400 rpm, the ECM controls the spark timing through the EST mode. In the Direct Ignition system, to properly control the ignition timing, the ECM relies on the the following information from the various sensors.

1. Engine load (manifold pressure or vacuum).
2. Atmospheric (barometric) pressure.
3. Engine temperature.
4. Manifold air temperature.
5. Crankshaft position.
6. Engine speed (rpm).

Direct Ignition System Components

➡ **The Direct Ignition System/EST is used with TBI and Ported fuel injection systems.**

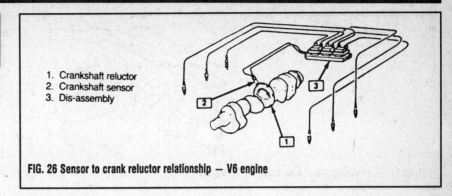

1. Crankshaft reluctor
2. Crankshaft sensor
3. Dis-assembly

FIG. 26 Sensor to crank reluctor relationship — V6 engine

CRANKSHAFT SENSOR

♦ SEE FIGS. 26-27

A magnetic crankshaft sensor (Hall Effect switch) is used and is remotely mounted on the opposite side of the engine from the DIS module. The sensor protrudes in to the engine block, within 0.050 in. (1.27mm) of the crankshaft reluctor.

The reluctor is a special wheel cast into the crankshaft with seven slots machined into it, six of them being evenly spaced at 60° apart. A seventh slot is spaced 10° from one of the other slots and serves as a generator of a "sync-pulse". As the reluctor rotates as part of the crankshaft, the slots change the magnetic field of the sensor, creating an induced voltage pulse.

Based on the crankshaft sensor pulses, the DIS module sends reference signals to the ECM, which are used to indicate crankshaft position and engine speed. The DIS module will continue to send these reference pulses to the ECM at a rate of one per each 120° of crankshaft rotation. The ECM activates the fuel injectors, based on the recognition of every other reference pulse, beginning at a crankshaft position 120° after piston top dead center (TDC). By comparing the time between the pulses, the DIS module can recognize the pulse representing the seventh slot (sync-pulse) which starts the calculation of ignition coil sequencing. The second crankshaft pulse following the sync-pulse signals the DIS module to fire the No.2-5 ignition coil, the fourth crankshaft pulse signals the module to fire No.3-6 ignition coil and the sixth crankshaft pulse signals the module to fire the 1-4 ignition coil.

IGNITION COILS

There are two separate coils for the four cylinder engines and three separate coils for the V6 engines, mounted to the coil/module assembly. Spark distribution is synchronized by a signal from the crankshaft sensor which the ignition module uses to trigger each coil at the proper time. Each coil provides the spark for two spark plugs.

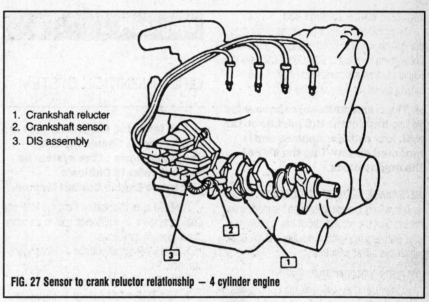

1. Crankshaft reluctor
2. Crankshaft sensor
3. DIS assembly

FIG. 27 Sensor to crank reluctor relationship — 4 cylinder engine

Two types of ignition coil assemblies are used, Type I and Type II During the diagnosis of the systems, the correct type of ignition coil assembly must be identified and the diagnosis directed to that system.

Type I module/coil assembly has three twin tower ignition coils, combined into a single coil pack unit. This unit is mounted to the DIS module. ALL THREE COILS MUST BE REPLACED AS A UNIT. A separate current source through a fused circuit to the module terminal **P** is used to power the ignition coils.

Type II coil/module assembly has three separate coils that are mounted to the DIS module. EACH COIL CAN BE REPLACED SEPARATELY. A fused low current source to the module terminal **M**, provides power for the sensors, ignition coils and internal module circuitry.

DIS MODULE

♦ SEE FIG. 28

The DIS module monitors the crankshaft sensor signal and based on these signals, sends a reference signal to the ECM so that correct spark and fuel injector control can be maintained during all driving conditions. During cranking, the DIS module monitors the sync-pulse to begin the ignition firing sequence. Below 400 rpm, the module controls the spark advance by triggering each of the ignition coils at a predetermined interval, based on engine speed only. Above 400 rpm, the ECM controls the spark timing (EST) and compensates for all driving conditions. The DIS module must receive a sync-pulse and then a crank signal, in that order, to enable the engine to start.

The DIS module is not repairable. When a module is replaced, the remaining DIS components must be transferred to the new module.

DIRECT IGNITION ELECTRONIC SPARK TIMING (EST) CIRCUITS

This system uses the same EST to ECM circuits that the distributor type systems with EST use. The following is a brief description for the EST circuits.

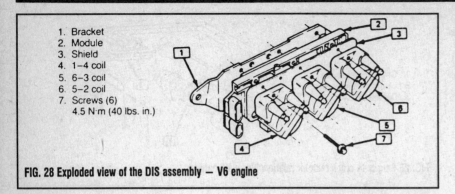

1. Bracket
2. Module
3. Shield
4. 1–4 coil
5. 6–3 coil
6. 5–2 coil
7. Screws (6)
   4.5 N·m (40 lbs. in.)

FIG. 28 Exploded view of the DIS assembly — V6 engine

DIS REFERENCE, CIRCUIT 430

The crankshaft sensor generates a signal to the ignition module, which results in a reference pulse being sent to the ECM. The ECM uses this signal to calculate crankshaft position and engine speed for injector pulse width.

➡ **The crankshaft sensor is mounted to the base of the DIS module on the 2.5L four cylinder engines and is mounted directly into the side of the engine block.**

REFERENCE GROUND CIRCUIT 453

This wire is grounded through the module and insures that the ground circuit has no voltage drop between the ignition module and the ECM, which can affect performance.

BY-PASS, CIRCUIT 424

At approximately 400 rpm, the ECM applies 5 volts to this circuit to switch spark timing control from the DIS module to the ECM. An open or grounded by pass circuit will set a code 42 and result in the engine operating in a back-up ignition timing mode (module timing) at a calculated timing value. This may cause poor performance and reduced fuel economy.

ELECTRONIC SPARK TIMING (EST), CIRCUIT 423

The DIS module sends a reference signal to the ECM when the engine is cranking. While the engine is under 400 rpm, the DIS module controls the ignition timing. When the engine speed exceeds 400 rpm, the ECM applies 5 volts to the By-pass line to switch the timing to the ECM control (EST).

An open or ground in the EST circuit will result in the engine continuing to run, but in a back-up ignition timing mode (module timing mode) at a calculated timing value and the SERVICE ENGINE SOON light will not be on. If the EST fault is still present, the next time the engine is restarted, a code 42 will be set and the engine will operate in the module timing mode. This may cause poor performance and reduced fuel economy.

Diagnosis

DIRECT IGNITION SYSTEM

➡ **The following diagnostic aids are quick checks. Should more in-depth diagnosis of the system be needed, refer to Chilton's Electronic Engine Control Manual.**

The ECM uses information from the MAP and Coolant sensors, in addition to rpm to calculate spark advance as follows;

1. Low MAP output voltage = More spark advance.
2. Cold engine = More spark advance.
3. High MAP output voltage = Less spark advance.
4. Hot engine = Less spark advance.

Therefore, detonation could be caused by low MAP output or high resistance in the coolant sensor circuit.

Poor performance could be caused by high MAP output or low resistance in the coolant sensor circuit.

If the engine cranks but will not operate, or starts, then immediately stalls, diagnosis must be accomplished to determine if the failure is in the DIS system or the fuel system.

CHECKING EST PERFORMANCE

The ECM will set timing at a specified value when the diagnostic **TEST** terminal in the ALDL connector is grounded. To check for EST operation, run the engine at 1500 rpm with the terminal ungrounded. Then ground the **TEST** terminal. If the EST is operating, there should be a noticeable engine rpm change. A fault in the EST system will set a trouble code 42.

CODE 12

Code 12 is used during the diagnostic circuit check procedure to test the diagnostic and code display ability of the ECM. This code indicates that the ECM is not receiving the engine rpm (reference) signal. This occurs with the ignition key in the ON position and the engine not operating.

SETTING IGNITION TIMING

Because the reluctor wheel is an integral part of the crankshaft and the crankshaft sensor is mounted in a fixed position, timing adjustment is not possible.

DIS Assembly

REMOVAL & INSTALLATION

1. Disconnect the negative battery cable.
2. Disconnect the electrical wires from the DIS assembly.
3. Mark the location of the spark plug wires on the DIS assembly and remove the wires.
4. Remove the DIS assembly mounting bolts and remove the assembly from the block.

➡ **With the coil pack removed, the coils can each be removed and the ignition module can be removed as well.**

To install:

5. Install the DIS assembly on the block.
6. Reconnect the plug wires to their original location.
7. Connect the DIS assembly wiring.
8. Connect the negative battery cable.
9. If equipped with the 3.1L engine, perform the idle learn procedure to allow the ECM memory to be updated with the correct IAC valve pintle position and provide for a stable idle speed.
   a. Install a Tech 1 scan tool.
   b. Turn the ignition to the **ON** position, engine not running.
   c. Select **IAC SYSTEM**, then **IDLE LEARN** in the **MISC TEST** mode.
   d. Proceed with idle learn as directed by the scan tool.

Crankshaft Sensor

REMOVAL & INSTALLATION

♦ SEE FIGS. 29-30

1. Disconnect the negative battery cable.
2. Disconnect the sensor harness plug.
3. Remove the sensor-to-block bolt and remove the sensor from the engine.
4. To install the sensor, position the sensor in the block and install the sensor bolt. Torque the sensor bolt to 71 inch lbs.
5. Reconnect the sensor harness plug.

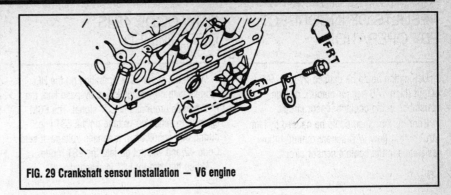

FIG. 29 Crankshaft sensor installation — V6 engine

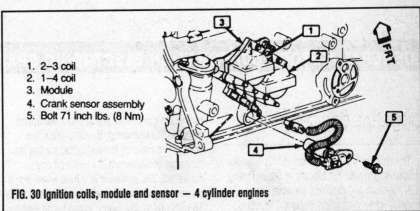

1. 2–3 coil
2. 1–4 coil
3. Module
4. Crank sensor assembly
5. Bolt 71 inch lbs. (8 Nm)

FIG. 30 Ignition coils, module and sensor — 4 cylinder engines

GENERAL MOTORS CORPORATION ELECTRONIC SPARK TIMING (EST) SYSTEM

GENERAL DESCRIPTION

The High Energy Ignition (HEI) system controls fuel combustion by providing the spark to ignite the compressed air/fuel mixture, in the combustion chamber, at the correct time. To provide improved engine performance, fuel economy and control of the exhaust emissions, the ECM controls distributor spark advance (timing) with the Electronic Spark Timing (EST) system.

The standard High Energy Ignition (HEI) system has a modified distributor module which is used in conjunction with the EST system. The module has seven terminals instead of the four used without EST. Two different terminal arrangements are used, depending upon the distributor used with a particular engine application.

To properly control ignition/combustion timing, the ECM needs to know the following information:

1. Crankshaft position.
2. Engine speed (rpm).
3. Engine load (manifold pressure or vacuum).
4. Atmospheric (barometric) pressure.
5. Engine temperature.
6. Transmission gear position (certain models)

The EST system consists of the distributor module, ECM and its connecting wires. The distributor has four wires from the HEI module connected to a four terminal connector, which mates with a four wire connector from the ECM.

These circuits perform the following functions:

1. Distributor reference at terminal **B**. This provides the ECM with rpm and crankshaft position information.
2. Reference ground at terminal **D**. This wire is grounded in the distributor and makes sure the ground circuit has no voltage drop, which could affect performance. If this circuit is open, it could cause poor performance.
3. By-pass at terminal **C**. At approximately 400 rpm, the ECM applies 5 volts to this circuit to switch the spark timing control from the HEI module to the ECM. An open or grounded bypass circuit will set a Code 42 and the engine

will run at base timing, plus a small amount of advance built into the HEI module.

4. EST at terminal **A**. This triggers the HEI module. The ECM does not know what the actual timing is, but it does know when it gets its reference signal. It then advances or retards the spark timing from that point. Therefore, if the base timing is set incorrectly, the entire spark curve will be incorrect.

An open circuit in the EST circuit will set a Code 42 and cause the engine to run on the HEI module timing. This will cause poor performance and poor fuel economy. A ground may set a Code 42, but the engine will not run.

The ECM uses information from the MAP or VAC and coolant sensors, in addition to rpm, in order to calculate spark advance as follows:

1. Low MAP output voltage (high VAC sensor output voltage) would require MORE spark advance.
2. Cold engine would require MORE spark advance.
3. High MAP output voltage (low VAC sensor output voltage) would require LESS spark advance.
4. Hot engine would require LESS spark advance.

RESULTS OF INCORRECT EST OPERATION

Detonation could be caused by low MAP output (high VAC sensor output), or high resistance in the coolant sensor circuit.

Poor performance could be caused by high MAP output (low VAC sensor output) or low resistance in the coolant sensor circuit.

HOW CODE 42 IS DETERMINED

When the systems is operating on the HEI module with no voltage in the by-pass line, the HEI module grounds the EST signal. The ECM expects to sense no voltage on the EST line during this condition. If it senses voltage, it sets Code 42 and will not go into the EST mode.

When the rpm for EST is reached (approximately 400 rpm), the ECM applies 5 volts to the by-pass line and the EST should no longer be grounded in the HEI module, so the EST voltage should be varying.

If the by-pass line is open, the HEI module will not switch to the EST mode, so the EST voltage will be low and Code 42 will be set.

If the EST line is grounded, the HEI module will switch to the EST, but because the line is grounded, there will be no EST signal and the engine will not operate. A Code 42 may or may not be set.

GENERAL MOTORS CORPORATION ELECTRONIC SPARK CONTROL (ESC) SYSTEM

GENERAL DESCRIPTION

The Electronic Spark Control (ESC) operates in conjunction with the Electronic Spark Timing (EST) system and modifies (retards) the spark advance when detonation occurs. The retard mode is held for approximately 20 seconds after which the spark control will again revert to the Electronic Spark Timing (EST) system. There are three basic components of the Electronic Spark Control (ESC) system.

SENSOR

The Electronic Spark Control (ESC) sensor detects the presence (or absence) and intensity of the detonation by the vibration characteristics of the engine. The output is an electrical signal that goes to the controller. A sensor failure would allow no spark retard.

DISTRIBUTOR

The distributor is an HEI/EST unit with an electronic module, modified so it can respond to the ESC controller signal. This command is delayed when detonation is occurring, thus providing the level of spark retard required. The amount of spark retard is a function of the degree of detonation.

CONTROLLER

The Electronic Spark Control (ESC) controller

processes the sensor signal into a command signal to the distributor, to adjust the spark timing. The process is continuous, so that the presence of detonation is monitored and controlled. The controller is a hard wired signal processor and amplifier which operates from 6-16 volts. Controller failure would be no ignition, no retard or full retard. The controller has no memory storage.

CODE 43

Should a Code 43 be set in the ECM memory, it would indicate that the ESC system retard signal has been sensed by the ECM for too long a period of time. When voltage at terminal L of the ECM is low, spark timing is retarded. Normal voltage in the non-retarded mode is approximately 7.5 volts or more.

BASIC IGNITION TIMING

➡ **Late model vehicles, both 4 cylinder and 6 cylinder engines, have distributorless ignition systems (DIS). Because the reluctor wheel is an integral part of the crankshaft, and the crankshaft sensor is mounted in a fixed position, timing adjustment is not possible.**

Basic ignition timing is critical to the proper operation of the ESC system. ALWAYS FOLLOW THE VEHICLE EMISSION CONTROL INFORMATION LABEL PROCEDURES WHEN ADJUSTING IGNITION TIMING.

Some engines will incorporate a magnetic

timing probe hole for use with special electronic timing equipment. Consult the manufacturer's instructions for the use of this electronic timing equipment.

Ignition timing is the measurement, in degrees of crankshaft rotation, of the point at which the spark plugs fire in each of the cylinders. It is measured in degrees before or after Top Dead Center (TDC) of the compression stroke.

Because it takes a fraction of a second for the spark plug to ignite the mixture in the cylinder, the spark plug must fire a little before the piston reaches TDC. Otherwise, the mixture will not completely ignited as the piston passes TDC and the full power of the explosion will not be used by the engine.

The timing measurement is given in degrees of crankshaft rotation before the piston reaches TDC (BTDC). If the setting for the ignition timing is 5° BTDC, the spark plug must fire 5° before each piston reaches TDC. This only holds true, however, when the engine is at idle speed.

As the engine speed increases, the pistons go faster. The spark plugs have to ignite the fuel even sooner if it is to be completely ignited when the piston reaches TDC.

If the ignition is set too far advanced (BTDC), the ignition and expansion of the fuel in the cylinder will occur too soon and tend to force the piston down while it is still traveling up. This causes engine ping. If the ignition spark is set too far retarded, after TDC (ATDC), the piston will have already passed TDC and started on its way down when the fuel is ignited. This will cause the piston to be forced down for only a portion of its travel. This will result in poor engine performance and lack of power.

Ignition timing for this engine should be accomplished using the averaging method in which the timing of each cylinder can be brought into closer agreement with the base timing specification.

The averaging method involves the use of a double notched crankshaft pulley. When timing the engine, the coil wire, instead of the Number 1 plug wire, should be used to trigger the timing light. The notch for the No. 1 cylinder is scribed across all three edges of the double sheave pulley. Another notch located 180° away from the No. 1 cylinder notch is scribed only across the center section of the pulley to make it distinguishable from the No. 1 cylinder notch.

Since the trigger signal for the timing light is picked up at the coil wire, each spark firing results in a flash from the timing light. A slight jiggling of the timing notch may be apparent since each cylinder firing is being displayed. Optimum timing of all cylinders is accomplished by centering the total apparent notch width about the correct timing specification.

There are three basic types of timing light available. The first is a simple neon bulb with two wire connections (one for the spark plug and one for the plug wire, connecting the light in series). This type of light is quite dim, and must be held closely to the marks to be seen, but it is quite inexpensive. The second type of light operates from the car's battery. Two alligator clips connect to the battery terminals, while a third wire connects to the spark plug with an adapter. This type of light is more expensive, but the xenon bulb provides a nice bright flash which can even be seen in sunlight. The third type replaces the battery source with 110 volt house current. Some timing lights have other functions built into them, such as dwell meters, tachometers, or remote starting switches. These are convenient, in that they reduce the tangle of wires under the hood, but may duplicate the functions of tools you already have.

Because your car has electronic ignition, you should use a timing light with an inductive pickup. This pickup simply clamps around the Number 1 spark plug wire (in this case, the coil wire), eliminating the adapter. It is not susceptible to crossfiring or false triggering, which may occur with a conventional light due to the greater voltages produced by HEI.

Ignition Timing

ADJUSTMENT

1.8L, 2.0L OHV engine

1982–86

◆ SEE FIG. 31

1. REFER TO THE INSTRUCTIONS ON THE EMISSION CONTROL STICKER INSIDE THE ENGINE COMPARTMENT. FOLLOW ALL INSTRUCTIONS ON THE LABEL.

2. Locate the timing marks on the crankshaft pulley and the front of the engine.

3. Clean off the marks so that you can see them. Chalk or white paint will help to make them more visible.

4. Attach a tachometer to the engine as detailed previously.

5. Disconnect the 4-terminal EST connector at the distributor so that the engine will switch to the bypass timing mode (please refer to Section 4 for more information).

6. Attach a timing light as per the manufacturer's instructions. Clamp the inductive pick-up around the HIGH TENSION COIL WIRE (not the No. 1 spark plug wire) at the distributor. Before installing the pick-up on the wire, it will be necessary to peel back the protective plastic cover which encases the wire.

7. Loosen the distributor clamp bolt slightly so that the distributor may be rotated as necessary to adjust timing.

8. Check that all wires are clear of the fan and then start the engine. Allow the engine to reach normal operating temperature.

9. Aim the timing light at the marks. A slight jiggling of the notch on the pulley may appear due to the fact that each cylinder is being displayed as it fires. The apparent notch width cannot be reduced by a timing adjustment.

10. Center the total apparent notch width about the correct timing mark on the indicator by rotating the distributor housing. This will insure that the average cylinder timing is as close to specifications as possible. Once again, the apparent notch width cannot be reduced by timing adjustment.

11. Turn off the engine and tighten the distributor lock bolt. Start the engine and recheck the timing. Sometimes the distributor will move a little during the tightening process. If the ignition timing is within 1° of the correct setting, that is close enough; a tolerance of up to 2° is permitted by the manufacturer.

12. Turn off the engine and disconnect the timing light and the tachometer. Reconnect the 4-terminal EST connector.

2.0L (VIN 1) 2.2L, 2.8L AND 3.1L Engines

1987–92

The ignition timing on engines with distributorless ignitions, is controlled by the Electronic Control Module (ECM). No adjustments are possible.

2.0L (VIN K AND M) Engines

AVERAGING METHOD

1. REFER TO THE UNDERHOOD EMISSION CONTROL LABEL AND FOLLOW ALL OF THE TIMING INSTRUCTIONS IF THEY DIFFER FROM BELOW.

2. Warm the engine to normal operating temperature.

3. Place the transmission in **N** or **P**. Apply the parking brake and block wheels.

4. Air conditioning, cooling fan and choke must be **OFF**. Do not remove the air cleaner, except as noted.

5. Ground the ALCL connector under the dash by installing a jumper wire between the **A** and **B** terminals. The Check Engine light should begin flashing.

6. Connect an inductive timing light to the No. 1 spark plug wire lead and record timing.

7. Connect an inductive timing light to the No. 4 spark plug wire lead and record timing.

8. Add the 2 timing numbers and divide by 2 to obtain "average timing".

For example: No. 1 timing = 4 degrees and No. 4 timing = 8 degrees; 4 + 8 = 12 ÷ 2 = 6 degrees average timing. If a change is necessary, subtract the average timing from the timing specification to determine the amount of timing change to No. 1 cylinder. For example: if the timing specification is 8 degrees and the average timing is 6 degrees, advance the No. 1 cylinder 2 degrees to set the timing.

9. To correct the timing, loosen the distributor hold-down clamp, adjust the distributor and retighten the hold-down bolt.

10. Once the timing is properly set, remove the jumper wire from the ALCL connector.

11. If necessary to clear the ECM memory, disconnect the ECM harness from the positive battery pigtail for 10 seconds with the key in the **OFF** position.

Tachometer Hook-up

OHV Engines

1982–86

◆ SEE FIGS. 32-33

Due to the relative inaccessibility of the ignition coil, a separate tachometer hookup has been provided. It is taped to the main wiring harness in the back of the engine compartment, near the firewall. Connect one tachometer lead to this terminal and the other lead to a suitable ground. On some tachometers, the leads must be connected to the terminal and then to the positive battery terminal.

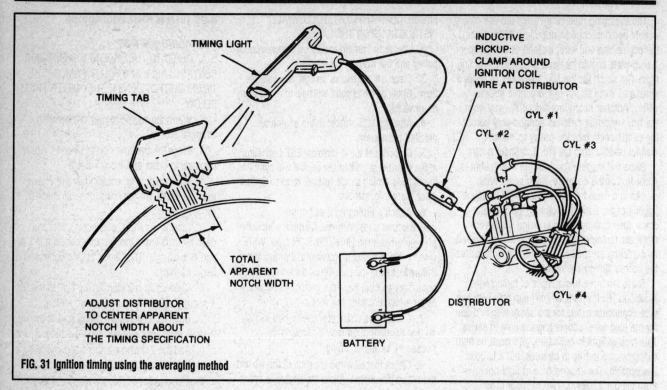

FIG. 31 Ignition timing using the averaging method

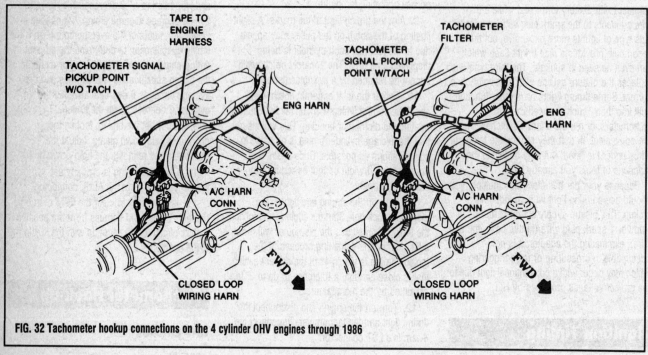

FIG. 32 Tachometer hookup connections on the 4 cylinder OHV engines through 1986

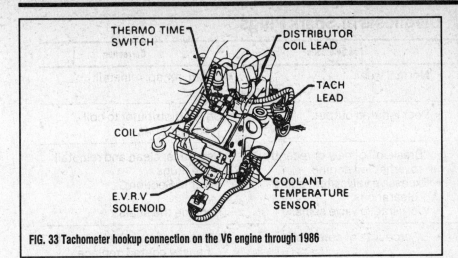

FIG. 33 Tachometer hookup connection on the V6 engine through 1986

※※ CAUTION

Never ground the TACH terminal; serious module and ignition coil damage will result. If there is any doubt as to the correct tachometer hookup, check with the tachometer manufacturer.

OHC Engines

There is a terminal marked TACH on the distributor cap. Connect one tachometer lead to this terminal and the other lead to a ground. On some tachometer, the leads must be connected to the TACH terminal and to the battery positive terminal.

※※ CAUTION

Never ground the TACH terminal; If there is any doubt as to the correct tachometer hookup, check with the tachometer manufacturer.

Valve Adjustment

All models utilize an hydraulic valve lifter system to obtain zero lash. No adjustment is necessary. An initial adjustment is required anytime that the lifters are removed or the valve train is disturbed, this procedure is covered in Section 3.

Idle Speed and Mixture Adjustment

Carbureted Engines

All carbureted vehicles are equipped with an Idle Speed Control (ISC) motor which is in turn controlled by the Electronic Control Module (ECM). All idle speeds are programmed into the ECM's memory and then relayed to the ISC motor as any given situation requires. Curb idle is pre-set at the factory and not routinely adjustable. Although curb idle is not to be adjusted under normal conditions, it can be adjusted, but only upon replacement of the ISC (for further details, refer to Section 5).

The idle mixture screws are concealed under staked-in plugs. Idle mixture is not considered to be a normal tune-up procedure, because of the sensitivity of emission control adjustments. Mixture adjustment requires not only the special tools with which to remove the concealing plugs, but also the addition of an artificial enrichment substance (generally propane) which must be introduced into the carburetor by means of a finely calibrated metering valve. These tools are not generally available and require a certain amount of expertise to use, therefore, mixture adjustments are purposely not covered in this book. If you suspect that your car's carburetor requires a mixture adjustment, we strongly recommend that the job be referred to a qualified service technician.

Fuel Injected Engines

The fuel injected vehicles are controlled by a computer which supplies the correct amount of fuel during all engine operating conditions; no adjustment is necessary.

TORQUE SPECIFICATIONS

Component	U.S.	Metric
Battery cable negative bolt:	11 ft. lbs.	15 Nm
Ignition wire harness retaining bolt:	90 inch lbs.	10 Nm
Ignition wire harness bracket nut:	10 ft. lbs.	13 Nm
Spark plugs:	11 ft. lbs.	15 Nm

Diagnosis of Spark Plugs

Problem	Possible Cause	Correction
Brown to grayish-tan deposits and slight electrode wear.	• Normal wear.	• Clean, regap, reinstall.
Dry, fluffy black carbon deposits.	• Poor ignition output.	• Check distributor to coil connections.
Wet, oily deposits with very little electrode wear.	• "Break-in" of new or recently overhauled engine. • Excessive valve stem guide clearances. • Worn intake valve seals.	• Degrease, clean and reinstall the plugs. • Refer to Section 3. • Replace the seals.
Red, brown, yellow and white colored coatings on the insulator. Engine misses intermittently under severe operating conditions.	• By-products of combustion.	• Clean, regap, and reinstall. If heavily coated, replace.
Colored coatings heavily deposited on the portion of the plug projecting into the chamber and on the side facing the intake valve.	• Leaking seals if condition is found in only one or two cylinders.	• Check the seals. Replace if necessary. Clean, regap, and reinstall the plugs.
Shiny yellow glaze coating on the insulator.	• Melted by-products of combustion.	• Avoid sudden acceleration with wide-open throttle after long periods of low speed driving. Replace the plugs.
Burned or blistered insulator tips and badly eroded electrodes.	• Overheating.	• Check the cooling system. • Check for sticking heat riser valves. Refer to Section 1. • Lean air-fuel mixture. • Check the heat range of the plugs. May be too hot. • Check ignition timing. May be over-advanced. • Check the torque value of the plugs to ensure good plug-engine seat contact.
Broken or cracked insulator tips.	• Heat shock from sudden rise in tip temperature under severe operating conditions. Improper gapping of plugs.	• Replace the plugs. Gap correctly.

3

ENGINE AND ENGINE OVERHAUL

THE ENGINE ELECTRICAL SYSTEM

The engine electrical system can be broken down into three separate and distinct systems:
1. The starting system
2. The charging system
3. The ignition system.

Battery and Starting System

The battery is the first link in the chain of mechanisms which work together to provide cranking of the automobile engine. In most modern cars, the battery is a lead-acid electrochemical device consisting of six 2 volt (2V) subsections connected in series so the unit is capable of producing approximately 12V of electrical pressure. Each subsection, or sell, consists of a series of positive and negative plates held a short distance apart in a solution of sulfuric acid and water. The two types of plates are of dissimilar metals. This causes a chemical reaction to be set up, and it is this reaction which produces current flow from the battery when its positive and negative terminals are connected to an electrical appliance such as a lamp or motor. The continued transfer of electrons would eventually convert the sulfuric acid in the electrolyte to water, and make the two plates identical in chemical composition. As electrical energy is removed from the battery, its voltage output tend to drop. Thus, measuring battery voltage and battery electrolyte composition are two ways of checking the ability of the unit to supply power. During the starting of the engine, electrical energy is removed from the battery. However, if the charging circuit is in good condition and the operating conditions are normal, the power removed from the battery will be replaced by the generator (or alternator) which will force electrons back through the battery, reversing the normal flow, and restoring the battery to its original chemical state.

The battery and starting motor are linked by very heavy electrical cables designed to minimize resistance to the flow of current. Generally, the major power supply cable that leaves the battery goes directly to the starter, while other electrical system needs are supplied by a smaller cable. During the starter operation, power flows from the battery to the starter and is grounded through the car's frame and the battery's negative ground strap.

The starting motor is a specially designed, direct current electric motor capable of producing a very great amount of power for its size. One thing that allows the motor to produce a great deal of power is its tremendous rotating speed. It drives the engine through a tiny pinion gear (attached to the starter's armature), which drives the very large flywheel ring gear at a greatly reduced speed. Another factor allowing it to produce so much power is that only intermittent operation is required of it. Thus, little allowance for air circulation is required, and the windings can be built into a very small space.

The starter solenoid is a magnetic device which employs the small current supplied by the starting switch circuit of the ignition switch. This magnetic action moves a plunger which mechanically engages the starter and electrically closes the heavy switch which connects it to the battery. The starting switch circuit consists of the starting switch contained within the ignition switch, a transmission neutral safety switch or clutch pedal switch, and the wiring necessary to connect these with the starter solenoid or relay.

A pinion, which is a small gear, is mounted to a one-way drive clutch. this clutch is splined to the starter armature shaft. When the ignition switch is moved to the start position, the solenoid plunger slides the pinion toward the flywheel ring gear via a collar and spring. If the teeth on the pinion and flywheel match properly, the pinion will engage the flywheel immediately. IF the gear teeth butt one another, the spring will be compressed and will force the gears to mesh as soon as the starter turns far enough to allow them to do so. As the solenoid plunger reaches the end of its travel, it closes the contacts that connect the battery and starter and then the engine is cranked.

As soon as the engine starts, the flywheel ring gear begins turning fast enough to drive the pinion at an extremely high rate of speed. At this point, the one-way clutch begins allowing the pinion to spin faster that the starter shaft so that the starter will not operate at excessive speed. When the ignition switch is released from the starter position, the solenoid is de-energized, and a spring contained within the solenoid assembly pulls the gear out of mesh and interrupts the current flow to the starter.

Some starters employ a separate relay, mounted away from the starter, to switch the motor and solenoid current on and off. The relay thus replaces the solenoid electrical switch, but does not eliminate the need for a solenoid mounted on the starter used to mechanically engage the starter drive gears. The relay is used to reduce the amount of current the starting switch must carry.

The Charging System

The automobile charging system provides electrical power for operation of the vehicle's ignition and starting systems and all the electrical accessories. The battery serves as an electrical surge of storage tank, storing (in chemical form) the energy originally produced by the engine driven generator. The system also provides a means of regulating generator output to protect the battery from being overcharged and to avoid excessive voltage to the accessories.

The storage battery is a chemical device incorporating parallel lead plates in a tank containing a sulfuric acid-water solution. Adjacent plates are slightly dissimilar, and the chemical reaction of the two dissimilar plates produces electrical energy when the battery is connected to a load such as the starter motor. The chemical reaction is reversible, so that when the generator is producing a voltage (electrical pressure) greater then that produced by the battery, electricity is forced into the battery, and the battery is returned to its fully charged state.

The vehicle's generator is driven mechanically, through V belts, by the engine crankshaft. It consists of two coils of fine wire, one stationary (the stator), and one movable (the rotor). The rotor may also be known as the armature and consists of fine wire wrapped around an iron core which is mounted on a shaft. The electricity which flows through the two coils of wire (provided initially by the battery in some cases) creates an intense magnetic field around both rotor and stator, and the interaction between the two fields creates voltage, allowing the generator to power the accessories and charge the battery.

There are two types of generators; the earlier is the direct current (DC) type. The current produced by the DC generator is generated in the armature and carried off the spinning armature by stationary brushes contacting the commutator. The commutator is a series of smooth metal contact plates on the end of the armature. The commutator plates, which are separated from one another by a very short gap, are connected to the armature circuits so that current will flow in one direction only in wires carrying the generator output. The generator stator consists of two stationary coils of wire which draw some of the output current of the generator to form a powerful magnetic field and create the interaction of fields which generates the voltage. The generator field is wired in series with the regulator.

Newer automobiles use alternating current generators or alternators because they are more efficient, can be rotated at higher speeds, and have fewer brush problems, In an alternator, the field rotates while all the current produced passes only through the stator windings. The brushes bear against continuous slip rings rather than a commutator. This causes the current produced to periodically reverse the direction of its flow. Diodes (electrical one-way switches) block the flow of current from traveling in the wrong direction. A series of diodes is wired together to permit the alternating flow of the stator to be converted to a pulsating, but uni-directional flow of current from traveling in the wrong direction. A series of diodes is wires together to permit the alternating flow of the stator to be converted to a pulsating, but unidirectional flow at the alternator output. The alternator's field is wires in series with the voltage regulator.

The regulator consist of several circuits. Each circuit has a core, or magnetic coil of wire, which operates a switch. Each switch is con-nected to ground through on or more resistors. The coil of wire responds directly to system volt-age. When the voltage reaches the required level, the magnetic field created by the winding of wire closes the switch and inserts a resistance into the generator field circuit, thus reducing the output. The contacts of the switch cycle open and close many times each second to precisely control voltage.

While alternators are self-limiting as far as maximum current is concerned. DC generators employ a current regulating circuit which responds directly to the total amount of current flowing through the generator circuit rather than to the output voltage. The current regulator is similar to the voltage regulator except all system current must flow through the energizing coil on its way to the various accessories.

SAFETY PRECAUTIONS

Observing these precautions will ensure safe handling of the electrical system components, and will avoid damage to the vehicle's electrical system:

a. Be absolutely sure of the polarity of a booster battery before making connections. Connect the cables positive to positive, and negative to negative. Connect positive cables first and then make the last connection to ground on the body of the booster vehicle so that arcing cannot ignite hydrogen gas that may have accumulated near the battery. Even momentary connection of a booster battery with the polarity reversed will damage alternator diodes.

b. Disconnect both vehicle battery cables before attempting to charge a battery.

c. Never ground the alternator or generator output or battery terminal. Be cautious when using metal tools around a battery to avoid creating a short circuit between the terminals.

d. Never ground the field circuit between the alternator and regulator.

e. Never run an alternator or generator without load unless the field circuit is disconnected.

f. Never attempt to polarize an alternator.

g. Keep the regulator cover in place when taking voltage and current limiter readings.

h. Use insulated tools when adjusting the regulator.

i. Whenever DC generator-to-regulator wires have been disconnected, the generator must be repolarized. To do this with an exter-nally grounded, light duty generator, momentarily place a jumper wires between the battery terminal and the generator terminal of the regulator. With an internally grounded heavy duty unit, disconnect the wire to the regulator field terminal and touch the regulator battery terminal with it.

ENGINE ELECTRICAL

Ignition Coil

The High Energy Ignition distributor is used on all engines. The ignition coil is either mounted to the top of the distributor cap or is externally mounted on the engine, having a secondary circuit high tension wire connecting the coil to the distributor cap and interconnecting primary wiring as part of the engine harness.

The Direct Ignition System (DIS) does not use the conventional distributor and ignition coil. The system consists of ignition module, crankshaft sensor or combination sensor, along with the related connecting wires and Electronic Spark Timing (EST) portion of the Electronic Control Module (ECM).

TESTING

Distributor With Separate Coil Type One

1. Disconnect the primary wiring connectors and secondary coil wire from the ignition coil.
2. Using an ohmmeter on the high scale, connect one lead to a grounding screw and the second lead to one of the primary coil terminals.
3. The reading should be infinite. If not, replace the ignition coil.
4. Using the low scale, place the ohmmeter leads on both the primary coil terminals.
5. The reading should be very low or zero. If not, replace the ignition coil.

6. Using the high scale, place one ohmmeter lead on the high tension output terminal and the other lead on a primary coil terminal.
7. The reading should NOT be infinite. If it is, replace the ignition coil.

Distributor With Separate Coil Type Two

1. Using an ohmmeter set on the high scale, place one lead on a ground of the ignition coil.
2. Place the second lead into one of the rearward terminals of the ignition coil primary connector.
3. The ohmmeter scale should read infinite. If not, replace the ignition coil.
4. Using the low scale, place the ohmmeter

leads into each of the outer terminals of the coil connector.

5. The reading should be zero or very low. If not, replace the ignition coil.

6. Using the high scale, place one ohmmeter lead on the coil secondary terminal and the second lead into the rearward terminal of the ignition coil primary connector.

7. The reading should not be infinite. If so, replace the ignition coil.

Distributor With Separate Coil Type Three w/Tang Drive

1. Using an ohmmeter set on the high scale, place one lead on a ground of the ignition coil.

2. Place the second lead into one of the rearward terminals of the ignition coil primary connector.

3. The ohmmeter scale should read infinite. If not, replace the ignition coil.

4. Using the low scale, place the ohmmeter leads into each of the outer terminals of the coil connector.

5. The reading should be zero or very low. If not, replace the ignition coil.

6. Using the high scale, place one ohmmeter lead on the coil secondary terminal and the second lead into the rearward terminal of the ignition coil primary connector.

7. The reading should not be infinite. If so, replace the ignition coil.

Direct Ignition System (DIS)

There are two separate coils for the 4-cylinder engines and three separate coils for the V6 engines, mounted to the coil/module assembly. Spark distribution is synchronized by a signal from the crankshaft sensor which the ignition module uses to trigger each coil at the proper time. Each coil provides the spark for two spark plugs.

Two types of ignition coil assemblies are used, Type I and Type II. During the diagnosis of the systems, the correct type of ignition coil assembly must be identified and the diagnosis directed to that system.

Type I module/coil assembly has three twin tower ignition coils, combined into a single coil pack unit. This unit is mounted to the DIS module. ALL THREE COILS MUST BE REPLACED AS A UNIT. A separate current source through a fused circuit to the module terminal **P** is used to power the ignition coils.

Type II coil/module assembly has three separate coils that are mounted to the DIS module. EACH COIL CAN BE REPLACED SEPARATELY. A fused low current source to the module terminal **M**, provides power for the sensors, ignition coils and internal module circuitry.

Ignition Module

DISTRIBUTOR WITH SEPARATE COIL TYPE ONE

➡ **This type distributor has no vacuum or centrifugal advance mechanism and has the pickup coil mounted above the module. This distributor is used with the EST system.**

Because of the complexity of the internal circuitry of the HEI/EST module, it is recommended the module be tested with an accurate module tester.

It is imperative that silicone lubricant be used under the module when it is installed, to prevent module failure due to overheating.

➡ **The module and the Hall Effect switch (if used) can be removed from the distributor without disassembly. To remove the pickup coil, the distributor shaft must be removed to expose a waved retaining ring (C-washer) holding the pickup coil in place.**

DISTRIBUTOR WITH SEPARATE COIL TYPE TWO

➡ **This type distributor has no vacuum or centrifugal advance mechanisms and the module has two outside terminal connections for the wiring harness. This distributor is used with the EST system.**

Because of the complexity of the internal circuitry of the HEI/EST module, it is recommended the module be tested with an accurate module tester.

It is imperative that silicone lubricant be used under the module when it is installed, to prevent module failure due to overheating.

➡ **The module can be removed without distributor disassembly. To remove the pickup coil, the distributor shaft must be removed. A retainer can then be removed from the top of the pole piece and the pickup coil removed.**

DISTRIBUTOR WITH SEPARATE COIL TYPE THREE W/ TANG DRIVE

➡ **This distributor is used with the EST system. The unit is mounted horizontally to the valve cover housing and is driven by the camshaft, through a tang on the distributor shaft.**

Because of the complexity of the internal circuitry of the HEI/EST module, it is recommended the module be tested with an accurate module tester.

It is imperative that silicone lubricant be used under the module when it is installed, to prevent module failure due to overheating.

➡ **The module can be removed without distributor disassembly. The distributor shaft and C-clip must be removed before the pickup coil can be removed. Before removing the roll pin from the distributor tang drive to shaft, a spring must first be removed.**

Distributor

REMOVAL & INSTALLATION

1.8L and 2.0L OHV Engines

♦ SEE FIG. 1

➡ **On Chevrolet V6 models the distributor body is involved in the engine lubricating system. The lubricating circuit to the right bank valve train can be interrupted by misalignment of the distributor body. See Firing Order illustrations for correct distributor positioning.**

The 1987–92 Chevrolet built 4-cylinder 2.0L and V6 2.8L engines do not have a distributor. For an explanation of this type of ignition system refer to (DIS) Ignition System in Section 2.

1. Disconnect the negative battery cable.

2. Tag and disconnect all wires leading from the distributor cap.

3. Remove the air cleaner housing as previously detailed.

4. Remove the distributor cap.

5. Disconnect the AIR pipe-to-exhaust manifold hose at the air management valve.

6. Unscrew the rear engine lift bracket bolt and nut, lift it off the stud and then position the entire assembly out of the way to facilitate better access to the distributor.

7. Mark the position of the distributor, relative to the engine block and then scribe a mark on the distributor body indicating the initial position of the rotor.

8. Remove the holddown nut and clamp from the base of the distributor. Remove the distributor from the engine. The drive gear on the distributor shaft is helical and the shaft will rotate slightly as the distributor is removed. Note and mark the position of the rotor at this second position. Do not crank the engine while the distributor is removed.

9. To install the distributor, rotate the shaft until the rotor aligns with the second mark you made (when the shaft stopped moving). Lubricate the drive gear with clean engine oil and install the distributor into the engine. As the distributor is installed, the rotor should move to the first mark that you made. This will ensure proper timing. If the marks do not align properly, remove the distributor and try again.

10. Install the clamp and holddown nut.

➡ **You may wish to use a magnet attached to an extension bar to position the clamp on the stud.**

11. Installation of the remaining components is in the reverse order of removal. Check the ignition timing.

1.8L and 2.0L OHC Engines

◆ SEE FIG. 2

1. Disconnect the battery ground.

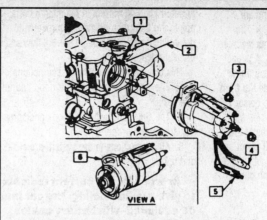

1. Stud
2. 20 ± 1.0
3. Nut
4. EST connector
5. Coil Connector
6. Distributor

FIG. 2 Distributor mounting on 1.8L and 2.0 OHC engines

2. Mark the spark plug wires and remove the wires and coil.

3. Matchmark the position of the rotor, distributor body and cylinder head.

4. Disconnect the wiring from the distributor.

5. Remove the two distributor holddown nuts.

6. Remove the distributor.

7. Installation is the reverse of removal. Torque the holddown nuts to 13 ft. lbs. If the engine was rotated while the distributor was out, refer to the necessary service procedures.

INSTALLATION IF THE ENGINE WAS DISTURBED

IF THE ENGINE WAS CRANKED WHILE THE DISTRIBUTOR WAS REMOVED, YOU WILL HAVE TO PLACE THE ENGINE ON TDC OF THE COMPRESSION STROKE TO OBTAIN PROPER IGNITION TIMING.

1. Remove the No. 1 spark plug.

2. Place your thumb over the spark plug hole. Crank the engine slowly until compression is felt. It will be easier if you have someone rotate the engine by hand, using a wrench on the crankshaft pulley.

3. Align the timing mark on the crankshaft pulley with the **0°** mark on the timing scale attached to the front of the engine. This places the engine at TDC of the compression stroke.

4. Turn the distributor shaft until the rotor points to the No. 1 spark plug tower on the cap.

5. Install the distributor into the engine. Be sure to align the distributor-to-engine block mark made earlier.

6. Perform all necessary remaining service steps.

Alternator

The alternating current generator (alternator) supplies a continuous output of electrical energy at all engine speeds. The alternator generates electrical energy for the engine and all electrical components, and recharges the battery by supplying it with current. This unit consists of four main assemblies: two end frame assemblies, a rotor assembly, and a stator assembly. The rotor is supported in the drive end frame by a ball bearing and at the other end by a roller bearing. These bearings are lubricated during manufacture and require no maintenance. There are six diodes in the end frame assembly. Diodes are electrical check valves that change the alternating current supplied from the stator windings to a direct current (DC), delivered to the output (BAT) terminal. Three diodes are negative and are mounted flush with the end

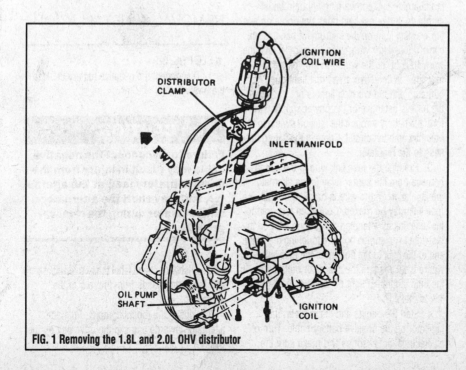

IGNITION COIL WIRE

DISTRIBUTOR CLAMP

INLET MANIFOLD

FWD

OIL PUMP SHAFT

IGNITION COIL

FIG. 1 Removing the 1.8L and 2.0L OHV distributor

frame; the other three are positive and are mounted into a strip called a heat sink. The positive diodes are easily identified as the ones within small cavities or depressions. A capacitor, or condenser, mounted on the end frame protects the rectifier bridge and diode trio from high voltages, and suppresses radio noise. This capacitor requires no maintenance.

Two models of the SI series alternator are used on J-cars. The 10 SI and 15 SI are of similar construction; the 15 SI is slightly larger, uses different stator windings, and produces more current.

ALTERNATOR PRECAUTIONS

1. When installing a battery, make sure that the positive and negative cables are not reversed.

2. When jump-starting the car, be sure that like terminals are connected. This also applies to using a battery charger. Reversed polarity will burn out the alternator and regulator in a matter of seconds.

3. Never operate the alternator with the battery disconnected or on an otherwise uncontrolled open circuit.

4. Do not short across or ground any alternator or regulator terminals.

5. Do not try to polarize the alternator.

6. Do not apply full battery voltage to the field (brown) connector.

7. Always disconnect the battery ground cable before disconnecting the alternator lead.

8. Always disconnect the battery (negative cable first) when charging it.

9. Never subject the alternator to excessive heat or dampness. If you are steam cleaning the engine, cover the alternator.

10. Never use arc-welding equipment on the car with the alternator connected.

CHARGING SYSTEM TROU-BLESHOOTING

There are many possible ways in which the charging system can malfunction. Often the source of a problem is difficult to diagnose, requiring special equipment and a good deal of experience. This is usually not the case, however, where the charging system fails completely and causes the dash board warning light to come on or the battery to become dead. To troubleshoot a complete system failure only two pieces of equipment are needed: a test light,

to determine that current is reaching a certain point; and a current indicator (ammeter), to determine the direction of the current flow and its measurement in amps.

This test works under three assumptions:

1. The battery is known to be good and fully charged.

2. The alternator belt is in good condition and adjusted to the proper tension.

3. All connections in the system are clean and tight.

➡ **In order for the current indicator to give a valid reading, the car must be equipped with battery cables which are of the same gauge size and quality as original equipment battery cables.**

1. Turn off all electrical components on the car. Make sure the doors of the car are closed. If the car is equipped with a clock, disconnect the clock by removing the lead wire from the rear of the clock. Disconnect the positive battery cable from the battery and connect the ground wire on a test light to the disconnected positive battery cable. Touch the probe end of the test light to the positive battery post. The test light should not light. If the test light does light, there is a short or open circuit on the car.

2. Disconnect the voltage regulator wiring harness connector at the voltage regulator. Turn on the ignition key. Connect the wire on a test light to a good ground (engine bolt). Touch the probe end of a test light to the ignition wire connector into the voltage regulator wiring connector. This wire corresponds to the **I** terminal on the regulator. If the test light goes on, the charging system warning light circuit is complete. If the test light does not come on and the warning light on the instrument panel is on, either the resistor wire, which is parallel with the warning light, or the wiring to the voltage regulator, is defective. If the test light does not come on and the warning light is not on, either the bulb is defective or the power supply wire form the battery through the ignition switch to the bulb has an open circuit. Connect the wiring harness to the regulator.

3. Examine the fuse link wire in the wiring harness from the starter relay to the alternator. If the insulation on the wire is cracked or split, the fuse link may be melted. Connect a test light to the fuse link by attaching the ground wire on the test light to an engine bolt and touching the probe end of the light to the bottom of the fuse link wire where it splices into the alternator output wire. If the bulb in the test light does not light, the fuse link is melted.

4. Start the engine and place a current indicator on the positive battery cable. Turn off all electrical accessories and make sure the

doors are closed. If the charging system is working properly, the gauge will show a draw of less than 5 amps. If the system is not working properly, the gauge will show a draw of more than 5 amps. A charge moves the needle toward the battery, a draw moves the needle away from the battery. Turn the engine off.

5. Disconnect the wiring harness from the voltage regulator at the regulator at the regulator connector. Connect a male spade terminal (solderless connector) to each end of a jumper wire. Insert one end of the wire into the wiring harness connector which corresponds to the **A** terminal on the regulator. Insert the other end of the wire into the wiring harness connector which corresponds to the **F** terminal on the regulator. Position the connector with the jumper wire installed so that it cannot contact any metal surface under the hood. Position a current indicator gauge on the positive battery cable. Have an assistant start the engine. Observe the reading on the current indicator. Have your assistant slowly raise the speed of the engine to about 2,000 rpm or until the current indicator needle stops moving, whichever comes first. Do not run the engine for more than a short period of time in this condition. If the wiring harness connector or jumper wire becomes excessively hot during this test, turn off the engine and check for a grounded wire in the regulator wiring harness. If the current indicator shows a charge of about three amps less than the output of the alternator, the alternator is working properly. If the previous tests showed a draw, the voltage regulator is defective. If the gauge does not show the proper charging rate, the alternator is defective.

REMOVAL & INSTALLATION

◆ SEE FIGS. 3-9

1. Disconnect the negative battery cable at the battery.

❋❋ CAUTION

Failure to disconnect the negative cable may result in injury from the positive battery lead at the alternator, and may short the alternator and regulator during the removal process.

2. Disconnect and label the two terminal plug and the battery leads from the rear of the alternator.

3. Loosen the mounting bolts. Push the alternator inwards and slip the drive belt off the pulley.

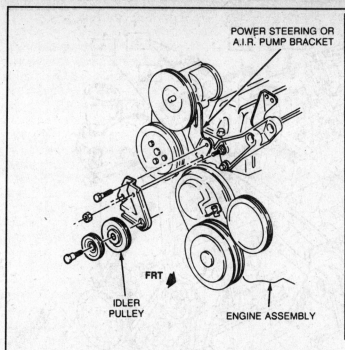
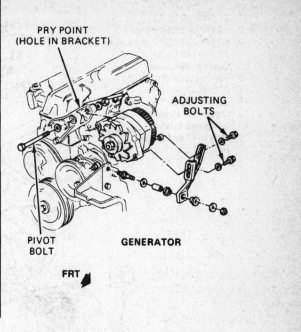

FIG. 3 Alternator installation details — 1982–86 1.8L and 2.0L OHV engines

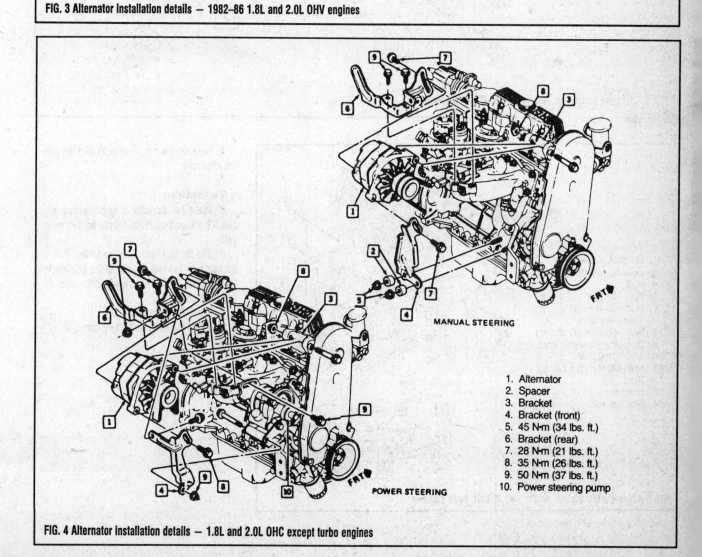

1. Alternator
2. Spacer
3. Bracket
4. Bracket (front)
5. 45 N·m (34 lbs. ft.)
6. Bracket (rear)
7. 28 N·m (21 lbs. ft.)
8. 35 N·m (26 lbs. ft.)
9. 50 N·m (37 lbs. ft.)
10. Power steering pump

FIG. 4 Alternator installation details — 1.8L and 2.0L OHC except turbo engines

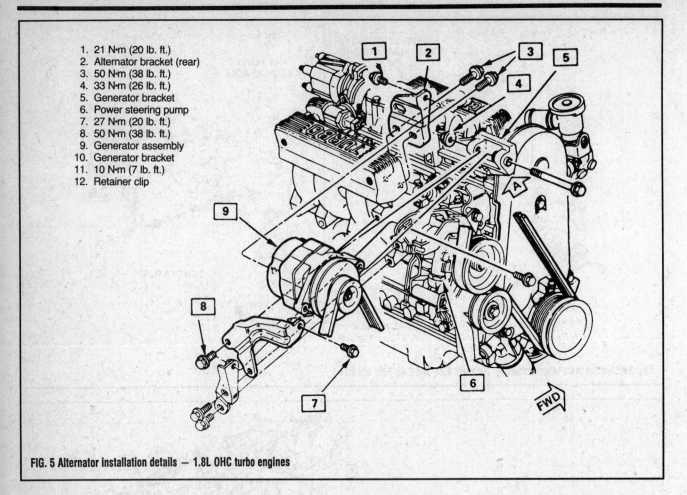

1. 21 N·m (20 lb. ft.)
2. Alternator bracket (rear)
3. 50 N·m (38 lb. ft.)
4. 33 N·m (26 lb. ft.)
5. Generator bracket
6. Power steering pump
7. 27 N·m (20 lb. ft.)
8. 50 N·m (38 lb. ft.)
9. Generator assembly
10. Generator bracket
11. 10 N·m (7 lb. ft.)
12. Retainer clip

FIG. 5 Alternator installation details — 1.8L OHC turbo engines

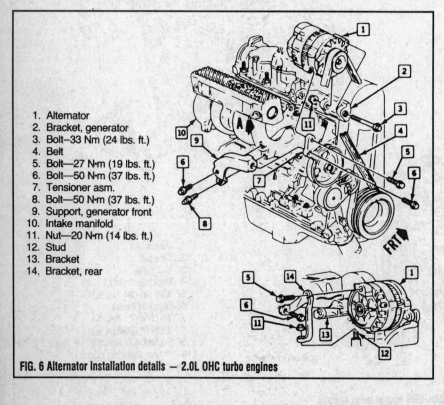

1. Alternator
2. Bracket, generator
3. Bolt–33 Nm (24 lbs. ft.)
4. Belt
5. Bolt—27 N·m (19 lbs. ft.)
6. Bolt—50 N·m (37 lbs. ft.)
7. Tensioner asm.
8. Bolt—50 N·m (37 lbs. ft.)
9. Support, generator front
10. Intake manifold
11. Nut—20 N·m (14 lbs. ft.)
12. Stud
13. Bracket
14. Bracket, rear

FIG. 6 Alternator installation details — 2.0L OHC turbo engines

4. Remove the mounting bolts and remove the alternator.

To Install:

5. Place the alternator in its brackets and install the mounting bolts. Do not tighten them yet.

6. Slip the belt back over the pulley. Pull outwards on the unit and adjust the belt tension (see Section 1). Tighten the mounting and adjusting bolts.

7. Install the electrical leads.

8. Install the negative battery cable.

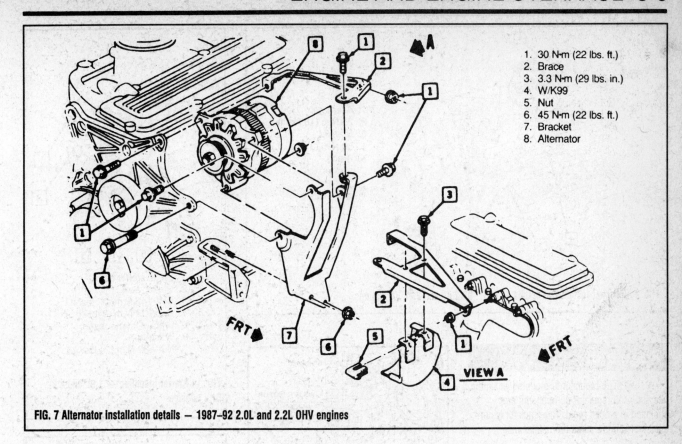

1. 30 N·m (22 lbs. ft.)
2. Brace
3. 3.3 N·m (29 lbs. in.)
4. W/K99
5. Nut
6. 45 N·m (22 lbs. ft.)
7. Bracket
8. Alternator

FIG. 7 Alternator installation details — 1987–92 2.0L and 2.2L OHV engines

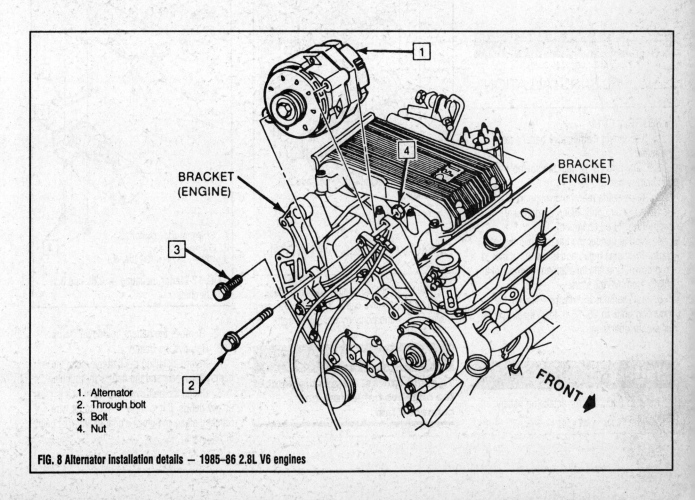

1. Alternator
2. Through bolt
3. Bolt
4. Nut

FIG. 8 Alternator installation details — 1985–86 2.8L V6 engines

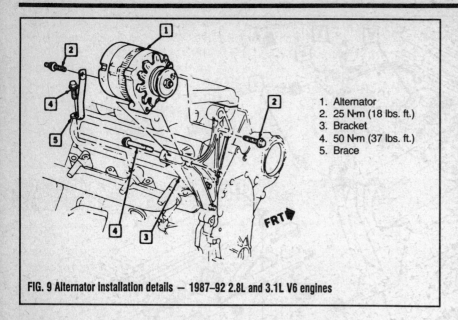

1. Alternator
2. 25 N·m (18 lbs. ft.)
3. Bracket
4. 50 N·m (37 lbs. ft.)
5. Brace

FIG. 9 Alternator installation details — 1987–92 2.8L and 3.1L V6 engines

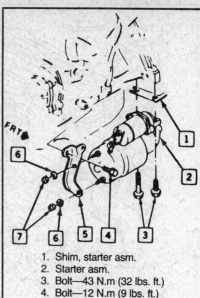

1. Shim, starter asm.
2. Starter asm.
3. Bolt—43 N.m (32 lbs. ft.)
4. Bolt—12 N.m (9 lbs. ft.)
5. Bracket, starter asm.
6. Washer
7. Nut—32 N.m (24 lbs. ft.)

FIG. 11 Starter mounting — 1.8L and 2.0L OHV engines

Regulator

A solid state regulator is mounted within the alternator. All regulator components are enclosed in a solid mold. The regulator is non-adjustable and requires no maintenance.

Starter

REMOVAL & INSTALLATION

♦ SEE FIGS. 10-12

1. Disconnect the negative battery cable at the battery.

2. Label and disconnect the solenoid wires and battery cable.

3. Remove the rear motor support bracket. Remove the air conditioning compressor support rod (if so equipped).

4. Working under the car, remove the two starter-to-engine bolts, and allow the starter to drop down. Note the location and number of any shims. Remove the starter.

5. Installation is the reverse. Tighten the mounting bolts to 25–35 ft. lbs. Check system for proper operation.

Battery

Refer to Section 1 for details on battery maintenance.

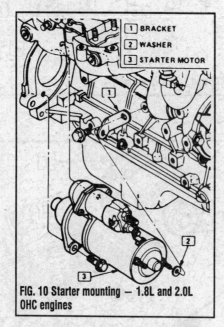

1. BRACKET
2. WASHER
3. STARTER MOTOR

FIG. 10 Starter mounting — 1.8L and 2.0L OHC engines

REMOVAL & INSTALLATION

1. Disconnect the negative (ground) cable first, then the positive cable. The side terminal cables are retained only by the center bolt.

✳✳ CAUTION

To avoid sparks, always disconnect the negative cable first, and connect it last.

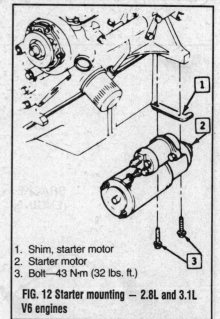

1. Shim, starter motor
2. Starter motor
3. Bolt—43 N·m (32 lbs. ft.)

FIG. 12 Starter mounting — 2.8L and 3.1L V6 engines

2. Remove the battery holddown clamp.

3. Remove the battery.

4. Before installing the battery, clean the battery terminals and the cables thoroughly.

5. Check the battery tray to be sure it is clear of any debris. If it is rusty, it should be wire-brushed clean and given a coat of anti-rust paint, or replaced.

6. Install the battery in the tray, being sure it is centered in the lip.

7. Install the holddown clamp. Tighten to 6 ft. lbs., which is tight enough to hold the battery in place, but loose enough to prevent the case from cracking.

8. Connect the positive, then the negative battery cables. Installation torque for the cables is 9 ft. lbs. Give the terminals a light external coat of grease after installation to retard corrosion.

➡ **Make absolutely sure that the battery is connected properly before you turn on the ignition switch. Reversed polarity can burn out the alternator and regulator in a matter of seconds.**

ENGINE MECHANICAL

These cars use 5 different 4-cylinder engines. Three are built by Chevrolet: a 1835.5cc (1.8L) 112 cid, a 1986.8cc (2.0L) 121 cid, and a 2196.3cc (2.2L) 134 cid. All of these Chevrolet-built engines are of the overhead valve configuration (OHV). That means that the camshaft is in the block and the rest of the valve train is on top of the head. The two other engines are Pontiac (Brazil) built. The 1797.9cc (1.8L) 110 cid and the (2.0) 122 overhead cam engines (OHC). This means that the camshaft and valve components are all located in the engine head. The 3 Chevrolet-built engines are virtually identical in all aspects except displacement.

The Pontiac-built engines are quite different in most respects.

In the 1985 Model year, a 2838.4cc (2.8L), 173 cid V6 engine was introduced. This engine is a high output version of the Chevy-built V6, using MFI (multi-port fuel injection). In 1990 the 3148.8cc (3.1L) 192 cid engine replaced the 2.8L engine. Both V6 engines are basically identical except for the cubic inch displacement.

Engine Overhaul Tips

Most engine overhaul procedures are fairly standard. In addition to specific parts replacement procedures and complete specifications for your individual engine, this section also is a guide to accept rebuilding procedures. Examples of standard rebuilding practice are shown and should be used along with specific details concerning your particular engine.

Competent and accurate machine shop services will ensure maximum performance, reliability and engine life.

In most instances it is more profitable for the do-it-yourself mechanic to remove, clean and inspect the component, buy the necessary parts and deliver these to a shop for actual machine work.

On the other hand, much of the rebuilding work (crankshaft, block, bearings, piston rods, and other components) is well within the scope of the do-it-yourself mechanic.

TOOLS

The tools required for an engine overhaul or parts replacement will depend on the depth of your involvement. With a few exceptions, they will be the tools found in a mechanic's tool kit (see Section 1). More in-depth work will require any or all of the following:

• a dial indicator (reading in thousandths) mounted on a universal base
• micrometers and telescope gauges
• jaw and screw-type pullers
• scraper
• valve spring compressor
• ring groove cleaner
• piston ring expander and compressor
• ridge reamer
• cylinder hone or glaze breaker
• Plastigage®
• engine stand

The use of most of these tools is illustrated in this section. Many can be rented for a one-time use from a local parts jobber or tool supply house specializing in automotive work.

Occasionally, the use of special tools is called for. See the information on Special Tools and Safety Notice in the front of this book before substituting another tool.

INSPECTION TECHNIQUES

Procedures and specifications are given in this section for inspecting, cleaning and assessing the wear limits of most major components. Other procedures such as Magnaflux® and Zyglo® can be used to locate material flaws and stress cracks. Magnaflux® is a magnetic process applicable only to ferrous materials. The Zyglo® process coats the material with a fluorescent dye penetrant and can be used on any material Check for suspected surface cracks can be more readily made using spot check dye. The dye is sprayed onto the suspected area, wiped off and the area sprayed with a developer. Cracks will show up brightly.

OVERHAUL TIPS

Aluminum has become extremely popular for use in engines, due to its low weight. Observe the following precautions when handling aluminum parts:

• Never hot tank aluminum parts (the caustic hot tank solution will eat the aluminum.
• Remove all aluminum parts (identification tag, etc.) from engine parts prior to the tanking.
• Always coat threads lightly with engine oil or anti-seize compounds before installation, to prevent seizure.
• Never overtorque bolts or spark plugs especially in aluminum threads.

Stripped threads in any component can be repaired using any of several commercial repair kits (Heli-Coil®, Microdot®, Keenserts®, etc.).

When assembling the engine, any parts that will be frictional contact must be prelubed to provide lubrication at initial start-up. Any product specifically formulated for this purpose can be used, but engine oil is not recommended as a prelube.

When semi-permanent (locked, but removable) installation of bolts or nuts is desired, threads should be cleaned and coated with Loctite® or other similar, commercial non-hardening sealant.

REPAIRING DAMAGED THREADS

Several methods of repairing damaged threads are available. Heli-Coil® (shown here), Keenserts® and Microdot® are among the most widely used. All involve basically the same principle — drilling out stripped threads, tapping the hole and installing a prewound insert — making welding, plugging and oversize fasteners unnecessary.

Two types of thread repair inserts are usually supplied: a standard type for most Inch Coarse, Inch Fine, Metric Course and Metric Fine thread sizes and a spark lug type to fit most spark plug port sizes. Consult the individual manufacturer's catalog to determine exact applications. Typical thread repair kits will contain a selection of prewound threaded inserts, a tap (corresponding to the outside diameter threads of the insert) and an installation tool. Spark plug inserts usually differ because they require a tap equipped with pilot threads and a combined reamer/tap section. Most manufacturers also supply blister-packed thread repair inserts separately in addition to a master kit containing a variety of taps and inserts plus installation tools.

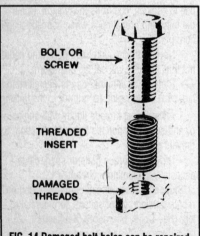

FIG. 14 Damaged bolt holes can be repaired with thread repair inserts

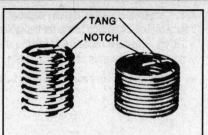

FIG. 15 Standard thread repair insert (left) and spark plug thread insert (right)

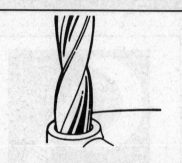

FIG. 16 Drill out the damaged threads with specified drill. Drill completely through the hole or to the bottom of a blind hole

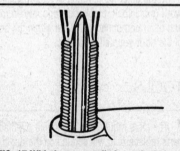

FIG. 17 With the tap supplied, tap the hole to receive the thread insert. Keep the tap well oiled and back it out frequently to avoid clogging the threads

Before effecting a repair to a threaded hole, remove any snapped, broken or damaged bolts or studs. Penetrating oil can be used to free frozen threads. The offending item can be removed with locking pliers or with a screw or stud extractor. After the hole is clear, the thread can be repaired, as shown in the series of accompanying illustrations.

Checking Engine Compression

◆ SEE FIG. 19

A noticeable lack of engine power, excessive

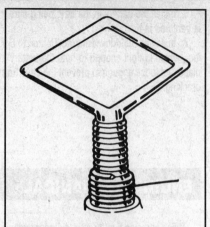

FIG. 18 Screw the threaded insert onto the installation tool until the tang engages the slot. Screw the insert into the tapped hole until it is $^1/_4$–$^1/_2$ turn below the top surface. After installation break off the tang with a hammer and punch.

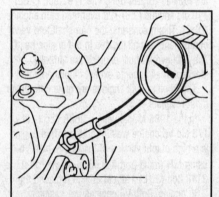

FIG. 19 The screw-in type compression gauge is more accurate

oil consumption and/or poor fuel mileage measured over an extended period are all indicators of internal engine war. Worn piston rings, scored or worn cylinder bores, blown head gaskets, sticking or burnt valves and worn valve seats are all possible culprits here. A check of each cylinder's compression will help you locate the problems.

As mentioned in the Tools and Equipment (Section 1), a screw-in type compression gauge is more accurate that the type you simply hold against the spark plug hole, although it takes slightly longer to use. It's worth it to obtain a more accurate reading. Follow the procedures below.

1. Warm up the engine to normal operating temperature.

2. Remove all the spark plugs.

3. Disconnect the **BAT** terminal and if so equipped, the four terminal connector from the

HEI distributor. On 1987 and later Cavaliers, disconnect the ECM fuse.

4. Fully open the throttle either by operating the throttle linkage by hand or by having an assistant floor the accelerator pedal.

5. Screw the compression gauge into the no.1 spark plug hole until the fitting is snug.

➡ **Be careful not to crossthread the plug hole. On aluminum cylinder heads use extra care, as the threads in these heads are easily ruined.**

6. Ask an assistant to depress the accelerator pedal fully on both carbureted and fuel injected vehicles. Then, while you read the compression gauge, ask the assistant to crank the engine two or three times in short bursts using the ignition switch.

7. Read the compression gauge at the end of each series of cranks, and record the highest of these readings. Repeat this procedure for each of the engine's cylinders. Compare the highest reading of each cylinder to the compression pressure specification in the Tune-Up Specifications chart in Section 2. The specs in this chart are maximum values.

A cylinder's compression pressure is usually acceptable if it is not less than 70% of maximum. And no cylinder should be less than 100 lbs.

8. If a cylinder is unusually low, pour a tablespoon of clean engine oil into the cylinder through the spark plug hole and repeat the compression test. If the compression comes up after adding the oil, it appears that the cylinder's piston rings or bore are damaged or worn. If the pressure remains low, the valves may not be seating properly (a valve job is needed), or the head gasket may be blown near that cylinder. If compression in any two adjacent cylinders is low, and if the addition of oil doesn't help the compression, there is leakage past the head gasket. Oil and coolant water in the combustion chamber can result from this problem. There may be evidence of water droplets on the engine dipstick when a head gasket has blown.

GENERAL ENGINE SPECIFICATIONS

Year	VIN	No. Cylinder Displacement cu. in. (liter)	Fuel System Type	Net Horsepower @ rpm	Net Torque @ rpm (ft. lbs.)	Bore × Stroke (in.)	Compression Ratio	Oil Pressure @ rpm
1982	G	4-110 (1.8)	2 bbl	88 @ 5100	100 @ 2800	3.50 × 2.91	9.0:1	45 @ 2400
	B	4-122 (2.0)	2 bbl	90 @ 5100	111 @ 2800	3.50 × 3.15	9.0:1	45 @ 2400
1983	0	4-110 (1.8)	TBI	84 @ 5200	102 @ 2800	3.34 × 3.13	8.8:1	45 @ 2400
	J	4-110 (1.8)	MFI Turbo	150 @ 5600	150 @ 2800	3.34 × 3.13	8.0:1	65 @ 2500
	P	4-121 (2.0)	TBI	86 @ 4900	100 @ 3000	3.50 × 3.15	9.3:1	68 @ 1200
	B	4-121 (2.0)	TBI	86 @ 4900	110 @ 3000	3.50 × 3.15	9.3:1	45 @ 2400
1984	0	4-110 (1.8)	TBI	84 @ 5200	102 @ 2800	3.34 × 3.13	8.8:1	45 @ 2400
	J	4-110 (1.8)	MFI Turbo	150 @ 5600	150 @ 2800	3.34 × 3.13	8.0:1	65 @ 2500
	P	4-121 (2.0)	TBI	86 @ 4900	100 @ 3000	3.50 × 3.15	9.3:1	68 @ 1200
1985	0	4-110 (1.8)	TBI	84 @ 5200	102 @ 2800	3.34 × 3.13	8.8:1	45 @ 2400
	J	4-110 (1.8)	MFI Turbo	150 @ 5600	150 @ 2800	3.34 × 3.13	8.0:1	65 @ 2500
	P	4-121 (2.0)	TBI	86 @ 4900	100 @ 3000	3.50 × 3.15	9.3:1	68 @ 1200
	W	6-173 (2.8)	MFI	120 @ 4800	155 @ 3600	3.50 × 2.99	8.9:1	50 @ 2400
1986	0	4-110 (1.8)	TBI	84 @ 5200	102 @ 2800	3.34 × 3.13	8.8:1	45 @ 2400
	J	4-110 (1.8)	MFI Turbo	150 @ 5600	150 @ 2800	3.34 × 3.13	8.0:1	65 @ 2500
	P	4-121 (2.0)	TBI	86 @ 4900	100 @ 3000	3.50 × 3.15	9.3:1	68 @ 1200
	W	6-173 (2.8)	MFI	120 @ 4800	155 @ 3600	3.50 × 2.99	8.9:1	50 @ 2400
1987	M	4-121 (2.0)	MFI Turbo	160 @ 5600	160 @ 2800	3.38 × 3.38	8.0:1	65 @ 2500
	1	4-121 (2.0)	TBI (HO)	90 @ 5600	108 @ 3200	3.50 × 3.15	9.0:1	63–77 @ 1200
	K	4-121 (2.0)	TBI	102 @ 5200	130 @ 2800	3.38 × 3.38	8.8:1	45 @ 2000
	W	6-173 (2.8)	MFI	120 @ 4800	155 @ 3600	3.50 × 2.99	8.9:1	50 @ 2400

GENERAL ENGINE SPECIFICATIONS

Year	VIN	No. Cylinder Displacement cu. in. (liter)	Fuel System Type	Net Horsepower @ rpm	Net Torque @ rpm (ft. lbs.)	Bore × Stroke (in.)	Compression Ratio	Oil Pressure @ rpm
1988	M	4-121 (2.0)	MFI Turbo	160 @ 5600	160 @ 2800	3.38 × 3.38	8.0:1	65 @ 2500
	1	4-121 (2.0)	TBI (HO)	90 @ 5600	108 @ 3200	3.50 × 3.15	9.0:1	63–77 @ 1200
	K	4-121 (2.0)	TBI	102 @ 5200	130 @ 2800	3.38 × 3.38	8.8:1	45 @ 2000
	W	6-173 (2.8)	MFI	120 @ 4800	155 @ 3600	3.50 × 2.99	8.9:1	50 @ 2400
1989	M	4-121 (2.0)	MFI Turbo	160 @ 5600	160 @ 2800	3.38 × 3.38	8.0:1	65 @ 2500
	1	4-121 (2.0)	TBI	90 @ 5600	108 @ 3200	3.50 × 3.15	9.0:1	63–77 @ 1200
	K	4-121 (2.0)	TBI	102 @ 5200	130 @ 2800	3.38 × 3.38	8.8:1	45 @ 2000
	W	6-173 (2.8)	MFI	120 @ 4800	155 @ 3600	3.50 × 2.99	8.9:1	50 @ 2400
1990	K	4-121 (2.0)	TBI	102 @ 5200	108 @ 3200	3.39 × 3.39	8.8:1	NA
	M	4-121 (2.0)	MFI Turbo	160 @ 5600	160 @ 2800	3.39 × 3.39	8.0:1	NA
	G	4-134 (2.2)	TBI	95 @ 5200	120 @ 3200	3.50 × 3.46	9.0:1	56 @ 3000
	T	6-192 (3.1)	MFI	140 @ 4500	180 @ 3600	3.50 × 3.31	8.8:1	15 @ 1100
1991	K	4-121 (2.0)	TBI	96 @ 4800	118 @ 3600	3.39 × 3.39	8.8:1	NA
	G	4-134 (2.2)	TBI	95 @ 5200	120 @ 3200	3.50 × 3.46	8.85:1	56 @ 3000
	T	6-192 (3.1)	MFI	140 @ 4500	180 @ 3600	3.50 × 3.31	8.8:1	15 @ 1100
1992	H	4-121 (2.0)	MFI	111 @ 5200	125 @ 3600	3.38 × 3.38	9.2:1	NA
	4	4-134 (2.2)	MFI	110 @ 5200	176 @ 3200	3.50 × 3.46	8.85:1	56 @ 3000
	T	6-192 (3.1)	MFI	140 @ 4200	180 @ 3200	3.50 × 3.31	8.8:1	15 @ 1100

NOTE: Horsepower and torque are SAE net figures. They are measured at the rear of the transmission with all accessories installed and operating. Since the figures vary when a given engine is installed in different models, some are representative rather than exact.

VALVE SPECIFICATIONS

Year	VIN	No. Cylinder Displacement cu. in. (liter)	Seat Angle (deg.)	Face Angle (deg.)	Spring Test Pressure (lbs.)	Spring Installed Height (in.)	Stem-to-Guide Clearance (in.) Intake	Stem-to-Guide Clearance (in.) Exhaust	Stem Diameter (in.) Intake	Stem Diameter (in.) Exhaust
1982	G	4-110 (1.8)	46	45	183 @ 1.33	1.60	0.0011–0.0026	0.0014–0.0031	0.3139–0.3144	0.3129–0.3136
	B	4-121 (2.0)	46	45	183 @ 1.33	1.60	0.0011–0.0026	0.0014–0.0031	0.3139–0.3144	0.3129–0.3136
1983	0	4-110 (1.8)	46	46	NA	NA	0.0006–0.0016	0.0012–0.0024	NA	NA
	J	4-110 (1.8)	46	46	NA	NA	0.0006–0.0016	0.0012–0.0024	NA	NA
	P	4-121 (2.0)	46	45	183 @ 1.33	1.60	0.0011–0.0026	0.0014–0.0031	0.3139–0.3144	0.3129–0.3136
	B	4-121 (2.0)	46	45	183 @ 1.33	1.60	0.0011–0.0026	0.0014–0.0031	0.3139–0.3144	0.3129–0.3136
1984	0	4-110 (1.8)	46	46	NA	NA	0.0006–0.0016	0.0012–0.0024	NA	NA
	J	4-110 (1.8)	46	46	NA	NA	0.0006–0.0016	0.0012–0.0024	NA	NA
	P	4-121 (2.0)	46	45	183 @ 1.33	1.60	0.0011–0.0026	0.0014–0.0031	0.3139–0.3144	0.3129–0.3136

VALVE SPECIFICATIONS

Year	VIN	No. Cylinder Displacement cu. in. (liter)	Seat Angle (deg.)	Face Angle (deg.)	Spring Test Pressure (lbs.)	Spring Installed Height (in.)	Stem-to-Guide Clearance (in.) Intake	Stem-to-Guide Clearance (in.) Exhaust	Stem Diameter (in.) Intake	Stem Diameter (in.) Exhaust
1985	0	4-110 (1.8)	46	46	NA	NA	0.0006–0.0016	0.0012–0.0024	NA	NA
	J	4-110 (1.8)	46	46	NA	NA	0.0006–0.0016	0.0012–0.0024	NA	NA
	P	4-121 (2.0)	46	45	183 @ 1.33	1.60	0.0011–0.0026	0.0014–0.0031	0.3139–0.3144	0.3129–0.3136
	W	6-173 (2.8)	46	45	195 @ 1.18	1.57	0.0010–0.0027	0.0010–0.0027	NA	NA
1986	0	4-110 (1.8)	46	46	NA	NA	0.0006–0.0016	0.0012–0.0024	NA	NA
	J	4-110 (1.8)	46	46	NA	NA	0.0006–0.0016	0.0012–0.0024	NA	NA
	P	4-121 (2.0)	46	45	183 @ 1.33	1.60	0.0011–0.0026	0.0014–0.0031	0.3139–0.3144	0.3129–0.3136
	W	6-173 (2.8)	46	45	195 @ 1.18	1.57	0.0010–0.0027	0.0010–0.0027	NA	NA
1987	M	4-121 (2.0)	45	46	NA	NA	0.0006–0.0020	0.0010–0.0024	NA	NA
	1	4-121 (2.0)	46	45	183 @ 1.33	1.60	0.0011–0.0026	0.0014–0.0030	NA	NA
	K	4-121 (2.0)	45	46	NA	NA	0.0006–0.0020	0.0010–0.0024	NA	NA
	W	6-173 (2.8)	46	45	195 @ 1.18	1.57	0.0010–0.0027	0.0010–0.0027	NA	NA
1988	M	4-121 (2.0)	45	46	NA	NA	0.0006–0.0020	0.0010–0.0024	NA	NA
	1	4-121 (2.0)	46	45	183 @ 1.33	1.60	0.0011–0.0026	0.0014–0.0030	0.0490–0.0560	0.0630–0.0750
	K	4-121 (2.0)	45	46	NA	NA	0.0006–0.0020	0.0010–0.0024	NA	NA
	W	6-173 (2.8)	46	45	195 @ 1.18	1.57	0.0010–0.0027	0.0010–0.0027	0.0610–0.0730	0.0670–0.0790
1989	M	4-121 (2.0)	45	46	165–179 @ 1.043	1.47	0.0006–0.0017	0.0012–0.0024	NA	NA
	1	4-121 (2.0)	46	45	208–222 @ 1.22	1.61	0.0011–0.0026	0.0014–0.0030	NA	NA
	K	4-121 (2.0)	45	46	165–197 @ 1.043	1.47	0.0006–0.0017	0.0012–0.0024	NA	NA
	W	6-173 (2.8)	46	45	215– @ 1.291	1.57	0.0010–0.0027	0.0010–0.0027	NA	NA
1990	K	4-121 (2.0)	45	46	165–197 @ 1.043	1.47	0.0006–0.0017	0.0012–0.0024	0.2755–0.2760	0.2747–0.2753
	M	4-121 (2.0)	45	46	165–179 @ 1.043	1.47	0.0006–0.0017	0.0012–0.0024	0.2755–0.2760	0.2747–0.2753
	G	4-134 (2.2)	46	45	208–222 @ 1.22	1.61	0.0011–0.0026	0.0014–0.0021	NA	NA
	T	6-192 (3.1)	46	45	215– @ 1.291	1.57	0.0010–0.0027	0.0010–0.0027	NA	NA

VALVE SPECIFICATIONS

Year	VIN	No. Cylinder Displacement cu. in. (liter)	Seat Angle (deg.)	Face Angle (deg.)	Spring Test Pressure (lbs.)	Spring Installed Height (in.)	Stem-to-Guide Clearance (in.) Intake	Exhaust	Stem Diameter (in.) Intake	Exhaust
1991	K	4-121 (2.0)	45	46	165–197 @ 1.043	1.47	0.0006–0.0017	0.0012–0.0024	0.2755–0.2760	0.2747–0.2753
	G	4-134 (2.2)	46	45	208–222 @ 1.22	1.61	0.0011–0.0026	0.0014–0.0031	NA	NA
	T	6-192 (3.1)	46	45	215– @ 1.291	1.57	0.0010–0.0027	0.0010–0.0027	NA	NA
1992	H	4-121 (2.0)	45	46	165–197 @ 1.043	1.47	0.0006–0.0017	0.0012–0.0024	0.2755–0.2760	0.2747–0.2753
	4	4-134 (2.2)	46	45	NA	NA	0.0011–0.0026	0.0014–0.0031	NA	NA
	T	6-192 (3.1)	46	45	215– @ 1.291	1.57	0.0010–0.0027	0.0010–0.0027	NA	NA

CAMSHAFT SPECIFICATIONS

All measurements given in inches.

Year	VIN	No. Cylinder Displacement cu. in. (liter)	Journal Diameter 1	2	3	4	5	Elevation In.	Ex.	Bearing Clearance	Camshaft End Play
1982	G	4-110 (1.8)	1.8677–1.8696	1.8677–1.8696	1.8677–1.8696	1.8677–1.8696	1.8677–1.8696	0.2625	0.2625	0.0010–0.0039	NA
	B	4-121 (2.0)	1.8677–1.8696	1.8677–1.8696	1.8677–1.8696	1.8677–1.8696	1.8677–1.8696	0.2600	0.2600	0.0010–0.0039	NA
1983	0	4-110 (1.8)	1.6714–1.6720	1.6812–1.6816	1.6911–1.6917	1.7009–1.7015	1.7108–1.7114	0.2409	0.2409	NA	0.0160–0.0640
	J	4-110 (1.8)	1.6714–1.6720	1.6812–1.6816	1.6911–1.6917	1.7009–1.7015	1.7108–1.7114	0.2409	0.2409	NA	0.0160–0.0640
	P	4-121 (2.0)	1.8677–1.8696	1.8677–1.8696	1.8677–1.8696	1.8677–1.8696	1.8677–1.8696	0.2600	0.2600	0.0010–0.0039	NA
	B	4-121 (2.0)	1.8677–1.8696	1.8677–1.8696	1.8677–1.8696	1.8677–1.8696	1.8677–1.8696	0.2600	0.2600	0.0010–0.0039	NA
1984	0	4-110 (1.8)	1.6714–1.6720	1.6812–1.6816	1.6911–1.6917	1.7009–1.7015	1.7108–1.7114	0.2409	0.2409	NA	0.0160–0.0640
	J	4-110 (1.8)	1.6714–1.6720	1.6812–1.6816	1.6911–1.6917	1.7009–1.7015	1.7108–1.7114	0.2409	0.2409	NA	0.0160–0.0640
	P	4-121 (2.0)	1.8677–1.8696	1.8677–1.8696	1.8677–1.8696	1.8677–1.8696	1.8677–1.8696	0.2600	0.2600	0.0010–0.0039	NA
1985	0	4-110 (1.8)	1.6714–1.6720	1.6812–1.6816	1.6911–1.6917	1.7009–1.7015	1.7108–1.7114	0.2409	0.2409	NA	0.0160–0.0640
	J	4-110 (1.8)	1.6714–1.6720	1.6812–1.6816	1.6911–1.6917	1.7009–1.7015	1.7108–1.7114	0.2409	0.2409	NA	0.0160–0.0640
	P	4-121 (2.0)	1.8677–1.8696	1.8677–1.8696	1.8677–1.8696	1.8677–1.8696	1.8677–1.8696	0.2600	0.2600	0.0010–0.0039	NA
	W	6-173 (2.8)	1.8678–1.8815	1.8678–1.8815	1.8678–1.8815	1.8678–1.8815	1.8678–1.8815	0.2626	0.2732	NA	NA

CAMSHAFT SPECIFICATIONS

All measurements given in inches.

Year	VIN	No. Cylinder Displacement cu. in. (liter)	Journal Diameter 1	2	3	4	5	Elevation In.	Ex.	Bearing Clearance	Camshaft End Play
1986	O	4-110 (1.8)	1.6714–1.6720	1.6812–1.6816	1.6911–1.6917	1.7009–1.7015	1.7108–1.7114	0.2409	0.2409	NA	0.0160–0.0640
	J	4-110 (1.8)	1.6714–1.6720	1.6812–1.6816	1.6911–1.6917	1.7009–1.7015	1.7108–1.7114	0.2409	0.2409	NA	0.0160–0.0640
	P	4-121 (2.0)	1.8677–1.8696	1.8677–1.8696	1.8677–1.8696	1.8677–1.8696	1.8677–1.8696	0.2600	0.2600	0.0010–0.0039	NA
	W	6-173 (2.8)	1.8678–1.8815	1.8678–1.8815	1.8678–1.8815	1.8678–1.8815	1.8678–1.8815	0.2626	0.2732	NA	NA
1987	M	4-121 (2.0)	1.6714–1.6720	1.6812–1.6816	1.6911–1.6917	1.7009–1.7015	1.7108–1.7114	0.2409	0.2409	0.0008	0.0160–0.0640
	1	4-121 (2.0)	1.8670–1.8690	1.8670–1.8690	1.8670–1.8690	1.8670–1.8690	1.8670–1.8690	0.2600	0.2600	0.0010–0.0040	NA
	K	4-121 (2.0)	1.6714–1.6720	1.6812–1.6816	1.6911–1.6917	1.7009–1.7015	1.7108–1.7114	0.2409	0.2409	0.0008	0.0160–0.0640
	W	6-173 (2.8)	1.8678–1.8815	1.8678–1.8815	1.8678–1.8815	1.8678–1.8815	1.8678–1.8815	0.2626	0.2732	NA	NA
1988	M	4-121 (2.0)	1.6714–1.6720	1.6812–1.6816	1.6911–1.6917	1.7009–1.7015	1.7108–1.7114	0.2409	0.2409	0.0008	0.0160–0.0640
	1	4-121 (2.0)	1.8670–1.8690	1.8670–1.8690	1.8670–1.8690	1.8670–1.8690	1.8670–1.8690	0.2600	0.2600	0.0010–0.0040	NA
	K	4-121 (2.0)	1.6714–1.6720	1.6812–1.6816	1.6911–1.6917	1.7009–1.7015	1.7108–1.7114	0.2409	0.2409	0.0008	0.0160–0.0640
	W	6-173 (2.8)	1.8678–1.8696	1.8678–1.8696	1.8678–1.8696	1.8678–1.8696	1.8678–1.8696	0.2626	0.2732	0.0010–0.0030	NA
1989	M	4-121 (2.0)	1.6706–1.6712	1.6812–1.6818	1.6911–1.6917	1.7009–1.7015	1.7100–1.7106	0.2625	0.2625	0.0011–0.0035	0.0016–0.0063
	1	4-121 (2.0)	1.8670–1.8690	1.8670–1.8690	1.8670–1.8690	1.8670–1.8690	1.8670–1.8690	0.2600	0.2600	0.0010–0.0040	NA
	K	4-121 (2.0)	1.6706–1.6712	1.6812–1.6818	1.6911–1.6917	1.7009–1.7015	1.7100–1.7106	0.2366	0.2515	0.0011–0.0035	0.0016–0.0063
	W	6-173 (2.8)	1.8678–1.8815	1.8678–1.8815	1.8678–1.8815	1.8678–1.8815	1.8678–1.8815	0.2626	0.2732	0.0010–0.0040	NA
1990	K	4-121 (2.0)	1.6706–1.6712	1.6812–1.6818	1.6911–1.6917	1.7009–1.7015	1.7100–1.7106	0.2366	0.2515	0.0011–0.0035	0.0016–0.0063
	M	4-121 (2.0)	1.6706–1.6717	1.6812–1.6818	1.6911–1.6917	1.7009–1.7015	1.7100–1.7106	0.2625	0.2625	0.0011–0.0035	0.0016–0.0063
	G	4-134 (2.2)	1.8670–1.8690	1.8670–1.8690	1.8670–1.8690	1.8670–1.8690	1.8670–1.8690	0.2590	0.2590	0.0010–0.0040	NA
	T	6-192 (3.1)	1.8678–1.8815	1.8678–1.8815	1.8678–1.8815	1.8678–1.8815	1.8678–1.8815	0.2626	0.2626	0.0010–0.0040	NA
1991	K	4-121 (2.0)	1.6706–1.6712	1.6812–1.6818	1.6911–1.6917	1.7009–1.7015	1.7100–1.7106	0.2366	0.2515	0.0011–0.0035	0.0016–0.0063
	G	4-134 (2.2)	1.8670–1.8690	1.8670–1.8690	1.8670–1.8690	1.8670–1.8690	1.8670–1.8690	0.2590	0.2590	0.0010–0.0040	NA
	T	6-192 (3.1)	1.8677–1.8815	1.8677–1.8815	1.8677–1.8815	1.8677–1.8815	1.8677–1.8815	0.2626	0.2626	0.0010–0.0040	NA

CAMSHAFT SPECIFICATIONS

All measurements given in inches.

Year	VIN	No. Cylinder Displacement cu. in. (liter)	Journal Diameter 1	2	3	4	5	Elevation In.	Ex.	Bearing Clearance	Camshaft End Play
1992	H	4-121 (2.0)	1.6706–1.6712	1.6812–1.6818	1.6911–1.6917	1.7009–1.7015	1.7100–1.7106	0.2626	0.2626	0.0011–0.0035	0.0016–0.0063
	4	4-132 (2.2)	1.8670–1.8690	1.8670–1.8690	1.8670–1.8690	1.8670–1.8690	1.8670–1.8690	0.2590	0.2590	0.0010–0.0040	NA
	T	6-192 (3.1)	1.8677–1.8815	1.8677–1.8815	1.8677–1.8815	1.8677–1.8815	1.8677–1.8815	0.2626	0.2732	0.0010–0.0040	NA

CRANKSHAFT AND CONNECTING ROD SPECIFICATIONS

All measurements are given in inches.

Year	VIN	No. Cylinder Displacement cu. in. (liter)	Crankshaft Main Brg. Journal Dia.	Main Brg. Oil Clearance	Shaft End-play	Thrust on No.	Connecting Rod Journal Diameter	Oil Clearance	Side Clearance
1982	G	4-110 (1.8)	2.4944–2.4954②	0.0006–0.0018③	0.0019–0.0071	4	1.9983–1.9993	0.0009–0.0031	0.0039–0.0240
	B	4-121 (2.0)	2.4944–2.4954②	0.0006–0.0018③	0.0019–0.0071	4	1.9983–1.9993	0.0009–0.0031	0.0039–0.0240
1983	0	4-110 (1.8)	①	0.0006–0.0016	0.0027–0.0118	3	1.9278–1.9286	0.0007–0.0024	0.0027–0.0095
	J	4-110 (1.8)	①	0.0006–0.0016	0.0027–0.0118	3	1.9278–1.9286	0.0007–0.0024	0.0027–0.0095
	P	4-121 (2.0)	2.4944–2.4954②	0.0006–0.0018③	0.0019–0.0071	4	1.9983–1.9993	0.0009–0.0031	0.0039–0.0240
	B	4-121 (2.0)	2.4944–2.4954②	0.0006–0.0018③	0.0019–0.0071	4	1.9983–1.9993	0.0009–0.0031	0.0039–0.0240
1984	0	4-110 (1.8)	①	0.0006–0.0016	0.0027–0.0118	3	1.9278–1.9286	0.0007–0.0024	0.0027–0.0095
	J	4-110 (1.8)	①	0.0006–0.0016	0.0027–0.0118	3	1.9278–1.9286	0.0007–0.0024	0.0027–0.0095
	P	4-121 (2.0)	2.4944–2.4954②	0.0006–0.0018③	0.0019–0.0071	4	1.9983–1.9993	0.0009–0.0031	0.0039–0.0240
1985	0	4-110 (1.8)	①	0.0006–0.0016	0.0027–0.0118	3	1.9278–1.9286	0.0007–0.0024	0.0027–0.0095
	J	4-110 (1.8)	①	0.0006–0.0016	0.0027–0.0118	3	1.9278–1.9286	0.0007–0.0024	0.0027–0.0095
	P	4-121 (2.0)	2.4944–2.4954②	0.0006–0.0018③	0.0019–0.0071	4	1.9983–1.9993	0.0009–0.0031	0.0039–0.0240
	W	6-173 (2.8)	2.6473–2.6482	0.0016–0.0033	0.0024–0.0083	3	1.9983–1.9994	0.0014–0.0037	0.0063–0.0173
1986	0	4-110 (1.8)	①	0.0006–0.0016	0.0027–0.0118	3	1.9278–1.9286	0.0007–0.0024	0.0027–0.0095
	J	4-110 (1.8)	①	0.0006–0.0016	0.0027–0.0118	3	1.9278–1.9286	0.0007–0.0024	0.0027–0.0095
	P	4-121 (2.0)	2.4944–2.4954②	0.0006–0.0018③	0.0019–0.0071	4	1.9983–1.9993	0.0009–0.0031	0.0039–0.0240
	W	6-173 (2.8)	2.6473–2.6482	0.0016–0.0033	0.0024–0.0083	3	1.9983–1.9994	0.0014–0.0037	0.0063–0.0173

CRANKSHAFT AND CONNECTING ROD SPECIFICATIONS

All measurements are given in inches.

Year	VIN	No. Cylinder Displacement cu. in. (liter)	Crankshaft				Connecting Rod		
			Main Brg. Journal Dia.	Main Brg. Oil Clearance	Shaft End-play	Thrust on No.	Journal Diameter	Oil Clearance	Side Clearance
1987	M	4-121 (2.0)	①	0.0006–0.0016	0.0030–0.0120	3	1.9278–1.9286	0.0007–0.0024	0.0027–0.0095
	1	4-121 (2.0)	2.4945–2.4954	0.0006–0.0019	0.0020–0.0080	4	1.9983–1.9994	0.0010–0.0031	0.0040–0.0150
	K	4-121 (2.0)	①	0.0006–0.0016	0.0030–0.0120	3	1.9278–1.9286	0.0007–0.0024	0.0027–0.0095
	W	6-173 (2.8)	2.6473–2.6482	0.0016–0.0033	0.0024–0.0083	3	1.9983–1.9994	0.0014–0.0037	0.0063–0.0173
1988	M	4-121 (2.0)	①	0.0006–0.0016	0.0030–0.0120	3	1.9278–1.9286	0.0007–0.0024	0.0027–0.0095
	1	4-121 (2.0)	2.4945–2.4954	0.0006–0.0019	0.0020–0.0080	4	1.9983–1.9994	0.0010–0.0031	0.0040–0.0150
	K	4-121 (2.0)	①	0.0006–0.0016	0.0030–0.0120	3	1.9278–1.9286	0.0007–0.0024	0.0027–0.0095
	W	6-173 (2.8)	2.6473–2.6482	0.0016–0.0033	0.0024–0.0083	3	1.9983–1.9994	0.0014–0.0037	0.0063–0.0173
1989	M	4-121 (2.0)	①	0.0006–0.0016	0.0030–0.0120	3	1.9278–1.9286	0.0007–0.0024	0.0027–0.0095
	1	4-121 (2.0)	2.4945–2.4954	0.0006–0.0019	0.0020–0.0080	4	1.9983–1.9994	0.0010–0.0031	0.0040–0.0150
	K	4-121 (2.0)	①	0.0006–0.0016	0.0030–0.0120	3	1.9278–1.9286	0.0007–0.0024	0.0027–0.0095
	W	6-173 (2.8)	2.6473–2.6482	0.0016–0.0033	0.0024–0.0083	3	1.9983–1.9994	0.0014–0.0037	0.0063–0.0173
1990	K	4-121 (2.0)	①	0.0006–0.0016	0.0028–0.0120	3	1.9279–1.9287	0.0007–0.0025	0.0028–0.0095
	M	4-121 (2.0)	①	0.0006–0.0016	0.0028–0.0118	3	1.9279–1.9287	0.0007–0.0025	0.0028–0.0095
	G	4-134 (2.2)	2.4945–2.4954	0.0006–0.0019	0.0020–0.0070	4	1.9983–1.9994	0.00098–0.0031	0.0039–0.0149
	T	6-192 (3.1)	2.6473–2.6483	0.0012–0.0030	0.0024–0.0083	3	1.9983–1.9994	0.0011–0.0034	0.0140–0.0270
1991	K	4-121 (2.0)	2.2828–2.2833	0.0006–0.0016	0.0028–0.0118	3	1.9279–1.9287	0.0007–0.0025	0.0028–0.0095
	G	4-134 (2.2)	2.4945–2.4954	0.0006–0.0019	0.0020–0.0070	4	1.9983–1.9994	0.00098–0.0031	0.0039–0.0149
	T	6-192 (3.1)	2.6473–2.6483	0.0012–0.0030	0.0024–0.0083	3	1.9983–1.9994	0.0011–0.0034	0.0140–0.0270
1992	H	4-121 (2.0)	2.2828–2.2833	0.0006–0.0016	0.0028–0.0118	3	1.9279–1.9287	0.0007–0.0025	0.0028–0.0095
	4	4-134 (2.2)	2.4945–2.4954	0.0006–0.0019	0.0020–0.0070	4	1.9983–1.9994	0.00098–0.0031	0.0039–0.0149
	T	6-192 (3.1)	2.6473–2.6483	0.0012–0.0030	0.0024–0.0083	3	1.9983–1.9994	0.0011–0.0034	0.0140–0.0270

① Bearings are identified by color:
  Brown 2.2830–2.2832;
  Green 2.2827–2.2830
② No. 5: 2.4936–2.4946
③ No. 5: 0.0014–0.0027

PISTON AND RING SPECIFICATIONS

All measurements are given in inches.

| Year | VIN | No. Cylinder Displacement cu. in. (liter) | Piston Clearance | Ring Gap | | | Ring Side Clearance | | |
				Top Compression	Bottom Compression	Oil Control	Top Compression	Bottom Compression	Oil Control
1982	G	4-110 (1.8)	0.0008–0.0018	0.0098–0.0197	0.0098–0.0197	Snug	0.0012–0.0027	0.0012–0.0027	0.0078
	B	4-121 (2.0)	0.0008–0.0018	0.0098–0.0197	0.0098–0.0197	Snug	0.0012–0.0027	0.0012–0.0027	0.0078
1983	0	4-110 (1.8)	0.0004–0.0012	0.0010–0.0020	0.0010–0.0020	0.0010–0.0020	0.0020–0.0030	0.0010–0.0024	Snug
	J	4-110 (1.8)	0.0004–0.0012	0.0010–0.0020	0.0010–0.0020	0.0010–0.0020	0.0020–0.0030	0.0010–0.0024	Snug
	P	4-121 (2.0)	0.0008–0.0018	0.0098–0.0197	0.0098–0.0197	Snug	0.0012–0.0027	0.0012–0.0027	0.0078
	B	4-121 (2.0)	0.0008–0.0018	0.0098–0.0197	0.0098–0.0197	Snug	0.0012–0.0027	0.0012–0.0027	0.0078
1984	0	4-110 (1.8)	0.0004–0.0012	0.0010–0.0020	0.0010–0.0020	0.0010–0.0020	0.0020–0.0030	0.0010–0.0024	Snug
	J	4-110 (1.8)	0.0004–0.0012	0.0010–0.0020	0.0010–0.0020	0.0010–0.0020	0.0020–0.0030	0.0010–0.0024	Snug
	P	4-121 (2.0)	0.0007–0.0017	0.0098–0.0197	0.0098–0.0197	Snug	0.0012–0.0027	0.0012–0.0027	0.0078
1985	0	4-110 (1.8)	0.0004–0.0012	0.0010–0.0020	0.0010–0.0020	0.0010–0.0020	0.0020–0.0030	0.0010–0.0024	Snug
	J	4-110 (1.8)	0.0004–0.0012	0.0010–0.0020	0.0010–0.0020	0.0010–0.0020	0.0020–0.0030	0.0010–0.0024	Snug
	P	4-121 (2.0)	0.0007–0.0017	0.0098–0.0197	0.0098–0.0197	Snug	0.0012–0.0027	0.0012–0.0027	0.0078
	W	6-173 (2.8)	0.0007–0.0017	0.0098–0.0197	0.0098–0.0197	Snug	0.0012–0.0027	0.0012–0.0027	0.0078 Max.
1986	0	4-110 (1.8)	0.0004–0.0012	0.0120–0.0200	0.0120–0.0200	0.0160–0.0550	0.0020–0.0040	0.0010–0.0024	0.0047
	J	4-110 (1.8)	0.0004–0.0012	0.0120–0.0200	0.0120–0.0200	0.0160–0.0550	0.0020–0.0040	0.0010–0.0024	0.0047
	P	4-121 (2.0)	0.0008–0.0018	0.0098–0.0197	0.0098–0.0197	Snug	0.0012–0.0027	0.0012–0.0027	0.0078
	W	6-173 (2.8)	0.0007–0.0017	0.0098–0.0197	0.0098–0.0197	0.0200–0.0550	0.0012–0.0027	0.0016–0.0037	0.0078 Max.
1987	M	4-121 (2.0)	0.0012–0.0020	0.0120–0.0200	0.0120–0.0200	0.0160–0.0550	0.0020–0.0030	0.0010–0.0024	0.0047
	1	4-121 (2.0)	0.0098–0.0220	0.0100–0.0200	0.0100–0.0200	0.0100–0.0500	0.0010–0.0030	0.0010–0.0030	0.0006–0.0090
	K	4-121 (2.0)	0.0012–0.0020	0.0120–0.0200	0.0120–0.0200	0.0160–0.0550	0.0020–0.0030	0.0010–0.0024	0.0047
	W	6-173 (2.8)	0.0020–0.0028	0.0100–0.0200	0.0100–0.0200	0.0200–0.0550	0.0010–0.0030	0.0010–0.0030	0.0078 Max.

PISTON AND RING SPECIFICATIONS

All measurements are given in inches.

Year	VIN	No. Cylinder Displacement cu. in. (liter)	Piston Clearance	Ring Gap			Ring Side Clearance		
				Top Compression	Bottom Compression	Oil Control	Top Compression	Bottom Compression	Oil Control
1988	M	4-121 (2.0)	0.0012–0.0020	0.0120–0.0200	0.0120–0.0200	0.0160–0.0550	0.0020–0.0030	0.0010–0.0024	0.0047
	1	4-121 (2.0)	0.00098–0.0022	0.0100–0.0200	0.0100–0.0200	0.0100–0.0500	0.0010–0.0030	0.0010–0.0030	0.0006–0.0090
	K	4-121 (2.0)	0.0004–0.0012	0.0120–0.0200	0.0120–0.0200	0.0160–0.0550	0.0020–0.0030	0.0010–0.0024	Snug
	W	6-173 (2.8)	0.0022–0.0028	0.0100–0.0200	0.0100–0.0200	0.0100–0.0500	0.0020–0.0035	0.0020–0.0035	0.0080 Max.
1989	M	4-121 (2.0)	0.0012–0.0020	0.0098–0.0177	0.0118–0.0197	NA 0.0036	0.0024–0.0032	0.0019	NA
	1	4-121 (2.0)	0.00098–0.0022	0.0100–0.0200	0.0100–0.0200	0.0100–0.0500	0.0019–0.0027	0.0019–0.0027	0.0019–0.0082
	K	4-121 (2.0)	0.0004–0.0012	0.0980–0.1770	0.1180–0.1970	NA	0.0024–0.0036	0.0019–0.0032	NA
	W	6-178 (2.8)	0.00093–0.0022	0.0100–0.0200	0.0100–0.0200	0.0010–0.0030	0.0020–0.0035	0.0020–0.0035	0.0080 Max.
1990	K	4-121 (2.0)	0.0004–0.0012	0.0098–0.0177	0.0118–0.0197	NA	0.0024–0.0036	0.0019–0.0032	NA
	M	4-121 (2.0)	0.0004–0.0012	0.0098–0.0177	0.0118–0.0197	NA	0.0024–0.0036	0.0019–0.0032	NA
	G	4-134 (2.2)	0.0007–0.0017	0.0100–0.0200	0.0100–0.0200	0.0100–0.0500	0.0019–0.0027	0.0019–0.0027	0.0019–0.0082
	T	6-192 (3.1)	0.00093–0.00222	0.0100–0.0200	0.0200–0.0280	0.0010–0.0300	0.0020–0.0350	0.0020–0.0350	0.0080 Max.
1991	K	4-121 (2.0)	0.0004–0.0012	0.0098–0.0177	0.0118–0.0197	NA	0.0024–0.0036	0.0019–0.0032	NA
	G	4-134 (2.2)	0.0007–0.0017	0.0100–0.0200	0.0100–0.0200	0.0100–0.0500	0.0019–0.0027	0.0019–0.0027	0.0019–0.0082
	T	6-192 (3.1)	0.00093–0.00222	0.0100–0.0200	0.0200–0.0280	0.0010–0.0300	0.0020–0.0035	0.0020–0.0035	0.0080 Max.
1992	H	4-121 (2.0)	0.0004–0.0012	0.0098–0.0177	0.0118–0.0197	NA	0.0024–0.0036	0.0019–0.0032	NA
	4	4-134 (2.2)	0.0007–0.0017	0.0100–0.0200	0.0100–0.0200	0.0100–0.0050	0.0019–0.0027	0.0019–0.0027	0.0019–0.0082
	T	6-192 (3.1)	0.00093–0.00222	0.0100–0.0200	0.0200–0.0280	0.0100–0.0300	0.0020–0.0035	0.0020–0.0035	0.0080 Max.

TORQUE SPECIFICATIONS
All readings in ft. lbs.

Year	VIN	No. Cylinder Displacement cu. in. (liter)	Cylinder Head Bolts	Main Bearing Bolts	Rod Bearing Bolts	Crankshaft Pulley Bolts	Flywheel Bolts	Manifold Intake	Manifold Exhaust	Spark Plugs	Lug Nut
1982	G	4-110 (1.8)	65–75	63–74	34–40	66–84	45–55	20–25	22–28	15	100
	B	4-121 (2.0)	65–75	63–77	34–43	66–89	45–63②	18–25	20–30	15	100
1983	O	4-110 (1.8)	①	57	39	20⑥	45	25	16	15	100
	J	4-110 (1.8)	①	57	39	20⑥	45	25	16	15	100
	P	4-121 (2.0)	65–75	63–77	34–43	68–89	45–63②	18–25	20–30	15	100
	B	4-121 (2.0)	65–75	63–77	34–43	68–89	45–63②	18–25	20–30	15	100
1984	O	4-110 (1.8)	①	57	39	20⑥	45	25	16	15	100
	J	4-110 (1.8)	①	57	39	20⑥	45	25	16	15	100
	P	4-121 (2.0)	65–75	63–77	34–43	68–89	45–63②	18–25	20–30	15	100
1985	O	4-110 (1.8)	①	57	39	20⑥	45	25	16	15	100
	J	4-110 (1.8)	①	57	39	20⑥	45	25	16	15	100
	P	4-121 (2.0)	65–75	63–77	34–43	68–89	45–63②	18–25	34–44	7–20	100
	W	6-173 (2.8)	65–90	70	34–45	75	45	13–25	19–31	15	100
1986	O	4-110 (1.8)	①	57	39	20⑥	45	25	16	15	100
	J	4-110 (1.8)	①	57	39	20⑥	45	25	16	15	100
	P	4-121 (2.0)	73–85	63–77	34–43	68–89	45–63②	18–25	34–44	7–20	100
	W	6-173 (2.8)	65–90	70	34–45	75	45	13–25	19–31	15	100
1987	M	4-121 (2.0)	①	④	⑤	20⑥	48	16	16	7–15	100
	1	4-121 (2.0)	③	63–77	34–43	68–89	45–63②	18–25	16–13	7–20	100
	K	4-121 (2.0)	①	④	⑤	20⑥	48	16	16	7–15	100
	W	6-173 (2.8)	⑧	70	34–45	75	45	25⑪	15–23	10–25	
1988	M	4-121 (2.0)	①	④	⑤	20⑥	⑦	16	16	25	100
	1	4-121 (2.0)	③	63–70	34–43	66–89	47–63②	19–25	6–13	7–20	100
	K	4-121 (2.0)	①	④	⑤	20⑥	⑦	16	16	25	100
	W	6-173 (2.8)	⑧	63–83	34–40	67–85	46	⑪	15–23	10–25	
1989	M	4-121 (2.0)	①	④	⑤	⑬	⑦	18	⑭	15	100
	1	4-121 (2.0)	③	63–77	34–43	⑨	47–63②	15–22	6–13	15	100
	K	4-121 (2.0)	①	④	⑤	⑬	⑦	16	⑭	15	100
	W	6-173 (2.8)	⑧	73	39	76	⑩	⑪	18	⑫	
1990	K	4-121 (2.0)	①	④	⑤	⑬	⑦	16	⑭	15	100
	M	4-121 (2.0)	①	④	⑤	⑬	⑦	18	⑭	15	100
	G	4-134 (2.2)	⑯	70	38	85	⑰	18	⑮	11	100
	T	6-192 (3.1)	⑧	73	39	76	⑰	⑪	18	11	100
1991	K	4-121 (2.0)	①	④	⑤	⑬	⑦	16	⑭	15	100
	G	4-134 (2.2)	⑱	70	38	77	⑰	18	⑮	11	100
	T	6-192 (3.1)	⑧	73	39	76	⑰	⑪	18	11	100

TORQUE SPECIFICATIONS
All readings in ft. lbs.

Year	VIN	No. Cylinder Displacement cu. in. (liter)	Cylinder Head Bolts	Main Bearing Bolts	Rod Bearing Bolts	Crankshaft Pulley Bolts	Flywheel Bolts	Manifold		Spark Plugs	Lug Nut
								Intake	Exhaust		
1992	H	4-121 (2.0)	①	④	⑤	15	⑦	16	16	11	100
	4	4-134 (2.2)	⑱	70	38	77	55	22	10	11	100
	T	6-192 (3.1)	⑧	73	39	76	⑰	⑪	18	11	100

CAUTION: Verify the correct original equipment engine is in the vehicle by referring to the VIN engine code before torquing any bolts.

① Torque bolts to 18 ft. lbs., then turn each bolt 60°, in sequence, 3 times for a 180° rotation, then run the engine to normal operating temperature and turn each bolt, in sequence, an additional 30°–50°.

② Auto. Trans.: 45–59

③ Long: 73–83
Short: 62–70

④ 44 ft. lbs. plus a 40° to 50° turn

⑤ 26 ft. lbs. plus a 40° to 45° turn

⑥ Crankshaft pulley to sprocket bolts

⑦ Manual transaxle: 48 ft. lbs. plus 30 degree turn
Automatic transaxle: 48 ft. lbs.

⑧ Coat threads with sealer, torque to 33 ft. lbs. plus an additional 90 degrees (¼ turn)

⑨ Crankshaft pulley center 66–89 ft. lbs., crankshaft pulley outer 30–40 ft. lbs.

⑩ Automatic transaxle: 46 ft. lbs., manual transaxle: 59 ft. lbs.

⑪ Tighten in sequence to 15 ft. lbs., retighten to 24 ft. lbs.

⑫ Tapered seat plugs: 15 ft. lbs., without tapered seat: 25 ft. lbs.

⑬ Crankshaft pulley to sprocket bolts: 150 inch lbs.

⑭ 115 inch lbs.

⑮ Nuts: 115 inch lbs., studs: 89 inch lbs.

⑯ Step 1—Tighten all bolts initially to 41 ft. lbs.
Step 2—Tighten all bolts an additional 45 degrees in sequence
Step 3—Tighten all bolts an additional 45 degrees in sequence
Step 4—Tighten the long bolts—8, 4, 1, 5 and 9 an additional 20 degrees and tighten the short bolts—7, 3, 2, 6 and 10 an additional 10 degrees.

⑰ Automatic transaxle: 52 ft. lbs., manual transaxle: 55 ft. lbs.

⑱ Tighten bolts in sequence as follows:
Long bolts 46 ft. lbs.
Short bolts 43 ft. lbs.
Tighten all bolts in sequence an additional 90 degrees.

Standard Torque Specifications and Fastener Markings

In the absence of specific torques, the following chart can be used as a guide to the maximum safe torque of a particular size/grade of fastener.

- There is no torque difference for fine or coarse threads.
- Torque values are based on clean, dry threads. Reduce the value by 10% if threads are oiled prior to assembly.
- The torque required for aluminum components or fasteners is considerably less.

U.S. Bolts

SAE Grade Number	1 or 2			5			6 or 7		
Number of lines always 2 less than the grade number.									
Bolt Size (Inches)—(Thread)	Ft./Lbs.	Kgm	Nm	Ft./Lbs.	Kgm	Nm	Ft./Lbs.	Kgm	Nm
¼ — 20	5	0.7	6.8	8	1.1	10.8	10	1.4	13.5
— 28	6	0.8	8.1	10	1.4	13.6			
5/16 — 18	11	1.5	14.9	17	2.3	23.0	19	2.6	25.8
— 24	13	1.8	17.6	19	2.6	25.7			
⅜ — 16	18	2.5	24.4	31	4.3	42.0	34	4.7	46.0
— 24	20	2.75	27.1	35	4.8	47:5			
7/16 — 14	28	3.8	37.0	49	6.8	66.4	55	7.6	74.5
— 20	30	4.2	40.7	55	7.6	74.5			
½ — 13	39	5.4	52.8	75	10.4	101.7	85	11.75	115.2
— 20	41	5.7	55.6	85	11.7	115.2			
9/16 — 12	51	7.0	69.2	110	15.2	149.1	120	16.6	162.7
— 18	55	7.6	74.5	120	16.6	162.7			
⅝ — 11	83	11.5	112.5	150	20.7	203.3	167	23.0	226.5
— 18	95	13.1	128.8	170	23.5	230.5			
¾ — 10	105	14.5	142.3	270	37.3	366.0	280	38.7	379.6
— 16	115	15.9	155.9	295	40.8	400.0			
⅞ — 9	160	22.1	216.9	395	54.6	535.5	440	60.9	596.5
— 14	175	24.2	237.2	435	60.1	589.7			
1 — 8	236	32.5	318.6	590	81.6	799.9	660	91.3	894.8
— 14	250	34.6	338.9	660	91.3	849.8			

Metric Bolts

Relative Strength Marking	4.6, 4.8			8.8		
Bolt Markings						
Bolt Size Thread Size x Pitch (mm)	Ft./Lbs.	Kgm	Nm	Ft./Lbs.	Kgm	Nm
6 x 1.0	2–3	.2–.4	3–4	3–6	.4–.8	5–8
8 x 1.25	6–8	.8–1	8–12	9–14	1.2–1.9	13–19
10 x 1.25	12–17	1.5–2.3	16–23	20–29	2.7–4.0	27–39
12 x 1.25	21–32	2.9–4.4	29–43	35–53	4.8–7.3	47–72
14 x 1.5	35–52	4.8–7.1	48–70	57–85	7.8–11.7	77–110
16 x 1.5	51–77	7.0–10.6	67–100	90–120	12.4–16.5	130–160
18 x 1.5	74–110	10.2–15.1	100–150	130–170	17.9–23.4	180–230
20 x 1.5	110–140	15.1–19.3	150–190	190–240	26.2–46.9	160–320
22 x 1.5	150–190	22.0–26.2	200–260	250–320	34.5–44.1	340–430
24 x 1.5	190–240	26.2–46.9	260–320	310–410	42.7–56.5	420–550

Engine

REMOVAL & INSTALLATION

✹✹ CAUTION

When draining the coolant, keep in mind that cats and dogs are attracted by the ethylene glycol anti-freeze, and are quite likely to drink any that is left in an uncovered container or in puddles on the ground. This will prove fatal in sufficient quantity. Always drain the coolant into a sealable container. Coolant should be reused unless it is contaminated or several years old.

1.8L, 2.0L and 2.2L OHV Engines

1982–84

◆ SEE FIGS. 20-21

➡ **This procedure will require the use of a special powertrain alignment tool.**

1. Disconnect the battery cables at the battery, negative cable first.
2. Remove the air cleaner. Drain the cooling system.
3. Remove the power steering pump (if so equipped) and position it out of the way. Leave the lines connected. Remove the windshield washer bottle.
4. If the car is equipped with air conditioning, remove the relay bracket at the bulkhead connector. Remove the bulkhead connector and then separate the wiring harness connections.
5. If equipped with cruise control, remove the servo bracket and position it out of the way.
6. Tag and disconnect all vacuum hoses and wires.
7. Remove the master cylinder at the vacuum booster.
8. Remove all heater and radiator hoses and position them out of the way.
9. Remove the fan assembly. Remove the horn.
10. Disconnect the carburetor or TBI body linkage. Raise the front of the car and support it with jackstands.
11. Release the fuel system pressure (see Section 1) and disconnect the fuel line at the intake manifold.

12. Remove the air conditioning brace (if so equipped).
13. Remove the exhaust shield. Remove the starter.
14. Disconnect the exhaust pipe at the manifold. Remove the wheels.
15. Disconnect the stabilizer bar from the lower control arms. Remove the ball joints from the steering knuckle.
16. Remove the drive axles at the transaxle and then remove the transaxle strut.
17. If equipped with air conditioning, remove the inner fender shield. Remove the drive belt, tag and disconnect the wires and then remove the compressor. Do not disconnect any of the refrigerant lines.
18. Remove the rear engine mount nuts and plate.
19. If equipped with an automatic transaxle, remove the oil filter.
20. Disconnect the speedometer cable and lower the vehicle.
21. If equipped with an automatic transaxle, remove the oil cooler at the transaxle.
22. Remove the front engine mount nuts.
23. Disconnect the clutch cable on the manual transaxle. Disconnect the detent cable on the automatic transaxle.
24. Install an engine lifting device, remove the transaxle mount and bracket. Lift the engine out of the car.

To install:

25. Install the engine mount alignment bolt (M6 × 1 × 65) to ensure proper power train alignment.
26. Lower the engine into the car, leaving the lifting device attached.
27. Install the transaxle bracket. Install the mount to the side frame and secure with NEW mount bolts.
28. With the weight not yet on the mounts, tighten the transaxle bolts. Tighten the right front mount nuts.
29. Lower the engine fully onto the mounts, remove the lifting device and then raise the front of the car.
30. Installation of the remaining components is in the reverse order of removal. Check the powertrain alignment bolt; if excessive force is required to remove the bolt, loosen the transaxle adjusting bolts and realign the powertrain. Adjust the drive belts and the clutch cable (if equipped with manual transaxle).

1985–89

◆ SEE FIGS. 22-23

1. Disconnect the battery.
2. Drain the cooling system.
3. Remove the air cleaner.
4. Disconnect the accelerator cable and T.V. cables.

5. Disconnect the ECM harness at the engine.
6. Disconnect and tag all necessary vacuum hoses.
7. Disconnect the radiator hoses at the engine.
8. Disconnect the heater hoses at the engine.
9. Remove the exhaust heat shield.
10. If equipped with air conditioning, remove the adjustment bolt at the motor mount.
11. Disconnect the engine wiring harness at the bulkhead.
12. Remove the windshield washer bottle.
13. Remove the alternator belt or serpentine, if so equipped.
14. Relieve the fuel system pressure as outlined in Section 1 and disconnect the fuel hoses.
15. Raise the vehicle.
16. If equipped with air conditioning, remove the air conditioning brace.
17. Remove the inner fender splash shield.
18. If equipped with air conditioning, remove the air conditioning compressor.
19. Remove the flywheel splash shield.
20. Disconnect the starter wires.
21. Remove the front starter brace and starter.
22. Remove the torque converter bolts.
23. Remove the crankshaft pulley using Tool J-24420 or equivalent.
24. Remove the oil filter.
25. Disconnect the engine to transmission support bracket.
26. Disconnect the right rear motor mount.
27. Disconnect the exhaust pipe at the manifold.
28. Disconnect the exhaust pipe at at the center hanger and loosen the muffler hanger.
29. Disconnect the T.V and shift cable bracket.
30. Remove the lower two bell housing bolts.
31. Lower the car.
32. Remove the right front motor mount nuts.
33. Remove the alternator and if necessary, the adjusting brace.
34. Disconnect the master cylinder from the booster, set aside and suitably support.
35. Install a lifting device.
36. Remove the right front motor mount bracket.
37. Remove the remaining upper bellhousing bolts.
38. Remove the power steering pump while lifting the engine.
39. Remove the engine.

To Install

1. Install the engine.
2. Install the power steering pump while lowering the engine.
3. Install the upper bellhousing bolts.
4. Install the right front motor mount bracket.

5. Remove the lifting device.

6. Connect the master cylinder from the booster, set aside and suitably support.

7. Install the alternator and if removed, the adjusting brace.

8. Install the right front motor mount nuts.

9. Raise the car.

10. Install the remaining two bell housing bolts.

11. Connect the T.V and shift cable bracket.

12. Connect the exhaust pipe at at the center hanger and loosen the muffler hanger.

13. Connect the exhaust pipe at the manifold.

14. Connect the right rear motor mount. If the rear engine mount bracket is removed, the following procedure should be used to ensure proper engine mount bracket locations:

a. Loosely install the engine mount bracket.

b. Raise the engine and transaxle.

c. Torque the engine mount nuts and bolts to the specifications shown.

15. Connect the engine to transmission support bracket.

16. Install the oil filter.

17. Install the crankshaft pulley using Tool J 24420 or equivalent.

18. Install the torque converter bolts.

19. Install the front starter brace and starter.

20. Connect the starter wires.

21. Install the flywheel splash shield.

22. If equipped with air conditioning, install the air conditioning compressor.

23. Install the inner fender splash shield.

24. If equipped with air conditioning, install the air conditioning brace.

25. Lower the vehicle.

26. Connect the fuel hoses.

27. Install the alternator belt or serpentine belt, if so equipped.

28. Install the windshield washer bottle.

29. Connect the engine wiring harness at the bulkhead.

30. Install the exhaust heat shield.

31. Connect the heater hoses at the engine.

32. Connect the radiator hoses at the engine.

33. Connect all vacuum hoses.

34. Connect the ECM harness at the engine.

35. Connect the accelerator cable and T.V. cables.

36. Install the air cleaner.

37. Fill the cooling system.

38. Connect the battery.

1990–92

➡ **The following procedure is for the engine and transaxle assembly. On the 1992 model year, slight variations may occur due to extra connections, etc., but the basic procedure should work.**

1. Disconnect the battery.

2. Drain the cooling system.

3. Relieve the fuel system pressure.

4. Disconnect the hood lamp wiring, if so equipped and remove the hood.

5. Disconnect the throttle body intake duct.

6. Remove the rear sight shields.

7. Disconnect the upper radiator hose.

9. Disconnect the brake booster vacuum hose.

10. Disconnect the alternator top brace and wiring.

11. Disconnect and tag the upper engine harness from the engine.

12. Discharge the A/C system as outlined in Section 1.

13. Disconnect the A/C compressor to condenser and accumulator lines.

14. Raise and support the vehicle safely.

15. Remove the left splash shield.

16. Disconnect the exhaust system.

17. Disconnect and tag the lower engine wiring.

18. Remove the flywheel inspection cover.

19. Remove the front wheels.

20. Disconnect the lower radiator hose.

21. Disconnect the heater hoses from the heater core.

22. Remove the brake calipers from the steering knuckle and wire up out of the way as outlined in Section 9.

23. Disconnect the tie rods from the struts.

24. Lower the vehicle.

25. Remove the clutch slave cylinder.

26. With the fuel system pressure released, place an absorbant shop towel around the connections and disconnect the fuel lines.

27. Disconnect the transaxle linkage at the transaxle.

28. Disconnect the accelerator cables from the TBI unit.

29. Disconnect the cruise control cables from the TBI unit.

30. Disconnect the throttle valve cables from the TBI, on vehicles equipped with an automatic transaxle.

31. Disconnect the automatic transaxle cooling lines.

32. Disconnect the power steering hoses from the power steering pump.

33. Remove the center suspension support bolts.

34. Align Engine/Transaxle Frame Handler tool No. J 36295 or equivalent under the suspension supports, engine and transaxle; lower vehicle to dolly and add support under the engine.

35. Safely support the rear of the vehicle.

36. Disconnect the upper transaxle mount.

37. Remove the upper strut bolts and nuts.

38. Disconnect the front engine mount.

39. Disconnect the rear engine mount.

40. Remove the 4 rear suspension support bolts.

41. Remove the 4 front suspension support bolts and wire the bolt holes together to prevent axle separation.

42. Raise the vehicle and remove the engine and transaxle assembly on tool No. J 36295 or equivalent.

To install:

43. Lower the vehicle and install the engine and transaxle assembly using tool No. J 36295 or equivalent.

44. Install the suspension supports bolts and tighten to 65 ft. lbs. for the front and rear suspension supports and 66 ft. lbs. for the center suspension support.

45. Install the transaxle mount but do not tighten.

46. Install the rear engine mount but do not tighten.

47. Install the front engine mount but do not tighten.

48. Torque the manual transaxle mounting bolts as follows:

• Front transaxle strut to body bolts to 40 ft. lbs.

• Rear transaxle mount to body bolts to 23 ft. lbs.

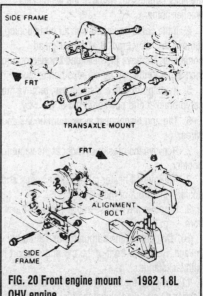

FIG. 20 Front engine mount — 1982 1.8L OHV engine

49. Torque the automatic transaxle mount bolts to 22 ft. lbs.

50. Torque the front and rear engine mount bolts, please refer to the engine mount illustration.

➡ **All engine mount bolts that have been removed must be cleaned and a new thread locking compound applied to the threads before reinstallation.**

51. Install the power steering hoses.

52. Connect the accelerator, cruise control and T.V. cables to the TBI.

53. Connect the transaxle cooling lines to the automatic transaxle.

54. Connect the transaxle linkage.

55. Reconnect the fuel lines.

56. Reconnect the clutch slave cylinder.

57. Raise and support the vehicle safely.

58. Install the tie rods.

59. Install the calipers to the steering knuckle.

60. Install the heater hoses to the heater core.

61. Install the lower radiator hose.

62. Install the A/C compressor.

63. Install the flywheel inspection cover.

64. Install the engine splash shield.

65. Install the front wheel and torque the wheel stud nuts to 100 ft. lbs.

66. Lower the vehicle.

67. Install the upper engine wiring.

68. Install the compressor to condenser and accumulator lines.

69. Install the brake booster vacuum hose.

70. Install the upper radiator hose.

71. Raise and support the vehicle safely.

72. Install the lower engine wiring.

73. Reconnect the exhaust system.

74. Lower the vehicle.

75. Connect the TBI wiring.

76. Install the air cleaner assembly.

77. Recharge the A/C system.

78. Check and adjust the wheel alignment.

79. Install the hood and connect the battery.

1.8L, 2.0L OHC Engines

➡ **This procedure requires the use of a special tool.**

1. Remove battery cables.

2. Drain cooling system.

3. Remove air cleaner.

4. Disconnect engine electrical harness at bulkhead.

5. Disconnect electrical connector at brake cylinder.

6. Remove throttle cable from bracket and E.F.I. assembly.

7. Remove vacuum hoses from E.F.I. assembly.

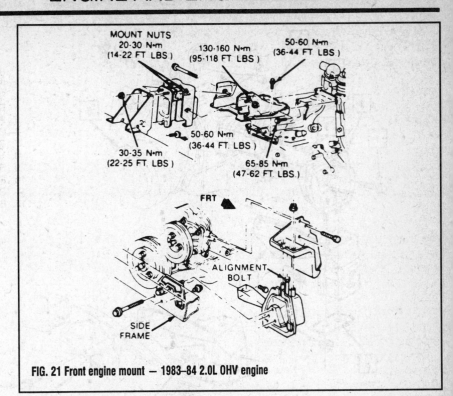

FIG. 21 Front engine mount — 1983–84 2.0L OHV engine

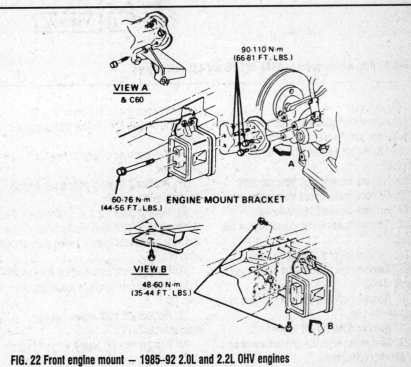

FIG. 22 Front engine mount — 1985–92 2.0L and 2.2L OHV engines

8. Remove power steering high pressure hose at cut-off switch.

9. Remove vacuum hoses at map sensor and canister.

10. Disconnect air conditioning relay cluster switches.

11. Remove power steering return hose at pump.

12. Disconnect ECM wire connections and feed harness through bulkhead and lay harness over engine.

13. Remove upper and lower radiator hoses from engine.

14. Remove electrical connections from temperature switch at thermostat housing.

15. Disconnect transmission shift cable at transmission.

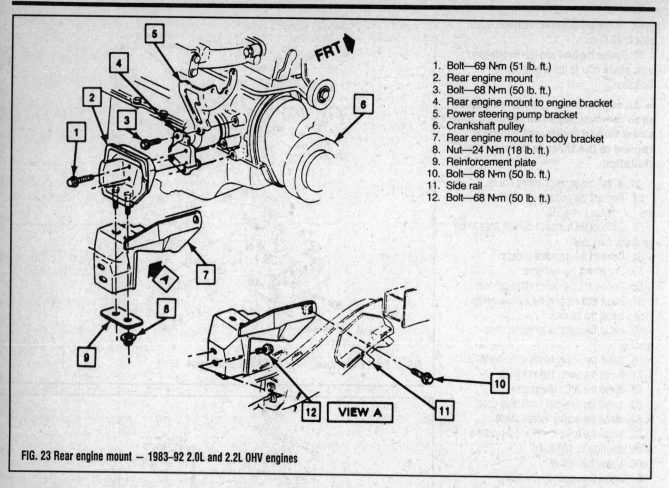

1. Bolt—69 N·m (51 lb. ft.)
2. Rear engine mount
3. Bolt—68 N·m (50 lb. ft.)
4. Rear engine mount to engine bracket
5. Power steering pump bracket
6. Crankshaft pulley
7. Rear engine mount to body bracket
8. Nut—24 N·m (18 lb. ft.)
9. Reinforcement plate
10. Bolt—68 N·m (50 lb. ft.)
11. Side rail
12. Bolt—68 N·m (50 lb. ft.)

FIG. 23 Rear engine mount — 1983–92 2.0L and 2.2L OHV engines

16. Hoist car.
17. Remove speedometer cable at transmission and bracket.
18. Disconnect exhaust pipe at exhaust manifold.
19. Remove exhaust pipe from converter.
20. Remove heater hoses from heater core.
21. Remove fuel lines at flex hoses.
22. Remove transmission cooler lines at flex hoses.
23. Remove left and right front wheels.
24. Remove right hand spoiler section and splash shield.
25. Remove right and left brake calipers and support with wire.
26. Remove right and left tie rod ends.
27. Disconnect electrical connections at air conditioning compressor.
28. Remove air conditioning compressor and mounting brackets, support air conditioning compressor with wire in wheel opening.
29. Remove front suspension support attachment bolts (6 bolts each side).
30. Lower car.
31. Support front of vehicle by placing two short jackstands under core support.
32. Position front post hoist to the rear of cowl.

33. Position a 4 in. (102mm) × 4 in. (102mm) × 6 ft. (2m) timber on front post hoist.
34. Raise vehicle enough to remove jackstands.
35. Position a 4-wheel dolly under engine and transaxle assembly.
36. Position three (3) 4 in. (102mm) × 4 in. (102mm) 12 in. (305mm) blocks under engine and transaxle assembly only, letting support rails hang free.
37. Lower vehicle onto 4-wheel dolly slightly.
38. Remove rear transaxle mount attachment bolts (2).
39. Remove left front engine mount attachment bolts (3).
40. Remove two (2) engine support to body attachment bolts behind right-hand inner axle U-joint.
41. Remove one (1) attaching bolt and nut from right-hand chassis side rail to engine mount bracket.
42. Remove six (6) strut attachment nuts.
43. Raise vehicle letting engine, transaxle and suspension resting on 4-wheel dolly.
Reverse the removal procedure for engine installation with the following exceptions.

1. With one man's assistance, position engine and transaxle assembly in chassis.
2. Install transaxle and left front mounts to side rail bolts loosely.
3. Install a M6 × 1 × 65 alignment bolt in left front mount to prevent powertrain misalignment.
4. Torque transaxle mount bolts to 42 ft. lbs. and left front mount bolts to 18 ft. lbs.
5. Install right rear mount to body bolts and torque to 38 ft. lbs.
6. Install right rear mount to chassis side rail bolt and nut torque to 38 ft. lbs.
7. Place a floor jack under control arms, jack struts into position and install retaining nuts.
8. Raise vehicle.
9. Using a transmission jack or suitable lifting equipment, raise control arms and attach tie rod ends.

2.8L and 3.1L V6 Engine

1985–88
▶ SEE FIGS. 24-27
1. Disconnect the negative battery cable. Drain the cooling system and remove the air cleaner assembly.
2. Remove the air flow sensor. Remove the

exhaust crossover heat shield and remove the crossover pipe.

3. Remove the serpentine belt tensioner and belt.

4. Remove the power steering pump mounting bracket. Disconnect the heater pipe at the power steering pump mounting bracket.

5. Disconnect the radiator hoses from the engine.

6. Disconnect the accelerator and throttle valve cable at the throttle valve.

7. Remove the alternator. Tag and disconnect the wiring harness at the engine.

8. Relieve the fuel pressure (see Section 1) and disconnect the fuel hose. Disconnect the coolant bypass and the overflow hoses at the engine.

9. Tag and remove the vacuum hoses to the engine.

10. Raise the vehicle and support it safely.

11. Remove the inner fender splash shield. Remove the harmonic balancer.

12. Remove the flywheel cover. Remove the starter bolts. Tag and disconnect the electrical connections to the starter. Remove the starter.

13. Disconnect the wires at the oil sending unit.

14. Remove the air conditioning compressor and related brackets.

15. Disconnect the exhaust pipe at the rear of the exhaust manifold.

16. Remove the flex plate-to-torque converter bolts.

17. Remove the transaxle-to-engine bolts. Remove the engine-to-rear mount frame nuts.

18. Disconnect the shift cable bracket at the transaxle. Remove the lower bell housing bolts.

19. Lower the vehicle and disconnect the heater hoses at the engine.

20. Install a suitable engine lifting device. While supporting the engine and transaxle, remove the upper bell housing bolts.

21. Remove the front mounting bolts.

22. Remove the master cylinder from the booster.

23. Remove the engine assembly from the vehicle.

To Install

1. Install the engine and remove the engine lifting device.

2. Install the master cylinder to the booster.

3. Install the front mounting bolts.

4. Install the upper bell housing bolts.

5. Connect the heater hoses at the engine.

6. Connect the shift cable bracket at the transaxle. Install the lower bell housing bolts.

7. Install the transaxle-to-engine bolts. Install the engine-to-rear mount frame nuts.

8. Install the flex plate-to-torque converter bolts.

9. Connect the exhaust pipe at the rear of the exhaust manifold.

10. Install the air conditioning compressor and related brackets.

11. Connect the wires at the oil sending unit.

12. Install the flywheel cover. Install the starter bolts. Connect the electrical connections to the starter. Install the starter.

13. Install the inner fender splash shield. Install the harmonic balancer.

14. Lower the vehicle.

15. Install the vacuum hoses to the engine.

16. Connect the fuel hose. Connect the coolant bypass and the overflow hoses at the engine.

17. Install the alternator. Connect the wiring harness at the engine.

18. Connect the accelerator and throttle valve cable at the throttle valve.

19. Connect the radiator hoses to the engine.

20. Install the power steering pump mounting bracket. Connect the heater pipe at the power steering pump mounting bracket.

21. Install the serpentine belt tensioner and belt.

22. Install the air flow sensor. Install the exhaust crossover heat shield and crossover pipe.

23. Connect the negative battery cable. Fill the cooling system and install the air cleaner assembly.

1989–92

1. Disconnect the negative battery cable. Drain the cooling system and remove the air cleaner assembly.

2. Remove the air cleaner and duct assembly.

3. Disconnect the exhaust manifold/crossover assembly.

4. Remove the serpentine belt tensioner and idler, if equipped.

5. Disconnect the radiator hoses from the engine.

6. Disconnect the cables from the bracket at the plenum.

7. Remove the alternator. Tag and disconnect the wiring harness at the engine.

8. Relieve the fuel pressure (see Section 1) and disconnect the fuel hose.

9. Disconnect the coolant bypass and the overflow hoses at the engine.

10. Support the engine using J 28467–A engine support fixture or equivalent.

11. Raise and support the vehicle safely.

12. Remove the inner fender splash shield.

13. Remove the flywheel cover.

14. Remove the starter bolts. Tag and disconnect the electrical connections to the starter. Remove the starter.

15. Remove the air conditioning compressor and related brackets.

16. Disconnect the exhaust pipe at the rear of the exhaust manifold.

17. Remove the flywheel-to-torque converter bolts.

18. Disconnect the engine mounts.

19. If equipped with a manual transaxle, disconnect the intermediate shaft bracket to the engine.

20. Disconnect the shift cable bracket at the transaxle. Remove the lower bell housing bolts.

21. Lower the vehicle and disconnect the heater hoses at the engine.

22. Install a suitable engine lifting device. While supporting the engine and transaxle, remove the J 28467–A engine support fixture.

23. Support the transaxle and remove the transaxle bolts.

24. Remove the engine assembly from the vehicle.

To Install

25. Install J 28467–A engine support fixture, or equivalent.

26. Remove the engine lifting device.

27. Support the transaxle and install the transaxle bolts.

28. Connect the heater hoses at the engine.

29. Raise and support the vehicle safely.

30. Install the lower bell housing bolts.

31. Install the shift cable bracket at the transaxle.

32. If equipped with a manual transaxle, connect the intermediate shaft bracket to the engine.

33. Reconnect the engine mounts and torque as follows:

- Front engine mount to bracket bolt to 50 ft. lbs.
- Front engine mount to frame bolt (top) to 54 ft. lbs.
- Front engine mount to frame bolt (bottom) to 61 ft. lbs.
- Engine mount bracket to body lower bolt to 47 ft. lbs.
- Engine mount bracket to body upper bolt to 74 ft. lbs.
- Rear engine mount to engine bolt to 40 ft. lbs.
- Rear engine bracket to body bolt to 45 ft. lbs.

➡ **All engine mount bolts that have been removed must be cleaned and a new thread locking compound applied to the threads before reinstallation.**

34. Install the flywheel-to-torque converter bolts.

35. Connect the exhaust pipe at the rear of the exhaust manifold.

36. Install the air conditioning compressor.
37. Install the starter.
38. Install the flywheel cover.
39. Install the inner fender splash shield.
40. Lower the vehicle and remove J 28467–A engine support fixture, or equivalent.
41. Connect the coolant bypass and the overflow hoses at the engine.
42. Reconnect the fuel lines.
43. Reconnect the wiring harness at the engine.
44. Install the alternator.
45. Connect the cables from the bracket at the plenum.
46. Install the radiator hoses.
47. Install the serpentine belt tensioner and idler, if equipped.
48. Refill the cooling system.
49. Install the air cleaner and duct assembly.
50. Connect the battery.

Rocker Arm Cover

REMOVAL & INSTALLATION

1.8L, 2.0L and 2.2L OHV Engines

1982–86

▶ SEE FIGS. 28-29

1. Disconnect the negative battery cable.
2. Remove the air cleaner.
3. Disconnect the canister purge line and the PCV valve.
4. Disconnect (mark location of spark plug wires for correct installation) the spark plug wires at the spark plugs and pull the wires away from the rocker arm cover.
5. Loosen the accelerator linkage bracket.
6. Remove the rocker arm cover bolts.
7. Remove the rocker arm cover. If the cover adheres to the cylinder head, lightly tap the end of the cover with a rubber mallet. If necessary, carefully pry until loose.

➡ **Do not distort the sealing flange.**

8. Clean the sealing surfaces of the head and the cover.
9. Place a ⅛ in. (3mm) wide bead of RTV sealant all around the rocker arm cover sealing surface.

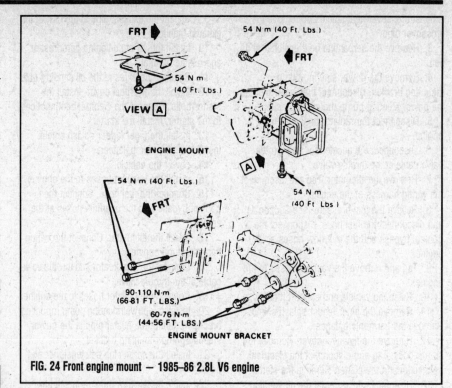

FIG. 24 Front engine mount — 1985–86 2.8L V6 engine

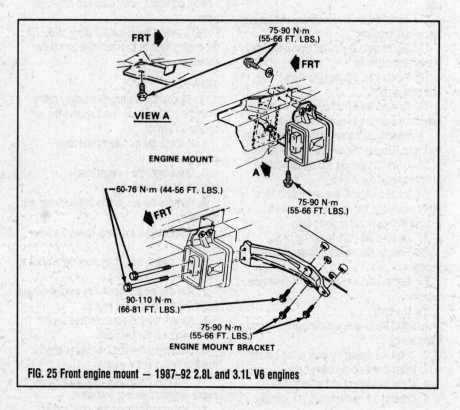

FIG. 25 Front engine mount — 1987–92 2.8L and 3.1L V6 engines

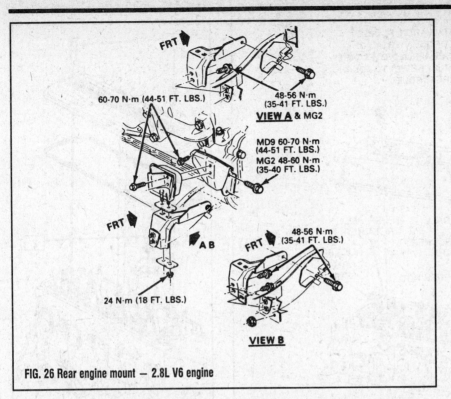

FIG. 26 Rear engine mount — 2.8L V6 engine

➡ **When going around the attaching bolt holes, always flow the RTV on the inboard side of the bolt holes.**

➡ **Keep the sealant out of the bolt holes as this could cause a "Hydraulic lock" condition which could damage the head casting.**

11. Install the remaining parts and reconnect the battery cable.

1987–92
◆ SEE FIG. 30
1. Disconnect the negative battery cable.
2. Disconnect the AIR hose at the TBI and air cleaner.
3. Remove the hose from the intake to the cover.
4. Remove the rocker arm cover bolts and remove the cover.
5. Clean the sealing surfaces of the head and the cover.
6. Install a new gasket, reposition the cover and torque the bolts EVENLY to 8 ft. lbs.
7. Install all hoses removed and connect the negative battery cable.

V6 Engine

1984–86
LEFT
1. Disconnect the negative battery cable.
2. Remove the coil at the bracket.
3. Disconnect the PCV hose.
4. Disconnect the spark plug wires at the

10. Install the valve cover and torque the bolts to 8 ft. lbs. EVENLY while the sealant is still wet.

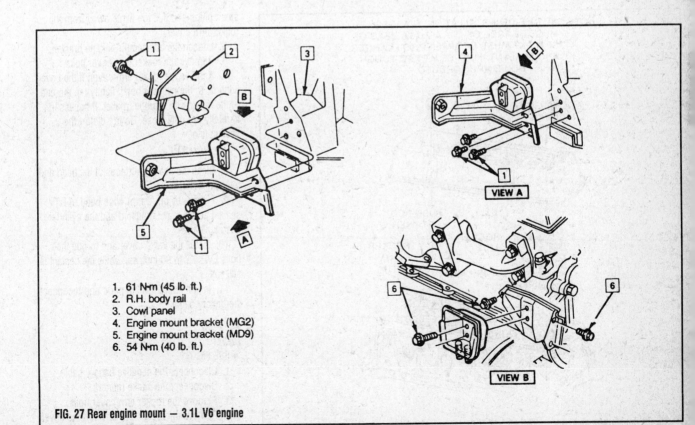

1. 61 N·m (45 lb. ft.)
2. R.H. body rail
3. Cowl panel
4. Engine mount bracket (MG2)
5. Engine mount bracket (MD9)
6. 54 N·m (40 lb. ft.)

FIG. 27 Rear engine mount — 3.1L V6 engine

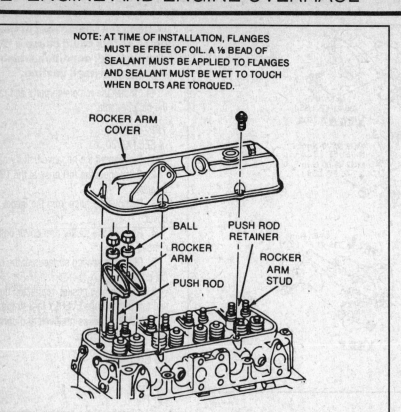

NOTE: AT TIME OF INSTALLATION, FLANGES MUST BE FREE OF OIL. A ⅛ BEAD OF SEALANT MUST BE APPLIED TO FLANGES AND SEALANT MUST BE WET TO TOUCH WHEN BOLTS ARE TORQUED.

ROCKER ARM COVER

BALL

ROCKER ARM

PUSH ROD

PUSH ROD RETAINER

ROCKER ARM STUD

FIG. 28 Rocker arm and cover, 1982–83 1.8L and 2.0L OHV engine

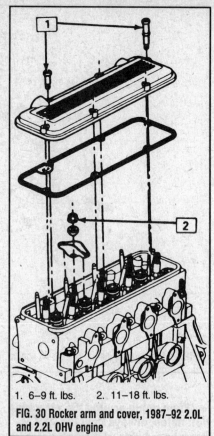

1. 6–9 ft. lbs.   2. 11–18 ft. lbs.

FIG. 30 Rocker arm and cover, 1987–92 2.0L and 2.2L OHV engine

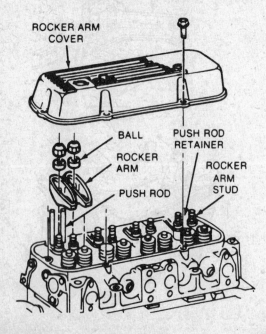

NOTE: AT TIME OF INSTALLATION, FLANGES MUST BE FREE OF OIL. A 2.0–3.0 BEAD OF SEALANT MUST BE APPLIED TO FLANGES AND SEALANT MUST BE WET TO TOUCH WHEN BOLTS ARE TORQUED.

ROCKER ARM COVER

BALL

ROCKER ARM

PUSH ROD

PUSH ROD RETAINER

ROCKER ARM STUD

FIG. 29 Rocker arm and cover, 1984–86 2.0L OHV engine

spark plugs and pull the wires away from the rocker arm cover.

5. Loosen the accelerator linkage bracket.

6. Remove the rocker arm cover bolts.

7. Remove the rocker arm cover. If the cover adheres to the cylinder head, lightly tap the end of the cover with a rubber mallet. If necessary, carefully pry until loose. Do not distort the sealing flange.

To Install:

8. Clean the sealing surfaces of the head and the cover.

9. Place a ⅛ in. (3mm) wide bead of RTV sealant at the intake manifold and the cylinder head split line.

10. Install the valve cover and torque the bolts EVENLY to 90 inch lbs. while the sealant is still wet.

11. Install the remaining parts and reconnect the battery cable.

1984–86
RIGHT
◆ SEE FIG. 31

1. Disconnect the negative battery cable.

2. Disconnect the intake runners.

3. Remove the rocker arm cover bolts.

4. Remove the rocker arm cover. If the cover adheres to the cylinder head, lightly tap the end

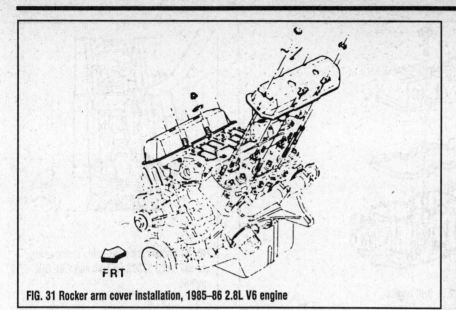

FIG. 31 Rocker arm cover installation, 1985–86 2.8L V6 engine

12. If the cover adheres to the cylinder head, lightly tap the end of the cover with a soft rubber mallet or palm of the hand. Do not distort or scratch the sealing flange.

To install:

13. Clean the sealing surfaces of the head and the cover.

14. Install a new gasket and make sure it is seated properly in the rocker cover groove.

15. Apply RTV sealant in the notch.

16. Install the rocker cover and tighten the retaining bolts EVENLY to 89 inch lbs.

17. Install the remaining parts and reconnect the battery cable.

Camshaft Carrier Cover

REMOVAL & INSTALLATION

OHC Engines

▶ SEE FIG. 33

1. Disconnect the negative battery cable. Remove the air cleaner on non-turbo models.

2. Disconnect the breather hoses.

3. Disconnect the induction tube on turbo models.

4. Remove the bolts and remove the cover.

To install:

5. Clean the sealing surfaces on the camshaft carrier and cover.

6. Reposition the cover with a new gasket and torque the retainer bolts EVENLY to 71 inch lbs.

---

of the cover with a rubber mallet. If necessary, carefully pry until loose. Do not distort the sealing flange.

To install:

5. Clean the sealing surfaces of the head and the cover.

6. Place a 1/8 in. (3mm) wide bead of RTV sealant at the intake manifold and the cylinder head split line.

7. Install the valve cover and torque the bolts EVENLY to 90 inch lbs. while the sealant is still wet.

8. Install the remaining parts and reconnect the battery cable.

1987–92 LEFT

1. Disconnect the negative battery cable.

2. Remove the bracket tube at the cover.

3. Remove the plug wire cover.

4. Disconnect the heater hose at the filler neck.

5. Remove the cover bolts and remove the cover.

6. If the cover adheres to the cylinder head, lightly tap the end of the cover with a soft rubber mallet or palm of the hand. Do not distort or scratch the sealing flange.

To install:

7. Clean the sealing surfaces of the head and the cover.

8. Install a new gasket and make sure it is seated properly in the rocker cover groove.

9. Apply RTV sealant in the notch.

10. Install the rocker cover and tighten the retaining bolts EVENLY to 89 inch lbs.

11. Install the remaining parts and reconnect the battery cable.

1987–92 RIGHT

▶ SEE FIG. 32

1. Disconnect the negative battery cable.

2. Disconnect the brake booster vacuum line at the bracket.

3. Disconnect the cable bracket at the plenum.

4. Remove the vacuum line bracket at the cable bracket.

5. Disconnect the lines at the alternator brace stud.

6. Disconnect the rear alternator brace.

7. Remove the serpentine belt.

8. Disconnect the alternator and lay to one side.

9. Remove the PCV valve.

10. Loosen the alternator bracket.

11. Remove the rocker cover bolts, plug wires and rocker cover.

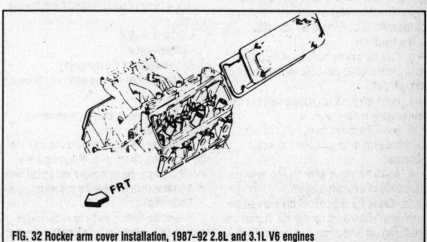

FIG. 32 Rocker arm cover installation, 1987–92 2.8L and 3.1L V6 engines

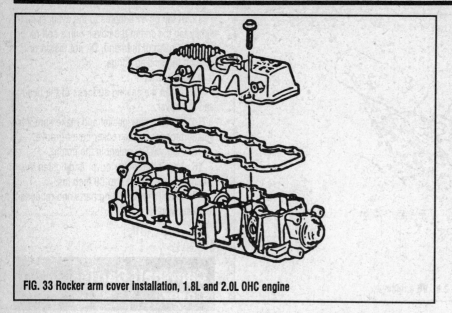

FIG. 33 Rocker arm cover installation, 1.8L and 2.0L OHC engine

FIG. 34 Compressing the valve spring using special tool J 33302 on 1.8L and 2.0L OHC engines

7. Install the air cleaner and breather hoses.
8. Install the induction tube on turbo models

Rocker Arms and Pushrods

REMOVAL & INSTALLATION

1.8L, 2.0L and 2.1L OHV Engines

1982–86

1. Remove the air cleaner. Remove the rocker arm cover.
2. Remove the rocker arm nut and ball. Lift the rocker arm off the stud. Always keep the rocker arm assemblies together and install them on the same stud. Remove the pushrods.

To install:

3. Coat the bearing surfaces of the rocker arms and the rocker arm balls with Molykote® or its equivalent.
4. Install the pushrods making sure that they seat properly in the lifter.
5. Install the rocker arms, balls and nuts. Tighten the rocker arm nuts until all lash is eliminated.
6. Adjust the valves when the lifter is on the base circle of a camshaft lobe:

   a. Crank the engine until the mark on the crankshaft pulley lines up with the **O** mark on the timing tab. Make sure that the engine is in the No. 1 firing position. Place your fingers on the No. 1 rocker arms as the mark on the

crank pulley comes near the **O** mark. If the valves are not moving, the engine is in the No. 1 firing position. If the valves move, the engine is in the No. 4 firing position; rotate the engine one complete revolution and it will be in the No. 1 position.

   b. When the engine is in the No. 1 firing position, adjust the following valves:
   • Exhaust — 1,3
   • Intake — 1,2

   c. Back the adjusting nut out until lash can be felt at the pushrod, then turn the nut until all lash is removed (this can be determined by rotating the pushrod while turning the adjusting nut). When all lash has been removed, turn the nut in 1½ additional turns, this will center the lifter plunger.

   d. Crank the engine one complete revolution until the timing tab and the **O** mark are again in alignment. Now the engine is in the No. 4 firing position. Adjust the following valves:
   • Exhaust — 2,4
   • Intake — 3,4

7. Installation of the remaining components is the reverse order of removal.

1987–92

1. Remove the air cleaner. Remove the rocker arm cover.
2. Remove the rocker arm nut and ball. Lift the rocker arm off the stud. Always keep the rocker arm assemblies together and install them on the same stud. Remove the pushrods.

To install:

3. Coat the bearing surfaces of the rocker arms and the rocker arm balls with Molykote® or its equivalent.
4. Install the pushrods making sure that they seat properly in the lifter.

5. Install the rocker arms, balls and nuts. Tighten the rocker arm nuts to 22 ft. lbs.
6. Install the rocker cover.

1.8L and 2.0L OHC Engines

▶ SEE FIGS. 34-35

➡ **A special tool is required for this procedure.**

1. Remove the camshaft carrier cover.
2. Using a valve train compressing fixture, tool J-33302, depress all the lifters at once.
3. Remove the rocker arms, placing them on the workbench in the same order that they were removed.
4. Remove the hydraulic valve lash compensators keeping them in the order in which they were removed.
5. Installation is the reverse of removal. Rocker arms and compensators must be replaced in the exact same position as when they were removed.

2.8L and 3.1L V6 Engines

1985–86

▶ SEE FIGS. 36-37

1. Remove the rocker arm covers as outlined earlier.
2. Remove the rocker arm nuts, rocker arm balls, rocker arms and push rods and place in a rack so that they may be reinstalled in the same location.

To install:

3. Coat the bearing surfaces of the rocker arms and the rocker arm balls with Molykote® or its equivalent.
4. Install the pushrods making sure that they seat properly in the lifter.

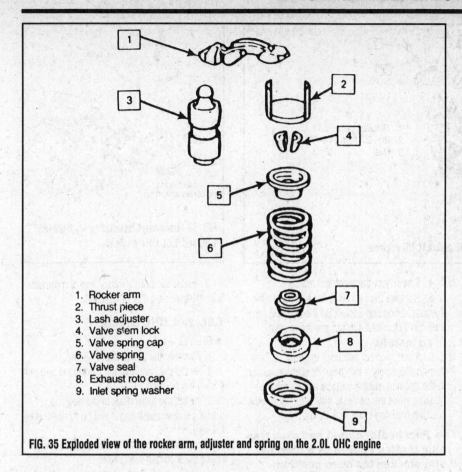

1. Rocker arm
2. Thrust piece
3. Lash adjuster
4. Valve stem lock
5. Valve spring cap
6. Valve spring
7. Valve seal
8. Exhaust roto cap
9. Inlet spring washer

FIG. 35 Exploded view of the rocker arm, adjuster and spring on the 2.0L OHC engine

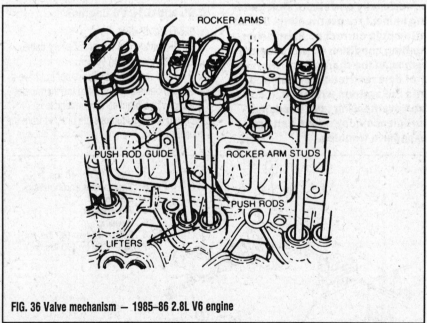

FIG. 36 Valve mechanism — 1985–86 2.8L V6 engine

FIG. 37 Adjusting the valve lash — 1985–86 2.8L V6 engine

one complete revolution and it will be in the No. 1 position.

b. When the engine is in the No. 1 firing position, adjust the following valves:
- Exhaust — 1,2,3
- Intake — 1,5,6

c. Back the adjusting nut out until lash can be felt at the pushrod, then turn the nut until all lash is removed (this can be determined by rotating the pushrod while turning the adjusting nut). When all lash has been removed, turn the nut in $1\frac{1}{2}$ additional turns, this will center the lifter plunger.

d. Crank the engine one complete revolution until the timing tab and the **O** mark are again in alignment. Now the engine is in the No. 4 firing position. Adjust the following valves:
- Exhaust — 4,5,6
- Intake — 2,3,4

7. Installation of the remaining components is the reverse order of removal.

1987–92
▶ SEE FIG. 38

1. Remove the rocker arm covers as outlined earlier.

2. Remove the rocker arm nuts, rocker arm balls, rocker arms, push rod guides and push rods and place in a rack so that they may be reinstalled in the same location.

➡ **Intake pushrods are marked orange and are 6 in. (152.4mm) long. Exhaust pushrods are marked blue and are $6\frac{3}{8}$ in. (161.9mm) long.**

3. Coat the bearing surfaces of the rocker arms and the rocker arm balls with Molykote® or its equivalent.

4. Install the pushrods making sure that they seat properly in the lifter.

5. Install the rocker arms, balls and nuts. Tighten the rocker arm nuts until all lash is eliminated.

6. Adjust the valves when the lifter is on the base circle of a camshaft lobe:

a. Crank the engine until the mark on the crankshaft pulley lines up with the **O** mark on the timing tab. Make sure that the engine is in the No. 1 firing position. Place your fingers on the No. 1 rocker arms as the mark on the crank pulley comes near the **O** mark. If the valves are not moving, the engine is in the No. 1 firing position. If the valves move, the engine is in the No. 4 firing position; rotate the engine

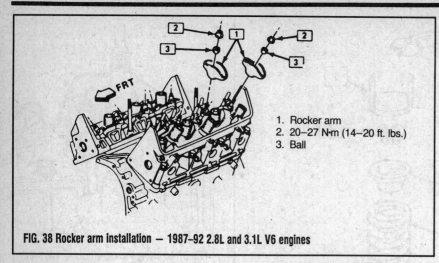

FIG. 38 Rocker arm installation — 1987–92 2.8L and 3.1L V6 engines

1. Rocker arm
2. 20–27 N·m (14–20 ft. lbs.)
3. Ball

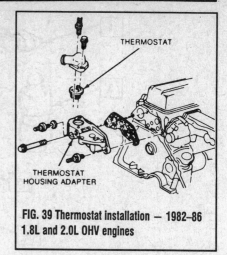

FIG. 39 Thermostat installation — 1982–86 1.8L and 2.0L OHV engines

5. Install the pushrod guides, rocker arms, pivot balls and nuts.

6. Tighten the rocker arm nuts to 14–20 ft. lbs.

Thermostat

REMOVAL & INSTALLATION

❄❄ CAUTION

When draining the coolant, keep in mind that cats and dogs are attracted by the ethylene glycol antifreeze, and are quite likely to drink any that is left in an uncovered container or in puddles on the ground. This will prove fatal in sufficient quantity. Always drain the coolant into a sealable container. Coolant should be reused unless it is contaminated or several years old.

1.8L, 2.0L and 2.2L OHV Engines

♦ SEE FIGS. 39-40

The thermostat is located inside a housing on the back of the cylinder head. It is not necessary to remove the radiator hose from the thermostat housing when removing the thermostat.

1. Disconnect the negative battery cable.
2. Drain the cooling system and remove the air cleaner.
3. On some models it may be necessary to disconnect the A.I.R. pipe at the upper check valve and the bracket at the water outlet.

4. Disconnect the electrical lead.
5. Remove the two retaining bolts from the thermostat housing and lift up the housing with the house attached. Lift out the thermostat.

To install:

6. Insert (correct position) the new thermostat. Apply a thin bead of silicone sealer to the housing mating surface and install the housing while the sealer is still wet. Tighten the housing retaining bolts to 6 ft. lbs.

➡ **Poor heater output and slow warmup is often caused by a thermostat stuck in the open position; occasionally one sticks shut causing immediate overheating. Do not attempt to correct a chronic overheating condition by permanently removing the thermostat. Thermostat flow restriction is designed into the system; without it, localized overheating (due to coolant turbulence) may occur, causing expensive troubles.**

7. Installation of the remaining components is in the reverse order of removal.

1.8L, 2.0L OHC Engines

♦ SEE FIG. 41

1. Remove the thermostat housing.
2. Grasp the handle of the thermostat and pull it from the housing.
3. Install the thermostat in the housing, pushing it down as far as it will go to make sure it's seated.
4. Install the housing on the engine, using a new gasket coated with sealer.

2.8L and 3.1L V6 Engines

♦ SEE FIGS. 42-43

1. Disconnect the negative battery cable.
2. Drain the cooling system.
3. Some models with cruise control have a vacuum modulator attached to the thermostat housing with a bracket. If your vehicle is equipped as such, remove the bracket from the housing.

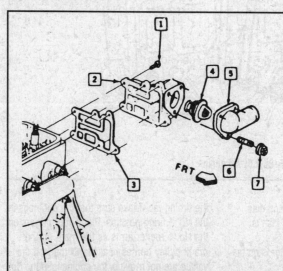

1. Bolt—10 Nm (8 lbs. ft.)
2. Thermostat and housing
3. Gasket
4. Thermostat
5. Housing
6. Stud—10 Nm (90 lbs. in.)
7. Nut—10 Nm (90 lbs. in.)

FIG. 40 Thermostat installation — 1987–92 2.0L and 2.2L OHV engines

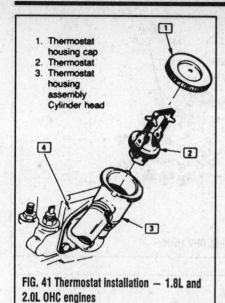

1. Thermostat housing cap
2. Thermostat
3. Thermostat housing assembly
   Cylinder head

FIG. 41 Thermostat Installation — 1.8L and 2.0L OHC engines

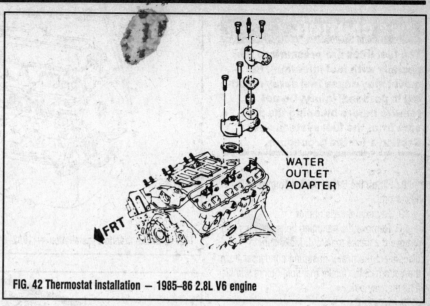

WATER OUTLET ADAPTER

FRT

FIG. 42 Thermostat installation — 1985–86 2.8L V6 engine

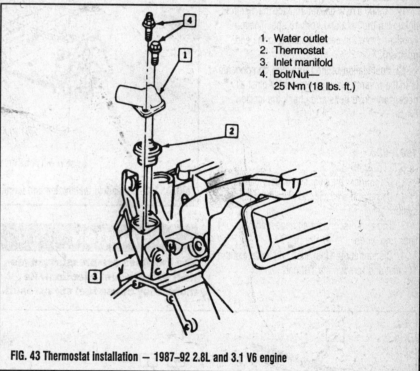

1. Water outlet
2. Thermostat
3. Inlet manifold
4. Bolt/Nut—
   25 N·m (18 lbs. ft.)

FIG. 43 Thermostat installation — 1987–92 2.8L and 3.1 V6 engine

4. Unbolt the water outlet from the intake manifold, remove the outlet and lift the thermostat out of the manifold.

To install:

5. Clean both of the mating surfaces and run a 1/8 in. (3mm) wide bead of R.T.V. (room temperature vulcanizing) sealer in the groove of the water outlet.

6. Install the thermostat (spring towards engine) and bolt the water outlet into place while the R.T.V. sealer is still wet. Torque the bolts to 18 ft. lbs. The remainder of the installation is the reverse of removal. Check for leaks after the car is started and correct as required.

Intake Manifold

REMOVAL & INSTALLATION

> **✳✳ CAUTION**
>
> When draining the coolant, keep in mind that cats and dogs are attracted by the ethylene glycol antifreeze, and are quite likely to drink any that is left in an uncovered container or in puddles on the ground. This will prove fatal in sufficient quantity. Always drain the coolant into a sealable container. Coolant should be reused unless it is contaminated or several years old.

1.8, 2.0L and 2.2L OHV Engines

1985–86

▶ SEE FIG. 44

1. Disconnect the negative battery cable.

2. Remove the air cleaner. Drain the cooling system.

3. Tag and disconnect all necessary vacuum lines and wires. Remove the idler pulley.

4. Remove the A.I.R. drive belt. If equipped with power steering, remove the drive belt and then remove the pump with the lines attached. Position the pump out of the way.

5. Remove the A.I.R. bracket-to-intake manifold bolt. Remove the air pump pulley.

6. If equipped with power steering, remove the A.I.R. through-bolt and then the power steering adjusting bracket.

7. Loosen the lower bolt on the air pump mounting bracket so that the bracket will rotate.

8. Disconnect the fuel lines at the carburetor or TBI unit. Disconnect the carburetor or TBI linkage and then remove the carburetor or TBI unit.

✳✳ CAUTION

The fuel lines are pressurized (especially with fuel injection). Removal may cause fuel spray resulting in personal injury. Do not remove before bleeding the pressure from the fuel system. See Section 1 for the procedure.

9. Lift off the Early Fuel Evaporation (EFE) heater grid.

10. Remove the distributor.

11. Remove the mounting bolts and nuts and remove the intake manifold. Make sure to disconnect the heater hose and condenser from the bottom of the intake manifold before you lift it all the way out.

To install:

12. Using a new gasket, replace the manifold, tightening the nuts and bolts to specification (working from the center position to the end position).

13. Installation of the remaining components is in the reverse order of removal. Adjust all necessary drive belts and check the ignition timing.

1987–92

♦ SEE FIGS. 45-46

1. Disconnect the negative battery cable.

2. Remove the air cleaner. Drain the cooling system.

3. Tag and disconnect all necessary vacuum lines and wires.

4. Disconnect the fuel lines and linkage at the TBI unit and remove the TBI unit.

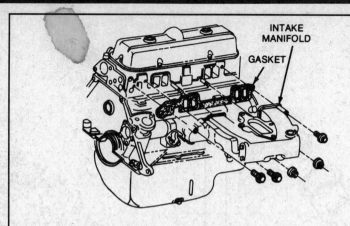

FIG. 44 Intake manifold installation — 1982–86 2.0L OHV engine

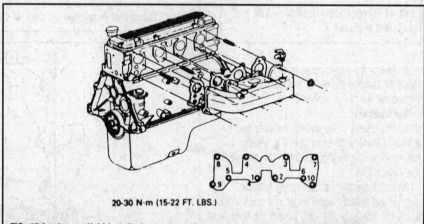

20-30 N·m (15-22 FT. LBS.)

FIG. 45 Intake manifold installation and torque sequence — 1987–88 2.0L OHV engine

✳✳ CAUTION

The fuel lines are pressurized (especially with fuel injection). Removal may cause fuel spray result- ing in personal injury. Do not remove before bleeding the pressure from the fuel system. See Section 1 for the procedure.

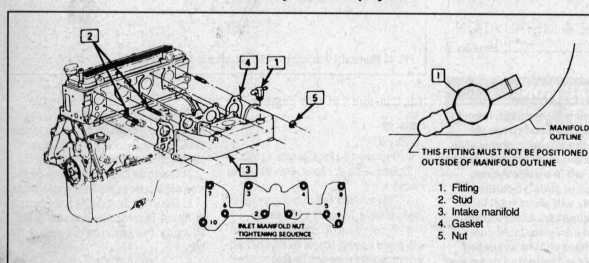

INLET MANIFOLD NUT TIGHTENING SEQUENCE

THIS FITTING MUST NOT BE POSITIONED OUTSIDE OF MANIFOLD OUTLINE

MANIFOLD OUTLINE

1. Fitting
2. Stud
3. Intake manifold
4. Gasket
5. Nut

FIG. 46 Intake manifold installation and torque sequence — 1989–92 2.0L and 2.2L OHV engine

5. Disconnect the power steering pump and lay aside.

6. Disconnect the coolant hose to the intake manifold.

7. Raise and support the vehicle safely.

8. Disconnect the accelerator and T.V. cables and cable bracket.

9. Remove the 6 intake manifold lower nuts.

10. Lower the vehicle.

11. Remove the intake manifold upper nuts and remove the intake manifold.

To install:

12. Clean the mating surfaces on the intake manifold and the cylinder head.

13. Install the intake manifold with a new gasket and tighten the manifold nuts in the proper sequence to 18 ft. lbs. (25 Nm).

14. Raise and support the vehicle safely.

15. Connect the coolant hoses and the accelerator and T.V. cables and cable bracket.

16. Lower the vehicle.

17. Install the TBI unit and connect the linkage and fuel lines.

18. Install the vacuum lines and wires.

19. Install the air cleaner assembly.

20. Fill the cooling system and connect the negative battery cable.

1992

▶ SEE FIGS. 46A-46B

1. Disconnect the negative battery cable.

2. Relieve the fuel system pressure.

3. Remove the air intake duct.

4. Drain the cooling system.

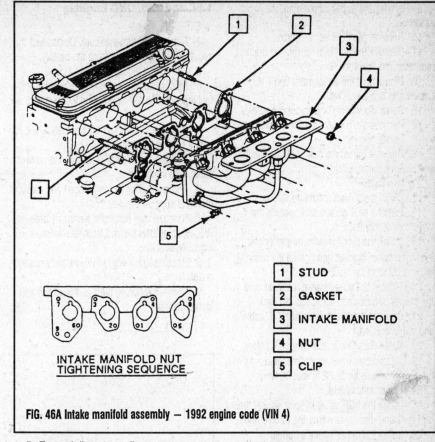

1	STUD
2	GASKET
3	INTAKE MANIFOLD
4	NUT
5	CLIP

FIG. 46A Intake manifold assembly — 1992 engine code (VIN 4)

5. Tag and disconnect all necessary vacuum lines and wires.

6. Disconnect the throttle linkage.

7. Remove the power steering pump and lay it aside without disconnecting the fluid lines.

8. Disconnect the MAP sensor and EGR solenoid valve.

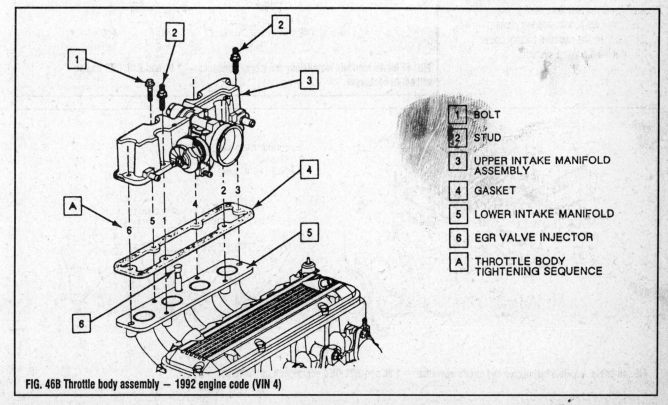

1	BOLT
2	STUD
3	UPPER INTAKE MANIFOLD ASSEMBLY
4	GASKET
5	LOWER INTAKE MANIFOLD
6	EGR VALVE INJECTOR
A	THROTTLE BODY TIGHTENING SEQUENCE

FIG. 46B Throttle body assembly — 1992 engine code (VIN 4)

9. Remove the upper intake manifold assembly.

10. Remove the EGR valve injector.

11. Remove the fuel injector retainer bracket, regulator and injectors.

12. Disconnect the accelerator and T.V. cables and cable bracket.

13. Raise the vehicle and support it safely.

14. Remove the 6 intake manifold lower nuts.

15. Lower the vehicle.

16. Remove the intake manifold upper nuts and remove the manifold.

To install:

17. Clean the gasket mounting surfaces.

18. Install a new gasket and position the lower intake manifold.

19. Install the fuel injectors, regulator and injector retainer bracket and tighten the retaining bolts to 22 inch lbs. (3.5 Nm).

20. Tighten the upper intake manifold nuts in the proper sequence to 22 ft. lbs. 30 Nm).

21. Connect the accelerator and T.V. cables and cable bracket.

22. Raise the vehicle and support it safely.

23. Tighten the lower intake manifold nuts in the proper sequence to 22 ft. lbs. 30 Nm).

24. Lower the vehicle.

25. Install the EGR valve injector so that the port is facing directly towards the throttle body.

26. Install the upper intake manifold assembly.

27. Connect the MAP sensor and EGR solenoid valve.

28. Connect the vacuum lines and wires.

29. Install the air intake duct.

30. Install the power steering pump.

31. Connect the negative battery cable.

32. Refill the coolant system.

1.8L and 2.0L OHC Engines

▶ SEE FIGS. 47-48

1. Release the fuel pressure. Disconnect the negative battery terminal from the battery.

2. Remove induction tube and hoses.

3. Disconnect and tag wiring to throttle body, fuel injectors, M.A.P sensor and wastegate, if so equipped.

4. Disconnect and tag PCV hose and vacuum hoses on throttle body.

5. Remove throttle cable and cruise control cable if so equipped.

6. Remove wiring to ignition coil and remove manifold support bracket.

7. Remove rear bolt from alternator bracket, P/S adjusting bracket and front alternator adjusting bracket.

8. Remove fuel lines to fuel rail and regulator outlet.

9. Remove retaining nuts and washers and intake manifold.

To install:

10. To install, use new gasket and reverse the removal procedures. Torque intake manifold retaining nuts and washers EVENLY in sequence to 20–25 ft. lbs. for 1982–86 and 16 ft. lbs. for 1987–92.

➡ **The rear adjusting bracket must be the last part secured to prevent distorting the accessory drive system this will prevent the belt from coming off.**

2.8L and 3.1L V6 Engines

1985–88

▶ SEE FIGS. 49-50

1. Disconnect the negative battery cable. Release the fuel pressure.

2. Disconnect the accelerator cable bracket at the plenum.

3. Disconnect the throttle body and the EGR pipe from the EGR valve. Remove the plenum assembly.

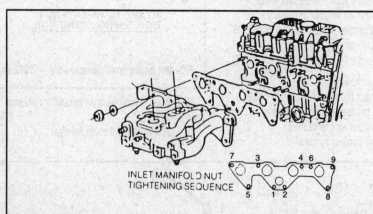

INLET MANIFOLD NUT TIGHTENING SEQUENCE

FIG. 47 Intake manifold installation and torque sequence — 1.8L and 2.0L OHC engine without turbocharger

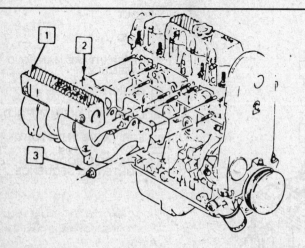

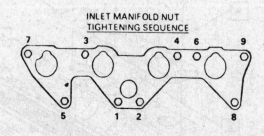

1. Intake manifold
2. Gasket
3. Nut (18 ft. lbs.)

INLET MANIFOLD NUT TIGHTENING SEQUENCE

FIG. 48 Intake manifold installation and torque sequence — 1.8L and 2.0L OHC engine with turbocharger

4. Disconnect the fuel line along the fuel rail.

5. Disconnect the serpentine drive belt. Remove the power steering pump mounting bracket.

6. Remove the heater pipe at the power steering pump bracket.

7. Tag and disconnect the wiring at the alternator and remove the alternator.

8. Disconnect the wires from the cold start injector assembly. Remove the injector assembly from the intake manifold.

9. Disconnect the idle air vacuum hose at the throttle body. Disconnect the wires at the injectors.

10. Remove the fuel rail, breather tube and the fuel runners from the engine.

11. Tag and disconnect the coil wires.

12. Remove the rocker arm covers. Drain the cooling system, the disconnect the radiator hose at the thermostat housing. Disconnect the heater hose from the thermostat housing and the thermostat wiring.

13. Remove the distributor.

14. Remove the thermostat assembly housing.

15. Remove the intake manifold bolts and remove the intake manifold from the engine.

To Install:

1. The gaskets are marked for right and left side installation; do not interchange them. Clean the sealing surface of the engine block, and apply a 3/16 in. (5mm) wide bead of silicone sealer to each ridge.

2. Install the new gaskets onto the heads. The gaskets will have to be cut slightly to fit past the center pushrods. Do not cut any more material than necessary. Hold the gaskets in place by extending the ridge bead of sealer 1/4 in. (6mm) onto the gasket ends.

3. Install the intake manifold. The area between the ridges and the manifold should be completely sealed.

4. Install the retaining bolts and nuts, and tighten in sequence to 23 ft. lbs. Do not overtighten; the manifold is made from aluminum, and can be warped or cracked with excessive force.

5. The rest of installation is the reverse of removal. Adjust the ignition timing after installation, and check the coolant level after the engine has warmed up.

1989–92

◆ SEE FIG. 51

1. Disconnect the negative battery cable.

2. Disconnect the cables at the plenum.

3. Disconnect the brake vacuum pipe at the plenum.

3. Disconnect the throttle body and the EGR pipe from the EGR valve. Remove the plenum assembly.

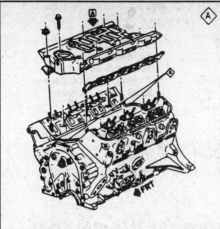

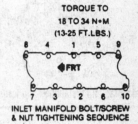

NOTE APPLY A SMOOTH CONTINUOUS BEAD APPROX. 2.0-3.0 WIDE AND 3.0-5.0 THICK ON BOTH SURFACES. BEAD CONFIGURATION MUST INSURE COMPLETE SEALING OF WATER AND OIL. SURFACE MUST BE FREE OF OIL AND DIRT TO INSURE ADEQUATE SEAL.

TORQUE TO
18 TO 34 N•M
(13-25 FT.LBS.)

INLET MANIFOLD BOLT/SCREW & NUT TIGHTENING SEQUENCE

FIG. 49 Intake manifold installation — 1985–86 2.8L V6 engine

1. Intake manifold
2. Gasket
3. 25 N·m (18 lbs. ft.)
4. Sealer

FIG. 50 Intake manifold installation — 1987–88 2.8L V6 engine

4. Release the fuel system pressure and disconnect the fuel line along the fuel rail.

5. Disconnect the serpentine drive belt.

6. Remove the alternator and move to one side. Loosen the alternator bracket.

7. Disconnect the power steering pump and move to one side.

8. Disconnect the idle air vacuum hose at the throttle body.

9. Disconnect the the wires at the injectors.

10. Remove the fuel rail, breather tube and the fuel runners from the engine.

11. Tag and disconnect the plug wires at the manifold.

12. Remove the rocker arm covers — refer to the necessary service procedure. Drain the cooling system, the disconnect the radiator hose at the thermostat housing. Disconnect the heater hose from the thermostat housing and tag and disconnect the thermostat wiring.

13. Remove the intake manifold bolts and remove the intake manifold from the engine.

➡ **Retain the Belleville washer in the same orientation on the 4 center bolts.**

14. Loosen the rocker arms and remove the pushrods.

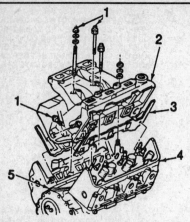

1. Tighten in proper sequence to 15 ft. lbs. (20Nm), then retighten to 24 ft. lbs. (33Nm)

⑦ ④ ③ ⑥
⑧ ① ② ⑤

2. Intake manifold
3. Gasket
4. Cylinder head
5. Sealer

FIG. 51 Intake manifold installation and torque sequence — 1989–92 2.8L and 3.1 V6 engine

➡ **Intake pushrods are marked orange and are 6 in. (152.4mm) long. Exhaust pushrods are marked blue and are 6³/₈ in. (161.9mm) long.**

15. Remove the intake gasket.

To install:

16. Clean the gasket material and grease from the mating surfaces.

17. Place a bead of RTV sealant on each ridge where the front and rear of the intake manifold contact the block.

18. Install the new intake manifold gasket.

19. Install the pushrods and make sure they are seated in the lifter.

➡ **Intake pushrods are marked orange and are 6 in. (152.4mm) long. Exhaust pushrods are marked blue and are 6³/₈ in. (161.9mm) long.**

20. Install the rocker arm nuts and tighten to 18 ft. lbs.

21. Install the intake manifold and retaining bolts. Torque the bolts to 15 ft. lbs. in the proper sequence shown, then retighten in sequence to 24 ft. lbs.

22. Install the heater pipe to the manifold.

23. Connect the coolant sensor and any other necessary wiring.

24. Install the upper radiator hose.

25. Install the rocker arm covers.

26. Install the breather tube.

27. Install the fuel rail and the wires to the injectors.

28. Connect the idle air vacuum hose at the throttle body.

29. Install the alternator and bracket.

30. Install the power steering gear and pump.

31. Connect the power steering line at the alternator bracket.

32. Install the serpentine drive belt.

33. Connect the fuel lines to the fuel rail and to the bracket.

34. Install the plenum, plug harness and EGR valve.

35. Install the throttle body.

36. Connect cables at the plenum.

37. Connect the negative battery cable and fill the cooling system.

Exhaust Manifold

REMOVAL & INSTALLATION

1.8L, 2.0L and 2.2L OHV Engines

◆ SEE FIGS. 52-55

1. Disconnect the negative terminal from the battery.

2. Disconnect the oxygen sensor wire.

3. Remove the serpentine belt or alternator drive belt.

4. Remove the alternator-to-bracket bolts and support the alternator (with the wires attached) out of the way.

5. If equipped with A.I.R. or Pulsair system (1982–84), disconnect the pipes and hoses.

6. Raise and support the vehicle safely.

7. Disconnect the exhaust pipe-to-exhaust manifold bolts and lower the vehicle.

8. Remove the exhaust manifold-to-cylinder head bolts.

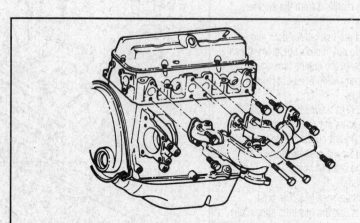

FIG. 52 Exhaust manifold installation, 1982–84 1.8L and 2.0L OHV engine

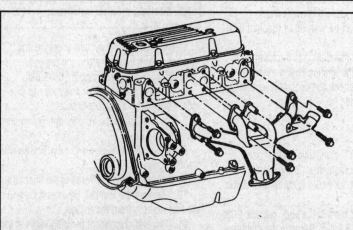

FIG. 53 Exhaust manifold installation, 1985–86 2.0L OHV engine

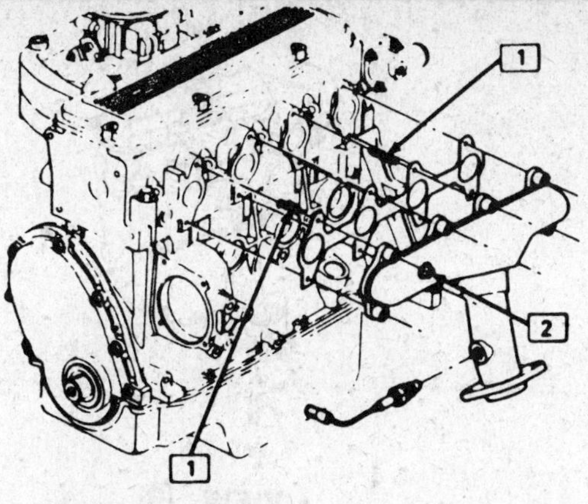

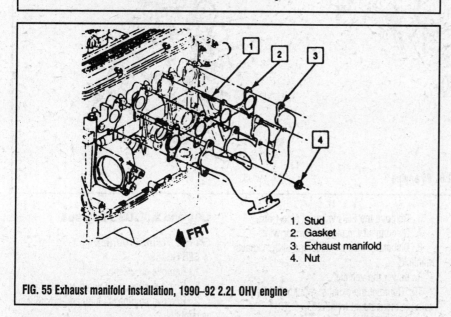

1. 5–15 N·m (3–11 ft. lbs.)
2. 8–18 N·m (6–13 ft. lbs.)

FIG. 54 Exhaust manifold installation, 1987–89 2.0L OHV engine

1. Stud
2. Gasket
3. Exhaust manifold
4. Nut

FIG. 55 Exhaust manifold installation, 1990–92 2.2L OHV engine

9. Remove the exhaust manifold from the exhaust pipe flange and the manifold from the vehicle.

To install:

10. Using a gasket scraper, clean the gasket mounting surfaces.

11. To install, use new gaskets and reverse the removal procedures. Torque the exhaust manifold-to-cylinder head nuts to 3–12 ft. lbs. and the bolts to 6–13 ft. lbs. Start the engine and check for exhaust leaks.

2.8L and 3.1L Engine

1985–86
LEFT SIDE
♦ SEE FIG. 56

1. Disconnect the negative battery cable.
2. Remove the air cleaner assembly.
3. Remove the air flow sensor. Remove the engine heat shield.

4. Remove the crossover pipe at the manifold.
5. Remove the exhaust manifold bolts.
6. Remove the exhaust manifold.

To install:

7. Clean the surfaces of the cylinder head and manifold.
8. Place the manifold into position, loosely install the manifold bolts, then install the exhaust crossover pipe to the manifold.
9. Tighten the manifold bolts EVENLY to 25 ft. lbs.
10. Install the heat shield and the mass flow sensor.
11. Install the air cleaner and the negative battery cable.

RIGHT SIDE

1. Disconnect the negative battery cable.
2. Remove the air cleaner assembly.

3. Remove the air flow sensor. Remove the engine heat shield.
4. Disconnect the crossover pipe at the manifold.
5. Disconnect the accelerator and throttle valve cable at the throttle lever and the plenum. Move aside to gain working clearance.
6. Disconnect the power steering line at the power steering pump.
7. Remove the EGR valve assembly.
8. Raise the vehicle and support safely.
9. Disconnect the exhaust pipe at the exhaust manifold.
10. Lower the vehicle.
11. Remove the manifold bolts. Remove the exhaust manifold.

To install:

12. Clean the surfaces of the cylinder head and manifold.
13. Place the manifold into position and loosely install the manifold bolts.
14. Raise and support the vehicle safely.
15. Install the exhaust pipe at the manifold.
16. Lower the vehicle.
17. Tighten the manifold bolts EVENLY to 25 ft. lbs.
18. Install the EGR valve and related parts.
19. Connect the power steering line at the power steering pump.
20. Connect the accelerator and throttle valve cable at the throttle lever and the plenum.
21. Connect the crossover pipe at the manifold.
22. Install the engine heat shield.
23. Install the mass air flow sensor.
24. Install the air cleaner assembly and connect the negative battery cable.

1987–92
LEFT SIDE

1. Disconnect the negative battery cable.
2. Remove the air cleaner inlet hose.
3. Remove the mass air flow sensor, on models so equipped.
4. Drain the coolant and remove the coolant by-pass pipe and engine heat shield.

⁑ CAUTION

When draining the coolant, keep in mind that cats and dogs are attracted by the ethylene glycol antifreeze, and are quite likely to drink any that is left in an uncovered container or in puddles on the ground. This will prove fatal in sufficient quantity. Always drain the coolant into a sealable container. Coolant should be reused unless it is contaminated or several years old.

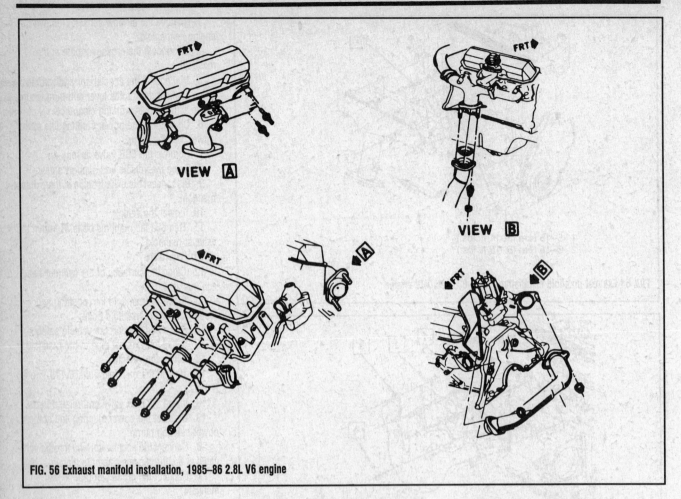

FIG. 56 Exhaust manifold installation, 1985–86 2.8L V6 engine

5. Disconnect the exhaust crossover pipe at the manifold.

6. Remove the exhaust manifold bolts and remove the exhaust manifold/crossover assembly.

To Install:

7. Clean the surfaces of the cylinder head and manifold.

8. Place the manifold into position and loosely install the manifold bolts.

9. Install the exhaust crossover pipe to the manifold.

10. Tighten the exhaust manifold bolts EVENLY to 18 ft. lbs.

11. Install the heat shield and coolant pipe.

12. Fill the cooling system.

13. Install the air cleaner inlet hose.

14. Connect the negative battery cable.

RIGHT SIDE

♦ SEE FIGS. 57-58

1. Disconnect the negative battery cable.

2. Raise and support the vehicle safely.

3. Remove the heat shield.

4. Disconnect the exhaust pipe at the crossover.

5. Lower the vehicle.

6. Remove the EGR valve or pipe from.

7. Disconnect the oxygen sensor wire.

8. Disconnect the exhaust pipe at the exhaust manifold.

9. Lower the vehicle.

10. Remove the exhaust manifold bolts and remove the exhaust manifold.

To Install:

11. Clean the surfaces of the cylinder head and manifold.

12. Install the manifold gasket, place the manifold into position and loosely install the manifold bolts.

13. Install the crossover at the manifold.

14. Tighten the manifold bolts EVENLY to 25 ft. lbs.

15. Install the EGR valve or pipe and connect the oxygen sensor wire.

16. Raise and support the vehicle safely.

17. Install the engine heat shield.

18. Install the exhaust pipe to the crossover.

19. Lower the vehicle.

20. Install the negative battery cable. and check for leaks.

1.8L and 2.0L OHC Engines

EXCEPT TURBOCHARGER

♦ SEE FIG. 59

1. Remove air cleaner.

2. Remove spark plug wires and retainers.

3. Remove oil dipstick tube and breather assembly.

4. Disconnect oxygen sensor wire.

5. Disconnect exhaust pipe from manifold flange.

6. Remove exhaust manifold to cylinder head attaching nuts and remove manifold and gasket.

7. Installation is the reverse of removal. Torque the bolts EVENLY to 16-19 ft. lbs.

WITH TURBOCHARGER

♦ SEE FIG. 60

1. Disconnect the negative battery cable. Remove the turbo induction tube.

2. Disconnect (mark for correct installation) the spark plug wires.

3. Remove the bolts and nuts between the turbo and exhaust manifold.

4. Remove the bolts and nuts and remove the manifold and gasket.

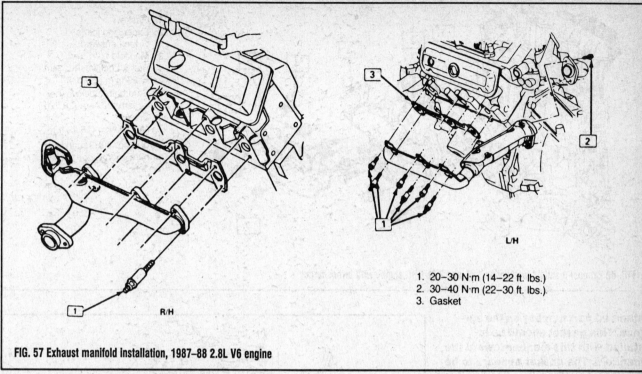

1. 20–30 N·m (14–22 ft. lbs.)
2. 30–40 N·m (22–30 ft. lbs.)
3. Gasket

FIG. 57 Exhaust manifold installation, 1987–88 2.8L V6 engine

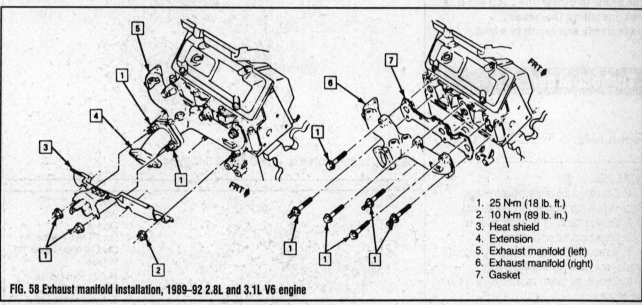

1. 25 N·m (18 lb. ft.)
2. 10 N·m (89 lb. in.)
3. Heat shield
4. Extension
5. Exhaust manifold (left)
6. Exhaust manifold (right)
7. Gasket

FIG. 58 Exhaust manifold installation, 1989–92 2.8L and 3.1L V6 engine

To install:

5. Clean the mating surfaces at the cylinder head and manifold.

6. Install the manifold with a new gasket and torque the nuts EVENLY to 16 ft. lbs.

7. Install the turbocharger to the exhaust manifold and torque the nuts EVENLY to 18 ft. lbs.

8. Install the spark plug wires and the turbo induction tube.

➡ **Before installing a new gasket on the 1.8L MFI Turbo engine (code J), check for the location of the**

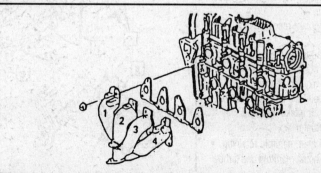

FIG. 59 Exhaust manifold installation and torque sequence 1.8L and 2.0L OHC engine without turbocharger

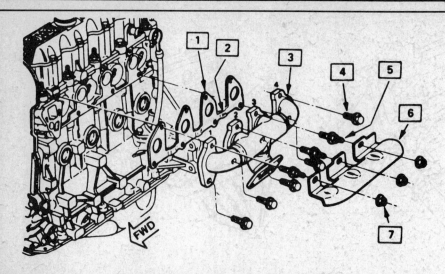

1. Gasket
2. Expansion joints face outward
3. Manifold asm.
4. Bolt & Lockwasher asm. 27 N·m (20 lb. ft.)
5. Stud bolt & lockwasher asm. 27 N·m (20 lb.ft.)
6. Shield
7. Nut 22 N·m (16 lb. ft.)

Torque no. 2 & 3 manifold runners prior to no. 1 & 4 runners

FIG. 60 Exhaust manifold installation 1.8L and 2.0L OHC engine with turbocharger

stamped part number on the surface. This gasket should be installed with this number toward the manifold. The gasket appears to be the same in either direction but it is not. Installing the gasket backwards will result in a leak.

Turbocharger

REMOVAL & INSTALLATION

◆ SEE FIGS. 61-62

1. Disconnect the negative battery cable. Raise the car and support it with jackstands.
2. Remove the lower fan retaining screw.
3. Disconnect the exhaust pipe.
4. Remove the rear air conditioning support bracket and loosen the remaining bolts.
5. Remove the turbo support bracket bolt to the engine.
6. Disconnect the oil drain hose at the turbo.
7. Lower the vehicle.
8. Disconnect the coolant recovery pipe and move to one side.
9. Disconnect the induction tube.
10. Disconnect the cooling fan.
11. Disconnect the oxygen sensor.
12. Disconnect the oil feed pipe at the union.
13. Disconnect the air intake duct and vacuum hose at the actuator.
14. Remove the exhaust manifold retaining nuts and remove the exhaust manifold and turbocharger.

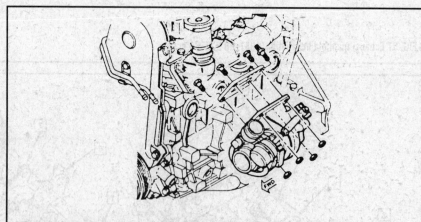

FIG. 61 Turbocharger mounting — 1983–86 1.8L OHC engine

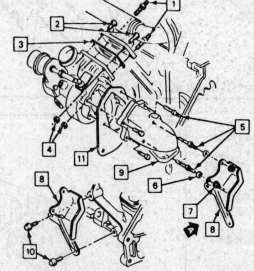
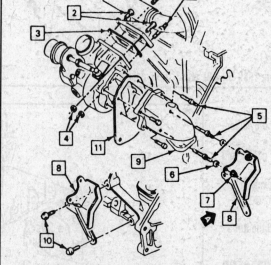

1. Stud
2. Bolt
3. Gasket
4. Nut 25 N·m (18 lbs. ft.)
5. Stud 25 N·m (18 lbs. ft.)
6. Washer
7. Nut 25 N·m (18 lbs. ft.)
8. Support bracket
9. Exhuast outlet elbow
10. Bolt 50 N·m (37 lbs. ft.)
11. Adapter plate

FIG. 62 Turbocharger mounting — 1987–90 2.0L OHC engine

To install:

15. Install the exhaust manifold and turbocharger. Torque the bolts EVENLY to 16 ft. lbs.

16. Install the exhaust manifold retaining nuts.

17. Connect the air intake duct and vacuum hose at the actuator.

18. Connect the oil feed pipe at the union.

19. Connect the oxygen sensor.

20. Connect the cooling fan.

21. Connect the induction tube.

22. Connect the coolant recovery pipe and move to one side.

23. Lower the vehicle.

24. Connect the oil drain hose at the turbo.

25. Install the turbo support bracket bolt to the engine.

26. Install the rear air conditioning support bracket.

27. Connect the exhaust pipe.

28. Install the lower fan retaining screw.

Radiator

REMOVAL & INSTALLATION

♦ SEE FIGS. 62A-62B

1. Disconnect the negative battery cable.
2. Drain the cooling system.

❈❈ CAUTION

When draining the coolant, keep in mind that cats and dogs are attracted by the ethylene glycol antifreeze, and are quite likely to drink any that is left in an uncovered container or in puddles on the ground. This will prove fatal in sufficient quantity. Always drain the coolant into a sealable container. Coolant should be reused unless it is contaminated or several years old.

3. Disconnect the electrical lead at the fan motor.

4. Remove the fan frame-to-radiator support attaching bolts and then remove the fan assembly.

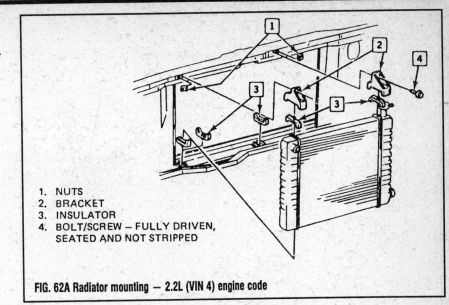

1. NUTS
2. BRACKET
3. INSULATOR
4. BOLT/SCREW – FULLY DRIVEN, SEATED AND NOT STRIPPED

FIG. 62A Radiator mounting — 2.2L (VIN 4) engine code

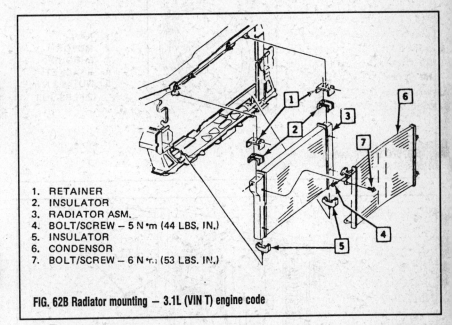

1. RETAINER
2. INSULATOR
3. RADIATOR ASM.
4. BOLT/SCREW – 5 N•m (44 LBS. IN.)
5. INSULATOR
6. CONDENSOR
7. BOLT/SCREW – 6 N•m (53 LBS. IN.)

FIG. 62B Radiator mounting — 3.1L (VIN T) engine code

5. Disconnect the upper and lower radiator hoses and the coolant recovery hose from the radiator.

6. Disconnect the transmission oil cooler lines from the radiator and wire them out of the way.

7. If equipped with A/C, remove the 4 radiator to condenser bolts and the radiator tank to refrigerent line clamp bolt.

8. Remove the radiator-to-radiator support attaching bolts and clamps. Remove the radiator.

To install:

9. Place the radiator in the vehicle so that the bottom is located in the lower mounting pads. Tighten the attaching bolts and clamps.

10. Connect the transmission oil cooler lines and tighten the bolts to 20 ft. lbs.

11. Installation of the remaining components is in the reverse order of removal. Fill the coolant system, check for coolant leaks.

Electric Cooling Fan

REMOVAL & INSTALLATION

♦ SEE FIGS. 62C-62D

➡ **The electric cooling fan can start**

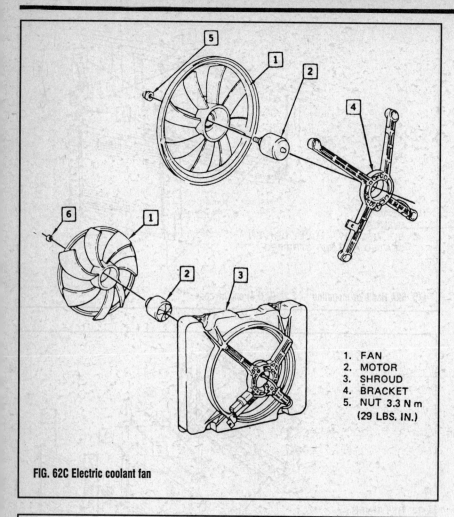

FIG. 62C Electric coolant fan

1. FAN
2. MOTOR
3. SHROUD
4. BRACKET
5. NUT 3.3 N·m
   (29 LBS. IN.)

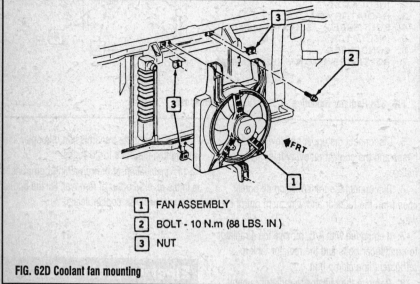

1. FAN ASSEMBLY
2. BOLT - 10 N.m (88 LBS. IN)
3. NUT

FIG. 62D Coolant fan mounting

whether or not the engine is running. After replacing electric coolant fan, verify that the fan is moving the air in the proper direction.

4-Cylinder Engines

1. Disconnect the negative battery cable.
2. Remove the air cleaner duct.
3. Disconnect the wiring harness from the motor and the fan frame.

4. Remove the fan assembly from the radiator support.

5. Installation is the reverse of the removal procedure. Torque the fan assembly motor-to-fan 29 inch lbs. and fan-to-radiator support bolt 80 inch lbs.

6-Cylinder Engines

1. Disconnect the negative battery cable. Drain engine coolant to level below the upper radiator hose.

❊❊ CAUTION

When draining the coolant, keep in mind that cats and dogs are attracted by the ethylene glycol antifreeze, and are quite likely to drink any that is left in an uncovered container or in puddles on the ground. This will prove fatal in sufficient quantity. Always drain the coolant into a sealable container. Coolant should be reused unless it is contaminated or several years old.

2. Remove the air cleaner duct.
3. Remove the air cleaner assembly.
4. Mark latch position for reassembly, then remove the main hood latch assembly.
5. Disconnect the upper radiator hose and position aside. On automatic transaxle equipped vehicles, position transaxle cooler lines aside.
6. Disconnect the electrical wiring harness connector at the coolant fan. Remove the fan assembly from the radiator support.
7. Installation is the reverse of the removal procedure. Torque the fan assembly motor-to-fan 29 inch lbs. and fan-to-radiator support bolt 80 inch lbs.

Water Pump

REMOVAL & INSTALLATION

❊❊ CAUTION

When draining the coolant, keep in mind that cats and dogs are attracted by the ethylene glycol antifreeze, and are quite likely to drink any that is left in an uncovered container or in puddles

on the ground. This will prove fatal in sufficient quantity. Always drain the coolant into a sealable container. Coolant should be reused unless it is contaminated or several years old.

1.8L, 2.0L and 2.2L OHV Engines

◆ SEE FIGS. 63-65

1. Disconnect the negative battery cable.
2. Drain the cooling system.
3. Remove all accessory drive belts or the serpentine belt.
4. Remove the alternator.
5. Unscrew the water pump pulley mounting bolts and then pull off the pulley.
6. Remove the mounting bolts and remove the water pump.

To Install:

7. Place a 1/8 in. (3mm) wide bead of RTV sealant on the water pump sealing surface or install a new gasket, on models so equipped . While the sealer is still wet, install the pump and tighten the bolts to 13–18 ft. lbs.
8. Installation of the remaining components is in the reverse order of removal. Fill the cooling system to the proper level.

1.8L and 2.0L OHC Engines

◆ SEE FIG. 66

1. Remove the timing belt as described later.
2. Remove the timing belt rear protective covers.
3. Remove the hose from the pump.
4. Unbolt and remove the pump.
5. Installation is the reverse of removal. Torque the bolts to 19 ft. lbs.

2.8L and 3.1L V6 Engines

◆ SEE FIGS. 67-68

1. Disconnect battery negative cable.
2. Drain cooling system.
3. Disconnect the serpentine belt at the water pump pulley.
4. On 1985–86 models, disconnect the wires at the air conditioning pressure cycling switch and remove the cycling switch.
5. Remove the water pump pulley.
6. Remove the pump retaining bolts and remove the water pump.

To install:

7. Clean the gasket surfaces.
8. Install the gasket and water pump and tighten the pump to block bolts to 18 ft. lbs.
9. Install the water pump pulley.
10. Install the air conditioning pressure cycling switch on 1985–86 models.
11. Install the serpentine belt.

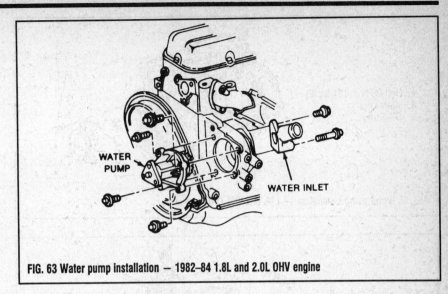

FIG. 63 Water pump installation — 1982–84 1.8L and 2.0L OHV engine

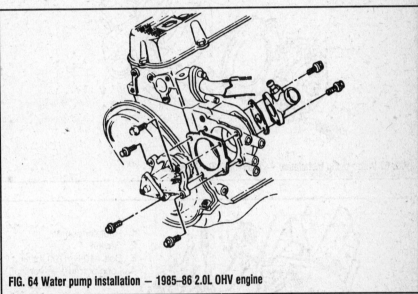

FIG. 64 Water pump installation — 1985–86 2.0L OHV engine

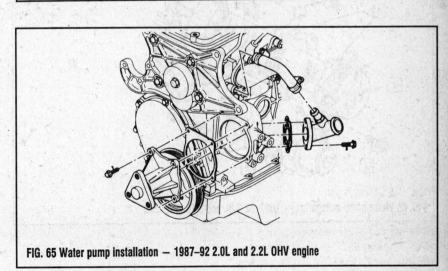

FIG. 65 Water pump installation — 1987–92 2.0L and 2.2L OHV engine

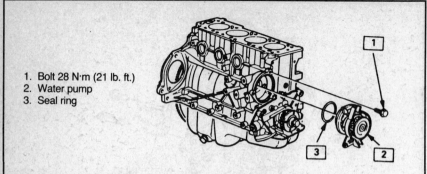

1. Bolt 28 N·m (21 lb. ft.)
2. Water pump
3. Seal ring

FIG. 66 Water pump installation — 1.8L and 2.0L OHC engine

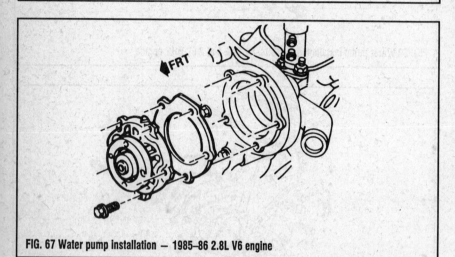

◄FRT

FIG. 67 Water pump installation — 1985-86 2.8L V6 engine

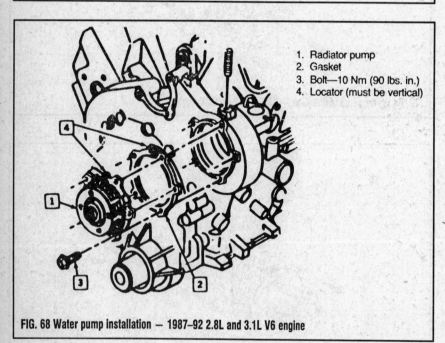

1. Radiator pump
2. Gasket
3. Bolt—10 Nm (90 lbs. in.)
4. Locator (must be vertical)

FIG. 68 Water pump installation — 1987–92 2.8L and 3.1L V6 engine

12. Fill the cooling system.
13. Reconnect the battery, start the engine and check for leaks.

Cylinder Head

REMOVAL & INSTALLATION

❋❋ CAUTION

When draining the coolant, keep in mind that cats and dogs are attracted by the ethylene glycol antifreeze, and are quite likely to drink any that is left in an uncovered container or in puddles on the ground. This will prove fatal in sufficient quantity. Always drain the coolant into a sealable container. Coolant should be reused unless it is contaminated or several years old.

1.8L, 2.0L and 2.2L OHV Engines

1982–86
◆ SEE FIG. 69

➡ **The engine should be overnight cold before removing the cylinder head.**

1. Disconnect the negative battery cable. Release the fuel pressure.
2. Drain the cooling system into a clean container; the coolant can be reused if it is still good.
3. Remove the air cleaner. Raise and support the front of the vehicle.
4. Remove the exhaust shield. Disconnect the exhaust pipe.
5. Remove the heater hose from the intake manifold and then lower the car.
6. Unscrew the mounting bolts and remove the engine lift bracket (includes air management).
7. Remove (mark for correct installation) the distributor. Disconnect the vacuum manifold at the alternator bracket.
8. Tag and disconnect the remaining vacuum lines at the intake manifold and thermostat.
9. Remove the air management pipe at the exhaust check valve.
10. Disconnect the accelerator linkage at the

carburetor or T.B.I. unit and then remove the linkage bracket.

11. Tag and disconnect all necessary wires. Remove the upper radiator hose at the thermostat.

12. Remove the bolt attaching the dipstick tube and hot water bracket.

13. Remove the idler pulley. Remove the A.I.R. and power steering pump drive belts.

14. Remove the A.I.R. bracket-to-intake manifold bolt. If equipped with power steering, remove the air pump pulley, the A.IR. through-bolt and the power steering adjusting bracket.

15. Loosen the A.I.R. mounting bracket lower bolt so that the bracket will rotate.

16. Disconnect and plug the fuel line at the carburetor.

17. Remove the alternator. Remove the alternator brace from the head and then remove the upper mounting bracket.

18. Remove the cylinder head cover. Remove the rocker arms and pushrods.

19. Remove the cylinder head bolts in the order given in the illustration. Remove the cylinder head with the carburetor or T.B.I. unit, intake and exhaust manifolds still attached.

To install:

20. To install, the gasket surfaces on both the head and the block must be clean of any foreign matter and free of any nicks or heavy scratches. Cylinder bolt threads in the block and the bolt must be clean.

21. Place a new cylinder head gasket in position over the dowel pins on the block. Carefully guide the cylinder head into position.

22. Coat the cylinder bolts with sealing compound and install them finger tight.

23. Using a torque wrench, torque as follows:

a. 1982–85 — gradually tighten the bolts to 65–75 ft. lbs. in the sequence shown in the illustration.

b. 1986 — gradually tighten the bolts to 73–85 ft. lbs. in the sequence shown in the illustration.

24. Install the rocker arms and pushrods and adjust the valve lash.

25. Install the cylinder head cover.

26. Install the alternator brace on the head. Install the upper mounting bracket.

27. Install the alternator.

28. Connect the fuel line at the carburetor.

29. Install the A.I.R. bracket-to-intake manifold bolt. If equipped with power steering, install the air pump pulley, the A.IR. through-bolt and the power steering adjusting bracket.

30. Install the idler pulley. Install the A.I.R. and power steering pump drive belts.

31. Install the bolt attaching the dipstick tube and hot water bracket.

32. Connect all wires.

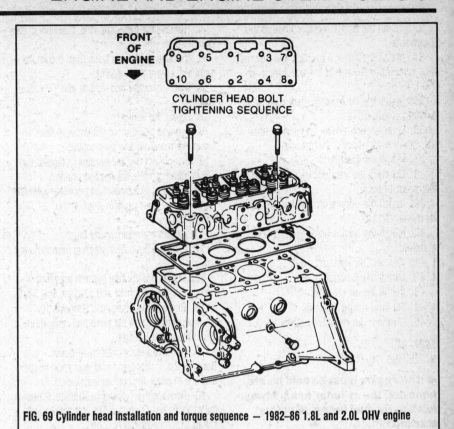

FRONT OF ENGINE

CYLINDER HEAD BOLT TIGHTENING SEQUENCE

FIG. 69 Cylinder head installation and torque sequence — 1982–86 1.8L and 2.0L OHV engine

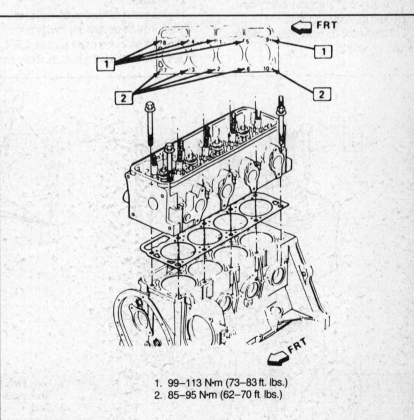

FRT

FRT

1. 99–113 N·m (73–83 ft. lbs.)
2. 85–95 N·m (62–70 ft. lbs.)

FIG. 70 Cylinder head installation and torque sequence — 1987–89 2.0L and 2.2L OHV engine

33. Install the upper radiator hose at the thermostat.

34. Install the linkage bracket and connect the accelerator linkage at the carburetor or T.B.I.

35. Install the air management pipe at the exhaust check valve.

36. Connect the remaining vacuum lines at the intake manifold and thermostat.

37. Install the distributor.

38. Connect the vacuum manifold at the alternator bracket.

39. Install the engine lift bracket (includes air management).

40. Install the heater hose at the intake manifold.

41. Connect the exhaust pipe.

42. Install the exhaust shield.

43. Install the air cleaner.

44. Fill the cooling system.

45. Connect the negative battery cable.

1987–92
♦ SEE FIGS. 70-71

➡ **The engine must be cold before removing the cylinder head. Always release the fuel pressure before starting repair.**

1. Disconnect the negative battery cable.
2. Drain the cooling system.
3. Remove the TBI cover. Raise and safely support the vehicle.

4. Remove the exhaust shield. Disconnect the exhaust pipe.

5. Remove the heater hose from the intake manifold. Lower the vehicle.

6. Disconnect the accelerator and TV cable bracket.

7. Lower the vehicle.

8. Tag and disconnect the vacuum lines at the intake manifold and thermostat.

9. Disconnect the accelerator linkage at the TBI unit and remove the linkage bracket.

10. Tag and disconnect all necessary wires. Remove the upper radiator hose at the thermostat.

11. Remove the serpentine belt.

12. Remove the power steering pump and lay aside.

13. Make sure the fuel system pressure is released and disconnect and plug the fuel lines.

14. Remove the alternator. Remove the alternator brace from the head and remove the upper mounting bracket.

15. Remove the cylinder head cover. Remove the rocker arms and pushrods keeping all parts in order for correct installation.

16. Remove the cylinder head bolts. Remove the cylinder head with the TBI unit, intake and exhaust manifolds still attached.

To install:

17. The gasket surfaces on both the head and the block must be clean of any foreign matter and free of any nicks or heavy scratches. Bolt threads in the block and the bolts must be clean.

18. Place a new cylinder head gasket in position over the dowel pins on the block. Carefully guide the cylinder head into position.

19. Coat the cylinder bolts with sealing compound and install them finger tight.

20. Using a torque wrench, torque as follows:
   a. 1987–89 — tighten the long bolts to 73–83 ft lbs. in the sequence shown in the illustration and tighten the short bolts to 62–70 ft lbs. in the sequence shown in the illustration.
   b. 1990 — Tighten in 4 steps as follows:
   • Tighten all bolts in sequence to 41 ft. lbs.
   • Tighten all bolts an additional 45° in sequence.
   • Tighten all bolts an additional 45° in sequence.
   • Tighten the long bolts — 8, 4, 1, 1, 5 and 9 an additional 20° and tighten the short bolts — 7, 3, 2, 6 and 10 an additional 10°.

➡ **The short bolts, exhaust side, should end up with a total rotation of 100° and the long bolts, intake side, should end up with a total rotation of 110°.**

   c. 1991–92 — Tighten in 3 steps as follows:
   • Tighten the long bolts in sequence to 46 ft. lbs.
   • Tighten the short bolts in sequence to 43 ft. lbs.

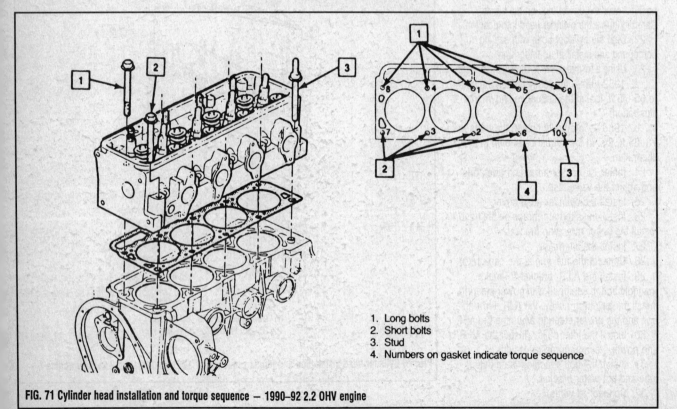

1. Long bolts
2. Short bolts
3. Stud
4. Numbers on gasket indicate torque sequence

FIG. 71 Cylinder head installation and torque sequence — 1990–92 2.2 OHV engine

• Tighten all bolts in sequence an additional 90°.

21. Reinstall the alternator. Install the power steering pump and brackets.

22. Reconnect the fuel lines and the hoses. Connect the exhaust pipe to the manifold.

23. Install the valve cover and connect the linkage at the TBI unit. Install the air cleaner and fill all the fluids.

24. Run the engine and check for leaks.

1.8L 1nd 2.0L OHC Engines

♦ SEE FIGS. 72-74

1. Remove air cleaner or induction tube (turbo engines). Release the fuel pressure.

2. Drain cooling system.

3. Remove alternator and pivot bracket at camshaft carrier housing.

4. Disconnect power steering pump and bracket and lay to one side.

5. Disconnect ignition coil electrical connections and remove coil.

6. Disconnect spark plug wires and distributor cap and remove.

7. Remove throttle cable from bracket at intake manifold.

8. Disconnect throttle cable, downshift cable and T.V. cable from E.F.I. assembly.

9. Disconnect E.C.M. connectors from E.F.I. assembly.

10. Remove vacuum brake hose at filter.

11. Disconnect inlet and return fuel lines at flex joints.

✳✳ CAUTION

The fuel lines are pressurized (especially Turbo Engines). Removal may cause fuel spray resulting in personal injury. Do not remove before bleeding the pressure from the fuel system. See Section 1 for the procedure.

12. Remove water pump bypass hose at intake manifold and water pump.

13. Disconnect ECM harness connectors at intake manifold.

14. Disconnect heater hose from intake manifold.

15. Disconnect exhaust pipe at exhaust manifold. On turbo engines, disconnect the exhaust manifold at the turbo connection.

16. Disconnect breather hose at camshaft carrier.

17. Remove upper radiator hose.

18. Disconnect engine electrical harness and wires from thermostat housing.

19. Remove timing cover.

20. Remove timing probe holder.

21. Loosen water pump retaining bolts and remove timing belt.

22. Loosen camshaft carrier and cylinder head attaching bolts a little at a time in sequence shown.

➡ **Camshaft carrier and cylinder head bolts should only be removed when engine is cold.**

23. Remove camshaft carrier assembly.

24. Remove cylinder head, intake manifold and exhaust manifold as an assembly.

To install:

25. Install a new cylinder head gasket in position on the block.

26. Apply a continuous bead of sealer to the cam carrier.

27. Install the cylinder head, reassembled with the intake and exhaust manifolds, if removed.

28. Install the camshaft carrier on the cylinder head and tighten the bolts, in following sequence, to the correct torque.

a. Tighten all bolts in sequence to 18 ft. lbs.

b. Tighten all bolts an additional 180° in 3 steps of 60° each.

29. Install timing belt.

30. Install timing probe holder.

31. Install timing cover.

32. Connect engine electrical harness and wires at thermostat housing.

33. Install upper radiator hose.

34. Connect breather hose at camshaft carrier.

35. Connect exhaust pipe at exhaust manifold. On turbo engines, connect the exhaust manifold at the turbo connection.

36. Connect heater hose at intake manifold.

37. Connect ECM harness connectors at intake manifold.

38. Install water pump bypass hose at intake manifold and water pump.

39. Connect inlet and return fuel lines at flex joints.

40. Install vacuum brake hose at filter.

41. Connect E.C.M. connectors at E.F.I. assembly.

42. Connect throttle cable, downshift cable and T.V. cable at E.F.I. assembly.

43. Install throttle cable at bracket on intake manifold.

44. Connect spark plug wires and install the distributor cap.

45. Connect ignition coil electrical connections and install coil.

46. Install power steering pump and bracket.

47. Install alternator and pivot bracket on camshaft carrier housing.

48. Fill cooling system.

49. Install air cleaner or induction tube (turbo engines).

2.8L and 3.1L V6 Engines

1985–86
LEFT SIDE

♦ SEE FIG. 75

1. Disconnect the negative battery cable.

2. Drain the coolant from the block and lower the car.

3. Remove the intake manifold.

4. Remove the exhaust crossover at the intake manifold.

5. Remove the air cleaner cover and air cleaner.

6. Disconnect the MAP sensor.

7. Remove the exhaust crossover heat shield.

8. Disconnect the exhaust crossover at the left manifold.

9. Remove the oil level indicator tube.

10. Disconnect the wiring harness at the left head.

11. Loosen the rocker arm bolts and remove the pushrods.

12. Remove the cylinder head bolts and cylinder head.

To install:

13. Clean all gasket surfaces and bolts.

14. Place the new head gasket in position over the dowel pins with the words "This side Up" facing upward.

15. Coat the cylinder head bolts with sealer and torque to 77 ft. lbs. in the sequence shown.

16. Install the pushrods in the lifter seats and loosely retain with the rocker arms.

17. Install the intake manifold and gaskets.

18. Install the MAP sensor.

19. Install the exhaust manifold.

20. Install the spark plug wires.

21. Fill the cooling system.

22. Install the oil level indicator tube.

23. Install the air cleaner and cover.

24. Adjust the drive belt and the valve lash.

RIGHT SIDE

1. Disconnect the negative battery cable.

2. Drain the cooling system.

3. Remove the intake manifold.

4. Raise and support the vehicle safely.

5. Remove the exhaust crossover at the right manifold.

6. Lower the vehicle.

7. Loosen the rocker arm bolts and remove the pushrods.

8. Remove the air cleaner cover and air cleaner.

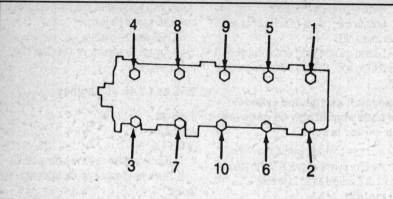

FIG. 72 Camshaft carrier and head bolt loosening sequence — 1.8L and 2.0L OHC engines

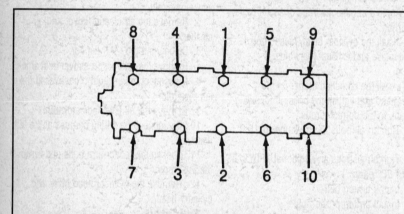

FIG. 73 Camshaft carrier and head bolt tightening sequence — 1.8L and 2.0L OHC engines

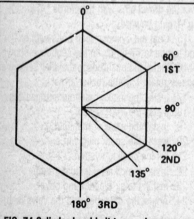

FIG. 74 Cylinder head bolt torque degree sequence — 1.8L and 2.0L OHC engines

over the dowel pins with the words "This side Up" facing upward.

15. Coat the cylinder head bolts with sealer and torque to 77 ft. lbs. in the sequence shown.

16. Install the pushrods in the lifter seats and loosely retain with the rocker arms.

17. Install the intake manifold and gaskets.

18. Install the MAP sensor.

19. Install the exhaust manifold.

20. Install the spark plug wires.

21. Fill the cooling system.

22. Install the oil level indicator tube.

23. Install the air cleaner and cover.

24. Adjust the drive belt and the valve lash.

1987–92
LEFT SIDE
▶ SEE FIG. 76

1. Relieve the fuel system pressure and disconnect the negative battery cable. Drain the cooling system. Remove the rocker cover.

2. Remove the intake manifold. Disconnect the exhaust crossover at the right exhaust manifold.

3. Disconnect the oil level indicator tube bracket.

4. Loosen the rocker arms nuts enough to remove the pushrods.

5. Starting with the outer bolts, remove the cylinder head bolts. Remove the cylinder head with the exhaust manifold.

6. Clean and inspect the surfaces of the cylinder head, block and intake manifold. Clean the threads in the block and the threads on the bolts.

To install:

7. Align the new gasket over the dowels on the block with the note **THIS SIDE UP** facing the cylinder head.

11. Loosen the rocker arm bolts and remove the pushrods.

12. Remove the cylinder head bolts and cylinder head.

To install:

13. Clean all gasket surfaces and bolts.

14. Place the new head gasket in position

9. Remove the MAP sensor.

10. Remove the exhaust crossover heat shield.

11. Disconnect the exhaust crossover at the right manifold.

12. Disconnect the spark plug wiring harness at the right head.

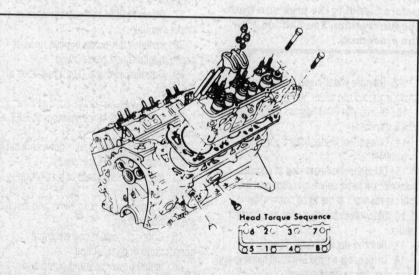

FIG. 75 Cylinder head installation and torque sequence — 1985–86 2.8L V6 engine

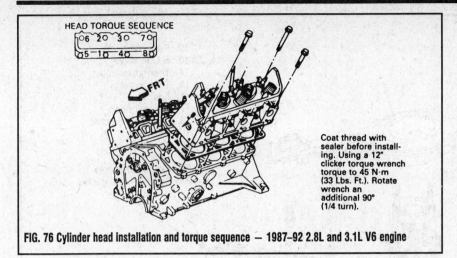

HEAD TORQUE SEQUENCE

6 20 30 70

5 10 40 8

FRT

Coat thread with sealer before installing. Using a 12" clicker torque wrench torque to 45 N·m (33 Lbs. Ft.). Rotate wrench an additional 90° (1/4 turn).

FIG. 76 Cylinder head installation and torque sequence — 1987–92 2.8L and 3.1L V6 engine

8. Install the cylinder head and exhaust manifold crossover assembly on the engine.

9. Coat the cylinder head bolts with a proper sealer and install the bolts hand tight.

10. Torque the bolts, in the correct sequence, to 33 ft. lbs., then rotate an additional 90° (1/4 turn).

11. Install the pushrods in the same order they were removed.

➡ **Intake pushrods are marked orange and are 6 in. (152.4mm) long. Exhaust pushrods are marked blue and are 6³/₈ in. (161.9mm) long.**

12. Install the rocker arms. The correct rocker arm torque is 14–20 ft. lbs.

13. Install the intake manifold using a new gasket and following the correct sequence, torque the bolts to the correct specification.

14. The remainder of the installation is the reverse of the removal.

RIGHT SIDE

1. Disconnect the negative battery cable. Drain the cooling system.

2. Raise and safely support the vehicle. Disconnect the exhaust manifold from the exhaust pipe.

3. Lower the vehicle. Disconnect the exhaust manifold from the cylinder head and remove the manifold.

4. Remove the rocker cover. Remove the intake manifold.

5. Loosen the rocker arms enough so the pushrods can be removed. Note the position of the pushrods for assembly.

6. Starting with the outer bolts, remove the cylinder head bolts and remove the cylinder head.

7. Inspect and clean the surfaces of the cylinder head, engine block and intake manifold.

8. Clean the threads in the engine block and the threads on the cylinder head bolts.

To install:

9. Align the new gasket on the dowels on the engine block with the note **THIS SIDE UP** facing the cylinder head.

10. Install the cylinder head on the engine. Coat the head bolts with a proper sealer. Install and tighten the bolts hand tight.

11. Torque the bolts, in sequence, to 33 ft. lbs., then rotate an additional 90° (1/4 turn).

12. Install the pushrods in the same order as they were removed.

➡ **Intake pushrods are marked orange and are 6 in. (152.4mm) long. Exhaust pushrods are marked blue and are 6³/₈ in. (161.9mm) long.**

13. Install the rocker arms. The correct rocker arm torque is 14–20 ft. lbs. (1987–88), 18 ft. lbs. (1989–92).

14. Install the intake manifold using a new gasket. Following the correct sequence, torque the bolts to the proper specification.

15. The remainder of the installation is the reverse of the removal.

RESURFACING

Cylinder Head Flatness

When the cylinder head is removed, check the flatness of the cylinder head gasket surfaces.

1. Place a straightedge across the gasket surface of the cylinder head. Using feeler gauges, determine the clearance at the center of the straightedge.

2. If warpage exceeds 0.003 in. (0.076mm) in a 6 in. (152mm) span, or 0.006 in. (0.152mm) over the total length, the cylinder head must be resurfaced.

3. If necessary to refinish the cylinder head gasket surface, do not plane or grind off more than 0.254mm (0.010 in.) from the original gasket surface.

➡ **When milling the cylinder heads of V6 engines, the intake manifold mounting position is altered, and must be corrected by milling the manifold flange a proportionate amount. Consult an experienced machinist about this service.**

CLEANING AND INSPECTION

1. Clean all carbon from the combustion chambers and valve ports.

2. Thoroughly clean the valve guides.

3. Clean all carbon and sludge from the pushrods, rocker arms and pushrod guides.

4. Clean the valve stems and heads on a buffing wheel.

5. Clean the carbon deposits from the head gasket mating surface.

6. Inspect the cylinder head for cracks in the exhaust ports, combustion chambers or external cracks to the water jacket.

7. Inspect the valves for burned heads, cracked faces or damaged stems.

8. Measure the valve stem clearance as follows:

a. Clamp a dial indicator on ones side of the cylinder head. Locate the indicator so that movement of the valve stem from side to side (crosswise to the head) will cause direct movement of the indicator stem. The indicator stem must contact the side of the valve stem just above the guide.

b. Drop the valve head 1.5mm off the valve seat.

c. Move the stem of the valve from side to side, using light pressure to obtain a clearance reading. If the clearance exceeds specifications, it will be necessary to ream the valve guides for oversize valves. Service valves are available as follows:

• 1.8L and 2.0L (OHV), 2.8L and 3.1L engines — standard, 0.089mm, 0.394mm and 0.775mm O.S. sizes.

• 2.2L (OHV) engine — standard, 0.075mm, 0.150mm and 0.300mm O.S. sizes.

• 1.8L and 2.0L (OHC) engine — standard, 0.075mm, 0.150mm and 0.250mm O.S. sizes.

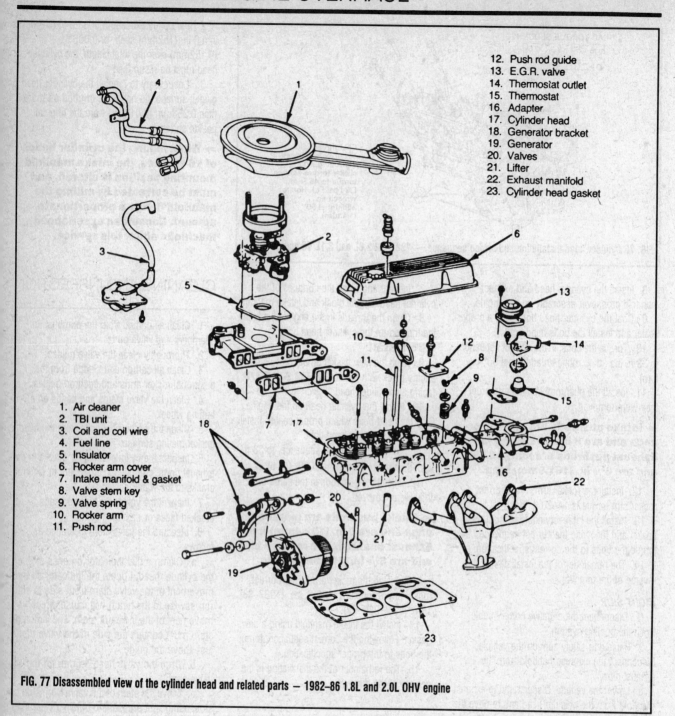

12. Push rod guide
13. E.G.R. valve
14. Thermostat outlet
15. Thermostat
16. Adapter
17. Cylinder head
18. Generator bracket
19. Generator
20. Valves
21. Lifter
22. Exhaust manifold
23. Cylinder head gasket

1. Air cleaner
2. TBI unit
3. Coil and coil wire
4. Fuel line
5. Insulator
6. Rocker arm cover
7. Intake manifold & gasket
8. Valve stem key
9. Valve spring
10. Rocker arm
11. Push rod

FIG. 77 Disassembled view of the cylinder head and related parts — 1982–86 1.8L and 2.0L OHV engine

➡ **If valve guides must be reamed this service is available at most machine shops.**

9. Check the valve spring tension with tool J-8056, spring tester. Springs should be compressed to the specified height and checked against the specifications chart. Springs should be replaced if not within (10 lbs. of the specified load (without dampers).

10. Inspect the rocker arms studs for wear or damage.

➡ **If a dial indicator is not available to you, take your cylinder head to a qualified machine shop for inspection**

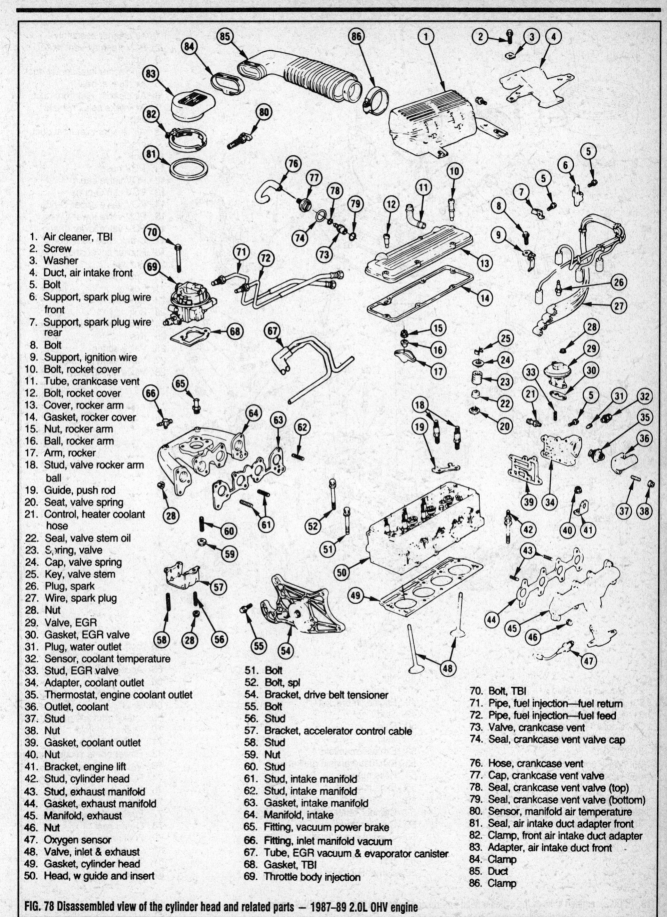

1. Air cleaner, TBI
2. Screw
3. Washer
4. Duct, air intake front
5. Bolt
6. Support, spark plug wire front
7. Support, spark plug wire rear
8. Bolt
9. Support, ignition wire
10. Bolt, rocket cover
11. Tube, crankcase vent
12. Bolt, rocket cover
13. Cover, rocker arm
14. Gasket, rocker cover
15. Nut, rocker arm
16. Ball, rocker arm
17. Arm, rocker
18. Stud, valve rocker arm ball
19. Guide, push rod
20. Seat, valve spring
21. Control, heater coolant hose
22. Seal, valve stem oil
23. Spring, valve
24. Cap, valve spring
25. Key, valve stem
26. Plug, spark
27. Wire, spark plug
28. Nut
29. Valve, EGR
30. Gasket, EGR valve
31. Plug, water outlet
32. Sensor, coolant temperature
33. Stud, EGR valve
34. Adapter, coolant outlet
35. Thermostat, engine coolant outlet
36. Outlet, coolant
37. Stud
38. Nut
39. Gasket, coolant outlet
40. Nut
41. Bracket, engine lift
42. Stud, cylinder head
43. Stud, exhaust manifold
44. Gasket, exhaust manifold
45. Manifold, exhaust
46. Nut
47. Oxygen sensor
48. Valve, inlet & exhaust
49. Gasket, cylinder head
50. Head, w guide and insert

51. Bolt
52. Bolt, spl
54. Bracket, drive belt tensioner
55. Bolt
56. Stud
57. Bracket, accelerator control cable
58. Stud
59. Nut
60. Stud
61. Stud, intake manifold
62. Stud, intake manifold
63. Gasket, intake manifold
64. Manifold, intake
65. Fitting, vacuum power brake
66. Fitting, inlet manifold vacuum
67. Tube, EGR vacuum & evaporator canister
68. Gasket, TBI
69. Throttle body injection

70. Bolt, TBI
71. Pipe, fuel injection—fuel return
72. Pipe, fuel injection—fuel feed
73. Valve, crankcase vent
74. Seal, crankcase vent valve cap
76. Hose, crankcase vent
77. Cap, crankcase vent valve
78. Seal, crankcase vent valve (top)
79. Seal, crankcase vent valve (bottom)
80. Sensor, manifold air temperature
81. Seal, air intake duct adapter front
82. Clamp, front air intake duct adapter
83. Adapter, air intake duct front
84. Clamp
85. Duct
86. Clamp

FIG. 78 Disassembled view of the cylinder head and related parts – 1987–89 2.0L OHV engine

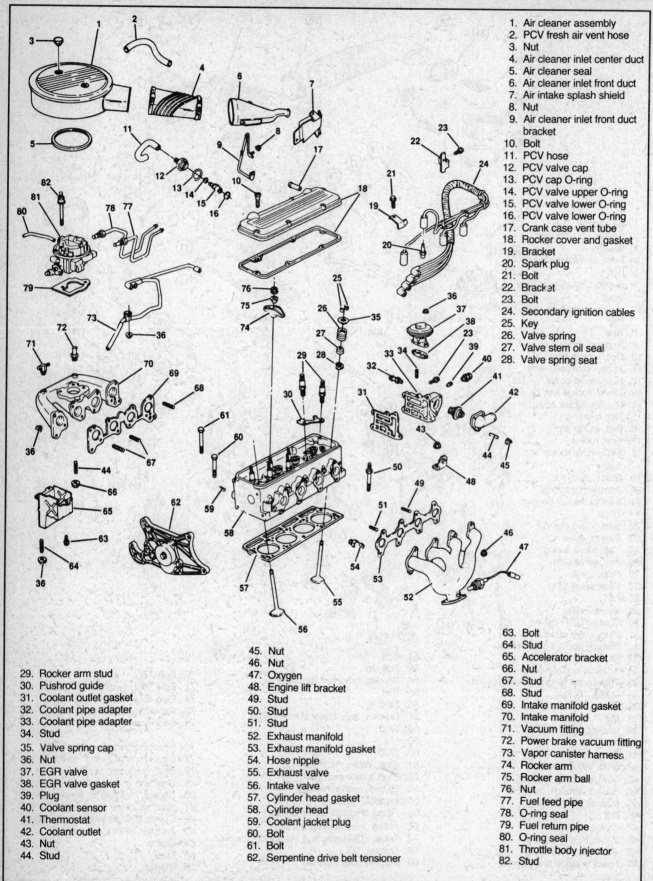

1. Air cleaner assembly
2. PCV fresh air vent hose
3. Nut
4. Air cleaner inlet center duct
5. Air cleaner seal
6. Air cleaner inlet front duct
7. Air intake splash shield
8. Nut
9. Air cleaner inlet front duct bracket
10. Bolt
11. PCV hose
12. PCV valve cap
13. PCV cap O-ring
14. PCV valve upper O-ring
15. PCV valve lower O-ring
16. PCV valve lower O-ring
17. Crank case vent tube
18. Rocker cover and gasket
19. Bracket
20. Spark plug
21. Bolt
22. Bracket
23. Bolt
24. Secondary ignition cables
25. Key
26. Valve spring
27. Valve stem oil seal
28. Valve spring seat

29. Rocker arm stud
30. Pushrod guide
31. Coolant outlet gasket
32. Coolant pipe adapter
33. Coolant pipe adapter
34. Stud
35. Valve spring cap
36. Nut
37. EGR valve
38. EGR valve gasket
39. Plug
40. Coolant sensor
41. Thermostat
42. Coolant outlet
43. Nut
44. Stud

45. Nut
46. Nut
47. Oxygen
48. Engine lift bracket
49. Stud
50. Stud
51. Stud
52. Exhaust manifold
53. Exhaust manifold gasket
54. Hose nipple
55. Exhaust valve
56. Intake valve
57. Cylinder head gasket
58. Cylinder head
59. Coolant jacket plug
60. Bolt
61. Bolt
62. Serpentine drive belt tensioner

63. Bolt
64. Stud
65. Accelerator bracket
66. Nut
67. Stud
68. Stud
69. Intake manifold gasket
70. Intake manifold
71. Vacuum fitting
72. Power brake vacuum fitting
73. Vapor canister harness
74. Rocker arm
75. Rocker arm ball
76. Nut
77. Fuel feed pipe
78. O-ring seal
79. Fuel return pipe
80. O-ring seal
81. Throttle body injector
82. Stud

FIG. 79 Disassembled view of the cylinder head and related parts — 1990–92 2.2L OHV engine

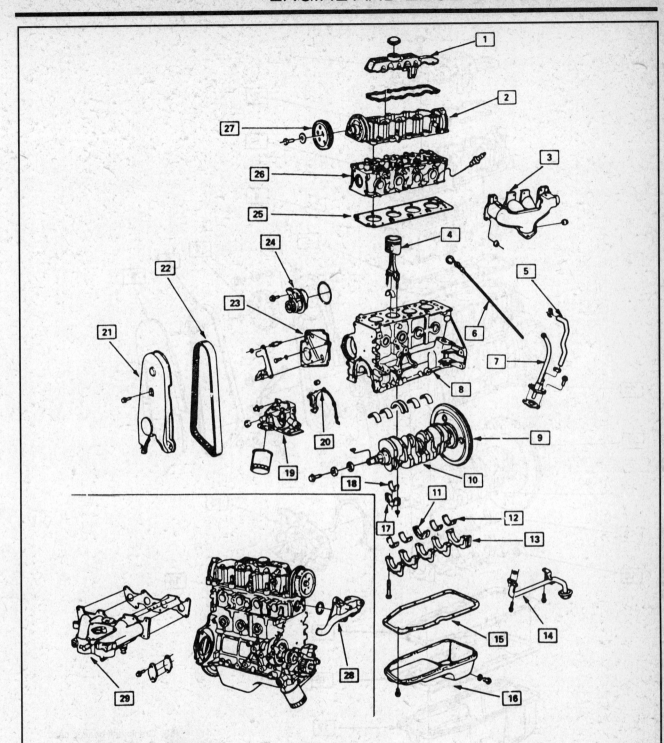

1. Camshaft cover
2. Camshaft carrier
3. Exhaust manifold (VIN code O)
4. Piston
5. Vent tube (VIN code O)
6. Oil dipstick
7. Tube
8. Cylinder block
9. Flywheel
10. Crankshaft

11. Main thrust bearing
12. Main bearings
13. Main bearing caps
14. Oil pump pickup tube
15. Gasket
16. Oil pan
17. Connecting rod cap
18. Connecting rod bearing
19. Oil pump
20. Gasket

21. Front cover
22. Timing belt
23. Rear cover
24. Water pump
25. Head gasket
26. Cylinder head
27. Camshaft sprocket
28. Water crossover
29. Intake manifold (VIN code O)

FIG. 80 Disassembled view of the engine assembly — 1.8L OHC engine

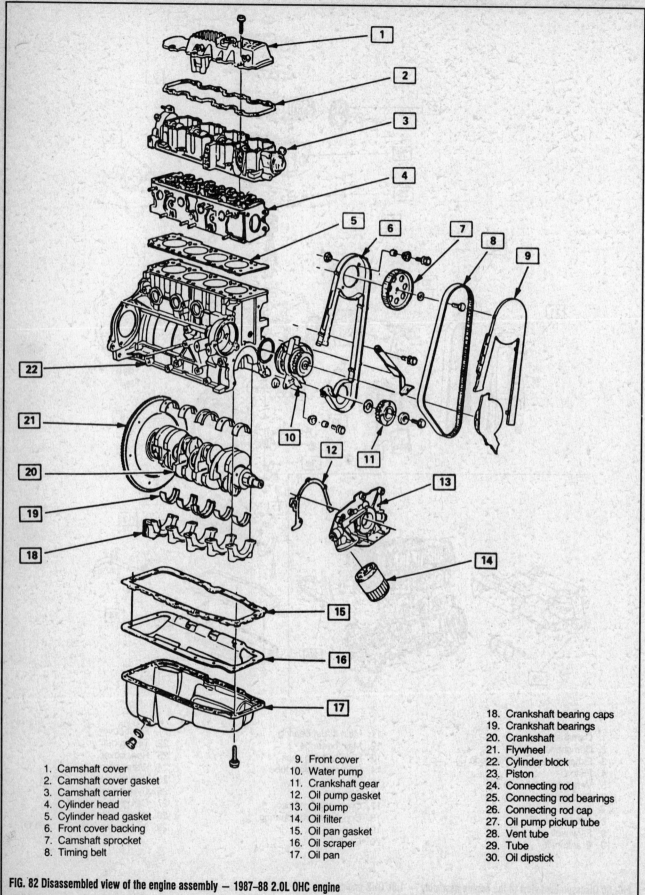

1. Camshaft cover
2. Camshaft cover gasket
3. Camshaft carrier
4. Cylinder head
5. Cylinder head gasket
6. Front cover backing
7. Camshaft sprocket
8. Timing belt
9. Front cover
10. Water pump
11. Crankshaft gear
12. Oil pump gasket
13. Oil pump
14. Oil filter
15. Oil pan gasket
16. Oil scraper
17. Oil pan
18. Crankshaft bearing caps
19. Crankshaft bearings
20. Crankshaft
21. Flywheel
22. Cylinder block
23. Piston
24. Connecting rod
25. Connecting rod bearings
26. Connecting rod cap
27. Oil pump pickup tube
28. Vent tube
29. Tube
30. Oil dipstick

FIG. 82 Disassembled view of the engine assembly — 1987–88 2.0L OHC engine

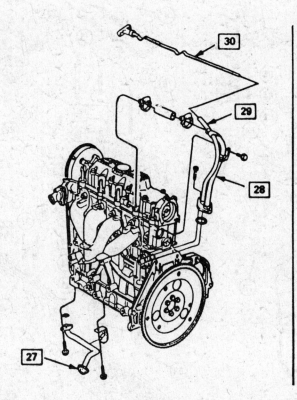

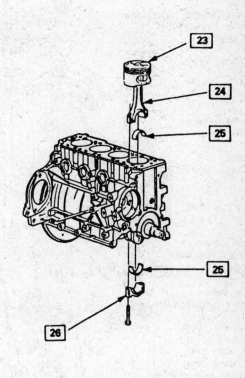

FIG. 83 Disassembled view of the engine assembly — 1987–88 2.0L OHC engine (cont.)

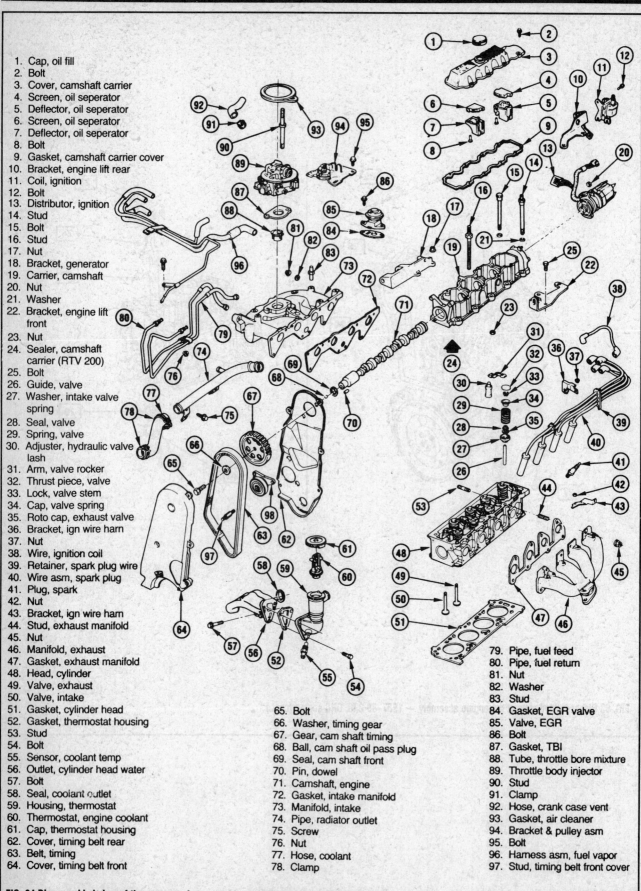

1. Cap, oil fill
2. Bolt
3. Cover, camshaft carrier
4. Screen, oil seperator
5. Deflector, oil seperator
6. Screen, oil seperator
7. Deflector, oil seperator
8. Bolt
9. Gasket, camshaft carrier cover
10. Bracket, engine lift rear
11. Coil, ignition
12. Bolt
13. Distributor, ignition
14. Stud
15. Bolt
16. Stud
17. Nut
18. Bracket, generator
19. Carrier, camshaft
20. Nut
21. Washer
22. Bracket, engine lift front
23. Nut
24. Sealer, camshaft carrier (RTV 200)
25. Bolt
26. Guide, valve
27. Washer, intake valve spring
28. Seal, valve
29. Spring, valve
30. Adjuster, hydraulic valve lash
31. Arm, valve rocker
32. Thrust piece, valve
33. Lock, valve stem
34. Cap, valve spring
35. Roto cap, exhaust valve
36. Bracket, ign wire harn
37. Nut
38. Wire, ignition coil
39. Retainer, spark plug wire
40. Wire asm, spark plug
41. Plug, spark
42. Nut
43. Bracket, ign wire harn
44. Stud, exhaust manifold
45. Nut
46. Manifold, exhaust
47. Gasket, exhaust manifold
48. Head, cylinder
49. Valve, exhaust
50. Valve, intake
51. Gasket, cylinder head
52. Gasket, thermostat housing
53. Stud
54. Bolt
55. Sensor, coolant temp
56. Outlet, cylinder head water
57. Bolt
58. Seal, coolant outlet
59. Housing, thermostat
60. Thermostat, engine coolant
61. Cap, thermostat housing
62. Cover, timing belt rear
63. Belt, timing
64. Cover, timing belt front

65. Bolt
66. Washer, timing gear
67. Gear, cam shaft timing
68. Ball, cam shaft oil pass plug
69. Seal, cam shaft front
70. Pin, dowel
71. Camshaft, engine
72. Gasket, intake manifold
73. Manifold, intake
74. Pipe, radiator outlet
75. Screw
76. Nut
77. Hose, coolant
78. Clamp

79. Pipe, fuel feed
80. Pipe, fuel return
81. Nut
82. Washer
83. Stud
84. Gasket, EGR valve
85. Valve, EGR
86. Bolt
87. Gasket, TBI
88. Tube, throttle bore mixture
89. Throttle body injector
90. Stud
91. Clamp
92. Hose, crank case vent
93. Gasket, air cleaner
94. Bracket & pulley asm
95. Bolt
96. Harness asm, fuel vapor
97. Stud, timing belt front cover

FIG. 84 Disassembled view of the upper engine assembly – 1989–91 2.0L OHC (VIN Code K) engine

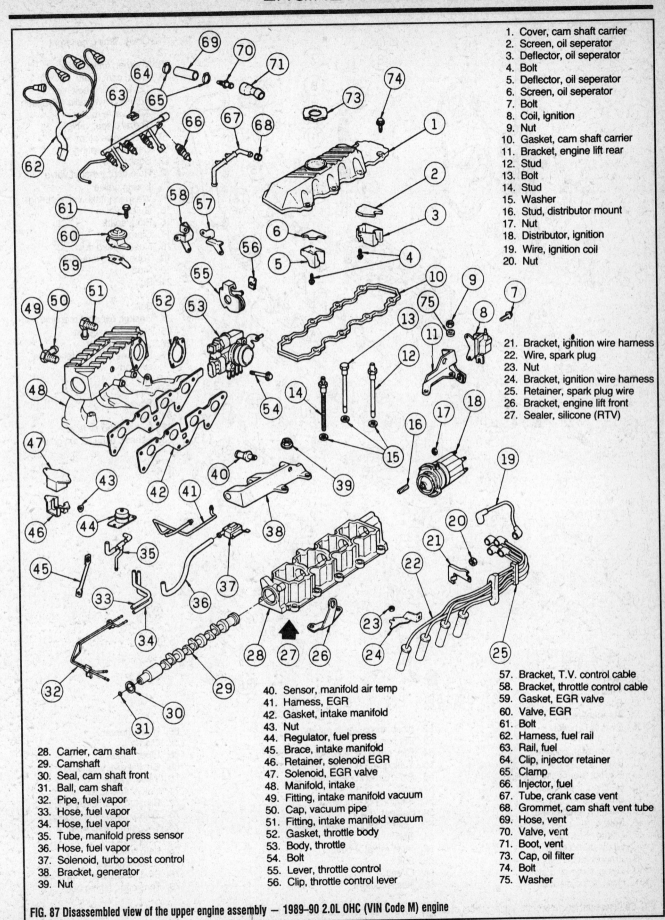

1. Cover, cam shaft carrier
2. Screen, oil seperator
3. Deflector, oil seperator
4. Bolt
5. Deflector, oil seperator
6. Screen, oil seperator
7. Bolt
8. Coil, ignition
9. Nut
10. Gasket, cam shaft carrier
11. Bracket, engine lift rear
12. Stud
13. Bolt
14. Stud
15. Washer
16. Stud, distributor mount
17. Nut
18. Distributor, ignition
19. Wire, ignition coil
20. Nut
21. Bracket, ignition wire harness
22. Wire, spark plug
23. Nut
24. Bracket, ignition wire harness
25. Retainer, spark plug wire
26. Bracket, engine lift front
27. Sealer, silicone (RTV)

28. Carrier, cam shaft
29. Camshaft
30. Seal, cam shaft front
31. Ball, cam shaft
32. Pipe, fuel vapor
33. Hose, fuel vapor
34. Hose, fuel vapor
35. Tube, manifold press sensor
36. Hose, fuel vapor
37. Solenoid, turbo boost control
38. Bracket, generator
39. Nut
40. Sensor, manifold air temp
41. Harness, EGR
42. Gasket, intake manifold
43. Nut
44. Regulator, fuel press
45. Brace, intake manifold
46. Retainer, solenoid EGR
47. Solenoid, EGR valve
48. Manifold, intake
49. Fitting, intake manifold vacuum
50. Cap, vacuum pipe
51. Fitting, intake manifold vacuum
52. Gasket, throttle body
53. Body, throttle
54. Bolt
55. Lever, throttle control
56. Clip, throttle control lever

57. Bracket, T.V. control cable
58. Bracket, throttle control cable
59. Gasket, EGR valve
60. Valve, EGR
61. Bolt
62. Harness, fuel rail
63. Rail, fuel
64. Clip, injector retainer
65. Clamp
66. Injector, fuel
67. Tube, crank case vent
68. Grommet, cam shaft vent tube
69. Hose, vent
70. Valve, vent
71. Boot, vent
73. Cap, oil filter
74. Bolt
75. Washer

FIG. 87 Disassembled view of the upper engine assembly — 1989–90 2.0L OHC (VIN Code M) engine

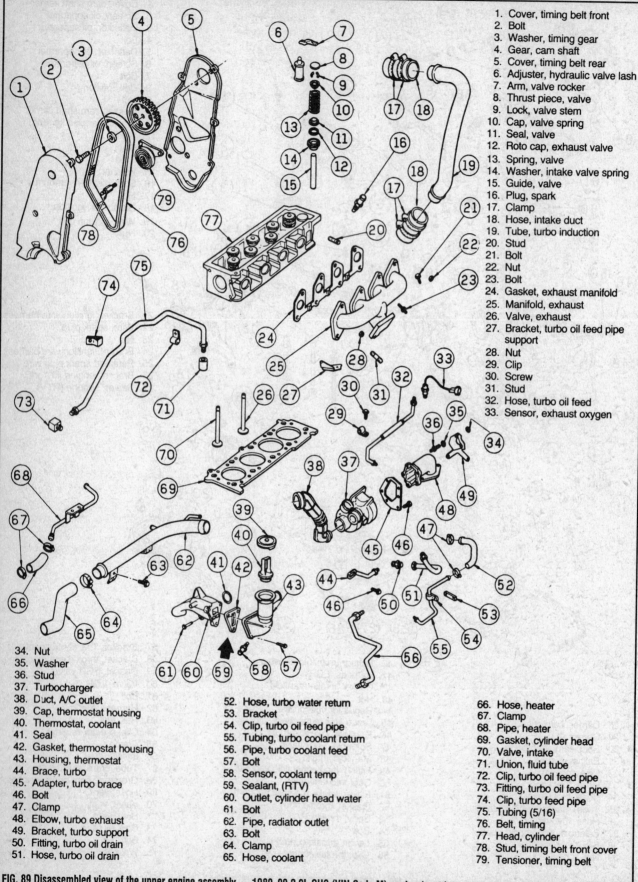

1. Cover, timing belt front
2. Bolt
3. Washer, timing gear
4. Gear, cam shaft
5. Cover, timing belt rear
6. Adjuster, hydraulic valve lash
7. Arm, valve rocker
8. Thrust piece, valve
9. Lock, valve stem
10. Cap, valve spring
11. Seal, valve
12. Roto cap, exhaust valve
13. Spring, valve
14. Washer, intake valve spring
15. Guide, valve
16. Plug, spark
17. Clamp
18. Hose, intake duct
19. Tube, turbo induction
20. Stud
21. Bolt
22. Nut
23. Bolt
24. Gasket, exhaust manifold
25. Manifold, exhaust
26. Valve, exhaust
27. Bracket, turbo oil feed pipe support
28. Nut
29. Clip
30. Screw
31. Stud
32. Hose, turbo oil feed
33. Sensor, exhaust oxygen

34. Nut
35. Washer
36. Stud
37. Turbocharger
38. Duct, A/C outlet
39. Cap, thermostat housing
40. Thermostat, coolant
41. Seal
42. Gasket, thermostat housing
43. Housing, thermostat
44. Brace, turbo
45. Adapter, turbo brace
46. Bolt
47. Clamp
48. Elbow, turbo exhaust
49. Bracket, turbo support
50. Fitting, turbo oil drain
51. Hose, turbo oil drain

52. Hose, turbo water return
53. Bracket
54. Clip, turbo oil feed pipe
55. Tubing, turbo coolant return
56. Pipe, turbo coolant feed
57. Bolt
58. Sensor, coolant temp
59. Sealant, (RTV)
60. Outlet, cylinder head water
61. Bolt
62. Pipe, radiator outlet
63. Bolt
64. Clamp
65. Hose, coolant

66. Hose, heater
67. Clamp
68. Pipe, heater
69. Gasket, cylinder head
70. Valve, intake
71. Union, fluid tube
72. Clip, turbo oil feed pipe
73. Fitting, turbo oil feed pipe
74. Clip, turbo feed pipe
75. Tubing (5/16)
76. Belt, timing
77. Head, cylinder
78. Stud, timing belt front cover
79. Tensioner, timing belt

FIG. 89 Disassembled view of the upper engine assembly – 1989–90 2.0L OHC (VIN Code M) engine (cont.)

J-5892

ENGAGE AT LEAST 3 THREADS

FIG. 81 Valve spring compressing tool

Valves and Springs

REMOVAL & INSTALLATION

♦ SEE FIG. 81

1. Block the head on its side, or install a pair of head-holding brackets made especially for valve removal.

2. Use a socket slightly larger than the valve stem and keepers, place the socket over the valve stem and gently hit the socket with a plastic hammer to break loose any varnish buildup.

3. Remove the valve keepers, retainer, spring shield and valve spring using a valve spring compressor (the locking C-clamp type is the easiest kind to use).

4. Put the parts in a separate container numbered for the cylinder being worked on; do not mix them with other parts removed.

5. Remove and discard the valve stem oil seals. A new seal will be used at assembly time.

6. Remove the valves from the cylinder head and place them, in order, through numbered holes punched in a stiff piece of cardboard or wood valve holding stick.

➡ **The exhaust valve stems, on some engines, are equipped with small metal caps. Take care not to lose the caps. Make sure to reinstall them at assembly time. Replace any caps that are worn.**

7. Use an electric drill and rotary wire brush to clean the intake and exhaust valve ports, combustion chamber and valve seats. In some cases, the carbon will need to be chipped away. Use a blunt pointed drift for carbon chipping. Be careful around the valve seat areas.

8. Use a wire valve guide cleaning brush and safe solvent to clean the valve guides.

9. Clean the valves with a revolving wires brush. Heavy carbon deposits may be removed with the blunt drift.

➡ **When using a wire brush to clean carbon on the valve ports, valves etc., be sure that the deposits are actually removed, rather than burnished.**

10. Wash and clean all valve springs, keepers, retaining caps etc., in safe solvent.

11. Clean the head with a brush and some safe solvent and wipe dry.

12. Check the head for cracks. Cracks in the cylinder head usually start around an exhaust valve seat because it is the hottest part of the combustion chamber. If a crack is suspected but cannot be detected visually have the area checked with dye penetrant or other method by the machine shop.

13. After all cylinder head parts are reasonably clean, check the valve stem-to-guide clearance. If a dial indicator is not on hand, a visual inspection can give you a fairly good idea if the guide, valve stem or both are worn.

14. Insert the valve into the guide until slight away from the valve seat. Wiggle the valve sideways. A small amount of wobble is normal, excessive wobble means a worn guide or valve stem. If a dial indicator is on hand, mount the indicator so that the stem of the valve is at 90° to the valve stem, as close to the valve guide as possible. Move the valve off the seat, and measure the valve guide-to-stem clearance by rocking the stem back and forth to actuate the dial indicator. Measure the valve stem using a micrometer and compare to specifications to determine whether stem or guide wear is causing excessive clearance.

15. The valve guide, if worn, must be repaired before the valve seats can be resurfaced. The machine shop will be able to handle the guide reaming for you. In some cases, if the guide is not too badly worn, knurling may be all that is required.

16. Reface, or have the valves and valve seats refaced. The valve seats should be a true 46° angle (OHV) engines and 46° angle (OHC) engines. Remove only enough material to clean up any pits or grooves. Be sure the valve seat is not too wide or narrow. Use a 60° grinding wheel to remove material from the bottom of the seat for raising and a 30° grinding wheel to remove material from the top of the seat to narrow.

17. After the valves are refaced by machine, hand lap them to the valve seat. Clean the grinding compound off and check the position of face-to-seat contact. Contact should be close to the center of the valve face. If contact is close to the top edge of the valve, narrow the seat; if too close to the bottom edge, raise the seat.

18. Valves should be refaced to a true angle of 45° (OHV) engines and 46° (OHC) engines. Remove only enough metal to clean up the valve face or to correct runout. If the edge of a valve head, after machining, is $\frac{1}{32}$ in. (0.8mm) or less replace the valve. The tip of the valve stem should also be dressed on the valve grinding machine, however, do not remove more than 0.010 in. (0.254mm).

19. After all valve and valve seats have been machined, check the remaining valve train parts (springs, retainers, keepers, etc.) for wear. Check the valve springs for straightness and tension.

20. Install the valves in the cylinder head and metal caps.

21. Install new valve stem oil seals.

22. Install the valve keepers, retainer, spring shield and valve spring using a valve spring compressor (the locking C-clamp type is the easiest kind to use).

23. Check the valve spring installed height, shim or replace as necessary.

CHECKING VALVE SPRINGS

Place the valve spring on a flat surface next to a carpenter's square. Measure the height of the spring, and rotate the spring against the edge of the square to measure distortion. If the spring height varies (by comparison) by more than $\frac{1}{16}$ in. (1.6mm) or if the distortion exceeds $\frac{1}{16}$ in. (1.6mm), replace the spring.

Have the valve springs tested for spring pressure at the installed and compressed (installed height minus valve lift) height using a valve spring tester. Springs should be within one pound, plus or minus each other. Replace springs as necessary.

VALVE SPRING INSTALLED HEIGHT

After installing the valve spring, measure the distance between the spring mounting pad and the lower edge of the spring retainer. Compare the measurement to specifications. If the installed height is incorrect, add shim washers between the spring mounting pad and the spring. Use only washers designed for valve springs, available at most parts houses.

Check the installed height of the valve springs, using a narrow thin scale. On the OHV 4-cylinder engine, measure from the top of the spring seat to the bottom of the cap.

On the V6 engine measure from the top of the spring damper "feet" to the bottom inside of the oil shedder for exhaust and from the top of the spring shim to the bottom of the valve cap for the intake. If this is found to exceed the specified height, install an additional valve spring seat shim approximately 0.7mm thick.

➡ **At no time should the valve spring be shimmed to give an installed height under the minimum specified.**

VALVE STEM OIL SEALS

When installing valve stem oil seals, ensure that a small amount of oil is able to pass the seal to lubricate the valve stems and guide walls, otherwise, excessive wear will occur.

On the V6 engine, check each valve stem oil seal by placing the valve stem leak detector tool J-23994, over the end of the valve stem and against the cap. Operate the vacuum pump and make sure no air leaks past the seal.

VALVE SEATS

If the valve seat is damaged or burnt and cannot be serviced by refacing, it may be possible to have the seat machined and an insert installed. Consult an automotive machine shop for their advice.

VALVE GUIDES

Worn valve guides can, in most cases, be reamed to accept a valve with an oversized stem. Valve guides that are not excessively worn

or distorted may, in some cases, be knurled rather than reamed. However, if the valve stem is worn reaming for an oversized valve stem is the answer since a new valve would be required.

Knurling is a process in which metal is displaced and raised, thereby reducing clearance. Knurling also produces excellent oil control. The possibility of knurling instead of reaming the valve guides should be discussed with a machinist.

Valve Lifters

REMOVAL & INSTALLATION

4-Cylinder Engines

1. Disconnect the negative battery cable.
2. Remove the rocker cover.
3. Loosen rocker arm nut and position rocker arm aside. Remove the pushrod — keep all parts in order for correct installation.
4. With a suitable tool remove the lifter assembly form the bore.
5. Installation is the reverse of the removal procedure. Soak engine lifters in clean engine oil before installation.

6-Cylinder Engines

1. Disconnect the negative battery cable. Drain the engine coolant.

❄❄ CAUTION

When draining the coolant, keep in mind that cats and dogs are attracted by the ethylene glycol antifreeze, and are quite likely to drink any that is left in an uncovered container or in puddles on the ground. This will prove fatal in sufficient quantity. Always drain the coolant into a sealable container. Coolant should be reused unless it is contaminated or several years old.

2. Remove the intake manifold assembly — refer to the necessary service procedures in this section.
3. Remove the rocker arm nut, rocker arm and pushrod. Keep all parts in order for correct installation.
4. With a suitable tool remove the lifter assembly form the bore.

5. Installation is the reverse of the removal procedure. Soak engine lifters in clean engine oil before installation.

Oil Pan

REMOVAL & INSTALLATION

1.8L, 2.0L and 2.2L OHV Engines

➡ SEE FIGS. 85-86
1. Disconnect the negative battery cable.
2. Drain the crankcase. Raise and support the front of the vehicle.

❄❄ CAUTION

The EPA warns that prolonged contact with used engine oil may cause a number of skin disorders, including cancer! You should make every effort to minimize your exposure to used engine oil. Protective gloves should be worn when changing the oil. Wash your hands and any other exposed skin areas as soon as possible after exposure to used engine oil. Soap and water, or waterless hand cleaner should be used.

3. On 1982–86 models ,remove the air conditioning brace at the starter and air conditioning bracket.
4. Remove the exhaust shield and disconnect the exhaust pipe at the manifold.
5. Remove the starter motor and position it out of the way.
6. Remove the flywheel cover.
7. On 1982–90 models, remove the 4 right support bolts. Lower the support slightly to gain clearance for oil pan removal.
8. On cars equipped with automatic transmission, remove the oil filter and extension.
9. Remove the oil pan bolts and remove the oil pan.
   To Install:
10. Prior to oil pan installation, check that the sealing surfaces on the pan, cylinder block and front cover are clean and free of oil. If installing the old pan, be sure that all old RTV has been removed.
11. Apply a 1/8 in. (3mm) bead of RTV sealant to the oil pan sealing surface. Use a new oil pan rear seal and apply a thin coat of RTV

sealant to the ends of the gasket down to the ears and install the pan in place.

12. On 1982–86 models, tighten the front bolts to 7–13 ft. lbs., the rear bolts to 11–18 ft. lbs., the stud to 5–7 ft. lbs., and all others to 4–9 ft. lbs. On 1987–92 models tighten the bolts to 77 inch lbs.

13. On cars equipped with automatic transmission, replace the oil filter adapter seal and replace the oil filter adapter.

14. Install the remaining components is in the reverse order of removal.

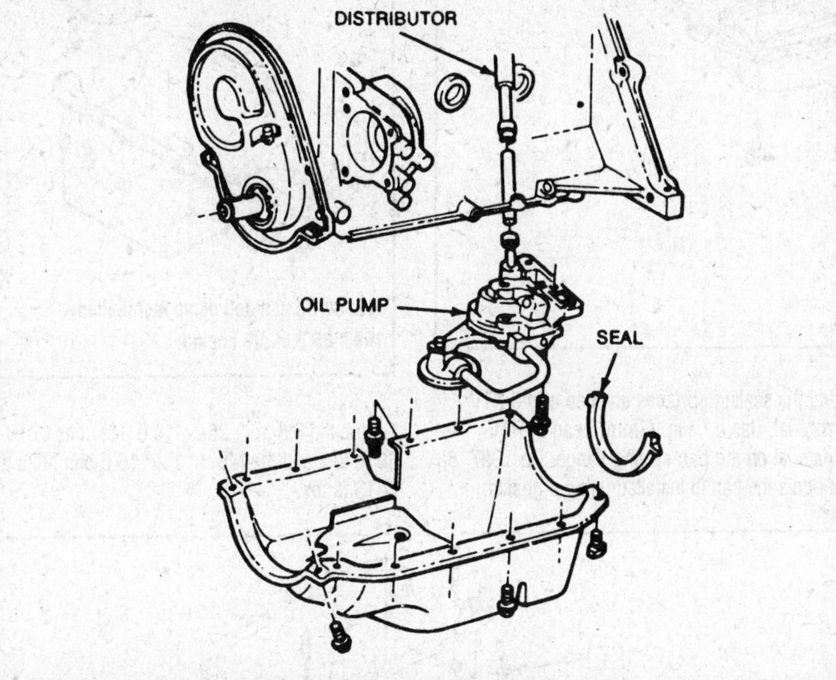

1.8L and 2.0L OHC Engines

▶ SEE FIGS. 88-88A
1. Raise and support the car safely.
2. Remove right front wheel.
3. Remove right hand splash shield.
4. Position jackstands at jacking points.
5. Drain engine oil.

⁂ CAUTION

The EPA warns that prolonged contact with used engine oil may cause a number of skin disorders, including cancer! You should make every effort to minimize your exposure to used engine oil. Protective gloves should be worn when changing the oil. Wash your hands and any other exposed skin areas as soon as possible after exposure to used engine oil. Soap and water, or waterless hand cleaner should be used.

6. If necessary on some models, remove lower air conditioning bracket strut rod attachment bolt and swing aside.

7. Remove exhaust pipe to manifold attachment bolts. On turbo models, disconnect the exhaust pipe at the wastegate.

8. Remove flywheel dust cover.

9. Remove oil pan bolts and remove the oil pan.

10. Clean the sealing surfaces, install the oil pan with a new gasket and apply RTV as shown in the illustration. Install the bolts to the oil pan with Loctite® on the threads. Torque the pan bolts to 48 inch lbs.

FIG. 85 Oil pan installation — 1982–86 1.8L and 2.0L OHV engine

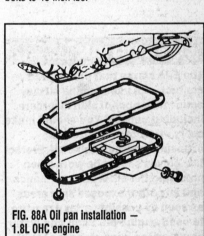

FIG. 88A Oil pan installation — 1.8L OHC engine

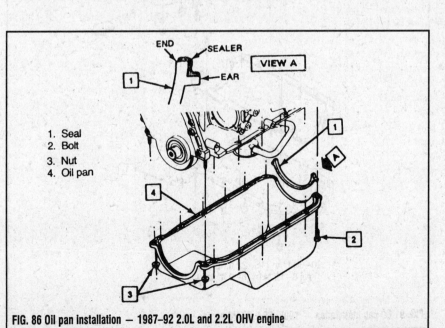

1. Seal
2. Bolt
3. Nut
4. Oil pan

FIG. 86 Oil pan installation — 1987–92 2.0L and 2.2L OHV engine

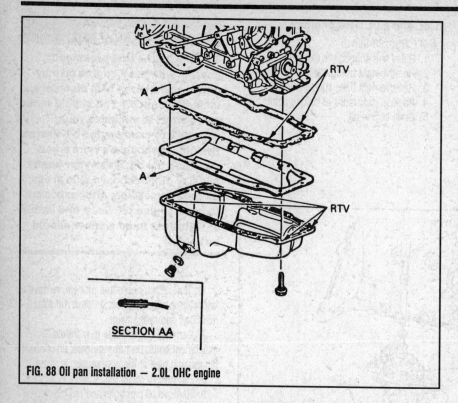

SECTION AA

FIG. 88 Oil pan installation — 2.0L OHC engine

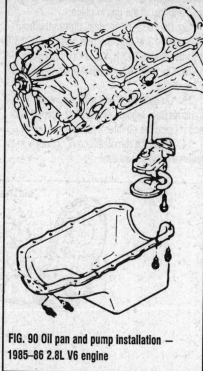

FIG. 90 Oil pan and pump installation —
1985–86 2.8L V6 engine

2.8L and 3.1L Engines

1985–88

▶ SEE FIGS. 90-91

1. Disconnect the battery ground.
2. Raise and support the car on jackstands.
3. Drain the oil.

❋❋ CAUTION

The EPA warns that prolonged contact with used engine oil may cause a number of skin disorders, including cancer! You should make every effort to minimize your exposure to used engine oil. Protective gloves should be worn when changing the oil. Wash your hands and any other exposed skin areas as soon as possible after exposure to used engine oil. Soap and water, or waterless hand cleaner should be used.

4. Remove the bellhousing cover.
5. Remove the starter.
6. Remove the oil pan bolts and remove the oil pan.

To install:

7. Installation is the reverse of removal. On 1985–86 models, the pan is installed using RTV gasket material in place of a gasket. Make sure

that the sealing surfaces are free of old RTV material. Use a 1/8 in. (3mm) bead of RTV material on the pan sealing flange. On 1987–88 models the pan is installed using a gasket.

Torque the M8 × 1.25 × 14.0 pan bolts to 15–30 ft. lbs. and the M6 × 1 × 16.0 pan bolts to 6–15 ft. lbs.

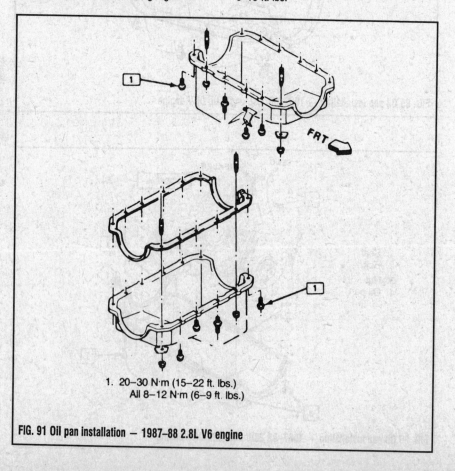

1. 20–30 N·m (15–22 ft. lbs.)
   All 8–12 N·m (6–9 ft. lbs.)

FIG. 91 Oil pan installation — 1987–88 2.8L V6 engine

1989–92

▶ SEE FIGS. 92-93

1. Disconnect the negative battery cable.

2. Remove the serpentine belt and the tensioner.

3. Support the engine with tool J–28467 or equivalent.

4. Raise and safely support the vehicle. Drain the engine oil.

5. Remove the starter shield and the flywheel cover. Remove the starter.

6. Remove the engine to frame mount retaining nuts.

7. Lower the vehicle.

8. Support the engine using tool J–28467–A or equivalent, then raise and support the vehicle safely.

9. Remove the right tire and wheel assembly. Remove the right inner fender splash shield.

10. Remove the oil pan retaining bolts and nuts and remove the oil pan.

To install:

11. Clean the gasket mating surfaces.

12. Install a new gasket on the oil pan. Apply silicon sealer to the portion of the pan that contacts the rear of the block.

13. Install the oil pan retaining nuts. Tighten the nuts to 89 inch lbs.

14. Install the oil pan retaining bolts. Tighten the rear bolts to 18 inch lbs. and the remaining bolts to 89 inch lbs.

15. Install the right inner fender splash shield.

16. Lower the vehicle and remove the engine support tool.

17. Raise and support the vehicle safely.

18. Install the engine to frame mounting nuts.

19. Install the starter and splash shield. Install the flywheel shield.

20. Lower the vehicle and fill the crankcase with oil, install the belt tensioner and belt and connect the negative battery cable. Run the engine to normal operating temperature and check for leaks.

Oil Pump

REMOVAL & INSTALLATION

1.8L, 2.0L and 2.2L OHV Engines

1. Remove the engine oil pan.

2. Remove the pump to rear bearing cap bolt and remove the pump and extension shaft.

3. Remove the extension shaft and retainer.

To install:

4. Heat the retainer in hot water prior to assembling the extension shaft.

5. Install the extension to the oil pump, being careful not to crack the retainer.

6. Install pump to rear bearing cap bolt and torque is 26–38 ft. lbs.

7. Install the oil pan.

1.8L and 2.0L OHC Engines

1. Remove the crankshaft sprocket.

2. Remove the timing belt rear covers.

3. Disconnect the oil pressure switch wires.

4. Remove the oil pan.

5. Remove the oil filter.

6. Unbolt and remove the oil pick-up tube.

7. Unbolt and remove the oil pump.

8. On the 2.0L engine, pry out the front oil seal.

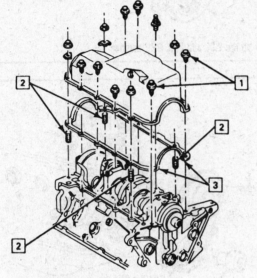

1. 25 N·m (18 lb. ft.)
2. 17 N·m (13 lb. ft.) all others 10 N·m (89 lb. in.)
3. Sealer (1052917)

FIG. 92 Oil pan installation — 1989 2.8L V6 engine

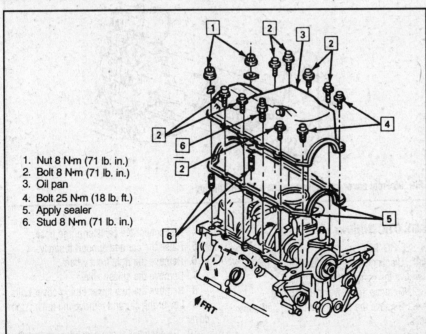

1. Nut 8 N·m (71 lb. in.)
2. Bolt 8 N·m (71 lb. in.)
3. Oil pan
4. Bolt 25 N·m (18 lb. ft.)
5. Apply sealer
6. Stud 8 N·m (71 lb. in.)

FIG. 93 Oil pan installation — 1990–92 3.1L V6 engine

9. Installation is the reverse of removal. Use new gaskets in all instances. On the 2.0L engine, install a new front seal using tool J33083 Seal Installer. Torque the oil pump bolts to 60 inch lbs. Install the bolts to the oil pan with Loctite® on the threads. Torque the pan bolts to 48 inch lbs., and the oil pickup tube bolts to 60 inch lbs.

2.8L and 3.1L OHV V6 Engines

1. Remove the oil pan as described earlier.
2. Unbolt and remove the oil pump and pickup.
3. Installation is the reverse of removal. Torque to 30 ft. lbs.

Timing Belt/Chain Front Cover

REMOVAL & INSTALLATION

1.8L, 2.0L and 2.2L OHV Engines

♦ SEE FIGS. 94–95

➡ **The following procedure requires the use of a special tool.**

1. Remove the engine drive belts (1982–86) or the serpentine belt and tensioner (1987–92).
2. Although not absolutely necessary, removal of the right front inner fender splash shield will facilitate access to the front cover.
3. Unscrew the center bolt from the crankshaft pulley and slide the pulley and hub from the crankshaft.
4. On some models, if necessary, remove the alternator lower bracket.
5. Remove the oil pan-to-front cover bolts.
6. Remove the front cover-to-block bolts and then remove the front cover. If the front cover is difficult to remove, use a plastic mallet.
   To install:
7. The surfaces of the block and front cover must be clean and free of oil. on 1982–86 models, apply a 1/8 in. (3mm) wide bead of RTV sealant to the cover. The sealant must be wet to the touch when the bolts are torqued down. On 1987–92 models a gasket is used. Torque the bolts to 6–9 ft. lbs.

➡ **When applying RTV sealant to the front cover, be sure to keep it out of the bolt holes.**

8. Position the front cover on the block using a centering tool (J-23042) and tighten the screws.
9. Installation of the remaining components is in the reverse order of removal.

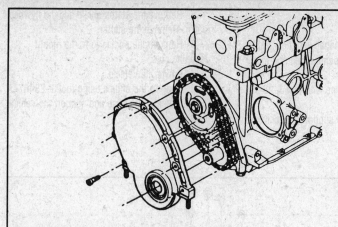
FIG. 94 Front cover on the 2.0L and 2.2L OHV engines

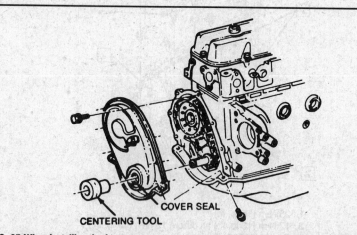
FIG. 95 When installing the front cover a centering tool can aid in positioning on the OHV 4 cylinder engines

CENTERING TOOL
COVER SEAL

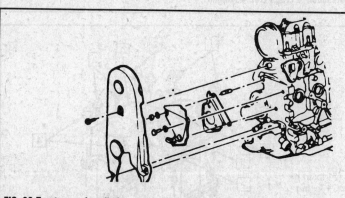
FIG. 96 Front cover installation on the 1.8L OHC engine

1.8L OHC Engine

♦ SEE FIG. 96

1. Disconnect the negative battery cable. Remove the generator pivot bolts.
2. Remove the power steering belt.
3. Remove the two upper timing belt cover bolts.
4. Disconnect the canister purge hose.
5. Raise the car and support it safely.
6. Remove the right front wheel.
7. Remove the splash shield.
8. Remove the two lower timing cover bolts.
9. Lower the car and remove the timing belt cover.
10. Reverse the above procedure to install.

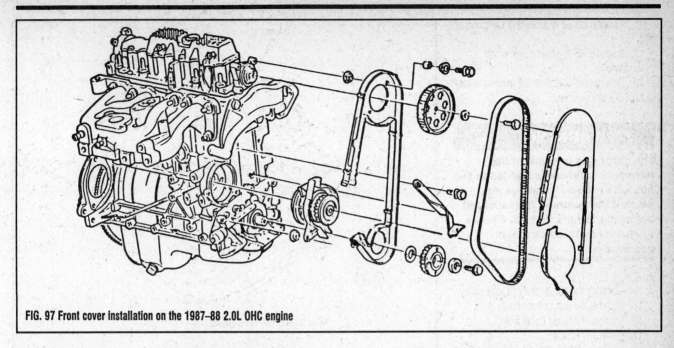

FIG. 97 Front cover installation on the 1987–88 2.0L OHC engine

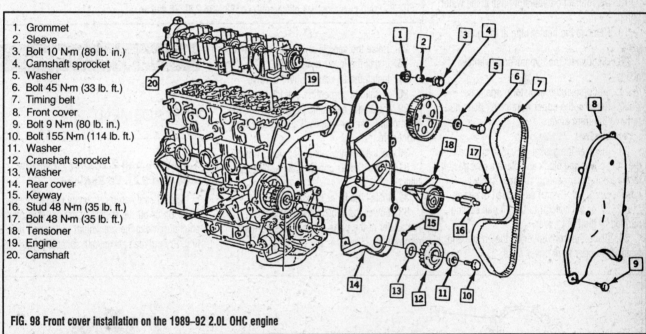

1. Grommet
2. Sleeve
3. Bolt 10 N·m (89 lb. in.)
4. Camshaft sprocket
5. Washer
6. Bolt 45 N·m (33 lb. ft.)
7. Timing belt
8. Front cover
9. Bolt 9 N·m (80 lb. in.)
10. Bolt 155 N·m (114 lb. ft.)
11. Washer
12. Cranshaft sprocket
13. Washer
14. Rear cover
15. Keyway
16. Stud 48 N·m (35 lb. ft.)
17. Bolt 48 N·m (35 lb. ft.)
18. Tensioner
19. Engine
20. Camshaft

FIG. 98 Front cover installation on the 1989–92 2.0L OHC engine

2.0L OHC Engine

♦ SEE FIGS. 97-98

1. Disconnect the negative battery cable. Remove the belt, tensioner bolt and tensioner.
2. Unsnap the cover (upper first).
3. To install, snap the cover (lower first).
4. Install the tensioner and bolt then the serpentine belt. Torque the timing belt cover bolts and nuts to 89 inch lbs. (54 Nm).

2.8L and 3.1L V6 Engines

♦ SEE FIGS. 99-100

1. Disconnect the battery ground cable.
2. Drain the cooling system.

✷✷ CAUTION

When draining the coolant, keep in mind that cats and dogs are attracted by the ethylene glycol antifreeze, and are quite likely to drink any that is left in an uncovered container or in puddles on the ground. This will prove fatal in sufficient quantity. Always drain the coolant into a sealable container. Coolant should be reused unless it is contaminated or several years old.

3. On 1985–86 models, disconnect the MAP sensor and the EGR solenoid.
4. On 1985–86 models, remove the coolant recovery tank.
5. Remove the serpentine belt adjustment pulley.
6. Remove the alternator and disconnect the electrical wires.
7. Remove the power steering pump bracket.
8. Disconnect the heater pipe at the P/S bracket.
9. Jack up the car and support it safely.
10. Remove the inner splash shield.

11. Remove the air conditioning compressor belt.

12. Remove the flywheel cover at the transaxle.

13. Remove the harmonic balancer with tool J-23523-1 or equivalent.

❊❊ WARNING

The outer ring (weight) of the harmonic balancer is bonded to the hub with rubber. Breakage may occur if the balancer is hammered back onto the crankshaft. A press or special installation tool is necessary.

14. Remove the serpentine belt idler pulley.

15. Remove the pan to front cover bolts.

16. Remove the lower cover bolts.

17. Lower the vehicle.

18. Disconnect the radiator hose at the water pump.

19. Remove the heater pipe at the goose neck.

20. Disconnect the bypass and overflow hoses.

21. Disconnect the canister purge hose.

22. Remove the upper front cover bolts and remove the front cover.

To Install

23. Clean all the gasket mounting surfaces on the front cover and block and place a new gasket to the front cover sealing surface. Apply a continuous 1/8 in. (3mm) wide bead of sealer (1052357 or equivalent) to the oil pan sealing surface of the front cover.

24. Place the front cover on the engine and install the upper front cover bolts.

25. Raise the vehicle and support it safely.

26. Install the lower cover bolts.

27. Install the oil pan to cover screws.

28. Install the serpentine belt idler pulley.

29. Install the harmonic balancer. (See the Harmonic Balancer Removal and Installation procedure.)

30. Install the flywheel cover on the transaxle.

31. Install the air conditioning compressor belt.

32. Install the inner splash shield.

33. Lower the vehicle and install the remainder of the parts in the reverse order of removal.

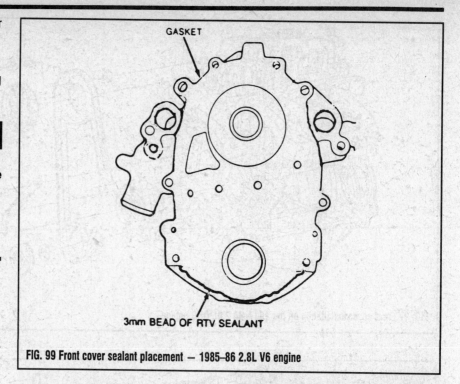

FIG. 99 Front cover sealant placement — 1985–86 2.8L V6 engine

Timing Cover Oil Seal

REPLACEMENT

1.8L, 2.0L and 2.2L OHV Engines 2.8L and 3.1L V6 Engines

The oil seal can be replaced with the cover either on or off the engine. If the cover is on the engine, remove the crankshaft pulley and hub first. Pry out the seal using a suitable prying tool,

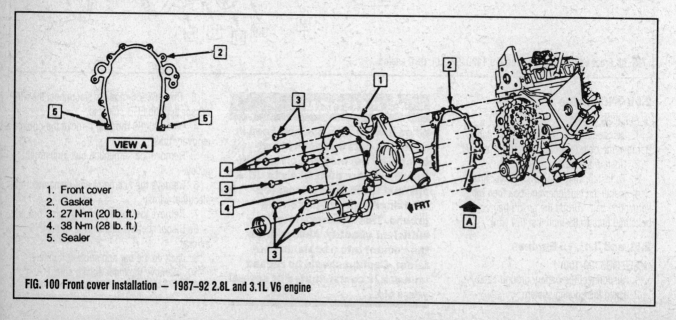

1. Front cover
2. Gasket
3. 27 N·m (20 lb. ft.)
4. 38 N·m (28 lb. ft.)
5. Sealer

FIG. 100 Front cover installation — 1987–92 2.8L and 3.1L V6 engine

being careful not to distort the seal mating surface. Install the new seal so that the open side or lip side is towards the engine. Press it into place with a seal driver made for the purpose. Chevrolet recommends a tool, J-35468 Seal Centering Tool. Install the hub if removed.

Timing Chain and Sprockets

REMOVAL & INSTALLATION

1.8L and 2.0L and 2.2L OHV Engines

◆ SEE FIGS. 101-103

1. Remove the front cover as previously detailed.

2. Place the No. 1 piston at TDC of the compression stroke so that the marks on the camshaft and crankshaft sprockets are in alignment (see illustration).

3. Loosen the timing chain tensioner nut as far as possible without actually removing it.

4. Remove the camshaft sprocket bolts and remove the sprocket and chain together. If the sprocket does not slide from the camshaft easily, a light blow with a soft mallet at the lower edge of the sprocket will dislodge it.

5. Use a gear puller (J-2288-8-20) and remove the crankshaft sprocket.

To Install:

6. Press the crankshaft sprocket back onto the crankshaft.

7. Install the timing chain over the camshaft sprocket and then around the crankshaft sprocket. Make sure that the marks on the two sprockets are in alignment (see illustration). Lubricate the thrust surface with Molykote® or its equivalent.

8. Align the dowel in the camshaft with the dowel hole in the sprocket and then install the sprocket onto the camshaft. Use the mounting bolts to draw the sprocket onto the camshaft and then tighten to 66–68 ft. lbs.

9. Lubricate the timing chain with clean engine oil. Tighten the chain tensioner.

10. Installation of the remaining components is in the reverse order of removal.

2.8L and 3.1L Engines

◆ SEE FIGS. 104-106

1. Remove the front cover.

2. Place the No. 1 piston at TDC and the

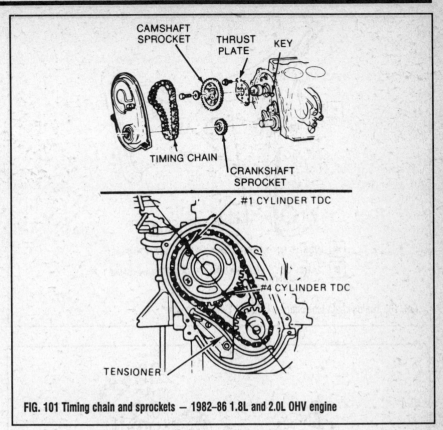

FIG. 101 Timing chain and sprockets — 1982–86 1.8L and 2.0L OHV engine

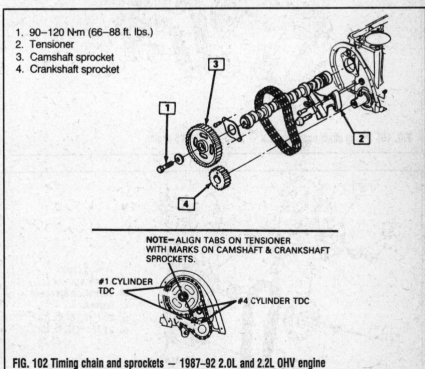

1. 90–120 N•m (66–88 ft. lbs.)
2. Tensioner
3. Camshaft sprocket
4. Crankshaft sprocket

NOTE— ALIGN TABS ON TENSIONER WITH MARKS ON CAMSHAFT & CRANKSHAFT SPROCKETS.

FIG. 102 Timing chain and sprockets — 1987–92 2.0L and 2.2L OHV engine

stamped timing marks on both sprockets are closest to one another and in line between the shaft centers (No. 4 firing position).

3. Take out the three bolts that hold the camshaft sprocket to the camshaft. This

sprocket is a light press fit on the camshaft and will come off readily. If the sprocket does not come off easily, a light blow on the lower edge of the sprocket with a plastic mallet should dislodge the sprocket. The chain comes off with

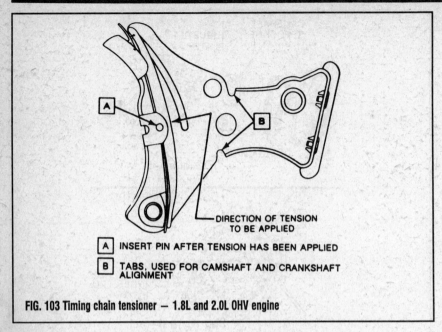

DIRECTION OF TENSION
TO BE APPLIED

A INSERT PIN AFTER TENSION HAS BEEN APPLIED

B TABS, USED FOR CAMSHAFT AND CRANKSHAFT
ALIGNMENT

FIG. 103 Timing chain tensioner — 1.8L and 2.0L OHV engine

FIG. 104 Timing chain and sprockets — 1985–86 2.8L V6 engine

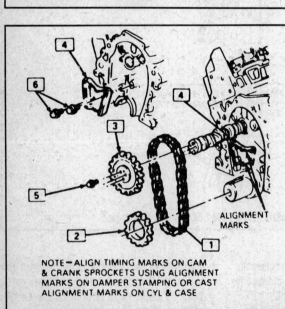

1. Timing chain
2. Crank sprocket
3. Camshaft sprocket
4. Damper
5. 28 N·m (21 lb. ft.)
6. 21 N·m (15 lb. ft.)

ALIGNMENT
MARKS

NOTE—ALIGN TIMING MARKS ON CAM
& CRANK SPROCKETS USING ALIGNMENT
MARKS ON DAMPER STAMPING OR CAST
ALIGNMENT MARKS ON CYL & CASE

FIG. 105 Timing chain and sprockets — 1987–92 2.8L and 3.1L V6 engine

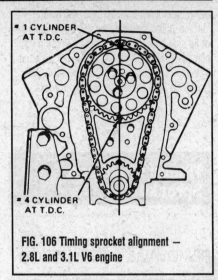

● 1 CYLINDER
AT T.D.C.

● 4 CYLINDER
AT T.D.C.

FIG. 106 Timing sprocket alignment —
2.8L and 3.1L V6 engine

the camshaft sprocket. A gear puller will be required to remove the crankshaft sprocket.

To install:

4. Without disturbing the position of the engine, mount the new crank sprocket on the shaft, then mount the chain over the camshaft sprocket. Arrange the camshaft sprocket in such a way that the timing marks will line up between the shaft centers and the camshaft locating dowel will enter the dowel hole in the cam sprocket.

5. Place the cam sprocket, with its chain mounted over it, in position on the front of the camshaft and pull up with the three bolts that hold it to the camshaft. Torque the bolts to 18 ft. lbs. (25 Nm).

6. Lubricate the timing chain with oil.

7. After the sprockets are in place, turn the engine two full revolutions to make certain that the timing marks are in correct alignment between the shaft centers.

Timing Belt

REMOVAL & INSTALLATION

1.8L and 2.0L OHC Engine

1983–88
◆ SEE FIGS. 107-109A

➡ **The following procedure requires the use of a special adjustment tool J33039 and tension gauge J26486-A or their equivalents.**

1. Remove the timing belt front cover.
2. Raise and support the vehicle safely.
3. Remove the crankshaft pulley as previously described.
4. Check that the camshaft sprocket lines up with mark on the camshaft carrier on the 1.8L engine and the mark on the camshaft sprocket must line up with the mark on the rear timing belt cover on the 2.0L engine. The timing mark on the crankshaft pulley should line up with the 10° BTDC mark on the indicator scale.
5. Lower the vehicle.
6. Remove timing probe holder.
7. Loosen the water pump retaining bolts and rotate the water pump to loosen the timing belt.
8. Remove the timing belt.

To Install:

9. Install timing belt on sprockets.
10. Install the crankshaft pulley.
11. Check if the mark on the camshaft sprocket lines up with mark on the camshaft carrier, on the 1.8L engine. The timing mark on the crankshaft pulley should line up at 10° BTDC on the indicator scale.

❄❄ WARNING

Do not turn the camshaft. Use only the crankshaft nut to turn. Turning the nut on the camshaft directly can damage the camshaft bearings.

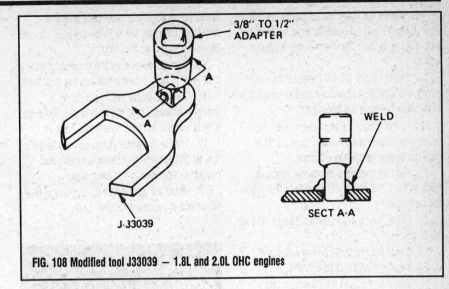

FIG. 108 Modified tool J33039 — 1.8L and 2.0L OHC engines

Belt Size	19mm
INITIAL ADJUSTMENT	
New Belt	22 lbs.
Used Belt	18 lbs.
CHECKING VALUE	
New Belt	18–27 lbs.
Used Belt	13–22 lbs.

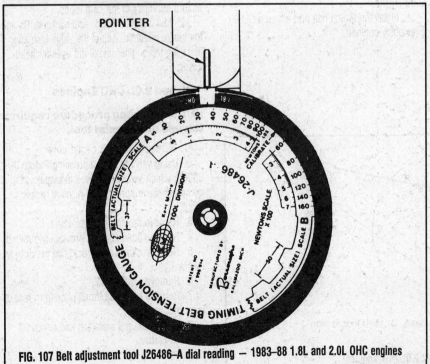

FIG. 107 Belt adjustment tool J26486–A dial reading — 1983–88 1.8L and 2.0L OHC engines

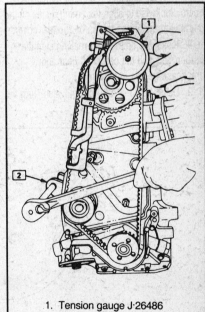

1. Tension gauge J·26486
2. Adjustment tool J·33039

FIG. 109 Timing belt adjustment — 1.8L and 2.0L OHC engines

12. Rotate the water pump clockwise using Tool J-33039 until all slack is removed from the belt. Slightly tighten the water pump retaining bolts.

13. Install Tool J-26486 between the water pump and camshaft sprockets so that the pointer is midway between the sprockets.

14. If the tension is incorrect, loosen the water pump and rotate it using Tool J-33039 until the proper tension is obtained.

15. Fully torque the water pump retaining bolts to 18 ft. lbs. taking care not to further rotate the water pump.

16. Install timing probe holder. Torque nuts to 19 ft. lbs.

17. Install the timing belt front cover and torque the attaching bolts to 5 ft. lbs.

18. Install and adjust the generator and power steering belt. Refill the cooling system, if necessary.

1989–92

◆ SEE FIG. 110

1. Disconnect the negative battery cable.

2. Remove the serpentine belt and timing belt cover.

3. Loosen the water pump bolts and release tension with tool J–33039 or equivalent.

4. Raise and support the vehicle safely.

5. Remove the crankshaft pulley.

6. Lower the vehicle and remove the timing belt.

To Install:

7. Turn the crankshaft and the camshaft gears clockwise to align the timing marks on the gears with the timing marks on the rear cover.

8. Install the timing belt, making sure the portion between the camshaft gear and crankcase gear is in tension.

9. Using tool J–33039 or equivalent, turn the water pump eccentric clockwise until the tensioner contacts the high torque stop. Tighten the water pump screws slightly.

10. Turn the engine by the crankshaft gear bolt 720° to fully seat the belt into the gear teeth.

11. Turn the water pump eccentric counterclockwise until the hole in the tensioner arm is aligned with the hole in the base.

12. Torque the water pump screws to 18 ft. lbs. while checking that the tensioner holes remain as adjusted in the prior step.

13. Install the crankshaft pulley, timing belt cover and the serpentine drive belt.

Timing Belt Rear Cover

REMOVAL & INSTALLATION

1.8L and 2.0L OHC Engines

1. Remove the timing belt from the crankshaft sprocket as outlined in this section.

2. Remove the timing belt rear cover attaching bolts and the rear cover.

3. Install the rear cover and torque the attaching bolts to 19 ft. lbs. 25 Nm on the 1.8L engine, 54 inch lbs. (6 Nm) on the 1987–88 2.0L engine and 89 inch lbs. (10 Nm) on the 1989–92 2.0L engine.

4. Install the timing belt and adjust as previously outlined.

Camshaft

REMOVAL & INSTALLATION

1.8L, 2.0L and 2.2L OHV Engine

1. Remove the engine.

2. Remove the cylinder head cover, pivot the rocker arms to the sides, and remove the pushrods, keeping them in order. Remove the valve lifters, keeping them in order. There are special tools which make lifter removal easier.

3. Remove the front cover.

4. Remove the distributor, if so equipped.

5. Remove the fuel pump and its pushrod.

6. Remove the timing chain and sprocket as described earlier in this section.

7. Carefully pull the camshaft from the block, being sure that the camshaft lobes do not contact the bearings.

To install:

8. To install, lubricate the camshaft journals with clean engine oil. Lubricate the lobes with Molykote® or the equivalent.

9. Install the camshaft into the engine, being extremely careful not to contact the bearings with the cam lobes.

10. Install the timing chain and sprocket. Install the fuel pump and pushrod. Install the timing cover. Install the distributor.

11. Install the valve lifters. If a new camshaft has been installed, new lifters should be used to ensure durability of the cam lobes.

12. Install the pushrods and rocker arms and the intake manifold. Adjust the valve lash after installing the engine. Install the cylinder head cover.

1.8L and 2.0L OHC Engines

➡ **The following procedure requires the use of a special tool.**

1. Remove camshaft carrier cover.

2. Using valve train compressing Fixture J-33302, which holds the valves in place, compress valve springs and remove rocker arms.

3. Remove timing belt front cover.

4. Remove timing belt as previously outlined.

5. Remove camshaft sprocket as previously outlined.

6. Remove distributor.

7. Remove camshaft thrust plate from rear of camshaft carrier.

8. Slide camshaft rearward and remove it from the carrier.

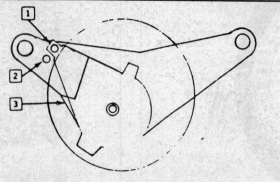

1. Tensioner arm 2. Hole in base 3. High torque stop

FIG. 110 Timing belt tensioner positions — 1989–92 2.0L OHC engines

To Install:

9. Install a new camshaft carrier front oil seal using Tool J-33085.

10. Place camshaft in the carrier.

❋❋ WARNING

Take care not to damage the carrier front oil seal when installing the camshaft.

11. Install camshaft thrust plate retaining bolts. Torque bolts to 70 inch lbs.

12. Check camshaft end play, which should be within 0.016-0.064mm.

13. Install distributor.

14. Install camshaft sprocket as previously described.

15. Install timing belt as previously described.

16. Install timing belt front cover.

17. Using valve train compressing fixture J-33302, compress valve springs and replace rocker arms.

18. Install camshaft carrier cover as previously described.

2.8L and 3.1L V6 Engines

1. Remove the engine assembly as outlined earlier.

2. Remove intake manifold, valve lifters and timing chain cover as described in this section. If the car is equipped with air conditioning, unbolt the condenser and move it aside without disconnecting any lines.

3. Remove fuel pump and pump pushrod.

4. Remove camshaft sprocket bolts, sprocket and timing chain. A light blow to the lower edge of a tight sprocket should free it (use a plastic mallet).

5. Install two bolts in cam bolt holes and pull cam from block.

To Install:

6. Lubricate the camshaft journals with engine oil and reverse removal procedure aligning the sprocket timing marks.

➡ **If a new camshaft is being installed, coat the camshaft lobes with GM Engine Oil Supplement (E.O.S.), or equivalent.**

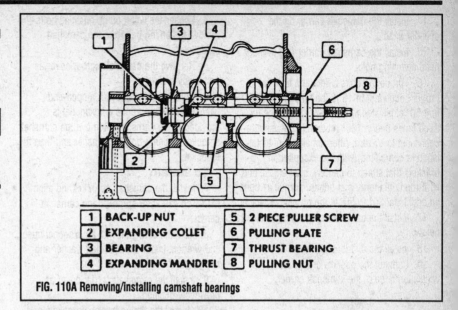

1	BACK-UP NUT	5	2 PIECE PULLER SCREW
2	EXPANDING COLLET	6	PULLING PLATE
3	BEARING	7	THRUST BEARING
4	EXPANDING MANDREL	8	PULLING NUT

FIG. 110A Removing/installing camshaft bearings

Camshaft Bearings

REMOVAL & INSTALLATION

➡ SEE FIG. 110A

1. Remove the camshaft assembly — refer to the necessary service procedures.

2. To remove the camshaft bearings use a special tool (refer to the illustrations) select the proper pilot, nut and thrust washer.

3. Pull out camshaft bearings.

4. To install the camshaft bearings place the bearing onto the tool and index the oil holes of the bearing with the oil passages in the cylinder block. Pull bearing into proper place.

➡ **Proper alignment of the oil holes is critical. Restriction of the oil flow will cause severe engine damage.**

Camshaft Carrier

REMOVAL & INSTALLATION

1.8L and 2.0L OHC Engines

➡ **Whenever the camshaft carrier bolts are loosened, it is necessary to replace the cylinder head gasket. To do this, see the previous instructions under Cylinder Head Removal and Installation.**

1. Disconnect the positive crankcase ventilation hose from the camshaft carrier.

2. Remove the distributor.

3. Remove the camshaft sprocket as previously outlined.

4. Loosen the camshaft carrier and cylinder head attaching bolts a little at a time in the sequence shown in the "Cylinder Head Removal and Installation" procedure.

➡ **Camshaft carrier and cylinder head bolts should be loosened only when the engine is cold.**

5. Remove the camshaft carrier.

6. Remove the camshaft thrust plate from the rear of the camshaft carrier.

7. Slide the camshaft rearward and remove it from the carrier.

8. Remove the carrier front oil seal.

To Install:

9. Install a new carrier front oil seal using Tool J-33085.

10. Place the camshaft in the carrier.

❋❋ WARNING

Take care not to damage the carrier front oil seal when installing the camshaft.

11. Install the camshaft thrust plate and the retaining bolts. Torque the bolts to 70 inch lbs.

12. Check camshaft end-play which should be within 0.04-0.16mm.

13. Clean the sealing surfaces on cylinder head and carrier. Apply a continuous 3mm bead of RTV sealer.

14. Install the camshaft carrier on the cylinder head.

15. Install the camshaft carrier and cylinder head attaching bolts.

16. Torque the bolts a little at a time in the proper sequence, to 18 ft. lbs. Then turn each bolt 60° clockwise in the proper sequence for three times until a 180° rotation is obtained, or equivalent to 1/2 turn. After remainder of installation is completed (with the exception of brackets that attach to carrier), start engine and let it run until thermostat opens. Torque all bolts an additional 30° to 50° in the proper sequence.

17. Install the camshaft sprocket as outlined below.

18. Install the distributor.

19. Connect the positive crankcase ventilation hose to the camshaft carrier.

Camshaft Sprocket

REMOVAL & INSTALLATION

1.8L and 2.0L OHC Engines

▶ SEE FIG. 111

1. Remove the timing belt front cover.

2. Align the mark on camshaft sprocket with mark on or camshaft carrier or rear timing belt cover.

3. Remove timing probe holder.

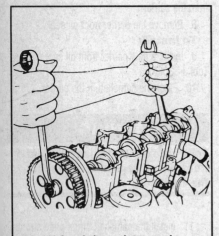

FIG. 111 Camshaft sprocket removal — 1.8L and 2.0L OHC engines

4. Loosen the water pump retaining bolts and remove the timing belt from the camshaft sprocket.

5. Remove the camshaft carrier cover as previously outlined.

6. Hold the camshaft with a open-end wrench. For this purpose a hexagonal is provided in the camshaft. Remove the camshaft sprocket retaining bolt and washer and then the sprocket.

To Install:

7. Install the camshaft sprocket and align marks on camshaft sprocket and camshaft carrier.

8. Hold the camshaft with a hexagonal open-end wrench. Install the sprocket washer and retaining bolt. Torque to 34 ft. lbs.

9. Install the camshaft carrier cover as previously outlined.

10. Install the timing belt on sprockets and adjust as previously outlined.

11. Install timing probe holder, if so equipped, and torque the nuts to 19 ft. lbs.

12. Install timing belt front cover.

Crankshaft Sprocket

REMOVAL & INSTALLATION

1.8L and 2.0L OHC Engines

1. Remove the timing belt from the crankshaft sprocket as previously described.

2. Remove the crankshaft sprocket to crankshaft attaching bolt and the thrust washer.

3. Remove the sprocket.

To Install:

4. Position the sprocket over the key on end of crankshaft.

5. Install the thrust washer and the attaching bolt. Torque to 115 ft. lbs. (through 1983), 107 ft. lbs. plus a 45° rotation (1984-87), 96 ft. lbs. plus a 45° rotation (1988) and 114 ft. lbs. (1989-92).

6. Install the timing belt and adjust as previously described.

Pistons and Connecting Rod

REMOVAL

1. Remove the engine assembly from the car, see Engine Removal and Installation service procedures.

2. Remove the intake manifold, cylinder head or heads.

3. Remove the oil pan.

4. Remove the oil pump assembly.

5. Stamp the cylinder number on the machined surfaces of the bolt bosses of the connecting rod and cap for identification when reinstalling. If the pistons are to be removed from the connecting rod, mark the cylinder number on the piston with a silver pencil or quick drying paint for proper cylinder identification and cap to rod location. The 2.8L and 3.1L V6 engines are numbered 1-3-5 on the right bank, 2-4-6 on the left bank.

6. Examine the cylinder bore above the ring travel. If a ridge exists, remove the ridge with a ridge reamer before attempting to remove the piston and rod assembly.

7. Remove the rod bearing cap and bearing.

8. Install a guide hose over threads of rod bolts. This is to prevent damage to bearing journal and rod bolt threads.

9. Remove the rod and piston assembly through the top of the cylinder bore.

10. Remove any other rod and piston assemblies in the same manner.

CLEANING AND INSPECTION

Connecting Rods

Wash connecting rods in cleaning solvent and dry with compressed air. Check for twisted or bent rods and inspect for nicks or cracks. Replace connecting rods that are damaged.

Pistons

Clean varnish from piston skirts and pins with a cleaning solvent. DO NOT WIRE BRUSH ANY PART OF THE PISTON. Clean the ring grooves with a groove cleaner and make sure oil ring holes and slots are clean.

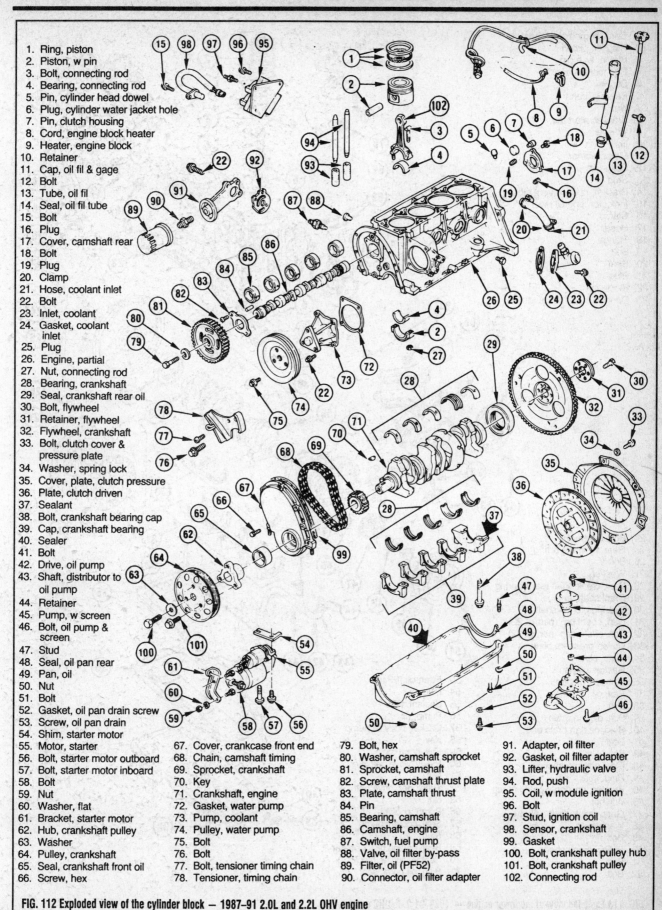

1. Ring, piston
2. Piston, w pin
3. Bolt, connecting rod
4. Bearing, connecting rod
5. Pin, cylinder head dowel
6. Plug, cylinder water jacket hole
7. Pin, clutch housing
8. Cord, engine block heater
9. Heater, engine block
10. Retainer
11. Cap, oil fil & gage
12. Bolt
13. Tube, oil fil
14. Seal, oil fil tube
15. Bolt
16. Plug
17. Cover, camshaft rear
18. Bolt
19. Plug
20. Clamp
21. Hose, coolant inlet
22. Bolt
23. Inlet, coolant
24. Gasket, coolant inlet
25. Plug
26. Engine, partial
27. Nut, connecting rod
28. Bearing, crankshaft
29. Seal, crankshaft rear oil
30. Bolt, flywheel
31. Retainer, flywheel
32. Flywheel, crankshaft
33. Bolt, clutch cover & pressure plate
34. Washer, spring lock
35. Cover, plate, clutch pressure
36. Plate, clutch driven
37. Sealant
38. Bolt, crankshaft bearing cap
39. Cap, crankshaft bearing
40. Sealer
41. Bolt
42. Drive, oil pump
43. Shaft, distributor to oil pump
44. Retainer
45. Pump, w screen
46. Bolt, oil pump & screen
47. Stud
48. Seal, oil pan rear
49. Pan, oil
50. Nut
51. Bolt
52. Gasket, oil pan drain screw
53. Screw, oil pan drain
54. Shim, starter motor
55. Motor, starter
56. Bolt, starter motor outboard
57. Bolt, starter motor inboard
58. Bolt
59. Nut
60. Washer, flat
61. Bracket, starter motor
62. Hub, crankshaft pulley
63. Washer
64. Pulley, crankshaft
65. Seal, crankshaft front oil
66. Screw, hex

67. Cover, crankcase front end
68. Chain, camshaft timing
69. Sprocket, crankshaft
70. Key
71. Crankshaft, engine
72. Gasket, water pump
73. Pump, coolant
74. Pulley, water pump
75. Bolt
76. Bolt
77. Bolt, tensioner timing chain
78. Tensioner, timing chain

79. Bolt, hex
80. Washer, camshaft sprocket
81. Sprocket, camshaft
82. Screw, camshaft thrust plate
83. Plate, camshaft thrust
84. Pin
85. Bearing, camshaft
86. Camshaft, engine
87. Switch, fuel pump
88. Valve, oil filter by-pass
89. Filter, oil (PF52)
90. Connector, oil filter adapter

91. Adapter, oil filter
92. Gasket, oil filter adapter
93. Lifter, hydraulic valve
94. Rod, push
95. Coil, w module ignition
96. Bolt
97. Stud, ignition coil
98. Sensor, crankshaft
99. Gasket
100. Bolt, crankshaft pulley hub
101. Bolt, crankshaft pulley
102. Connecting rod

FIG. 112 Exploded view of the cylinder block — 1987–91 2.0L and 2.2L OHV engine

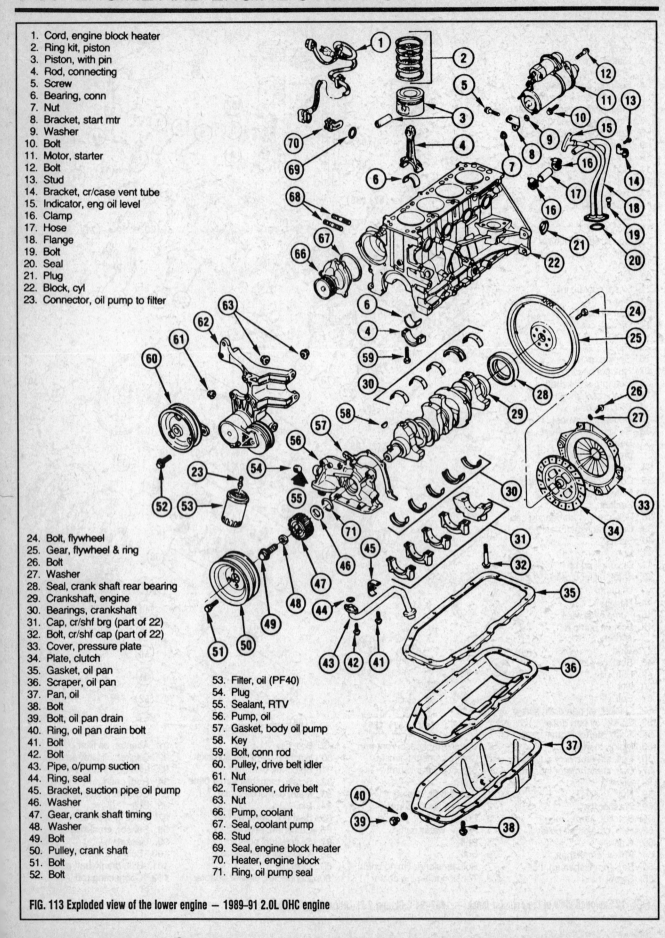

1. Cord, engine block heater
2. Ring kit, piston
3. Piston, with pin
4. Rod, connecting
5. Screw
6. Bearing, conn
7. Nut
8. Bracket, start mtr
9. Washer
10. Bolt
11. Motor, starter
12. Bolt
13. Stud
14. Bracket, cr/case vent tube
15. Indicator, eng oil level
16. Clamp
17. Hose
18. Flange
19. Bolt
20. Seal
21. Plug
22. Block, cyl
23. Connector, oil pump to filter

24. Bolt, flywheel
25. Gear, flywheel & ring
26. Bolt
27. Washer
28. Seal, crank shaft rear bearing
29. Crankshaft, engine
30. Bearings, crankshaft
31. Cap, cr/shf brg (part of 22)
32. Bolt, cr/shf cap (part of 22)
33. Cover, pressure plate
34. Plate, clutch
35. Gasket, oil pan
36. Scraper, oil pan
37. Pan, oil
38. Bolt
39. Bolt, oil pan drain
40. Ring, oil pan drain bolt
41. Bolt
42. Bolt
43. Pipe, o/pump suction
44. Ring, seal
45. Bracket, suction pipe oil pump
46. Washer
47. Gear, crank shaft timing
48. Washer
49. Bolt
50. Pulley, crank shaft
51. Bolt
52. Bolt

53. Filter, oil (PF40)
54. Plug
55. Sealant, RTV
56. Pump, oil
57. Gasket, body oil pump
58. Key
59. Bolt, conn rod
60. Pulley, drive belt idler
61. Nut
62. Tensioner, drive belt
63. Nut
66. Pump, coolant
67. Seal, coolant pump
68. Stud
69. Seal, engine block heater
70. Heater, engine block
71. Ring, oil pump seal

FIG. 113 Exploded view of the lower engine — 1989–91 2.0L OHC engine

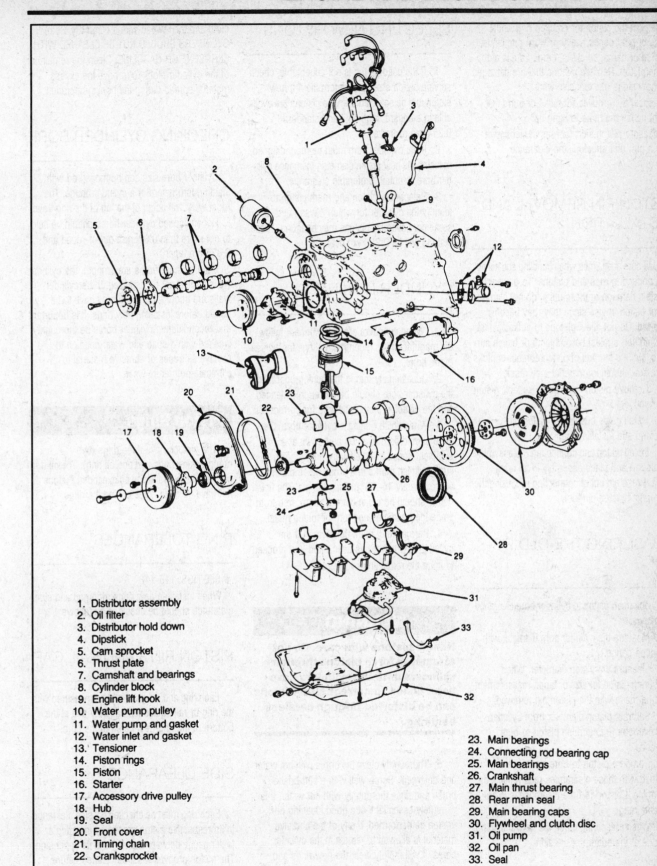

1. Distributor assembly
2. Oil filter
3. Distributor hold down
4. Dipstick
5. Cam sprocket
6. Thrust plate
7. Camshaft and bearings
8. Cylinder block
9. Engine lift hook
10. Water pump pulley
11. Water pump and gasket
12. Water inlet and gasket
13. Tensioner
14. Piston rings
15. Piston
16. Starter
17. Accessory drive pulley
18. Hub
19. Seal
20. Front cover
21. Timing chain
22. Cranksprocket

23. Main bearings
24. Connecting rod bearing cap
25. Main bearings
26. Crankshaft
27. Main thrust bearing
28. Rear main seal
29. Main bearing caps
30. Flywheel and clutch disc
31. Oil pump
32. Oil pan
33. Seal

FIG. 114 Exploded view of the cylinder block — 1982–86 1.8L and 2.0L OHV engine

Inspect the piston for cracked ring lands, skirts or pin bosses, wavy or worn ring lands, scuffed or damaged skirts, eroded areas at top of the piston. Replace pistons that are damaged or show signs of excessive wear.

Inspect the grooves for nicks or burrs that might cause the rings to hang up.

Measure piston skirt (across center line of piston pin) and check piston clearance.

PISTON PIN REMOVAL AND INSTALLATION

Use care at all times when handling and servicing connecting rods and pistons. To prevent possible damage to these units, do not clamp rod or piston in vise since they may become distorted. Do not allow pistons to strike against one another, against hard objects or bench surfaces, since distortion of piston contour or nicks in the soft aluminum material may result.

1. Remove piston rings using suitable piston ring remover.

2. Install guide bushing of piston pin removing and installing tool.

3. Install piston and connecting rod assembly on support and place assembly in an arbor press. Press pin out of connecting rod, using the appropriate piston pin tool.

MEASURING THE OLD PISTONS

Check used piston to cylinder bore clearance as follows:

1. Measure the cylinder bore diameter with a telescope gauge.

2. Measure the piston diameter. When measuring piston for size or taper, measurement must be made with the piston pin removed.

3. Subtract piston diameter from cylinder bore diameter to determine piston-to-bore clearance.

4. Compare piston-to-bore clearance obtained with those clearances recommended. Determine if piston-to-bore clearance is in acceptable range.

5. When measuring taper, the largest reading must be at the bottom of the skirt.

SELECTING NEW PISTONS

1. If the used piston is not acceptable, check service piston sizes and determine if a new piston can be selected. Service pistons are available in standard, high limit and standard 0.254mm oversize.

2. If the cylinder bore must be reconditioned, measure the new piston diameter, then hone cylinder bore to obtain preferable clearance.

3. Select new piston and mark piston to identify the cylinder for which it was fitted. On some cars oversize pistons may be found. These pistons will be 0.254mm oversize.

CYLINDER HONING

1. When cylinders are being honed, follow the manufacturer's recommendations for the use of the hone.

2. Occasionally during the honing operation, the cylinder bore should be thoroughly cleaned and the selected piston checked for correct fit.

3. When finish honing a cylinder bore, the hone should be moved up and down at a sufficient speed to obtain very fine uniform surface finish marks in a cross hatch pattern of approximately 45–65° included angle. The finish marks should be clean but not sharp, free from embedded particles and torn or folded metal.

4. Permanently mark the piston for the cylinder to which it has been fitted and proceed to hone the remaining cylinders.

※※ WARNING

Handle pistons with care. Do not attempt to force pistons through cylinders until the cylinders have been honed to correct size. Pistons can be distorted through careless handling.

5. Thoroughly clean the bores with hot water and detergent. Scrub well with a stiff bristle brush and rinse thoroughly with hot water. It is extremely essential that a good cleaning operation be performed. If any of the abrasive material is allowed to remain in the cylinder bores, it will rapidly wear the new rings and cylinder bores. The bores should be swabbed several times with light engine oil and a clean

cloth and then wiped with a clean dry cloth. CYLINDERS SHOULD NOT BE CLEANED WITH KEROSENE OR GASOLINE! Clean the remainder of the cylinder block to remove the excess material spread during the honing operation.

CHECKING CYLINDER BORE

Cylinder bore size can be measured with inside micrometers or a cylinder gauge. The most wear will occur at the top of the ring travel.

Reconditioned cylinder bores should be held to not more than 0.025mm out-of-round and 0.025mm taper.

If the cylinder bores are smooth, the cylinder walls should not be deglazed. If the cylinder walls are scored, the walls may have to be honed before installing new rings. It is important that reconditioned cylinder bores be thoroughly washed with a soap and water solution to remove all traces of abrasive material to eliminate premature wear.

Piston Rings

The pistons have three rings (two compression rings and one oil ring). The oil ring consists of two rails and an expander. Pistons do not have oil drain holes behind the rings.

RING TOLERANCES

♦ SEE FIGS. 115-118

When installing new rings, ring gap and side clearance should be check as as follows:

PISTON RING AND RAIL GAP

Each ring and rail gap must be measured with the ring or rail positioned squarely and at the bottom of the ring-travel area of the bore.

SIDE CLEARANCE

Each ring must be checked for side clearance in its respective piston groove by inserting a feeler gauge between the ring and its upper land. The piston grooves must be cleaned before checking ring for side clearance. See PISTON RING CLEARANCE CHART in this section for ring side clearance specifications. To check oil

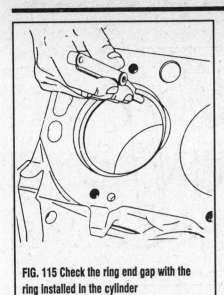

FIG. 115 Check the ring end gap with the ring installed in the cylinder

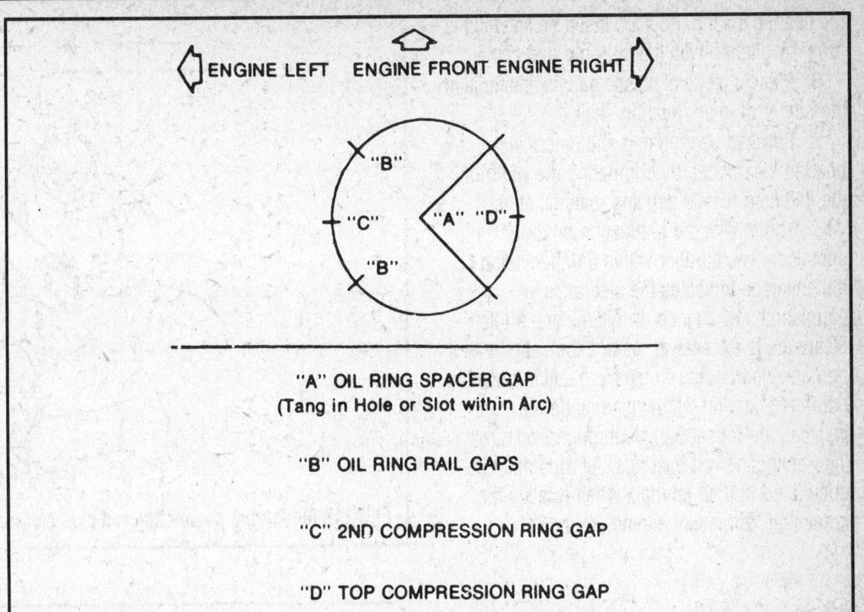

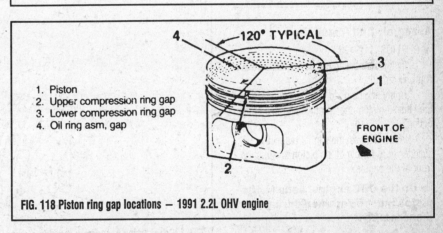

ENGINE LEFT
ENGINE FRONT
ENGINE RIGHT
"B"
"C"
"A"
"D"
"B"
"A" OIL RING SPACER GAP
(Tang in Hole or Slot within Arc)
"B" OIL RING RAIL GAPS
"C" 2ND COMPRESSION RING GAP
"D" TOP COMPRESSION RING GAP

FIG. 117 Piston ring gap locations – except 1991 2.2L OHV engine

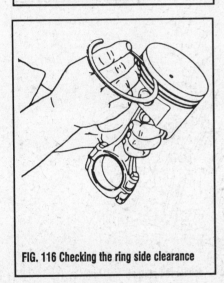

FIG. 116 Checking the ring side clearance

120° TYPICAL
4
3
1
2
1. Piston
2. Upper compression ring gap
3. Lower compression ring gap
4. Oil ring asm, gap
FRONT OF ENGINE

FIG. 118 Piston ring gap locations – 1991 2.2L OHV engine

ring side clearance, the oil rings must be installed on the piston.

RING INSTALLATION

For service ring specifications and detailed installation productions, refer to the instructions furnished with the parts package.

CONNECTING ROD BEARINGS

Removal, Inspection, Installation

If you have already removed the connecting rod and piston assemblies from the engine, follow only steps 3-7 of the following procedure.

The connecting rod bearings are designed to have a slight projection above the rod and cap faces to insure a positive contact. The bearings can be replaced with removing the rod and piston assembly from the engine.

1. Remove the oil pan, see Oil Pan. It may be necessary to remove the oil pump to provide access to rear connecting rod bearings.
2. With the connecting rod journal at the bottom, stamp the cylinder number on the machined surfaces of connecting rod and cap for identification when reinstalling, then remove caps.
3. Inspect journals for roughness and wear. Slight roughness may be removed with a fine grit polishing cloth saturated with engine oil. Burrs may be removed with a fine oil stone by moving the stone on the journal circumference.

WARNING

Do not move the stone back and forth across the journal. If the journals are scored or ridged, the crankshaft must be replaced.

4. The connecting rod journals should be checked for out-of-round and correct size with a micrometer.

➡ Crankshaft rod journals will normally be standard size. If any undersized crankshafts are used, all will be 0.254mm undersize and 0.254mm will be stamped on the number 4 counterweight.

If plastic gauging material is to be used:

5. Clean oil from the journal bearing cap, connecting rod and outer and inner surface of

the bearing inserts. Position insert so that tang is properly aligned with notch in rod and cap.

6. Place a piece of plastic gauging material in the center of lower bearing shell.

7. Remove bearing cap and determine bearing clearances by comparing the width of the flattened plastic gauging material at its widest point with the graduation on the container. The number within the graduation on the envelope indicates the clearance in thousandths of an inch or millimeters. If this clearance is excessive, replace the bearing and recheck clearance with plastic gauging material. Lubricate bearing with engine oil before installation. Repeat Steps 2 through 7 on remaining connecting rod bearings. All rods must be connected to their journals when rotating the crankshaft to prevent engine damage.

PISTON AND CONNECTING ROD

Assembly And Installation

♦ SEE FIGS. 119-123

1. Install connecting rod bolt guide hose over rod bolt threads.

2. Apply engine oil to the rings and piston, then install piston ring compressing tool on the piston.

3. Install the assembly in its respective cylinder bore (arrow of the piston towards the front of the engine).

➡ **On the OHC engine, code M, the piston must be marked during disassembly.**

4. Lubricate the crankshaft journal with engine oil and install connecting rod bearing and cap, with bearing index tang in rod and cap on same side. On the OHC engines the identification numbers must be on the same side and facing the water pump.

➡ **When more than one rod and piston assembly is being installed, the connecting rod cap attaching nuts should only be tightened enough to keep each rod in position until all have been installed. This will aid installation of remaining piston assemblies.**

5. Torque rod bolt nuts to specifications — refer to the "Torque Specifications Chart".

6. Install all other removed parts.

7. Install the engine in the car, see Engine Removal and Installation.

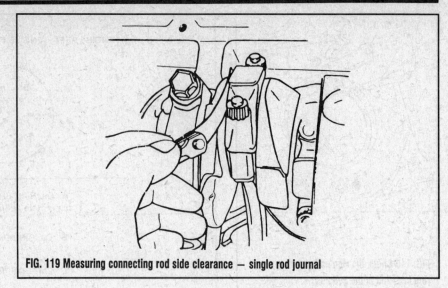

FIG. 119 Measuring connecting rod side clearance — single rod journal

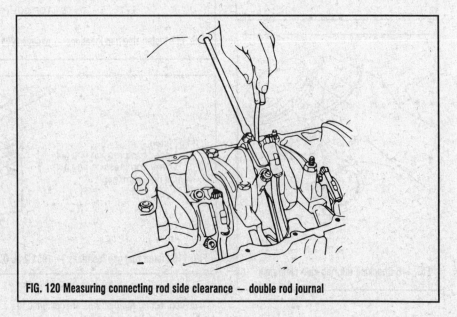

FIG. 120 Measuring connecting rod side clearance — double rod journal

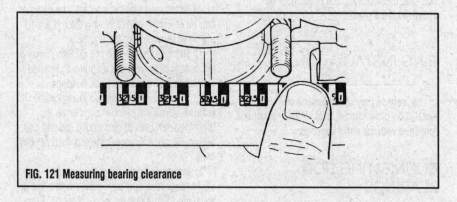

FIG. 121 Measuring bearing clearance

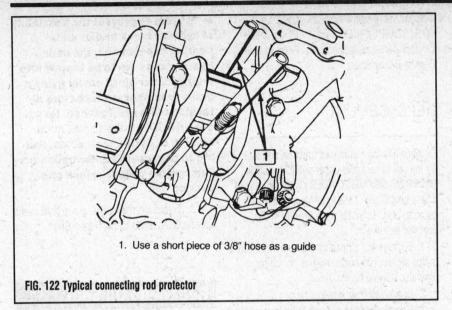

1. Use a short piece of 3/8" hose as a guide

FIG. 122 Typical connecting rod protector

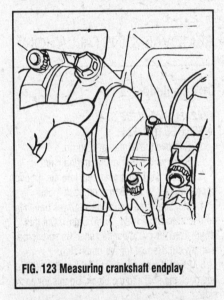

FIG. 123 Measuring crankshaft endplay

Engine Core Plugs (Freeze Plugs)

REMOVAL

✳✳ CAUTION

When draining the coolant, keep in mind that cats and dogs are attracted by the ethylene glycol antifreeze, and are quite likely to drink any that is left in an uncovered container or in puddles

on the ground. This will prove fatal in sufficient quantity. Always drain the coolant into a sealable container. Coolant should be reused unless it is contaminated or several years old.

Drain the cooling system. Using a blunt tool such as a drift or a screwdriver and a hammer, strike the bottom edge of the cup plug. With the cup plug rotated, grasp firmly with pliers or other suitable tool remove the plug.

➡ **Do not drive cup plug into the block assembly casting as restricted cooling can result.**

INSTALLATION

Thoroughly clean inside of cup plug hole in cylinder block or head. Be sure to remove old sealer. Lightly coat inside of cup plug hole with sealer. Make certain the new plug is cleaned of all oil and grease. Using proper drive tool, drive plug into hole. Refill the cooling system.

Crankshaft

REMOVAL

1. Remove the engine assembly as previously outlined.
2. Remove the engine front cover.
3. Remove the timing chain and sprockets.

4. Remove the oil pan.
5. Remove the oil pump.
6. Stamp the cylinder number on the machined surfaces of the bolt bosses of the connecting rods and caps for identification when reinstalling. If the pistons are to be removed from the connecting rod, mark cylinder number on piston with a silver pencil or quick-drying paint for proper cylinder identification and cap to rod location.
7. Remove the connecting rod caps and install thread protectors.
8. Mark the main bearing caps so that they can be installed in their original positions.
9. Remove all the main bearing caps.
10. Note position of keyway in crankshaft so it can be installed in the same position.
11. Lift crankshaft out of block. Rods will pivot to the center of the engine when the crankshaft is removed.
12. Remove both halves of the rear main oil seal.

INSTALLATION

1. Measure the crankshaft journals with a micrometer to determine the correct size rod and main bearings to be used. Whenever a new or reconditioned crankshaft is installed, new connecting rod bearings and main bearings should be installed. See Main Bearings and Rod Bearings.
2. Clean all oil passages in the block (and crankshaft if it is being reused).

➡ **A new rear main seal should be installed anytime the crankshaft is removed or replaced.**

3. Install sufficient oil pan bolts in the block to align with the connecting rod bolts. Use rubber bands between the bolts to position the connecting rods as required. Connecting rod position can be adjusted by increasing the tension on the rubber bands with additional turns around the pan bolts or thread protectors.
4. Position the upper half of main bearings in the block and lubricate with engine oil.
5. Position crankshaft keyway in the same position as removed and lower into block. The connecting rods will follow the crank pins into the correct position as the crankshaft is lowered.
6. Lubricate the thrust flanges with 1050169 Lubricant or equivalent. Install caps with lower half of bearings lubricated with engine oil. Lubricate cap bolts with engine oil and install, but do not tighten.
7. With a block of wood, bump shaft in each direction to align thrust flanges of main bearing. After bumping shaft in each direction, wedge the

shaft to the front and hold it while torquing the thrust bearing cap bolts.

❋❋ WARNING

In order to prevent the possibility of cylinder block and/or main bearing cap damage, the main bearing caps are to be tapped into their cylinder block cavity using a brass or leather mallet before attaching bolts are installed. Do not use attaching bolts to pull main bearing caps into their seats. Failure to observe this information may damage the cylinder block or a bearing cap.

8. Torque all main bearing caps to specifications — refer to the Torque Specification Chart.

9. Remove the connecting rod bolt thread protectors and lubricate the connecting rod bearings with engine oil.

10. Install the connecting rod bearing caps in their original position. Torque the nuts to specification — refer to the Torque Specifications Chart.

11. Complete the installation by reversing the removal steps.

Main Bearings

CHECKING BEARING CLEARANCE

1. Remove bearing cap and wipe oil from crankshaft journal and outer and inner surfaces of bearing shell.

2. Place a piece of plastic gauging material in the center of bearing.

3. Use a floor jack or other means to hold crankshaft against upper bearing shell. This is necessary to obtain accurate clearance readings when using plastic gauging material.

4. Reinstall bearing cap and bearing. Place engine oil on cap bolts and install Torque bolts to specification.

5. Remove bearing cap and determine bearing clearance by comparing the width of the flattened plastic gauging material at its widest point with graduations on the gauging material container. The number within the graduation on the envelope indicates the clearance in millimeters or thousandths of an inch. If the

clearance is greater than allowed, REPLACE BOTH BEARING SHELLS AS A SET. Recheck clearance after replacing shells. Refer to Main Bearing Replacement.

REPLACEMENT

Main bearing clearances must be corrected by the use of selective upper and lower shells. UNDER NO CIRCUMSTANCES should the use of shims behind the shells to compensate for wear be attempted. To install main bearing shells, proceed as follows:

1. Remove the oil pan as outlined elsewhere in this section. On some models, the oil pump may also have to be removed.

2. Loosen all main bearing caps.

3. Remove bearing cap and remove lower shell.

4. Insert a flattened cotter pin or roll out pin in the oil passage hole in the crankshaft, then rotate the crankshaft in the direction opposite to cranking rotation. The pin will contact the upper shell and roll it out.

5. The main bearing journals should be checked for roughness and wear. Slight roughness may be removed with a fine grit polishing cloth saturated with engine oil. Burrs may be removed with a fine oil stone. If the journals are scored or ridged, the crankshaft must be replaced.

The journals can be measured for out-of-round with the crankshaft installed by using a crankshaft caliper and inside micrometer or a main bearing micrometer. The upper bearing shell must be removed when measuring the crankshaft journals. Maximum out-of-round of the crankshaft journals must not exceed 0.037mm.

6. Clean crankshaft journals and bearing caps thoroughly before installing new main bearings.

7. Apply special lubricant, No. 1050169 or equivalent, to the thrust flanges of bearing shells.

8. Place new upper shell on crankshaft journal with locating tang in correct position and rotate shaft to turn it into place using cotter pin or roll out pin as during removal.

9. Place new bearing shell in bearing cap.

10. Install a new oil seal in the rear main bearing cap and block.

11. Lubricate the removed or replaced main bearings with engine oil. Lubricate the thrust surface with lubricant 1050169 or equivalent.

12. Lubricate the main bearing cap bolts with engine oil.

➡ In order to prevent the possibility of cylinder block and/or main bearing cap damage, the main bearing caps are to be tapped into their cylinder block cavity using a brass or leather mallet before attaching bolts are installed. Do not use attaching bolts to pull main bearing caps into their seats. Failure to observe this information may damage the cylinder block or a bearing cap.

13. Torque the main bearing cap bolts to the specifications noted in the Torque Chart.

Rear Main Oil Seal

REMOVAL & INSTALLATION

OHV Engines

1982-84 TWO PIECE SEAL

◆ SEE FIGS. 124-125

1. Remove the oil pan and pump.

2. Remove the rear main bearing cap.

3. Gently pack the upper seal into the groove approximately 1/4 in. (6mm) on each side.

4. Measure the amount the seal was driven in on one side and add 1/16 in. (0.8mm). Cut this length from the old lower cap seal. Be sure to get a sharp cut. Repeat for the other side.

5. Place the piece of cut seal into the groove and pack the seal into the block. Do this for each side.

6. Install a piece of Plastigage® or the equivalent on the bearing journal. Install the rear cap and tighten to 75 ft. lbs. Remove the cap and check the gauge for bearing clearance. If out of specification, the ends of the seal may be frayed or not flush, preventing the cap from proper seating. Correct as required.

7. Clean the journal, and apply a thin film of sealer to the mating surfaces of the cap and tighten to 70 ft. lbs. Install the pan and pump.

➡ Some 1982 1.8L engines (Code G), experience a rear main seal oil leak. To correct this condition a new crankshaft part No. 14086053 and a one piece rear main seal kit part No. 14081761 has been released for service. The one piece seal kit contains an installation tool, rear main seal, and an instruction sheet.

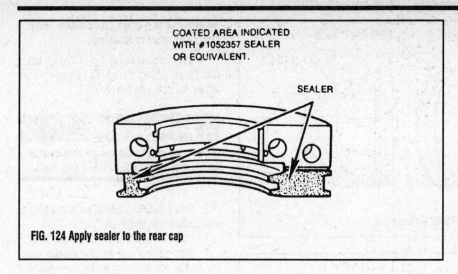

COATED AREA INDICATED WITH #1052357 SEALER OR EQUIVALENT.

SEALER

FIG. 124 Apply sealer to the rear cap

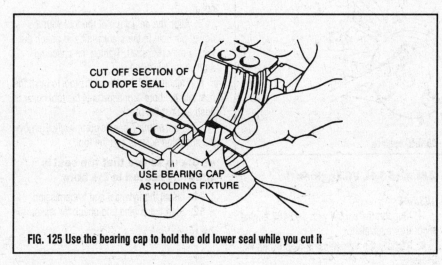

CUT OFF SECTION OF OLD ROPE SEAL

USE BEARING CAP AS HOLDING FIXTURE

FIG. 125 Use the bearing cap to hold the old lower seal while you cut it

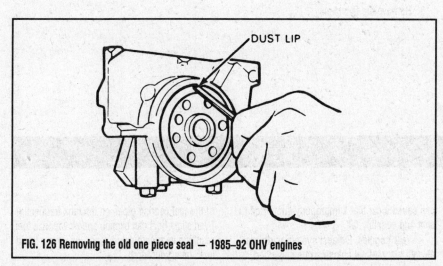

DUST LIP

FIG. 126 Removing the old one piece seal — 1985–92 OHV engines

1985-92
ONE PIECE SEAL
◆ SEE FIGS. 126-127

1. Jack up the engine and support it safely.
2. Remove the transmission as outlined in Section 7.
3. Remove the flywheel.

➡ **Now is the time to confirm that the rear seal is leaking.**

4. Insert a suitable pry tool in through the dust lip and pry out the seal by moving the tool around the seal until it is removed.

➡ **Use care not to damage the crankshaft seal surface with a pry tool.**

5. Before installing, lubricate the seal bore to seal surface with engine oil.
6. Install the new seal using tool J-34686.
7. Slide the new seal over the mandrel until the dust lip bottoms squarely against the tool collar.
8. Align the dowel pin of the tool with the dowel pin hole in the crankshaft and attach the tool to the crankshaft. Tighten the attaching screws to 2-5 ft. lbs.
9. Tighten the T-handle of the tool to push the seal into the bore. Continue until the tool collar is flush against the block.
10. Loosen the T-handle completely. Remove the attaching screws and the tool.

➡ **Check to see that the seal is squarely seated in the bore.**

11. Install the flywheel and transmission.
12. Start the engine and check for leaks.

1.8L and 2.0 OHC Engines
◆ SEE FIG. 128

➡ **The rear main bearing oil seal is a one piece unit and can be replaced without removing the oil pan or the crankshaft.**

1. Remove the transaxle assembly as outlined in Section 7.
2. Remove the flywheel retaining bolts and remove the flywheel.
3. If equipped with manual transaxle, remove the pressure plate and disc.
4. Pry out the rear main seal.
5. Clean the block and crankcase to seal mating surfaces.
6. Position the rear main seal to the block and press evenly into place using tool J33084 (1983–86) or tool J–36227 (1987–92). Lubricate the outside of the seal to aid assembly.

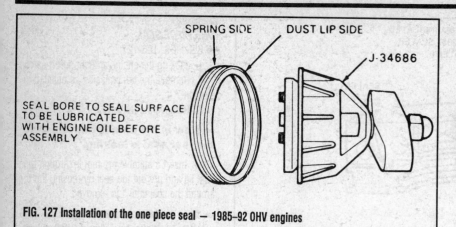

SPRING SIDE   DUST LIP SIDE

J-34686

SEAL BORE TO SEAL SURFACE
TO BE LUBRICATED
WITH ENGINE OIL BEFORE
ASSEMBLY

FIG. 127 Installation of the one piece seal — 1985-92 OHV engines

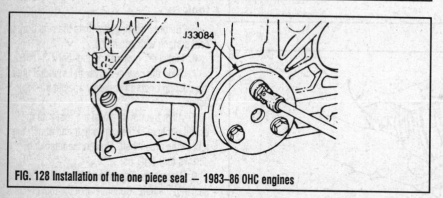

J33084

FIG. 128 Installation of the one piece seal — 1983-86 OHC engines

7. Use new bolts and install the flywheel and torque the bolts to 44 ft. lbs. (1983-86) or 48 ft. lbs. plus a 30° turn (1987-92).

8. On automatic transaxle models, install the flexplate and torque to 48 ft. lbs.

9. Install the pressure plate and disc, if equipped with manual transaxle.

10. Install the transaxle assembly as outlined in Section 7.

2.8L and 3.1L V6 Engines

1985-92

1. Support the engine with J-28467 engine support or equivalent.

2. Remove the transmission as outlined in Section 7.

3. Remove the flywheel.

➡ **Now is the time to confirm that the rear seal is leaking.**

4. Insert a suitable pry tool in through the dust lip and pry out the seal by moving the tool around the seal until it is removed.

✳✳ WARNING

Use care not to damage the crankshaft seal surface with a pry tool.

5. Before installing, lubricate the seal bore to seal surface with engine oil.

6. Install the new seal using tool J-34686.

7. Slide the new seal over the mandrel until the dust lip bottoms squarely against the tool collar.

8. Align the dowel pin of the tool with the dowel pin hole in the crankshaft and attach the tool to the crankshaft. Tighten the attaching screws to 2-5 ft. lbs.

9. Tighten the T-handle of the tool to push the seal into the bore. Continue until the tool collar is flush against the block.

10. Loosen the T-handle completely. Remove the attaching screws and the tool.

➡ **Check to see that the seal is squarely seated in the bore.**

11. Install the flywheel and transmission.

12. Start the engine and check for leaks.

EXHAUST SYSTEM

Safety Precautions

For a number of reasons, exhaust system work can be the most dangerous type of work you can do on your car. Always observe the following precautions:

• Support the car extra securely. Not only will you often be working directly under it, but you'll frequently be using a lot of force, say, heavy hammer blows, to dislodge rusted parts. This

can cause a car that's improperly supported to shift and possibly fall.

• Wear goggles. Exhaust system parts are always rusty. Metal chips can be dislodged, even when you're only turning rusted bolts. Attempting to pry pipes apart with a chisel makes the chips fly even more frequently.

• If you're using a cutting torch, keep it a great distance from either the fuel tank or lines. Stop what you're doing and feel the temperature

of the fuel bearing pipes on the tank frequently. Even slight heat can expand and/or vaporize fuel, resulting in accumulated vapor, or even a liquid leak, near your torch.

• Watch where your hammer blows fall and make sure you hit squarely. You could easily tap a brake or fuel line when you hit an exhaust system part with a glancing blow. Inspect all lines and hoses in the area where you've been working.

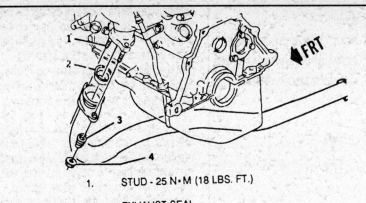

1.   STUD - 25 N•M (18 LBS. FT.)

2.   EXHAUST SEAL

3.   SPRING

4.   NUT - 35 N•M (26 LBS. FT.)

FIG. 129 Manifold attachment — 2.2L (VIN 4) engine code

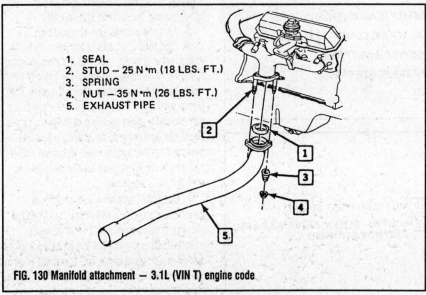

1.   SEAL
2.   STUD — 25 N•m (18 LBS. FT.)
3.   SPRING
4.   NUT — 35 N•m (26 LBS. FT.)
5.   EXHAUST PIPE

FIG. 130 Manifold attachment — 3.1L (VIN T) engine code

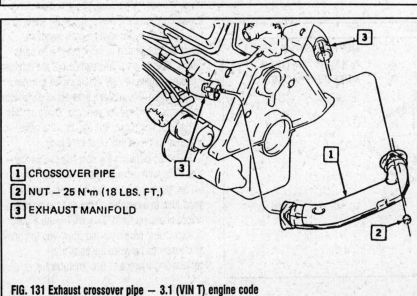

1. CROSSOVER PIPE

2. NUT — 25 N•m (18 LBS. FT.)

3. EXHAUST MANIFOLD

FIG. 131 Exhaust crossover pipe — 3.1 (VIN T) engine code

✳✳ CAUTION

Be very careful when working on or near the catalytic converter. External temperatures can reach 1,500°F (816°C) and more, causing severe burns. Removal or installation should be performed only on a cold exhaust system.

Special Tools

A number of special exhaust system tools can be rented from auto supply houses or local stores that rent special equipment. A common one is a tail pipe expander, designed to enable you to join pipes of identical diameter.

It may also be quite helpful to use solvents designed to loosen rusted bolts or flanges. Soaking rusted parts the night before you do the job can speed the work of freeing rusted parts considerably. Remember that these solvents are often flammable. Apply only to parts after they are cool!

COMPONENT RE-PLACEMENT

▶ SEE FIGS. 129-136

System components may be welded or clamped together. The system consists of a head pipe, catalytic converter, intermediate pipe, muffler and tail pipe, in that order from the engine to the back of the car.

The head pipe is bolted to the exhaust manifold, except on turbocharged engines, in which case it is bolted to the turbocharger outlet elbow. Various hangers suspend the system from the floor pan. When assembling exhaust system parts, the relative clearances around all system parts is extremely critical. Observe all clearances during assembly. In the event that the system is welded, the various parts will have to be cut apart for removal. In these cases, the cut parts may not be reused. To cut the parts, a hacksaw is the best choice. An oxy-acetylene cutting torch may be faster but the sparks are DANGEROUS near the fuel tank, and, at the very least, accidents could happen, resulting in damage to other under-car parts, not to mention yourself!

The following replacement steps relate to clamped parts:

1. Raise and support the car on jackstands.

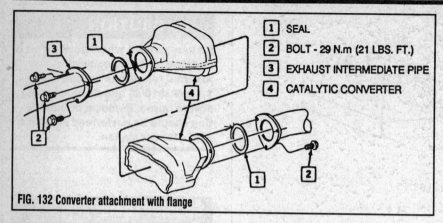

1. SEAL
2. BOLT - 29 N.m (21 LBS. FT.)
3. EXHAUST INTERMEDIATE PIPE
4. CATALYTIC CONVERTER

FIG. 132 Converter attachment with flange

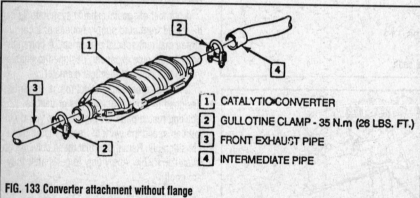

1. CATALYTIC CONVERTER
2. GULLOTINE CLAMP - 35 N.m (26 LBS. FT.)
3. FRONT EXHAUST PIPE
4. INTERMEDIATE PIPE

FIG. 133 Converter attachment without flange

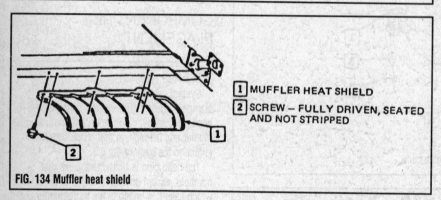

1. MUFFLER HEAT SHIELD
2. SCREW – FULLY DRIVEN, SEATED AND NOT STRIPPED

FIG. 134 Muffler heat shield

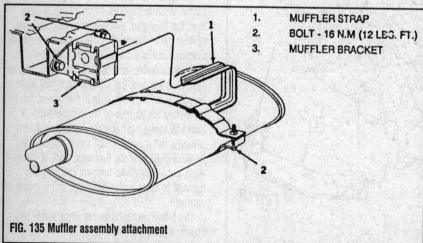

1. MUFFLER STRAP
2. BOLT - 16 N.M (12 LBS. FT.)
3. MUFFLER BRACKET

FIG. 135 Muffler assembly attachment

It's much easier on you if you can get the car up on 4 stands. Some pipes need lots of clearance for removal and installation. If the system has been in the car for a long time, spray the clamped joints with a rust dissolving solutions such as WD-40® or Liquid Wrench®, and let it set according to the instructions on the can.

2. Remove the nuts from the U-bolts; don't be surprised if the U-bolts break while removing the nuts. Age and rust account for this. Besides, you shouldn't reuse old U-bolts. When unbolting the headpipe from the exhaust manifold, make sure that the bolts are free before trying to remove them. If you snap a stud in the exhaust manifold, the stud will have to be removed with a bolt extractor, which often necessitates the removal of the manifold itself. On J-cars, the headpipe uses a necked collar for sealing purposes at the manifold, eliminating the need for a gasket. On turbocharged engines, however, a gasket is used at the joint between the headpipe and the turbocharger outlet.

3. After the clamps are removed from the joints, first twist the parts at the joints to break loose rust and scale, then pull the components apart with a twisting motion. If the parts twist freely but won't pull apart, check the joint. The clamp may have been installed so tightly that it has caused a slight crushing of the joint. In this event, the best thing to do is secure a chisel designed for the purpose and, using the chisel and a hammer, peel back the female pipe end until the parts are freed.

4. Once the parts are freed, check the condition of the pipes which you had intended keeping. If their condition is at all in doubt, replace them too. You went to a lot of work to get one or more components out. You don't want to have to go through that again in the near future. If you are retaining a pipe, check the pipe end. If it was crushed by a clamp, it can be restored to its original diameter using a pipe expander, which can be rented at most good auto parts stores. Check, also, the condition of the exhaust system hangers. If ANY deterioration is noted, replace them. Oh, and one note about parts: use only parts designed for your car. Don't use fits-all parts or flex pipes. The fits-all parts never fit and the flex pipes don't last very long.

5. When installing the new parts, coat the pipe ends with exhaust system lubricant. It makes fitting the parts much easier. It's also a good idea to assemble all the parts in position before clamping them. This will ensure a good fit, detect any problems and allow you to check all clearances between the parts and surrounding frame and floor members.

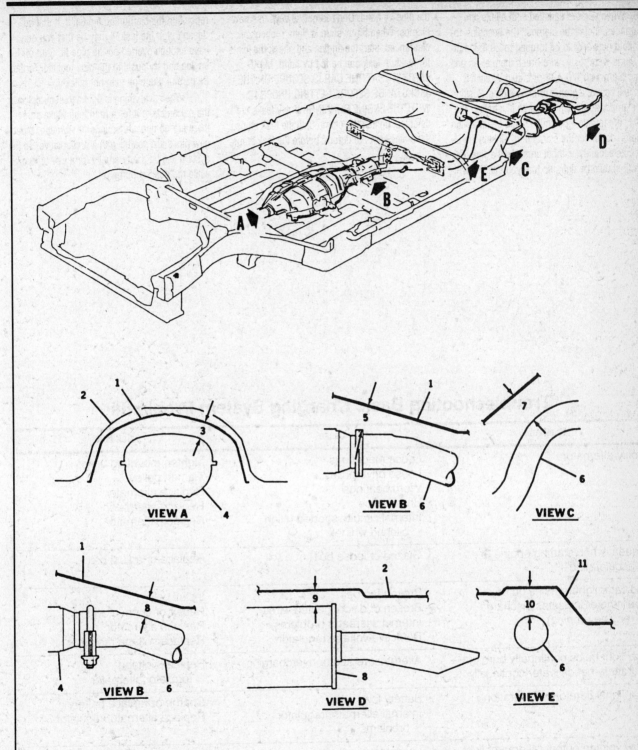

1. CONVERTER SHIELD
2. UNDERBODY
3. 18 MM TO 35 MM (3/4" TO 1-9/16")
4. CONVERTER
5. 11 MM MIN. (7/16")
6. INTERMEDIATE EXHAUST PIPE
7. 42 MM TO 54 MM (1-11/16" TO 2-3/16")
8. 18 MM MIN. (3/4")
9. 15 MM TO 35 MM (5/8" TO 1-9/16")
10. 30 MM MIN. (1-7/32")
11. FUEL TANK

FIG. 136 Exhaust system to body clearance — 1992 Cavalier

6. When you are satisfied with all fits and clearances, install the clamps. The headpipe-to-manifold nuts should be torqued to 20 ft. lbs. If the studs were rusty, wire-brush them clean and spray them with WD-40® or Liquid Wrench®. This will ensure a proper torque reading. Position the clamps on the slip points as illustrated. The slits in the female pipe ends should be under the U-bolts, not under the clamp end. Tighten the U-bolt nuts securely, without crushing the pipe. The pipe fit should be tight, so that you can't swivel the pipe by hand. Don't forget: always use new clamps. When the system is tight, recheck all clearances. Start the engine and check the joints for leaks. A leak can be felt by hand. MAKE CERTAIN THAT THE CAR IS SECURE ON THE JACKSTANDS BEFORE GETTING UNDER IT WITH THE ENGINE RUNNING!! If any leaks are detected, tighten the clamp until the leak stops. If the pipe starts to deform before the leak stops, reposition the clamp and tighten it. If that still doesn't stop the leak, it may be that you don't have enough overlap on the pipe fit. Shut off the engine and try pushing the pipe together further. Be careful; the pipe gets hot quickly.

7. When everything is tight and secure, lower the car and take it for a road test. Make sure there are no unusual sounds or vibration. Most new pipes are coated with a preservative, so the system will be pretty smelly for a day or two while the coating burns off.

Troubleshooting Basic Charging System Problems

Problem	Cause	Solution
Noisy alternator	• Loose mountings • Loose drive pulley • Worn bearings • Brush noise • Internal circuits shorted (High pitched whine)	• Tighten mounting bolts • Tighten pulley • Replace alternator • Replace alternator • Replace alternator
Squeal when starting engine or accelerating	• Glazed or loose belt	• Replace or adjust belt
Indicator light remains on or ammeter indicates discharge (engine running)	• Broken fan belt • Broken or disconnected wires • Internal alternator problems • Defective voltage regulator	• Install belt • Repair or connect wiring • Replace alternator • Replace voltage regulator
Car light bulbs continually burn out—battery needs water continually	• Alternator/regulator overcharging	• Replace voltage regulator/alternator
Car lights flare on acceleration	• Battery low • Internal alternator/regulator problems	• Charge or replace battery • Replace alternator/regulator
Low voltage output (alternator light flickers continually or ammeter needle wanders)	• Loose or worn belt • Dirty or corroded connections • Internal alternator/regulator problems	• Replace or adjust belt • Clean or replace connections • Replace alternator or regulator

Troubleshooting Basic Starting System Problems

Problem	Cause	Solution
Starter motor rotates engine slowly	• Battery charge low or battery defective	• Charge or replace battery
	• Defective circuit between battery and starter motor	• Clean and tighten, or replace cables
	• Low load current	• Bench-test starter motor. Inspect for worn brushes and weak brush springs.
	• High load current	• Bench-test starter motor. Check engine for friction, drag or coolant in cylinders. Check ring gear-to-pinion gear clearance.
Starter motor will not rotate engine	• Battery charge low or battery defective	• Charge or replace battery
	• Faulty solenoid	• Check solenoid ground. Repair or replace as necessary.
	• Damage drive pinion gear or ring gear	• Replace damaged gear(s)
	• Starter motor engagement weak	• Bench-test starter motor
	• Starter motor rotates slowly with high load current	• Inspect drive yoke pull-down and point gap, check for worn end bushings, check ring gear clearance
	• Engine seized	• Repair engine
Starter motor drive will not engage (solenoid known to be good)	• Defective contact point assembly	• Repair or replace contact point assembly
	• Inadequate contact point assembly ground	• Repair connection at ground screw
	• Defective hold-in coil	• Replace field winding assembly
Starter motor drive will not disengage	• Starter motor loose on flywheel housing	• Tighten mounting bolts
	• Worn drive end busing	• Replace bushing
	• Damaged ring gear teeth	• Replace ring gear or driveplate
	• Drive yoke return spring broken or missing	• Replace spring
Starter motor drive disengages prematurely	• Weak drive assembly thrust spring	• Replace drive mechanism
	• Hold-in coil defective	• Replace field winding assembly
Low load current	• Worn brushes	• Replace brushes
	• Weak brush springs	• Replace springs

Troubleshooting Engine Mechanical Problems

Problem	Cause	Solution
External oil leaks	• Fuel pump gasket broken or improperly seated	• Replace gasket
	• Cylinder head cover RTV sealant broken or improperly seated	• Replace sealant; inspect cylinder head cover sealant flange and cylinder head sealant surface for distortion and cracks
	• Oil filler cap leaking or missing	• Replace cap
External oil leaks	• Oil filter gasket broken or improperly seated	• Replace oil filter
	• Oil pan side gasket broken, improperly seated or opening in RTV sealant	• Replace gasket or repair opening in sealant; inspect oil pan gasket flange for distortion
	• Oil pan front oil seal broken or improperly seated	• Replace seal; inspect timing case cover and oil pan seal flange for distortion
	• Oil pan rear oil seal broken or improperly seated	• Replace seal; inspect oil pan rear oil seal flange; inspect rear main bearing cap for cracks, plugged oil return channels, or distortion in seal groove
	• Timing case cover oil seal broken or improperly seated	• Replace seal
	• Excess oil pressure because of restricted PCV valve	• Replace PCV valve
	• Oil pan drain plug loose or has stripped threads	• Repair as necessary and tighten
	• Rear oil gallery plug loose	• Use appropriate sealant on gallery plug and tighten
	• Rear camshaft plug loose or improperly seated	• Seat camshaft plug or replace and seal, as necessary
	• Distributor base gasket damaged	• Replace gasket
Excessive oil consumption	• Oil level too high	• Drain oil to specified level
	• Oil with wrong viscosity being used	• Replace with specified oil
	• PCV valve stuck closed	• Replace PCV valve
	• Valve stem oil deflectors (or seals) are damaged, missing, or incorrect type	• Replace valve stem oil deflectors
	• Valve stems or valve guides worn	• Measure stem-to-guide clearance and repair as necessary
	• Poorly fitted or missing valve cover baffles	• Replace valve cover
	• Piston rings broken or missing	• Replace broken or missing rings
	• Scuffed piston	• Replace piston
	• Incorrect piston ring gap	• Measure ring gap, repair as necessary
	• Piston rings sticking or excessively loose in grooves	• Measure ring side clearance, repair as necessary
	• Compression rings installed upside down	• Repair as necessary
	• Cylinder walls worn, scored, or glazed	• Repair as necessary

Troubleshooting Engine Mechanical Problems (cont.)

Problem	Cause	Solution
	• Piston ring gaps not properly staggered	• Repair as necessary
	• Excessive main or connecting rod bearing clearance	• Measure bearing clearance, repair as necessary
No oil pressure	• Low oil level	• Add oil to correct level
	• Oil pressure gauge, warning lamp or sending unit inaccurate	• Replace oil pressure gauge or warning lamp
	• Oil pump malfunction	• Replace oil pump
	• Oil pressure relief valve sticking	• Remove and inspect oil pressure relief valve assembly
	• Oil passages on pressure side of pump obstructed	• Inspect oil passages for obstruction
	• Oil pickup screen or tube obstructed	• Inspect oil pickup for obstruction
	• Loose oil inlet tube	• Tighten or seal inlet tube
Low oil pressure	• Low oil level	• Add oil to correct level
	• Inaccurate gauge, warning lamp or sending unit	• Replace oil pressure gauge or warning lamp
	• Oil excessively thin because of dilution, poor quality, or improper grade	• Drain and refill crankcase with recommended oil
	• Excessive oil temperature	• Correct cause of overheating engine
	• Oil pressure relief spring weak or sticking	• Remove and inspect oil pressure relief valve assembly
	• Oil inlet tube and screen assembly has restriction or air leak	• Remove and inspect oil inlet tube and screen assembly. (Fill inlet tube with lacquer thinner to locate leaks.)
	• Excessive oil pump clearance	• Measure clearances
	• Excessive main, rod, or camshaft bearing clearance	• Measure bearing clearances, repair as necessary
High oil pressure	• Improper oil viscosity	• Drain and refill crankcase with correct viscosity oil
	• Oil pressure gauge or sending unit inaccurate	• Replace oil pressure gauge
	• Oil pressure relief valve sticking closed	• Remove and inspect oil pressure relief valve assembly
Main bearing noise	• Insufficient oil supply	• Inspect for low oil level and low oil pressure
	• Main bearing clearance excessive	• Measure main bearing clearance, repair as necessary
	• Bearing insert missing	• Replace missing insert
	• Crankshaft end play excessive	• Measure end play, repair as necessary
	• Improperly tightened main bearing cap bolts	• Tighten bolts with specified torque
	• Loose flywheel or drive plate	• Tighten flywheel or drive plate attaching bolts
	• Loose or damaged vibration damper	• Repair as necessary

Troubleshooting Engine Mechanical Problems (cont.)

Problem	Cause	Solution
Connecting rod bearing noise	• Insufficient oil supply	• Inspect for low oil level and low oil pressure
	• Carbon build-up on piston	• Remove carbon from piston crown
	• Bearing clearance excessive or bearing missing	• Measure clearance, repair as necessary
	• Crankshaft connecting rod journal out-of-round	• Measure journal dimensions, repair or replace as necessary
	• Misaligned connecting rod or cap	• Repair as necessary
	• Connecting rod bolts tightened improperly	• Tighten bolts with specified torque
Piston noise	• Piston-to-cylinder wall clearance excessive (scuffed piston)	• Measure clearance and examine piston
	• Cylinder walls excessively tapered or out-of-round	• Measure cylinder wall dimensions, rebore cylinder
	• Piston ring broken	• Replace all rings on piston
	• Loose or seized piston pin	• Measure piston-to-pin clearance, repair as necessary
	• Connecting rods misaligned	• Measure rod alignment, straighten or replace
	• Piston ring side clearance excessively loose or tight	• Measure ring side clearance, repair as necessary
	• Carbon build-up on piston is excessive	• Remove carbon from piston
Valve actuating component noise	• Insufficient oil supply	• Check for: (a) Low oil level (b) Low oil pressure (c) Plugged push rods (d) Wrong hydraulic tappets (e) Restricted oil gallery (f) Excessive tappet to bore clearance
	• Push rods worn or bent	• Replace worn or bent push rods
	• Rocker arms or pivots worn	• Replace worn rocker arms or pivots
	• Foreign objects or chips in hydraulic tappets	• Clean tappets
	• Excessive tappet leak-down	• Replace valve tappet
	• Tappet face worn	• Replace tappet; inspect corresponding cam lobe for wear
	• Broken or cocked valve springs	• Properly seat cocked springs; replace broken springs
	• Stem-to-guide clearance excessive	• Measure stem-to-guide clearance, repair as required
	• Valve bent	• Replace valve
	• Loose rocker arms	• Tighten bolts with specified torque
	• Valve seat runout excessive	• Regrind valve seat/valves
	• Missing valve lock	• Install valve lock
	• Push rod rubbing or contacting cylinder head	• Remove cylinder head and remove obstruction in head
	• Excessive engine oil (four-cylinder engine)	• Correct oil level

Troubleshooting the Cooling System

Problem	Cause	Solution
High temperature gauge indication—overheating	• Coolant level low	• Replenish coolant
	• Fan belt loose	• Adjust fan belt tension
	• Radiator hose(s) collapsed	• Replace hose(s)
	• Radiator airflow blocked	• Remove restriction (bug screen, fog lamps, etc.)
	• Faulty radiator cap	• Replace radiator cap
	• Ignition timing incorrect	• Adjust ignition timing
	• Idle speed low	• Adjust idle speed
	• Air trapped in cooling system	• Purge air
	• Heavy traffic driving	• Operate at fast idle in neutral intermittently to cool engine
	• Incorrect cooling system component(s) installed	• Install proper component(s)
	• Faulty thermostat	• Replace thermostat
	• Water pump shaft broken or impeller loose	• Replace water pump
	• Radiator tubes clogged	• Flush radiator
	• Cooling system clogged	• Flush system
	• Casting flash in cooling passages	• Repair or replace as necessary. Flash may be visible by removing cooling system components or removing core plugs.
	• Brakes dragging	• Repair brakes
	• Excessive engine friction	• Repair engine
	• Antifreeze concentration over 68%	• Lower antifreeze concentration percentage
	• Missing air seals	• Replace air seals
	• Faulty gauge or sending unit	• Repair or replace faulty component
	• Loss of coolant flow caused by leakage or foaming	• Repair or replace leaking component, replace coolant
	• Viscous fan drive failed	• Replace unit
Low temperature indication—undercooling	• Thermostat stuck open	• Replace thermostat
	• Faulty gauge or sending unit	• Repair or replace faulty component
Coolant loss—boilover	• Overfilled cooling system	• Reduce coolant level to proper specification
	• Quick shutdown after hard (hot) run	• Allow engine to run at fast idle prior to shutdown
	• Air in system resulting in occasional "burping" of coolant	• Purge system
	• Insufficient antifreeze allowing coolant boiling point to be too low	• Add antifreeze to raise boiling point
	• Antifreeze deteriorated because of age or contamination	• Replace coolant
	• Leaks due to loose hose clamps, loose nuts, bolts, drain plugs, faulty hoses, or defective radiator	• Pressure test system to locate source of leak(s) then repair as necessary

Troubleshooting the Cooling System (cont.)

Problem	Cause	Solution
Coolant loss—boilover	• Faulty head gasket • Cracked head, manifold, or block • Faulty radiator cap	• Replace head gasket • Replace as necessary • Replace cap
Coolant entry into crankcase or cylinder(s)	• Faulty head gasket • Crack in head, manifold or block	• Replace head gasket • Replace as necessary
Coolant recovery system inoperative	• Coolant level low • Leak in system • Pressure cap not tight or seal missing, or leaking • Pressure cap defective • Overflow tube clogged or leaking • Recovery bottle vent restricted	• Replenish coolant to FULL mark • Pressure test to isolate leak and repair as necessary • Repair as necessary • Replace cap • Repair as necessary • Remove restriction
Noise	• Fan contacting shroud • Loose water pump impeller • Glazed fan belt • Loose fan belt • Rough surface on drive pulley • Water pump bearing worn • Belt alignment	• Reposition shroud and inspect engine mounts • Replace pump • Apply silicone or replace belt • Adjust fan belt tension • Replace pulley • Remove belt to isolate. Replace pump. • Check pulley alignment. Repair as necessary.
No coolant flow through heater core	• Restricted return inlet in water pump • Heater hose collapsed or restricted • Restricted heater core • Restricted outlet in thermostat housing • Intake manifold bypass hole in cylinder head restricted • Faulty heater control valve • Intake manifold coolant passage restricted	• Remove restriction • Remove restriction or replace hose • Remove restriction or replace core • Remove flash or restriction • Remove restriction • Replace valve • Remove restriction or replace intake manifold

NOTE: *Immediately after shutdown, the engine enters a condition known as heat soak. This is caused by the cooling system being inoperative while engine temperature is still high. If coolant temperature rises above boiling point, expansion and pressure may push some coolant out of the radiator overflow tube. If this does not occur frequently it is considered normal.*

Troubleshooting the Serpentine Drive Belt

Problem	Cause	Solution
Tension sheeting fabric failure (woven fabric on outside circumference of belt has cracked or separated from body of belt)	• Grooved or backside idler pulley diameters are less than minimum recommended • Tension sheeting contacting (rubbing) stationary object • Excessive heat causing woven fabric to age • Tension sheeting splice has fractured	• Replace pulley(s) not conforming to specification • Correct rubbing condition • Replace belt • Replace belt
Noise (objectional squeal, squeak, or rumble is heard or felt while drive belt is in operation)	• Belt slippage • Bearing noise • Belt misalignment • Belt-to-pulley mismatch • Driven component inducing vibration • System resonant frequency inducing vibration	• Adjust belt • Locate and repair • Align belt/pulley(s) • Install correct belt • Locate defective driven component and repair • Vary belt tension within specifications. Replace belt.
Rib chunking (one or more ribs has separated from belt body)	• Foreign objects imbedded in pulley grooves • Installation damage • Drive loads in excess of design specifications • Insufficient internal belt adhesion	• Remove foreign objects from pulley grooves • Replace belt • Adjust belt tension • Replace belt
Rib or belt wear (belt ribs contact bottom of pulley grooves)	• Pulley(s) misaligned • Mismatch of belt and pulley groove widths • Abrasive environment • Rusted pulley(s) • Sharp or jagged pulley groove tips • Rubber deteriorated	• Align pulley(s) • Replace belt • Replace belt • Clean rust from pulley(s) • Replace pulley • Replace belt
Longitudinal belt cracking (cracks between two ribs)	• Belt has mistracked from pulley groove • Pulley groove tip has worn away rubber-to-tensile member	• Replace belt • Replace belt
Belt slips	• Belt slipping because of insufficient tension • Belt or pulley subjected to substance (belt dressing, oil, ethylene glycol) that has reduced friction • Driven component bearing failure • Belt glazed and hardened from heat and excessive slippage	• Adjust tension • Replace belt and clean pulleys • Replace faulty component bearing • Replace belt
"Groove jumping" (belt does not maintain correct position on pulley, or turns over and/or runs off pulleys)	• Insufficient belt tension • Pulley(s) not within design tolerance • Foreign object(s) in grooves	• Adjust belt tension • Replace pulley(s) • Remove foreign objects from grooves

Troubleshooting the Serpentine Drive Belt (cont.)

Problem	Cause	Solution
"Groove jumping" (belt does not maintain correct position on pulley, or turns over and/or runs off pulleys)	• Excessive belt speed • Pulley misalignment • Belt-to-pulley profile mismatched • Belt cordline is distorted	• Avoid excessive engine acceleration • Align pulley(s) • Install correct belt • Replace belt
Belt broken (Note: identify and correct problem before replacement belt is installed)	• Excessive tension • Tensile members damaged during belt installation • Belt turnover • Severe pulley misalignment • Bracket, pulley, or bearing failure	• Replace belt and adjust tension to specification • Replace belt • Replace belt • Align pulley(s) • Replace defective component and belt
Cord edge failure (tensile member exposed at edges of belt or separated from belt body)	• Excessive tension • Drive pulley misalignment • Belt contacting stationary object • Pulley irregularities • Improper pulley construction • Insufficient adhesion between tensile member and rubber matrix	• Adjust belt tension • Align pulley • Correct as necessary • Replace pulley • Replace pulley • Replace belt and adjust tension to specifications
Sporadic rib cracking (multiple cracks in belt ribs at random intervals)	• Ribbed pulley(s) diameter less than minimum specification • Backside bend flat pulley(s) diameter less than minimum • Excessive heat condition causing rubber to harden • Excessive belt thickness • Belt overcured • Excessive tension	• Replace pulley(s) • Replace pulley(s) • Correct heat condition as necessary • Replace belt • Replace belt • Adjust belt tension

TORQUE SPECIFICATIONS

Component	U.S.	Metric
1982 1.8L OHV V.I.N. CODE G		
Camshaft sprocket:	66-85 ft. lbs.	90-115 Nm
Cylinder head:	66-75 ft. lbs.	88-107 Nm
Connecting rod cap:	34-40 ft. lbs.	46-54 Nm
Crankshaft pulley:	20-30 ft. lbs.	27-41 Nm
Crankshaft pulley hub:	66-84 ft. lbs.	90-115 Nm
Exhaust manifold:	22-28 ft. lbs.	30-38 Nm
Flywheel:	45-55 ft. lbs.	61-75 Nm
Intake manifold:	20-25 ft. lbs.	27-34 Nm
Main bearing caps:	63-74 ft. lbs.	27-34 Nm
Transaxle-to-engine block:	48-63 ft. lbs.	65-85 Nm

TORQUE SPECIFICATIONS

Component	U.S.	Metric
1982-83 2.0L OHV V.I.N. CODE B		
Camshaft sprocket:	66-85 ft. lbs.	90-115 Nm
Cylinder head:	66-75 ft. lbs.	88-107 Nm
Connecting rod cap:	34-40 ft. lbs.	46-54 Nm
Crankshaft pulley:	20-30 ft. lbs.	27-41 Nm
Crankshaft pulley hub:	66-84 ft. lbs.	90-115 Nm
Exhaust manifold:	22-28 ft. lbs.	30-38 Nm
Flywheel:	45-55 ft. lbs.	61-75 Nm
Intake manifold:	20-25 ft. lbs.	27-34 Nm
Main bearing caps:	63-74 ft. lbs.	27-34 Nm
Transaxle-to-engine block:	48-63 ft. lbs.	65-85 Nm
1983-86 2.0L OHV V.I.N. CODE P		
Camshaft sprocket:	66-85 ft. lbs.	90-115 Nm
Cylinder head:	66-75 ft. lbs.	88-107 Nm
Connecting rod cap:	34-40 ft. lbs.	46-54 Nm
Crankshaft pulley:	20-30 ft. lbs.	27-41 Nm
Crankshaft pulley hub:	66-84 ft. lbs.	90-115 Nm
Exhaust manifold:	22-28 ft. lbs.	30-38 Nm
Flywheel:	45-55 ft. lbs.	61-75 Nm
Intake manifold:	20-25 ft. lbs.	27-34 Nm
Main bearing caps:	63-74 ft. lbs.	27-34 Nm
Transaxle-to-engine block:	48-63 ft. lbs.	65-85 Nm
1983-86 1.8L OHC V.I.N. CODES 0 AND J		
Camshaft carrier cover bolts:	5 ft. lbs.	7 Nm
Camshaft carrier and cylinder head attaching bolts:	See Text	
Camshaft sprocket retaining bolt:	34 ft. lbs.	45 Nm
Camshaft thrust plate bolts:	70 inch lbs.	8 Nm
Crankshaft pulley to sprocket bolts:	20 ft. lbs.	27 Nm
Crankshaft sprocket to retaining bolt:	107 ft. lbs. plus 45° rotation	145 Nm
Connecting rod cap bolts:	39 ft. lbs.	53 Nm
Exhaust manifold-to-cylinder head:	16 ft. lbs.	22 Nm
Flywheel retaining bolts:	45 ft. lbs.	60 Nm
Intake manifold-to-cylinder head:	25 ft. lbs.	34 Nm
Main bearing cap bolts:	57 ft. lbs.	77 Nm
Water pump retaining bolts:	19 ft. lbs.	25 Nm
1985-89 2.8L OHV V.I.N. CODE W		
Camshaft sprocket:	15-20 ft. lbs.	20-27 Nm
Cylinder head assembly:	See Text	
Camshaft rear cover:	6-9 ft. lbs.	8-12 Nm
Connecting rod caps:	34-40 ft. lbs.	46-54 Nm
Exhaust manifold:	15-23 ft. lbs.	20-30 Nm
Water pump:	6-9 ft. lbs.	8-12 Nm
Intake manifold:	25 ft. lbs.	32 Nm
Timing chain dampener:	14-19 ft. lbs.	18-24 Nm
Rocker arm nuts:	15-20 ft. lbs.	20-27 Nm

TORQUE SPECIFICATIONS

Component	U.S.	Metric
Oil pan retaining bolts		
Size M8 bolts:	15-23 ft. lbs.	20-30 Nm
Size M6 bolts:	6-9 ft. lbs.	8-22 Nm
Main bearing caps:	63-83 ft. lbs.	85-112 Nm

1987-89 2.0L OHV V.I.N. CODE 1

Component	U.S.	Metric
Camshaft thrust plate:	4-14 ft. lbs.	6-18 Nm
Camshaft sprocket:	66-88 ft. lbs.	90-120 Nm
Connecting rod cap:	34-43 ft. lbs.	46-58 Nm
Crankshaft pulley center:	66-89 ft. lbs.	90-120 Nm
Cylinder head (long):	73-83 ft. lbs.	99-113 Nm
Cylinder head (short):	62-70 ft. lbs.	85-95 Nm
Exhaust manifold:	6-13 ft. lbs.	8-18 Nm
Intake manifold:	15-22 ft. lbs.	20-30 Nm
Main bearing caps:	63-77 ft. lbs.	85-105 Nm
Rocker arm nut:	11-18 ft. lbs.	15-25 Nm
Water pump:	15-22 ft. lbs.	20-30 Nm

1987-91 2.0L OHC V.I.N. CODES K AND M

Component	U.S.	Metric
Camshaft carrier cover bolts:	6 ft. lbs.	8 Nm
Camshaft carrier and cylinder head attaching bolts:	See Text	
Camshaft sprocket retaining bolt:	34 ft. lbs.	45 Nm
Camshaft thrust plate bolts:	70 inch lbs.	8 Nm
Crankshaft pulley to sprocket bolts:	20 ft. lbs.	27 Nm
Crankshaft sprocket to retaining bolt:	107 ft. lbs. plus 45° rotation	145 Nm
Connecting rod cap bolts:	26 ft. lbs. plus a 40-45° turn	53 Nm
Exhaust manifold-to-cylinder head:	16 ft. lbs.	22 Nm
Flywheel retaining bolts:	48 ft. lbs. plus a 30° turn	60 Nm
Intake manifold-to-cylinder head:	16 ft. lbs.	22 Nm
Main bearing cap bolts:	44 ft. lbs. plus a 40-50° turn	77 Nm
Water pump retaining bolts:	19 ft. lbs.	25 Nm

1990-91 2.2L OHV V.I.N. CODE G

Component	U.S.	Metric
Camshaft thrust plate:	106 inch lbs.	12 Nm
Camshaft sprocket:	77 ft. lbs.	105 Nm
Connecting rod cap:	38 ft. lbs.	52 Nm
Crankshaft pulley and hub bolt:	77 ft. lbs.	105 Nm
Cylinder head assembly:	See Text	
Exhaust manifold:	115 inch lbs.	13 Nm
Intake manifold:	18 ft. lbs.	25 Nm
Main bearing caps:	70 ft. lbs.	95 Nm
Rocker arm nut:	22 ft. lbs.	30 Nm
Water pump:	18 ft. lbs.	25 Nm
Serpentine drive belt tensioner:	37 ft. lbs.	50 Nm

TORQUE SPECIFICATIONS

Component	U.S.	Metric
1990-92 3.1L OHV V.I.N. CODE T		
Exhaust manifold to cylinder head:	18 ft. lbs.	25 Nm
Rocker arm nut:	18 ft. lbs.	25 Nm
Crankshaft balancer assembly:	76 ft. lbs.	103 Nm
Camshaft sprocket bolt:	21 ft. lbs.	28 Nm
Timing chain dampener bolt:	15 ft. lbs.	21 Nm
Connecting rod nut:	39 ft. lbs.	53 Nm
Main bearing cap bolt:	73 ft. lbs.	99 Nm
Intake manifold assembly:	See Text	
Cylinder head assembly:	See Text	
Oil pan retaining nuts and bolts:	89 inch lbs.	10 Nm
1992 2.0L OHC V.I.N. CODE H		
Camshaft carrier cover bolts:	84 inch lbs.	9.5 Nm
Camshaft carrier and cylinder head attaching bolts:	See Text	
Camshaft sprocket retaining bolt:	34 ft. lbs.	45 Nm
Camshaft thrust plate bolts:	71 inch lbs.	8 Nm
Crankshaft pulley to sprocket bolts:	15 ft. lbs.	21 Nm
Crankshaft sprocket to retaining bolt:	114 ft. lbs.	155 Nm
Connecting rod cap bolts:	26 ft. lbs. plus a 40-45° turn	53 Nm
Exhaust manifold-to-cylinder head:	16 ft. lbs.	22 Nm
Flywheel retaining bolts:	48 ft. lbs. plus a 30° turn	65 Nm
Intake manifold-to-cylinder head:	16 ft. lbs.	22 Nm
Main bearing cap bolts:	44 ft. lbs. plus a 40-50° turn	60 Nm
Serpentine drive belt tensioner:	35 ft. lbs.	48 Nm
1992 2.2L OHV V.I.N. CODE 4		
Camshaft thrust plate:	106 inch lbs.	12 Nm
Camshaft sprocket:	77 ft. lbs.	105 Nm
Connecting rod cap:	38 ft. lbs.	52 Nm
Crankshaft pulley and hub bolt:	77 ft. lbs.	105 Nm
Cylinder head assembly:	See Text	
Exhaust manifold:	115 inch lbs.	13 Nm
Intake manifold:	22 ft. lbs.	30 Nm
Main bearing caps:	70 ft. lbs.	95 Nm
Rocker arm nut:	22 ft. lbs.	30 Nm
Water pump:	18 ft. lbs.	25 Nm
Serpentine drive belt tensioner:	37 ft. lbs.	50 Nm

ENGINE MECHANICAL SPECIFICATIONS

Component	U.S.	Metric
1982 1.8L OHV V.I.N. CODE G		
Piston clearance:	0.0079-0.0181 in.	0.020-0.046 mm
Piston ring		
Compression (groove clearance):		
Top	0.0012-0.0027 in.	0.030-0.068 mm
2nd	0.0012-0.0027 in.	0.030-0.068 mm
Gap		
Top	0.0098-0.0197 in.	0.25-0.50 mm
2nd	0.0098-0.0197 in.	0.25-0.50 mm
Oil (groove clearance gap):	0.199 mm	
Piston pin		
Diameter:	0.9053-0.9056 in	22.9937-23.0015 mm
Clearance:	0.00026-0.00036 in.	0.0065-0.0091 mm
Fit in rod:	0.00075-0.0020 in.	0.019-0.052 mm (press)
Crankshaft		
Main Journal		
Diameter:	2.4937-2.4946 in	63.340-63.364 mm
Taper:	0.00019 in.	0.005 mm (max.)
Out of round:	0.00019 in.	0.005 mm (max.)
Crankshaft end play:	0.00197-0.00708 in.	0.05-0.18 mm
Crankshaft pin:		
Diameter:	1.9990-2.0000 in.	50.775-50.800 mm
Taper:	0.000197 in.	0.005 mm (max.)
Out of round:	0.000197 in.	0.005 mm (max.)
Rod bearing clearance:	0.00098-0.00311 in.	0.025-0.079 mm
Rod side clearance:	0.0039-0.0240 in.	0.10-0.61 mm
Valve lash:	1-1½ turn from zero lash	
Valve seat runout:	0.00197 in.	0.05 mm
Stem clearance		
Intake:	0.0011-0.0026 in.	0.028-0.066 mm
Exhaust:	0.0014-0.0031 in.	0.035-0.078 mm
1982-83 2.0L OHV V.I.N. CODE B		
Piston clearance:	0.00079-0.00181 in.	0.020-0.046 mm
Piston ring		
Compression (groove clearance):		
Top	0.0012-0.0268 in.	0.030-0.68 mm
2nd	0.0012-0.0268 in.	0.030-0.68 mm
Gap		
Top	0.0098-0.0197 in.	0.25-0.50 mm
2nd	0.0098-0.0197 in.	0.25-0.50 mm
Oil (groove clearance gap):	0.0078 in.	0.199 mm
Piston pin		
Diameter:	0.9053-0.9056 in.	22.9937-23.0015 mm
Clearance:	0.0026-0.0036 in.	0.0065-0.0091 mm
Fit in rod:	0.00075-0.00205 in.	0.019-0.052 mm (press)
Crankshaft		
Main Journal		
Diameter # 1, 2, 3, 4:	2.4945-2.4954 in.	63.360-63.384 mm
Diameter # 5:	2.4937-2.4946 in.	63.340-63.364 mm
Taper:	0.00019 in.	0.005 mm (max.)
Out of round:	0.00019 in.	0.005 mm (max.)
Crankshaft end play:	0.00197-0.00708 in.	0.05-0.18 mm
Crankshaft pin:		
Diameter:	1.9983-1.9994 in.	50.758-50.784 mm
Taper:	0.00019 in.	0.005 mm (max.)
Out of round:	0.00019 in.	0.005 mm (max.)
Rod bearing clearance:	0.00098-0.00311 in.	0.025-0.079 mm
Rod side clearance:	0.0039-0.0240 in.	0.10-0.61 mm

ENGINE MECHANICAL SPECIFICATIONS

Component	U.S.	Metric
Valve lash:	1-1½ turn from zero lash	
Valve seat runout:	0.0019 in.	0.05 mm
Stem clearance		
Intake:	0.0011-0.0026 in.	0.028-0.066 mm
Exhaust:	0.0014-0.0031 in.	0.035-0.078 mm
1983-86 2.0L OHV V.I.N. CODE P		
Piston clearance:	0.00079-0.00181 in.	0.020-0.046 mm
Piston ring		
Compression (groove clearance):		
Top	0.0012-0.0268 in.	0.030-0.68 mm
2nd	0.0012-0.0268 in.	0.030-0.68 mm
Gap		
Top	0.0098-0.0197 in.	0.25-0.50 mm
2nd	0.0098-0.0197 in.	0.25-0.50 mm
Oil (groove clearance gap):	0.0078 in.	0.199 mm
Piston pin		
Diameter:	0.9053-0.9056 in.	22.9937-23.0015 mm
Clearance:	0.00026-0.00036 in.	0.0065-0.0091 mm
Fit in rod:	0.00075-0.00205 in.	0.019-0.052 mm (press)
Crankshaft		
Main Journal		
Diameter # 1, 2, 3, 4:	2.4945-2.4954 in.	63.360-63.384 mm
Diameter # 5:	2.4937-2.4946 in.	63.340-63.364 mm
Taper:	0.00019 in.	0.005 mm (max.)
Out of round:	0.00019 in.	0.005 mm (max.)
Crankshaft end play:	0.0019-0.0083 in.	0.05-0.21 mm
Crankshaft pin:		
Diameter:	1.9983-1.9994 in.	50.758-50.784 mm
Taper:	0.00019 in.	0.005 mm (max.)
Out of round:	0.00019 in.	0.005 mm (max.)
Rod bearing clearance:	0.00098-0.00311 in.	0.025-0.079 mm
Rod side clearance:	0.0039-0.0240 in.	0.10-0.61 mm
Valve lash:	1-1½ turn from zero lash	
Valve seat runout:	0.0019 in.	0.05 mm
Stem clearance		
Intake:	0.0011-0.0026 in.	0.028-0.066 mm
Exhaust:	0.0014-0.0031 in.	0.035-0.078 mm
1983-86 1.8L OHC V.I.N. CODES 0 AND J		
Piston clearance		
Top (V.I.N. 0):	0-0.00079 in.	0-0.02 mm
Top (V.I.N. J):	0.00039-0.00118 in.	0.01-0.03 mm
Piston ring		
Compression (groove clearance):		
Top	0.0024-0.0036 in.	0.06-0.092 mm
2nd	0.0012-0.0024 in.	0.030-0.062 mm
Gap		
Top	0.012-0.020 in.	0.30-0.50 mm
2nd	0.012-0.020 in.	0.30-0.50 mm
Oil (groove clearance gap):	0.016-0.055 in.	0.40-1.40 mm
Piston pin		
Fit in rod:	Press	
Fit in piston:	0.00019 in.	0.005 mm

ENGINE MECHANICAL SPECIFICATIONS

Component	U.S.	Metric
Crankshaft		
Main Journal (diameter)		
Brown:	2.2829-2.2837 in.	57.988-57.995 mm
Green:	2.2828-2.2830 in.	57.982-57.988 mm
Taper:	0.00019 in.	0.005 mm (max.)
Out of round:	0.00019 in.	0.005 mm (max.)
Crankshaft end play:	0.0028-0.0118 in.	0.07-0.30 mm
Crankshaft pin:		
Diameter:	1.9280-1.9286 in.	48.971-48.987 mm
Taper:	0.00019 in.	0.005 mm (max.)
Out of round:	0.00019 in.	0.005 mm (max.)
Rod bearing clearance:	0.00075-0.02480 in.	0.019-0.063 mm
Rod side clearance:	0.0028-0.0095 in.	0.070-0.242 mm
Valve seat runout:	0.0019 in.	0.05 mm
Stem clearance		
Intake:	0.0006-0.0017 in.	0.015-0.042 mm
Exhaust:	0.0012-0.0024 in.	0.030-0.060 mm

1985-89 2.8L OHV V.I.N. CODE W

Component	U.S.	Metric
Piston clearance:	0.0022-0.0028 in.	0.057-0.072 mm
Piston ring		
Compression (groove clearance):		
1st	0.0020-0.0035 in.	0.050-0.090 mm
2nd	0.0020-0.0035 in.	0.050-0.90 mm
Gap		
1st	0.0098-0.0197 in.	0.25-0.50 mm
2nd	0.0098-0.0197 in.	0.25-0.50 mm
Oil (groove clearance gap):	0.0079 in.	0.20 mm
Piston pin		
Diameter:	0.9052-0.9034 in.	22.9915-22.9464 mm
Clearance:	0.0038-0.0085 in.	0.0096-0.215 mm
Fit in rod:	0.0008-0.0020 in.	0.020-0.0515 mm (press)
Crankshaft		
Main Journal		
Diameter:	2.6473-2.6482 in.	67.241-67.265 mm
Taper:	0.0003 in.	0.008 mm (max.)
Out of round:	0.00019 in.	0.005 mm (max.)
Crankshaft end play:	0.0024-0.0083 in.	0.06-0.21 mm
Crankshaft pin:		
Diameter:	1.9983-1.9994 in.	50.758-50.784 mm
Taper:	0.0003 in.	0.008 mm (max.)
Out of round:	0.00019 in.	0.005 mm (max.)
Rod bearing clearance:	0.0013-0.0031 in.	0.032-0.079 mm
Rod side clearance:	0.014-0.027 in.	0.36-0.68 mm
Valve seat runout:	0.00098 in.	0.025 mm
Stem clearance		
Intake:	0.0010-0.0027 in.	0.026-0.068 mm
Exhaust:	0.0010-0.0027 in.	0.026-0.068 mm

1987-89 2.0L OHV V.I.N. CODE 1

Component	U.S.	Metric
Piston clearance:	0.00098-0.0022 in.	0.025-0.055 mm
Piston ring		
Groove clearance		
Compression:	0.0012-0.0027 in.	0.030-0.070 mm
Oil:	0.00059-0.0089 in.	0.015-0.227 mm
Gap		
Compression:	0.0098-0.0197 in.	0.25-0.50 mm
Oil:	0.0098-0.0512 in.	0.25-1.3 mm

ENGINE MECHANICAL SPECIFICATIONS

Component	U.S.	Metric
Piston pin		
Diameter:	0.8000-0.8004 in.	20.32-20.33 mm
Press fit in rod:	0.0008-0.0020 in.	0.021-0.051 mm
Fit in piston:	0.00039-0.00087 in.	0.0099-0.022 mm
Crankshaft		
Main Journal		
Diameter:	2.4945-2.4954 in.	63.360-63.384 mm
Taper:	0.00019 in.	0.005 mm (max.)
Out of round:	0.00019 in.	0.005 mm (max.)
Crankshaft end play:	0.0019-0.0083 in.	0.05-0.21 mm
Crankshaft pin:		
Diameter:	1.9983-1.9994 in.	50.758-50.784 mm
Taper:	0.00019 in.	0.005 mm (max.)
Out of round:	0.00019 in.	0.005 mm (max.)
Rod bearing clearance:	0.00098-0.00311 in.	0.025-0.079 mm
Rod side clearance:	0.0039-0.0150 in.	0.10-0.38 mm
Valve seat runout:	0.0019 in.	0.05 mm
Stem clearance		
Intake:	0.0011-0.0026 in.	0.028-0.066 mm
Exhaust:	0.0014-0.0031 in.	0.035-0.078 mm

1987-91 2.0L OHC V.I.N. CODES K AND M

Component	U.S.	Metric
Piston clearance		
Top (V.I.N. K):	0.00039-0.00118 in.	0.010-0.030 mm
Top (V.I.N. M):	0.00118-0.00197 in.	0.030-0.050 mm
Piston ring		
Compression (groove clearance):		
Top	0.0024-0.0036 in.	0.06-0.092 mm
2nd	0.0012-0.0024 in.	0.03-0.062 mm
Gap		
Top	0.00118-0.00197 in.	0.30-0.50 mm
2nd	0.00118-0.00197 in.	0.30-0.50 mm
Oil control:	0.016-0.055 in.	0.40-1.40 mm
Piston pin		
Fit in rod:	Press	
Fit in piston:	0.00043-0.00055 in.	0.011-0.014 mm
Crankshaft		
Main Journal (diameter)		
Brown:	2.2830-2.2833 in.	57.988-57.995 mm
Green:	2.2828-2.2830 in.	57.982-57.988 mm
Taper:	0.00019 in.	0.005 mm (max.)
Out of round:	0.00019 in.	0.005 mm (max.)
Crankshaft end play:	0.0028-0.012 in.	0.07-0.30 mm
Crankshaft pin:		
Diameter:	1.9280-1.9286 in.	48.971-48.987 mm
Taper:	0.00019 in.	0.005 mm (max.)
Out of round:	0.00019 in.	0.005 mm (max.)
Rod bearing clearance:	0.00075-0.0025 in.	0.019-0.063 mm
Rod side clearance:	0.0027-0.0095 in.	0.070-0.242 mm
Valve seat runout:	0.0019 in.	0.05 mm
Stem clearance		
Intake:	0.0006-0.0016 in.	0.015-0.042 mm
Exhaust:	0.0012-0.0024 in.	0.030-0.060 mm

1990-91 2.2L OHV V.I.N. CODE G

Component	U.S.	Metric
Piston clearance:	0.0006-0.0018 in.	0.015-0.045 mm

ENGINE MECHANICAL SPECIFICATIONS

Component	U.S.	Metric
Piston ring		
Groove clearance		
Compression:	0.0020-0.0027 in.	0.05-0.07 mm
Oil:	0.0020-0.0083 in.	0.05-0.21 mm
Gap		
Compression:	0.0098-0.0200 in.	0.25-0.50 mm
Oil:	0.0098-0.0500 in.	0.25-1.27 mm
Piston pin		
Diameter:	0.8000-0.8002 in.	20.320-20.325 mm
Press fit in rod:	0.00098-0.0018 in.	0.025-0.045 mm
Fit in piston:	0.00039-0.00087 in.	0.010-0.022 mm
Crankshaft		
Main Journal		
Diameter:	2.4945-2.4954 in.	63.360-63.384 mm
Taper:	0.00019 in.	0.005 mm (max.)
Out of round:	0.00019 in.	0.005 mm (max.)
Crankshaft end play:	0.0020-0.0070 in.	0.0511-0.1780 mm
Crankshaft pin:		
Diameter:	1.9983-1.9994 in.	50.758-50.784 mm
Taper:	0.00019 in.	0.005 mm (max.)
Out of round:	0.00019 in.	0.005 mm (max.)
Rod bearing clearance:	0.00098-0.0031 in.	0.025-0.079 mm
Rod side clearance:	0.0039-0.015 in.	0.10-0.38 mm
Valve seat runout:	0.0019 in.	0.05 mm
Stem clearance		
Intake:	0.0011-0.0026 in.	0.028-0.066 mm
Exhaust:	0.0014-0.0032 in.	0.035-0.081 mm

1990-92 3.1L OHV V.I.N. CODE T

Component	U.S.	Metric
Piston clearance:	0.0009-0.0022 in.	0.0235-0.0565 mm
Piston ring		
Compression (groove clearance):		
1st	0.0019-0.0354 in.	0.050-0.90 mm
2nd	0.0019-0.0354 in.	0.050-0.90 mm
Gap		
1st	0.0098-0.0197 in.	0.25-0.50 mm
2nd	0.0197-0.0279 in.	0.50-0.71 mm
Oil (groove clearance gap):	0.008 in.	0.20 mm
Piston pin		
Diameter:	0.9052-0.9034 in.	22.9915-22.9464 mm
Clearance:	0.0038-0.0085 in.	0.096-0.215 mm
Fit in rod:	0.00065-0.0183 in.	0.0165-0.464 mm (press)
Crankshaft		
Main Journal		
Diameter:	2.6473-2.6482 in.	67.241-67.265 mm
Taper:	0.00019 in.	0.005 mm (max.)
Out of round:	0.00019 in.	0.005 mm (max.)
Crankshaft end play:	0.0024-0.0083 in.	0.06-0.21 mm
Crankshaft pin:		
Diameter:	1.9983-1.9994 in.	50.758-50.784 mm
Taper:	0.00019 in.	0.005 mm (max.)
Out of round:	0.00019 in.	0.005 mm (max.)
Rod bearing clearance:	0.0011-0.0034 in.	0.028-0.086 mm
Rod side clearance:	0.014-0.027 in.	0.36-0.68 mm

ENGINE MECHANICAL SPECIFICATIONS

Component	U.S.	Metric
Valve seat runout:	0.00098 in.	0.025 mm
Stem clearance		
Intake:	0.0010-0.0027 in.	0.026-0.068 mm
Exhaust:	0.0010-0.0027 in.	0.026-0.068 mm

1992 2.0L OHC V.I.N. CODE H

Piston clearance:	0.00039-0.0012 in.	0.010-0.030 mm
Piston ring		
Compression (groove clearance):		
Top	0.0024-0.0036 in.	0.0609-0.0914 mm
2nd	0.0019-0.0032 in.	0.0482-0.0812 mm
Gap		
Top	0.0098-0.018 in.	0.25-0.45 mm
2nd	0.012-0.019 in.	0.30-0.50 mm
Piston pin		
Fit in piston:	0.0004-0.0006 in.	0.011-0.014 mm
Fit in rod:	Press	
Crankshaft		
Main Journal (diameter):	2.2828-2.2833 in.	57.982-57.995 mm
Taper:	0.00019 in.	0.005 mm (max.)
Out of round:	0.00019 in.	0.005 mm (max.)
Crankshaft end play	0.0028-0.0119 in.	0.07-0.302 mm
Crankshaft pin:		
Diameter:	1.9280-1.9287 in.	48.970-48.988 mm
Taper:	0.00019 in.	0.005 mm (max.)
Out of round:	0.00019 in.	0.005 mm (max.)
Rod bearing clearance:	0.0007-0.0025 in.	0.019-0.063 mm
Rod side clearance:	0.0028-0.0095 in.	0.070-0.242 mm
Valve seat runout:	0.0019 in.	0.05 mm
Stem clearance		
Intake:	0.0006-0.0017 in.	0.015-0.042 mm
Exhaust:	0.0012-0.0024 in.	0.030-0.060 mm

1992 2.2L OHV V.I.N. CODE 4

Piston clearance:	0.0006-0.0018 in.	0.015-0.045 mm
Piston ring		
Groove clearance		
Compression:	0.0019-0.0028 in.	0.05-0.07 mm
Oil:	0.0019-0.0083 in.	0.05-0.21 mm
Gap		
Compression:	0.0098-0.0197 in.	0.25-0.50 mm
Oil:	0.0098-0.0500 in.	0.25-1.27 mm
Piston pin		
Diameter:	0.8000-0.8002 in.	20.320-20.325 mm
Press fit in rod:	0.00098-0.00178 in.	0.025-0.045 mm
Fit in piston:	0.00039-0.00087 in.	0.010-0.022 mm
Crankshaft		
Main Journal		
Diameter:	2.4945-2.4954 in.	63.360-63.384 mm
Taper:	0.00019 in.	0.005 mm (max.)
Out of round:	0.00019 in.	0.005 mm (max.)
Crankshaft end play:	0.0020-0.0070 in.	0.0511-0.1780mm

ENGINE MECHANICAL SPECIFICATIONS

Component	U.S.	Metric
Crankshaft pin		
Diameter:	1.9983-1.9994 in.	50.758-50.784 mm
Taper:	0.00019 in.	0.005 mm (max.)
Out of round:	0.00019 in.	0.005 mm (max.)
Rod bearing clearance:	0.00098-0.0031 in.	0.025-0.079 mm
Rod side clearance:	0.0039-0.015 in.	0.10-0.38 mm
Valve seat runout:	0.0019 in.	0.05 mm
Stem clearance		
Intake:	0.0011-0.0026 in.	0.028-0.066 mm
Exhaust:	0.0014-0.0032 in.	0.035-0.081 mm

4

EMISSION CONTROLS

AIR POLLUTION

The earth's atmosphere, at or near sea level, consists of 78% nitrogen, 21% oxygen and 1% other gases, approximately. If it were possible to remain in this state, 100% clean air would result. However, many varied causes allow other gases and particulates to mix with the clean air, causing the air to become unclean or polluted.

Certain of these pollutants are visible while others are invisible, with each having the capability of causing distress to the eyes, ears, throat, skin and respiratory system. Should these pollutants be concentrated in a specific area and under the right conditions, death could result due to the displacement or chemical change of the oxygen content in the air. These pollutants can cause much damage to the environment and to the many man made objects that are exposed to the elements.

To better understand the causes of air pollution, the pollutants can be categorized into 3 separate types, natural, industrial and automotive.

Natural Pollutants

Natural pollution has been present on earth before man appeared and is still a factor to be considered when discussing air pollution, although it causes only a small percentage of the present overall pollution problem existing in our country. It is the direct result of decaying organic matter, wind born smoke and particulates from such natural events as plains and forest fires (ignited by heat or lightning), volcanic ash, sand and dust which can spread over a large area of the countryside.

Such a phenomenon of natural pollution has been recent volcanic eruptions, with the resulting plume of smoke, steam and volcanic ash blotting out the sun's rays as it spreads and rises higher into the atmosphere, where the upper air currents catch and carry the smoke and ash, while condensing the steam back into water vapor. As the water vapor, smoke and ash traveled on their journey, the smoke dissipates into the atmosphere while the ash and moisture settle back to earth in a trail hundred of miles long. In many cases, lives are lost and millions of dollars of property damage result, and ironically, man can only stand by and watch it happen.

Industrial Pollution

Industrial pollution is caused primarily by industrial processes, the burning of coal, oil and natural gas, which in turn produces smoke and fumes. Because the burning fuels contain much sulfur, the principal ingredients of smoke and fumes are sulfur dioxide (SO_2) and particulate matter. This type of pollutant occurs most severely during still, damp and cool weather, such as at night. Even in its less severe form, this pollutant is not confined to just cities. Because of air movements, the pollutants move for miles over the surrounding countryside, leaving in its path a barren and unhealthy environment for all living things.

Working with Federal, State and Local mandated rules, regulations and by carefully monitoring the emissions, industries have greatly reduced the amount of pollutant emitted from their industrial sources, striving to obtain an acceptable level. Because of the mandated industrial emission clean up, many land areas and streams in and around the cities that were formerly barren of vegetation and life, have now begun to move back in the direction of nature's intended balance.

Automotive Pollutants

The third major source of air pollution is the automotive emissions. The emissions from the internal combustion engine were not an appreciable problem years ago because of the small number of registered vehicles and the nation's small highway system. However, during the early 1950's, the trend of the American people was to move from the cities to the surrounding suburbs. This caused an immediate problem in the transportation areas because the majority of the suburbs were not afforded mass transit conveniences. This lack of transportation created an attractive market for the automobile manufacturers, which resulted in a dramatic increase in the number of vehicles produced and sold, along with a marked increase in highway construction between cities and the suburbs. Multi-vehicle families emerged with much emphasis placed on the individual vehicle per family member. As the increase in vehicle ownership and usage occurred, so did the pollutant levels in and around the cities, as the suburbanites drove daily to their businesses and employment in the city and its fringe area, returning at the end of the day to their homes in the suburbs.

It was noted that a fog and smoke type haze was being formed and at times, remained in suspension over the cities and did not quickly dissipate. At first this "smog", derived from the words "smoke" and "fog", was thought to result from industrial pollution but it was determined that the automobile emissions were largely to blame. It was discovered that as normal automobile emissions were exposed to sunlight for a period of time, complex chemical reactions would take place.

It was found the smog was a photo chemical layer and was developed when certain oxides of nitrogen (NOx) and unburned hydrocarbons (HC) from the automobile emissions were exposed to sunlight and was more severe when the smog would remain stagnant over an area in which a warm layer of air would settle over the top of a cooler air mass at ground level, trapping and holding the automobile emissions, instead of the emissions being dispersed and diluted through normal air flows. This type of air stagnation was given the name "Temperature Inversion".

Temperature Inversion

In normal weather situations, the surface air is warmed by the heat radiating from the earth's surface and the sun's rays and will rise upward, into the atmosphere, to be cooled through a convection type heat expands with the cooler upper air. As the warm air rises, the surface pollutants are carried upward and dissipated into the atmosphere.

When a temperature inversion occurs, we find the higher air is no longer cooler but warmer than the surface air, causing the cooler surface air to become trapped and unable to move. This warm air blanket can extend from above ground level to a few hundred or even a few thousand feet into the air. As the surface air is trapped, so are the pollutants, causing a severe smog condition. Should this stagnant air mass extend to a few thousand feet high, enough air movement with the inversion takes place to allow the smog layer to rise above ground level but the pollutants still cannot dissipate. This inversion can remain for days over an area, with only the smog level rising or lowering from ground level to a few hundred feet high. Meanwhile, the pollutant levels increases, causing eye irritation, respirator problems, reduced visibility, plant damage and in some cases, cancer type diseases.

This inversion phenomenon was first noted in the Los Angeles, California area. The city lies in a basin type of terrain and during certain weather conditions, a cold air mass is held in the basin while a warmer air mass covers it like a lid.

Because this type of condition was first documented as prevalent in the Los Angeles area, this type of smog was named Los Angeles Smog, although it occurs in other areas where a large concentration of automobiles are used and the air remains stagnant for any length of time.

Internal Combustion Engine Pollutants

Consider the internal combustion engine as a machine in which raw materials must be placed so a finished product comes out. As in any machine operation, a certain amount of wasted material is formed. When we relate this to the internal combustion engine, we find that by putting in air and fuel, we obtain power from this mixture during the combustion process to drive the vehicle. The by-product or waste of this power is, in part, heat and exhaust gases with which we must concern ourselves.

HEAT TRANSFER

The heat from the combustion process can rise to over 4000°F (2204°C). The dissipation of this heat is controlled by a ram air effect, the use of cooling fans to cause air flow and having a liquid coolant solution surrounding the combustion area and transferring the heat of combustion through the cylinder walls and into the coolant. The coolant is then directed to a thin-finned, multi-tubed radiator, from which the excess heat is transferred to the outside air by 1 or all of the 3 heat transfer methods, conduction, convection or radiation.

The cooling of the combustion area is an important part in the control of exhaust emissions. To understand the behavior of the combustion and transfer of its heat, consider the air/fuel charge. It is ignited and the flame front burns progressively across the combustion chamber until the burning charge reaches the cylinder walls. Some of the fuel in contact with the walls is not hot enough to burn, thereby snuffing out or Quenching the combustion process. This leaves unburned fuel in the combustion chamber. This unburned fuel is then forced out of the cylinder along with the exhaust gases and into the exhaust system.

Many attempts have been made to minimize the amount of unburned fuel in the combustion chambers due to the snuffing out or "Quenching", by increasing the coolant temperature and lessening the contact area of the coolant around the combustion area. Design limitations within the combustion chambers prevent the complete burning of the air/fuel charge, so a certain amount of the unburned fuel is still expelled into the exhaust system, regardless of modifications to the engine.

EXHAUST EMISSIONS

Composition Of The Exhaust Gases

The exhaust gases emitted into the atmosphere are a combination of burned and unburned fuel. To understand the exhaust emission and its composition review some basic chemistry.

When the air/fuel mixture is introduced into the engine, we are mixing air, composed of nitrogen (78%), oxygen (21%) and other gases (1%) with the fuel, which is 100% hydrocarbons (HC), in a semi-controlled ratio. As the combustion process is accomplished, power is produced to move the vehicle while the heat of combustion is transferred to the cooling system. The exhaust gases are then composed of nitrogen, a diatomic gas (N_2), the same as was introduced in the engine, carbon dioxide (CO_2), the same gas that is used in beverage carbonation and water vapor (H_2O). The nitrogen (N_2), for the most part passes through the engine unchanged, while the oxygen (O_2) reacts (burns) with the hydrocarbons (HC) and produces the carbon dioxide (CO_2) and the water vapors (H_2O). If this chemical process would be the only process to take place, the exhaust emissions would be harmless. However, during the combustion process, other pollutants are formed and are considered dangerous. These pollutants are carbon monoxide (CO), hydrocarbons (HC), oxides of nitrogen (NOx) oxides of sulfur (SOx) and engine particulates.

Lead (Pb), is considered 1 of the particulates and is present in the exhaust gases whenever leaded fuels are used. Lead (Pb) does not dissipate easily. Levels can be high along roadways when it is emitted from vehicles and can pose a health threat. Since the increased usage of unleaded gasoline and the phasing out of leaded gasoline for fuel, this pollutant is gradually diminishing. While not considered a major threat lead is still considered a dangerous pollutant.

HYDROCARBONS

Hydrocarbons (HC) are essentially unburned fuel that have not been successfully burned during the combustion process or have escaped into the atmosphere through fuel evaporation. The main sources of incomplete combustion are rich air/fuel mixtures, low engine temperatures and improper spark timing. The main sources of hydrocarbon emission through fuel evaporation come from the vehicle's fuel tank and carburetor bowl.

To reduce combustion hydrocarbon emission, engine modifications were made to minimize dead space and surface area in the combustion chamber. In addition the air/fuel mixture was made more lean through improved carburetion, fuel injection and by the addition of external controls to aid in further combustion of the hydrocarbons outside the engine. Two such methods were the addition of an air injection system, to inject fresh air into the exhaust manifolds and the installation of a catalytic converter, a unit that is able to burn traces of hydrocarbons without affecting the internal combustion process or fuel economy.

To control hydrocarbon emissions through fuel evaporation, modifications were made to the fuel tank and carburetor bowl to allow storage of the fuel vapors during periods of engine shut-down, and at specific times during engine operation, to purge and burn these same vapors by blending them with the air/fuel mixture.

CARBON MONOXIDE

Carbon monoxide is formed when not enough oxygen is present during the combustion process to convert carbon (C) to carbon dioxide (CO_2). An increase in the carbon monoxide (CO) emission is normally accompanied by an increase in the hydrocarbon (HC) emission because of the lack of oxygen to completely burn all of the fuel mixture.

Carbon monoxide (CO) also increases the rate at which the photo chemical smog is formed by speeding up the conversion of nitric oxide (NO) to nitrogen dioxide (NO_2). To accomplish this, carbon monoxide (CO) combines with oxygen (O_2) and nitrogen dioxide (NO_2) to produce carbon dioxide (CO_2) and nitrogen dioxide (NO_2). ($CO + O_2 + NO = CO_2 + NO_2$).

The dangers of carbon monoxide, which is an odorless, colorless toxic gas are many. When carbon monoxide is inhaled into the lungs and passed into the blood stream, oxygen is replaced by the carbon monoxide in the red blood cells, causing a reduction in the amount of oxygen being supplied to the many parts of the body. This lack of oxygen causes headaches, lack of coordination, reduced mental alertness and should the carbon monoxide concentration be high enough, death could result.

NITROGEN

Normally, nitrogen is an inert gas. When heated to approximately 2500°F (1371°C) through the combustion process, this gas becomes active and causes an increase in the nitric oxide (NOx) emission.

Oxides of nitrogen (NOx) are composed of approximately 97–98% nitric oxide (NO_2). Nitric oxide is a colorless gas but when it is passed into the atmosphere, it combines with oxygen and forms nitrogen dioxide (NO_2). The nitrogen dioxide then combines with chemically active hydrocarbons (HC) and when in the presence of sunlight, causes the formation of photo chemical smog.

OZONE

To further complicate matters, some of the nitrogen dioxide (NO_2) is broken apart by the sunlight to form nitric oxide and oxygen. (NO_2 + sunlight = NO + O). This single atom of oxygen then combines with diatomic (meaning 2 atoms) oxygen (O_2) to form ozone (O_3). Ozone is 1 of the smells associated with smog. It has a pungent and offensive odor, irritates the eyes and lung tissues, affects the growth of plant life and causes rapid deterioration of rubber products. Ozone can be formed by sunlight as well as electrical discharge into the air.

The most common discharge area on the automobile engine is the secondary ignition electrical system, especially when inferior quality spark plug cables are used. As the surge of high voltage is routed through the secondary cable, the circuit builds up an electrical field around the wire, acting upon the oxygen in the surrounding air to form the ozone. The faint glow along the cable with the engine running that may be visible on a dark night, is called the "corona discharge." It is the result of the electrical field passing from a high along the cable, to a low in the surrounding air, which forms the ozone gas. The combination of corona and ozone has been a major cause of cable deterioration. Recently, different types and better quality insulating materials have lengthened the life of the electrical cables.

Although ozone at ground level can be harmful, ozone is beneficial to the earth's inhabitants. By having a concentrated ozone layer called the 'ozonosphere', between 10 and 20 miles (16–32km) up in the atmosphere much of the ultra violet radiation from the sun's rays are absorbed and screened. If this ozone layer were not present, much of the earth's surface would be burned, dried and unfit for human life.

There is much discussion concerning the ozone layer and its density. A feeling exists that this protective layer of ozone is slowly diminishing and corrective action must be directed to this problem. Much experimenting is presently being conducted to determine if a problem exists and if so, the short and long term effects of the problem and how it can be remedied.

OXIDES OF SULFUR

Oxides of sulfur (SOx) were initially ignored in the exhaust system emissions, since the sulfur content of gasoline as a fuel is less than $\frac{1}{10}$ of 1%. Because of this small amount, it was felt that it contributed very little to the overall pollution problem. However, because of the difficulty in solving the sulfur emissions in industrial pollutions and the introduction of catalytic converter to the automobile exhaust systems, a change was mandated. The automobile exhaust system, when equipped with a catalytic converter, changes the sulfur dioxide (SO_2) into the sulfur trioxide (SO_3).

When this combines with water vapors (H_2O), a sulfuric acid mist (H_2SO_4) is formed and is a very difficult pollutant to handle and is extremely corrosive. This sulfuric acid mist that is formed, is the same mist that rises from the vents of an automobile storage battery when an active chemical reaction takes place within the battery cells.

When a large concentration of vehicles equipped with catalytic converters are operating in an area, this acid mist will rise and be distributed over a large ground area causing land, plant, crop, paints and building damage.

PARTICULATE MATTER

A certain amount of particulate matter is present in the burning of any fuel, with carbon constituting the largest percentage of the particulates. In gasoline, the remaining percentage of particulates is the burned remains of the various other compounds used in its manufacture. When a gasoline engine is in good internal condition, the particulate emissions are low but as the engine wears internally, the particulate emissions increase. By visually inspecting the tail pipe emissions, a determination can be made as to where an engine defect may exist. An engine with light gray smoke emitting from the tail pipe normally indicates an increase in the oil consumption through burning due to internal engine wear. Black smoke would indicate a defective fuel delivery system, causing the engine to operate in a rich mode. Regardless of the color of the smoke, the internal part of the engine or the fuel delivery system should be repaired to a "like new" condition to prevent excess particulate emissions.

Diesel and turbine engines emit a darkened plume of smoke from the exhaust system because of the type of fuel used. Emission control regulations are mandated for this type of emission and more stringent measures are being used to prevent excess emission of the particulate matter. Electronic components are being introduced to control the injection of the fuel at precisely the proper time of piston travel, to achieve the optimum in fuel ignition and fuel usage. Other particulate after-burning components are being tested to achieve a cleaner particular emission.

Good grades of engine lubricating oils should be used, meeting the manufacturers specification. "Cut-rate" oils can contribute to the particulate emission problem because of their low "flash" or ignition temperature point. Such oils burn prematurely during the combustion process causing emissions of particulate matter.

The cooling system is an important factor in the reduction of particulate matter. With the cooling system operating at a temperature specified by the manufacturer, the optimum of combustion will occur. The cooling system must be maintained in the same manner as the engine oiling system, as each system is required to perform properly in order for the engine to operate efficiently for a long time.

Other Automobile Emission Sources

Before emission controls were mandated on the internal combustion engines, other sources of engine pollutants were discovered, along with the exhaust emission. It was determined the engine combustion exhaust produced 60% of the total emission pollutants, fuel evaporation from the fuel tank and carburetor vents produced 20%, with the another 20% being produced through the crankcase as a by-product of the combustion process.

CRANKCASE EMISSIONS

Crankcase emissions are made up of water, acids, unburned fuel, oil fumes and particulates. The emissions are classified as hydrocarbons (HC) and are formed by the small amount of unburned, compressed air/fuel mixture entering the crankcase from the combustion area during the compression and power strokes, between the cylinder walls and piston rings. The head of the compression and combustion help to form the remaining crankcase emissions.

Since the first engines, crankcase emissions were allowed to go into the air through a road draft tube, mounted on the lower side of the engine block. Fresh air came in through an open oil filler cap or breather. The air passed through the crankcase mixing with blow-by gases. The motion of the vehicle and the air blowing past the open end of the road draft tube caused a low pressure area at the end of the tube. Crankcase emissions were simply drawn out of the road draft tube into the air.

To control the crankcase emission, the road draft tube was deleted. A hose and/or tubing was routed from the crankcase to the intake manifold so the blow-by emission could be burned with the air/fuel mixture. However, it was found that intake manifold vacuum, used to draw the crankcase emissions into the manifold, would vary in strength at the wrong time and not allow the proper emission flow. A regulating type valve was needed to control the flow of air through the crankcase.

Testing, showed the removal of the blow-by gases from the crankcase as quickly as possible, was most important to the longevity of the engine. Should large accumulations of blow-by gases remain and condense, dilution of the engine oil would occur to form water, soots, resins, acids and lead salts, resulting in the formation of sludge and varnishes. This condensation of the blow-by gases occur more frequently on vehicles used in numerous starting and stopping conditions, excessive idling and when the engine is not allowed to attain normal operating temperature through short runs. The crankcase purge control or PCV system will be described in detail later in this section.

FUEL EVAPORATIVE EMISSIONS

Gasoline fuel is a major source of pollution, before and after it is burned in the automobile engine. From the time the fuel is refined, stored, pumped and transported, again stored until it is pumped into the fuel tank of the vehicle, the gasoline gives off unburned hydrocarbons (HC) into the atmosphere. Through redesigning of the storage areas and venting systems, the pollution factor has been diminished but not eliminated, from the refinery standpoint. However, the automobile still remained the primary source of vaporized, unburned hydrocarbon (HC) emissions.

Fuel pumped form an underground storage tank is cool but when exposed to a warner ambient temperature, will expand. Before controls were mandated, an owner would fill the fuel tank with fuel from an underground storage tank and park the vehicle for some time in warm area, such as a parking lot. As the fuel would warm, it would expand and should no provisions or area be provided for the expansion, the fuel would spill out the filler neck and onto the ground, causing hydrocarbon (HC) pollution and creating a severe fire hazard. To correct this condition, the vehicle manufacturers added overflow plumbing and/or gasoline tanks with built in expansion areas or domes.

However, this did not control the fuel vapor emission from the fuel tank and the carburetor bowl. It was determined that most of the fuel evaporation occurred when the vehicle was stationary and the engine not operating. Most vehicles carry 5–25 gallons (19–95 liters) of gasoline. Should a large concentration of vehicles be parked in one area, such as a large parking lot, excessive fuel vapor emissions would take place, increasing as the temperature increases.

To prevent the vapor emission from escaping into the atmosphere, the fuel system is designed to trap the fuel vapors while the vehicle is stationary, by sealing the fuel system from the atmosphere. A storage system is used to collect and hold the fuel vapors from the carburetor and the fuel tank when the engine is not operating. When the engine is started, the storage system is then purged of the fuel vapors, which are drawn into the engine and burned with the air/fuel mixture.

The components of the fuel evaporative system will be described in detail later in this section.

EMISSION CONTROLS

There are three sources of automotive pollutants: crankcase fumes, exhaust gases, and gasoline evaporation. The pollutants formed from these substances fall into three categories: unburnt hydrocarbons (HC), carbon monoxide (CO), and oxides of nitrogen (NOx). The equipment that is used to limit these pollutants is commonly called emission control equipment.

Positive Crankcase Ventilation System

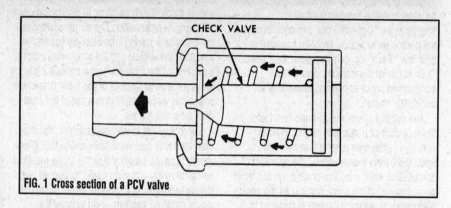

FIG. 1 Cross section of a PCV valve

♦ SEE FIGS. 1-1B

All vehicles are equipped with a positive crankcase ventilation (PCV) system to control crankcase blow-by vapors. The system functions as follows:

When the engine is running, a small portion of the gases which are formed in the combustion chamber leak by the piston rings and enter the crankcase. Since these gases are under pressure, they tend to escape from the crankcase and enter the atmosphere. If these gases are allowed to remain in the crankcase for any period of time, they contaminate the engine oil and cause sludge to build up in the crankcase. If the gases are allowed to escape into the atmosphere, they pollute the air with unburned hydrocarbons. The job of the

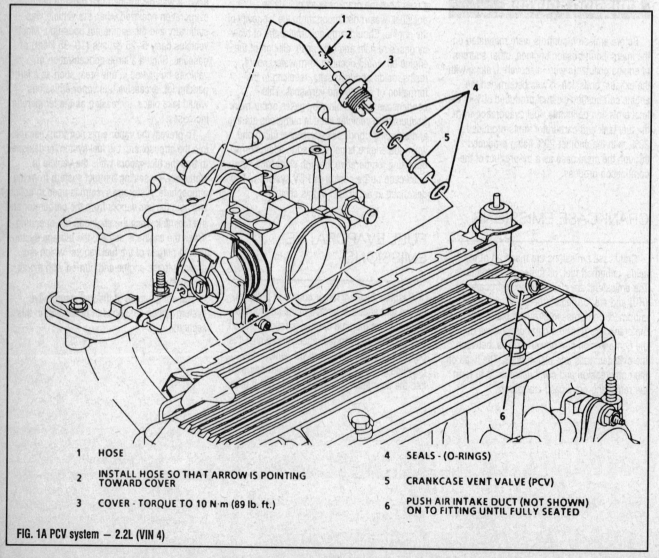

1	HOSE	4	SEALS - (O-RINGS)
2	INSTALL HOSE SO THAT ARROW IS POINTING TOWARD COVER	5	CRANKCASE VENT VALVE (PCV)
3	COVER - TORQUE TO 10 N·m (89 lb. ft.)	6	PUSH AIR INTAKE DUCT (NOT SHOWN) ON TO FITTING UNTIL FULLY SEATED

FIG. 1A PCV system — 2.2L (VIN 4)

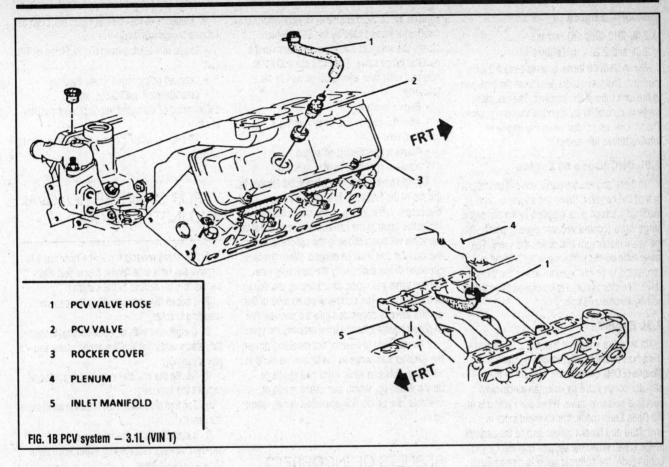

1   PCV VALVE HOSE

2   PCV VALVE

3   ROCKER COVER

4   PLENUM

5   INLET MANIFOLD

FIG. 1B PCV system — 3.1L (VIN T)

crankcase emission control equipment is to recycle these gases back into the engine combustion chamber where they are reburned.

The crankcase (blow-by gases are recycled in the following way: as the engine is running, clean, filtered air is drawn through the air filter and into the crankcase. As the air passes through the crankcase, it picks up the combustion gases and carries them out of the crankcase, through the oil separator, through the PCV valve, and into the induction system. As they enter the intake manifold, they are drawn into the combustion chamber where they are reburned.

The most critical component in the system is the PCV valve. This valve controls the amount of gases which are recycled into the combustion chamber. At low engine speeds, the valve is partially closed, limiting the flow of gases into the intake manifold. As engine speed increases, the valve opens to admit greater quantities of gases into the intake manifold. If the valve should become blocked or plugged, the gases will be prevented from escaping from the crankcase by the normal route. Since these gases are under pressure, they will find their own way out of the crankcase. This alternate route is usually a weak oil seal or gasket in the engine. As the gas

escapes by the gasket, it also creates an oil leak. Besides causing oil leaks, a clogged PCV valve also allows these gases to remain in the crankcase for an extended period of time, promoting the formation of sludge in the engine.

SERVICE

Inspect the PCV system hose and connections at each tune-up and replace any deteriorated hoses. Check the PCV valve at every tune-up and replace it at 30,000 mile intervals. Replacement procedures are in Section 1.

Always replace the PCV valve instead of trying to clean the PCV valve. On later models, replace the seals as necessary.

Evaporative Emission Control System

The basic Evaporative Emission Control System (EEC) used on all vehicles is the carbon canister storage method. The system is used to

reduce emissions of fuel vapors from the car's fuel system. Evaporated fuel vapors are stored for burning during combustion rather than being vented into the atmosphere when the engine is not running. To accomplish this, the fuel tank and the carburetor float bowl, on those models so equipped, are vented through a vapor canister containing activated charcoal. The canister absorbs these vapors in a bed of activated charcoal and retains them until the canister is purged or cleared by air drawn through the filter at its bottom. The absorbing occurs when the car is not running, while the purging or cleaning occurs when the car is running. The amount of vapor being drawn into the engine at any given time is too small to have an effect on either fuel economy or engine performance.

1.8L OHV Engine

On vehicles equipped with the 1.8L engine (Carburetor), the ECM controls the vacuum to the purge valve in the charcoal canister with a solenoid valve. When the system is in the Open Loop mode, the solenoid valve is energized and blocks all vacuum to the canister purge valve. When the system is in the Closed Loop mode, the solenoid valve is de-energized and vacuum is then supplied to operate the purge valve. This releases the fuel vapors, collected in the canister, into the intake manifold.

1.8L OHC Engine

2.0L OHC (Code K) Engine
2.0L and 2.2L OHV Engines

The system on these engines uses a 2 tube canister. The fuel vapors vent from the fuel tank to the tank tube of the canister. The canister purge is controlled by a ported vacuum source. The vapors are purged when the engine is running above idle speed.

2.0L OHC (Code M) Engine

On these engines the purge valve is an integral part of the canister. When the engine is running, manifold vacuum is is supplied to the top of the purge valve (control vacuum signal), which lifts the valve diaphragm and opens the valve. The lower tube on the purge valve (PCV) tube is connected to ported vacuum above the throttle valve. The rate of purge is controlled through this port by throttle position.

2.8L Engine

On vehicles equipped with the 2.8L engine (Port Fuel Injection), the Electronic Control Module (ECM) controls the vacuum to the canister purge valve by using an electrically operated solenoid valve. When the system is in the Open Loop mode, the solenoid valve is energized and blocks all vacuum to the canister purge valve. When the system is in the Closed Loop mode, the solenoid valve is de-energized and vacuum is then supplied to operate the purge valve. This releases the fuel vapors, collected in the canister, into the induction system.

The fuel tank pressure control valve located in the engine compartment, is a spring biased diaphragm valve, which is normally closed. When the vapor in the fuel tank exceeds 6.0 kPa, the valve will open allowing the vapors to vent to the canister and then be purged. When the tank pressure drops sufficiently the tank pressure control valve will close, thus keeping the vapors in the fuel tank. The control vacuum tube of the control valve is connected into the canister line to prevent contamination from entering the valve.

If the solenoid is open or not receiving power, the canister can purge to the intake manifold at all times. This can allow extra fuel at idle or during warm-up, which can cause rough or unstable idle, or too rich operation during warm-up.

3.1L Engine

On vehicles equipped with the 3.1L engine (Port Fuel Injection), the Electronic Control Module (ECM) opens a normally opened pulse width modulated solenoid valve which controls vacuum to the purge valve in the charcoal canister. Under cold engine or idle conditions the solenoid is turned **ON** by the ECM, which closes the solenoid and blocks vacuum to the canister purge valve. The ECM turns **OFF** the solenoid valve and allows purge during the following:

• Engine is warm
• After the engine has been running a specified time
• Above a specified road speed
• Above a specified throttle opening

The fuel tank pressure control valve located in the top of the fuel tank, is a spring biased diaphragm valve, which is normally closed. When the vapor in the fuel tank exceeds 6.0 kPa, the valve will open allowing the vapors to vent to the canister and then be purged. When the tank pressure drops sufficiently the tank pressure control valve will close, thus keeping the vapors in the fuel tank. The control vacuum tube of the control valve is connected into the canister line to prevent contamination from entering the valve.

If the solenoid is open or not receiving power, the canister can purge to the intake manifold at all times. This can allow extra fuel at idle or during warm-up, which can cause rough or unstable idle, or too rich operation during warm-up.

RESULTS OF INCORRECT OPERATION

1. Poor idling, stalling and poor derivability can be caused by the following:
• Damaged canister
• Hoses split, cracked and/or not connected to the proper tubes

2. Evidence of fuel loss or vapor odor can be caused by the following:
• Liquid fuel leaking from the fuel lines or TBI unit
• Cracked or damaged vapor canister
• Disconnected, misrouted, kinked, deteriorated or damaged vapor pipe or canister hoses
• Air cleaner or air cleaner gasket improperly seated

VAPOR CANISTER REMOVAL AND INSTALLATION

1. On some models it may be necessary to remove the right side fender fascia and filler panels to gain access to the canister.
2. Loosen the screw holding the canister retaining bracket.
3. If equipped with air conditioning, loosen the attachments holding the accumulator and pipe assembly.
4. Rotate the canister retaining bracket and remove the canister.
5. Tag and disconnect the hoses leading from the canister.
6. Installation is in the reverse order of removal. Always replace any vapor hose thats shows signs of wear.

FILTER REPLACEMENT

♦ SEE FIG. 2

➡ **On most 1982–87 4 cylinder**

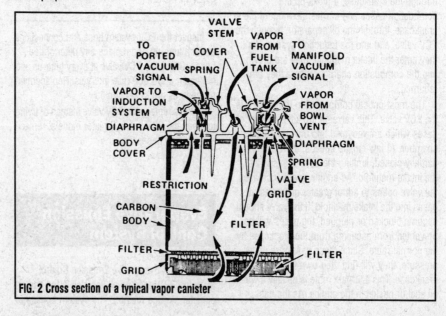

FIG. 2 Cross section of a typical vapor canister

engines it is possible to replace the filter at the bottom of the canister. Check for new filter availability before removing.

1. Remove the vapor canister.
2. Pull the filter out from the bottom of the canister.
3. Install a new filter and then replace the canister.

Exhaust Emission Controls

Exhaust emission control systems constitute the largest body of emission control devices installed on these vehicles. Included in this category are: Thermostatic Air Cleaner (THERMAC); Air Management System; Early Fuel Evaporation System (EFE); Exhaust Gas Recirculation (EGR); Computer Command Control System (CCC); Deceleration Valve; Mixture Control Solenoid (M/C); Throttle Position Sensor (TPS); Idle Speed Control (ISC); Electronic Spark Timing (EST); Transmission Converter Clutch (TCC); Catalytic Converter and the Oxygen Sensor System. A brief description of each system and any applicable service procedures follows.

Thermostatic Air Cleaner (THERMAC)

◆ SEE FIGS. 3-4

All 4 cylinder engines, through 1986, use the THERMAC system except those equipped with ported fuel injection. This system is designed to warm the air entering the carburetor when underhood temperatures are low, and to maintain a controlled air temperature into the carburetor at all times. By allowing preheated air to enter the carburetor, the amount of time the choke is on is reduced, resulting in better fuel economy and lower emissions. Engine warm-up time is also reduced.

The THERMAC system is composed of the air cleaner body, a filter, sensor unit, vacuum diaphragm, damper door, and associated hoses and connections. Heat radiating from the exhaust manifold is trapped by a heat stove and is ducted to the air cleaner to supply heated air to the carburetor. A movable door in the air cleaner case snorkel allows air to be drawn in from the heat stove (cold operation). The door position is controlled by the vacuum motor, which receives intake manifold vacuum as modulated by the temperature sensor.

SYSTEM CHECKS

1. Check the vacuum hoses for leaks, kinks, breaks, or improper connections and correct any defects.
2. With the engine off, check the position of the damper door within the snorkel. A mirror can be used to make this job easier. The damper door should be open to admit outside air.
3. Apply at least 7 in.Hg of vacuum to the damper diaphragm unit. The door should close. If it doesn't, check the diaphragm linkage for binding and correct hookup.
4. With the vacuum still applied and the door closed, clamp the tube to trap the vacuum. If the door doesn't remain closed, there is a leak in the diaphragm assembly.

Air Management System

1982–84

◆ SEE FIGS. 5-6

The AIR management system, is used to provide additional oxygen to continue the combustion process after the exhaust gases leave the combustion chamber. Air is injected

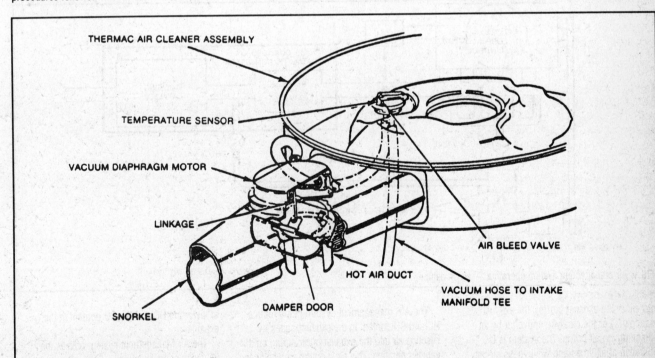

FIG. 3 Typical THERMAC air cleaner

THERMAC AIR CLEANER ASSEMBLY
TEMPERATURE SENSOR
VACUUM DIAPHRAGM MOTOR
LINKAGE
SNORKEL
DAMPER DOOR
HOT AIR DUCT
AIR BLEED VALVE
VACUUM HOSE TO INTAKE MANIFOLD TEE

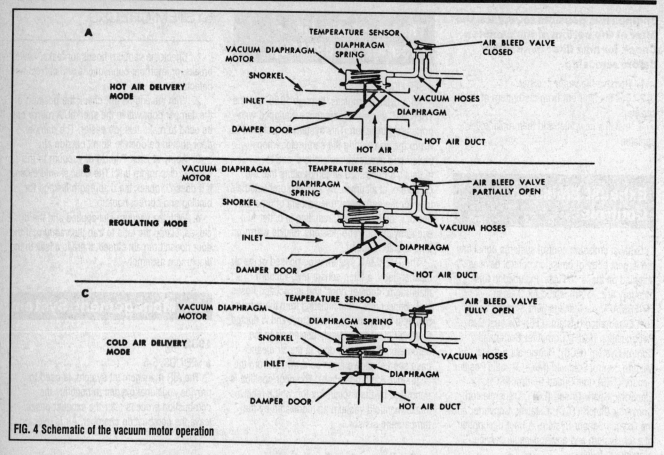

FIG. 4 Schematic of the vacuum motor operation

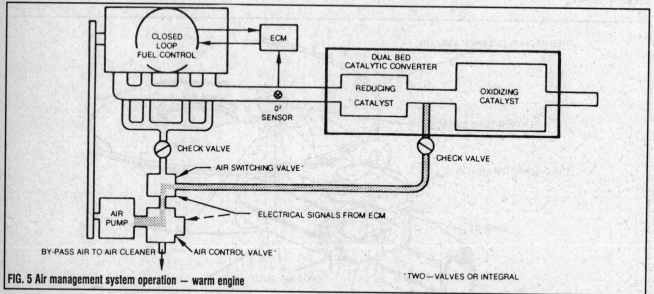

FIG. 5 Air management system operation — warm engine   *TWO—VALVES OR INTEGRAL

into either the exhaust port(s), the exhaust manifold(s) or the catalytic converter by an engine driven air pump. The system is in operation at all times and will bypass air only momentarily during deceleration and at high speeds. The bypass function is performed by the Air Management Valve, while the check valve protects the air pump by preventing any backflow of exhaust gases.

The AIR management system helps reduce HC and CO content in the exhaust gases by injecting air into the exhaust ports during cold engine operation. This air injection also helps the catalytic converter to reach the proper temperature quicker during warmup. When the engine is warm (Closed Loop), the AIR system injects air into the beds of a three-way converter

to lower the HC and the CO content in the exhaust.

The Air Management system utilizes the following components:
1. An engine driven AIR pump
2. AIR management valves (Air Control, Air Switching)
3. Air flow and control hoses
4. Check valves

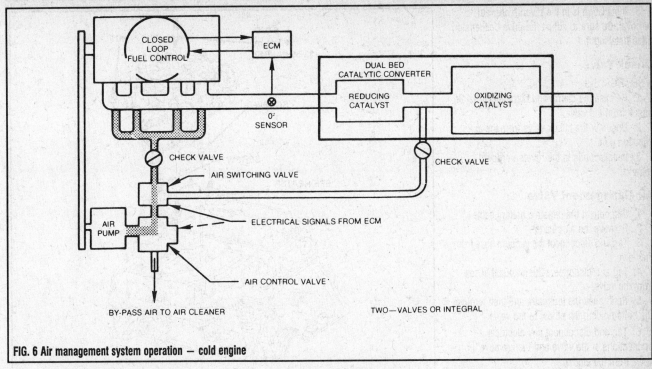

FIG. 6 Air management system operation — cold engine

5. A dual-bed, three-way catalytic converter

The belt driven, vane-type air pump is located at the front of the engine and supplies clean air to the AIR system for purposes already stated. When the engine is cold, the Electronic Control Module (ECM) energizes an AIR control solenoid. This allows air to flow to the AIR switching valve. The AIR switching valve is then energized to direct air to the exhaust ports.

When the engine is warm, the ECM de-energizes the AIR switching valve, thus directing the air between the beds of the catalytic converter. This provides additional oxygen for the oxidizing catalyst in the second bed to decrease HC and CO, while at the same time keeping oxygen levels low in the first bed, enabling the reducing catalyst to effectively decrease the levels of NOx.

If the AIR control valve detects a rapid increase in manifold vacuum (deceleration), certain operating modes (wide open throttle, etc.) or if the ECM self-diagnostic system detects any problem in the system, air is diverted to the air cleaner or directly into the atmosphere.

The primary purpose of the ECM's divert mode is to prevent backfiring. Throttle closure at the beginning of deceleration will temporarily create air/fuel mixtures which are too rich to burn completely. These mixtures become burnable when they reach the exhaust if combined with the injection air. The next firing of the engine will ignite this mixture causing an exhaust backfire. Momentary diverting of the injection air from the exhaust prevents this.

The AIR management system check valves

and hoses should be checked periodically for any leaks, cracks or deterioration.

REMOVAL & INSTALLATION

Air Pump

♦ SEE FIG. 7

1. Remove the AIR management valves and/or adapter at the pump.

2. Loosen the air pump adjustment bolt and remove the drive belt.

3. Unscrew the pump mounting bolts and then remove the pump pulley.

4. Unscrew the pump mounting bolts and then remove the pump.

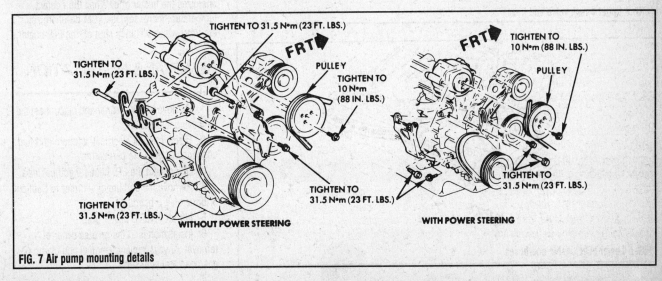

FIG. 7 Air pump mounting details

5. Installation is in the reverse order of removal. Be sure to adjust the drive belt tension after installing it.

Check Valve

♦ SEE FIGS. 8-9

1. Release the clamp and disconnect the air hoses from the valve.

2. Unscrew the check valve from the air injection pipe.

3. Installation is in the reverse order of removal.

Air Management Valve

1. Disconnect the negative battery cable.

2. Remove the air cleaner.

3. Tag and disconnect the vacuum hose from the valve.

4. Tag and disconnect the air outlet hoses from the valve.

5. Bend back the lock tabs and then remove the bolts holding the elbow to the valve.

6. Tag and disconnect any electrical connections at the valve and then remove the valve from the elbow.

7. Installation is in the reverse order of removal.

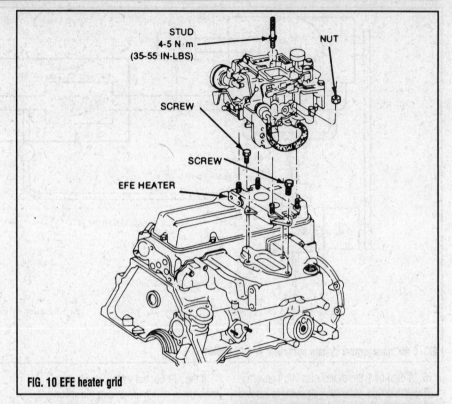

FIG. 10 EFE heater grid

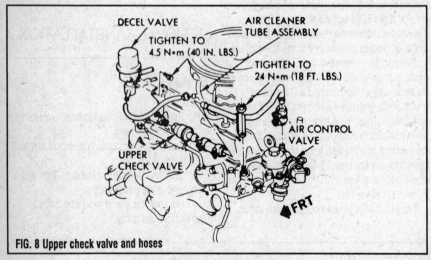

FIG. 8 Upper check valve and hoses

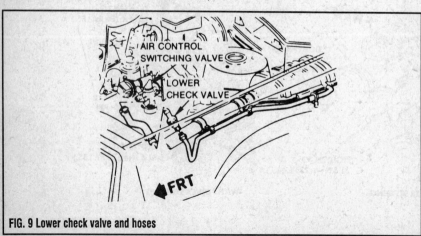

FIG. 9 Lower check valve and hoses

Early Fuel Evaporation (EFE)

♦ SEE FIG. 10

All carbureted models are equipped with this system to reduce engine warm-up time, improve driveability and reduce emissions. The system is electric and uses a ceramic heater grid located underneath the primary bore of the carburetor as part of the carburetor insulator/gasket. When the ignition switch is turned on and the engine coolant temperature is low, voltage is applied to the EFE relay by the ECM. The EFE relay in turn energizes the heater grid. When the coolant temperature increases, the ECM de-energizes the relay which will then shut off the EFE heater.

REMOVAL & INSTALLATION

1. Remove the air cleaner and disconnect the negative battery cable.

2. Disconnect all electrical, vacuum and fuel connections from the carburetor.

3. Disconnect the EFE heater electrical lead.

4. Remove the carburetor — refer to Section 5 for service procedures.

5. Lift off the EFE heater grid.

6. Installation is in the reverse order of removal. Always replace any fuel line clamp or gas hose as necessary.

EFE HEATER RELAY REPLACEMENT

♦ SEE FIG. 11

1. Disconnect the negative battery cable.

2. Remove the retaining bracket on the right fender skirt.

3. Tag and disconnect all electrical connections.

4. Unscrew the retaining bolts and remove the relay.

5. Installation is in the reverse order of removal.

Exhaust Gas Recirculation (EGR)

DESCRIPTION

♦ SEE FIGS. 12-15

All models are equipped with this system, which is used to lower the NOx (oxides of nitrogen) emission levels caused by high combustion temperature.

It does this by introducing exhaust gas, which contains very little oxygen, into the intake manifold. The exhaust gas will not support combustion, but does occupy volume, reducing the total amount of air/fuel mixture which burns in the cylinder. This reduces combustion temperatures.

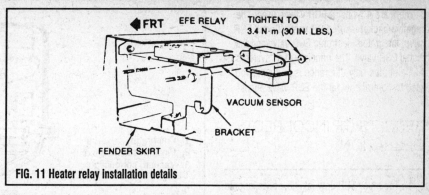

FIG. 11 Heater relay installation details

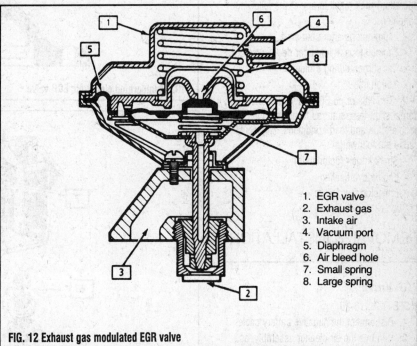

1. EGR valve
2. Exhaust gas
3. Intake air
4. Vacuum port
5. Diaphragm
6. Air bleed hole
7. Small spring
8. Large spring

FIG. 12 Exhaust gas modulated EGR valve

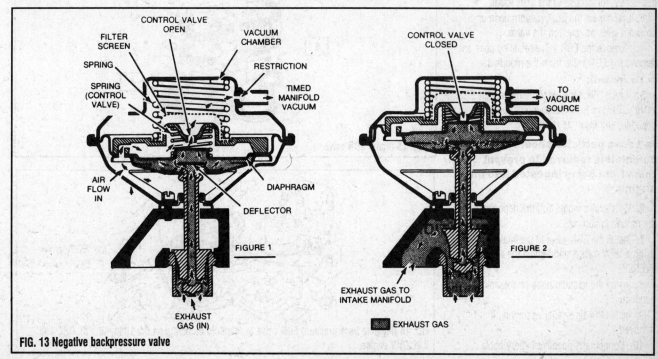

FIG. 13 Negative backpressure valve

There are 4 types of EGR valves used; The negative backpressure EGR valve, Ported EGR valve, Integrated Electronic EGR valve and the Digital EGR valve. The principle of all systems is the same; the only difference is in the method used to control how far the EGR valve opens.

RESULTS OF INCORRECT OPERATION

1. Too much EGR flow (at idle, cruise, or cold operation) may result in any of the following conditions:
- Engine stops after cold start
- Engine stops at idle after deceleration
- Car surges during cruise
- Rough idle

2. Too little or no EGR flow allows combustion temperatures to get too high during acceleration and load conditions. This could cause the following:
- Spark knock (detonation)
- Engine overheating
- Emission test failure

REMOVAL & INSTALLATION

EGR Valve

◆ SEE FIGS. 16–20

1. Disconnect the negative battery cable.
2. Remove the air cleaner assembly, as necessary, for access to the EGR valve.
3. Disconnect the EGR vacuum hose or solenoid wire, as required the valve.
4. Remove the EGR valve retaining bolts and remove the EGR valve from the manifold.

To Install:

5. If reinstalling the old valve inspect the EGR valve passages for excessive build-up of deposits, and clean as necessary.

➡ **Loose particles should be completely removed to prevent them from being ingested into the engine.**

6. With a wire wheel buff the deposits from the mounting surfaces.
7. Install the EGR valve to the intake manifold using a NEW gasket and tighten the bolts EVENLY.
8. Install the vacuum hose or solenoid wire connector.
9. Install the air cleaner assembly, if removed.
10. Connect the negative battery cable.

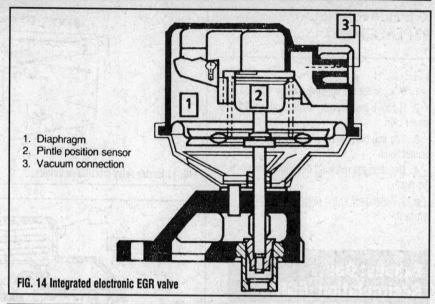

1. Diaphragm
2. Pintle position sensor
3. Vacuum connection

FIG. 14 Integrated electronic EGR valve

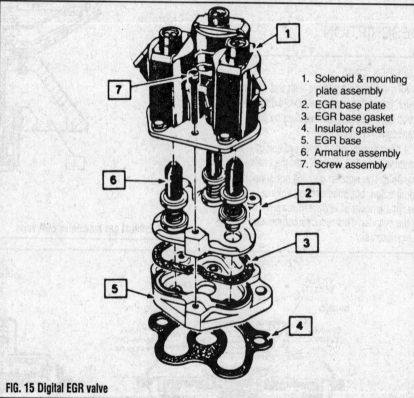

1. Solenoid & mounting plate assembly
2. EGR base plate
3. EGR base gasket
4. Insulator gasket
5. EGR base
6. Armature assembly
7. Screw assembly

FIG. 15 Digital EGR valve

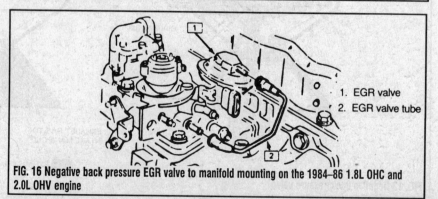

1. EGR valve
2. EGR valve tube

FIG. 16 Negative back pressure EGR valve to manifold mounting on the 1984–86 1.8L OHC and 2.0L OHV engine

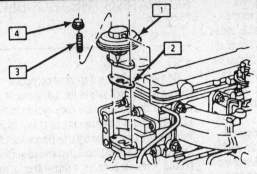

1. EGR valve
2. Gasket
3. Stud 25 N·m (19 lb. ft.)
4. Nut 25 N·m (19 lb. ft.)

FIG. 17 Negative back pressure EGR valve to manifold mounting on the 1987–92 2.0L OHV engine

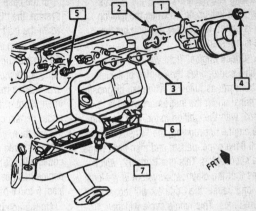

1. EGR valve
2. Valve gasket
3. Tube gasket
4. Nut (3) 25 N·m (19 lb. ft.)
5. Bolt (2) 25 N·m (19 lb. ft.)
6. EGR tube
7. Tube nut 25 N·m (19 lb. ft.)

FIG. 18 Integrated electronic EGR valve manifold mounting — 1985–89 2.8L engine

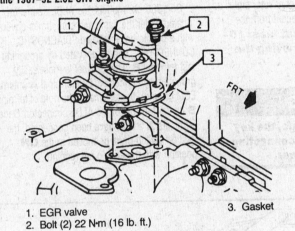

1. EGR valve
2. Bolt (2) 22 N·m (16 lb. ft.)
3. Gasket

FIG. 19 Negative back pressure EGR valve to manifold mounting on the 1987–92 2.0L OHC Non turbocharged engine

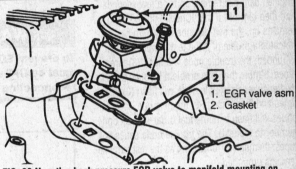

1. EGR valve asm
2. Gasket

FIG. 20 Negative back pressure EGR valve to manifold mounting on the 1987–91 2.0L OHC turbocharged engine

Computer Command Control System (CCC)

The Computer Command Control System (CCC) is an electronically controlled exhaust emission system that can monitor and control a large number of interrelated emission control systems. It can monitor up to 15 various engine/vehicle operating conditions and then use this information to control as many as 9 engine related systems. The system is thereby making constant adjustments to maintain good vehicle performance under all normal driving conditions while at the same time allowing the catalytic converter to effectively control the emissions of HC, CO and NOx.

In addition, the system has a built in diagnostic system that recognizes and identifies possible operational problems and alerts the driver through a "Check Engine" light in the instrument panel. The light will remain on until

the problem is corrected. The system also has built in back-up systems that in most cases of an operational problem will allow for the continued operation of the vehicle in a near normal manner until the repairs can be made.

BASIC TROUBLESHOOTING

➡ **The following explains how to activate the Trouble Code signal light in the instrument cluster. This is not a full fledged CCC system troubleshooting and isolation procedure.**

Before suspecting the CCC system, or any of its components as being faulty, check the ignition system (distributor, timing, spark plugs and wires). Check the engine compression, the air cleaner and any of the emission control components that are not controlled by the ECM.

Also check the intake manifold, the vacuum hoses and hose connectors for any leaks. Check the carburetor or throttle body and mounting bolts for tightness.

The following symptoms could indicate a possible problem area with the CCC system:
1. Detonation
2. Stalling or rough idling when the engine is cold
3. Stalling or rough idling when the engine is hot
4. Missing
5. Hesitation
6. Surging
7. Poor gasoline mileage
8. Sluggish or spongy performance
9. Hard starting when engine is cold
10. Hard starting when the engine is hot
11. Objectionable exhaust odors
12. Engine cuts out
13. Improper idle speed

As a bulb and system check, the "Check Engine" light will come on when the ignition switch is turned to the **ON** position but the engine is not started.

The "Check Engine" light will also produce the trouble code/codes by a series of flashes which translate as follows: When the diagnostic test terminal under the instrument panel is grounded, with the ignition in the **ON** position and the engine not running, the "Check Engine" light will flash once, pause, and then flash twice in rapid succession. This is a Code 12, which indicates that the diagnostic system is working. After a long pause, the Code 12 will repeat itself two more times. This whole cycle will then repeat itself until the engine is started or the ignition switch is turned **OFF**.

➡ **Remove the ground from the test terminal before starting the engine.**

When the engine is started, the "Check Engine" light will remain on for a few seconds and then turn off. If the "Check Engine" light remains on, the self-diagnostic system has detected a problem. If the test terminal is then grounded, the trouble code will flash (3) three times. If more than one problem is found to be in existence, each trouble code will flash (3) three times and then change to the next one. Trouble codes will flash in numerical order (lowest code number to highest). The trouble code series will repeat themselves for as long as the test terminal remains grounded.

A trouble code indicates a problem with a given circuit. For example, trouble code 14 indicates a problem in the cooling sensor circuit. This includes the coolant sensor, its electrical harness and the Electronic Control Module (ECM).

Since the self-diagnostic system cannot diagnose every possible fault in the system, the absence of a trouble code does not necessarily mean that the system is trouble-free. To determine whether or not a problem with the system exists that does not activate a trouble code, a system performance check must be made.

In the case of an intermittent fault in the system, the "Check Engine" light will go out when the fault goes away, but the trouble code will remain in the memory of the ECM. Therefore, if a trouble code can be obtained even though the "Check Engine" light is not on, it must still be evaluated. It must be determined if the fault is intermittent or if the engine must be operating under certain conditions (acceleration, deceleration, etc.) before the "Check Engine" light will come on. In some cases, certain trouble codes will not be recorded in the ECM until the engine has been operated at part throttle for at least 5 to 18 minutes.

On the computer system, depending on how the vehicle is equipped, a trouble code will be stored until the ECM harness connector pigtail or inline fuse has been disconnected from the battery with the key OFF **for at least 10–30 seconds or by removing the ECM fuse.**

✳ WARNING

To prevent ECM damage, the key must be OFF when disconnecting or reconnecting ECM power.

ACTIVATING THE TROUBLE CODE

◆ SEE FIGS. 21-22

On 1982 models, a 5 terminal connector, located on the right side of the fues panel, is used to activate the trouble code system in the ECM. This same connector is use at assembly and known as the Assembly Line Diagnostic Link (ALDL) or Assembly Line Communication Link (ALCL). A trouble code test terminal **D** is located in the 5 terminal connector and a ground terminal **E**, is located next to this terminal. With the ignition **ON**, car not running, jump the test terminal to ground.

On 1983–92 models, the ALDL connector, located under the dash, and sometimes covered with a plastic cover labeled "DIAGNOSTIC CONNECTOR", can be activated by grounding test terminal **B**. The terminal is most easily grounded by connecting it to terminal **A** (internal ECM ground), the terminal to the right of terminal **B** on the top row of the ALDL connector. Once terminals **A** and **B** have been connected, the ignition switch must be moved to the **ON** position with the engine not running.

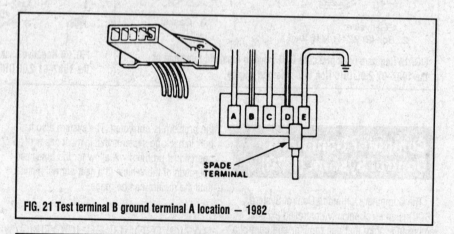

FIG. 21 Test terminal B ground terminal A location — 1982

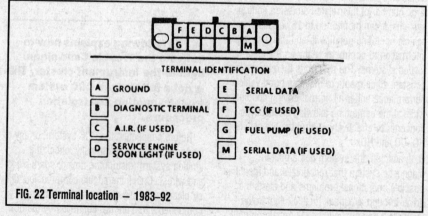

TERMINAL IDENTIFICATION

A	GROUND	**E**	SERIAL DATA
B	DIAGNOSTIC TERMINAL	**F**	TCC (IF USED)
C	A.I.R. (IF USED)	**G**	FUEL PUMP (IF USED)
D	SERVICE ENGINE SOON LIGHT (IF USED)	**M**	SERIAL DATA (IF USED)

FIG. 22 Terminal location — 1983–92

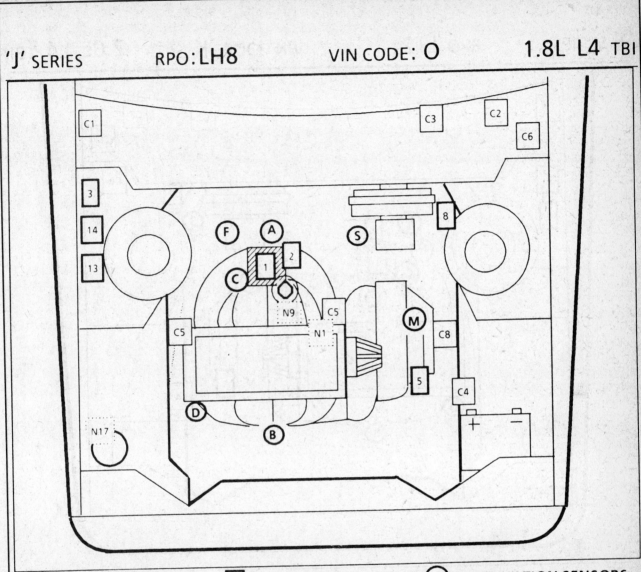

'J' SERIES   RPO: LH8   VIN CODE: O   1.8L L4 TBI

▢ COMPUTER HARNESS

C1 Electronic Control Module (ECM)
C2 ALCL diagnostic connector
C3 "SERVICE ENGINE SOON" light
C4 ECM power
C5 ECM harness ground
C6 Fuse panel
C8 Fuel pump test connector

NOT ECM CONNECTED

N1 Crankcase vent valve (PCV)
N9 Exhaust Gas Recirculation valve
N17 Fuel vapor canister

▢ CONTROLLED DEVICES

1 Fuel injector solenoid
2 Idle air control valve
3 Fuel pump relay
5 Trans. Conv. Clutch connector
8 Engine fan relay
13 A/C compressor relay
14 A/C fan relay

◯ Exhaust Gas Recirculation valve

◯ INFORMATION SENSORS

A Manifold pressure (M.A.P.)
B Exhaust oxygen
C Throttle position
D Coolant temperature
F Vehicle speed
M P/N switch/neutral start
S P/S pressure switch

FIG. 21A Component locations — 1. 8L TBI (VIN 0)

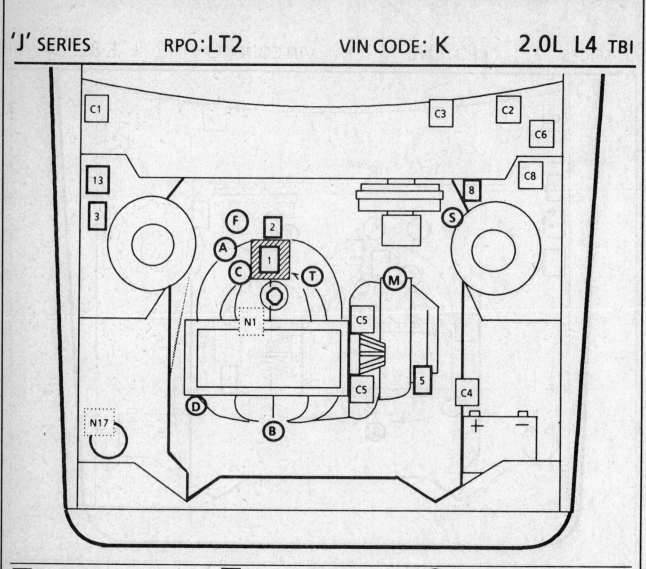

'J' SERIES   RPO: LT2   VIN CODE: K   2.0L L4 TBI

⬜ COMPUTER HARNESS

C1 Electronic Control Module (ECM)
C2 ALDL diagnostic connector
C3 "SERVICE ENGINE SOON" light
C4 ECM power
C5 ECM harness grounds
C6 Fuse panel
C8 Fuel pump test connector

⬚ NOT ECM CONNECTED

N1 Crankcase vent valve (PCV)
N17 Fuel vapor canister

⬡ Exhaust Gas Recirculation valve

⬜ CONTROLLED DEVICES

1 Fuel injector solenoid
2 Idle air control valve
3 Fuel pump relay
5 Trans. Conv. Clutch connector
8 Engine fan relay
13 A/C compressor relay

◯ INFORMATION SENSORS

A Manifold pressure (M.A.P.)
    (Mounted On Air Cleaner)
B Exhaust oxygen
C Throttle position
D Coolant temperature
F Vehicle speed
M P/N switch/neutral start
S P/S pressure switch
T Manifold Air Temperature
    (Mounted On Air Cleaner)

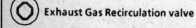

FIG. 21B Component locations — 2.0L OHC (VIN K)

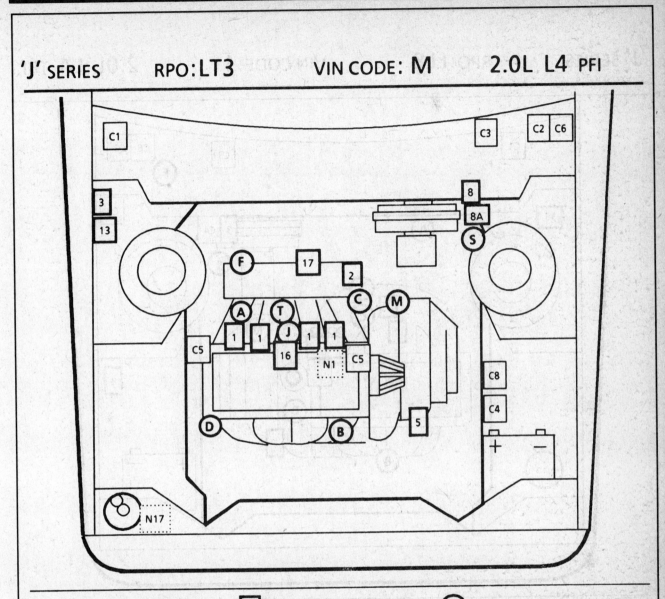

'J' SERIES   RPO:**LT3**   VIN CODE: **M**   **2.0L L4** PFI

COMPUTER HARNESS

C1 Electronic Control Module (ECM)
C2 ALDL diagnostic connector
C3 "SERVICE ENGINE SOON" light
C4 ECM power (2)
C5 ECM harness grounds
C6 Fuse panel
C8 Fuel pump test connector

NOT ECM CONNECTED

N1 Crankcase vent valve (PCV) (inside PCV hose)
N17 Fuel vapor canister

CONTROLLED DEVICES

1 Fuel injectors
2 Idle air control valve
3 Fuel pump relay
5 Trans. Converter Clutch connector
8 Low speed cooling fan relay
8a High Speed cooling fan relay
13 A/C compressor relay
16 Wastegate solenoid
17 EGR Relay (Below Manifold)

INFORMATION SENSORS

A Manifold pressure (M.A.P.)
B Exhaust oxygen
C Throttle position
D Coolant temperature
F PM Generator
J ESC knock (Below Manifold)
M P/N switch/park neutral
S Power Steering Pressure Switch
T Manifold Air Temperature

FIG. 21C Component locations — 2.0L TURBO (VIN M)

'J' SERIES   RPO: LL8   VIN CODE: 1   2.0L L4 TBI

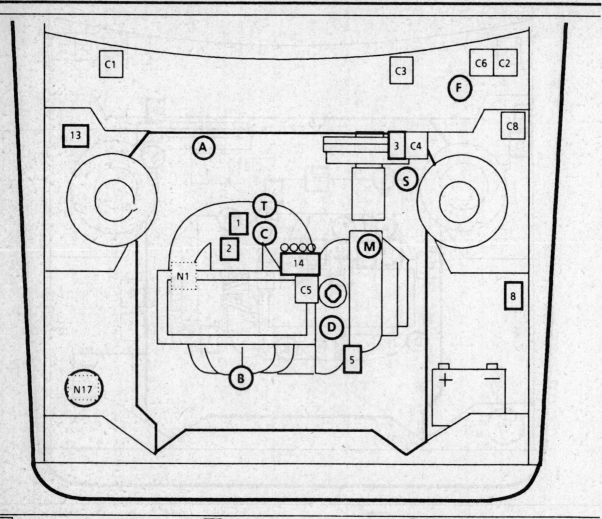

☐ **COMPUTER HARNESS**
- C1   Electronic Control Module (ECM)
- C2   ALDL Diagnostic Connector
- C3   "Service Engine Soon" light
- C4   ECM Power Fuse
- C5   ECM Harness Grounds
- C6   Fuse Panel
- C8   Fuel Pump Test Connector

⬚ **NOT ECM CONNECTED**
- N1   Crankcase Vent Valve (PCV)
- N17   Fuel Vapor Canister

⬡   Exhaust Gas Recirculation valve

☐ **CONTROLLED DEVICES**
- 1   Fuel Injector Solenoid
- 2   Idle Air Control Valve
- 3   Fuel Pump Relay
- 5   TCC Solenoid Connector
- 8   Cooling Fan Relay
- 13   A/C Compressor Relay
- 14   Direct Ignition System Assembly

◯ **INFORMATION SENSORS**
- A   Manifold Pressure (MAP)
- B   Exhaust Oxygen
- C   Throttle Position
- D   Coolant Temperature
- F   Vehicle Speed
- M   P/N Switch
- S   P/S Pressure Switch
- T   MAT Sensor

FIG. 21D Component locations — 2.0L TBI (VIN 1)

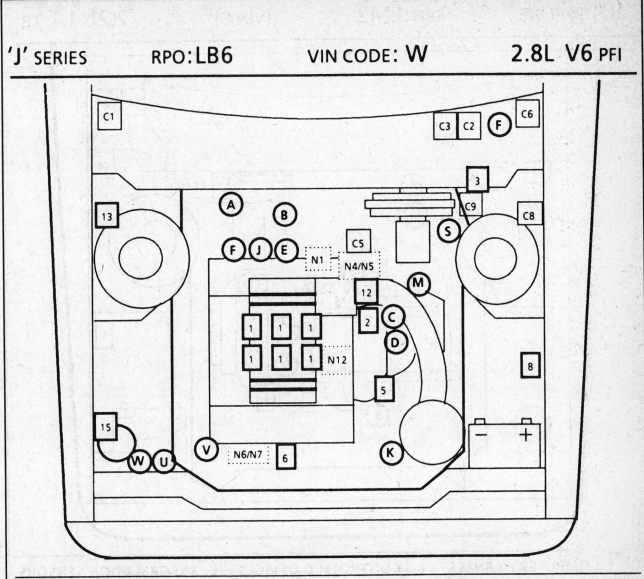

'J' SERIES RPO: LB6 VIN CODE: W 2.8L V6 PFI

FIG. 21E Component locations — 2.8L PFI (VIN W)

☐ COMPUTER HARNESS

- **C1** Electronic Control Module (ECM)
- **C2** ALDL diagnostic connector
- **C3** "SERVICE ENGINE SOON" light
- **C5** ECM harness ground
- **C6** Fuse panel
- **C8** Fuel pump test connector
- **C9** Fuel pump / ECM fuse

☐ NOT ECM CONNECTED

- **N1** Crankcase vent valve (PCV)
- **N4** Engine temp. switch (telltale)
- **N5** Engine temp. sensor (gage)
- **N6** Oil press. switch (telltale)
- **N7** Oil press. sensor (gage)
- **N12** Fuel pressure connector

☐ CONTROLLED DEVICES

- **1** Fuel injector
- **2** Idle air control motor
- **3** Fuel pump relay
- **5** Trans. Converter Clutch connector
- **6** Direct Ignition System (DIS)
- **8** Engine fan relay
- **9.** Air Control Solenoid (M/T only)
- **12** Exh. Gas Recirc. valve
- **13** A/C compressor relay
- **15** Fuel vapor canister solenoid

◯ INFORMATION SENSORS

- **A** Manifold Pressure (MAP)
- **B** Exhaust oxygen
- **C** Throttle position
- **D** Coolant temperature
- **E** Crank Shaft Sensor
- **F** Vehicle speed
- **J** Knock (ESC)
- **K** MAT
- **M** P/N switch
- **S** P/S pressure switch
- **U** A/C pressure fan switch
- **V** A/C Low Press. switch (mounted in compressor)
- **W** A/C Hi Press. cut-out sw.

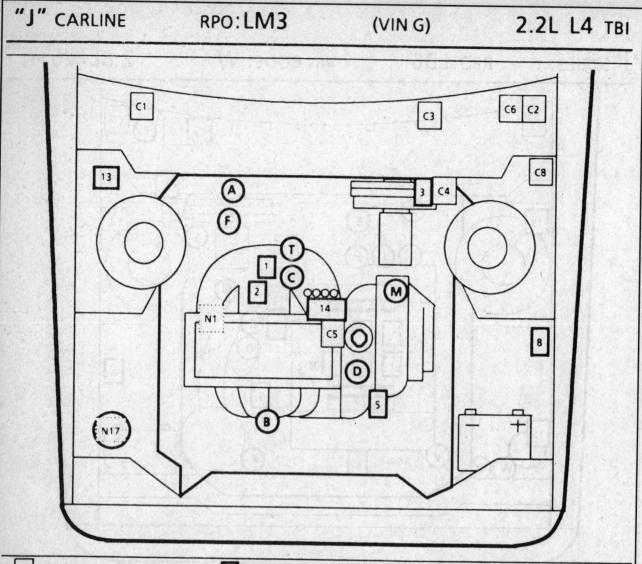

"J" CARLINE   RPO: **LM3**   (VIN G)   **2.2L L4** TBI

□ COMPUTER HARNESS

C1	Electronic Control Module (ECM)
C2	ALDL Diagnostic Connector
C3	"Service Engine Soon" light
C4	ECM Power Fuse
C5	ECM Harness Grounds
C6	Fuse Panel
C8	Fuel Pump Test Connector

☐ NOT ECM CONNECTED

N1	Crankcase Vent Valve (PCV)
N17	Fuel Vapor Canister

⬡ Exhaust Gas Recirculation (EGR) Valve

□ CONTROLLED DEVICES

1	Fuel Injector Solenoid
2	Idle Air Control (IAC) Valve
3	Fuel Pump Relay
5	Torque Converter Clutch (TCC) Solenoid Connector
8	Cooling Fan Relay
13	A/C Compressor Relay
14	Direct Ignition System (DIS) Assembly

○ INFORMATION SENSORS

A	Manifold Absolute Pressure (MAP)
B	Oxygen (O_2) Sensor
C	Throttle Position Sensor (TPS)
D	Coolant Temperature Sensor (CTS)
F	Vehicle Speed Sensor (VSS)
M	Park/Neutral (P/N) Switch
T	Intake Air Temperature (IAT) Sensor (In Air Cleaner Assembly)

FIG. 21F Component locations — 2. 2L TBI (VIN G)

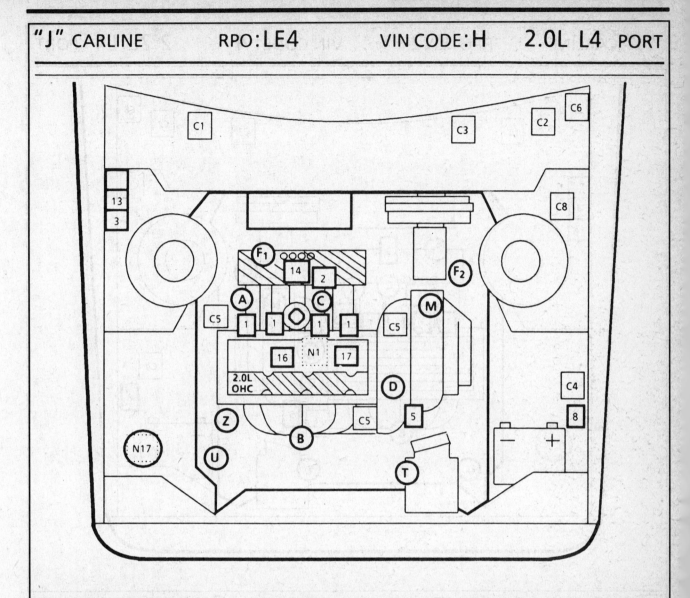

| "J" CARLINE | RPO: LE4 | VIN CODE: H | 2.0L L4 PORT |

COMPUTER HARNESS

- C1 Electronic Control Module (ECM)
- C2 ALDL Diagnostic Connector
- C3 "Check Engine" light
- C4 Power Feed Connector
- C5 ECM Harness Grounds
- C6 Fuse Panel
- C8 Fuel Pump Test Connector

NOT ECM CONNECTED

- N1 Crankcase Vent Valve (PCV)
- N17 Fuel Vapor Canister

CONTROLLED DEVICES

- 1 Fuel Injector
- 2 Idle Air Control (IAC) Valve
- 3 Fuel Pump Relay*
- 5 TCC Solenoid
- 8 Cooling Fan Relay
- 13 A/C Compressor Relay*
- 14 Direct Ignition System (DIS) Coil Assy.
  (Under Intake Plenum)
- 16 Computer Controlled Purge (CCP) Solenoid
- 17 Exhaust Gas Recirculation (EGR) Solenoid
- ⬡ Exhaust Gas Recirculation (EGR) Valve

INFORMATION SENSORS

- A Manifold Absolute Pressure (MAP) Sensor
- B Oxygen (O_2) Sensor
- C Throttle Position Sensor (TPS)
- D Coolant Temperature Sensor (CTS)
- F_1 Vehicle Speed (Auto Trans.)
- F_2 Vehicle Speed (Manual Trans.)
- M Park/Neutral (P/N) Switch
- T Intake Air Temperature (IAT) Sensor (In Air Cleaner Assy.)
- U A/C Pressure Sensor
- Z Crankshaft Position Sensor

* Actual location may vary.

FIG. 21G Component locations — 2.0L PFI (VIN H)

"J" CARLINE   RPO: **LN2**   VIN CODE: **4**   **2.2L L4** PORT

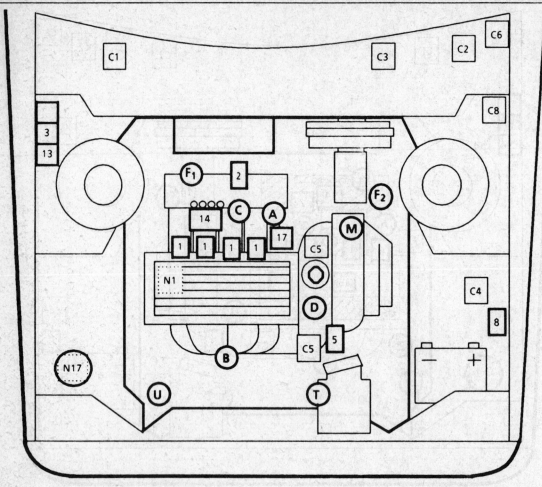

☐ **COMPUTER HARNESS**

C1	Electronic Control Module (ECM)
C2	ALDL Diagnostic Connector
C3	"Check Engine" Light
C4	Power Feed Connector
C5	ECM Harness Grounds
C6	Fuse Panel
C8	Fuel Pump Test Connector

▢ **NOT ECM CONNECTED**

N1	Crankcase Vent Valve (PCV)
N17	Fuel Vapor Canister

*   Actual location may vary

☐ **CONTROLLED DEVICES**

1	Fuel Injector
2	Idle Air Control (IAC) Valve
3	Fuel Pump Relay*
5	Torque Converter Clutch (TCC) Solenoid
8	Cooling Fan Relay
13	A/C Compressor Relay*
14	Direct Ignition System (DIS) Assembly (under intake manifold)
17	Exhaust Gas Recirculation (EGR) Solenoid

⬡ Exhaust Gas Recirculation (EGR) Valve

○ **INFORMATION SENSORS**

A	Manifold Absolute Pressure (MAP) Sensor
B	Oxygen (O_2) Sensor
C	Throttle Position Sensor (TPS)
D	Coolant Temperature Sensor (CTS)
F_1	Vehicle Speed (Auto Trans.)
F_2	Vehicle Speed (Manual Trans.)
M	Park/Neutral (P/N) Switch
T	Intake Air Temperature (IAT) Sensor (On Air Cleaner Assembly)
U	A/C Pressure Sensor

FIG. 21H Component locations – 2. 2L PFI (VIN 4)

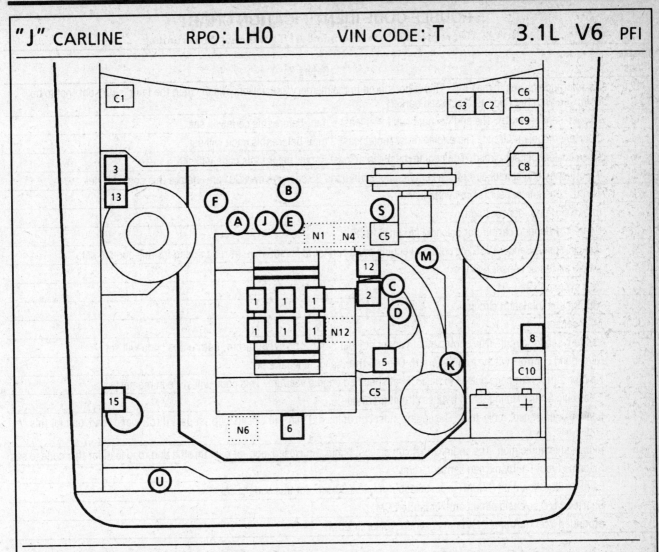

"J" CARLINE   RPO: **LH0**   VIN CODE: **T**   **3.1L V6** PFI

☐ **COMPUTER HARNESS**
- **C1** Electronic Control Module (ECM)
- **C2** ALDL diagnostic connector
- **C3** "SERVICE ENGINE SOON" light
- **C5** ECM harness ground
- **C6** Fuse panel
- **C8** Fuel pump test connector
- **C9** Fuel pump/ECM fuse
- **C10** ECM Power Feed

⋯ **NOT ECM CONNECTED**
- **N1** Positive Crankcase Ventilation (PCV) valve
- **N4** Engine temperature sensor gage and (telltale)
- **N6** Fuel pump/oil pressure sensor gage and (telltale)
- **N12** Fuel pressure connector

☐ **CONTROLLED DEVICES**
- **1** Fuel injector
- **2** Idle Air Control (IAC) motor
- **3** Fuel pump relay
- **5** Trans. Converter Clutch connector
- **6** Direct Ignition System (DIS)
- **8** Cooling fan relay
- **12** Exh. Gas Recirc. valve
- **13** A/C compressor relay
- **15** Fuel vapor canister solenoid

◯ **INFORMATION SENSORS**
- **A** Manifold Air Pressure (MAP)
- **B** Exhaust oxygen (O_2)
- **C** Throttle Position Sensor (TPS)
- **D** Coolant Temperature Sensor (CTS)
- **E** Crank Shaft Sensor
- **F** Vehicle Speed Sensor (VSS)
- **J** Electronic Spark Control (ESC)
- **K** Intake Air Temperature (IAT)
- **M** P/N switch
- **S** P/S pressure switch
- **U** A/C pressure sensor

FIG. 21I Component locations — 3. 1L PFI (VIN T)

TROUBLE CODE IDENTIFICATION CHART

NOTE: Always ground the test terminal AFTER the engine is running.

Trouble Code	Refers To:
12	No reference pulses to the ECM. This is not stored in the memory and will only flash when the fault is present (not to be confused with the Code 12 discussed earlier).
13	Oxygen sensor circiut. The engine must run for at least 5 min. before this code will set.
14	Shortened coolant circuit. The engine must run at least 2 min. before this code will set.
15	Open coolant sensor circuit. The engine must run at least 5 min. before this code will set.
21	Throttle position sensor circuit. The engine must run up to 25 sec., below 800 rpm, before this code will set.
22	Throttle position sensor (signal voltage low)
23	Intake air temp. sensor (high)
23	Open or grounded carburetor solenoid circuit. (1982)
24	Vehicle Speed Sensor (VSS) circuit. The engine must run for at least 5 min. at road speed for this code to set.
25	Intake air temp. sensor (low)
32	EGR system (1990–91)
32	Altitude Compensator circuit.
33	MAP sensor
34	Vacuum sensor circuit. The engine must run for at least 5 min., below 800 rpm, before this code will set.
35	Idle speed control switch circuit shorted. Over ½ throttle for at least 2 sec.
41	No distributor reference pulses to the ECM at specified engine vacuum. This code will store in memory.
42	Electronic Spark Timing (EST) bypass circuit grounded.
44	Lean oxygen sensor indication. The engine must run at least 5 min., in closed loop, at part throttle and road load for this code to set.
45	Rich system indication. The engine must run at least 5 min., in closed loop, at part throttle and road load for this code to set.
44 & 45	(at same time) Faulty oxygen sensor circuit.
51	Faulty calibration until (PROM) or installation. It takes 30 sec. for this code to set.
54	Shorted M/C solenoid circuit and/or faulty ECM.
55	Grounded Vref (terminal 21), faulty oxygen sensor or ECM.

Oxygen Sensor

An oxygen sensor is used on all models. The sensor protrudes into the exhaust stream and monitors the oxygen content of the exhaust gases. The difference between the oxygen content of thc exhaust gases and that of the outside air generates a voltage signal to the ECM. The ECM monitors this voltage and, depending upon the value of the signal received, issues a command to adjust for a rich or a lean condition.

No attempt should ever be made to measure the voltage output of the sensor. The current drain of any conventional voltmeter would be such that it would permanently damage the sensor. No jumpers, test leads or any other electrical connections should ever be made to the sensor. Use these tools ONLY on the ECM side of the wiring harness connector AFTER disconnecting it from the sensor.

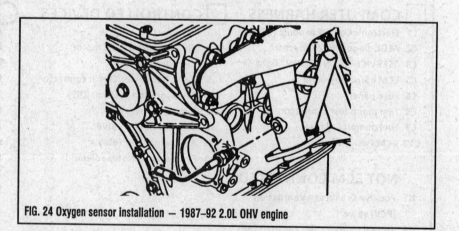

FIG. 24 Oxygen sensor installation — 1987–92 2.0L OHV engine

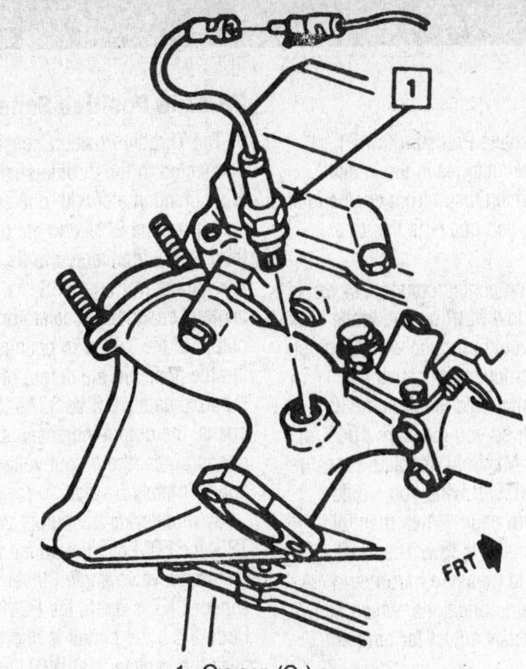

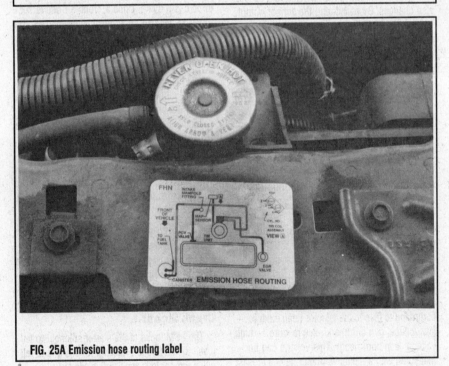

1. Oxygen (O₂) sensor

FIG. 25 Oxygen sensor installation — 1987–92 2.8L and 3.1L V6 engine

FIG. 25A Emission hose routing label

REMOVAL & INSTALLATION

♦ SEE FIGS. 24-25

The oxygen sensor must be replaced every 30,000 miles (48,000 km.). The sensor may be difficult to remove when the engine temperature is below 120°F (49°C). Excessive removal force may damage the threads in the exhaust manifold or pipe; follow the removal procedure carefully.

1. Locate the oxygen sensor. It protrudes from the center of the exhaust manifold at the front of the engine compartment (it looks somewhat like a spark plug).

2. Disconnect the electrical connector from the oxygen sensor.

3. Spray a commercial heat riser solvent onto the sensor threads and allow it to soak in for at least five minutes.

4. Carefully unscrew and remove the sensor.

To install:

5. First coat the new sensor's threads with G.M. anti-seize compound No. 5613695 or the equivalent. This is not a conventional anti-seize paste. The use of a regular compound may electrically insulate the sensor, rendering it inoperative. You must coat the threads with an electrically conductive anti-seize compound.

6. Installation torque is 30 ft. lbs. (42 Nm.). Do not overtighten.

7. Reconnect the electrical connector. Be careful not to damage the electrical pigtail. Check the sensor boot for proper fit and installation.

ELECTRONIC ENGINE CONTROLS

The Electronic Control Module (ECM) is designed to maintain and monitor a large number of interrelated emission control systems. It can monitor up to 15 various engine/vehicle operating conditions and then use this information to control as many as 9 engine related systems. The system is thereby making constant adjustments to maintain good vehicle performance under all normal driving conditions while at the same time allowing the catalytic converter to effectively control the emissions of HC, CO and NOx.

In addition, the system has a built in diagnostic system that recognizes and identifies possible operational problems and alerts the driver through a "Check Engine" light in the instrument panel. The light will remain on until the problem is corrected. The system also has built in back-up systems that in most cases of an operational problem will allow for the continued operation of the vehicle in a near normal manner until the repairs can be made.

INFORMATION SENSORS

Engine Coolant Temperature Sensor

The coolant sensor is a thermister (a resistor) which changes value based on temperature) mounted in the engine coolant stream. Low coolant temperature produces a high resistance (100,000Ω at −40°C/−40°F) while high temperature causes low resistance (70Ω at 130°C/266°F).

The ECM supplies a 5 volt signal to the coolant sensor thru a resistor in the ECM and measures the voltage. The voltage will be high when the engine is cold, and low when the engine is hot. By measuring the voltage, the ECM knows the engine coolant temperature. Engine coolant temperature affects most systems the ECM controls.

A failure in the coolant sensor circuit should set either a Code 14 or Code 15. Remember, these codes indicate a failure in the coolant temperature circuit, so proper use of the chart will lead to either repairing a wiring problem or replacing the sensor, to properly repair a problem.

MAP Sensor

The Manifold Absolute Pressure (MAP) Sensor measures the changes in the intake manifold pressure which result from engine load and speed changes, and converts this to a voltage output.

A closed throttle on engine coastdown would produce a relatively low MAP output, while a wide-open throttle would produce a high output. This high output is produced because the pressure inside the manifold is the same as outside the manifold, so you measure 100% of outside air pressure. Manifold Absolute Pressure (MAP) is the OPPOSITE of what you would measure on a vacuum gage. When manifold pressure is high, vacuum is low. The MAP sensor is also used to measure barometric pressure under certain conditions, which allows the ECM to automatically adjust for different altitudes.

The ECM sends a 5 volts reference signal to the MAP sensor. As the manifold pressure changes, the electrical resistance of the sensor also changes. By monitoring the sensor output voltage, the ECM knows the manifold pressure. A higher pressure, low vacuum (high voltage) requires more fuel, while a lower pressure, higher vacuum (low voltage) requires less fuel.

The ECM uses the MAP sensor to control fuel delivery and ignition timing.

A failure in the MAP sensor circuit should set a Code 33 or Code 34.

Oxygen (O_2) Sensor

The exhaust Oxygen (O_2) sensor is mounted in the exhaust system where it can monitor the oxygen content of the exhaust gas stream. The oxygen content in the exhaust reacts with the oxygen sensor to produce a voltage output. This voltage ranges from approximately 0.010 volt (high O_2 — lean mixture) to 0.9 volt (low O_2 — rich mixture).

By monitoring the voltage output of the O_2 sensor, the ECM will know what fuel mixture command to give to the injector (lean mixture — low voltage; rich command, rich mixture — high voltage, lean command). This voltage can be measured with a digital voltmeter having at least 10 megohms input impedance. Use of standard shop type voltmeters will result in very inaccurate readings.

An open O_2 sensor circuit, should set a Code 13. A shorted sensor circuit should set a Code 44. A high voltage in the circuit should set a Code 45. When any of these codes are set, the car will run in the "Open Loop" mode.

Throttle Position Sensor (TPS)

The Throttle Position Sensor (TPS) is connected to the throttle shaft on the TBI unit. It is a potentiometer with one end connected to 5 volts from the ECM and the other to ground. A third wire is connected to the ECM to measure the voltage from the TPS. As the throttle valve angle is changed (accelerator pedal moved), the output of the TPS also changes. At a closed throttle position, the output of the TPS is low (approximately 0.5 volt). As the throttle valve opens, the output increases so that, at wide-open throttle, the output voltage should be approximately 5 volts.

By monitoring the output voltage from the TPS, the ECM can determine fuel delivery based on throttle valve angle (driver demand). If the sensor CKT is open, the ECM will set a Trouble Code 22. If the circuit is shorted, the ECM will think the vehicle is at WOT, and a Trouble Code 21 will be set. A broken or loose TPS can cause intermittent bursts of fuel from the injector, and an unstable idle, because the ECM thinks the throttle is moving. Once a Trouble Code is set, the ECM will use an artificial value for TPS, and some vehicle performance will return.

Knock Sensor

The knock sensor is mounted in the engine block. When abnormal engine vibrations (spark knock) are present, the sensor produces a voltage signal, which is sent to the ESC module.

Park/Neutral Switch

The Park/Neutral (P/N) switch indicates to the ECM when the transmission is in park or neutral. This information is used for the TCC, and the IAC valve operation.

➡ **Vehicle should not be driven with Park/Neutral (P/N) switch disconnected as idle quality will be affected and a possible false Code 24 VSS.**

Crank Signal

The ECM looks at the starter solenoid to tell when the engine is cranking. It uses this to tell when the car is in the Starting Mode.

If this signal is not available, the car may be hard to start in extremely cold weather.

Air Conditioner Request Signal

This signal tells the ECM that the A/C selector switch is turned "ON" and that the high side low pressure switch is closed. The ECM uses this to adjust the idle speed when the air conditioning is working.

Vehicle Speed Sensor (VSS)

The Vehicle Speed Sensor (VSS) sends a pulsing voltage signal the the ECM, which the ECM converts to miles per hour. This sensor mainly controls the operation the TCC system.

Distributor Reference Signal

The distributor sends a signal to the ECM to tell it both engine rpm and crankshaft position.

DIAGNOSIS

Since the ECM can have a failure which may effect only one circuit, following the diagnostic procedures in this section can reliably tell when a failure has occurred in the ECM. Also, a Code 55 indicates a failure of the ECM.

If a diagnostic chart indicates that the ECM connections or ECM is the cause of a problem, and the ECM is replaced, but does not correct the problem, one of the following may be the reason:

• There is a problem with the ECM terminal connections — the diagnostic chart will say ECM connections or ECM. The terminals may have to be removed from the connector in order to check them properly.

• The ECM or PROM is not correct for the application — The incorrect ECM or PROM may cause a malfunction and may or may not set a code.

• The problem is intermittent — This means that the problem is not present at the time the system is being checked. In this case, make a careful physical inspection of all portions of the system involved.

• Shorted solenoid, relay coil or harness — Solenoids and relays are turned "ON" and "OFF" by the ECM using internal electronic switches called "drivers." Each driver is part of a group of four called "Quad-Drivers."

A shorted solenoid, relay coil or harness may cause an ECM to fail, and a replacement ECM to fail when it is installed. Use a short tester, J 34696, BT 8405, or equivalent, as a fast, accurate means of checking for a short circuit.

• The PROM may be faulty — Although the PROM rarely fails, it operates as part of the ECM. Therefore, it could be the cause of the problem. Substitute a known good PROM.

• The replacement ECM may be faulty — After the ECM is replaced, the system should be rechecked for proper operation. If the diagnostic chart again indicates the ECM is the problem, substitute a known good ECM. Although this is a rare condition, it could happen.

ECM

A faulty ECM will be determined in the diagnostic charts, or by a Code 55.

PROM

An incorrect or faulty PROM, which is part of the ECM, may set a Code 51.

ECM Inputs

All of the sensors and input switches can be diagnosed by the use of a "Scan" tool. Following is a short description of how the sensors and switches can be diagnosed by the use of "Scan." The "Scan" can also be used to compare the values for a normal running engine with the engine you're diagnosing.

Coolant Temperature Sensor (CTS)

A "Scan" tool displays engine temperature in degrees centigrade and farenheit. After the engine is started, the temperature should rise steadily between 88–106°C (190–222°F), then stabilize when thermostat opens. A fault in the coolant sensor circuit should set a Code 14 or 15. The code charts also contain a chart to check for sensor resistance values relative to temperature.

MAP Sensor

A "Scan" tool reads manifold pressure and will display volts and kPa of pressure.

Key "ON," engine stopped, (no vacuum), MAP will read high voltage or pressure, while at idle (high vacuum), MAP will read low voltage or pressure. Likewise, on acceleration, MAP will read high and on deceleration, will read low.

A failure in the MAP sensor, or circuit, should result in a Code 33 or 34.

Oxygen (O₂) Sensor

The "Scan" has several positions that will indicate the state of the exhaust gases, O_2 voltage, integrator, and block learn.

A problem in the O_2 sensor circuit should set a Code 13 (open circuit), Code 44 (lean O_2 indication), Code 45 (rich O_2 indication). Refer to applicable chart, if any of these codes were stored in memory

Throttle Position Sensor (TPS)

A "Scan" tool displays throttle position in volts. For example, the 3.1L should read under 1.25 volts, with throttle closed and ignition on, or at idle. Voltage should increase at a steady rate as throttle is moved toward WOT.

The ECM has the ability to auto-zero the TPS voltage, if it is below about 1.25 volts. This means that any voltage less than 1.25 volts will be determined by the ECM to be 0% throttle. Some "Scan" tools have the ability to read the

percentage of throttle angle and should read 0%, when the throttle is closed. A failure in the TPS, or circuit, should set a Code 21 or 22.

Vehicle Speed Sensor (VSS)

A "Scan" tool reading should closely match with speedometer reading, with drive wheels turning. A failure in the VSS circuit should set a Code 24.

P/N Switch

A "Scan" tool should read "P–N–," when in park or neutral and "R–D–L," when in drive. This reading may vary with different makes of tools.

A/C Request Signal

If the low pressure switch is closed and A/C is "ON," the A/C clutch should indicate "ON".

Distributor Reference Signal

A "Scan" tool will read this signal and is displayed in rpm.

Knock Signal

A "Scan" tool will indicate when the ESC module signals the ECM that knock is present.

BASIC KNOWLEDGE AND TOOLS REQUIRED

To use this manual most effectively, a general understanding of basic electrical circuits and circuit testing tools is required. You should be familiar with wiring diagrams, the meaning of voltage, ohms, amps, the basic theories of electricity, and understand what happens in an open or shorted wire.

To perform system diagnosis, the use of a TECH 1 Diagnostic Computer or equivalent "Scan" tool is required. A tachometer, test light, ohmmeter, digital voltmeter with 10 megohms impedance, vacuum gauge, and jumper wires are also required. Please become acquainted with the tools and their use before attempting to diagnose a vehicle.

DIAGNOSTIC INFORMATION

The diagnostic "tree" charts and functional checks in this manual are designed to locate a faulty circuit or component through logic based on the process of elimination.

"Service Engine Soon" Light

This light is on the instrument panel and has the following functions.

• It informs the driver that a problem has occurred and that the vehicle should be taken for service as soon as reasonably possible.

• It displays "Codes" stored by the ECM which help the technician diagnose system problems.

• It indicates "Open Loop" or "Closed Loop" operation.

As a bulb and system check, the light will come "ON" with the key "ON" and the engine not running. When the engine is started, the light will turn "OFF". If the light remains "ON", the self-diagnostic system has detected a problem. If the problem goes away, the light will go out in most cases after 10 seconds, but a Code will remain stored in the ECM.

When the light remains "ON" while the engine is running, or when a malfunction is suspected due to a drive ability or emissions problem, a "Diagnostic Circuit Check" must be performed. These checks will expose malfunctions which may not be detected if other diagnostics are performed prematurely.

Intermittent "Service Engine Soon" Light

In the case of an "intermittent" problem, the "Service Engine Soon" light will light for ten (10) seconds and then will go out. However, the corresponding code will be stored in the memory of the ECM until the battery voltage to the ECM has been removed. When unexpected codes appear during the code reading process, one can assume that these codes were set by an intermittent malfunction and could be helpful in diagnosing the system.

An intermittent code may or may not re-set. If it is an intermittent failure, a Diagnostic Code Chart is not used. A physical inspection of the applicable sub-system most often will resolve the problem.

Reading Codes

The provision for communicating with the ECM is the Assembly Line Diagnostic Link (ALDL) connector. It is located under the instrument panel and is sometimes covered by a plastic cover labeled "DIAGNOSTIC CONNECTOR." It is used in the assembly plant to receive information in checking that the engine is operating properly before it leaves the plant. The code(s) stored in the ECM's memory can be read either through TECH 1 Diagnostic Computer, a hand-held diagnostic scanner plugged into the ALDL connector or by counting the number of flashes of the "Service Engine Soon" light when the diagnostic terminal of the ALDL connector is grounded. The ALDL connector terminal "B" (diagnostic terminal) is the second terminal from the right of the ALDL

connector's top row. The terminal is most easily grounded by connecting it to terminal "A" (internal ECM ground), the terminal to the right of terminal "B" on top row of the ALDL connector.

Once terminals "A" and "B" have been connected, the ignition switch must be moved to the "ON" position, with the engine not running. At this point, the "Service Engine Soon" light should flash Code 12 three times consecutively. This would be the following flash sequence: "flash, pause, flash-flash, long pause, flash, pause, flash-flash, long pause, flash, pause, flash-flash." Code 12 indicates that the ECM's diagnostic system is operating. If Code 12 is not indicated, a problem is present within the diagnostic system itself, and should be addressed by consulting the appropriate diagnostic chart.

Following the output of Code 12, the "Service Engine Soon" light will indicate a diagnostic code three times if a code is present, or it will simply continue to output Code 12. If more than one diagnostic code has been stored in the ECM's memory, the codes will be output from the lowest to the highest, with each code being displayed three times.

Clearing Codes

To clear the codes from the memory of the ECM, either to determine if the malfunction will occur again or because repair has been completed, the ECM power feed must be disconnected for at least thirty (30) seconds. Depending on how the vehicle is equipped, the ECM power feed can be disconnected at the positive battery terminal "pigtail," the inline fuseholder that originates at the positive connection at the battery, or the ECM fuse in the fuse block. (The negative battery terminal may be disconnected, but other on-board memory data, such as preset radio tuning, will also be lost.)

❄ WARNING

To prevent ECM damage, the key must be "OFF when disconnecting or reconnecting ECM power.

➡ **When using a hand-held TECH 1 Diagnostic Computer, or "Scan" tool to read the codes, clearing the diagnostic codes is done in the same manner as in the above procedure.**

Diagnostic Mode

When the Diagnostic terminal is grounded with the ignition "ON" and the engine "OFF," the system will enter what is called the Diagnostic Mode. In this mode the ECM will:

1. Display a Code 12 by flashing the "Service Engine Soon" light (indicating the system is operating correctly).

2. Display any stored codes by flashing the "Service Engine Soon" light. Each code will be flashed three times, then Code 12 will be flashed again.

3. Energize all ECM controlled relays and solenoids except fuel pump relay. This allows checking circuits which may be difficult to energize without driving the vehicle and being under particular operating conditions.

4. The IAC valve moves to its fully extended position on most models, blocking the idle air passage. This is useful in checking the minimum idle speed.

Field Service Mode

If the diagnostic terminal is grounded with the engine running, the system will enter the Field Service mode. In this mode, the "Service Engine Soon" light will indicate whether the system is in "Open Loop" or "Closed Loop."

In "Open Loop" the "Service Engine Soon" light flashes two and one-half times per second.

In "Closed Loop," the light flashes once per second. Also, in "Closed Loop," the light will stay "OFF" most of the time if the system is running lean. It will stay "ON" most of the time if the system is running rich.

While the system is in Field Service Mode, new codes cannot be stored in the ECM and the "Closed Loop" timer is bypassed.

ECM Learning Ability

The ECM has a "learning" ability which allows it to make corrections for minor variations in the fuel system to improve driveability. If the battery is disconnected, to clear diagnostic codes or for other repair, the "learning" process resets and begins again. A change may be noted in the vehicle's performance. To "teach" the vehicle, ensure that the engine is at operating temperature. The vehicle should be driven at part throttle, with moderate acceleration and idle conditions until normal performance returns.

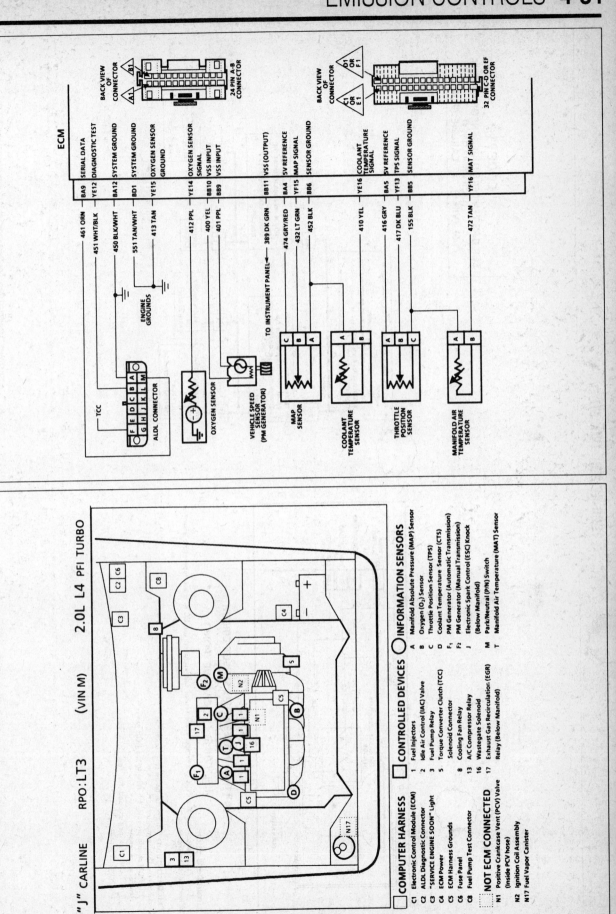

1990-92 2.0L (VIN M)

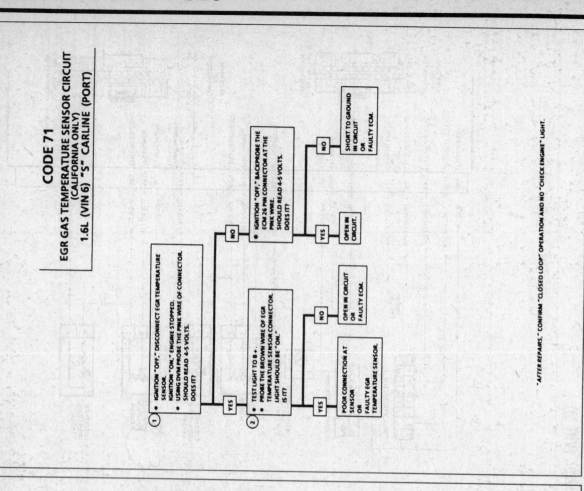

CODE 71

EGR GAS TEMPERATURE SENSOR CIRCUIT
(CALIFORNIA ONLY)
1.6L (VIN 6) "S" CARLINE (PORT)

Circuit Description:

Code 71 indicates that the EGR gas temperature sensor has signaled the ECM of a temperature above or below the calibrated range.

Test Description: Number(s) below refer to circled number(s) on the diagnostic chart.

1. The ECM should provide 4-5 volts to the EGR gas temperature sensor.
2. The ECM provides ground for the EGR gas temperature sensor.

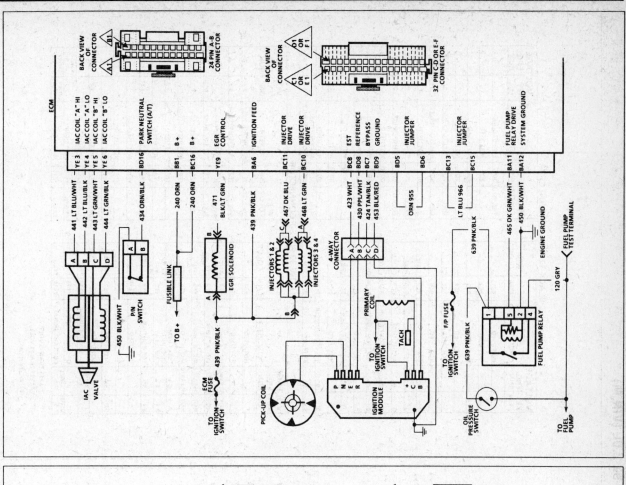

1990-92 2.0L (VIN M)

1990-92 2.0L (VIN M)

PORT FUEL INJECTION ECM CONNECTOR IDENTIFICATION

This ECM voltage chart is for use with a digital voltmeter to further aid in diagnosis. The voltages you get may vary due to low battery charge or other reasons, but they should be very close.

THE FOLLOWING CONDITIONS MUST BE MET BEFORE TESTING:

• Engine at operating temperature • Engine idling in "Closed Loop" (For "Engine Run" column) in park or neutral • Test terminal not grounded • "Scan" tool not installed
• B+ indicates battery or charging system voltage

32 PIN C-D CONNECTOR — BACK VIEW OF CONNECTOR (BLACK)

24 PIN A-B CONNECTOR — BACK VIEW OF CONNECTOR (BLACK)

32 PIN E-F CONNECTOR — BACK VIEW OF CONNECTOR (YELLOW)

BLACK 32 PIN C-D CONNECTOR

WIRE COLOR	PIN	CIRCUIT	VOLTAGE KEY ENG. "ON"	VOLTAGE ENG RUN
	BC1	NOT USED		
	BC2	NOT USED		
	BC3	NOT USED		
	BC4	NOT USED		
	BC5	NOT USED		
	BC6	NOT USED		
TAN	BC7	BYPASS	0*	varies 4.7
WHT	BC8	EST	0*	1.2
DK BLU	BC9	A/C REQUEST	0	0
LT GRN	BC10	INJECTOR DRIVER	B+	B+
DK BLU	BC11	INJECTOR DRIVER	B+	B+
	BC12	NOT USED		
LT BLU	BC13	INJECTOR JUMPER	0*	0*
	BC14	NOT USED		
LT BLU	BC15	INJECTOR JUMPER	0*	0*
ORN	BC16	BATTERY	B+	B+
TAN/WHT	BD1	ECM GROUND	0*	0
	BD2	NOT USED		
	BD3	NOT USED		
	BD4	NOT USED		
ORN	BD5	INJECTOR JUMPER	0*	0*
ORN	BD6	INJECTOR JUMPER	0*	0*
	BD7	NOT USED		
PPL/WHT	BD8	REFERENCE	0*	varies 1.0
BLK/RED	BD9	IGN. GROUND	0*	0*
	BD10	NOT USED		
	BD11	NOT USED		
	BD12	NOT USED		
	BD13	NOT USED		
	BD14	NOT USED		
	BD15	NOT USED		
ORN/BLK	BD16	PARK/NEUTRAL AUTO TRANS. ONLY	0*	0*

YELLOW 32 PIN E-F CONNECTOR

WIRE COLOR	PIN	CIRCUIT	VOLTAGE KEY ENG. "ON"	VOLTAGE ENG RUN
	YE1	NOT USED		
	YE2	NOT USED		
LT BLU/WHT	YE3	IAC "A" HIGH	NOT USEABLE	
LT BLU/WHT	YE4	IAC "A" LOW	NOT USEABLE	
LT GRN/WHT	YE5	IAC "B" HIGH	NOT USEABLE	
LT GRN/BLK	YE6	IAC "B" LOW	NOT USEABLE	
BRN/WHT	YE7	"SES" LAMP	.1	
DK GRN/WHT	YE8	COOLING FAN RELAY	B+	
TAN/LT GRN	YE9	EGR CONTROL	B+	
	YE10	NOT USED		
	YE11	NOT USED		
WHT/BLK	YE12	ALDL DIAG. ENABLE	5.0	5.0
	YE13	NOT USED		
PPL	YE14	O² SENSOR SIGNAL	varies .1-.9	varies .1-3
TAN	YE15	O² SENSOR GROUND	0*	0*
YEL	YE16	COOLANT SIGNAL	varies 1.5	varies 1.5
DK GRN/WHT	YF1	A/C CONTROL RELAY	B+	B+
GRY	YF2	WASTE GATE SOL.	B+	.5
	YF3	NOT USED		
TAN/BLK	YF4	TCC SOLENOID	0*	0*
	YF5	NOT USED		
	YF6	NOT USED		
	YF7	NOT USED		
	YF8	NOT USED		
DK BLU	YF9	ESC SIGNAL	2.4	2.4
	YF10	NOT USED		
	YF11	NOT USED		
	YF12	NOT USED		
DK BLU	YF13	TPS SIGNAL	.84	.84
	YF14	NOT USED		
LT GRN	YF15	MAP SIGNAL	2.2	varies .8
TAN	YF16	MAT SIGNAL	2.4	varies 2.2

BLACK 24 PIN A-B CONNECTOR

WIRE COLOR	PIN	CIRCUIT	VOLTAGE KEY ENG. "ON"	VOLTAGE ENG RUN
	BA1	NOT USED		
	BA2	NOT USED		
	BA3	NOT USED		
GRY	BA4	5 VOLTS REFERENCE	5.0	5.0
GRY	BA5	5 VOLTS REFERENCE	5.0	5.0
PNK/BLK	BA6	IGN POWER	B+	B+
	BA7	NOT USED		
	BA8	NOT USED		
ORN	BA9	SERIAL DATA	4.8	4.8
	BA10	NOT USED		
DK GRN/WHT	BA11	FUEL PUMP RELAY	B+ 2 sec.	B+
BLK/WHT	BA12	ECM GROUND	0	0
ORN	BB1	BATTERY	B+	B+
	BB2	NOT USED		
	BB3	NOT USED		
	BB4	NOT USED		
BLK/YEL	BB5	MAT & TPS GROUND	0	0
BLK	BB6	MAP & COOLANT GROUND	0	0
	BB7	NOT USED		
	BB8	NOT USED		
PPL	BB9	VSS INPUT	0	0
YEL	BB10	VSS INPUT	0	0
DK GRN	BB11	VSS TO I/P	3.8	9.5
RED	BB12	VSS OUTPUT	0	0

ENGINE   2.0L TURBO LT 3

* Less than 5 Volt
▽ Less than 1 Volt
① A/C Fan "OFF"

1990-92 2.0L (VIN M)

DIAGNOSTIC CIRCUIT CHECK

The Diagnostic Circuit Check is an organized approach to identifying a problem created by an electronic engine control system malfunction. It must be the starting point for any driveability complaint diagnosis because it directs the service technician to the next logical step in diagnosing the complaint.

The "Scan" data listed in the table may be used for comparison after completing the diagnostic circuit check and finding the on-board diagnostics functioning properly with no trouble codes displayed. The "Typical Data Values" are an average of display values recorded from normally operating vehicles and are intended to represent what a normally functioning system would typically display.

A "SCAN" TOOL THAT DISPLAYS FAULTY DATA SHOULD NOT BE USED, AND THE PROBLEM SHOULD BE REPORTED TO THE MANUFACTURER. THE USE OF A FAULTY "SCAN" TOOL CAN RESULT IN MISDIAGNOSIS AND UNNECESSARY PARTS REPLACEMENT.

Only the parameters listed below are used in this manual for diagnosis. If a "Scan" tool reads other parameters, the values are not recommended by General Motors for use in diagnosis. If use of the "Scan" tool to diagnosis ECM inputs, refer to the applicable component diagnosis section in if all values are within the range illustrated, refer to symptoms

"SCAN" TOOL DATA

Test Under Following Conditions: Idle, Upper Radiator Hose Hot, Closed Throttle, Park or Neutral, "Closed Loop", All Accessories "OFF".

"SCAN" Position	Units Displayed	Typical Data Value
Engine Speed	RPM	+ 50 RPM from desired rpm in drive (AUTO) ± 100 RPM from desired rpm in neutral (MANUAL)
Desired Idle	RPM	ECM idle command (varies with temperature)
Coolant Temperature	Degrees Celsius	85 - 105
MAT Temperature	Degrees Celsius	10 - 90 (varies with underhood temperature and sensor location)
MAP	kPa/Volts	1 - 2 Volts (varies with manifold and barometric pressures)
Baro	kPa/Volts	Varies with barometric pressure
Throttle Position	Volts	.4 - 1.25
Throttle Angle	0 - 100%	0
Oxygen Sensor	Millivolts	100 - 1000
Injector Pulse width	Milliseconds	.8 - 3.0
Spark Advance	Degrees	Varies
Fuel Integrator	Counts	110 - 145
Block Learn	Counts	118 - 138
Open/Closed Loop	Open/Closed	"Closed Loop" (may enter "Open Loop" with extended idle)
Knock Retard	Degrees	0
Knock Signal	Yes/No	No
Exhaust Recirculation	0 - 100%	0
Boost Pressure	kPa	100
Wastegate Duty Cycle	0 - 100%	1 - 50
Park/Neutral Switch	Counts (Steps) P/N and R-D-L	Park/Neutral (P/N)
VSS	MPH/kPa	0
Torque Conv. Clutch	"ON"/"OFF"	"OFF"
Battery Voltage	Volts	13.5 - 14.5
A/C Request	Yes/No	No
A/C Clutch	"ON"/"OFF"	"OFF"
Cooling Fan Relay	"ON"/"OFF"	"OFF"

DIAGNOSTIC CIRCUIT CHECK
2.0L TURBO (VIN M) "J" CARLINE (PORT)

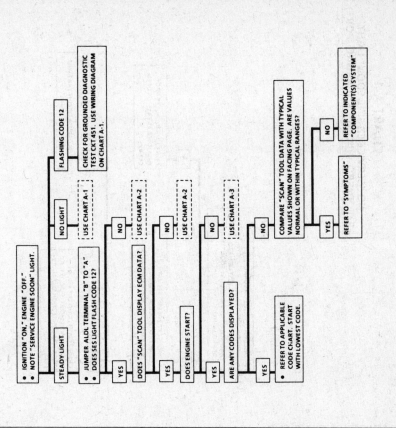

1990-92 2.0L (VIN M)

CHART A-1

NO "SERVICE ENGINE SOON" LIGHT
2.0L TURBO (VIN M) "J" CARLINE (PORT)

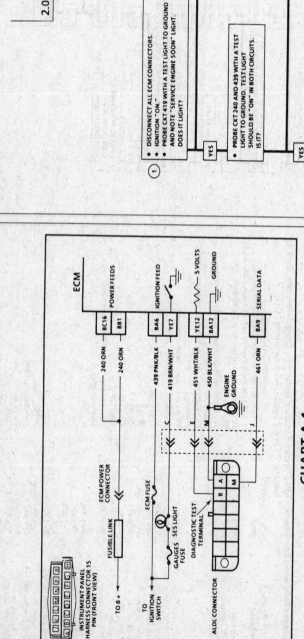

① • DISCONNECT ALL ECM CONNECTORS.
• IGNITION "ON."
• PROBE CKT 419 WITH A TEST LIGHT TO GROUND AND NOTE "SERVICE ENGINE SOON" LIGHT. DOES IT LIGHT?

YES | **NO**

YES branch:
• PROBE CKT 240 AND 439 WITH A TEST LIGHT TO GROUND. TEST LIGHT SHOULD BE "ON" IN BOTH CIRCUITS. IS IT?

NO branch:
FAULTY BULB, FAULTY GAGE FUSE, OPEN CKT 419, OR OPEN CKT 439.

YES | **NO**

YES branch:
CHECK ECM GROUND CKT 450. IF ECM GROUND CIRCUIT IS OK, IT IS A POOR ECM CONNECTION OR FAULTY ECM.

NO branch:
REPAIR OPEN IN CIRCUIT THAT WILL NOT LIGHT TEST LIGHT.

CLEAR CODES AND CONFIRM "CLOSED LOOP" OPERATION AND NO "SERVICE ENGINE SOON" LIGHT.

ECM

BC16	240 ORN	POWER FEEDS
BB1	240 ORN	
BA6	439 PNK/BLK	IGNITION FEED
YE7	419 BRN/WHT	
YE12	451 WHT/BLK	5 VOLTS
BA12	450 BLK/WHT	GROUND
BA9	461 ORN	SERIAL DATA

ENGINE GROUND

INSTRUMENT PANEL HARNESS CONNECTOR 15 PIN (FRONT VIEW)

TO B +

FUSIBLE LINK

ECM POWER CONNECTOR

TO IGNITION SWITCH

ECM FUSE

GAUGES SES LIGHT FUSE

DIAGNOSTIC TEST TERMINAL

ALDL CONNECTOR

CHART A-1

NO "SERVICE ENGINE SOON" LIGHT
2.0L TURBO (VIN M) "J" CARLINE (PORT)

Circuit Description:

There should always be a steady "Service Engine Soon" light when the ignition is "ON" and the engine is "OFF." Battery voltage is supplied directly to the light bulb. The electronic control module (ECM) controls the light and turns it "ON" by providing a ground path through CKT 419 to the ECM.

Test Description: Numbers below refer to circled numbers on the diagnostic chart.

1. Probing CKT 419 to ground creates an alternate ground. If the "Service Engine Soon" light illuminates, this verifies that the trouble is not in the lamp portion of the circuit.

Diagnostic Aids:

If engine runs OK, check the following:
• Faulty light bulb.
• CKT 419 open.
• Gage fuse blown. This will result in no oil or generator lights, seat belt reminder, etc.

If "Engine Cranks But Won't Run," use CHART A-3.

1990-92 2.0L (VIN M)

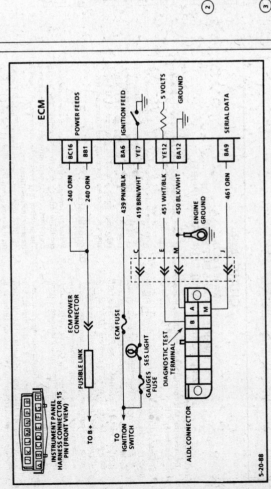

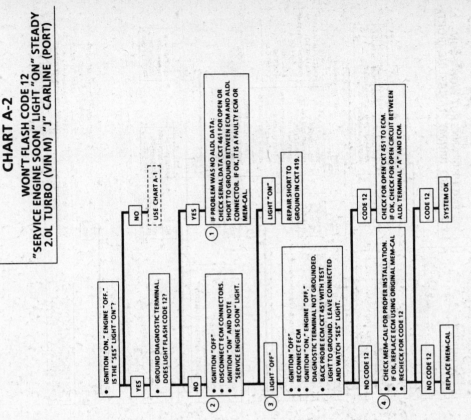

CHART A-2

WON'T FLASH CODE 12
"SERVICE ENGINE SOON" LIGHT "ON" STEADY
2.0L TURBO (VIN M) "J" CARLINE (PORT)

Circuit Description:

There should always be a steady "Service Engine Soon" light when the ignition is "ON" and engine stopped. Battery voltage is supplied directly to the light bulb. The electronic control module (ECM) will turn the light "ON" by grounding CKT 419 at the ECM.

With the diagnostic terminal grounded, the light should flash a Code 12 followed by any trouble code(s) stored in memory.

A steady light suggests a short to ground in the light control CKT 419 or an open in diagnostic CKT 451.

Test Description: Numbers below refer to circled numbers on the diagnostic chart.

1. If there is a problem with the ECM that causes a "Scan" tool to not read serial data, then the ECM should not flash a Code 12. If Code 12 does flash, be sure that the "Scan" tool is functioning properly on another vehicle. If the "Scan" tool is functioning properly and CKT 461 is OK, the Mem-Cal or ECM may be at fault for the no ALDL symptom.

2. If the light goes "OFF" when the ECM connector is disconnected, then CKT 419 is not shorted to ground.

3. This step will check for an open diagnostic CKT 451.

4. At this point the "Service Engine Soon" light wiring is OK. The problem is a faulty ECM or Mem-Cal. If Code 12 does not flash, the ECM should be replaced using the original Mem-Cal. Replace the Mem-Cal only after trying an ECM, as a defective Mem-Cal is an unlikely cause of the problem.

1990-92 2.0L (VIN M)

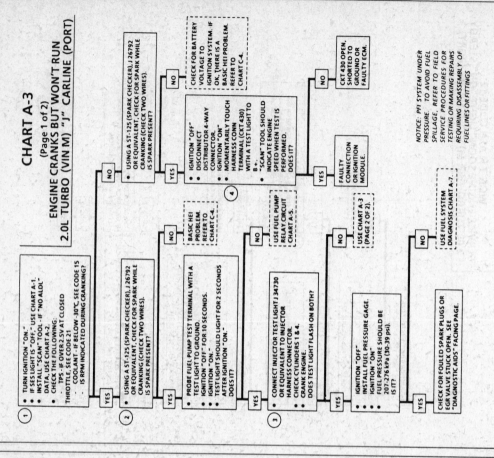

CHART A-3
(Page 1 of 2)
ENGINE CRANKS BUT WON'T RUN
2.0L TURBO (VIN M) "J" CARLINE (PORT)

(1)
- TURN IGNITION "ON."
- IF SES LIGHT IS "OFF," USE CHART A-1.
- INSTALL "SCAN" TOOL. IF "NO ALDL" DATA, USE CHART A-2.
- CHECK THE FOLLOWING:
  TPS: IF OVER 2.5V AT CLOSED THROTTLE, SEE CODE 21
  COOLANT: IF BELOW -30°C, SEE CODE 15
- IS RPM INDICATED DURING CRANKING?

(2) USING A ST-125 (SPARK CHECKER), J 26792 OR EQUIVALENT, CHECK FOR SPARK WHILE CRANKING (CHECK TWO WIRES). IS SPARK PRESENT?

USING A ST-125 (SPARK CHECKER), J 26792 OR EQUIVALENT, CHECK FOR SPARK WHILE CRANKING (CHECK TWO WIRES). IS SPARK PRESENT?

- PROBE FUEL PUMP TEST TERMINAL WITH A TEST LIGHT TO GROUND.
- IGNITION "OFF" FOR 10 SECONDS.
- IGNITION "ON."
- TEST LIGHT SHOULD LIGHT FOR 2 SECONDS AFTER IGNITION "ON."
DOES IT?

- IGNITION "OFF."
- DISCONNECT DISTRIBUTOR 4-WAY CONNECTOR.
- IGNITION "ON."
- MOMENTARILY TOUCH HARNESS CONN TERMINAL (CKT 430) WITH A TEST LIGHT TO B+.
- "SCAN" TOOL SHOULD INDICATE ENGINE SPEED WHEN TEST IS PERFORMED. DOES IT?

CHECK FOR BATTERY VOLTAGE TO IGNITION SYSTEM. IF OK, THERE IS A BASIC HEI PROBLEM. REFER TO CHART C-4.

BASIC HEI PROBLEM. REFER TO CHART C-4.

(3)
- CONNECT INJECTOR TEST LIGHT J 34730 OR EQUIVALENT TO INJECTOR HARNESS CONNECTOR.
- CHECK CYLINDERS 1 & 4.
- CRANK ENGINE.
DOES TEST LIGHT FLASH ON BOTH?

USE FUEL PUMP RELAY CIRCUIT CHART A-5.

FAULTY CONNECTION OR IGNITION MODULE.

- IGNITION "OFF."
- INSTALL FUEL PRESSURE GAGE.
- IGNITION "ON."
- FUEL PRESSURE SHOULD BE 207-276 kPa (30-39 psi).
IS IT?

USE CHART A-3 (PAGE 2 OF 2).

CKT 430 OPEN, SHORTED TO GROUND OR FAULTY ECM.

CHECK FOR FOULED SPARK PLUGS OR EGR VALVE STUCK OPEN. SEE "DIAGNOSTIC AIDS" FACING PAGE.

USE FUEL SYSTEM DIAGNOSIS CHART A-7.

NOTICE: PFI SYSTEM UNDER PRESSURE. TO AVOID FUEL SPILLAGE. REFER TO FIELD SERVICE PROCEDURES FOR TESTING OR MAKING REPAIRS REQUIRING DISASSEMBLY OF FUEL LINES OR FITTINGS.

CLEAR CODES AND CONFIRM "CLOSED LOOP" OPERATION AND NO "SERVICE ENGINE SOON" LIGHT.

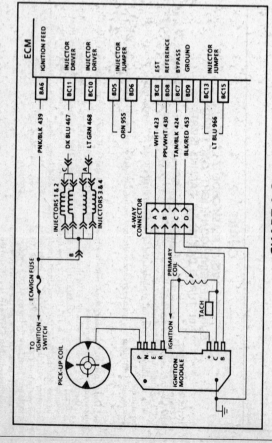

ECM
- IGNITION FEED — BA6
- INJECTOR DRIVER — BC11
- INJECTOR DRIVER — BC10
- INJECTOR JUMPER — BD5
- INJECTOR JUMPER — BD6
- EST — BC8
- REFERENCE — BD8
- BYPASS — BC7
- GROUND — BD9
- INJECTOR JUMPER — BC13
- INJECTOR JUMPER — BC15

PNK/BLK 439 · DK BLU 467 · LT GRN 468 · ORN 955 · WHT 423 · PPL/WHT 430 · TAN/BLK 424 · BLK/RED 453 · LT BLU 966

INJECTORS 1 & 2 · INJECTORS 3 & 4 · 4-WAY CONNECTOR (A B C D) · PRIMARY COIL · TACH · IGNITION MODULE (P N E R + C B) · PICK-UP COIL · TO IGNITION SWITCH · ECM/IGN FUSE

CHART A-3
(Page 1 of 2)
ENGINE CRANKS BUT WON'T RUN
2.0L TURBO (VIN M) "J" CARLINE (PORT)

Circuit Description:
Before using this chart, battery condition, engine cranking speed, and fuel quantity should be checked and verified as being OK.

Test Description: Numbers below refer to circled numbers on the diagnostic chart.

1. A "Service Engine Soon" light "ON" is a basic test to determine if there is battery voltage and ignition voltage supplied to the ECM. No ALDL data may be due to an ECM problem. CHART A-2 will diagnose the ECM. If TPS voltage is over 2.5 volts, the engine may be in the "clear flood" mode, which will cause starting problems. The engine will not start without reference pulses and, therefore, the "Scan" tool should indicate engine speed during cranking.

2. If engine speed was indicated during crank, the ignition module is receiving a 'crank signal, but "no spark" at this test indicates the ignition module is not triggering the coil or there is a secondary ignition problem.

3. The test light should flash, indicating the ECM is controlling the injectors. The brightness of the light is not important. However, the test light should be a J 34730 or equivalent.

4. This test will determine if the ignition module is not generating the reference pulse, or if the wiring or ECM are at fault. By touching and removing a test light to battery voltage on CKT 430, a reference pulse should be generated. If engine speed is indicated, the ECM and wiring are OK.

Diagnostic Aids:

- Water or foreign material can cause a no' start condition during freezing weather. The engine may start after .5 or 6 minutes in a heated shop. The problem may recur after an overnight park in freezing temperatures.

An EGR sticking open can cause a low air/fuel ratio during cranking. Unless the system enters "clear flood" at the first indication of a flooding condition it can result in a no start.

Fuel pressure: Low fuel pressure can result in a very lean air/fuel ratio. See CHART A-7.

1990-92 2.0L (VIN M)

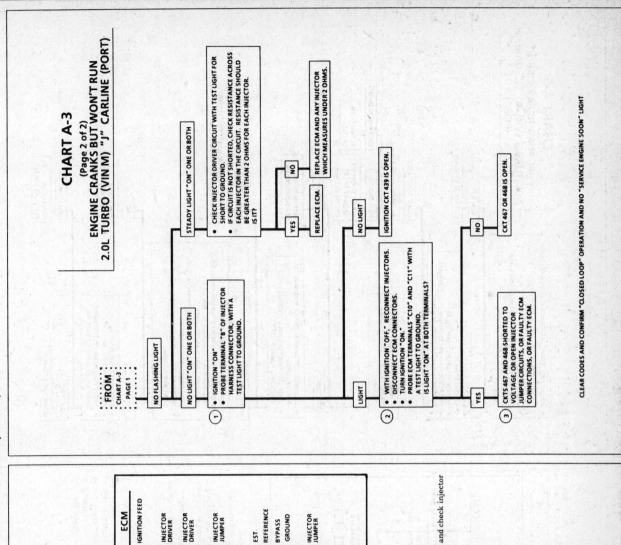

CHART A-3

(Page 2 of 2)

ENGINE CRANKS BUT WON'T RUN
2.0L TURBO (VIN M) "J" CARLINE (PORT)

FROM
CHART A-3
PAGE 1

NO FLASHING LIGHT

NO LIGHT "ON" ONE OR BOTH

STEADY LIGHT "ON" ONE OR BOTH

1. • IGNITION "ON"
   • PROBE TERMINAL "B" OF INJECTOR HARNESS CONNECTOR, WITH A TEST LIGHT TO GROUND.

• CHECK INJECTOR DRIVER CIRCUIT WITH TEST LIGHT FOR SHORT TO GROUND.
• IF CIRCUIT IS NOT SHORTED, CHECK RESISTANCE ACROSS EACH INJECTOR IN THE CIRCUIT. RESISTANCE SHOULD BE GREATER THAN 2 OHMS FOR EACH INJECTOR.
IS IT?

NO → REPLACE ECM AND ANY INJECTOR WHICH MEASURES UNDER 2 OHMS.

YES → REPLACE ECM.

LIGHT

2. • WITH IGNITION "OFF," RECONNECT INJECTORS.
   • DISCONNECT ECM CONNECTORS.
   • TURN IGNITION "ON."
   • PROBE ECM TERMINALS "C10" AND "C11" WITH A TEST LIGHT TO GROUND.
   IS LIGHT "ON" AT BOTH TERMINALS?

NO LIGHT → IGNITION CKT 439 IS OPEN.

3. NO → CKT 467 OR 468 IS OPEN.

   YES → CKTS 467 AND 468 SHORTED TO VOLTAGE, OR OPEN INJECTOR JUMPER CIRCUITS, OR FAULTY ECM CONNECTIONS, OR FAULTY ECM.

CLEAR CODES AND CONFIRM "CLOSED LOOP" OPERATION AND NO "SERVICE ENGINE SOON" LIGHT

ECM

IGNITION FEED — BA6 — PNK/BLK 439

INJECTOR DRIVER — BC11 — DK BLU 467

INJECTOR DRIVER — BC10 — LT GRN 468

INJECTOR JUMPER — BD5

— BD6 — ORN 955

EST. — BC8 — WHT 423

REFERENCE — BD8 — PPL/WHT 430

BYPASS — BC7 — TAN/BLK 424

GROUND — BD9 — BLK/RED 453

INJECTOR JUMPER — BC13 — LT BLU 966

— BC15

TO IGNITION SWITCH

ECM/IGN FUSE

INJECTORS 1 & 2

INJECTORS 3 & 4

PICK-UP COIL

P N E R

IGNITION MODULE

+ C B

4-WAY CONNECTOR
A B C D

PRIMARY COIL

IGNITION

TACH

CHART A-3

(Page 2 of 2)

ENGINE CRANKS BUT WON'T RUN
2.0L TURBO (VIN M) "J" CARLINE (PORT)

Test Description: Numbers below refer to circled numbers on the diagnostic chart.

1. This step checks for ignition voltage at the injector harness connector. Disconnect harness connector before probing terminal "B." Reconnect connector after test.

2. Checks for open CKT 467 or 468 from connector to ECM. Be sure injector harness is connected.

3. Disconnect ECM C-D connector and check injector jumper circuits with a DVM.

1990-92 2.0L (VIN M)

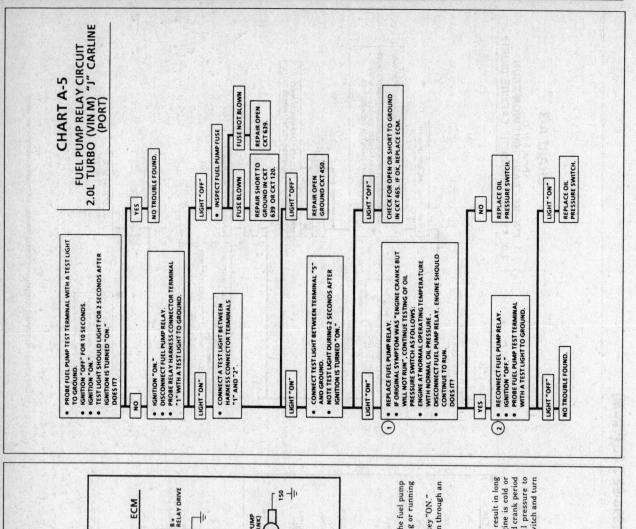

CHART A-5
FUEL PUMP RELAY CIRCUIT
2.0L TURBO (VIN M) "J" CARLINE (PORT)

CHART A-5
FUEL PUMP RELAY CIRCUIT
2.0L TURBO (VIN M) "J" CARLINE (PORT)

Circuit Description:

When the ignition switch is turned "ON," the Electronic Control Module (ECM) will activate the fuel pump relay and run the in-tank fuel pump. The fuel pump will operate as long as the engine is cranking or running and the ECM is receiving ignition reference pulses.

If there are no reference pulses, the ECM will shut "OFF" the fuel pump within 2 seconds after key "ON."

Should the fuel pump relay or the 12V relay drive from the ECM fail, the fuel pump will be run through an oil pressure switch back-up circuit.

Test Description: Numbers below refer to circled numbers on the diagnostic chart.

1. This test will determine if the oil pressure switch is closing and supplying voltage to the fuel pump when the relay is not functioning.
2. This test will determine if the oil pressure switch is stuck open.

Diagnostic Aids:

An inoperative fuel pump relay can result in long cranking times, particularly if the engine is cold or engine oil pressure is low. The extended crank period is caused by the time necessary for oil pressure to build enough to close the oil pressure switch and turn "ON" the fuel pump.

1990-92 2.0L (VIN M)

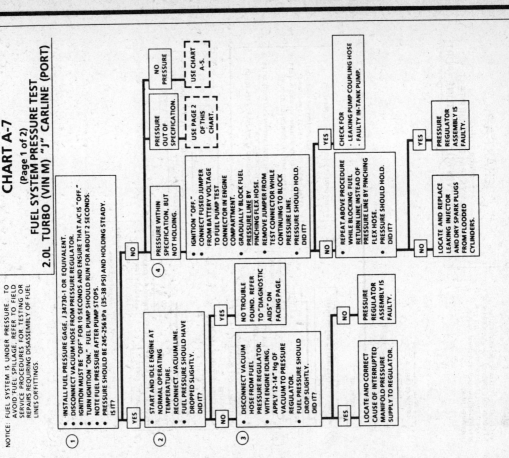

CHART A-7
(Page 1 of 2)
FUEL SYSTEM PRESSURE TEST
2.0L TURBO (VIN M) "J" CARLINE (PORT)

NOTICE: FUEL SYSTEM IS UNDER PRESSURE. TO AVOID FUEL SPILLAGE, REFER TO FIELD SERVICE PROCEDURES FOR TESTING OR REPAIRS REQUIRING DISASSEMBLY OF FUEL LINES OR FITTINGS.

1. • INSTALL FUEL PRESSURE GAGE, J 34730-1 OR EQUIVALENT.
   • DISCONNECT VACUUM HOSE FROM PRESSURE REGULATOR.
   • IGNITION MUST BE "OFF." FOR 10 SECONDS AND ENSURE THAT A/C IS "OFF."
   • TURN IGNITION "ON." FUEL PUMP SHOULD RUN FOR ABOUT 2 SECONDS.
   • NOTE FUEL PRESSURE AFTER PUMP STOPS.
   • PRESSURE SHOULD BE 245-256 kPa (35-38 PSI) AND HOLDING STEADY.
   IS IT?

   NO → PRESSURE WITHIN SPECIFICATION, BUT NOT HOLDING.
   NO → PRESSURE OUT OF SPECIFICATION. → USE PAGE 2 OF THIS CHART.
   NO PRESSURE → USE CHART A-5.

4. • IGNITION "OFF."
   • CONNECT FUSED JUMPER FROM BATTERY VOLTAGE TO FUEL PUMP TEST CONNECTOR IN ENGINE COMPARTMENT.
   • GRADUALLY BLOCK FUEL PRESSURE LINE BY PINCHING FLEX HOSE.
   • REMOVE JUMPER FROM TEST CONNECTOR WHILE CONTINUING TO BLOCK PRESSURE LINE.
   • PRESSURE SHOULD HOLD. DID IT?

   YES → REPEAT ABOVE PROCEDURE WHILE BLOCKING FUEL RETURN LINE INSTEAD OF PRESSURE LINE BY PINCHING FLEX HOSE.
   PRESSURE SHOULD HOLD. DID IT?

   YES → CHECK FOR
   - LEAKING PUMP COUPLING HOSE
   - FAULTY IN-TANK PUMP.

   NO → LOCATE AND REPLACE LEAKING INJECTOR AND/DRY SPARK PLUGS FROM FLOODED CYLINDERS.

   YES → PRESSURE REGULATOR ASSEMBLY IS FAULTY.

2. START AND IDLE ENGINE AT NORMAL OPERATING TEMPERATURE. RECONNECT VACUUM LINE. FUEL PRESSURE SHOULD HAVE DROPPED SLIGHTLY. DID IT?

   YES → NO TROUBLE FOUND. REFER TO "DIAGNOSTIC AIDS" ON FACING PAGE.

3. DISCONNECT VACUUM HOSE FROM FUEL PRESSURE REGULATOR. WITH ENGINE IDLING, APPLY 12-14" Hg OF VACUUM TO FUEL PRESSURE REGULATOR. FUEL PRESSURE SHOULD DROP SLIGHTLY. DID IT?

   NO → LOCATE AND CORRECT CAUSE OF INTERRUPTED MANIFOLD PRESSURE SUPPLY TO REGULATOR.

   YES → PRESSURE REGULATOR ASSEMBLY IS FAULTY.

   NO → PRESSURE REGULATOR ASSEMBLY IS FAULTY.

CLEAR CODES AND CONFIRM "CLOSED LOOP" OPERATION AND NO "SERVICE ENGINE SOON" LIGHT.

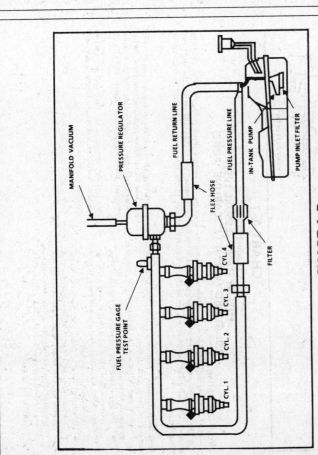

MANIFOLD VACUUM
PRESSURE REGULATOR
FUEL RETURN LINE
FLEX HOSE
FUEL PRESSURE LINE
IN-TANK PUMP
PUMP INLET FILTER
FILTER
FUEL PRESSURE GAGE TEST POINT
CYL. 1   CYL. 2   CYL. 3   CYL. 4

CHART A-7
(Page 1 of 2)
FUEL SYSTEM PRESSURE TEST
2.0L TURBO (VIN M) "J" CARLINE (PORT)

Circuit Description:

The fuel pump delivers fuel to the fuel rail and injectors, where the system pressure is controlled to 245 to 256 kPa (35 to 38 psi) by the pressure regulator. Excess fuel is returned to the fuel tank. When the engine is stopped, the pump can be energized by applying battery voltage to the test terminal located in the engine compartment.

Test Description: Numbers below refer to circled numbers on the diagnostic chart.

1. Use pressure gage J 34730-1. Wrap a shop towel around the fuel pressure tap to absorb any small amount of fuel leakage that may occur when installing the gage. (The pressure will not leak down after the fuel pump is stopped on a correctly functioning system.)

2. While the engine is idling, manifold pressure is low (vacuum). When applied to the fuel regulator diaphragm, the pressure will result in a lower fuel pressure at about 190-200 kPa (25-30 psi).

3. The application of vacuum to the pressure regulator should result in a fuel pressure drop.

4. Pressure leak-down may be caused by one of the following:
   • In-tank fuel pump check valve not holding
   • Pump coupling hose leaking
   • Fuel pressure regulator valve leaking
   • Injector sticking open

Diagnostic Aids:

Improper fuel system pressure may contribute to one or all of the following symptoms:
   • Cranks but won't run
   • Code 44 or 45
   • Cutting out (May feel like ignition problem)
   • Hesitation, loss of power or poor fuel economy
   Refer to "Symptoms"

1990-92 2.0L (VIN M)

CHART A-7
(Page 2 of 2)
FUEL SYSTEM PRESSURE TEST
2.0L TURBO (VIN M) "J" CARLINE (PORT)

NOTICE: FUEL SYSTEM IS UNDER PRESSURE TO AVOID FUEL SPILLAGE, REFER TO FIELD SERVICE PROCEDURES FOR TESTING OR REPAIRS REQUIRING DISASSEMBLY OF FUEL LINES OR FITTINGS.

FROM CHART A-7 PAGE 1
PRESSURE OUT OF SPEC. 207-276 kPa (30-39 PSI)

HIGH PRESSURE

(7) · DISCONNECT VACUUM LINE TO PRESSURE REGULATOR.
· DISCONNECT FUEL RETURN LINE FLEXIBLE HOSE. ATTACH A 3/16 I.D. FLEX HOSE TO PRESSURE REGULATOR SIDE OF RETURN LINE AND INSERT THE OTHER END INTO AN APPROVED GASOLINE CONTAINER.
· NOTE FUEL PRESSURE WITHIN 2 SECONDS AFTER IGNITION IS TURNED "ON".
· PRESSURE SHOULD BE 245-256 kPa (35-36 PSI). IS IT?

YES → LOCATE AND REPAIR RESTRICTED FUEL RETURN LINE.

NO → PRESSURE REGULATOR ASSEMBLY IS FAULTY.

LOW PRESSURE

(5) · CHECK FOR RESTRICTED IN-LINE FILTER. IS FILTER OK?

NO → REPLACE FILTER AND RE-TEST.

YES

(6) · IGNITION "OFF."
· APPLY BATTERY VOLTAGE TO FUEL PUMP TEST CONNECTOR.
· GRADUALLY BLOCK FUEL RETURN LINE BY PINCHING FLEXIBLE HOSE AND NOTE PRESSURE.
· PRESSURE SHOULD BE ABOVE 450 kPa (65 psi). IS IT?

NO → CHECK IN-TANK PUMP ASSEMBLY FOR
- FAULTY FUEL PUMP
- LEAKING COUPLING HOSE
- INCORRECT PUMP.

YES → PRESSURE REGULATOR ASSEMBLY IS FAULTY.

CLEAR CODES AND CONFIRM "CLOSED LOOP" OPERATION AND NO "SERVICE ENGINE SOON" LIGHT.

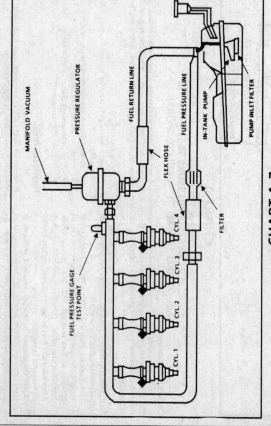

MANIFOLD VACUUM — PRESSURE REGULATOR — FUEL RETURN LINE — FLEX HOSE — FUEL PRESSURE LINE — IN-TANK PUMP — PUMP INLET FILTER — FILTER — CYL. 4 — CYL. 3 — CYL. 2 — CYL. 1 — FUEL PRESSURE GAGE TEST POINT

CHART A-7
(Page 2 of 2)
FUEL SYSTEM PRESSURE TEST
2.0L TURBO (VIN M) "J" CARLINE (PORT)

Circuit Description:
The fuel pump delivers fuel to the fuel rail and injectors, where the system pressure is controlled to 245 to 256 kPa (35 to 36 psi) by the pressure regulator. Excess fuel is returned to the fuel tank. When the engine is stopped, the pump can be energized by applying battery voltage to the test terminal located in the engine compartment.

Test Description: Numbers below refer to circled numbers on the diagnostic chart.

5. Pressure less than 245 kPa (35 psi) may be caused by one of two problems.
   · The regulated fuel pressure is too low. The system will be running lean and may set Code 44. Also, hard cold starting and overall poor performance is possible.
   · Restricted flow is causing a pressure drop. Normally, a vehicle with a fuel pressure loss at idle will not be driveable. However, if the pressure drop occurs only while driving, the engine will surge and then stop as pressure begins to drop rapidly.

6. Restricting the fuel return line allows the fuel pump to build above regulated pressure. When battery voltage is applied to the pump test terminal, pressure should be above 450 kPa (65 psi).

7. This test determines if the high fuel pressure is due to a restricted fuel return line or a pressure regulator problem.

1990-92 2.0L (VIN M)

CODE 13
OXYGEN (O₂) SENSOR CIRCUIT
(OPEN CIRCUIT)
2.0L TURBO (VIN M) "J" CARLINE (PORT)

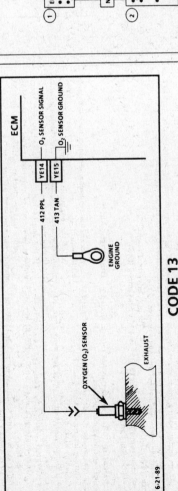

OXYGEN (O₂) SENSOR

ECM

YE14 — O₂ SENSOR SIGNAL
YE15 — O₂ SENSOR GROUND

412 PPL
413 TAN

ENGINE GROUND

EXHAUST

6-21-89

Circuit Description:

The ECM supplies a voltage of about .45 volt between terminals "YE14" and "YE15". (If measured with a 10 megohm digital voltmeter, this may read as low as .32 volt.) The O₂ sensor varies the voltage within a range of about 1 volt if the exhaust is rich, down through about .10 volt if exhaust is lean.

The sensor is like an open circuit and produces no voltage when it is below 316°C (600°F). An open sensor circuit or cold sensor causes "Open Loop" operation.

Test Description: Numbers below refer to circled numbers on the diagnostic chart.

1. Code 13 will set:
   - Engine at normal operating temperature
   - O₂ signal voltage steady between .35 and .55 volt
   - Throttle position sensor signal above 6.5%
   - All conditions must be met for about 60 seconds.

   If the conditions for a Code 13 exist, the system will not go "Closed Loop."

2. This will determine if the sensor is at fault or the wiring or ECM is the cause of the Code 13.

3. In doing this test use only a high impedance digital volt ohm meter. This test checks the continuity of CKTs 412 and 413 because if CKT 413 is open, the ECM voltage on CKT 412 will be over .6 volt (600 mV).

Diagnostic Aids:

Normal "Scan" voltage varies between 100 mV to 999 mV (.1 and 1.0 volt) while in "Closed Loop." Code 13 will set in 3 seconds if all criteria have been met and the system will go "Open Loop."

Refer to "Intermittents"

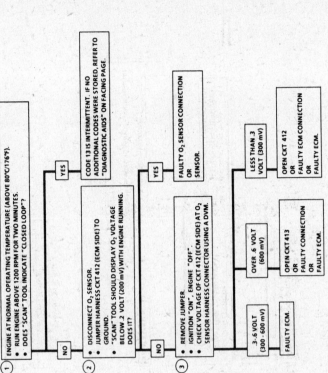

CODE 13
OXYGEN (O₂) SENSOR CIRCUIT
(OPEN CIRCUIT)
2.0L TURBO (VIN M) "J" CARLINE (PORT)

1
ENGINE AT NORMAL OPERATING TEMPERATURE (ABOVE 80°C/176°F).
- RUN ENGINE ABOVE 1200 RPM FOR TWO MINUTES.
- DOES "SCAN" TOOL INDICATE "CLOSED LOOP"?

NO → **2**
DISCONNECT O₂ SENSOR.
JUMPER HARNESS CKT 412 (ECM SIDE) TO GROUND.
"SCAN" TOOL SHOULD DISPLAY O₂ VOLTAGE BELOW .2 VOLT (200 mV) WITH ENGINE RUNNING. DOES IT?

YES → CODE 13 IS INTERMITTENT. IF NO ADDITIONAL CODES WERE STORED, REFER TO "DIAGNOSTIC AIDS" ON FACING PAGE.

NO → **3**
- REMOVE JUMPER.
- IGNITION "ON", ENGINE "OFF".
- CHECK VOLTAGE OF CKT 412 (ECM SIDE) AT O₂ SENSOR HARNESS CONNECTOR USING A DVM.

YES → FAULTY O₂ SENSOR CONNECTION OR SENSOR.

.3 - .6 VOLT (300 - 600 mV) → FAULTY ECM.

OVER .6 VOLT (600 mV) → OPEN CKT 413 OR FAULTY CONNECTION OR FAULTY ECM.

LESS THAN .3 VOLT (300 mV) → OPEN CKT 412 OR FAULTY ECM CONNECTION OR FAULTY ECM.

CLEAR CODES AND CONFIRM "CLOSED LOOP" OPERATION AND NO "SERVICE ENGINE SOON" LIGHT.

1990-92 2.0L (VIN M)

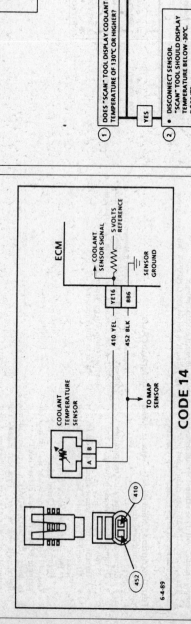

6-4-89

CODE 14

COOLANT TEMPERATURE SENSOR (CTS) CIRCUIT
(HIGH TEMPERATURE INDICATED)
2.0L TURBO (VIN M) "J" CARLINE (PORT)

Circuit Description:

The Coolant Temperature Sensor (CTS) uses a thermistor to control the signal voltage to the ECM. The ECM applies a voltage on CKT 410 to the sensor. When the engine is cold, the sensor (thermistor) resistance is high, therefore, the ECM will see high signal voltage.

As the engine warms, the sensor resistance becomes less and the voltage drops. At normal engine operating temperature, the voltage will measure about 1.5 to 2.0 volts at the ECM terminal "YE16".

Coolant temperature is one of the inputs used to control:

- Fuel Delivery
- Electronic Spark Timing (EST)
- Cooling Fan
- Torque Converter Clutch (TCC)
- Idle Air Control (IAC)

Test Description: Numbers below refer to circled numbers on the diagnostic chart.

1. Checks to see if code was set as result of hard failure or intermittent condition.
   Code 14 will set if:
   - Engine has been running for more than 10 seconds.
   - Signal voltage indicates a coolant temperature above 135°C (275°F) for 3 seconds.

2. This test simulates conditions for a Code 15. If the ECM recognizes the open circuit (high voltage), and displays a low temperature, the ECM and wiring are OK.

Diagnostic Aids:

A "Scan" tool reads engine temperature in degrees centigrade.

After the engine is started, the temperature should rise steadily to about 90°, then stabilize, when the thermostat opens.

If the engine has been allowed to cool to an ambient temperature (overnight), coolant and MAT temperature may be checked with a "Scan" tool and should read close to each other.

When a Code 14 is set, the ECM will turn "ON" the engine cooling fan.

A Code 14 will result if CKT 410 is shorted to ground.

CODE 14

COOLANT TEMPERATURE SENSOR (CTS) CIRCUIT
(HIGH TEMPERATURE INDICATED)
2.0L TURBO (VIN M) "J" CARLINE (PORT)

1 DOES "SCAN" TOOL DISPLAY COOLANT TEMPERATURE OF 130°C OR HIGHER?

YES / NO

2 DISCONNECT SENSOR. "SCAN" TOOL SHOULD DISPLAY TEMPERATURE BELOW -30°C. DOES IT?

YES / NO

REPLACE SENSOR.

- NO → CODE 14 IS INTERMITTENT. IF NO ADDITIONAL CODES WERE STORED, REFER TO "DIAGNOSTIC AIDS" ON FACING PAGE.

- NO → CKT 410 SHORTED TO GROUND,
  OR
  CKT 410 SHORTED TO SENSOR GROUND CIRCUIT
  OR
  FAULTY ECM.

DIAGNOSTIC AID

COOLANT SENSOR TEMPERATURE VS. RESISTANCE VALUES (APPROXIMATE)		
°F	°C	OHMS
210	100	185
160	70	450
100	38	1,800
70	20	3,400
40	4	7,500
20	-7	13,500
0	-18	25,000
-40	-40	100,700

CLEAR CODES AND CONFIRM "CLOSED LOOP" OPERATION AND NO "SERVICE ENGINE SOON" LIGHT.

1990-92 2.0L (VIN M)

CODE 15
COOLANT TEMPERATURE SENSOR (CTS) CIRCUIT
(LOW TEMPERATURE INDICATED)
2.0L TURBO (VIN M) "J" CARLINE (PORT)

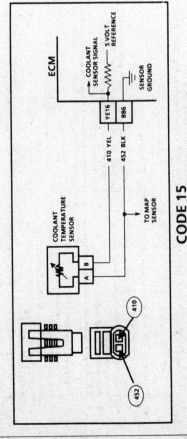

Circuit Description:

The Coolant Temperature Sensor (CTS) uses a thermistor to control the signal voltage to the ECM. The ECM applies a voltage on CKT 410 to the sensor. When the engine is cold, the sensor (thermistor) resistance is high, therefore, the ECM will see high signal voltage.

As the engine warms, the sensor resistance becomes less, and the voltage drops. At normal engine operating temperature, the voltage will measure about 1.5 to 2.0 volts at the ECM terminal "YE16".

Coolant temperature is one of the inputs used to control

- Fuel Delivery
- Electronic Spark Timing (EST)
- Cooling Fan
- Torque Converter Clutch (TCC)
- Idle Air Control (IAC)

Test Description: Numbers below refer to circled numbers on the diagnostic chart.

1. Checks to see if code was set as result of hard failure or intermittent condition. Code 15 will set if:
   - Engine has been running for more than 50 seconds.
   - Signal voltage indicates a coolant temperature below -30°C (-22°F).
2. This test simulates conditions for a Code 14. If the ECM recognizes the grounded circuit (low voltage) and displays a high temperature, the ECM and wiring are OK.
3. This test will determine if there is a wiring problem or a faulty ECM. If CKT 452 is open, there may also be a Code 21 stored.

Diagnostic Aids:

A "Scan" tool reads engine temperature in degrees centigrade.

After the engine is started, the temperature should rise steadily to about 90°C (194°F), then stabilize when the thermostat opens.

If the engine has been allowed to cool to an ambient temperature (overnight), coolant and MAT temperature may be checked with a "Scan" tool and should read close to each other.

When a Code 15 is set, the ECM will turn "ON" the engine cooling fan.

A Code 15 will result if CKTs 410 or 452 are open. If Code 15 is intermittent,

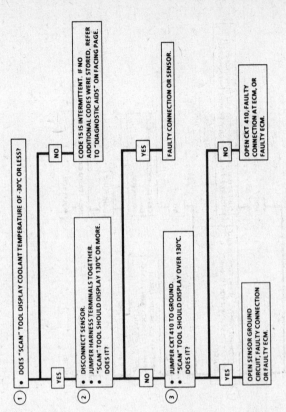

CODE 15

1. • DOES "SCAN" TOOL DISPLAY COOLANT TEMPERATURE OF -30°C OR LESS?

   NO → CODE 15 IS INTERMITTENT. IF NO ADDITIONAL CODES WERE STORED, REFER TO "DIAGNOSTIC AIDS" ON FACING PAGE.

2. • DISCONNECT SENSOR.
   • JUMPER HARNESS TERMINALS TOGETHER.
   • "SCAN" TOOL SHOULD DISPLAY 130°C OR MORE. DOES IT?

   YES → FAULTY CONNECTION OR SENSOR.

3. • JUMPER CKT 410 TO GROUND.
   • "SCAN" TOOL SHOULD DISPLAY OVER 130°C. DOES IT?

   NO → OPEN CKT 410, FAULTY CONNECTION AT ECM, OR FAULTY ECM.

   YES → OPEN SENSOR GROUND CIRCUIT, FAULTY CONNECTION OR FAULTY ECM.

DIAGNOSTIC AID

COOLANT SENSOR TEMPERATURE TO RESISTANCE VALUES (APPROXIMATE)		
°F	°C	OHMS
210	100	185
160	70	450
100	38	1,800
70	20	3,400
40	4	7,500
20	-7	13,500
0	-18	25,000
-40	-40	100,700

CLEAR CODES AND CONFIRM "CLOSED LOOP" OPERATION AND NO "SERVICE ENGINE SOON" LIGHT.

1990-92 2.0L (VIN M)

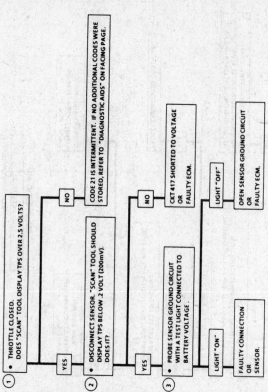

CODE 21

THROTTLE POSITION SENSOR (TPS) CIRCUIT
(SIGNAL VOLTAGE HIGH)
2.0L TURBO (VIN M) "J" CARLINE (PORT)

1. • THROTTLE CLOSED.
   • DOES "SCAN" TOOL DISPLAY TPS OVER 2.5 VOLTS?

   YES / NO

   NO → CODE 21 IS INTERMITTENT. IF NO ADDITIONAL CODES WERE STORED, REFER TO "DIAGNOSTIC AIDS" ON FACING PAGE.

2. • DISCONNECT SENSOR. "SCAN" TOOL SHOULD DISPLAY TPS BELOW .2 VOLT (200mV).
   DOES IT?

   YES / NO

   NO → CKT 417 SHORTED TO VOLTAGE OR FAULTY ECM.

3. • PROBE SENSOR GROUND CIRCUIT WITH A TEST LIGHT CONNECTED TO BATTERY VOLTAGE.

   LIGHT "ON" → FAULTY CONNECTION OR SENSOR.

   LIGHT "OFF" → OPEN SENSOR GROUND CIRCUIT OR FAULTY ECM.

CLEAR CODES AND CONFIRM "CLOSED LOOP" OPERATION AND NO "SERVICE ENGINE SOON" LIGHT.

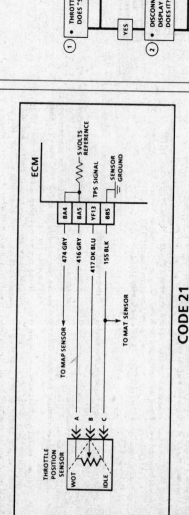

CODE 21

THROTTLE POSITION SENSOR (TPS) CIRCUIT
(SIGNAL VOLTAGE HIGH)
2.0L TURBO (VIN M) "J" CARLINE (PORT)

Circuit Description:

The Throttle Position Sensor (TPS) provides a voltage signal that changes relative to the throttle valve. Signal voltage will vary from less than 1.0 volt at idle to about 4.6 volts at wide open throttle (WOT).

The TPS signal is one of the most important inputs used by the ECM for fuel control and for many of the ECM controlled outputs.

Test Description: Numbers below refer to circled numbers on the diagnostic chart.

1. This step checks to see if Code 21 is the result of a hard failure or an intermittent condition.
   A Code 21 will set if:
   • TPS reading above 2.5 volts
   • MAP reading below 70 kPa (M/T) or 81 kPa (A/T)
   • Engine speed less than 1300 rpm
   • All of the above conditions are present for 10 seconds

2. This step simulates conditions for a Code 22. If the ECM recognizes the change of state, the ECM and CKTs 416 and 417 are OK.

3. This step isolates a faulty sensor, ECM, or an open CKT 155.

Diagnostic Aids:

A "Scan" tool displays throttle position in volts. Closed throttle voltage should be less than 1.0 volt. TPS voltage should increase at a steady rate as throttle is moved to WOT.

A Code 21 will result if CKT 155 is open or CKT 417 is shorted to voltage. If Code 21 is intermittent, refer to "Intermittents" in Section "B".

1990-92 2.0L (VIN M)

CODE 22

THROTTLE POSITION SENSOR (TPS) CIRCUIT
(SIGNAL VOLTAGE LOW)
2.0L TURBO (VIN M) "J" CARLINE (PORT)

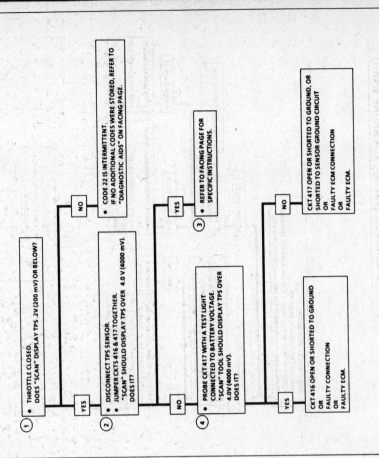

1. THROTTLE CLOSED. DOES "SCAN" DISPLAY TPS .2V (200 mV) OR BELOW?

NO → • CODE 22 IS INTERMITTENT. IF NO ADDITIONAL CODES WERE STORED, REFER TO "DIAGNOSTIC AIDS" ON FACING PAGE.

YES →

2. • DISCONNECT TPS SENSOR. • JUMPER CKTS 416 & 417 TOGETHER. "SCAN" SHOULD DISPLAY TPS OVER 4.0 V (4000 mV). DOES IT?

YES → (3) REFER TO FACING PAGE FOR SPECIFIC INSTRUCTIONS.

NO →

4. PROBE CKT 417 WITH A TEST LIGHT CONNECTED TO BATTERY VOLTAGE. "SCAN" TOOL SHOULD DISPLAY TPS OVER 4.0V (4000 mV). DOES IT?

NO → CKT 417 OPEN OR SHORTED TO GROUND, OR SHORTED TO SENSOR GROUND CIRCUIT OR FAULTY ECM CONNECTION OR FAULTY ECM.

YES → CKT 416 OPEN OR SHORTED TO GROUND OR FAULTY CONNECTION OR FAULTY ECM.

CLEAR CODES AND CONFIRM "CLOSED LOOP" OPERATION AND NO "SERVICE ENGINE SOON" LIGHT.

ECM
5 VOLTS REFERENCE
TPS SIGNAL
SENSOR GROUND

BA4 — 474 GRY — TO MAP SENSOR
BA5 — 416 GRY
YF13 — 417 DK BLU
BB5 — 155 BLK

TO MAT SENSOR

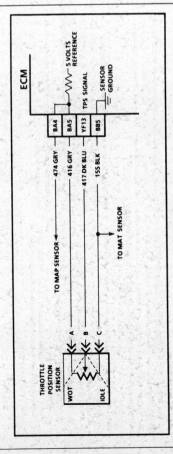

THROTTLE POSITION SENSOR
WOT — A B C — IDLE

CODE 22

THROTTLE POSITION SENSOR (TPS) CIRCUIT
(SIGNAL VOLTAGE LOW)
2.0L TURBO (VIN M) "J" CARLINE (PORT)

Circuit Description:

The Throttle Position Sensor (TPS) provides a voltage signal that changes relative to the throttle valve. Signal voltage will vary from less than 1.0 volt at idle to about 4.5 volts at wide open throttle (WOT).

The TPS signal is one of the most important inputs used by the ECM for fuel control and for many of the ECM controlled outputs.

Test Description: Numbers below refer to circled numbers on the diagnostic chart.

1. Code 22 will set if:
   - Engine is running
   - TPS signal voltage is less than .2 volt for 4 seconds
2. Simulates Code 21: (high voltage). If ECM recognizes the high signal voltage the ECM and wiring are OK.
3. With closed throttle, ignition "ON" or at idle, voltage at "YF13" should be .36-.44 volt. If not, replace the TPS.
4. Simulates a high signal voltage. Checks CKT 417 for an open.

Diagnostic Aids:

A "Scan" tool reads throttle position in volts. Voltage should increase at a steady rate as throttle is moved toward WOT.

Also some "Scan" tools will read throttle angle 0% = closed throttle, 100% = WOT.

An open or short to ground in CKTs 416 or 417 will result in a Code 22.

- **Poor Connection or Damaged Harness.** Inspect ECM harness connectors for backed out terminal "YF13", improper mating, broken locks, improperly formed or damaged terminals, poor terminal to wire connection, and damaged harness.
- **Intermittent Test.** If connections and harness check OK, monitor TPS voltage display while moving related connectors and wiring harness. If the failure is induced, the display will change. This may help to isolate the location of the malfunction.
- **TPS Scaling.** Observe TPS voltage display while depressing accelerator pedal with engine stopped and ignition "ON." Display should vary from closed throttle TPS voltage when throttle was closed, to over 4.5 volts (4500 mV) when throttle is held at wide open throttle position.

1990-92 2.0L (VIN M)

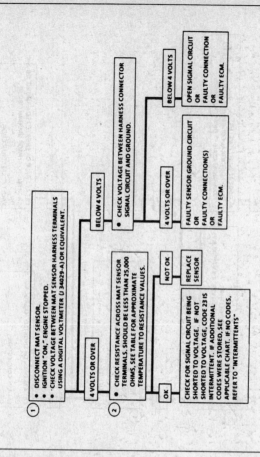

CODE 23

MANIFOLD AIR TEMPERATURE (MAT) SENSOR CIRCUIT
(LOW TEMPERATURE INDICATED)
2.0L TURBO (VIN M) "J" CARLINE (PORT)

(1)
- DISCONNECT MAT SENSOR.
- IGNITION "ON," ENGINE STOPPED.
- CHECK VOLTAGE BETWEEN MAT SENSOR HARNESS TERMINALS USING A DIGITAL VOLTMETER (J 34029-A) OR EQUIVALENT.

4 VOLTS OR OVER

(2)
- CHECK RESISTANCE ACROSS MAT SENSOR TERMINALS. SHOULD BE LESS THAN 25,000 OHMS. SEE TABLE FOR APPROXIMATE TEMPERATURE TO RESISTANCE VALUES.

OK

CHECK FOR SIGNAL CIRCUIT BEING SHORTED TO VOLTAGE. IF NOT SHORTED TO VOLTAGE, CODE 23 IS INTERMITTENT. IF ADDITIONAL CODES WERE STORED, SEE APPLICABLE CHART. IF NO CODES, REFER TO "INTERMITTENTS".

NOT OK

REPLACE SENSOR

BELOW 4 VOLTS

- CHECK VOLTAGE BETWEEN HARNESS CONNECTOR SIGNAL CIRCUIT AND GROUND.

4 VOLTS OR OVER

FAULTY SENSOR GROUND CIRCUIT OR FAULTY CONNECTION(S) OR FAULTY ECM.

BELOW 4 VOLTS

OPEN SIGNAL CIRCUIT OR FAULTY CONNECTION OR FAULTY ECM.

MAT SENSOR TEMPERATURE TO RESISTANCE VALUES (APPROXIMATE)		
°F	°C	OHMS
210	100	185
160	70	450
100	38	1,800
70	20	3,400
40	4	7,500
20	-7	13,500
0	-18	25,000
-40	-40	100,700

CLEAR CODES AND CONFIRM "CLOSED LOOP" OPERATION AND NO "SERVICE ENGINE SOON" LIGHT.

CODE 23

MANIFOLD AIR TEMPERATURE (MAT) SENSOR CIRCUIT
(LOW TEMPERATURE INDICATED)
2.0L TURBO (VIN M) "J" CARLINE (PORT)

ECM

MAT SENSOR SIGNAL
5 VOLTS REFERENCE
SENSOR GROUND

YF16
BB5

472 TAN
155 BLK

MAT SENSOR
A B

TO TPS SENSOR

470

472

4-28-88

Circuit Description:

The Manifold Air Temperature Sensor (MAT) uses a thermistor to control the signal voltage to the ECM. The ECM applies a voltage (about 5 volts) on CKT 472 to the sensor. When the air is cold the sensor (thermistor) resistance is high, therefore the ECM will see a high signal voltage. If the air is warm, the sensor resistance is low, therefore, the ECM will detect a low voltage.

Test Description: Numbers below refer to circled numbers on the diagnostic chart.

Code 23 will set if:
- A signal voltage indicates a manifold air temperature below −30°C (−22°F)
- Boost conditions have been present for longer than 10 seconds.

Due to the conditions necessary to set a Code 23, the "Service Engine Soon" light will only stay "ON" while the fault is present.

1. A "Scan" tool may not be used to diagnose this fault, due to the ECM transmitting "default" (substitute) values while the fault is present. A Code 23 will set due to an open sensor, wire, or connection. This test will determine if the wiring and ECM are OK.

2. If the resistance is greater than 25,000 ohms, replace the sensor.

1990-92 2.0L (VIN M)

CODE 24

VEHICLE SPEED SENSOR (VSS) CIRCUIT
2.0L TURBO (VIN M) "J" CARLINE (PORT)

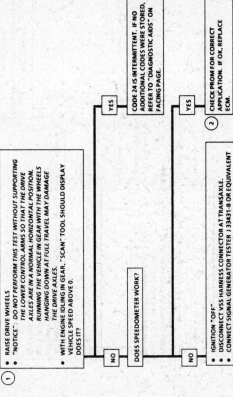

DISREGARD CODE 24 IF SET WHILE DRIVE WHEELS ARE NOT TURNING.

1. • RAISE DRIVE WHEELS
   • "NOTICE": DO NOT PERFORM THIS TEST WITHOUT SUPPORTING THE LOWER CONTROL ARMS SO THAT THE DRIVE AXLES ARE IN A NORMAL HORIZONTAL POSITION. RUNNING THE VEHICLE IN GEAR WITH THE WHEELS HANGING DOWN AT FULL TRAVEL MAY DAMAGE THE DRIVE AXLES.
   • WITH ENGINE IDLING IN GEAR, "SCAN" TOOL SHOULD DISPLAY VEHICLE SPEED ABOVE 0.
   DOES IT?

NO → DOES SPEEDOMETER WORK?

YES → CODE 24 IS INTERMITTENT. IF NO ADDITIONAL CODES WERE STORED, REFER TO "DIAGNOSTIC AIDS" ON FACING PAGE.

DOES SPEEDOMETER WORK?

NO →
• IGNITION "OFF".
• DISCONNECT VSS HARNESS CONNECTOR AT TRANSAXLE.
• CONNECT SIGNAL GENERATOR TESTER J 33431-B OR EQUIVALENT TO VSS HARNESS CONNECTOR.
• IGNITION "ON", TOOL "ON" AND SET TO GENERATE A VSS SIGNAL.
• "SCAN" TOOL SHOULD DISPLAY VEHICLE SPEED ABOVE 0.
DOES IT?

YES → 2 CHECK PROM FOR CORRECT APPLICATION. IF OK, REPLACE ECM.

2 CHECK PROM FOR CORRECT APPLICATION. IF OK, REPLACE ECM.

NO → CKT 400 OR 401 OPEN, SHORTED TO GROUND, SHORTED TOGETHER, FAULTY CONNECTIONS, OR FAULTY ECM.

YES → REPLACE VEHICLE SPEED SENSOR.

CLEAR CODES AND CONFIRM "CLOSED LOOP" OPERATION AND NO "SERVICE ENGINE SOON" LIGHT.

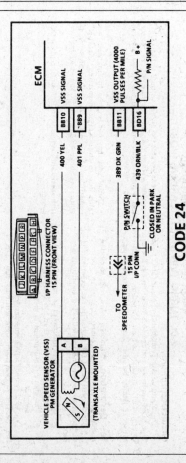

VEHICLE SPEED SENSOR (VSS)
PM GENERATOR

(TRANSAXLE MOUNTED)

A
B

TO SPEEDOMETER

P/N SWITCH

15 PIN
I/P CONN

CLOSED IN PARK OR NEUTRAL

I/P HARNESS CONNECTOR
15 PIN (FRONT VIEW)

ECM

400 YEL — BB10 — VSS SIGNAL
401 PPL — BB9 — VSS SIGNAL
389 DK GRN — BB11 — VSS OUTPUT (4000 PULSES PER MILE)
439 ORN/BLK — BD16 — B+ / P/N SIGNAL

CODE 24

VEHICLE SPEED SENSOR (VSS) CIRCUIT
2.0L TURBO (VIN M) "J" CARLINE (PORT)

Circuit Description:

Vehicle speed information is provided to the ECM by the Vehicle Speed Sensor (VSS), which is a Permanent Magnet (PM) generator, located in the transaxle. The PM generator produces a pulsing voltage whenever vehicle speed is over 3 mph. The AC voltage level and the number of pulses increases with vehicle speed. The ECM then converts the pulsing voltage to mph which is used for calculations, and the mph can be displayed with a "Scan" tool.

The function of VSS buffer used in past model years has been incorporated into the ECM. The ECM then supplies the necessary signal for the instrument panel (4000 pulses per mile) for operating the speedometer and the odometer. If the vehicle is equipped with cruise control the ECM also provides a signal (2000 pulses per mile) to the cruise control module.

Test Description: Numbers below refer to circled numbers on the diagnostic chart.

1. Code 24 will set if vehicle speed equals 0 mph when:
   • Engine speed is between 1600 and 4400 rpm
   • TPS indicates closed throttle
   • Low load condition (low air flow)
   • Not in park or neutral
   • All conditions met for 5 seconds
   These conditions are met during a road load deceleration. Disregard Code 24 that sets when drive wheels are not turning.
   • The PM generator only produces a signal if drive wheels are turning greater than 3 mph.
   Before replacing ECM, check Mem-Cal for proper application.

Diagnostic Aids:

"Scan" should indicate a vehicle speed whenever the drive wheels are turning greater than 3 mph.

A problem in CKT 381 or 389 will not affect the VSS input or the readings on a "Scan."

Check CKTs 400 and 401 to ensure that the connections are clean and tight and that the harness is routed correctly. Refer to "Intermittents" in Section "B".

(A/T) A faulty or misadjusted park/neutral switch can result in a false Code 24. Use a "Scan" and check for proper signal while in drive. Refer to CHART C-1A for P/N switch diagnosis check.

1990-92 2.0L (VIN M)

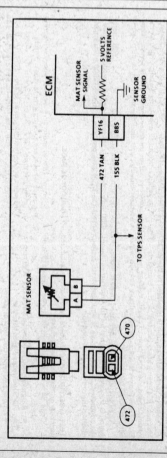

CODE 25
MANIFOLD AIR TEMPERATURE (MAT) SENSOR CIRCUIT
(HIGH TEMPERATURE INDICATED)
2.0L TURBO (VIN M) "J" CARLINE (PORT)

Circuit Description:

The Manifold Air Temperature Sensor (MAT) uses a thermistor to control the signal voltage to the ECM. The ECM applies a voltage (4-6 volts) on CKT 472 to the sensor. When manifold air is cold, the sensor (thermistor) resistance is high, therefore, the ECM will detect a high signal voltage. If the air warms, the sensor resistance becomes less, and the voltage drops.

Test Description: Numbers below refer to circled numbers on the diagnostic chart.

1. A "Scan" tool may not be used to diagnose this fault due to the ECM transmitting "default" (substitute) values while the fault is present. If voltage is above 4 volts, the ECM and wiring are OK.

2. If the resistance is less than 100 ohms, replace the sensor.

Code 25 will set if the engine is not experiencing turbocharger boost and the following conditions are met:

- Signal voltage indicates a manifold air temperature greater than 135°C (275°F).
- The above requirement is met for at least 30 seconds.

Due to the conditions necessary to set a Code 25, the "Service Engine Soon" light will only stay "ON" while the fault is present.

CODE 25
MANIFOLD AIR TEMPERATURE (MAT) SENSOR CIRCUIT
(HIGH TEMPERATURE INDICATED)
2.0L TURBO (VIN M) "J" CARLINE (PORT)

NOTE: A "SCAN" TOOL MAY NOT BE USED TO DIAGNOSE THIS FAULT, DUE TO THE ECM TRANSMITTING "DEFAULT" (SUBSTITUTE) VALUES WHEN THE FAULT IS PRESENT.

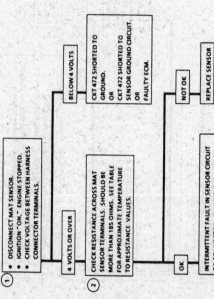

(1) DISCONNECT MAT SENSOR.
- IGNITION "ON," ENGINE STOPPED.
- CHECK VOLTAGE BETWEEN HARNESS CONNECTOR TERMINALS.

4 VOLTS OR OVER

BELOW 4 VOLTS

(2) CHECK RESISTANCE ACROSS MAT SENSOR TERMINALS. SHOULD BE MORE THAN 185 OHMS. SEE TABLE FOR APPROXIMATE TEMPERATURE TO RESISTANCE VALUES.

CKT 472 SHORTED TO GROUND.
OR
CKT 472 SHORTED TO SENSOR GROUND CIRCUIT.
OR
FAULTY ECM.

OK

NOT OK

REPLACE SENSOR

INTERMITTENT FAULT IN SENSOR CIRCUIT OR CONNECTOR. IF ADDITIONAL CODES WERE STORED, SEE APPLICABLE CHART. IF NO CODES, REFER TO "INTERMITTENTS."

CLEAR CODES AND CONFIRM "CLOSED LOOP" OPERATION AND NO "SERVICE ENGINE SOON" LIGHT.

MAT SENSOR		
TEMPERATURE TO RESISTANCE VALUES (APPROXIMATE)		
°F	°C	OHMS
210	100	185
160	70	450
100	38	1,600
70	20	3,400
40	4	7,500
20	-7	13,500
0	-18	25,000
-40	-40	100,700

1990-92 2.0L (VIN M)

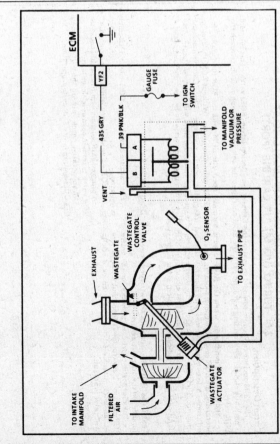

CODE 31
TURBO WASTEGATE OVERBOOST
2.0L TURBO (VIN M) "J" CARLINE (PORT)

Circuit Description:

On turbo charged engines, the exhaust gases pass from the exhaust manifold through the turbocharger, turning the turbine blades. The compressor side of the turbocharger also turns, pulling air through the air filter and pushing the air into the intake manifold, pressurizing the intake manifold.

The wastegate is normally closed, but opens to bypass exhaust gas to prevent an overboost condition. The wastegate will open when pressure is applied to the actuator, and is controlled by a wastegate control solenoid valve pulsed "ON" and "OFF" by the ECM. Under normal driving conditions, the control solenoid is energized all the time which closes "OFF" the manifold pressure to the wastegate actuator. This allows for a rapid increase in boost pressure. A boost increase will be detected by the MAP sensor, and the ECM will pulse the wastegate control valve. Manifold pressure will then be allowed to pass to the wastegate actuator, and the actuator will open the wastegate. This will prevent an overboost condition on heavy acceleration. As boost pressure decreases, the ECM closes the control valve and the wastegate actuator pressure bleeds "OFF" through the vent in the control valve. If an overboost does exist as indicated by the MAP sensor, the ECM will reduce fuel delivery to prevent damage to the engine.

Test Description: Numbers below refer to circled numbers on the diagnostic chart.

1. A Code 31 will set when the manifold pressure exceeds 143 kPa of boost for two seconds, and a Code 33 has not previously been set. Code 31 will set, but the "Service Engine Soon" light will stay "ON" only while the overboost exists. The light will stay "ON" for 10 seconds after the condition exists and then go "OUT."

An overboost condition could be caused by
- CKT 435 shorted to ground
- A sticking wastegate actuator or wastegate
- A control valve stuck in the closed position
- A cut or pinched hose
- A faulty ECM

- An extremely dirty air filter
  With ignition shut "OFF," the control valve solenoid is open.

2. After the 103 kPa (15 psi) is applied to valve and then the pressure source is removed, the actuator should slowly move back and close the wastegate. If the pressure does not bleed "OFF," the vent in the control valve solenoid could be plugged.

3. With the ignition "ON" and the diagnostic terminal grounded, the control valve solenoid should be energized. This closes "OFF" the manifold to the wastegate actuator.

4. Checks the electrical control portion of the system. With key "ON" and engine not running, the solenoid should not be energized.

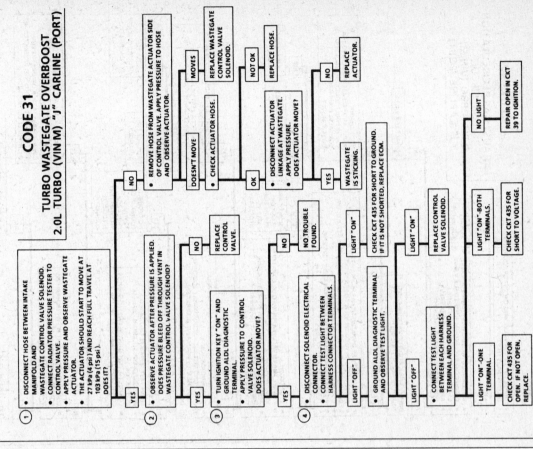

CODE 31
TURBO WASTEGATE OVERBOOST
2.0L TURBO (VIN M) "J" CARLINE (PORT)

1. • DISCONNECT HOSE BETWEEN INTAKE MANIFOLD AND WASTEGATE CONTROL VALVE SOLENOID.
   • CONNECT RADIATOR PRESSURE TESTER TO CONTROL VALVE.
   • APPLY PRESSURE AND OBSERVE WASTEGATE ACTUATOR.
   • THE ACTUATOR SHOULD START TO MOVE AT 27 kPa (4 psi) AND REACH FULL TRAVEL AT 103 kPa (15 psi).
   DOES IT?

   NO → • REMOVE HOSE FROM WASTEGATE ACTUATOR SIDE OF CONTROL VALVE. APPLY PRESSURE TO HOSE AND OBSERVE ACTUATOR.
   - **MOVES** → REPLACE WASTEGATE CONTROL VALVE SOLENOID.
   - **DOESN'T MOVE** → • CHECK ACTUATOR HOSE.
     - **NOT OK** → REPLACE HOSE.
     - **OK** → • DISCONNECT ACTUATOR LINKAGE AT WASTEGATE. APPLY PRESSURE. DOES ACTUATOR MOVE?
       - **YES** → WASTEGATE IS STICKING.
       - **NO** → REPLACE ACTUATOR.

   YES →

2. • OBSERVE ACTUATOR AFTER PRESSURE IS APPLIED. DOES PRESSURE BLEED OFF THROUGH VENT IN WASTEGATE CONTROL VALVE SOLENOID?

   NO → REPLACE CONTROL VALVE.

   YES →

3. • TURN IGNITION KEY "ON" AND GROUND ALDL DIAGNOSTIC TERMINAL.
   • APPLY PRESSURE TO CONTROL VALVE SOLENOID.
   DOES ACTUATOR MOVE?

   NO → NO TROUBLE FOUND.

   YES →

4. • DISCONNECT SOLENOID ELECTRICAL CONNECTOR.
   • CONNECT TEST LIGHT BETWEEN HARNESS CONNECTOR TERMINALS.

   - **LIGHT "OFF"** → • GROUND ALDL DIAGNOSTIC TERMINAL AND OBSERVE TEST LIGHT.
     - **LIGHT "ON"** → CHECK CKT 435 FOR SHORT TO GROUND. IF IT IS NOT SHORTED, REPLACE ECM.
   - **LIGHT "ON"** → REPLACE CONTROL VALVE SOLENOID.

   • CONNECT TEST LIGHT BETWEEN EACH HARNESS TERMINAL AND GROUND.
   - **LIGHT "ON"—ONE TERMINAL.** → CHECK CKT 435 FOR OPEN. IF NOT OPEN, REPLACE.
   - **LIGHT "ON"—BOTH TERMINALS.** → CHECK CKT 435 FOR SHORT TO VOLTAGE.
     - **NO LIGHT** → REPAIR OPEN IN CKT 39 TO IGNITION.

CLEAR CODES AND CONFIRM "CLOSED LOOP" OPERATION AND NO "SERVICE ENGINE SOON" LIGHT.

1990-92 2.0L (VIN M)

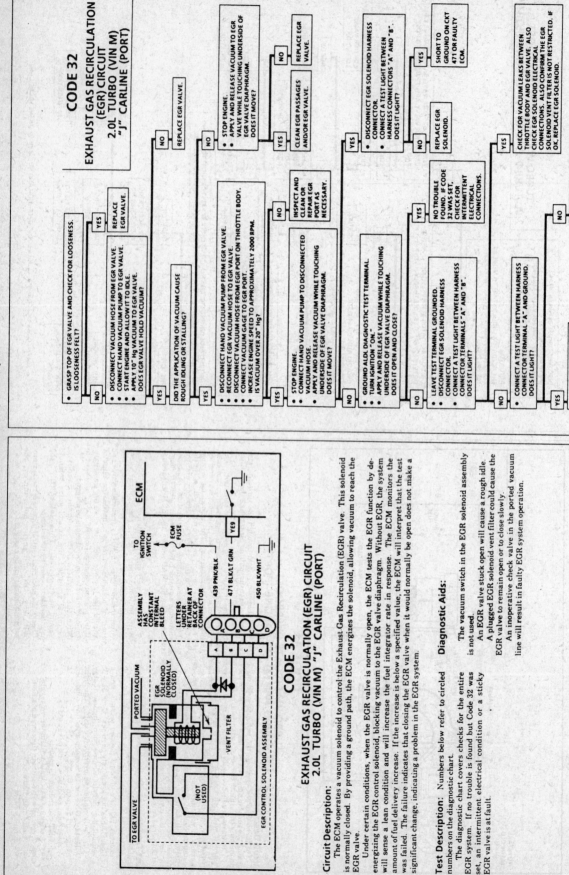

CODE 32
EXHAUST GAS RECIRCULATION (EGR) CIRCUIT
2.0L TURBO (VIN M) "J" CARLINE (PORT)

Circuit Description:

The ECM operates a vacuum solenoid to control the Exhaust Gas Recirculation (EGR) valve. This solenoid is normally closed. By providing a ground path, the ECM energizes the solenoid, allowing vacuum to reach the EGR valve.

Under certain conditions, when the EGR valve is normally open, the ECM tests the EGR function by de-energizing the EGR control solenoid, blocking vacuum to the EGR valve diaphragm. Without EGR, the system will sense a lean condition and will increase the fuel integrator rate in response. The ECM monitors the amount of fuel delivery increase. If the increase is below a specified value, the ECM will interpret that the test was failed. The failure indicates that closing the EGR valve when it would normally be open does not make a significant change, indicating a problem in the EGR system.

Test Description: Numbers below refer to circled numbers on the diagnostic chart.

The diagnostic chart covers checks for the entire EGR system. If no trouble is found but Code 32 was set, an intermittent electrical condition or a sticky EGR valve is at fault.

Diagnostic Aids:

The vacuum switch in the EGR solenoid assembly is not used.

An EGR valve stuck open will cause a rough idle.

A plugged EGR solenoid vent filter could cause the EGR valve to remain open or to close slowly.

An inoperative check valve in the ported vacuum line will result in faulty EGR system operation.

1990-92 2.0L (VIN M)

CODE 33
MANIFOLD ABSOLUTE PRESSURE (MAP) SENSOR CIRCUIT
(SIGNAL VOLTAGE HIGH - LOW VACUUM)
2.0L TURBO (VIN M) "J" CARLINE (PORT)

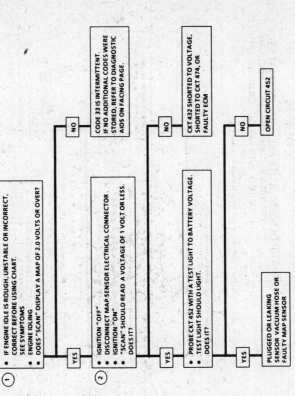

ECM
- BA5 — 416 GRY — TO TPS
- BA4 — 474 GRY — 5 VOLTS REFERENCE
- YF15 — 432 LT GRN — MAP SIGNAL
- BB6 — 452 BLK — SENSOR GROUND

MAP SENSOR
MANIFOLD ABSOLUTE PRESSURE (VACUUM)
A B C
TO COOLANT SENSOR

Circuit Description:
The Manifold Absolute Pressure (MAP) sensor responds to changes in manifold pressure (vacuum). The ECM receives this information as a signal voltage that will vary from about 1-1.5 volts at closed throttle idle, to 4-4.5 volts at wide open throttle (low vacuum or boost).
If the MAP sensor fails, the ECM will substitute a fixed MAP value and use the Throttle Position Sensor (TPS) to control fuel delivery.

Test Description: Numbers below refer to circled numbers on the diagnostic chart.
1. This step will determine if Code 33 is the result of a hard failure or an intermittent condition.
A Code 33 will set if:
- MAP signal voltage is too high (low vacuum)
- TPS less than 2%
- These conditions for a time longer than 5 seconds

2. This step simulates conditions for a Code 34. If the ECM recognizes the change, the ECM and CKTs 474 and 432 are OK. If CKT 452 is open, there may also be a stored Code 23.

Diagnostic Aids:
With the ignition "ON" and the engine stopped, the manifold pressure is equal to atmospheric pressure and the signal voltage will be high. This information is used by the ECM as an indication of vehicle altitude and is referred to as BARO. Comparison of this BARO reading with a known good vehicle with the same sensor is a good way to check accuracy of a "suspect" sensor. Reading should be the same ± .4 volt.
A Code 33 will result if CKT 452 is open, or if CKT 432 is shorted to voltage or to CKT 474. If Code 33 is intermittent,

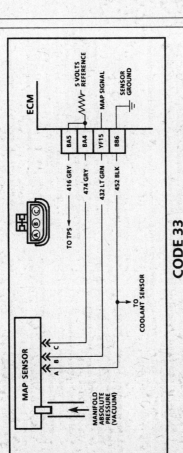

(1)
- IF ENGINE IDLE IS ROUGH, UNSTABLE OR INCORRECT, CORRECT BEFORE USING CHART. SEE SYMPTOMS
- ENGINE IDLING
- DOES "SCAN" DISPLAY A MAP OF 2.0 VOLTS OR OVER?

NO → CODE 33 IS INTERMITTENT. IF NO ADDITIONAL CODES WERE STORED, REFER TO DIAGNOSTIC AIDS ON FACING PAGE.

(2)
- IGNITION "OFF"
- DISCONNECT MAP SENSOR ELECTRICAL CONNECTOR.
- IGNITION "ON"
- "SCAN" SHOULD READ A VOLTAGE OF 1 VOLT OR LESS. DOES IT?

NO → CKT 432 SHORTED TO VOLTAGE, SHORTED TO CKT 474, OR FAULTY ECM

- PROBE CKT 452 WITH A TEST LIGHT TO BATTERY VOLTAGE. TEST LIGHT SHOULD LIGHT. DOES IT?

NO → OPEN CIRCUIT 452

YES → PLUGGED OR LEAKING SENSOR VACUUM HOSE OR FAULTY MAP SENSOR

1990-92 2.0L (VIN M)

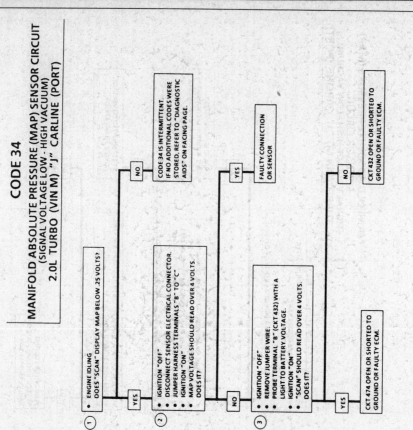

CODE 34

MANIFOLD ABSOLUTE PRESSURE (MAP) SENSOR CIRCUIT
(SIGNAL VOLTAGE LOW - HIGH VACUUM)
2.0L TURBO (VIN M) "J" CARLINE (PORT)

① ENGINE IDLING
DOES "SCAN" DISPLAY MAP BELOW .25 VOLTS?

- YES
- NO → CODE 34 IS INTERMITTENT. IF NO ADDITIONAL CODES WERE STORED, REFER TO "DIAGNOSTIC AIDS" ON FACING PAGE.

② IGNITION "OFF".
- DISCONNECT SENSOR ELECTRICAL CONNECTOR.
- JUMPER HARNESS TERMINALS "B" TO "C".
- IGNITION "ON".
- MAP VOLTAGE SHOULD READ OVER 4 VOLTS. DOES IT?

- NO
- YES → FAULTY CONNECTION OR SENSOR

③ IGNITION "OFF".
- REMOVE JUMPER WIRE.
- PROBE TERMINAL "B" (CKT 432) WITH A LIGHT TO BATTERY VOLTAGE.
- IGNITION "ON".
- "SCAN" SHOULD READ OVER 4 VOLTS. DOES IT?

- YES → CKT 474 OPEN OR SHORTED TO GROUND OR FAULTY ECM.
- NO → CKT 432 OPEN OR SHORTED TO GROUND OR FAULTY ECM.

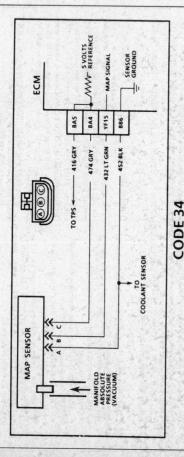

CODE 34

MANIFOLD ABSOLUTE PRESSURE (MAP) SENSOR CIRCUIT
(SIGNAL VOLTAGE LOW - HIGH VACUUM)
2.0L TURBO (VIN M) "J" CARLINE (PORT)

MAP SENSOR

MANIFOLD ABSOLUTE PRESSURE (VACUUM)

TO COOLANT SENSOR

416 GRY — TO TPS
474 GRY
432 LT GRN
452 BLK

ECM
BA5
BA4 — 5 VOLTS REFERENCE
YF15 — MAP SIGNAL
BB6 — SENSOR GROUND

Circuit Description:

The Manifold Absolute Pressure (MAP) sensor responds to changes in manifold pressure (vacuum). The ECM receives this information as a signal voltage that will vary from less than 1.0 volt at closed throttle idle, to 4-4.5 volts at wide open throttle.

If the MAP sensor fails, the ECM will substitute a fixed MAP value and use the Throttle Position Sensor (TPS) to control fuel delivery.

Test Description: Numbers below refer to circled numbers on the diagnostic chart.

1. This step determines if Code 34 is the result of a hard failure or an intermittent condition.
   A Code 34 will set when:
   - MAP signal voltage is too low
   - Engine speed below 1200 rpm and/or TPS greater than 20%

2. Jumpering harness terminals "B" to "C", 5 volts to signal, will determine if the sensor is at fault or if there is a problem with the ECM or wiring. The "Scan" tool may not display battery voltage. The important thing is that the ECM recognizes the voltage as more than 4 volts, indicating that the ECM and CKT 432 are OK.

3. [continuation]

Diagnostic Aids:

With the ignition "ON" and the engine stopped, the manifold pressure is equal to atmospheric pressure and the signal voltage will be high. This information is used by the ECM as an indication of vehicle altitude and is referred to as BARO. Comparison of this BARO reading with a known good vehicle with the same sensor is a good way to check accuracy of a "suspect" sensor. Reading should be the same ± .4 volt.

A Code 34 will result if CKTs 474 or 432 are open or shorted to ground.

If CKT 416 is shorted to ground, there may also be a stored Code 22.

If Code 34 is intermittent,

1990-92 2.0L (VIN M)

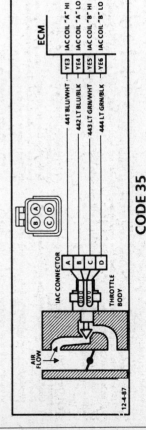

ECM

441 BLU/WHT	YE3 IAC COIL "A" HI
442 LT BLU/BLK	YE4 IAC COIL "A" LO
443 LT GRN/WHT	YE5 IAC COIL "B" HI
444 LT GRN/BLK	YE6 IAC COIL "B" LO

CODE 35
IDLE SPEED ERROR
2.0L TURBO (VIN M) "J" CARLINE (PORT)

Circuit Description:

The ECM controls engine idle speed with the IAC valve. To increase idle speed, the ECM retracts the IAC valve pintle away from its seat, allowing more air to bypass the throttle bore. To decrease idle speed, it extends the IAC valve pintle towards its seat, reducing bypass air flow. A "Scan" tool will read the IAC valve in counts. Higher the counts indicate more air bypass (higher idle). The lower the counts indicate less air is allowed to bypass (lower idle). Code 35 will set when the closed throttle engine speed is 225 rpm above or below the desired (commanded) idle speed for 20 seconds. Review the general description of the IAC operation in section "C2".

Test Description: Numbers below refer to circled numbers on the diagnostic chart.

1. The Tech 1 rpm control mode is used to extend and retract the IAC valve. The valve should move smoothly within the specified range. If the idle speed is commanded (IAC extended) too low (below 700 rpm), the engine may stall. this may be normal and would not indicate a problem. Retracting the IAC beyond its controlled range (above 1500 rpm) will cause a delay before the rpm's start dropping. This too is normal.

2. This test uses the Tech 1 to command the IAC controlled idle speed. The ECM issues commands to obtain commanded idle speed. the node lights each should flash red and green to indicate a good circuit as the ECM issues commands. While the sequence of color is not important if either light is "OFF" or does not flash red and green, check the circuits for faults, beginning with poor terminal contacts.

Diagnostic Aids:

A slow, unstable, or fast idle may be caused by a non-IAC system problem that cannot be overcome by the IAC valve. Out of control range IAC "Scan" tool counts will be above 60 if idle is too low, and zero counts if idle is too high. The following checks should be made to repair a non-IAC system problem:

- **Vacuum Leak (High Idle)**
  If idle is too high, stop the engine. Start engine with IAC with tester. Fully extend (low) IAC until idle speed is above 800 rpm, locate and correct vacuum leak including PCV system. Also check for binding of throttle blade or linkage.

- **System too lean (High Air/Fuel Ratio)**
  The idle speed may be too high or too low. Engine speed may vary up and down and disconnecting the IAC valve does not help. Code 44 may be set. "Scan" O₂ voltage will be less than 300 mV (.3 volts). Check for low regulated fuel pressure, water in the fuel or a restricted injector.

- **System too rich (Low Air/Fuel Ratio)**
  The idle speed will be too low. "Scan" tool IAC Counts will usually be above 80. System is obviously rich and may exhibit black smoke in exhaust. "Scan" tool O₂ voltage will be fixed above 800 mV (.8 volt). Check for high fuel pressure, leaking or sticking injector. Silicone contaminated O₂ "Scan" voltage will be slow to respond.

- **Throttle Body**
  Remove IAC valve and inspect bore for foreign material.

- **IAC Valve Electrical Connections**
  IAC valve connections should be carefully checked for proper contact.

- **PCV Valve**
  An incorrect or faulty PCV valve may result in an incorrect idle speed. Refer to "Rough, Unstable, Incorrect Idle or Stalling" in "Symptoms,".

- If intermittent poor driveability or idle symptoms are resolved by disconnecting the IAC, carefully recheck connections, valve terminal resistance, or replace IAC.

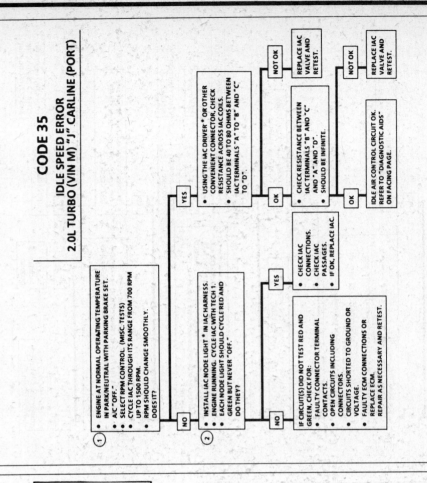

CODE 35
IDLE SPEED ERROR
2.0L TURBO (VIN M) "J" CARLINE (PORT)

(1)
- ENGINE AT NORMAL OPERATING TEMPERATURE IN PARK/NEUTRAL WITH PARKING BRAKE SET.
- A/C "OFF."
- SELECT RPM CONTROL. (MISC. TESTS)
- CYCLE IAC THROUGH ITS RANGE FROM 700 RPM UP TO 1500 RPM.
- RPM SHOULD CHANGE SMOOTHLY. DOES IT?

(2)
- INSTALL IAC NODE LIGHT * IN IAC HARNESS.
- ENGINE RUNNING. CYCLE IAC WITH TECH 1.
- EACH NODE LIGHT SHOULD CYCLE RED AND GREEN BUT NEVER "OFF." DO THEY?

NO (from 1) →
- IF CIRCUIT(S) DID NOT TEST RED AND GREEN, CHECK FOR:
- FAULTY CONNECTOR TERMINAL CONTACTS.
- OPEN CIRCUITS INCLUDING CONNECTORS.
- CIRCUITS SHORTED TO GROUND OR VOLTAGE.
- FAULTY ECM CONNECTIONS OR REPLACE ECM.
- REPAIR AS NECESSARY AND RETEST.

YES (from 2) →
- CHECK IAC CONNECTIONS.
- CHECK IAC PASSAGES.
- IF OK, REPLACE IAC.

YES (from 1) →
- USING THE IAC DRIVER * OR OTHER CONVENIENT CONNECTOR, CHECK RESISTANCE ACROSS IAC COILS.
- SHOULD BE 40 TO 80 OHMS BETWEEN IAC TERMINALS "A" TO "B" AND "C" TO "D".

NOT OK → REPLACE IAC VALVE AND RETEST.

OK →
- CHECK RESISTANCE BETWEEN IAC TERMINALS "B" AND "C" AND "A" AND "D".
- SHOULD BE INFINITE.

NOT OK → REPLACE IAC VALVE AND RETEST.

OK → IDLE AIR CONTROL CIRCUIT OK. REFER TO "DIAGNOSTIC AIDS" ON FACING PAGE.

* IAC DRIVER AND NODE LIGHT REQUIRED KIT 222-L FROM: CONCEPT TECHNOLOGY, INC. J 37027 FROM: KENT-MOORE, INC.

CLEAR CODES, CONFIRM "CLOSED LOOP" OPERATION, NO "SERVICE ENGINE SOON" LIGHT, PERFORM IAC RESET PROCEDURE PER APPLICABLE SERVICE MANUAL AND VERIFY CONTROLLED IDLE SPEED IS CORRECT.

1990-92 2.0L (VIN M)

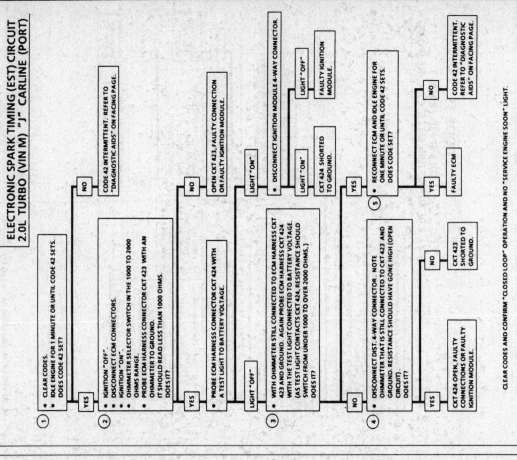

CODE 42

ELECTRONIC SPARK TIMING (EST) CIRCUIT
2.0L TURBO (VIN M) "J" CARLINE (PORT)

(1)
- CLEAR CODES.
- IDLE ENGINE FOR 1 MINUTE OR UNTIL CODE 42 SETS.
  DOES CODE 42 SET?

NO → CODE 42 INTERMITTENT. REFER TO "DIAGNOSTIC AIDS" ON FACING PAGE.

(2)
- IGNITION "OFF".
- DISCONNECT ECM CONNECTORS.
- IGNITION "ON".
- OHMMETER SELECTOR SWITCH IN THE 1000 TO 2000 OHMS RANGE.
- PROBE ECM HARNESS CONNECTOR CKT 423 WITH AN OHMMETER TO GROUND.
  IT SHOULD READ LESS THAN 1000 OHMS.
  DOES IT?

NO → OPEN CKT 423, FAULTY CONNECTION OR FAULTY IGNITION MODULE.

YES → PROBE ECM HARNESS CONNECTOR CKT 424 WITH A TEST LIGHT TO BATTERY VOLTAGE.

LIGHT "OFF" →

(3)
- WITH OHMMETER STILL CONNECTED TO ECM HARNESS CKT 423 AND GROUND. AGAIN PROBE ECM HARNESS CKT 424 WITH THE TEST LIGHT CONNECTED TO BATTERY VOLTAGE. (AS TEST LIGHT CONTACTS CKT 424, RESISTANCE SHOULD SWITCH FROM UNDER 1000 TO OVER 2000 OHMS.)
  DOES IT?

LIGHT "ON" → DISCONNECT IGNITION MODULE 4-WAY CONNECTOR.

LIGHT "ON" → CKT 424 SHORTED TO GROUND.

LIGHT "OFF" → FAULTY IGNITION MODULE.

(4)
- DISCONNECT DIST. 4-WAY CONNECTOR. NOTE OHMMETER THAT'S STILL CONNECTED TO CKT 423 AND GROUND. RESISTANCE SHOULD HAVE GONE HIGH (OPEN CIRCUIT).
  DOES IT?

NO →

YES → CKT 424 OPEN, FAULTY CONNECTIONS OR FAULTY IGNITION MODULE.

NO → CKT 423 SHORTED TO GROUND.

(5)
- RECONNECT ECM AND IDLE ENGINE FOR ONE MINUTE OR UNTIL CODE 42 SETS.
  DOES CODE SET?

YES → FAULTY ECM.

NO → CODE 42 INTERMITTENT. REFER TO "DIAGNOSTIC AIDS" ON FACING PAGE.

CLEAR CODES AND CONFIRM "CLOSED LOOP" OPERATION AND NO "SERVICE ENGINE SOON" LIGHT.

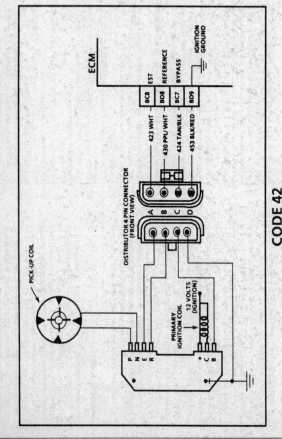

CODE 42

ELECTRONIC SPARK TIMING (EST) CIRCUIT
2.0L TURBO (VIN M) "J" CARLINE (PORT)

Circuit Description:

The ignition module sends a reference signal (CKT 430) to the ECM when the engine is cranking. While the engine speed is under 400 rpm, the ignition module will control ignition timing. When the engine speed exceeds 400 rpm, the ECM applies 5 volts to the bypass line (CKT 424) to switch the timing to ECM control (EST CKT 423).

When the system is running "ON" the ignition module, that is, no voltage on the bypass line, the ignition module grounds the EST signal. The ECM expects to see no voltage on the EST line during this condition. If it sees a voltage, it sets Code 42 and will not go into the EST mode.

When the rpm for EST is reached (about 400 rpm), voltage will be applied to the bypass line, the EST should no longer be grounded in the ignition module, so the EST voltage should be varying.

If the bypass line is open or grounded, the ignition module will not switch to EST mode, so the EST voltage will be low and Code 42 will be set.

If the EST line is grounded, the ignition module will switch to EST but, because the line is grounded, there will be no EST signal. A Code 42 will be set.

Test Description: Numbers below refer to circled numbers on the diagnostic chart.

1. Confirms Code 42 and that the fault causing the code is present.

2. Checks for a normal EST ground path through the ignition module. An EST CKT 423 shorted to ground will also read less than 500 ohms, however, this will be checked later.

3. As the test light voltage touches terminal "C7", the module should switch, causing the ohmmeter

to "overrange" if the meter is in the 1000-2000 ohms position.
Selecting the 10-20,000 ohms position will indicate above 5000 ohms. The important thing is that the module "switched."

4. The module did not switch and this step checks for
   - EST CKT 423 shorted to ground
   - Bypass CKT 424 open
   - Faulty ignition module connection or module

5. Confirms that Code 42 is a faulty ECM and not an intermittent in CKTs 423 or 424.

(Wiring diagram labels: PICK-UP COIL; DISTRIBUTOR 4 PIN CONNECTOR (FRONT VIEW); PRIMARY IGNITION COIL; 12 VOLTS (IGNITION); ECM; BC8 EST 423 WHT; BD8 REFERENCE 430 PPL/WHT; BC7 BYPASS 424 TAN/BLK; BD9 IGNITION GROUND 453 BLK/RED)

1990-92 2.0L (VIN M)

CODE 43
ELECTRONIC SPARK CONTROL (ESC) CIRCUIT
2.0L TURBO (VIN M) "J" CARLINE (PORT)

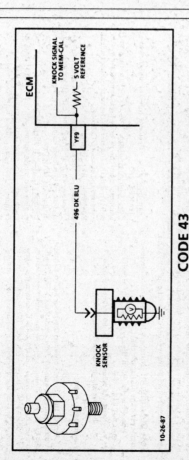

10-26-87

ECM
KNOCK SIGNAL TO MEM-CAL
5 VOLT REFERENCE
YF9
496 DK BLU
KNOCK SENSOR

Circuit Description:

The knock sensor is used to detect engine detonation and the ECM will retard the electronic spark timing based on the signal being received. The circuitry within the knock sensor causes the ECM 5 volts to be pulled down so that under a no knock condition, CKT 496 would measure about 2.5 volts. The knock sensor produces an A/C signal which rides on the 2.5 volts, DC voltage. The amplitude and signal frequency is dependent upon the knock level.

If CKT 496 becomes open or shorted to ground the voltage will either go above 3.5 volts or below 1.5 volts. If either of these conditions are met for about 5 seconds, a Code 43 will be stored.

Test Description: Numbers below refer to circled numbers on the diagnostic chart.

1. Code 43 will set when
   • Coolant temperature is over 90°C
   • MAT temperature is over 0°C
   • High engine load based on MAP and rpm
   • Voltage on CKT 496 goes above 3.5 volts or below 1.5 volts
   • All conditions present for 5 seconds
   If an audible knock is heard from the engine, repair the internal engine problem, as normally no knock should be detected at idle.

2. If tapping on the engine lift hook does not produce a knock signal, try tapping engine closer to sensor before proceeding.

3. The ECM has a 5 volts pull-up resistor, which should be present at the knock sensor terminal.

4. This test determines if the knock sensor is faulty or if the ESC portion of the Mem-Cal is faulty.

Diagnostic Aids:

Check CKT 496 for a potential open or short to ground. Also check for proper installation of Mem-Cal.

Refer to "Intermittents"

CODE 43
ELECTRONIC SPARK CONTROL (ESC) CIRCUIT
2.0L TURBO (VIN M) "J" CARLINE (PORT)

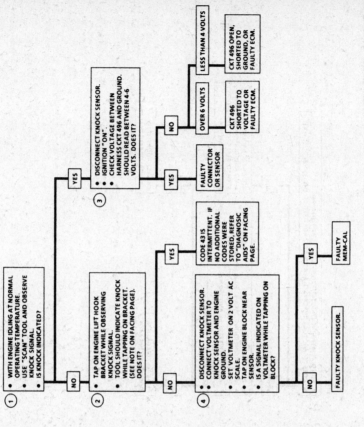

(1) WITH ENGINE IDLING AT NORMAL OPERATING TEMPERATURE. USE "SCAN" TOOL AND OBSERVE KNOCK SIGNAL. IS KNOCK INDICATED?

NO →

(2) TAP ON ENGINE LIFT HOOK BRACKET WHILE OBSERVING KNOCK SIGNAL. TOOL SHOULD INDICATE KNOCK WHILE TAPPING ON BRACKET. (SEE NOTE ON FACING PAGE). DOES IT?

YES →

(3) DISCONNECT KNOCK SENSOR. IGNITION "ON". CHECK VOLTAGE BETWEEN HARNESS CKT 496 AND GROUND. SHOULD READ BETWEEN 4-6 VOLTS. DOES IT?

YES → FAULTY CONNECTOR OR SENSOR

NO → OVER 6 VOLTS → CKT 496 SHORTED TO VOLTAGE OR FAULTY ECM.

LESS THAN 4 VOLTS → CKT 496 OPEN, SHORTED TO GROUND, OR FAULTY ECM.

(4) DISCONNECT KNOCK SENSOR. CONNECT VOLTMETER TO KNOCK SENSOR AND ENGINE GROUND. SET VOLTMETER ON 2 VOLT AC SCALE. TAP ON ENGINE BLOCK NEAR SENSOR. IS A SIGNAL INDICATED ON VOLTMETER WHILE TAPPING ON BLOCK?

YES → CODE 43 IS INTERMITTENT. IF NO ADDITIONAL CODES WERE STORED, REFER TO "DIAGNOSTIC AIDS" ON FACING PAGE. → YES → FAULTY MEM-CAL

NO → FAULTY KNOCK SENSOR.

CLEAR CODES AND CONFIRM "CLOSED LOOP" OPERATION AND NO "SERVICE ENGINE SOON" LIGHT

1990-92 2.0L (VIN M)

CODE 44

OXYGEN (O₂) SENSOR CIRCUIT
(LEAN EXHAUST INDICATED)
2.0L TURBO (VIN M) "J" CARLINE (PORT)

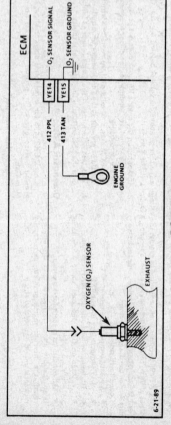

ECM

O₂ SENSOR SIGNAL — YE14 — 412 PPL

O₂ SENSOR GROUND — YE15 — 413 TAN

ENGINE GROUND

EXHAUST

OXYGEN (O₂) SENSOR

6-21-89

CODE 44

OXYGEN (O₂) SENSOR CIRCUIT
(LEAN EXHAUST INDICATED)
2.0L TURBO (VIN M) "J" CARLINE (PORT)

Circuit Description:

The ECM supplies a voltage of about .45 volt between terminals "YE14" and "YE15". (If measured with a 10 megohm digital voltmeter, this may read as low as .32 volt.) The O₂ sensor varies the voltage within a range of about 1 volt if the exhaust is rich, down through about .10 volt if exhaust is lean.

The sensor is like an open circuit and produces no voltage when it is below about 316°C (600°F). An open sensor circuit or cold sensor causes "Open Loop" operation.

Test Description: Numbers below refer to circled numbers on the diagnostic chart.

1. Code 44 is set when the O₂ sensor signal voltage on CKT 412:
   - Remains below .2 volt for 60 seconds or more
   - And the system is operating in "Closed Loop"

Diagnostic Aids:

Using the "Scan," observe the block learn values at different rpm and air flow conditions. The "Scan" also displays the block learn values, so the block learn values can be checked in each of the cells to determine when the Code 44 may have been set. If the conditions for Code 44 exists, the block learn values will be around 150.

- O₂ Sensor Wire. Sensor pigtail may be mispositioned and contacting the exhaust manifold.
- Check for intermittent ground in wire between connector and sensor.

- Lean Injector(s). Perform injector balance test CHART C-2A.
- Fuel Contamination. Water, even in small amounts, near the in-tank fuel pump inlet can be delivered to the injectors. The water causes a lean exhaust and can set a Code 44.
- Fuel Pressure. System will be lean if pressure is too low. It may be necessary to monitor fuel pressure while driving the car at various road speeds and/or loads to confirm. See Fuel System diagnosis CHART A-7.
- Exhaust Leaks. If there is an exhaust leak, the engine can cause outside air to be pulled into the exhaust and past the sensor. Vacuum or crankcase leaks can cause a lean condition.
- If the above are OK, it is a faulty oxygen sensor.

---

①
- RUN WARM ENGINE (75°C/167°F TO 95°C/203°F) AT 1200 RPM.
- DOES "SCAN" TOOL INDICATE O₂ SENSOR VOLTAGE FIXED BELOW .35 VOLT (350 mV)?

YES →
- DISCONNECT O₂ SENSOR.
- WITH ENGINE IDLING, "SCAN" TOOL SHOULD DISPLAY O₂ SENSOR VOLTAGE BETWEEN .35 VOLT AND .55 VOLT (350 mV AND 550 mV).
  DOES IT?

YES → REFER TO "DIAGNOSTIC AIDS" ON FACING PAGE.

NO → CKT 412 SHORTED TO GROUND OR FAULTY ECM.

NO → CODE 44 IS INTERMITTENT. IF NO ADDITIONAL CODES WERE STORED, REFER TO "DIAGNOSTIC AIDS" ON FACING PAGE.

CLEAR CODES AND CONFIRM "CLOSED LOOP" OPERATION AND NO "SERVICE ENGINE SOON" LIGHT.

1990-92 2.0L (VIN M)

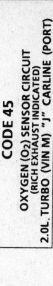

EXHAUST

OXYGEN (O₂) SENSOR

6-21-89

CODE 45

OXYGEN (O₂) SENSOR CIRCUIT
(RICH EXHAUST INDICATED)
2.0L TURBO (VIN M) "J" CARLINE (PORT)

Circuit Description:

The ECM supplies a voltage of about .45 volt between terminals "YE14" and "YE15". (If measured with a 10 megohm digital voltmeter, this may read as low as .32 volt.) The O₂ sensor varies the voltage within a range of about 1 volt if the exhaust is rich, down through about .10 volt if exhaust is lean.

The sensor is like an open circuit and produces no voltage when it is below about 316°C (600°F). An open sensor circuit or cold sensor causes "Open Loop" operation.

Test Description: Numbers below refer to circled numbers on the diagnostic chart.

1. Code 45 is set when the O₂ sensor voltage:
   - Remains above .75 volt for 50 seconds; and the system is in "Closed Loop."

Diagnostic Aids:

Using the "Scan," observe the block learn values at different rpm and air flow conditions. The "Scan" also displays the block cells, so the block learn values can be checked in each of the cells to determine when the Code 45 may have been set. If the conditions for Code 45 exists, the block learn values will be around 115.

- **Fuel Pressure.** System will go rich if pressure is too high. The ECM can compensate for some increase. However, if it gets too high, a Code 45 may be set. See Fuel System diagnosis CHART A-7.
- **Rich Injector.** Perform injector balance test CHART C-2A.
- **Leaking Injector.** See CHART A-7.
- Check for fuel contaminated oil.
- **HEI Shielding.** An open ignition ground CKT 453 may result in EMI, or induced electrical "noise." The ECM looks at this "noise" as reference pulses.

The additional pulses result in a higher than actual engine speed signal. The ECM then delivers too much fuel, causing system to go rich. Engine tachometer will also show higher than actual engine speed, which can help in diagnosing this problem.

- **Canister purge.** Check canister for fuel saturation. If full of fuel, check canister control and hoses. See "Canister Purge," Section "C3."
- **MAP Sensor.** An output that causes the ECM to sense a higher than normal manifold pressure can cause the system to go rich. Disconnecting the MAP sensor will allow the ECM to set a fixed value for the sensor. Substitute a different MAP sensor if the rich condition is gone while the sensor is disconnected.
- Check for leaking fuel pressure regulator diaphragm by checking vacuum line to regulator for fuel.
- **TPS.** An intermittent TPS output will cause the system to go rich, due to a false indication of the engine accelerating.
- **EGR.** An EGR staying open (especially at idle) will cause the O₂ sensor to indicate a rich exhaust, and this could result in a Code 45.

CODE 45

OXYGEN (O₂) SENSOR CIRCUIT
(RICH EXHAUST INDICATED)
2.0L TURBO (VIN M) "J" CARLINE (PORT)

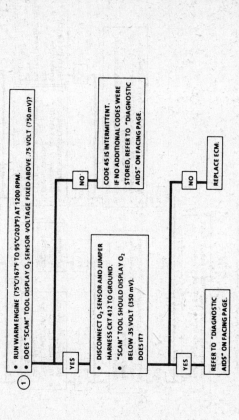

(1)
- RUN WARM ENGINE (75°C/167°F TO 95°C/203°F) AT 1200 RPM.
- DOES "SCAN" TOOL DISPLAY O₂ SENSOR VOLTAGE FIXED ABOVE .75 VOLT (750 mV)?

YES
- DISCONNECT O₂ SENSOR AND JUMPER HARNESS CKT 412 TO GROUND.
- "SCAN" TOOL SHOULD DISPLAY O₂ BELOW .35 VOLT (350 mV). DOES IT?

NO → CODE 45 IS INTERMITTENT. IF NO ADDITIONAL CODES WERE STORED, REFER TO "DIAGNOSTIC AIDS" ON FACING PAGE.

YES → REFER TO "DIAGNOSTIC AIDS" ON FACING PAGE.

NO → REPLACE ECM.

CODE 51

PROM ERROR
(FAULTY OR INCORRECT PROM)
2.0L TURBO (VIN M) "J" CARLINE (PORT)

CHECK THAT ALL PINS ARE FULLY INSERTED IN THE SOCKET AND THAT PROM IS PROPERLY SEATED. IF OK, REPLACE PROM, CLEAR MEMORY, AND RECHECK. IF CODE 51 REAPPEARS, REPLACE ECM.

CLEAR CODES AND CONFIRM "CLOSED LOOP" OPERATION AND NO "SERVICE ENGINE SOON" LIGHT.

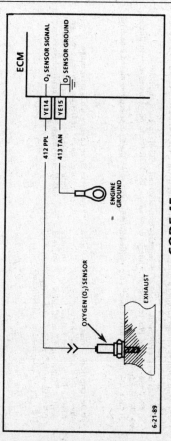

1990-92 2.0L (VIN M)

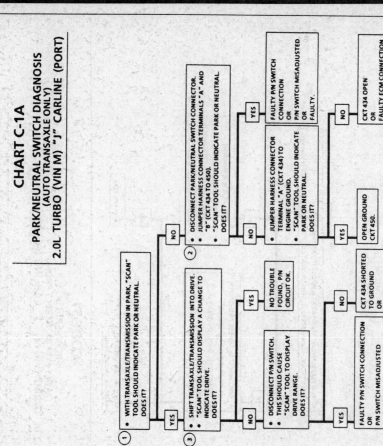

CHART C-1A
PARK/NEUTRAL SWITCH DIAGNOSIS
(AUTO TRANSAXLE ONLY)
2.0L TURBO (VIN M) "J" CARLINE (PORT)

HARNESS CONNECTOR

A B C D E F G

FRONT VIEW

ECM

BD16 — B+

P/N SIGNAL

A — ORN/BLK 434

B — BLK/WHT 450

PARK/NEUTRAL SWITCH

R N D L

P

CIRCUIT TO GROUND IN PARK AND NEUTRAL

NEUTRAL START AND BACK-UP SWITCH TRANSAXLE MOUNTED

P/N SWITCH CONNECTOR

A G

CHART C-1A
PARK/NEUTRAL SWITCH DIAGNOSIS
(AUTO TRANSAXLE ONLY)
2.0L TURBO (VIN M) "J" CARLINE (PORT)

Circuit Description:

The Park/Neutral switch contacts are a part of the neutral start switch they are closed to ground in park or neutral and open in drive ranges.

The ECM supplies voltage through a current limiting resistor to CKT 434 and senses a closed switch when the voltage on CKT 434 drops to less than one volt.

The ECM uses the P/N signal as one of the inputs to control idle air, VSS diagnostics, and EGR.

If CKT 434 indicates P/N (grounded), while in drive range, the EGR would be inoperative, resulting in possible detonation.

If CKT 434 indicates drive (open) a dip in the idle may exist when the gear selector is moved into drive range.

Test Description: Numbers below refer to circled numbers on the diagnostic chart.

1. Checks for a closed switch to ground in park position. Different makes of "Scan" tools will read P/N differently. Refer to tool operator's manual for type of display used for a specific tool.

2. Checks for an open switch in drive range.

3. Be sure "Scan" indicates drive, even while wiggling shifter, to test for an intermittent o misadjusted switch in drive or overdrive range.

Flowchart (CHART C-1A — PARK/NEUTRAL SWITCH DIAGNOSIS)

(1) • WITH TRANSAXLE/TRANSMISSION IN PARK, "SCAN" TOOL SHOULD INDICATE PARK OR NEUTRAL. DOES IT?

→ YES → (3)

→ NO → (2) • DISCONNECT PARK/NEUTRAL SWITCH CONNECTOR.
• JUMPER HARNESS CONNECTOR TERMINALS "A" AND "B" (CKT 434 TO 450).
• "SCAN" TOOL SHOULD INDICATE PARK OR NEUTRAL. DOES IT?

→ YES → • JUMPER HARNESS CONNECTOR TERMINAL "A" (CKT 434) TO ENGINE GROUND.
• "SCAN" TOOL SHOULD INDICATE PARK OR NEUTRAL. DOES IT?

→ YES → FAULTY P/N SWITCH CONNECTION OR P/N SWITCH MISADJUSTED OR FAULTY.

→ NO → OPEN GROUND CKT 450.

→ NO → • DISCONNECT P/N SWITCH. THIS SHOULD CAUSE "SCAN" TOOL TO DISPLAY DRIVE RANGE. DOES IT? → NO → CKT 434 OPEN OR FAULTY ECM CONNECTION OR ECM.

(3) • SHIFT TRANSAXLE/TRANSMISSION INTO DRIVE. "SCAN" TOOL SHOULD DISPLAY A CHANGE TO INDICATE DRIVE. DOES IT?

→ YES → NO TROUBLE FOUND, P/N CIRCUIT OK.

→ NO → • DISCONNECT P/N SWITCH. THIS SHOULD CAUSE "SCAN" TOOL TO DISPLAY DRIVE RANGE. DOES IT?

→ YES → FAULTY P/N SWITCH CONNECTION OR P/N SWITCH MISADJUSTED OR FAULTY.

→ NO → CKT 434 SHORTED TO GROUND OR FAULTY ECM.

1990-92 2.0L (VIN M)

CHART C-1D
MANIFOLD ABSOLUTE PRESSURE (MAP) OUTPUT CHECK
2.0L TURBO (VIN M) "J" CARLINE (PORT)

Circuit Description:

The Manifold Absolute Pressure (MAP) sensor measures manifold pressure (vacuum) and sends that signal to the ECM. The MAP sensor is mainly used to calculate engine load, which is a fundamental input for spark and fuel calculations. The MAP sensor is also used to determine barometric pressure.

Test Description: Numbers below refer to circled numbers on the diagnostic chart.

1. Checks MAP sensor output voltage to the ECM. With the ignition "ON" and the engine stopped, the manifold pressure is equal to atmospheric pressure and the signal voltage will be high. This voltage, without engine running, represents a barometric reading to the ECM. Comparison of this BARO reading with a known good vehicle with the same sensor is a good way to check accuracy of a "suspect" sensor. Readings should be the same ± .4 volt.

2. Applying 34 kPa (10 inches Hg) vacuum to the MAP sensor should cause the voltage to be 1.2-2.3 volts less than the voltage at step 1. Upon applying vacuum to the sensor, the change in voltage should be instantaneous. A slow voltage change indicates a faulty sensor.

3. Check vacuum hose to sensor for leaking or restriction. Be sure no other vacuum devices are connected to the MAP hose.

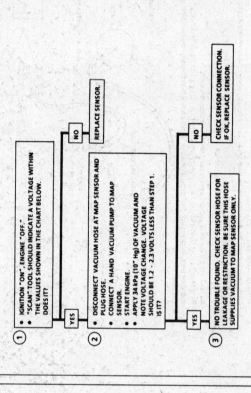

CHART C-1D
MANIFOLD ABSOLUTE PRESSURE (MAP) OUTPUT CHECK
2.0L TURBO (VIN M) "J" CARLINE (PORT)

① • IGNITION "ON", ENGINE "OFF."
 • "SCAN" TOOL SHOULD INDICATE A VOLTAGE WITHIN THE VALUES SHOWN IN THE CHART BELOW. DOES IT?

 — NO → REPLACE SENSOR.

② • DISCONNECT VACUUM HOSE AT MAP SENSOR AND PLUG HOSE.
 • CONNECT A HAND VACUUM PUMP TO MAP SENSOR.
 • START ENGINE.
 • APPLY 34 kPa (10" Hg) OF VACUUM AND NOTE VOLTAGE CHANGE. VOLTAGE SHOULD BE 1.2 - 2.3 VOLTS LESS THAN STEP 1. IS IT?

 — NO → CHECK SENSOR CONNECTION. IF OK, REPLACE SENSOR.

③ NO TROUBLE FOUND. CHECK SENSOR HOSE FOR LEAKAGE OR RESTRICTION. BE SURE THIS HOSE SUPPLIES VACUUM TO MAP SENSOR ONLY.

| ALTITUDE | | |
Meters	Feet	VOLTAGE RANGE
Below 305	Below 1,000	3.8-5.5V
305—610	1,000-2,000	3.6-5.3V
610—914	2,000-3,000	3.5-5.1V
914-1219	3,000-4,000	3.3-5.0V
1219-1524	4,000-5,000	3.2-4.8V
1524-1829	5,000-6,000	3.0-4.6V
1829-2133	6,000-7,000	2.9-4.5V
2133-2438	7,000-8,000	2.8-4.3V
2438-2743	8,000-9,000	2.6-4.2V
2743-3048	9,000-10,000	2.5-4.0V

LOW ALTITUDE = HIGH PRESSURE = HIGH VOLTAGE

CLEAR CODES AND CONFIRM "CLOSED LOOP" OPERATION AND NO "SERVICE ENGINE SOON" LIGHT.

1990-92 2.0L (VIN M)

CHART C-2A
INJECTOR BALANCE TEST

The injector balance tester is a tool used to turn the injector on for a precise amount of time, thus spraying a measured amount of fuel into the manifold. This causes a drop in fuel rail pressure that we can record and compare between each injector. All injectors should have the same amount of pressure drop (± 10 kpa). Any injector with a pressure drop that is 10 kpa (or more) greater or less than the average drop of the other injectors should be considered faulty and replaced.

STEP 1

Engine "cool down" period (10 minutes) is necessary to avoid irregular readings due to "Hot Soak" fuel boiling. With ignition "OFF" connect fuel gauge J 347301 or equivalent to fuel pressure tap Wrap a shop towel around fitting while connecting gage to avoid fuel spillage.

Disconnect harness connectors at all injectors, and connect injector tester J 34730-3, or equivalent, to one injector. On Turbo equipped engines, use adaptor harness furnished with injector tester to energize injectors that are not accessible. Follow manufacturers instructions for use of adaptor harness. Ignition must be "OFF" at least 10 seconds to complete ECM shutdown cycle. Fuel pump should run about 2 seconds after ignition is turned "ON". At this point, insert clear tubing attached to vent valve into a suitable container and bleed air from gauge and hose to insure accurate gauge operation. Repeat this step until all air is bled from gauge.

STEP 2

Turn ignition "OFF" for 10 seconds and then "ON" again to get fuel pressure to its maximum. Record this initial pressure reading. Energize tester one time and note pressure drop at its lowest point (Disregard any slight pressure increase after drop hits low point). By subtracting this second pressure reading from the initial pressure, we have the actual amount of injector pressure drop.

STEP 3

Repeat step 2 on each injector and compare the amount of drop. Usually, good injectors will have virtually the same drop. Retest any injector that has a pressure difference of 10kPa, either more or less than the average of the other injectors on the engine. Replace any injector that also fails the retest. If the pressure drop of all injectors is within 10kPa of this average, the injectors appear to be flowing properly. Reconnect them and review "Symptoms", Section

NOTE: *The entire test should not be repeated more than once without running the engine to prevent flooding. (This includes any retest on faulty injectors).*

CHART C-2A
INJECTOR BALANCE TEST
2.0L TURBO (VIN M)
"J" CARLINE (PORT)

NOTE: If injectors are suspected of being dirty, they should be cleaned using an approved tool and procedure prior to performing this test. The fuel pressure test in Chart A-7, should be completed prior to this test.

Step 1. If engine is at operating temperature, allow a 10 minute "cool down" period then connect fuel pressure gauge and injector tester.
1. Ignition "OFF."
2. Connect fuel pressure gauge and injector tester.
3. Ignition "ON."
4. Bleed off air in gauge. Repeat until all air is bled from gauge.

Step 2. Run test:
1. Ignition "OFF" for 10 seconds.
2. Ignition "ON". Record gauge pressure. (Pressure must hold steady, if not see the Fuel System diagnosis, Chart A-7.
3. Turn injector on, by depressing button on injector tester, and note pressure at the instant the gauge needle stops.

Step 3.
1. Repeat step 2 on all injectors and record pressure drop on each. Retest injectors that appear faulty (Any injectors that have a 10 kPa difference, either more or less, in pressure from the average). If no problem is found, review "Symptoms" Section

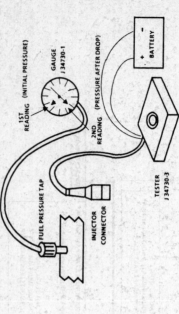

GAUGE J 34730-1
1ST READING (INITIAL PRESSURE)
2ND READING (PRESSURE AFTER DROP)
FUEL PRESSURE TAP
INJECTOR CONNECTOR
TESTER J34730-3
BATTERY

— EXAMPLE —

CYLINDER	1	2	3	4	5	6
1ST READING	225	225	225	225	225	225
2ND READING	100	100	100	90	100	115
AMOUNT OF DROP	125	125	125	135	125	110
	OK	OK	OK	FAULTY, RICH (TOO MUCH) (FUEL DROP)	OK	FAULTY, LEAN (TOO LITTLE) (FUEL DROP)

1990-92 2.0L (VIN M)

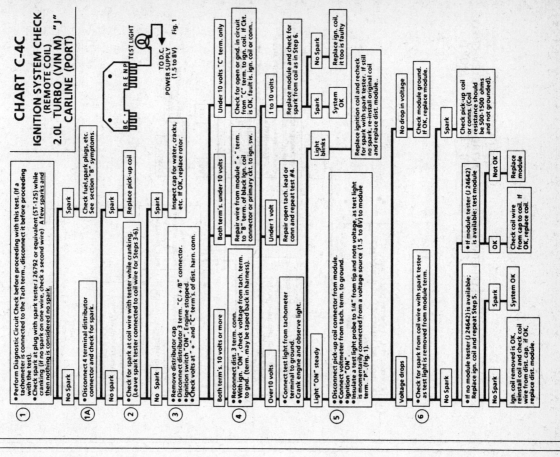

CHART C-4C

IGNITION SYSTEM CHECK (REMOTE COIL)

2.0L TURBO (VIN M) "J" CARLINE (PORT)

Fig. 1

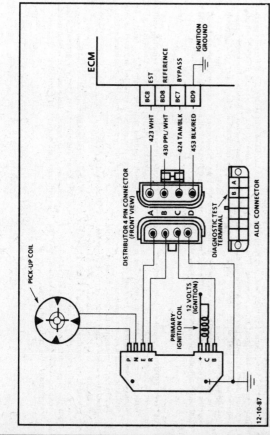

12-10-87

CHART C-4C

IGNITION SYSTEM CHECK (REMOTE COIL)

2.0L TURBO (VIN M) "J" CARLINE (PORT)

Test Description: Numbers below refer to circled numbers on the diagnostic chart.

1. Two wires are checked to ensure that an open is not present in a spark plug wire.

1A. If spark occurs with 4 terminal distributor connector disconnected, pick-up coil output is too low for EST operation.

2. A spark indicates the problem must be the distributor cap or rotor.

3. Normally, there should be battery voltage at the "C" and "+" terminals. Low voltage would indicate an open or a high resistance circuit from the distributor to the coil or ignition switch. If "C" terminal voltage was low, but "+" terminal voltage is 10 volts or more, circuit from "C" terminal to ignition coil or ignition coil primary winding is open.

4. Checks for a shorted module or grounded circuit from the ignition coil to the module. The distributor module should be turned "OFF". Normal voltage should be about 12 volts.

   If the module is turned "ON", the voltage would be low, but above 1 volt. This could cause the ignition coil primary circuit to be turned "ON", causing the ignition coil to fail from excessive heat.

   With an open ignition coil primary winding, a small amount of voltage will leak through the module from the "BATT" to the "tach" terminal. Applying voltage (1.5 to 8 volts) to module terminal "P" should turn the module "ON" and the tachometer terminal voltage should drop to about 7-9 volts. This test will determine whether the module or coil is faulty or if the pick-up coil is not generating the proper signal to turn the module "ON." This test can be performed by using a DC battery with a rating of 1.5 to 8 volts. The use of the test light is mainly to allow the "P" terminal to be probed more easily.

5. Some digital multi-meters can also be used to trigger the module by selecting ohms, usually the diode position. In this position the meter may have a voltage across its terminals which can be used to trigger the module. The voltage in the ohms position can be checked by using a second meter or by checking the manufacturer's specification of the tool being used.

   This should turn "OFF" the module and cause a spark. If no spark occurs, the fault is most likely in the ignition coil because most module problems would have been found before this point in the procedure. A module tester (J 24642) could determine which is at fault.

6. Checks for spark from coil with spark tester as test light is removed from module term.

1990-92 2.0L (VIN M)

CHART C-5

ELECTRONIC SPARK CONTROL (ESC) SYSTEM CHECK
2.0L TURBO (VIN M) "J" CARLINE (PORT)

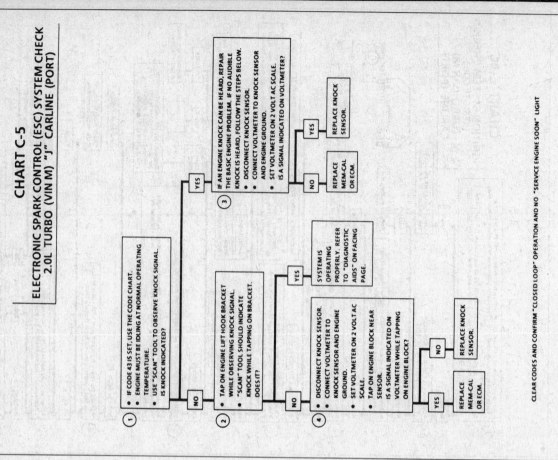

1.
- IF CODE 43 IS SET, USE THE CODE CHART.
- ENGINE MUST BE IDLING AT NORMAL OPERATING TEMPERATURE.
- USE "SCAN" TOOL TO OBSERVE KNOCK SIGNAL.
IS KNOCK INDICATED?

2.
- TAP ON ENGINE LIFT HOOK BRACKET WHILE OBSERVING KNOCK SIGNAL.
- "SCAN" TOOL SHOULD INDICATE KNOCK WHILE TAPPING ON BRACKET.
DOES IT?

3.
IF AN ENGINE KNOCK CAN BE HEARD, REPAIR THE BASIC ENGINE PROBLEM. IF NO AUDIBLE KNOCK IS HEARD, FOLLOW THE STEPS BELOW.
- DISCONNECT KNOCK SENSOR.
- CONNECT VOLTMETER TO KNOCK SENSOR AND ENGINE GROUND.
- SET VOLTMETER ON 2 VOLT AC SCALE.
IS A SIGNAL INDICATED ON VOLTMETER?

4.
- DISCONNECT KNOCK SENSOR.
- CONNECT VOLTMETER TO KNOCK SENSOR AND ENGINE GROUND.
- SET VOLTMETER ON 2 VOLT AC SCALE.
- TAP ON ENGINE BLOCK NEAR SENSOR.
IS A SIGNAL INDICATED ON VOLTMETER WHILE TAPPING ON ENGINE BLOCK?

SYSTEM IS OPERATING PROPERLY. REFER TO "DIAGNOSTIC AIDS" ON FACING PAGE.

REPLACE KNOCK SENSOR.

REPLACE MEM-CAL OR ECM.

CLEAR CODES AND CONFIRM "CLOSED LOOP" OPERATION AND NO "SERVICE ENGINE SOON" LIGHT

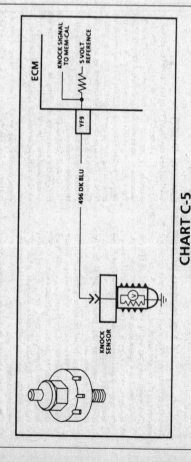

CHART C-5

ELECTRONIC SPARK CONTROL (ESC) SYSTEM CHECK
2.0L TURBO (VIN M) "J" CARLINE (PORT)

Circuit Description:

The ESC knock sensor is used to detect engine detonation and the ECM will retard the electronic spark timing based on the signal being received. The circuitry, within the knock sensor, causes the ECM's 5 volts to be pulled down so that under a no knock condition, CKT 496 would measure about 2.5 volts. The knock sensor produces an A/C signal, which rides on the 2.5 volts DC voltage. The amplitude and frequency are dependent upon the knock level.

The Mem-Cal, used with this engine, contains the functions which were part of remotely mounted ESC modules used on other GM vehicles. The ESC portion of the Mem-Cal then sends a signal to other parts of the ECM which adjusts the spark timing to retard the spark and reduce the detonation.

Test Description: Numbers below refer to circled numbers on the diagnostic chart.

1. With engine idling, there should not be a knock signal present at the ECM, because detonation is not likely under a no load condition.

2. Tapping on the engine lift, hood bracket should simulate a knock signal to determine if the sensor is capable of detecting detonation. If no knock is detected, try tapping on engine block closer to sensor before replacing sensor.

3. If the engine has an internal problem, which is creating a knock, the knock sensor may be responding to the internal failure.

4. This test determines if the knock sensor is faulty, or, if the ESC portion of the Mem-Cal is faulty. If it is determined that the Mem-Cal is faulty, be sure that it is properly installed and latched into place. If not properly installed, repair and retest.

Diagnostic Aids:

While observing knock signal on the "Scan," there should be an indication that knock is present, when detonation can be heard. Detonation is most likely to occur under high engine load conditions.

1990-92 2.0L (VIN M)

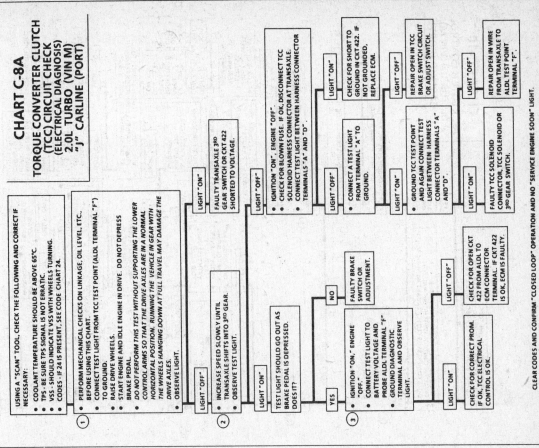

CHART C-8A
TORQUE CONVERTER CLUTCH (TCC) CIRCUIT CHECK (ELECTRICAL DIAGNOSIS) 2.0L TURBO (VIN M) "J" CARLINE (PORT)

USING A "SCAN" TOOL, CHECK THE FOLLOWING AND CORRECT IF NECESSARY:
- COOLANT TEMPERATURE SHOULD BE ABOVE 65°C.
- TPS - BE SURE TPS SIGNAL IS NOT ERRATIC.
- VSS - SHOULD INDICATE VSS WITH WHEELS TURNING.
- CODES - IF 24 IS PRESENT, SEE CODE CHART 24.

(1) PERFORM MECHANICAL CHECKS ON LINKAGE, OIL LEVEL, ETC., BEFORE USING THIS CHART.
- CONNECT TEST LIGHT FROM TCC TEST POINT (ALDL TERMINAL "F") TO GROUND.
- RAISE DRIVE WHEELS.
- START ENGINE AND IDLE ENGINE IN DRIVE. DO NOT DEPRESS BRAKE PEDAL.
- DO NOT PERFORM THIS TEST WITHOUT SUPPORTING THE LOWER CONTROL ARMS SO THAT THE DRIVE AXLES ARE IN A NORMAL HORIZONTAL POSITION. RUNNING THE VEHICLE IN GEAR WITH THE WHEELS HANGING DOWN AT FULL TRAVEL MAY DAMAGE THE DRIVE AXLES.
- OBSERVE LIGHT.

LIGHT "ON" → FAULTY TRANSAXLE 3RD GEAR SWITCH OR CKT 422 SHORTED TO VOLTAGE.

LIGHT "OFF"

(2) INCREASE SPEED SLOWLY UNTIL TRANSAXLE SHIFTS INTO 3RD GEAR. OBSERVE TEST LIGHT.

LIGHT "ON" → TEST LIGHT SHOULD GO OUT AS BRAKE PEDAL IS DEPRESSED. DOES IT?

- **NO** → FAULTY BRAKE SWITCH OR ADJUSTMENT.
- **YES**

(3) IGNITION "ON," ENGINE "OFF."
- CONNECT TEST LIGHT TO BATTERY VOLTAGE AND PROBE ALDL TERMINAL "F".
- GROUND DIAGNOSTIC TERMINAL AND OBSERVE LIGHT.

LIGHT "ON" → CHECK FOR CORRECT PROM. IF OK, TCC ELECTRICAL CONTROL IS OK.

LIGHT "OFF" → CHECK FOR OPEN CKT 422 FROM ALDL TO ECM CONNECTOR TERMINAL. IF CKT 422 IS OK, ECM IS FAULTY.

LIGHT "OFF" (from step 2)
- IGNITION "ON," ENGINE "OFF."
- CHECK FOR BLOWN FUSE. IF OK, DISCONNECT TCC SOLENOID HARNESS CONNECTOR AT TRANSAXLE.
- CONNECT TEST LIGHT BETWEEN HARNESS CONNECTOR TERMINALS "A" AND "D".

LIGHT "ON" → CHECK FOR SHORT TO GROUND IN CKT 422. IF NOT GROUNDED, REPLACE ECM.

LIGHT "OFF" → CONNECT A TEST LIGHT FROM TERMINAL "A" TO GROUND.

LIGHT "ON" → GROUND TCC TEST POINT AND AGAIN CONNECT TEST LIGHT BETWEEN HARNESS CONNECTOR TERMINALS "A" AND "D".

LIGHT "OFF" → REPAIR OPEN IN TCC BRAKE SWITCH CIRCUIT OR ADJUST SWITCH.

LIGHT "ON" → FAULTY TCC SOLENOID CONNECTOR, TCC SOLENOID OR 3RD GEAR SWITCH.

LIGHT "OFF" → REPAIR OPEN IN WIRE FROM TRANSAXLE TO ALDL TEST POINT TERMINAL "F".

CLEAR CODES AND CONFIRM "CLOSED LOOP" OPERATION AND NO "SERVICE ENGINE SOON" LIGHT.

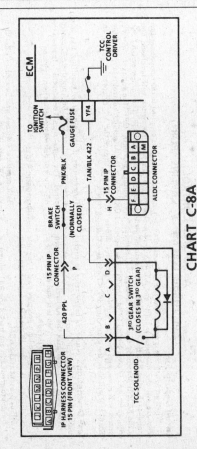

CHART C-8A
TORQUE CONVERTER CLUTCH (TCC) CIRCUIT CHECK (ELECTRICAL DIAGNOSIS) 2.0L TURBO (VIN M) "J" CARLINE (PORT)

Circuit Description:
The purpose of the Torque Converter Clutch (TCC) is to eliminate the power loss of the torque converter when the vehicle is in a cruise condition. This allows the convenience of the automatic transmission and the fuel economy of a manual transmission.

Voltage is supplied to the TCC solenoid through the brake switch and transmission third gear apply switch. The ECM will engage TCC by grounding CKT 422 to energize the solenoid.

TCC will engage under the following conditions:
- Vehicle speed exceeds 30 mph (48 km/h)
- Engine temperature is above 70°C (158°F)
- Throttle position sensor output is not changing faster than a calibrated rate (steady throttle).
- Transaxle third gear switch is closed
- Brake switch is closed

Test Description: Numbers below refer to circled numbers on the diagnostic chart.
1. Light "OFF" confirms that transaxle third gear apply switch is open.
2. At 48 km/h (30 mph), the transmission third gear switch should close. Test light will light and confirm battery supply, and close brake switch.
3. Grounding the diagnostic terminal, with engine "OFF," should energize the TCC solenoid. This test checks the capability of the ECM to control the solenoid.

Diagnostic Aids:
An engine coolant thermostat that is stuck open or opens at too low a temperature may result in an inoperative TCC.

1990-92 2.0L (VIN M)

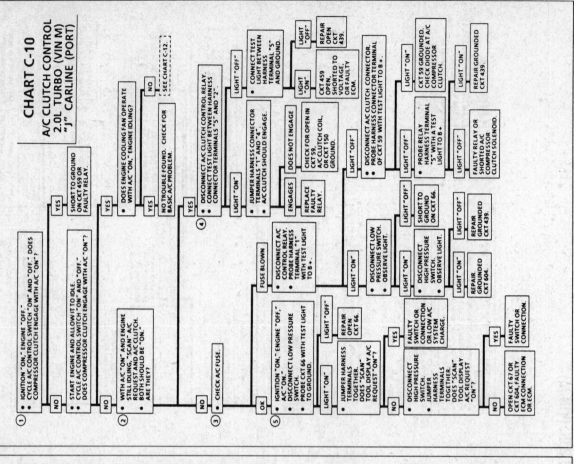

CHART C-10
A/C CLUTCH CONTROL
2.0L TURBO (VIN M) "J" CARLINE (PORT)

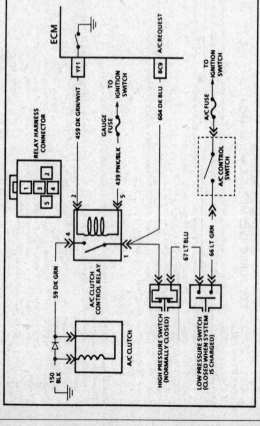

CHART C-10
A/C CLUTCH CONTROL
2.0L TURBO (VIN M) "J" CARLINE (PORT)

Circuit Description:

When an A/C mode is selected on the A/C control switch, ignition voltage is supplied to the compressor low pressure switch. If there is sufficient A/C refrigerant charge, the low pressure switch will be closed and complete the circuit to the closed high pressure cut-off switch and to CKTs 67 and 366. The voltage on CKT 366 to the ECM is shown by the "Scan" tool as A/C request "ON" (voltage present), "OFF" (no voltage). When a request for A/C is seen by the ECM, the ECM will ground CKT 459 of the A/C clutch control relay, the relay contact will close, and current will flow from CKT 366 to CKT 59 and engage the A/C compressor clutch. A "Scan" tool will show the grounding of CKT 459 as A/C clutch "ON."

Test Description: Numbers below refer to circled numbers on the diagnostic chart.

1. The ECM will energize the A/C relay only when the engine is running. This test will determine if the relay or CKT 459 is faulty.

2. The low pressure and high pressure switches must be closed so that the A/C request signal (12 volts) will be present at the ECM.

3. A short to ground in any part of the A/C request or A/C clutch control circuits could be the cause of the blown fuse.

4. With the engine idling and A/C "ON," the ECM should be grounding CKT 459, causing the test light to be "ON."

5. Determines if the signal is reaching the low pressure switch on CKT 66 from the A/C control panel. The signal should be present only when the A/C mode or defrost mode has been selected.

Diagnostic Aids:

Both pressure switches are located on the high side of the A/C system. The low pressure switch will be closed at 40-47 psi and allow A/C clutch operation. Below 37 psi, the low pressure switch will be open and the A/C clutch will not operate.

At about 430 psi, the high pressure switch will open to disengage the A/C clutch and prevent system damage.

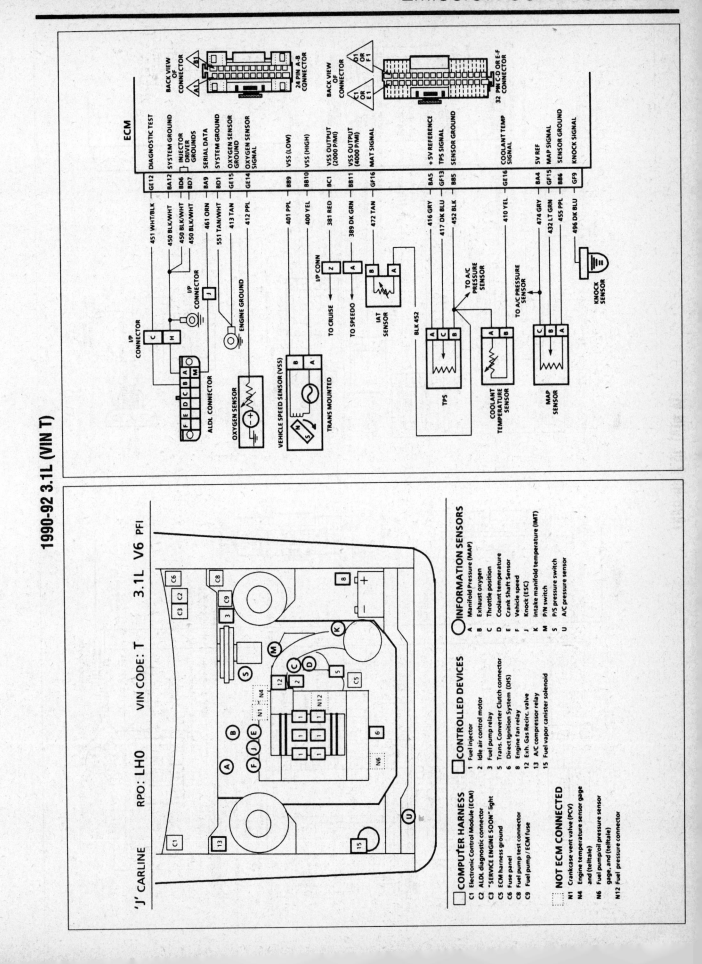

1990-92 3.1L (VIN T)

'J' CARLINE   RPO: LH0   VIN CODE: T   3.1L V6 PFI

☐ **COMPUTER HARNESS**
C1 Electronic Control Module (ECM)
C2 ALDL diagnostic connector
C3 "SERVICE ENGINE SOON" light
C5 ECM harness ground
C6 Fuse panel
C8 Fuel pump test connector
C9 Fuel pump / ECM fuse

NOT ECM CONNECTED
N1 Crankcase vent valve (PCV)
N4 Engine temperature sensor gage and (telltale)
N6 Fuel pump/oil pressure sensor gage, and (telltale)
N12 Fuel pressure connector

☐ **CONTROLLED DEVICES**
1 Fuel injector
2 Idle air control motor
3 Fuel pump relay
5 Trans. Converter Clutch connector
6 Direct Ignition System (DIS)
8 Engine fan relay
13 A/C compressor relay
15 Fuel vapor canister solenoid

○ **INFORMATION SENSORS**
A Manifold Pressure (MAP)
B Exhaust oxygen
C Throttle position
D Coolant temperature
E Crank Shaft Sensor
F Vehicle speed
J Knock (ESC)
K Intake manifold temperature (IMT)
M P/N switch
S P/S pressure switch
U A/C pressure sensor

1990-92 3.1L (VIN T)

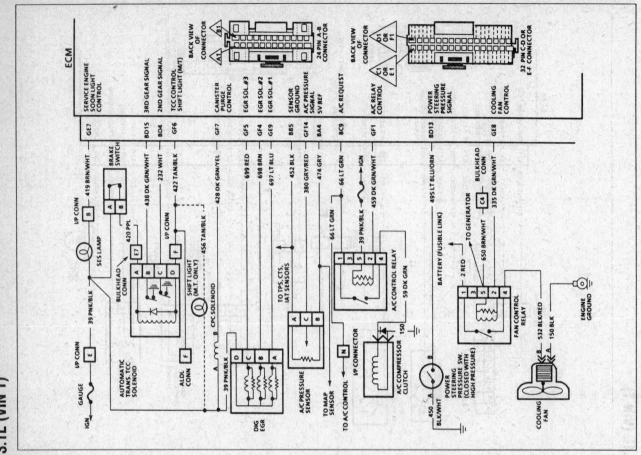

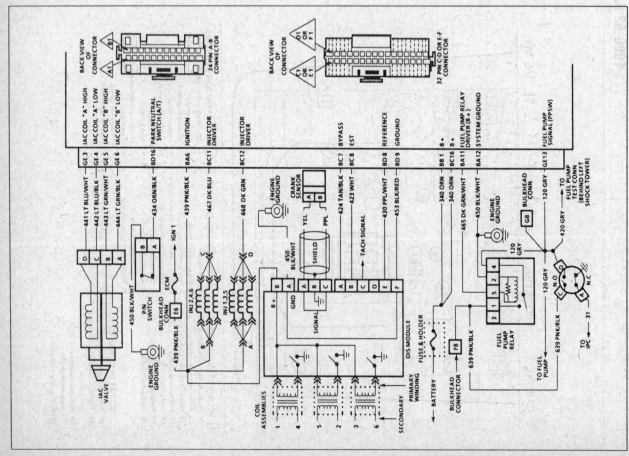

1990-92 3.1L (VIN T)

Top Tables

WIRE COLOR	PIN	CIRCUIT	KEY "ON"	ENG. "RUN"
TAN/WHT	BD1	SYSTEM GROUND	0*	0*
	BD2			
	BD3			
WHT	BD4	2ND GEAR SIGNAL	B+	B+
	BD5			
BLK/WHT	BD6	INJ DRIVE GROUND	0*	0*
BLK/WHT	BD7	INJ DRIVE GROUND	0*	0*
PPL/WHT	BD8	REFERENCE	0*	2.3
BLK/RED	BD9	REFERENCE GROUND	0*	0*
	BD10			
	BD11			
	BD12			
LT BLU/ORN	BD13	(WITH HIGH P/S PRESSURE) P.S.P.S.	0* / B+	0* / B+
	BD14			
DK GRN/WHT	BD15	3RD GEAR SIGNAL	B+	B+
ORN/BLK	BD16	P/N SWITCH	0*	0*

WIRE COLOR	PIN	CIRCUIT	KEY "ON"	ENG. "RUN"
DK GRN/WHT	GF1	A/C RELAY "ON" CONTROL "OFF"	0* / B+	0* / B+
	GF2			
	GF3			
BRN	GF4	EGR SOL. #2	B+	B+
RED	GF5	EGR SOL #3	B+	B+
TAN/BLK	GF6	TCC CONTROL A/T SHIFT LIGHT M/T	0* / B+	0* / B+
DK GRN/YEL	GF7	PURGE CONTROL	0*	0*
	GF8			
DK BLU	GF9	ESC SIGNAL	2.5	2.5 ③
	GF10			
	GF11			
	GF12			
DK BLU	GF13	TPS SIGNAL	.29-.98	.29-.98
GRY/RED	GF14	A/C PRESS. SENSOR	③	③
LT GRN	GF15	MAP SIGNAL	4.57	③
TAN	GF16	IAT SIGNAL	⑤	⑤

4. 12V First two seconds.
5. Varies with temperature.
*. Less than 1 volt.

PIN	WIRE COLOR	CIRCUIT	KEY "ON"	ENG. "RUN"
BC1	RED	VSS OUTPUT 2000 P/MI	0* ①	
BC2				
BC3				
BC4	PPL	IF USED/BRAKE SWITCH	B+	B+
BC5				
BC6				
BC7	TAN/BLK	BYPASS	0*	5
BC8	WHT	EST	0*	1.3
BC9	LT GRN	A/C REQUEST	0*	0*
BC10				
BC11	DK BLU	INJECTOR 2,4,6	B+	B+
BC12	DK GRN	INJECTOR 1,3,5	B+	B+
BC13				
BC14				
BC15				
BC16	ORN	BATTERY	B+	B+

PIN	WIRE COLOR	CIRCUIT	KEY "ON"	ENG. "RUN"
GE1			NOT USEABLE	
GE2	LT BLU/WHT	IAC "A" HIGH	NOT USEABLE	
GE3	LT BLU/BLK	IAC "A" LOW	NOT USEABLE	
GE4	LT GRN/WHT	IAC "B" HIGH	NOT USEABLE	
GE5	LT GRN/BLK	IAC "B" LOW	NOT USEABLE	
GE6				
GE7	BRN/WHT	SERVICE ENGINE SOON LIGHT	0*	B+
GE8	BRN/WHT	"ON" FAN CONTROL "OFF"-RELAY	0* / B+	0* / B+
GE9	LT BLU	EGR SOL #1	B+	B+
GE10				
GE11				
GE12	WHT/BLK	DIAG TERMINAL	5	5
GE13	GRY	FUEL PUMP SIGNAL	.35-.55	.1 ③ / .9 ③
GE14	PPL	O₂ SIGNAL	0*	0*
GE15	TAN	O₂ GND	0*	0*
GE16	YEL	COOLANT TEMP	⑤	⑤

1. Increases with speed (measure on A/C scale).
2. Normal operating temperature.
3. Varies.

PORT FUEL INJECTION ECM CONNECTOR IDENTIFICATION

This ECM voltage chart is for use with a digital voltmeter to further aid in diagnosis. The voltages you get may vary due to low battery charge or other reasons, but they should be very close.

THE FOLLOWING CONDITIONS MUST BE MET BEFORE TESTING:

• Engine at operating temperature • Engine idling in "Closed Loop" (For "Engine Run" column) in park or neutral • Test terminal not grounded • ALDL tool not installed

32 PIN C-D CONNECTOR
BACK VIEW OF CONNECTOR (BLACK)

24 PIN A-B CONNECTOR
BACK VIEW OF CONNECTOR (BLACK)

32 PIN E-F CONNECTOR
BACK VIEW OF CONNECTOR (GREEN)

WIRE COLOR	PIN	CIRCUIT	KEY "ON" RUN	ENG "RUN"
ORN	BA1			
	BA2			
	BA3			
GRY	BA4	5V REF (MAP)	5	5
GRY	BA5	5V REF (TPS)	5	5
PNK/BLK	BA6	IGNITION	B+	B+
	BA7			
	BA8			
ORN	BA9	SERIAL DATA	4.8	4.8 ③
DK GRN/WHT	BA10	FUEL PUMP RELAY DRIVER	B+	B+
	BA11			
BLK/WHT	BA12	SYSTEM GROUND	0*	0* ④

WIRE COLOR	PIN	CIRCUIT	KEY "ON" RUN	ENG "RUN"
ORN	BB1	BATTERY	B+	B+
	BB2			
	BB3			
	BB4			
BLK	BB5	SENSOR GROUND	0*	0*
PPL	BB6	SENSOR GROUND	0*	0*
	BB7			
	BB8			
PPL	BB9	VSS (LOW)	0*	①
YEL	BB10	VSS (HIGH)	0*	②
DK GRN	BB11	VSS OUTPUT 4000 P/MI	10	11.7
	BB12			

1. Increases with speed (measure on A/C scale).
2. Normal operating temperature.
3. Varies.
4. 12V First two seconds.
5. Varies with temperature.
*. Less than 1 volt.

ENGINE 3.1L LHO "T"
CARLINE "J"

1990-92 3.1L (VIN T)

DIAGNOSTIC CIRCUIT CHECK

The Diagnostic Circuit Check is and organized approach to identifying a problem created by an Electronic Engine Control System Malfunction. It must be the starting point for any driveability complaint diagnosis, because it directs the Service Technician to the next logical step in diagnosing the complaint.

The "Scan Data" listed in the table may be used for comparison, after completing the Diagnostic Circuit Check and finding the on-board diagnostics functioning properly and no trouble codes displayed. The "Typical Values" are an average of display values recorded from normally operating vehicles and are intended to represent what a normally functioning system would typically display.

A "SCAN" TOOL THAT DISPLAYS FAULTY DATA SHOULD NOT BE USED, AND THE PROBLEM SHOULD BE REPORTED TO THE MANUFACTURER. THE USE OF A FAULTY "SCAN" CAN RESULT IN MISDIAGNOSIS AND UNNECESSARY PARTS REPLACEMENT.

Only the parameters listed below are used in this manual for diagnosis. If a "Scan" reads other parameters the values are not recommended by General Motors for use in diagnosis. For more description on the values and use of the "Scan" to diagnose ECM inputs, refer to the applicable diagnosis section. If all values are within the range illustrated, refer to "Symptoms" in Section

"SCAN" DATA

"SCAN" Position	Units Displayed	Typical Data Value
Engine Speed	Rpm	± 100 from desired rpm (± 50 rpm in drive)
Desired Rpm	Rpm	ECM idle command (varies with temp.)
Coolant Temp	°C/°F	85 - 109°C, (185 - 223°F)
IAT	°C/°F	10° - 80° (50°F - 176°F) depends on underhood temp.
MAP	kPa, Volts	29 - 48kPa (1-2 volts) depends on Vac. & Baro pressure.
Baro	kPa, Volts	58-114kPa (2.5-5.5) depends on altitude & Baro pressure.
Throttle Position	Volts	29 - 98
Throttle Angle	0 - 100%	0
Oxygen Sensor	M/Volts	100 - 1000 and varying
Inj. Pulse Width	M/Sec	1-4 and varying
Spark Advance	# of Degrees	Varies
Engine Speed	Rpm	± 100 rpm from desired rpm (± 50 rpm in drive)
Block Learn	Counts	Varies
Open/Closed Loop	Open/Closed	Closed Loop (may go open with extended idle)
Block Learn Cell	Cell Number	0 or 1 (depends on Air Flow & rpm)
Knock Retard	Degrees of Retard	0*
EGR 1/EGR 2	Yes/No	No
EGR 3	Off/On	Off (On when commanded by ECM)
Idle Air Control	Off/On	Off (On when commanded by ECM)
Park/Neutral	Counts (steps)	5 - 50
MPH/KPH	P/N and RDL	Park/Neutral (P/N)
Torque Converter Clutch	MPH/KPH	0
Battery Voltage	On/Off	Off (On with TCC commanded)
Fuel Pump Volts	Volts	13.5 - 14.5 volts
Crank rpm	Volts	13.5 - 14.5 volts
Battery Voltage	Rpm	Varies
A/C Request	Volts	13.5 - 14.5 volts
A/C Clutch	Yes/No	No (Yes, with A/C requested)
A/C Clutch	On/Off	Off (On, with A/C commanded on)
A/C Pressure	On/Off	Off (On, with A/C commanded on)
Fan 1 (Fan 2 if applicable)	psi/Volt	Varies (depends on temperature)
Coolant Temp.	On/Off	109°C, 228°F with A/C Off/106°C (223°F) with A/C On.
Power Steering	C°/F°	85° - 109° (185°F - 223°F)
Purge Duty Cycle	Normal/Hi Press.	Normal
Park/Neutral	0-100	0%
2nd Gear (3T40) (4T60)	P/N and RDL	Park/Neutral (P/N)
3rd Gear (3T40) (4T60)	Yes/No	No (Yes, when in 2nd , 3rd , or 4th gear)
4th Gear (4T60)	Yes/No	No (Yes, when in 3rd, or 4th gear)
PROM ID	Yes/No	No (Yes, when in 4th gear)
Time from Start	0-999	Varies
	Hrs/Min	Varies

*Note: If maximum retard is indicated, go to CHART C-5

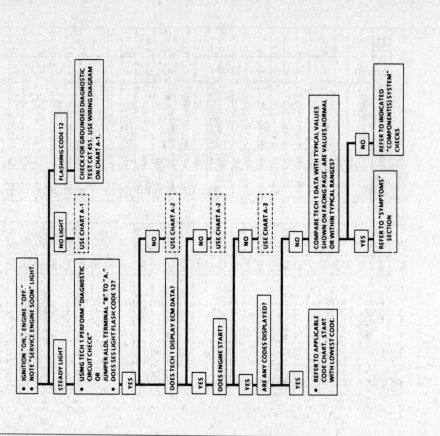

DIAGNOSTIC CIRCUIT CHECK
3.1L (VIN T) "J" CARLINE (PORT)

- IGNITION "ON." ENGINE "OFF."
- NOTE "SERVICE ENGINE SOON" LIGHT.

STEADY LIGHT → NO LIGHT → FLASHING CODE 12

NO LIGHT:
USE CHART A-1

FLASHING CODE 12:
CHECK FOR GROUNDED DIAGNOSTIC TEST CKT 451. USE WIRING DIAGRAM ON CHART A-1.

- USING TECH 1 PERFORM "DIAGNOSTIC CIRCUIT CHECK"
  OR
- JUMPER ALDL TERMINAL "B" TO "A."
- DOES SES LIGHT FLASH CODE 12?

YES → NO: USE CHART A-1

DOES TECH 1 DISPLAY ECM DATA?
YES → NO: USE CHART A-2

DOES ENGINE START?
YES → NO: USE CHART A-2

ARE ANY CODES DISPLAYED?
YES → NO: USE CHART A-3

- REFER TO APPLICABLE CODE CHART. START WITH LOWEST CODE.

COMPARE TECH 1 DATA WITH TYPICAL VALUES SHOWN ON FACING PAGE. ARE VALUES NORMAL OR WITHIN TYPICAL RANGES?

YES → REFER TO "SYMPTOMS" SECTION

NO → REFER TO INDICATED "COMPONENT(S) SYSTEM" CHECKS

1990-92 3.1L (VIN T)

CHART A-1

NO "SERVICE ENGINE SOON" LIGHT
3.1L (VIN T) "J" CARLINE (PORT)

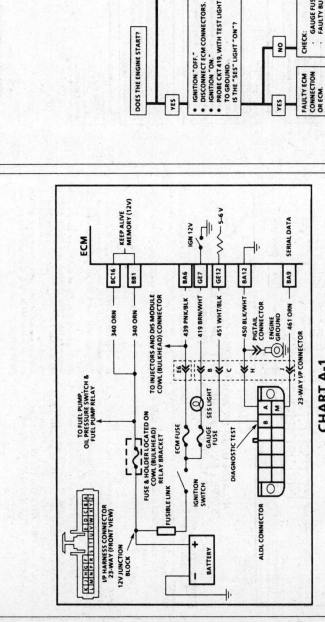

DOES THE ENGINE START?

YES → IGNITION "OFF."
• DISCONNECT ECM CONNECTORS.
• IGNITION "ON."
• PROBE CKT 419, WITH TEST LIGHT TO GROUND.
IS THE "SES" LIGHT "ON"?

NO → IS THE 20A CONTINUOUS BATTERY FUSE (IN HOLDER) AND ECM FUSE OK?

NO (from "SES" light) → CHECK:
• GAUGE FUSE.
• FAULTY BULB.
• OPEN CKT 419.
• CKT 419 SHORTED TO VOLTAGE.
• OPEN IGNITION FEED TO BULB.

YES (from "SES" light) → FAULTY ECM CONNECTION OR ECM.

NO (battery fuse) → LOCATE AND CORRECT SHORT TO GROUND IN CIRCUIT THAT HAD A BLOWN FUSE. ①

YES (battery fuse) →
• IGNITION "OFF."
• IGNITION "ON."
• PROBE CKT 340 & 439 WITH TEST LIGHT TO GROUND.
IS THE LIGHT "ON" ON BOTH CIRCUITS?

NO → REPAIR OPEN IN CIRCUIT THAT DID NOT LIGHT THE TEST LIGHT.

YES → FAULTY ECM GROUNDS OR ECM. ②

"AFTER REPAIRS," CONFIRM "CLOSED LOOP" OPERATION AND NO "SERVICE ENGINE SOON" LIGHT.

ECM

BC16
BB1 — KEEP ALIVE MEMORY (12V)
BA6
GE7 — IGN 12V
GE12 — 5-6 v
BA12
BA9 — SERIAL DATA

340 ORN — TO FUEL PUMP OIL PRESSURE SWITCH & FUEL PUMP RELAY
340 ORN
439 PNK/BLK
419 BRN/WHT
451 WHT/BLK
450 BLK/WHT — PIGTAIL CONNECTOR — ENGINE GROUND
461 ORN — 23-WAY I/P CONNECTOR

TO INJECTORS AND DIS MODULE COWL (BULKHEAD) CONNECTOR

E6
E5
B
C
H
J

I/P HARNESS CONNECTOR 23-WAY (FRONT VIEW)
12V JUNCTION BLOCK

FUSE & HOLDER LOCATED ON COWL (BULKHEAD) RELAY BRACKET

FUSIBLE LINK

IGNITION SWITCH

ECM FUSE
GAUGE FUSE
SES LIGHT

DIAGNOSTIC TEST

BATTERY

ALDL CONNECTOR
B A M

CHART A-1

NO "SERVICE ENGINE SOON" LIGHT
3.1L (VIN T) "J" CARLINE (PORT)

Circuit Description:

There should always be a steady "Service Engine Soon" light when the ignition is "ON" and engine stopped. Battery is supplied directly to the light bulb. The Electronic Control Module (ECM) will control the light and turn it "ON" by providing a ground path through CKT 419 to the ECM.

Test Description: Number(s) refer to circled number(s) on the diagnostic chart.

1. If the fuse in holder is blown, refer to facing page of Code 54 for complete circuit.

2. Using a test light connected to 12 volts, probe each of the system ground circuits to be sure a good ground is present. See ECM terminal end view in front of this section for ECM pin locations of ground circuits.

Diagnostic Aids:

Engine runs OK, check:
• Faulty light bulb
• CKT 419 open
• Gauges fuse blown. This will result in no oil or generator lights, seat belt reminder, etc.

Engine cranks but will not run:
• Continuous battery - fuse or fusible link open
• ECM ignition fuse open
• Battery CKT 340 to ECM open
• Ignition CKT 439 to ECM open
• Poor connection to ECM

1990-92 3.1L (VIN T)

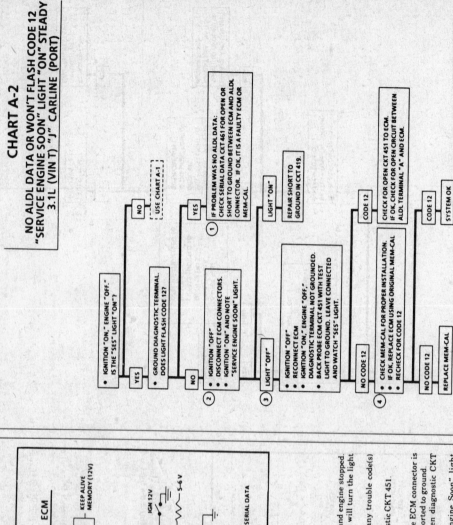

CHART A-2

NO ALDL DATA OR WON'T FLASH CODE 12
"SERVICE ENGINE SOON" LIGHT "ON" STEADY
3.1L (VIN T) "J" CARLINE (PORT)

Circuit Description:

There should always be a steady "Service Engine Soon" light when the ignition is "ON" and engine stopped. Battery ignition voltage is supplied to the light bulb. The Electronic Control Module (ECM) will turn the light "ON" by grounding CKT 419 at the ECM.

With the diagnostic terminal grounded, the light should flash a Code 12, followed by any trouble code(s) stored in memory.

A steady light suggests a short to ground in the light control CKT 419 or an open in diagnostic CKT 451.

Test Description: Number(s) refer to circled number(s) on the diagnostic chart.

1. If there is a problem with the ECM that causes a "Scan" tool to not read serial data, the ECM should not flash a Code 12. If Code 12 is flashing check for CKT 451 short to ground. If Code 12 does flash be sure that the "Scan" tool is functioning properly on another vehicle. If the "Scan" is functioning properly and CKT 461 is OK, the MEM-CAL or ECM may be at fault for the NO ALDL symptom.

2. If the light goes "OFF" when the ECM connector is disconnected, CKT 419 is not shorted to ground.

3. This step will check for an open diagnostic CKT 451.

4. At this point the "Service Engine Soon" light wiring is OK. The problem is a faulty ECM or MEM-CAL. If Code 12 does not flash, the ECM should be replaced using the original MEM-CAL. Replace the MEM-CAL only after trying an ECM, as a defective MEM-CAL is an unlikely cause of the problem.

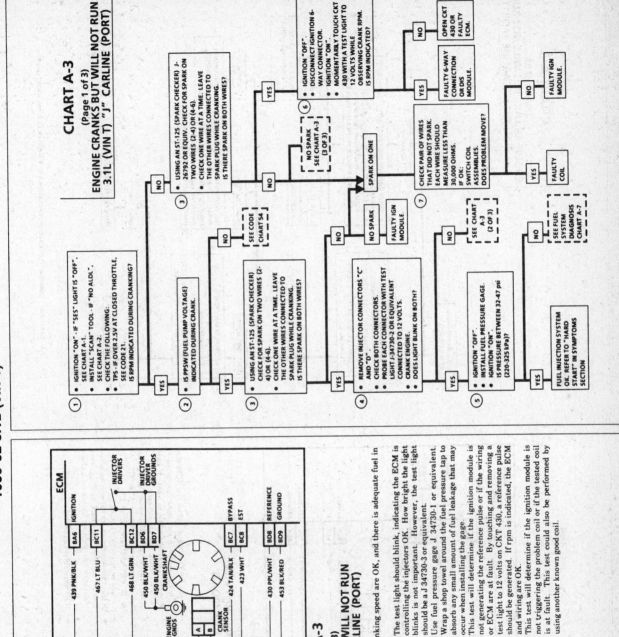

CHART A-3
(Page 1 of 3)
ENGINE CRANKS BUT WILL NOT RUN
3.1L (VIN T) "J" CARLINE (PORT)

1990-92 3.1L (VIN T)

CHART A-3
(Page 1 of 3)
ENGINE CRANKS BUT WILL NOT RUN
3.1L (VIN T) "J" CARLINE (PORT)

Circuit Description:

This chart assumes that battery condition and engine cranking speed are OK, and there is adequate fuel in the tank.

Test Description: Number(s) refer to circled number(s) on the diagnostic chart.

1. A "Service Engine Soon" light "ON" is a basic test to determine if there is a 12 volt supply and ignition 12 volts to ECM. No AIDL or due to an ECM problem and CHART A-2 will diagnose the ECM. If TPS is over 2.5 volts, the engine may be in the clear flood mode which will cause starting problems. The engine will not start without reference pulses and therefore the "Scan" should read rpm (reference) during crank.

2. For the first two seconds with ignition "ON" or whenever reference pulses are being received, PPSW should indicate fuel pump circuit voltage (8 to 12 volts).

3. Because the direct ignition system uses two plugs and wires to complete the circuit of each coil, the opposite spark should be left connected. If rpm was indicated during crank, the ignition module is receiving a crank signal, but no spark at this test indicates the ignition module is not triggering the coils.

4. The test light should blink, indicating the ECM is controlling the injectors OK. How bright the light blinks is not important. However, the test light should be a J 34730-3 or equivalent.

5. Use fuel pressure gage J 34730-1 or equivalent. Wrap a shop towel around the fuel pressure tap to absorb any small amount of fuel leakage that may occur when installing the gage.

6. This test will determine if the ignition module is not generating the reference pulse or if the wiring or ECM are at fault. By touching and removing a test light to 12 volts on CKT 430, a reference pulse should be generated. If rpm is indicated, the ECM and wiring are OK.

7. This test will determine if the ignition module is not triggering the problem coil or if the tested coil is at fault. This test could also be performed by using another known good coil.

1990-92 3.1L (VIN T)

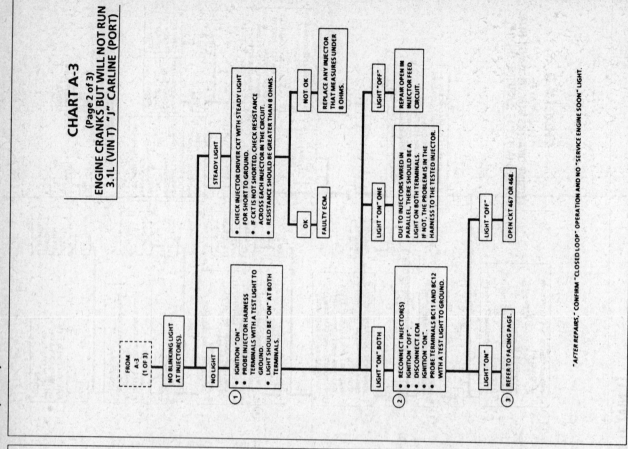

CHART A-3
(Page 2 of 3)
ENGINE CRANKS BUT WILL NOT RUN
3.1L (VIN T) "J" CARLINE (PORT)

Test Description: Number(s) refer to circled number(s) on the diagnostic chart.

1. Checks for 12 volt supply to injectors. Because the injectors are wired in parallel there should be a light "ON" on both terminals.

2. Checks continuity of CKT 467 and 468.

3. All checks made to this point would indicate that the ECM is at fault. However, there is a possibility of CKT 467 or 468 being shorted to a voltage source either in the engine harness or in the injector harness.

• To test for this condition:
  • Disconnect the injector 4-way connector.
  • Ignition "ON."

• Probe CKTs 467 and 468 on the ECM side of harness with a test light connected to ground. There should be no light. If light is "ON," repair short to voltage.

• If OK, check the resistance of the injector harness between terminals "A" & "C", "A" & "D", "B" & "D" and "B" & "C". Should be more than 4 ohms. If less than 4 ohms, check harness for wires shorted together and check each injector resistance. (Resistance should be 8 ohms or more.)

• If all OK, replace ECM

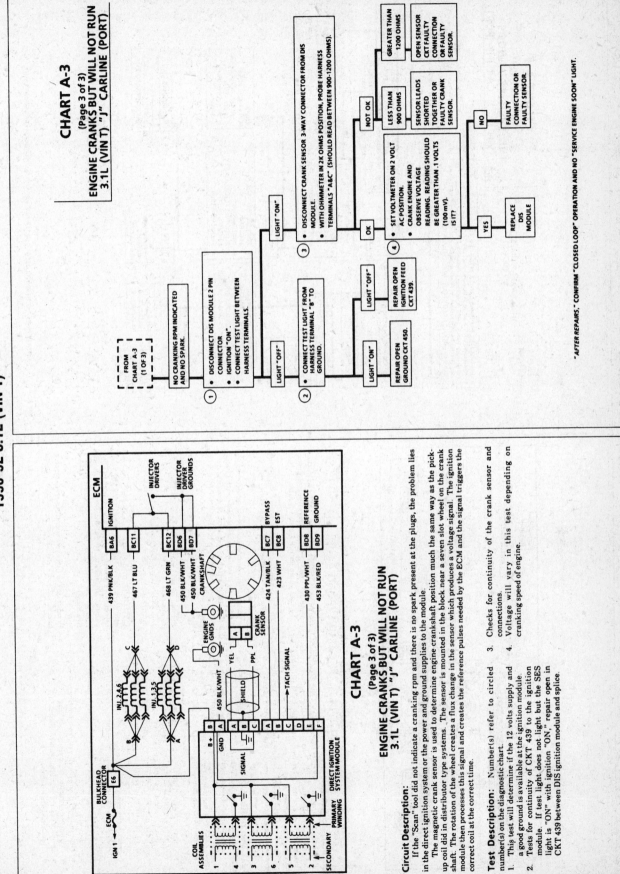

1990-92 3.1L (VIN T)

CHART A-3
(Page 3 of 3)
ENGINE CRANKS BUT WILL NOT RUN
3.1L (VIN T) "J" CARLINE (PORT)

Circuit Description:

If the "Scan" tool did not indicate a cranking rpm and there is no spark present at the plugs, the problem lies in the direct ignition system or the power and ground supplies to the module.

The magnetic crank sensor is used to determine engine crankshaft position much the same way as the pick-up coil did in distributor type systems. The sensor is mounted in the block near a seven slot wheel on the crank shaft. The rotation of the wheel creates a flux change in the sensor which produces a voltage signal. The ignition module then processes this signal and creates the reference pulses needed by the ECM and the signal triggers the correct coil at the correct time.

Test Description: Number(s) refer to circled number(s) on the diagnostic chart.

1. This test will determine if the 12 volts supply and a good ground is available at the ignition module.

2. Tests for continuity of CKT 439 to the ignition module. If test light does not light but the SES light is "ON" with ignition "ON", repair open in CKT 439 between DIS ignition module and splice.

3. Checks for continuity of the crank sensor and connections.

4. Voltage will vary in this test depending on cranking speed of engine.

"AFTER REPAIRS," CONFIRM "CLOSED LOOP" OPERATION AND NO "SERVICE ENGINE SOON" LIGHT.

1990-92 3.1L (VIN T)

CHART A-7
(Page 1 of 2)
FUEL SYSTEM DIAGNOSIS
3.1L (VIN T) "J" CARLINE (PORT)

THIS CHART ASSUMES THERE IS NO CODE 54

FROM CHART A-3

(1)
- INSTALL FUEL PRESSURE GAGE, J-34730-1 OR EQUIVALENT.
- IGNITION "OFF" FOR 10 SECONDS. A/C "OFF".
- IGNITION "ON". FUEL PUMP WILL RUN FOR ABOUT 2 SECONDS. NOTE FUEL PRESSURE, WITH PUMP RUNNING SHOULD BE 280-325 kPa (40.5-47 psi) AND HOLD STEADY WHEN PUMP STOPS.

OK

(2) START AND IDLE ENGINE AT NORMAL OPERATING TEMPERATURE. PRESSURE SHOULD BE LOWER BY 21-69 kPa (3-10 psi).

OK

NO TROUBLE FOUND. REVIEW "SYMPTOMS SECTION".

NOT OK

- APPLY 10 INCHES OF VACUUM TO PRESSURE REGULATOR. FUEL PRESSURE SHOULD DROP 21-69 kPa (3-10 psi).

OK — REPAIR VACUUM SOURCE TO REGULATOR

NOT OK — REPLACE REGULATOR ASSEMBLY

NOT OK

(3) PRESSURE, BUT NOT HOLDING

- IGNITION "OFF" FOR 10 SECONDS.
- IGNITION "ON".
- BLOCK FUEL PRESSURE LINE BY PINCHING FLEX HOSE. PRESSURE SHOULD HOLD.

NOT HOLDING

- IGNITION "OFF" FOR 10 SECONDS.
- IGNITION "ON".
- BLOCK FUEL RETURN LINE BY PINCHING HOSE. RECHECK PRESSURE.

HOLDS — FAULTY FUEL PRESSURE REGULATOR

NOT HOLDING — CHECK:
- LEAKING PUMP COUPLING HOSE OR PULSATOR.
- FAULTY IN-TANK PUMP.

HOLDS — (4) LOCATE AND CORRECT LEAKING INJECTOR(S).

PRESSURE, BUT LESS THAN 280 kPa (40.5 psi).

SEE CHART A-7 (2 of 2)

PRESSURE, BUT ABOVE 325 kPa (47 psi).

NO PRESSURE — **SEE CHART A-5 (1 of 2)**

NOTE:
THE IGNITION MAY HAVE TO BE CYCLED "ON" MORE THAN ONCE TO OBTAIN MAXIMUM PRESSURE. ALSO, IT'S NORMAL FOR THE PRESSURE TO DROP SLIGHTLY WHEN THE PUMP STOPS.

"AFTER REPAIRS," CONFIRM "CLOSED LOOP" OPERATION AND NO "SERVICE ENGINE SOON" LIGHT.

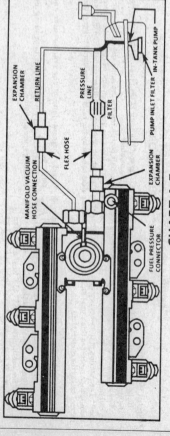

EXPANSION CHAMBER
RETURN LINE
MANIFOLD VACUUM HOSE CONNECTION
FLEX HOSE
PRESSURE LINE
FILTER
FUEL PRESSURE CONNECTOR
EXPANSION CHAMBER
PUMP INLET FILTER IN-TANK PUMP

CHART A-7
(Page 1 of 2)
FUEL SYSTEM DIAGNOSIS
3.1L (VIN T) "J" CARLINE (PORT)

Circuit Description:

When the ignition switch is turned "ON," the Electronic Control Module (ECM) will turn "ON" the in-tank fuel pump. It will remain "ON" as long as the engine is cranking or running, and the ECM is receiving reference pulses. If there are no reference pulses, the ECM will shut "OFF" the fuel pump within 2 seconds after ignition "ON" or engine stops.

The pump will deliver fuel to the fuel rail and injectors, then to the pressure regulator, where the system pressure is controlled to about 234 to 325 kPa (34 to 47 psi). Excess fuel is then returned to the fuel tank.

Test Description: Number(s) refer to circled number(s) on the diagnostic chart.

1. Wrap a shop towel around the fuel pressure connector to absorb any small amount of fuel leakage that may occur when installing the gage. Ignition "ON" pump pressure should be 280-325 kPa (40.5-47 psi). This pressure is controlled by spring pressure within the regulator assembly.

2. When the engine is idling, the manifold pressure is low (high vacuum) and is applied to the fuel regulator diaphragm. This will offset the spring and result in a lower fuel pressure. This idle pressure will vary somewhat depending on barometric pressure, however, the pressure idling should be less indicating pressure regulator control.

3. Pressure that continues to fall is caused by one of the following:
   - In-tank fuel pump check valve not holding
   - Pump coupling hose or pulsator leaking
   - Fuel pressure regulator valve leaking
   - Injector(s) sticking open

4. An injector sticking open can best be determined by checking for a fouled or saturated spark plug(s). If a leaking injector can not be determined by a fouled or saturated spark plug, the following procedure should be used.
   - Remove plenum and remove fuel rail bolts. Follow the procedures in the Fuel Control Section of this manual, but leave fuel lines connected.
   - Lift fuel rail out just enough to leave injector nozzles in the ports.

   CAUTION: Be sure injector(s) are not allowed to spray on engine and that injector retaining clips are intact. This should be carefully followed to prevent fuel spray on engine which would cause a fire hazard.

   - Pressurize the fuel system and observe injector nozzles.

1990-92 3.1L (VIN T)

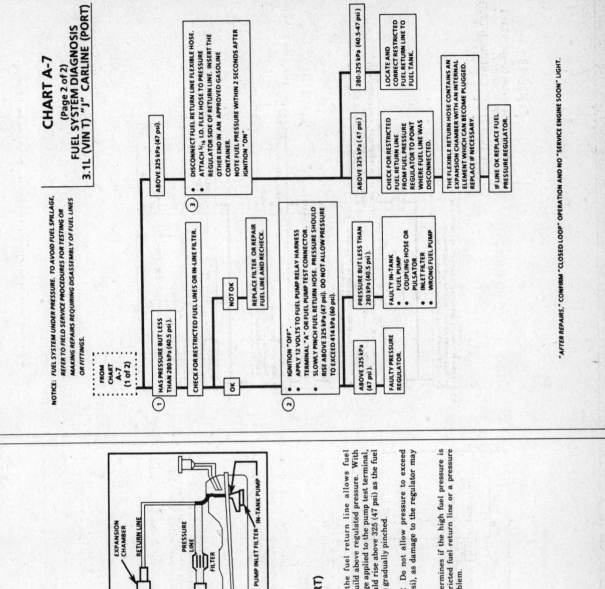

CHART A-7
(Page 2 of 2)
FUEL SYSTEM DIAGNOSIS
3.1L (VIN T) "J" CARLINE (PORT)

Test Description: Number(s) refer to circled number(s) on the diagnostic chart.

1. Pressure but less than 280 kPa (40.5 psi) falls into two areas:

   • Regulated pressure but less than 280 kPa (40.5 psi). Amount of fuel to injectors OK but pressure is too low. System will be lean running and may set Code 44. Also, hard starting cold and overall poor performance.

   • Restricted flow causing pressure drop - Normally, a vehicle with a fuel pressure of less than 165 kPa (24 psi) at idle will not be driveable. However, if the pressure drop occurs only while driving, the engine will normally surge then stop running as pressure begins to drop rapidly. This is most likely caused by a restricted fuel line or plugged filter.

2. Restricting the fuel return line allows fuel pressure to build above regulated pressure. With battery voltage applied to the pump test terminal, pressure should rise above 325 (47 psi) as the fuel return hose is gradually pinched.

   NOTICE: Do not allow pressure to exceed 414 (60 psi), as damage to the regulator may result.

3. This test determines if the high fuel pressure is due to a restricted fuel return line or a pressure regulator problem.

1990-92 3.1L (VIN T)

CODE 13

OXYGEN SENSOR (O₂) CIRCUIT
(OPEN CIRCUIT)
3.1L (VIN T) "J" CARLINE (PORT)

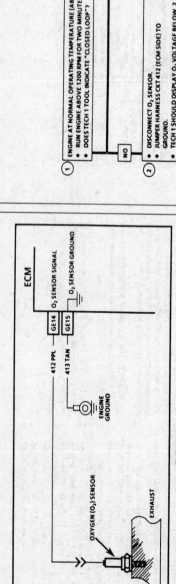

①
- ENGINE AT NORMAL OPERATING TEMPERATURE (ABOVE 80°C/176°F).
- RUN ENGINE ABOVE 1200 RPM FOR TWO MINUTES.
- DOES TECH 1 TOOL INDICATE "CLOSED LOOP"?

NO → ②

YES → CODE 13 IS INTERMITTENT. IF NO ADDITIONAL CODES WERE STORED, REFER TO "DIAGNOSTIC AIDS" ON FACING PAGE.

②
- DISCONNECT O₂ SENSOR.
- JUMPER HARNESS CKT 412 (ECM SIDE) TO GROUND.
- TECH 1 SHOULD DISPLAY O₂ VOLTAGE BELOW 2 VOLT (200 mV) WITH ENGINE RUNNING. DOES IT?

NO → ③

YES → FAULTY O₂ SENSOR CONNECTION OR SENSOR.

③
- REMOVE JUMPER.
- IGNITION "ON," ENGINE "OFF."
- CHECK VOLTAGE OF CKT 412 (ECM SIDE) AT O₂ SENSOR HARNESS CONNECTOR USING A DVM.

3 - 6 VOLT (300 - 600 mV)	OVER .6 VOLT (600 mV)	LESS THAN 3 VOLT (300 mV)
FAULTY ECM.	OPEN CKT 413 OR FAULTY CONNECTION OR FAULTY ECM.	OPEN CKT 412 OR FAULTY ECM CONNECTION OR FAULTY ECM.

"AFTER REPAIRS," REFER TO CODE CRITERIA ON FACING PAGE AND CONFIRM CODE DOES NOT RESET.

ECM
- GE14 — O₂ SENSOR SIGNAL
- GE15 — O₂ SENSOR GROUND
- 412 PPL
- 413 TAN
- ENGINE GROUND
- OXYGEN (O₂) SENSOR
- EXHAUST

CODE 13

OXYGEN (O₂) SENSOR CIRCUIT
(OPEN CIRCUIT)
3.1L (VIN T) "J" CARLINE (PORT)

Circuit Description:

The ECM supplies a voltage of about .45 volt between terminals "GE14" and "GE15". (If measured with a 10 megohm digital voltmeter, this may read as low as .32 volt.) The Oxygen (O₂) sensor varies the voltage within a range of about 1 volt if the exhaust is rich, down through about .10 volt if exhaust is lean.

The sensor is like an open circuit and produces no voltage when it is below 315°C (600°F). An open sensor circuit or cold sensor causes "Open Loop" operation.

Test Description: Number(s) refer to circled number(s) on the diagnostic chart.

1. Code 13 will set:
   - Engine at normal operating temperature
   - At least 2 minutes engine time after start
   - O₂ signal voltage steady between .35 and .55 volt.
   - Throttle position sensor signal above 4%
   - All conditions must be met for about 60 seconds.

   If the conditions for a Code 13 exist, the system will not go "Closed Loop."

2. This will determine if the sensor is at fault or the wiring or ECM is the cause of the Code 13.

3. In doing this test use only a high impedance digital volt ohm meter. This test checks the continuity of CKTs 412 and 413 because if CKT 413 is open the ECM voltage on CKT 412 will be over .6 volt (600 mV).

Diagnostic Aids:

Normal "Scan" voltage varies between 100 mV to 999 mV (.1 and 1.0 volt) while in "Closed Loop." Code 13 sets in one minute if voltage remains between .35 and .55 volt, but the system will go "Open Loop" in about 15 seconds.

Refer to "Intermittents" in "Symptoms," Section

1990-92 3.1L (VIN T)

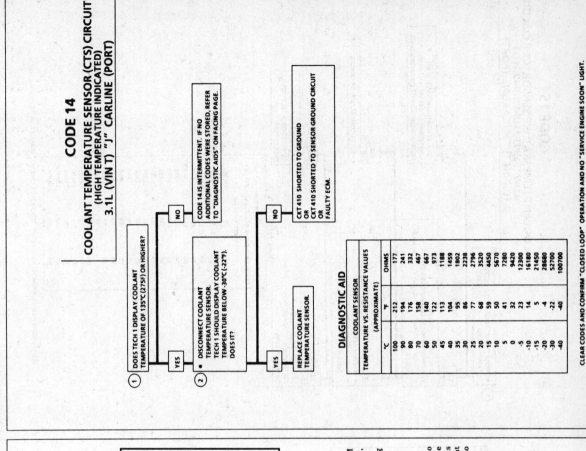

CODE 14
COOLANT TEMPERATURE SENSOR (CTS) CIRCUIT
(HIGH TEMPERATURE INDICATED)
3.1L (VIN T) "J" CARLINE (PORT)

1. DOES TECH 1 DISPLAY COOLANT TEMPERATURE OF 135°C (275F) OR HIGHER?

   NO → CODE 14 IS INTERMITTENT. IF NO ADDITIONAL CODES WERE STORED, REFER TO "DIAGNOSTIC AIDS" ON FACING PAGE.

   YES →

2. • DISCONNECT COOLANT TEMPERATURE SENSOR. TECH 1 SHOULD DISPLAY COOLANT TEMPERATURE BELOW -30°C (-22°F). DOES IT?

   NO → CKT 410 SHORTED TO GROUND OR CKT 410 SHORTED TO SENSOR GROUND CIRCUIT OR FAULTY ECM.

   YES → REPLACE COOLANT TEMPERATURE SENSOR.

DIAGNOSTIC AID

COOLANT SENSOR
TEMPERATURE VS. RESISTANCE VALUES
(APPROXIMATE)

°C	°F	OHMS
100	212	177
90	194	241
80	176	332
70	158	467
60	140	667
50	122	973
45	113	1188
40	104	1459
35	95	1802
30	86	2238
25	77	2796
20	68	3520
15	59	4450
10	50	5670
5	41	7280
0	32	9420
-5	23	12300
-10	14	16180
-15	5	21450
-20	-4	28680
-30	-22	52700
-40	-40	100700

CLEAR CODES AND CONFIRM "CLOSED LOOP" OPERATION AND NO "SERVICE ENGINE SOON" LIGHT.

COOLANT TEMPERATURE SENSOR (CTS)

410 YEL — COOLANT SENSOR SIGNAL
452 BLK — SENSOR GROUND

GE16 · B85

ECM — 5 VOLTS

TO TPS, IAT AND A/C PRESSURE SENSOR

455 · 410

CODE 14
COOLANT TEMPERATURE SENSOR (CTS) CIRCUIT
(HIGH TEMPERATURE INDICATED)
3.1L (VIN T) "J" CARLINE (PORT)

Circuit Description:

The Coolant Temperature Sensor (CTS) uses a thermistor to control the signal voltage to the ECM. The ECM applies a voltage on CKT 410 to the sensor. When the engine is cold, the sensor (thermistor) resistance is high, therefore, the ECM will see high signal voltage.

As the engine warms, the sensor resistance becomes less, and the voltage drops. At normal engine operating temperature (85°C to 95°C) the voltage will measure about 1.5 to 2.0 volts.

Test Description: Number(s) refer to circled number(s) on the diagnostic chart.

1. Code 14 will set if:
   - Signal voltage indicates a coolant temperature above 135°C (275°F) for 1 second.

2. This test will determine if CKT 410 is shorted to ground which will cause the conditions for Code 14.

Diagnostic Aids:

Check harness routing for a potential short to ground in CKT 410. "Scan" tool displays engine temperature in degrees centigrade. After engine is started, the temperature should rise steadily to about 90°C then stabilize when thermostat opens. Refer to "Intermittents" in "Symptoms," Section

1990-92 3.1L (VIN T)

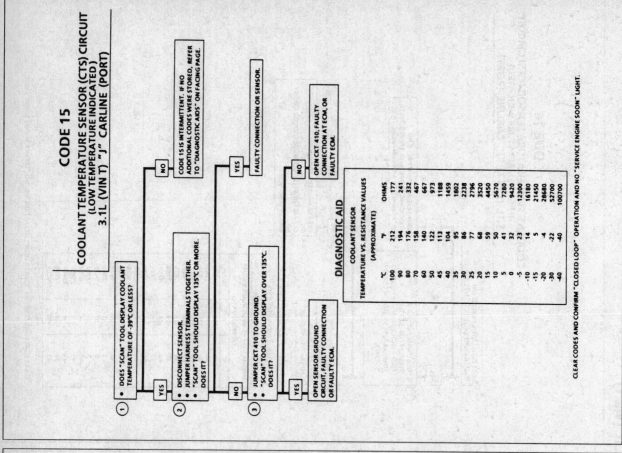

CODE 15
COOLANT TEMPERATURE SENSOR (CTS) CIRCUIT
(LOW TEMPERATURE INDICATED)
3.1L (VIN T) "J" CARLINE (PORT)

1. • DOES "SCAN" TOOL DISPLAY COOLANT TEMPERATURE OF -39°C OR LESS?

    YES / NO

    NO → CODE 15 IS INTERMITTENT. IF NO ADDITIONAL CODES WERE STORED, REFER TO "DIAGNOSTIC AIDS" ON FACING PAGE.

2. • DISCONNECT SENSOR.
    • JUMPER HARNESS TERMINALS TOGETHER.
    • "SCAN" TOOL SHOULD DISPLAY 135°C OR MORE. DOES IT?

    YES / NO

    YES → FAULTY CONNECTION OR SENSOR.

3. • JUMPER CKT 410 TO GROUND.
    • "SCAN" TOOL SHOULD DISPLAY OVER 135°C. DOES IT?

    YES / NO

    NO → OPEN CKT 410, FAULTY CONNECTION AT ECM, OR FAULTY ECM.

    YES → OPEN SENSOR GROUND CIRCUIT, FAULTY CONNECTION OR FAULTY ECM.

DIAGNOSTIC AID

COOLANT TEMPERATURE VS. RESISTANCE VALUES (APPROXIMATE)

°C	°F	OHMS
100	212	177
90	194	241
80	176	332
70	158	467
60	140	667
50	122	973
45	113	1188
40	104	1459
35	95	1802
30	86	2238
25	77	2796
20	68	3520
15	59	4450
10	50	5670
5	41	7280
0	32	9420
-5	23	12300
-10	14	16180
-15	5	21450
-20	-4	28680
-30	-22	52700
-40	-40	100700

CLEAR CODES AND CONFIRM "CLOSED LOOP" OPERATION AND NO "SERVICE ENGINE SOON" LIGHT.

ECM
COOLANT SENSOR SIGNAL — 5 VOLTS
SENSOR GROUND
GE16 — 410 YEL
BB5 — 452 BLK
COOLANT TEMPERATURE SENSOR (CTS)
TO TPS, IAT AND A/C PRESSURE SENSOR
455 · 410

CODE 15
COOLANT TEMPERATURE SENSOR (CTS) CIRCUIT
(LOW TEMPERATURE INDICATED)
3.1L (VIN T) "J" CARLINE (PORT)

Circuit Description:

The Coolant Temperature Sensor (CTS) uses a thermistor to control the signal voltage to the ECM. The ECM applies a voltage on CKT 410 to the sensor. When the engine is cold the sensor (thermistor) resistance is high, therefore the ECM will see high signal voltage.

As the engine warms, the sensor resistance becomes less, and the voltage drops. At normal engine operating temperature (85°C to 95°C) the voltage will measure about 1.5 to 2.0 volts at the ECM.

Test Description: Number(s) refer to circled number(s) on the diagnostic chart.

1. • Code 15 will set if:
   • Signal voltage indicates an open circuit (a coolant temperature less than -39°C) for 1 second at normal ambient temperature.

2. This test simulates a Code 14. If the ECM recognizes the low signal voltage, (high temperature) and the "Scan" reads 135°C, the ECM and wiring are OK.

3. This test will determine if CKT 410 is open. There should be 5 volts present at sensor connector if measured with a DVOM.

Diagnostic Aids:

A "Scan" tool reads engine temperature in degrees centigrade. After engine is started the temperature should rise steadily to about 90°C then stabilize when thermostat opens.

A faulty connection or an open in CKT 410 or 452 will result in a Code 15.

If Code 21 or 23 is also set, check CKT 452 for faulty wiring or connections. Check terminals at sensor for good contact.

Refer to "Intermittents" in "Symptoms," Section.

1990-92 3.1L (VIN T)

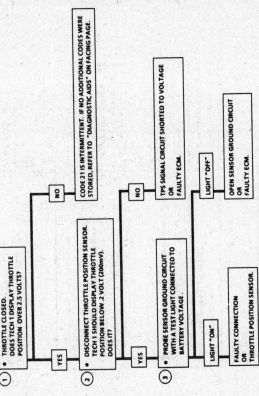

CODE 21

THROTTLE POSITION SENSOR (TPS) CIRCUIT
(SIGNAL VOLTAGE HIGH)
3.1L (VIN T) "J" CARLINE (PORT)

1. THROTTLE CLOSED. DOES TECH 1 DISPLAY THROTTLE POSITION OVER 2.5 VOLTS?

   - YES
   - NO → CODE 21 IS INTERMITTENT. IF NO ADDITIONAL CODES WERE STORED, REFER TO "DIAGNOSTIC AIDS" ON FACING PAGE.

2. DISCONNECT THROTTLE POSITION SENSOR. TECH 1 SHOULD DISPLAY THROTTLE POSITION BELOW .2 VOLT (200mV). DOES IT?

   - YES
   - NO → TPS SIGNAL CIRCUIT SHORTED TO VOLTAGE OR FAULTY ECM.

3. PROBE SENSOR GROUND CIRCUIT WITH A TEST LIGHT CONNECTED TO BATTERY VOLTAGE.

   - LIGHT "ON" → FAULTY CONNECTION OR THROTTLE POSITION SENSOR.
   - LIGHT "OFF" → OPEN SENSOR GROUND CIRCUIT OR FAULTY ECM.

CLEAR CODES AND CONFIRM "CLOSED LOOP" OPERATION AND NO "SERVICE ENGINE SOON" LIGHT.

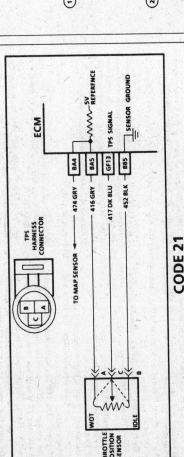

CODE 21

THROTTLE POSITION SENSOR (TPS) CIRCUIT
(SIGNAL VOLTAGE HIGH)
3.1L (VIN T) "J" CARLINE (PORT)

Circuit Description:

The Throttle Position Sensor (TPS) provides a voltage signal that changes relative to the throttle blade. Signal voltage will vary from about .29 at idle to about 4.8 volts at wide open throttle and is nonadjustable.

The TPS signal is one of the most important inputs used by the ECM for fuel control and for most of the ECM control outputs.

Test Description: Number(s) refer to circled number(s) on the diagnostic chart.

1. Code 21 will set if:
   - Engine is running
   - TPS signal voltage is greater than 3.7 volts
   - Air flow is less than 17 GM/sec
   - All conditions met for 10 seconds

   OR
   - TPS signal voltage over 4.5 volts with ignition "ON."

   TPS: The TPS has an auto zeroing feature. If the voltage reading is within the range of .29 to .98 volt, the ECM will use that value as closed throttle. If the voltage reading is out of the auto zero range on an existing or replacement TPS, make sure the cruise control and throttle cables are not being held open. If OK, replace TPS.

2. With the TPS sensor disconnected the TPS voltage should go low, if the ECM and wiring is OK.

3. Probing CKT 452 with a test light checks the 5 volts return circuit. Faulty sensor ground circuit will cause a Code 21.

Diagnostic Aids:

A "Scan" tool reads throttle position in volts. Voltage should increase at a steady rate as throttle is moved toward WOT.

Also, some "Scan" tools will read throttle angle. 0% = closed throttle, 100% = WOT.

An open in CKT 452 will result in a Code 21. Refer to "Intermittents" in "Symptoms," Section

1990-92 3.1L (VIN T)

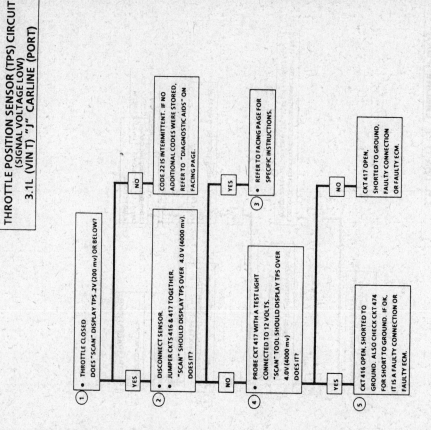

CODE 22
THROTTLE POSITION SENSOR (TPS) CIRCUIT
(SIGNAL VOLTAGE LOW)
3.1L (VIN T) "J" CARLINE (PORT)

① THROTTLE CLOSED
DOES "SCAN" DISPLAY TPS .2V (200 mv) OR BELOW?

NO → CODE 22 IS INTERMITTENT. IF NO ADDITIONAL CODES WERE STORED, REFER TO "DIAGNOSTIC AIDS" ON FACING PAGE.

YES

② DISCONNECT SENSOR.
JUMPER CKTS 416 & 417 TOGETHER.
"SCAN" SHOULD DISPLAY TPS OVER 4.0 V (4000 mv).
DOES IT?

YES → ③ REFER TO FACING PAGE FOR SPECIFIC INSTRUCTIONS.

NO

④ PROBE CKT 417 WITH A TEST LIGHT CONNECTED TO 12 VOLTS.
"SCAN" TOOL SHOULD DISPLAY TPS OVER 4.0V (4000 mv)
DOES IT?

NO → CKT 417 OPEN.
SHORTED TO GROUND,
FAULTY CONNECTION
OR FAULTY ECM.

YES

⑤ CKT 416 OPEN, SHORTED TO GROUND. ALSO CHECK CKT 474 FOR SHORT TO GROUND. IF OK, IT IS A FAULTY CONNECTION OR FAULTY ECM.

CLEAR CODES AND CONFIRM "CLOSED LOOP" OPERATION AND NO "SERVICE ENGINE SOON" LIGHT.

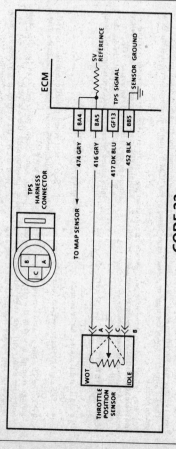

CODE 22
THROTTLE POSITION SENSOR (TPS) CIRCUIT
(SIGNAL VOLTAGE LOW)
3.1L (VIN T) "J" CARLINE (PORT)

Circuit Description:
The Throttle Position Sensor (TPS) provides a voltage signal that changes relative to the throttle blade. Signal voltage will vary from about .29 at idle to about 4.8 volts at Wide Open Throttle (WOT) and is nonadjustable.
The TPS signal is one of the most important inputs used by the ECM for fuel control and for most of the ECM control outputs.

Test Description: Number(s) refer to circled number(s) on the diagnostic chart.

1. Code 22, will set if:
   • Engine running
   • TPS signal voltage is less than about .2 volt for 3 seconds

2. Simulates Code 21: (high voltage) If the ECM recognizes the high signal voltage, the ECM and wiring are OK.

3. TPS check: The TPS has an auto zeroing feature. If the voltage reading is within the range of .29 to .98 volt, the ECM will use that value as closed throttle. If the voltage reading is out of the auto zero range on an existing or replacement TPS, make sure the cruise control and throttle cables are not being held open. If OK, replace TPS.

4. This simulates a high signal voltage to check for an open in CKT 417.

5. CKTs 416 and 474 share a common 5 volts buffered reference signal. If either of these circuits is shorted to ground, Code 22 will set. To determine if the MAP sensor is causing the 22 problem, disconnect it to see if Code 22 resets. Be sure TPS is connected and clear codes before testing.

Diagnostic Aids:
A "Scan" tool reads throttle position in volts. Voltage should increase at a steady rate as throttle is moved toward WOT.
Also, some "Scan" tools will read throttle angle.
0% = closed throttle, 100% = WOT
An open or short to ground in CKTs 416 or 417 will result in a Code 22. Also, a short to ground in CKT 474 will result in a Code 22.
Refer to "Intermittents" in "Symptoms," Section

1990-92 3.1L (VIN T)

CODE 23

INTAKE AIR TEMPERATURE (IAT) SENSOR CIRCUIT
(LOW TEMPERATURE INDICATED)
3.1L (VIN T) "J" CARLINE (PORT)

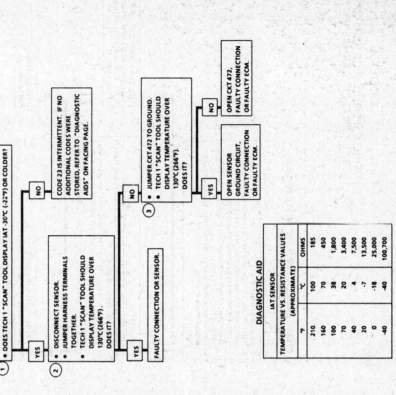

DIAGNOSTIC AID

IAT SENSOR		
TEMPERATURE VS. RESISTANCE VALUES (APPROXIMATE)		
°F	°C	OHMS
210	100	185
160	70	450
100	38	1,800
70	20	3,400
40	4	7,500
20	-7	13,500
0	-18	25,000
-40	-40	100,700

CLEAR CODES AND CONFIRM "CLOSED LOOP" OPERATION AND NO "SERVICE ENGINE SOON" LIGHT.

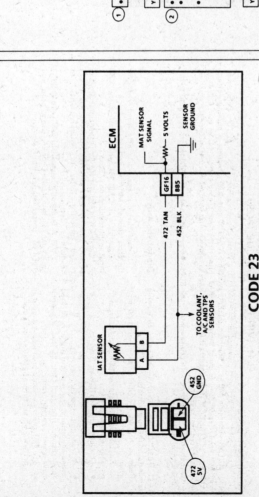

CODE 23

INTAKE AIR TEMPERATURE (IAT) SENSOR CIRCUIT
(LOW TEMPERATURE INDICATED)
3.1L (VIN T) "J" CARLINE (PORT)

Circuit Description:

The Intake Air Temperature (IAT) sensor uses a thermistor to control the signal voltage to the ECM. The ECM applies a voltage (about 5 volts) on CKT 472 to the sensor. When the air is cold the sensor (thermistor) resistance is high, therefore the ECM will see a high signal voltage. If the air is warm the sensor resistance is low, therefore, the ECM will see a low voltage.

The IAT sensor is located in the air cleaner.

Test Description: Number(s) refer to circled number(s) on the diagnostic chart.

1. Code 23 will set if:
   - A signal voltage indicates a intake air temperature below -35°C (-31°F) for 10 seconds.
   - Time since engine start is 4 minutes or longer
   - No VSS
2. A Code 23 will set due to an open sensor, wire or connection. This test will determine if the wiring and ECM are OK.
3. This will determine if the signal CKT 472 or the sensor ground, CKT 452 is open.

Diagnostic Aids:

A "Scan" tool reads temperature of the air entering the engine and should read close to ambient air temperature when engine is cold, and rises as underhood temperature increases.

A faulty connection, or an open in CKT 472 or 452 will result in a Code 23.

Refer to "Intermittents" in "Symptoms," Section

1990-92 3.1L (VIN T)

CODE 24
VEHICLE SPEED SENSOR (VSS) CIRCUIT
3.1L (VIN T) "J" CARLINE (PORT)

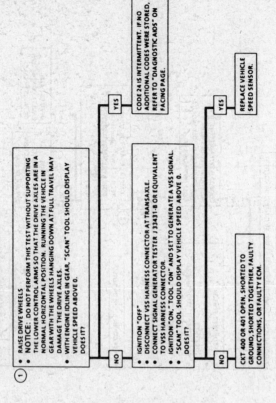

DISREGARD CODE 24 IF SET WHILE DRIVE WHEELS ARE NOT TURNING.

(1)
- RAISE DRIVE WHEELS
- NOTICE: DO NOT PERFORM THIS TEST WITHOUT SUPPORTING THE LOWER CONTROL ARMS SO THAT THE DRIVE AXLES ARE IN A NORMAL HORIZONTAL POSITION. RUNNING THE VEHICLE IN GEAR WITH THE WHEELS HANGING DOWN AT FULL TRAVEL MAY DAMAGE THE DRIVE AXLES.
- WITH ENGINE IDLING IN GEAR, "SCAN" TOOL SHOULD DISPLAY VEHICLE SPEED ABOVE 0.
  DOES IT?

NO

- IGNITION "OFF"
- DISCONNECT VSS HARNESS CONNECTOR AT TRANSAXLE.
- CONNECT SIGNAL GENERATOR TESTER J 33431-B OR EQUIVALENT TO VSS HARNESS CONNECTOR.
- IGNITION "ON", TOOL "ON" AND SET TO GENERATE A VSS SIGNAL.
- "SCAN" TOOL SHOULD DISPLAY VEHICLE SPEED ABOVE 0.
  DOES IT?

NO

CKT 400 OR 401 OPEN, SHORTED TO GROUND, SHORTED TOGETHER, FAULTY CONNECTIONS, OR FAULTY ECM.

YES → CODE 24 IS INTERMITTENT. IF NO ADDITIONAL CODES WERE STORED, REFER TO "DIAGNOSTIC AIDS" ON FACING PAGE.

YES → REPLACE VEHICLE SPEED SENSOR.

CLEAR CODES AND CONFIRM "CLOSED LOOP" OPERATION AND NO "SERVICE ENGINE SOON" LIGHT.

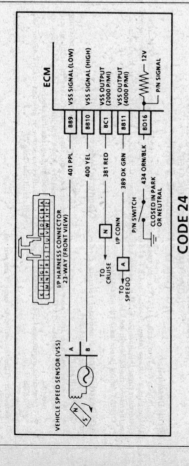

ECM

401 PPL	BB9 — VSS SIGNAL (LOW)
400 YEL	BB10 — VSS SIGNAL (HIGH)
381 RED	BC1 — VSS OUTPUT (2000 P/MI)
389 DK GRN	BB11 — VSS OUTPUT (4000 P/MI)
434 ORN/BLK	BD16 — 12v — P/N SIGNAL

J/P HARNESS CONNECTOR
23-WAY (FRONT VIEW)

VEHICLE SPEED SENSOR (VSS)

TO CRUISE — N — U/P CONN
TO SPEEDO — A
P/N SWITCH
CLOSED IN PARK OR NEUTRAL

CODE 24
VEHICLE SPEED SENSOR (VSS) CIRCUIT
3.1L (VIN T) "J" CARLINE (PORT)

Circuit Description:

Vehicle speed information is provided to the ECM by the Vehicle Speed Sensor (VSS), which is a Permanent Magnet (PM) generator and it is mounted in the transaxle. The PM generator produces a pulsing voltage whenever vehicle speed is over about 3 mph. The A/C voltage level and the number of pulses increases with vehicle speed. The ECM then converts the pulsing voltage to mph which is used for calculations and the mph can be displayed with a "Scan" tool.

If the vehicle is equipped with cruise control, the ECM also provides a signal (2000 pulses per mile) to the cruise control module.

Test Description: Number(s) refer to circled number(s) on the diagnostic chart.

1. Code 24 will set if vehicle speed equals 0 mph when:
   - Engine speed is between 2200 and 4400 rpm
   - TPS is less than 2%
   - Low load condition (low air flow)
   - Not in park or neutral
   - All conditions met for 3 seconds

   These conditions are met during a road load deceleration. Disregard Code 24 that sets when drive wheels are not turning.
   - The PM generator only produces a signal if drive wheels are turning greater than 3 mph.

Diagnostic Aids:

"Scan" should indicate a vehicle speed whenever the drive wheels are turning greater than 3 mph.

A problem in CKT 381 will not affect the VSS input or the readings on a "Scan."

Check CKTs 400 and 401 for proper connections to be sure they're clean and tight and the harness is routed correctly. Refer to "Intermittents" in "Symptoms," Section

(A/T) A faulty or misadjusted Park/Neutral (P/N) switch can result in a false Code 24. Use a "Scan" and check for proper signal while in drive.

1990-92 3.1L (VIN T)

CODE 25
INTAKE AIR TEMPERATURE (IAT) SENSOR CIRCUIT
(HIGH TEMPERATURE INDICATED)
3.1L (VIN T) "J" CARLINE (PORT)

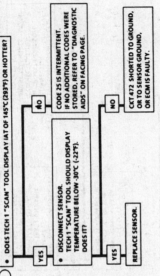

IAT SENSOR

A B

472 TAN
452 BLK

TO COOLANT, A/C AND TPS SENSORS

ECM
MAT SENSOR SIGNAL
5 VOLTS
SENSOR GROUND

GF16 BB5

452 GND
472 5V

Circuit Description:

The Intake Air Temperature (IAT) sensor uses a thermistor to control the signal-voltage to the ECM. The ECM applies a voltage (about 5 volts) on CKT 472 to the sensor. When intake air is cold, the sensor (thermistor) resistance is high, therefore, the ECM will see a high signal voltage. As the air warms, the sensor resistance becomes less, and the voltage drops.

The IAT sensor is located in the air cleaner.

Test Description: Number(s) refer to circled number(s) on the diagnostic chart.

1. Code 25 will set if:
   - Signal voltage indicates an intake air temperature greater than 145°C (293°F) for 2 seconds
   - Time since engine start is 4 minutes or longer
   - A vehicle speed is present

Diagnostic Aids:

A "Scan" tool reads temperature of the air entering the engine and should read close to ambient air temperature, when engine is cold, and rises as underhood temperature increases.

A faulty connection, or an open in CKT 472 or 452 will result in a Code 23.

Refer to "Intermittents" in "Symptoms," Section

---

1. • DOES TECH 1 "SCAN" TOOL DISPLAY IAT OF 145°C (293°F) OR HOTTER?

YES → DISCONNECT SENSOR. TECH 1 "SCAN" TOOL SHOULD DISPLAY TEMPERATURE BELOW -30°C (-22°F). DOES IT?

NO → CODE 25 IS INTERMITTENT. IF NO ADDITIONAL CODES WERE STORED, REFER TO "DIAGNOSTIC AIDS" ON FACING PAGE.

YES → REPLACE SENSOR.

NO → CKT 472 SHORTED TO GROUND, OR TO SENSOR GROUND, OR ECM IS FAULTY.

DIAGNOSTIC AID

IAT SENSOR
TEMPERATURE VS. RESISTANCE VALUES
(APPROXIMATE)

°F	°C	OHMS
210	100	185
160	70	450
100	38	1,800
70	20	3,400
40	4	7,500
20	-7	13,500
0	-18	25,000
-40	-40	100,700

CLEAR CODES AND CONFIRM "CLOSED LOOP" OPERATION AND NO "SERVICE ENGINE SOON" LIGHT.

1990-92 3.1L (VIN T)

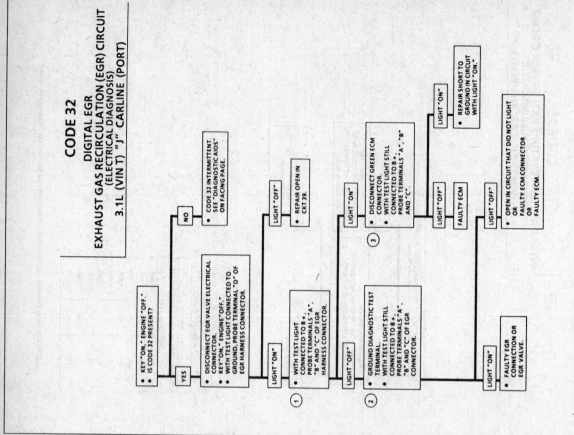

CODE 32
DIGITAL EGR
EXHAUST GAS RECIRCULATION (EGR) CIRCUIT
(ELECTRICAL DIAGNOSIS)
3.1L (VIN T) "J" CARLINE (PORT)

TOP VIEW OF EGR VALVE

Circuit Description:

The ECM is programmed with an Exhaust Gas Recirculation (EGR) diagnostic check to monitor flow through each individual valve in the three solenoid EGR valve.

When the vehicle is in the decel mode with the valves normally closed, the ECM opens each valve in succession (while keeping previous valves open) and manifold pressure is monitored for an appropriate increase associated with each valve's application. Should the calibrated response in manifold pressure not be seen by the ECM, a Code 32 will set.

Test Description: Number(s) refer to circled number(s) on the diagnostic chart.

1. This test determines if there is power to the EGR valve.
2. This test will determine if there is an open circuit in the EGR wiring or if the EGR valve is at fault.
3. This test will determine if there is a short to ground in any circuit going to the EGR valve or if the ECM is at fault.

Diagnostic Aids:

An intermittent may be caused by a poor connection, rubbed-through wire insulation, or a wire broken inside the insulation.

* THESE STEPS MUST BE DONE VERY QUICKLY AS THE ECM WILL COMPENSATE FUEL DELIVERY.

1990-92 3.1L (VIN T)

CODE 33

MANIFOLD ABSOLUTE PRESSURE (MAP) SENSOR CIRCUIT
(SIGNAL VOLTAGE HIGH - LOW VACUUM)
3.1L (VIN T) "J" CARLINE (PORT)

(1)
- IF ENGINE IDLE IS ROUGH, UNSTABLE OR INCORRECT, CORRECT BEFORE USING CHART. SEE "SYMPTOMS" SECTION'.
- ENGINE IDLING.
- DOES "SCAN" DISPLAY A MAP OF 4.0 VOLTS OR OVER?

NO → CODE 33 IS INTERMITTENT. IF NO ADDITIONAL CODES WERE STORED, REFER TO "DIAGNOSTIC AIDS" ON FACING PAGE.

YES

(2)
- IGNITION "OFF".
- DISCONNECT MAP SENSOR ELECTRICAL CONNECTOR.
- IGNITION "ON".
- "SCAN" SHOULD READ A VOLTAGE OF 1 VOLT OR LESS. DOES IT?

NO → CKT 432 SHORTED TO VOLTAGE, SHORTED TO CKT 474, OR FAULTY ECM.

YES

- PROBE CKT 455 WITH A TEST LIGHT TO 12 VOLTS. TEST LIGHT SHOULD LIGHT. DOES IT?

NO → OPEN CKT 455.

YES → PLUGGED OR LEAKING SENSOR VACUUM HOSE OR FAULTY MAP SENSOR. REFER TO "DIAGNOSTIC AIDS" ON FACING PAGE.

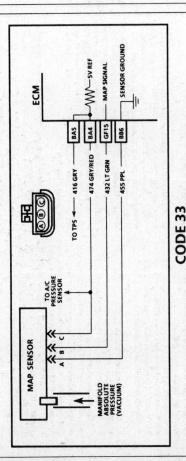

CODE 33

MANIFOLD ABSOLUTE PRESSURE (MAP) SENSOR CIRCUIT
(SIGNAL VOLTAGE HIGH - LOW VACUUM)
3.1L (VIN T) "J" CARLINE (PORT)

Circuit Description:

The Manifold Absolute Pressure (MAP) sensor responds to changes in manifold pressure (vacuum). The ECM receives this information as a signal voltage that will vary from about 1 to 1.5 volts at idle (high vacuum) to 4 - 4.5 volts at wide open throttle (low vacuum).

Test Description: Number(s) refer to circled number(s) on the diagnostic chart.

1. Code 33 will set when:
   - Engine running
   - Manifold pressure greater than 74 kPa (A/C "OFF"), 83.4 kPa (A/C "ON")
   - Throttle angle less than 2%
   - Conditions met for 4.8 seconds
   Engine misfire, or a low unstable idle, may set Code 33.
2. With the MAP sensor disconnected, the ECM should see a low voltage if the ECM and wiring is OK.

Diagnostic Aids:

With the ignition "ON" and the engine stopped, the manifold pressure is equal to atmospheric pressure and the signal voltage will be high. This information is used by the ECM as an indication of vehicle altitude. Comparison of this reading with a known good vehicle with the same sensor is a good way to check accuracy of a "suspect" sensor. Readings should be the same ± .4 volt.
- Check all connections.
- Disconnect sensor from bracket and twist sensor by hand (only) to check for intermittent connections. Output changes greater than .1 volt indicates a bad connector or connections. If OK, replace sensor.
- Refer to CHART C-1D, MAP sensor voltage output check for further diagnosis.

1990-92 3.1L (VIN T)

MAP SENSOR

MANIFOLD ABSOLUTE PRESSURE (VACUUM)

TO A/C PRESSURE SENSOR

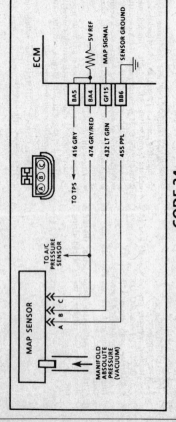

ECM

TO TPS ← 416 GRY — BA5
474 GRY/RED — BA4 — 5V REF
432 LT GRN — GF15 — MAP SIGNAL
455 PPL — BB6 — SENSOR GROUND

CODE 34

MANIFOLD ABSOLUTE PRESSURE (MAP) SENSOR CIRCUIT
(SIGNAL VOLTAGE LOW - HIGH VACUUM)
3.1L (VIN T) "J" CARLINE (PORT)

Circuit Description:

The Manifold Absolute Pressure (MAP) sensor responds to changes in manifold pressure (vacuum). The ECM receives this information as a signal voltage that will vary from about 1 to 1.5 volts at idle (high vacuum) to 4-4.5 volts at wide open throttle (low vacuum).

Test Description: Number(s) refer to circled number(s) on the diagnostic chart.

1. Code 34 will set if:
   - When engine rpm less than 1200
   - Manifold pressure reading less than 13 kPa
   - Conditions met for 1 second

   or
   - Engine rpm greater than 1200
   - Throttle angle over 20%
   - Manifold pressure less than 13 kPa
   - Conditions met for 1 second

2. This tests to see if the sensor is at fault for the low voltage or if there is a ECM or wiring problem.

3. This simulates a high signal voltage to check for an open in CKT 432. If the test light is bright during this test, CKT 432 is probably shorted to ground. If "Scan" reads over 4 volts at this test, CKT 474 can be checked by measuring the voltage at terminal "C" (should be 5 volts.).

Diagnostic Aids:

An intermittent open in CKT 432 or 474 will result in a Code 34. With the ignition "ON" and the engine "OFF," the manifold pressure is equal to atmospheric pressure and the signal voltage will be high. This information is used by the ECM as an indication of vehicle altitude.

Comparison of this reading with a known good vehicle with the same sensor is a good way to check accuracy of a "suspect" sensor. Readings should be the same ± .4 volt. Also CHART C-1D can be used to test the MAP sensor. Refer to "Intermittents" in "Symptoms," Section

NOTE: Make sure electrical connector remains securely fastened.

- Check all connections.
- Disconnect sensor from bracket and twist sensor by hand (only) to check for intermittent connections. Output changes greater than .1 volt indicates a bad connector or connections. If OK, replace sensor.
- Refer to CHART C-1D, MAP sensor voltage output check for further diagnosis.
- Refer to "Intermittents" in "Symptoms," Section

CODE 34

MANIFOLD ABSOLUTE PRESSURE (MAP) SENSOR CIRCUIT
(SIGNAL VOLTAGE LOW - HIGH VACUUM)
3.1L (VIN T) "J" CARLINE (PORT)

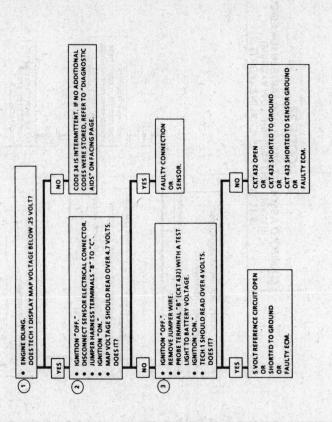

(1)
- ENGINE IDLING.
- DOES TECH 1 DISPLAY MAP VOLTAGE BELOW .25 VOLT?

NO → CODE 34 IS INTERMITTENT. IF NO ADDITIONAL CODES WERE STORED, REFER TO "DIAGNOSTIC AIDS" ON FACING PAGE.

YES

(2)
- IGNITION "OFF."
- DISCONNECT SENSOR ELECTRICAL CONNECTOR. JUMPER HARNESS TERMINALS "B" TO "C".
- IGNITION "ON."
- MAP VOLTAGE SHOULD READ OVER 4.7 VOLTS. DOES IT?

YES → FAULTY CONNECTION OR SENSOR.

NO

(3)
- IGNITION "OFF."
- REMOVE JUMPER WIRE.
- PROBE TERMINAL "B" (CKT 432) WITH A TEST LIGHT TO BATTERY VOLTAGE.
- IGNITION "ON."
- TECH 1 SHOULD READ OVER 4 VOLTS. DOES IT?

YES → 5 VOLT REFERENCE CIRCUIT OPEN
OR
SHORTED TO GROUND
OR
FAULTY ECM.

NO → CKT 432 OPEN
OR
CKT 432 SHORTED TO GROUND
OR
CKT 432 SHORTED TO SENSOR GROUND
OR
FAULTY ECM.

1990-92 3.1L (VIN T)

CODE 35
IDLE AIR CONTROL (IAC)
3.1L (VIN T) "J" CARLINE (PORT)

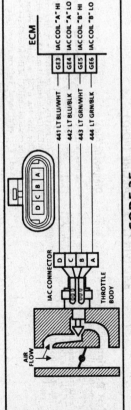

ECM

GE3	IAC COIL "A" HI
GE4	IAC COIL "A" LO
GE5	IAC COIL "B" HI
GE6	IAC COIL "B" LO

441 LT BLU/WHT
442 LT BLU/BLK
443 LT GRN/WHT
444 LT GRN/BLK

IAC CONNECTOR

THROTTLE BODY

AIR FLOW

Circuit Description:

Code 35 will set when the closed throttle engine speed is 200 rpm above or below the desired (commanded) idle speed for 50 seconds. Review the general description of the Idle Air Control (IAC) operation in "Fuel Metering System."

Test Description: Numbers below refer to circled numbers on the diagnostic chart.

1. The Tech 1 rpm control mode is used to extend and retract the IAC valve. The valve should move smoothly within the specified range. If the idle speed is commanded (IAC extended) too low (below 700 rpm), the engine may stall. This may be normal and would not indicate a problem. Retracting the IAC beyond its controlled range (above 1500 rpm) will cause a delay before the rpm's start dropping. This too is normal.

2. This test uses the Tech 1 to command the IAC controlled idle speed. The ECM issues commands to obtain commanded idle speed. The node lights each should flash red and green to indicate a good circuit as the ECM issues commands. While the sequence of color is not important if either light is "OFF" or does not flash red and green, check the circuits for faults, beginning with poor terminal contacts.

Diagnostic Aids:

- A slow, unstable, or fast idle may be caused by a non-IAC system problem that cannot be overcome by the IAC system. Out of control range IAC "Scan" tool counts will be above 60 if idle is too low and zero counts if idle is too high. The following checks should be made to repair a non-IAC system problem:

- Vacuum Leak (High Idle)
  If idle is too high, stop the engine. Fully extend (low) IAC with tester. Start engine. If idle speed is above 800 rpm, locate and correct vacuum leak including PCV system. Also check for binding of throttle blade or linkage.

- System too lean (High Air/Fuel Ratio)
  The idle speed may be too high or too low. Engine speed may vary up and down and disconnecting the IAC valve does not help. Code 44 may be set. "Scan" O₂ voltage will be less than 300 mV (.3 volt). Check for low regulated fuel pressure, water in the fuel or a restricted injector.

- System too rich (Low Air/Fuel Ratio)
  The idle speed will be too low. "Scan" tool IAC counts will usually be above 80. System is obviously rich and may exhibit black smoke in exhaust. "Scan" tool O₂ voltage will be fixed above 800 mV (.8 volt).
  Check for high fuel pressure, leaking or sticking injector. Silicone contaminated O₂ sensors "Scan" voltage will be slow to respond.

- Throttle Body
  Remove IAC valve and inspect bore for foreign material.

- IAC Valve Electrical Connections
  IAC valve connections should be carefully checked for proper contact.

- PCV Valve
  An incorrect or faulty PCV valve may result in an incorrect idle speed.
  Refer to "Rough, Unstable, Incorrect Idle or Stalling," in "Symptoms," Section
  If intermittent poor driveability or idle symptoms are resolved by disconnecting the IAC, carefully recheck connections, valve terminal resistance, or replace IAC.

---

① INSTALL TECH 1
- ENGINE AT NORMAL OPERATING TEMPERATURE IN PARK/NEUTRAL WITH PARKING BRAKE SET.
- A/C "OFF".
- SELECT RPM CONTROL. (MISC. TESTS)
- CYCLE IAC THROUGH ITS RANGE FROM 700 RPM UP TO 1500 RPM.
- RPM SHOULD CHANGE SMOOTHLY.
DOES IT?

NO →

② INSTALL IAC NODE LIGHT * IN IAC HARNESS.
- ENGINE RUNNING. CYCLE IAC WITH TECH 1.
- EACH NODE LIGHT SHOULD CYCLE RED AND GREEN BUT NEVER "OFF."
DO THEY?

YES ↑

YES →

USING THE IAC DRIVER * OR OTHER CONVENIENT CONNECTOR, CHECK RESISTANCE ACROSS IAC COILS.
SHOULD BE 40 TO 80 OHMS BETWEEN IAC TERMINALS "A" TO "B" AND "C" TO "D".

OK ↓

CHECK RESISTANCE BETWEEN IAC TERMINALS "B" AND "C" AND "A" AND "D".
- SHOULD BE INFINITE.

OK ↓

IDLE AIR CONTROL CIRCUIT OK. REFER TO "DIAGNOSTIC AIDS" ON FACING PAGE.

NOT OK →

REPLACE IAC VALVE AND RETEST.

NOT OK →

REPLACE IAC VALVE AND RETEST.

NO →

IF CIRCUIT(S) DID NOT TEST RED AND GREEN, CHECK FOR:
- FAULTY CONNECTOR TERMINAL CONTACTS.
- OPEN CIRCUITS INCLUDING CONNECTORS.
- CIRCUITS SHORTED TO GROUND OR VOLTAGE.
- FAULTY ECM CONNECTIONS OR REPLACE ECM.
REPAIR AS NECESSARY AND RETEST.

YES →

CHECK IAC CONNECTIONS.
CHECK IAC PASSAGES.
IF OK, REPLACE IAC.

---

* IAC DRIVER AND NODE LIGHT REQUIRED KIT 222-L FROM: CONCEPT TECHNOLOGY, INC. J 37027 FROM: KENT-MOORE, INC.

CLEAR CODES, CONFIRM "CLOSED LOOP" OPERATION, NO "SERVICE ENGINE SOON" LIGHT. PERFORM IAC RESET PROCEDURE PER APPLICABLE SERVICE MANUAL AND VERIFY CONTROLLED IDLE SPEED IS CORRECT.

1990-92 3.1L (VIN T)

CODE 41

CYLINDER SELECT ERROR
(FAULTY OR INCORRECT MEM-CAL)
3.1L (VIN T) "J" CARLINE (PORT)

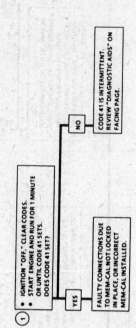

1. • IGNITION "OFF." CLEAR CODES.
   • START ENGINE AND RUN FOR 1 MINUTE OR UNTIL CODE 41 SETS.
   DOES CODE 41 SET?

YES

FAULTY CONNECTIONS DUE TO MEM-CAL NOT LOCKED IN PLACE, OR INCORRECT MEM-CAL INSTALLED.

NO

CODE 41 IS INTERMITTENT. REVIEW "DIAGNOSTIC AIDS" ON FACING PAGE.

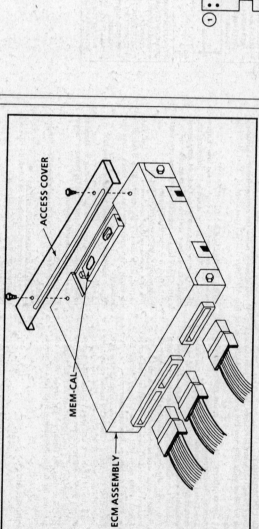

- ACCESS COVER
- MEM-CAL
- ECM ASSEMBLY

CODE 41

CYLINDER SELECT ERROR
(FAULTY OR INCORRECT MEM-CAL)
3.1L (VIN T) "J" CARLINE (PORT)

Test Description: Number(s) refer to circled number(s) on the diagnostic chart.

1. The ECM used for this engine can also be used for other engines, and the difference is in the MEM-CAL. If a Code 41 sets, the incorrect MEM-CAL has been installed or it is faulty and it must be replaced.

Diagnostic Aids:

Check MEM-CAL to be sure locking tabs are secure. Also check the pins on both the MEM-CAL and ECM to assure they are making proper contact. Check the MEM-CAL part number to assure it is the correct part. If the MEM-CAL part number it must be replaced. It is also possible that the ECM is faulty, however it should not be replaced until all of the above have been checked. For additional information refer to "Intermittents" in "Symptoms," Section

1990-92 3.1L (VIN T)

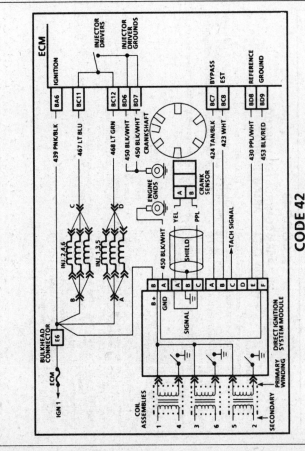

CODE 42

ELECTRONIC SPARK TIMING (EST) CIRCUIT
3.1L (VIN T) "J" CARLINE (PORT)

Circuit Description:

When the system is running on the ignition module, that is, no voltage on the bypass line, the ignition module grounds the Electronic Spark Timing (EST) signal. The ECM expects to see no voltage on the EST line during this condition. If it sees a voltage, it sets Code 42 and will not go into the EST mode.

When the rpm for EST is reached (about 400 rpm) and bypass voltage applied, the EST should no longer be grounded in the ignition module, so the EST voltage should be varying.

If the bypass line is open or grounded, the ignition module will not switch to EST mode, so the EST voltage will be low and Code 42 will be set.

If the EST line is grounded, the ignition module will switch to EST, but because the line is grounded, there will be no EST signal. A Code 42 will be set.

Test Description: Number(s) refer to circled number(s) on the diagnostic chart.

1. Code 42 means the ECM has seen an open or short to ground in the EST or bypass circuits. This test confirms Code 42 and that the fault causing the code is present.

2. Checks for a normal EST ground path through the ignition module. An EST CKT 423 shorted to ground will also read less than 500 ohms; however, this will be checked later.

3. As the test light voltage touches CKT 424, the module should switch, causing the ohmmeter to "overrange," if the meter is in the 1000-2000 ohms position. Selecting the 10-20,000 ohms position will indicate above 5000 ohms. The important thing is that the module "switched."

4. The module did not switch and this step checks for:
   - EST CKT 423 shorted to ground
   - Bypass CKT 424 open
   - Faulty ignition module connection or module
5. Confirms that Code 42 is a faulty ECM and not an intermittent in CKTs 423 or 424.

Diagnostic Aids:

The "Scan" tool does not have any ability to help diagnose a Code 42 problem.

A MEM-CAL not fully seated in the ECM can result in a Code 42.

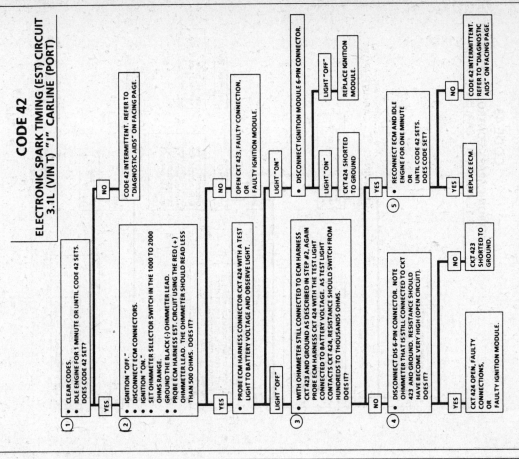

CODE 42

ELECTRONIC SPARK TIMING (EST) CIRCUIT
3.1L (VIN T) "J" CARLINE (PORT)

① - CLEAR CODES.
- IDLE ENGINE FOR 1 MINUTE OR UNTIL CODE 42 SETS.
DOES CODE 42 SET?

NO → CODE 42 INTERMITTENT. REFER TO "DIAGNOSTIC AIDS" ON FACING PAGE.

YES ↓

② - IGNITION "OFF."
- DISCONNECT ECM CONNECTORS.
- IGNITION "ON."
- SET OHMMETER SELECTOR SWITCH IN THE 1000 TO 2000 OHMS RANGE.
- GROUND THE BLACK (–) OHMMETER LEAD.
- PROBE ECM HARNESS EST. CIRCUIT USING THE RED (+) OHMMETER LEAD. THE OHMMETER SHOULD READ LESS THAN 500 OHMS. DOES IT?

NO → OPEN CKT 423, FAULTY CONNECTION, OR FAULTY IGNITION MODULE.

YES ↓

- PROBE ECM HARNESS CONNECTOR CKT 424 WITH A TEST LIGHT TO BATTERY VOLTAGE AND OBSERVE LIGHT.

LIGHT "ON" → DISCONNECT IGNITION MODULE 6-PIN CONNECTOR.

LIGHT "OFF" ↓

③ - WITH OHMMETER STILL CONNECTED TO ECM HARNESS CKT 423 AND GROUND AS DESCRIBED IN STEP #2, AGAIN PROBE ECM HARNESS CKT 424 WITH THE TEST LIGHT CONNECTED TO BATTERY VOLTAGE. AS TEST LIGHT CONTACTS CKT 424, RESISTANCE SHOULD SWITCH FROM HUNDREDS TO THOUSANDS OHMS. DOES IT?

LIGHT "OFF" → REPLACE IGNITION MODULE.
LIGHT "ON" → CKT 424 SHORTED TO GROUND.

NO ↓

④ - DISCONNECT DIS 6-PIN CONNECTOR. NOTE OHMMETER THAT IS STILL CONNECTED TO CKT 423 AND GROUND. RESISTANCE SHOULD HAVE BECOME VERY HIGH (OPEN CIRCUIT). DOES IT?

YES ↓   NO → CKT 423 SHORTED TO GROUND.

CKT 424 OPEN, FAULTY CONNECTIONS, OR FAULTY IGNITION MODULE.

⑤ - RECONNECT ECM AND IDLE ENGINE FOR ONE MINUTE OR UNTIL CODE 42 SETS. DOES CODE SET?

YES → REPLACE ECM.
NO → CODE 42 INTERMITTENT. REFER TO "DIAGNOSTIC AIDS" ON FACING PAGE.

CLEAR CODES AND CONFIRM "CLOSED LOOP" OPERATION AND NO "SERVICE ENGINE SOON" LIGHT.

1990-92 3.1L (VIN T)

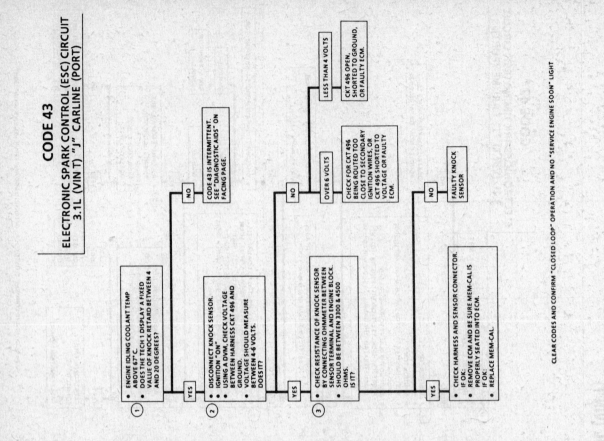

CODE 43

ELECTRONIC SPARK CONTROL (ESC) CIRCUIT
3.1L (VIN T) "J" CARLINE (PORT)

CODE 43

ELECTRONIC SPARK CONTROL (ESC) CIRCUIT
3.1L (VIN T) "J" CARLINE (PORT)

Circuit Description:

The knock sensor is used to detect engine detonation, and the ECM will retard the Electronic Spark Timing (EST) based on the signal being received. The circuitry within the knock sensor causes the ECM 5 volts to be pulled down so that, under a no knock condition, CKT 496 would measure about 2.5 volts. The knock sensor produces an A/C signal which rides on the 2.5 volts DC voltage. The amplitude and signal frequency is dependent upon the knock level.

If CKT 496 becomes open or shorted to ground, the voltage will either go above 4.6 volts or below .64 volt. If either of these conditions are met for about 10 seconds, a Code 43 will be stored.

Test Description: Number(s) refer to circled number(s) on the diagnostic chart.

1. This step determines if conditions for Code 43 still exist (voltage on CKT 496 above 4.6 volts or below .64 volt). The system is designed to retard the spark 15°, if either condition exists.
2. The ECM has a 5 volt pull-up resistor, which applies 5 volts to CKT 496. The 5 volts signal should be present at the knock sensor terminal during these test conditions.
3. This step determines if the knock sensor resistance is 3900 ohms ± 15%. If the resistance is between 3300 to 4500 ohms, the sensor is OK.

Diagnostic Aids:

If CKT 496 is not open or shorted to ground and the voltage reading is below 4 volts, the most likely cause is an open circuit in the ECM. It is possible that a faulty MEM-CAL could be drawing the 5 volt signal down and it should be replaced, if a replacement ECM did not correct the problem.

Refer to "Intermittents" in "Symptoms," Section

1990-92 3.1L (VIN T)

CODE 44

OXYGEN (O₂) SENSOR CIRCUIT
(LEAN EXHAUST INDICATED)
3.1L (VIN T) "J" CARLINE (PORT)

CODE 44

OXYGEN (O₂) SENSOR CIRCUIT
(LEAN EXHAUST INDICATED)
3.1L (VIN T) "J" CARLINE (PORT)

Circuit Description:

The ECM supplies a voltage of about .45 volt between terminals "GE14" and "GE15". (If measured with a 10 megohm digital voltmeter, this may read as low as .32 volt.) The Oxygen (O₂) sensor varies the voltage within a range of about 1 volt if the exhaust is rich, down through about .10 volt if exhaust is lean.

The sensor is like an open circuit and produces no voltage when it is below about 315°C (600°F). An open sensor circuit or cold sensor causes "Open Loop" operation.

Test Description: Number(s) refer to circled number(s) on the diagnostic chart.

1. Code 44 is set when the O₂ sensor signal voltage on CKT 412:
   - Remains below .2 volt for 60 seconds or more
   - And the system is operating in "Closed Loop"

Diagnostic Aids:

Using the "Scan," observe the block learn values at different rpm and air flow conditions. The "Scan" also displays the block learn cells, so the block learn values can be checked in each of the cells to determine when the Code 44 may have been set. If the conditions for Code 44 exists, the block learn values will be around 150.

- O₂ sensor wire. Sensor pigtail may be mispositioned and contacting the exhaust manifold.
- Check for intermittent ground in wire between connector and sensor.

- **MAP sensor.** A shifted "Low" MAP sensor could cause the fuel system to go lean.
- **Lean injector(s).** Perform injector balance test CHART C-2A.
- **Fuel contamination.** Water, even in small amounts, near the in-tank fuel pump inlet can be delivered to the injectors. The water causes a lean exhaust and can set a Code 44.
- **Fuel pressure.** System will be lean if pressure is too low. It may be necessary to monitor fuel pressure while driving the car at various road speeds and/or loads to confirm. See fuel system diagnosis CHART A-7.
- **Exhaust leaks.** If there is an exhaust leak, the engine can cause outside air to be pulled into the exhaust and past the sensor. Vacuum or crankcase leaks can cause a lean condition.
- If the above are OK, it is a faulty oxygen sensor.

ECM
O₂ SENSOR SIGNAL — GE14 — 412 PPL
O₂ SENSOR GROUND — GE15 — 413 TAN
ENGINE GROUND

OXYGEN (O₂) SENSOR
EXHAUST

---

① • RUN WARM ENGINE (75°C/167°F TO 95°C/203°F) AT 1200 RPM.
• DOES TECH 1 INDICATE O₂ SENSOR VOLTAGE FIXED BELOW .35 VOLT (350 mV)?

YES → • DISCONNECT O₂ SENSOR.
• WITH ENGINE IDLING, TECH 1 SHOULD DISPLAY O₂ SENSOR VOLTAGE BETWEEN .35 VOLT AND .55 VOLT (350 mV AND 550 mV). DOES IT?

NO → CODE 44 IS INTERMITTENT. IF NO ADDITIONAL CODES WERE STORED, REFER TO "DIAGNOSTIC AIDS" ON FACING PAGE.

YES → REFER TO "DIAGNOSTIC AIDS" ON FACING PAGE.

NO → CKT 412 SHORTED TO GROUND OR FAULTY ECM.

CLEAR CODES AND CONFIRM "CLOSED LOOP" OPERATION AND NO "SERVICE ENGINE SOON" LIGHT.

1990-92 3.1L (VIN T)

CODE 45

OXYGEN (O₂) SENSOR CIRCUIT
(RICH EXHAUST INDICATED)
3.1L (VIN T) "J" CARLINE (PORT)

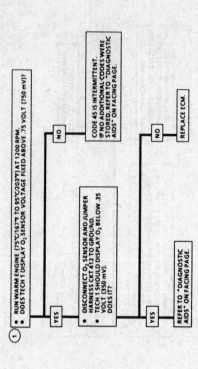

① • RUN WARM ENGINE (75°C/167°F TO 95°C/203°F) AT 1200 RPM.
 • DOES TECH 1 DISPLAY O₂ SENSOR VOLTAGE FIXED ABOVE .75 VOLT (750 mV)?

YES → • DISCONNECT O₂ SENSOR AND JUMPER HARNESS CKT 412 TO GROUND.
 TECH 1 SHOULD DISPLAY O₂ BELOW .35 VOLT (350 mV). DOES IT?

 NO → CODE 45 IS INTERMITTENT. IF NO ADDITIONAL CODES WERE STORED, REFER TO "DIAGNOSTIC AIDS" ON FACING PAGE.

 YES → REFER TO "DIAGNOSTIC AIDS" ON FACING PAGE.

 NO → REPLACE ECM.

CLEAR CODES AND CONFIRM "CLOSED LOOP" OPERATION AND NO "SERVICE ENGINE SOON" LIGHT.

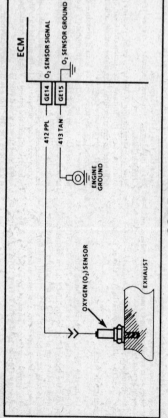

CODE 45

OXYGEN (O₂) SENSOR CIRCUIT
(RICH EXHAUST INDICATED)
3.1L (VIN T) "J" CARLINE (PORT)

Circuit Description:

The ECM supplies a voltage of about .45 volt between terminals "GE14" and "GE15". (If measured with a 10 megohm digital voltmeter, this may read as low as .32 volt.) The Oxygen (O₂) sensor varies the voltage within a range of about 1 volt, if the exhaust is rich, down through about .10 volt, if exhaust is lean.

The sensor produces no voltage when it is below about 315°C (600°F). An open sensor circuit or cold sensor causes "Open Loop" operation.

Test Description: Number(s) refer to circled number(s) on the diagnostic chart.

1. Code 45 is set when the O₂ sensor signal voltage or CKT 412.
 • Remains above .7 volt for 50 seconds; and in "Closed Loop".
 • Engine time after start is 1 minute or more.
 • Throttle angle between 3% and 45%.

Diagnostic Aids:

Using the "Scan," observe the block learn values at different rpm and air flow conditions. The "Scan" also displays the block cells, so the block learn values can be checked in each of the cells to determine when the Code 45 may have been set. If the conditions for Code 45 exists, the block learn values will be around 115.

Fuel pressure. System will go rich, if pressure is too high. The ECM can compensate for some increase. However, if it gets too high, a Code 45 may be set. See fuel system diagnosis CHART A-7.

 Rich injector. Perform injector balance test CHART C-2A.

 Leaking injector. See CHART A-7.

 • Check for fuel contaminated oil.

Check For:

 • Short to voltage on CKT 412

 HEI shielding. An open ground CKT 453 (ignition system) may result in EMI, or induced electrical "noise." The ECM looks at this "noise" as reference pulses. The additional pulses result in a higher than actual engine speed signal. The ECM then delivers too much fuel, causing system to go rich. Engine tachometer will also show higher than actual engine speed, which can help in diagnosing this problem.

 Canister purge. Check for fuel saturation. If full of fuel, check canister control and hoses. See "Canister Purge," in "Evaporative Emission Control System," Section

 MAP sensor. A shifted "High" MAP sensor could cause the fuel system to go rich.

 Fuel pressure regulator. Check for leaking fuel pressure regulator diaphragm by checking vacuum line to regulator for fuel.

 TPS. An intermittent TPS output will cause the system to go rich, due to a false indication of the engine accelerating.

 EGR. An EGR staying open (especially at idle) will cause the O₂ sensor to indicate a rich exhaust.

1990-92 3.1L (VIN T)

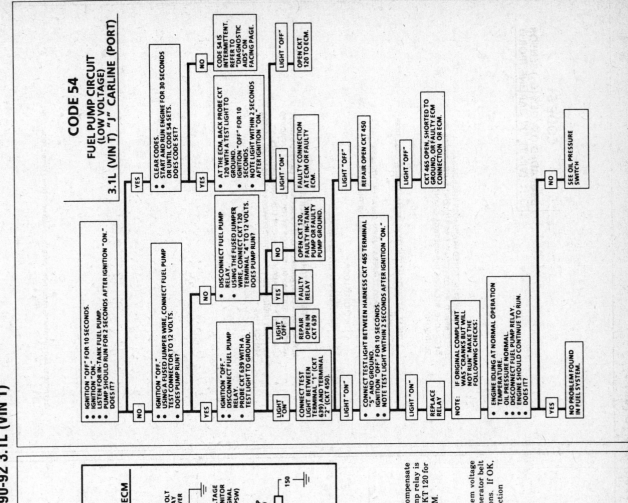

CODE 54

FUEL PUMP CIRCUIT
(LOW VOLTAGE)
3.1L (VIN T) "J" CARLINE (PORT)

Circuit Description:

The status of the fuel pump CKT 120 is monitored by the ECM at terminal "GE13" and is used to compensate fuel delivery based on system voltage. This signal is also used to store a trouble code, if the fuel pump relay is defective or fuel pump voltage is lost, while the engine is running. There should be about 12 volts on CKT 120 for 2 seconds, after the ignition is turned "ON," or any time references pulses are being received by the ECM.

Diagnostic Aids:

Code 54 will set, if the voltage at terminal "GE13" is less than 4 volts for .4 seconds since the last reference pulse was received. This code is designed to detect a faulty relay, causing extended crank time, and the code will help the diagnosis of an engine that "CRANKS BUT WILL NOT RUN."

If a fault is detected during start-up, the "Service Engine Soon" light will stay "ON" until the ignition is cycled "OFF." However, if the voltage is detected below 2 volts with the engine running, the light will only remain "ON" while the condition exists.

Check sources of intermittent low system voltage such as; loose battery connections, poor generator belt or belt tension or loose generator connections. If OK, refer to "Intermittents" in "Symptoms," Section

1990-92 3.1L (VIN T)

CODE 51
CODE 52
CODE 53

3.1L (VIN T) "J" CARLINE (PORT)

CODE 51
MEM-CAL ERROR
(FAULTY OR INCORRECT MEM-CAL)

CHECK THAT ALL PINS ARE FULLY INSERTED IN THE SOCKET AND THAT MEM-CAL IS PROPERLY LATCHED. IF OK, REPLACE MEMICAL, CLEAR MEMORY, AND RECHECK. IF CODE 51 REAPPEARS, REPLACE ECM.

CLEAR CODES AND CONFIRM "CLOSED LOOP" OPERATION AND NO "SERVICE ENGINE SOON" LIGHT.

CODE 52
CALPAK ERROR
(FAULTY OR INCORRECT CALPAK)

CHECK THAT THE MEM-CAL IS FULLY SEATED AND LATCHED INTO THE MEM-CAL SOCKET. IF OK, REPLACE MEM-CAL, CLEAR MEMORY, AND RECHECK. IF CODE 52 REAPPEARS, REPLACE ECM.

CLEAR CODES AND CONFIRM "CLOSED LOOP" OPERATION AND NO "SERVICE ENGINE SOON" LIGHT.

CODE 53
SYSTEM OVER VOLTAGE

THIS CODE INDICATES THERE IS A BASIC GENERATOR PROBLEM.

- CODE 53 WILL SET, IF VOLTAGE AT ECM IGNITION INPUT PIN IS GREATER THAN 16.9 VOLTS FOR 10 SECONDS.
- CHECK AND REPAIR CHARGING SYSTEM.

CLEAR CODES AND CONFIRM "CLOSED LOOP" OPERATION AND NO "SERVICE ENGINE SOON" LIGHT.

CODE 61
DEGRADED OXYGEN (O_2) SENSOR
3.1L (VIN T) "J" CARLINE (PORT)

IF A CODE 61 IS STORED IN MEMORY THE ECM HAS DETERMINED THE OXYGEN SENSOR IS CONTAMINATED OR DEGRADED, BECAUSE THE VOLTAGE CHANGE TIME IS SLOW OR SLUGGISH.

THE ECM PERFORMS THE OXYGEN SENSOR RESPONSE TIME TEST WHEN:

COOLANT TEMPERATURE IS GREATER THAN 85°C.

MAT TEMPERATURE IS GREATER THAN 10°C.

IN CLOSED LOOP.

IN DECEL FUEL CUT-OFF MODE.

IF A CODE 61 IS STORED THE OXYGEN SENSOR SHOULD BE REPLACED. A CONTAMINATED SENSOR CAN BE CAUSED BY FUEL ADDITIVES, SUCH AS SILICON, OR BY USE OF NON-GM APPROVED LUBRICANTS OR SEALANTS. SILICON CONTAMINATION IS USUALLY INDICATED BY A WHITE POWDERY SUBSTANCE ON THE SENSOR FINS.

CLEAR CODES AND CONFIRM "CLOSED LOOP" OPERATION AND NO "SERVICE ENGINE SOON" LIGHT.

1990-92 3.1L (VIN T)

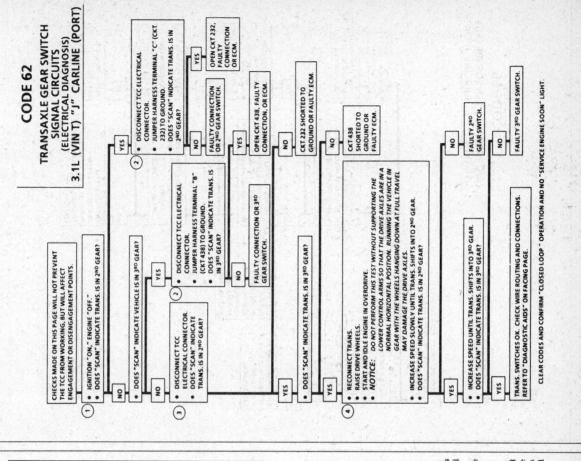

CODE 62

TRANSAXLE GEAR SWITCH SIGNAL CIRCUITS (ELECTRICAL DIAGNOSIS) 3.1L (VIN T) "J" CARLINE (PORT)

1. CHECKS MADE ON THIS PAGE WILL NOT PREVENT THE TCC FROM WORKING, BUT WILL AFFECT ENGAGEMENT OR DISENGAGEMENT POINTS.
   - IGNITION "ON," ENGINE "OFF."
   - DOES "SCAN" INDICATE TRANS. IS IN 2ND GEAR?

   YES → 2. DISCONNECT TCC ELECTRICAL CONNECTOR. JUMPER HARNESS TERMINAL "C" (CKT 232) TO GROUND. DOES "SCAN" INDICATE TRANS. IS IN 2ND GEAR?
   - YES → OPEN CKT 232, FAULTY CONNECTION OR ECM.
   - NO → FAULTY CONNECTION OR 2ND GEAR SWITCH.

   NO → DOES "SCAN" INDICATE VEHICLE IS IN 3RD GEAR?
   - YES → 2. DISCONNECT TCC ELECTRICAL CONNECTOR. JUMPER HARNESS TERMINAL "B" (CKT 438) TO GROUND. DOES "SCAN" INDICATE TRANS. IS IN 3RD GEAR?
     - NO → FAULTY CONNECTION OR 3RD GEAR SWITCH.
     - YES → OPEN CKT 438, FAULTY CONNECTION, OR ECM.

   NO → 3. DISCONNECT TCC ELECTRICAL CONNECTOR. DOES "SCAN" INDICATE TRANS. IS IN 2ND GEAR?
   - YES → DOES "SCAN" INDICATE TRANS. IS IN 3RD GEAR?
     - NO → CKT 232 SHORTED TO GROUND OR FAULTY ECM.
     - YES → DOES "SCAN" INDICATE TRANS. IS IN 3RD GEAR?
       - NO → CKT 438 SHORTED TO GROUND OR FAULTY ECM.
       - YES → 4. RECONNECT TRANS. RAISE DRIVE WHEELS. START AND IDLE ENGINE IN OVERDRIVE.
         NOTICE: DO NOT PERFORM THIS TEST WITHOUT SUPPORTING THE LOWER CONTROL ARMS SO THAT THE DRIVE AXLES ARE IN A NORMAL HORIZONTAL POSITION. RUNNING THE VEHICLE IN GEAR WITH THE WHEELS HANGING DOWN AT FULL TRAVEL MAY DAMAGE THE DRIVE AXLES.
         - INCREASE SPEED SLOWLY UNTIL TRANS. SHIFTS INTO 2ND GEAR. DOES "SCAN" INDICATE TRANS. IS IN 2ND GEAR?
           - NO → FAULTY 2ND GEAR SWITCH.
           - YES → INCREASE SPEED UNTIL TRANS. SHIFTS INTO 3RD GEAR. DOES "SCAN" INDICATE TRANS. IS IN 3RD GEAR?
             - NO → FAULTY 3RD GEAR SWITCH.
             - YES → TRANS. SWITCHES OK. CHECK WIRE ROUTING AND CONNECTIONS. REFER TO "DIAGNOSTIC AIDS" ON FACING PAGE.

   CLEAR CODES AND CONFIRM "CLOSED LOOP" OPERATION AND NO "SERVICE ENGINE SOON" LIGHT.

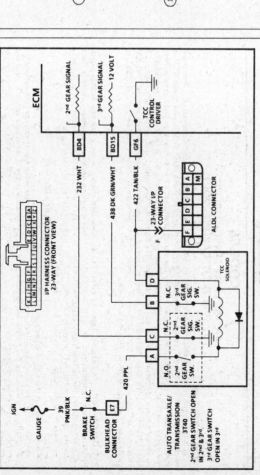

ECM
- 2nd GEAR SIGNAL — BD4 — 232 WHT
- 3rd GEAR SIGNAL — BD15 — 438 DK GRN/WHT
- 12 VOLT — GF6 — 422 TAN/BLK
- TCC CONTROL DRIVER

I/P HARNESS CONNECTOR 23-WAY (FRONT VIEW)
KJHGFEDCBA / LMNPRSTUVWXYZ

23-WAY I/P CONNECTOR
FEDCBA / M
ALDL CONNECTOR

IGN
GAUGE
BRAKE SWITCH — N.C.
39 PNK/BLK
BULKHEAD CONNECTOR — E7
420 PPL

AUTO TRANSAXLE/TRANSMISSION 3T40
2ND GEAR SWITCH OPEN IN 2ND & 3rd
3RD GEAR SWITCH OPEN IN 3RD

TCC SOLENOID
N.C. 3rd GEAR SIG. SW.
N.C. 2nd GEAR SIG. SW.

N.O. = 2nd gear switch open
       2nd gear signal switch closed
       3rd gear signal switch closed
1st Gear = 2nd gear switch open
       2nd gear signal switch closed
       3rd gear signal switch opens
2nd Gear = 2nd gear switch closed
       3rd gear signal switch closed
3rd Gear = 2nd gear switch closed
       3rd gear signal switch opens

CODE 62

TRANSAXLE GEAR SWITCH SIGNAL CIRCUITS (ELECTRICAL DIAGNOSIS) 3.1L (VIN T) "J" CARLINE (PORT)

Circuit Description:

The 2nd gear signal switch in this vehicle should be open in 2nd and 3rd gear. The ECM uses this 2nd gear signal to disengage the TCC when downshifting.

The 3rd gear switch should be open in 3rd gear.

Test Description: Number(s) refer to circled number(s) on the diagnostic chart.

1. Some "Scan" tools display the state of these switches in different ways. Be familiar with the type of tool being used. Since both switches should be in the closed state during this test, the tool should read the same for either the 2nd or 3rd gear switch.

2. Determines whether the switch or signal circuit is open. The circuit can be checked for an open by measuring the voltage (with a voltmeter) at the TCC connector (should be about 12 volts).

3. Because the switch(s) should be grounded in this step, disconnecting the TCC connector should cause the "Scan" switch state to change.

4. The switch state should change when the vehicle shifts into 2nd gear.

Diagnostic Aids:

If vehicle is road tested because of a TCC related problem, be sure the switch states do not change while in 3rd gear because the TCC will disengage. If switches change state, carefully check wire routing and connections.

1990-92 3.1L (VIN T)

CODE 66

A/C PRESSURE SENSOR CIRCUIT
3.1L (VIN T) "J" CARLINE (PORT)

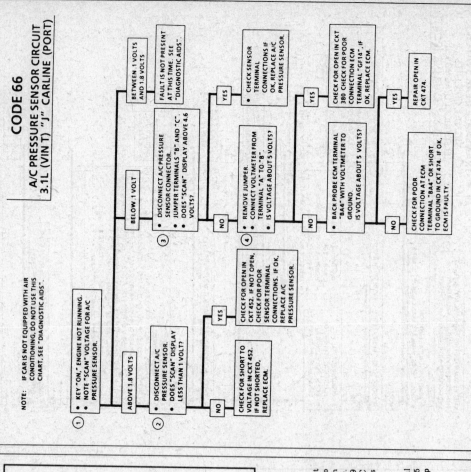

NOTE: IF CAR IS NOT EQUIPPED WITH AIR CONDITIONING, DO NOT USE THIS CHART, SEE "DIAGNOSTIC AIDS".

(1) KEY "ON," ENGINE NOT RUNNING. NOTE "SCAN" VOLTAGE FOR A/C PRESSURE SENSOR.

- ABOVE 1.8 VOLTS
- BETWEEN .1 VOLTS AND 1.8 VOLTS → FAULT IS NOT PRESENT AT THIS TIME. SEE "DIAGNOSTIC AIDS".
- BELOW .1 VOLT

(2) DISCONNECT A/C PRESSURE SENSOR. DOES "SCAN" DISPLAY LESS THAN 1 VOLT?

- YES → CHECK FOR OPEN IN CKT 452. IF NOT OPEN, CHECK FOR POOR SENSOR TERMINAL CONNECTIONS. IF OK, REPLACE A/C PRESSURE SENSOR.
- NO → CHECK FOR SHORT TO VOLTAGE IN CKT 452. IF NOT SHORTED, REPLACE ECM.

(3) DISCONNECT A/C PRESSURE SENSOR CONNECTOR. JUMPER TERMINALS "B" AND "C". DOES "SCAN" DISPLAY ABOVE 4.6 VOLTS?

- YES → CHECK SENSOR TERMINAL CONNECTIONS. IF OK, REPLACE A/C PRESSURE SENSOR.
- NO

(4) REMOVE JUMPER. CONNECT VOLTMETER FROM TERMINAL "A" TO "B". IS VOLTAGE ABOUT 5 VOLTS?

- YES → CHECK FOR OPEN IN CKT 380 CHECK FOR POOR CONNECTION ECM TERMINAL "GF14". IF OK, REPLACE ECM.
- NO → BACK PROBE ECM TERMINAL "BA4" WITH VOLTMETER TO GROUND. IS VOLTAGE ABOUT 5 VOLTS?
  - YES → REPAIR OPEN IN CKT 474.
  - NO → CHECK FOR POOR CONNECTION AT ECM TERMINAL "BA4" OR SHORT TO GROUND IN CKT 474. IF OK, ECM IS FAULTY.

CLEAR CODES AND CONFIRM "CLOSED LOOP" OPERATION AND NO "SERVICE ENGINE SOON" LIGHT.

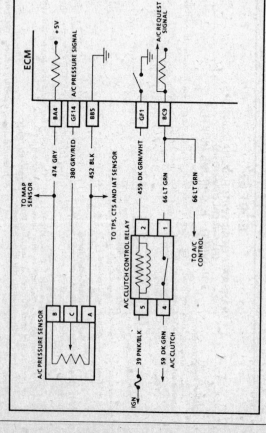

CODE 66

A/C PRESSURE SENSOR CIRCUIT
3.1L (VIN T) "J" CARLINE (PORT)

Circuit Description:

The A/C pressure sensor responds to changes in A/C refrigerant system high side pressure. This input indicates how much load the A/C compressor is putting on the engine and is one of the factors used by the ECM to determine IAC valve position for idle speed control. The circuit consists of a 5 volts reference and a ground, both provided by the ECM, and a signal line to the ECM. The signal is a voltage which is proportional to the pressure. The sensor's range of operation is 0 to 450 psi. At 0 psi, the signal will be about .1 volt, varying up to about 4.9 volts at 450 psi or above. Code 66 sets if the voltage is above 4.9 volts or below .1 volt 5 seconds or more. The A/C compressor is disabled by the ECM if Code 66 is present, or if pressure is above or below calibrated values described in "A/C Clutch Circuit Diagnosis," Section

Test Description: Number(s) refer to circled number(s) on the diagnostic chart.

1. This step checks the voltage signal being received by the ECM from the A/C pressure sensor. The normal operating range is between .1 volt and 4.9 volts.

2. Checks to see if the high voltage signal is from a shorted sensor or a short to voltage in the circuit. Normally, disconnecting the sensor would make a normal circuit go to near zero volt.

3. Checks to see if low voltage signal is from the sensor or the circuit. Jumpering the sensor signal CKT 380 to 5 volts, checks the circuit, connections, and ECM.

4. This step checks to see if the low voltage signal was due to an open in the sensor circuit or the 5 volts reference circuit since the prior step eliminated the pressure sensor.

Diagnostic Aids:

Code 66 sets when signal voltage falls outside the normal possible range of the sensor and is not due to a refrigerant system problem. If problem is intermittent, check for opens or shorts in harness or poor connections. If OK, replace A/C pressure sensor. If Code 66 re-sets, replace ECM.

1990-92 3.1L (VIN T)

ECM CONNECTOR "A" (24 PIN BLACK)

PIN FUNCTION	CKT #	WIRE COLOR	COMPONENT CONNECTOR CAVITY	NORMAL VOLTAGES KEY "ON"	NORMAL VOLTAGES ENG RUN	CODES AFFECT.	POSSIBLE SYMPTOMS FROM FAULTY CIRCUIT
BA1	N/C						
BA2	N/C						
BA3	N/C						
BA4 MAP 5 VOLTS REF	474	GRY	MAP SENSOR CONNECTOR "C"	5	5	33 (9) 34 66	LACK OF POWER. ROUGH IDLE, SURGE, NO A/C
BA5 TPS 5 VOLTS REF.	416	GRY	TPS CONNECTOR "A"	5	5	21 (9) 22	HIGH IDLE.
BA6 IGNITION FEED	439	PNK/BLK	**	B +	B +	NONE	INJECTOR (9) ECM FUSE. NO DATA. CRANK WILL NOT START. REFER TO "DIAGNOSTIC CIRCUIT CHECK."
BA7	N/C						
BA8	N/C						
BA9 SERIAL DATA	461	ORN	ALDL CONNECTOR "M" I/P CONNECTOR "J"	4.8 (3)	4.8	NONE	NO ALDL DATA. REFER TO "DIAGNOSTIC CIRCUIT CHECK."
BA10	N/C						
BA11 FUEL PUMP RELAY DRIVER	465	DK GRN/WHT	FUEL PUMP RELAY CONNECTOR "S"	0* (4)	B +	NONE	HARD TO START. LONG CRANK TIME. REFER TO CHART A-7.
BA12 SYSTEM GROUND	450	BLK/WHT	ALDL CONNECTOR "A" I/P CONNECTOR "H"	0*	0*	NONE	CRANKS WILL NOT START, IF BOTH SYSTEM GROUNDS OPEN. CHECK GROUNDS AT ENGINE BLOCK, DIS MODULE, P/S PRESSURE SWITCH, FPR, INJECTOR DRIVER GROUNDS TRANSMISSION NEUTRAL SAFETY SWITCH. REFER TO "DIAGNOSTIC CIRCUIT CHECK." **

(1) INCREASES WITH VEHICLE SPEED (MEASURE A/C SCALE)
(2) NORMAL OPERATING TEMPERATURE
(3) VARIES
(4) 12 VOLTS FOR FIRST TWO SECONDS
(5) VARIES WITH TEMPERATURE
(6) 12 VOLTS 4T60 TRANS.
(7) 12 VOLTS WHEN COMMANDED "ON"
(8) OPEN
(9) OPEN/GROUNDED CIRCUIT
(10) GROUNDED CIRCUIT
(11) LESS THAN 1 VOLT
* LESS THAN .5 VOLT (500 mV)

ECM CONNECTOR "B" (24 PIN BLACK)

PIN FUNCTION	CKT #	WIRE COLOR	COMPONENT CONNECTOR CAVITY	NORMAL VOLTAGES KEY "ON"	NORMAL VOLTAGES ENG RUN	CODES AFFECT.	POSSIBLE SYMPTOMS FROM FAULTY CIRCUIT
BB1 BATTERY	340	ORN	**	B +	B +	NONE	IF B1 AND C16 OPEN, NO START REFER TO "DIAGNOSTIC CIRCUIT CHECK."
BB2	N/C						
BB3	N/C						
BB4	N/C						
BB5 SENSOR GROUND TPS, CTS, A/C PRESSURE AND IAT	452	BLK	TPS CONNECTOR "B" CTS CONNECTOR "A" A/C PRESSURE SENSOR CONNECTOR "A" IAT SENSOR CONNECTOR "A"	0*	0*	14 (9) 21 23 66	HIGH IDLE, SAG OR HESITATION NO A/C.
BB6 SENSOR GROUND MAP	455	PPL	MAP SENSOR CONNECTOR "A"	0*	0*	33 (8)	ROUGH OR UNSTABLE IDLE, HARD TO START, POOR PERFORMANCE REFER TO MAP CHART C-1D
BB7	N/C						
BB8	N/C						
BB9 VSS (LOW)	401	PPL	VEHICLE SPEED SENSOR (VSS) CONNECTOR "B"	0*	(1)	24 (9)	NO VSS SIGNAL, INOPERATIVE SPEEDOMETER, INOPERATIVE CRUISE CONTROL
BB10 VSS (HIGH)	400	YEL	VEHICLE SPEED SENSOR (VSS) CONNECTOR "A"	0*	(1)	24 (5)	NO VSS SIGNAL, INOPERATIVE SPEEDOMETER, INOPERATIVE CRUISE CONTROL
BB11 VSS OUTPUT (4000 P/MI)	389	DK GRN	TO SPEEDOMETER I/P CONNECTOR "N"	10	11.7	24 (9)	NO VSS SIGNAL, INOPERATIVE SPEEDOMETER, INOPERATIVE CRUISE CONTROL. **
BB12	N/C						

(1) INCREASES WITH VEHICLE SPEED (MEASURE ON A/C SCALE)
(2) NORMAL OPERATING TEMPERATURE
(3) VARIES
(4) 12 VOLTS FOR FIRST TWO SECONDS
(5) VARIES WITH TEMPERATURE
(6) 12 VOLTS 4T60 TRANS.
(7) 12 VOLTS WHEN COMMANDED "ON"
(8) OPEN
(9) OPEN/GROUNDED CIRCUIT
(10) GROUNDED CIRCUIT
(11) LESS THAN 1 VOLT
* LESS THAN .5 VOLT (500 mV)

1990-92 3.1L (VIN T)

ECM CONNECTOR "D" (32 PIN BLACK)

PIN FUNCTION	CKT #	WIRE COLOR	COMPONENT CONNECTOR CAVITY	NORMAL VOLTAGES KEY "ON"	NORMAL VOLTAGES ENG RUN	CODES AFFECT.	POSSIBLE SYMPTOMS FROM FAULTY CIRCUIT
BD1 SYSTEM GROUND	551	TAN/WHT	ENGINE BLOCK	0*	0*	NONE	NO SYMPTOM. IF BD1 AND BA12 OPEN, NO START. REFER TO "DIAGNOSTIC CIRCUIT CHECK."
BD2 N/C							
BD3 N/C							
BD4 2nd GEAR SIGNAL (3T40)	232	WHT	TCC SOLENOID CONNECTOR "C"	B+	B+	62	POOR FUEL ECONOMY "CHUGGLE" OR "SURGE" CONDITION.
BD5 N/C							
BD6 INJECTOR DRIVER GROUND	450	BLK/WHT	DIS MODULE TWO PIN CONN. "A" SPLICE TO ECM PIN BA12 AND BD7	0*	0*	NONE	NO SYMPTOM, LOSS OF BOTH GROUNDS, NO START. REFER TO "DIAGNOSTIC CIRCUIT CHECK."
BD7 INJECTOR DRIVER GROUND	450	BLK/WHT	DIS MODULE TWO PIN CONN. "A" SPLICE TO ECM PIN BA12 AND BD6	0*	0*	NONE	NO SYMPTOM, LOSS OF BOTH GROUNDS, NO START. REFER TO "DIAGNOSTIC CIRCUIT CHECK.".
BD8 REFERENCE	430	PPL/WHT	DIS MODULE SIX PIN CONNECTOR "E"	0*	2,3	NONE	NO START. REFER TO "DIAGNOSTIC CIRCUIT CHECK."
BD9 REFERENCE GROUND	453	BLK/RED	DIS MODULE SIX PIN CONNECTOR "F"	0*	0*	NONE	POOR PERFORMANCE. (8)
BD10 N/C							
BD11 N/C							
BD12							
BD13 P.S.P.S. SIGNAL	495	LT BLU/ORN	POWER STEERING PRESS. SW CONN. "B"	B+	B+	NONE	STALLING AROUND CORNER, RETARD TIMING AT IDLE, ROUGH IDLE. REFER TO CHART C-1E.
BD14							
BD15 3rd GEAR SIGNAL	438	DK GRN/WHT	TCC SOLENOID CONNECTOR "B"	B+	B+	62	POOR FUEL ECONOMY, "CHUGGLE" OR "SURGE" CONDITION.
BD16 P/N SWITCH	434	ORN/BLK	P/N SWITCH CONNECTOR "A"	0*	0*	NONE	POOR FUEL ECONOMY, STALL, INCORRECT IDLE.

(1) INCREASES WITH VEHICLE SPEED (MEASURE ON A/C SCALE)
(2) NORMAL OPERATING TEMPERATURE
(3) VARIES
(4) 12 VOLTS FOR FIRST TWO SECONDS
(5) VARIES WITH TEMPERATURE
(6) 12 VOLTS 4T60 TRANS.
(7) 12 VOLTS WHEN COMMANDED "ON"
(8) OPEN CIRCUIT
(9) OPEN/GROUNDED CIRCUIT
(10) GROUNDED CIRCUIT
(11) LESS THAN 1 VOLT
* LESS THAN 5 VOLT (500 mV)

ECM CONNECTOR "C" (32 PIN BLACK)

PIN FUNCTION	CKT #	WIRE COLOR	COMPONENT CONNECTOR CAVITY	NORMAL VOLTAGES KEY "ON"	NORMAL VOLTAGES ENG RUN	CODES AFFECT.	POSSIBLE SYMPTOMS FROM FAULTY CIRCUIT
BC1 VSS OUTPUT (2000 P/MI)	381	RED	TO CRUISE CONTROL I/P CONN "K"	(11)	(11)	NONE	NO VSS SIGNAL, INOPERATIVE SPEEDOMETER, INOPERATIVE CRUISE CONTROL
BC2 N/C							
BC3 N/C			BRAKE SWITCH CONNECTOR "B"				
BC4 BRAKE SWITCH IF USED	420	PPL	TCC CONNECTOR "A"	B+	B+	62	NO TCC OR 2nd GEAR SWITCH REFER TO CODE.
BC5 N/C							
BC6 N/C							
BC7 BYPASS	424	TAN/BLK	DIS MODULE SIX PIN CONN. "A"	0*	5	42 (9)	SURGE, HESITATION, LACK OF PERFORMANCE.
BC8 EST	423	WHT	DIS MODULE SIX PIN CONN. "B"	0*	1 3	42 (9)	SURGE, HESITATION, RUNS ROUGH, STALLS, LACK OF PERFORMANCE.
BC9 A/C REQUEST	66	LT GRN	A/C RELAY CONNECTOR "I"	"ON" B+ "OFF" 0*	"ON" B+ "OFF" 0*	NONE	NO A/C CLUTCH ENGAGEMENT. (8)
BC10 N/C							
BC11 INJECTOR DRIVERS 2,4,6	467	DK BLU	FUEL INJECTOR CONN "C"	B+	B+	NONE	HARD TO START, POOR PERFORMANCE, ROUGH IDLE. REFER TO CHART A-7. REFER TO CHART C-2A
BC12 INJECTOR DRIVERS 1,3,5	468	DK GRN	FUEL INJECTOR CONN "D"	B+	B+	NONE	HARD TO START, POOR PERFORMANCE, ROUGH IDLE. REFER TO CHART A-7. REFER TO CHART C-2A
BC13 N/C							
BC14 N/C							
BC15 N/C							
BC16 BATTERY	340	ORN	**	B+	B+	NONE	IF C16 AND B1 ARE OPEN, NO START. REFER TO "DIAGNOSTIC CIRCUIT CHECK."

(1) INCREASES WITH VEHICLE SPEED (MEASURE ON A/C SCALE)
(2) NORMAL OPERATING TEMPERATURE
(3) VARIES
(4) 12 VOLTS FOR FIRST TWO SECONDS
(5) VARIES WITH TEMPERATURE
(6) 12 VOLTS 4T60 TRANS
(7) 1 VOLT WHEN COMMANDED "ON"
(8) OPEN CIRCUIT
(9) OPEN/GROUNDED CIRCUIT
(10) GROUNDED CIRCUIT
(11) LESS THAN 1 VOLT
* LESS THAN 5 VOLT (500 mV)

1990-92 3.1L (VIN T)

ECM CONNECTOR "E" (32 PIN GREEN)

PIN FUNCTION	CKT #	WIRE COLOR	COMPONENT CONNECTOR CAVITY	NORMAL VOLTAGES KEY "ON"	NORMAL VOLTAGES ENG RUN	CODES AFFECT	POSSIBLE SYMPTOMS FROM FAULTY CIRCUIT
GE1 N/C							
GE2 N/C							
GE3 IAC COIL "A" HIGH	441	LT BLU/WHT	IAC VALVE CONN "D"	NOT USEABLE	USEABLE	35	STALLING, ROUGH UNSTABLE OR INCORRECT IDLE. REFER TO CHART C-2C.
GE4 IAC COIL "A" LOW	442	LT BLU/BLK	IAC VALVE CONN "C"	NOT USEABLE	USEABLE	35	STALLING, ROUGH UNSTABLE OR INCORRECT IDLE. REFER TO CHART C-2C.
GE5 IAC COIL "B" HIGH	443	LT GRN/WHT	IAC VALVE CONN "B"	NOT USEABLE	USEABLE	35	STALLING, ROUGH UNSTABLE OR INCORRECT IDLE. REFER TO CHART C-2C.
GE6 IAC COIL "B" LOW	444	LT GRN/BLK	IAC VALVE CONN "A"	NOT USEABLE	USEABLE	35	STALLING, ROUGH UNSTABLE OR INCORRECT IDLE. REFER TO CHART C-2C.
GE7 SERVICE ENGINE SOON LIGHT	419	BRN/WHT	I/P CONN "B"	0*	B+	NONE	BULB CHECK, NO SES LIGHT. (8) LIGHT "ON" ALL THE TIME. DOES NOT FLASH. (10) REFER TO "DIAGNOSTIC CIRCUIT CHECK."
GE8 COOLING FAN CONTROL	335	DK GRN/WHT	COOLING FAN RELAY CONN "2"	"ON" 0* "OFF" B+	"ON" 0* "OFF" B+	NONE	INOPERATIVE FAN, FAN RUNS ALL THE TIME.
GE9 EGR SOL #1	697	LT BLU	DIGITAL EGR SOLENOID CONN "A"	0	0 (7)	32	ROUGH IDLE, SPARK KNOCK. STALLS AFTER COLD START, SURGE DURING CRUISE
GE10 N/C							
GE11 N/C							
GE12 DIAG. TEST TERMINAL	451	WHT/BLK	ALDL CONN "B" I/P CONN "C"	5	5	NONE	NO ALDL DATA OR WILL NOT FLASH CODE 12. (9) REFER TO "DIAGNOSTIC CIRCUIT CHECK."
GE13 FUEL PUMP SIGNAL	120	GRY	FUEL PUMP RELAY CONN "4" I/P CONN "D"	(4)	B+	54	HARD TO START. REFER TO CHART A-7.
GE14 OXYGEN (O₂) SENSOR SIGNAL	412	PPL	OXYGEN (O₂) SENSOR	35-55	1-9 (3)	1345 61	RICH EXHAUST, EXHAUST ODOR, ROUGH OR INCORRECT IDLE. HESITATION, POOR PERFORMANCE.
GE15 OXYGEN (O₂) SENSOR GROUND	413	TAN	ENGINE BLOCK	0*	0*	1344 (9)	ROUGH OR INCORRECT IDLE. LEAN EXHAUST, POOR PERFORMANCE
GE16 COOLANT TEMP SIGNAL	410	YEL	CTS CONN "B"	(5)	(5)	1415 (9)	HARD TO START, ROUGH IDLE, LACK OF PERFORMANCE, EXHAUST ODOR.

(1) INCREASES WITH VEHICLE SPEED (MEASURE ON A/C SCALE)
(2) NORMAL OPERATING TEMPERATURE
(3) VARIES
(4) 12 VOLTS FOR FIRST TWO SECONDS
(5) VARIES WITH TEMPERATURE
(6) 12 VOLTS 4T60 TRANS.
(7) 12 VOLTS WHEN COMMANDED "ON"
(8) OPEN CIRCUIT
(9) OPEN/GROUNDED CIRCUIT
(10) GROUNDED CIRCUIT
(11) LESS THAN 1 VOLT
* LESS THAN 5 VOLT (500 mV)

ECM CONNECTOR "F" (32 PIN GREEN)

PIN FUNCTION	CKT #	WIRE COLOR	COMPONENT CONNECTOR CAVITY	NORMAL VOLTAGES KEY "ON"	NORMAL VOLTAGES ENG RUN	CODES AFFECT	POSSIBLE SYMPTOMS FROM FAULTY CIRCUIT
GF1 A/C RELAY CONTROL	459	DK GRN/WHT	A/C CONTROL RELAY CONNECTOR "F"	"ON" 0* "OFF" B+	"ON" 0* "OFF" B+	NONE	INOPERATIVE A/C.
GF2 N/C							
GF3 N/C							
GF4 EGR SOLENOID #2	698	BRN	DIGITAL EGR SOLENOID CONNECTOR "B"	0	0 (7)	32	ROUGH IDLE, SPARK KNOCK, STALLS AFTER COLD START, SURGE DURING CRUISE. REFER TO SECTION "C7"
GF5 EGR SOLENOID #3	699	RED	DIGITAL EGR SOLENOID CONNECTOR "C"	0	0 (7)	32	ROUGH IDLE, SPARK KNOCK, STALLS AFTER COLD START, SURGE DURING CRUISE.
GF6 TCC CONTROL A/T SHIFT LIGHT MT	422	TAN/BLK	TCC SOLENOID CONNECTOR "D" ALDL CONNECTOR "F" I/P CONNECTOR "E"	0* B+	0* (6) B+	62	NO TCC. POOR FUEL ECONOMY, CHUGGLE OR SURGE CONDITION.
GF7 CANISTER PURGE CONTROL	428	DK GRN/YEL	CCP SOLENOID CONNECTOR "B"	0*	0*	NONE	FUEL LOSS OR FUEL VAPOR ODOR, POOR IDLE, STALLING, POOR DRIVEABILITY.
GF8 N/C							
GF9 ESC KNOCK SIGNAL	496	DK BLU	KNOCK SENSOR	2.5	2.5 (3)	43 (9)	LACK OF PERFORMANCE. SPARK KNOCK.
GF10 N/C							
GF11 N/C							
GF12 N/C							
GF13 TPS SIGNAL	417	DK BLU	TPS CONNECTOR "C"	29-98	29-98	22 (9)	LACK OF PERFORMANCE. ROUGH IDLE. SURGE. HIGH IDLE.
GF14 A/C PRESSURE SENSOR	380	GRY/RED	A/C PRESSURE SENSOR CONNECTOR "C"	(3)	(3)	66	NO A/C
GF15 MAP SIGNAL	432	LT GRN	MAP SENSOR CONNECTOR "B"	4.57	(3)	34 (9)	LACK OF PERFORMANCE. ROUGH IDLE. SURGE. REFER TO CHART C-1D
GF16 IAT SIGNAL	472	TAN	IAT SENSOR CONNECTOR "B"	(5)	(5)	25 (9)	POOR PERFORMANCE. HARD TO START.

(1) INCREASES WITH VEHICLE SPEED (MEASURE A/C SCALE)
(2) NORMAL OPERATING TEMPERATURE
(3) VARIES
(4) 12 VOLTS FOR FIRST TWO SECONDS
(5) VARIES WITH TEMPERATURE
(6) 12 VOLTS 4T60 TRANS.
(7) 12 VOLTS WHEN COMMANDED "ON"
(8) OPEN
(9) OPEN/GROUNDED CIRCUIT
(10) GROUNDED CIRCUIT
(11) LESS THAN 1 VOLT
* LESS THAN 5 VOLT (500 mV)

1990-92 3.1L (VIN T)

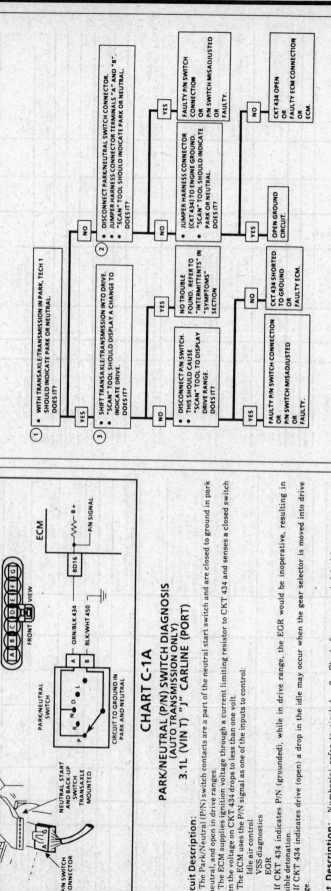

CHART C-1A

PARK/NEUTRAL (P/N) SWITCH DIAGNOSIS
(AUTO TRANSMISSION ONLY)
3.1L (VIN T) "J" CARLINE (PORT)

1. • WITH TRANSAXLE/TRANSMISSION IN PARK, TECH 1 SHOULD INDICATE PARK OR NEUTRAL. DOES IT?

3. • SHIFT TRANSAXLE/TRANSMISSION INTO DRIVE. "SCAN" TOOL SHOULD DISPLAY A CHANGE TO INDICATE DRIVE. DOES IT?

YES → • DISCONNECT P/N SWITCH. THIS SHOULD CAUSE "SCAN" TOOL TO DISPLAY DRIVE RANGE. DOES IT?

→ **YES** NO TROUBLE FOUND. REFER TO "INTERMITTENTS" IN "SYMPTOMS" SECTION

→ **NO** | **YES** FAULTY P/N SWITCH CONNECTION OR P/N SWITCH MISADJUSTED OR FAULTY. | **NO** CKT 434 SHORTED TO GROUND OR FAULTY ECM.

NO → ② • DISCONNECT PARK/NEUTRAL SWITCH CONNECTOR. • JUMPER HARNESS CONNECTOR TERMINALS "A" AND "B". • "SCAN" TOOL SHOULD INDICATE PARK OR NEUTRAL. DOES IT?

→ **YES** FAULTY P/N SWITCH CONNECTION OR P/N SWITCH MISADJUSTED OR FAULTY.

→ **NO** • JUMPER HARNESS CONNECTOR (CKT 434) TO ENGINE GROUND. • "SCAN" TOOL SHOULD INDICATE PARK OR NEUTRAL. DOES IT?

→ **YES** OPEN GROUND CIRCUIT.

→ **NO** CKT 434 OPEN OR FAULTY ECM CONNECTION OR ECM.

"AFTER REPAIRS," CONFIRM "CLOSED LOOP" OPERATION AND NO "SERVICE ENGINE SOON" LIGHT.

P/N SWITCH CONNECTOR

NEUTRAL START AND BACK-UP SWITCH TRANSAXLE MOUNTED

HARNESS CONNECTOR
(A B C D E F G)
FRONT VIEW

ECM
B+
P/N SIGNAL
BD16

PARK/NEUTRAL SWITCH
A — ORN/BLK 434
B — BLK/WHT 450
CIRCUIT TO GROUND IN PARK AND NEUTRAL

CHART C-1A

PARK/NEUTRAL (P/N) SWITCH DIAGNOSIS
(AUTO TRANSMISSION ONLY)
3.1L (VIN T) "J" CARLINE (PORT)

Circuit Description:

The Park/Neutral (P/N) switch contacts are a part of the neutral start switch and are closed to ground in park or neutral, and open in drive ranges.

The ECM supplies ignition voltage through a current limiting resistor to CKT 434 and senses a closed switch when the voltage on CKT 434 drops to less than one volt.

The ECM uses the P/N signal as one of the inputs to control:
- Idle air control
- VSS diagnostics
- EGR

If CKT 434 indicates P/N (grounded), while in drive range, the EGR would be inoperative, resulting in possible detonation.

If CKT 434 indicates drive (open) a drop in the idle may occur when the gear selector is moved into drive range.

Test Description: Number(s) refer to circled number(s) on the diagnostic chart.

1. Checks for a closed switch to ground in park position. Different makes of "Scan" tools will read P/N differently. Refer to tool operator's manual for type of display used for a specific tool.

2. Checks for an open switch in drive range.

3. Be sure "Scan" indicates drive, even while wiggling shifter, to test for an intermittent or misadjusted switch in drive range.

1990-92 3.1L (VIN T)

CHART C-1D

MANIFOLD ABSOLUTE PRESSURE (MAP) OUTPUT CHECK
3.1L (VIN T) "J" CARLINE (PORT)

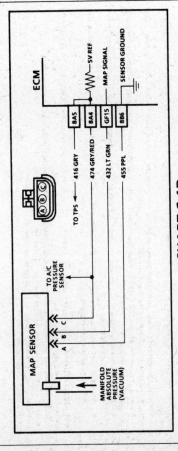

ECM

- 416 GRY — TO TPS
- 474 GRY/RED — 5V REF
- 432 LT GRN — MAP SIGNAL
- 455 PPL — SENSOR GROUND

(BA5, BA4, GF15, BB6)

MAP SENSOR — A B C — TO A/C PRESSURE SENSOR

MANIFOLD ABSOLUTE PRESSURE (VACUUM)

Circuit Description:

The Manifold Absolute Pressure (MAP) sensor measures the changes in the intake manifold pressure which result from engine load (intake manifold vacuum) and rpm changes; and converts these into a voltage output. The ECM sends a 5 volt reference voltage to the MAP sensor. As the manifold pressure changed, the output voltage of the sensor also changes. By monitoring the sensor output voltage, the ECM knows the manifold pressure. A lower pressure (low voltage) output voltage will be about 1 - 2 volts at idle. While higher pressure (high voltage) output voltage will be about 4 - 4.8 at Wide Open Throttle (WOT). The MAP sensor is also used, under certain conditions, to measure barometric pressure, allowing the ECM to make adjustments for different altitudes. The ECM used the MAP sensor to control fuel delivery and ignition timing.

Test Description: Number(s) refer to circled number(s) on the diagnostic chart.

⚡ Important
- Be sure to use the same Diagnostic Test Equipment for all measurements

1. When comparing "Scan" readings to a known good vehicle, it is important to compare vehicles that use a MAP sensor having the same color insert or having the same "Hot Stamped" number. See figures on facing page.

2. Applying 34 kPa (10" Hg) vacuum to the MAP sensor should cause the voltage to change. Subtract second reading from the first. Voltage value should be greater than 1.5 volts. Upon applying vacuum to the sensor, the change in voltage should be instantaneous. A slow voltage change indicates a faulty sensor.

3. Check vacuum hose to sensor for leaking or restriction. Be sure that no other vacuum devices are connected to the MAP hose.

NOTE: Make sure electrical connector remains securely fastened.

4. Disconnect sensor from bracket and twist sensor by hand (only) to check for intermittent connection. Output changes greater than .1 volt indicate a bad connector or connection If OK, replace sensor

---

CHART C-1D

MANIFOLD ABSOLUTE PRESSURE (MAP) OUTPUT CHECK
3.1L (VIN T) "J" CARLINE (PORT)

NOTE: THIS CHART ONLY APPLIES TO MAP SENSORS HAVING GREEN OR BLACK COLOR KEY INSERT (SEE BELOW).

① IGNITION "ON," ENGINE "OFF."
- TECH 1 SHOULD INDICATE A MAP SENSOR VOLTAGE.
- COMPARE THIS READING WITH THE READING OF A KNOWN GOOD VEHICLE. SEE FACING PAGE TEST DESCRIPTION, STEP 1.
- VOLTAGE READING SHOULD BE WITHIN, ± .4 VOLT.
- IS IT?

YES → ② / NO → REPLACE SENSOR.

② DISCONNECT AND PLUG VACUUM SOURCE TO MAP SENSOR.
- CONNECT A HAND VACUUM PUMP TO MAP SENSOR.
- START ENGINE.
- NOTE MAP SENSOR VOLTAGE.
- APPLY 34 kPa (10" Hg) OF VACUUM AND NOTE VOLTAGE CHANGE.
- SUBTRACT SECOND READING FROM THE FIRST. VOLTAGE VALUE SHOULD BE GREATER THAN 1.5 VOLTS.
- IS IT?

YES → ③ / NO → CHECK SENSOR CONNECTION. IF OK, REPLACE SENSOR.

③ NO TROUBLE FOUND. CHECK SENSOR VACUUM SOURCE FOR LEAKAGE OR RESTRICTION. BE SURE THIS SOURCE SUPPLIES VACUUM TO MAP SENSOR ONLY.

④ CHECK SENSOR CONNECTION. IF OK, REPLACE SENSOR.

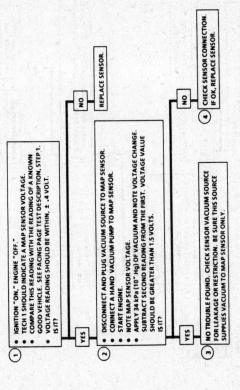

COLOR KEYED INSERT

Figure 1 - Color Key Insert

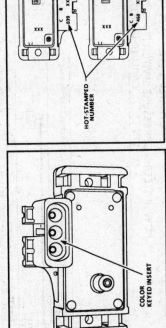

HOT-STAMPED NUMBER

039   460

Figure 2 - Hot-Stamped Number

"AFTER REPAIRS," CONFIRM "CLOSED LOOP" OPERATION AND NO "SERVICE ENGINE SOON" LIGHT.

1990-92 3.1L (VIN T)

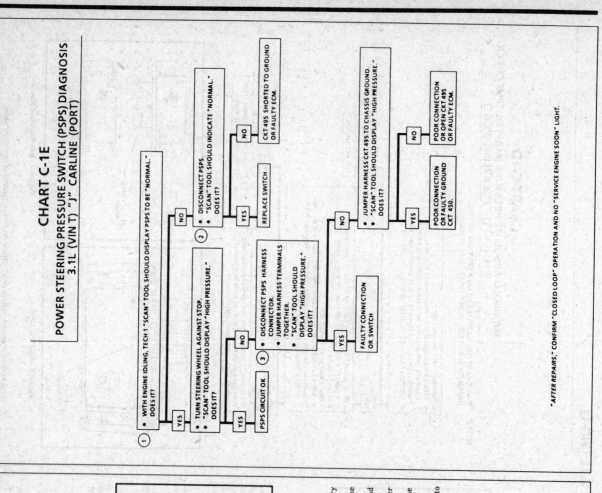

CHART C-1E

POWER STEERING PRESSURE SWITCH (PSPS) DIAGNOSIS
3.1L (VIN T) "J" CARLINE (PORT)

Circuit Description:

The Power Steering Pressure Switch (PSPS) is normally open to ground and CKT 495 will be near the battery voltage.

Turning the steering wheel increases power steering oil pressure and its load on an idling engine. The pressure switch will close before the load can cause an idle problem.

Closing the switch causes CKT 495 to read less than 1 volt. The ECM will increase the idle air rate and disengage the A/C relay.

- A pressure switch that will not close or an open CKT 495 or 450, may cause the engine to stop when power steering loads are high.
- A switch that will not open, or a CKT 495 shorted to ground, may affect idle quality and will cause the A/C relay to be de-energized.

Test Description: Number(s) refer to circled number(s) on the diagnostic chart.

1. Different makes of "Scan" tools may display the state of this switch in different ways. Refer to "Scan" tool operator's manual to determine how this input is indicated.

2. Checks to determine if CKT 495 is shorted to ground.

3. This should simulate a closed switch.

1990-92 3.1L (VIN T)

CHART C-2A
INJECTOR BALANCE TEST

The injector balance tester is a tool used to turn the injector on for a precise amount of time, thus spraying a measured amount of fuel into the manifold. This causes a drop in fuel rail pressure that we can record and compare between each injector. All injectors should have the same amount of pressure drop ($\pm$ 10 kPa). Any injector with a pressure drop that is 10 kPa (or more) greater or less than the average drop of the other injectors should be considered faulty and replaced.

STEP 1

Engine "cool down" period (10 minutes) is necessary to avoid irregular readings due to "Hot Soak" fuel boiling. With ignition "OFF" connect fuel gauge J 347301 or equivalent to fuel pressure tap. Wrap a shop towel around fitting while connecting gage to avoid fuel spillage.

Disconnect harness connectors at all injectors, and connect injector tester J 34730-3, or equivalent, to one injector. On Turbo equipped engines, use adaptor harness furnished with injector tester to energize injectors that are not accessible. Follow manufacturers instructions for use of adaptor harness. Ignition must be "OFF" at least 10 seconds to complete ECM shutdown cycle. Fuel pump should run about 2 seconds after ignition is turned "ON". At this point, insert clear tubing attached to vent valve into a suitable container and bleed air from gauge and hose to insure accurate gauge operation. Repeat this step until all air is bled from gauge.

STEP 2

Turn ignition "OFF" for 10 seconds and then "ON" again to get fuel pressure to its initial pressure reading. Record this initial pressure reading. Energize tester one time and note pressure drop at its lowest point (Disregard any slight pressure increase after drop hits low point.) By subtracting this second pressure reading from the initial pressure, we have the actual amount of injector pressure drop.

STEP 3

Repeat step 2 on each injector and compare the amount of drop. Usually, good injectors will have virtually the same drop. Retest any injector that has a pressure difference of 10 kPa, either more or less than the average of the other injectors on the engine. Replace any injector that also fails the retest. If the pressure drop of all injectors is within 10 kPa of this average, the injectors appear to be flowing properly. Reconnect them and review "Symptoms"

NOTE: *The entire test should not be repeated more than once without running the engine to prevent flooding. (This includes any retest on faulty injectors).*

CHART C-2A
INJECTOR BALANCE TEST
3.1L (VIN T) "J" CARLINE (PORT)

NOTE: The fuel pressure test

CHART A-7, should be completed prior to this test.

Step 1. If engine is at operating temperature, allow a 10 minute "cool down" period then connect fuel pressure gauge and injector tester.
1. Ignition "OFF".
2. Connect fuel pressure gauge and injector tester.
3. Ignition "ON".
4. Bleed off air in gauge. Repeat until all air is bled from gauge.

Step 2. Run test:
1. Ignition "OFF" for 10 seconds.
2. Ignition "ON". Record gauge pressure. (Pressure must hold steady, if not see the Fuel System diagnosis, Chart A-7.
3. Turn injector on, by depressing button on injector tester, and note pressure at the instant the gauge needle stops.

Step 3.
1. Repeat step 2 on all injectors and record pressure drop on each.
Retest injectors that appear faulty (Any injectors that have a 10 kPa difference, either more or less, in pressure from the average). If no problem is found, review "Symptoms" Section

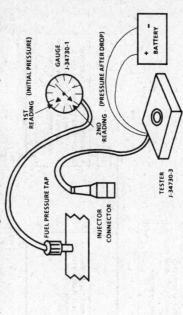

— EXAMPLE —

CYLINDER	1	2	3	4	5	6
1ST READING	225	225	225	225	225	225
2ND READING	100	100	100	90	100	115
AMOUNT OF DROP	125	125	125	135	125	110
	OK	OK	OK	FAULTY, RICH (TOO MUCH) (FUEL DROP)	OK	FAULTY, LEAN (TOO LITTLE) (FUEL DROP)

1990-92 3.1L (VIN T)

CHART C-2B
IDLE AIR CONTROL (IAC) CIRCUIT
3.1L (VIN T) "J" CARLINE (PORT)

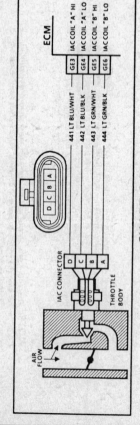

ECM

GE3	IAC COIL "A" HI
GE4	IAC COIL "A" LO
GE5	IAC COIL "B" HI
GE6	IAC COIL "B" LO

441 LT BLU/WHT
442 LT BLU/BLK
443 LT GRN/WHT
444 LT GRN/BLK

IAC CONNECTOR
D C B A

THROTTLE BODY
AIR FLOW

Circuit Description:

The ECM controls engine idle speed with the Idle Air Control (IAC) valve. To increase idle speed, the ECM retracts the IAC valve pintle away from its seat, allowing more air to bypass the throttle bore. To decrease idle speed, it extends the IAC valve pintle towards its seat, reducing bypass air flow. A "Scan" tool will read the ECM commands to the IAC valve in counts. Higher the counts indicate more air bypass (higher idle). The lower the counts indicate less air is allowed to bypass (lower idle).

Test Description: Number(s) refer to circled number(s) on the diagnostic chart.

1. The Tech 1 rpm control mode is used to extend and retract the IAC valve. The valve should move smoothly within the specified range. If the idle speed is commanded (IAC extended) too low (below 700 rpm), the engine may stall. This may be normal and would not indicate a problem. Retracting the IAC beyond its controlled range (above 1500 rpm) will cause a delay before the rpm's start dropping. This too is normal.

2. This test uses the Tech 1 to command the IAC controlled idle speed. The ECM issues commands to obtain commanded idle speed. The node lights each should flash red and green to indicate a good circuit as the ECM issues commands. While the sequence of color is not important if either light is "OFF" or does not flash red and green, check the circuits for faults, beginning with poor terminal contacts.

Diagnostic Aids:

A slow, unstable or fast idle may be caused by a non-IAC system problem that cannot be overcome by the IAC "Scan" tool. Out of control range IAC "Scan" tool counts will be above 60 if idle is too low and zero counts if idle is too high. The following checks should be made to repair a non-IAC system problem:

• Vacuum Leak (High Idle)

If idle is too high, stop the engine. Fully extend (low) IAC with tester. Start engine. If idle speed is above 800 rpm, locate and correct vacuum leak including PCV system. Also check for binding of throttle blade or linkage.

• System too lean (High Air/Fuel Ratio)

The idle speed may be too high or too low. Engine speed may vary up and down and disconnecting the IAC valve does not help. Code 44 may be set. "Scan" O2 voltage will be less than 300 mV (.3 volt). Check for low regulated fuel pressure, water in the fuel or a restricted injector.

• System too rich (Low Air/Fuel Ratio)

The idle speed will be too low. "Scan" tool IAC counts will usually be above 80. System is obviously rich and may exhibit black smoke in exhaust. "Scan" tool O2 voltage will be fixed above 800 mV (.8 volt).

Check for high fuel pressure, leaking or sticking injector. Silicone contaminated O2 sensors "Scan" voltage will be slow to respond.

• Throttle Body

Remove IAC valve and inspect bore for foreign material.

• IAC Valve Electrical Connections

IAC valve connections should be carefully checked for proper contact.

• PCV Valve

An incorrect or faulty PCV valve may result in an incorrect idle speed.

Refer to "Rough, Unstable, Incorrect Idle or Stalling" in "Symptoms," Section "6E3-B".

If intermittent poor driveability or idle symptoms are resolved by disconnecting the IAC, carefully recheck connections, valve terminal resistance or replace IAC.

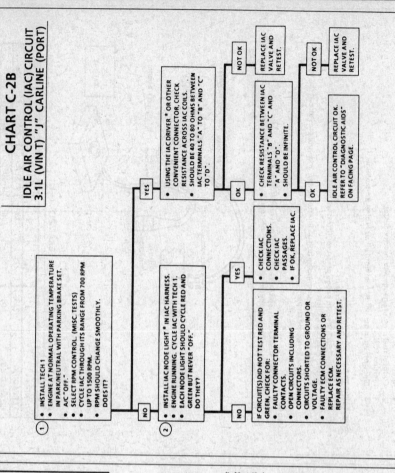

CHART C-2B

**IDLE AIR CONTROL (IAC) CIRCUIT
3.1L (VIN T) "J" CARLINE (PORT)**

(1)
• INSTALL TECH 1
• ENGINE AT NORMAL OPERATING TEMPERATURE IN PARK/NEUTRAL WITH PARKING BRAKE SET.
• A/C "OFF".
• SELECT RPM CONTROL. (MISC. TESTS)
• CYCLE IAC THROUGH ITS RANGE FROM 700 RPM UP TO 1500 RPM.
• RPM SHOULD CHANGE SMOOTHLY. DOES IT?

NO → (2)

YES → USING THE IAC DRIVER * OR OTHER CONVENIENT CONNECTOR, CHECK RESISTANCE ACROSS IAC COILS. SHOULD BE 40 TO 80 OHMS BETWEEN IAC TERMINALS "A" TO "B" AND "C" TO "D".

NOT OK → REPLACE IAC VALVE AND RETEST.

OK → CHECK RESISTANCE BETWEEN IAC TERMINALS "B" AND "C" AND "A" AND "D". SHOULD BE INFINITE.

NOT OK → REPLACE IAC VALVE AND RETEST.

OK → IDLE AIR CONTROL CIRCUIT OK. REFER TO "DIAGNOSTIC AIDS" ON FACING PAGE.

(2)
• INSTALL IAC NODE LIGHT * IN IAC HARNESS.
• ENGINE RUNNING. CYCLE IAC WITH TECH 1.
• EACH NODE LIGHT SHOULD CYCLE RED AND GREEN BUT NEVER "OFF."
DO THEY?

NO → IF CIRCUIT(S) DID NOT TEST RED AND GREEN, CHECK FOR:
• FAULTY CONNECTOR TERMINAL CONTACTS.
• OPEN CIRCUITS INCLUDING CONNECTORS.
• CIRCUITS SHORTED TO GROUND OR VOLTAGE.
• FAULTY ECM CONNECTIONS OR REPLACE ECM.
REPAIR AS NECESSARY AND RETEST.

YES → CHECK IAC CONNECTIONS.
CHECK IAC PASSAGES.
IF OK, REPLACE IAC.

* IAC DRIVER AND NODE LIGHT REQUIRED KIT 222-L FROM: CONCEPT TECHNOLOGY, INC. J37027 FROM: KENT-MOORE, INC.

CLEAR CODES, CONFIRM "CLOSED LOOP" OPERATION, NO "SERVICE ENGINE SOON" LIGHT, PERFORM IAC RESET PROCEDURE PER APPLICABLE SERVICE MANUAL AND VERIFY CONTROLLED IDLE SPEED IS CORRECT.

1990-92 3.1L (VIN T)

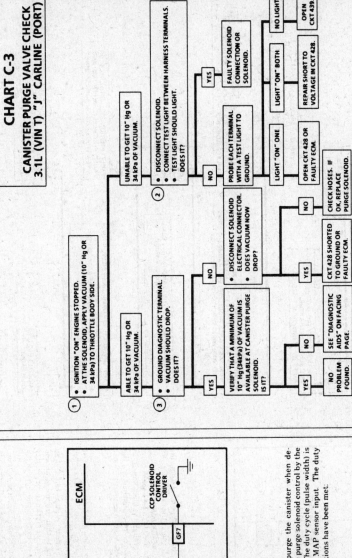

CHART C-3

CANISTER PURGE VALVE CHECK
3.1L (VIN T) "J" CARLINE (PORT)

① IGNITION "ON" ENGINE STOPPED.
• AT THE SOLENOID, APPLY VACUUM (10" Hg OR 34 kPa) TO THROTTLE BODY SIDE.

UNABLE TO GET 10" Hg OR 34 kPa OF VACUUM.

ABLE TO GET 10" Hg OR 34 kPa OF VACUUM.

② DISCONNECT SOLENOID.
• CONNECT TEST LIGHT BETWEEN HARNESS TERMINALS.
• TEST LIGHT SHOULD LIGHT.
DOES IT?

   YES → FAULTY SOLENOID CONNECTION OR SOLENOID.

   NO → PROBE EACH TERMINAL WITH A TEST LIGHT TO GROUND.

     LIGHT "ON" ONE → OPEN CKT 428 OR FAULTY ECM.

     LIGHT "ON" BOTH → REPAIR SHORT TO VOLTAGE IN CKT 428.

     NO LIGHT → OPEN CKT 439.

③ GROUND DIAGNOSTIC TERMINAL.
• VACUUM SHOULD DROP.
DOES IT?

   NO → DISCONNECT SOLENOID ELECTRICAL CONNECTOR. DOES VACUUM NOW DROP?

     YES → CKT 428 SHORTED TO GROUND OR FAULTY ECM.

     NO → CHECK HOSES. IF OK, REPLACE PURGE SOLENOID.

   YES → VERIFY THAT A MINIMUM OF 10" Hg (34 kPa) OF VACUUM IS AVAILABLE AT CANISTER PURGE SOLENOID. IS IT?

     YES → NO PROBLEM FOUND.

     NO → SEE "DIAGNOSTIC AIDS" ON FACING PAGE.

"AFTER REPAIRS," CONFIRM "CLOSED LOOP" OPERATION AND NO "SERVICE ENGINE SOON" LIGHT.

ECM

CCP SOLENOID CONTROL DRIVER

GF7

428 DK GRN/YEL

E   39 PNK/BLK

I/P CONNECTOR

GAUGE 10 AMP

IGN

TO CANISTER

PORTED MANIFOLD VACUUM

N.O.

B   A

CANISTER PURGE SOLENOID

I/P HARNESS CONNECTOR 23-WAY (FRONT VIEW)

CHART C-3

CANISTER PURGE VALVE CHECK
3.1L (VIN T) "J" CARLINE (PORT)

Circuit Description:

Canister purge is controlled by a solenoid that allows manifold vacuum to purge the canister when de-energized. The ECM supplies a ground to energize the solenoid (purge "OFF"). The purge solenoid control by the ECM is pulse width modulated (turned "ON" and "OFF" several times a second) The duty cycle (pulse width) is determined by the amount of air flow and the engine vacuum as determined by the MAP sensor input. The duty cycle is calculated by the ECM and the output commanded when the following conditions have been met:

• Engine run time after start more than 3 minutes
• Coolant temperature above 80°C
• Vehicle speed above 5 mph
• Throttle "OFF" idle (about 3%)

Also, if the diagnostic "test" terminal is grounded with the engine stopped, the purge solenoid is de-energized (purge "ON").

Test Description: Number(s) refer to circled number(s) on the diagnostic chart.

1. Checks to see if the solenoid is opened or closed. The solenoid is normally energized in this step, so it should be closed.

2. Checks for a complete circuit. Normally there is ignition voltage on CKT 39 and the ECM provides a ground on CKT 428.

3. Completes functional check by grounding test terminal. This should normally de-energize the solenoid opening the valve which should allow the vacuum to drop (purge "ON").

1990-92 3.1L (VIN T)

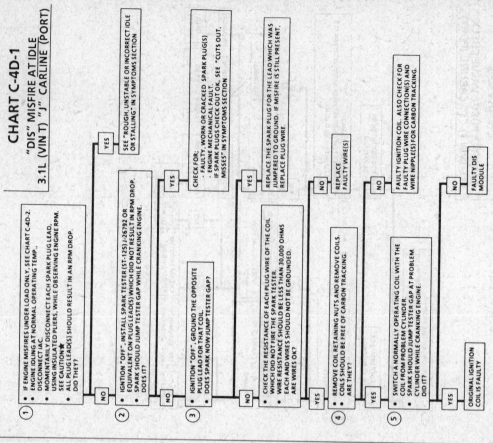

CHART C-4D-1
"DIS" MISFIRE AT IDLE
3.1L (VIN T) "J" CARLINE (PORT)

(1)
- IF ENGINE MISFIRES UNDER LOAD ONLY, SEE CHART C-4D-2.
- ENGINE IDLING AT NORMAL OPERATING TEMP.,
- DISCONNECT IAC.
- MISMOMENTARILY DISCONNECT EACH SPARK PLUG LEAD, USING INSULATED PLIERS, WHILE OBSERVING ENGINE RPM. SEE CAUTION★
- ALL PLUG LEAD(S) SHOULD RESULT IN AN RPM DROP. DID THEY?

→ NO

→ YES → SEE "ROUGH, UNSTABLE OR INCORRECT IDLE OR STALLING" IN SYMPTOMS SECTION

(2)
- IGNITION "OFF". INSTALL SPARK TESTER (ST-125) OR EQUIVALENT ON PLUG LEAD(S) WHICH DID NOT RESULT IN RPM DROP.
- SPARK SHOULD JUMP TESTER GAP WHILE CRANKING ENGINE. DOES IT?

→ NO

→ YES → CHECK FOR:
- FAULTY, WORN OR CRACKED SPARK PLUG(S)
- ENGINE MECHANICAL FAULT.
IF SPARK PLUGS CHECK OUT OK, SEE "CUTS OUT, MISSES" IN SYMPTOMS SECTION

(3)
- IGNITION "OFF". GROUND THE OPPOSITE PLUG LEAD FOR THAT COIL.
- DOES SPARK NOW JUMP TESTER GAP?

→ YES → REPLACE THE SPARK PLUG FOR THE LEAD WHICH WAS JUMPERED TO GROUND. IF MISFIRE IS STILL PRESENT, REPLACE PLUG WIRE.

→ NO

- CHECK THE RESISTANCE OF EACH PLUG WIRE OF THE COIL WHICH DID NOT FIRE THE SPARK TESTER.
- WIRE RESISTANCE SHOULD BE LESS THAN 30,000 OHMS EACH AND WIRES SHOULD NOT BE GROUNDED.
- ARE WIRES OK?

→ NO → REPLACE FAULTY WIRE(S)

→ YES

(4)
- REMOVE COIL RETAINING NUTS AND REMOVE COILS.
- COILS SHOULD BE FREE OF CARBON TRACKING. ARE THEY?

→ NO → FAULTY IGNITION COIL. ALSO CHECK FOR FAULTY PLUG WIRE CONNECTION(S) AND WIRE NIPPLE(S) FOR CARBON TRACKING.

→ YES

(5)
- SWITCH A NORMALLY OPERATING COIL WITH THE COIL FROM PROBLEM CYLINDER.
- SPARK SHOULD JUMP TESTER GAP AT PROBLEM CYLINDER WHILE CRANKING ENGINE. DID IT?

→ YES → ORIGINAL IGNITION COIL IS FAULTY

→ NO → FAULTY DIS MODULE

★CAUTION: When handling secondary spark plug leads with engine running, insulated pliers must be used and care exercised to prevent a possible electrical shock.

"AFTER REPAIRS," CONFIRM "CLOSED LOOP" OPERATION AND NO "SERVICE ENGINE SOON" LIGHT.

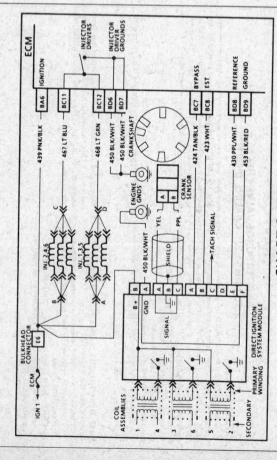

CHART C-4D-1
"DIS" MISFIRE AT IDLE
3.1L (VIN T) "J" CARLINE (PORT)

Circuit Description:

The Direct Ignition System (DIS) uses a waste spark method of distribution. In this type of system, the ignition module triggers the #1/4 coil pair resulting in both #1 and #4 spark plugs firing at the same time. #1 cylinder is on the compression stroke at the same time #4 is on the exhaust stroke, resulting in a lower energy requirement to fire #4 spark plug. This leaves the remainder of the high voltage to be used to fire #1 spark plug. On this application, the crank sensor is mounted on the engine block and protrudes through the block to within approximately .050" of the crankshaft reluctor. Since the reluctor is a machined portion of the crankshaft and the crank sensor is mounted in a fixed position on the block, timing adjustments are not possible or necessary.

Test Description: Number(s) refer to circled number(s) on the diagnostic chart.

1. If the "Misfire" complaint exists under load only, diagnostic CHART C-4D-2 must be used. Engine rpm should drop approximately equally on all plug leads.

2. A spark test such as a ST-125 must be used because it is essential to verify adequate available secondary voltage at the spark plug (25,000 volts).

3. If the spark jumps the test gap after grounding the opposite plug wire, it indicates excessive resistance in the plug which was bypassed

A faulty or poor connection at that plug could also result in the miss condition. Also check for carbon deposits inside the spark plug boot.

4. If carbon tracking is evident, replace coil and be sure plug wires relating to that coil are clean and tight. Excessive wire resistance or faulty connections could have caused the coil to be damaged.

5. If the no spark condition follows the suspected coil, that coil is faulty. Otherwise, the ignition module is the cause of no spark. This test could also be performed by substituting a known good coil for the one causing the no spark condition.

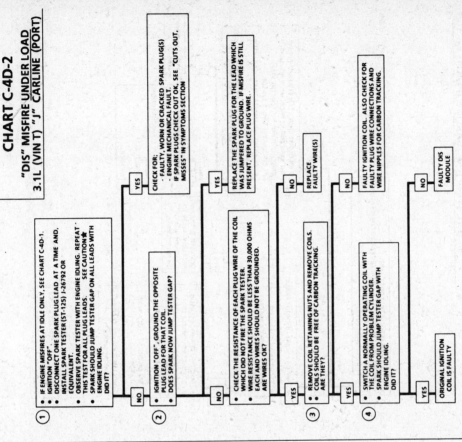

CHART C-4D-2
"DIS" MISFIRE UNDER LOAD
3.1L (VIN T) "J" CARLINE (PORT)

(1)
- IF ENGINE MISFIRES AT IDLE ONLY, SEE CHART C-4D-1.
- IGNITION "OFF".
- DISCONNECT ONE SPARK PLUG LEAD AT A TIME AND, INSTALL SPARK TESTER (ST-125) J-26792 OR EQUIVALENT.
- OBSERVE SPARK TESTER WITH ENGINE IDLING. REPEAT THIS TEST FOR ALL PLUG LEADS.   SEE CAUTION★
- SPARK SHOULD JUMP TESTER GAP ON ALL LEADS WITH ENGINE IDLING.
DID IT?

→ YES → CHECK FOR:
- FAULTY, WORN OR CRACKED SPARK PLUG(S)
- ENGINE MECHANICAL FAULT.
IF SPARK PLUGS CHECK OUT OK, SEE "CUTS OUT, MISSES" IN SYMPTOMS SECTION

↓ NO

(2)
- IGNITION "OFF", GROUND THE OPPOSITE PLUG LEAD FOR THAT COIL.
- DOES SPARK NOW JUMP TESTER GAP?

→ YES → REPLACE THE SPARK PLUG FOR THE LEAD WHICH WAS JUMPERED TO GROUND. IF MISFIRE IS STILL PRESENT, REPLACE PLUG WIRE.

↓ NO

- CHECK THE RESISTANCE OF EACH PLUG WIRE OF THE COIL WHICH DID NOT FIRE THE SPARK TESTER.
- WIRE RESISTANCE SHOULD BE LESS THAN 30,000 OHMS EACH AND WIRES SHOULD NOT BE GROUNDED.
ARE WIRES OK?

→ NO → REPLACE FAULTY WIRE(S)

↓ YES

(3)
- REMOVE COIL RETAINING NUTS AND REMOVE COILS. COILS SHOULD BE FREE OF CARBON TRACKING. ARE THEY?

→ NO → FAULTY IGNITION COIL. ALSO CHECK FOR FAULTY PLUG WIRE CONNECTIONS AND WIRE NIPPLES FOR CARBON TRACKING.

↓ YES

(4)
- SWITCH A NORMALLY OPERATING COIL WITH THE COIL FROM PROBLEM CYLINDER.
- SPARK SHOULD JUMP TESTER GAP WITH ENGINE IDLING.
DID IT?

→ NO → FAULTY DIS MODULE

↓ YES

ORIGINAL IGNITION COIL IS FAULTY

★CAUTION: When handling secondary spark plug leads with engine running, insulated pliers must be used and care exercised to prevent a possible electrical shock.

"AFTER REPAIRS," CONFIRM "CLOSED LOOP" OPERATION AND NO "SERVICE ENGINE SOON" LIGHT.

1990-92 3.1L (VIN T)

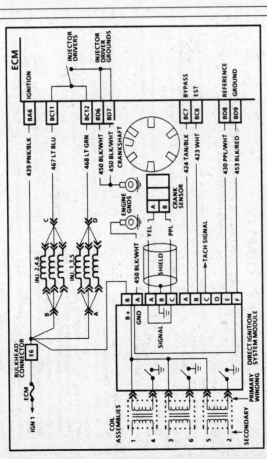

CHART C-4D-2
"DIS" MISFIRE UNDER LOAD
3.1L (VIN T) "J" CARLINE (PORT)

Circuit Description:

The Direct Ignition System (DIS) uses a waste spark method of distribution. In this type of system, the ignition module triggers the #1/4 coil pair resulting in both #1 and #4 spark plugs firing at the same time. #1 cylinder is on the compression stroke at the same time #4 is on the exhaust stroke, resulting in a lower energy requirement to fire #4 spark plug. This leaves the remainder of the high voltage to be used to fire #1 spark plug. On this application, the crank sensor is mounted to the engine block and protrudes through the block to within approximately .050" of the crankshaft reluctor. Since the reluctor is a machined portion of the crankshaft and the crank sensor is mounted in a fixed position on the block, timing adjustments are not possible or necessary.

Test Description: Number(s) refer to circled number(s) on the diagnostic chart.

1. If the "Misfire" complaint exists at idle only, diagnostic CHART C-4D-1 must be used. A spark tester such as a ST-125 must be used because it is essential to verify adequate available secondary voltage at the spark plug (25,000 volts). Spark should jump the test gap on all 4 leads. This simulates a "load" condition.
2. If the spark jumps the tester gap after grounding the opposite plug wire, it indicates excessive resistance in the plug which was bypassed.

A faulty or poor connection at that plug could also result in the miss condition. Also check for carbon deposits inside the spark plug boot.

3. If carbon tracing is evident, replace coil and be sure plug wires relating to that coil are clean and tight. Excessive wire resistance or faulty connections could have caused the coil to be damaged.
4. If the no spark condition follows the suspected coil, that coil is faulty. Otherwise, the ignition module is the cause of no spark. This test could also be performed by substituting a known good coil for the one causing the no spark condition.

1990-92 3.1L (VIN T)

CHART C-5
ELECTRONIC SPARK CONTROL (ESC) SYSTEM CHECK
3.1L (VIN T) "J" CARLINE (PORT)

① IF CODE 43 IS SET, USE THE CODE CHART.
ENGINE MUST BE IDLING AT NORMAL OPERATING TEMPERATURE.
• USE TECH 1 TO OBSERVE KNOCK SIGNAL.
IS KNOCK INDICATED?

NO → ② TAP ON ENGINE LIFT HOOK BRACKET WHILE OBSERVING KNOCK SIGNAL. TECH 1 SHOULD INDICATE KNOCK WHILE TAPPING ON BRACKET. DOES IT?

YES → ③ IF AN ENGINE KNOCK CAN BE HEARD, REPAIR THE BASIC ENGINE PROBLEM. IF NO AUDIBLE KNOCK IS HEARD, FOLLOW THE STEPS:
• DISCONNECT KNOCK SENSOR.
• CONNECT VOLTMETER TO KNOCK SENSOR AND ENGINE GROUND.
• SET VOLTMETER ON 2 VOLT AC SCALE.
IS A SIGNAL INDICATED ON VOLTMETER?

YES → REPLACE KNOCK SENSOR.

NO → CHECK CKT 496 FOR BEING NEAR A SPARK PLUG WIRE OR A FAULTY ECM CONNECTION OR FAULTY ECM OR MEM-CAL.

② YES → SYSTEM IS OPERATING PROPERLY. REFER TO "DIAGNOSTIC AIDS" ON FACING PAGE.

② NO → ④ DISCONNECT KNOCK SENSOR. CONNECT VOLTMETER TO KNOCK SENSOR AND ENGINE GROUND. SET VOLTMETER ON 2 VOLT AC SCALE. TAP ON ENGINE BLOCK NEAR SENSOR. IS A SIGNAL INDICATED ON VOLTMETER WHILE TAPPING ON ENGINE BLOCK?

YES → REPLACE MEM-CAL OR ECM.

NO → REPLACE KNOCK SENSOR.

"AFTER REPAIRS," CONFIRM "CLOSED LOOP" OPERATION AND NO "SERVICE ENGINE SOON" LIGHT.

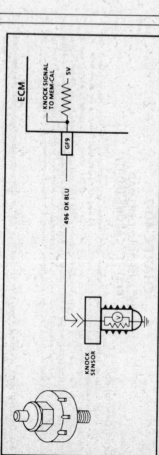

CHART C-5
ELECTRONIC SPARK CONTROL (ESC) SYSTEM CHECK
3.1L (VIN T) "J" CARLINE (PORT)

Circuit Description:

The knock sensor is used to detect engine detonation and the ECM will retard the electronic spark timing based on the signal being received. The circuitry, within the knock sensor, causes the ECMs 5 volts to be pulled down so that under a no knock condition, CKT 496 would measure about 2.5 volts. The knock sensor produces an A/C signal, which rides on the 2.5 volts DC voltage. The amplitude and frequency are dependent upon the knock level.

The MEM-CAL used with this engine contains the functions which were part of remotely mounted ESC modules used on other GM vehicles. The ESC portion of the MEM-CAL then sends a signal to other parts of the ECM which adjusts the spark timing to retard the spark and reduce the detonation.

Test Description: Number(s) refer to circled number(s) on the diagnostic chart.

1. With engine idling, there should not be a knock signal present at the ECM, because detonation is not likely under a no load condition.

2. Tapping on the engine lift bracket should simulate a knock signal to determine if the sensor is capable of detecting detonation. If no knock is detected, try tapping on engine block closer to sensor before replacing sensor.

3. If the engine has an internal problem which is creating a knock, the knock sensor may be responding to the internal failure.

4. This test determines if the knock sensor is faulty or if the ESC portion of the MEM-CAL is faulty. If it is determined that the MEM-CAL is faulty, be sure that it is properly installed and latched into place. If not properly installed, repair and retest.

Diagnostic Aids:

While observing knock signal on the "Scan," there should be an indication that knock is present, when detonation can be heard. Detonation is most likely to occur under high engine load conditions.

1990-92 3.1L (VIN T)

CHART C-7

EXHAUST GAS RECIRCULATION (EGR) FLOW CHECK
3.1L (VIN T) "J" CARLINE (PORT)

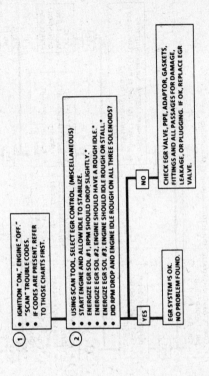

TOP VIEW OF EGR VALVE

ECM

EGR #3 — GF5 — 699 RED
EGR #1 — GE9 — 697 LT BLU
EGR #2 — GF4 — 698 BRN

39 PNK/BLK

10 AMP
GAUGE FUSE

E
CONN
UP

TO IGNITION

CHART C-7

EXHAUST GAS RECIRCULATION (EGR) FLOW CHECK
3.1L (VIN T) "J" CARLINE (PORT)

Circuit Description:

The digital Exhaust Gas Recirculation (EGR) valve is designed to accurately supply EGR to an engine independent of intake manifold vacuum. The valve controls EGR flow from the exhaust to the intake manifold through three orifices which increment in size to produce seven combinations. When a solenoid is energized, the armature with attached shaft and swivel pintle is lifted opening the orifice.

The flow accuracy is dependent on metering orifice size only, which results in improved control.

Test Description: Number(s) refer to circled number(s) on the diagnostic chart.

1. Codes should be diagnosed using appropriate chart before preparing a functional check.

2. This step activates each solenoid individually. As you energize #1 or #2 solenoid, the engine rpm should drop. #3 solenoid has the large port and may stall the engine when energized.

NOTE: If the digital Exhaust Gas Recirculation (EGR) valve shows signs of excessive heat, a melted condition. Check the exhaust system for blockage (possibly a plugged converter) using the procedure found on CHART B-1. If the exhaust system is restricted, repair the cause, one of which might be an injector which is open due to one of the following: a. stuck, b. grounded driver circuit, c. possibly defective ECM. If this condition is found, the oil should be checked for possible fuel contamination.

1.
- IGNITION "ON," ENGINE "OFF."
- "SCAN" TROUBLE CODES.
- IF CODES ARE PRESENT, REFER TO THOSE CHARTS FIRST.

2.
- USING SCAN TOOL, SELECT EGR CONTROL. (MISCELLANEOUS)
- START ENGINE AND ALLOW IDLE TO STABILIZE.
- ENERGIZE EGR SOL. #1, RPM SHOULD DROP SLIGHTLY.*
- ENERGIZE EGR SOL. #2, ENGINE SHOULD HAVE A ROUGH IDLE.*
- ENERGIZE EGR SOL. #3, ENGINE SHOULD IDLE ROUGH OR STALL.*
- DID RPM DROP AND ENGINE IDLE ROUGH ON ALL THREE SOLENOIDS?

YES
EGR SYSTEM IS OK. NO PROBLEM FOUND.

NO
CHECK EGR VALVE, PIPE, ADAPTOR, GASKETS, FITTINGS AND ALL PASSAGES FOR DAMAGE, LEAKAGE, OR PLUGGING. IF OK, REPLACE EGR VALVE.

* THESE STEPS MUST BE DONE VERY QUICKLY, AS THE ECM WILL ADJUST THE IDLE AIR CONTROL VALVE TO CORRECT IDLE SPEED.

* "AFTER REPAIRS," CONFIRM "CLOSED LOOP" OPERATION AND NO "SERVICE ENGINE SOON" LIGHT.

1990-92 3.1L (VIN T)

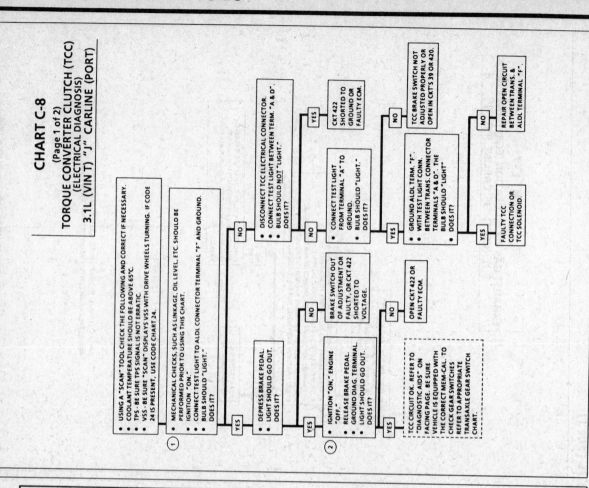

CHART C-8
(Page 1 of 2)

**TORQUE CONVERTER CLUTCH (TCC)
(ELECTRICAL DIAGNOSIS)
3.1L (VIN T) "J" CARLINE (PORT)**

Circuit Description:

The purpose of the automatic transmission Torque Converter Clutch (TCC) feature is to eliminate the power loss of the torque converter when the vehicle is in a cruise condition. This allows the convenience of the automatic transmission and the fuel economy of a manual transmission. The heart of the system is a solenoid located inside the automatic transmission which is controlled by the ECM.

When the solenoid coil is activated ("ON"), the torque converter clutch is applied which results in straight through mechanical coupling from the engine to transmission. When the transmission solenoid is deactivated, the torque converter clutch is released, which allows the torque converter to operate in the conventional manner (fluidic coupling between engine and transmission).

The TCC will engage on a warm engine under given road load in 3rd gear. TCC will engage when:

- Brake switch closed
- Coolant temperature is above 65°C
- Vehicle speed above a calibrated value (about 28 mph 45km/h)
- Throttle position not changing, indicating a steady speed

Test Description: Number(s) refer to circled number(s) on the diagnostic chart.

1. This test checks the continuity of the TCC circuit from the fuse to the ALDL connector.
2. When the brake pedal is released, the light should come back "ON" and then go "OFF" when the diagnostic terminal is grounded. This tests CKT 422 and the TCC driver in the ECM.

Diagnostic Aids:

A "Scan" tool only indicates when the ECM has turned "ON" the TCC driver and this does not confirm that the TCC has engaged. To determine if TCC is functioning properly, engine rpm should decrease when the "Scan" indicates the TCC driver has turned "ON." A thermostat that is stuck open or opens at too low a temperature may result in an inoperative TCC.

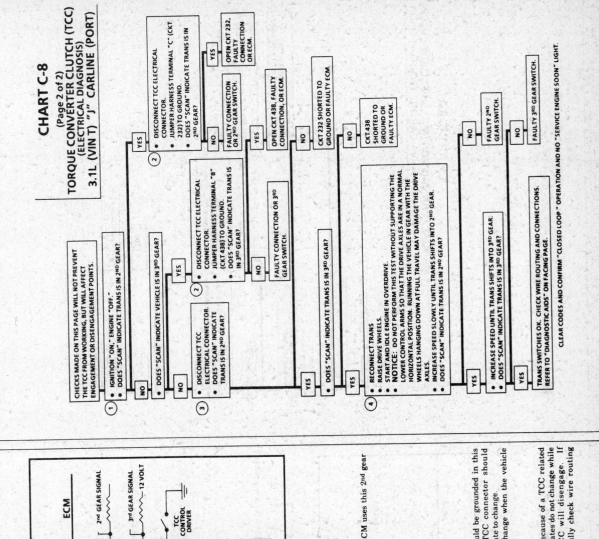

CHART C-8
(Page 2 of 2)
TORQUE CONVERTER CLUTCH (TCC)
(ELECTRICAL DIAGNOSIS)
3.1L (VIN T) "J" CARLINE (PORT)

1990-92 3.1L (VIN T)

CHART C-8
(Page 2 of 2)
TORQUE CONVERTER CLUTCH (TCC)
(ELECTRICAL DIAGNOSIS)
3.1L (VIN T) "J" CARLINE (PORT)

Circuit Description:

The 2nd gear signal switch in this vehicle should be open in 2nd and 3rd gear. The ECM uses this 2nd gear signal to disengage the Torque Converter Clutch (TCC) when going into a downshift.

The 3rd gear switch should be open in 3rd gear.

1st Gear	= 2nd gear switch open
	= 3rd gear signal switch closed
2nd Gear	= 2nd gear switch closed
	= 3rd gear signal switch closed
3rd Gear	= 2nd gear signal switch opens
	= 3rd gear signal switch opens

Test Description: Number(s) refer to circled number(s) on the diagnostic chart.

1. Some "Scan" tools display the state of these switches in different ways. Be familiar with the type of tool being used. Since both switches should be in the closed state during this test, the tool should read the same for either the 2nd or 3rd gear switch.

2. Determines whether the switch or signal circuit is open. The circuit can be checked for an open by measuring the voltage (with a voltmeter) at the TCC connector (should be about 12 volts).

3. Because the switch(s) should be grounded in this step, disconnecting the TCC connector should cause the "Scan" switch state to change.

4. The switch state should change when the vehicle shifts into 2nd gear.

Diagnostic Aids:

If vehicle is road tested because of a TCC related problem, be sure the switch states do not change while in 3rd gear because the TCC will disengage. If switches change state, carefully check wire routing and connections.

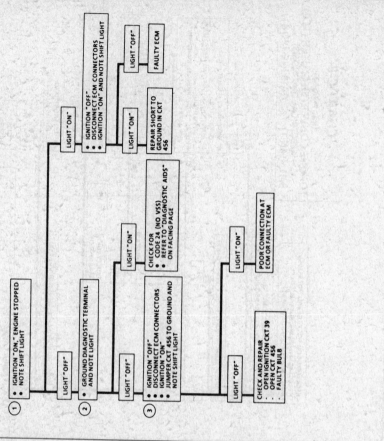

CHART C-8A

MANUAL TRANSMISSION (M/T) SHIFT LIGHT CHECK
3.1L (VIN T) "J" CARLINE (PORT)

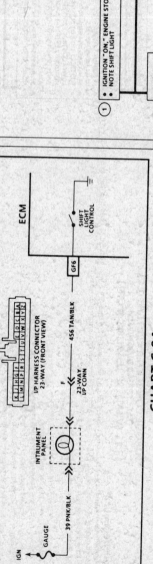

CHART C-8A

MANUAL TRANSMISSION (M/T) SHIFT LIGHT CHECK
3.1L (VIN T) "J" CARLINE (PORT)

Circuit Description:

The shift light indicates the best transmission shift point for maximum fuel economy. The light is controlled by the ECM and is turned "ON" by grounding CKT 422.

The ECM uses information from the following inputs to control the shift light.

- Coolant temperature must be above 16°C (61°F)
- TPS above 4%
- VSS
- Rpm above about 1900
- Air Flow - The ECM uses rpm, MAP and VSS to calculate what gear the vehicle is in.

It's this calculation that determines when the shift light should be turned "ON." The shift light will only stay "ON" 5 seconds after the conditions were met to turn it "ON."

Test Description: Number(s) refer to circled number(s) on the diagnostic chart.

1. This should not turn "ON" the shift light. If the light is "ON," there is a short to ground in CKT 456 wiring or a fault in the ECM.

2. When the diagnostic terminal is grounded, the ECM should ground CKT 456 and the shift light should come "ON."

3. This checks the shift light circuit up to the ECM connector. If the shift light illuminates, then the ECM connector is faulty or the ECM does not have the ability to ground the circuit or has incorrect or faulty PROM.

Diagnostic Aids:

A loss of vehicle speed input to the ECM should set a Code 24.

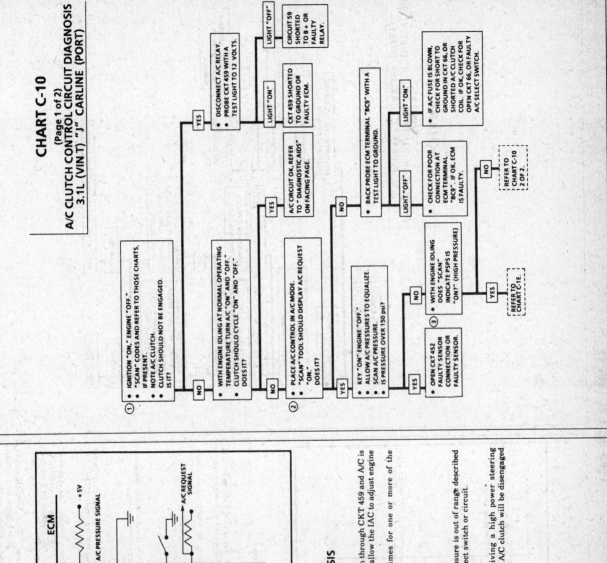

1990-92 3.1L (VIN T)

CHART C-10
(Page 1 of 2)
A/C CLUTCH CONTROL CIRCUIT DIAGNOSIS
3.1L (VIN T) "J" CARLINE (PORT)

Circuit Description:

The A/C clutch control relay is energized when the ECM provides a ground path through CKT 459 and A/C is requested. A/C clutch is delayed about .3 seconds after A/C is requested. This will allow the IAC to adjust engine rpm for the additional load.

The ECM will temporarily disengage the A/C clutch relay for calibrated times for one or more of the following:

- Hot engine restart
- Wide open throttle (TPS over 90%)
- Power steering pressure high (open power steering pressure switch)
- Engine rpm greater than about 6000 rpm
- During IAC reset

The A/C clutch relay will remain disengaged when a Code 66 is present, if pressure is out of range described previously in this section or there is no A/C request signal due to an open A/C select switch or circuit.

Test Description: Number(s) refer to circled number(s) on the diagnostic chart.

1. The ECM will only energize the A/C relay when the engine is running. This test will determine if the relay or CKT 459 is faulty.

2. Determines if the signal is reaching the ECM through CKT 66 from the A/C control panel. Signal should only be present when an A/C mode or defrost mode has been selected.

3. If the ECM is receiving a high power steering pressure signal, the A/C clutch will be disengaged by the ECM.

1990-92 3.1L (VIN T)

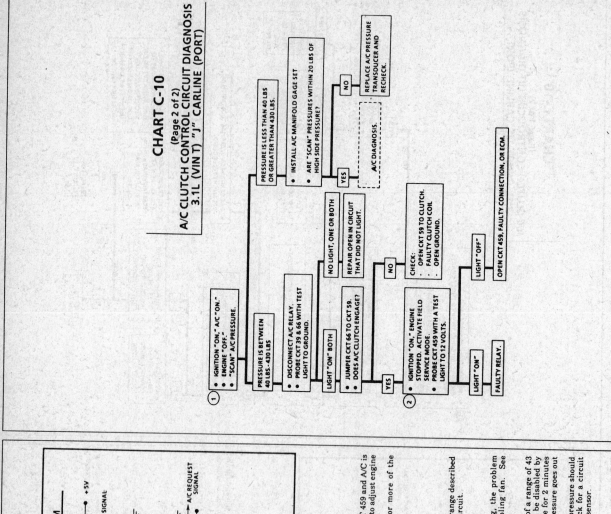

CHART C-10
(Page 2 of 2)
A/C CLUTCH CONTROL CIRCUIT DIAGNOSIS
3.1L (VIN T) "J" CARLINE (PORT)

Circuit Description:

The A/C clutch control relay is energized when the ECM provides a ground path through CKT 459 and A/C is requested. A/C clutch is delayed about .3 seconds after A/C is requested. This will allow the IAC to adjust engine rpm for the additional load.

The ECM will temporarily disengage the A/C clutch relay for calibrated times for one or more of the following:

- Hot engine restart
- Wide open throttle (TPS over 90%)
- Power steering pressure high (open power steering pressure switch)
- Engine rpm greater than about 6000 rpm
- During IAC reset

The A/C clutch relay will remain disengaged when a Code 66 is present, if pressure is out of range described previously in this section or there is no A/C request signal due to an open A/C select switch or circuit.

Test Description: Number(s) refer to circled number(s) on the diagnostic chart.

1. Determines if the pressure transducer is out of range causing the compressor clutch to be disengaged.

2. With the engine stopped and field service mode activated, the ECM should be grounding CKT 459, which should cause the test light to be "ON."

Diagnostic Aids:

If complaint is insufficient cooling, the problem may be caused by an inoperative cooling fan. See CHART C-12 for cooling fan diagnosis.

A/C pressure outside of a range of 43 to 428 psi will cause the compressor to be disabled by the ECM. Observe "Scan" A/C pressure for 2 minutes with engine idling and A/C "ON." If pressure goes out of range,

measure and diagnose. "Scan" pressure should be within 20 psi of actual. If not, check for a circuit problem using Code 66 chart or replace sensor.

1990-92 3.1L (VIN T)

CHART C-12
(Page 1 of 2)
COOLANT FAN CONTROL CIRCUIT DIAGNOSIS
3.1L (VIN T) "J" CARLINE (PORT)

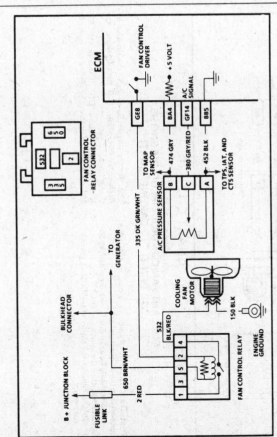

- IGN. "ON," ENGINE "OFF," A/C "OFF."
- SCAN INDICATES COOLANT TEMP. BELOW 100°C.
- COOLING FAN SHOULD BE "OFF." IS IT?

① GROUND DIAGNOSTIC TERMINAL. FAN SHOULD TURN "ON." DOES IT?

UNGROUND DIAGNOSTIC TERMINAL. START AND IDLE ENGINE. A/C "OFF." FAN SHOULD BE "OFF" (WHILE TEMP. UNDER 100°C), AND "ON" WHEN OVER ABOUT 109°C. IS IT?

NO — DISCONNECT FAN RELAY. FAN SHOULD STOP. DOES IT?
- YES — PROBE CKT 335 WITH A TEST LIGHT TO 12 VOLTS.
  - NO — CKT 532 SHORTED TO VOLTAGE.
  - LIGHT "OFF" — FAULTY RELAY
  - LIGHT "ON" — CKT 335 SHORTED TO GROUND OR FAULTY ECM.

NO — REFER TO CHART C-12 (2 OF 2)

NO — FAULTY ECM

WITHOUT A/C

WITH A/C

② ENGINE IDLING, A/C "OFF." USE A "SCAN" TOOL AND CHECK A/C PRESSURE SENSOR. DOES "SCAN" INDICATE PRESSURE ABOVE 300 psi?
- YES — DISCONNECT A/C PRESSURE SENSOR. DOES SCAN INDICATE ZERO A/C PRESSURE.
  - YES — OPEN CKT 452 OR FAULTY SENSOR CONN OR FAULTY SENSOR
  - NO — CKT 380 SHORTED TO VOLTAGE OR FAULTY ECM

③ ENGINE IDLING, A/C "ON." IF A/C IS INOP, SEE CHART C-10. FAN SHOULD TURN "ON" WHEN A/C PRESSURE EXCEEDS ABOUT 200 psi (1380 kPa) DOES IT?

④

NO — DISCONNECT A/C PRESSURE SENSOR. MEASURE VOLTAGE BETWEEN CONNECTOR TERMINAL "B" AND "A". VOLTMETER SHOULD READ 5 VOLTS. DOES IT?
- YES — MEASURE VOLTAGE BETWEEN CONNECTOR TERMINAL "B" AND "C." VOLTMETER SHOULD READ 5 VOLTS, DOES IT?
  - YES — FAULTY SENSOR
  - NO — CKT 380 OPEN OR SHORTED TO GROUND FAULTY ECM CONNECTION OR ECM.
- NO — MEASURE VOLTAGE BETWEEN CONNECTOR TERMINAL "B" AND GROUND OR TERMINAL "A" AND GROUND. VOLTMETER SHOULD READ 5 VOLTS. DOES IT?
  - YES — CKT 452 OPEN FAULTY ECM CONNECTION OR ECM.
  - NO — CKT 474 OPEN OR SHORTED TO GROUND, FAULTY ECM CONNECTION OR ECM.

NO TROUBLE FOUND. REFER TO "DIAGNOSTIC AIDS" OF FACING PAGE.

ECM

FAN CONTROL DRIVER
GE8 — FAN CONTROL RELAY CONNECTOR
BA4 — +5 VOLT
GF14 — A/C SIGNAL
BB5

532
335 DK GRN/WHT
474 GRY — TO MAP SENSOR
380 GRY/RED
452 BLK — TO TPS, IAT, AND CTS SENSOR

A/C PRESSURE SENSOR — B, C, A

FAN CONTROL RELAY CONNECTOR

B+ JUNCTION BLOCK
BULKHEAD CONNECTOR
TO GENERATOR

FUSIBLE LINK
2 RED
650 BRN/WHT

532
BLK/RED

COOLING FAN MOTOR
150 BLK
ENGINE GROUND

FAN CONTROL RELAY

CHART C-12
(Page 1 of 2)
COOLANT FAN CONTROL CIRCUIT DIAGNOSIS
3.1L (VIN T) "J" CARLINE (PORT)

Circuit Description:
The electric cooling fan is controlled by the ECM based on inputs from the coolant temperature sensor, the A/C pressure sensor and vehicle speed. The ECM controls the fan by grounding CKT 335, which energizes the fan control relay. Battery voltage is then supplied to the fan motor.

The ECM grounds CKT 335 when coolant temperature is over about 109°C (228°F) or when A/C has been requested and the A/C pressure sensor indicates high A/C pressure, 200 psi (1380 kPa). Once the ECM turns the relay "ON," it will keep it "ON" for a minimum of 30 seconds or until vehicle speed exceeds 70 mph.

Also, if Code 14 or 15 sets or the ECM is in back up, the fan will run at all times.

Test Description: Number(s) refer to circled number(s) on the diagnostic chart.

1. With the diagnostic terminal grounded, the cooling fan control driver will close, which should energize the fan control relay.
2. If the A/C fan control switch or circuit is open, the fan would run whenever A/C is requested.
3. With A/C clutch engaged, the A/C fan control switch should open when A/C high pressure exceeds about 200 psi (1380 kPa). This signal should cause the ECM to energize the fan control relay.
4. Disconnecting the A/C pressure sensor will cause a Code 66 to set. After finishing this step, be sure to clear codes.

Diagnostic Aids:

If the owner complained of an overheating problem, it must be determined if the complaint was due to an actual boilover or the hot light (temperature gage) indicated over heating.

If the gage (light) indicates overheating but no boilover is detected, the gage circuit should be checked. The gage accuracy can also be checked by comparing the coolant sensor reading using a "Scan" tool and comparing its reading with the gage reading.

If the engine is actually overheating and the gage indicates overheating but the cooling fan is not coming "ON," the coolant sensor has probably shifted out of calibration and should be replaced.

If the engine is overheating and the cooling fan is "ON," the cooling system should be checked.

1990-92 3.1L (VIN T)

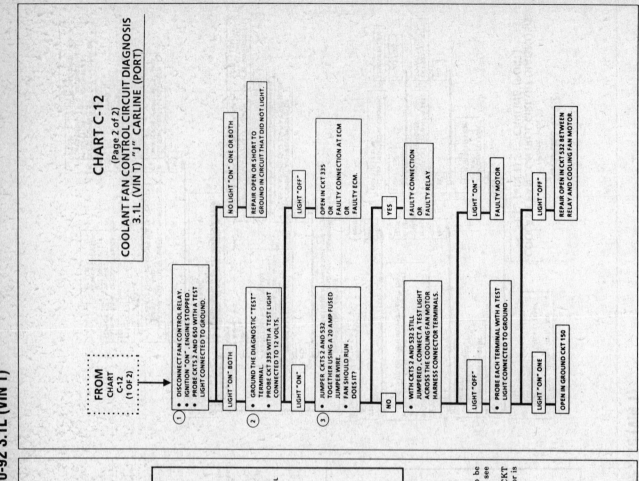

CHART C-12
(Page 2 of 2)
COOLANT FAN CONTROL CIRCUIT DIAGNOSIS
3.1L (VIN T) "J" CARLINE (PORT)

Test Description: Number(s) refer to circled number(s) on the diagnostic chart.

1. 12 volts should be available to both terminal "2" & CKT 532 when the ignition is "ON."

2. This test checks the ability of the ECM to ground CKT 335.

The "Service Engine Soon" light should also be flashing at this point. If it isn't flashing, see CHART A-2.

3. If the fan does not turn "ON" at this point, CKT 532 or CKT 150 is open or the cooling fan motor is faulty.

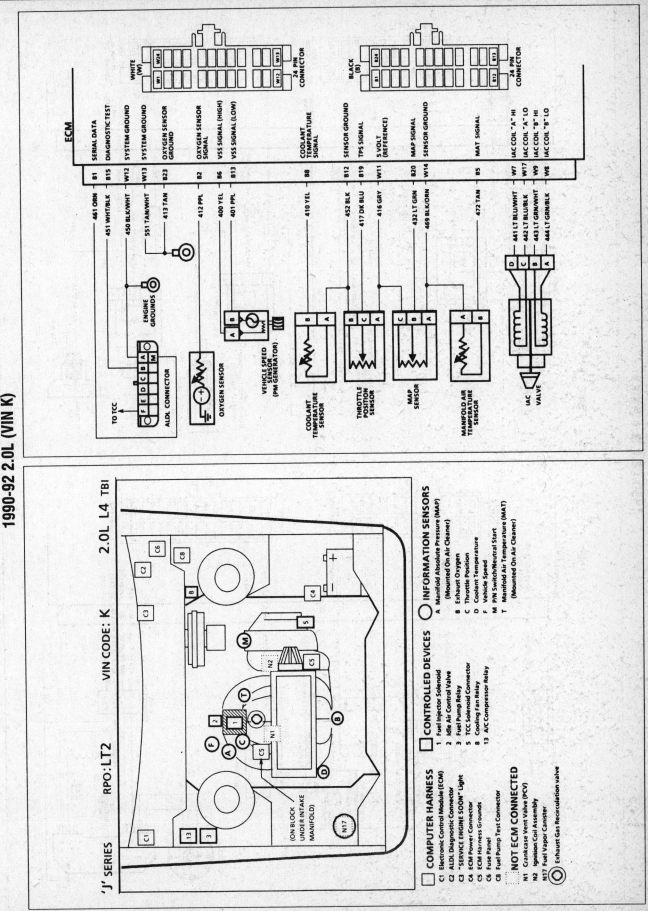

'J' SERIES **RPO: LT2** **VIN CODE: K** **2.0L L4 TBI**

1990-92 2.0L (VIN K)

COMPUTER HARNESS
- C1 Electronic Control Module (ECM)
- C2 ALDL Diagnostic Connector
- C3 "SERVICE ENGINE SOON" Light
- C4 ECM Power Connector
- C5 ECM Harness Grounds
- C6 Fuse Panel
- C8 Fuel Pump Test Connector

NOT ECM CONNECTED
- N1 Crankcase Vent Valve (PCV)
- N2 Ignition Coil Assembly
- N17 Fuel Vapor Canister
- ◎ Exhaust Gas Recirculation valve

CONTROLLED DEVICES
- 1 Fuel Injector Solenoid
- 2 Idle Air Control Valve
- 3 Fuel Pump Relay
- 5 TCC Solenoid Connector
- 8 Cooling Fan Relay
- 13 A/C Compressor Relay

INFORMATION SENSORS
- A Manifold Absolute Pressure (MAP) (Mounted On Air Cleaner)
- B Exhaust Oxygen
- C Throttle Position
- D Coolant Temperature
- F Vehicle Speed
- M P/N Switch/Neutral Start
- T Manifold Air Temperature (MAT) (Mounted On Air Cleaner)

1990-92 2.0L (VIN K)

ECM

WHITE (W)
W24 · W1 · W12 · W13
24 PIN CONNECTOR

BLACK (B)
B24 · B1 · B12 · B13
24 PIN CONNECTOR

B+ — W10
B+ — W15
FUEL PUMP RELAY DRIVE (B+) — W24
SYSTEM GROUND — W12

A/C SIGNAL FOR FAN — B24
A/C REQUEST — W2
A/C RELAY CONTROL — B3
COOLING FAN CONTROL — B21

240 ORN
240 ORN
465 DK GRN/WHT
450 BLK/WHT
ENGINE GROUND
120 GRY
FUEL PUMP TEST CONNECTOR

603 DK GRN/WHT
HTR/AC FUSE
TO IGNITION SWITCH

604 DK BLU/WHT
HTR/AC FUSE
39 PNK/BLK
459 DK GRN/WHT
TO IGNITION SWITCH

59 DK GRN

2 RED
FUSIBLE LINK
TO B+
TO ALTERNATOR
650 BRN/WHT
TO IGNITION SWITCH
ALT FUSE
335 DK BRN/WHT

FUSIBLE LINK
TO B+
F/P FUSE
TO IGNITION SWITCH
639 PNK/BLK

FUEL PUMP RELAY
TO FUEL PUMP

OIL PRESSURE SWITCH

A/C LOW PRESSURE SWITCH (CLOSED WHEN A/C IS CHARGED)
66 LT GRN
A/C CONTROL SWITCH

A/C CONTROL RELAY
A/C HIGH PRESSURE SWITCH (NORMALLY CLOSED)
150 BLK
A/C COMPRESSOR CLUTCH

COOLING FAN CONTROL RELAY
532 BLK/RED
150 BLK
COOLING FAN

ECM

WHITE (W)
W24 · W1 · W12 · W13
24 PIN CONNECTOR

BLACK (B)
B24 · B1 · B12 · B13
24 PIN CONNECTOR

PARK NEUTRAL SWITCH (A/T) — W18
SERVICE ENGINE SOON LIGHT CONTROL — B22
TCC OR SHIFT LIGHT — B7
IGNITION — W16
INJECTOR DRIVER — W1
EST — W6
REFERENCE — B9
BY-PASS — W19
GROUND — B16

434 ORN/BLK
419 BRN/WHT
420 PPL
422 TAN/BLK
456 TAN/BLK
439 PNK/BLK
467 DK BLU
423 WHT
430 PPL/WHT
424 TAN/BLK
453 BLK/RED

450 BLK/WHT
P/N SWITCH
GAUGES FUSE
TO IGNITION SWITCH

39 PNK/BLK
SES LAMP
BRAKE SWITCH
3RD GEAR SWITCH
AUTOMATIC TRANSMISSION TCC SOLENOID
ALDL CONNECTOR
SHIFT LIGHT (M/T ONLY)

ECM FUSE
TO IGNITION SWITCH
RED
INJECTOR

4-WAY CONNECTOR
A · B · C · D
PRIMARY COIL
TO IGNITION SWITCH
TACH
PICK-UP COIL
P N E R
IGNITION MODULE

1990-92 2.0L (VIN K)

DIAGNOSTIC CIRCUIT CHECK

The Diagnostic Circuit Check is an organized approach to identifying a problem created by an electronic engine control system malfunction. It must be the starting point for any driveability complaint diagnosis because it directs the service technician to the next logical step in diagnosing the complaint.

The "Scan" data listed in the table may be used for comparison after completing the diagnostic circuit check and finding the on-board diagnostics functioning properly with no trouble codes displayed. The "Typical Data Values" are an average of display values recorded from normally operating vehicles and are intended to represent what a normally functioning system would typically display.

A "SCAN" TOOL THAT DISPLAYS FAULTY DATA SHOULD NOT BE USED, AND THE PROBLEM SHOULD BE REPORTED TO THE MANUFACTURER. THE USE OF A FAULTY "SCAN" TOOL CAN RESULT IN MISDIAGNOSIS AND UNNECESSARY PARTS REPLACEMENT.

Only the parameters listed below are used in this manual for diagnosis. If a "Scan" tool reads other parameters, the values are not recommended by General Motors for use in diagnosis. For more description on the values and use of the "Scan" tool to diagnosis ECM inputs, refer to the applicable component diagnosis section. If all values are within the range illustrated, refer to "Symptoms"

"SCAN" TOOL DATA

Test Under Following Conditions: Idle, Upper Radiator Hose Hot, Closed Throttle, Park or Neutral, "Closed Loop," All Accessories "OFF."

"SCAN" Position	Units Displayed	Typical Data Value
Engine Speed	RPM	ECM Idle command (varies with temperature)
Desired Idle	RPM	± 100 RPM from desired RPM (± 50 RPM in drive)
Coolant Temp	°C	85° - 105°
Mani Air Temp	°C	10° - 80° (varies with underhood temp.)
MAP	Volts	1-2 (depends on Vac. and Baro. pressure)
Open/Closed Loop	Open Loop/Closed Loop	"Closed Loop" (May enter "Open Loop" with extended idle)
Throt Position	Volts	.45 - 1.25
Throttle Angle	0-100%	0
Oxygen Sensor	mV	100-1000 (varies continuously)
Inj. Pulse Width	MSec	.8 - 3.0
Spark Advance	# of Degrees	Varies
Engine Speed	RPM	ECM Idle Command (varies with temp.)
Fuel Integrator	Counts	118-138
Block Learn	Counts	Varies
Idle Air Control	Counts/Steps	5 - 50
Park/Neutral	P/N and RDL	P/N
VSS	MPH/KPH	0
Torque Conv. CL.	On/Off	Off
Battery Voltage	Volts	13.5 - 14.5
Cool. Fan Relay	On/Off	Off (below 108°)
A/C Request	Yes/No	No
A/C Clutch	On/Off	Off
Power Steering	Normal/High Press	Not Used
Shift Light (M/T)	On/Off	Off

FUEL INJECTION ECM CONNECTOR IDENTIFICATION

This ECM voltage chart is for use with a digital voltmeter to further aid in diagnosis. The voltages you get may vary due to low battery charge or other reasons, but they should be very close.

THE FOLLOWING CONDITIONS MUST BE MET BEFORE TESTING:
- Engine at operating temperature • Engine idling in Closed Loop (for "Engine Run" column)
- Test terminal not grounded • "Scan" tool not installed • All voltages shown "B+" indicates battery or charging voltage.

WHITE (W) 24 PIN CONNECTOR

PIN	CIRCUIT	WIRE COLOR	KEY "ON"	ENG. "RUN"
W1	INJECTOR DRIVE	DK BLU	B+	B+
W2	A/C REQUEST	DK BLU	0*	0*
W3	VSS OUTPUT 2000 PPM	RED GRY/BLK	0*	0*
W4	CRUISE			
W5	NOT USED			
W6	EST	WHT	0	1.1
W7	IAC "A"-HI	LT BLU/WHT	(4)	(4)
W8	IAC "A"-LOW	LT GRN/BLK	(4)	(4)
W9	IAC "B"-LOW	LT GRN/WHT	(4)	(4)
W10	12V BATT	ORN	B+	B+
W11	5 VOLT REFERENCE	GRY	5.0	5.0
W12	ECM GROUND	BLK/WHT	0*	0*
W13	ECM GND	BLK/WHT	0*	0*
W14	MAP/MAT GND	ORN/TAN/WHT	0*	0*
W15	12V BATT.	ORN	B+	B+
W16	12 V IGN.	PNK/BLK	B+	B+
W17	IAC "A"-LOW	LT BLU/BLK	(4)	(4)
W18	P/N SWITCH	ORN/BLK	0*	
W19	BY-PASS	TAN/BLK	0*	4.7
W20	CRUISE	GRY		
W21	CRUISE	DK BLU		
W22	VSS OUTPUT 4000 PPM (IF USED)	DK GRN	0*	0*
W23	NOT USED			
W24	FUEL PUMP	DK GRN/WHT	(2)	B+

BLACK (B) 24 PIN CONNECTOR

PIN	CIRCUIT	WIRE COLOR	KEY "ON"	ENG. "RUN"
B1	SERIAL DATA	ORN	3.9	3.9
B2	OXYGEN SENSOR SIGNAL	PPL	33-55	1.9
B3	A/C CLUTCH RELAY	DK GRN/WHT	B+	B+
B4	NOT USED			
B5	MAT SIGNAL	TAN	1.3	1.3
B6	MAGNETIC VSS (IF USED)	PPL TAN	.13	.13
B7	TCC OR SHIFTLITE	BLK/BLK	B+	B+
B8	COOLANT SIGNAL	YEL	1.9	1.9
B9	IGNITION REF. HI	PPL WHT		
B10	CRUISE	LT GRN		
B11	COOLANT AND TPS GND	DK BLU/WHT	0*	0*
B12	CRUISE	BLK		
B13	MAGNETIC VSS (IF USED)	YEL	0*	0*
B14	CRUISE	BRN		
B15	ALDL DIAG.	BRN	5.0	5.0
B16	IGNITION GROUND	BLK/RED WHT/BLK	0*	0*
B17	NOT USED			
B18	NOT USED			
B19	TPS SIGNAL	DK BLU	.6	.6
B20	MAP SIGNAL	LT GRN	4.8	1.1
B21	ENG. COOLING FAN	DK GRN/WHT	B+	B+
B22	SERVICE ENG. SOON LITE	BRN/WHT	B+	B+
B23	OXYGEN SENSOR GROUND	TAN/WHT	0*	0*
B24	A/C SIGNAL FOR FAN	DK GRN/WHT	0*	0*

* All voltages shown "0" should read less than 5 volt.
① A/C, Fan "OFF"
② Reads battery voltage for 2 seconds after ignition "ON" then should read 0 volts
③ Varies depending on temparature
④ Not usable

1990-92 2.0L (VIN K)

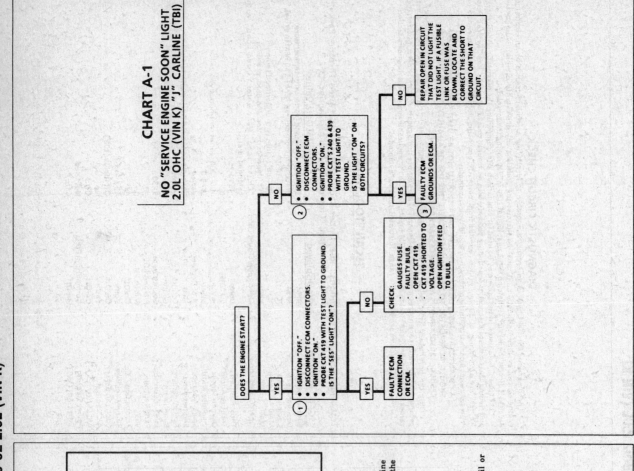

CHART A-1
NO "SERVICE ENGINE SOON" LIGHT
2.0L OHC (VIN K) "J" CARLINE (TBI)

Circuit Description:

There should always be a steady "Service Engine Soon" light, when the ignition is "ON" and engine stopped. Battery is supplied directly to the light bulb. The Electronic Control Module (ECM) will control the light and turn it "ON" by providing a ground path through CKT 419 to the ECM.

Test Description: Numbers below refer to circled numbers on the diagnostic chart.

1. Battery feed CKT 240 is protected by a fusible link at the battery.
2. If CKTs 439 and 440 have voltage, the ECM grounds or the ECM are faulty.
3. Using a test light connected to 12 volts, probe each of the system ground circuits to be sure a good ground is present. See ECM terminal end view in front of this section for ECM pin locations of ground circuits.

Diagnostic Aids:

Engine runs OK, check:
- Faulty light bulb
- CKT 419 open
- Gage fuse blown. This will result in no oil or generator lights, seat belt reminder, etc.

Engine cranks, but will not run.
- Continuous battery - fuse or fusible link open
- ECM ignition fuse open
- Battery CKT 240 to ECM open
- Ignition CKT 439 to ECM open
- Poor connection to ECM

1990-92 2.0L (VIN K)

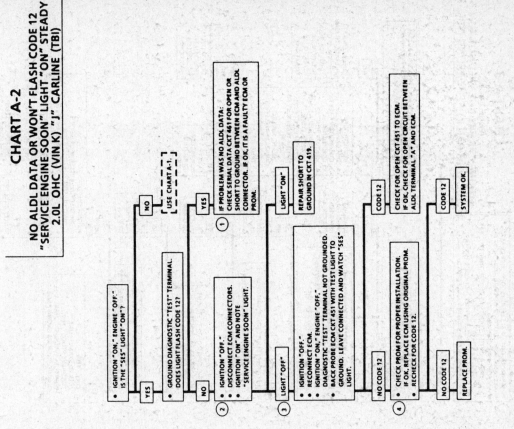

CHART A-2

NO ALDL DATA OR WON'T FLASH CODE 12
"SERVICE ENGINE SOON" LIGHT "ON" STEADY
2.0L OHC (VIN K) "J" CARLINE (TBI)

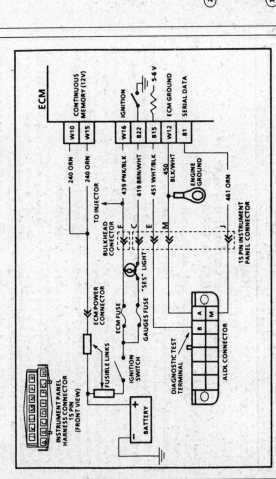

CHART A-2

NO ALDL DATA OR WON'T FLASH CODE 12
"SERVICE ENGINE SOON" LIGHT "ON" STEADY
2.0L OHC (VIN K) "J" CARLINE (TBI)

Circuit Description:

There should always be a steady "Service Engine Soon" light when the ignition is "ON" and engine stopped. Battery is supplied directly to the light bulb. The Electronic Control Module (ECM) will turn the light "ON" by grounding CKT 419 at the ECM.

With the diagnostic terminal grounded, the light should flash a Code 12, followed by any trouble code(s) stored in memory.

A steady light suggests a short to ground in the light control CKT 419, or an open in diagnostic CKT 451.

Test Description: Numbers below refer to circled numbers on the diagnostic chart.

1. If there is a problem with the ECM that causes a "Scan" tool to not read Serial data, then the ECM should not flash a Code 12. If Code 12 does flash, be sure that the "Scan" tool is working properly on another vehicle. If the "Scan" tool is functioning properly and CKT 461 is OK, the PROM, or ECM, may be at fault for the NO ALDL symptom.

2. If the light goes "OFF" when the ECM connector is disconnected, then CKT 419 is not shorted to ground.

3. This step will check for an open diagnostic CKT 451.

4. At this point, the "Service Engine Soon" light wiring is OK. The problem is a faulty ECM or PROM. If Code 12 does flash, the ECM should be replaced using the original PROM. Replace the PROM only after trying an ECM, as a defective PROM is an unlikely cause of the problem.

1990-92 2.0L (VIN K)

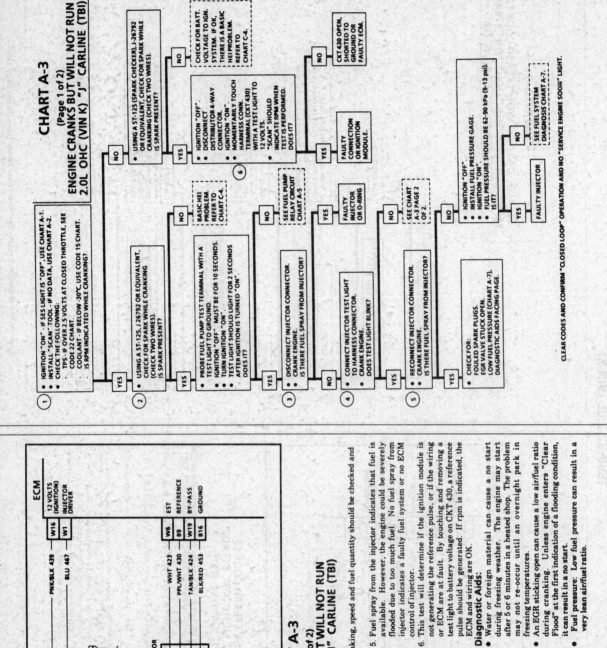

CHART A-3
(Page 1 of 2)
ENGINE CRANKS BUT WILL NOT RUN
2.0L OHC (VIN K) "J" CARLINE (TBI)

Circuit Description:

Before using this chart, battery condition, engine cranking, speed and fuel quantity should be checked and verified as being OK.

Test Description: Numbers below refer to circled numbers on the diagnostic chart.

1. A "Service Engine Soon" light "ON" is a basic test to determine if there is battery voltage and ignition 12 volts to the ECM. No ALDL may be due to an ECM problem, and CHART A-2 will diagnose the ECM. If TPS is over 2.5 volts, the engine may be in the clear flood mode, which will cause starting problems. The engine will not start without reference pulses and, therefore, the "Scan" should read rpm (reference) during cranking.

2. If rpm was indicated during crank, the ignition module is receiving a crank signal, but "No Spark" at this test indicates the ignition module is not triggering the coil.

3. While cranking engine, there should be no fuel spray with injector disconnected. Replace the injector, if it sprays fuel or drips like a leaking water faucet.

4. The test light should "blink," indicating the ECM is controlling the injector OK. How bright the light "blinks" is not important. However, the test light should be a BT 8329 or equivalent.

5. Fuel spray from the injector indicates that fuel is available. However, the engine could be severely flooded due to too much fuel. No fuel spray from injector indicates a faulty fuel system or no ECM control of injector.

6. This test will determine if the ignition module is not generating the reference pulse, or if the wiring or ECM are at fault. By touching and removing a test light to battery voltage on CKT 430, a reference pulse should be generated. If rpm is indicated, the ECM and wiring are OK.

Diagnostic Aids:

• Water or foreign material can cause a no start during freezing weather. The engine may start after 5 or 6 minutes in a heated shop. The problem may not re-occur until an overnight park in freezing temperatures.

• An EGR sticking open can cause a low air/fuel ratio during cranking. Unless engine enters "Clear Flood" at the first indication of a flooding condition, it can result in a no start.

• Fuel pressure: Low fuel pressure can result in a very lean air/fuel ratio.

1990-92 2.0L (VIN K)

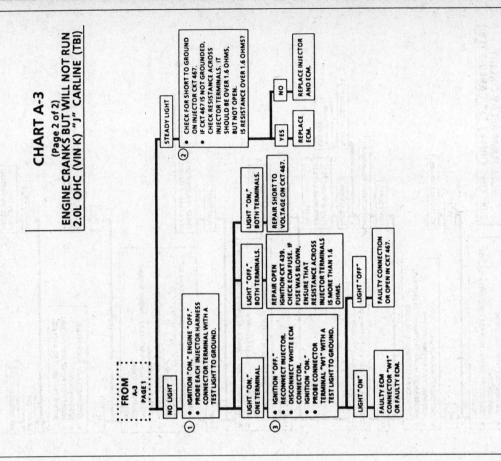

CHART A-3
(Page 2 of 2)
ENGINE CRANKS BUT WILL NOT RUN
2.0L OHC (VIN K) "J" CARLINE (TBI)

Circuit Description:

Ignition voltage is supplied to the fuel injector on CKT 439. The injector will be pulsed (turned "ON" and "OFF") when the ECM opens and grounds injector drive CKT 467.

Test Description: Numbers below refer to the circled numbers on the diagnostic chart.

1. This check determines if injector connector has ignition voltage and on only one terminal.

2. A faulty ECM may result in damage to the injector.

3. A test light connected from ECM harness terminal "W1" to ground should light due to continuity through the injector.

CLEAR CODES AND CONFIRM "CLOSED LOOP" OPERATION AND NO "SERVICE ENGINE SOON" LIGHT.

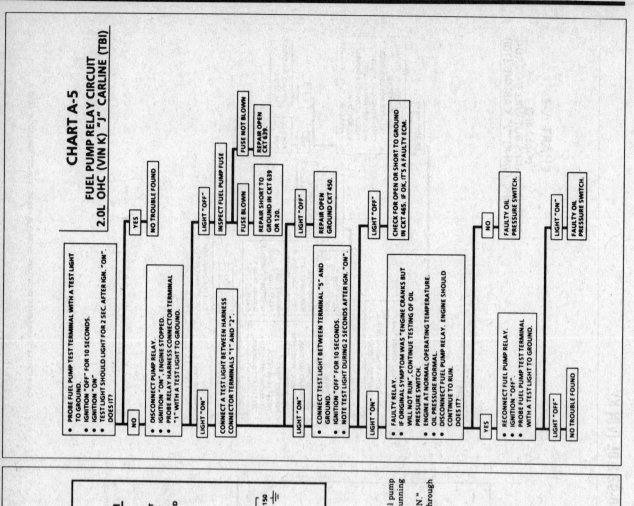

1990-92 2.0L (VIN K)

CHART A-5

FUEL PUMP RELAY CIRCUIT
2.0L OHC (VIN K) "J" CARLINE (TBI)

Circuit Description:

When the ignition switch is turned "ON," the Electronic Control Module (ECM) will activate the fuel pump relay and run the in-tank fuel pump. The fuel pump will operate as long as the engine is cranking or running and the ECM is receiving ignition reference pulses.

If there are no reference pulses, the ECM will shut "OFF" the fuel pump within 2 seconds after key "ON."

Should the fuel pump relay, or the 12 volt relay drive from the ECM fail, the fuel pump will be run through an oil pressure switch back-up circuit.

Diagnostic Aids:

An inoperative fuel pump relay can result in long cranking times, particularly if the engine is cold or engine oil pressure is low. The extended crank period is caused by the time necessary for oil pressure to build enough to close the oil pressure switch and turn "ON" the fuel pump. The fuel pump part of the oil pressure switch closes at about 28 kPa (4 psi).

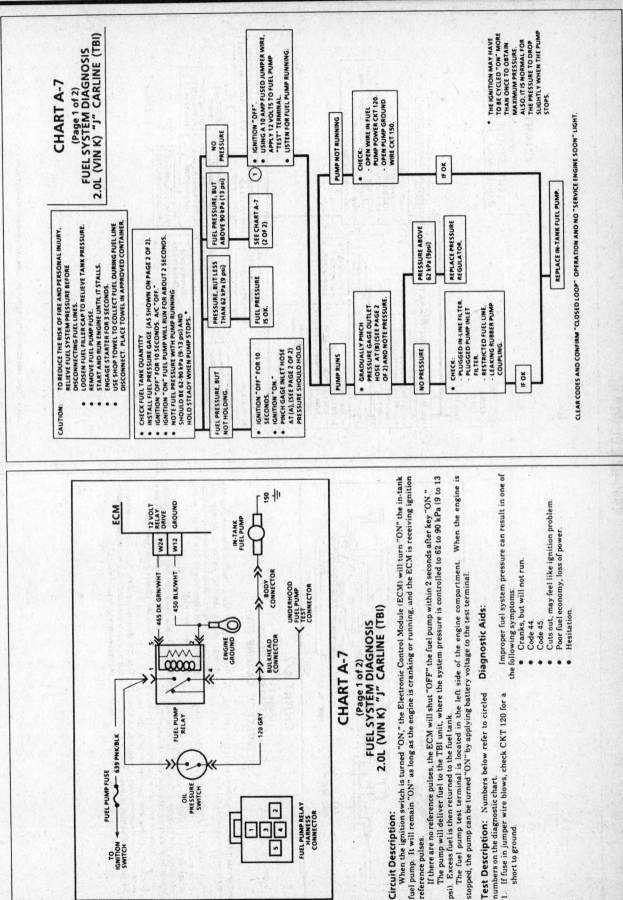

1990-92 2.0L (VIN K)

CHART A-7
(Page 1 of 2)
FUEL SYSTEM DIAGNOSIS
2.0L (VIN K) "J" CARLINE (TBI)

CHART A-7
(Page 1 of 2)
FUEL SYSTEM DIAGNOSIS
2.0L (VIN K) "J" CARLINE (TBI)

Circuit Description:

When the ignition switch is turned "ON," the Electronic Control Module (ECM) will turn "ON" the in-tank fuel pump. It will remain "ON" as long as the engine is cranking or running, and the ECM is receiving ignition reference pulses.

If there are no reference pulses, the ECM will shut "OFF" the fuel pump within 2 seconds after key "ON."

The pump will deliver fuel to the TBI unit, where the system pressure is controlled to 62 to 90 kPa (9 to 13 psi). Excess fuel is then returned to the fuel tank.

The fuel pump test terminal is located in the left side of the engine compartment. When the engine is stopped, the pump can be turned "ON" by applying battery voltage to the test terminal.

Test Description: Numbers below refer to circled numbers on the diagnostic chart.

1. If fuse in jumper wire blows, check CKT 120 for a short to ground.

Diagnostic Aids:

Improper fuel system pressure can result in one of the following symptoms:

- Cranks, but will not run.
- Code 44.
- Code 45.
- Cuts out, may feel like ignition problem.
- Poor fuel economy, loss of power.
- Hesitation.

1990-92 2.0L (VIN K)

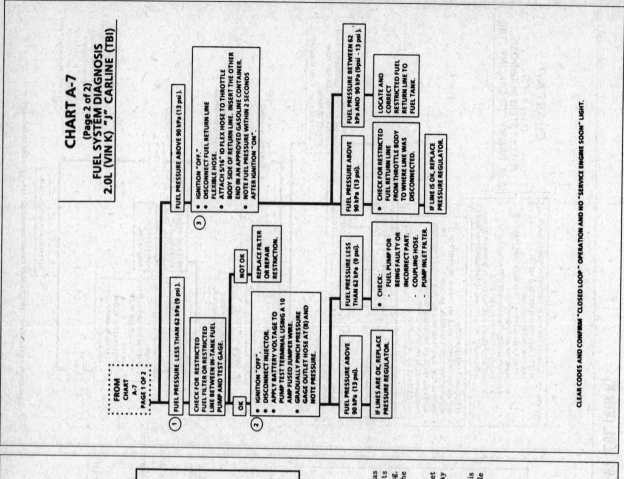

CHART A-7
(Page 2 of 2)
FUEL SYSTEM DIAGNOSIS
2.0L (VIN K) "J" CARLINE (TBI)

Test Description: Numbers below refer to circled numbers on the diagnostic chart.

Tool Required: J 29658-B or BT-8205 - Fuel Pressure Gage

1. Pressure below 62 kPa (9 psi) may cause a lean condition, and may set a Code 44. It could also cause hard starting cold and poor driveability. Low fuel pressure may allow the engine to run at idle or low speeds, but may cause the engine to surge or stall when more fuel is required (such as accelerating or at high speed).

2. Restricting fuel flow at the fuel pressure gage (as shown) causes the fuel pump to develop its maximum pressure. With the fuel pump running, pressure should rise above 90 kPa (13 psi) as the gage hose is restricted.

NOTICE: Do Not block the fuel return line (outlet side of TBI unit) as excessive pressure may damage the TBI pressure regulator.

3. This test determines if the high fuel pressure is due to a restricted fuel return line, or a throttle body pressure regulator problem.

1990-92 2.0L (VIN K)

CODE 13
OXYGEN SENSOR CIRCUIT
(OPEN CIRCUIT)
2.0L OHC (VIN K) "J" CARLINE (TBI)

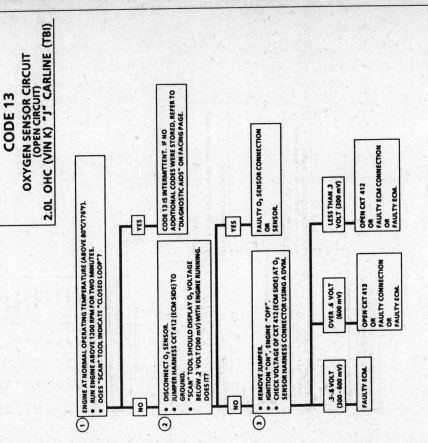

1. ENGINE AT NORMAL OPERATING TEMPERATURE (ABOVE 80°C/176°F).
   • RUN ENGINE ABOVE 1200 RPM FOR TWO MINUTES.
   • DOES "SCAN" TOOL INDICATE "CLOSED LOOP"?

   YES → CODE 13 IS INTERMITTENT. IF NO ADDITIONAL CODES WERE STORED, REFER TO "DIAGNOSTIC AIDS" ON FACING PAGE.

   NO

2. DISCONNECT O₂ SENSOR.
   JUMPER HARNESS CKT 412 (ECM SIDE) TO GROUND.
   "SCAN" TOOL SHOULD DISPLAY O₂ VOLTAGE BELOW .2 VOLT (200 mV) WITH ENGINE RUNNING. DOES IT?

   YES → FAULTY O₂ SENSOR CONNECTION OR SENSOR.

   NO

3. REMOVE JUMPER.
   IGNITION "ON", ENGINE "OFF".
   CHECK VOLTAGE OF CKT 412 (ECM SIDE) AT O₂ SENSOR HARNESS CONNECTOR USING A DVM.

   LESS THAN .3 VOLT (300 mV) → OPEN CKT 412 OR FAULTY ECM CONNECTION OR FAULTY ECM.

   .3-.6 VOLT (300-600 mV) → FAULTY ECM.

   OVER .6 VOLT (600 mV) → OPEN CKT 413 OR FAULTY CONNECTION OR FAULTY ECM.

CLEAR CODES AND CONFIRM "CLOSED LOOP" OPERATION AND NO "SERVICE ENGINE SOON" LIGHT.

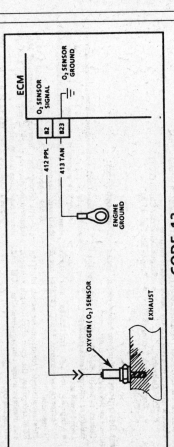

CODE 13
OXYGEN SENSOR CIRCUIT
(OPEN CIRCUIT)
2.0L OHC (VIN K) "J" CARLINE (TBI)

Circuit Description:

The ECM supplies a voltage of about of .45 volt between terminals "B2" and "B23". (If measured with 10 megohm digital voltmeter, this may read as low as .32 volt).

The Oxygen (O₂) sensor varies the voltage within a range of about 1 volt, if the exhaust is rich, down through about .10 volt, if exhaust is lean.

The sensor is like an open circuit and produces no voltage, when it is below 316°C (600°F). An open sensor circuit, or cold sensor, causes "Open Loop" operation.

Test Description: Numbers below refer to circled numbers on the diagnostic chart.

1. Code 13 will set if:
   • Engine at normal operating temperature.
   • At least 40 seconds engine run time after start.
   • O₂ signal voltage steady between .35 and .55 volt.
   • Throttle angle above 7%.
   • All conditions must be met for about 3 seconds.

   If the conditions for a Code 13 exist, the system will not go "Closed Loop".

2. This test determines if the O₂ sensor is the problem, or, if the ECM and wiring are at fault.

3. In doing this test, use only a high impedance digital volt ohmmeter. This test checks the continuity of CKTs 412 and 413. If CKT 413 is open, the ECM voltage on CKT 412 will be over .6 volt (600 mV).

Diagnostic Aids:

Normal "Scan" voltage varies between 100 mV to 999 mV (.1 and 1.0 volt), while in "Closed Loop." Code 13 sets within one minute, if voltage remains between .35 and .55 volt, but the system will go "Open Loop" in about 15 seconds.

Verify a clean, tight ground connection for CKT 413. Open CKT(s) 412 or 413 will result in a Code 13.

If Code 13 is intermittent, refer to "Symptoms".

ECM

B2 — O₂ SENSOR SIGNAL
B23 — O₂ SENSOR GROUND

412 PPL
413 TAN

ENGINE GROUND

OXYGEN (O₂) SENSOR

EXHAUST

1990-92 2.0L (VIN K)

CODE 14

COOLANT TEMPERATURE SENSOR (CTS) CIRCUIT
(HIGH TEMPERATURE INDICATED)
2.0L OHC (VIN K) "J" CARLINE (TBI)

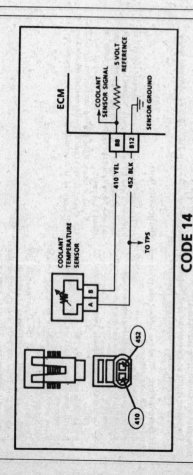

ECM

410 YEL — COOLANT SENSOR SIGNAL — 5 VOLT REFERENCE

452 BLK — SENSOR GROUND

B8

B12

COOLANT TEMPERATURE SENSOR

TO TPS

452

410

CODE 14

COOLANT TEMPERATURE SENSOR (CTS) CIRCUIT
(HIGH TEMPERATURE INDICATED)
2.0L OHC (VIN K) "J" CARLINE (TBI)

Circuit Description:

The Coolant Temperature Sensor (CTS) uses a thermistor to control the signal voltage to the ECM. The ECM applies a voltage on CKT 410 to the sensor. When the engine is cold, the sensor (thermistor) resistance is high, therefore, the ECM will see high signal voltage.

As the engine warms, the sensor resistance becomes less and the voltage drops. At normal engine operating temperature, the voltage will measure about 1.5 to 2.0 volts at the ECM terminal "B8".

Coolant temperature is one of the inputs used to control:

- Fuel Delivery
- Engine Spark Timing (EST)
- Cooling Fan
- Torque Converter Clutch (TCC)
- Engine Idle Speed (IAC)

Test Description: Numbers below refer to circled numbers on the diagnostic chart.

1. Checks to see if code was set as result of hard failure or intermittent condition.
   Code 14 will set if:
   - Signal voltage indicates a coolant temperature above 135°C (275°F) for 2 seconds.

2. This test simulates conditions for a Code 15. If the ECM recognizes the open circuit (high voltage), and displays a low temperature, the ECM and wiring are OK.

Diagnostic Aids:

A "Scan" tool reads engine temperature in degrees centigrade.

After the engine is started, the temperature should rise steadily to about 90°C, then stabilize when the thermostat opens.

If the engine has been allowed to cool to an ambient temperature (overnight), coolant and MAT temperature may be checked with a "Scan" tool and should read close to each other.

When a Code 14 is set, the ECM will turn "ON" the engine cooling fan.

A Code 14 will result if CKT 410 is shorted to ground.

If Code 14 is intermittent, refer to "Symptoms"

---

1. DOES "SCAN" TOOL DISPLAY COOLANT TEMPERATURE OF 130°C (266°F) OR HIGHER?

   NO → CODE 14 IS INTERMITTENT. IF NO ADDITIONAL CODES WERE STORED, REFER TO "DIAGNOSTIC AIDS"

   YES

2. • DISCONNECT SENSOR.
   • "SCAN" TOOL SHOULD DISPLAY TEMPERATURE BELOW -30°C (-22°F). DOES IT?

   NO → CKT 410 SHORTED TO GROUND.
   OR
   CKT 410 SHORTED TO SENSOR GROUND CIRCUIT
   OR
   FAULTY ECM.

   YES

   REPLACE SENSOR.

DIAGNOSTIC AID

COOLANT SENSOR		
TEMPERATURE VS. RESISTANCE VALUES		
(APPROXIMATE)		
°F	°C	OHMS
210	100	185
160	70	450
100	38	1,800
70	20	3,400
40	4	7,500
20	-7	13,500
0	-18	25,000
-40	-40	100,700

CLEAR CODES AND CONFIRM "CLOSED LOOP" OPERATION AND NO "SERVICE ENGINE SOON" LIGHT.

1990-92 2.0L (VIN K)

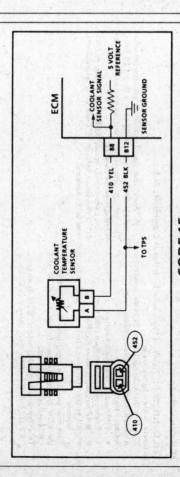

CODE 15

COOLANT TEMPERATURE SENSOR (CTS) CIRCUIT
(LOW TEMPERATURE INDICATED)
2.0L OHC (VIN K) "J" CARLINE (TBI)

Circuit Description:

The Coolant Temperature Sensor (CTS) uses a thermistor to control the signal voltage to the ECM. The ECM applies a voltage on CKT 410 to the sensor. When the engine is cold, the sensor (thermistor) resistance is high, therefore, the ECM will see high signal voltage.

As the engine warms, the sensor resistance becomes less and the voltage drops. At normal engine operating temperature, the voltage will measure about 1.5 to 2.0 volts at the ECM terminal "B8"

Coolant temperature is one of the inputs used to control:
- Fuel Delivery
- Engine Spark Timing (EST)
- Cooling Fan
- Torque Converter Clutch (TCC)
- Engine Idle Speed (IAC)

Test Description: Numbers below refer to circled numbers on the diagnostic chart.

1. Checks to see if code was set as a result of hard failure or intermittent condition. Code 15 will set if:
   - The engine has been running for 2 minutes.
   - Signal voltage indicates a coolant temperature below -30°C (-22°F).

2. This test simulates conditions for a Code 14. If the ECM recognizes the grounded circuit (low voltage), and displays a high temperature, the ECM and wiring are OK.

3. This test will determine if there is a wiring problem or a faulty ECM. If CKT 452 is open, there may also be a Code 21 stored.

Diagnostic Aids:

A "Scan" tool reads engine temperature in degrees centigrade. After the engine is started, the temperature should rise steadily to about 90°C, then stabilize when the thermostat opens.

If the engine has been allowed to cool to an ambient temperature (overnight), coolant and MAT temperatures may be checked with a "Scan" tool and should read close to each other.

When a Code 15 is set, the ECM will turn "ON" the engine cooling fan.

A Code 15 will result if CKT(s) 410 or 452 are open. If Code 15 is intermittent, refer to "Symptoms".

CODE 15

COOLANT TEMPERATURE SENSOR (CTS) CIRCUIT
(LOW TEMPERATURE INDICATED)
2.0L OHC (VIN K) "J" CARLINE (TBI)

1. • DOES "SCAN" TOOL DISPLAY COOLANT TEMPERATURE OF -30°C (-22°F) OR LESS?

   NO → CODE 15 IS INTERMITTENT. IF NO ADDITIONAL CODES WERE STORED, REFER TO "DIAGNOSTIC AIDS"

   YES ↓

2. • DISCONNECT SENSOR.
   • JUMPER HARNESS TERMINALS TOGETHER.
   • "SCAN" TOOL SHOULD DISPLAY 130°C (266°F) OR MORE.
     DOES IT?

   YES → FAULTY CONNECTION OR SENSOR.

   NO ↓

3. • JUMPER CKT 410 TO GROUND.
   • "SCAN" TOOL SHOULD DISPLAY OVER 130°C (266°F).
     DOES IT?

   NO → OPEN CKT 410, FAULTY CONNECTION AT ECM, OR FAULTY ECM.

   YES ↓

   OPEN SENSOR GROUND CIRCUIT, FAULTY CONNECTION OR FAULTY ECM.

DIAGNOSTIC AID

COOLANT SENSOR		
TEMPERATURE TO RESISTANCE VALUES (APPROXIMATE)		
°F	°C	OHMS
210	100	185
160	70	450
100	38	1,800
70	20	3,400
40	4	7,500
20	-7	13,500
0	-18	25,000
-40	-40	100,700

CLEAR CODES AND CONFIRM "CLOSED LOOP" OPERATION AND NO "SERVICE ENGINE SOON" LIGHT.

1990-92 2.0L (VIN K)

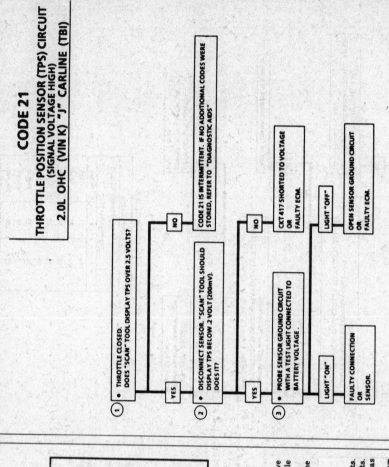

CODE 21

THROTTLE POSITION SENSOR (TPS) CIRCUIT
(SIGNAL VOLTAGE HIGH)
2.0L OHC (VIN K) "J" CARLINE (TBI)

Circuit Description:

The Throttle Position Sensor (TPS) provides a voltage signal that changes relative to the throttle valve position. Signal voltage will vary from less than 1.25 volts at idle to about 4.5 volts at Wide Open Throttle (WOT).

The TPS signal is one of the most important inputs used by the ECM for fuel control and for many of the ECM controlled outputs.

Test Description: Numbers below refer to circled numbers on the diagnostic chart.

1. This step checks to see if Code 21 is the result of a hard failure or an intermittent condition.
   A Code 21 will set if
   - TPS reading is above 2.5 volts
   - Engine speed is less than 1800 rpm
   - MAP reading is below 65 kPa
   - All of the above conditions are present for 2 seconds

2. This step simulates conditions for a Code 22. If the ECM recognizes the change, the ECM and CKTs 416 and 417 are OK.

3. This step isolates a faulty sensor, ECM, or an open CKT 452. If CKT 452 is open, there may also be a Code 15 stored.

Diagnostic Aids:

A "Scan" tool displays throttle position in volts. Closed throttle voltage should be less than 1.25 volts. TPS voltage should increase at a steady rate as throttle is moved to WOT.

A Code 21 will result if CKT 452 is open or CKT 417 is shorted to voltage. If Code 21 is intermittent, refer to "Symptoms"

1990-92 2.0L (VIN K)

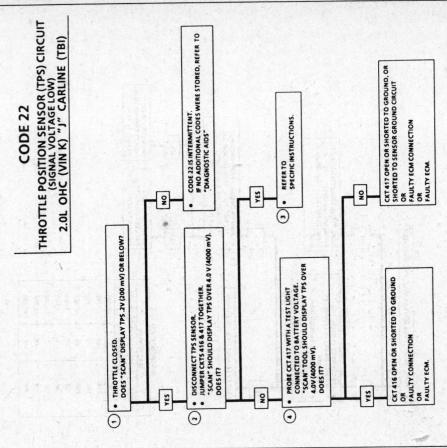

CODE 22

THROTTLE POSITION SENSOR (TPS) CIRCUIT
(SIGNAL VOLTAGE LOW)
2.0L OHC (VIN K) "J" CARLINE (TBI)

Circuit Description:

The Throttle Position Sensor (TPS) provides a voltage signal that changes, relative to the throttle valve position. Signal voltage will vary from less than 1.25 volts at idle to about 4.5 volts at Wide Open Throttle (WOT).

The TPS signal is one of the most important inputs used by the ECM for fuel control and for many of the ECM controlled outputs.

Test Description: Numbers below refer to circled numbers on the diagnostic chart.

1. This step checks to see if Code 22 is the result of a hard failure or an intermittent condition.
   A Code 22 will set if
   • The engine is running.
   • TPS voltage is below .2 volt (200 mV)
2. This step simulates conditions for a Code 21. If a Code 21 is set, or the "Scan" tool displays over 4 volts, the ECM and wiring are OK.
3. The "Scan" tool may not display 5 volts. The important thing is that the ECM recognizes the voltage as over 4 volts, indicating that CKT 417 and the ECM are OK.
4. If CKT 416 is open or shorted to ground, there may also be a stored Code 34.

Diagnostic Aids:

A "Scan" tool displays throttle position in volts. Closed throttle voltage should be less than 1.25 volts. TPS voltage should increase at a steady rate as throttle is moved to WOT.

An open or grounded 416 or 417 will result in a Code 22.

If Code 22 is intermittent, refer to "Symptoms"

CODE 22

THROTTLE POSITION SENSOR (TPS) CIRCUIT
(SIGNAL VOLTAGE LOW)
2.0L OHC (VIN K) "J" CARLINE (TBI)

(1) • THROTTLE CLOSED.
DOES "SCAN" DISPLAY TPS .2V (200 mV) OR BELOW?

YES

(2) • DISCONNECT TPS SENSOR.
JUMPER CKTS 416 & 417 TOGETHER.
"SCAN" SHOULD DISPLAY TPS OVER 4.0 V (4000 mV).
DOES IT?

NO

(4) • PROBE CKT 417 WITH A TEST LIGHT CONNECTED TO BATTERY VOLTAGE.
"SCAN" TOOL SHOULD DISPLAY TPS OVER 4.0V (4000 mV).
DOES IT?

YES — CKT 416 OPEN OR SHORTED TO GROUND
OR
FAULTY CONNECTION
OR
FAULTY ECM.

NO (from 1) — CODE 22 IS INTERMITTENT.
IF NO ADDITIONAL CODES WERE STORED, REFER TO "DIAGNOSTIC AIDS"

YES (from 2) — **(3)** REFER TO SPECIFIC INSTRUCTIONS.

NO (from 4) — CKT 417 OPEN OR SHORTED TO GROUND, OR SHORTED TO SENSOR GROUND CIRCUIT
OR
FAULTY ECM CONNECTION
OR
FAULTY ECM.

CLEAR CODES AND CONFIRM "CLOSED LOOP" OPERATION AND NO "SERVICE ENGINE SOON" LIGHT.

THROTTLE POSITION SENSOR CONNECTOR

A
B

TO MAP SENSOR

TO COOLANT TEMPERATURE SENSOR

THROTTLE POSITION SENSOR

A
C
B

WOT
IDLE

416 GRY
417 DK BLU
452 BLK

ECM

W11 — 5 VOLT REFERENCE
B19 — TPS SIGNAL
B12 — SENSOR GROUND

1990-92 2.0L (VIN K)

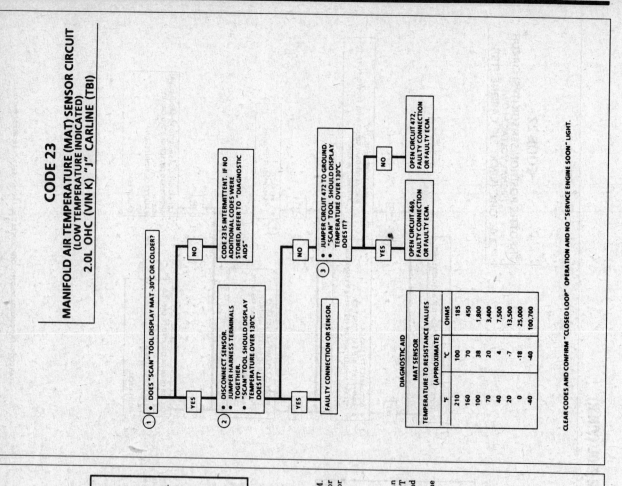

CODE 23

MANIFOLD AIR TEMPERATURE (MAT) SENSOR CIRCUIT
(LOW TEMPERATURE INDICATED)
2.0L OHC (VIN K) "J" CARLINE (TBI)

Circuit Description:

The Manifold Air Temperature (MAT) sensor uses a thermistor to control the signal voltage to the ECM. The ECM applies a voltage (4-6 volts) on CKT 472 to the sensor. When manifold air is cold, the sensor (thermistor) resistance is high, therefore, the ECM will see a high signal voltage. As the air warms, the sensor resistance becomes less and the voltage drops.

Test Description: Numbers below refer to circled numbers on the diagnostic chart.

1. This step checks to see if Code 23 is the result of a hard failure or, an intermittent condition.
   A Code 23 will set if:
   - Engine has been running for longer than 2 minutes.
   - Signal voltage indicates a MAT temperature less than -38° C (-36°F).

2. This test simulates conditions for a Code 25. If the "Scan" tool displays a high temperature, the ECM and wiring are OK.

3. This step checks continuity of CKT(s) 472 or 469. If CKT 469 is open there may also be a Code 33.

Diagnostic Aids:

If the engine has been allowed to cool to an ambient temperature (overnight), coolant and MAT temperatures may be checked with a "Scan" tool and should read close to each other.

A Code 23 will result if CKT(s) 472 or 469 become open.

If Code 23 is intermittent, refer to "Symptoms"

CODE 23

MANIFOLD AIR TEMPERATURE (MAT) SENSOR CIRCUIT
(LOW TEMPERATURE INDICATED)
2.0L OHC (VIN K) "J" CARLINE (TBI)

1. • DOES "SCAN" TOOL DISPLAY MAT -30°C OR COLDER?

- NO → CODE 23 IS INTERMITTENT. IF NO ADDITIONAL CODES WERE STORED, REFER TO "DIAGNOSTIC AIDS"

- YES →

2. • DISCONNECT SENSOR.
   • JUMPER HARNESS TERMINALS TOGETHER.
   • "SCAN" TOOL SHOULD DISPLAY TEMPERATURE OVER 130°C.
   DOES IT?

- YES → FAULTY CONNECTION OR SENSOR.

- NO →

3. • JUMPER CIRCUIT 472 TO GROUND.
   • "SCAN" TOOL SHOULD DISPLAY TEMPERATURE OVER 130°C.
   DOES IT?

- YES → OPEN CIRCUIT 469, FAULTY CONNECTION OR FAULTY ECM.

- NO → OPEN CIRCUIT 472, FAULTY CONNECTION OR FAULTY ECM.

DIAGNOSTIC AID

MAT SENSOR
TEMPERATURE TO RESISTANCE VALUES
(APPROXIMATE)

°F	°C	OHMS
210	100	185
160	70	450
100	38	1,800
70	20	3,400
40	4	7,500
20	-7	13,500
0	-18	25,000
-40	-40	100,700

CLEAR CODES AND CONFIRM "CLOSED LOOP" OPERATION AND NO "SERVICE ENGINE SOON" LIGHT.

ECM

MAT SENSOR SIGNAL
5 VOLT REFERENCE
SENSOR GROUND

B5
W14

472 TAN
469 BLK/ORN

TO MAP SENSOR

MAT SENSOR
A B

469
472

1990-92 2.0L (VIN K)

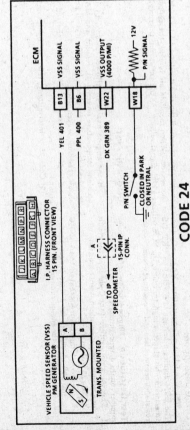

CODE 24

**VEHICLE SPEED SENSOR (VSS) CIRCUIT
2.0L OHC (VIN K) "J" CARLINE (TBI)**

Circuit Description:

Vehicle speed information is provided to the ECM by the Vehicle Speed Sensor (VSS), which is a Permanent Magnet (PM) generator, located in the transaxle. The PM generator produces a pulsing voltage whenever vehicle speed is over 3 mph. The A/C voltage level and the number of pulses increases with vehicle speed. The ECM then converts the pulsing voltage to a mph signal. The mph signal can now be displayed with a "Scan" tool and can also be used for calculations.

The function of the VSS buffer used in past model years has been incorporated into the ECM. The ECM then supplies the necessary signal to the instrument panel (4000 pulses per mile), for operating the speedometer and the odometer.

Test Description: Numbers below refer to circled numbers on the diagnostic chart.

1. Code 24 will set if vehicle speed equals 0 mph when:
   - Engine speed is between 1800 and 4400 rpm
   - TPS is at 0% (closed throttle).
   - Low load condition (low MAP voltage, high manifold vacuum)
   - Not in Park or Neutral
   - All conditions met for 3 seconds

   These conditions are met during a road load deceleration. Disregard Code 24 that sets when drive wheels are not turning.
   The PM generator only produces a signal if the drive wheels are turning greater than 3 mph.

2. Before replacing the ECM the PROM should be checked for correct application.

Diagnostic Aids:

"Scan" should indicate a vehicle speed whenever the drive wheels are turning greater than 3 mph.

A problem in CKT 389 will not affect the VSS input or the readings on a "Scan" tool.

Check CKTs 400 and 401 for proper connections to be sure they are clean and tight and the harness is routed correctly. Refer to "Intermittents"

(A/T) - A faulty or misadjusted Park/Neutral switch can result in a false Code 24. Use a "Scan" tool and check for proper signal while in drive. Refer to CHART C-1A for Park/Neutral (P/N) switch check.

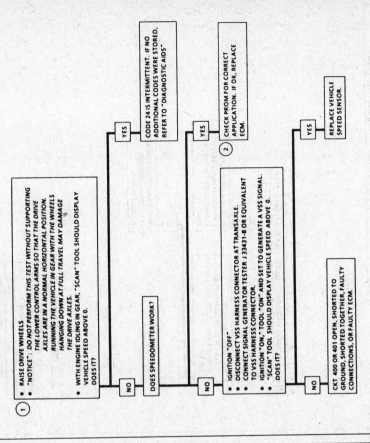

CODE 24

**VEHICLE SPEED SENSOR (VSS) CIRCUIT
2.0L OHC (VIN K) "J" CARLINE (TBI)**

DISREGARD CODE 24 IF SET WHILE DRIVE WHEELS ARE NOT TURNING.

1. • RAISE DRIVE WHEELS
   • "NOTICE": DO NOT PERFORM THIS TEST WITHOUT SUPPORTING THE LOWER CONTROL ARMS SO THAT THE DRIVE AXLES ARE IN A NORMAL HORIZONTAL POSITION. RUNNING THE VEHICLE IN GEAR WITH THE WHEELS HANGING DOWN AT FULL TRAVEL MAY DAMAGE THE DRIVE AXLES.
   • WITH ENGINE IDLING IN GEAR, "SCAN" TOOL SHOULD DISPLAY VEHICLE SPEED ABOVE 0.
   DOES IT?

   YES → CODE 24 IS INTERMITTENT. IF NO ADDITIONAL CODES WERE STORED, REFER TO "DIAGNOSTIC AIDS"

   NO → DOES SPEEDOMETER WORK?

   YES → CHECK PROM FOR CORRECT APPLICATION. IF OK, REPLACE ECM.

   NO →
   • IGNITION "OFF"
   • DISCONNECT VSS HARNESS CONNECTOR AT TRANSAXLE.
   • CONNECT SIGNAL GENERATOR TESTER J 33431-B OR EQUIVALENT TO VSS HARNESS CONNECTOR.
   • IGNITION "ON", TOOL "ON" AND SET TO GENERATE A VSS SIGNAL.
   • "SCAN" TOOL SHOULD DISPLAY VEHICLE SPEED ABOVE 0.
   DOES IT?

   YES → (2)

   NO → CKT 400 OR 401 OPEN, SHORTED TO GROUND, SHORTED TOGETHER, FAULTY CONNECTIONS, OR FAULTY ECM.

   YES → REPLACE VEHICLE SPEED SENSOR.

CLEAR CODES AND CONFIRM "CLOSED LOOP" OPERATION AND NO "SERVICE ENGINE SOON" LIGHT.

CODE 25

MANIFOLD AIR TEMPERATURE (MAT) SENSOR CIRCUIT
(HIGH TEMPERATURE INDICATED)
2.0L OHC (VIN K) "J" CARLINE (TBI)

DOES "SCAN" TOOL DISPLAY MAT AT 145°C (293°F) OR HOTTER?

- YES
- NO

- DISCONNECT SENSOR.
  "SCAN" TOOL SHOULD DISPLAY TEMPERATURE BELOW -30°C (-22°F). DOES IT?

- CODE 25 IS INTERMITTENT. IF NO ADDITIONAL CODES WERE STORED, REFER TO "DIAGNOSTIC AIDS"

- YES
- NO

- REPLACE SENSOR.

- CKT 472 SHORTED TO GROUND, OR TO SENSOR GROUND, OR ECM IS FAULTY.

DIAGNOSTIC AID

MAT SENSOR
TEMPERATURE VS. RESISTANCE VALUES
(APPROXIMATE)

°F	°C	OHMS
210	100	185
160	70	450
100	38	1,800
70	20	3,400
40	4	7,500
20	-7	13,500
0	-18	25,000
-40	-40	100,700

CLEAR CODES AND CONFIRM "CLOSED LOOP" OPERATION AND NO "SERVICE ENGINE SOON" LIGHT.

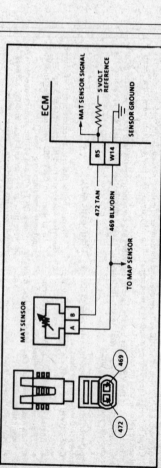

CODE 25

MANIFOLD AIR TEMPERATURE (MAT) SENSOR CIRCUIT
(HIGH TEMPERATURE INDICATED)
2.0L OHC (VIN K) "J" CARLINE (TBI)

Circuit Description:

The Manifold Air Temperature (MAT) sensor uses a thermistor to control the signal voltage to the ECM. The ECM applies a voltage (4-6 volts) on CKT 472 to the sensor. When manifold air is cold, the sensor (thermistor) resistance is high, therefore, the ECM will see a high signal voltage. As the air warms, the sensor resistance becomes less and the voltage drops.

Test Description: Numbers below refer to circled numbers on the diagnostic chart.

1. This check determines if the Code 25 is the result of a hard failure or an intermittent condition. A Code 25 will set if:
   - A MAT temperature greater than 135°C (275°F) is detected for a time longer than 2 seconds, with the engine running

Diagnostic Aids:

If the engine has been allowed to cool to an ambient temperature (overnight), coolant and MAT temperatures may be checked with a "Scan" tool and should read close to each other.

A Code 25 will result if CKT 472 is shorted to ground.

If Code 25 is intermittent, refer to "Symptoms"

1990-92 2.0L (VIN K)

CODE 32

EXHAUST GAS RECIRCULATION (EGR) SYSTEM FAILURE
2.0L OHC (VIN K) "J" CARLINE (TBI)

IF CODES 21, 22, 33, OR 34 ARE PRESENT, REPAIR CAUSES FOR THOSE CODES BEFORE USING THIS CHART.

- FIRMLY GRASP TOP OF EGR VALVE AND CHECK FOR LOOSENESS BY TRYING TO ROTATE VALVE IN BOTH DIRECTIONS. IS LOOSENESS FELT?

→ YES → REPLACE EGR VALVE ASSEMBLY.

→ NO

- PLACE TRANSMISSION IN "PARK" OR "NEUTRAL."
- RUN WARM ENGINE AT IDLE. ENGINE TEMPERATURE MUST BE ABOVE 90°C (195°F).
- PUSH UP ON UNDERSIDE OF EGR VALVE DIAPHRAGM. ENGINE SPEED SHOULD DROP. DOES IT?

→ YES

- CHECK FOR MOVEMENT OF EGR VALVE DIAPHRAGM AS ENGINE SPEED IS INCREASED FROM IDLE TO 2000 RPM. DOES DIAPHRAGM MOVE?

→ NO → CLEAN EGR VALVE OR PASSAGES. REPLACE VALVE IF NECESSARY.

→ YES → REFER TO "DIAGNOSTIC AIDS"

- CHECK VACUUM AT EGR VALVE AS ENGINE SPEED IS INCREASED FROM IDLE TO 2000 RPM.

VACUUM IS UNDER 20 kPa (6"Hg)

→ VACUUM IS OVER 20 kPa (6"Hg) → REPLACE EGR VALVE.

CHECK VACUUM HOSES FOR RESTRICTIONS, LEAKS, AND CONNECTIONS.

CLEAR CODES AND CONFIRM "CLOSED LOOP" OPERATION AND NO "SERVICE ENGINE SOON" LIGHT.

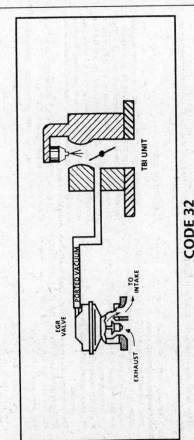

CODE 32

EXHAUST GAS RECIRCULATION (EGR) SYSTEM FAILURE
2.0L OHC (VIN K) "J" CARLINE (TBI)

Code Description:

A properly operating EGR system will directly affect the air/fuel requirements of the engine. Since the exhaust gas introduced into the air/fuel mixture is an inert gas (contains very little or no oxygen), less fuel is required to maintain a correct air/fuel ratio. If the EGR system were to become inoperative, the inert exhaust gas would be replaced with air and the air/fuel mixture would be leaner. The ECM would compensate for the lean condition by adding fuel, resulting in higher block learn values.

The engine control system operates within two block learn cells, a closed throttle cell, and an open throttle cell. Since EGR is not used at idle, the closed throttle cell would not be affected by EGR system operation. The open throttle cell is affected by EGR operation and, when the EGR system is operating properly, the block learn values in both cells should be close to being the same. If the EGR system was inoperative, the block learn value in the open throttle cell would change (become higher) to compensate for the resulting lean system, but the block learn value in the closed throttle cell would not change.

This change or difference in block learn values is used to monitor EGR system performance. When the change becomes too great, a Code 32 is set.

Diagnostic Aids:

The Code 32 chart is a functional check of the EGR system. If the EGR system works properly, but a Code 32 has been set, check other items that could result in high block learn values in the open throttle cell, but not in the closed throttle cell.

CHECK:

EGR Passages
Restricted or blocked

MAP Sensor
A MAP sensor may shift in calibration enough to affect fuel delivery. Use CHART C-1D, MAP output check.

1990-92 2.0L (VIN K)

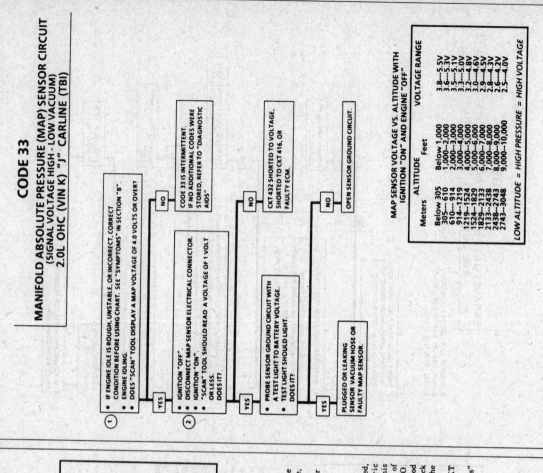

CODE 33

MANIFOLD ABSOLUTE PRESSURE (MAP) SENSOR CIRCUIT
(SIGNAL VOLTAGE HIGH - LOW VACUUM)
2.0L OHC (VIN K) "J" CARLINE (TBI)

Circuit Description:

The Manifold Absolute Pressure (MAP) sensor responds to changes in manifold pressure (vacuum). The ECM receives this information as a signal voltage that will vary from about 1 to 1.5 volts, at closed throttle idle, to 4 – 4.5 volts at wide open throttle (low vacuum).

If the MAP sensor fails, the ECM will substitute a fixed MAP value and use the Throttle Position Sensor (TPS) to control fuel delivery.

Test Description: Numbers below refer to circled numbers on the diagnostic chart.

1. This step will determine if Code 33 is the result of a hard failure or an intermittent condition. A Code 33 will set if
   - MAP signal indicates greater than 84 kPa (low vacuum)
   - TPS less than 2%
   - These conditions for a time longer than 5 seconds

2. This step simulates conditions for a Code 34. If the ECM recognizes the change, the ECM and CKTs 416 and 432, are OK. If CKT 469 is open, there may, also, be a stored Code 23.

Diagnostic Aids:

With the ignition "ON" and the engine stopped, the manifold pressure is equal to atmospheric pressure and the signal voltage will be high. This information is used by the ECM as an indication of vehicle altitude and is referred to as BARO. Comparison of this BARO reading with a known good vehicle with the same sensor is a good way to check accuracy of a "suspect" sensor. Readings should be the same ± .4 volt.

A Code 33 will result if CKT 469 is open, or if CKT 432 is shorted to voltage or to CKT 416.

If Code 33 is intermittent, refer to "Symptoms"

1990-92 2.0L (VIN K)

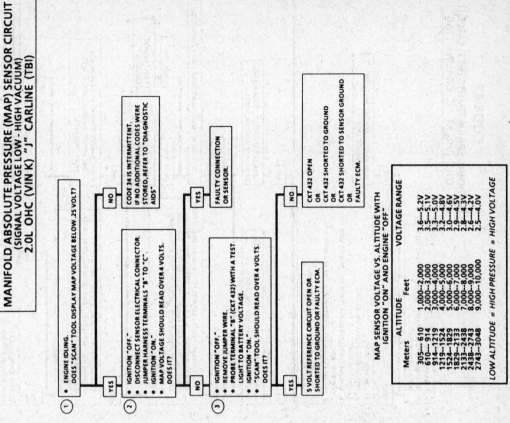

CODE 34

MANIFOLD ABSOLUTE PRESSURE (MAP) SENSOR CIRCUIT
(SIGNAL VOLTAGE LOW - HIGH VACUUM)
2.0L OHC (VIN K) "J" CARLINE (TBI)

① ENGINE IDLING.
• DOES "SCAN" TOOL DISPLAY MAP VOLTAGE BELOW .25 VOLT?

YES

NO → CODE 34 IS INTERMITTENT.
IF NO ADDITIONAL CODES WERE STORED, REFER TO "DIAGNOSTIC AIDS"

② • IGNITION "OFF."
• DISCONNECT SENSOR ELECTRICAL CONNECTOR.
• JUMPER HARNESS TERMINALS "B" TO "C."
• IGNITION "ON."
• MAP VOLTAGE SHOULD READ OVER 4 VOLTS.
DOES IT?

NO

YES → FAULTY CONNECTION OR SENSOR.

③ • IGNITION "OFF."
• REMOVE JUMPER WIRE.
• PROBE TERMINAL "B" (CKT 432) WITH A TEST LIGHT TO BATTERY VOLTAGE.
• IGNITION "ON."
• "SCAN" TOOL SHOULD READ OVER 4 VOLTS.
DOES IT?

YES

NO → CKT 432 OPEN
OR
CKT 432 SHORTED TO GROUND
OR
CKT 432 SHORTED TO SENSOR GROUND
OR
FAULTY ECM.

5 VOLT REFERENCE CIRCUIT OPEN OR SHORTED TO GROUND OR FAULTY ECM.

MAP SENSOR VOLTAGE VS. ALTITUDE WITH IGNITION "ON" AND ENGINE "OFF"

ALTITUDE		VOLTAGE RANGE
Meters	Feet	
305——610	1,000–2,000	3.6—5.2V
610——914	2,000–3,000	3.5—5.1V
914——1219	3,000–4,000	3.3—5.0V
1219—1524	4,000–5,000	3.2—4.8V
1524—1829	5,000–6,000	3.0—4.6V
1829—2133	6,000–7,000	2.9—4.5V
2133—2438	7,000–8,000	2.8—4.3V
2438—2743	8,000–9,000	2.6—4.2V
2743—3048	9,000–10,000	2.5—4.0V

LOW ALTITUDE = HIGH PRESSURE = HIGH VOLTAGE

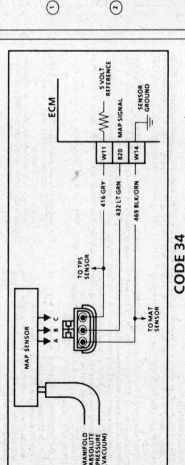

CODE 34

MANIFOLD ABSOLUTE PRESSURE (MAP) SENSOR CIRCUIT
(SIGNAL VOLTAGE LOW - HIGH VACUUM)
2.0L OHC (VIN K) "J" CARLINE (TBI)

Circuit Description:

The Manifold Absolute Pressure (MAP) sensor responds to changes in manifold pressure (vacuum). The ECM receives this information as a signal voltage that will vary from about 1 to 1.5 volts at closed throttle idle, to 4—4.5 volts at wide open throttle.

If the MAP sensor fails, the ECM will substitute a fixed MAP value and use the Throttle Position Sensor (TPS) to control fuel delivery.

Test Description: Numbers below refer to circled numbers on the diagnostic chart.

1. This step determines if Code 34 is the result of a hard failure or an intermittent condition. A Code 34 will set when
   • Engine rpm is greater than 1200 rpm
   • TPS is greater the 20%
   • MAP signal voltage is too low

2. Jumpering harness terminals "B" to "C," 5 volts to signal, will determine if the sensor is at fault, or if there is a problem with the ECM or wiring. The "Scan" tool may not display 5 volts. The important thing is that the ECM recognizes the voltage as more than 4 volts, indicating that the ECM and CKT 432 are OK.

Diagnostic Aids:

With the ignition "ON," and the engine stopped, the manifold pressure is equal to atmospheric pressure and the signal voltage will be high. This information is used by the ECM as an indication of vehicle altitude and is referred to as BARO. Comparison of this BARO reading with a known good vehicle with the same sensor is a good way to check accuracy of a "suspect" sensor. Readings should be the same ± .4 volts.

A Code 34 will result if CKT(s) 416 or 432 are open or shorted to ground.

If Code 34 is intermittent, refer to "Symptoms"

1990-92 2.0L (VIN K)

CODE 42

ELECTRONIC SPARK TIMING (EST) CIRCUIT 2.0L OHC (VIN K) "J" CARLINE (TBI)

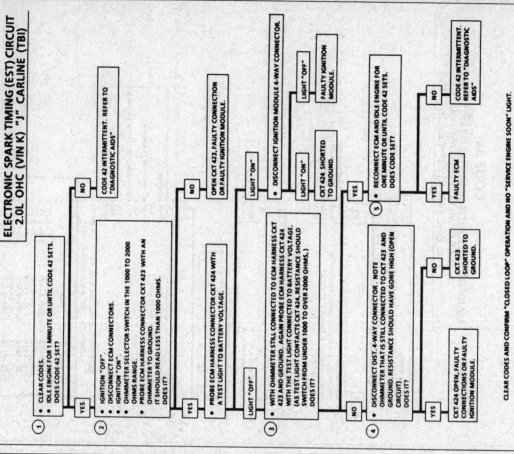

1. CLEAR CODES.
   IDLE ENGINE FOR 1 MINUTE OR UNTIL CODE 42 SETS.
   DOES CODE 42 SET?

   - YES
   - NO → CODE 42 INTERMITTENT. REFER TO "DIAGNOSTIC AIDS"

2. IGNITION "OFF".
   DISCONNECT ECM CONNECTORS.
   IGNITION "ON".
   OHMMETER SELECTOR SWITCH IN THE 1000 TO 2000 OHMS RANGE.
   PROBE ECM HARNESS CONNECTOR CKT 423 WITH AN OHMMETER TO GROUND.
   IT SHOULD READ LESS THAN 1000 OHMS.
   DOES IT?

   - YES
   - NO → OPEN CKT 423, FAULTY CONNECTION OR FAULTY IGNITION MODULE.

   PROBE ECM HARNESS CONNECTOR CKT 424 WITH A TEST LIGHT TO BATTERY VOLTAGE.

   - LIGHT "OFF"
   - LIGHT "ON" → DISCONNECT IGNITION MODULE 4-WAY CONNECTOR.
     - LIGHT "OFF"
     - LIGHT "ON" → CKT 424 SHORTED TO GROUND.
     - FAULTY IGNITION MODULE.

3. WITH OHMMETER STILL CONNECTED TO ECM HARNESS CKT 423 AND GROUND. AGAIN PROBE ECM HARNESS CKT 424 WITH THE TEST LIGHT CONNECTED TO BATTERY VOLTAGE. (AS TEST LIGHT CONTACTS CKT 424, RESISTANCE SHOULD SWITCH FROM UNDER 1000 TO OVER 2000 OHMS.)
   DOES IT?

   - YES
   - NO

4. DISCONNECT DIST. 4-WAY CONNECTOR. NOTE OHMMETER THAT IS STILL CONNECTED TO CKT 423 AND GROUND. RESISTANCE SHOULD HAVE GONE HIGH (OPEN CIRCUIT).
   DOES IT?

   - YES → CKT 423 SHORTED TO GROUND.
   - NO → CKT 424 OPEN, FAULTY CONNECTIONS OR FAULTY IGNITION MODULE.

5. RECONNECT ECM AND IDLE ENGINE FOR ONE MINUTE OR UNTIL CODE 42 SETS.
   DOES CODE SET?

   - YES → FAULTY ECM
   - NO → CODE 42 INTERMITTENT. REFER TO "DIAGNOSTIC AIDS"

CLEAR CODES AND CONFIRM "CLOSED LOOP" OPERATION AND NO "SERVICE ENGINE SOON" LIGHT.

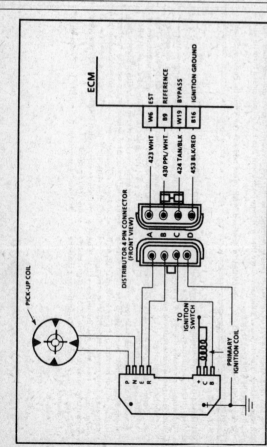

ECM

W6	EST	423 WHT
B9	REFERENCE	430 PPL/WHT
W19	BYPASS	424 TAN/BLK
B16	IGNITION GROUND	453 BLK/RED

DISTRIBUTOR 4 PIN CONNECTOR (FRONT VIEW)

A B C D

PICK-UP COIL

TO IGNITION SWITCH

PRIMARY IGNITION COIL

CODE 42

ELECTRONIC SPARK TIMING (EST) CIRCUIT 2.0L OHC (VIN K) "J" CARLINE (TBI)

Circuit Description:

The ignition module sends a reference signal (CKT 430) to the ECM, when the engine is cranking. While the engine speed is under 400 rpm, the ignition module will control ignition timing. When the engine speed exceeds 400 rpm, the ECM applies 5 volts to the bypass line (CKT 424) to switch the timing to ECM control (EST CKT 423).

When the system is running on the ignition module, that is, no voltage on the bypass line, the ignition module grounds the EST signal. The ECM expects to sense or detect a voltage. If it senses or detects a voltage, it sets Code 42 and will not go into the EST mode.

When the rpm for EST is reached (about 400 rpm), voltage will be applied to the bypass line. The EST should no longer be grounded in the ignition module, so the EST voltage should be varying.

If the bypass line is open or grounded, the ignition module will not switch to EST mode, so the EST voltage will be low and Code 42 will be set.

If the EST line is grounded, the ignition module will switch to EST but, because the line is grounded, there will be no EST signal. A Code 42 will be set.

Test Description: Numbers below refer to circled numbers on the diagnostic chart.

1. Code 42 means the ECM has detected an open or short to ground in the EST or bypass circuits. This test confirms Code 42 and that the fault causing the code is present.

2. Checks for a normal EST ground path through the ignition module. An EST CKT 423, shorted to ground, will also read less than 500 ohms, however, this will be checked later.

3. As the test light voltage touches CKT 424, the module should switch, causing the ohmmeter to "overrange" if the meter is in the 1000-2000 ohms position. Selecting the 10-20,000 ohms position will indicate above 5000 ohms. The important thing is that the module "switched".

4. The module did not switch and this step checks for:
   - EST CKT 423 shorted to ground
   - Bypass CKT 424 open
   - Faulty ignition module connection or module

5. Confirms that Code 42 is a faulty ECM and not an intermittent in CKT(s) 423 or 424.

Diagnostic Aids:

The "Scan" tool does not have any ability to help diagnose a Code 42 problem.

If Code 42 is intermittent, refer to "Symptoms"

1990-92 2.0L (VIN K)

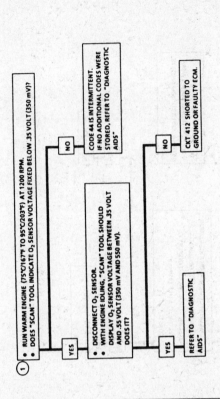

CODE 44

OXYGEN SENSOR CIRCUIT
(LEAN EXHAUST INDICATED)
2.0L OHC (VIN K) "J" CARLINE (TBI)

① • RUN WARM ENGINE (75°C/167°F TO 95°C/203°F) AT 1200 RPM.
 • DOES "SCAN" TOOL INDICATE O_2 SENSOR VOLTAGE FIXED BELOW .35 VOLT (350 mV)?

YES

 • DISCONNECT O_2 SENSOR.
 • WITH ENGINE IDLING, "SCAN" TOOL SHOULD DISPLAY O_2 SENSOR VOLTAGE BETWEEN .35 VOLT AND .55 VOLT (350 mV AND 550 mV).
   DOES IT?

YES

REFER TO "DIAGNOSTIC AIDS"

NO

CODE 44 IS INTERMITTENT. IF NO ADDITIONAL CODES WERE STORED, REFER TO "DIAGNOSTIC AIDS"

NO

CKT 412 SHORTED TO GROUND OR FAULTY ECM.

CLEAR CODES AND CONFIRM "CLOSED LOOP" OPERATION AND NO "SERVICE ENGINE SOON" LIGHT.

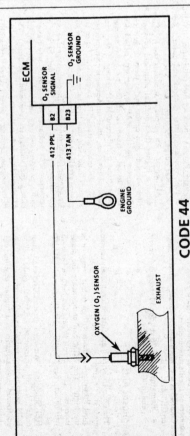

OXYGEN (O_2) SENSOR

EXHAUST

ENGINE GROUND

412 PPL
413 TAN

ECM

B2 — O_2 SENSOR SIGNAL

B23 — O_2 SENSOR GROUND

CODE 44

OXYGEN SENSOR CIRCUIT
(LEAN EXHAUST INDICATED)
2.0L OHC (VIN K) "J" CARLINE (TBI)

Circuit Description:

The ECM supplies a voltage of about .45 volt between terminals "B2" and "B23". (If measured with a 10 megohm digital voltmeter, this may read as low as .32 volt.) The O_2 sensor varies the voltage within a range of about 1 volt, if the exhaust is rich, down through about .10 volt, if exhaust is lean.

The sensor is like an open circuit and produces no voltage, when it is below about 316°C (600°F). An open sensor circuit or cold sensor causes "Open Loop" operation.

Test Description: Numbers below refer to circled numbers on the diagnostic chart.

1. Code 44 is set, when the O_2 sensor signal voltage on CKT 412:
   • Remains below .2 volt for 50 seconds or more;
   • And the system is operating in "Closed Loop"

Diagnostic Aids:

Using the "Scan," observe the block learn value at different rpms. The "Scan" also displays the block learn cells, so the block learn values can be checked in each of the cells, to determine when the Code 44 may have been set. If the conditions for Code 44 exists, the block learn values will be around 150.

 • O_2 Sensor Wire - Sensor pigtail may be mispositioned and contacting the exhaust manifold.
 • Check for ground in wire between connector and sensor.

 • Fuel Contamination - Water, even in small amounts, near the in-tank fuel pump inlet can be delivered to the injector. The water causes a lean exhaust and can set a Code 44.
 • Fuel Pressure - System will be lean if pressure is too low. It may be necessary to monitor fuel pressure, while driving the car at various road speeds and/or loads to confirm. See "Fuel System Diagnosis," CHART A-7.
 • Exhaust Leaks - If there is an exhaust leak, the engine can cause outside air to be pulled into the exhaust and past the sensor. Vacuum or crankcase leaks can cause a lean condition. If Code 44 intermittent, refer to "Symptoms"

1990-92 2.0L (VIN K)

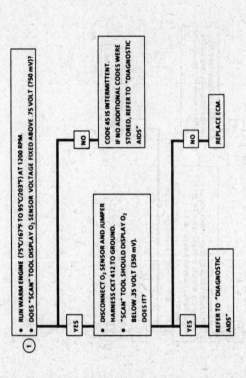

CODE 45
OXYGEN SENSOR CIRCUIT
(RICH EXHAUST INDICATED)
2.0L OHC (VIN K) "J" CARLINE (TBI)

①
- RUN WARM ENGINE (75°C/167°F TO 95°C/203°F) AT 1200 RPM.
- DOES "SCAN" TOOL DISPLAY O_2 SENSOR VOLTAGE FIXED ABOVE .75 VOLT (750 mV)?

YES
- DISCONNECT O_2 SENSOR AND JUMPER HARNESS CKT 412 TO GROUND.
- "SCAN" TOOL SHOULD DISPLAY O_2 BELOW .35 VOLT (350 mV). DOES IT?

NO → CODE 45 IS INTERMITTENT. IF NO ADDITIONAL CODES WERE STORED, REFER TO "DIAGNOSTIC AIDS"

YES → REFER TO "DIAGNOSTIC AIDS"

NO → REPLACE ECM.

CLEAR CODES AND CONFIRM "CLOSED LOOP" OPERATION AND NO "SERVICE ENGINE SOON" LIGHT.

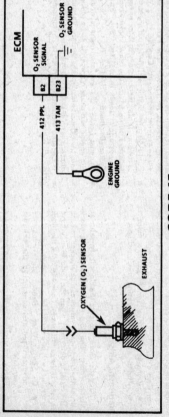

CODE 45
OXYGEN SENSOR CIRCUIT
(RICH EXHAUST INDICATED)
2.0L OHC (VIN K) "J" CARLINE (TBI)

Circuit Description:

The ECM supplies a voltage of about .45 volt between terminals "B2" and "B23". (If measured with a 10 megohm digital voltmeter, this may read as low as .32 volt.) The O_2 sensor varies the voltage within a range of about 1 volt, if the exhaust is rich, down through about .10 volt, if exhaust is lean.

The sensor is like an open circuit and produces no voltage, when it is below about 316°C (600°F). An open sensor circuit, or cold sensor, causes "Open Loop" operation.

Test Description: Numbers below refer to circled numbers on the diagnostic chart.

1. Code 45 is set, when the O_2 sensor signal voltage on CKT 412:
   - Remains above .75 volt for 50 seconds or more; and in "Closed Loop".

Diagnostic Aids:

The Code 45, or rich exhaust, is most likely caused by one of the flowing:

- **Fuel Pressure** - System will go rich if pressure is too high. The ECM can compensate for some increase. However, if it gets too high, a Code 45 will be set. See "Fuel System Diagnosis" CHART A-7.

- **HEI Shielding** - An open ground CKT 453 may result in EMI, or induced electrical "noise." The ECM looks at this "noise" as reference pulses. The additional pulses result in a higher than actual engine speed signal. The ECM then delivers too much fuel, causing system to go rich. Engine tachometer will also show higher than actual engine speed, which can help in diagnosing this problem.

- **Canister Purge** - Check for fuel saturation. If full of fuel, check canister control and hoses. See "Canister Purge," Section "C3".

- **MAP Sensor** - An output that causes the ECM to sense a higher than normal manifold pressure (low vacuum) can cause the system to go rich. Disconnecting the MAP sensor will allow the ECM to set a fixed value for the MAP sensor. Substitute a different MAP sensor if the rich condition is gone, while the sensor is disconnected.

- **TPS** - An intermittent TPS output will cause the system to go rich, due to a false indication of the engine accelerating.

- **O_2 Sensor Contamination** - Inspect oxygen sensor for silicone contamination from fuel, or use of improper RTV sealant. The sensor may have a white, powdery coating and result in a high, but false signal voltage (rich exhaust indication). The ECM will then reduce the amount of fuel delivered to the engine, causing a severe surge driveability problem.

- **EGR** - Valve sticking open at idle, usually accompanied by a rough idle, stall complaint. If Code 45 is intermittent, refer to "Symptoms"

1990-92 2.0L (VIN K)

CODE 51

2.0L OHC (VIN K) "J" CARLINE (TBI)

CODE 51

PROM ERROR
(FAULTY OR INCORRECT PROM)

CHECK THAT ALL PINS ARE FULLY INSERTED IN THE SOCKET AND THAT PROM IS PROPERLY SEATED. IF OK, REPLACE PROM, CLEAR MEMORY, AND RECHECK. IF CODE 51 REAPPEARS, REPLACE ECM.

CLEAR CODES AND CONFIRM "CLOSED LOOP" OPERATION AND NO "SERVICE ENGINE SOON" LIGHT.

CODE 53

2.0L OHC (VIN K) "J" CARLINE (TBI)

CODE 53

SYSTEM OVER VOLTAGE

- THIS CODE INDICATES THAT THERE IS A BASIC GENERATOR PROBLEM.
- CODE 53 WILL SET IF BATTERY VOLTAGE AT THE ECM IS GREATER THAN 16.9 VOLTS FOR AT LEAST 50 SECONDS.
- CHECK AND REPAIR CHARGING SYSTEM.

CLEAR CODES AND CONFIRM "CLOSED LOOP" OPERATION AND NO "SERVICE ENGINE SOON" LIGHT.

1990-92 2.0L (VIN K)

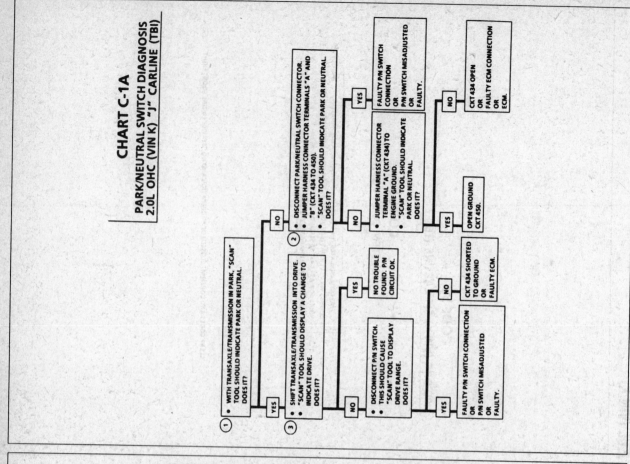

CHART C-1A

**PARK/NEUTRAL SWITCH DIAGNOSIS
2.0L OHC (VIN K) "J" CARLINE (TBI)**

Circuit Description:

The Park/Neutral (P/N) switch contacts are a part of the neutral start switch and are closed to ground in park or neutral, and open in drive ranges.

The ECM supplies ignition voltage through a current limiting resistor to CKT 434 and senses a closed switch when the voltage on CKT 434 drops to less than one volt.

The ECM uses the P/N signal as one of the inputs to control idle air control and VSS diagnostics.

Test Description: Numbers below refer to circled numbers on the diagnostic chart.

1. Checks for a closed switch to ground in park position. Different "Scan" tools may display P/N differently. Refer to tool operator's manual for the display used.

2. Checks for an open switch in drive range.

3. Be sure "Scan" tool indicates drive even while wiggling shifter to test for an intermittent or maladjusted switch in drive range.

1990-92 2.0L (VIN K)

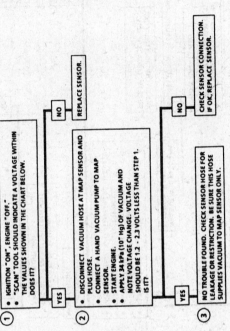

CHART C-1D
MANIFOLD ABSOLUTE PRESSURE (MAP) OUTPUT CHECK
2.0L OHC (VIN K) "J" CARLINE (TBI)

ECM

- 5 VOLT REFERENCE — W11 — 416 GRY
- MAP SIGNAL — B20 — 432 LT GRN
- SENSOR GROUND — W14 — 469 BLK/ORN

MAP SENSOR — A B C

MANIFOLD ABSOLUTE PRESSURE (VACUUM)

TO TPS SENSOR
TO MAT SENSOR

Circuit Description:

The Manifold Absolute Pressure (MAP) sensor senses manifold pressure and sends that signal to the ECM. The MAP sensor is mainly used to calculate engine load, which is a fundamental input for spark and fuel calculations. The MAP sensor is also used to determine barometric pressure.

Test Description: Numbers below refer to circled numbers on the diagnostic chart.

1. Checks MAP sensor output voltage to the ECM. This voltage, without engine running, represents a barometer reading to the ECM. Comparison of this BARO reading with a known good vehicle with the same sensor is a good way to check the accuracy of a "suspect" sensor. Readings should be within .4 volt.

2. Applying 34 kPa (10" Hg) vacuum to the MAP sensor should cause the voltage to be 1.2 to 2.3 volts less than the voltage at step 1. Upon applying vacuum to the sensor, the change in voltage should be instantaneous. A slow voltage change indicates a faulty sensor.

3. Check vacuum hose to sensor for leaking or restriction. Be sure no other vacuum devices are connected to the MAP hose.

CHART C-1D
MANIFOLD ABSOLUTE PRESSURE (MAP) OUTPUT CHECK
2.0L OHC (VIN K) "J" CARLINE (TBI)

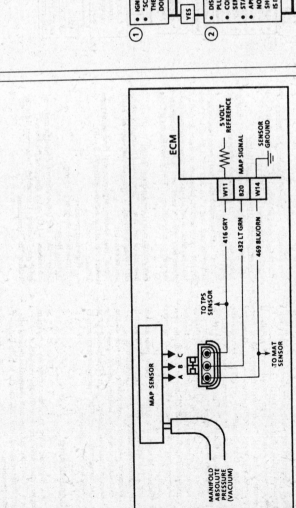

1. IGNITION "ON", ENGINE "OFF."
   - "SCAN" TOOL SHOULD INDICATE A VOLTAGE WITHIN THE VALUES SHOWN IN THE CHART BELOW. DOES IT?

   NO → REPLACE SENSOR.

2. - DISCONNECT VACUUM HOSE AT MAP SENSOR AND PLUG HOSE.
   - CONNECT A HAND VACUUM PUMP TO MAP SENSOR.
   - START ENGINE.
   - APPLY 34 kPa (10" Hg) OF VACUUM AND NOTE VOLTAGE CHANGE. VOLTAGE SHOULD BE 1.2 - 2.3 VOLTS LESS THAN STEP 1. IS IT?

   NO → CHECK SENSOR CONNECTION. IF OK, REPLACE SENSOR.

3. NO TROUBLE FOUND. CHECK SENSOR HOSE FOR LEAKAGE OR RESTRICTION. BE SURE THIS HOSE SUPPLIES VACUUM TO MAP SENSOR ONLY.

ALTITUDE		VOLTAGE RANGE
Meters	Feet	
Below 305	Below 1,000	3.8—5.5V
305—610	1,000—2,000	3.6—5.3V
610—914	2,000—3,000	3.5—5.1V
914—1219	3,000—4,000	3.3—5.0V
1219—1524	4,000—5,000	3.2—4.8V
1524—1829	5,000—6,000	3.0—4.6V
1829—2133	6,000—7,000	2.9—4.5V
2133—2438	7,000—8,000	2.8—4.3V
2438—2743	8,000—9,000	2.6—4.2V
2743—3048	9,000—10,000	2.5—4.0V

LOW ALTITUDE = HIGH PRESSURE = HIGH VOLTAGE

CLEAR CODES AND CONFIRM "CLOSED LOOP" OPERATION AND NO "SERVICE ENGINE SOON" LIGHT.

1990-92 2.0L (VIN K)

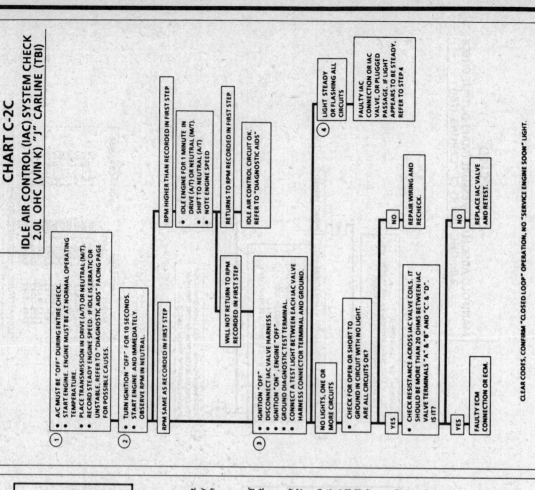

CHART C-2C

IDLE AIR CONTROL (IAC) SYSTEM CHECK
2.0L OHC (VIN K) "J" CARLINE (TBI)

①
- A/C MUST BE "OFF" DURING ENTIRE CHECK.
- START ENGINE. ENGINE MUST BE AT NORMAL OPERATING TEMPERATURE.
- PLACE TRANSMISSION IN DRIVE (A/T) OR NEUTRAL (M/T).
- RECORD STEADY ENGINE SPEED. IF IDLE IS ERRATIC OR UNSTABLE, REFER TO "DIAGNOSTIC AIDS" FACING PAGE FOR POSSIBLE CAUSES.

②
- TURN IGNITION "OFF" FOR 10 SECONDS.
- START ENGINE AND IMMEDIATELY OBSERVE RPM IN NEUTRAL.

RPM SAME AS RECORDED IN FIRST STEP

RPM HIGHER THAN RECORDED IN FIRST STEP
- IDLE ENGINE FOR 1 MINUTE IN DRIVE (A/T) OR NEUTRAL (M/T). SHIFT TO NEUTRAL (A/T).
- NOTE ENGINE SPEED.

RETURNS TO RPM RECORDED IN FIRST STEP

IDLE AIR CONTROL CIRCUIT OK. REFER TO "DIAGNOSTIC AIDS"

WILL NOT RETURN TO RPM RECORDED IN FIRST STEP

③
- IGNITION "OFF"
- DISCONNECT IAC VALVE HARNESS.
- IGNITION "ON". ENGINE "OFF"
- GROUND DIAGNOSTIC TEST TERMINAL.
- CONNECT A TEST LIGHT BETWEEN EACH IAC VALVE HARNESS CONNECTOR TERMINAL AND GROUND.

NO LIGHTS, ONE OR MORE CIRCUITS

- CHECK FOR OPEN OR SHORT TO GROUND IN CIRCUIT WITH NO LIGHT. ARE ALL CIRCUITS OK?

YES
- CHECK RESISTANCE ACROSS IAC VALVE COILS. IT SHOULD BE MORE THAN 20 OHMS BETWEEN IAC VALVE TERMINALS "A" & "B" AND "C" & "D" IS IT?

NO — REPAIR WIRING AND RECHECK.

YES — FAULTY ECM CONNECTION OR ECM.

LIGHT STEADY OR FLASHING ALL CIRCUITS

④
FAULTY IAC CONNECTION OR IAC VALVE, OR PLUGGED PASSAGE. IF LIGHT APPEARS TO BE STEADY, REFER TO STEP 4.

NO — REPLACE IAC VALVE AND RETEST.

CLEAR CODES, CONFIRM "CLOSED LOOP" OPERATION, NO "SERVICE ENGINE SOON" LIGHT.

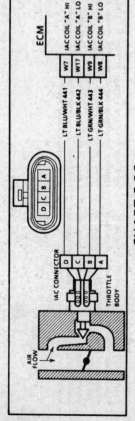

ECM

LT BLU/WHT 441	W7 IAC COIL "A" HI
LT BLU/BLK 442	W17 IAC COIL "A" LO
LT GRN/WHT 443	W9 IAC COIL "B" HI
LT GRN/BLK 444	W8 IAC COIL "B" LO

IAC CONNECTOR

D C B A

THROTTLE BODY

AIR FLOW

CHART C-2C

IDLE AIR CONTROL (IAC) SYSTEM CHECK
2.0L (VIN K) "J" CARLINE (TBI)

Circuit Description:

The ECM controls idle rpm with the IAC valve. To increase idle rpm, the ECM moves the IAC valve out allowing more air to pass by the throttle plate. To decrease rpm, it moves the IAC valve in, reducing air flow by the throttle plate. A "Scan" tool will read the ECM commands to the IAC valve in counts. The higher the counts, the more air allowed (higher idle). The lower the counts, the less air allowed (lower idle).

Test Description: Numbers below refer to circled numbers on the diagnostic chart.

1. Continue with test, even if engine will not idle. If idle is too low, "Scan" will display 80 or more counts, or steps. If idle is high, it will display "0" counts. Occasionally an erratic or unstable idle may occur. Engine speed may vary 200 rpm or more up and down. Disconnect IAC. If the condition is unchanged, the IAC is not at fault.

2. When the engine was stopped, the IAC valve retracted (more air) to a fixed "Park" position for increased air flow and idle speed during the next engine start. A "Scan" will display 100 or more counts.

3. Be sure to disconnect the IAC valve prior to this test. The test light will confirm the ECM signals by a steady or flashing light on all circuits.

4. There is a remote possibility that one of the circuits is shorted to voltage which would have been indicated by a steady light. Disconnect ECM and turn the ignition "ON" and probe terminals to check for this condition.

Diagnostic Aids:

An incorrect idle may be caused by a system problem that cannot be controlled by the IAC. A "Scan" tool may be used to monitor desired idle, actual engine speed, and IAC counts to help isolate a system problem.

For example, a vacuum leak may be indicated if the desired idle is 900 rpm, IAC counts are at 0, but the actual engine speed is 1500 rpm.

- **System too lean (High Air/Fuel Ratio)**
  Idle speed may be too high or too low. Engine speed may vary up and down, disconnecting IAC does not help. May set Code 44.
  "Scan" and/or voltmeter will read an oxygen sensor output less than 300 mV (.3 volt). Check for low regulated fuel pressure or water in fuel. A lean exhaust, with an oxygen sensor output fixed above 800 mV (.8 volt) will be a contaminated sensor, usually silicone. This may also set a Code 45.

- **System too rich (Low Air/Fuel Ratio)**
  Idle speed counts usually above 80. System obviously rich and may exhibit black smoke exhaust.
  "Scan" tool and/or voltmeter will read an oxygen sensor signal fixed above 800 mV (.8 volt). Check:
  - High fuel pressure.
  - Injector leaking or sticking.

- **Throttle Body**
  Remove IAC and inspect bore for foreign material or evidence of IAC valve dragging the bore. Refer to "Rough, Unstable, Incorrect Idle or Stalling" in "Symptoms"

1990-92 2.0L (VIN K)

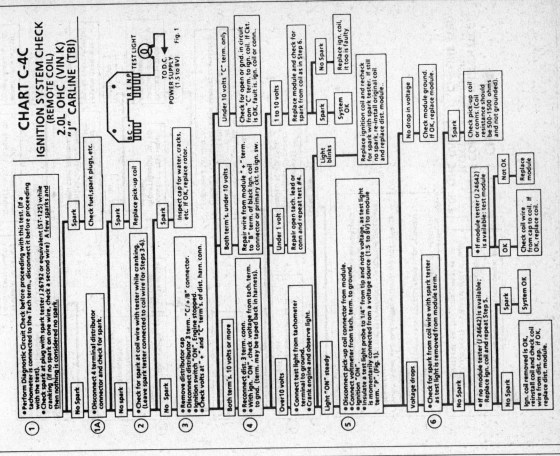

CHART C-4C
IGNITION SYSTEM CHECK
(REMOTE COIL)
2.0L OHC (VIN K)
"J" CARLINE (TBI)

① • Perform Diagnostic Circuit Check before proceeding with this test. (If a tachometer is connected to the Tach term., disconnect it before proceeding with the test).
• Check spark at plug with spark tester (J 26792 or equivalent (ST-125) while cranking (if spark on one wire, check a second wire). A few sparks and then nothing is considered no spark.

No Spark → Spark → Check fuel, spark plugs, etc.

1A • Disconnect 4 terminal distributor connector and check for spark.

No spark → Spark → Replace pick-up coil

② • Check for spark at coil wire with tester while cranking. (Leave spark tester connected to coil wire for Steps 3-6).

No Spark → Spark → Inspect cap for water, cracks, etc. If OK, replace rotor.

③ • Remove distributor cap.
• Disconnect distributor 3 term. "C / + /B" connector.
• Ignition switch "ON". Engine stopped.
• Check volts at "+", and "C" term's. of dist. harn. conn.

Both term's. 10 volts or more → Both term's. under 10 volts → Repair wire from module "+" term. to "B" term. of black ign. coil connector or primary ckt. to ign. sw.

Under 10 volts "C" term. only → Check for open or grnd. in circuit from "C" term. to ign. coil. If Ckt is OK, fault is. ign. coil or conn...

④ • Reconnect dist. 3 term. conn.
• With ign. "ON". check voltage from tach. term. to grnd. (term. may be taped back in harness).

Over 10 volts → Repair open tach. lead or conn and repeat test #4.

Under 1 volt → 1 to 10 volts → Replace module and check for spark from coil as in Step 6.

No Spark → Replace ign. coil, it too is faulty

⑤ • Connect test light from tachometer terminal to ground.
• Crank engine and observe light.

Light "ON" steady → • Disconnect pick-up coil connector from module.
• Connect voltmeter from tach. term. to ground.
• Insulate a test light probe to 1/4" from tip and note voltage, as test light is momentarily connected from a voltage source (1.5 to 8V) to module term. "P". (Fig. 1).

Light blinks → Replace ignition coil and recheck for spark from coil with spark tester. If still no spark, re-install original coil and replace dist. module...

Spark → System OK

No drop in voltage → Check module ground. If OK, replace module.

Voltage drops → Spark → Check pick-up coil or conn. (Coil resistance should be 500-1500 ohms and not grounded)

⑥ • Check for spark from coil wire with spark tester as test light is removed from module term.

No Spark → • If module tester (J 24642) is available: Replace ign. coil and repeat Step 5.

Spark → System OK

• If module tester (J 24642) is available: test module

OK → Check coil wire from cap to coil. If OK, replace coil.

Not OK → Replace module

Ign. coil removed is OK, re-install coil and check coil wire from dist. cap. If OK, replace dist. module.

TO D.C. POWER SUPPLY (1.5 to 8V) Fig. 1

B. C. R E N P TEST LIGHT

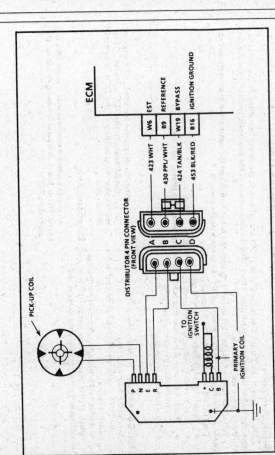

PICK-UP COIL

ECM

W6	EST	423 WHT
B9	REFERENCE	430 PPL/WHT
W19	BYPASS	424 TAN/BLK
B16	IGNITION GROUND	453 BLK/RED

DISTRIBUTOR 4 PIN CONNECTOR (FRONT VIEW)

A B C D

TO IGNITION SWITCH

PRIMARY IGNITION COIL

CHART C-4C
IGNITION SYSTEM CHECK
(REMOTE COIL)
2.0L OHC (VIN K) "J" CARLINE (TBI)

Test Description: Numbers below refer to circled numbers on the diagnostic chart.

1. Two wires are checked to ensure that an open is not present in a spark plug wire.

1A. If spark occurs with 4 terminal distributor connector disconnected, pick-up coil output is too low for EST operation.

2. A spark indicates the problem must be the distributor cap or rotor.

3. Normally, there should be battery voltage at the "C" and "+" terminals. Low voltage would indicate an open or a high resistance circuit from the distributor to the coil or ignition switch. If "C" terminal voltage was low, but "+" terminal voltage is 10 volts or more, circuit from "C" terminal to ignition coil or ignition coil primary winding is open.

4. Checks for a shorted module or grounded circuit from the ignition coil to the module. The distributor module should be turned "OFF." Normal voltage should be about 12 volts. If the module is turned "ON," the voltage would be low, but above 1 volt. This could cause the ignition coil to fail from excessive heat. With an open ignition coil primary winding, a small amount of voltage will leak through the module from the "Bat." to the "Tach" terminal.

5. Applying voltage (1.5 to 8 volts) to module terminal "P" should turn the module "ON" and the tachometer terminal voltage should drop to about 7-9 volts. This test will determine whether the module or coil is faulty or if the pick-up coil is not generating the proper signal to turn the module "ON." This test can be performed by using a DC battery with a rating of 1.5 to 8 volts. The use of the test light is mainly to allow the "P" terminal to be probed more easily.

Some digital multi-meters can also be used to trigger the module by selecting ohms, usually the diode position. In this position the meter may have a voltage across its terminals which can be used to trigger the module. The voltage in the ohms position can be checked by using a second meter or by checking the manufacturer's specification of the tool being used.

6. This should turn "OFF" the module and cause a spark. If no spark occurs, the fault is most likely in the ignition coil because most module problems would have been found before this point in the procedure. A module tester (J 24642) could determine which is at fault.

1990-92 2.0L (VIN K)

CHART C-8A
TORQUE CONVERTER CLUTCH (TCC)
(ELECTRICAL DIAGNOSIS)
2.0L OHC (VIN K) "J" CARLINE (TBI)

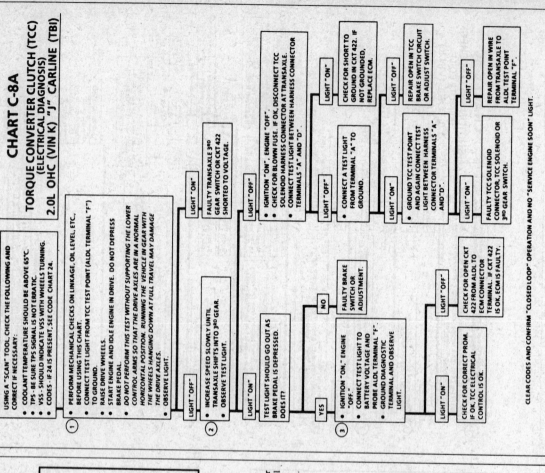

USING A "SCAN" TOOL, CHECK THE FOLLOWING AND CORRECT IF NECESSARY:
- COOLANT TEMPERATURE SHOULD BE ABOVE 65°C.
- TPS - BE SURE TPS SIGNAL IS NOT ERRATIC.
- VSS - SHOULD INDICATE VSS WITH WHEELS TURNING.
- CODES - IF 24 IS PRESENT, SEE CODE CHART 24.

(1) PERFORM MECHANICAL CHECKS ON LINKAGE, OIL LEVEL, ETC., BEFORE USING THIS CHART.
CONNECT TEST LIGHT FROM TCC TEST POINT (ALDL TERMINAL "F") TO GROUND.
RAISE DRIVE WHEELS.
START ENGINE AND IDLE ENGINE IN DRIVE. DO NOT DEPRESS BRAKE PEDAL.
DO NOT PERFORM THIS TEST WITHOUT SUPPORTING THE LOWER CONTROL ARMS SO THAT THE DRIVE AXLES ARE IN A NORMAL HORIZONTAL POSITION. RUNNING THE VEHICLE IN GEAR WITH THE WHEELS HANGING DOWN AT FULL TRAVEL MAY DAMAGE THE DRIVE AXLES.
OBSERVE LIGHT.

LIGHT "ON" → FAULTY TRANSAXLE 3RD GEAR SWITCH OR CKT 422 SHORTED TO VOLTAGE.

LIGHT "OFF"

(2) INCREASE SPEED SLOWLY UNTIL TRANSAXLE SHIFTS INTO 3RD GEAR.
OBSERVE TEST LIGHT.

LIGHT "OFF" → IGNITION "ON", ENGINE "OFF".
CHECK FOR BLOWN FUSE. IF OK, DISCONNECT TCC SOLENOID HARNESS CONNECTOR AT TRANSAXLE.
CONNECT TEST LIGHT BETWEEN HARNESS CONNECTOR TERMINALS "A" AND "D".

LIGHT "ON" → CHECK FOR SHORT TO GROUND IN CKT 422. IF NOT GROUNDED, REPLACE ECM.

LIGHT "OFF" → CONNECT A TEST LIGHT FROM TERMINAL "A" TO GROUND.

LIGHT "ON" → GROUND TCC TEST POINT AND AGAIN CONNECT TEST LIGHT BETWEEN HARNESS CONNECTOR TERMINALS "A" AND "D".

LIGHT "OFF" → REPAIR OPEN IN TCC BRAKE SWITCH CIRCUIT OR ADJUST SWITCH.

LIGHT "ON"

LIGHT "OFF" → FAULTY TCC SOLENOID CONNECTOR, TCC SOLENOID OR 3RD GEAR SWITCH.

LIGHT "ON" → REPAIR OPEN IN WIRE FROM TRANSAXLE TO ALDL TEST POINT TERMINAL "F".

LIGHT "ON"

TEST LIGHT SHOULD GO OUT AS BRAKE PEDAL IS DEPRESSED. DOES IT?

NO → FAULTY BRAKE SWITCH OR ADJUSTMENT.

YES

(3) IGNITION "ON", ENGINE "OFF".
CONNECT TEST LIGHT TO BATTERY VOLTAGE AND PROBE ALDL TERMINAL "F". GROUND DIAGNOSTIC TERMINAL AND OBSERVE LIGHT.

LIGHT "OFF" → CHECK FOR OPEN CKT 422 FROM ALDL TO ECM CONNECTOR TERMINAL. IF CKT 422 IS OK, ECM IS FAULTY.

LIGHT "ON" → CHECK FOR CORRECT PROM. IF OK, TCC ELECTRICAL CONTROL IS OK.

CLEAR CODES AND CONFIRM "CLOSED LOOP" OPERATION AND NO "SERVICE ENGINE SOON" LIGHT.

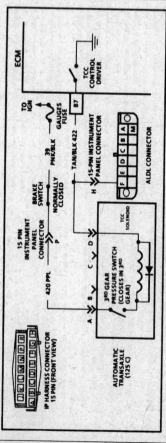

CHART C-8A
TORQUE CONVERTER CLUTCH (TCC)
(ELECTRICAL DIAGNOSIS)
2.0L OHC (VIN K) "J" CARLINE (TBI)

Circuit Description:
The purpose of the Torque Converter Clutch (TCC) is to eliminate the power loss of the torque converter when the vehicle is in a cruise condition. This allows the convenience of the automatic transaxle and the fuel economy of a manual transaxle.

Voltage is supplied to the TCC solenoid through the brake switch and transaxle third gear apply switch. The ECM will engage TCC by grounding CKT 422 to energize the solenoid.

The TCC will engage under the following conditions:
- Vehicle speed exceeds 30 mph (48 km/h)
- Engine coolant temperature exceeds 70°C (156°F)
- Throttle position is not changing faster than a calibrated rate (steady throttle)
- Transaxle third gear switch is closed
- Brake switch is closed

Test Description: Numbers below refer to circled numbers on the diagnostic chart.

1. Light "OFF" confirms transaxle third gear apply switch is open.

2. At 48 km/h (30 mph), the transaxle third gear switch should close. Test light will light and confirm battery supply and close brake switch.

3. Grounding the diagnostic terminal, with engine "OFF," should energize the TCC solenoid. This test checks the capability of the ECM to control the solenoid.

Diagnostic Aids:

An engine coolant thermostat that is stuck open or opens at too low a temperature may result in an inoperative TCC.

1990-92 2.0L (VIN K)

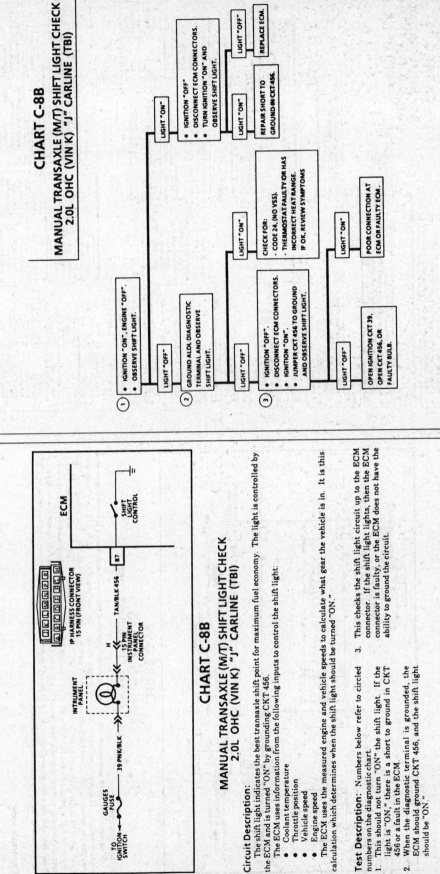

CHART C-8B

MANUAL TRANSAXLE (M/T) SHIFT LIGHT CHECK
2.0L OHC (VIN K) "J" CARLINE (TBI)

Circuit Description:

The shift light indicates the best transaxle shift point for maximum fuel economy. The light is controlled by the ECM and is turned "ON" by grounding CKT 456.

The ECM uses information from the following inputs to control the shift light:
- Coolant temperature
- Throttle position
- Vehicle speed
- Engine speed

The ECM uses the measured engine and vehicle speeds to calculate what gear the vehicle is in. It is this calculation which determines when the shift light should be turned "ON."

Test Description: Numbers below refer to circled numbers on the diagnostic chart.

1. This should not turn "ON" the shift light. If the light is "ON," there is a short to ground in CKT 456 or a fault in the ECM.
2. When the diagnostic terminal is grounded, the ECM should ground CKT 456, and the shift light should be "ON."
3. This checks the shift light circuit up to the ECM connector. If the shift light lights, then the ECM connector is faulty, or the ECM does not have the ability to ground the circuit.

CHART C-8B

MANUAL TRANSAXLE (M/T) SHIFT LIGHT CHECK
2.0L OHC (VIN K) "J" CARLINE (TBI)

Diagram labels: TO IGNITION SWITCH — GAUGES FUSE — 39 PNK/BLK — INTRUMENT PANEL — IP HARNESS CONNECTOR 15 PIN (FRONT VIEW) — 15 PIN INSTRUMENT PANEL CONNECTOR — TAN/BLK 456 — B7 — ECM — SHIFT LIGHT CONTROL

Flowchart:

① • IGNITION "ON", ENGINE "OFF". • OBSERVE SHIFT LIGHT.
- LIGHT "ON" → • IGNITION "OFF". • DISCONNECT ECM CONNECTORS. • TURN IGNITION "ON" AND OBSERVE SHIFT LIGHT.
  - LIGHT "OFF" → REPLACE ECM.
  - LIGHT "ON" → REPAIR SHORT TO GROUND IN CKT 456.
- LIGHT "OFF" → ②

② • GROUND ALDL DIAGNOSTIC TERMINAL AND OBSERVE SHIFT LIGHT.
- LIGHT "ON" → CHECK FOR: - CODE 24, (NO VSS). - THERMOSTAT FAULTY OR HAS INCORRECT HEAT RANGE. IF OK, REVIEW SYMPTOMS
- LIGHT "OFF" → ③

③ • IGNITION "OFF". • DISCONNECT ECM CONNECTORS. • IGNITION "ON". • JUMPER CKT 456 TO GROUND AND OBSERVE SHIFT LIGHT.
- LIGHT "ON" → POOR CONNECTION AT ECM OR FAULTY ECM.
- LIGHT "OFF" → OPEN IGNITION CKT 39, OPEN CKT 456, OR FAULTY BULB.

1990-92 2.0L (VIN K)

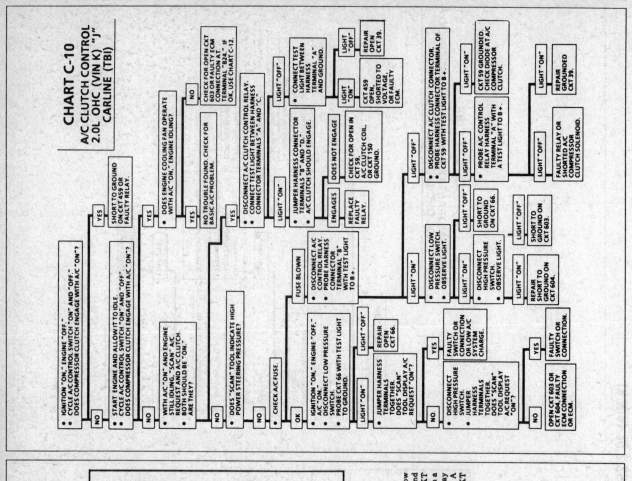

CHART C-10
A/C CLUTCH CONTROL
2.0L OHC (VIN K) "J" CARLINE (TBI)

Circuit Description:

When an A/C mode is selected on the A/C control switch, ignition voltage is supplied to the compressor low pressure switch. If there is sufficient A/C refrigerant charge, the low pressure switch will be closed and complete the circuit to the closed high pressure cut-off switch and to CKTs 603 and 604. The voltage on CKT 604 to the ECM is shown by the "Scan" tool as A/C request "ON" (voltage present), "OFF" (no voltage). When a request for A/C is sensed by the ECM, the ECM will ground CKT 459 of the A/C clutch control relay, the relay contact will close, and current will flow from CKT 604 to CKT 59 and engage the A/C compressor clutch. A "Scan" tool will show the grounding of CKT 459 as A/C clutch "ON." If voltage is sensed by the ECM on CKT 603, the cooling fan will be turned "ON."

Diagnostic Aids:

Both pressure switches are located at the rear of the A/C compressor. The low pressure switch connector can be identified by a blue insert and the high pressure switch connector by a red insert.

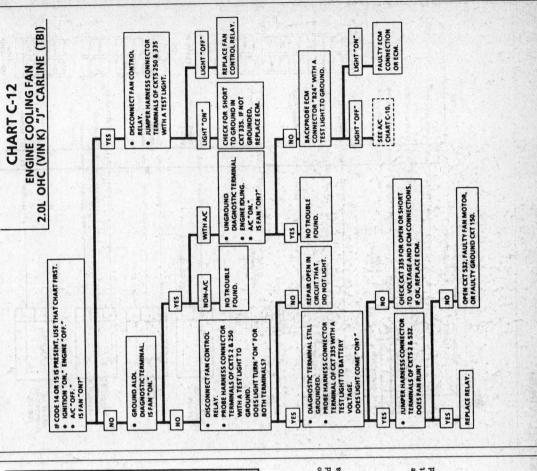

CHART C-12
ENGINE COOLING FAN
2.0L OHC (VIN K) "J" CARLINE (TBI)

1990-92 2.0L (VIN K)

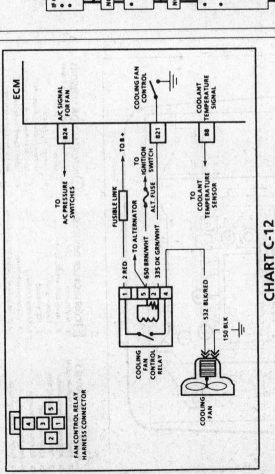

CHART C-12
ENGINE COOLING FAN
2.0L OHC (VIN K) "J" CARLINE (TBI)

Circuit Description:

Battery voltage to operate the cooling fan motor is supplied to relay terminal "1". Ignition voltage to energize the relay is supplied to relay terminal "5". When the ECM grounds CKT 335, the relay is energized and the cooling fan is turned "ON." When the engine is running, the ECM will energize the cooling fan relay if a coolant temperature sensor code (14 or 15) has been set, or under the following conditions:

- A/C is "ON" and vehicle speed is less than 30 mph (48 km/h).
- Coolant temperature is greater than 108°C (230°F).

Diagnostic Aids:

If the vehicle has an overheating problem, it must be determined if the complaint was due to an actual boil over, the coolant temperature warning light, or the temperature gage indicated overheating.

If the gage or light indicates overheating but no boil over is detected, the gage circuit should be checked. The gage accuracy can be checked by comparing the coolant sensor reading using a "Scan" tool with the gage reading.

If the engine is actually overheating and the gage indicates overheating, but the cooling fan is not turning "ON," the coolant sensor has probably shifted out of calibration and should be replaced.

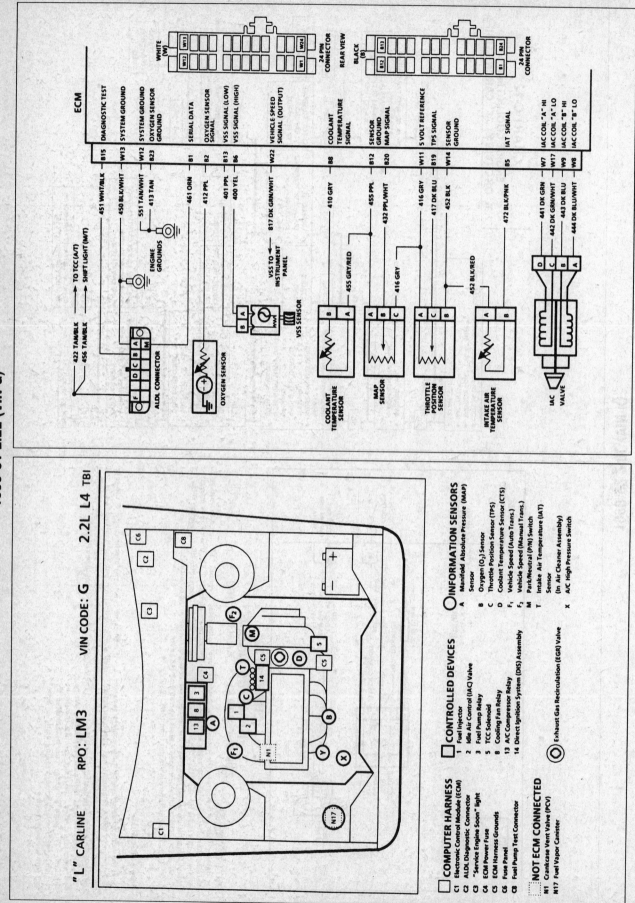

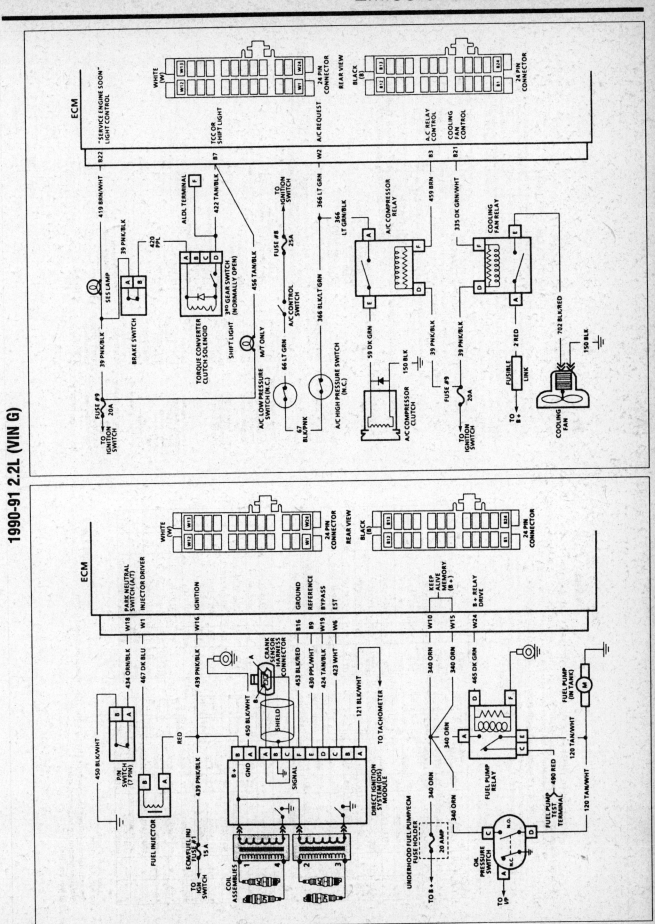

1990-91 2.2L (VIN G)

DIAGNOSTIC CIRCUIT CHECK

The Diagnostic Circuit Check is an organized approach to identifying a problem created by an electronic engine control system malfunction. It must be the starting point for any drivability complaint diagnosis because it directs the service technician to the next logical step in diagnosing the complaint.

The Tech 1 data listed in the table may be used for comparison after completing the diagnostic circuit check and finding the on-board diagnostics functioning properly with no trouble codes displayed. The "Typical Data Values" are an average of display values recorded from normally operating vehicles and are intended to represent what a normally functioning system would typically display.

A "SCAN" TOOL THAT DISPLAYS FAULTY DATA SHOULD NOT BE USED, AND THE PROBLEM SHOULD BE REPORTED TO THE MANUFACTURER. THE USE OF A FAULTY "SCAN" TOOL CAN RESULT IN MISDIAGNOSIS AND UNNECESSARY PARTS REPLACEMENT.

Only the parameters listed below are used in this manual for diagnosis. If a "Scan" tool reads other parameters, the values are not recommended by General Motors for use in diagnosis.

If all values are within the range illustrated, refer to "Symptoms"

TECH 1 TOOL DATA

Test Under Following Conditions: Idle, Upper Radiator Hose Hot, Closed Throttle, Park or Neutral, "Closed Loop", All Accessories "OFF."

"SCAN" Position	Units Displayed	Typical Data Value
Engine Speed	Rpm	± 50 RPM from desired rpm in drive (A/T), ± 100 RPM from desired rpm in neutral (M/T)
Desired Idle	Rpm	ECM idle command (varies with temp.)
Coolant Temperature	Degrees Celsius	85° - 105°
IAT/MAT	Degrees Celsius	10° - 90° (varies with underhood temp. and sensor location)
MAP	kPa/Volts	29-48 kPa/1 - 2 volts (varies with manifold and barometric pressures)
Open/Closed Loop	Open/Closed	"Closed Loop" (may enter "Open Loop" with extended idle)
Throt Position	Volts	.30 - 1.33
Throttle Angle	0 - 100%	0
Oxygen Sensor	Millivolts	100 - 999 (varies continuously)
Inj. Pulse Width	Milliseconds	8 - 3.0
Spark Advance	Degrees	Varies
Engine Speed	Rpm	± 50 RPM from desired rpm in drive (A/T), ± 100 RPM from desired rpm in neutral (M/T)
Fuel Integrator	Counts	110-145
Block Learn	Counts	118-138
Idle Air Control	Counts (steps)	1 - 50
P/N Switch	P-N and R-D-L	Park/Neutral (P/N)
MPH/KPH	"ON"/"OFF"	0
TCC	0-255	)796
Crank Rpm	Rpm	13.5 - 14.5
Ign/Batt Voltage	Volts	"OFF" (coolant temperature below 102°C)
Cooling Fan Relay	"ON"/"OFF"	No
A/C Request	"YES"/"NO"	"OFF"
A/C Clutch	"ON"/"OFF"	"OFF"
Power Steering	Normal/High Pressure	Normal
Shift Light (M/T)	"ON"/"OFF"	"OFF"

FUEL INJECTION ECM CONNECTOR IDENTIFICATION

This ECM voltage chart is for use with a digital voltmeter to further aid in diagnosis. The voltages you get may vary due to low battery charge or other reasons, but they should be very close.

THE FOLLOWING CONDITIONS MUST BE MET BEFORE TESTING:
- Engine at operating temperature • Engine idling in "Closed Loop" (for "Engine Run" column)
- Test terminal not grounded • "Scan" tool not installed • All voltages shown "B +" indicates battery or charging voltage.

VOLTAGE — WHITE (W) 24 PIN CONNECTOR — W1–W12

KEY "ON"	ENG. RUN	CIRCUIT	PIN	WIRE COLOR
B+	B+	INJECTOR DRIVER	W1	DK BLU
0*	0*	A/C REQUEST	W2	LT GRN
		NOT USED	W3	
		CRUISE LIGHT	W4	GRY/BLK
		NOT USED	W5	
0	1.1	EST	W6	WHT
④	④	IAC "A" HI	W7	DK GRN
④	④	IAC "B" LOW	W8	DK BLU/WHT
④	④	IAC "B" HI	W9	DK BLU
B+	B+	BATTERY	W10	ORN
5.0	5.0	5 V REF	W11	GRY
0*	0*	ECM GROUND	W12	TAN/WHT

VOLTAGE — WHITE (W) 24 PIN CONNECTOR — W13–W24

KEY "ON"	ENG. RUN	CIRCUIT	PIN	WIRE COLOR
②	B+	FUEL PUMP	W24	DK GRN
		NOT USED	W23	
0*	0*	VSS OUTPUT 4000 PPM (IF FUSED)	W22	DK GRN/WHT
		CRUISE SET	W21	DK BLU
0*	4.5	CRUISE ENABLE	W20	GRY
0*	0*	BYPASS	W19	TAN/BLK
④	④	P/N SWITCH	W18	ORN/BLK
④	④	IAC "A" LOW	W17	DK GRN/WHT
B+	B+	IGNITION	W16	PNK/BLK
B+	B+	BATTERY	W15	ORN
0*	0*	SENSOR GROUND	W14	BLK
0*	0*	ECM GROUND	W13	BLK/WHT

WHITE (W) — 24 PIN CONNECTOR — REAR VIEW

BLACK (B) 24 PIN CONNECTOR — B1–B12

KEY "ON"	ENG. RUN	CIRCUIT	PIN	WIRE COLOR
4.5	4.5	SERIAL DATA	B1	ORN
B+	.01-33 1-9	O₂ SIGNAL	B2	PPL
B+	B+	A/C CLUTCH RELAY	B3	BRN
		NOT USED	B4	
1.3	1.3	IAT SIGNAL	B5	BLK/PNK
.13	.13	VSS SIGNAL (HIGH)	B6	YEL
0*/B+	B+	TCC OR SHIFT LIGHT	B7	TAN/BLK
1.9	1.9	CTS SIGNAL	B8	GRY
A.6	3.05	REF HI	B9	PPL/WHT
		CRUISE SOLENOID	B10	LT GRN
		CRUISE SOLENOID	B11	DK BLU
0*	0*	SENSOR GROUNDS	B12	PPL

BLACK (B) 24 PIN CONNECTOR — B13–B24

KEY "ON"	ENG. RUN	CIRCUIT	PIN	WIRE COLOR
		NOT USED	B24	
0*	0*	O₂ GROUND	B23	TAN/BRN/WHT
0*	B+	SES LIGHT	B22	
B+	B+	COOLANT FAN	B21	DK GRN/WHT
4.75	1.1	MAP SIGNAL	B20	PPL/WHT
.6	.6	TPS SIGNAL	B19	DK BLU
		NOT USED	B18	
		REF LO	B17	
5.0	5.0	ALDI DIAG.	B16	BLK/RED
0*	0*	BRAKE SIGNAL	B15	WHT/BLK
0*	0*	VSS SIGNAL (LOW)	B14	BRN
		VSS SIGNAL (LOW)	B13	PPL

BLACK (B) — 24 PIN CONNECTOR

ENGINE 2.2L

* Less than .5 volt.
① A/C, Fan "OFF"
② Reads battery voltage for 2 seconds after ignition "ON" then should read 0 volts
③ Varies depending on temperature
④ Not useable

1990-91 2.2L (VIN G)

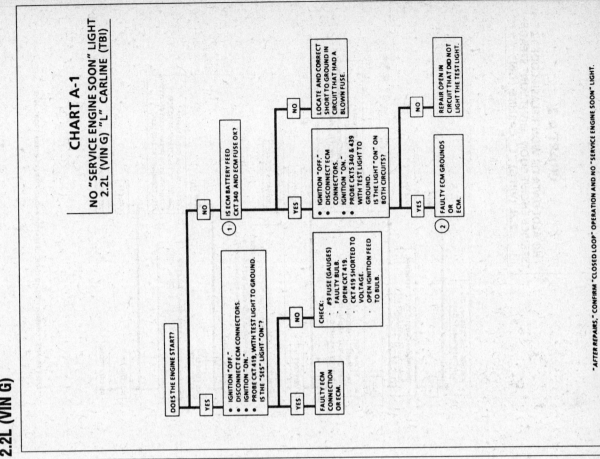

CHART A-1
NO "SERVICE ENGINE SOON" LIGHT
2.2L (VIN G) "L" CARLINE (TBI)

"AFTER REPAIRS," CONFIRM "CLOSED LOOP" OPERATION AND NO "SERVICE ENGINE SOON" LIGHT.

CHART A-1
NO "SERVICE ENGINE SOON" LIGHT
2.2L (VIN G) "L" CARLINE (TBI)

Circuit Description:

There should always be a steady "Service Engine Soon" light, when the ignition is "ON" and engine "OFF." Ignition battery voltage is supplied directly to the light bulb. The Electronic Control Module (ECM) will control the light and turn it "ON" by providing a ground path through CKT 419.

Test Description: Number(s) below refer to circled number(s) on the diagnostic chart.

1. Battery feed CKT 340 is protected by an underhood ECM fuse.

2. Using a test light connected to B+, probe each of the system ground circuits to be sure a good ground is present. See ECM terminal end view in front of this section for ECM pin locations of ground circuits.

Diagnostic Aids:

If engine runs correctly, check for the following

* Faulty light bulb
* CKT 419 open.
* Gauges fuse blown. This will result in no oil or generator lights, seat belt reminder, etc.

If "Engine Cranks But Will Not Run," use CHART A-3

1990-91 2.2L (VIN G)

CHART A-2

NO ALDL DATA OR WON'T FLASH CODE 12
"SERVICE ENGINE SOON" LIGHT "ON" STEADY
2.2L (VIN G) "L" CARLINE (TBI)

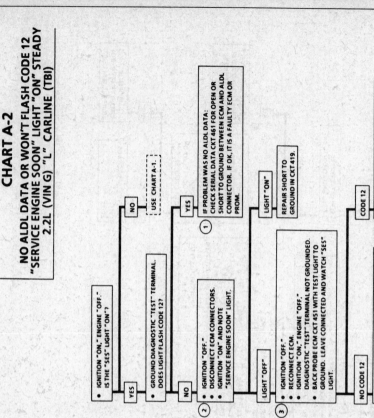

- IGNITION "ON," ENGINE "OFF." IS THE "SES" LIGHT "ON"?
  - YES → GROUND DIAGNOSTIC "TEST" TERMINAL. DOES LIGHT FLASH CODE 12?
  - NO → USE CHART A-1.

- **(2)** IGNITION "OFF."
  - DISCONNECT ECM CONNECTORS.
  - IGNITION "ON" AND NOTE "SERVICE ENGINE SOON" LIGHT.
  - NO → YES → IF PROBLEM WAS NO ALDL DATA: CHECK SERIAL DATA CKT 461 FOR OPEN OR SHORT TO GROUND BETWEEN ECM AND ALDL CONNECTOR. IF OK, IT IS A FAULTY ECM OR PROM.
    - **(1)**

- LIGHT "OFF" → LIGHT "ON" → REPAIR SHORT TO GROUND IN CKT 419.

- **(3)** IGNITION "OFF."
  - RECONNECT ECM.
  - IGNITION "ON," ENGINE "OFF."
  - DIAGNOSTIC "TEST" TERMINAL NOT GROUNDED.
  - BACK PROBE ECM CKT 451 WITH TEST LIGHT TO GROUND. LEAVE CONNECTED AND WATCH "SES" LIGHT.
    - NO CODE 12 → CODE 12 → CHECK PROM FOR PROPER INSTALLATION. IF OK, REPLACE ECM USING ORIGINAL PROM.
      - RECHECK FOR CODE 12.
      - **(4)**

- **(4)** CODE 12 → CHECK FOR OPEN CKT 451 FROM DIAGNOSTIC TEST TERMINAL TO ECM. IF OK, CHECK FOR OPEN CIRCUIT BETWEEN ALDL TERMINAL "A" AND ECM.
  - NO CODE 12 → REPLACE PROM.
  - CODE 12 → SYSTEM OK.

"AFTER REPAIRS," CONFIRM "CLOSED LOOP" OPERATION AND NO "SERVICE ENGINE SOON" LIGHT.

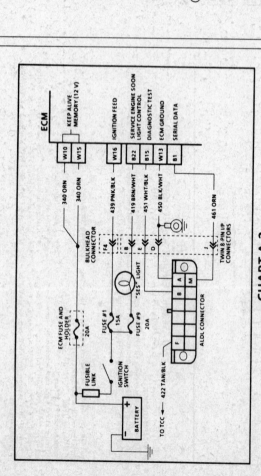

ECM

KEEP ALIVE MEMORY (12 V)	W10
	W15
IGNITION FEED	W16
SERVICE ENGINE SOON LIGHT CONTROL	B22
DIAGNOSTIC TEST	B15
ECM GROUND	W13
SERIAL DATA	B1

340 ORN
340 ORN
439 PNK/BLK
419 BRN/WHT
451 WHT/BLK
450 BLK/WHT
461 ORN

ECM FUSE AND HOLDER
20A

FUSE #1
15A

FUSE #9
20A

FUSIBLE LINK

IGNITION SWITCH

BATTERY

TO TCC

422 TAN/BLK

BULKHEAD CONNECTOR
F4

"SES" LIGHT

ALDL CONNECTOR

TWIN 8-PIN UP CONNECTORS

CHART A-2

NO ALDL DATA OR WON'T FLASH CODE 12
"SERVICE ENGINE SOON" LIGHT "ON" STEADY
2.2L (VIN G) "L" CARLINE (TBI)

Circuit Description:

There should always be a steady "Service Engine Soon" light when the ignition is "ON" and the engine is "OFF." Ignition battery voltage is supplied directly to the light bulb. The Electronic Control Module (ECM) will control the light and turn it "ON" by providing a ground path through CKT 419 to the ECM.

With the diagnostic terminal grounded, the light should flash a Code 12, followed by any trouble code(s) stored in memory. A steady light suggests a short to ground in the light control CKT 419, or an open in diagnostic CKT 451.

Test Description: Number(s) below refer to circled number(s) on the diagnostic chart.

1. If there is a problem with the ECM that causes a "Scan" tool to not read data from the ECM, then the ECM should not flash a Code 12. If Code 12 does not flash, be sure the "Scan" tool is working properly on another vehicle. If the "Scan" tool is functioning properly and CKT 461 is OK, the PROM or ECM may be at fault for the "NO ALDL DATA" symptom.

2. The "Service Engine Soon" light should not be "ON" with ignition "ON" and the ECM disconnected.

3. This step will check for an open diagnostic CKT 451.

4. At this point, the "Service Engine Soon" light wiring is OK. The problem is a faulty ECM or PROM. If Code 12 does not flash, the ECM should be replaced using the original PROM. Replace the PROM only after trying an ECM, as a defective PROM is an unlikely cause of the problem.

1990-91 2.2L (VIN G)

CHART A-3
(Page 1 of 3)
ENGINE CRANKS BUT WON'T RUN
2.2L (VIN G) "L" CARLINE (TBI)

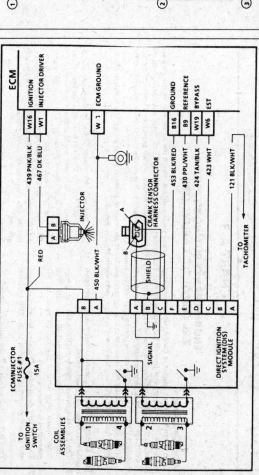

ECM

W16	IGNITION	
W1	INJECTOR DRIVER	
W 3	ECM GROUND	
B16	GROUND	
B9	REFERENCE	
W19	BYPASS	
W6	EST	

439 PNK/BLK
467 DK BLU
453 BLK/RED
430 PPL/WHT
424 TAN/BLK
423 WHT
121 BLK/WHT

TO IGNITION SWITCH
ECM/INJECTOR FUSE #1
15A

INJECTOR
A B
RED
450 BLK/WHT

CRANK SENSOR HARNESS CONNECTOR
SHIELD

COIL ASSEMBLIES
1 4
2 3

SIGNAL

DIRECT IGNITION SYSTEM (DIS) MODULE

TO TACHOMETER

CHART A-3
(Page 1 of 3)
ENGINE CRANKS BUT WON'T RUN
2.2L (VIN G) "L" CARLINE (TBI)

Circuit Description:

Before using this chart, battery condition, engine cranking speed, and fuel quantity should be checked and verified as being OK.

Test Description: Number(s) below refer to circled number(s) on the diagnostic chart.

1. A "Service Engine Soon" light "ON" is a basic test to determine if there is battery and ignition voltage at the ECM. No ALDL data may be due to an ECM problem, and CHART A-2 will diagnose the ECM. If TPS is over 2.5 volts, the engine may be in the clear flood mode, which will cause starting problems. The engine will not start without crank sensor reference pulses. The Tech 1 "Scan" tool should display rpm during cranking if pulses are received at the ECM. Crank rpm should be used if available.

2. Because the direct ignition system uses two plugs and wires to complete the circuit of each coil, the opposite spark plug wire should be left connected. If rpm was indicated during crank; the ignition module is receiving a crank signal, but "No Spark" at this test indicates the ignition module is not triggering the coil.

3. While cranking the engine, there should be no fuel spray with the injector electrical connector disconnected. Replace the injector if it sprays fuel or drips.

4. The test light should flash, indicating the ECM is controlling the injector. How bright the light flashes is not important. However, the test light should be a BT 8329 or equivalent.

5. Fuel spray from the injector indicates that fuel is available. However, the engine could be severely flooded due to too much fuel. No fuel spray from injector indicates a faulty fuel system or injector.

Diagnostic Aids:

- Water or foreign material can cause a no start condition during freezing weather. The engine may start after approximately 5 minutes in a heated shop. The problem may not recur until an overnight park in freezing temperatures.
- An EGR valve sticking open can cause a rich air/fuel charge during cranking. Unless engine enters "Clear Flood" at the first indication of a flooding condition, it can result in a no start.
- Fuel Pressure: Low fuel pressure can result in a very lean air/fuel charge. See CHART A-7.

① • IGNITION "ON" - IF "SES" LIGHT IS "OFF," USE CHART A-1.
  • INSTALL "SCAN" TOOL - IF NO DATA, USE CHART A-2.
  • CHECK THE FOLLOWING:
    - TPS - IF OVER 2.5V AT CLOSED THROTTLE, USE CODE 22 CHART.
    - COOLANT - IF BELOW -30°C, USE CODE 15 CHART.
    - RPM - IF NO RPM WHILE CRANKING, USE CHART A-3 (Page 2 of 3).

• PROBE FUEL PUMP TEST TERMINAL WITH A TEST LIGHT TO BATTERY VOLTAGE.
• IGNITION "OFF" FOR 10 SECONDS.
• IGNITION "ON."
• TEST LIGHT SHOULD TURN "OFF" FOR ABOUT 2 SECONDS AFTER IGNITION IS TURNED "ON." DOES IT?

YES → ②
NO → USE FUEL PUMP RELAY CIRCUIT CHART A-5.

② • CRANK ENGINE AND CHECK FOR SPARK WITH ST-125 ON SPARK PLUG WIRES 1&2 OR 3&4.
  • CHECK ONE WIRE AT A TIME. LEAVE THE OTHER WIRES CONNECTED TO THE SPARK PLUGS DURING CRANKING. IS THERE SPARK ON BOTH WIRES?

YES → ③
NO → SPARK ON ONE → USE CHART A-3 (Page 2 of 3).
NO SPARK → REPLACE IGNITION MODULE.

③ • DISCONNECT INJECTOR CONNECTOR.
  • CRANK ENGINE. IS THERE FUEL SPRAY FROM INJECTOR?

YES → FAULTY INJECTOR OR O-RING.
NO → ④

④ • CONNECT INJECTOR TEST LIGHT TO HARNESS CONNECTOR.
  • CRANK ENGINE.
  • DOES TEST LIGHT FLASH?

YES → ⑤
NO → USE CHART A-3 (Page 3 of 3).

⑤ • RECONNECT INJECTOR CONNECTOR.
  • CRANK ENGINE.
  • IS THERE FUEL SPRAY FROM INJECTOR?

YES → • CHECK FOR
  • FOULED SPARK PLUGS.
  • EGR VALVE STUCK OPEN.
  • LOW FUEL PRESSURE USE CHART A-7.

NO → • IGNITION "OFF."
  • INSTALL FUEL PRESSURE GAGE.
  • IGNITION "ON."
  • FUEL PRESSURE SHOULD BE 62-90 kPa (9-13 psi). IS IT?

YES → REPLACE INJECTOR.
NO → USE FUEL SYSTEM DIAGNOSIS CHART A-7.

*AFTER REPAIRS, "CONFIRM "CLOSED LOOP" OPERATION AND NO "SERVICE ENGINE SOON" LIGHT.

1990-91 2.2L (VIN G)

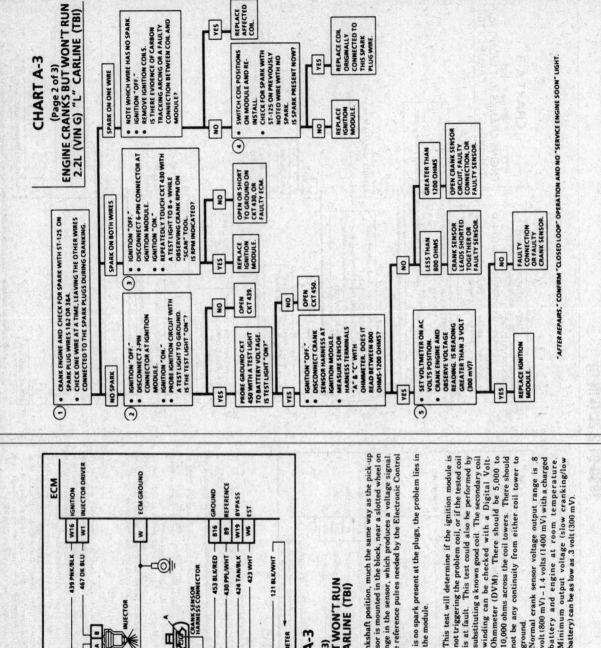

CHART A-3
(Page 2 of 3)
ENGINE CRANKS BUT WON'T RUN
2.2L (VIN G) "L" CARLINE (TBI)

Circuit Description:

A magnetic crank sensor is used to determine engine crankshaft position, much the same way as the pick-up coil did in High Energy Ignition (HEI) type systems. The sensor is mounted in the block, near a slotted wheel on the crankshaft. The rotation of the wheel creates a flux change in the sensor, which produces a voltage signal. The DIS ignition module processes this signal and creates the reference pulses needed by the Electronic Control Module (ECM) to trigger the correct coil at the correct time.

If the "Scan" tool did not indicate cranking rpm, and there is no spark present at the plugs, the problem lies in the direct ignition system or the power and ground supplies to the module.

Test Description: Number(s) below refer to circled number(s) on the diagnostic chart.

1. The Direct Ignition System (DIS) uses two plugs and wires to complete the circuit of each coil. The other spark plug wire in the circuit must be left connected to create a spark.

2. This test will determine if battery ignition voltage and a good ground is available at the DIS ignition module.

3. This test will determine if the ignition module is not generating the reference pulse, or if the wiring or ECM are at fault. By touching and removing a test light to 12 volts on CKT 430, a reference pulse should be generated. If rpm is indicated, the ECM and wiring are OK.

4. This test will determine if the ignition module is not triggering the problem coil, or if the tested coil is at fault. This test could also be performed by substituting a known good coil. The secondary coil winding can be checked with a Digital Volt-Ohmmeter (DVM). There should be 5,000 to 10,000 ohms across the coil towers. There should not be any continuity from either coil tower to ground.

5. Normal crank sensor voltage range is .8 volt (800 mV) - 1.4 volts (1400 mV) with a charged battery and engine at room temperature. Minimum output voltage (slow cranking/low battery) can be as low as .3 volt (300 mV).

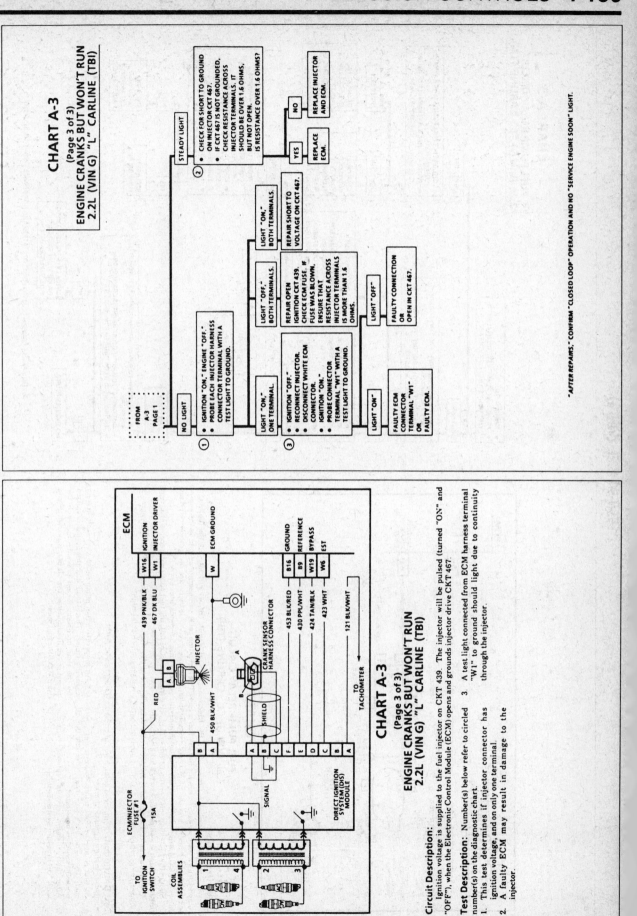

1990-91 2.2L (VIN G)

CHART A-3
(Page 3 of 3)
ENGINE CRANKS BUT WON'T RUN
2.2L (VIN G) "L" CARLINE (TBI)

"AFTER REPAIRS," CONFIRM "CLOSED LOOP" OPERATION AND NO "SERVICE ENGINE SOON" LIGHT.

CHART A-3
(Page 3 of 3)
ENGINE CRANKS BUT WON'T RUN
2.2L (VIN G) "L" CARLINE (TBI)

Circuit Description:
Ignition voltage is supplied to the fuel injector on CKT 439. The injector will be pulsed (turned "ON" and "OFF"), when the Electronic Control Module (ECM) opens and grounds injector drive CKT 467.

Test Description: Number(s) below refer to circled number(s) on the diagnostic chart.
1. This test determines if injector connector has ignition voltage, and on only one terminal.
2. A faulty ECM may result in damage to the injector.
3. A test light connected from ECM harness terminal "W1" to ground should light due to continuity through the injector.

1990-91 2.2L (VIN G)

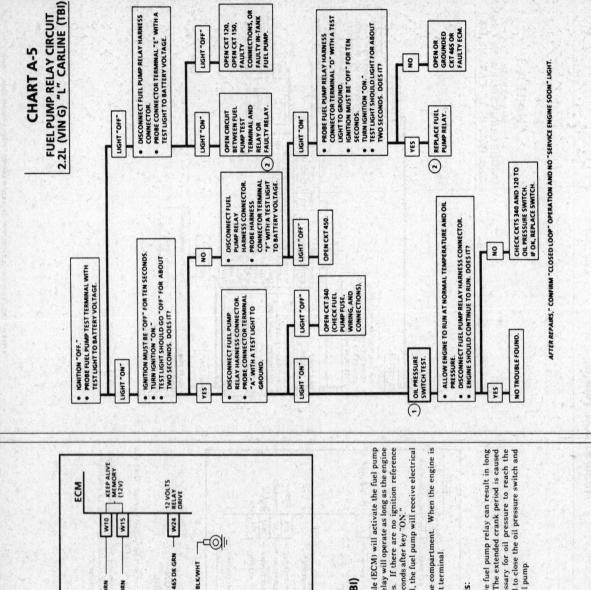

CHART A-5

FUEL PUMP RELAY CIRCUIT
2.2L (VIN G) "L" CARLINE (TBI)

Circuit Description:

When the ignition switch is turned "ON," the Electronic Control Module (ECM) will activate the fuel pump relay with a 12 volts signal and run the in-tank fuel pump. The fuel pump relay will operate as long as the engine is cranking or running and the ECM is receiving ignition reference pulses. If there are no ignition reference pulses, the ECM will no longer supply the fuel pump relay signal within 2 seconds after key "ON."

Should the fuel pump relay or the 12 volts relay drive from the ECM fail, the fuel pump will receive electrical current through the oil pressure switch back-up circuit.

The fuel pump test terminal is located in the engine compartment. When the engine is stopped, the pump can be turned "ON" by applying battery voltage to the test terminal.

Test Description: Number(s) below refer to circled number(s) on the diagnostic chart.

1. At this point, the fuel pump relay is operating correctly. The back-up circuit through the oil pressure switch is now tested.

2. After the fuel pump relay is replaced, continue with "Oil Pressure Switch Test."

Diagnostic Aids:

An inoperative fuel pump relay can result in long cranking times. The extended crank period is caused by the time necessary for oil pressure to reach the pressure required to close the oil pressure switch and turn "ON" the fuel pump.

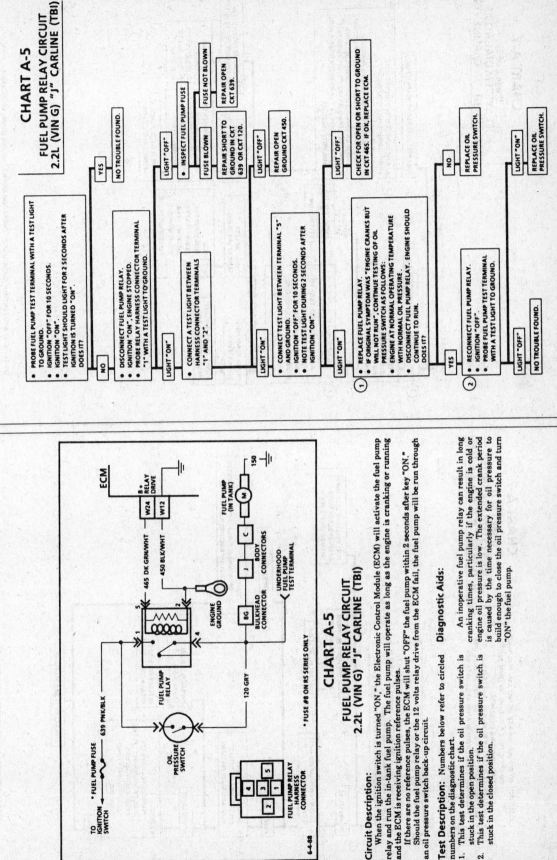

1990-91 2.2L (VIN G)

CHART A-5
FUEL PUMP RELAY CIRCUIT
2.2L (VIN G) "J" CARLINE (TBI)

Circuit Description:

When the ignition switch is turned "ON," the Electronic Control Module (ECM) will activate the fuel pump relay and run the in-tank fuel pump. The fuel pump will operate as long as the engine is cranking or running and the ECM is receiving ignition reference pulses.

If there are no reference pulses, the ECM will shut "OFF" the fuel pump within 2 seconds after key "ON."

Should the fuel pump relay or the 12 volts relay drive from the ECM fail, the fuel pump will be run through an oil pressure switch back-up circuit.

Test Description: Numbers below refer to circled numbers on the diagnostic chart.

1. This test determines if the oil pressure switch is stuck in the open position.

2. This test determines if the oil pressure switch is stuck in the closed position.

Diagnostic Aids:

An inoperative fuel pump relay can result in long cranking times, particularly if the engine is cold or engine oil pressure is low. The extended crank period is caused by the time necessary for oil pressure to build enough to close the oil pressure switch and turn "ON" the fuel pump.

1990-91 2.2L (VIN G)

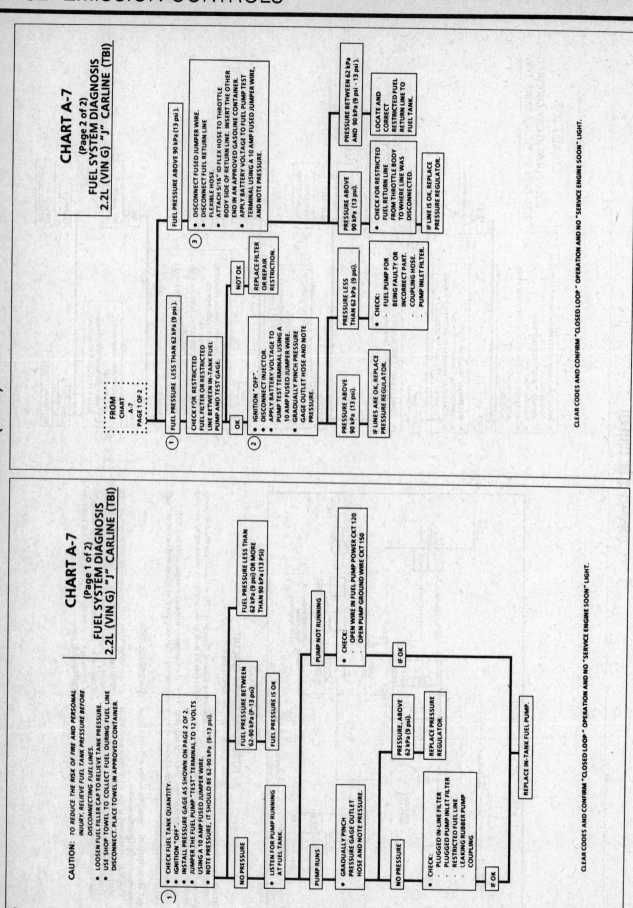

CHART A-7
(Page 1 of 2)
FUEL SYSTEM DIAGNOSIS
2.2L (VIN G) "J" CARLINE (TBI)

CHART A-7
(Page 2 of 2)
FUEL SYSTEM DIAGNOSIS
2.2L (VIN G) "J" CARLINE (TBI)

CAUTION: TO REDUCE THE RISK OF FIRE AND PERSONAL INJURY, RELIEVE FUEL TANK PRESSURE BEFORE DISCONNECTING FUEL LINES.
• LOOSEN FUEL FILLER CAP TO RELIEVE TANK PRESSURE.
• USE SHOP TOWEL TO COLLECT FUEL DURING FUEL LINE DISCONNECT. PLACE TOWEL IN APPROVED CONTAINER.

CLEAR CODES AND CONFIRM "CLOSED LOOP" OPERATION AND NO "SERVICE ENGINE SOON" LIGHT.

1990-91 2.2L (VIN G)

CODE 13
OXYGEN (O₂) SENSOR CIRCUIT
(OPEN CIRCUIT)

1.
- ENGINE AT NORMAL OPERATING TEMPERATURE (ABOVE 80°C/176°F).
- RUN ENGINE ABOVE 1200 RPM FOR TWO MINUTES.
- DOES TECH 1 TOOL INDICATE "CLOSED LOOP"?

→ YES → CODE 13 IS INTERMITTENT.

→ NO →

2.
- DISCONNECT O₂ SENSOR.
- JUMPER HARNESS CKT 412 (ECM SIDE) TO GROUND.
- TECH 1 SHOULD DISPLAY O₂ VOLTAGE BELOW .2 VOLT (200 mV) WITH ENGINE RUNNING. DOES IT?

→ YES → FAULTY O₂ SENSOR CONNECTION OR SENSOR.

→ NO →

3.
- REMOVE JUMPER.
- IGNITION "ON," ENGINE "OFF."
- CHECK VOLTAGE OF CKT 412 (ECM SIDE) AT O₂ SENSOR HARNESS CONNECTOR USING A DVM.

- .3 - 6 VOLT (300 - 600 mV) → FAULTY ECM.
- OVER .6 VOLT (600 mV) → OPEN CKT 413 OR FAULTY CONNECTION OR FAULTY ECM.
- LESS THAN .3 VOLT (300 mV) → OPEN CKT 412 OR FAULTY ECM CONNECTION OR FAULTY ECM.

"AFTER REPAIRS," REFER TO CODE CRITERIA AND CONFIRM CODE DOES NOT RESET.

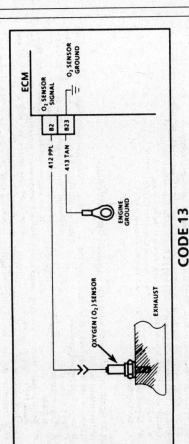

CODE 13
OXYGEN (O₂) SENSOR CIRCUIT
(OPEN CIRCUIT)

Circuit Description:

The Electronic Control Module (ECM) supplies a voltage of about .45 volt between terminals "B2" and "B23". (If measured with a 10 megohm digital voltmeter, this may read as low as .32 volt).

When the O₂ sensor reaches operating temperature, it varies this voltage from about .1 volt (exhaust is lean) to about .9 volt (exhaust is rich).

The sensor is like an open circuit and produces no voltage when it is below 316°C (600°F). An open sensor circuit, or cold sensor, causes "Open Loop" operation.

Test Description: Numbers below refer to circled numbers on the diagnostic chart.

1. Code 13 will set under the following conditions:
   - Engine at normal operating temperature.
   - At least 1 minute has elapsed since engine start-up.
   - O₂ signal voltage is steady between .35 and .55 volt.
   - Throttle angle is above 7%.
   - All above conditions are met for about 20 seconds.

   If the conditions for a Code 13 exist, the system will not operate in "Closed Loop."

2. This test determines if the O₂ sensor is the problem or if the ECM and wiring are at fault.

3. In doing this test, use only a 10 megohm digital voltmeter. This test checks the continuity of CKTs 412 and 413. If CKT 413 is open, the ECM voltage on CKT 412 will be over .6 volt (600 mV).

Diagnostic Aids:

Normal Tech 1 "Scan" tool O₂ sensor voltage varies between 100 mV to 999 mV (.1 and 1.0 volt) while in "Closed Loop." Code 13 sets in one minute if sensor signal voltage remains between .35 and .55 volt, but the system will go to "Open Loop" in about 15 seconds.

Verify a clean, tight ground connection for CKT 413. Open CKT(s) 412 or 413 will result in a Code 13. If Code 13 is intermittent, refer to "Symptoms,"

1990-91 2.2L (VIN G)

CODE 14
COOLANT TEMPERATURE SENSOR (CTS) CIRCUIT
(HIGH TEMPERATURE INDICATED)

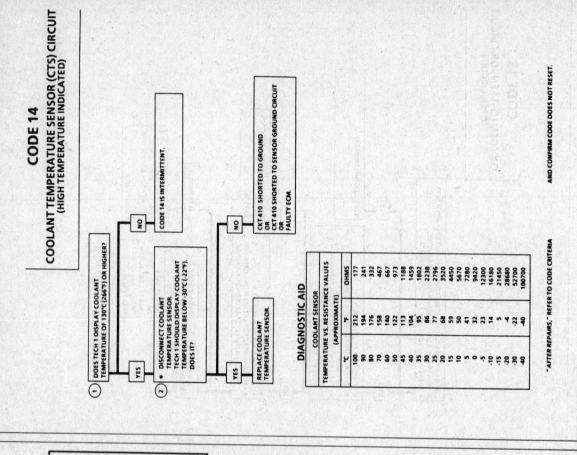

① DOES TECH 1 DISPLAY COOLANT TEMPERATURE OF 130°C (266°F) OR HIGHER?

- YES
- NO → CODE 14 IS INTERMITTENT.

② • DISCONNECT COOLANT TEMPERATURE SENSOR.
TECH 1 SHOULD DISPLAY COOLANT TEMPERATURE BELOW -30°C (-22°F).
DOES IT?

- YES → REPLACE COOLANT TEMPERATURE SENSOR.
- NO → CKT 410 SHORTED TO GROUND
OR
CKT 410 SHORTED TO SENSOR GROUND CIRCUIT
OR
FAULTY ECM.

DIAGNOSTIC AID

**COOLANT SENSOR
TEMPERATURE VS. RESISTANCE VALUES
(APPROXIMATE)**

°C	°F	OHMS
100	212	177
90	194	241
80	176	332
70	158	467
60	140	667
50	122	973
45	113	1188
40	104	1459
35	95	1802
30	86	2238
25	77	2796
20	68	3520
15	59	4450
10	50	5670
5	41	7280
0	32	9420
-5	23	12300
-10	14	16180
-15	5	21450
-20	-4	28680
-30	-22	52700
-40	-40	100700

"AFTER REPAIRS," REFER TO CODE CRITERIA AND CONFIRM CODE DOES NOT RESET.

CODE 14
COOLANT TEMPERATURE SENSOR (CTS) CIRCUIT
(HIGH TEMPERATURE INDICATED)

ECM

COOLANT SENSOR SIGNAL — B8
5 VOLT REFERENCE
SENSOR GROUND — B12

COOLANT TEMPERATURE SENSOR

410 GRY
455 PPL

TO MAP SENSOR

A B
455
410

Circuit Description:

The Coolant Temperature Sensor (CTS) uses a thermistor to control the signal voltage to the Electronic Control Module (ECM). The ECM applies a voltage on CKT 410 to the sensor. When the engine is cold, the sensor (thermistor) resistance is high. The ECM will then sense a high signal voltage.

As the engine warms up, the sensor resistance decreases and the voltage drops. At normal engine operating temperature, the voltage will measure about 1.5 to 2.0 volts at ECM terminal "B8".

Coolant temperature is one of the inputs used to control the following:
- Fuel delivery
- Electronic Spark Timing (EST)
- Cooling fan
- Torque Converter Clutch (TCC)
- Idle Air Control (IAC)

Test Description: Number(s) below refer to circled number(s) on the diagnostic chart.

1. Checks to see if code was set as result of hard failure or intermittent condition.
Code 14 will set if:
- Engine has been running for more than 10 seconds.
- Signal voltage indicates a coolant temperature above 135°C (275°F) for 3 seconds.

2. This test simulates conditions for a Code 15. If the ECM recognizes the open circuit (high voltage), and displays a low temperature, the ECM and wiring are OK.

Diagnostic Aids:

A Tech 1 "Scan" tool reads engine temperature in degrees celsius. After the engine is started, the temperature should rise steadily to about 90°C (194°F), then stabilize when the thermostat opens.

If the engine has been allowed to cool to an ambient temperature (overnight), coolant and IAT temperature may be checked with a "Scan" tool and should read close to each other.

When a Code 14 is set, the ECM will turn "ON" the engine cooling fan.

A Code 14 will result if CKT 410 is shorted to ground.

If Code 14 is intermittent refer to "Symptoms."

1990-91 2.2L (VIN G)

CODE 15

COOLANT TEMPERATURE SENSOR (CTS) CIRCUIT
(LOW TEMPERATURE INDICATED)

Circuit Description:

The Coolant Temperature Sensor (CTS) uses a thermistor to control the signal voltage to the Electronic Control Module (ECM). The ECM applies a voltage on CKT 410 to the sensor. When the engine is cold, the sensor (thermistor) resistance is high. The ECM will then sense a high signal voltage.

As the engine warms up, the sensor resistance decreases and the voltage drops. At normal engine operating temperature, the voltage will measure about 1.5 to 2.0 volts at ECM terminal "B8".

Coolant temperature is one of the inputs used to control the following:
- Fuel delivery
- Electronic Spark Timing (EST)
- Cooling fan
- Torque Converter Clutch (TCC)
- Idle Air Control (IAC)

Test Description: Number(s) below refer to circled number(s) on the diagnostic chart.

1. Check to see if code was set as result of hard failure or intermittent condition. Code 15 will set if:
   - Engine has been running for more than 120 seconds.
   - Signal voltage indicates a coolant temperature below -30°C (-22°F).
2. This test simulates conditions for a Code 14. If the ECM recognizes the grounded circuit (low voltage), and displays a high temperature, the ECM and wiring are OK.
3. This test will determine if there is a wiring problem or a faulty ECM. If CKT 452 is open, there may also be a Code 33 stored.

Diagnostic Aids:

A Tech 1 "Scan" tool reads engine temperature in degrees celsius. After the engine is started, the temperature should rise steadily to about 90°C (194°F), then stabilize, when the thermostat opens.

If the engine has been allowed to cool to an ambient temperature (overnight), coolant and Intake Air Temperature (IAT) temperature may be checked with a "Scan" tool and should read close to each other. When a Code 15 is set, the ECM will turn "ON" the engine cooling fan.

A Code 15 will result: if CKTs 410 or 455 are open. If Code 15 is intermittent, refer to "Symptoms."

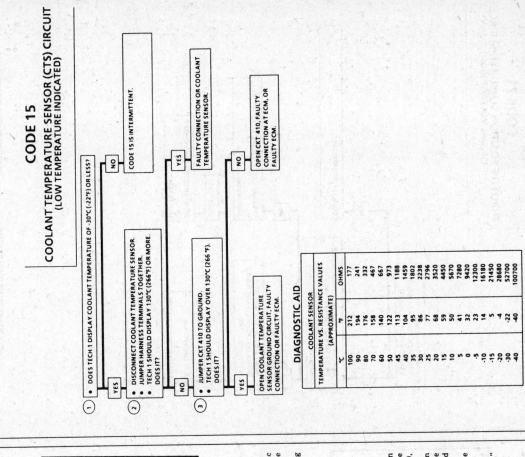

CODE 15

COOLANT TEMPERATURE SENSOR (CTS) CIRCUIT
(LOW TEMPERATURE INDICATED)

1. DOES TECH 1 DISPLAY COOLANT TEMPERATURE OF -30°C (-22°F) OR LESS?

   - YES →
   - NO → CODE 15 IS INTERMITTENT.

2. DISCONNECT COOLANT TEMPERATURE SENSOR. JUMPER HARNESS TERMINALS TOGETHER. TECH 1 SHOULD DISPLAY 130°C (266°F) OR MORE. DOES IT?

   - YES → FAULTY CONNECTION OR COOLANT TEMPERATURE SENSOR.
   - NO →

3. JUMPER CKT 410 TO GROUND. TECH 1 SHOULD DISPLAY OVER 130°C (266°F). DOES IT?

   - YES → OPEN COOLANT TEMPERATURE SENSOR GROUND CIRCUIT, FAULTY CONNECTION OR FAULTY ECM.
   - NO → OPEN CKT 410, FAULTY CONNECTION AT ECM, OR FAULTY ECM.

DIAGNOSTIC AID

COOLANT SENSOR
TEMPERATURE VS. RESISTANCE VALUES
(APPROXIMATE)

°C	°F	OHMS
100	212	177
90	194	241
80	176	332
70	158	467
60	140	667
50	122	973
45	113	1188
40	104	1459
35	95	1802
30	86	2238
25	77	2796
20	68	3520
15	59	4450
10	50	5670
5	41	7280
0	32	9420
-5	23	12300
-10	14	16180
-15	5	21450
-20	-4	28680
-30	-22	52700
-40	-40	100700

"AFTER REPAIRS," REFER TO CODE CRITERIA AND CONFIRM CODE DOES NOT RESET.

ECM

COOLANT SENSOR SIGNAL

5 VOLT REFERENCE

SENSOR GROUND

B8

B12

410 GRY

455 PPL

COOLANT TEMPERATURE SENSOR

A B

TO MAP SENSOR

455

410

1990-91 2.2L (VIN G)

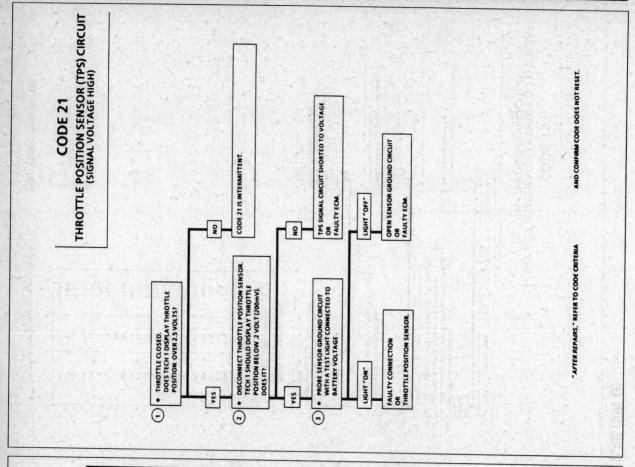

CODE 21

THROTTLE POSITION SENSOR (TPS) CIRCUIT
(SIGNAL VOLTAGE HIGH)

Circuit Description:

The Throttle Position Sensor (TPS) provides a voltage signal that changes relative to the throttle valve. Signal voltage will vary from less than 1.33 volts at idle to about 4.5 volts at Wide Open Throttle (WOT).

The TPS signal is one of the most important inputs used by the Electronic Control Module (ECM) for fuel control and for many of the ECM controlled outputs.

Test Description: Number(s) below refer to circled number(s) on the diagnostic chart.

1. This step checks to see if Code 21 is the result of a hard failure or an intermittent condition.
   A Code 21 will set under the following conditions:
   - TPS reading above 2.5 volts.
   - MAP reading below 55 kPa.
   - All of the above conditions present for 5 seconds.

2. This step simulates conditions for a Code 22. If the ECM recognizes the change of state, the ECM and CKTs 416 and 417 are OK.

3. This step isolates a faulty sensor, ECM, or an open CKT 452. If CKT 452 is open, there may also be a Code 23 stored.

Diagnostic Aids:

A Tech 1 "Scan" tool displays throttle position in volts. Closed throttle voltage should be between .30 and 1.33 volts. TPS voltage should increase at a steady rate as throttle is moved to WOT.

A Code 21 will result if CKT 452 is open or CKT 417 is shorted to voltage. If Code 21 is intermittent, refer to "Symptoms."

1990-91 2.2L (VIN G)

CODE 22

THROTTLE POSITION SENSOR (TPS) CIRCUIT
(SIGNAL VOLTAGE LOW)

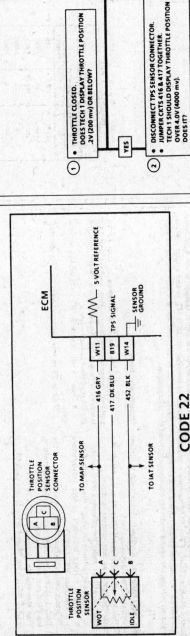

Circuit Description:

The Throttle Position Sensor (TPS) provides a voltage signal that changes relative to the throttle valve. Signal voltage will vary from less than 1.33 volts at idle to about 5 volts at Wide Open Throttle (WOT).

The TPS signal is one of the most important inputs used by the Electronic Control Module (ECM) for fuel control and many ECM controlled outputs.

Test Description: Number(s) below refer to circled number(s) on the diagnostic chart.

1. Code 22 will set if:
   - Engine is running.
   - TPS signal voltage is less than .20 volt.
   The TPS has an auto zeroing feature. If the voltage reading is within the range of about .3 to 1.33 volts, the ECM will use that value as closed throttle. If the voltage reading is out of the auto zero range at closed throttle, check for a binding throttle cable or damaged linkage, if OK, continue with diagnosis.
2. Simulates Code 21: (high voltage). If the ECM recognizes the high signal voltage then the ECM and wiring are OK.
3. This simulates a high signal voltage to check for an open in CKT 417. The Tech 1 "Scan" tool will not read up to battery voltage, but what is important is that the ECM recognizes the signal on CKT 417.

Diagnostic Aids:

A Tech 1 "Scan" tool reads throttle position in volts. With ignition "ON" or at idle, TPS signal voltage should read from about .3 to 1.33 volts with the throttle closed and increase at a steady rate as throttle is moved toward WOT.

An open or short to ground in CKT 416 or CKT 417 will result in a Code 22.

Refer to "Intermittents" in "Symptoms,"

---

1. THROTTLE CLOSED. DOES TECH 1 DISPLAY THROTTLE POSITION .2V (200 mv) OR BELOW?

  - YES →
  - NO → • CODE 22 IS INTERMITTENT.

2. DISCONNECT TPS SENSOR CONNECTOR. JUMPER CKTS 416 & 417 TOGETHER. TECH 1 SHOULD DISPLAY THROTTLE POSITION OVER 4.0V (4000 mv). DOES IT?

  - NO →
  - YES → • FAULTY SENSOR CONNECTION OR FAULTY SENSOR.

3. PROBE CKT 417 WITH A TEST LIGHT CONNECTED TO BATTERY VOLTAGE. TECH 1 SHOULD DISPLAY THROTTLE POSITION OVER 4.0V (4000 mv). DOES IT?

  - YES → CKT 416 OPEN OR SHORTED TO GROUND OR FAULTY CONNECTION OR FAULTY ECM.
  - NO → CKT 417 OPEN OR SHORTED TO GROUND, OR SHORTED TO THROTTLE POSITION SENSOR GROUND CIRCUIT OR FAULTY ECM CONNECTION OR FAULTY ECM.

*"AFTER REPAIRS," REFER TO CODE CRITERIA   AND CONFIRM CODE DOES NOT RESET.

1990-91 2.2L (VIN G)

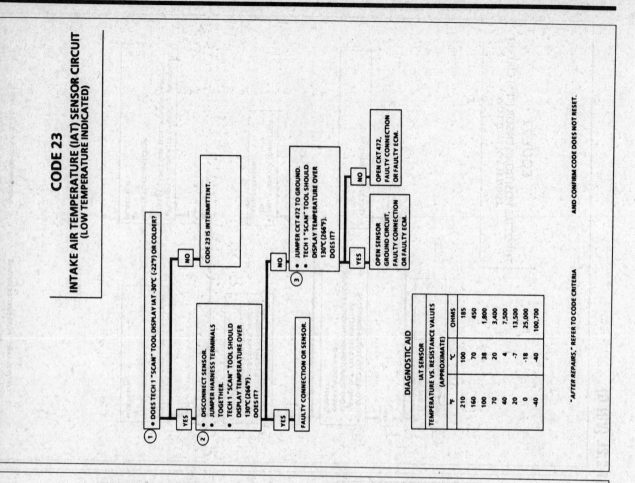

CODE 23

INTAKE AIR TEMPERATURE (IAT) SENSOR CIRCUIT
(LOW TEMPERATURE INDICATED)

Circuit Description:

The Intake Air Temperature (IAT) sensor uses a thermistor to control the signal voltage to the Electronic Control Module (ECM). The ECM applies a reference voltage (4-6 volts) on CKT 472 to the sensor. When manifold air is cold, the sensor (thermistor) resistance is high. The ECM will then sense a high signal voltage. As the air warms, the sensor resistance becomes less and the voltage drops.

Test Description: Number(s) below refer to circled number(s) on the diagnostic chart.

1. This step checks to see if Code 23 is the result of a hard failure or an intermittent condition.
   Code 23 will set under the following conditions:
   - Engine is running for longer than 2 minutes.
   - Signal voltage indicates an IAT temperature less than -30°C (-22°F).

2. This test simulates conditions for a Code 25. If the Tech 1 "Scan" tool displays a high temperature, the ECM and wiring are OK.

3. This step checks continuity of CKTs 472 and 452. If CKT 452 is open, there may also be a Code 21.

Diagnostic Aids:

If the engine has been allowed to cool to an ambient temperature (overnight), coolant and IAT temperatures may be checked with a "Scan" tool and should read close to each other.

A Code 23 will result if CKTs 472 or 452 become open.

If Code 23 is intermittent, refer to "Symptoms."

1990-91 2.2L (VIN G)

CODE 24

VEHICLE SPEED SENSOR (VSS) CIRCUIT

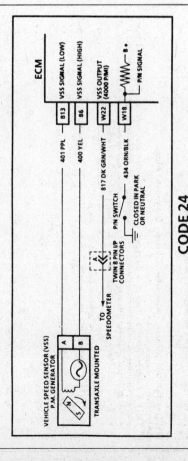

Circuit Description:

Vehicle speed information is provided to the Electronic Control Module (ECM) by the Vehicle Speed Sensor (VSS), which is a Permanent Magnet (PM) generator, and it is mounted in the transaxle. The PM generator produces a pulsing voltage, whenever vehicle speed is over about 3 mph. The AC voltage level and the number of pulses increases with vehicle speed. The ECM, then, converts the pulsing voltage to mph, which is used for calculations, and the mph can be displayed with a Tech 1 "Scan" tool.

The function of VSS buffer used in past model years has been incorporated into the ECM. The ECM then supplies the necessary signal for the instrument panel (4000 pulses per mile) for operating the speedometer and the odometer. If the vehicle is equipped with cruise control, the ECM also provides a signal (2000 pulses per mile) to the cruise control module.

Test Description: Number(s) below refer to circled number(s) on the diagnostic chart.

1. Code 24 will set if vehicle speed equals 0 mph when:
   - Engine speed is between 1200 and 4400 rpm.
   - MAP is less than 24 kPa.
   - Low load condition (low MAP voltage, high manifold vacuum).
   - Transmission not in park or neutral.
   - All above conditions are met for 5 seconds.

   These conditions are met during a road load deceleration.

   Disregard a Code 24 that sets when the drive wheels are not turning. This can be caused by a faulty park/neutral switch circuit.

   The PM generator only produces a signal if the drive wheels are turning greater than 3 mph.

2. Before replacing ECM, make sure that the correct PROM is installed for the application.

Diagnostic Aids:

Tech 1 "Scan" tool should indicate a vehicle speed whenever the drive wheels are turning greater than 3 mph.

A problem in CKT 938 will not affect the VSS input or the readings on a "Scan" tool.

Check CKTs 400 and 401 for proper connections to be sure they are clean and tight and the harness is routed correctly. Refer to "Intermittents" in "Symptoms."

(A/T) - A faulty or misadjusted park/neutral switch can result in a false Code 24. Use a "Scan" tool and check for the proper signal while in a drive range. P/N switch check.

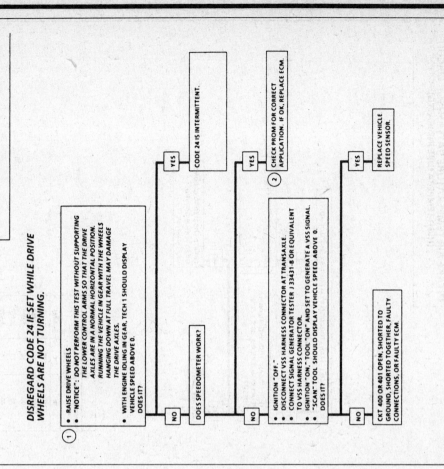

1990-91 2.2L (VIN G)

CODE 25

INTAKE AIR TEMPERATURE (IAT) SENSOR CIRCUIT
(HIGH TEMPERATURE INDICATED)

Circuit Description:

The Intake Air Temperature (IAT) sensor uses a thermistor to control the signal voltage to the Electronic Control Module (ECM). The ECM applies a reference voltage (4-6 volts) on CKT 472 to the sensor. When intake air is cold, the sensor (thermistor) resistance is high. The ECM will then sense a high signal voltage. As the air warms, the sensor resistance becomes less and the voltage drops.

Test Description: Number(s) below refer to circled number(s) on the diagnostic chart.

1. This check determines if the Code 25 is the result of a hard failure or an intermittent condition. A Code 25 will set under the following conditions:
   - Engine has been running longer than 8.5 minutes.
   - An IAT temperature greater than 135°C (275°F) is detected for a time longer than 2 seconds.
   - VSS signal present.

Diagnostic Aids:

If the engine has been allowed to cool to an ambient temperature (overnight), coolant and IAT temperatures may be checked with a "Scan" tool and should read close to each other.

A Code 25 will result if CKT 472 is shorted to ground.

If Code 25 is intermittent, refer to "Symptoms."

CODE 25

INTAKE AIR TEMPERATURE (IAT) SENSOR CIRCUIT
(HIGH TEMPERATURE INDICATED)

1 • DOES TECH 1 "SCAN" TOOL DISPLAY IAT OF 145°C (293°F) OR HOTTER?

YES	**NO**

NO → CODE 25 IS INTERMITTENT.

• DISCONNECT SENSOR
TECH 1 "SCAN" TOOL SHOULD DISPLAY TEMPERATURE BELOW -30°C (-22°F).
DOES IT?

YES	**NO**

NO → CKT 472 SHORTED TO GROUND, OR TO SENSOR GROUND, OR ECM IS FAULTY.

REPLACE SENSOR.

DIAGNOSTIC AID

IAT SENSOR
TEMPERATURE VS. RESISTANCE VALUES
(APPROXIMATE)

°F	°C	OHMS
210	100	185
160	70	450
100	38	1,800
70	20	3,400
40	4	7,500
20	-7	13,500
0	-18	25,000
-40	-40	100,700

"AFTER REPAIRS," REFER TO CODE CRITERIA

CONFIRM CODE DOES NOT RESET.

ECM

IAT SENSOR SIGNAL

5 VOLT REFERENCE

SENSOR GROUND

B5   472 BLK/PNK

W14   452 BLK

TO TPS

IAT SENSOR

A   B

452

472

1990-91 2.2L (VIN G)

CODE 32
EXHAUST GAS RECIRCULATION (EGR) SYSTEM FAILURE

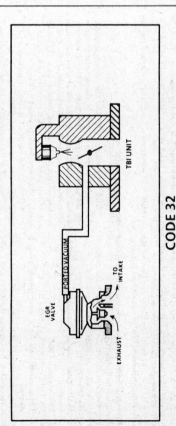

Code Description:

A properly operating Exhaust Gas Recirculation (EGR) system will directly affect the air/fuel mixture requirements of the engine. Since the exhaust gas introduced into the air/fuel mixture cannot be used in combustion (contains very little oxygen), less fuel is required to maintain a correct air/fuel ratio. If the EGR system were to fail in a closed position, the exhaust gas would be replaced with air, and the air/fuel mixture would be leaner. The Electronic Control Module (ECM) would compensate for the lean condition by adding fuel, resulting in higher block learn values.

The fuel control on this engine is conducted within 16 block learn cells. Since EGR is not used at idle, the closed throttle cell would not be affected by EGR system operation. The other block learn cells are affected by EGR operation, and, when the EGR system is operating properly, the block learn values in all cells should be close to the same. If the EGR system becomes inoperative, the block learn values in the open throttle cells would change to compensate for the resulting lean mixtures, but the block learn value in the closed throttle cell would not change.

The difference in block learn values between the idle (closed throttle) cell and cell 10 is used to monitor EGR system performance. When the difference between the two block learn values is greater than 12 and the block learn value in cell 10 is greater than 140, Code 32 is set. The system operates in block learn cell 10 during a cruise condition at approximately 55 mph.

Diagnostic Aids:

The Code 32 chart is a functional check of the EGR system. If the EGR system works properly, but a Code 32 has been set, check other items that could result in high block learn values in block learn cell 10, but not in the closed throttle cell.

Check for restricted or blocked EGR passages. Perform a MAP output check. Follow the procedure in CHART C-1D.

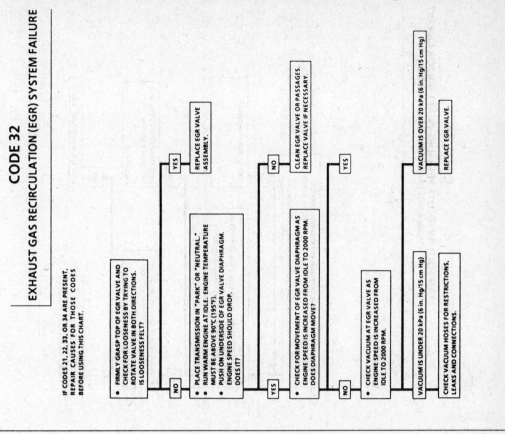

CODE 32
EXHAUST GAS RECIRCULATION (EGR) SYSTEM FAILURE

IF CODES 21, 22, 33, OR 34 ARE PRESENT, REPAIR CAUSES FOR THOSE CODES BEFORE USING THIS CHART.

- FIRMLY GRASP TOP OF EGR VALVE AND CHECK FOR LOOSENESS BY TRYING TO ROTATE VALVE IN BOTH DIRECTIONS. IS LOOSENESS FELT?

NO →
- PLACE TRANSMISSION IN "PARK" OR "NEUTRAL."
- RUN WARM ENGINE AT IDLE. ENGINE TEMPERATURE MUST BE ABOVE 90°C (195°F).
- PUSH ON UNDERSIDE OF EGR VALVE DIAPHRAGM. ENGINE SPEED SHOULD DROP. DOES IT?

YES → REPLACE EGR VALVE ASSEMBLY.

YES →
- CHECK FOR MOVEMENT OF EGR VALVE DIAPHRAGM AS ENGINE SPEED IS INCREASED FROM IDLE TO 2000 RPM. DOES DIAPHRAGM MOVE?

NO → CLEAN EGR VALVE OR PASSAGES. REPLACE VALVE IF NECESSARY.

YES →
- CHECK VACUUM AT EGR VALVE AS ENGINE SPEED IS INCREASED FROM IDLE TO 2000 RPM.

VACUUM IS UNDER 20 kPa (6 in. Hg/15 cm Hg) → CHECK VACUUM HOSES FOR RESTRICTIONS, LEAKS AND CONNECTIONS.

VACUUM IS OVER 20 kPa (6 in. Hg/15 cm Hg) → REPLACE EGR VALVE.

1990-91 2.2L (VIN G)

CODE 33
MANIFOLD ABSOLUTE PRESSURE (MAP) SENSOR CIRCUIT
(SIGNAL VOLTAGE HIGH - LOW VACUUM)

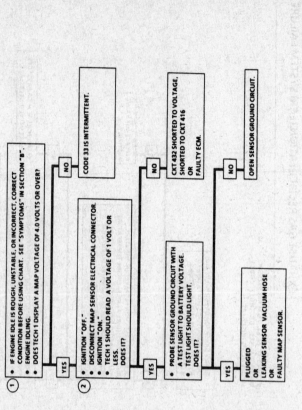

① • IF ENGINE IDLE IS ROUGH, UNSTABLE, OR INCORRECT, CORRECT CONDITION BEFORE USING CHART. SEE "SYMPTOMS" IN SECTION "B".
• ENGINE IDLING.
• DOES TECH 1 DISPLAY A MAP VOLTAGE OF 4.0 VOLTS OR OVER?

YES | NO → CODE 33 IS INTERMITTENT.

② • IGNITION "OFF."
• DISCONNECT MAP SENSOR ELECTRICAL CONNECTOR.
• IGNITION "ON."
• TECH 1 SHOULD READ A VOLTAGE OF 1 VOLT OR LESS. DOES IT?

YES | NO → CKT 432 SHORTED TO VOLTAGE, SHORTED TO CKT 416 OR FAULTY ECM.

• PROBE SENSOR GROUND CIRCUIT WITH A TEST LIGHT TO BATTERY VOLTAGE.
• TEST LIGHT SHOULD LIGHT. DOES IT?

YES | NO → OPEN SENSOR GROUND CIRCUIT.

YES → PLUGGED OR LEAKING SENSOR VACUUM HOSE OR FAULTY MAP SENSOR.

"AFTER REPAIRS," REFER TO CODE CRITERIA

CONFIRM CODE DOES NOT RESET.

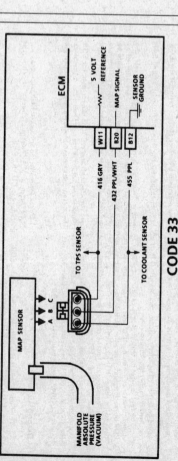

CODE 33
MANIFOLD ABSOLUTE PRESSURE (MAP) SENSOR CIRCUIT
(SIGNAL VOLTAGE HIGH - LOW VACUUM)

Circuit Description:
The Manifold Absolute Pressure (MAP) sensor responds to changes in manifold pressure (vacuum). The ECM receives this information as a signal voltage that will vary from about 1 to 1.5 volts at closed throttle idle, to 4.5-4.8 volts at wide open throttle (low vacuum).
If the MAP sensor fails, the Electronic Control Module (ECM) will substitute a fixed MAP value and use the Throttle Position Sensor (TPS) to control fuel delivery.

Test Description: Number(s) below refer to circled number(s) on the diagnostic chart.
1. This step will determine if Code 33 is the result of a hard failure or an intermittent condition. A Code 33 will set if:
   • MAP signal voltage is too high (low manifold vacuum).
   • TPS less than 12%.
   • No VSS signal (vehicle stopped)
   • These conditions for a time longer than 5 seconds.
2. This step simulates conditions for a Code 34. If the ECM recognizes the change, the ECM and CKTs 416 and 432 are OK.

Diagnostic Aids:
With the ignition "ON" and the engine stopped, the manifold pressure is equal to atmospheric pressure and the signal voltage will be high. This information is used by the ECM as an indication of vehicle altitude and is referred to as BARO. Comparison of this BARO reading with a known good vehicle with the same sensor is a good way to check accuracy of a "suspect" sensor. Readings should be equal ± .4 volt.
A Code 33 will result if CKT 455 is open, or if CKT 432 is shorted to voltage or to CKT 416.
If Code 33 is intermittent, refer to "Symptoms."

• Check all connections.
• Disconnect sensor from bracket and twist sensor by hand (only) to check for intermittent connections. Output changes greater than .1 volt indicates a faulty connection or connector. If OK, replace sensor.
• Refer to CHART C-1D, MAP sensor voltage vs. atmospheric pressure for further diagnosis.

CODE 34

MANIFOLD ABSOLUTE PRESSURE (MAP) SENSOR CIRCUIT
(SIGNAL VOLTAGE LOW - HIGH VACUUM)

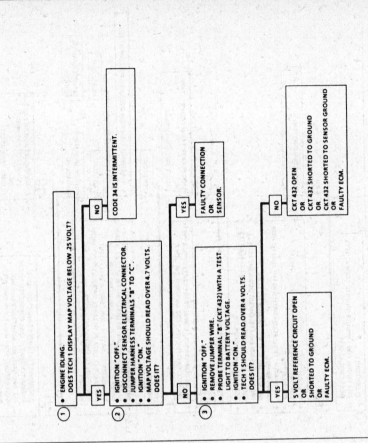

1.
- ENGINE IDLING.
- DOES TECH 1 DISPLAY MAP VOLTAGE BELOW .25 VOLT?

NO → CODE 34 IS INTERMITTENT.

2.
- IGNITION "OFF."
- DISCONNECT SENSOR ELECTRICAL CONNECTOR.
- JUMPER HARNESS TERMINALS "B" TO "C".
- IGNITION "ON."
- MAP VOLTAGE SHOULD READ OVER 4.7 VOLTS. DOES IT?

YES → FAULTY CONNECTION OR SENSOR.

3.
- IGNITION "OFF."
- REMOVE JUMPER WIRE.
- PROBE TERMINAL "B" (CKT 432) WITH A TEST LIGHT TO BATTERY VOLTAGE.
- IGNITION "ON."
- TECH 1 SHOULD READ OVER 4 VOLTS. DOES IT?

YES → 5 VOLT REFERENCE CIRCUIT OPEN OR SHORTED TO GROUND OR FAULTY ECM.

NO → CKT 432 OPEN OR CKT 432 SHORTED TO GROUND OR CKT 432 SHORTED TO SENSOR GROUND OR FAULTY ECM.

"AFTER REPAIRS," REFER TO CODE CRITERIA   CONFIRM CODE DOES NOT RESET.

1990-91 2.2L (VIN G)

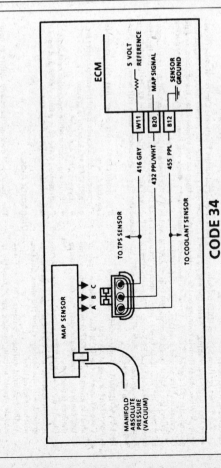

CODE 34

MANIFOLD ABSOLUTE PRESSURE (MAP) SENSOR CIRCUIT
(SIGNAL VOLTAGE LOW - HIGH VACUUM)

Circuit Description:

The Manifold Absolute Pressure (MAP) sensor responds to changes in manifold pressure (vacuum). The ECM receives this information as a signal voltage that will vary from about 1 to 1.5 volts at closed throttle (idle), to 4.5-4.8 volts at wide open throttle (low vacuum).

If the MAP sensor fails, the Electronic Control Module (ECM) will substitute a fixed MAP value and use the Throttle Position Sensor (TPS) to control fuel delivery.

Test Description: Number(s) below refer to circled number(s) on the diagnostic chart.

1. This step determines if Code 34 is the result of a hard failure or an intermittent condition.
   A Code 34 will set under the following conditions:
   - MAP signal voltage is too low
   - Engine speed is over 1200 rpm
2. Jumpering harness terminals "B" to "C" 5 volts to signal, will determine if the sensor is at fault, or if there is a problem with the ECM or wiring.
3. The Tech 1 "Scan" tool may not display 5 volts. What is important is that the ECM recognizes the voltage as more than 4 volts, indicating that the ECM and CKT 432 are OK.

Diagnostic Aids:

An intermittent open in CKT 432 or CKT 416 will result in a Code 34. With the ignition "ON" and the engine "OFF," the manifold pressure is equal to atmospheric pressure and the signal voltage will be high. This information is used by the ECM as an indications of vehicle altitude.

Comparison of this reading with a known good vehicle with same sensor is a good way to check accuracy of a "suspect" sensor. Reading should be the same ± .4 volt. Also CHART C-1D can be used to test the MAP sensor. Refer to "Intermittents" in "Symptoms,"
- Check all connections.
- Disconnect sensor from bracket and twist sensor by hand (only) to check for intermittent connections. Output changes greater than .1 volt indicates a bad connector or connection. If OK, replace sensor.

NOTE: Make sure electrical connector remains securely fastened.

- Refer to CHART C-1D, MAP sensor voltage vs. atmospheric pressure for further diagnosis.

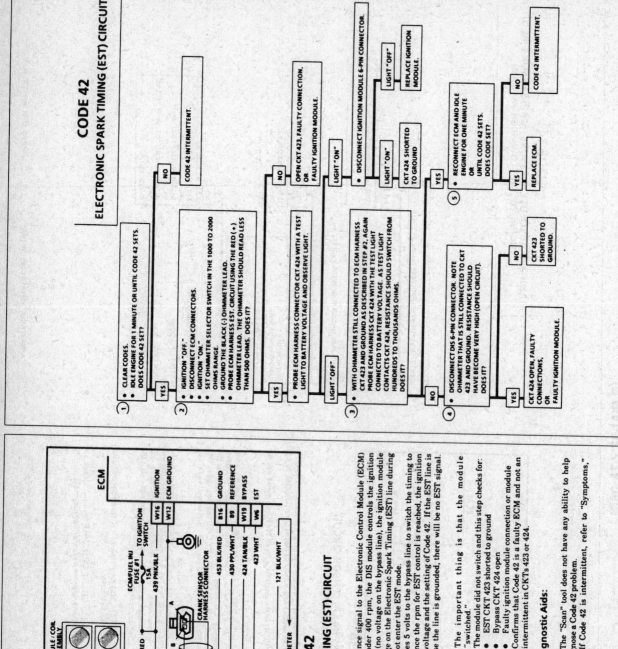

CODE 42

ELECTRONIC SPARK TIMING (EST) CIRCUIT

Circuit Description:

The Direct Ignition System (DIS) module sends a reference signal to the Electronic Control Module (ECM) when the engine is cranking. While the engine speed is under 400 rpm, the DIS module controls the ignition timing. When the system is running on the ignition module (no voltage on the bypass line), the ignition module grounds the EST signal. The ECM expects to sense no voltage on the Electronic Spark Timing (EST) line during this condition. If it senses a voltage, it sets Code 42 and will not enter the EST mode.

When the engine speed exceeds 400 rpm, the ECM applies 5 volts to the bypass line to switch the timing to ECM control (EST). If the bypass line is open or grounded, once the rpm for EST control is reached, the ignition module will not switch to EST mode. This results in low EST voltage and the setting of Code 42. If the EST line is grounded, the ignition module will switch to EST, but because the line is grounded, there will be no EST signal. A Code 42 will be set.

Test Description: Number(s) below refer to circled number(s) on the diagnostic chart.

1. Code 42 means the ECM has sensed an open or short to ground in the EST or bypass circuits. This test confirms Code 42 and that the fault causing the code is present.

2. Checks for a normal EST ground path through the ignition module. An EST CKT 423, shorted to ground, will also read less than 500 ohms, but this will be checked later.

3. As the test light voltage contacts CKT 424, the module should switch, causing the ohmmeter to "overrange" if the meter is in the 1000-2000 ohms position. Selecting the 10 - 20,000 ohms position will indicate a reading above 5000 ohms.

The important thing is that the module "switched."

4. The module did not switch and this step checks for:
   - EST CKT 423 shorted to ground
   - Bypass CKT 424 open
   - Faulty ignition module connection or module

5. Confirms that Code 42 is a faulty ECM and not an intermittent in CKTs 423 or 424.

Diagnostic Aids:

The "Scan" tool does not have any ability to help diagnose a Code 42 problem.

If Code 42 is intermittent, refer to "Symptoms."

1990-91 2.2L (VIN G)

CODE 44
OXYGEN SENSOR CIRCUIT
(LEAN EXHAUST INDICATED)

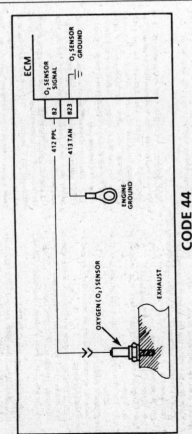

Circuit Description:

The Electronic Control Module (ECM) supplies a voltage of about .45 volt between terminals "B2" and "B23". (If measured with a 10 megohm digital voltmeter, this may read as low as .32 volt). When the O_2 sensor reaches operating temperature, it varies this voltage from about .1 volt (exhaust is lean) to about .9 volt (exhaust is rich). An open sensor circuit, or cold sensor, causes "Open Loop" operation.

The sensor is like an open circuit and produces no voltage when it is below 360°C (600°F).

Test Description: Number(s) below refer to circled number(s) on the diagnostic chart.

1. Code 44 is set when the O_2 sensor signal voltage on CKT 412 remains below .3 volt for 50 seconds or more and the system is operating in "Closed Loop."

Diagnostic Aids:

Using the "Scan" tool, observe the block learn value at different engine speeds. If the conditions for Code 44 exists, the block learn values will be around 150 or higher.
Check the following possible causes:
- O_2 **Sensor Wire.** Sensor pigtail may be mispositioned and contacting the exhaust manifold.
- Check for ground in wire between connector and sensor.
- **Fuel Contamination.** Water, even in small amounts, near the in-tank fuel pump inlet can be delivered to the injector. The water causes a lean exhaust and can set a Code 44.
- **Fuel Pressure.** System will be lean if fuel pressure is too low. It may be necessary to monitor fuel pressure while driving the car at various road speeds and/or loads to confirm. See "Fuel System Diagnosis," CHART A-7.
- **Exhaust Leaks.** If there is an exhaust leak, the engine can cause outside air to be pulled into the exhaust and past the sensor. Vacuum or crankcase leaks can cause a lean condition.
- If Code 44 is intermittent, refer to "Symptoms,"
- A cracked or otherwise damaged O_2 sensor may set an intermittent Code 44.

CODE 44
OXYGEN SENSOR CIRCUIT
(LEAN EXHAUST INDICATED)

(1) RUN WARM ENGINE (75°C/167°F TO 95°C/203°F) AT 1200 RPM.
- DOES TECH 1 INDICATE O_2 SENSOR VOLTAGE FIXED BELOW .35 VOLT (350 mV)?

YES
- DISCONNECT O_2 SENSOR.
- WITH ENGINE IDLING, TECH 1 SHOULD DISPLAY O_2 SENSOR VOLTAGE BETWEEN .35 VOLT AND .55 VOLT (350 mV AND 550 mV). DOES IT?

NO → CODE 44 IS INTERMITTENT.

YES → CKT 412 SHORTED TO GROUND OR FAULTY ECM.

NO → "AFTER REPAIRS," REFER TO CODE CRITERIA

CONFIRM CODE DOES NOT RESET.

1990-91 2.2L (VIN G)

CODE 45
OXYGEN SENSOR CIRCUIT (RICH EXHAUST INDICATED)

① RUN WARM ENGINE (75°C/167°F TO 95°C/203°F) AT 1200 RPM.
• DOES TECH 1 DISPLAY O₂ SENSOR VOLTAGE FIXED ABOVE .75 VOLT (750 mV)?

- **YES** →
  - DISCONNECT O₂ SENSOR AND JUMPER HARNESS CKT 412 TO GROUND. TECH 1 SHOULD DISPLAY O₂ BELOW .35 VOLT (350 mV). DOES IT?
    - **YES** → REPLACE ECM.
    - **NO** → CODE 45 IS INTERMITTENT.
- **NO** → CODE 45 IS INTERMITTENT.

"AFTER REPAIRS," REFER TO CODE CRITERIA — CONFIRM CODE DOES NOT RESET.

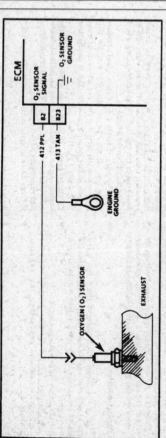

ECM
O₂ SENSOR SIGNAL — B2 — 412 PPL
O₂ SENSOR GROUND — B23 — 413 TAN — ENGINE GROUND

OXYGEN (O₂) SENSOR
EXHAUST

CODE 45
OXYGEN SENSOR CIRCUIT (RICH EXHAUST INDICATED)

Circuit Description:

The Electronic Control Module (ECM) supplies a voltage of about .45 volt between terminals "B2" and "B23". (If measured with a 10 megohm digital voltmeter, this may read as low as .32 volt.) When the O₂ sensor reaches operating temperature, it varies this voltage from about .1 volt (exhaust is lean) to about .9 volt (exhaust is rich).

The sensor is like an open circuit and produces no voltage when it is below 360°C (600°F). An open sensor circuit, or cold sensor, causes "Open Loop" operation.

Test Description: Number(s) below refer to circled number(s) on the diagnostic chart.

1. Code 45 is set when the O₂ sensor signal voltage on CKT 412 remains above .7 volt under the following conditions:
   • 30 seconds or more.
   • System is operating in "Closed Loop."
   • Engine run time after start is 1 minute or more.
   • Throttle angle less than 2% or greater than 20%.

Diagnostic Aids:

Code 45, or rich exhaust, is most likely caused by one of the following:

• **Fuel Pressure.** System will go rich, if pressure is too high. The ECM can compensate for some increase. However, if it gets too high, a Code 45 will be set. See "Fuel System Diagnosis," CHART A-7.

• **Leaking Injector.** See CHART A-7.

• **HEI Shielding.** An open ground CKT 453 may result in EMI, or induced electrical "noise." The ECM looks at this "noise" as reference pulses. The additional pulses result in a higher than actual engine speed signal. The ECM then delivers too much fuel causing the system to go rich. The engine tachometer will also show higher than actual engine speed, which can help in diagnosing this problem.

• **Canister Purge.** Check for fuel saturation. If full of fuel, check canister control and hoses.

• **MAP Sensor.** An output that causes the ECM to sense a higher than normal manifold pressure (low vacuum) can cause the system to go rich. Disconnecting the Manifold Absolute Pressure (MAP) sensor will allow the ECM to set a fixed value for the MAP sensor. Substitute a different MAP sensor if the rich condition is gone, while the sensor is disconnected.

• **TPS.** An intermittent Throttle Position Sensor (TPS) output will cause the system to operate richly due to a false indication of the engine accelerating.

• **O₂ Sensor Contamination.** Inspect oxygen sensor for silicone contamination from fuel, or use of improper RTV sealant. The sensor may have a white, powdery coating and result in a high but false signal voltage (rich exhaust indication). The ECM will then reduce the amount of fuel delivered to the engine causing a severe surge driveability problem.

• **EGR Valve.** Exhaust Gas Recirculation (EGR) sticking open at idle is usually accompanied by a rough idle and/or stall condition.
If Code 45 is intermittent, refer to "Symptoms,"

1990-91 2.2L (VIN G)

CODE 51
PROM ERROR
(FAULTY OR INCORRECT PROM)
2.2L (VIN G) "L" CARLINE (TBI)

CHECK THAT ALL PINS ARE FULLY INSERTED IN THE SOCKET AND THAT PROM IS PROPERLY SEATED. IF OK, REPLACE PROM, CLEAR MEMORY, AND RECHECK. IF CODE 51 REAPPEARS, REPLACE ECM.

2.2L (VIN G) "L" CARLINE (TBI) WHITE (W) 24 PIN ECM CONNECTOR

PIN FUNCTION	CKT #	WIRE COLOR	COMPONENT/ CONNECTOR CAVITY	NORMAL VOLTAGE KEY "ON"	NORMAL VOLTAGE ENG RUN**	CODES AFFECT	POSSIBLE SYMPTOMS FROM FAULTY CIRCUIT
W1 INJECTOR DRIVER	467	DK BLU	FUEL INJECTOR "B"	B+	B+		(5) CRANKS, BUT WON'T RUN
W2 A/C REQUEST	366	LT GRN	A/C RELAY "A"	0*	0*		(3) NO A/C COOLING. A/C CLUTCH INOPERATIVE
W4 CRUISE R/A	87	GRY/BLK					REFER TO ELECTRICAL DIAGNOSIS
W6 EST	423	WHT	"DIS" MODULE "C"	0*	1.1V	42	(5) STUMBLES, UNSTABLE IDLE.
W7 IAC "A" HI	441	DK GRN	IAC VALVE "D"	NOT USABLE	NOT USABLE	35	(5) UNSTABLE. INCORRECT IDLE.
W8 IAC "B" LO	444	DK BLU/ WHT	IAC VALVE "A"	NOT USABLE	NOT USABLE	35	(5) UNSTABLE. INCORRECT IDLE.
W9 IAC "B" HI	443	DK BLU	IAC VALVE "B"	NOT USABLE	NOT USABLE	35	(5) UNSTABLE. INCORRECT IDLE.
W10 ECM MEMORY (B+)	340	ORN	F/P ECM FUSE	B+	B+		(3) NO EFFECT. IF W15 IS ALSO OPEN. NO START. (4) BLOWN FUEL PUMP/ECM FUSE, NO START.
W11 5 VOLT REF. TPS & MAP	416	GRY	TPS "A" MAP "C"	5.0V	5.0V	22, 34	(5) STUMBLES, HESITATES; FUEL INTEGRATOR REMOVING FUEL (LOW COUNTS)
W12 ECM GROUND	551	TAN/WHT	ENGINE GROUND	0*	0*		(3) NO EFFECT. IF W13 IS ALSO OPEN. NO START
W13 ECM GROUND	450	BLK/WHT	ENGINE GROUND	0*	0*		(3) NO EFFECT. IF W12 IS ALSO OPEN, NO START.
W14 MAP, IAT SENSOR GROUND	452	BLK	TPS "B" IAT "A"	0*	0*	33	(3) POOR PERFORMANCE. STRONG EXHAUST ODOR
W15 ECM MEMORY (B+)	340	ORN	F/P ECM FUSE	B+	B+		(3) NO EFFECT. IF W10 IS ALSO OPEN, NO START
W16 IGNITION FEED	439	PNK/BLK	ECM FUSE "DIS" MODULE "B"	B+	B+		(3) NO START
W17 IAC "A" LO	442	DK GRN/ WHT	IAC VALVE "C"	NOT USABLE	NOT USABLE	35	(5) UNSTABLE. INCORRECT IDLE
W18 PARK/NEUTRAL SWITCH	434	ORN/BLK	P/N SWITCH "A"	0* P-N B+ R-DL	0* P-N B+ R-DL		(5) INCORRECT IDLE
W19 IGNITION BYPASS	424	TAN/BLK	"DIS" MODULE "D"	0*	4.5V	42	(5) POOR PERFORMANCE
W20 CRUISE ENABLE	397	GRY					REFER TO ELECTRICAL DIAGNOSIS
W21 CRUISE S/C	84	DK BLU					REFER TO ELECTRICAL DIAGNOSIS
W22 VSS OUTPUT	817	DK GRN/ WHT	BULK HEAD CONNECTOR A7	0*	0*		(5) SPEEDOMETER INOPERATIVE
W24 FUEL PUMP RELAY DRIVE	465	DK GRN	FUEL PUMP RELAY "D"	(6)	B+		(5) LONG CRANKING TIME WHEN COLD

NOTICE: The voltages may vary due to battery charge or other reasons, but they should be very close.

* All voltages shown 0* should read less than .5 volt.

* All voltages shown are typical with engine at idle, Closed Throttle, Normal Operating Temperature, Park or Neutral and "Closed Loop." All accessories "OFF."

** Changes with IAC valve activity (when moving throttle slightly up and down).

(1) Varies
(2) Open circuit
(3) Grounded circuit
(4) Open or grounded circuit
(5) Open or grounded circuit
(6) Reads B + for 2 seconds after ignition "ON," then should read 0 volts.

"AFTER REPAIRS," CONFIRM "CLOSED LOOP" OPERATION AND NO "SERVICE ENGINE SOON" LIGHT.

1990-91 2.2L (VIN G)

2.2L (VIN G) "L" CARLINE (TBI) BLACK (B) 24 PIN ECM CONNECTOR

PIN FUNCTION	CKT #	WIRE COLOR	COMPONENT/ CONNECTOR CAVITY	NORMAL VOLTAGE KEY "ON"	ENG. RUN**	CODES AFFECT.	POSSIBLE SYMPTOMS FROM FAULTY CIRCUIT
B1 SERIAL DATA	461	ORN	I/P CONNECTOR "F"	4.5V	4.5V		(5) NO TECH 1 DATA
B2 OXYGEN (O2) SENSOR SIGNAL	412	PPL	O2 SENSOR	33-.55V	1-.9V		(5) OPEN LOOP, STRONG EXHAUST ODOR
B3 A/C COMPRESSOR RELAY	459	BRN	A/C COMPRESSOR RELAY "F"	B+	B+		(3) A/C CLUTCH INOPERATIVE (4) BLOWN ENGINE CONTROL FUSE A/C CLUTCH INOPERATIVE
B5 IAT SIGNAL	472	BLK/PNK	IAT SENSOR "B"	1.3V	1.3V	23,25	(3) POSSIBLE STRONG EXHAUST, TECH 1 READS -38°C (-36°F). (4) TECH 1 READS 179°C (354°F)
B6 VSS SIGNAL (LOW)	400	YEL	PM GENERATOR "A"	0*	0*	24	(5) POOR FUEL ECONOMY, TCC DISENGAGED AT ALL TIMES, SPEEDOMETER INOPERATIVE
B7 TCC CONTROL SHIFT LIGHT	422 456	TAN/BLK	TCC SOLENOID "D" ALDL "F"	0*	0*		(3) POOR FUEL ECONOMY, TCC DOES NOT ENGAGE TECH 1 SHOWS TCC "ON". (4) TCC ENGAGES TOO SOON IN 3rd GEAR, LUGS ENGINE AT HIGHWAY SPEEDS
B8 COOLANT TEMPERATURE SIGNAL	410	GRY	CTS "B"	1.9V	1.9V	14,15	(3) INCORRECT IDLE, COOLING FAN RUNS AT ALL TIMES, TECH 1 READS 39°C (38°F). (4) SAME AS OPEN EXCEPT TECH 1 READS 151°C (304°F)
B9 IGNITION REFERENCE HI	430	PPL/WHT	"DIS" MODULE "E"	4.6V	3.05V		(5) NO START
B10 CRUISE (VAC)	402	LT GRN					REFER TO ELECTRICAL DIAGNOSIS
B11 CRUISE (VENT)	403	DK BLU					REFER TO ELECTRICAL DIAGNOSIS
B12 CTS & TPS GROUND	455	PPL	CTS "A" MAP "A"	0*	0*	15,21	(3) INCORRECT IDLE, HESITATION. TECH 1 READS TPS - 5V, CTS 39°C (102°F)

NOTICE: The voltages may vary due to battery charge or other reasons, but should be very close.

* All voltages shown 0* should read less than .5 volt.
** All voltages shown are typical with engine at Idle, Closed Throttle, Normal Operating Temperature, Park or Neutral and "Closed Loop." All accessories "OFF."
(A) A/C select switch "OFF."
(B) Varies depending on temperature
(1) Changes with IAC valve activity (when moving throttle slightly up and down).
(2) Varies
(3) Open circuit
(4) Grounded circuit
(5) Open or grounded circuit

2.2L (VIN G) "L" CARLINE (TBI) BLACK 24 PIN "B" ECM CONNECTOR

PIN FUNCTION	CKT #	WIRE COLOR	COMPONENT/ CONNECTOR CAVITY	NORMAL VOLTAGE KEY "ON"	ENG RUN**	CODES AFFECT.	POSSIBLE SYMPTOMS FROM FAULTY CIRCUIT
B13 VSS SIGNAL (HIGH)	401	PPL	PM GENERATOR "B"	0*	0*	24	(3) POOR FUEL ECONOMY, TCC INOPERATIVE.
B14 CRUISE/BRAKE SWITCH	86	BRN					REFER TO ELECTRICAL DIAGNOSIS
B15 DIAGNOSTIC TEST	451	WHT/BLK	ALDL "B"	5.0V	5.0V		(4) FIELD SERVICE MODE ACTIVE, "SES" LIGHT FLASHES RICH/LEAN.
B16 IGNITION REF LO	453	BLK/RED	DIS" MODULE "F"	0*	0*		(5) NO EFFECT
B19 TPS SIGNAL	417	DK BLU	TPS "C"	.6V	6V IDLE	21,22	(5) POOR PERFORMANCE, BACKFIRE, HESITATION.
B20 MAP SIGNAL	432	PPL/WHT	MAP SENSOR "B"	4.75V	1.1V	33,34	(5) INCORRECT IDLE, CHUGGLE, POOR PERFORMANCE.
B21 COOLING FAN RELAY	335	DK GRN/ WHT	COOLING FAN RELAY "F"	B+	B+		(3) POSSIBLE OVERHEATING, SPARK KNOCK. (4) COOLING FAN RUNS AT ALL TIMES.
B22 "SERVICE ENGINE SOON" LIGHT	419	BRN/WHT	TWIN 8-PIN I/P CONNECTOR "B"	0*	B+		(4) "SES" LIGHT "ON" AT ALL TIMES
B23 OXYGEN (O2) SENSOR GROUND	413	TAN	ENGINE GROUND	0*	0*	13	(3) OPEN LOOP, TECH 1 READS (O2) SENSOR VOLTAGE FIXED AT 400-500 mV.

NOTICE: Voltages may vary due to low battery charge or other reasons, but should be very close.

* All voltages shown 0* should read less than .5 volt.
** All voltages shown are typical with engine at Idle, Closed Throttle, Normal Operating Temperature, Park or Neutral and "Closed Loop." All accessories "OFF."
(A) A/C Select Switch "OFF."
(B) Varies depending on temperature
(1) Changes with IAC valve activity (when moving throttle slightly up and down).
(2) Varies
(3) Open circuit
(4) Grounded circuit
(5) Open or grounded circuit

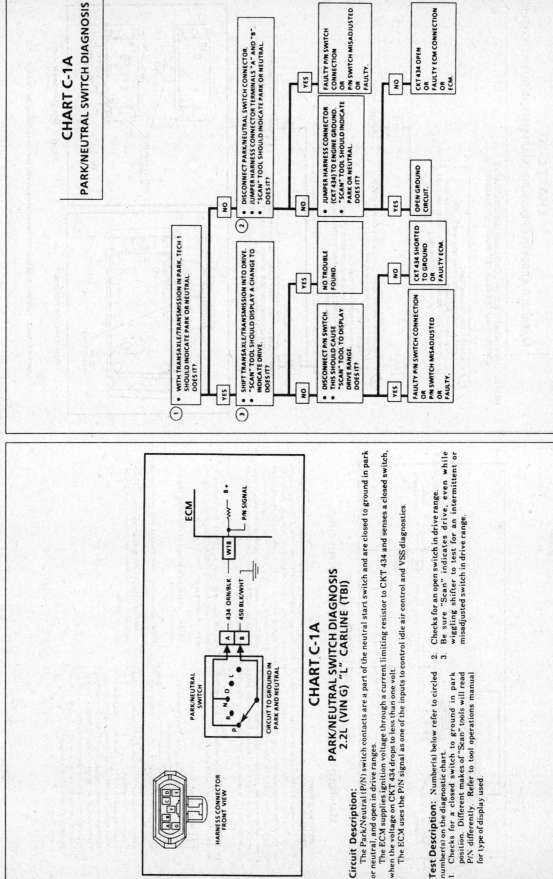

CHART C-1A
PARK/NEUTRAL SWITCH DIAGNOSIS

1990-91 2.2L (VIN G)

① WITH TRANSAXLE/TRANSMISSION IN PARK, TECH 1 SHOULD INDICATE PARK OR NEUTRAL.
   DOES IT?

② • DISCONNECT PARK/NEUTRAL SWITCH CONNECTOR.
   • JUMPER HARNESS CONNECTOR TERMINALS "A" AND "B".
   • "SCAN" TOOL SHOULD INDICATE PARK OR NEUTRAL.
     DOES IT?

③ • SHIFT TRANSAXLE/TRANSMISSION INTO DRIVE.
   • "SCAN" TOOL SHOULD DISPLAY A CHANGE TO INDICATE DRIVE.
     DOES IT?

• JUMPER HARNESS CONNECTOR (CKT 434) TO ENGINE GROUND.
• "SCAN" TOOL SHOULD INDICATE PARK OR NEUTRAL.
  DOES IT?

FAULTY P/N SWITCH CONNECTION OR P/N SWITCH MISADJUSTED OR FAULTY.

CKT 434 OPEN OR FAULTY ECM CONNECTION OR ECM.

OPEN GROUND CIRCUIT.

NO TROUBLE FOUND.

• DISCONNECT P/N SWITCH.
• THIS SHOULD CAUSE "SCAN" TOOL TO DISPLAY DRIVE RANGE.
  DOES IT?

FAULTY P/N SWITCH CONNECTION OR P/N SWITCH MISADJUSTED OR FAULTY.

CKT 434 SHORTED TO GROUND OR FAULTY ECM.

YES / NO

ECM

B+
P/N SIGNAL

W18

434 ORN/BLK
450 BLK/WHT

A
B

PARK/NEUTRAL SWITCH

R N D L
P

CIRCUIT TO GROUND IN PARK AND NEUTRAL

HARNESS CONNECTOR FRONT VIEW

CHART C-1A
PARK/NEUTRAL SWITCH DIAGNOSIS
2.2L (VIN G) "L" CARLINE (TBI)

Circuit Description:
The Park/Neutral (P/N) switch contacts are a part of the neutral start switch and are closed to ground in park or neutral, and open in drive ranges.

The ECM supplies ignition voltage through a current limiting resistor to CKT 434 and senses a closed switch, when the voltage on CKT 434 drops to less than one volt.

The ECM uses the P/N signal as one of the inputs to control idle air control and VSS diagnostics.

Test Description: Number(s) below refer to circled number(s) on the diagnostic chart.
1. Checks for a closed switch to ground in park position. Different makes of "Scan" tools will read P/N differently. Refer to tool operations manual for type of display used.
2. Checks for an open switch in drive range.
3. Be sure "Scan" indicates drive, even while wiggling shifter to test for an intermittent or misadjusted switch in drive range.

"AFTER REPAIRS," CONFIRM "CLOSED LOOP" OPERATION AND NO "SERVICE ENGINE SOON" LIGHT.

1990-91 2.2L (VIN G)

CHART C-1D
MANIFOLD ABSOLUTE PRESSURE (MAP) SENSOR OUTPUT CHECK

NOTE: THIS CHART ONLY APPLIES TO MAP SENSORS HAVING GREEN OR BLACK COLOR KEY INSERT (SEE BELOW).

① • IGNITION "ON," ENGINE "OFF."
• TECH 1 SHOULD INDICATE A MAP SENSOR VOLTAGE.
• COMPARE THIS READING WITH THE READING OF A KNOWN GOOD VEHICLE. SEE FACING PAGE TEST DESCRIPTION, STEP 1.
• VOLTAGE READING SHOULD BE WITHIN, ± .4 VOLT.
IS IT?

NO → REPLACE SENSOR.

YES

② • DISCONNECT AND PLUG VACUUM SOURCE TO MAP SENSOR.
• CONNECT A HAND VACUUM PUMP TO MAP SENSOR.
• START ENGINE.
• NOTE MAP SENSOR VOLTAGE.
• APPLY 34 kPa (10" Hg) OF VACUUM AND NOTE VOLTAGE CHANGE. SUBTRACT SECOND READING FROM THE FIRST. VOLTAGE VALUE SHOULD BE GREATER THAN 1.5 VOLTS.
IS IT?

NO → ④ CHECK SENSOR CONNECTION. IF OK, REPLACE SENSOR.

YES

③ NO TROUBLE FOUND. CHECK SENSOR VACUUM SOURCE FOR LEAKAGE OR RESTRICTION. BE SURE THIS SOURCE SUPPLIES VACUUM TO MAP SENSOR ONLY.

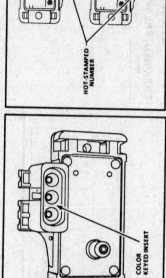

COLOR KEYED INSERT

Figure 1 - Color Key Insert

HOT-STAMPED NUMBER

Figure 2 - Hot-Stamped Number

"AFTER REPAIRS," CONFIRM "CLOSED LOOP" OPERATION AND NO "SERVICE ENGINE SOON" LIGHT.

CHART C-1D
MANIFOLD ABSOLUTE PRESSURE (MAP) SENSOR OUTPUT CHECK

MAP SENSOR

MANIFOLD ABSOLUTE PRESSURE (VACUUM)

A B C

TO TPS SENSOR

TO COOLANT SENSOR

416 GRY

432 PPL/WHT

455 PPL

ECM

W11 — 5 VOLT REFERENCE

B20 — MAP SIGNAL

B12 — SENSOR GROUND

Circuit Description:

The Manifold Absolute Pressure (MAP) sensor measures the changes in the intake manifold pressure which result from engine load (intake manifold vacuum) and rpm changes; and converts these into a voltage output. The ECM sends a 5 volts reference voltage to the MAP sensor. As the manifold pressure changed, the output voltage of the sensor also changes. By monitoring the sensor signal voltage, the ECM determines the manifold pressure. a lower pressure (low voltage) output voltage will be about 1 - 2 volts at idle. While higher pressure (high voltage) output voltage will be about 4 - 4.8 at Wide Open Throttle (WOT). The MAP sensor is also used, under certain conditions, to measure barometric pressure, allowing the ECM to make adjustments for different altitudes. The ECM uses the MAP sensor to control fuel delivery and ignition timing

Test Description: Number(s) below refer to circled number(s) on the diagnostic chart.

📋 **Important**

• Be sure to use the same Diagnostic Test Equipment for all measurements.

1. When comparing "Scan" readings to a known good vehicle, it is important to compare vehicles that use a MAP sensor having the same color insert or having the same "Hot Stamped" number. See figures on facing page.

2. Applying 34 kPa (10" Hg/25 cm Hg) vacuum to the MAP sensor should cause the voltage to change. Subtract second reading from the first. Voltage value should be greater than 1.5 volts. Upon applying vacuum to the sensor, the change in voltage should be instantaneous. A slow voltage change indicates a faulty sensor.

3. Check vacuum hose to sensor for leaking or restriction. Be sure that no other vacuum devices are connected to the MAP hose.

NOTE: Make sure electrical connector remains securely fastened.

4. Disconnect sensor from bracket and twist sensor by hand (only) to check for intermittent connection. Output changes greater than .1 volt indicate a bad connector or connection. If OK, replace sensor.

1990-91 2.2L (VIN G)

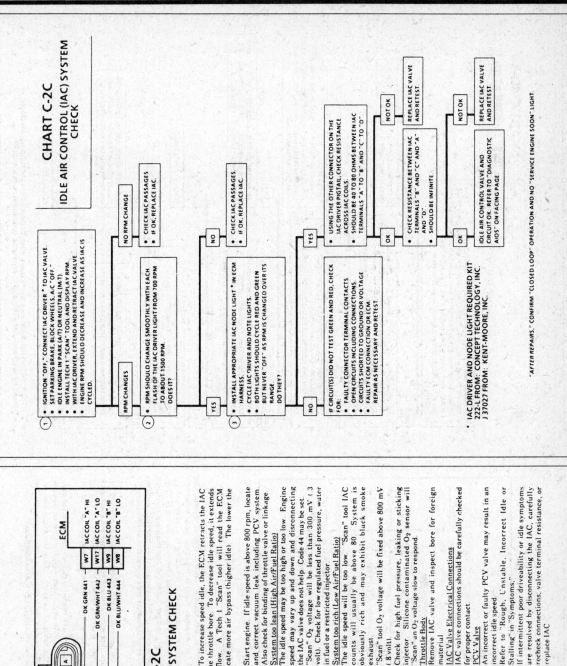

CHART C-2C
IDLE AIR CONTROL (IAC) SYSTEM CHECK

① IGNITION "OFF," CONNECT IAC DRIVER * TO IAC VALVE.
SET PARKING BRAKE, BLOCK WHEELS, A/C "OFF."
IDLE ENGINE IN PARK (A/T) OR NEUTRAL (M/T).
INSTALL TECH 1 "SCAN" TOOL AND DISPLAY RPM.
WITH IAC DRIVER, EXTEND AND RETRACT IAC VALVE.
ENGINE RPM SHOULD DECREASE AND INCREASE AS IAC IS
CYCLED.

RPM CHANGES → **NO RPM CHANGE** → • CHECK IAC PASSAGES. • IF OK, REPLACE IAC.

② RPM SHOULD CHANGE SMOOTHLY WITH EACH
FLASH OF THE IAC DRIVER LIGHT FROM 700 RPM
TO ABOUT 1500 RPM.
DOES IT?

YES / **NO** → • CHECK IAC PASSAGES. • IF OK, REPLACE IAC.

③ INSTALL APPROPRIATE IAC NODE LIGHT * IN ECM
HARNESS.
• CYCLE IAC DRIVER AND NOTE LIGHTS.
• BOTH LIGHTS SHOULD CYCLE RED AND GREEN
BUT NEVER "OFF" AS RPM IS CHANGED OVER ITS
RANGE.
DO THEY?

YES / **NO**

• USING THE OTHER CONNECTOR ON THE
IAC DRIVER PIGTAIL, CHECK RESISTANCE
ACROSS IAC COILS.
• SHOULD BE 40 TO 80 OHMS BETWEEN IAC
TERMINALS "A" TO "B" AND "C" TO "D".

OK / **NOT OK** → REPLACE IAC VALVE AND RETEST.

IF CIRCUIT(S) DID NOT TEST GREEN AND RED, CHECK
FOR:
• FAULTY CONNECTOR TERMINAL CONTACTS.
• OPEN CIRCUITS INCLUDING CONNECTIONS.
• CIRCUITS SHORTED TO GROUND OR VOLTAGE.
• FAULTY ECM CONNECTION OR ECM.
REPAIR AS NECESSARY AND RETEST.

• CHECK RESISTANCE BETWEEN IAC
TERMINALS "B" AND "C" AND "A"
AND "D".
• SHOULD BE INFINITE.

OK / **NOT OK** → REPLACE IAC VALVE AND RETEST.

IDLE AIR CONTROL VALVE AND
CIRCUIT OK. REFER TO "DIAGNOSTIC
AIDS" ON FACING PAGE.

* IAC DRIVER AND NODE LIGHT REQUIRED KIT
222-L FROM: CONCEPT TECHNOLOGY, INC.
J 37027 FROM: KENT-MOORE, INC.

"AFTER REPAIRS," CONFIRM "CLOSED LOOP" OPERATION AND NO "SERVICE ENGINE SOON" LIGHT

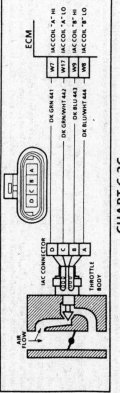

ECM

W7	DK GRN 441	IAC COIL "A" HI
W17	DK GRN/WHT 442	IAC COIL "A" LO
W9	DK BLU 443	IAC COIL "B" HI
W8	DK BLU/WHT 444	IAC COIL "B" LO

IAC CONNECTOR

THROTTLE BODY

AIR FLOW

CHART C-2C
IDLE AIR CONTROL (IAC) SYSTEM CHECK

Circuit Description:

The ECM controls engine idle speed with the IAC valve. To increase speed idle, the ECM retracts the IAC valve pintle away from its seat, allowing more air to bypass the throttle bore. To decrease idle speed, it extends the IAC valve pintle towards its seat, reducing bypass air flow. A Tech 1 "Scan" tool will read the ECM commands to the IAC valve in counts. Higher the counts indicate more air bypass (higher idle). The lower the counts indicate less air allowed to bypass (lower idle).

Test Description: Number(s) below refer to circled number(s) on the diagnostic chart.

1. The IAC tester is used to extend and retract the IAC valve. Valve movement is verified by an engine speed change. If no change in engine speed occurs, the valve can be retested when removed from the throttle body.

2. This step checks the quality of the IAC movement in Step 1. Between 700 rpm and about 1500 rpm, the engine speed should change smoothly with each flash of the tester light in both extend and retract. If the IAC valve is retracted beyond the control range (about 1500 rpm), it may take many flashes in the extend position before engine speed will begin to drop. This is normal on certain engines, fully extending IAC may cause engine stall. This may be normal.

3. Steps 1 and 2 verified proper IAC valve operation while this step checks the IAC circuits. Each lamp on the node light should flash red and green while the IAC valve is cycled. While the sequence of color is not important or if either light is "OFF" or does not flash red and green, check the circuits for faults, beginning with poor terminal contacts.

Diagnostic Aids:

• **Vacuum Leak (High Idle)**

A slow, unstable, or fast idle may be caused by a non-IAC system problem that cannot be overcome by the IAC valve. Out of control range IAC "Scan" tool counts will be above 60 if idle is too low, and zero counts if idle is too high. The following checks should be made to repair a non-IAC system problem.

If idle is too high, stop the engine. Fully extend (low) IAC with tester.

Start engine. If idle speed is above 800 rpm, locate and correct vacuum leak including PCV system. Also check for binding of throttle valve or linkage.

• **System too lean (High Air/Fuel Ratio)**

The idle speed may be too high or too low. Engine speed may vary up and down and disconnecting the IAC valve does not help. Code 44 may be set. "Scan" O2 voltage will be less than 300 mV (.3 volt). Check for low regulated fuel pressure, water in fuel or a restricted injector.

• **System too rich (Low Air/Fuel Ratio)**

The idle speed will be too low. "Scan" tool IAC counts will usually be above 80. System is obviously rich and may exhibit black smoke exhaust. "Scan" tool O2 voltage will be fixed above 800 mV (.8 volt). Check for high fuel pressure, leaking or sticking injector. Silicone contaminated O2 sensor will "Scan" an O2 voltage slow to respond.

• **Throttle Body**

Remove IAC valve and inspect bore for foreign material.

• **IAC Valve Electrical Connections**

IAC valve connections should be carefully checked for proper contact.

• **PCV Valve**

An incorrect or faulty PCV valve may result in an incorrect idle speed.

Refer to "Rough, Unstable, Incorrect Idle or Stalling" in "Symptoms."

If intermittent poor driveability or idle symptoms are resolved by disconnecting the IAC, carefully recheck connections, valve terminal resistance, or replace IAC

1990-91 2.2L (VIN G)

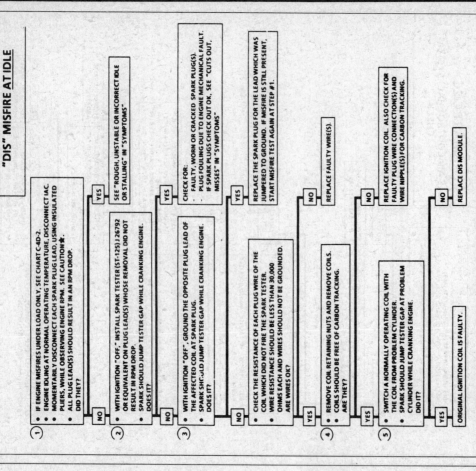

CHART C-4D-1
"DIS" MISFIRE AT IDLE

(1)
- IF ENGINE MISFIRES UNDER LOAD ONLY, SEE CHART C-4D-2.
- ENGINE IDLING AT NORMAL OPERATING TEMPERATURE, DISCONNECT IAC.
- MOMENTARILY DISCONNECT EACH SPARK PLUG LEAD, USING INSULATED PLIERS, WHILE OBSERVING ENGINE RPM. SEE CAUTION★.
- ALL PLUG LEAD(S) SHOULD RESULT IN AN RPM DROP.
  DID THEY?

YES → SEE "ROUGH, UNSTABLE OR INCORRECT IDLE OR STALLING" IN "SYMPTOMS"

(2)
- WITH IGNITION "OFF," INSTALL SPARK TESTER (ST-125) J 26792 OR EQUIVALENT ON PLUG LEAD(S) WHOSE REMOVAL DID NOT RESULT IN RPM DROP.
- SPARK SHOULD JUMP TESTER GAP WHILE CRANKING ENGINE. DOES IT?

YES → CHECK FOR:
- FAULTY, WORN OR CRACKED SPARK PLUG(S).
- PLUG FOULING DUE TO ENGINE MECHANICAL FAULT.
  IF SPARK PLUGS CHECK OUT OK, SEE "CUTS OUT, MISSES" IN "SYMPTOMS"

(3)
- WITH IGNITION "OFF," GROUND THE OPPOSITE PLUG LEAD OF THE AFFECTED COIL AT SPARK PLUG.
- SPARK SHOULD JUMP TESTER GAP WHILE CRANKING ENGINE. DOES IT?

YES → REPLACE THE SPARK PLUG FOR THE LEAD WHICH WAS JUMPERED TO GROUND. IF MISFIRE IS STILL PRESENT, START MISFIRE TEST AGAIN AT STEP #1.

(4)
- CHECK THE RESISTANCE OF EACH PLUG WIRE OF THE COIL WHICH DID NOT FIRE THE SPARK TESTER.
- WIRE RESISTANCE SHOULD BE LESS THAN 30,000 OHMS EACH AND WIRES SHOULD NOT BE GROUNDED.
  ARE WIRES OK?

NO → REPLACE FAULTY WIRE(S).

YES →
- REMOVE COIL RETAINING NUTS AND REMOVE COILS.
- COILS SHOULD BE FREE OF CARBON TRACKING. ARE THEY?

NO → REPLACE IGNITION COIL. ALSO CHECK FOR FAULTY PLUG WIRE CONNECTION(S) AND WIRE NIPPLE(S) FOR CARBON TRACKING.

(5)
- SWITCH A NORMALLY OPERATING COIL WITH THE COIL FROM PROBLEM CYLINDER.
- SPARK SHOULD JUMP TESTER GAP AT PROBLEM CYLINDER WHILE CRANKING ENGINE. DID IT?

YES → ORIGINAL IGNITION COIL IS FAULTY.

NO → REPLACE DIS MODULE.

★CAUTION: When handling secondary spark plug leads with engine running, insulated pliers must be used and care exercised to prevent a possible electrical shock.

"AFTER REPAIRS," CONFIRM "CLOSED LOOP" OPERATION AND NO "SERVICE ENGINE SOON" LIGHT.

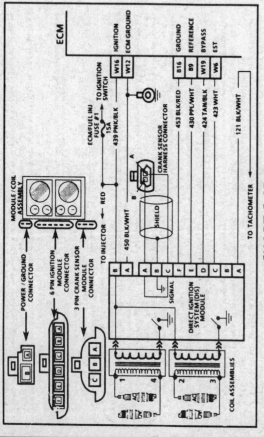

CHART C-4D-1
"DIS" MISFIRE AT IDLE

Circuit Description:

The Direct Ignition System (DIS) uses a waste spark method of distribution. In this type of system, the ignition module triggers the #1/4 coil pair resulting in both #1 and #4 spark plugs firing at the same time. #1 cylinder is on the compression stroke at the same time #4 is on the exhaust stroke, resulting in a lower energy requirement to fire #4 spark plug. This leaves the remainder of the high voltage to be used to fire #1 spark plug. The crank sensor is remotely mounted beside the module/coil assembly and protrudes through the block to within approximately .050" of the crankshaft reluctor. Since the reluctor is a machined portion of the crankshaft and the crankshaft sensor is mounted in a fixed position on the block, timing adjustments are not possible or necessary.

Test Description: Number(s) below refer to circled number(s) on the diagnostic chart.

1. If the "Misfire" complaint exists under load only, the diagnostic chart on page 2 must be used. Engine rpm should drop approximately equally on all plug leads.

2. A spark tester, such as a ST-125, must be used because it is essential to verify adequate available secondary voltage at the spark plug (25,000 volts).

3. If the spark jumps the tester gap after grounding the opposite plug wire, it indicates excessive resistance in the plug which was bypassed. A faulty or poor connection at that plug could also result in the miss condition. Also, check for carbon deposits inside the spark plug boot.

4. If carbon tracking is evident, replace coil and be sure plug wires relating to that coil are clean and tight. Excessive wire resistance or faulty connections could have caused the coil to be damaged.

5. If the no spark condition follows the suspected coil, that coil is faulty. Otherwise, the ignition module is the cause of no spark. This test could also be performed by substituting a known good coil for the one causing the no spark condition.

1990-91 2.2L (VIN G)

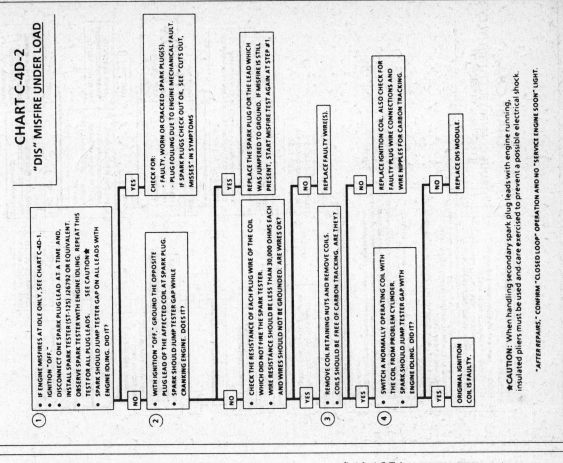

CHART C-4D-2
"DIS" MISFIRE UNDER LOAD

① • IF ENGINE MISFIRES AT IDLE ONLY, SEE CHART C-4D-1.
• IGNITION "OFF."
• DISCONNECT ONE SPARK PLUG LEAD AT A TIME AND, INSTALL SPARK TESTER (ST-125) J26792 OR EQUIVALENT.
• OBSERVE SPARK TESTER WITH ENGINE IDLING. REPEAT THIS TEST FOR ALL PLUG LEADS.   SEE CAUTION★
• SPARK SHOULD JUMP TESTER GAP ON ALL LEADS WITH ENGINE IDLING. DID IT?

NO ↓   YES →

YES → CHECK FOR:
- FAULTY, WORN OR CRACKED SPARK PLUG(S).
- PLUG FOULING DUE TO ENGINE MECHANICAL FAULT.
IF SPARK PLUGS CHECK OUT OK, SEE "CUTS OUT, MISSES" IN SYMPTOMS

② • WITH IGNITION "OFF," GROUND THE OPPOSITE PLUG LEAD OF THE AFFECTED COIL AT SPARK PLUG.
• SPARK SHOULD JUMP TESTER GAP WHILE CRANKING ENGINE. DOES IT?

NO ↓   YES →

YES → REPLACE THE SPARK PLUG FOR THE LEAD WHICH WAS JUMPERED TO GROUND. IF MISFIRE IS STILL PRESENT, START MISFIRE TEST AGAIN AT STEP #1.

CHECK THE RESISTANCE OF EACH PLUG WIRE OF THE COIL WHICH DID NOT FIRE THE SPARK TESTER.
• WIRE RESISTANCE SHOULD BE LESS THAN 30,000 OHMS EACH AND WIRES SHOULD NOT BE GROUNDED. ARE WIRES OK?

NO → REPLACE FAULTY WIRE(S).

③ • REMOVE COIL RETAINING NUTS AND REMOVE COILS.
• COILS SHOULD BE FREE OF CARBON TRACKING. ARE THEY?

YES ↓   NO →

NO → REPLACE IGNITION COIL. ALSO CHECK FOR FAULTY PLUG WIRE CONNECTIONS AND WIRE NIPPLES FOR CARBON TRACKING.

④ • SWITCH A NORMALLY OPERATING COIL WITH THE COIL FROM PROBLEM CYLINDER.
• SPARK SHOULD JUMP TESTER GAP WITH ENGINE IDLING. DID IT?

YES ↓   NO →

NO → REPLACE DIS MODULE.

ORIGINAL IGNITION COIL IS FAULTY.

★CAUTION: When handling secondary spark plug leads with engine running, insulated pliers must be used and care exercised to prevent a possible electrical shock.

"AFTER REPAIRS," CONFIRM "CLOSED LOOP" OPERATION AND NO "SERVICE ENGINE SOON" LIGHT.

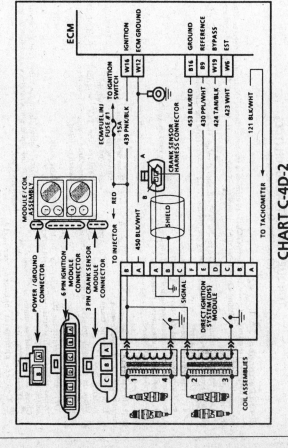

CHART C-4D-2
"DIS" MISFIRE UNDER LOAD

Circuit Description:

The Direct Ignition System (DIS) uses a waste spark method of distribution. In this type of system, the ignition module triggers the #1/4 coil pair resulting in both #1 and #4 spark plugs firing at the same time. #1 cylinder is on the compression stroke at the same time #4 is on the exhaust stroke, resulting in a lower energy requirement to fire #4 spark plug. This leaves the remainder of the high voltage to be used to fire #1 spark plug. The crank sensor is remotely mounted beside the module/coil assembly and protrudes through the block to within approximately .050" of the crankshaft reluctor. Since the reluctor is a machined portion of the crankshaft, and the crankshaft sensor is mounted in a fixed position on the block, timing adjustments are not possible or necessary.

Test Description: Number(s) below refer to circled number(s) on the diagnostic chart.

1. If the "Misfire" complaint exists at idle only, the diagnostic chart on page 1 must be used. A spark tester such as a ST-125 must be used because it is essential to verify adequate available secondary voltage at the spark plug (25,000 volts). Spark should jump the test gap on all 4 leads. This simulates a "load" condition.
2. If the spark jumps the tester gap after grounding the opposite plug wire, it indicates excessive resistance in the plug which was bypassed.

3. A faulty or poor connection at that plug could also result in the miss condition. Also, check for carbon deposits inside the spark plug boot.
   If carbon tracking is evident replace coil and be sure plug wires relating to that coil are clean and tight. Excessive wire resistance or faulty connections could have caused the coil to be damaged.
4. If the no spark condition follows the suspected coil, that coil is faulty. Otherwise, the ignition module is the cause of no spark. This test could also be performed by substituting a known good coil for the one causing the no spark condition.

1990-91 2.2L (VIN G)

CHART C-8A
TORQUE CONVERTER CLUTCH (TCC)
(ELECTRICAL DIAGNOSIS)

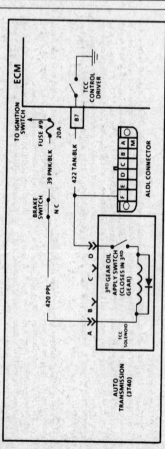

AUTO TRANSMISSION (3T40) — TCC SOLENOID — 3RD GEAR OIL APPLY SWITCH (CLOSES IN 3RD GEAR) — 420 PPL — BRAKE SWITCH — N.C. — 39 PNK/BLK — FUSE #9 20A — TO IGNITION SWITCH — ECM — TCC CONTROL DRIVER — B7 — 422 TAN/BLK — ALDL CONNECTOR — F E D C B A M

Circuit Description:

The purpose of the Torque Converter Clutch (TCC) is to eliminate the power loss of the torque converter when the vehicle is in a cruise condition. This allows the convenience of the automatic transaxle and the fuel economy of a manual transaxle.

Fused battery ignition voltage is supplied to the TCC solenoid through the brake switch and transaxle 3rd gear apply switch. The ECM will engage TCC by grounding CKT 422 to energize the solenoid.

TCC will engage when:
- Vehicle speed above 30 mph (48 km/h).
- Coolant temperature above 30°C (86°F).
- Throttle position sensor output not changing, indicating a steady road speed.
- Transaxle 3rd gear switch closed.
- Brake switch closed.

Test Description: Number(s) below refer to circled number(s) on the diagnostic chart.

1. Light "OFF" confirms transaxle 3rd gear apply switch is open.
2. When the transaxle 3rd gear switch closes, the test light should light.
3. Grounding the diagnostic terminal with engine "OFF" should energize the TCC solenoid. This test checks the capability of the ECM to control the solenoid.

Check TCC solenoid resistance as follows:
1. Disconnect TCC at transaxle.
2. Connect ohmmeter between transaxle connector opposite harness connector terminal "A" and "D".
3. Raise drive wheels.
4. Run engine in drive about 48 km/h (30 mph) to close 3rd gear apply switch.
5. Replace the TCC solenoid and ECM if resistance measures less than 20 ohms when switch is closed.

Diagnostic Aids:

An engine coolant thermostat that is stuck open, or opens at too low a temperature may result in an inoperative TCC.

CHART C-8A
TORQUE CONVERTER CLUTCH (TCC)
(ELECTRICAL DIAGNOSIS)

USING A TECH 1, CHECK THE FOLLOWING AND CORRECT IF NECESSARY:
- COOLANT TEMPERATURE SHOULD BE ABOVE 65°C.
- TPS - BE SURE TPS SIGNAL IS NOT ERRATIC.
- VSS - SHOULD INDICATE VSS WITH WHEELS TURNING.
- CODES - IF 24 IS PRESENT, SEE CODE CHART 24.

①
- PERFORM MECHANICAL CHECKS ON LINKAGE, OIL LEVEL, ETC., BEFORE USING THIS CHART.
- CONNECT TEST LIGHT FROM TCC TEST POINT (ALDL TERMINAL "F") TO GROUND.
- RAISE DRIVE WHEELS.
- START ENGINE AND IDLE ENGINE IN DRIVE. DO NOT DEPRESS BRAKE PEDAL.
- DO NOT PERFORM THIS TEST WITHOUT SUPPORTING THE LOWER CONTROL ARMS SO THAT THE DRIVE AXLES ARE IN A NORMAL HORIZONTAL POSITION. RUNNING THE VEHICLE IN GEAR WITH THE WHEELS HANGING DOWN AT FULL TRAVEL MAY DAMAGE THE DRIVE AXLES.
- OBSERVE LIGHT.

LIGHT "OFF"

LIGHT "ON" → FAULTY TRANSAXLE 3RD GEAR SWITCH OR CKT 422 SHORTED TO VOLTAGE.

② INCREASE SPEED SLOWLY UNTIL TRANSAXLE SHIFTS INTO 3RD GEAR. OBSERVE TEST LIGHT.

LIGHT "ON"

LIGHT "OFF" → TEST LIGHT SHOULD GO OUT AS BRAKE PEDAL IS DEPRESSED. DOES IT?

- IGNITION "ON," ENGINE "OFF."
- CHECK FOR BLOWN FUSE. IF OK, DISCONNECT TCC SOLENOID HARNESS CONNECTOR AT TRANSAXLE.
- CONNECT TEST LIGHT BETWEEN HARNESS CONNECTOR TERMINALS "A" AND "D".

LIGHT "OFF" → CONNECT A TEST LIGHT FROM TERMINAL "A" TO GROUND.

LIGHT "ON" → CHECK FOR SHORT TO GROUND IN CKT 422. IF NOT GROUNDED, REPLACE ECM.

LIGHT "OFF"

LIGHT "ON"

- GROUND TCC TEST POINT AND AGAIN CONNECT TEST LIGHT BETWEEN HARNESS CONNECTOR TERMINALS "A" AND "D".

LIGHT "OFF" → REPAIR OPEN IN TCC BRAKE SWITCH CIRCUIT OR ADJUST SWITCH.

LIGHT "ON"

LIGHT "OFF" → REPAIR OPEN IN WIRE FROM TRANSAXLE TO ALDL TEST POINT TERMINAL "F".

FAULTY TCC SOLENOID CONNECTOR, TCC SOLENOID OR 3RD GEAR SWITCH.

NO → FAULTY BRAKE SWITCH OR ADJUSTMENT.

YES

③
- IGNITION "ON," ENGINE "OFF."
- CONNECT TEST LIGHT TO BATTERY VOLTAGE AND PROBE ALDL TERMINAL "F".
- GROUND DIAGNOSTIC TERMINAL AND OBSERVE LIGHT.

LIGHT "ON" → CHECK FOR CORRECT PROM. IF OK, TCC ELECTRICAL CONTROL IS OK.

LIGHT "OFF" → CHECK FOR OPEN CKT 422 FROM ALDL TO ECM CONNECTOR TERMINAL. IF CKT 422 IS OK, ECM IS FAULTY.

"AFTER REPAIRS," CONFIRM "CLOSED LOOP" OPERATION AND NO "SERVICE ENGINE SOON" LIGHT.

1990-91 2.2L (VIN G)

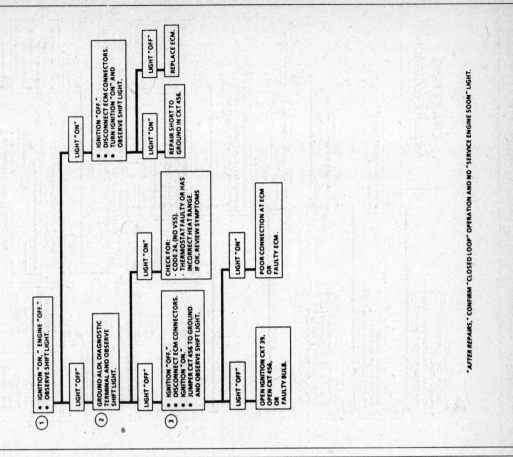

CHART C-8B

MANUAL TRANSAXLE (M/T) SHIFT LIGHT CHECK

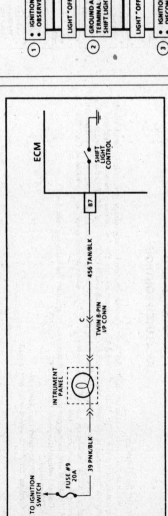

CHART C-8B

MANUAL TRANSAXLE (M/T) SHIFT LIGHT CHECK

Circuit Description:

The shift light indicates the best transaxle shift point for maximum fuel economy. The light is controlled by the ECM and is turned "ON" by grounding CKT 456.

The ECM uses information from the following inputs to control the shift light:

- CTS
- TPS
- VSS
- RPM

The ECM uses the measured rpm and the vehicle speed to calculate what gear the vehicle is in. It's this calculation that determines when the shift light should be turned "ON."

Test Description: Number(s) below refer to circled number(s) on the diagnostic chart.

1. This should not turn "ON" the shift light. If the light is "ON," there is a short to ground in CKT 456 wiring or a fault in the ECM.

2. When the diagnostic terminal is grounded, the ECM should ground CKT 456 and the shift light should come "ON."

3. This checks the shift light circuit up to the ECM connector. If the shift light illuminates, then the ECM connector is faulty or the ECM does not have the ability to ground the circuit.

1990-91 2.2L (VIN G)

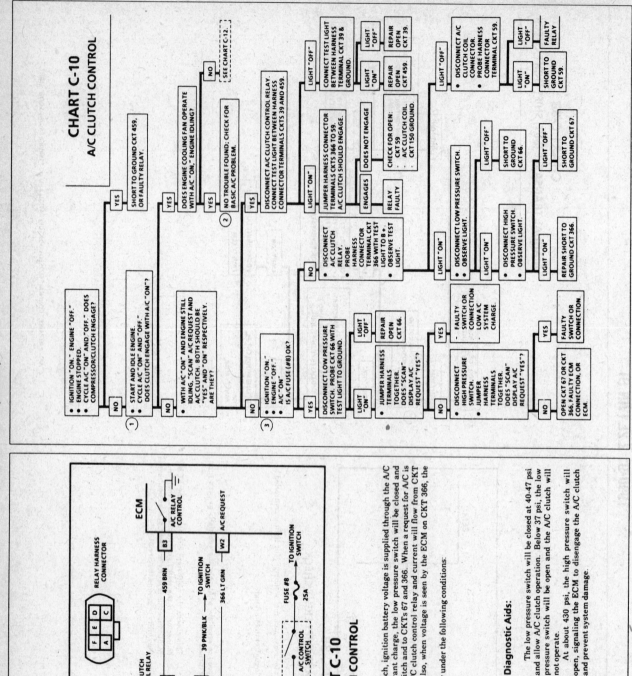

CHART C-10

A/C CLUTCH CONTROL

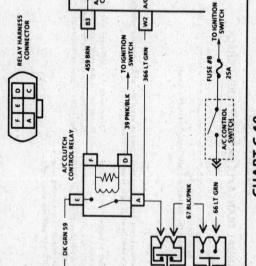

Circuit Description:

When an A/C mode is selected on the A/C control switch, ignition battery voltage is supplied through the A/C request circuit to the ECM. With sufficient A/C refrigerant charge, the low pressure switch will be closed and complete the circuit to the closed high pressure cut-off switch and to CKTs 67 and 366. When a request for A/C is sensed, the ECM will ground CKT 459 energizing the A/C clutch control relay and current will flow from CKT 366 to CKT 59 and engage the A/C compressor clutch. Also, when voltage is seen by the ECM on CKT 366, the cooling fan will be turned "ON."

The ECM will de-energize the A/C clutch control relay under the following conditions:

- Coolant temperature over 124°C (255°F)
- TPS at WOT
- Engine speed greater than 4800 rpm
- Ignition "OFF." (2 second delay on restart.)

Test Description: Number(s) below refer to circled number(s) on the diagnostic chart.

1. The A/C compressor clutch should not engage until 2 seconds after the engine is running.
2. Refer to AIR CONDITIONING DIAGNOSIS.
3. A blown A/C fuse could be caused by a short to ground from the ignition switch to the compressor.

Diagnostic Aids:

The low pressure switch will be closed at 40-47 psi and allow A/C clutch operation. Below 37 psi, the low pressure switch will be open and the A/C clutch will not operate.

At about 430 psi, the high pressure switch will open, signaling the ECM to disengage the A/C clutch and prevent system damage.

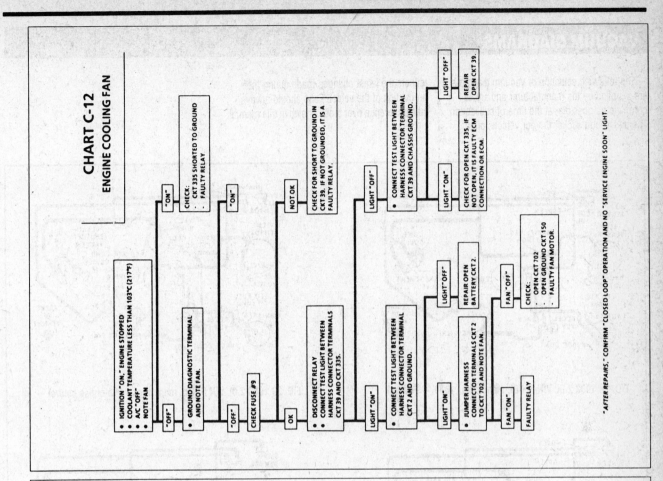

CHART C-12
ENGINE COOLING FAN

- IGNITION "ON," ENGINE STOPPED
- COOLANT TEMPERATURE LESS THAN 103°C (217°F)
- A/C "OFF"
- NOTE FAN

"OFF" → GROUND DIAGNOSTIC TERMINAL AND NOTE FAN.

"ON" → CHECK:
- CKT 335 SHORTED TO GROUND
- FAULTY RELAY

"OFF" → CHECK FUSE #9

"ON"

OK → DISCONNECT RELAY. CONNECT TEST LIGHT BETWEEN HARNESS CONNECTOR TERMINALS CKT 39 AND CKT 335.

NOT OK → CHECK FOR SHORT TO GROUND IN CKT 39. IF NOT GROUNDED, IT IS A FAULTY RELAY.

LIGHT "ON" → CONNECT TEST LIGHT BETWEEN HARNESS CONNECTOR TERMINAL CKT 2 AND GROUND.

LIGHT "OFF" → CONNECT TEST LIGHT BETWEEN HARNESS CONNECTOR TERMINAL CKT 39 AND CHASSIS GROUND.

LIGHT "ON" → CHECK FOR OPEN CKT 335. IF NOT OPEN, IT IS FAULTY ECM CONNECTION OR ECM.

LIGHT "OFF" → REPAIR OPEN CKT 39.

LIGHT "ON" → JUMPER HARNESS CONNECTOR TERMINALS CKT 2 TO CKT 702 AND NOTE FAN.

LIGHT "OFF" → REPAIR OPEN BATTERY CKT 2.

FAN "ON" → FAULTY RELAY

FAN "OFF" → CHECK:
- OPEN CKT 702
- OPEN GROUND CKT 150
- FAULTY FAN MOTOR

"AFTER REPAIRS," CONFIRM "CLOSED LOOP" OPERATION AND NO "SERVICE ENGINE SOON" LIGHT.

CHART C-12
ENGINE COOLING FAN

```
F E D
  C
A
RELAY
HARNESS
CONNECTOR

COOLING
FAN RELAY
E F D
A

2 RED → FUSIBLE LINK → TO BATTERY +

FUSE #9
20 A

39 PNK/BLK → TO IGNITION SWITCH

335 DK GRN/WHT → B21  COOLING FAN CONTROL   ECM

410 GRY → TO COOLANT SENSOR → B8  COOLANT TEMPERATURE SIGNAL

366 LT GRN → TO A/C SWITCH → W2  A/C REQUEST

702 BLK/RED
COOLING FAN

150 BLK
```

Circuit Description:

Battery voltage to operate the cooling fan motor is supplied to relay by CKT 2. Ignition voltage to energize the relay is supplied to relay by CKT 39. When the ECM grounds CKT 335, the relay is energized and the cooling fan is turned "ON." When the engine is running, the ECM will turn the cooling fan "ON" if:
- A/C is "ON."
- Coolant temperature greater than 108°C (230°F).
- Code 14 or 15, coolant sensor failure.
- Back-up fuel control mode is active.

Diagnostic Aids:

If the owner complained of an overheating problem, it must be determined if the complaint was due to an actual boil over, or the hot light, or temperature gage indicated over heating.

If the gage or light indicates overheating, but no boil over is detected, the gage circuit should be checked. The gage accuracy can also be checked by comparing the coolant sensor reading using a "Scan" tool and comparing its reading with the gage reading

If the engine is actually overheating and the gage indicates overheating, but the cooling fan is not coming "ON," the coolant sensor has probably shifted out of calibration and should be replaced

VACUUM DIAGRAMS

The following selection of vacuum diagrams are supplied by the manufacturer and are as complete as possible, at the time of publication. The underhood sticker in your vehicle, often reflects the latest changes made during the production of the vehicle, and should always take preference over those shown in this manual.

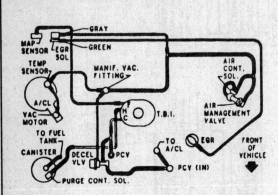

FIG. 28 1983 2.0L VIN P, TBI, man. trans., AMV — Federal

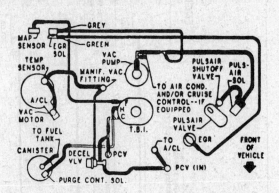

FIG. 29 1983 2.0L VIN P, TBI, man. trans., with cruise control — all

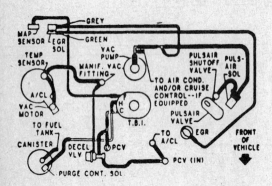

FIG. 30 1983 2.0L VIN P, TBI, auto. trans., without cruise control — all

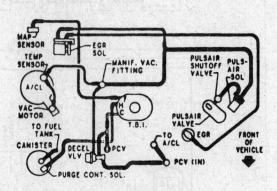

FIG. 31 1983 2.0L VIN P, TBI, man. trans., without cruise control — all

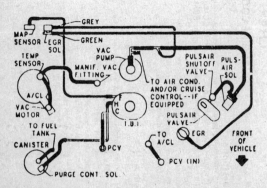

FIG. 32 1984 2.0L VIN O, TBI, man. & auto. trans., without cruise control — Calif.

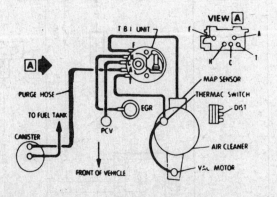

FIG. 33 1984 1.8L VIN O, TBI, man. & auto. trans., without cruise control — Calif.

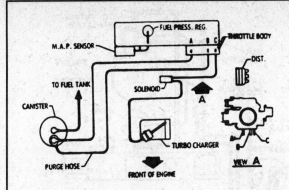

FIG. 34 1984 1.8L VIN J, TBI turbo, man. & auto. trans. — federal

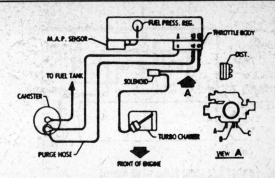

FIG. 35 1984 1.8L VIN J, TBI turbo, man. & auto. trans. — Calif.

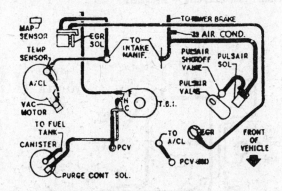

FIG. 36 1984 2.0L VIN P, TBI, man. & auto. trans. — Federal

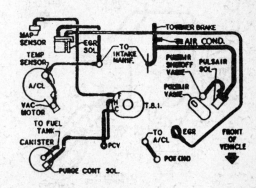

FIG. 37 1984 2.0L VIN P, TBI, man. & auto. trans. — Calif.

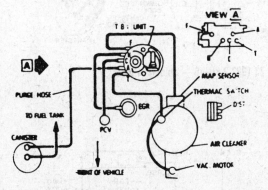

FIG. 39 1984 1.8L VIN O, TBI, man. & auto. trans. — Federal

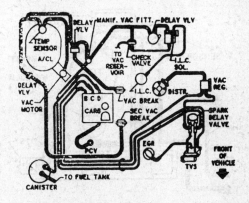

FIG. 40 1984 2.0L VIN P, 2-bbl, man. trans. — Canada

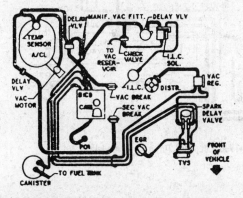

FIG. 41 1984 2.0L VIN P, 2-bbl, auto. trans. — Canada

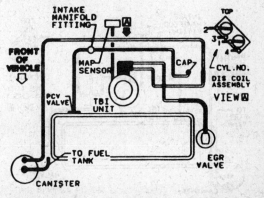

FIG. 69 1987 2.0L, OHC except Turbo — all models

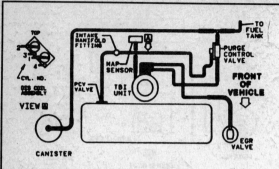

FIG. 70 1987 2.0L, OHC Turbo — all models

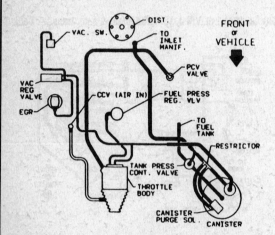

FIG. 72 1987 2.8L, V6 — manual trans.

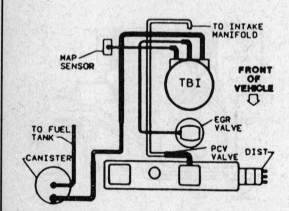

FIG. 74 1988 2.0L, OHC except Turbo — all models

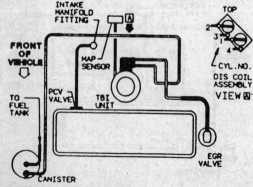

FIG. 76 1988 2.0L, OHV — all models

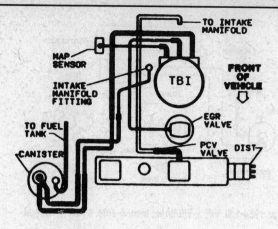

FIG. 71 1987 2.0L, OHV — all models

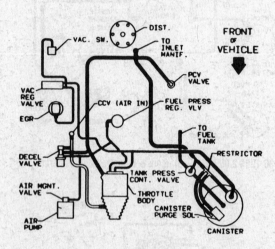

FIG. 73 1987 2.8L, V6 — automatic trans.

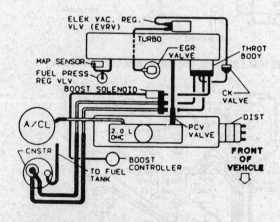

FIG. 75 1988 2.0L, OHC Turbo — all models

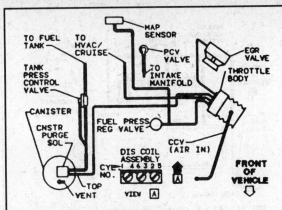

FIG. 77 1988 2.8L, V6 — all models

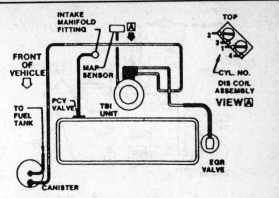

FIG. 78 1989 2.0L, OHV — all models

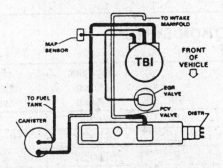

FIG. 79 1989 2.0L, OHC except Turbo — all models

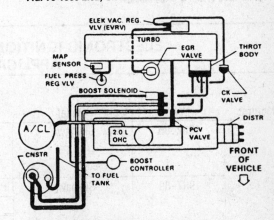

FIG. 80 1988 2.0L, OHC Turbo — all models

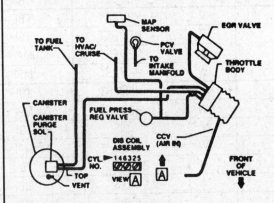

FIG. 81 1989 2.8L, V6 — all models

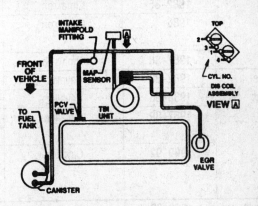

FIG. 82 1990 2.2L, OHV — all models

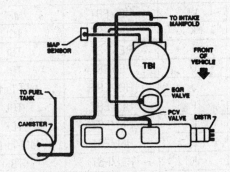

FIG. 83 1990 2.0L, OHC except Turbo — all models

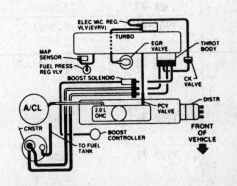

FIG. 84 1990 2.0L, OHC Turbo — all models

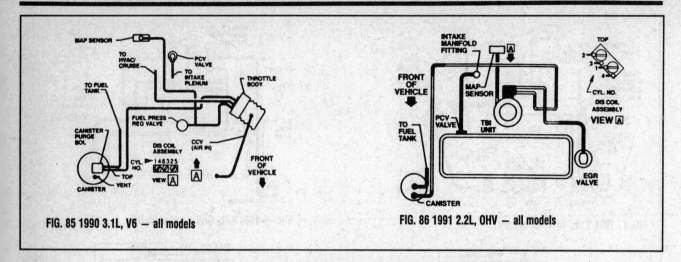

FIG. 85 1990 3.1L, V6 — all models

FIG. 86 1991 2.2L, OHV — all models

ELECTRONIC IGNITION/FUEL INJECTION SYSTEM
APPLICATION CHART

Manufacturer	Year	Model	Engine cu. in. (liter)	VIN	Electronic Ignition System	Fuel Injection System
Buick	1982–86	Skyhawk	110 (1.8)	O	HEI/EST	TBI
			110 (1.8)	J	HEI/EST	MPI-Turbo
			122 (2.0)	P	HEI/EST	TBI
	1987–89	Skyhawk	122 (2.0)	K	HEI/EST	TBI
			122 (2.0)	M	HEI/EST	MPI
			122 (2.0) HO	I	HEI/EST	TBI
Cadillac	1982–85	Cimarron	122 (2.0)	P	HEI/EST	TBI
	1986	Cimarron	122 (2.0)	P	HEI/EST	TBI
			173 (2.8)	W	HEI/EST	MPI
	1987–88	Cimarron	173 (2.8)	W	HEI/EST	MPI
Chevrolet	1982–86	Cavalier	122 (2.0)	P	HEI/EST	TBI
	1985–86	Cavalier	173 (2.8)	W	HEI/EST	MPI
	1987–89	Cavalier	122 (2.0)	I	DIS	TBI
			173 (2.8)	W	DIS	MPI
	1990–92	Cavalier	134 (2.2)	G	DIS	TBI
			134 (2.2)	4	DIS	MPI
			192 (3.1)	T	DIS	MPI
Oldsmobile	1982–86	Firenza	110 (1.8)	O	HEI/EST	TBI
			122 (2.0)	P	HEI/EST	TBI
	1986–87	Firenza	173 (2.8)	W	HEI/EST	MPI
	1987–88	Firenza	122 (2.0)	K	HEI/EST	TBI
			122 (2.0) HO	I	HEI/EST	TBI
Pontiac	1982–84	2000, Sunbird	110 (1.8)	O	HEI/EST	TBI
			110 (1.8)	J	HEI/EST	MPI-Turbo
			122 (2.0)	P	HEI/EST	TBI
	1985–86	Sunbird	110 (1.8)	O	HEI/EST	TBI
			110 (1.8)	J	HEI/EST	MPI-Turbo
	1987–92	Sunbird	122 (2.0)	K	HEI/EST	TBI
			122 (2.0) HO	M	HEI/EST	MPI-Turbo
			122 (2.0)	H	DIS	MPI

5

FUEL
SYSTEM

CARBURETED FUEL SYSTEM COMPONENTS

Mechanical Fuel Pump

A mechanical fuel pump is used on the 1982 carbureted engines. It is of the diaphragm-type and because of the design is serviced by replacement only. No adjustments or repairs are possible. The pump is operated by an eccentric on the camshaft.

TESTING THE FUEL PUMP

To determine if the fuel pump is in good condition, tests for both volume and pressure should be performed. The tests are made with the pump installed, and the engine at normal operating temperature and idle speed. Never replace a fuel pump without first performing these simple tests.

Be sure that the fuel filter has been changed at the specified interval, If in doubt, install a new filter then test the system.

1. Disconnect the fuel line at the carburetor and connect a fuel pump pressure gauge. Fill the carburetor float bowl with gasoline.

2. Start the engine and check the pressure with the engine at idle. If the pump has a vapor return hose, squeeze it off so that an accurate reading can be obtained. Pressure should not be below 4.5 psi.

3. If the pressure is incorrect, replace the pump. If it is ok, go on to the volume test.

Volume Test

4. Disconnect the pressure gauge. Run the fuel line into a graduated container.

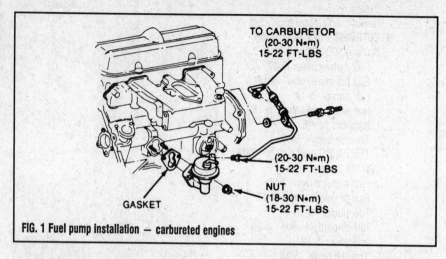

FIG. 1 Fuel pump installation — carbureted engines

TO CARBURETOR
(20-30 N•m)
15-22 FT-LBS

(20-30 N•m)
15-22 FT-LBS

NUT
(18-30 N•m)
15-22 FT-LBS

GASKET

5. Run the engine at idle until one pint of gasoline has been pumped. One pint should be delivered in 30 seconds or less. There is normally enough fuel in the carburetor float bowl to perform this test, but refill it if necessary.

6. If the delivery rate is below the minimum, check the lines for restrictions or leaks, then replace the pump.

REMOVAL & INSTALLATION

▶ SEE FIG. 1

The fuel pump is located at the center rear of the engine.

1. Disconnect the negative cable at the battery. Raise and support the car.

2. Disconnect the inlet hose from the pump. Disconnect the vapor return hose, if equipped.

3. Loosen the fuel line at the carburetor, then disconnect the outlet pipe from the pump.

4. Remove the two mounting bolts and remove the pump from the engine.

To Install:

5. Place a new gasket on the pump and install the pump on the engine. Tighten the two mounting bolts ALTERNATELY and EVENLY. Refer to the illustration.

6. Install the pump outlet pipe. This is easier if the pipe is disconnected from the carburetor. Tighten the fitting while backing up the pump nut with another wrench. Install the pipe at the carburetor.

7. Install the inlet and vapor hoses. Lower the car, connect the negative battery cable, start the engine, and check for fuel leaks.

CARBURETED FUEL SYSTEM

Carburetor

The Rochester E2SE is used on all 1982 models. It is a two barrel, two stage carburetor of downdraft design used in conjunction with the Computer Command Control system of fuel control. The carburetor has special design features for optimum air/fuel mixture control during all ranges of engine operation.

MODEL IDENTIFICATION

▶ SEE FIG. 2

General Motors Rochester carburetors are identified by their model code. The first number indicates the number of barrels, while one of the last letters indicates the type of choke used. These are V for the manifold mounted choke coil, C for the choke coil mounted in the carburetor body, and E for electric choke, also mounted on the carburetor. Model codes ending in A indicate an altitude-compensation carburetor.

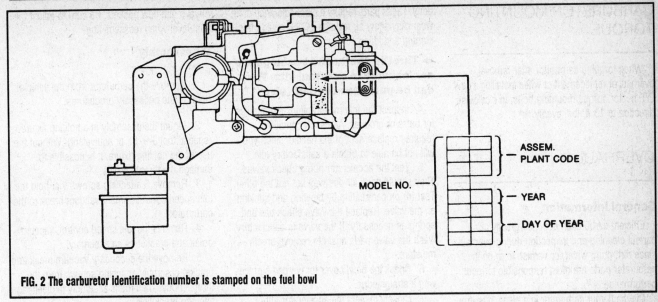

FIG. 2 The carburetor identification number is stamped on the fuel bowl

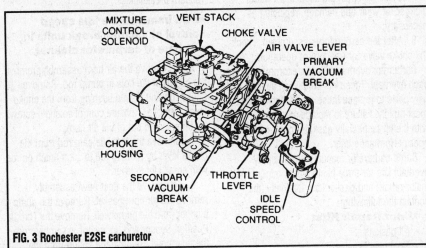

MIXTURE
CONTROL
SOLENOID

VENT STACK

CHOKE VALVE

AIR VALVE LEVER

PRIMARY
VACUUM
BREAK

CHOKE
HOUSING

SECONDARY
VACUUM
BREAK

THROTTLE
LEVER

IDLE
SPEED
CONTROL

FIG. 3 Rochester E2SE carburetor

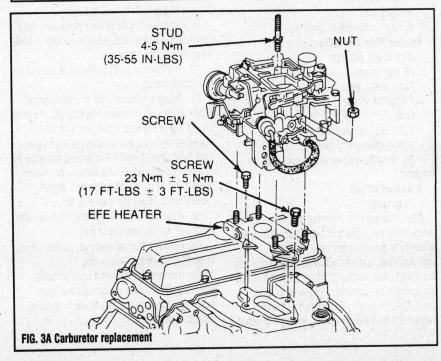

STUD
4-5 N•m
(35-55 IN-LBS)

NUT

SCREW

SCREW
23 N•m ± 5 N•m
(17 FT-LBS ± 3 FT-LBS)

EFE HEATER

FIG. 3A Carburetor replacement

REMOVAL & INSTALLATION

◆ SEE FIGS. 3-3B

1. Disconnect the negative battery cable. Remove the air cleaner and gasket.
2. Disconnect the fuel pipe and all vacuum lines.
3. Tag and disconnect all electrical connections.
4. Disconnect the downshift cable.
5. If equipped with cruise control, disconnect the linkage.
6. Unscrew the carburetor mounting bolts and remove the carburetor.

To Install:

7. Before installing the carburetor, fill the float bowl with gasoline to reduce the battery strain and the possibility of backfiring when the engine is started again.
8. Inspect the EFE heater for damage. Be sure that the throttle body and EFE mating surfaces are clean.
9. Install the carburetor and tighten the nuts alternately to the proper specifications. Refer to the section below.
10. Installation of the remaining components is in the reverse order of removal.

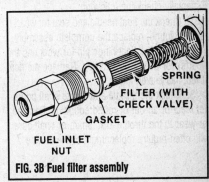

SPRING

FILTER (WITH
CHECK VALVE)

GASKET

FUEL INLET
NUT

FIG. 3B Fuel filter assembly

CARBURETOR MOUNTING TORQUE

When torquing carburetor after removal, overhaul or replacement or when installing a new EFE heater, torque mounting bolts, in clockwise direction to 13 ft. lbs. evenly.

OVERHAUL

General Information

Efficient carburetion depends greatly on careful cleaning and inspection during overhaul, since dirt, gum, water, or varnish in or on the carburetor parts are often responsible for poor performance.

Overhaul your carburetor in a clean, dust-free area. Carefully disassemble the carburetor, referring often to the exploded views and directions packaged with the rebuilding kit. Keep all similar and look-alike parts segregated during disassembly and cleaning to avoid accidental interchange during assembly. Make a note of all jet sizes.

When the carburetor is disassembled, wash all parts (except diaphragms, electric choke units, pump plunger, and any other plastic, leather, fiber, or rubber parts) in clean carburetor solvent. Do not leave parts in the solvent any longer than is necessary to sufficiently loosen the deposits. Excessive cleaning may remove the special finish from the float bowl and choke valve bodies, leaving these parts unfit for service. Rinse all parts in clean solvent and blow them dry with compressed air or allow them to air dry. Wipe clean all cork, plastic, leather, and fiber parts with a clean, lint-free cloth.

Blow out all passages and jets with compressed air and be sure that there are no restrictions or blockages. Never use wire or similar tools to clean jets, fuel passages, or air bleeds. Clean all jets and valves separately to avoid accidental interchange.

Check all parts for wear or damage. If wear or damage is found, replace the defective parts. Especially check the following:

1. Check the float needle and seat for wear. If wear is found, replace the complete assembly.

2. Check the float hinge pin for wear and the float(s) for dents or distortion. Replace the float if fuel has leaked into it.

3. Check the throttle and choke shaft bores for wear or an out-of-round condition. Damage or wear to the throttle arm, shaft, or shaft bore will often require replacement of the throttle

body. These parts require a close tolerance of fit; wear may allow air leakage, which could affect starting and idling.

➡ **Throttle shafts and bushings are not included in overhaul kits. They can be purchased separately.**

4. Inspect the idle mixture adjusting needles for burrs or grooves. Any such condition requires replacement of the needle, since you will not be able to obtain a satisfactory idle.

5. Test the accelerator pump check valves. They should pass air one way but not the other. Test for proper seating by blowing and sucking on the valve. Replace the valve check ball and spring as necessary. If the valve is satisfactory, wash the valve parts again to remove breath moisture.

6. Check the bowl cover for warped surfaces with a straightedge.

7. Closely inspect the accelerator pump plunger for wear and damage, replacing as necessary.

8. After the carburetor is assembled, check the choke valve for freedom of operation.

Carburetor overhaul kits are recommended for each overhaul. These kits contain all gaskets and new parts to replace those which deteriorate most rapidly. Failure to replace all parts supplied with the kit (especially gaskets) can result in poor performance later.

Some carburetor manufacturers supply overhaul kits for three basic types: minor repair; major repair; and gasket kits. Basically, the contain the following:

Minor Repair Kits:
- All gaskets
- Float needle valve
- All diagrams
- Spring for the pump diaphragm

Major Repair Kits:
- All jets and gaskets
- All diaphragms
- Float needle valve
- Pump ball valve
- Float
- Complete intermediate rod
- Intermediate pump lever
- Some cover hold-down screws and washers

Gasket Kits:
- All gaskets

After cleaning and checking all components, reassemble the carburetor, using new parts and referring to the exploded view. When reassembling, make sure that all screws and jets are tight in their seats, but do not overtighten as the tips will be distorted. Tighten all screws gradually, in rotation. Do not tighten needle valves into their seats; uneven jetting will result.

Always use new gaskets. Be sure to adjust the float level when reassembling.

Disassembly

◆ SEE FIGS. 3C-3T

1. Remove the carburetor from the vehicle. Refer to the necessary procedures.

2. Mount the assembly in a holding fixture (special tool J-9787 or equivalent). Without the use of the holding fixture, it is possible to damage the throttle valves.

3. Remove 3 attaching screws that hold the idle speed control/primary vacuum break to the carburetor.

4. Remove the idle speed control, vacuum break and bracket as an assembly.

5. Remove the secondary vacuum break and bracket assembly attaching screws from the throttle body. Then rotate assembly to disengage vacuum break link.

➡ **Do immerse the idle speed control or vacuum break units in any type of carburetor cleaner.**

6. To remove the air horn assembly, remove the clip from the hole in pump rod. Remove choke rod and plastic bushing from the choke lever. Remove 3 mixture control solenoid screws — lift solenoid out of the air horn.

7. Remove the fast idle cam rod from the choke lever by rotating rod to align notch on rod with small slot in lever.

8. To remove the float bowl assembly, remove the air horn gasket. Remove the pump plunger from the pump well. Remove the Throttle Position Sensor and connector assembly from the float bowl. Remove the spring from the bottom of the T. S. P. well in bowl.

9. Remove the plastic filler block over float valve. Remove the float assembly and float valve by pulling up on hinge pin.

10. Remove the plastic filler block insert from the float bowl cavity.

11. Using a removal tool or a wide-blade screwdriver (10mm wide) that fully fits the slots on the top of the float valve seat and the extended metering jet, remove the float valve seat (with gasket) and the extended metering jet from the float bowl. Do not remove or change adjustment of the small calibration screw located deep inside the metering jet.

12. Remove the plastic retainer holding pump discharge spring and check ball.

13. Remove the fuel inlet nut, gasket, check valve filter assembly and spring.

14. Remove the 4 throttle body to bowl attaching screws and remove throttle body assembly. Remove the throttle body to bowl insulator gasket.

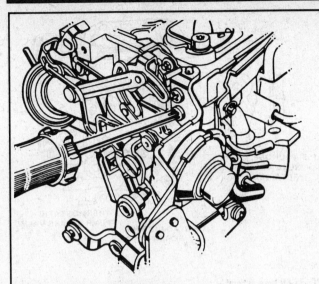

FIG. 3C Primary vacuum break removal

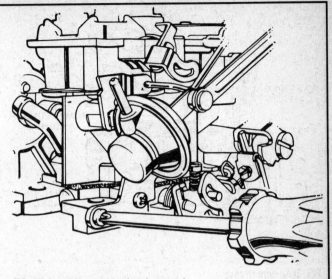

FIG. 3D Secondary vacuum break removal

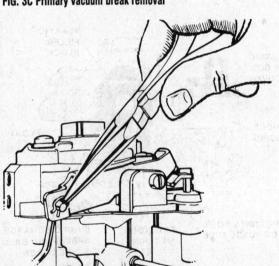

FIG. 3E Pump rod clip removal

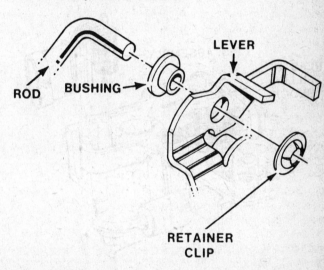

FIG. 3F Intermediate choke rod linkage

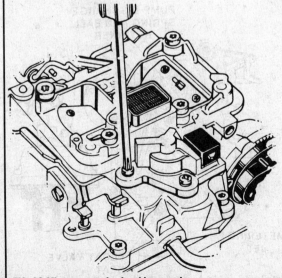

FIG. 3G Mixture control solenoid removal

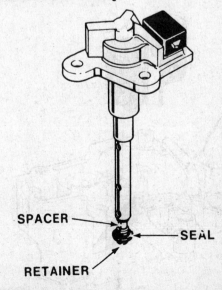

FIG. 3H Mixture control solenoid

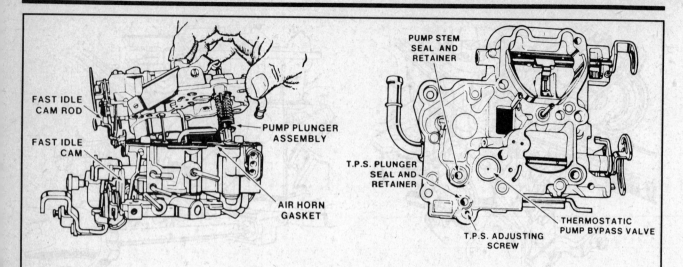

FAST IDLE CAM ROD

FAST IDLE CAM

PUMP PLUNGER ASSEMBLY

AIR HORN GASKET

FIG. 3I Air horn removal

PUMP STEM SEAL AND RETAINER

T.P.S. PLUNGER SEAL AND RETAINER

T.P.S. ADJUSTING SCREW

THERMOSTATIC PUMP BYPASS VALVE

FIG. 3J Air horn assembly

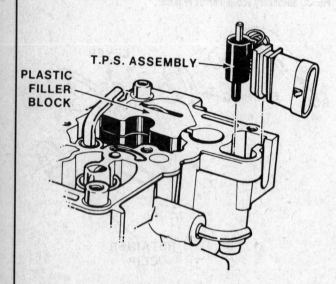

T.P.S. ASSEMBLY

PLASTIC FILLER BLOCK

FIG. 3K Throttle Position Sensor (T. P. S.) removal

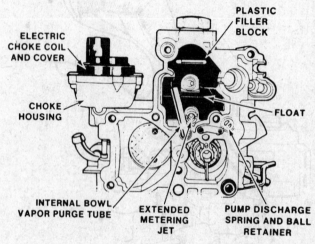

PLASTIC FILLER BLOCK

ELECTRIC CHOKE COIL AND COVER

CHOKE HOUSING

FLOAT

INTERNAL BOWL VAPOR PURGE TUBE

EXTENDED METERING JET

PUMP DISCHARGE SPRING AND BALL RETAINER

FIG. 3L Float bowl assembly

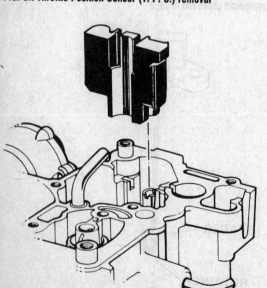

FIG. 3M Bowl plastic insert removal

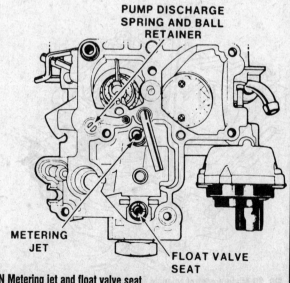

PUMP DISCHARGE SPRING AND BALL RETAINER

METERING JET

FLOAT VALVE SEAT

FIG. 3N Metering jet and float valve seat

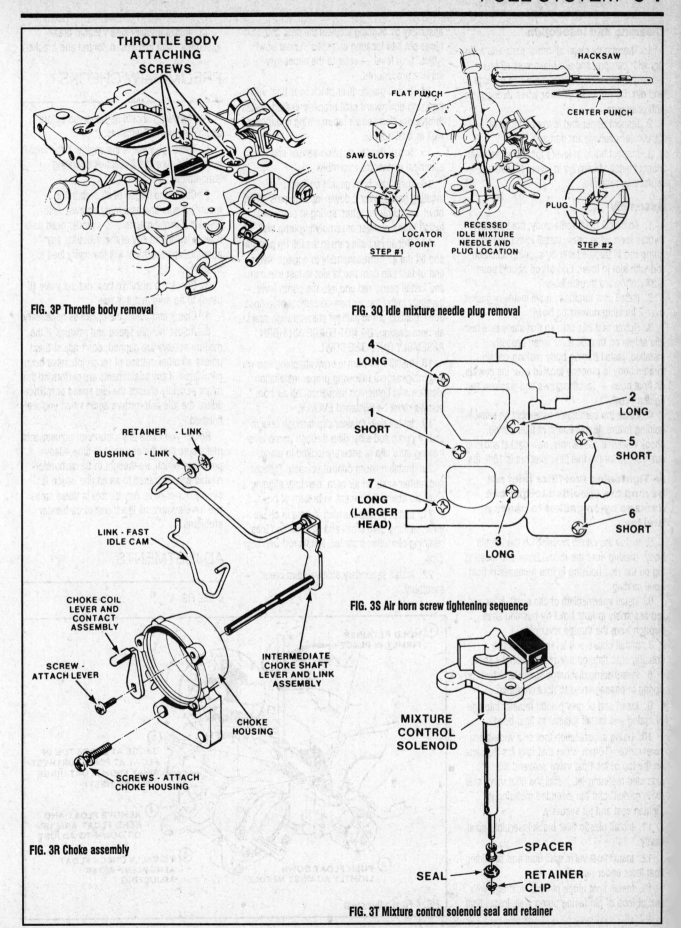

THROTTLE BODY ATTACHING SCREWS

FIG. 3P Throttle body removal

HACKSAW

FLAT PUNCH

SAW SLOTS

LOCATOR POINT

STEP #1

RECESSED IDLE MIXTURE NEEDLE AND PLUG LOCATION

CENTER PUNCH

PLUG

STEP #2

FIG. 3Q Idle mixture needle plug removal

4 LONG

1 SHORT

7 LONG (LARGER HEAD)

3 LONG

2 LONG

5 SHORT

6 SHORT

FIG. 3S Air horn screw tightening sequence

RETAINER - LINK

BUSHING - LINK

LINK - FAST IDLE CAM

CHOKE COIL LEVER AND CONTACT ASSEMBLY

SCREW - ATTACH LEVER

INTERMEDIATE CHOKE SHAFT LEVER AND LINK ASSEMBLY

CHOKE HOUSING

SCREWS - ATTACH CHOKE HOUSING

FIG. 3R Choke assembly

MIXTURE CONTROL SOLENOID

SPACER

SEAL

RETAINER CLIP

FIG. 3T Mixture control solenoid seal and retainer

Cleaning and Inspection

1. Thoroughly clean all metal parts and blow dry with compressed air. Make sure all fuel passages and metering parts are free of burrs and dirt. Do not pass drills or wires through jets and passages.

2. Inspect upper and lower surfaces of carburetor castings for damage.

3. Inspect holes in levers for excessive wear. Inspect plastic bushings in levers for damage — replace as required.

Assembly

1. To install the throttle body, hold primary throttle lever wide open, install lower end of pump rod in throttle lever by aligning notch on rod with slot in lever. End of rod should point outward toward throttle lever.

2. Install new throttle to bowl insulator gasket over 2 locating dowels on bowl.

3. Rotate fast idle cam so that steps face fast idle screw on throttle lever when properly installed, install throttle body making certain throttle body is properly located over the dowels on float bowl — install screws and washers and tighten evenly.

4. Place the carburetor assembly on suitable holding fixture. Install fuel inlet filter spring, check valve/filter assembly, new gasket and inlet nut. Torque for the fuel filter inlet nut is 18 ft. lbs.

➡ **Tightening fuel filter inlet nut beyond the specified torque can damage nylon gasket to cause a fuel leak.**

5. Install the choke housing on the throttle body, making sure the raised boss and locating lug on the rear housing fit into recesses in float bowl casting.

6. Install intermediate choke shaft, lever and rod assembly in float bowl by pushing shaft through from the throttle lever side.

7. Install choke coil lever inside choke housing onto flats on intermediate choke shaft.

8. Install pump discharge steel check ball and spring in passage next to float chamber.

9. Insert end of new plastic retainer into end of spring and install retainer in float bowl.

10. Using a installation tool or a wide-blade screwdriver (10mm wide) that fully fits the slots on the top of the float valve seat and the extended metering jet, install the float valve seat (with gasket) and the extended metering jet. Tighten seat and jet securely.

11. Install plastic filler block insert into bowl cavity.

12. Install float valve onto float arm by sliding float lever under pull clip.

13. Install float hinge pin into float arm with end of loop of pin facing pump well. Install float

assembly by aligning valve in the seat and float hinge pin into locating channels in float bowl. Adjust float level — refer to the necessary service procedures.

14. Install plastic filler block over float valve pressing downward until properly seated. Install throttle position sensor return spring in bottom of well in float bowl.

15. Install throttle position sensor and electrical connector assembly.

16. Install air horn gasket on float bowl, locating gasket over 2 dowel locating pins on the bowl. Install pump return spring in pump well. Install pump plunger assembly in pump well.

17. Rotate fast idle cam to the full Up position and tilt the air horn assembly to engage lower end of fast idle cam rod in slot in fast idle cam and install pump rod end into the pump lever — carefully lower the air horn assembly onto float bowl, guiding pump plunger stem through seal in air horn casting. DO NOT FORCE AIR HORN ASSEMBLY ONTO THE BOWL.

18. Install 7 air horn to bowl attaching screws and lockwashers following proper installation location and tightening sequence. All air horn screws must be tightened EVENLY.

19. Install new retainer clip through hole in end of pump rod extending through pump lever, making sure clip is securely locked in place.

20. Install mixture control solenoid (spacer and rubber seal) on air horn, carefully aligning solenoid stem with recess in bottom of bowl.

21. Install plastic bushing in hole in choke lever, making sure small end of bushing faces retaining clip when installed. Retain rod with new clip.

22. Install secondary side vacuum break assembly.

23. Install primary side vacuum break assembly (with idle speed control and bracket).

PRELIMINARY CHECKS

The following should be observed before attempting any adjustments.

1. Thoroughly warm the engine. If the engine is cold, be sure that it reaches operating temperature.

2. Check the torque of all carburetor mounting nuts and assembly screws. Also check the intake manifold-to-cylinder head bolts. If air is leaking at any of these points, any attempts at adjustment will inevitably lead to frustration.

3. Check the manifold heat control valve (if used) to be sure that it is free.

4. Check and adjust the choke as necessary.

5. Adjust the idle speed and mixture. If the mixture screws are capped, don't adjust them unless all other causes of rough idle have been eliminated. If any adjustments are performed that might possibly change the idle speed or mixture, adjust the idle and mixture again when you are finished.

Before you make any carburetor adjustments make sure that the engine is in tune. Many problems which are thought to be carburetor-related can be traced to an engine which is simply out-of-tune. Any trouble in these areas will have symptoms like those of carburetor problems.

ADJUSTMENTS

➡ SEE FIG. 4

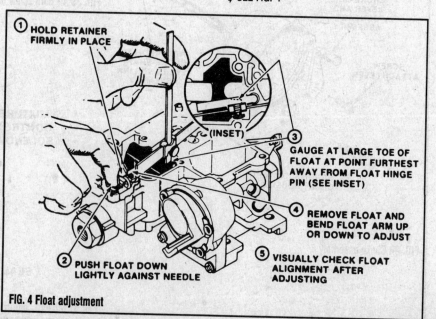

① HOLD RETAINER FIRMLY IN PLACE

(INSET)

③ GAUGE AT LARGE TOE OF FLOAT AT POINT FURTHEST AWAY FROM FLOAT HINGE PIN (SEE INSET)

④ REMOVE FLOAT AND BEND FLOAT ARM UP OR DOWN TO ADJUST

② PUSH FLOAT DOWN LIGHTLY AGAINST NEEDLE

⑤ VISUALLY CHECK FLOAT ALIGNMENT AFTER ADJUSTING

FIG. 4 Float adjustment

Float Adjustment

1. Remove the air horn from the throttle body.

2. Use your fingers to hold the retainer in place, and to push the float down into light contact with the needle.

3. Measure the distance from the toe of the float (furthest from the hinge) to the top of the carburetor (gasket removed).

4. To adjust, remove the float and gently bend the arm to specification. After adjustment, check the float alignment in the chamber.

Pump Adjustment

E2SE carburetors have a non-adjustable pump lever. No adjustments are either necessary or possible.

Fast Idle Adjustment

➧ SEE FIG. 5

1. Set the ignition timing and curb idle speed, and disconnect and plug hoses as directed on the emission control decal.

2. Place the fast idle screw on the highest step of the cam.

3. Start the engine and adjust the engine speed to specification with the fast idle screw.

Choke Coil Lever Adjustment

➧ SEE FIG. 6

1. Remove the three retaining screws and remove the choke cover and coil. On models with a riveted choke cover, drill out the three rivets and remove the cover and choke coil.

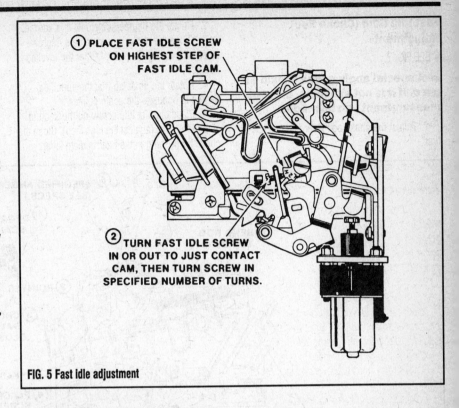

① PLACE FAST IDLE SCREW ON HIGHEST STEP OF FAST IDLE CAM.

② TURN FAST IDLE SCREW IN OR OUT TO JUST CONTACT CAM, THEN TURN SCREW IN SPECIFIED NUMBER OF TURNS.

FIG. 5 Fast idle adjustment

➡ **A choke stat cover retainer kit is required for reassembly.**

2. Place the fast idle screw on the high step of the cam.

3. Close the choke by pushing in on the intermediate choke lever.

4. Insert a drill or gauge of the specified size into the hole in the choke housing. The choke lever in the housing should be up against the side of the gauge.

5. If the lever does not just touch the gauge, bend the intermediate choke rod to adjust.

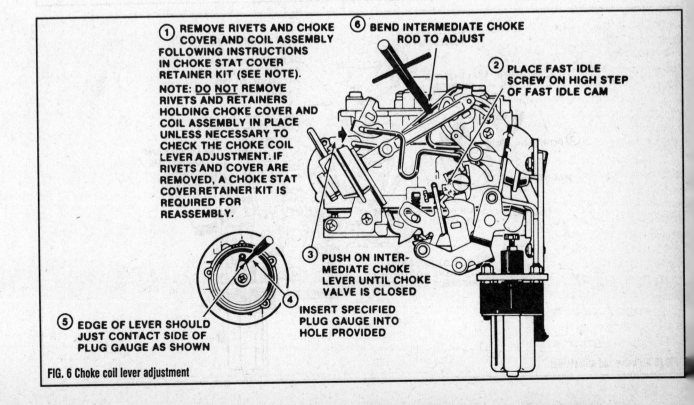

① REMOVE RIVETS AND CHOKE COVER AND COIL ASSEMBLY FOLLOWING INSTRUCTIONS IN CHOKE STAT COVER RETAINER KIT (SEE NOTE).
NOTE: <u>DO NOT</u> REMOVE RIVETS AND RETAINERS HOLDING CHOKE COVER AND COIL ASSEMBLY IN PLACE UNLESS NECESSARY TO CHECK THE CHOKE COIL LEVER ADJUSTMENT. IF RIVETS AND COVER ARE REMOVED, A CHOKE STAT COVER RETAINER KIT IS REQUIRED FOR REASSEMBLY.

⑥ BEND INTERMEDIATE CHOKE ROD TO ADJUST

② PLACE FAST IDLE SCREW ON HIGH STEP OF FAST IDLE CAM

③ PUSH ON INTERMEDIATE CHOKE LEVER UNTIL CHOKE VALVE IS CLOSED

④ INSERT SPECIFIED PLUG GAUGE INTO HOLE PROVIDED

⑤ EDGE OF LEVER SHOULD JUST CONTACT SIDE OF PLUG GAUGE AS SHOWN

FIG. 6 Choke coil lever adjustment

Fast Idle Cam (Choke Rod) Adjustment

♦ SEE FIG. 7

➡ **A special angle gauge should be used. If it is not available, a linear measurement can be made.**

1. Adjust the choke coil lever and fast idle first.

2. Rotate the degree scale until it is zeroed.

3. Close the choke and install the degree scale onto the choke plate. Center the leveling bubble.

4. Rotate the scale so that the specified degree is opposite the scale pointer.

5. Place the fast idle screw on the second step of the cam (against the high step). Close the choke by pushing in the intermediate lever.

6. Bend the fast idle cam rod at the U to adjust the angle to specifications.

Air Valve Rod Adjustment

♦ SEE FIG. 8

1. Seat the vacuum diaphragm with an outside vacuum source. Tape over the purge bleed hole if present.

2. Close the air valve.

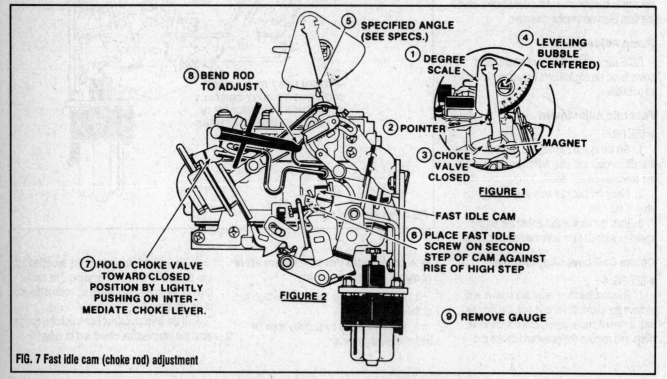

FIG. 7 Fast idle cam (choke rod) adjustment

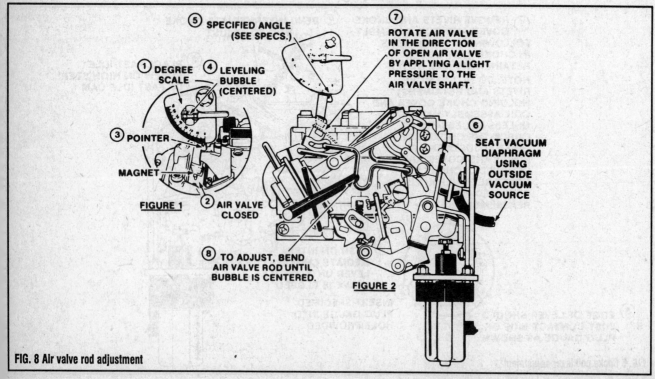

FIG. 8 Air valve rod adjustment

3. Insert the specified gauge between the rod and the end of the slot in the plunger.

4. Bend the rod to adjust the clearance.

Primary Side Vacuum Break Adjustment

♦ SEE FIG. 9

1. Follow Steps 1-4 of the Fast Idle Cam Adjustment.

2. Seat the choke vacuum diaphragm with an outside vacuum source.

3. Push in on the intermediate choke lever to close the choke valve, and hold closed during adjustment.

4. Adjust by using a 1/8 in. (3mm) hex wrench to turn the screw in the rear cover until the bubble is centered.

5. After adjusting, apply RTV silicone sealant over the screw to seal the setting.

Secondary Vacuum Break Adjustment

♦ SEE FIG. 10

1. Follow Steps 1-4 of the Fast Idle Cam Adjustment.

2. Seat the choke vacuum diaphragm with an outside vacuum source.

3. Push in on the intermediate choke lever to

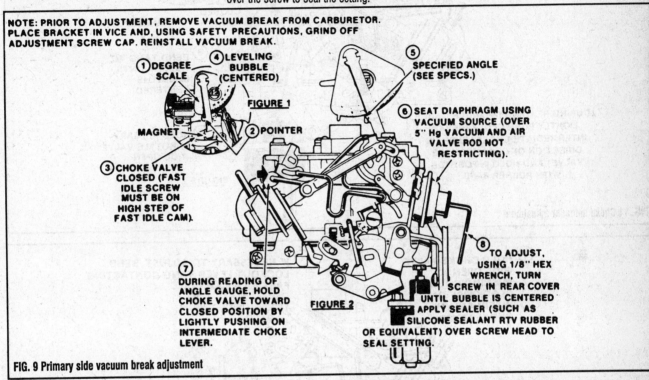

FIG. 9 Primary side vacuum break adjustment

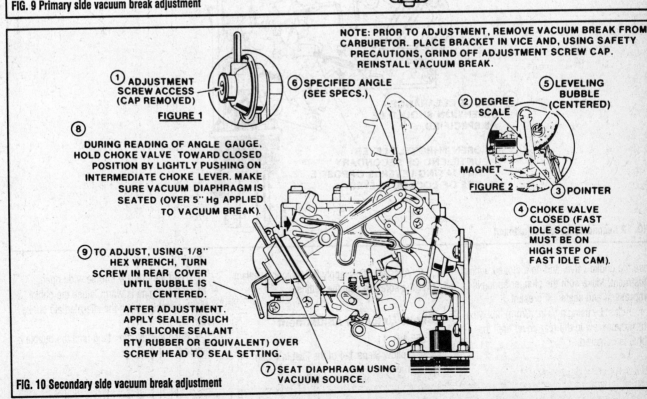

FIG. 10 Secondary side vacuum break adjustment

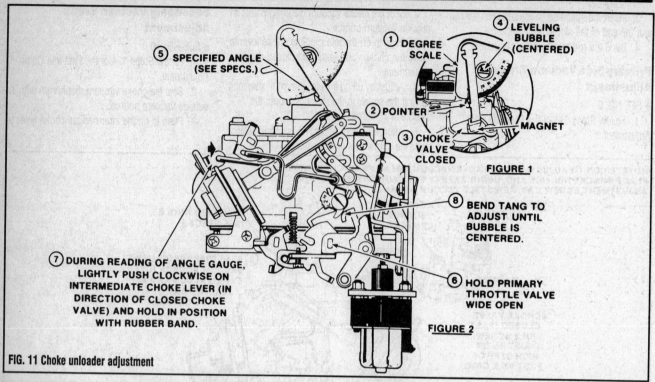

(5) SPECIFIED ANGLE (SEE SPECS.)

(4) LEVELING BUBBLE (CENTERED)

(1) DEGREE SCALE

(2) POINTER

(3) CHOKE VALVE CLOSED

MAGNET

FIGURE 1

(8) BEND TANG TO ADJUST UNTIL BUBBLE IS CENTERED.

(7) DURING READING OF ANGLE GAUGE, LIGHTLY PUSH CLOCKWISE ON INTERMEDIATE CHOKE LEVER (IN DIRECTION OF CLOSED CHOKE VALVE) AND HOLD IN POSITION WITH RUBBER BAND.

(6) HOLD PRIMARY THROTTLE VALVE WIDE OPEN

FIGURE 2

FIG. 11 Choke unloader adjustment

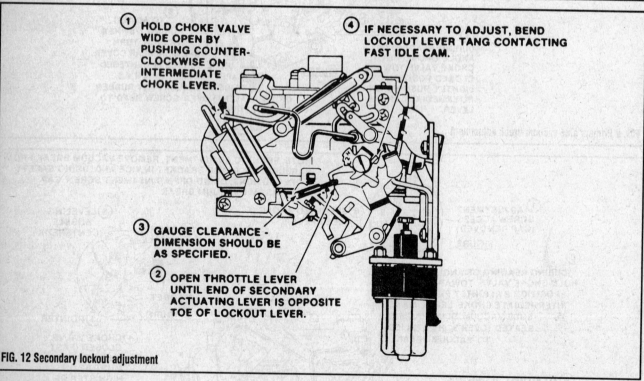

(1) HOLD CHOKE VALVE WIDE OPEN BY PUSHING COUNTER-CLOCKWISE ON INTERMEDIATE CHOKE LEVER.

(4) IF NECESSARY TO ADJUST, BEND LOCKOUT LEVER TANG CONTACTING FAST IDLE CAM.

(3) GAUGE CLEARANCE - DIMENSION SHOULD BE AS SPECIFIED.

(2) OPEN THROTTLE LEVER UNTIL END OF SECONDARY ACTUATING LEVER IS OPPOSITE TOE OF LOCKOUT LEVER.

FIG. 12 Secondary lockout adjustment

close the choke valve, and hold closed during adjustment. Make sure the plunger spring is compressed and seated, if present.

4. Adjust by using a 1/8 in. (3mm) hex wrench to turn the screw in the rear cover until the bubble is centered.

5. After adjusting, apply RTV silicone sealant over the screw to seal the setting.

Choke Unloader Adjustment

▶ SEE FIG. 11

1. Follow Steps 1-4 of the Fast Idle Cam Adjustment.

2. Hold the primary throttle wide open.

3. If the engine is warm, close the choke valve by pushing in on the intermediate choke lever.

4. Bend the unloader tang until the bubble is centered.

E2SE Carburetor Specifications

Year	Carburetor Identification	Float Level (in.)	Fast Idle (rpm)	Choke Coil Lever (in.)	Fast Idle Cam (deg.)	Air Valve Rod (deg.)	Primary Vacuum Break (deg/in.)	Choke Setting (notches)	Secondary Vacuum Break (deg/in.)	Choke Unloader (deg/in.)	Secondary Lockout (in.)
1982	17081600	5/16	①	.085	24	1	20/.110	①	27/.157	35/.220	.012
	17081601	5/16	①	.085	24	1	20/.110	①	27/.157	35/.220	.012
	17081607	5/16	①	.085	24	1	20/.110	①	27/.157	35/.220	.012
	17081700	5/16	①	.085	24	1	20/.110	①	27/.157	35/.220	.012
	17081701	5/16	①	.085	24	1	20/.110	①	27/.157	35/.220	.012

① See underhood emissions sticker

Secondary Lockout Adjustment

♦ SEE FIG. 12

1. Pull the choke wide open by pushing out on the intermediate choke lever.

2. Open the throttle until the end of the secondary actuating lever is opposite the toe of the lockout lever.

3. Gauge clearance between the lockout lever and secondary lever should be as specified.

4. To adjust, bend the lockout lever where it contacts the fast idle cam.

GM MODEL 300 AND 500 THROTTLE BODY (TBI) INJECTION SYSTEMS

The single bore, Model 300 throttle body unit used on the 1983-86 1.8L OHC engine and the Model 500 throttle body unit used on the 1983-86 2.0L OHV engine are similar systems.

In these throttle body systems, a single fuel injector mounted at the top of the throttle body sprays fuel down through the throttle valve and into the intake manifold. The throttle body resembles a carburetor in appearance but does away with much of the carburetor's complexity (choke system and linkage, power valves, accelerator pump, jets, fuel circuits, etc.), replacing these with the electrically operated fuel injector.

The injector is actually a solenoid which when activated lifts a pintle valve off its seat, allowing the pressurized (10 psi) fuel behind the valve to spray out. The nozzle of the injector is designed to atomize the fuel for complete air/fuel mixture.

The activating signal for the injector originates with the Electronic Control Module (ECM), which monitors engine temperature, throttle position, vehicle speed and several other engine-related conditions then continuously updates injector opening times in relation to the information given by these sensors.

The throttle body is also equipped with an idle air control valve. When the valve opens it allows air to bypass the throttle, which provides the additional air required to idle at elevated speed when the engine is cold. The idle air control motor also compensates for accessory loads and changing engine friction during break-in. The idle speed control valve is controlled by the ECM.

Fuel pressure for the system is provided by an in-tank fuel pump. The pump is a two-stage turbine designed powered by a DC motor. It is designed for smooth, quiet operation, high flow and fast priming. The design of the fuel inlet reduces the possibility of vapor lock under hot fuel conditions. The pump sends fuel forward through the fuel line to a stainless steel high-flow fuel filter mounted on the engine. From the filter the fuel moves to the throttle body. The fuel pump inlet is located in a reservoir in the fuel tank which insures a constant supply of fuel to the pump during hard cornering and on steep inclines. The fuel pump is controlled by a fuel pump relay, which in turn receives its signal from the ECM. A fuel pressure regulator inside the throttle body maintains fuel pressure at 10 psi and routes unused fuel back to the fuel tank through a fuel return line. On the dual throttle body system, a fuel pressure compensator is used on the second throttle body assembly to compensate for a momentary fuel pressure drop between the two units. This constant circulation of fuel through the throttle body prevents component overheating and vapor lock.

The electronic control module (ECM), also called a micro-computer, is the brain of the fuel injection system. After receiving input from various sensing elements in the system the ECM commands the fuel injector, idle air control motor, EST distributor, torque converter clutch and other engine actuators to operate in a pre-programmed manner to improve driveability and fuel economy while controlling emissions. The sensing elements update the computer every tenth of a second for general information and every 12.5 milliseconds for critical emissions and driveability information.

The ECM has limited system diagnostic capability. If certain system malfunctions occur, the diagnostic Check Engine light in the instrument panel will light, alerting the driver to the need for service.

Since both idle speed and mixture are controlled by the ECM on this system, no adjustments are possible or necessary.

FUEL PRESSURE RELEASE

✳✳ CAUTION

To reduce the risk of fire or personal injury, it is necessary to relieve the fuel system pressure before servicing the fuel system.

1983-86 1.8L and 2.0L (OHC)
1983-84 2.0L (OHV)

1. Remove the fuel pump fuse from the fuse block.

2. Crank the engine. The engine will run until it runs out of fuel. Crank the engine again for 3 seconds making sure it is out of fuel.

3. Turn the ignition off and replace the fuse.

1985-86 2.0L (OHV)

The TBI injection systems used on the 1985-86 engines contain a constant bleed feature in the pressure regulator that relieves pressure any time the engine is turned off. Therefore, no special relieve procedure is required, however, a small amount of fuel may be released when the fuel line is disconnected.

✳✳ CAUTION

To reduce the chance of personal injury, cover the fuel line with cloth to collect the fuel and then place the cloth in an approved container.

FUEL SYSTEM PRESSURE TEST

✳✳ CAUTION

To reduce the risk of fire and personal injury, it is necessary to relieve the fuel system pressure before servicing fuel system components (Refer to the appropriate procedure above).

1.8L and 2.0L OHV Engines

1. Remove the air cleaner. Plug the thermal vacuum port on the throttle body.

2. Remove the fuel line between the throttle body and filter.

3. Install a fuel pressure gauge between the throttle body and fuel filter. The gauge should be able to register at least 15 psi.

4. Start the car. The pressure reading should be 9-13 psi.

5. Depressurize the system and remove the gauge.

6. Assemble the system.

1.8L, 2.0L OHC Engines

1. Release the fuel system pressure.

✳✳ CAUTION

To reduce the risk of fire or personal injury, it is necessary to relieve the fuel system pressure before servicing the fuel system. Refer to Fuel System Pressure Release in the appropriate fuel injection system in this section.

2. Obtain two sections of 3/8 in. steel tubing. Each should be about 10 in. (254mm) long. Double flare one end of each section.

3. Install a flare nut on each section. Connect each of the above sections of tubing into the flare nut to flare nut adapters that are included in J-29658 gauge.

4. Attach the pipe and the adapter assemblies to the J-29658 gauge.

5. Jack up the car and support it safely.

6. Disconnect the front fuel feed hose from the fuel pipe on the body.

7. Install a 10 in. (254mm) length of 3/8 in. fuel hose on the fuel pipe on the body. Attach the other end of the hose onto one of the sections of the pipe mentioned in Step 2. Secure the hose connections with clamps.

8. Start the engine and check for leaks.

9. Observe the fuel pressure reading. It should be 9-13 psi.

10. Depressurize the fuel system and remove the gauge with adapters. Reconnect the fuel feed hose to the pipe and torque the clamp to 15 inch lbs.

11. Lower the car, start the engine and check for fuel leaks.

Fuel Pump

REMOVAL & INSTALLATION

1. Release the fuel system pressure.

✳✳ CAUTION

To reduce the risk of fire or personal injury, it is necessary to relieve the fuel system pressure before servicing the fuel system. Refer to Fuel System Pressure Release procedure above.

2. Disconnect the negative battery cable.

3. Jack up the car and support it safely.

4. Remove the fuel tank — refer to the necessary service procedures.

5. Remove the fuel lever sending unit and pump assembly by turning the cam lock ring counterclockwise. Lift the assembly from the fuel tank and remove the fuel pump from the fuel level sending unit.

6. Pull the fuel pump up into the attaching hose or pulsator while pulling outward away from the bottom support. After the pump is clear of the bottom support, pull the pump assembly out of the rubber connector or pulsator for removal.

To install:

7. Position and push the pump into the attaching hose.

8. Install the fuel level sending unit and pump assembly into the tank assembly. Use new O-ring during reassembly.

✳✳ WARNING

Be careful not to fold over or twist the strainer when installing the sending unit as it will restrict fuel flow. Also, be careful the strainer does not block full travel of the float arm.

9. Install the cam lock over the assembly and lock by turning clockwise.

10. Install the fuel tank. Check system for proper operation.

TOOLS

The system does not require special tools for diagnosis. A tachometer, test light, ohmmeter, digital voltmeter with 10 megohms impedance, vacuum pump, vacuum gauge and jumper wires are required for diagnosis. A test light or voltmeter must be used when specified in the procedures.

Idle Air Control Assembly

REMOVAL & INSTALLATION

♦ SEE FIG. 13
1. Remove the air cleaner.
2. Disconnect the electrical connection from the idle air control assembly.
3. Using a 1¼ in. (31.75mm) wrench or a special tool, remove the idle air control assembly from the throttle body.

✳✳ WARNING

Before installing a new assembly, measure the distance that the conical valve is extended. This measurement should be made from motor housing to end of cone. It should be greater than 1⅛ in. (28.6mm). If the cone is extended too far damage to the motor may result.

There are two different types of IAC assemblies that could be used on your car. Identify the replacement IAC assembly as either being type I (having a collar at the electric terminal) or Type II (without a collar). If the measured dimension is greater than 1⅛ in. (28.6mm), the distance must be reduced as follows:

TYPE I: Insert firm pressure on the conical valve to extract it. A slight side to side movement may be helpful.

TYPE II: Compress the retaining spring from the conical valve inward with a clockwise motion. Return the spring to the original position with the straight portion of the spring end aligned with the flat portion of the valve.

4. Install the new idle air control valve to the throttle body with a new gasket and tighten to 13 ft. lbs.

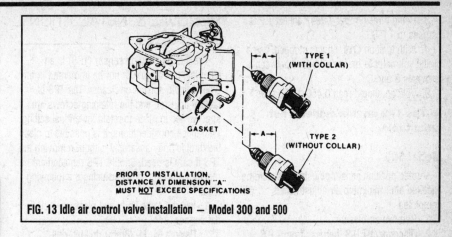

FIG. 13 Idle air control valve installation — Model 300 and 500

5. Install the electrical connection to the valve.
6. Install the air cleaner.

➡ **When the vehicle is operated at normal engine temperature at approximately 30 MPH, the ECM causes the valve pintle to seat in the throttle body.**

Fuel Pressure Regulator Compensator

REMOVAL & INSTALLATION

✳✳ CAUTION

To reduce the risk of fire and personal injury, it is necessary to relieve the fuel system pressure before servicing fuel system components (Refer to the appropriate procedure above).

1. Remove air cleaner.
2. Disconnect electrical connector to injector by squeezing on two tabs and pulling straight up.
3. Remove five screws securing fuel meter cover to fuel meter body. Notice location of two short screws during removal.

✳✳ CAUTION

Do not remove the four screws securing the pressure regulator to the fuel meter cover. The fuel pressure regulator includes a large spring under heavy tension which, if accidentally released, could cause personal injury. The fuel meter cover is only serviced as a complete assembly and includes the fuel pressure regulator preset and plugged at the factory.

✳✳ WARNING

DO NOT immerse the fuel meter cover (with pressure regulator) in any type of cleaner. Immersion in cleaner will damage the internal fuel pressure regulator diaphragms and gaskets.

4. Installation is the reverse of removal procedure.

Throttle Position Sensor

CHECK

Model 300

1. Remove air cleaner.
2. Disconnect T.P.S. harness from T.P.S.

3. Using three jumper wires connect T.P.S. harness to T.P.S.

4. With ignition **ON**, engine stopped, use a digital voltmeter to measure voltage between terminals B and C.

5. Voltage should read 0.450-1.250 volts.

➡ **The TPS on this model is not adjustable.**

Model 500

Throttle position sensor adjustment should be checked after minimum air adjustment is completed.

1. Remove air cleaner.
2. Disconnect T.P.S. harness from T.P.S.
3. Using three jumper wires connect T.P.S. harness to T.P.S.
4. With ignition **ON**, engine stopped, use a digital voltmeter to measure voltage between terminals B and C.
5. Voltage should read 0.525volts ± 0.075 volts.
6. Adjust T.P.S. if required.
7. With ignition **OFF**, remove jumpers and connect T.P.S. harness to T.P.S.
8. Install air cleaner.

Throttle Position Sensor

ADJUSTMENT

Model 500

1. After installing TPS to throttle body, install throttle body unit to engine.
2. Remove EGR valve and heat shield from engine.
3. Using three 6 in. (152mm) jumpers, connect TPS harness to TPS.
4. With ignition **ON**, engine stopped, use a digital voltmeter to measure voltage between TPS terminals B and C.
5. Loosen two TPS attaching screws and rotate throttle position sensor to obtain a voltage reading of 0.525 volts ± 0.075 volts.
6. With ignition **OFF**, remove jumpers and reconnect TPS harness to TPS.
7. Install EGR valve and heat shield to engine, using new gasket as necessary.
8. Install air cleaner gasket and air cleaner to throttle body unit.

REMOVAL & INSTALLATION

The throttle position sensor (TPS) is an electrical unit and must not be immersed in any type of liquid solvent or cleaner. The TPS is factory adjusted and the retaining screws are spot welded in place to retain the critical setting. With these considerations, it is possible to clean the throttle body assembly without removing the TPS if care is used. Should TPS replacement be required however, proceed using the following steps:

1. Invert throttle body and place on a clean, flat surface.
2. Using a $5/16$ in. (8mm) drill bit, drill completely through two (2) TPS screw access holes in base of throttle body to be sure of removing the spot welds holding TPS screws in place.
3. Remove the two TPS attaching screws, lockwashers, and retainers. Then, remove TPS sensor from throttle body. DISCARD SCREWS. New screws are supplied in service kits.
4. If necessary, remove screw holding Throttle Position Sensor actuator lever to end of throttle shaft.
5. Remove the Idle Air Control assembly and gasket from the throttle body.

❋❋ WARNING

DO NOT immerse the idle air control motor in any type of cleaner and it should always be removed before throttle body cleaning. Immersion in cleaner will damage the IAC assembly. It is replaced only as a complete assembly.

Further disassembly of the throttle body is not required for cleaning purposes. The throttle valve screws are permanently staked in place and should not be removed. The throttle body is serviced as a complete assembly.

ASSEMBLY

1. Place throttle body assembly on holding fixture to avoid damaging throttle valve.
2. Using a new sealing gasket, install idle air control motor in throttle body. Tighten motor securely.

❋❋ WARNING

DO NOT overtighten to prevent damage to valve.

3. If removed, install throttle position sensor actuator lever by aligning flats on lever with flats on end of shaft. Install retaining screw and tighten securely.

➡ **Install throttle position sensor after completion of assembly of the throttle body unit. Use thread locking compound supplied in service kit on attaching screws.**

Fuel Injector

REMOVAL & INSTALLATION

1. Remove the air cleaner.
2. Disconnect injector electrical connector by squeezing two tabs together and pulling straight up.

❋❋ WARNING

Use care in removing to prevent damage to the electrical connector pins on top of the injector, injector fuel filter and nozzle. The fuel injector is only serviced as a complete assembly. Do not immerse it in any type of cleaner.

3. Remove the fuel meter cover.
4. Using a small awl, gently pry up on the injector evenly and carefully remove it.
5. Installation is the reverse of removal, with the following recommendations.

Use Dexron®II transmission fluid to lubricate all O-rings. Install the steel backup washer in the recess of the fuel meter body. Then, install the O-ring directly above backup washer, pressing the O-ring into the recess.

❋❋ WARNING

Do not attempt to reverse this procedure and install backup washer and O-ring after injector is located in the cavity. To do so will prevent seating of the O-ring in the recess.

Fuel Meter Cover

REMOVAL & INSTALLATION

1. Remove the five fuel meter cover screws and lockwashers holding the cover on the fuel meter body.
2. Lift off fuel meter cover (with fuel pressure regulator assembly).
3. Remove the fuel meter cover gaskets.

✳✳ CAUTION

Do not remove the four screws securing the pressure regulator to the fuel meter cover. The fuel pressure regulator includes a large spring under heavy tension which, if accidentally released, could cause personal injury. The fuel meter cover is only serviced as a complete assembly and includes the fuel pressure regulator preset and plugged at the factory.

✳✳ WARNING

Do not immerse the fuel meter cover (with pressure regulator) in any type of cleaner. Immersion in cleaner will damage the internal fuel pressure regulator diaphragms and gaskets.

4. Remove the sealing ring (dust seal from the fuel meter body).
5. Installation is the reverse of removal.

Fuel Meter Body

REMOVAL & INSTALLATION

▶ SEE FIG. 14

1. Remove the fuel inlet and outlet nuts and gaskets from fuel meter body.
2. Remove three screws and lockwashers. Remove fuel meter body from throttle body assembly.

➡ **The air cleaner stud must have been removed previously.**

3. Remove fuel meter body insulator gasket.
4. Installation is the reverse of removal procedure.

Throttle Body

REMOVAL & INSTALLATION

1. Disconnect the battery cables at the battery.
2. Remove the air cleaner assembly, noting the connection points of the vacuum lines.
3. Disconnect the electrical connectors at the

FIG. 14 Removing the fuel meter body assembly — Model 300 and 500

injector, idle air control motor, and throttle position sensor.
4. Disconnect the vacuum lines from the TBI unit, noting the connection points. During installation, refer to the underhood emission control information decal for vacuum line routing information.
5. Disconnect the throttle and cruise control (if so equipped) cables at the TBI unit.
6. Disconnect the fuel return line.
7. Disconnect the fuel feed line.
8. Unbolt and remove the TBI unit.
9. Installation is the reverse of the previous steps. Torque the TBI retaining bolts alternately and evenly to the following specifications:

- 1983–85 with 2.0L OHV engine — 26 ft. lbs.
- 1986 with 2.0L OHV engine — 17 ft. lbs.
- 1983–86 with 1.8L OHC engine — 17 ft. lbs.

GM MODEL 700 THROTTLE BODY (TBI) INJECTION SYSTEM

The Model 700 throttle body system is used on the 1987-91 2.0L OHC (non-turbo) and the 1987–91 2.0L and 2.2L OHV engines.

FUEL SYSTEM PRESSURE RELEASE

✳✳ CAUTION

The fuel delivery pipe is under high

pressure even after the engine is stopped. Direct removal of the fuel line, may result in dangerous fuel spray. Make sure to release the fuel pressure according to the following procedures:

2.0L and 2.2L OHV Engines

1987

1. Release the fuel vapor pressure in the fuel

tank by removing the fuel tank cap and reinstalling it.
2. Disconnect the fuel pump at the rear body connector and wait until the engine stops.
3. Start the engine and allow it to run a few seconds until it runs out of fuel.
4. Once the engine is stopped, crank it a few times with the starter for about 3 seconds to dissipate the fuel in the lines.

1988–91

1. Disconnect the negative battery cable.
2. Release the fuel vapor pressure in the fuel

tank by removing the fuel tank cap and reinstalling it.

3. The internal constant bleed feature of the TBI Models 700, relieves the fuel pump system pressure when the engine is turned **OFF** and no further pressure relive procedure is required.

2.0L OHC Engine

1987–90

1. Release the fuel vapor pressure in the fuel tank by removing the fuel tank cap and reinstalling it.

2. Remove the fuel pump fuse from the fuse block.

3. Start the engine and allow it to run a few seconds until it runs out of fuel.

4. Once the engine is stopped, crank it a few times with the starter for about 3 seconds to dissipate the fuel in the lines.

5. If the fuel pressure can't be released in the above manner because the engine failed to run, disconnect the negative battery cable, cover the union bolt of the fuel line with an absorbent rag and loosen the union bolt slowly to release the fuel pressure gradually.

1991

1. Disconnect the negative battery cable.

2. Release the fuel vapor pressure in the fuel tank by removing the fuel tank cap and reinstalling it.

3. The internal constant bleed feature of this Model 700 TBI unit relieves the fuel pump system pressure when the engine is turned **OFF** and no further pressure relive procedure is required.

FUEL PRESSURE TESTING

1987–91

1. Turn the ignition to the **OFF** position.

2. Make sure the fuel tank quantity is sufficient.

3. Install pressure gauge J 29658–B or BT–8205 or equivalent to the fuel line as illustrated.

4. Apply battery voltage to the fuel pump test connector using a 10 amp fused jumper wire.

5. Note the fuel pressure which should be 9–13 psi.

Fuel Pump

REMOVAL & INSTALLATION

1. Release the fuel system pressure.

✳✳ CAUTION

To reduce the risk of fire or personal injury, it is necessary to relieve the fuel system pressure before servicing the fuel system. Refer to Fuel System Pressure Release procedure above.

2. Disconnect the negative battery cable.

3. Jack up the car and support it safely.

4. Remove the fuel tank.

5. Remove the fuel lever sending unit and pump assembly by turning the cam lock ring counterclockwise. Lift the assembly from the fuel tank and remove the fuel pump from the fuel level sending unit.

6. Pull the fuel pump up into the attaching hose or pulsator while pulling outward away from the bottom support. After the pump is clear of the bottom support, pull the pump assembly out of the rubber connector or pulsator for removal.

To Install:

7. Position and push the pump into the attaching hose.

8. Install the fuel level sending unit and pump assembly into the tank assembly. Use new O-ring during reassembly.

✳✳ WARNING

Be careful not to fold over or twist the strainer when installing the sending unit as it will restrict fuel flow. Also, be careful the strainer does not block full travel of the float arm.

9. Install the cam lock over the assembly and lock by turning clockwise.

10. Install the fuel tank. Check system for proper operation.

Throttle Body

REMOVAL & INSTALLATION

▶ SEE FIG. 15

1. Disconnect the battery cables at the battery.

2. Remove the air cleaner assembly, noting the connection points of the vacuum lines.

---

3. Disconnect the electrical connectors at the injector, idle air control motor, and throttle position sensor.

4. Disconnect the vacuum lines from the TBI unit, noting the connection points. During installation, refer to the underhood emission control information decal for vacuum line routing information.

5. Disconnect the throttle and cruise control (if so equipped) cables at the TBI unit.

6. Disconnect the fuel return line.

7. Disconnect the fuel feed line.

8. Unbolt and remove the TBI unit.

9. Installation is the reverse of the previous steps. Torque the TBI retaining bolts alternately and evenly to the following specifications:

- 1987–88 — 17 ft. lbs.
- 1989–91 — 18 ft. lbs.

Injector

REPLACEMENT

✳✳ WARNING

When removing the injectors, be careful not to damage the electrical connector pins (on top of the injector), the injector fuel filter and the nozzle. The fuel injector is serviced as a complete assembly ONLY. The injector is an electrical component and should not be immersed in any kind of cleaner.

1. Remove the air cleaner.

✳✳ CAUTION

To reduce the risk of fire and personal injury, it is necessary to relieve the fuel system pressure before servicing fuel system components (Refer to the appropriate procedure above).

2. Disconnect the electrical connector to the fuel injector.

3. Remove the injector retainer screw and retainer.

4. Using a fulcrum, place a suitable tool under the ridge opposite the connector end and carefully pry the injector out.

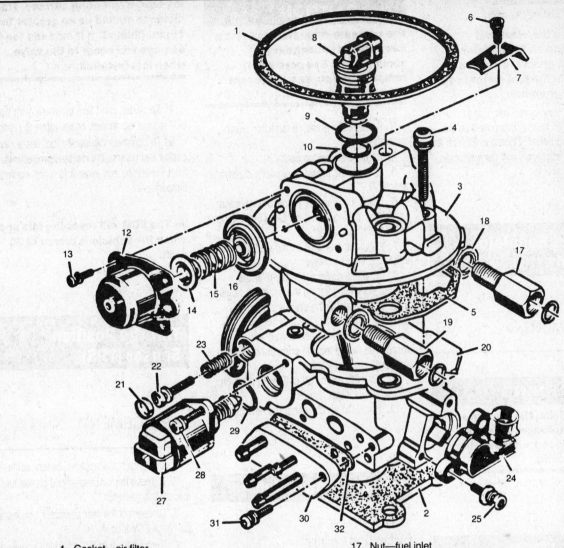

1. Gasket—air filter
2. Gasket—flange
3. Fuel meter assembly
4. Screw & washer assembly—fuel meter body attaching
5. Gasket—fuel meter body to throttle body
6. Screw—injector retainer
7. Retainer—injector
8. Fuel injector
9. O-ring—fuel injector—upper
10. O-ring—fuel injector—lower
11. Filter—injector
12. Pressure regulator cover assembly
13. Screw—pressure regulator attaching
14. Seat—spring
15. Spring—pressure regulator
16. Pressure regulator diaphragm assembly

17. Nut—fuel inlet
18. Seal—fuel nut
19. Nut—fuel outlet
20. Throttle body assembly
21. Plug—idle stop screw
22. Screw & washer assembly—idle stop
23. Spring—idle stop screw
24. Sensor—throttle position (TPS)
25. Screw & washer assembly—TPS attaching
26. Screw—TPS
27. Idle air control valve (IACV)
28. Screw—IACV attaching
29. O-ring—IACV
30. Tube module assembly
31. Screw—manifold assembly
32. Gasket—tubes manifold

FIG. 15 Exploded view of the Model 700 throttle body injection unit

5. Remove the upper and lower O-rings from the injector and in the fuel injector cavity and discard.

✵ WARNING

Be sure to replace the injector with

an identical part. Injectors from other models can fit in the Model 700, but are calibrated for different flow rates. There is a part number located on the top of the injector

6. Inspect the filter for evidence of contamination.

7. Lubricate the new upper and lower O-rings with automatic transmission fluid and place them on the injector. Make sur the upper O-ring is in the groove and the lower one is flush up against the filter.

8. Install the injector assembly by pushing it straight into the fuel injector cavity.

➡ **Make sure the electrical connector end on the injector is facing in the general direction to the cut-out in the fuel meter body for the wire grommet.**

9. Install the injector retainer, using appropriate thread locking compound on the retainer attaching screw. Tighten to 27 inch lbs.

10. With the engine off and the ignition on, check for fuel leaks

Pressure Regulator Assembly

REPLACEMENT

✳ WARNING

To prevent leaks, the pressure regulator diaphragm assembly must be replaced whenever the cover is removed.

✳ CAUTION

To reduce the risk of fire and personal injury, it is necessary to relieve the fuel system pressure before servicing fuel system components (Refer to the appropriate procedure above).

1. Remove the air cleaner and gasket and discard the gasket.

2. Remove the four pressure regulator attaching screws, while keeping the pressure regulator compressed.

✳ CAUTION

The pressure regulator contains a large spring under heavy compression. Use care when removing the screws to prevent personal injury.

3. Remove the pressure regulator cover assembly.

4. Remove the spring seat.

5. Remove the pressure regulator diaphragm assembly.

6. Install the pressure regulator diaphragm assembly, making sure it is seated in the groove in the fuel meter body.

7. Install the regulator spring seat and spring into the cover assembly.

8. Install the cover assembly over the diaphragm, while aligning the mounting holes.

9. While maintaining pressure on the regulator spring, install the four screw assemblies that have been coated with appropriate thread locking compound. Tighten the screws to 22 inch lbs.

10. With the engine off and the ignition on, check for fuel leaks.

11. Install the air cleaner and a new gasket.

Idle Air Control Valve

REPLACEMENT

1. Remove the air cleaner.

2. Disconnect the electrical connector from the idle air control valve.

3. Remove the retaining screws and remove the IAC valve.

✳ WARNING

Before installing a new idle air control valve, measure the distance that the valve extends (from the tip of the valve pintle and the flange mounting surface. The distance should be no greater than 1⅛ in. (28mm). If it extends too far, damage will occur to the valve when it is installed.

4. To adjust, exert firm pressure, with slight side to side movement, on the pintle to retract it.

5. To complete the installation, use a new gasket and reverse the removal procedures. Start the engine and allow it to reach operating temperature.

➡ **The ECM will reset the idle speed when the vehicle is driven at 30 mph.**

Throttle Position Sensor (TPS)

REPLACEMENT

1. Disconnect the negative battery cable.

2. Remove the air cleaner and gasket and discard the gasket.

3. Disconnect the rear alternator bracket and the metal PCV tube.

4. Remove the two TPS attaching screws and remove the TPS from the throttle body.

5. When installing, make sure the throttle body is closed and install the TPS on the shaft. Rotate counterclockwise to align the mounting holes.

6. Install the two TPS attaching screws and tighten to 18 inch lbs.

7. Install the metal PCV tube and the rear alternator bracket.

8. Install the air cleaner and new gasket.

9. Reconnect the negative battery cable.

BOTTOM FEED PORT (BFP) INJECTION SYSTEM

The Bottom Feed Port (BFP) injection system is used on the 2.2L OHV (VIN 4) engine in 1992.

FUEL SYSTEM PRESSURE RELEASE

1. Loosen the full filler cap to relieve the tank vapor pressure. Leave the cap loose at this time.
2. Raise and support the vehicle safely.
3. Disconnect the fuel pump electrical connector.
4. Lower the vehicle.
5. Start the engine and run until the fuel supply remaining in the fuel pipes is consumed. Engage the starter for 3 seconds to assure relief of any remaining pressure.
6. Raise and support the vehicle safely.
7. Connect the fuel pump electrical connector.
8. Lower the vehicle.
9. Tighten the fuel filler cap.
10. Disconnect the negative battery cable terminal to avoid possible fuel

discharge if an accidental attempt is made to start the engine.

Throttle Position Sensor (TPS)

REMOVAL & INSTALLATION

▶ SEE FIG. 15A
1. Disconnect the negative battery cable.
2. Disconnect the electrical connector from the TPS.
3. Remove the 2 TPS attaching screws and remove the TPS from the throttle body.
To Install:
5. When installing, make sure the throttle body is closed, position the TPS on the shaft and align the mounting holes.
6. Install the 2 TPS attaching screws and tighten to 18 inch lbs. (2.0 Nm).
7. Install the electrical connector.
8. Reconnect the negative battery cable.

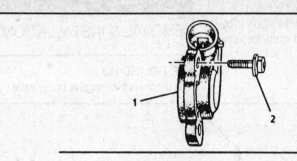

1 **THROTTLE POSITION SENSOR (TPS) (NONADJUSTABLE)**

2 **TPS ATTACHING SCREW ASSEMBLY**

FIG. 15A Throttle Position Sensor (TPS)

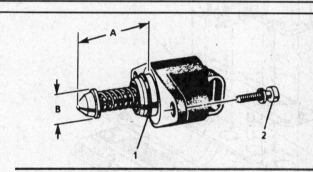

1 **IAC VALVE O-RING**

2 **IAC VALVE ATTACHING SCREW ASSEMBLY**

A **DISTANCE OF PINTLE EXTENSION**

B **DIAMETER OF PINTLE**

FIG. 15B Idle air control (IAC) valve

Idle Air Control (IAC) Valve

REMOVAL & INSTALLATION

▶ SEE FIG. 15B
1. Disconnect the negative battery cable.
2. Disconnect the electrical connector from the IAC valve.
3. Remove the IAC valve.
To Install:

❄ WARNING

Before installing a NEW idle air

control valve, measure the distance that the valve extends (from the tip of the valve pintle and the flange mounting surface. The distance should be no greater than 1¹/₈ in. (28mm). If it extends too far, damage will occur to the valve when it is installed.

4. To adjust, exert firm pressure, with slight side to side movement, on the pintle to retract it.
5. Lubricate the IAC valve O-ring with clean engine oil.
6. Install the IAC valve assembly, coat the screws with the appropriate thread locking material and tighten the retaining screws to 27 inch lbs. (3.0 Nm).
7. Connect the electrical connector.

8. Reset the IAC pintle position as follows:

a. Disconnect the negative battery cable for at least 10 seconds to clear the ECM memory, if not disconnected in Step 1.

b. Reconnect the negative battery cable.

c. Start the engine and check for proper idle operation.

Upper Manifold Assembly

REMOVAL & INSTALLATION

◆ SEE FIGS. 15C-15D

1. Disconnect the negative battery cable.

2. Remove the air intake duct.

3. Remove the accelerator cable splash shield from the accelerator cable bracket.

4. Disconnect the accelerator, cruise and transmission control cables.

5. Disconnect the vacuum harness from the top of the air inlet.

6. Disconnect the PCV and power brake

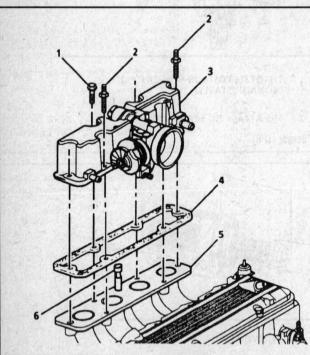

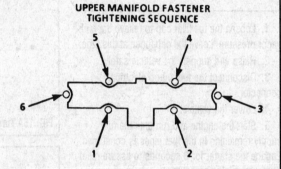

UPPER MANIFOLD FASTENER TIGHTENING SEQUENCE

1	BOLT
2	STUD
3	UPPER MANIFOLD ASSEMBLY
4	GASKET
5	LOWER MANIFOLD ASSEMBLY
6	EGR VALVE INJECTOR

FIG. 15C Upper manifold assembly — 2.2L (VIN 4)

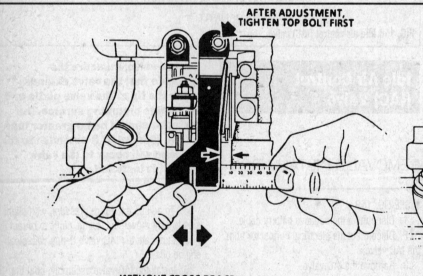

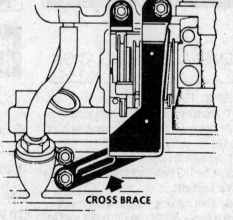

AFTER ADJUSTMENT, TIGHTEN TOP BOLT FIRST

WITHOUT CROSS BRACE:
ADJUST BRACKET TO PROVIDE 10mm ± 1mm (25/64" ± 1/32") CLEARANCE BETWEEN ACCELERATOR BRACKET AND THROTTLE BODY

CROSS BRACE

WITH CROSS BRACE:
NO ADJUSTMENT REQUIRED

FIG. 15D Accelerator bracket adjustment — 2.2L (VIN 4)

vacuum hoses from the vacuum tubes on the upper manifold.

7. Disconnect the electrical connectors at the MAP sensor, TPS and IAC valve.

8. Remove the bolts/nuts attaching the throttle cable bracket.

9. Position the EGR and injector wiring out of the way.

10. Remove the upper manifold and gasket and discard the gasket.

To Install:

11. Position the EGR valve injector so that the port faces directly towards the throttle bore.

12. Reposition the upper manifold assembly using a new gasket.

13. Reposition the EGR and injector wiring harness.

14. Install the upper manifold bolts/studs (in correct sequence — refer to the illustration) to 22 ft. lbs. (30 Nm).

15. Install the accelerator cable bracket with the attaching bolts/nuts finger tight at this time.

✳✳✳ WARNING

The accelerator bracket must be aligned with the accelerator cam to prevent cable wear, which could result in cable breakage.

16. Align the accelerator bracket as follows:

a. Place a steel rule across the bore of the throttle body, with one end in contact with the accelerator bracket.

b. Adjust the accelerator bracket to obtain a $\frac{25}{64}$ in. (9–11mm) gap between the bracket and the throttle body.

c. Tighten the top bolt first and tighten all bolts/nuts to 18 ft. lbs. (25 Nm).

17. Install the accelerator, cruise and transmission control cables.

18. Install the accelerator cable splash shield from the accelerator cable bracket.

19. Connect the electrical connectors at the MAP sensor, TPS, IAC valve and EGR vacuum solenoid.

20. Connect the vacuum harness to the top of the air inlet.

21. Connect the PCV and power brake vacuum hoses to the vacuum tubes on the upper manifold.

22. Connect the negative battery cable and turn the ignition **ON** for 2 seconds, **OFF** for 10 seconds, then **ON** and check for fuel leaks.

23. Install the air intake duct.

Lower Manifold Assembly

REMOVAL & INSTALLATION

▶ SEE FIG. 15E

1. Disconnect the negative battery cable.

2. Release the fuel system pressure.

3. Remove the upper manifold assembly.

4. Disconnect the quick connect fittings at the engine compartment fuel feed and return lines as follows:

a. Grasp both ends of one fuel line connection and twist $\frac{1}{4}$ turn in each direction to loosen any dirt in the quick connect fitting. Repeat for each fitting.

b. If compressed air is available, blow out the dirt from all quick connect fittings before removing.

c. Insert the correct size tool from J 37088–A tool set, into the female connector, then push inward to release the male connector.

d. Repeat for the other fitting.

5. Plug the fuel lines as required.

6. Remove the power steering pump brace.

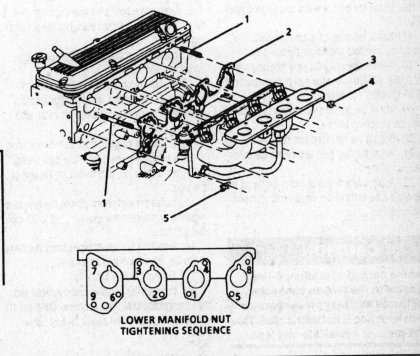

1	**STUD**
2	**GASKET**
3	**LOWER MANIFOLD ASSEMBLY**
4	**NUT**
5	**CLIP**

LOWER MANIFOLD NUT TIGHTENING SEQUENCE

FIG. 15E Lower manifold assembly — 2.2L (VIN 4)

7. Remove the engine fuel inlet pipe retainer nuts and retainers and disconnect the pipe and seal.

8. Remove the nut attaching the transmission fill tube on, automatic transaxles only.

Remove the lower manifold attaching nuts and remove the lower manifold. Discard the gasket.

To Install:

9. Transfer components to the replacement manifold as necessary.

10. Clean the gasket material from the sealing surfaces.

❊❊ WARNING

Use care when cleaning the machined aluminum surfaces. Sharp tools could damage the sealing surfaces.

11. Apply pipe sealant to the threaded ends of the EGR transfer pipe. Tighten the EGR transfer nuts to 20 ft.lbs. (27 Nm).

12. Position the EGR valve injector so that the port faces directly toward the throttle bore.

13. Position the lower manifold on the studs, install the nuts and tighten to 22 ft. lbs. (30 Nm) in the sequence shown in the illustration.

14. Install the nut attaching the transmission fill tube, on automatic transaxles.

15. Install a new fuel inlet pipe O-ring seal.

16. Install the inlet pipe nut and finger tighten only.

17. Install the support nut on the bottom of the lower manifold and finger tighten only.

18. Tighten the fuel inlet pipe retaining nut to 22 ft. lbs. (30 Nm). and the fuel pipe support nut to 89 inch lbs. (10 Nm).

19. Install the power steering pump brace with the attaching bolts.

20. Unplug the fuel feed and return lines.

21. Install the fuel feed and return line quick connect fittings.

22. Apply a few drops of clean engine oil to the male tube ends of the engine fuel feed and return pipes.

❊❊ CAUTION

During normal operation, O-rings, located in the female connector will swell and may prevent proper reconnection if not lubricated. This will prevent a possible fuel leak.

23. Push the connectors together to cause the retaining the retaining tabs/fingers to snap into place. Pull on both ends of each connection to make sure they are secure. Repeat for the other fitting.

24. Install the upper manifold assembly as outlined earlier in this section.

25. Tighten the fuel filler cap.

26. Connect the negative battery cable.

Pressure Regulator Assembly

REMOVAL & INSTALLATION

1. Relieve the fuel system pressure as outlined earlier.

2. Disconnect the negative battery cable.

3. Remove the vacuum hose from the regulator.

4. Place a rag under the connection and remove the fuel return pipe clamp.

5. Remove the fuel return pipe and O-ring from the regulator. Discard the O-ring.

6. Remove the pressure regulator bracket attaching screw.

7. Remove the pressure regulator assembly and O-ring. Discard the O-ring.

To Install:

8. Lubricate a new pressure regulator O-ring with clean engine oil, then install on the pressure regulator.

9. Install the pressure regulator assembly onto the manifold.

10. Install the pressure regulator bracket attaching screw coated with the appropriate thread locking material and tighten to 31 inch lbs. (3.5 Nm).

11. Install the vacuum hose to the regulator.

12. Lubricate a new fuel return pipe O-ring with clean engine oil, then install on the end of the pipe.

13. Install the fuel return pipe to the pressure regulator and tighten the attaching nut to 22 inch lbs. (30 Nm).

14. Install the fuel return pipe clamp attaching nut to the lower manifold assembly.

15. Tighten the fuel filler cap.

16. Connect the negative battery cable and turn the ignition **ON** for 2 seconds, **OFF** for 10 seconds, then **ON** and check for fuel leaks.

Bottom Feed Port Fuel Injectors

REMOVAL & INSTALLATION

❊❊ WARNING

Any time the injectors are removed for service, always remove the fuel pressure regulator to drain excess fuel, and prevent fuel from entering the engine cylinders. Flooded cylinders could result in engine damage.

1. Relieve the fuel system pressure as outlined earlier.

2. Disconnect the negative battery cable.

3. Remove the upper manifold assembly, as outlined earlier in this section.

❊❊ CAUTION

To reduce the chance of personal injury, cover the fuel line connections with a shop towel, when disconnecting.

4. Disconnect the fuel return line retaining bracket nut and move the return line away from the regulator.

5. Remove the pressure regulator assembly.

❊❊ WARNING

Do not try to remove the injectors by lifting up on the injector retaining bracket while the injectors are still installed in the in the bracket slots or damage to the bracket and/or injectors could result. Do not attempt to remove the bracket without first removing the pressure regulator.

6. Remove the injector retainer bracket attaching screws and carefully slide the bracket off to clear the injector slots and regulator.

7. Disconnect the injector electrical connectors.

8. Remove the fuel injector(s) and discard the O-ring seals.

✳ CAUTION

To reduce the risk fire and personal injury, make sure that the lower (small) O-ring of each injector does not remain in the lower manifold. If the O-ring is not removed with the injector, the replacement injector, with new O-rings, will not seat properly in the injector socket and could cause a fuel leak.

9. Cover the injector sockets to prevent dirt from entering the opening.

➡ **Each injector is calibrated with a different flow rate. Replace with the identical part numbers.**

To install:

10. Lubricate the new injector O-ring seals with clean engine oil and install on the injector assembly.

11. Install the injector assembly into the lower manifold injector socket, with the electrical connectors facing inward.

12. Carefully position the injector retainer bracket so that the injector retaining slots and regulator are aligned with the bracket slots.

13. Install the injector electrical connectors.

14. Install the pressure regulator assembly.

15. Install the injector retainer bracket retaining screws, coated with thread locking material and tighten to 31 inch lbs. (3.5 Nm).

16. Install the accelerator cable bracket with the attaching bolts/nuts finger tight at this time.

✳ WARNING

The accelerator bracket must be aligned with the accelerator cam to prevent cable wear, which could result in cable breakage.

17. Align the accelerator bracket as follows:

a. Place a steel rule across the bore of the throttle body, with one end in contact with the accelerator bracket.

b. Adjust the accelerator bracket to obtain a $^{25}/_{64}$ in. (9–11mm) gap between the bracket and the throttle body.

c. Tighten the top bolt first and tighten all bolts/nuts to 18 ft. lbs. (25 Nm).

18. Tighten the fuel filer cap.

19. Connect the negative battery cable and turn the ignition **ON** for 2 seconds, **OFF** for 10 seconds, then **ON** and check for fuel leaks.

20. Install the air intake duct.

GENERAL MOTORS MULTI-PORT (MFI) & SEQUENTIAL (SFI) FUEL INJECTION SYSTEMS

General Information

On 1985–92 2.8 and 3.1L V6 engines, multi-port fuel injection (MFI) system is available. The MFI system is controlled by an electronic control module (ECM) which monitors engine operations and generates output signals to provide the correct air/fuel mixture, ignition timing and engine idle speed control. Input to the control unit is provided by an oxygen sensor, coolant temperature sensor, detonation sensor, hot film air mass sensor and throttle position sensor. The ECM also receives information concerning engine rpm, road speed, transmission gear position, power steering and air conditioning.

On 1.8L, 2.0L OHC, turbocharged models, a sequential port fuel injection system (SFI) is used for more precise fuel control. With SFI, metered fuel is timed and injected sequentially through injectors into individual cylinder ports. Each cylinder receives one injection per working cycle (every two revolutions), just prior to the opening of the intake valve. The main difference between the two types of fuel injection systems is the manner in which fuel is injected. In the multiport system, all injectors work simultaneously, injecting half the fuel charge each engine revolution. The control units are different for SFI and MFI systems, but most other components are similar. In addition, the SFI system incorporates a new Computer Controlled Coil Ignition system that uses an electronic coil module that replaces the conventional distributor and coil used on most engines. An electronic spark control (ESC) is used to adjust the spark timing.

➡ **The 1992 2.0L (VIN 4) uses a Alternating Synchronous Double Fire Fuel Injection (ASDF) type system.**

Both systems use Bosch injectors, one at each intake port, rather than the single injector found on the earlier throttle body system. The injectors are mounted on a fuel rail and are activated by a signal from the electronic control module. The injector is a solenoid-operated valve which remains open depending on the width of the electronic pulses (length of the signal) from the ECM; the longer the open time, the more fuel is injected. In this manner, the air/fuel mixture can be precisely controlled for maximum performance with minimum emissions.

Fuel is pumped from the tank by a high pressure fuel pump, located inside the fuel tank. It is a positive displacement roller vane pump. The impeller serves as a vapor separator and pre-charges the high pressure assembly. A pressure regulator maintains 28-36 psi (28-50 psi on turbocharged engines) in the fuel line to the injectors and the excess fuel is fed back to the tank. On MFI systems, a fuel accumulator is used to dampen the hydraulic line hammer in the system created when all injectors open simultaneously.

The Mass Air Flow Sensor is used to measure the mass of air that is drawn into the engine cylinders. It is located just ahead of the air throttle in the intake system and consists of a heated film which measures the mass of air, rather than just the volume. A resistor is used to measure the temperature of the incoming air and the air mass sensor maintains the temperature of the film at 75° above ambient temperature. As the ambient (outside) air temperature rises, more energy is required to maintain the heated film at the higher temperature and the control unit uses this difference in required energy to calculate the mass of the incoming air. The control unit uses this information to determine the duration of fuel injection pulse, timing and EGR.

The throttle body incorporates an idle air control (IAC) that provides for a bypass channel through which air can flow. It consists of an orifice and pintle which is controlled by the ECM through a stepper motor. The IAC provides air flow for idle and allows additional air during cold start until the engine reaches operating temperature. As the engine temperature rises, the opening through which air passes is slowly closed.

The throttle position sensor (TPS) provides the control unit with information on throttle position, in order to determine injector pulse width and hence correct mixture. The TPS is connected to the throttle shaft on the throttle body and consists of a potentiometer with one end connected to a 5 volt source from the ECM and the other to ground. A third wire is connected to the ECM to measure the voltage output from the TPS which changes as the throttle valve angle is changed (accelerator pedal moves). At the closed throttle position, the output is low (approximately 0.4 volts); as the throttle valve opens, the output increases to a maximum 5 volts at wide open throttle (WOT). The TPS can be misadjusted open, shorted, or loose and if it is out of adjustment, the idle quality or WOT performance may be poor. A loose TPS can cause intermittent bursts of fuel from the injectors and an unstable idle because the ECM thinks the throttle is moving. This should cause a trouble code to be set. Once a trouble code is set, the ECM will use a preset value for TPS and some vehicle performance may return. A small amount of engine coolant is routed through the throttle assembly to prevent freezing inside the throttle bore during cold operation.

FUEL PRESSURE RELEASE

To reduce the risk of fire or personal injury, it is necessary to relieve the fuel system pressure before servicing the fuel system.

1.8L and 2.0L OHC Engines

1983-84

1. Remove the fuel pump fuse from the fuse block.
2. Crank the engine. The engine will run until it runs out of fuel. Crank the engine again for 3 seconds making sure it is out of fuel.
3. Turn the ignition **OFF** and replace the fuse.

1985-90

1. Disconnect the negative battery cable.
2. Disconnect the fuel filler cap.

3. Connect gauge J–34730–1 or equivalent, to the fuel pressure connection. Wrap a cloth around the fitting to absorb any fuel leakage.
4. Install the bleed hose into an approved container and open the valve to bleed system pressure.

1992 (VIN H)

1. Remove the fuel pump fuse from the fuse block.
2. Crank the engine. The engine will run until it runs out of fuel. Crank the engine again for 3 seconds making sure it is out of fuel.
3. Turn the ignition **OFF** and replace the fuse.

2.8L and 3.1L V6 Engines

1987–92

1. Disconnect the negative battery cable.
2. Disconnect the fuel filler cap.
3. Connect gauge J–34730–1 or equivalent, to the fuel pressure connection. Wrap a cloth around the fitting to absorb any fuel leakage.
4. Install the bleed hose into an approved container and open the valve to bleed system pressure.

FUEL SYSTEM PRESSURE TEST

1.8L and 2.0L OHC Engine

1984–85

1. Connect pressure gauge J-34370-1, or equivalent, to fuel pressure test point on the fuel rail. Wrap a rag around the pressure tap to absorb any leakage that may occur when installing the gauge.
2. Turn the ignition **OFF** for 10 seconds and the A/C **OFF**.
3. Turn the ignition **ON** and the fuel pump should run for about 2 seconds.
4. Note the fuel pressure after the pump stops. The pressure should be 30–40 psi and hold steady.

1986

1. Connect pressure gauge J-34370-1, or equivalent, to fuel pressure test point on the fuel rail. Wrap a rag around the pressure tap to absorb any leakage that may occur when installing the gauge.
2. Using a fused jumper, run the fuel pump by applying 12 volts to the fuel pump test terminal for several seconds.
3. Note the fuel pressure after the pump stops. The pressure should be 30–40 psi and hold steady.

1987–90

1. Connect pressure gauge J-34370-1, or equivalent, to fuel pressure test point on the fuel rail. Wrap a rag around the pressure tap to absorb any leakage that may occur when installing the gauge.
2. Disconnect the vacuum hose from the pressure regulator.
3. Turn the ignition **OFF** for 10 seconds and the A/C **OFF**.
4. Turn the ignition **ON** and the fuel pump should run for about 2 seconds.
5. Note the fuel pressure after the pump stops. The pressure should be 35–38 psi and hold steady.

2.8L and 3.1L Engine

1. Connect pressure gauge J-34370-1, or equivalent, to fuel pressure test point on the fuel rail. Wrap a rag around the pressure tap to absorb any leakage that may occur when installing the gauge.
2. Turn the ignition **OFF** for 10 seconds and the A/C **OFF**.
3. Turn the ignition **ON** and the fuel pump should run for about 2 seconds.
4. Note the fuel pressure after the pump stops. The pressure should be 40.5–47 psi and hold steady.

Fuel Pump

REMOVAL & INSTALLATION

1. Release the fuel system pressure.

❈❈❈ CAUTION

To reduce the risk of fire or personal injury, it is necessary to relieve the fuel system pressure before servicing the fuel system. Refer to Fuel System Pressure Release procedure above.

2. Disconnect the negative battery cable.
3. Jack up the car and support it safely.
4. Remove the fuel tank.
5. Remove the fuel lever sending unit and pump assembly by turning the cam lock ring counterclockwise. Lift the assembly from the fuel tank and remove the fuel pump from the fuel level sending unit.
6. Pull the fuel pump up into the attaching hose or pulsator while pulling outward away

from the bottom support. After the pump is clear of the bottom support, pull the pump assembly out of the rubber connector or pulsator for removal.

To Install:

7. Position and push the pump into the attaching hose.

8. Install the fuel level sending unit and pump assembly into the tank assembly. Use new O-ring during reassembly.

❋❋ WARNING

Be careful not to fold over or twist the strainer when installing the sending unit as it will restrict fuel flow. Also, be careful the strainer does not block full travel of the float arm.

9. Install the cam lock over the assembly and lock by turning clockwise.

10. Install the fuel tank.

Fuel Injectors

REMOVAL & INSTALLATION

1.8L, 2.0L OHC Engines

▶ SEE FIGS. 16-17

❋❋ WARNING

Use care in removing the fuel injectors to prevent damage to the electrical connector pins on the injector and the nozzle. The fuel injector is serviced as a complete assembly only and should not be immersed in any kind of cleaner.

1. Relieve fuel system pressure.
2. Remove the injector electrical connections.
3. Remove the fuel rail.
4. Separate the injector from the fuel rail.
5. Installation is the reverse of removal. Replace the O-rings when installing injectors into intake manifold.

2.8L V6 Engines

1985-86

Each port injector is located and held in

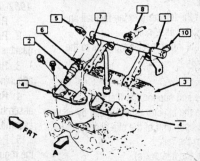

1. Fuel rail assembly
2. Injector
3. Intake manifold
4. Injector housing assembly
5. Injector retaining clip
6. Injector retaining groove
7. Injector cup flange
8. Injector control harness
9. Pressure regulator
10. Fuel pressure test point

FIG. 16 Exploded view of the fuel rail and injector assembly — 1983-87 1.8L and 2.0L OHC engine

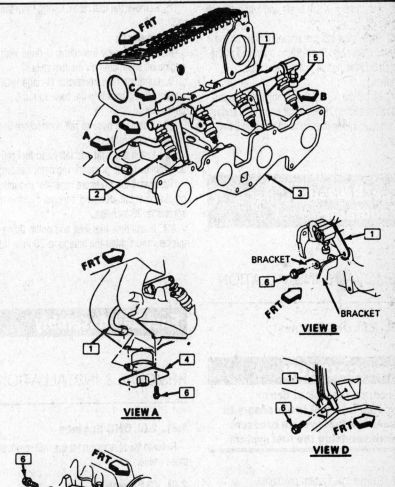

1. Fuel rail assembly
2. Injector
3. Intake manifold
4. Pressure regulator asm.
5. Fuel pressure gage test point
6. Bolt/screw (20-27 N·m)

FIG. 17 Exploded view of the fuel rail and injectors — 1988-90 2.0L OHC engine

position by a retainer clip that must be rotated to release and/or lock the injector in place.

1. Rotate the injector retaining clip(s) the the unlocked position.
2. Remove the port injectors.
3. Install new O-ring seals and lubricate with engine oil.
4. Position the injectors to the fuel rail and pressure regulator assembly.
5. Rotate the injector retaining clips to the locking position.

1987-92

1. Remove and support the fuel rail.
2. Remove the injector retaining clip by spreading the open end of the clip slightly and removing from the rail.
3. Remove the injector(s).
4. Remove the O-rings from both ends of the injectors.
5. Install new O-ring seals and lubricate with engine oil.
6. Place new injector retaining clips on the injector assembly. Position the open end of the clip so it is facing the injector electrical connector.
7. Install the injector assembly(ies) into the fuel rail socket(s). Push in far enough to engage the retainer clip with machined slots on the socket.

Fuel Pressure Regulator

REMOVAL & INSTALLATION

1.8L, 2.0L OHC Engines

❄❄❄ CAUTION

To reduce the risk of fire or personal injury, it is necessary to relieve the fuel system pressure before servicing the fuel system.

1. Relieve fuel system pressure.
2. Remove pressure regulator from fuel rail. Place a rag around the base of the regulator to catch any spilled fuel.
3. Installation is the reverse of removal procedure.

2.8L V6 engine

1985-86

The pressure regulator is factory adjusted and is not serviceable. Do not attempt to remove the regulator from the fuel rail.

1987-92

1. Remove and support the fuel rail.
2. Remove the fuel inlet and outlet fittings and gaskets.
3. Remove the pressure regulator bracket attaching screws and mounting bracket.
4. Remove the right and left hand fuel rail assemblies from the pressure regulator assembly.
5. Remove the base to rail connectors from the regulator or rails.
6. Disassemble connector O-rings from the base to rail connectors.
7. Remove the fuel return O-ring from the fuel rails.

To Install:

8. Lubricate new fuel return O-rings with engine oil and install on the fuel rails.
9. Lubricate new connector O-rings with engine oil and install to the base to rail connectors.
10. Install the base to rail connectors in the regulator assembly.
11. Install the right and left hand fuel rail assemblies to the pressure regulator assembly.
12. Install the pressure regulator mounting bracket with the attaching screws. Tighten the screws to 28 inch lbs.
13. Install new fuel inlet and outlet fitting gaskets and tighten the fittings to 20 inch lbs.

Fuel Rail Assembly

REMOVAL & INSTALLATION

1.8L, 2.0L OHC Engines

Refer to the illustration for fuel rail removal on these models.

2.8L V6 Engine

1985-86
♦ SEE FIG. 18
1. Disconnect the negative battery cable.

❄❄❄ CAUTION

To reduce the risk of fire or personal injury, it is necessary to relieve the fuel system pressure before servicing the fuel system.

2. Relieve fuel system pressure. Refer to the procedure above.
3. Remove the intake manifold plenum.
   a. Disconnect the vacuum lines.
   b. Remove the EGR-to-plenum nuts.
   c. Remove the two throttle body bolts.
   d. Remove the throttle cable to bracket bolts.
   e. Remove the plenum bolts and remove the plenum and gasket.
4. Remove the cold start valve and tube assembly.
5. Remove the retaining nut from the stud for the fuel lines at the head.
6. Disconnect the fuel lines at the rail.
7. Disconnect the vacuum line at the regulator.
8. Remove the rail retaining bolts.
9. Disconnect the injector electrical connectors.
10. Remove the fuel rail assembly.
11. To install use new injector O-rings and lubricate with engine oil.
12. Reverse the removal procedure.

1987-92
♦ SEE FIG. 19
1. Disconnect the negative battery cable.

❄❄❄ CAUTION

To reduce the risk of fire or personal injury, it is necessary to relieve the fuel system pressure before servicing the fuel system.

2. Relieve fuel system pressure. Refer to the procedure above.
3. Remove the intake manifold plenum.
   a. Disconnect the vacuum lines.
   b. Remove the EGR-to-plenum nuts.
   c. Remove the two throttle body bolts.
   d. Remove the throttle cable to bracket bolts.
   e. Remove the ignition wire plastic shield bolts.
   f. Remove the plenum bolts and remove the plenum and gasket.

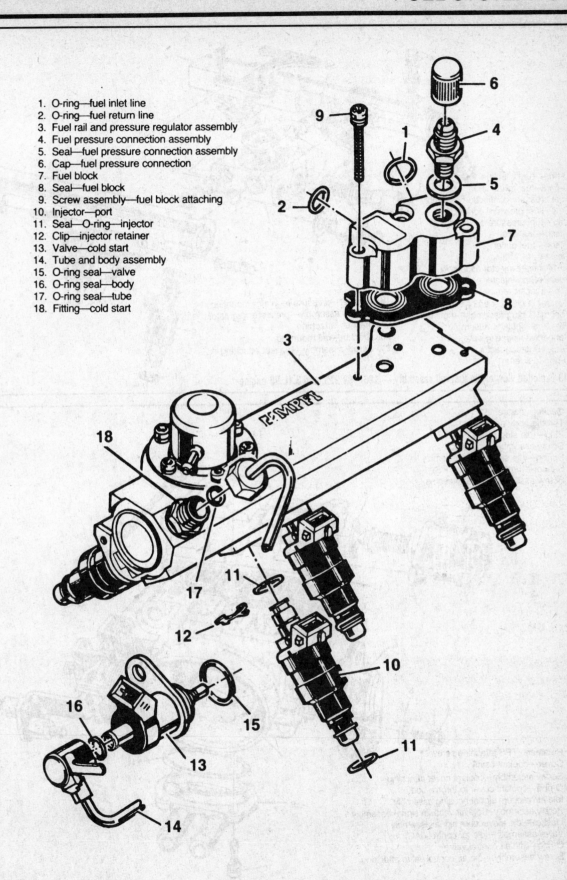

1. O-ring—fuel inlet line
2. O-ring—fuel return line
3. Fuel rail and pressure regulator assembly
4. Fuel pressure connection assembly
5. Seal—fuel pressure connection assembly
6. Cap—fuel pressure connection
7. Fuel block
8. Seal—fuel block
9. Screw assembly—fuel block attaching
10. Injector—port
11. Seal—O-ring—injector
12. Clip—injector retainer
13. Valve—cold start
14. Tube and body assembly
15. O-ring seal—valve
16. O-ring seal—body
17. O-ring seal—tube
18. Fitting—cold start

FIG. 18 Exploded view of the fuel rail assembly — 1985–86 2.8L V6 engine

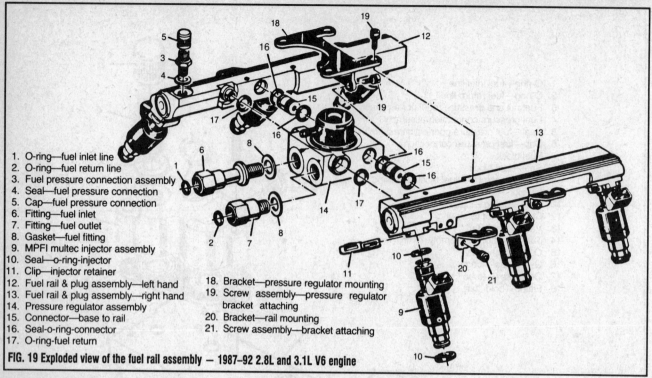

1. O-ring—fuel inlet line
2. O-ring—fuel return line
3. Fuel pressure connection assembly
4. Seal—fuel pressure connection
5. Cap—fuel pressure connection
6. Fitting—fuel inlet
7. Fitting—fuel outlet
8. Gasket—fuel fitting
9. MPFI multec injector assembly
10. Seal—o-ring-injector
11. Clip—injector retainer
12. Fuel rail & plug assembly—left hand
13. Fuel rail & plug assembly—right hand
14. Pressure regulator assembly
15. Connector—base to rail
16. Seal-o-ring-connector
17. O-ring-fuel return
18. Bracket—pressure regulator mounting
19. Screw assembly—pressure regulator bracket attaching
20. Bracket—rail mounting
21. Screw assembly—bracket attaching

FIG. 19 Exploded view of the fuel rail assembly — 1987–92 2.8L and 3.1L V6 engine

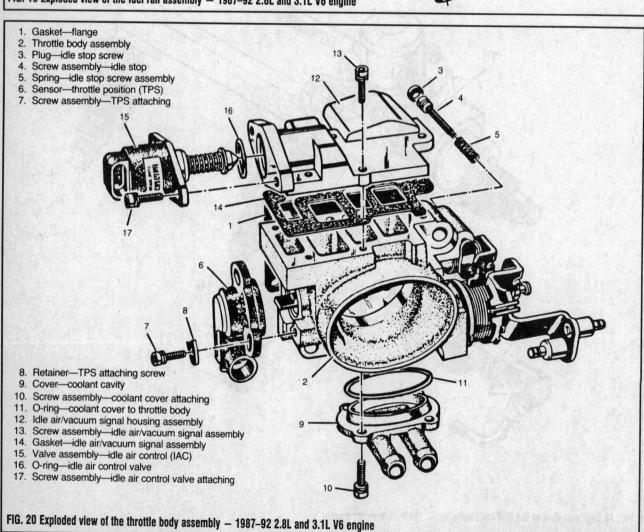

1. Gasket—flange
2. Throttle body assembly
3. Plug—idle stop screw
4. Screw assembly—idle stop
5. Spring—idle stop screw assembly
6. Sensor—throttle position (TPS)
7. Screw assembly—TPS attaching
8. Retainer—TPS attaching screw
9. Cover—coolant cavity
10. Screw assembly—coolant cover attaching
11. O-ring—coolant cover to throttle body
12. Idle air/vacuum signal housing assembly
13. Screw assembly—idle air/vacuum signal assembly
14. Gasket—idle air/vacuum signal assembly
15. Valve assembly—idle air control (IAC)
16. O-ring—idle air control valve
17. Screw assembly—idle air control valve attaching

FIG. 20 Exploded view of the throttle body assembly — 1987–92 2.8L and 3.1L V6 engine

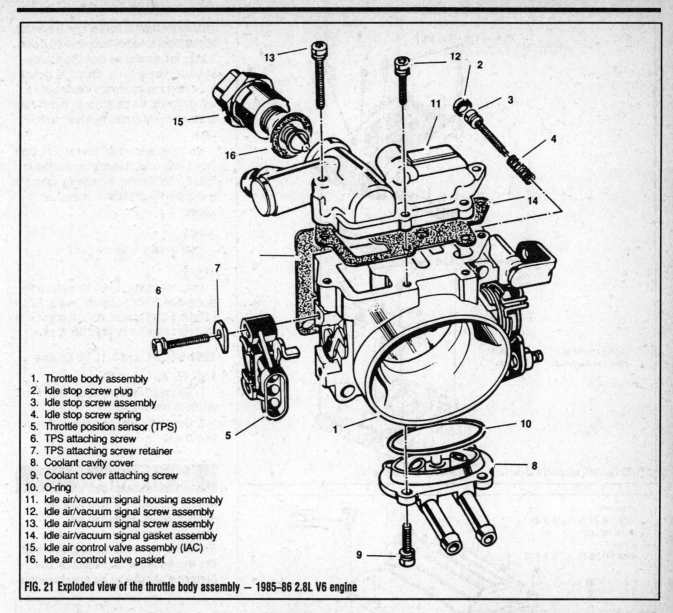

1. Throttle body assembly
2. Idle stop screw plug
3. Idle stop screw assembly
4. Idle stop screw spring
5. Throttle position sensor (TPS)
6. TPS attaching screw
7. TPS attaching screw retainer
8. Coolant cavity cover
9. Coolant cover attaching screw
10. O-ring
11. Idle air/vacuum signal housing assembly
12. Idle air/vacuum signal screw assembly
13. Idle air/vacuum signal screw assembly
14. Idle air/vacuum signal gasket assembly
15. Idle air control valve assembly (IAC)
16. Idle air control valve gasket

FIG. 21 Exploded view of the throttle body assembly — 1985–86 2.8L V6 engine

4. Remove the fuel line bracket bolt.
5. Disconnect the fuel lines at the rail.

❈ CAUTION

Wrap a cloth around the fuel lines to collect fuel, then place the fuel in an approved container.

6. Remove the fuel line O-rings.
7. Disconnect the vacuum line at the pressure regulator.
8. Remove the four rail retaining bolts.
9. Disconnect the injector electrical connectors.
10. Remove the fuel rail assembly.
11. Remove the O-ring seal from each of the spray tip end of the injector.

To Install:

12. Lubricate new the O-ring seals and install to each of the spray tip ends of the injector.
13. Install the fuel rail assembly in the intake manifold and tilt the rail assembly and install the injectors.
14. Install the fuel rail attaching bolts and tighten to 19 ft. lbs.
15. Install the injector electrical connectors.
16. Install the vacuum line at the pressure regulator.
17. Install new O-rings on the inlet and return fuel lines.
18. Use a back-up wrench and install the fuel inlet and outlet fittings.
19. Connect the negative battery cable.

Idle Air Control Valve

REMOVAL & INSTALLATION

1985–86 2.8L V6 engine
1983–90 2.0L OHC engine
1992 (VIN H)

◆ SEE FIG. 24

1. Remove electrical connector from idle air control valve.
2. Remove the idle air control valve using a suitable wrench.
3. Installation is the reverse of removal. Before installing the idle air control valve,

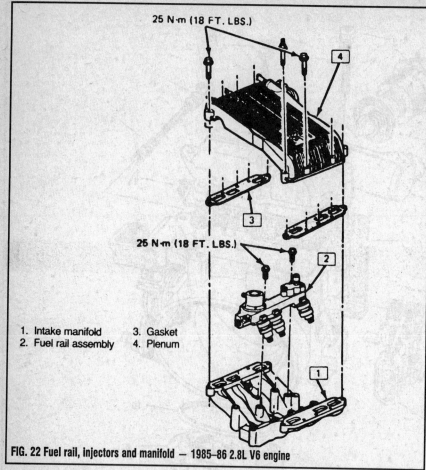

1. Intake manifold
2. Fuel rail assembly
3. Gasket
4. Plenum

25 N·m (18 FT. LBS.)

25 N·m (18 FT. LBS.)

FIG. 22 Fuel rail, injectors and manifold — 1985–86 2.8L V6 engine

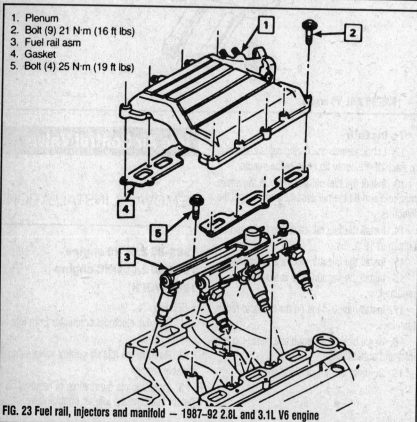

1. Plenum
2. Bolt (9) 21 N·m (16 ft lbs)
3. Fuel rail asm
4. Gasket
5. Bolt (4) 25 N·m (19 ft lbs)

FIG. 23 Fuel rail, injectors and manifold — 1987–92 2.8L and 3.1L V6 engine

measure the distance that the valve is extended. Measurement should be made from the motor housing to the end of the cone. The distance should not exceed 1⅛ in. (28mm), or damage to the valve may occur when installed. Use a new gasket and turn the ignition on then off again to allow the ECM to reset the idle air control valve.

Identify replacement IAC valve as being either Type 1 (with collar at electric terminal end) or Type 2 (without collar). If measuring distance is greater than specified above, proceed as follows:

TYPE 1

Press on valve firmly to retract it.

TYPE 2

Compress retaining spring from valve while turning valve in with a clockwise motion. Return spring to original position with straight portion of spring end aligned with flat surface of valve.

1987-92 2.8L and 3.1L V6 Engine

▶ SEE FIG. 25

1. Disconnect the electrical connector from the idle air control valve.

3. Remove the retaining screws and remove the IAC valve.

❊❊ WARNING

Before installing a new idle air control valve, measure the distance that the valve extends (from the tip of the valve pintle and the flange mounting surface. The distance should be no greater than

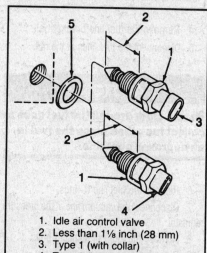

1. Idle air control valve
2. Less than 1⅛ inch (28 mm)
3. Type 1 (with collar)
4. Type 2 (without collar)
5. Gasket

FIG. 24 Idle air control valves used on the 1985–86 2.8L and 1983–90 2.0L OHC engine

28mm. If it extends too far, damage will occur to the valve when it is installed.

4. To adjust, exert firm pressure, with slight side to side movement, on the pintle to retract it.

5. To complete the installation, use a new seal lubricated with engine oil and install the IAC assembly. Tighten the screws to 30 inch lbs. Install the electrical connector. Start the engine and allow it to reach operating temperature.

➡ **The ECM will reset whenever the engine is started and then shut off.**

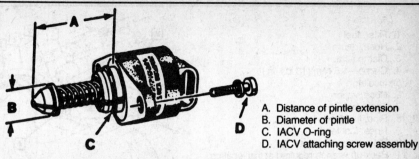

A. Distance of pintle extension
B. Diameter of pintle
C. IACV O-ring
D. IACV attaching screw assembly

FIG. 25 Idle air control valve used on the 1987–92 2.8L and 3.1L V6 engine

FUEL TANK

REMOVAL & INSTALLATION

♦ SEE FIGS. 26-29

1. Disconnect the negative cable at the battery. Raise and support the car.

2. Drain the tank. There is no drain plug; remaining fuel in the tank must be siphoned through the fuel feed line (the line to the fuel pump), because of the restrict in the filler neck.

3. Disconnect the hose and the vapor return hose from the level sending unit fittings.

4. Remove the ground wire screw.

5. Unplug the level sending unit electrical connector.

6. Disconnect the vent hose.

7. Unbolt the support straps, and lower and remove the tank. Installation is the reverse of removal.

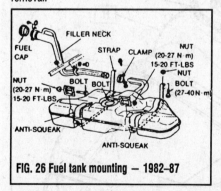

FIG. 26 Fuel tank mounting — 1982–87

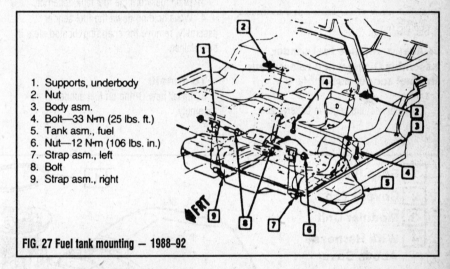

1. Supports, underbody
2. Nut
3. Body asm.
4. Bolt—33 N·m (25 lbs. ft.)
5. Tank asm., fuel
6. Nut—12 N·m (106 lbs. in.)
7. Strap asm., left
8. Bolt
9. Strap asm., right

FIG. 27 Fuel tank mounting — 1988–92

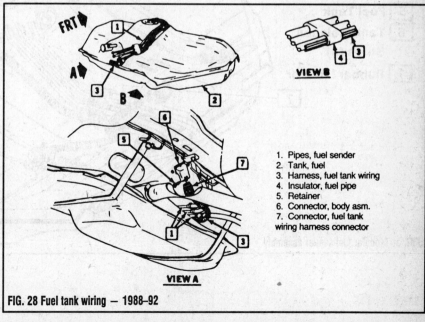

1. Pipes, fuel sender
2. Tank, fuel
3. Harness, fuel tank wiring
4. Insulator, fuel pipe
5. Retainer
6. Connector, body asm.
7. Connector, fuel tank wiring harness connector

FIG. 28 Fuel tank wiring — 1988–92

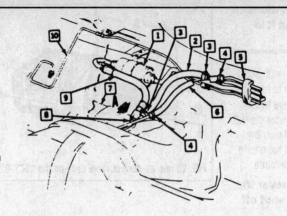

1. Filter, fuel
2. Hose, return
3. Clamp asm.
4. Clamp—1.5 N·m (13 lbs. in.)
5. Insulator
6. Hose, vapor
7. Tank, fuel
8. Pipe, fuel feed
9. Hose, fuel feed
10. Pipe, rear cross-over
11. Back-up wrench required at this location
12. Seal O-ring
13. Fitting—27 N·m (20 lbs. ft.)

VIEW A

FIG. 29 Fuel tank unit hoses — 1988–92

MODULAR FUEL SENDER ASSEMBLY REPLACEMENT

◆ SEE FIG. 30

➡ **Always replace fuel sender assembly O-ring when reinstalling the fuel sender assembly**

1. Disconnect the negative battery cable.

2. Relieve fuel system pressure — refer to the necessary service procedures.

3. Drain fuel from the fuel tank assembly.

4. While holding down the fuel sender assembly, remove the snap ring located slots in the retainer.

To Install:

5. Install new O-ring on fuel sender to tank assembly.

6. Align tab on front of sender with the slot on front of the retainer snapring.

7. Slowly apply pressure to top of the spring loaded sender until sender aligns flush with retainer on tank assembly.

8. Install snapring into correct position. Be sure that the snapring is fully seated in the retainer.

9. Install fuel tank, lower vehicle and refill the gas tank. Check system for proper operation.

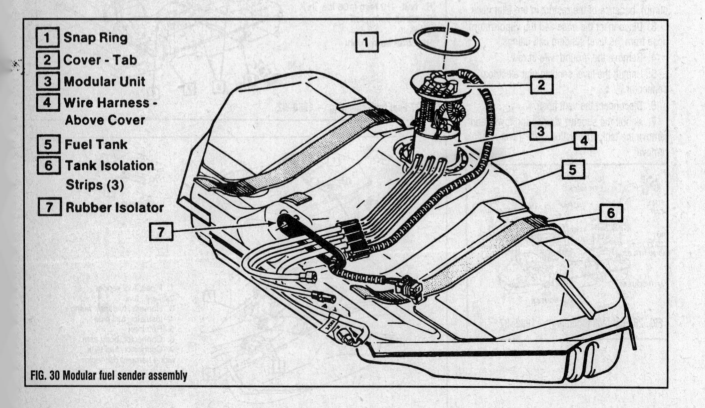

1	Snap Ring
2	Cover - Tab
3	Modular Unit
4	Wire Harness - Above Cover
5	Fuel Tank
6	Tank Isolation Strips (3)
7	Rubber Isolator

FIG. 30 Modular fuel sender assembly

6

CHASSIS ELECTRICAL

TROUBLESHOOTING ELECTRICAL SYSTEMS

With the rate at which both import and domestic manufacturers are incorporating electronic control systems into their production lines, it won't be long before every new vehicle is equipped with one or more on-board computer. These electronic components (with no moving parts) should theoretically last the life of the vehicle, provided nothing external happens to damage the circuits or memory chips.

While it is true that electronic components should never wear out, in the real world malfunctions do occur. It is also true that any computer-based system is extremely sensitive to electrical voltages and cannot tolerate careless or haphazard testing or service procedures. An inexperienced individual can literally do major damage looking for a minor problem by using the wrong kind of test equipment or connecting test leads or connectors with the ignition switch ON. When selecting test equipment, make sure the manufacturers instructions state that the tester is compatible with whatever type of electronic control system is being serviced. Read all instructions carefully and double check all test points before installing probes or making any test connections.

The following section outlines basic diagnosis techniques for dealing with computerized automotive control systems. Along with a general explanation of the various types of test equipment available to aid in servicing modern electronic automotive systems, basic repair techniques for wiring harnesses and connectors is given. Read the basic information before attempting any repairs or testing on any computerized system, to provide the background of information necessary to avoid the most common and obvious mistakes that can cost both time and money. Although the replacement and testing procedures are simple in themselves, the systems are not, and unless one has a thorough understanding of all components and their function within a particular computerized control system, the logical test sequence these systems demand cannot be followed. Minor malfunctions can make a big difference, so it is important to know how each component affects the operation of the overall electronic system to find the ultimate cause of a problem without replacing good components unnecessarily. It is not enough to use the correct test equipment; the test equipment must be used correctly.

Safety Precautions

✳✳✳ CAUTION

Whenever working on or around any computer based microprocessor control system, always observe these general precautions to prevent the possibility of personal injury or damage to electronic components.

• Never install or remove battery cables with the key ON or the engine running. Jumper cables should be connected with the key OFF to avoid power surges that can damage electronic control units. Engines equipped with computer controlled systems should avoid both giving and getting jump starts due to the possibility of serious damage to components from arcing in the engine compartment when connections are made with the ignition ON.

• Always remove the battery cables before charging the battery. Never use a high output charger on an installed battery or attempt to use any type of "hot shot" (24 volt) starting aid.

• Exercise care when inserting test probes into connectors to insure good connections without damaging the connector or spreading the pins. Always probe connectors from the rear (wire) side, NOT the pin side, to avoid accidental shorting of terminals during test procedures.

• Never remove or attach wiring harness connectors with the ignition switch ON, especially to an electronic control unit.

• Do not drop any components during service procedures and never apply 12 volts directly to any component (like a solenoid or relay) unless instructed specifically to do so. Some component electrical windings are designed to safely handle only 4 or 5 volts and can be destroyed in seconds if 12 volts are applied directly to the connector.

• Remove the electronic control unit if the vehicle is to be placed in an environment where temperatures exceed approximately 176°F (80°C), such as a paint spray booth or when arc or gas welding near the control unit location in the car.

ORGANIZED TROUBLESHOOTING

When diagnosing a specific problem, organized troubleshooting is a must. The complexity of a modern automobile demands that you approach any problem in a logical, organized manner. There are certain troubleshooting techniques that are standard:

1. Establish when the problem occurs. Does the problem appear only under certain conditions? Were there any noises, odors, or other unusual symptoms?

2. Isolate the problem area. To do this, make some simple tests and observations; then eliminate the systems that are working properly. Check for obvious problems such as broken wires, dirty connections or split or disconnected vacuum hoses. Always check the obvious before assuming something complicated is the cause.

3. Test for problems systematically to determine the cause once the problem area is isolated. Are all the components functioning properly? Is there power going to electrical switches and motors? Is there vacuum at vacuum switches and/or actuators? Is there a mechanical problem such as bent linkage or loose mounting screws? Doing careful, systematic checks will often turn up most causes on the first inspection without wasting time checking components that have little or no relationship to the problem.

4. Test all repairs after the work is done to make sure that the problem is fixed. Some causes can be traced to more than one component, so a careful verification of repair work is important to pick up additional malfunctions that may cause a problem to reappear or a different problem to arise. A blown fuse, for example, is a simple problem that may require more than another fuse to repair. If you don't look for a problem that caused a fuse to blow, for example, a shorted wire may go undetected.

Experience has shown that most problems tend to be the result of a fairly simple and obvious cause, such as loose or corroded connectors or air leaks in the intake system; making careful inspection of components during testing essential to quick and accurate troubleshooting. Special, hand held computerized testers designed specifically for diagnosing the system are available from a variety of aftermarket sources, as well as from the vehicle manufacturer, but care should be taken that any test equipment being used is designed to diagnose that particular computer controlled system accurately without damaging the control unit (ECU) or components being tested.

➡ **Pinpointing the exact cause of trouble in an electrical system can sometimes only be accomplished by the use of special test equipment. The following describes commonly used test equipment and explains how to put it to best use in diagnosis. In addition to the information covered below, the manufacturer's instructions booklet provided with the tester should be read and clearly understood before attempting any test procedures.**

TEST EQUIPMENT

Jumper Wires

Jumper wires are simple, yet extremely valuable, pieces of test equipment. Jumper wires are merely wires that are used to bypass sections of a circuit. The simplest type of jumper wire is merely a length of multistrand wire with an alligator clip at each end. Jumper wires are usually fabricated from lengths of standard automotive wire and whatever type of connector (alligator clip, spade connector or pin connector) that is required for the particular vehicle being tested. The well equipped tool box will have several different styles of jumper wires in several different lengths. Some jumper wires are made with three or more terminals coming from a common splice for special purpose testing. In cramped, hard-to-reach areas it is advisable to have insulated boots over the jumper wire terminals in order to prevent accidental grounding, sparks, and possible fire, especially when testing fuel system components.

Jumper wires are used primarily to locate open electrical circuits, on either the ground (-) side of the circuit or on the hot (+) side. If an electrical component fails to operate, connect the jumper wire between the component and a good ground. If the component operates only with the jumper installed, the ground circuit is open. If the ground circuit is good, but the component does not operate, the circuit between the power feed and component is open. You can sometimes connect the jumper wire directly from the battery to the hot terminal of the component, but first make sure the component uses 12 volts in operation. Some electrical

components, such as fuel injectors, are designed to operate on about 4 volts and running 12 volts directly to the injector terminals can burn out the wiring. By inserting an inline fuseholder between a set of test leads, a fused jumper wire can be used for bypassing open circuits. Use a 5 amp fuse to provide protection against voltage spikes. When in doubt, use a voltmeter to check the voltage input to the component and measure how much voltage is being applied normally. By moving the jumper wire successively back from the lamp toward the power source, you can isolate the area of the circuit where the open is located. When the component stops functioning, or the power is cut off, the open is in the segment of wire between the jumper and the point previously tested.

✱✱ CAUTION

Never use jumpers made from wire that is of lighter gauge than used in the circuit under test. If the jumper wire is of too small gauge, it may overheat and possibly melt. Never use jumpers to bypass high resistance loads (such as motors) in a circuit. Bypassing resistances, in effect, creates a short circuit which may, in turn, cause damage and fire. Never use a jumper for anything other than temporary bypassing of components in a circuit.

12 Volt Test Light

The 12 volt test light is used to check circuits and components while electrical current is flowing through them. It is used for voltage and ground tests. Twelve volt test lights come in different styles but all have three main parts; a ground clip, a probe, and a light. The most commonly used 12 volt test lights have picktype probes. To use a 12 volt test light, connect the ground clip to a good ground and probe wherever necessary with the pick. The pick should be sharp so that it can penetrate wire insulation to make contact with the wire, without making a large hole in the insulation. The wraparound light is handy in hard to reach areas or where it is difficult to support a wire to push a probe pick into it. To use the wrap around light, hook the wire to probed with the hook and pull the trigger. A small pick will be forced through the wire insulation into the wire core.

✱✱ CAUTION

Do not use a test light to probe electronic ignition spark plug or coil wires. Never use a pick-type test light to probe wiring on computer controlled systems unless specifically instructed to do so. Any wire insulation that is pierced by the test light probe should be taped and sealed with silicone after testing.

Like the jumper wire, the 12 volt test light is used to isolate opens in circuits. But, whereas the jumper wire is used to bypass the open to operate the load, the 12 volt test light is used to locate the presence of voltage in a circuit. If the test light glows, you know that there is power up to that point; if the 12 volt test light does not glow when its probe is inserted into the wire or connector, you know that there is an open circuit (no power). Move the test light in successive steps back toward the power source until the light in the handle does glow. When it does glow, the open is between the probe and point previously probed.

➡ **The test light does not detect that 12 volts (or any particular amount of voltage) is present; it only detects that some voltage is present. It is advisable before using the test light to touch its terminals across the battery posts to make sure the light is operating properly.**

Self-Powered Test Light

The self-powered test light usually contains a 1.5 volt penlight battery. One type of selfpowered test light is similar in design to the 12 volt test light. This type has both the battery and the light in the handle and pick-type probe tip. The second type has the light toward the open tip, so that the light illuminates the contact point. The self-powered test light is dual purpose piece of test equipment. It can be used to test for either open or short circuits when power is isolated from the circuit (continuity test). A powered test light should not be used on any computer controlled system or component unless specifically instructed to do so. Many engine sensors can be destroyed by even this small amount of voltage applied directly to the terminals.

Open Circuit Testing

To use the self-powered test light to check for open circuits, first isolate the circuit from the vehicle's 12 volt power source by disconnecting the battery or wiring harness connector. Connect the test light ground clip to a good ground and probe sections of the circuit sequentially with the test light. (start from either end of the circuit). If the light is out, the open is between the probe and the circuit ground. If the light is on, the open is between the probe and end of the circuit toward the power source.

Short Circuit Testing

By isolating the circuit both from power and from ground, and using a self-powered test light, you can check for shorts to ground in the circuit. Isolate the circuit from power and ground. Connect the test light ground clip to a good ground and probe any easy-to-reach test point in the circuit. If the light comes on, there is a short somewhere in the circuit. To isolate the short, probe a test point at either end of the isolated circuit (the light should be on). Leave the test light probe connected and open connectors, switches, remove parts, etc., sequentially, until the light goes out. When the light goes out, the short is between the last circuit component opened and the previous circuit opened.

➡ The 1.5 volt battery in the test light does not provide much current. A weak battery may not provide enough power to illuminate the test light even when a complete circuit is made (especially if there are high resistances in the circuit). Always make sure that the test battery is strong. To check the battery, briefly touch the ground clip to the probe; if the light glows brightly the battery is strong enough for testing. Never use a selfpowered test light to perform checks for opens or shorts when power is applied to the electrical system under test. The 12 volt vehicle power will quickly burn out the 1.5 volt light bulb in the test light.

Voltmeter

A voltmeter is used to measure voltage at any point in a circuit, or to measure the voltage drop across any part of a circuit. It can also be used to check continuity in a wire or circuit by indicating current flow from one end to the other. Voltmeters usually have various scales on the meter dial and a selector switch to allow the selection of different voltages. The voltmeter has a positive and a negative lead. To avoid damage to the meter, always connect the negative lead to the negative (-) side of circuit (to ground or nearest the ground side of the circuit) and connect the positive lead to the positive (+) side

of the circuit (to the power source or the nearest power source). Note that the negative voltmeter lead will always be black and that the positive voltmeter will always be some color other than black (usually red). Depending on how the voltmeter is connected into the circuit, it has several uses.

A voltmeter can be connected either in parallel or in series with a circuit and it has a very high resistance to current flow. When connected in parallel, only a small amount of current will flow through the voltmeter current path; the rest will flow through the normal circuit current path and the circuit will work normally. When the voltmeter is connected in series with a circuit, only a small amount of current can flow through the circuit. The circuit will not work properly, but the voltmeter reading will show if the circuit is complete or not.

Available Voltage Measurement

Set the voltmeter selector switch to the 20V position and connect the meter negative lead to the negative post of the battery. Connect the positive meter lead to the positive post of the battery and turn the ignition switch ON to provide a load. Read the voltage on the meter or digital display. A well charged battery should register over 12 volts. If the meter reads below 11.5 volts, the battery power may be insufficient to operate the electrical system properly. This test determines voltage available from the battery and should be the first step in any electrical trouble diagnosis procedure. Many electrical problems, especially on computer controlled systems, can be caused by a low state of charge in the battery. Excessive corrosion at the battery cable terminals can cause a poor contact that will prevent proper charging and full battery current flow.

Normal battery voltage is 12 volts when fully charged. When the battery is supplying current to one or more circuits it is said to be "under load". When everything is off the electrical system is under a "no-load" condition. A fully charged battery may show about 12.5 volts at no load; will drop to 12 volts under medium load; and will drop even lower under heavy load. If the battery is partially discharged the voltage decrease under heavy load may be excessive, even though the battery shows 12 volts or more at no load. When allowed to discharge further, the battery's available voltage under load will decrease more severely. For this reason, it is important that the battery be fully charged during all testing procedures to avoid errors in diagnosis and incorrect test results.

Voltage Drop

When current flows through a resistance, the voltage beyond the resistance is reduced (the

larger the current, the greater the reduction in voltage). When no current is flowing, there is no voltage drop because there is no current flow. All points in the circuit which are connected to the power source are at the same voltage as the power source. The total voltage drop always equals the total source voltage. In a long circuit with many connectors, a series of small, unwanted voltage drops due to corrosion at the connectors can add up to a total loss of voltage which impairs the operation of the normal loads in the circuit.

INDIRECT COMPUTATION OF VOLTAGE DROPS

1. Set the voltmeter selector switch to the 20 volt position.
2. Connect the meter negative lead to a good ground.
3. Probe all resistances in the circuit with the positive meter lead.
4. Operate the circuit in all modes and observe the voltage readings.

DIRECT MEASUREMENT OF VOLTAGE DROPS

1. Set the voltmeter switch to the 20 volt position.
2. Connect the voltmeter negative lead to the ground side of the resistance load to be measured.
3. Connect the positive lead to the positive side of the resistance or load to be measured.
4. Read the voltage drop directly on the 20 volt scale.

Too high a voltage indicates too high a resistance. If, for example, a blower motor runs too slowly, you can determine if there is too high a resistance in the resistor pack. By taking voltage drop readings in all parts of the circuit, you can isolate the problem. Too low a voltage drop indicates too low a resistance. If, for example, a blower motor runs too fast in the MED and/or LOW position, the problem can be isolated in the resistor pack by taking voltage drop readings in all parts of the circuit to locate a possibly shorted resistor. The maximum allowable voltage drop under load is critical, especially if there is more than one high resistance problem in a circuit because all voltage drops are cumulative. A small drop is normal due to the resistance of the conductors.

HIGH RESISTANCE TESTING

1. Set the voltmeter selector switch to the 4 volt position.
2. Connect the voltmeter positive lead to the positive post of the battery.
3. Turn on the headlights and heater blower to provide a load.
4. Probe various points in the circuit with the negative voltmeter lead.

5. Read the voltage drop on the 4 volt scale. Some average maximum allowable voltage drops are:

FUSE PANEL — 7 volts
IGNITION SWITCH — 5volts
HEADLIGHT SWITCH — 7 volts
IGNITION COIL (+) — 5 volts
ANY OTHER LOAD — 1.3 volts

➡ **Voltage drops are all measured while a load is operating; without current flow, there will be no voltage drop.**

Ohmmeter

The ohmmeter is designed to read resistance (ohms) in a circuit or component. Although there are several different styles of ohmmeters, all will usually have a selector switch which permits the measurement of different ranges of resistance (usually the selector switch allows the multiplication of the meter reading by 10, 100, 1000, and 10,000). A calibration knob allows the meter to be set at zero for accurate measurement. Since all ohmmeters are powered by an internal battery (usually 9 volts), the ohmmeter can be used as a self-powered test light. When the ohmmeter is connected, current from the ohmmeter flows through the circuit or component being tested. Since the ohmmeter's internal resistance and voltage are known values, the amount of current flow through the meter depends on the resistance of the circuit or component being tested.

The ohmmeter can be used to perform continuity test for opens or shorts (either by observation of the meter needle or as a selfpowered test light), and to read actual resistance in a circuit. It should be noted that the ohmmeter is used to check the resistance of a component or wire while there is no voltage applied to the circuit. Current flow from an outside voltage source (such as the vehicle battery) can damage the ohmmeter, so the circuit or component should be isolated from the vehicle electrical system before any testing is done. Since the ohmmeter uses its own voltage source, either lead can be connected to any test point.

➡ **When checking diodes or other solid state components, the ohmmeter leads can only be connected one way in order to measure current flow in a single direction. Make sure the positive (+) and negative () terminal connections are as described in the test procedures to verify the one-way diode operation.**

In using the meter for making continuity checks, do not be concerned with the actual resistance readings. Zero resistance, or any resistance readings, indicate continuity in the circuit. Infinite resistance indicates an open in the circuit. A high resistance reading where there should be none indicates a problem in the circuit. Checks for short circuits are made in the same manner as checks for open circuits except that the circuit must be isolated from both power and normal ground. Infinite resistance indicates no continuity to ground, while zero resistance indicates a dead short to ground.

RESISTANCE MEASUREMENT

The batteries in an ohmmeter will weaken with age and temperature, so the ohmmeter must be calibrated or "zeroed" before taking measurements. To zero the meter, place the selector switch in its lowest range and touch the two ohmmeter leads together. Turn the calibration knob until the meter needle is exactly on zero.

➡ **All analog (needle) type ohmmeters must be zeroed before use, but some digital ohmmeter models are automatically calibrated when the switch is turned on. Self-calibrating digital ohmmeters do not have an adjusting knob, but its a good idea to check for a zero readout before use by touching the leads together. All computer controlled systems require the use of a digital ohmmeter with at least 10 megohms impedance for testing. Before any test procedures are attempted, make sure the ohmmeter used is compatible with the electrical system or damage to the on-board computer could result.**

To measure resistance, first isolate the circuit from the vehicle power source by disconnecting the battery cables or the harness connector. Make sure the key is OFF when disconnecting any components or the battery. Where necessary, also isolate at least one side of the circuit to be checked to avoid reading parallel resistances. Parallel circuit resistances will always give a lower reading than the actual resistance of either of the branches. When measuring the resistance of parallel circuits, the total resistance will always be lower than the smallest resistance in the circuit. Connect the meter leads to both sides of the circuit (wire or component) and read the actual measured ohms on the meter scale. Make sure the selector switch is set to the proper ohm scale for the

circuit being tested to avoid misreading the ohmmeter test value.

✳✳ CAUTION

Never use an ohmmeter with power applied to the circuit. Like the selfpowered test light, the ohmmeter is designed to operate on its own power supply. The normal 12 volt automotive electrical system current could damage the meter.

Ammeters

An ammeter measures the amount of current flowing through a circuit in units called amperes or amps. Amperes are units of electron flow which indicate how fast the electrons are flowing through the circuit. Since Ohms Law dictates that current flow in a circuit is equal to the circuit voltage divided by the total circuit resistance, increasing voltage also increases the current level (amps). Likewise, any decrease in resistance will increase the amount of amps in a circuit. At normal operating voltage, most circuits have a characteristic amount of amperes, called "current draw" which can be measured using an ammeter. By referring to a specified current draw rating, measuring the amperes, and comparing the two values, one can determine what is happening within the circuit to aid in diagnosis. An open circuit, for example, will not allow any current to flow so the ammeter reading will be zero. More current flows through a heavily loaded circuit or when the charging system is operating.

An ammeter is always connected in series with the circuit being tested. All of the current that normally flows through the circuit must also flow through the ammeter; if there is any other path for the current to follow, the ammeter reading will not be accurate. The ammeter itself has very little resistance to current flow and therefore will not affect the circuit, but it will measure current draw only when the circuit is closed and electricity is flowing. Excessive current draw can blow fuses and drain the battery, while a reduced current draw can cause motors to run slowly, lights to dim and other components to not operate properly. The ammeter can help diagnose these conditions by locating the cause of the high or low reading.

Multimeters

Different combinations of test meters can be built into a single unit designed for specific tests. Some of the more common combination test devices are known as Volt/Amp testers, Tach/

Dwell meters, or Digital Multimeters. The Volt/Amp tester is used for charging system, starting system or battery tests and consists of a voltmeter, an ammeter and a variable resistance carbon pile. The voltmeter will usually have at least two ranges for use with 6, 12 and 24 volt systems. The ammeter also has more than one range for testing various levels of battery loads and starter current draw and the carbon pile can be adjusted to offer different amounts of resistance. The Volt/Amp tester has heavy leads to carry large amounts of current and many later models have an inductive ammeter pickup that clamps around the wire to simplify test connections. On some models, the ammeter also has a zero-center scale to allow testing of charging and starting systems without switching leads or polarity. A digital multimeter is a voltmeter, ammeter and ohmmeter combined in an instrument which gives a digital readout. These are often used when testing solid state circuits because of their high input impedance (usually 10 megohms or more).

The tach/dwell meter combines a tachometer and a dwell (cam angle) meter and is a specialized kind of voltmeter. The tachometer scale is marked to show engine speed in rpm and the dwell scale is marked to show degrees of distributor shaft rotation. In most electronic ignition systems, dwell is determined by the control unit, but the dwell meter can also be used to check the duty cycle (operation) of some electronic engine control systems. Some tach/dwell meters are powered by an internal battery, while others take their power from the car battery in use. The battery powered testers usually require calibration much like an ohmmeter before testing.

Special Test Equipment

A variety of diagnostic tools are available to help troubleshoot and repair computerized engine control systems. The most sophisticated of these devices are the console type engine analyzers that usually occupy a garage service bay, but there are several types of aftermarket electronic testers available that will allow quick circuit tests of the engine control system by plugging directly into a special connector located in the engine compartment or under the dashboard. Several tool and equipment manufacturers offer simple, hand held testers that measure various circuit voltage levels on command to check all system components for proper operation. Although these testers usually cost about $300-$500, consider that the average computer control unit (or ECM) can cost just as much and the money saved by not replacing perfectly good sensors or components in an attempt to correct a problem could justify

the purchase price of a special diagnostic tester the first time it's used.

These computerized testers can allow quick and easy test measurements while the engine is operating or while the car is being driven. In addition, the on-board computer memory can be read to access any stored trouble codes; in effect allowing the computer to tell you where it hurts and aid trouble diagnosis by pinpointing exactly which circuit or component is malfunctioning. In the same manner, repairs can be tested to make sure the problem has been corrected. The biggest advantage these special testers have is their relatively easy hookups that minimize or eliminate the chances of making the wrong connections and getting false voltage readings or damaging the computer accidentally.

➡ **It should be remembered that these testers check voltage levels in circuits; they don't detect mechanical problems or failed components if the circuit voltage falls within the preprogrammed limits stored in the tester PROM unit. Also, most of the hand held testers are designed to work only on one or two systems made by a specific manufacturer.**

A variety of aftermarket testers are available to help diagnose different computerized control systems. Owatonna Tool Company (OTC), for example, markets a device called the OTC Monitor which plugs directly into the assembly line diagnostic link (ALDL). The OTC tester makes diagnosis a simple matter of pressing the correct buttons and, by changing the internal PROM or inserting a different diagnosis cartridge, it will work on any model from full size to subcompact, over a wide range of years. An adapter is supplied with the tester to allow connection to all types of ALDL links, regardless of the number of pin terminals used. By inserting an updated PROM into the OTC tester, it can be easily updated to diagnose any new modifications of computerized control systems.

Wiring Harnesses

The average automobile contains about 1/2 mile of wiring, with hundreds of individual connections. To protect the many wires from damage and to keep them from becoming a confusing tangle, they are organized into bundles, enclosed in plastic or taped together and called wire harnesses. Different wiring harnesses serve different parts of the vehicle. Individual wires are color coded to help trace

them through a harness where sections are hidden from view.

A loose or corroded connection or a replacement wire that is too small for the circuit will add extra resistance and an additional voltage drop to the circuit. A ten percent voltage drop can result in slow or erratic motor operation, for example, even though the circuit is complete. Automotive wiring or circuit conductors can be in any one of three forms:

1. Single strand wire
2. Multistrand wire
3. Printed circuitry

Single strand wire has a solid metal core and is usually used inside such components as alternators, motors, relays and other devices. Multistrand wire has a core made of many small strands of wire twisted together into a single conductor. Most of the wiring in an automotive electrical system is made up of multistrand wire, either as a single conductor or grouped together in a harness. All wiring is color coded on the insulator, either as a solid color or as a colored wire with an identification stripe. A printed circuit is a thin film of copper or other conductor that is printed on an insulator backing. Occasionally, a printed circuit is sandwiched between two sheets of plastic for more protection and flexibility. A complete printed circuit, consisting of conductors, insulating material and connectors for lamps or other components is called a printed circuit board. Printed circuitry is used in place of individual wires or harnesses in places where space is limited, such as behind instrument panels.

Wire Gauge

Since computer controlled automotive electrical systems are very sensitive to changes in resistance, the selection of properly sized wires is critical when systems are repaired. The wire gauge number is an expression of the cross section area of the conductor. The most common system for expressing wire size is the American Wire Gauge (AWG) system.

Wire cross section area is measured in circular mils. A mil is $1/1000$ in. (0.001 in. [0.0254mm]); a circular mil is the area of a circle one mil in diameter. For example, a conductor $1/4$ in. (6mm) in diameter is 0.250 in. or 250 mils. The circular mil cross section area of the wire is 250 squared (250^2)or 62,500 circular mils. Imported car models usually use metric wire gauge designations, which is simply the cross section area of the conductor in square millimeters (mm^2).

Gauge numbers are assigned to conductors of various cross section areas. As gauge number increases, area decreases and the conductor becomes smaller. A 5 gauge conductor is smaller than a 1 gauge conductor and a 10 gauge is smaller than a 5 gauge. As the cross section area of a conductor decreases, resistance increases and so does the gauge number. A conductor with a higher gauge number will carry less current than a conductor with a lower gauge number.

➡ **Gauge wire size refers to the size of the conductor, not the size of the complete wire. It is possible to have two wires of the same gauge with different diameters because one may have thicker insulation than the other.**

12 volt automotive electrical systems generally use 10, 12, 14, 16 and 18 gauge wire. Main power distribution circuits and larger accessories usually use 10 and 12 gauge wire. Battery cables are usually 4 or 6 gauge, although 1 and 2 gauge wires are occasionally used. Wire length must also be considered when making repairs to a circuit. As conductor length increases, so does resistance. An 18 gauge wire, for example, can carry a 10 amp load for 10 feet without excessive voltage drop; however if a 15 foot wire is required for the same 10 amp load, it must be a 16 gauge wire.

An electrical schematic shows the electrical current paths when a circuit is operating properly. It is essential to understand how a circuit works before trying to figure out why it doesn't. Schematics break the entire electrical system down into individual circuits and show only one particular circuit. In a schematic, no attempt is made to represent wiring and components as they physically appear on the vehicle; switches and other components are shown as simply as possible. Face views of harness connectors show the cavity or terminal locations in all multi-pin connectors to help locate test points.

If you need to backprobe a connector while it is on the component, the order of the terminals must be mentally reversed. The wire color code can help in this situation, as well as a keyway, lock tab or other reference mark.

➡ **Wiring diagrams are not included in this book. As trucks have become more complex and available with longer option lists, wiring diagrams have grown in size and complexity. It has become almost impossible to provide a readable reproduction of a wiring diagram in a book this size. Information on ordering wiring diagrams from the vehicle manufacturer can be found in the owner's manual.**

WIRING REPAIR

Soldering is a quick, efficient method of joining metals permanently. Everyone who has the occasion to make wiring repairs should know how to solder. Electrical connections that are soldered are far less likely to come apart and will conduct electricity much better than connections that are only "pig-tailed" together. The most popular (and preferred) method of soldering is with an electrical soldering gun. Soldering irons are available in many sizes and wattage ratings. Irons with higher wattage ratings deliver higher temperatures and recover lost heat faster. A small soldering iron rated for no more than 50 watts is recommended, especially on electrical systems where excess heat can damage the components being soldered.

There are three ingredients necessary for successful soldering; proper flux, good solder and sufficient heat. A soldering flux is necessary to clean the metal of tarnish, prepare it for soldering and to enable the solder to spread into tiny crevices. When soldering, always use a resin flux or resin core solder which is noncorrosive and will not attract moisture once the job is finished. Other types of flux (acid core) will leave a residue that will attract moisture and cause the wires to corrode. Tin is a unique metal with a low melting point. In a molten state, it dissolves and alloys easily with many metals. Solder is made by mixing tin with lead. The most common proportions are 40/60, 50/50 and 60/40, with the percentage of tin listed first. Low priced solders usually contain less tin, making them very difficult for a beginner to use because more heat is required to melt the solder. A common solder is 40/60 which is well suited for allaround general use, but 60/40 melts easier, has more tin for a better joint and is preferred for electrical work.

Soldering Techniques

Successful soldering requires that the metals to be joined be heated to a temperature that will melt the solder — usually 360-460°F (182238°C). Contrary to popular belief, the purpose of the soldering iron is not to melt the solder itself, but to heat the parts being soldered to a temperature high enough to melt the solder when it is touched to the work. Melting flux-cored solder on the soldering iron will usually destroy the effectiveness of the flux.

➡ **Soldering tips are made of copper for good heat conductivity, but must be "tinned" regularly for quick transference of heat to the project and to prevent the solder from sticking to the iron. To "tin" the iron, simply heat it and touch the flux-cored solder to the tip; the solder will flow over the hot tip. Wipe the excess off with a clean rag, but be careful as the iron will be hot.**

After some use, the tip may become pitted. If so, simply dress the tip smooth with a smooth file and "tin" the tip again. An old saying holds that "metals well cleaned are half soldered." Flux-cored solder will remove oxides but rust, bits of insulation and oil or grease must be removed with a wire brush or emery cloth. For maximum strength in soldered parts, the joint must start off clean and tight. Weak joints will result in gaps too wide for the solder to bridge.

If a separate soldering flux is used, it should be brushed or swabbed on only those areas that are to be soldered. Most solders contain a core of flux and separate fluxing is unnecessary. Hold the work to be soldered firmly. It is best to solder on a wooden board, because a metal vise will only rob the piece to be soldered of heat and make it difficult to melt the solder. Hold the soldering tip with the broadest face against the work to be soldered. Apply solder under the tip close to the work, using enough solder to give a heavy film between the iron and the piece being soldered, while moving slowly and making sure the solder melts properly. Keep the work level or the solder will run to the lowest part and favor the thicker parts, because these require more heat to melt the solder. If the soldering tip overheats (the solder coating on the face of the tip burns up), it should be retinned. Once the soldering is completed, let the soldered joint stand until cool. Tape and seal all soldered wire splices after the repair has cooled.

Wire Harness and Connectors

The on-board computer (ECM) wire harness electrically connects the control unit to the various solenoids, switches and sensors used by the control system. Most connectors in the engine compartment or otherwise exposed to the elements are protected against moisture and dirt which could create oxidation and deposits on the terminals. This protection is important because of the very low voltage and current levels used by the computer and sensors. All connectors have a lock which secures the male and female terminals together, with a secondary lock holding the seal and terminal into the connector. Both terminal locks must be released when disconnecting ECM connectors.

These special connectors are weather-proof and all repairs require the use of a special terminal and the tool required to service it. This tool is used to remove the pin and sleeve terminals. If removal is attempted with an ordinary pick, there is a good chance that the terminal will be bent or deformed. Unlike standard blade type terminals, these terminals cannot be straightened once they are bent. Make certain that the connectors are properly seated and all of the sealing rings in place when connecting leads. On some models, a hinge-type flap provides a backup or secondary locking feature for the terminals. Most secondary locks are used to improve the connector reliability by retaining the terminals if the small terminal lock tangs are not positioned properly.

Molded-on connectors require complete replacement of the connection. This means splicing a new connector assembly into the harness. All splices in on-board computer systems should be soldered to insure proper contact. Use care when probing the connections or replacing terminals in them as it is possible to short between opposite terminals. If this happens to the wrong terminal pair, it is possible to damage certain components. Always use jumper wires between connectors for circuit checking and never probe through weatherproof seals.

Open circuits are often difficult to locate by sight because corrosion or terminal misalignment are hidden by the connectors. Merely wiggling a connector on a sensor or in the wiring harness may correct the open circuit condition. This should always be considered when an open circuit or a failed sensor is indicated. Intermittent problems may also be caused by oxidized or loose connections. When using a circuit tester for diagnosis, always probe connections from the wire side. Be careful not to damage sealed connectors with test probes.

All wiring harnesses should be replaced with identical parts, using the same gauge wire and connectors. When signal wires are spliced into a harness, use wire with high temperature insulation only. With the low voltage and current levels found in the system, it is important that the best possible connection at all wire splices be made by soldering the splices together. It is seldom necessary to replace a complete harness. If replacement is necessary, pay close attention to insure proper harness routing. Secure the harness with suitable plastic wire clamps to prevent vibrations from causing the harness to wear in spots or contact any hot components.

➡ Weatherproof connectors cannot be replaced with standard connectors. Instructions are provided with replacement connector and terminal packages. Some wire harnesses have mounting Indicators (usually pieces of colored tape) to mark where the harness is to be secured.

In making wiring repairs, it's important that you always replace damaged wires with wires that are the same gauge as the wire being replaced. The heavier the wire, the smaller the gauge number. Wires are color-coded to aid in identification and whenever possible the same color coded wire should be used for replacement. A wire stripping and crimping tool is necessary to install solderless terminal connectors. Test all crimps by pulling on the wires; it should not be possible to pull the wires out of a good crimp.

Wires which are open, exposed or otherwise damaged are repaired by simple splicing. Where possible, if the wiring harness is accessible and the damaged place in the wire can be located, it is best to open the harness and check for all possible damage. In an inaccessible harness, the wire must be bypassed with a new insert, usually taped to the outside of the old harness.

When replacing fusible links, be sure to use fusible link wire, NOT ordinary automotive wire. Make sure the fusible segment is of the same gauge and construction as the one being replaced and double the stripped end when crimping the terminal connector for a good contact. The melted (open) fusible link segment of the wiring harness should be cut off as close to the harness as possible, then a new segment spliced in as described. In the case of a damaged fusible link that feeds two harness wires, the harness connections should be replaced with two fusible link wires so that each circuit will have its own separate protection.

➡ Most of the problems caused in the wiring harness are due to bad ground connections. Always check all vehicle ground connections for corrosion or looseness before performing any power feed checks to eliminate the chance of a bad ground affecting the circuit.

Repairing Hard Shell Connectors

Unlike molded connectors, the terminal contacts in hard shell connectors can be replaced. Weatherproof hard-shell connectors with the leads molded into the shell have nonreplaceable terminal ends. Replacement usually involves the use of a special terminal removal tool that depress the locking tangs

(barbs) on the connector terminal and allow the connector to be removed from the rear of the shell. The connector shell should be replaced if it shows any evidence of burning, melting, cracks, or breaks. Replace individual terminals that are burnt, corroded, distorted or loose.

➡ The insulation crimp must be tight to prevent the insulation from sliding back on the wire when the wire is pulled. The insulation must be visibly compressed under the crimp tabs, and the ends of the crimp should be turned in for a firm grip on the insulation.

The wire crimp must be made with all wire strands inside the crimp. The terminal must be fully compressed on the wire strands with the ends of the crimp tabs turned in to make a firm grip on the wire. Check all connections with an ohmmeter to insure a good contact. There should be no measurable resistance between the wire and the terminal when connected.

Mechanical Test Equipment

Vacuum Gauge

Most gauges are graduated in inches of mercury (in.Hg), although a device called a manometer reads vacuum in inches of water (in. H_2O). The normal vacuum reading usually varies between 18 and 22 in.Hg at sea level. To test engine vacuum, the vacuum gauge must be connected to a source of manifold vacuum. Many engines have a plug in the intake manifold which can be removed and replaced with an adapter fitting. Connect the vacuum gauge to the fitting with a suitable rubber hose or, if no manifold plug is available, connect the vacuum gauge to any device using manifold vacuum, such as EGR valves, etc. The vacuum gauge can be used to determine if enough vacuum is reaching a component to allow its actuation.

Hand Vacuum Pump

Small, hand-held vacuum pumps come in a variety of designs. Most have a built-in vacuum gauge and allow the component to be tested without removing it from the vehicle. Operate the pump lever or plunger to apply the correct amount of vacuum required for the test specified in the diagnosis routines. The level of vacuum in inches of Mercury (in.Hg) is indicated on the pump gauge. For some testing, an additional vacuum gauge may be necessary.

Intake manifold vacuum is used to operate various systems and devices on late model vehicles. To correctly diagnose and solve problems in vacuum control systems, a vacuum source is necessary for testing. In some cases, vacuum can be taken from the intake manifold when the engine is running, but vacuum is normally provided by a hand vacuum pump.

These hand vacuum pumps have a built-in vacuum gauge that allow testing while the device is still attached to the component. For some tests, an additional vacuum gauge may be necessary.

HEATER

Blower Motor

REMOVAL & INSTALLATION

1982-91

▶ SEE FIGS. 1-4

1. Disconnect the negative battery cable.
2. Disconnect the electrical connections at the blower motor and blower resistor.

➡ **On the 3.1L engine remove the tower to tower brace assembly.**

3. On models through 1989, remove the plastic water shield from the right side of the cowl.
4. Remove the blower motor retaining screws and then pull the blower motor and cage out.

5. Hold the blower motor cage and remove the cage retaining nut from the blower motor shaft.
6. Remove the blower motor and cage.

To Install:

7. Install the cage on the new motor.
8. Check that the retaining nut is on tight, the motor rotates and the fan cage is not interferring with the motor.
9. Install the motor in the heater assembly (install tower to tower brace assembly if neceeasy) connect the wiring and check the motor operation in all speeds.

1992

2.0L AND 2.2L ENGINES

1. Disconnect the negative battery cable.
2. Mark and remove the electrical connections at blower motor.
3. Remove the blower motor cooling tube.
4. Remove the blower motor retaining screws. Remove the blower motor fan.

➡ **The blower motor and fan are serviced as an assembly.**

To Install:

5. Install the blower motor and fan assembly in the correct position.
6. Install and tighten evenly the fan assembly retaining screws.
7. Install blower motor cooling tube.
8. Connect the electrical connections and reconnect the negative battery cable. Check the blower motor operation in all speeds.

3.1L ENGINE

1. Disconnect the negative battery cable.
2. Remove the tower to tower brace. Mark and remove the electrical connections at blower motor.
3. Remove the blower motor cooling tube.
4. Remove the alternator assembly-refer to the necessary service procedures.
5. Remove the blower motor retaining screws. Remove the blower motor assembly.

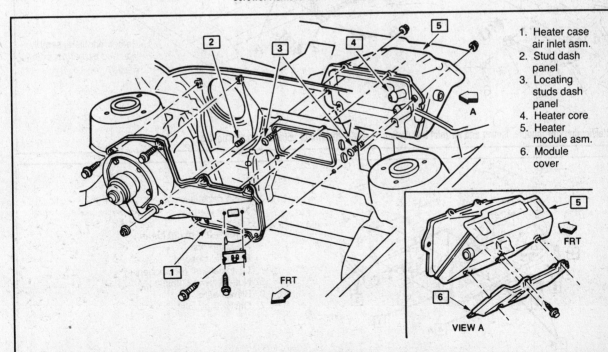

1. Heater case air inlet asm.
2. Stud dash panel
3. Locating studs dash panel
4. Heater core
5. Heater module asm.
6. Module cover

FIG. 1 Heater module and air inlet assembly — 1982–87 without air conditioning

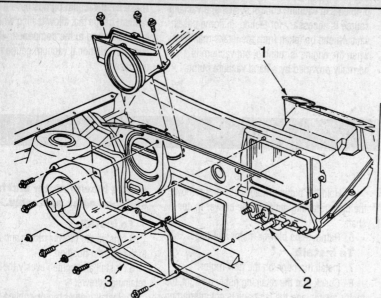

1. Heater & evaporator
2. Drain tube
3. Blower assembly

NOTICE: WHEN REMOVING
THE HEATER & EVAPORATOR
ASSEMBLY, PULL ASSEMBLY
STRAIGHT TOWARD INTERIOR
OF CAR UNTIL PLASTIC DRAIN
TUBE CLEARS COWL. IF
ASSEMBLY IS TILTED IN ANY
DIRECTION BEFORE THE TUBE
CLEARS THE COWL, THE TUBE
MAY BREAK.

FIG. 2 Heater evaporator assembly, blower assembly and air inlet installation — 1982–87 with air conditioning

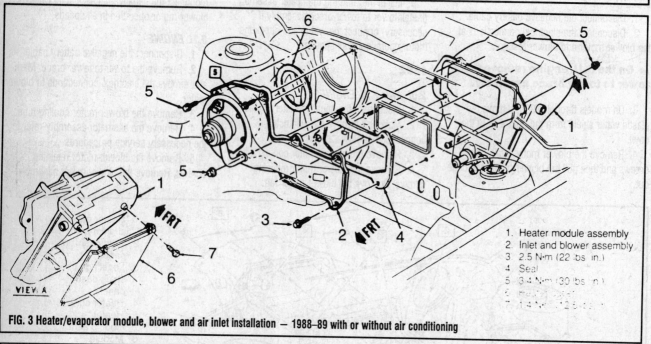

1. Heater module assembly
2. Inlet and blower assembly
3. 2.5 N·m (22 lbs. in.)
4. Seal
5. 3.4 N·m (30 lbs. in.)
6. Radial seal
7. 1.4 N·m (12 lbs. in.)

FIG. 3 Heater/evaporator module, blower and air inlet installation — 1988–89 with or without air conditioning

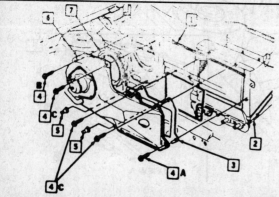

1. Dash panel asm.
2. Module asm.
3. Gasket
4. Screw—2 N·m (20 lbs. in.)
   A. Install first
   B. Install second
   C. Install last (no sequence)
5. Nut—3 N·m (27 lbs. ft.)
6. Blower asm.
7. Gasket—air inlet

FIG. 4 Blower case, air inlet and module assembly installation — 1990–92 with or without air conditioning

➡ **The blower motor and fan are serviced as an assembly.**

To Install:

5. Install the blower motor and fan assembly in the correct position.

6. Install and tighten evenly the fan assembly retaining screws.

7. Install the alternator assembly. Adjust the drive belt.

8. Install blower motor cooling tube.

9. Connect the electrical connections and install the tower to tower brace.

10. Reconnect the negative battery cable. Check the blower motor operation in all speeds.

Heater Core

REMOVAL & INSTALLATION

❄ CAUTION

When draining the coolant, keep in mind that cats and dogs are attracted by the ethylene glycol antifreeze, and are quite likely to drink any that is left in an uncovered container or in puddles on the ground. This will prove fatal in sufficient quantity. Always drain the coolant into a sealable container. Coolant should be reused unless it is contaminated or several years old.

Cars Without Air Conditioning

1982–87

1. Disconnect the negative battery cable and drain the cooling system.

2. Remove the heater inlet and outlet hoses from the heater core.

3. Remove the heater outlet deflector.

4. Remove the retaining screws and then remove the heater core cover.

5. Remove the heater core retaining straps and then remove the heater core.

6. Installation is the reverse of removal. Refill the cooling system. Check heater system for proper operation.

1988–92

1. Disconnect the negative battery cable and drain the cooling system.

2. Raise and support the vehicle safely.

3. Disconnect the rear lateral transaxle strut mount, if equipped.

4. Disconnect the drain tube from the heater case.

5. Disconnect the heater hoses from the heater core.

6. Lower the vehicle.

7. Remove the right and left sound insulators.

8. Remove the steering column opening filler. Disconnect the heater outlet deflector (floor air outlet duct).

9. Remove the heater core cover.

10. Remove the heater core retaining straps (clamps) and remove the heater core.

To Install:

11. Install the heater core and retaining straps (clamps).

12. Install the heater core cover.

13. Reconnect the heater outlet deflector (floor air outlet duct).

14. Install the right and left sound insulators. Install the steering column opening filler.

15. Raise and support the vehicle safely.

16. Connect the heater hoses (use new heater hose clamps if necessary) to the heater core.

17. Connect the drain tube to heater case.

18. Connect the rear lateral transaxle strut mount, if equipped.

19. Lower the vehicle.

20. Fill the cooling system and check for leaks. Check heater system for proper operation.

Cars With Air Conditioning

1982–87

1. Disconnect the negative battery cable and drain the cooling system.

2. Raise and support the front of the vehicle.

3. Disconnect the drain tube from the heater case.

4. Remove the heater hoses from the heater core.

5. Lower the car. Remove the right and left hush panels, the steering column trim cover, the heater outlet duct and the glove box.

6. Remove the heater core cover. Be sure to pull the cover straight to the rear so as not to damage the drain tube.

7. Remove the heater core clamps and then remove the core.

8. Reverse the above procedure to install, charge the A/C system (refer to Section 1), and fill the cooling system.

1988–92

1. Disconnect the negative battery cable and drain the cooling system.

2. Raise and support the vehicle safely.

3. Disconnect the rear lateral transaxle strut mount, if equipped.

4. Disconnect the drain tube from the heaterA/C module.

5. Disconnect the heater hoses from the heater core.

6. Lower the vehicle.

7. Remove the right and left sound insulators, steering column trim cover and the heater (floor) outlet duct.

8. Remove the heater core cover and pull straight rearward.

9. Remove the heater core clamps and remove the core.

To Install:

10. Install the heater core and clamps.

11. Install the heater core cover.

12. Install the heater (floor) outlet duct, steering column trim cover and the right and left sound insulators.

13. Raise and support the vehicle safely.

14. Connect the heater hoses to the heater core.

15. Connect the drain tube to the heater-A/C module.

16. Connect the rear lateral transaxle strut mount, if equipped.

17. Lower the vehicle.

18. Connect the negative battery cable.

19. Refill the cooling system. Check system for proper operation.

Temperature Control Cable

REMOVAL & INSTALLATION

◆ SEE FIGS. 5-7

1. Remove the right side sound insulator panel.

2. Remove the instrument panel (I/P) compartment.

3. Disconnect the cable at the module.

4. Remove the control panel trim plate and control panel assembly.

5. Disconnect the cable from the control assembly and remove the cable.

6. Installation is the reverse of the removal procedure. Adjust temperature control cable.

ADJUSTMENT

If the temperature control lever fails to move to full COLD or HOT, or a large amount of lever spring back is noticed when moving to either of the full positions, the cable clip may need adjustment. Failure to grip clip in the correct manner will damage its ability to hold position on the cable. The temperature control cable must be replaced if clip retention fails.

1. To adjust the clip, grip clip (in correct manner-refer to the illustration) at module end of cable while pulling temperature control lever to the correct full position (COLD or HOT) and connect.

2. Verify correct adjustment by observing for little or no spring back of the temperature control lever and listening for temperature door "slam" when the control lever is moved to full positions quickly.

Control Panel

REMOVAL & INSTALLATION

1. Disconnect the battery ground cable.
2. Remove the instrument panel trim plate.
3. Remove the control assembly retaining screws and pull the control assembly away from the instrument panel.
4. Disconnect the electrical and vacuum connectors.
5. Disconnect the temperature control cable from the control assembly and remove assembly.
6. Installation is the reverse of the removal procedure. Check system for proper operation.

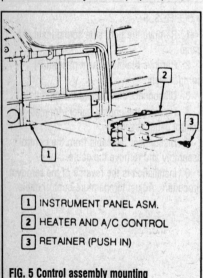

1. INSTRUMENT PANEL ASM.
2. HEATER AND A/C CONTROL
3. RETAINER (PUSH IN)

FIG. 5 Control assembly mounting

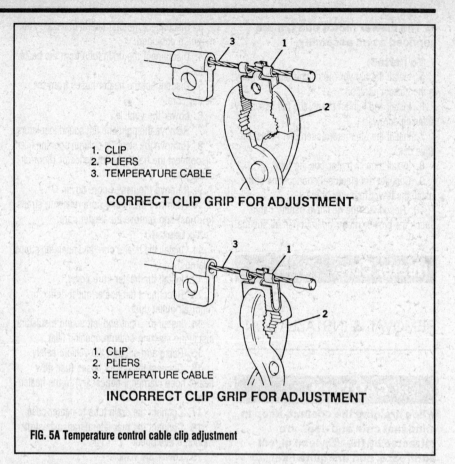

1. CLIP
2. PLIERS
3. TEMPERATURE CABLE

CORRECT CLIP GRIP FOR ADJUSTMENT

1. CLIP
2. PLIERS
3. TEMPERATURE CABLE

INCORRECT CLIP GRIP FOR ADJUSTMENT

FIG. 5A Temperature control cable clip adjustment

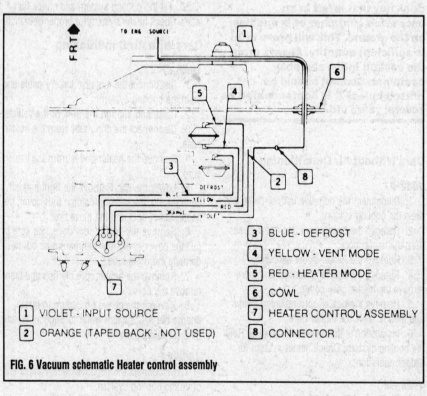

1. VIOLET - INPUT SOURCE
2. ORANGE (TAPED BACK - NOT USED)
3. BLUE - DEFROST
4. YELLOW - VENT MODE
5. RED - HEATER MODE
6. COWL
7. HEATER CONTROL ASSEMBLY
8. CONNECTOR

FIG. 6 Vacuum schematic Heater control assembly

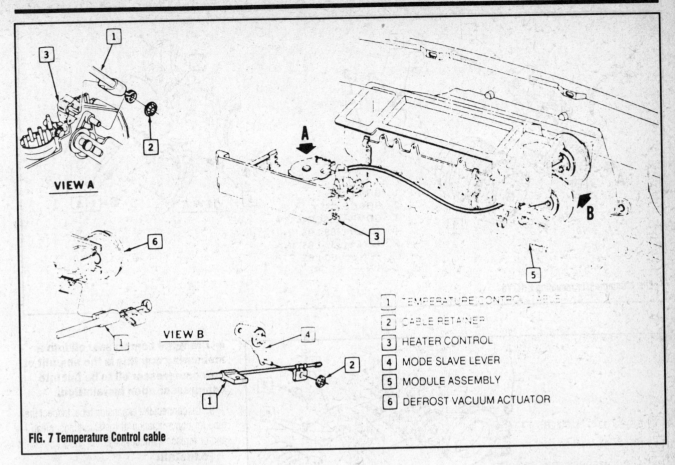

1 TEMPERATURE CONTROL CABLE
2 CABLE RETAINER
3 HEATER CONTROL
4 MODE SLAVE LEVER
5 MODULE ASSEMBLY
6 DEFROST VACUUM ACTUATOR

VIEW A

VIEW B

FIG. 7 Temperature Control cable

Blower Switch

REMOVAL & INSTALLATION

1. Disconnect the battery ground cable.

2. Remove the instrument panel (I/P) trim plate.

3. Remove the control assembly retaining screws and pull the control assembly away from the instrument panel.

4. Remove the blower switch knob.

5. Disconnect the electrical connector.

6. Remove the blower switch retaining screws and remove the switch.

7. Installation is the reverse of the removal procedure. Check system for proper operation.

AIR CONDITIONER

❄❄ CAUTION

Refer to SECTION 1 for discharging and charging of the A/C system; follow all safety precautions carefully!

Compressor

REMOVAL & INSTALLATION

♦ SEE FIGS. 8-10

1. Disconnect the battery ground cable.

2. Drain the system of all refrigerant using an approved Recovery/Recycling system (refer to Section 1).

3. Remove the compressor drive belt.

4. Raise and safely support vehicle on jack stands.

5. Remove the right air deflector and splash shield.

6. Disconnect the electrical connectors at the compressor switches.

7. Disconnect the compressor/condenser hose assembly at the rear of the compressor and discard the seals.

8. Remove the compressor attaching bolts and remove the compressor.

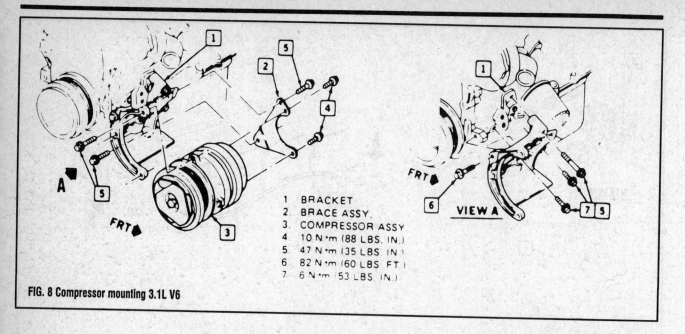

1 BRACKET
2 BRACE ASSY.
3 COMPRESSOR ASSY.
4 10 N·m (88 LBS. IN.)
5 47 N·m (35 LBS. IN.)
6 82 N·m (60 LBS. FT.)
7 6 N·m (53 LBS. IN.)

FIG. 8 Compressor mounting 3.1L V6

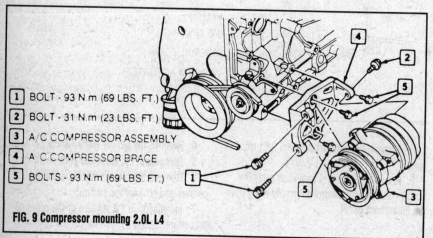

1 BOLT - 93 N.m (69 LBS. FT.)
2 BOLT - 31 N.m (23 LBS. FT.)
3 A/C COMPRESSOR ASSEMBLY
4 A/C COMPRESSOR BRACE
5 BOLTS - 93 N.m (69 LBS. FT.)

FIG. 9 Compressor mounting 2.0L L4

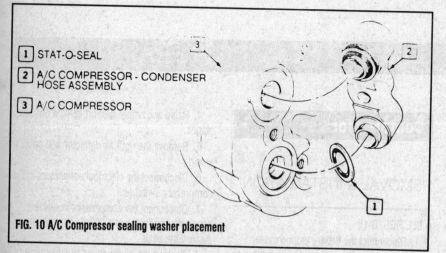

1 STAT-O-SEAL
2 A/C COMPRESSOR - CONDENSER HOSE ASSEMBLY
3 A/C COMPRESSOR

FIG. 10 A/C Compressor sealing washer placement

➡ **Drain the compressor oil into a measuring cup this is the amount of new compressor oil to be put into compressor upon installation.**

9. Disconnect the expansion tube. Inspect the tube for contamination or metal cuttings, clean and or replace as necessary.

To Install:

10. Ensure that the compressor (new or used) is completely drained of oil. Refill the compressor with new oil the same amount that was drained.

11. Position the compressor and install the attaching bolts.

12. Connect the condensor/compressor hose assembly at the rear of compressor using new sealing washers that don't need to be lubricated.

13. Connect the electrical connectors to the compressor clutch.

14. Install the drive belt and adjust as necessary.

15. Install the right air deflector and splash shield.

16. Lower the vehicle and connect the battery ground cable.

17. Evacuate, charge and leak test the A/C system (refer to Section 1).

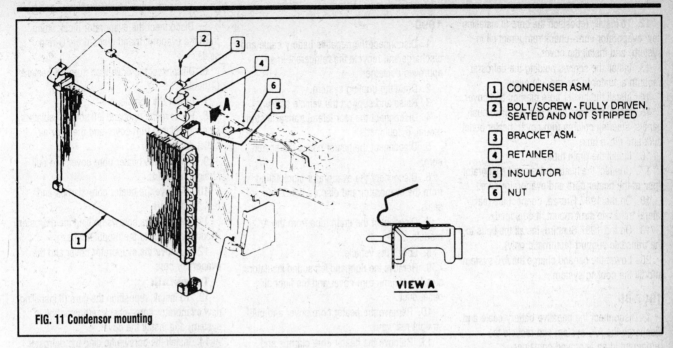

1. CONDENSER ASM.
2. BOLT/SCREW - FULLY DRIVEN, SEATED AND NOT STRIPPED
3. BRACKET ASM.
4. RETAINER
5. INSULATOR
6. NUT

VIEW A

FIG. 11 Condensor mounting

Condenser

REMOVAL & INSTALLATION

▶ SEE FIG. 11

➡ On some vehicles some steps can be omitted due different body styles and or vehicle optionsmodify the service procedure steps as necessary. Review the complete service procedure before starting this repair.

1. Disconnect the battery ground cable.
2. Drain the system of all refrigerant using an approved Recovery/Recycling system (refer to Section 1).

➡ On models so equipped, manually open headlamp doors (make sure negative battery cable is disconnected) by turning headlamp door actuator knob. Remove the 4 retaining bolts from the headlamp door actuators and pull actuator assemblies forward as far as possible. Remove the hood latch release cable and front end panel center brace.

3. Remove the right and left headlight trim.
4. Remove the center grille assembly.
5. Remove the right and left headlight housing.
6. Remove the hood bracket and latch assembly.

7. Disconnect the refrigerant lines from the condenser and discard the O-ring seals.
8. Remove the condenser air deflector shield if so equipped.
9. Remove the condenser mounting brackets and remove the condenser.

To install:

10. Position the condenser in vehicle and install the mounting brackets.
11. Install the condenser air deflector shield if so equipped.
12. Connect the refrigerant lines to the condenser using new O-ring seals.

➡ If necessary, install headlight actuator assemblies. Install the front end panel center brace and the hood latch release cable.

13. Install the hood latch and bracket assembly.
14. Install the headlight housings, center grille assembly, and headlight trim.
15. Connect the battery ground cable.
16. Evacuate and charge the A/C system (refer to Section 1).

Evaporator Core

REMOVAL & INSTALLATION

✳✳ CAUTION

When draining the coolant, keep in mind that cats and dogs are attracted by the ethylene glycol antifreeze, and are quite likely to drink any that is left in an uncovered container or in puddles on the ground. This will prove fatal in sufficent quantity. Always drain the coolant into a sealable container. Coolant should be reused unless it is contaminated or several years old.

1982-87

1. Disconnect the negative battery cable and discharge the A/C system and recycle the refrigerant in an approved container.
2. Jack up the car and support it safely.
3. On the 1987 Sunbird, remove the bolts to the transaxle support (automatic only).
4. On the 1987 Firenza, disconnect the rear lateral transaxle strut mount, if equipped.
5. Disconnect the heater hoses and evaporator lines at the heater core and evaporator core.
6. Remove the drain tube.
7. Remove the right hand and left hand hush panels, steering column trim cover, heater outlet duct and glove box.
8. Remove the heater core cover by pulling straight rearward on the cover to avoid breaking the drain tube.
9. Remove the heater core clamps and remove the heater core.
10. Remove the screws holding the defroster vacuum actuator to the module case.
11. Remove the evaporator cover and remove the evaporator core.

12. To install, reposition the core (if installing new evaporator core--check refrigerant oil in system) and install the cover.

13. Install the screws holding the defroster vacuum actuator to the module case.

14. Install the heater core clamps and cover.

15. Install the right hand and left hand hush panels, steering column trim cover, heater outlet duct and glove box.

16. Install the drain tube.

17. Connect the heater hoses and evaporator lines at the heater core and evaporator core.

18. On the 1987 Firenza, connect the rear lateral transaxle strut mount, if equipped.

19. On the 1987 Sunbird, install the bolts to the transaxle support (automatic only).

20. Lower the car and charge the A/C system and fill the cooling system.

1988-89

1. Disconnect the negative battery cable and discharge the A/C system and recycle the refrigerent in an approved container.

2. Drain the cooling system.

3. Raise and support the vehicle safely.

4. Disconnect the rear lateral transaxle strut mount, if equipped.

5. Disconnect the heater hoses and evaporator lines at the heater core and evaporator core.

6. Disconnect the drain tube.

7. Lower the vehicle.

8. Remove the right and left sound insulators, steering column trim cover, the heater outlet duct and the instrument panel compartment.

9. Remove the heater core cover and pull straight rearward.

10. Remove the heater core clamps and remove the core.

11. Remove the screws holding the defroster vacuum actuator to the module case.

12. Remove the evaporator cover and the evaporator core.

To Install:

13. To install, reposition the core (if installing new evaporator core--check refrigerant oil in system) and install the cover.

14. Install the screws holding the defroster vacuum actuator to the module case.

15. Install the heater core clamps and cover.

16. Install the steering column trim cover, glove box, right hand and left hand sound insulators and the heater outlet duct.

17. Install the drain tube.

18. Connect the heater hoses and evaporator lines at the heater core and evaporator core.

19. Connect the rear lateral transaxle strut mount, if equipped.

20. Evacuate and charge the A/C system.

21. Connect the negative battery cable.

22. Fill the cooling system.

1990

1. Disconnect the negative battery cable and discharge and recycle the refrigerent in an approved container.

2. Drain the cooling system.

3. Raise and support the vehicle safely.

4. Disconnect the rear lateral transaxle strut mount, if equipped.

5. Disconnect the heater hoses the heater core.

6. Disconnect the evaporator block fitting from the evaporator and discard the O-ring seals.

7. Disconnect the drain tube from the A/C module.

8. Lower the vehicle.

9. Remove the right and left sound insulators, steering column trim cover and the floor air outlet duct.

10. Remove the heater core cover and pull straight rearward.

11. Remove the heater core clamps and remove the core.

12. Remove the screws holding the defroster vacuum actuator to the module case.

13. Remove the evaporator cover and the evaporator core.

To Install:

14. To install, reposition the core (if installing new evaporator core--check refrigerant oil in system) and install the cover.

15. Install the screws holding the defroster vacuum actuator to the module case.

16. Install the heater core clamps and cover.

17. Install the floor air outlet duct, steering column trim cover and the right hand and left hand sound insulators.

18. Raise and support the vehicle safely.

19. Install the drain tube.

20. Connect the heater hoses at the heater core.

21. Connect the evaporator block fitting to the evaporator, using new O-ring seals lubricated in clean 525 refrigerent oil.

22. Connect the rear lateral transaxle strut mount, if equipped.

23. Evacuate and charge the A/C system.

24. Connect the negative battery cable.

25. Fill the cooling system.

1991-92

1. Disconnect the negative battery cable and discharge and recycle the refrigerent in an approved container.

2. Drain the cooling system.

3. Raise and support the vehicle safely.

4. Disconnect the heater hoses the heater core.

5. Disconnect the evaporator block fitting from the evaporator and discard the O-ring seals.

6. Disconnect the drain tube from the heaterA/C module.

7. Lower the vehicle.

8. Remove the right and left sound insulators, steering column trim cover and the floor air outlet duct.

9. Remove the heater core cover and pull straight rearward.

10. Remove the heater core clamps and remove the core.

11. Remove the screws holding the defroster vacuum actuator to the module case.

12. Remove the evaporator cover and the evaporator core.

To Install:

13. To install, reposition the core (if installing new evaporator core--check refrigerant oil in system) and install the cover.

14. Install the screws holding the defroster vacuum actuator to the module case.

15. Install the heater core clamps and cover.

16. Install the floor air outlet duct, steering column trim cover and the right hand and left hand sound insulators.

17. Raise and support the vehicle safely.

18. Install the drain tube.

19. Connect the heater hoses at the heater core.

20. Connect the evaporator block fitting to the evaporator, using new O-ring seals lubricated in clean 525 refrigerent oil.

21. Evacuate and charge the A/C system.

22. Connect the negative battery cable.

23. Fill the cooling system.

Control Panel

REMOVAL & INSTALLATION

1. Disconnect the battery ground cable.

2. Remove the steering column opening filler panel.

3. Remove the cigar lighter and control assembly trim plate.

4. Remove the control assembly retaining screws and pull the control assembly rearward.

5. Disconnect the electrical and vacuum connectors. Disconnect the temperature control cable from the control assembly and remove assembly.

6. Installation is the reverse of the removal procedure. Check heater-A/C system for proper operation.

Blower Switch

REMOVAL & INSTALLATION

1. Disconnect the battery ground cable.
2. Remove the instrument panel (I/P) trim plate.
3. Remove the control assembly retaining screws and pull the control assembly away from the instrument panel.
4. Remove the blower switch knob.
5. Disconnect the electrical connector.
6. Remove the blower switch retaining screws and remove the switch.
7. Installation is the reverse of the removal procedure. Check system for proper operation.

Expansion Valve

REMOVAL & INSTALLATION

◆ SEE FIG. 12

1. Drain the system of all refrigerant using an approved Recovery/Recycling system (refer to Section 1).
2. Disconnect the conection at the condenser and discard the O-ring seals.
3. Loosen the nut and seperate the front evaporator tube from the rear evaporator tube to access the expansion tube. Carefully remove the expansion tube with needle-nose pliers or special tool J-26549-89 expansion tube remover.

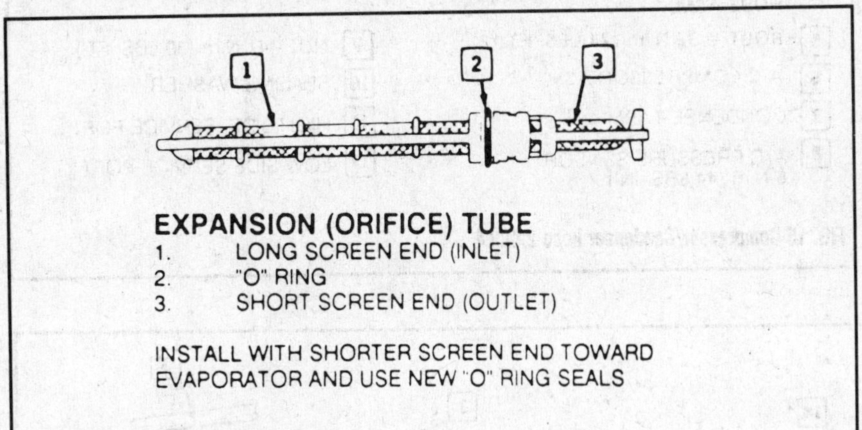

To Install:

4. Install the new expansion tube, with the short screen toward the evaporator.
5. Using new O-ring seals, assemble evaporator tube/condenser connection hand tight.
6. Torque the liquid line to 17 ft. lbs.
7. Torque the brazed nut connection to 12 ft. lbs.
8. Evacuate and charge the system (refer to Section 1).

Accumulator

REMOVAL & INSTALLATION

◆ SEE FIG. 13

1. Disconnect the battery ground cable.
2. Drain the system of all refrigerant using an approved Recovery/Recycling system (refer to Section 1).
3. Disconnect the refrigerant lines at the accumulator and discard the O-ring seals.
4. Remove the screws retaining bracket assembly to vehicle and remove the bracket and accumulator.
5. Installation is the reverse of the removal procedure.
6. Evacuate and charge the system (refer to Section 1).

Refrigerant Lines

DISCONNECT & CONNECT

◆ SEE FIGS. 14-16

Evaporator line

1. Drain the system of all refrigerant using an approved Recovery/Recycling system (refer to Section 1).
2. Disconnect the connection from the condenser and discard the O-ring seals.
3. Disconnect the line from the retaining clips on the body side rail. Disconnect the vacuum hoses from the vapor canister
4. Raise and safely support vehicle on jack stands. Disconnect the Block fitting from the evaporator and discard the O-ring seals.
5. Lower the vehicle and remove the evaporator tube.

EXPANSION (ORIFICE) TUBE
1. LONG SCREEN END (INLET)
2. "O" RING
3. SHORT SCREEN END (OUTLET)

INSTALL WITH SHORTER SCREEN END TOWARD EVAPORATOR AND USE NEW "O" RING SEALS

FIG. 12 Expansion Valve installation

1. ACCUMULATOR ASM.
2. BRACKET ASM.
3. BOLT/SCREW – 4 N·m (36 LBS. IN.)
4. RETAINER
5. CANISTER ASM.
6. BOLT/SCREW – FULLY DRIVEN, SEATED AND NOT STRIPPED
7. RETAINER
8. PARALLEL TO CENTER LINE OF CAR

VIEW A

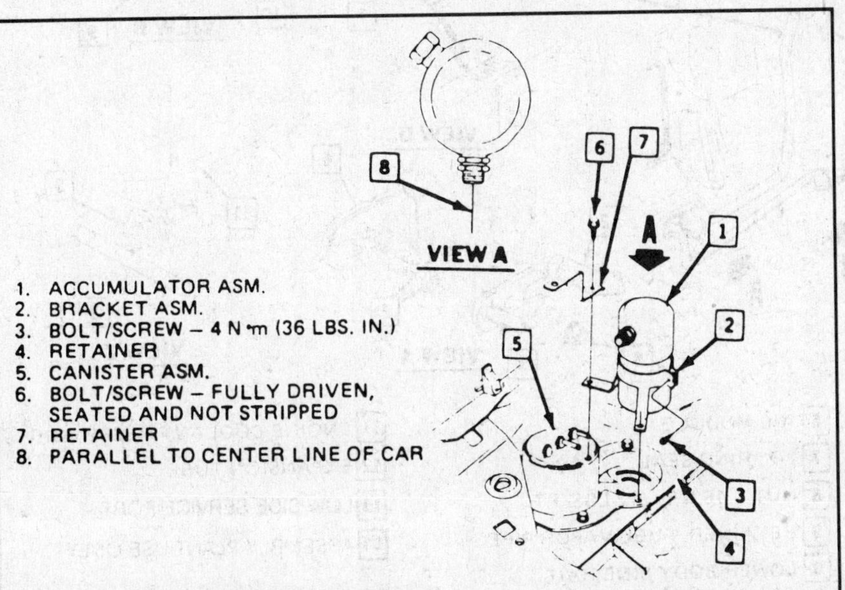

FIG. 13 Accumulator mounting

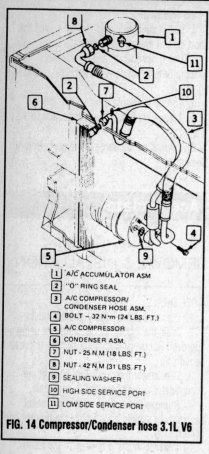

1. A/C ACCUMULATOR ASM
2. "O" RING SEAL
3. A/C COMPRESSOR/ CONDENSER HOSE ASM.
4. BOLT – 32 N·m (24 LBS. FT.)
5. A/C COMPRESSOR
6. CONDENSER ASM.
7. NUT - 25 N.M (18 LBS. FT.)
8. NUT - 42 N.M (31 LBS. FT.)
9. SEALING WASHER
10. HIGH SIDE SERVICE PORT
11. LOW SIDE SERVICE PORT

FIG. 14 Compressor/Condenser hose 3.1L V6

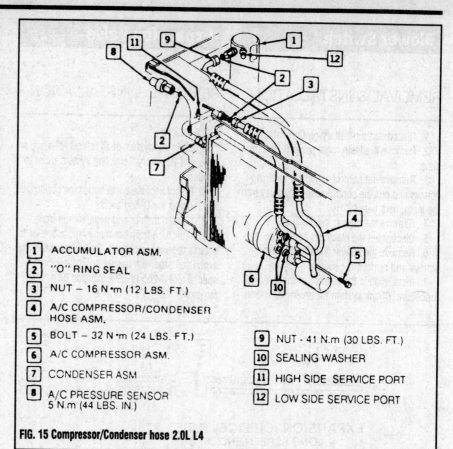

1. ACCUMULATOR ASM.
2. "O" RING SEAL
3. NUT – 16 N·m (12 LBS. FT.)
4. A/C COMPRESSOR/CONDENSER HOSE ASM.
5. BOLT – 32 N·m (24 LBS. FT.)
6. A/C COMPRESSOR ASM.
7. CONDENSER ASM
8. A/C PRESSURE SENSOR 5 N.m (44 LBS. IN.)
9. NUT - 41 N.m (30 LBS. FT.)
10. SEALING WASHER
11. HIGH SIDE SERVICE PORT
12. LOW SIDE SERVICE PORT

FIG. 15 Compressor/Condenser hose 2.0L L4

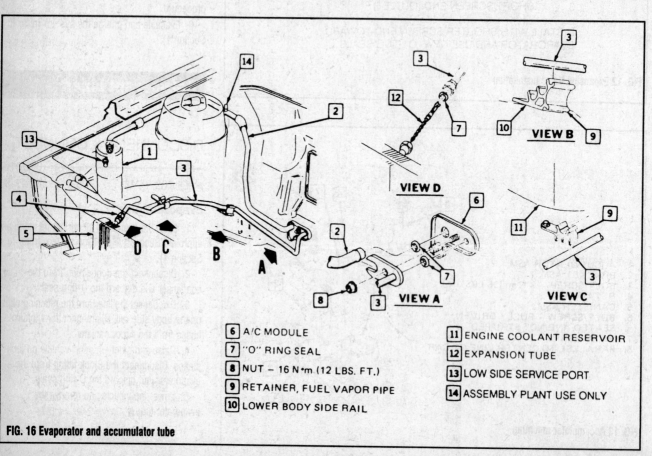

6. A/C MODULE
7. "O" RING SEAL
8. NUT – 16 N·m (12 LBS. FT.)
9. RETAINER, FUEL VAPOR PIPE
10. LOWER BODY SIDE RAIL
11. ENGINE COOLANT RESERVOIR
12. EXPANSION TUBE
13. LOW SIDE SERVICE PORT
14. ASSEMBLY PLANT USE ONLY

FIG. 16 Evaporator and accumulator tube

To Install:

6. Set the evaporator line into position.

7. Raise and safely support vehicle on jack stands. Connect the Block fitting to the evaporator using new O-ring seals.

8. Lower the vehicle. Connect the vacuum lines to the vapor canister.

9. Connect the refrigerant line to the retaining clips on the body side rail.

10. Connect the connection at the condenser using new O-ring seals.

11. Evacuate and charge the system (refer to Section 1).

Temperature Control Cable

REMOVAL & INSTALLATION

1. Disconnect the negative battery cable. Remove the right side sound insulator panel, instrument panel compartment and lower right side of the heater outlet duct.

2. Disconnect the cable at the temperature valve.

3. Remove the steering column opening filler and right hand side trim cover.

4. Remove the 4 screws attaching A/C control to panel. Disconnect temperature cable from the A/C control assembly.

5. Installation is the reverse of the removal procedure. Adjust temperature control cable.

ADJUSTMENT

If the temperature control lever fails to move to full COLD or HOT, or a large amount of lever spring back is noticed when moving to either of the full positions, the cable clip may need adjustment. Failure to grip clip in the correct manner will damage its ability to hold position on the cable. The temperature control cable must be replaced if clip retention fails.

1. To adjust the clip, grip clip (in correct manner-refer to the illustration in Heater section) at module end of cable while pulling temperature control lever to the correct full position (COLD or HOT) and connect.

2. Verify correct adjustment by observing for little or no spring back of the temperature control lever and listening for temperature door "slam" when the control lever is moved to full positions quickly.

Cycling Clutch Switch

REMOVAL & INSTALLATION

1. Drain the system of all refrigerant using an approved Recovery/Recycling system (refer to Section 1).

2. Disconnect the electrical connector from the switch in the rear head of the compressor.

3. Remove the switch retaining ring using internal snapring pliers.

4. Remove the switch from the compressor. Remove the o-ring seal from the switch cavity.

5. Installation is the reverse of the removal procedure, using new O-ring seals.

6. Evacuate and charge the system (refer to Section 1).

Air Conditioning Pressure Sensor

REMOVAL & INSTALLATION

1. Drain the system of all refrigerant using an approved Recovery/Recycling system (refer to Section 1) only if other work or service to the A/C system is necessary. The sensor is mounted on a Schrader-type valve; do not discharge the system if only the sensor is going to be replaced.

2. Disconnect the negative battery cable.

3. Remove the electrical connector at the sensor.

4. Remove the pressure sensor and discard the O-ring seal.

To Install:

5. Install new O-ring seal lubricated in clean refrigerant oil.

6. Install the pressure sensor. Torque sensor to 44 in. lbs.

7. Install the electrical connection. Reconnect the negative battery cable.

8. Evacuate and charge the system (refer to Section 1) only if necessary. Check system for proper operation.

CRUISE CONTROL

Control Switches

REMOVAL & INSTALLATION

Brake And/Or Clutch Pedal Switches

♦ SEE FIGS. 17-18

1. Remove the left sound insulator.

2. Disconnect the wiring harness connector or vacuum hose.

3. Pull the switch rearward to remove from the retainer in bracket.

To Install:

4. With brake or clutch pedal depressed, insert switch into retainer until switch seats on retainer. Audible "Clicks" can be heard as the switch is pushed forward through retainer.

5. Pull brake or clutch pedal fully rearward against pedal stop until "Clicks" can not be heard. Switch will be moved in retainer.

6. Release brake or clutch pedal and repeat Step 5 to assure that the switch is properly adjusted.

7. Install wiring harness connector or vacuum hose.

8. Install sound insulator.

Engagement Switch

The cruise control engagement switch is part of the turn signal lever assembly and is not serviceable by itself. The turn signal lever and cruise control switch must be replaced as an assembly. Refer to the necessary service procedures in Section 8.

➡ **On some models, the turn signal lever can be replaced without removing the switch assembly. Refer to the illustration in this section.**

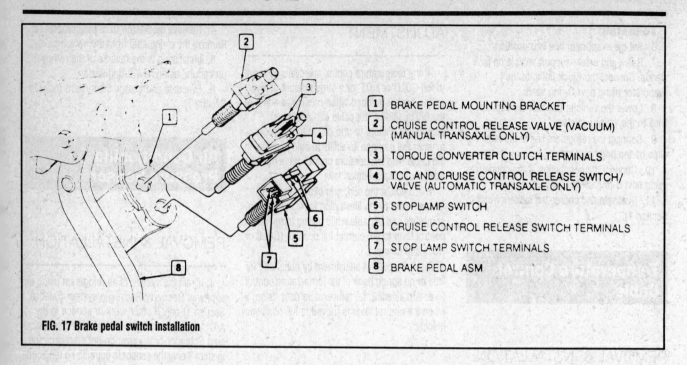

1	BRAKE PEDAL MOUNTING BRACKET
2	CRUISE CONTROL RELEASE VALVE (VACUUM) (MANUAL TRANSAXLE ONLY)
3	TORQUE CONVERTER CLUTCH TERMINALS
4	TCC AND CRUISE CONTROL RELEASE SWITCH/ VALVE (AUTOMATIC TRANSAXLE ONLY)
5	STOPLAMP SWITCH
6	CRUISE CONTROL RELEASE SWITCH TERMINALS
7	STOP LAMP SWITCH TERMINALS
8	BRAKE PEDAL ASM

FIG. 17 Brake pedal switch installation

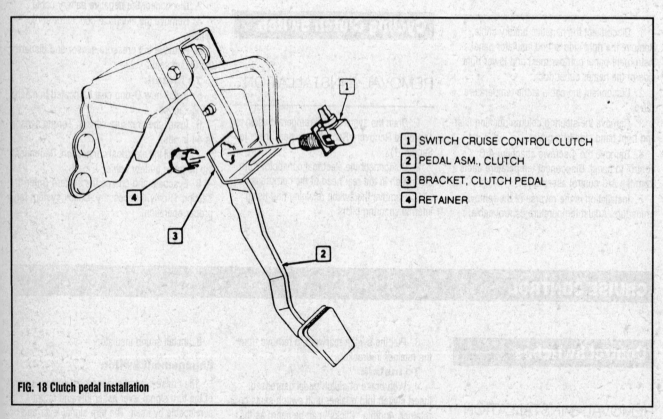

1	SWITCH CRUISE CONTROL CLUTCH
2	PEDAL ASM., CLUTCH
3	BRACKET, CLUTCH PEDAL
4	RETAINER

FIG. 18 Clutch pedal installation

Control Module

REMOVAL & INSTALLATION

♦ SEE FIG. 19

➡ **The cruise control module location may be located in different areas on some models and engines. The module is usually mounted in the lower left front area near the kickpanel left of the steering wheel, under the steering wheel on the filler panel or above the glove box area to the right side of the vehicle.**

   1. Disconnect the negative battey cable. Remove the four screws from steering column opening filler panel or remove the module from the mounting bracket.

   2. Disconnect the control module wiring connector.

   3. Remove the control module.

   4. Installation is the reverse of the removal procedure.

Servo Unit

REMOVAL & INSTALLATION

♦ SEE FIGS. 20-24

   1. Disconnect the electrical connector and the vacuum lines.

   2. Disconnect the throttle cable from the servo unit.

   3. Remove the three screws securing the servo unit and servo unit solenoid valve assembly to the mounting bracket and remove the servo.

   4. Installation is the reverse of the removal procedure. Do not stretch cable so as to make a particular tab hole connect to pin, this will prevent engine from returning to idle.

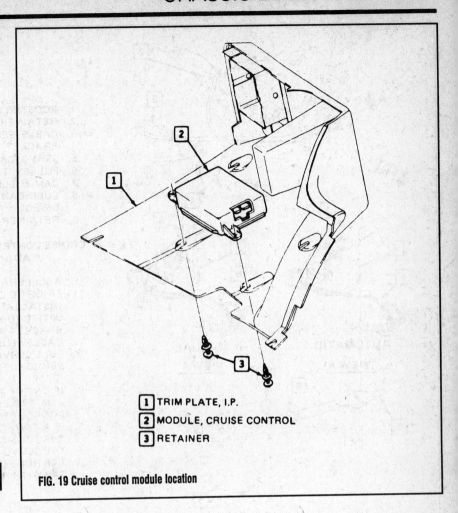

1 TRIM PLATE, I.P.
2 MODULE, CRUISE CONTROL
3 RETAINER

FIG. 19 Cruise control module location

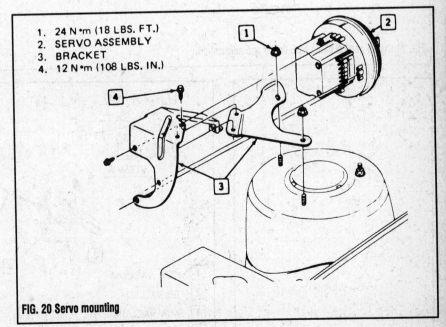

1. 24 N•m (18 LBS. FT.)
2. SERVO ASSEMBLY
3. BRACKET
4. 12 N•m (108 LBS. IN.)

FIG. 20 Servo mounting

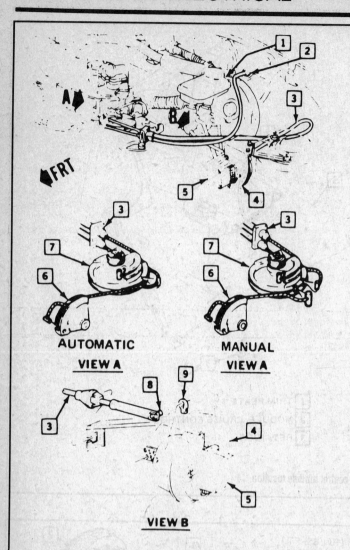

1. BOOSTER ASM., POWER BRAKE
2. RETAINER
3. CABLE, SERVO
4. BRACKET, SERVO
5. SERVO, CRUISE CONTROL
6. PULLEY, T.B.I.
7. CAM/PULLEY ASM.
8. LUBRICANT — APPLY (GM No. 9985377 OR EQUIVALENT) TO PIN.
9. RETAINER

CRUISE CONTROL CABLE INSTALLATION AND ADJUSTMENT PROCEDURE

1. ACCELERATOR CABLE MUST BE INSTALLED PRIOR TO CRUISE CONTROL CABLE INSTALLATION.
2. WITH CRUISE CABLE ATTACHED AT ENGINE BRACKET AND SERVO BRACKET, INSERT CABLE SLUG IN CRUISE PULLEY SLOT.
3. PULL SERVO ASM. END OF CABLE TOWARD SERVO WITHOUT MOVING IDLER PULLEY (CAM).
4. IF ONE OF THE SIX HOLES IN THE SERVO ASM. TAB LINES UP WITH CABLE PIN, CONNECT PIN TO TAB WITH RETAINER.
5. IF A TAB HOLE DOES NOT LINE UP WITH THE PIN, MOVE THE CABLE AWAY FROM THE SERVO ASM. UNTIL THE NEXT CLOSEST TAB HOLE LINES UP AND CONNECT PIN TO TAB WITH RETAINER.

FIG. 21 Cruise control cable installation and adjustment

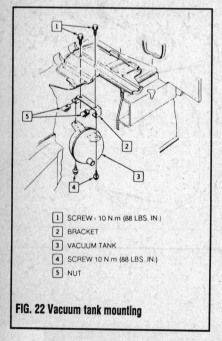

1	SCREW - 10 N.m (88 LBS. IN.)
2	BRACKET
3	VACUUM TANK
4	SCREW 10 N.m (88 LBS. IN.)
5	NUT

FIG. 22 Vacuum tank mounting

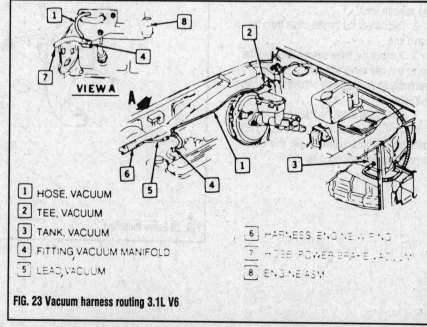

1	HOSE, VACUUM
2	TEE, VACUUM
3	TANK, VACUUM
4	FITTING, VACUUM MANIFOLD
5	LEAD, VACUUM
6	HARNESS, ENGINE WIRING
7	HOSE, POWER BRAKE VACUUM
8	ENGINE ASM.

FIG. 23 Vacuum harness routing 3.1L V6

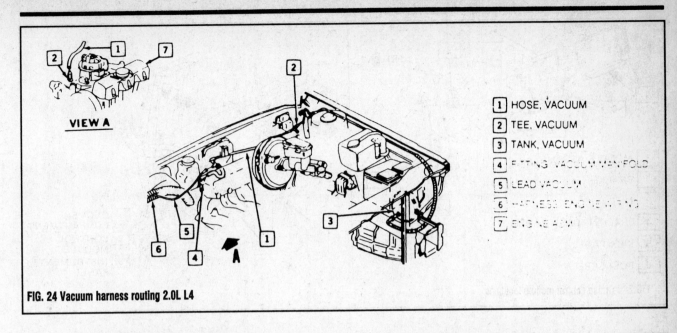

1	HOSE, VACUUM
2	TEE, VACUUM
3	TANK, VACUUM
4	FITTING VACUUM MANIFOLD
5	LEAD VACUUM
6	HARNESS ENGINE WIRING
7	ENGINE ASM

FIG. 24 Vacuum harness routing 2.0L L4

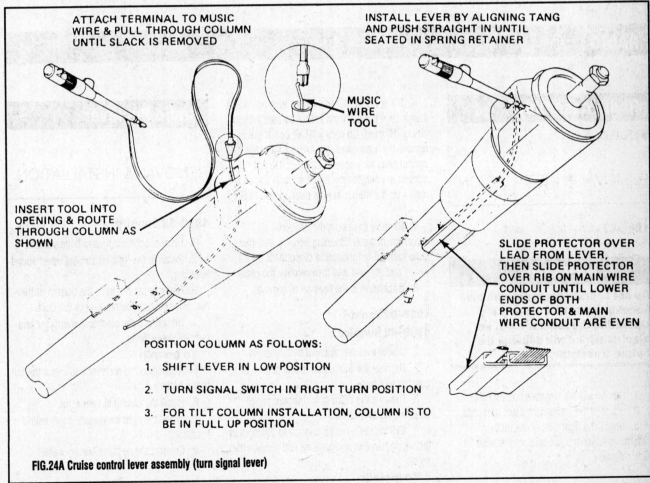

ATTACH TERMINAL TO MUSIC WIRE & PULL THROUGH COLUMN UNTIL SLACK IS REMOVED

INSTALL LEVER BY ALIGNING TANG AND PUSH STRAIGHT IN UNTIL SEATED IN SPRING RETAINER

MUSIC WIRE TOOL

INSERT TOOL INTO OPENING & ROUTE THROUGH COLUMN AS SHOWN

SLIDE PROTECTOR OVER LEAD FROM LEVER, THEN SLIDE PROTECTOR OVER RIB ON MAIN WIRE CONDUIT UNTIL LOWER ENDS OF BOTH PROTECTOR & MAIN WIRE CONDUIT ARE EVEN

POSITION COLUMN AS FOLLOWS:

1. SHIFT LEVER IN LOW POSITION

2. TURN SIGNAL SWITCH IN RIGHT TURN POSITION

3. FOR TILT COLUMN INSTALLATION, COLUMN IS TO BE IN FULL UP POSITION

FIG.24A Cruise control lever assembly (turn signal lever)

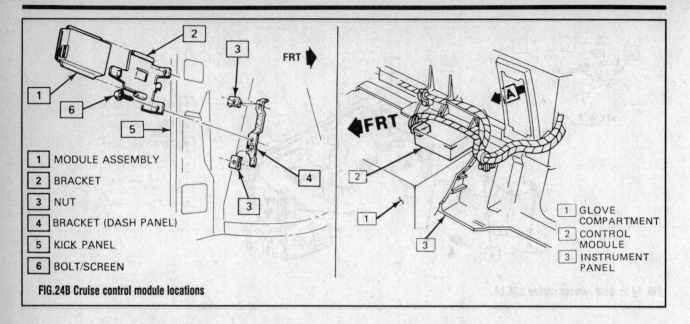

1 MODULE ASSEMBLY
2 BRACKET
3 NUT
4 BRACKET (DASH PANEL)
5 KICK PANEL
6 BOLT/SCREEN

1 GLOVE COMPARTMENT
2 CONTROL MODULE
3 INSTRUMENT PANEL

FIG.24B Cruise control module locations

RADIO

Radio Assembly

♦ SEE FIGS. 25-30

REMOVAL & INSTALLATION

1982–87

※※ WARNING

Do not operate the radio with the speaker leads disconnected. Operating the radio without an electrical load will damage the output transistors.

1. Disconnect the negative battery cable.
2. Remove the instrument panel trim plate.
3. Check the right side of the radio to determine whether a nut or a stud is used for side retention.

4. If a nut is used, remove the hush panel and then loosen the nut from below on cars without air conditioning. On cars with air conditioning, remove the hush panel, the A/C duct and the A/C control head for access to the nut. Do not remove the nut; loosen it just enough to pull the radio out. If a rubber stud is used, go on to Step 5.

5. Remove the two radio bracket-toinstrument panel attaching screws. Pull the radio forward far enough to disconnect the wiring and antenna and then remove the radio.

6. Installation is the reverse of removal.

1988–92 Except
1989–92 Sunbird

1. Disconnect the negative battery cable.
2. Remove the instrument panel cluster or console trim plate.
3. Remove the radio to instrument panel attaching screws or nuts.
4. Pull the radio out far enough to disconnect the wiring harness and antenna and remove the radio.

To Install:

5. Reposition the radio and connect the wiring harness and antenna.
6. Install the radio retaining screws or nuts.
7. Install the instrument panel cluster or console trim plate.
8. Connect the negative battery cable.

Radio Reciever

REMOVAL & INSTALLATION

1989–92 Sunbird

1. Disconnect the negative battery cable.
2. Remove the right instrument panel sound insulator.
3. Remove the nut from the bottom of the reciever securing the reciever to the duct.
4. Disconnect the electrical connector and remove the reciever.

To Install:

5. Reposition the reciever and install the nut to the bottom.
6. Install the electrical connector.
7. Install the right instrument panel sound insulator.
8. Connect the negative battery cable.

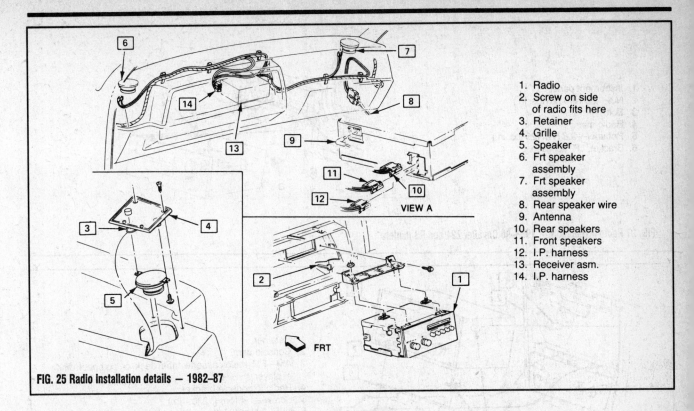

1. Radio
2. Screw on side of radio fits here
3. Retainer
4. Grille
5. Speaker
6. Frt speaker assembly
7. Frt speaker assembly
8. Rear speaker wire
9. Antenna
10. Rear speakers
11. Front speakers
12. I.P. harness
13. Receiver asm.
14. I.P. harness

FIG. 25 Radio installation details — 1982–87

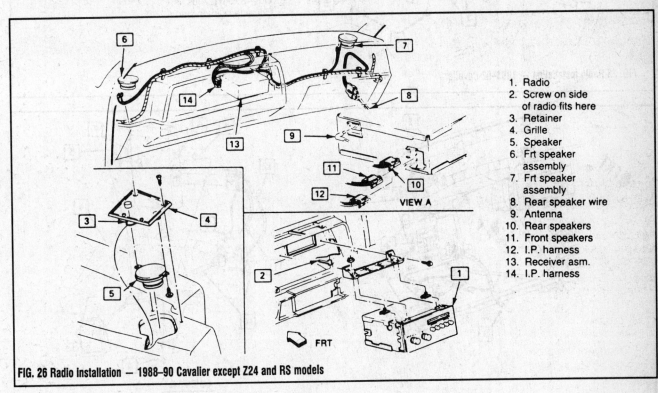

1. Radio
2. Screw on side of radio fits here
3. Retainer
4. Grille
5. Speaker
6. Frt speaker assembly
7. Frt speaker assembly
8. Rear speaker wire
9. Antenna
10. Rear speakers
11. Front speakers
12. I.P. harness
13. Receiver asm.
14. I.P. harness

FIG. 26 Radio installation — 1988–90 Cavalier except Z24 and RS models

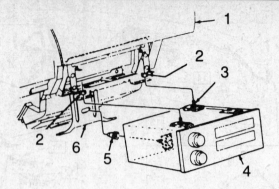

1. Instrument panel
2. Nut—2.8 N·m (25 lbs. in.)
3. Bolt
4. Radio asm.
5. Retainer—2.8 N·m (25 lbs. in.)
6. Bracket, I.P. accessory

FIG. 27 Radio installation — 1988–90 Cavalier Z24 and RS models

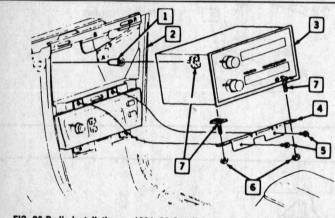

1. Retainer
2. Console asm.
3. AM—FM radio/cassette tape deck or compact disk player
4. Radio to console bracket
5. Screw—1.4 N·m (12 lbs. in.)
6. Nut—3 N·m (27 lbs. in.)
7. Threaded clip-on stud

FIG. 28 Radio installation — 1991–92 Cavalier

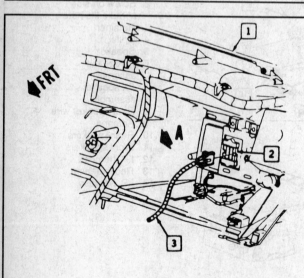
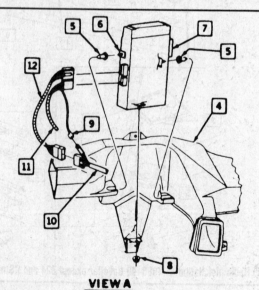

VIEW A

1. Instrument panel asm.
2. Radio control asm.
3. To receiver asm.
4. Air distributor asm.
5. Retainer
6. Stud
7. Radio receiver
8. Nut—9 N·m (6 lbs. ft.)
9. Compact disk lead
10. Lead from compact disk player or cassette player
11. To radio control asm.
12. Tape player/compact disk player wiring harness

FIG. 29 Radio receiver mounting — 1988–92 Sunbird

Radio Control Assembly

REMOVAL & INSTALLATION

1989–92 Sunbird

1. Disconnect the negative battery cable.
2. Remove the steering column closeout.
3. Remove the right instrument panel trim plate.

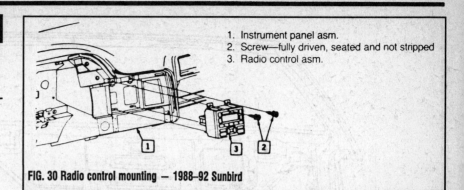

1. Instrument panel asm.
2. Screw—fully driven, seated and not stripped
3. Radio control asm.

FIG. 30 Radio control mounting — 1988–92 Sunbird

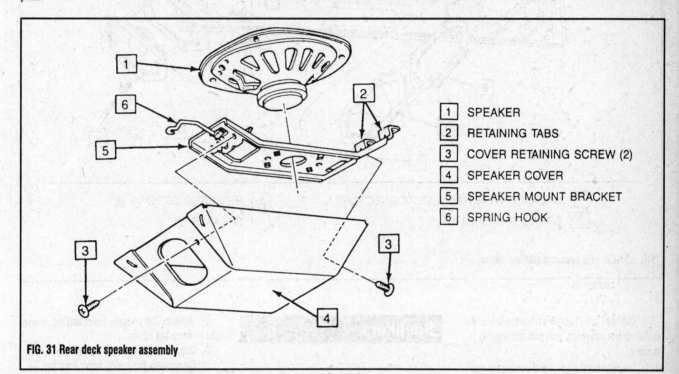

1	SPEAKER
2	RETAINING TABS
3	COVER RETAINING SCREW (2)
4	SPEAKER COVER
5	SPEAKER MOUNT BRACKET
6	SPRING HOOK

FIG. 31 Rear deck speaker assembly

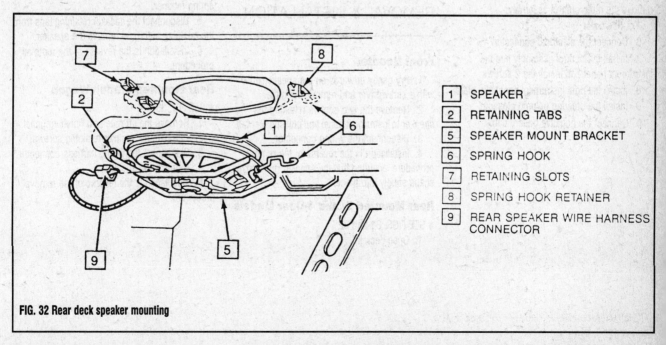

1	SPEAKER
2	RETAINING TABS
5	SPEAKER MOUNT BRACKET
6	SPRING HOOK
7	RETAINING SLOTS
8	SPRING HOOK RETAINER
9	REAR SPEAKER WIRE HARNESS CONNECTOR

FIG. 32 Rear deck speaker mounting

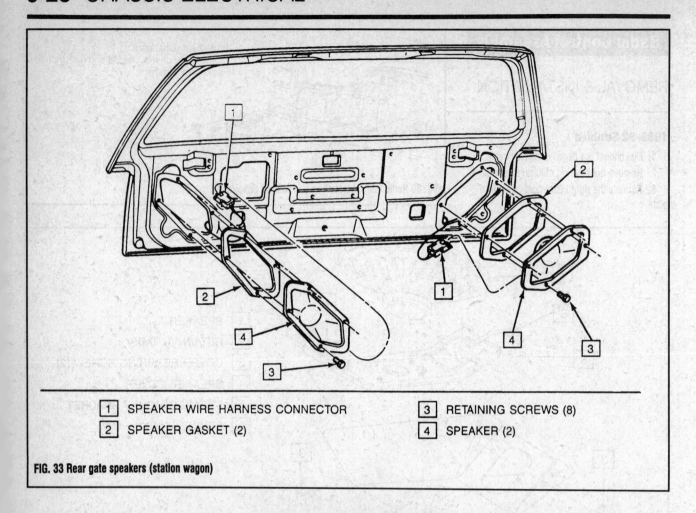

1	SPEAKER WIRE HARNESS CONNECTOR	3	RETAINING SCREWS (8)
2	SPEAKER GASKET (2)	4	SPEAKER (2)

FIG. 33 Rear gate speakers (station wagon)

4. Remove the 2 screws from the top of the radio control assembly and pull rearward to remove.

5. Disconnect the electrical connector and remove the radio control assembly.

To Install:

6. Connect the electrical connector.

7. Install the control assembly into the instrument panel and install the 2 screws.

8. Install the right instrument panel trim plate.

9. Install the steering column closeout.

10. Connect the negative battery cable.

Speakers

REMOVAL & INSTALLATION

Front Mounted

1. Pry gently upwards on the speaker grille with a screwdriver and remove the grille.

2. Remove the two screws retaining the speaker to instrument panel and pull speaker out.

3. Disconnect the wiring connector.

4. Installation is the reverse of the removal procedure, ensuring that the speaker grille cover snaps snugly into place.

Rear Mounted 2- and 4-Door Models

♦ SEE FIGS. 31 and 32

1. Open deck lid.

2. Remove the speaker cover retaing screws and remove the cover.

3. Disconnect the wiring harness connector.

4. Disconnect the spring hook from the spring retainer.

5. Disconnect the speaker retaining tabs from the retaining slots and remove the speaker.

6. Installation is the reverse of the removal procedure.

Rear Mounted Station Wagon

♦ SEE FIG. 33

1. Remove the lift gate trim finishing panel.

2. Remove the speaker retaining screws.

3. Disconnect the wiring harness connector.

4. Remove the speakers.

5. Installation is the reverse of the removal procedure.

WINDSHIELD WIPERS

♦ SEE FIGS. 34-38

Blade and Arm

REPLACEMENT

Wiper blade refill replacement procedures are detailed in Section 1.

➡ **Removal of the wiper arms requires the use of a special tool, G.M. J8966 or its equivalent. Versions of this tool are generally available in auto parts stores.**

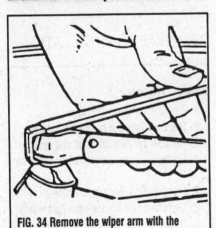

FIG. 34 Remove the wiper arm with the special tool

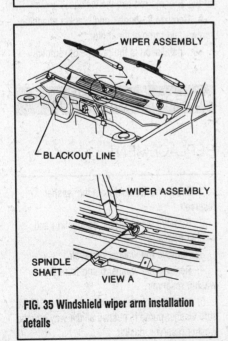

FIG. 35 Windshield wiper arm installation details

1. Insert the tool under the wiper arm and lever the arm off the shaft.
2. Disconnect the washer hose from the arm (if so equipped). Remove the arm.
3. Installation is the reverse of removal.

The proper park position is at the top of the blackout line on the glass. If the wiper arms and blades were in the proper position prior to removal, adjustment should not be required.

ADJUSTMENT

The only adjustment for the wiper arms is to remove an arm from the transmission shaft, rotate the arm the required distance and direction and then install the arm back in position so it is in line with the blackout line on the glass.

The wiper motor must be in the park position.

The correct blade-out wipe position on the driver's side is 28mm from the tip of the blade to the left windshield pillar moulding. The correct blade-down wipe position on the passenger side of the car is in line with the blackout line at the bottom of the glass.

Linkage

REMOVAL & INSTALLATION

1. Remove the wiper arms.
2. Remove the shroud top vent grille.

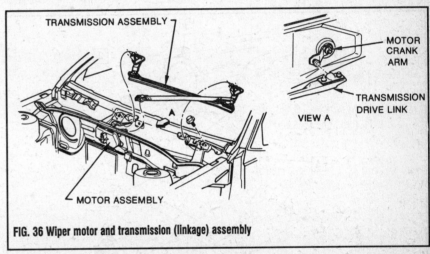

FIG. 36 Wiper motor and transmission (linkage) assembly

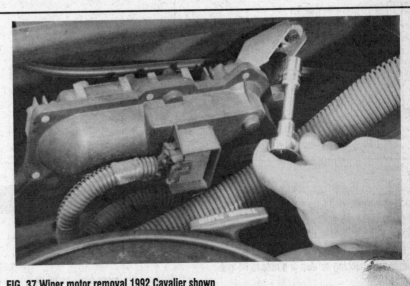

FIG. 37 Wiper motor removal 1992 Cavalier shown

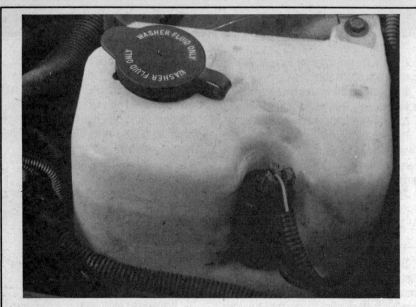

FIG. 38 Wiper washer fluid reservoir

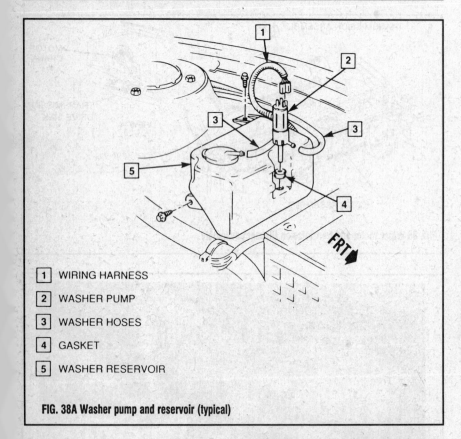

1 WIRING HARNESS

2 WASHER PUMP

3 WASHER HOSES

4 GASKET

5 WASHER RESERVOIR

FIG. 38A Washer pump and reservoir (typical)

3. Loosen (but do not remove) the drive linkto-crank arm attaching nuts.

4. Unscrew the linkage-to-cowl panel retaining screws and remove the linkage.

5. Installation is the reverse of removal. Torque the attaching screws and nuts to 64 inch lbs. (7 Nm).

Wiper Motor

REMOVAL & INSTALLATION

1. Remove the wiper arm and blade assemblies. Remove the shroud top vent grillle.

Loosen (but do not remove) the drive link-tocrank arm attaching nuts and detach the drive link from the motor crank arm.

2. Tag and disconnect all electrical leads from the wiper motor.

3. Unscrew the mounting bolts, rotate the motor up and outward and remove it.

4. Guide the crank arm through the opening in the body and then tighten the mounting bolts to 4-6 ft. lbs.

5. Install the drive link to the crank arm with the motor in the park position.

6. Installation of the remaining components is the reverse of removal.

Rear Window Wiper Motor

REMOVAL & INSTALLATION

Station Wagon

1. Turn the ignition switch OFF.

2. Pull the wiper arm from the pivot shaft.

3. Remove the pivot shaft nut and spacers.

4. Open the tailgate and remove the inner trim panel.

5. Remove the license plate housing.

6. Disconnect the license plate light wiring.

7. Disconnect the wiper motor wiring.

8. Remove the linkage arm locking clip, pry off the arm and remove the linkage.

9. Remove the motor and bracket attaching screws and remove the motor.

10. Installation is the reverse of removal.

Washer Pump

REPLACEMENT

1. Drain washer fluid from the washer reservoir.

2. Remove the electrical connection and washer hoses.

3. Remove the washer reservoir.

4. Remove the washer pump from the washer reservoir.

5. Installation is the reverse of removal. Make sure washer pump is pushed all the way into the washer reservoir gasket.

INSTRUMENTS AND SWITCHES

Instrument Cluster

REMOVAL & INSTALLATION

♦ SEE FIGS. 39-46

Cavalier

1982-90

1. Disconnect the negative battery cable.
2. Remove the speedometer cluster trim plate.
3. Remove the speedometer cluster attaching screws.
4. Lower the steering column. Pull the cluster away from the instrument panel and disconnect the speedometer cable.
5. Disconnect the vehicle speed sensor connector from the cluster. Disconnect all other electrical connectors as required.
6. Remove the cluster housing from the vehicle.
7. Installation is the reverse of the removal procedure.

1991-92

1. Disconnect the negative battery cable.

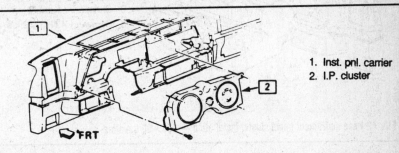

1. Inst. pnl. carrier
2. I.P. cluster

FIG. 39 Base instrument panel and cluster installation — 1982–88 Cavalier shown, other models similar

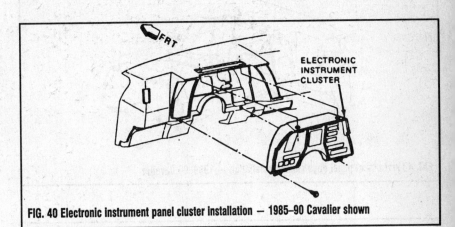

ELECTRONIC INSTRUMENT CLUSTER

FIG. 40 Electronic instrument panel cluster installation — 1985–90 Cavalier shown

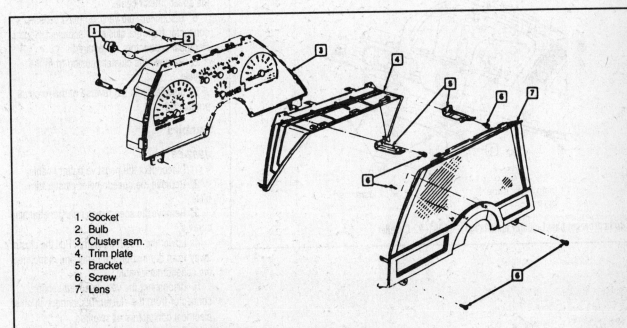

1. Socket
2. Bulb
3. Cluster asm.
4. Trim plate
5. Bracket
6. Screw
7. Lens

FIG. 41 Disassembled view of the gage instrument panel cluster — 1988–90 Cavalier

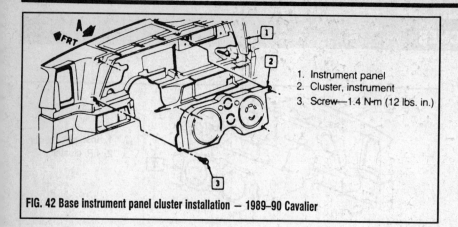

1. Instrument panel
2. Cluster, instrument
3. Screw—1.4 N·m (12 lbs. in.)

FIG. 42 Base instrument panel cluster installation — 1989–90 Cavalier

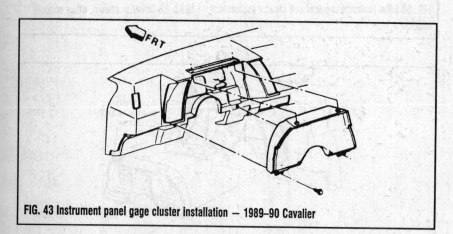

FIG. 43 Instrument panel gage cluster installation — 1989–90 Cavalier

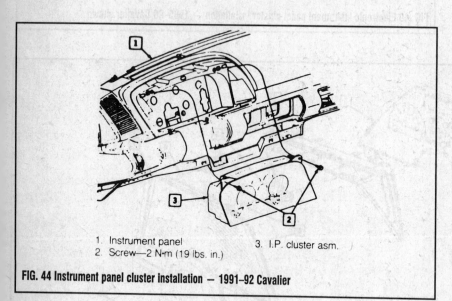

1. Instrument panel
2. Screw—2 N·m (19 lbs. in.)
3. I.P. cluster asm.

FIG. 44 Instrument panel cluster installation — 1991–92 Cavalier

2. Remove the 4 screws from the steering column opening filler and remove the steering column opening filler.

3. Pull down slightly on the steering column collar to gain access and remove the 2 screws from the bottom of the cluster extension and remove the extension.

4. Disconnect the electrical connectors from the instrument panel dimmer and interior lamp control switches.

5. Remove the 2 screws from the top of the cluster and pull the cluster rearward to remove.

To Install:

6. Reposition the cluster and install the 2 screws to the top of the cluster.

7. Connect the electrical connectors to the instrument panel dimmer and interior lamp control switches.

8. Reposition the cluster extension and install the 2 screws to the bottom of the cluster extension.

9. Reposition the steering column opening filler and install the 4 retaining screws.

10. Connect the negative battery cable.

Cimarron

1982-88

1. Disconnect the negative battery cable.

2. Remove the speedometer cluster trim plate.

3. Remove the speedometer cluster attaching screws.

4. Lower the steering column. Pull the cluster away from the instrument panel and disconnect the speedometer cable.

5. Disconnect the vehicle speed sensor connector from the cluster. Disconnect all other electrical connectors as required.

6. Remove the cluster housing from the vehicle.

7. Installation is the reverse of the removal procedure.

Sunbird

1982-88

1. Disconnect the negative battery cable.

2. Remove the speedometer cluster trim plate.

3. Remove the speedometer cluster attaching screws.

4. Lower the steering column. Pull the cluster away from the instrument panel and disconnect the speedometer cable.

5. Disconnect the vehicle speed sensor connector from the cluster. Disconnect all other electrical connectors as required.

6. Remove the cluster housing from the vehicle.

7. Installation is the reverse of the removal procedure.

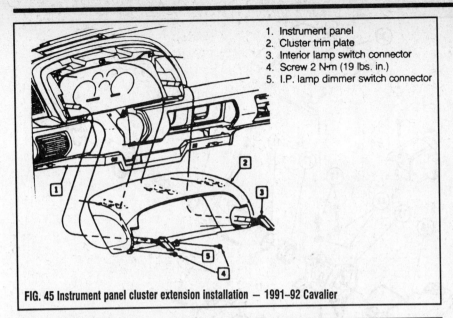

1. Instrument panel
2. Cluster trim plate
3. Interior lamp switch connector
4. Screw 2 N·m (19 lbs. in.)
5. I.P. lamp dimmer switch connector

FIG. 45 Instrument panel cluster extension installation — 1991–92 Cavalier

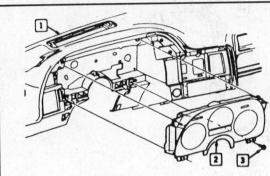

1. Instrument panel asm.
2. Cluster asm., I.P.
3. Screw—1.4 N·m (12 lbs. in.)

FIG. 46 Instrument panel cluster installation — 1989–92 Sunbird

1989–92

1. Disconnect the negative battery cable.
2. Remove the speedometer cluster trim plate.
3. Remove the 4 speedometer cluster attaching screws.
4. Remove the steering column opening filler cover which is retained by spring clips.
5. Pull the cluster away from the instrument panel and disconnect the speedometer cable.
6. Disconnect all other electrical connectors as required.
7. Remove the instrument cluster from the vehicle.
8. Installation is the reverse of the removal procedure.

Skyhawk and Firenza

1. Disconnect the negative battery cable.
2. Remove the steering column trim cover. Remove the left and right hand trim cover.
3. Remove the cluster trim cover.
4. Remove the screws attaching the lens and bezel to the cluster carrier.

5. Lower the steering wheel column by removing the 2 upper steering column attaching bolts.
6. Remove the screws attaching the cluster housing to the cluster carrier. Pull the cluster out slightly from the instrument panel and disconnect the speedometer cable. Disconnect all others connectors.
7. Remove the cluster housing from the vehicle.
8. Installation is the reverse of the removal procedure.

➡ **Some 1987–88 Firenza vehicles, equipped with manual control air conditioning, may exhibit metallic rattle or buzzing noise coming from the center of the instrument panel. Under certain road or engine load conditions, with the air conditioning ON, the metal defroster valve in the air conditioning module assembly may vibrate against the case causing the noise. The noise may be heard in all modes except defrost.**

Wiper Switch

REMOVAL & INSTALLATION

◆ SEE FIGS. 47-51

**All Models Except
1989–92 Sunbird
1991–92 Cavalier And
Dash Mounted Type Switch**

STANDARD STEERING COLUMNS

Remove the ignition and dimmer switch as outlined in Section 8 and remove the parts as shown in the illustration to remove the wiper switch.

ADJUSTABLE STEERING COLUMNS

The wiper switch is located inside the steering column cover. To gain access to the switch the steering wheel, turn signal switch and ignition lock will have to be removed. (Refer to Section 8 for these procedures). Remove the parts in the illustration, drive out the pivot pin with a punch and remove the switch.

1989–92 Sunbird

1. Disconnect the negative battery cable.
2. Remove the right side trim plate from the instrument panel.
3. Remove the windshield wiper switch housing attaching screw.
4. Disconnect the switch wiring harness connector and remove the switch.

To Install:

5. Connect the switch wiring harness connector.
6. Reposition the switch to the to the instrument panel and install the attaching screw.
7. Install the right side trim plate to the instrument panel.
8. Connect the negative battery cable.

1991–92 Cavalier

1. Disconnect the negative battery cable.
2. Remove the pad and horn lead, retainer and nut and remove the steering wheel from the column, using a suitable puller.
3. Remove the 2 lower column cover retaining screws.
4. Remove the 3 bottom retaining screws from lower column cover.
5. Separate the rose bud fastener (integral to wire harness) from the jacket assembly.
6. Remove the wipe/wash switch retaining screws.

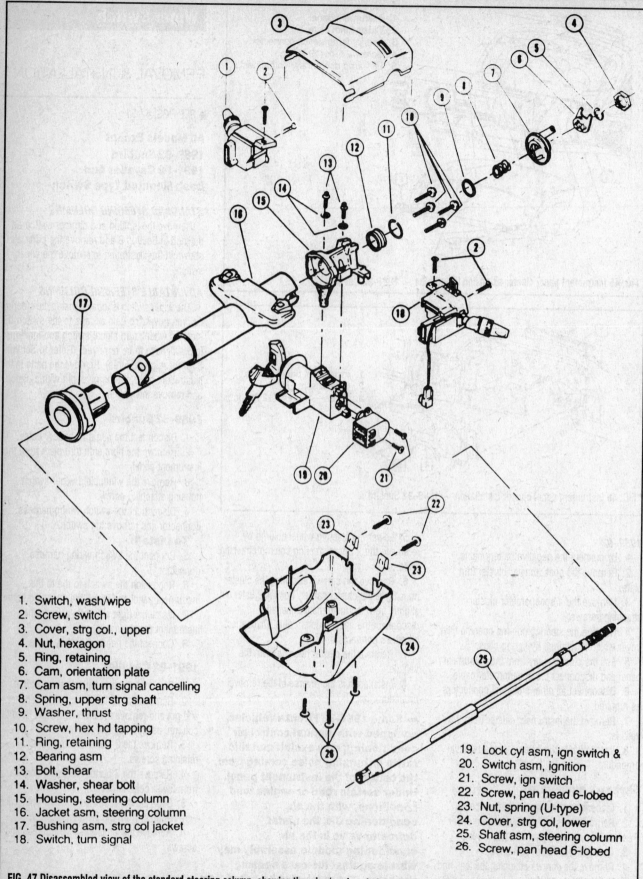

1. Switch, wash/wipe
2. Screw, switch
3. Cover, strg col., upper
4. Nut, hexagon
5. Ring, retaining
6. Cam, orientation plate
7. Cam asm, turn signal cancelling
8. Spring, upper strg shaft
9. Washer, thrust
10. Screw, hex hd tapping
11. Ring, retaining
12. Bearing asm
13. Bolt, shear
14. Washer, shear bolt
15. Housing, steering column
16. Jacket asm, steering column
17. Bushing asm, strg col jacket
18. Switch, turn signal

19. Lock cyl asm, ign switch &
20. Switch asm, ignition
21. Screw, ign switch
22. Screw, pan head 6-lobed
23. Nut, spring (U-type)
24. Cover, strg col, lower
25. Shaft asm, steering column
26. Screw, pan head 6-lobed

FIG. 47 Disassembled view of the standard steering column, showing the wipe/wash switch installation — 1991-92 Cavalier

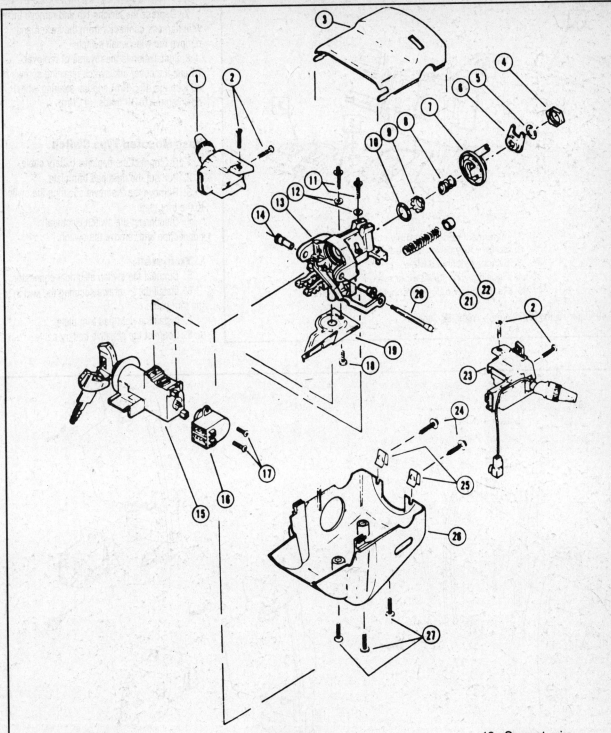

1. Switch, wash/wipe
2. Screw, switch
3. Cover, strg col, upper
4. Nut, hexagon
5. Ring, retaining
6. Cam, orientation plate
7. Cam asm, turn signal cancelling
8. Spring, upper bearing
9. Seat, inner race

10. Race, inner
11. Bolt, shear
12. Washer, shear bolt
13. Housing asm, steering column
14. Pin, pivot
15. Lock cyl asm, ign switch &
16. Switch asm, ignition
17. Screw, ign switch
18. Switch, wire support

19. Support, wire
20. Lever, tilt
21. Spring, wheel tilt
22. Retainer, spring
23. Switch, turn signal
24. Screw, pan head 6-lobed
25. Nut, spring (U-type)
26. Cover, strg col, lower
27. Screw, pan head 6-lobed

FIG. 48 Disassembled view of the tilt steering column, showing the wipe/wash switch installation – 1991–92 Cavalier

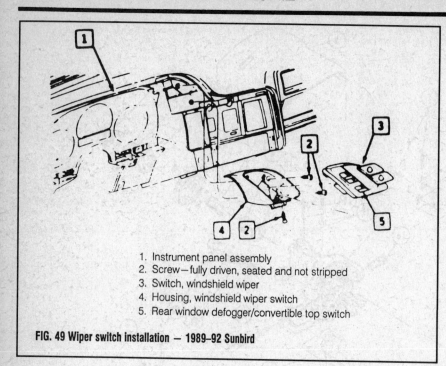

1. Instrument panel assembly
2. Screw—fully driven, seated and not stripped
3. Switch, windshield wiper
4. Housing, windshield wiper switch
5. Rear window defogger/convertible top switch

FIG. 49 Wiper switch installation — 1989–92 Sunbird

7. Depress the locking tab and remove the wire harness connector from the switch and remove the wipe/wash switch.

8. Installation is the reverse of removal. Torque the cover and switch retaining screws to 49 inch lbs. (5.5 Nm) and the steering wheel retaining nut to 30 ft. lbs. (41 Nm).

Dash Mounted Type Switch

1. Disconnect the negative battery cable.
2. Pull out the right pad trim plate.
3. Remove the 2 screws securing the switch to the trim plate.
4. Disconnect the switch electrical connection and remove the switch.

To Install:

5. Connect the switch electrical connector.
6. Install the 2 screws securing the switch to the trim plate.
7. Install the right pad trim plate.
8. Connect the negative battery cable.

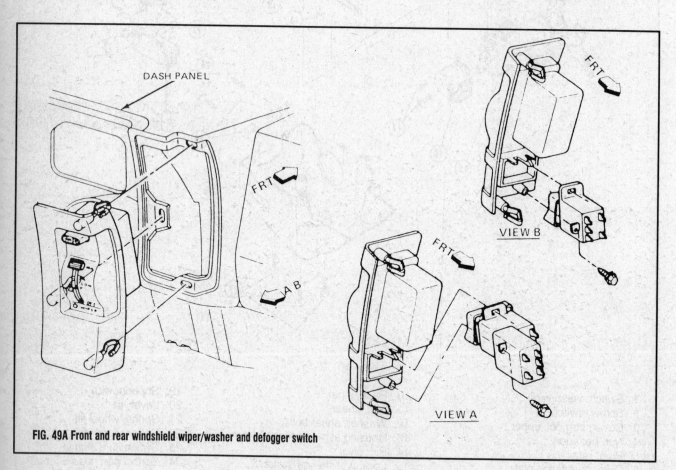

FIG. 49A Front and rear windshield wiper/washer and defogger switch

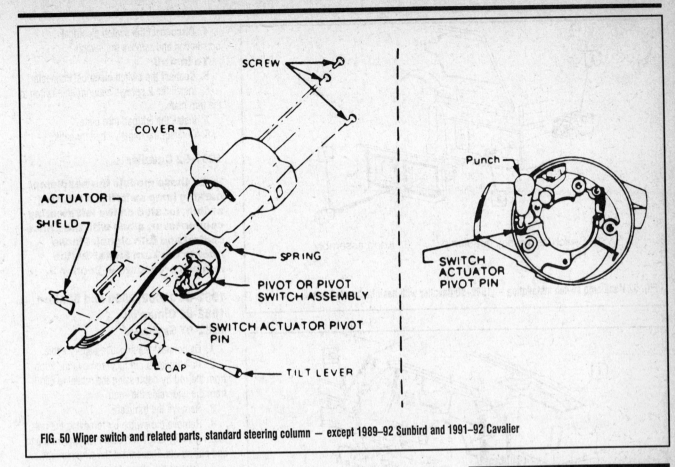

FIG. 50 Wiper switch and related parts, standard steering column — except 1989–92 Sunbird and 1991–92 Cavalier

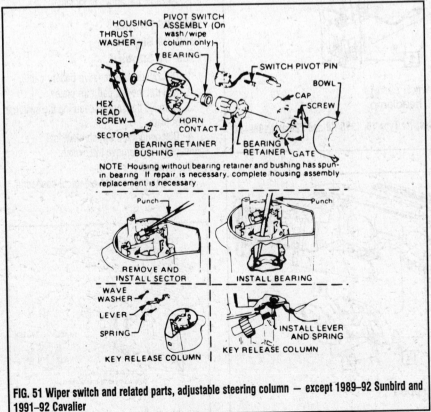

NOTE Housing without bearing retainer and bushing has spun-in bearing If repair is necessary, complete housing assembly replacement is necessary.

FIG. 51 Wiper switch and related parts, adjustable steering column — except 1989–92 Sunbird and 1991–92 Cavalier

Headlight Switch

REMOVAL & INSTALLATION

▶ SEE FIGS. 52-56

1982–90 All Cavalier except
1985–87 Cavalier Type 10
1988 RS and Z24
1989–90 Z24

1. Disconnect the negative battery cable.
2. Pull the knob out fully, remove the knob from the rod by depressing the retaining clip from the underside the knob.
3. Remove the trimplate.
4. Remove the switch by removing the nut, rotating the switch 180°, then tilting forward and and pulling out. Disconnect the wire harness.
5. Reverse the above to install.

1985–87 Cavalier Type 10
1988 RS and Z24
1989–90 Z24

1. Disconnect the negative battery cable.
2. Pull out the left pad trim plate.
3. Remove the 2 screws securing the switch to the trim plate.

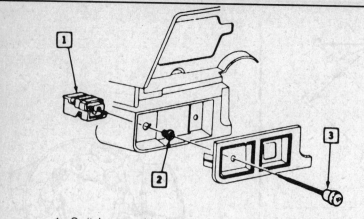

1. Switch assembly, headlamp
2. Nut
3. Knob assembly

FIG. 52 Headlamp switch installation — 1982–90 Cavalier with base instrument panel

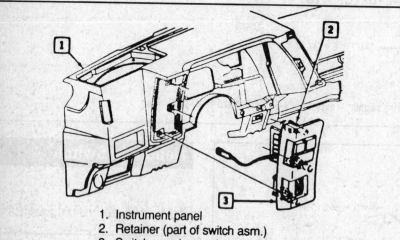

1. Instrument panel
2. Retainer (part of switch asm.)
3. Switch panel asm., headlamp

FIG. 53 Headlamp switch installation — 1985–87 Cavalier Type 10, 1988 RS and Z24 and 1989–90 Z24

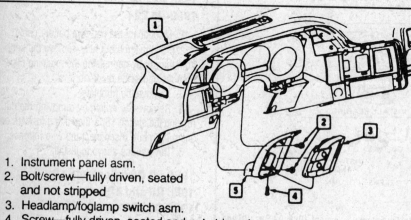

1. Instrument panel asm.
2. Bolt/screw—fully driven, seated and not stripped
3. Headlamp/foglamp switch asm.
4. Screw—fully driven, seated and not stripped
5. Headlamp switch panel housing

FIG. 54 Headlamp switch installation — 1989–92 Sunbird

4. Disconnect the switch electrical connection and remove the switch.

To Install:

5. Connect the switch electrical connector.
6. Install the 2 screws securing the switch to the trim plate.
7. Install the left pad trim plate.
8. Connect the negative battery cable.

1991–92 Cavalier

➡ On these models the headlamp/parking lamp switch is a rotating switch, located on the left steering column lever, along with the cruise control and turn signal. Please refer to the Turn Signal Switch removal procedure in Section 8.

1982–88 J2000, 2000 and Sunbird
1982–88 Cimarron
1982–87 Skyhawk

1. Disconnect the negative battery cable.
2. Pull the knob out fully, remove the knob from the rod by depressing the retaining clip from the underside the knob.
3. Remove the trimplate.
4. Remove the switch by removing the nut, rotating the switch 180°, then tilting forward and and pulling out. Disconnect the wire harness.
5. Reverse the above to install.

1982–89 Firenza
1982–89 Skyhawk
1989–92 Sunbird

1. Disconnect the negative battery cable.
2. Pull out the left pad trim plate.
3. Remove the screws securing the switch to the trim plate.
4. Disconnect the switch electrical connection and remove the switch.

To install:

5. Connect the switch electrical connector.

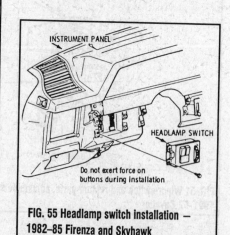

FIG. 55 Headlamp switch installation — 1982–85 Firenza and Skyhawk

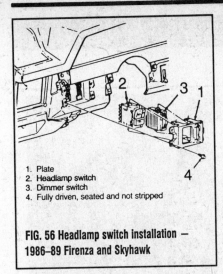

1. Plate
2. Headlamp switch
3. Dimmer switch
4. Fully driven, seated and not stripped

FIG. 56 Headlamp switch installation — 1986–89 Firenza and Skyhawk

6. Install the screws securing the switch to the trim plate.
7. Install the left pad trim plate.
8. Connect the negative battery cable.

Clock

REMOVAL & INSTALLATION

The clock is part of the radio. If the clock is found to be defective the radio will have to be removed and sent to an authorized facility for clock repair.

Speedometer Cable

♦ SEE FIGS. 57 and 58

REPLACEMENT

1. Reach behind the instrument cluster and push the speedometer cable casing toward the speedometer while depressing the retaining spring on the back of the instrument cluster case. Once the retaining spring has released, hold it in while pulling outward on the casing to disconnect the casing from the speedometer.

➡ **Removal of the steering column trim plate and/or the speedometer cluster may provide better access to the cable.**

2. Remove the cable casing sealing plug from the dash panel. Then, pull the casing down from behind the dash and remove the cable.

3. If the cable is broken and cannot be entirely removed from the top, support the car securely, and then unscrew the cable casing connector at the transaxle. Pull the bottom part of the cable out, and then screw the connector back onto the transaxle.

4. Lubricate the new cable. Insert it into the casing until it bottoms. Push inward while rotating it until the square portion at the bottom engages with the coupling in the transaxle, permitting the cable to move in another inch or so. Then, reconnect the cable casing to the speedometer and install the sealing plug into the dash panel.

Ignition Switch

The ignition switch removal and installation procedure is given in Section 8, under steering, because the steering wheel must be removed for access to the ignition switch.

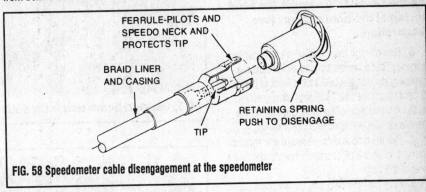

FIG. 58 Speedometer cable disengagement at the speedometer

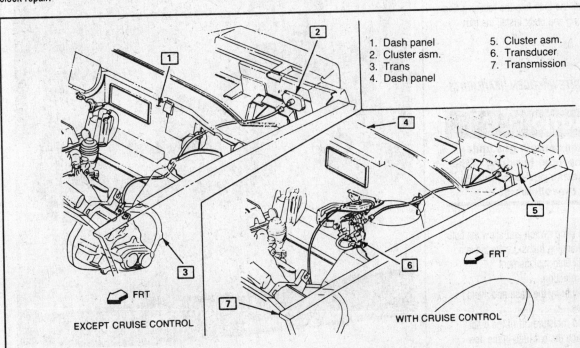

1. Dash panel
2. Cluster asm.
3. Trans
4. Dash panel
5. Cluster asm.
6. Transducer
7. Transmission

EXCEPT CRUISE CONTROL

WITH CRUISE CONTROL

FIG. 57 Speedometer cable routing — 1982–87

LIGHTING

Headlights

♦ SEE FIGS. 59-62

REMOVAL & INSTALLATION

1982–87

EXCEPT COMPOSITE HALOGEN HEADLIGHTS

1. Disconnect the negative battery cable.
2. Remove the headlamp trim panel (grille panel) attaching screws.

➡ **The trim panel retaining screws on the Cavalier are under the hood, on top of the front support (see illustration).**

3. Remove the four headlamp bulb retaining screws. These are the screws which hold the retaining ring for the bulb to the front of the car. Do not touch the two headlamp aiming screws, at the top and side of the retaining ring, or the headlamp aim will have to be readjusted.

4. Pull the bulb and ring forward and separate them. Unplug the electrical connector from the rear of the bulb.

5. Plug the new bulb into the electrical connector. Install the bulb into the retaining ring and install the ring and bulb. Install the trim panel.

1987–92

WITH COMPOSITE HALOGEN HEADLIGHTS

❈❈❈ CAUTION

Halogen bulbs contain gas under pressure. Improper handling of the bulb could cause personal injury. Please note the following:

• Turn off the lamp switch and allow the bulb to cool before changing bulbs. Leave the lamp switch **OFF** until bulb replacement.
• Wear eye protection.
• Handle the bulb by the base and avoid touching the glass.
• Keep dirt and moisture off of the bulb.
• Carefully place the old bulb in the new bulb's carton and dispose of properly.

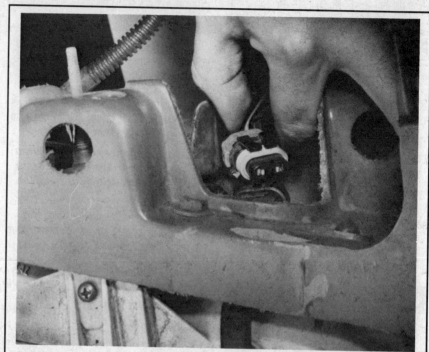

FIG. 59 Disconnect the wire conection from bulb on composite halogen lights

FIG. 60 Grasp bulb socket and twist on composite halogen lights

FIG. 61 Pull bulb out, donot touch bulb with fingers on composite halogen lights

1. Park the car on a level surface, at least 25 ft. from a wall that is perpendicular to the ground surface. Make sure there is no excess weight in the trunk, unless you normally travel with that amount of weight in the car. Bounce the car a few times to settle the suspension.

2. Measure and record the distance from the ground to the center of each headlight lens.

3. Measure and record the distance between lens centers (from one side to the other side).

4. Turn the headlights on and adjust so the hot-spots (lit area of most concentrated intensity) are the same height from the ground and distance from each other that the lens centers were in Steps 2 and 3. Adjusting screws are located on the inner side (horizontal aim) and top (vertical aim)of the lens.

5. Adjust each headlight so the hot-spot drops about 1 in. (25mm).

6. Adjust each headlight so it points to the right about 1 in. (25mm) on the wall; this will prevent glare in an oncoming driver's eyes.

7. Take your car to a service station and see how good you did !

Signal and Marker Lights

REMOVAL & INSTALLATION

Front Turn Signal and Parking Lights

Bulbs at the front of the car can normally be replaced from beneath the car or from under the hood. Some bulbs may require removal of the outer lens. Remove the socket from the lamp housing by twisting, then replace the bulb and reinstall the socket.

Rear Stop and turn Signal Lamps

▶ SEE FIGS. 63-67

Various methods are employed to remove and install the components of the tail lamp assemblies. Tail lamp bulbs can be replaced by removing the screws which retain the lamp assemblies to the rear end panel and then removing the lamp assemblies. On some models it will be necessary to remove the wing nut inside the rear compartment which retains the tail lamp to the body.

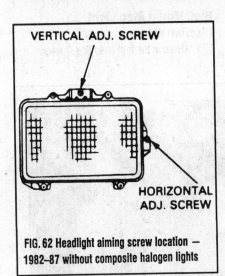

VERTICAL ADJ. SCREW

HORIZONTAL ADJ. SCREW

FIG. 62 Headlight aiming screw location — 1982–87 without composite halogen lights

• Keep halogen bulbs out of reach of children.

1. Open the hood.

2. Disconnect the negative battery cable.

3. Remove the socket by turning counterclockwise and pulling out.

4. Pull the bulb rearward with a vertical rocking motion.

5. With one hand, grip the wiring harness connector (not the wires). With the other hand, grip the base of the bulb (not the glass) and carefully pull the bulb base apart from the wiring harness connector.

To Install:

6. Carefully install the bulb socket to the lamp harness connector. Make sure the low beam connector is to the low beam lamp and the high beam connector is to the high beam lamp.

7. Align the bulb flange notch with the lamp housing keyway and insert the bulb into the lamp housing.

8. Install the socket into the housing and turn clockwise.

HEADLIGHT AIMING

Headlights should be checked for proper aim during your annual state inspection (each state has its own headlight aiming laws). If your state doesn't require state inspection, you should ideally have headlight aim checked annually, especially if you travel on rough road surfaces often. Headlights that are not aimed properly can create a dangerous situation by blinding oncoming drivers and by not illuminating the road properly for you. A universal do-it-yourself procedure that can be used in a pinch is given here, although it is not intended as the true method; expensive aiming tools are needed for that. If the headlights don't come close to straight ahead when aiming, something is properly broken; in fact if they are so far off as to catch your attention in the first place, a support piece probably broke.

FIG. 63 Remove the wing nuts on rear lights

Side Marker Lights

The rear quarter or front fender side marker lamp operates in conjuction with the tail lamp circuit. Some models use a wrap around front parking or tail lamp assembly which doubles as a side marker lamp.

On some models the side marker lamp is installed from the inside of the rear compartment or front fender but is retained with screws which are installed from outside the fender or quarter panel. The bulbs on these models can be replaced by reaching behind the front fender or opening the rear compartment and turning the socket to release it from the housing and pulling the bulb out from the socket.

High Mount Stop Light
(4-Door W/O Luggage Rack)

▶ SEE FIGS. 68-72

1. Remove the two mounting screws.
2. Disconnect the electrical connector.
3. Remove the two cover screws and remove the bulb.
4. Installation is the reverse of the removal procedure.

High Mount Stop Light
(Station Wagon)

1. Remove the four mounting screws.

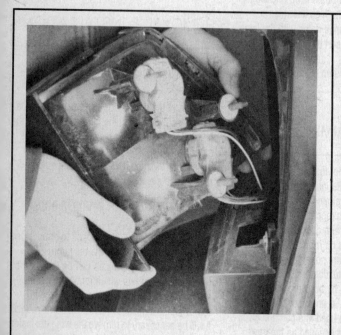

FIG. 64 Remove the rear light assembly

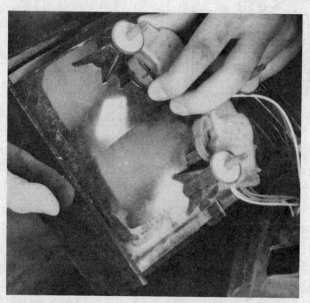

FIG. 65 Twist bulb socket

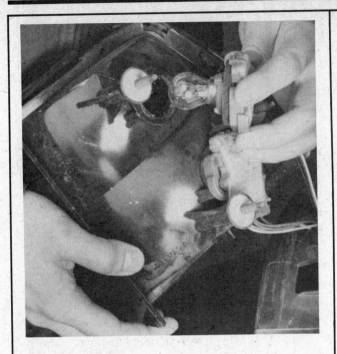

FIG. 66 Pull socket out

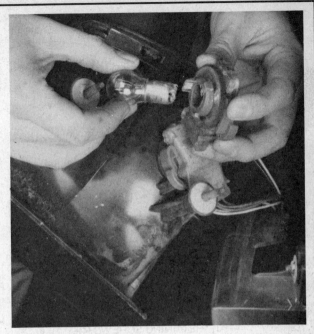

FIG. 67 Twist and remove bulb

2. Disconnect the electrical connector.

3. Remove the two cover screws and remove the bulb.

4. Installation is the reverse of the removal procedure.

High Mount Stop Light (With Luggage Rack or Aero Wing)

1. Remove the two cover screws and remove the bulb.

2. Installation is the reverse of the removal procedure.

Fog Lamps

REMOVAL & INSTALLATION

1. Remove the two screws from the lens retainers.

2. Remove the two lens retainers.

3. Remove the lens/bulb housing.

4. Disconnect the bulb retainer clip.

5. Disconnect the electrical connector and remove the bulb.

6. Installation is the reverse of the removal procedure.

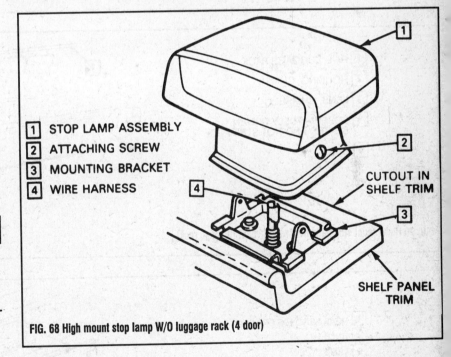

1. STOP LAMP ASSEMBLY
2. ATTACHING SCREW
3. MOUNTING BRACKET
4. WIRE HARNESS

CUTOUT IN SHELF TRIM

SHELF PANEL TRIM

FIG. 68 High mount stop lamp W/O luggage rack (4 door)

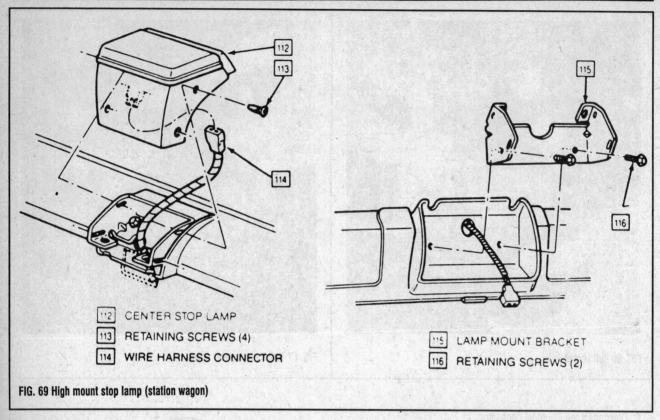

112 CENTER STOP LAMP

113 RETAINING SCREWS (4)

114 WIRE HARNESS CONNECTOR

115 LAMP MOUNT BRACKET

116 RETAINING SCREWS (2)

FIG. 69 High mount stop lamp (station wagon)

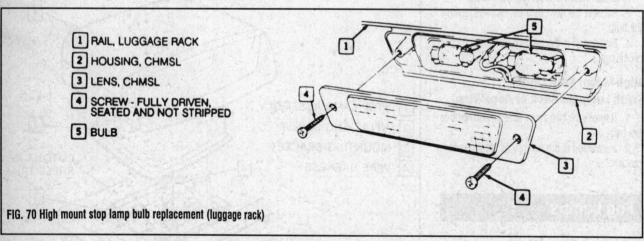

1 RAIL, LUGGAGE RACK

2 HOUSING, CHMSL

3 LENS, CHMSL

4 SCREW - FULLY DRIVEN, SEATED AND NOT STRIPPED

5 BULB

FIG. 70 High mount stop lamp bulb replacement (luggage rack)

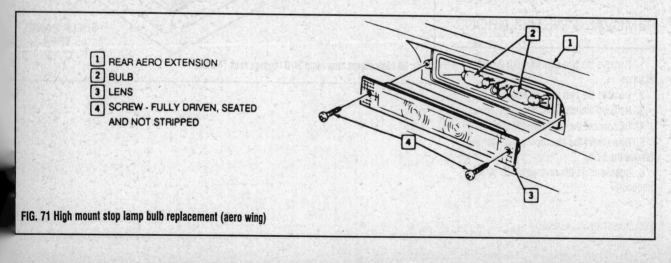

1 REAR AERO EXTENSION

2 BULB

3 LENS

4 SCREW - FULLY DRIVEN, SEATED AND NOT STRIPPED

FIG. 71 High mount stop lamp bulb replacement (aero wing)

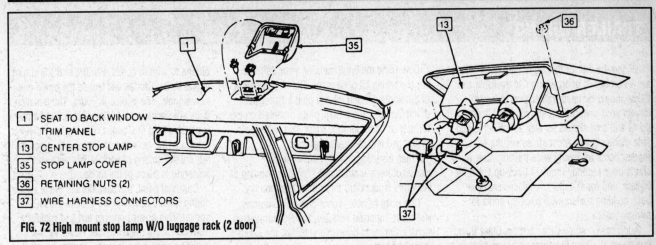

1   SEAT TO BACK WINDOW TRIM PANEL

13   CENTER STOP LAMP

35   STOP LAMP COVER

36   RETAINING NUTS (2)

37   WIRE HARNESS CONNECTORS

FIG. 72 High mount stop lamp W/O luggage rack (2 door)

APPLICATION	BULB NO.	QUANTITY	RATING CANDLEPOWER
FRONT LAMPS			
Headlamp — Inner—Std.	4651	2	50 Watts
— Inner—Halogen	H4651	2	50 Watts
— Outer	4652	2	60/40 Watts
Park & Turn Signal	2057	2	32
Sidemarker	194	2	2
REAR LAMPS			
Back-up	1156	2	32
License — Exc. Wagon	194	1	2
— Wagon	194	2	2
Sidemarker	194	2	2
Tail & Stop — Exc. Wagon	2057	2	2/32
Tail, Stop & Turn Signal — Wagon	2057	2	2/32
Turn Signal — Exc. Wagon	1156	2	32
High Mounted Stop — Exc. Conv. and Hatchback	1156	1	32
— Convertible	889	1	—
— Hatchback	906	4	6
INTERIOR ILLUMINATION			
A/C — Heater Control	168	1	3
Ash Tray	168	1	3
Auto Trans	168	1	3
Courtesy Lamp	906	2	6
Dome Lamp Std.	561	1	12
Dome & Reading — Dome	562	1	6
— Reading	90	1	6
Glove Box	194	1	2
Instrument Cluster	194/168	2/4	2/3
Luggage/Cargo — Exc. Wagon	1003	1	15
— Wagon	561	1	12
Radio Dial	194	1	2
Underhood Lamp	93	1	15
WARNING LIGHTS & INDICATORS			
Brake	194	1	2
Service Engine Soon	168	1	3
High Beam	194	1	2
Oil Pressure	194	1	2
Seat Belt	168	1	3
Tailgate Ajar	194	1	2
Door Ajar	194	1	2
Temperature	194	1	2
Turn Signal	194	2	2
Upshift	168	1	3
Volts (Battery)	194	1	2

Bulb usage chart all models

TRAILER WIRING

Wiring the car for towing is fairly easy. There are a number of good wiring kits available and these should be used, rather than trying to design your own. All trailers will need brake lights and turn signals as well as tail lights and side marker lights. Most states require extra marker lights for overly wide trailers. Also, most states have recently required back-up lights for trailers, and most trailer manufacturers have been building trailers with back-up lights for several years.

Additionally, some Class I, most Class II and just about all Class III trailers will have electric brakes.

Add to this number an accessories wire, to operate trailer internal equipment or to charge the trailer's battery, and you can have as many as seven wires in the harness.

Determine the equipment on your trailer and buy the wiring kit necessary. The kit will contain all the wires needed, plus a plug adapter set which included the female plug, mounted on the bumper or hitch, and the male plug, wired into, or plugged into the trailer harness.

When installing the kit, follow the manufacturer's instructions. The color coding of the wires is standard throughout the industry.

One point to note, some domestic vehicles, and most imported vehicles, have separate turn signals. On most domestic vehicles, the brake lights and rear turn signals operate with the same bulb. For those vehicles with separate turn signals, you can purchase an isolation unit so that the brake lights won't blink whenever the turn signals are operated, or, you can go to your local electronics supply house and buy four

diodes to wire in series with the brake and turn signal bulbs. Diodes will isolate the brake and turn signals. The choice is yours. The isolation units are simple and quick to install, but far more expensive than the diodes. The diodes, however, require more work to install properly, since they require the cutting of each bulb's wire and soldering in place of the diode.

One final point, the best kits are those with a spring loaded cover on the vehicle mounted socket. This cover prevents dirt and moisture from corroding the terminals. Never let the vehicle socket hang loosely. Always mount it securely to the bumper or hitch.

➡ **For more information on towing a trailer please refer to Section 1.**

CIRCUIT PROTECTION

Fuses

♦ SEE FIGS. 74 and 75

Fuses protect all the major electrical systems in the car. In case of an electrical overload, the fuse melts, breaking the circuit and stopping the flow of electricity.

If a fuse blows, the cause should be investigated and corrected before the installation of a new fuse. This, however, is easier to say than to do. Because each fuse protects a limited number of components, your job is narrowed down somewhat. Begin your investigation by looking for obvious fraying, loose connections, breaks in insulation, etc. Use the techniques outlined at the beginning of this Section. Electrical problems are almost always a real headache to solve, but if you are patient and persistent, and approach the problem logically (that is, don't start replacing electrical components randomly), you will eventually find the solution.

The amperage of each fuse and the circuit it protects are marked on the fusebox, which is located under the left side (driver's side) of the instrument panel.

FIG. 74 Fuse panel located underside of instrument panel on left side

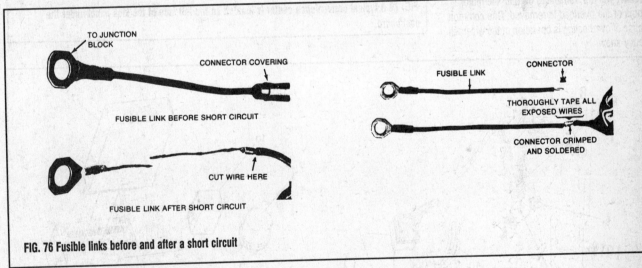

FIG. 75 Pull on fuse panel to gain access to fuses

Fusible Links

♦ SEE FIGS. 76-78

A fusible link is a protective device used in an electrical circuit. When the current increases beyond a certain amperage, the fusible metal of the wire link melts, thus breaking the electrical circuit and preventing further damage to other components and wiring. Whenever a fusible link is melted because of a short circuit, correct the cause before installing a new one.

To replace a fusible link, cut off the burned link beyond the original splice. Replace the link with a new one of the same rating. If the splice has two wires, two repair links are required, one for each wire. Connect the new fusible link to the wires, then crimp securely.

✳ WARNING

Use only replacements of the same electrical capacity as the original, available from your dealer. Replacements of a different electrical value will not provide adequate system protection.

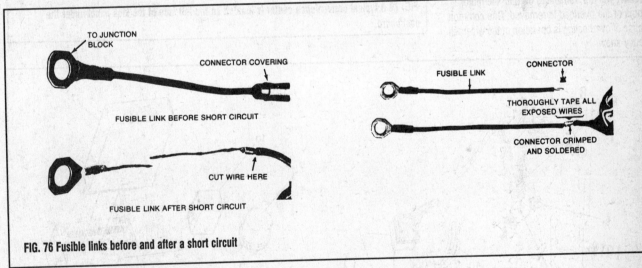

FIG. 76 Fusible links before and after a short circuit

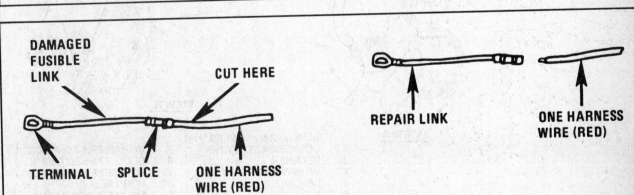

FIG. 77 Original fusible links with one wire

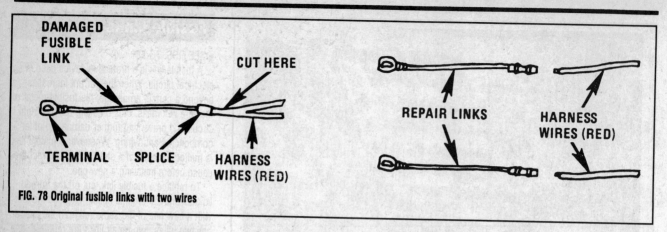

FIG. 78 Original fusible links with two wires

Circuit Breakers

◆ SEE FIG. 79

The headlights are protected by a circuit breaker in the headlamp switch. If the circuit breaker trips, the headlights will either flash on and off, or stay off altogether. The circuit breaker resets automatically after the overload is removed.

The windshield wipers are also protected by a circuit breaker. If the motor overheats, the circuit breaker will trip, remaining off until the motor cools or the overload is removed. One common cause of overheating is operation of the wipers in heavy snow.

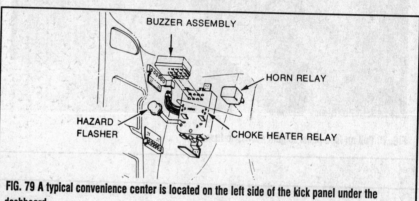

FIG. 79 A typical convenience center is located on the left side of the kick panel under the dashboard.

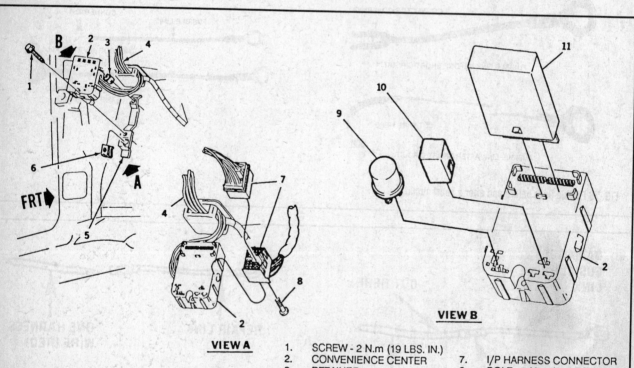

VIEW A

VIEW B

1.	SCREW - 2 N.m (19 LBS. IN.)		
2.	CONVENIENCE CENTER	7.	I/P HARNESS CONNECTOR
3.	RETAINER	8.	BOLT - 7 N.m (62 LBS. IN.)
4.	I/P HARNESS	9.	FLASHER ASM. HAZARD
5.	BRACKET	10.	HORN RELAY
6.	NUT	11.	MULTI-FUNCTION ALARM

FIG. 80 Convenience center (late model)

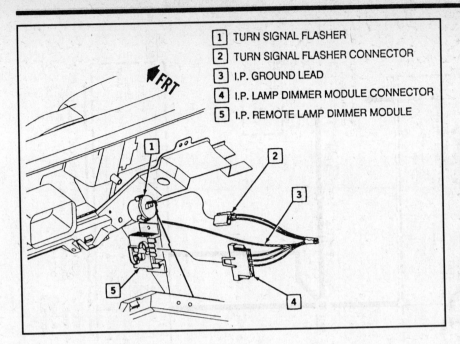

1 TURN SIGNAL FLASHER

2 TURN SIGNAL FLASHER CONNECTOR

3 I.P. GROUND LEAD

4 I.P. LAMP DIMMER MODULE CONNECTOR

5 I.P. REMOTE LAMP DIMMER MODULE

Their are also circuit breakers loacted in the fuse block for power windows and an (ACC) Accessory circuit breaker for such options as power seats, rear defogger, power door locks etc., located in the fuse box.

Flashers

♦ SEE FIG. 80-81

The hazard flasher is located in the convenience center', under the dash, on the left side kick panel. The horn relay and the buzzer assembly may be found here also. The turn signal flasher is installed in a clamp attached to the base of the steering column support inside the car. In all cases, replacement is made by unplugging the old unit and plugging in a new one.

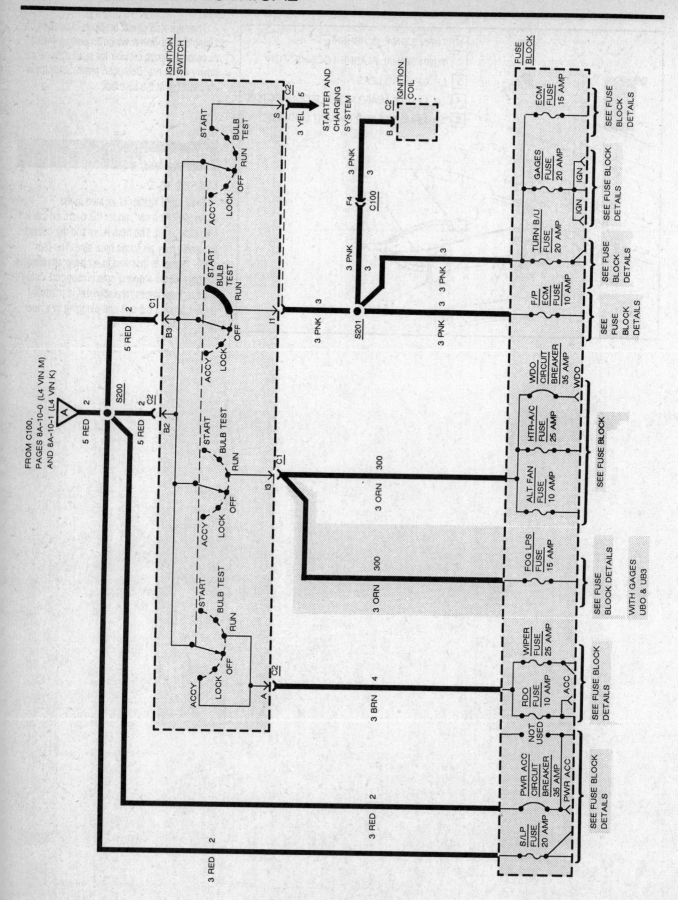

Power distribution 1982–89 All Models (con't).

FUSE	COLOR (AMPS)	SCHEMATICS
WIPER	WHT (25)	Wiper/Washer Wiper/Washer: Pulse
TURN B/U	YEL (20)	Exterior Lights Backup Lights
FOG LPS	BLU (15)	Headlights with Foglights
ALT/FAN	RED (10)	Starter and Charging System, Coolant Fan
WDO Circuit Breaker	(35)	Power Windows Convertible Roof
HTR-A/C	WHT (25)	Heater-Air Conditioning: Blower Controls
RDO	RED (10)	Radio Cruise Control

FUSE	COLOR (AMPS)	SCHEMATICS
ECM	BLU (15)	Throttle Body Injection -VIN K
		Multi-Port Fuel Injection -VIN M
RDO/CTSY	YEL (20)	Radio, Luggage Compartment Lid Realease, Horn, Warnings and Alarms, Interior Lights, Seatbelt Retractors, Convertible Roof, Power Door Locks
TAIL	YEL (20)	Light Switch Details, Headlights with Foglights
S/LP	YEL (20)	Exterior lights
PWR ACC Circuit Breaker	(35)	Power Door Locks, Rear Defogger
F/P ECM		Multi-Port Fuel Injection
INST LPS	TAN (5)	Interior Lights Dimming, Radio, Warnings and Alarms
GAGES	YEL (20)	Throttle Body Injection, Multi-Port Fuel Injection, Interior Lights, Rear Defogger, Instrument Panel, Warnings and Alarms, Air Conditioning

Fuse block details 1982–89 All Models.

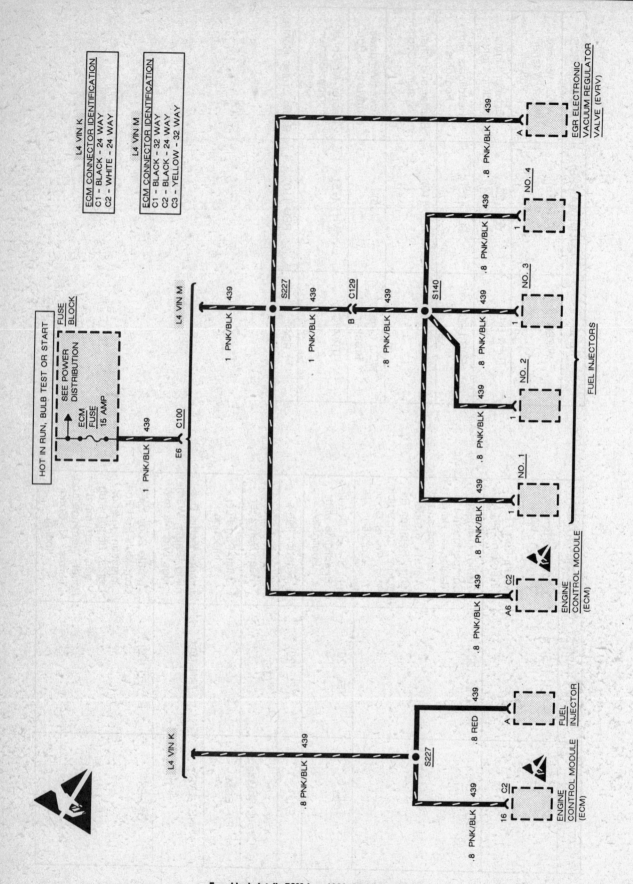

Fuse block details ECM fuse 1982–89 All Models.

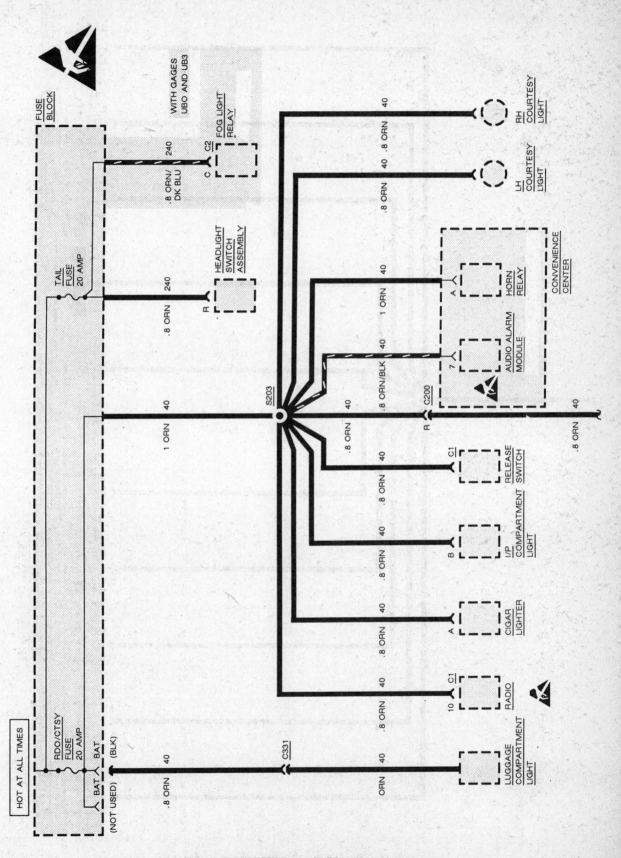

Fuse block details RDO/CTSY fuse and tail fuse 1982–89 All Models.

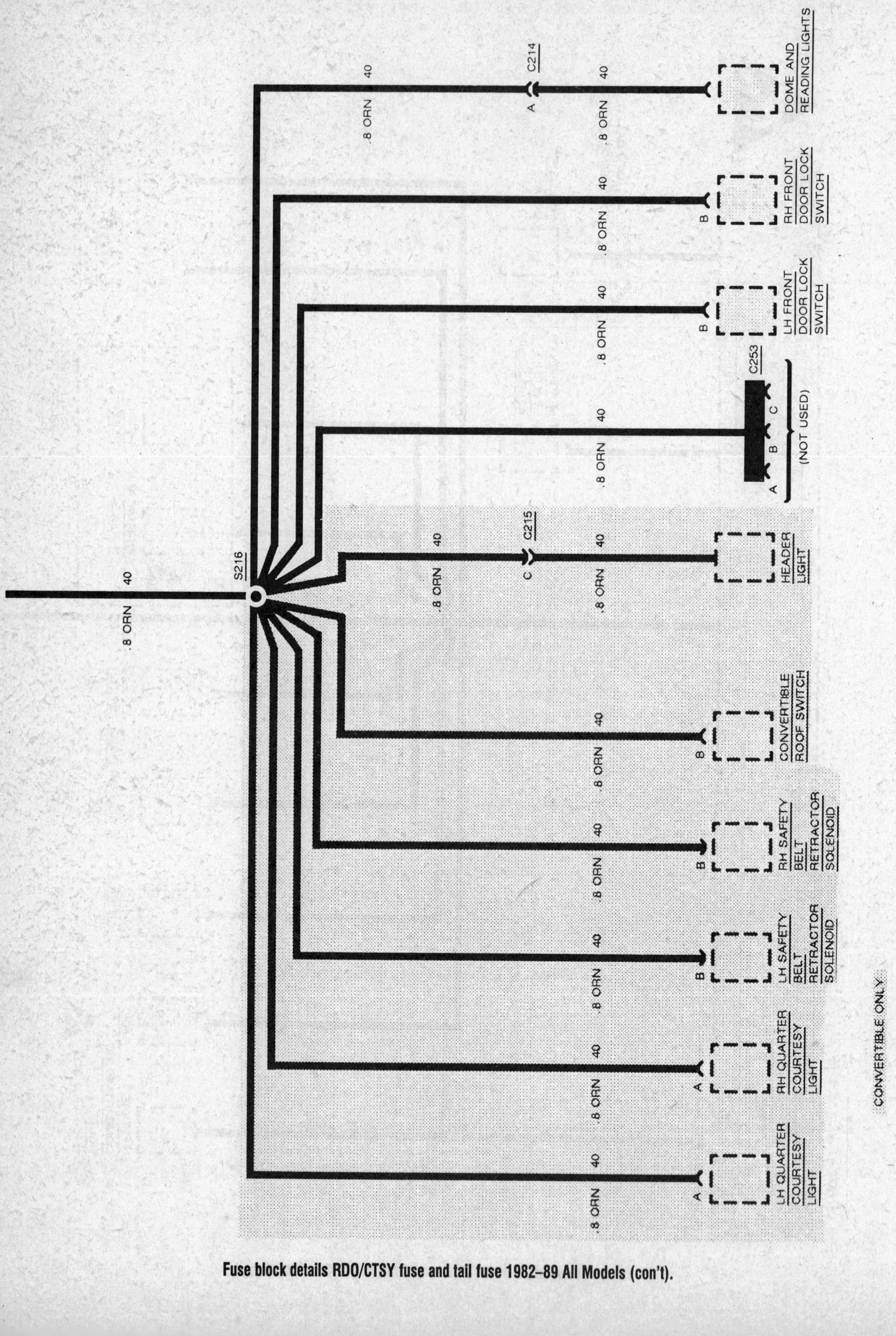

C214

DOME AND
READING LIGHTS

.8 ORN   40   A   40   .8 ORN

RH FRONT
DOOR LOCK
SWITCH

.8 ORN   40   B

LH FRONT
DOOR LOCK
SWITCH

.8 ORN   40   B

C253

C

B   (NOT USED)

.8 ORN   40   A

C215

HEADER
LIGHT

.8 ORN   40   C   40   .8 ORN

S216

.8 ORN   40

CONVERTIBLE
ROOF SWITCH

.8 ORN   40   B

RH SAFETY
BELT
RETRACTOR
SOLENOID

.8 ORN   40   B

LH SAFETY
BELT
RETRACTOR
SOLENOID

.8 ORN   40   B

RH QUARTER
COURTESY
LIGHT

.8 ORN   40   A

LH QUARTER
COURTESY
LIGHT

.8 ORN   40   A

CONVERTIBLE ONLY

Fuse block details RDO/CTSY fuse and tail fuse 1982–89 All Models (con't).

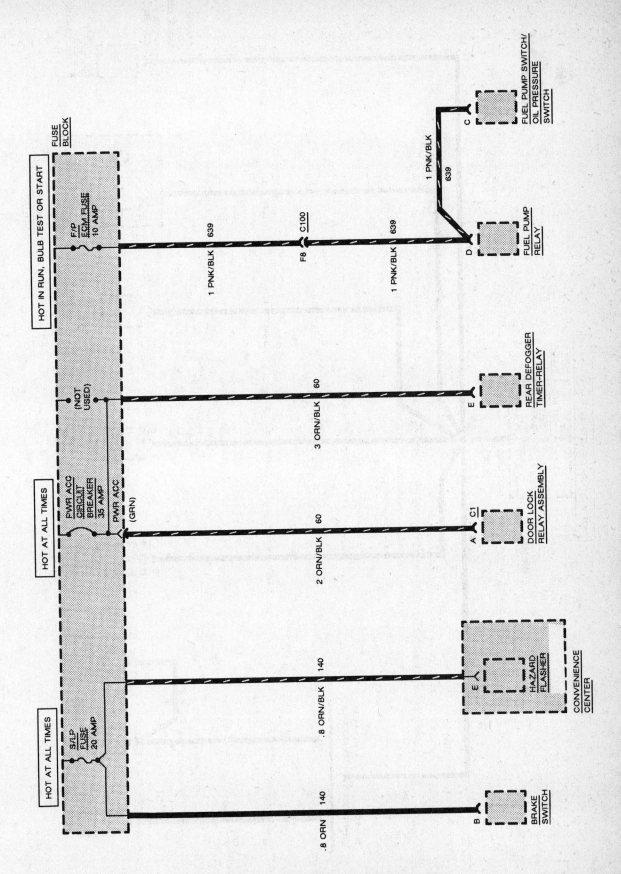

Fuse block details Power ACC circuit breaker 1982–89 All Models.

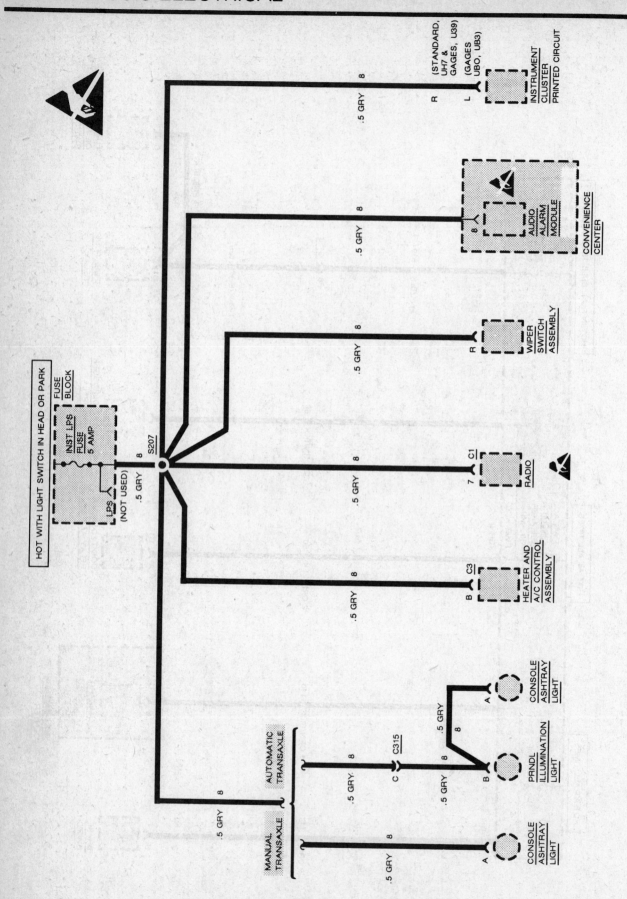

Fuse block details Instrument lamps fuse 1982–89 All Models.

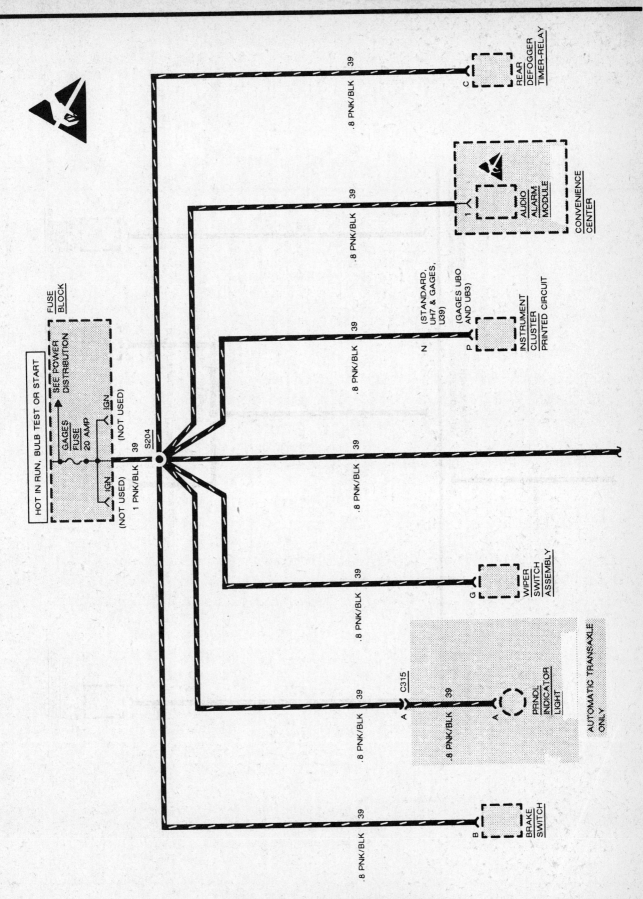

Fuse block details Gauges fuse 1982–89 All Models.

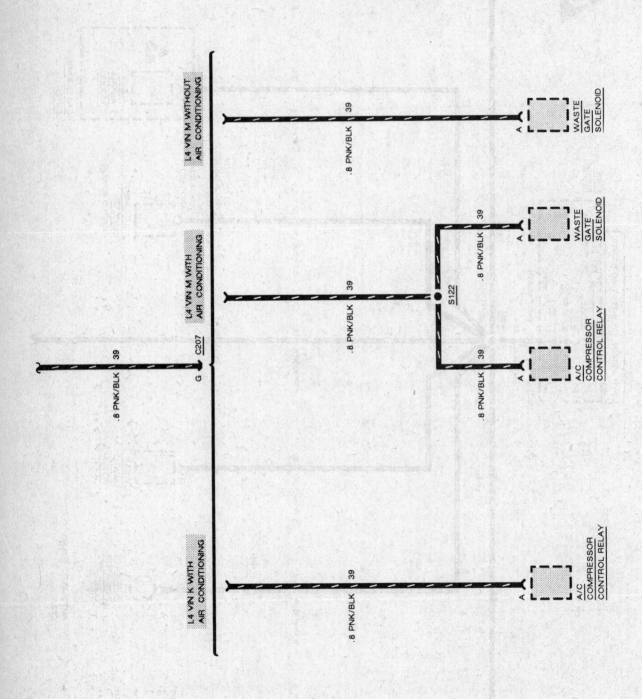

Fuse block details Gauges fuse 1982–89 All Models (con't).

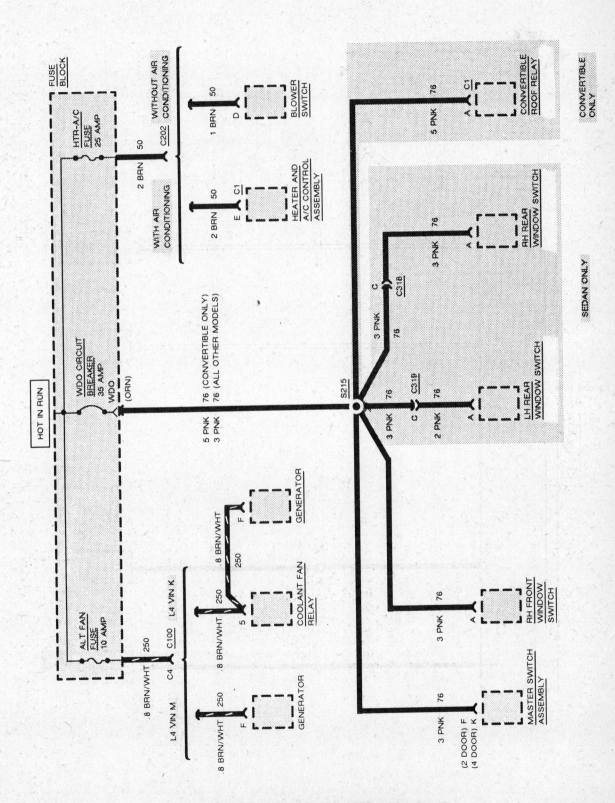

Fuse block details WDO circuit breaker 1982–89 All Models.

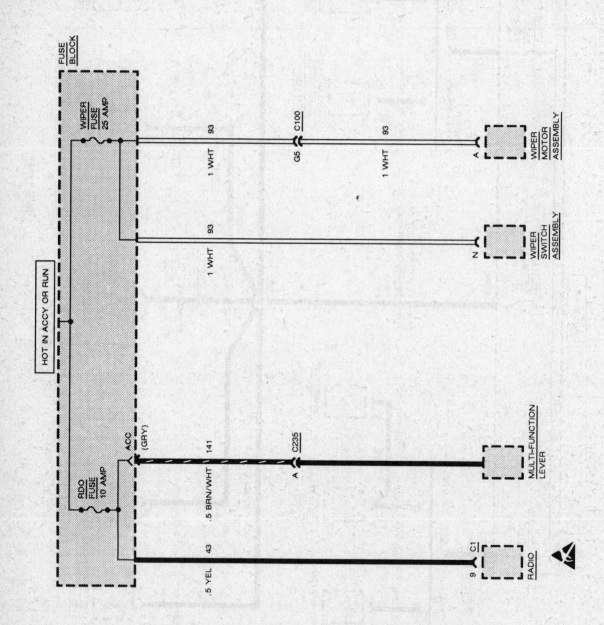

Fuse block details RDO fuse and Wiper fuse 1982–89 All Models.

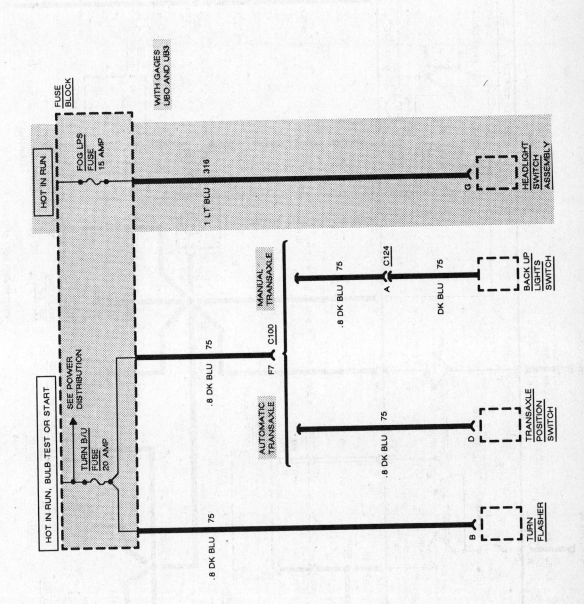

Fuse block details Turn B/U fuse and Fog lamp fuse 1982–89 All Models.

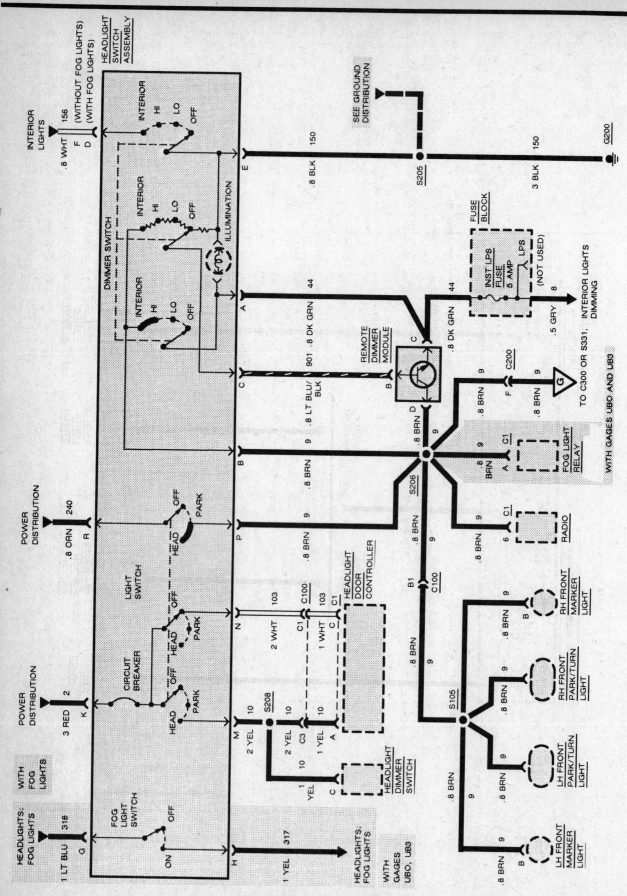

Light switch details 1982–89 All Models.

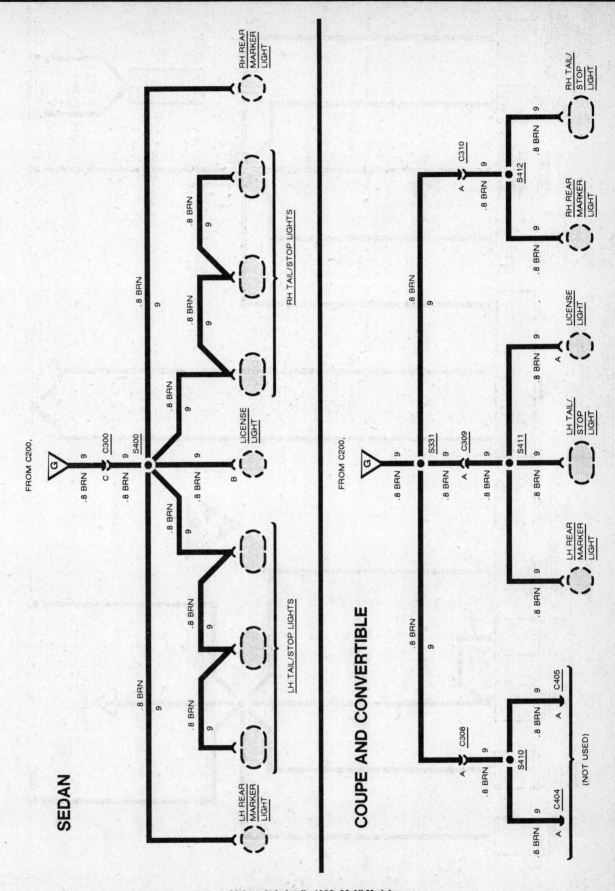

Light switch details 1982–89 All Models.

ENGINE GROUNDS: L4 VIN K

IDLE SPEED POWER STEERING PRESSURE SWITCH

B   450

FUEL PUMP RELAY

C   .5 BLK/WHT   450

BATTERY

1   G100 (ENGINE)

19 BLK

G101 (BODY)

3 BLK   G110

ASSEMBLY LINE DIAGNOSTIC LINK (ALDL) CONNECTOR

A   .8 BLK/WHT   450   M C207   .8 BLK/WHT   450   .8 BLK/WHT

S217

1 BLK/WHT   450

AUTOMATIC TRANSAXLE ONLY

TRANSAXLE POSITION SWITCH

B   .8 BLK/WHT   450   .8 BLK/WHT

ECM CONNECTOR IDENTIFICATION
C1 - BLACK - 24 WAY
C2 - WHITE - 24 WAY
ENGINE CONTROL MODULE (ECM)

C2   450

12   1 BLK/WHT

13   1 TAN/WHT   551

C1

23   .8 TAN   413   1 TAN/WHT

G111

WITH A/C

A/C CLUTCH DIODE   899

A/C COMPRESSOR CLUTCH

X   150   1 BLK

BLOWER RELAY

5   150   1 BLK

BLOWER MOTOR

C2   150 (WITH A/C)   150 (WITHOUT A/C)   3 BLK   1 BLK

S101

150   TO C100,

Z

BRAKE FLUID LEVEL SWITCH

A   150   .8 BLK

COOLANT FAN

A   150   2 BLK

G109

5 BLK   150

3 BLK   150

5 BLK   150   G112

Ground distribution L4 vin K 1982–89 All Models.

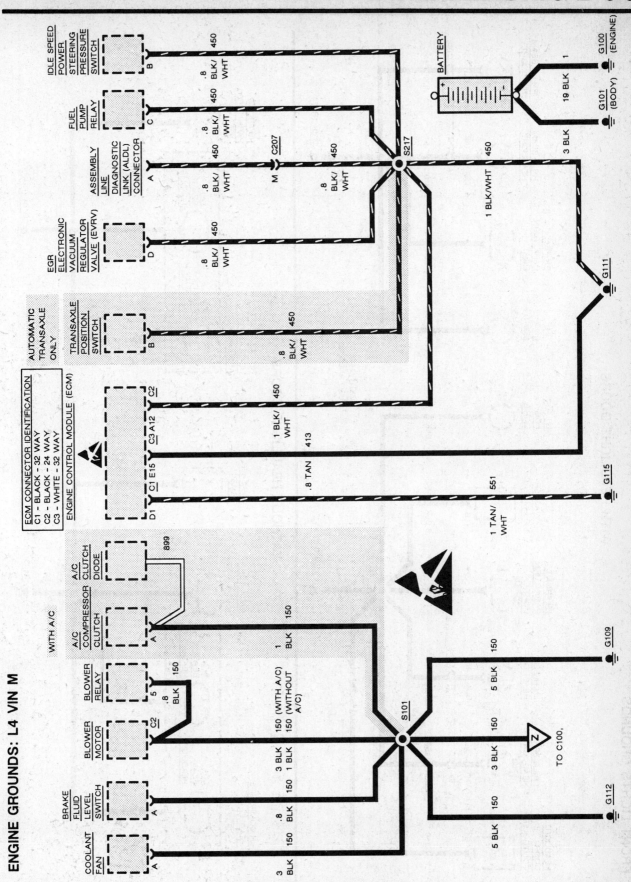

ENGINE GROUNDS: L4 VIN M

IDLE SPEED POWER STEERING PRESSURE SWITCH

FUEL PUMP RELAY

ASSEMBLY LINE DIAGNOSTIC LINK (ALDL) CONNECTOR

EGR ELECTRONIC VACUUM REGULATOR VALVE (EVRV)

AUTOMATIC TRANSAXLE ONLY

TRANSAXLE POSITION SWITCH

ECM CONNECTOR IDENTIFICATION
C1 - BLACK - 32 WAY
C2 - BLACK - 24 WAY
C3 - WHITE - 32 WAY
ENGINE CONTROL MODULE (ECM)

WITH A/C

A/C CLUTCH DIODE

A/C COMPRESSOR CLUTCH

BLOWER RELAY

BLOWER MOTOR

BRAKE FLUID LEVEL SWITCH

COOLANT FAN

BATTERY

G100 (ENGINE)
G101 (BODY)

.8 BLK/WHT 450

.8 BLK/WHT 450

.8 BLK/WHT 450

.8 BLK/WHT 450

.8 BLK/WHT 450

.8 BLK/WHT 450

M C207

S217

1 BLK/WHT 450

3 BLK

19 BLK

G111

1 BLK/WHT 450

413

.8 TAN

1 TAN/WHT 551

G115

899

1 BLK 150

.8 BLK 150

150 (WITH A/C)
150 (WITHOUT A/C)

3 BLK 1 BLK

.8 BLK 150

3 BLK 150

S101

5 BLK 150

5 BLK 150

3 BLK 150

5 BLK 150

G109

G112

TO C100,

Ground distribution L4 vin M 1982–89 All Models.

FRONT LIGHTS GROUNDS

WITH HEADLIGHT DOORS

RH LO BEAM HEADLIGHT — 151 — C103 — 151
1 BLK/WHT D

RH HI BEAM HEADLIGHT — 150 — A — 151 — S110 — 151 — G104 (RH)
1 BLK 1 BLK .8 BLK

RH FRONT PARK/TURN LIGHT — 151
.8 BLK

RH FOG LIGHT — 151
1 BLK

WITH GAGES UB0 AND UB3

LH FOG LIGHT — 150
1 BLK

WASHER PUMP — B — 150
.8 BLK

LH FRONT PARK/TURN LIGHT — 150 — S107 — 150 — G103 (LH)
.8 BLK 1 BLK

LH HI BEAM HEADLIGHT — 150 — A — C102 — 150
1 BLK 1 BLK

LH LO BEAM HEADLIGHT — 151 — D — 150
1 BLK/WHT 1 BLK

HEADLIGHT DOOR CONTROLLER — D — C1 — 150
1 BLK

WITHOUT HEADLIGHT DOORS

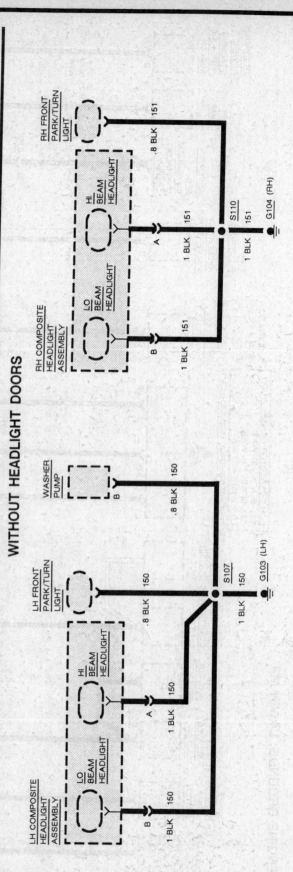

RH FRONT PARK/TURN LIGHT — 151
.8 BLK

RH COMPOSITE HEADLIGHT ASSEMBLY
HI BEAM HEADLIGHT — A — 151 — S110 — 151 — G104 (RH)
1 BLK 1 BLK
LO BEAM HEADLIGHT — B — 151
1 BLK

WASHER PUMP — B — 150
.8 BLK

LH FRONT PARK/TURN LIGHT — 150 — S107 — 150 — G103 (LH)
.8 BLK 1 BLK

LH COMPOSITE HEADLIGHT ASSEMBLY
HI BEAM HEADLIGHT — A — 150
1 BLK
LO BEAM HEADLIGHT — B — 150
1 BLK

Ground distribution 1982–89 All Models (con't).

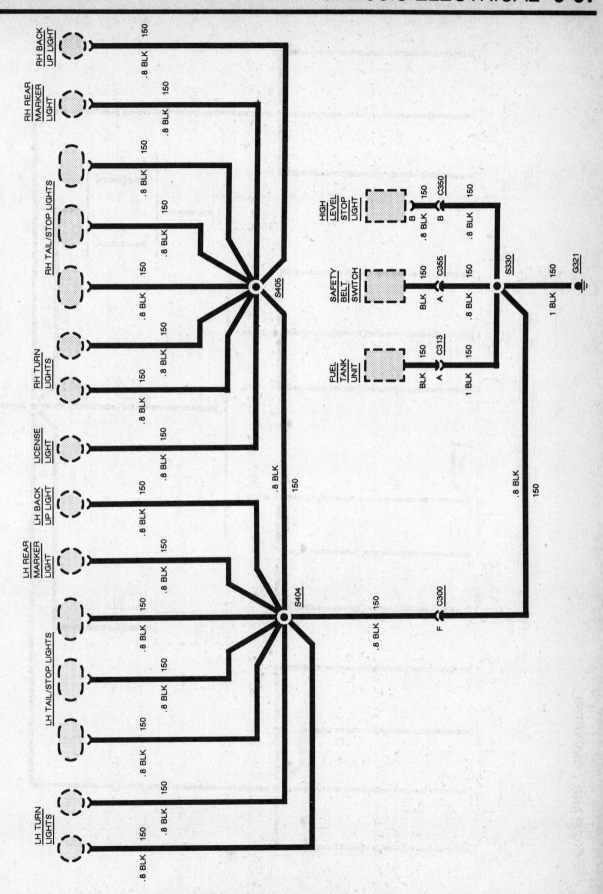

Ground distribution Sedan 1982–89 All Models (con't).

COUPE AND CONVERTIBLE

RH REAR MARKER LIGHT — 150 — .8 BLK

RH TURN LIGHT — 150 — .8 BLK — S413 — 150 — C310 — D

RH TAIL/ STOP LIGHT — 150 — .8 BLK

FUEL TANK UNIT — BLK — 150 — C313 — A

CONVERTIBLE — 150 — C203 — A — 1 BLK

COUPE — 1 BLK — 150 — .8 BLK — 150

HIGH LEVEL STOP LIGHT — B — 150 — .8 BLK

RH BACK UP LIGHT — B — 150 — .8 BLK — C405 — C — 150 — .8 BLK — S415 — 150 — .8 BLK

LH BACK UP LIGHT — B — 150 — .8 BLK — C404 — C — 150 — .8 BLK

COUPE WITH LUGGAGE CARRIER AND CONVERTIBLE

HIGH LEVEL STOP LIGHTS — A — .8 BLK — 150 — A — 150 — .8 BLK — S416 — 150 — .8 BLK

COUPE WITHOUT LUGGAGE CARRIER

.8 BLK — 150 — C308 — C — 150 — .8 BLK — S330 — 150 — G321 — 1 BLK

RH BACK UP LIGHT — B — 150 — .8 BLK — C405 — C — 150 — .8 BLK — S415 — 150 — .8 BLK

LH BACK UP LIGHT — B — 150 — .8 BLK — C404 — C — 150 — .8 BLK

SAFETY BELT SWITCH — BLK — 150 — C355 — A — 150 — .8 BLK

LICENSE LIGHT — B — 150 — .8 BLK

LH TURN LIGHT — 150 — .8 BLK

LH TAIL/ STOP LIGHT — 150 — .8 BLK — S414 — 150 — .8 BLK — C309 — D

LH REAR MARKER LIGHT — 150 — .8 BLK

.8 BLK — 150

Ground distribution Coupe and convertible 1982–89 All Models (con't).

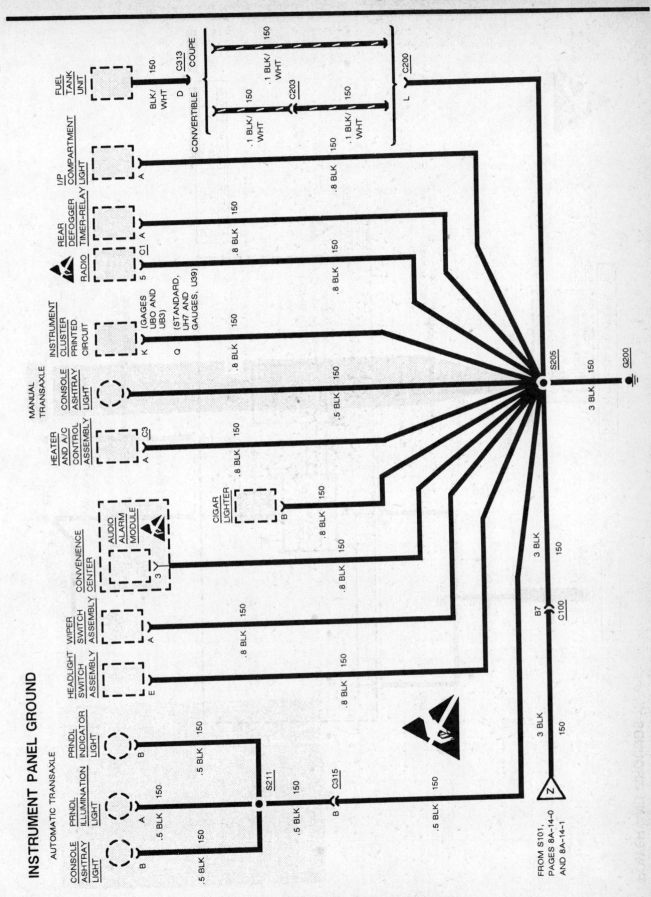

Ground distribution Instrument panel 1982–89 All Models.

POWER AND GROUNDS

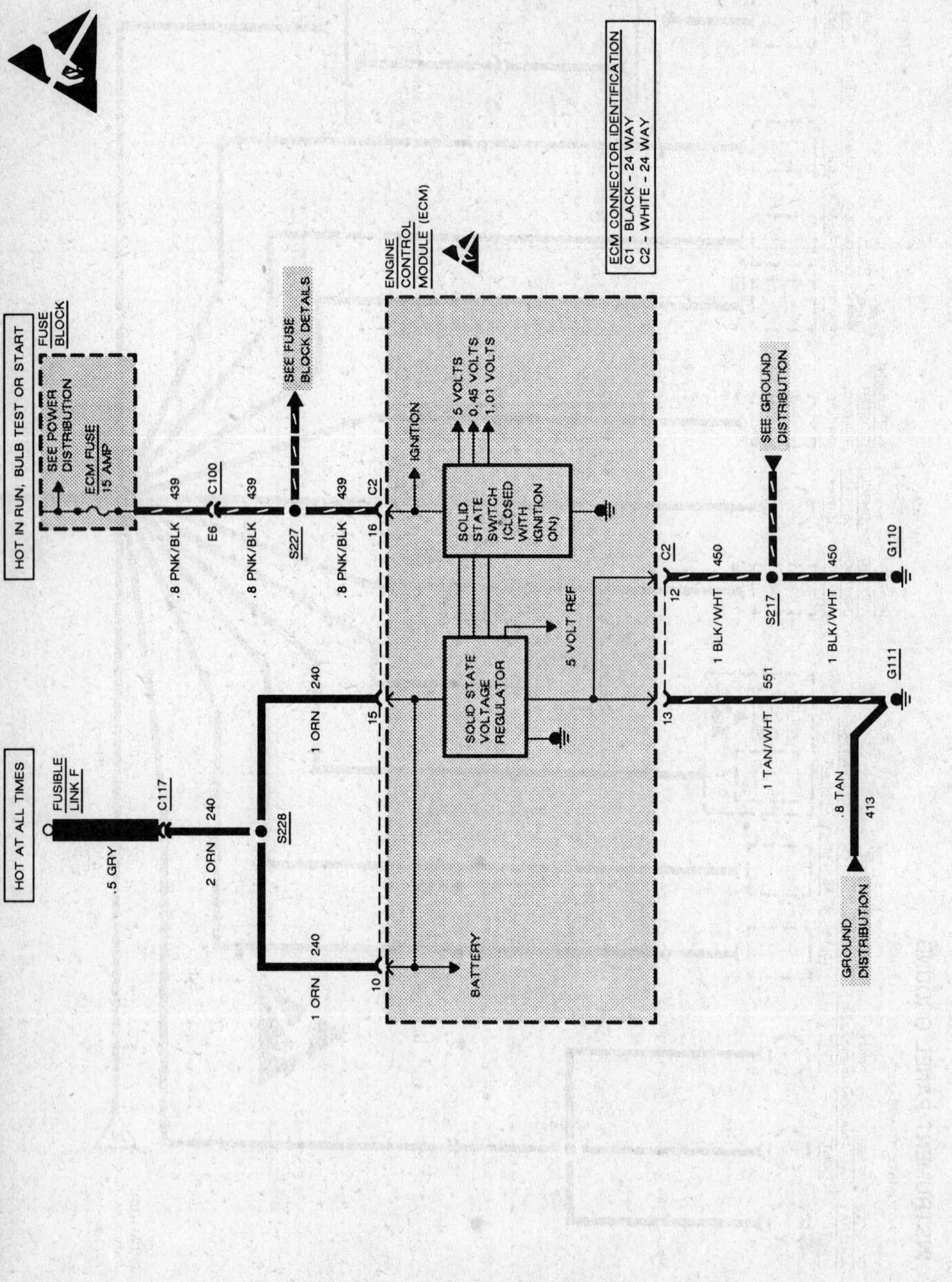

ECM CONNECTOR IDENTIFICATION
C1 – BLACK – 24 WAY
C2 – WHITE – 24 WAY

ENGINE CONTROL MODULE (ECM)

FUSE BLOCK

SEE POWER DISTRIBUTION

ECM FUSE 15 AMP

HOT IN RUN, BULB TEST OR START

SEE FUSE BLOCK DETAILS

5 VOLTS
0.45 VOLTS
1.01 VOLTS

IGNITION

SOLID STATE SWITCH (CLOSED WITH IGNITION ON)

SOLID STATE VOLTAGE REGULATOR

5 VOLT REF

SEE GROUND DISTRIBUTION

.8 PNK/BLK
439
E6
C100
439
.8 PNK/BLK
S227
439
.8 PNK/BLK
16
C2

240
1 ORN
15

FUSIBLE LINK F

HOT AT ALL TIMES

.5 GRY
C117
240
2 ORN
240
S228
1 ORN
240
1 ORN
10

BATTERY

C2
12
1 BLK/WHT
450
S217
1 BLK/WHT
450
G110

13
1 TAN/WHT
551
.8 TAN
413
G111

GROUND DISTRIBUTION

TBI L4 vin K Power and grounds 1982–89 All Models.

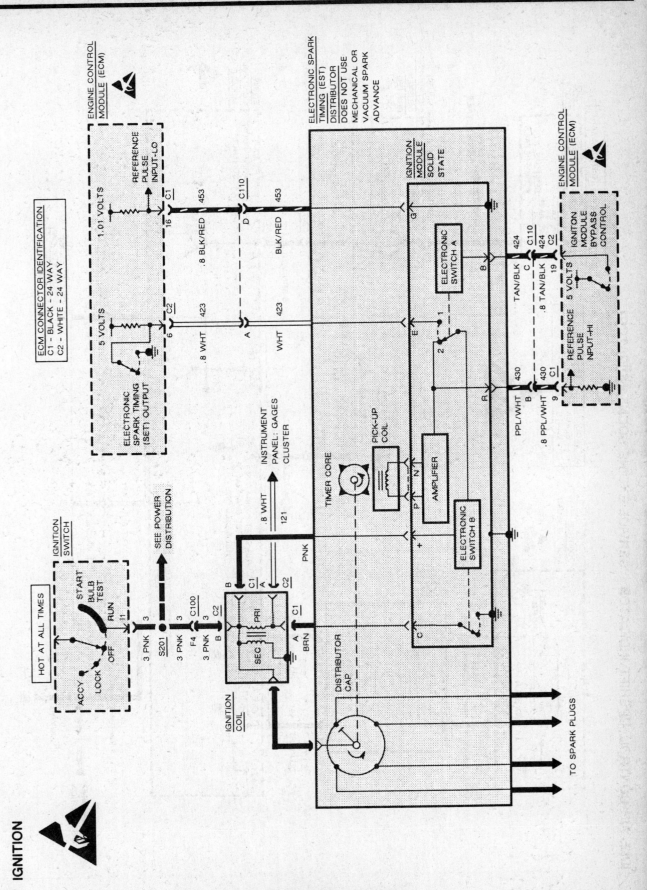

TBI L4 vin K Ignition 1982–89 All Models.

IDLE AIR CONTROL, UPSHIFT INDICATOR, "SERVICE ENGINE SOON" INDICATOR

ECM CONNECTOR IDENTIFICATION
C1 - BLACK - 24 WAY
C2 - WHITE - 24 WAY

FUSE BLOCK

HOT IN RUN, BULB TEST OR START

SEE POWER DISTRIBUTION

GAGES FUSE 20 AMP

SEE FUSE BLOCK DETAILS

1 PNK/BLK 39

S204

.8 PNK/BLK 39

P (GAGES U80 AND U83)
N (STANDARD, UH7 AND GAGES, U39)

INSTRUMENT CLUSTER PRINTED CIRCUIT

"SERVICE ENGINE SOON" INDICATOR

O (STANDARD, UH7 AND GAGES, UH9)
V (GAGES U80 AND U83)

C C207 419
17 C2 419

.5 BRN/WHT
.5 BRN/WHT

ENGINE CONTROL MODULE (ECM)

"SERVICE ENGINE SOON" INDICATOR CONTROL

SOLID STATE

UPSHIFT INDICATOR (MANUAL TRANSAXLE ONLY)

(STANDARD, UH7 AND GAGES, UH9)
(GAGES U80 AND U83)

I B 456
H 7 456

.8 TAN/BLK
.8 TAN/BLK

MANUAL TRANSAXLE ONLY

SOLID STATE

BATTERY UP SHIFT INDICATOR CONTROL (MANUAL TRANSAXLE ONLY)

5 VOLTS

DATA IN

SOLID STATE

DATA OUT

5 VOLTS

DIAGNOSTIC TEST

C1 461
C207 461

ASSEMBLY LINE DIAGNOSTIC LINK (ALDL) CONNECTOR

1 M
.5 ORN .5 ORN
J

15 451 451 B
E
.8 WHT/BLK .8 WHT/BLK

ENGINE CONTROL MODULE (ECM)

IDLE AIR CONTROL VALVE

BATTERY

IDLE AIR VALVE CONTROL

C2
8 444 A
.5 LT GRN/BLK

9 444 B
.5 LT GRN/WHT

STEPPER MOTOR

C 442 C2
17
.5 LT BLU/BLK

D 441 7
.5 LT BLU/WHT

IDLE AIR VALVE CONTROL

BATTERY

M 450 A
.8 BLK/WHT

.8 BLK/WHT S217 450
1 BLK/WHT G110

SEE GROUND DISTRIBUTION

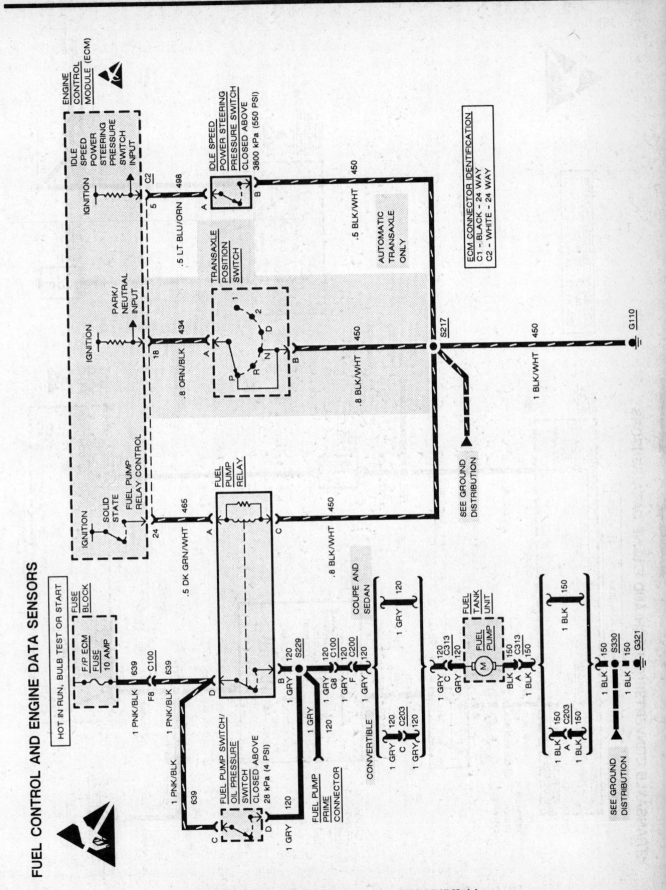

TBI L4 vin K Fuel control and Engine data sensors 1982–89 All Models.

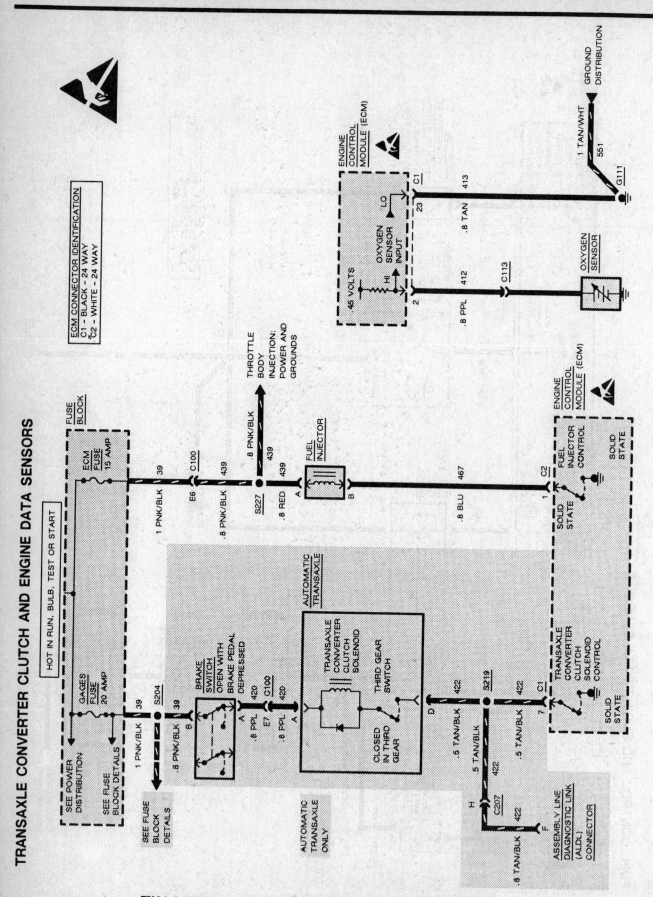

TBI L4 vin K Transaxle converter clutch and engine data sensors 1982–89 All Models.

ENGINE DATA SENSORS

TBI L4 vin K Engine data sensors 1982–89 All Models.

ENGINE DATA SENSORS AND CONTROLS

ECM CONNECTOR IDENTIFICATION
C1 – BLACK – 24 WAY
C2 – WHITE – 24 WAY

ENGINE CONTROL MODULE (ECM)

(NOT USED) N C207

.5 RED 381

3 C2

2000 PPM SPEED SIGNAL

A/C ON INPUT

2 C2

.8 DK BLU/WHT 604

AIR CONDITIONING: COMPRESSOR CONTROLS

VEHICLE SPEED SENSOR

389

.5 DK GRN

22

4000 PPM SPEED SIGNAL

COOLANT FAN A/C ENABLE

C1 24

.8 DK GRN/WHT 603

AIR CONDITIONING: COMPRESSOR CONTROLS

459

.8 DK GRN/WHT

C1 3

A/C COMPRESSOR RELAY CONTROL

SET / COAST INPUT

C2 21

84

.5 DK BLU

COOLANT FAN

335

.5 DK GRN/WHT

21

COOLANT FAN RELAY CONTROL

CRUISE ON INPUT

20

397

.5 GRY

CRUISE CONTROL

CRUISE CONTROL

87

.5 GRY/BLK

C2 4

RESUME/ ACCEL INPUT

VENT VALVE CONTROL

C1 11

403

.5 DK BLU/WHT

86

.5 BRN

C1 14

BRAKE INPUT

VACUUM VALVE CONTROL

10

402

.5 LT GRN

CRUISE CONTROL

TBI L4 vin K Engine data sensors and controls 1982–89 All Models.

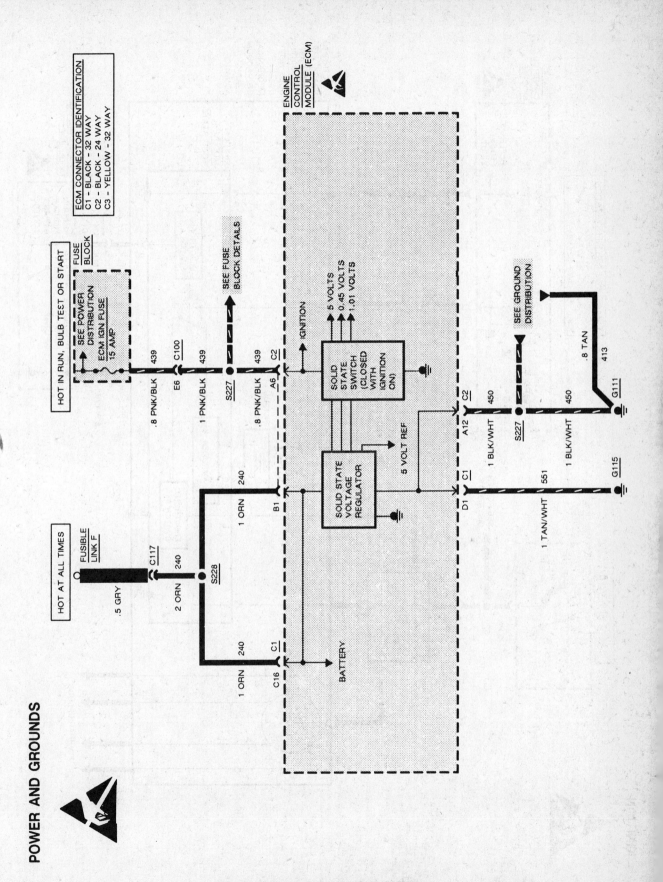

POWER AND GROUNDS

MPI L4 vin M Power and grounds 1982–89 All Models.

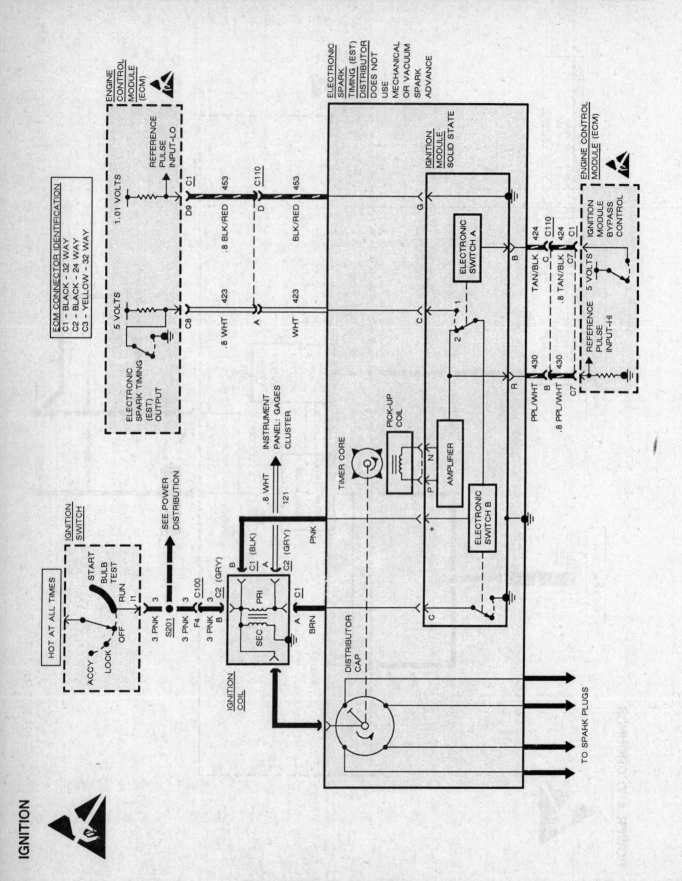

IGNITION

MPI L4 vin M Ignition 1982–89 All Models.

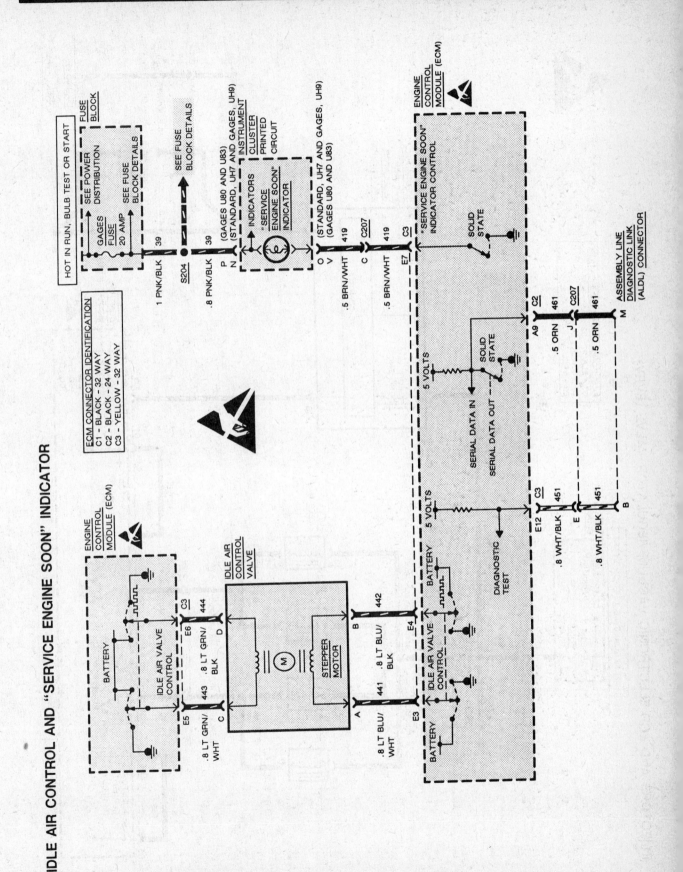

IDLE AIR CONTROL AND "SERVICE ENGINE SOON" INDICATOR

MPI L4 vin M Idle air control, Upshift and Service Engine Soon Indicators 1982–89 All Models.

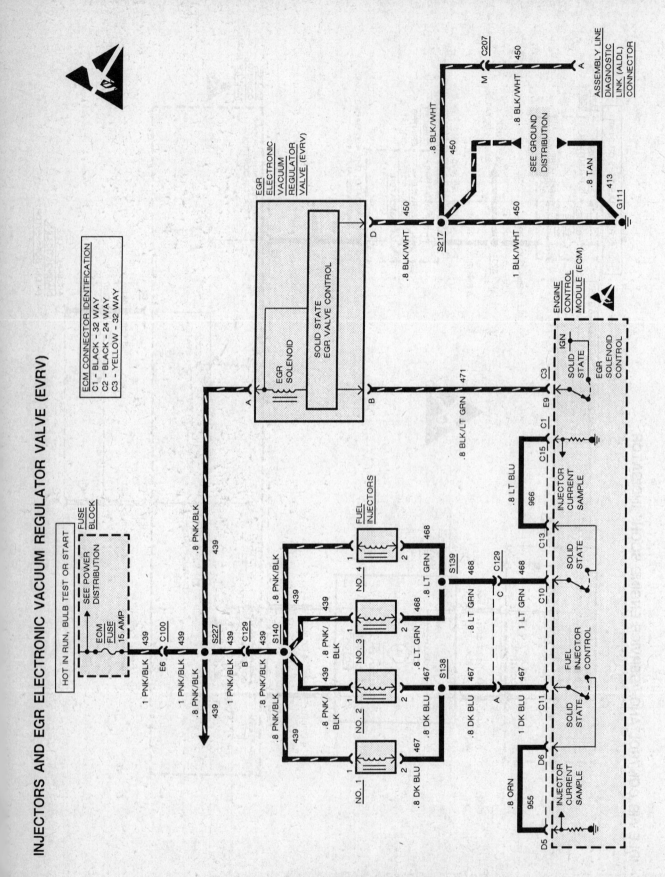

INJECTORS AND EGR ELECTRONIC VACUUM REGULATOR VALVE (EVRV)

MPI L4 vin M Injectors and EGR EVRV 1982–89 All Models.

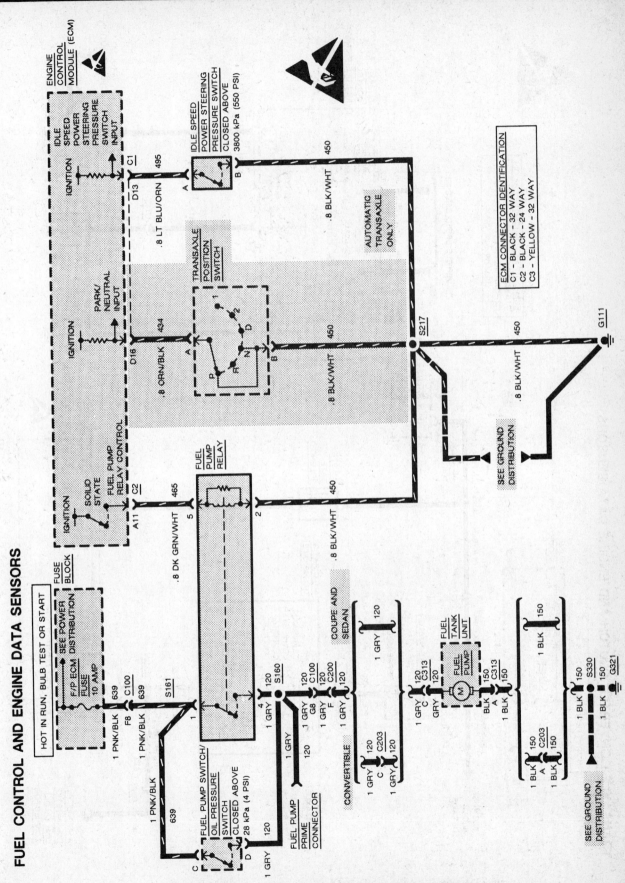

MPI L4 vin M Fuel control and Engine data sensors 1982–89 All Models.

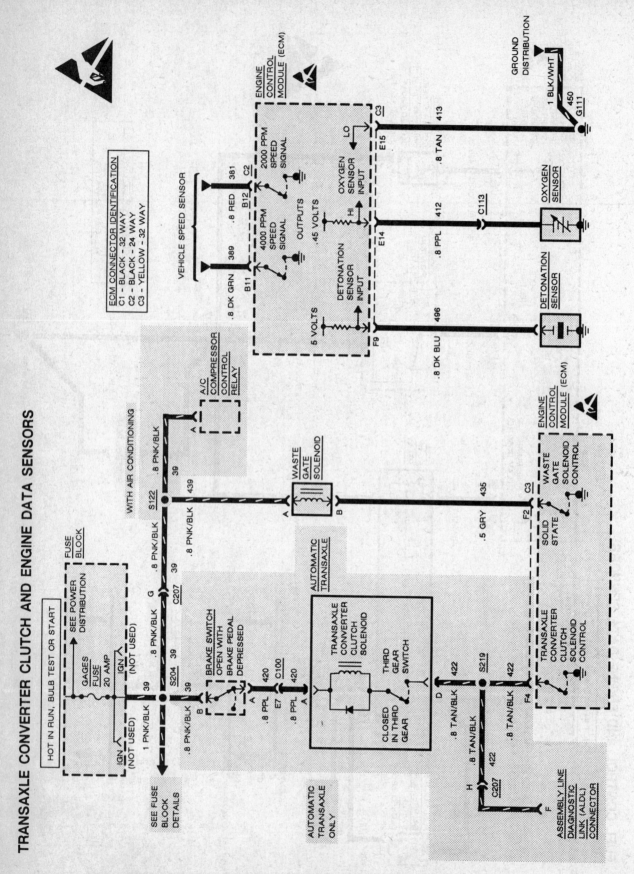

TRANSAXLE CONVERTER CLUTCH AND ENGINE DATA SENSORS

MPI L4 vin M Transaxle converter clutch and engine data sensors 1982–89 All Models.

ENGINE DATA SENSORS

ENGINE CONTROL MODULE (ECM)

ECM CONNECTOR IDENTIFICATION
C1 - BLACK - 32 WAY
C2 - BLACK - 24 WAY
C3 - YELLOW - 32 WAY

VEHICLE SPEED SENSOR INPUT

HI   C2
B10   8 YEL   400
LO
B9   8 PPL   401

VEHICLE SPEED SENSOR

PROGRAMMABLE READ ONLY MEMORY (PROM) PLUG-IN MODULE

ENGINE CONTROL MODULE (ECM)

A/C ON INPUT
604   C1
C9
A/C COMPRESSOR RELAY CONTROL

AIR CONDITIONING: COMPRESSOR CONTROLS

.8 DK BLU/ WHT

459   C3
F1
.8 DK GRN/ WHT

COOLANT FAN RELAY CONTROL

335   E8
COOLANT FAN
.8 DK GRN/ WHT

SOLID STATE

THROTTLE POSITION SENSOR (TPS)
B
A   C
417   F13
.8 DK BLU

THROTTLE POSITION SENSOR (TPS) INPUT

5 VOLT REF

MANIFOLD AIR TEMPERATURE (MAT) SENSOR INPUT

5 VOLTS

A5   .8 GRY   416

MANIFOLD AIR TEMPERATURE (MAT) SENSOR
99°C (210°F)- 185 OHMS
21°C (70°F)- 3400 OHMS
4°C (40°F)- 7500 OHMS
B   A
.8 BLK/YEL   155

C3   472   F16   .8 TAN
B
155   S137   155

.8 BLK/YEL   155   B5   C2
SENSOR GROUND

MANIFOLD ABSOLUTE PRESSURE (MAP) SENSOR
B
C   A
432   S218   432

COOLANT TEMPERATURE SENSOR (CTS) INPUT
5 VOLTS

5 VOLT REF

C2   474   A4   .8 GRY/RED

.8 LT GRN   432   .8 LT GRN   C3   F15
MANIFOLD ABSOLUTE PRESSURE (MAP) SENSOR INPUT

.8 LT GRN   432

COOLANT TEMPERATURE SENSOR (CTS)
99°C (210°F)- 185 OHMS
21°C (70°F)- 3400 OHMS
4°C (40°F)- 7500 OHMS
B   A
.8 BLK   452

INSTRUMENT PANEL: GAGES CLUSTER

C3   410   E16   .8 YEL
.8 BLK   452   S162   .8 BLK   452   B6   C2
SENSOR GROUND

MPI L4 vin M Engine data sensors 1982–89 All Models.

Starter system 1982–89 All Models.

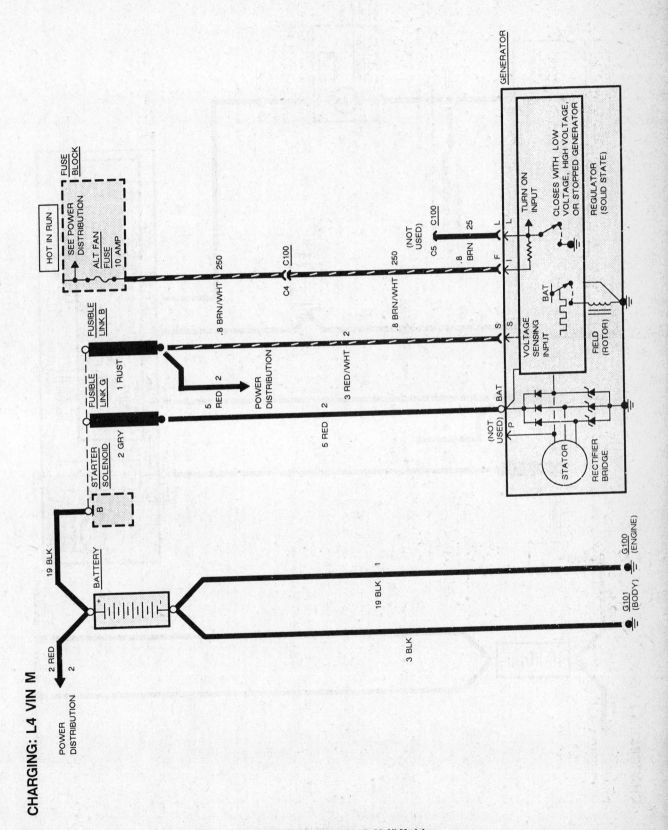

Charging system L4 vin M 1982–89 All Models.

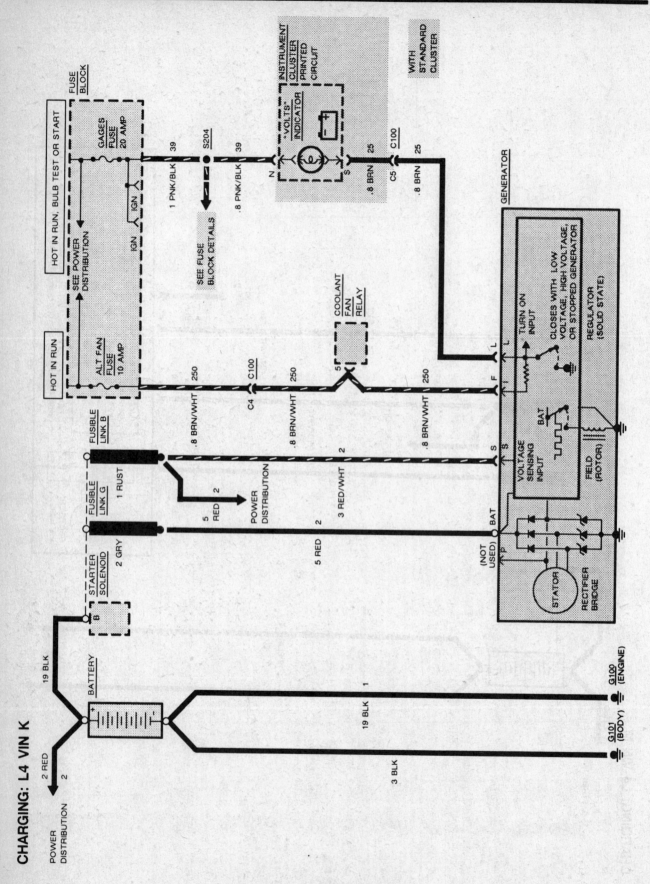

CHARGING: L4 VIN K

Charging system L4 vin K 1982–89 All Models.

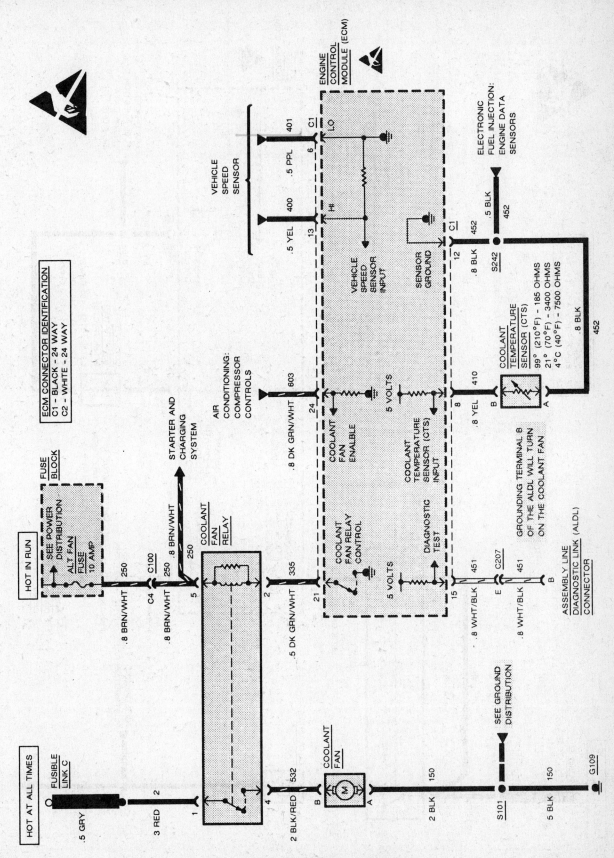

Coolant fan L4 vin K 1982–89 All Models.

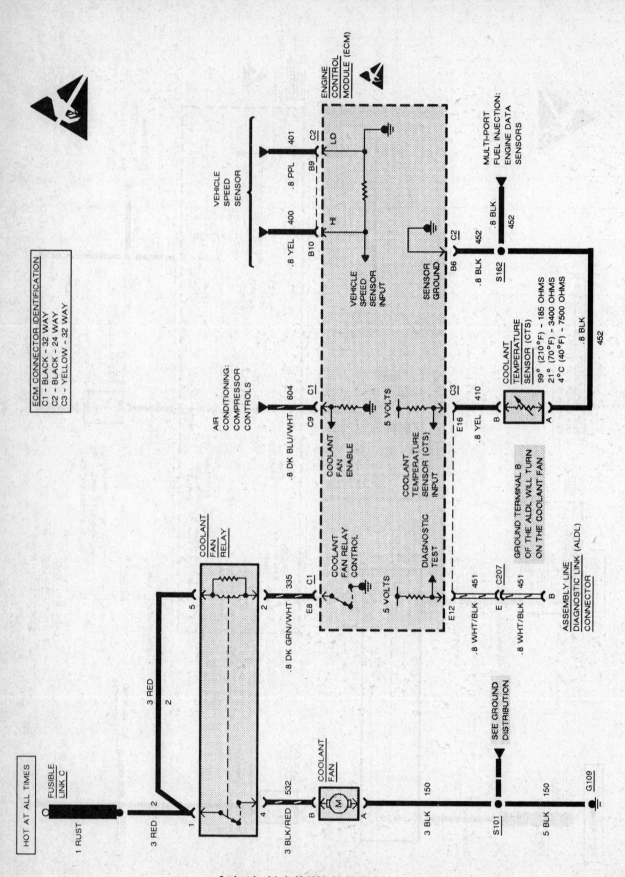

Coolant fan L4 vin M 1982–89 All Models.

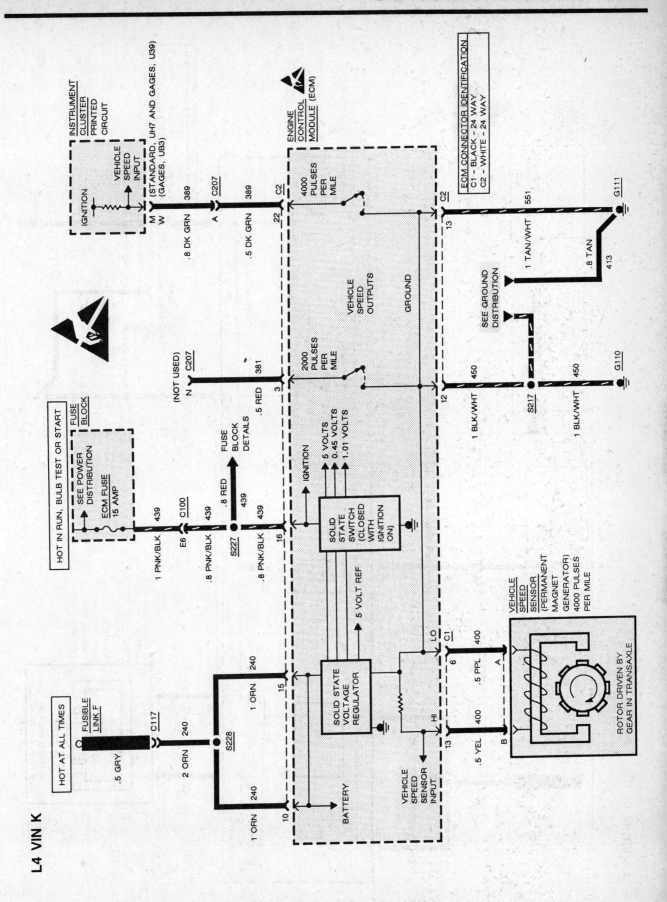

Vehicle speed sensor L4 vin K 1982–89 All Models.

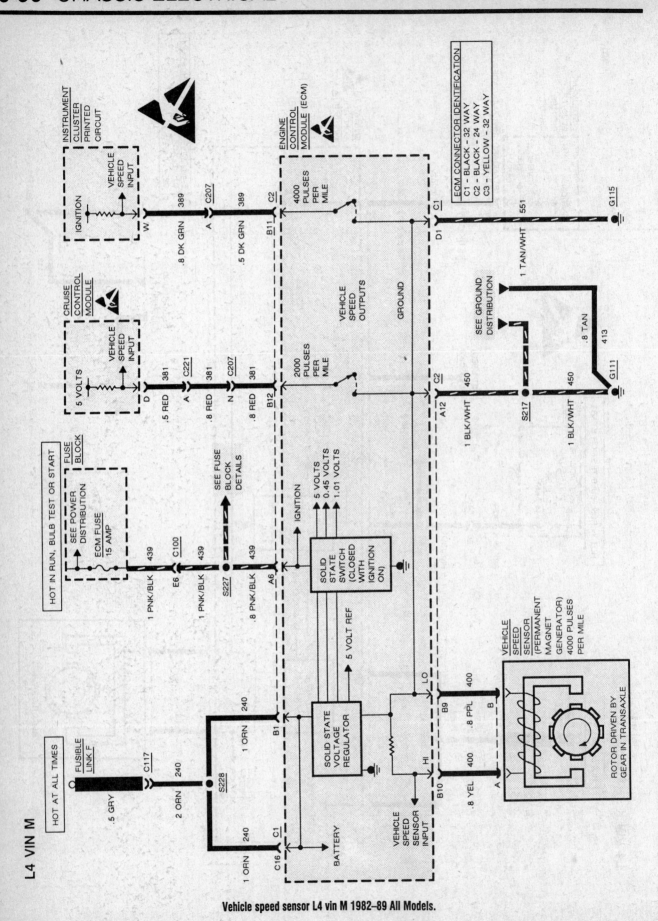

Vehicle speed sensor L4 vin M 1982–89 All Models.

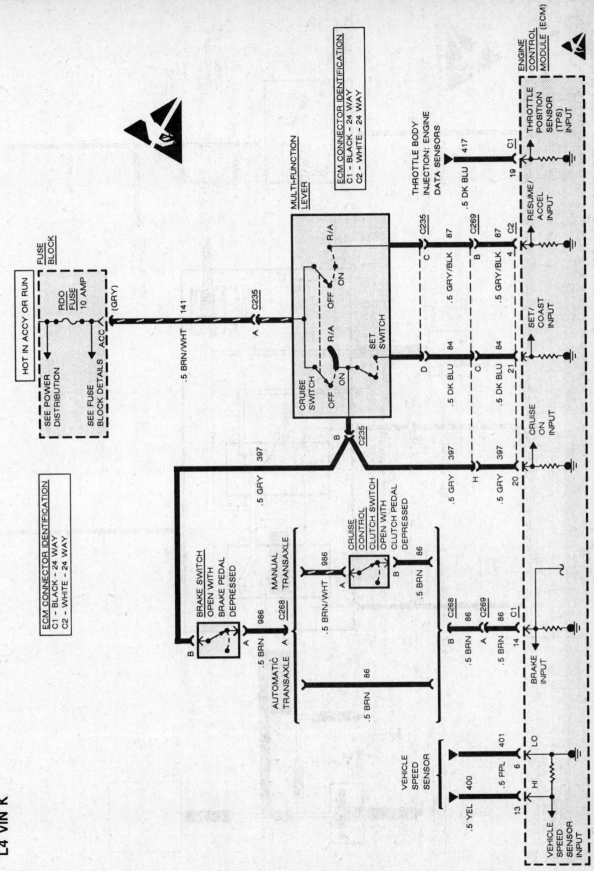

Cruise control L4 vin K 1982–89 All Models.

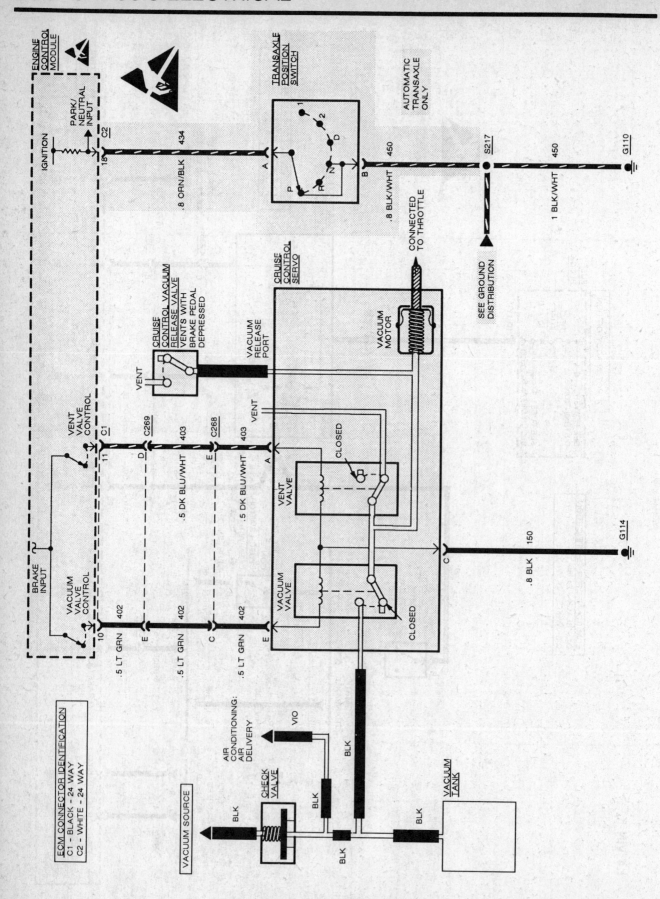

Cruise control L4 vin K 1982–89 All Models (con't).

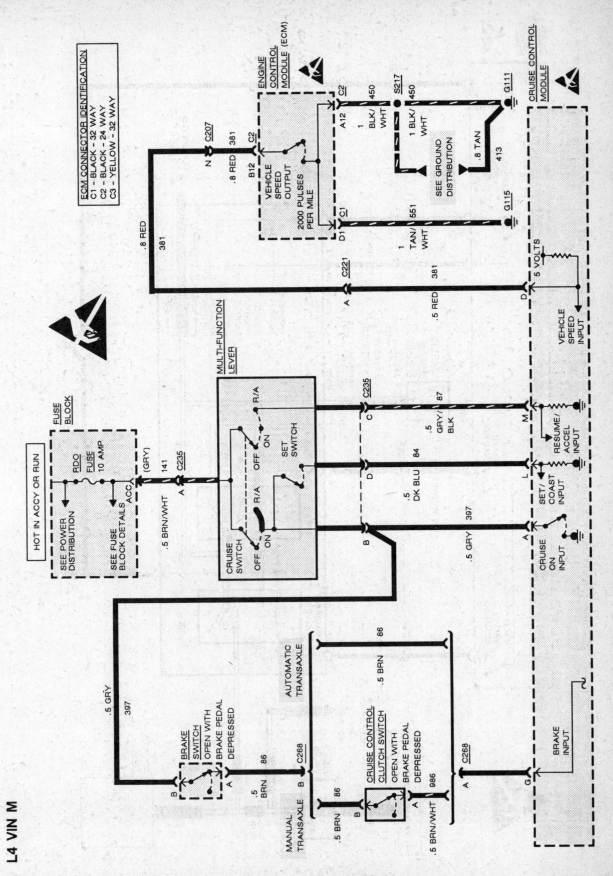

Cruise control L4 vin M 1982–89 All Models.

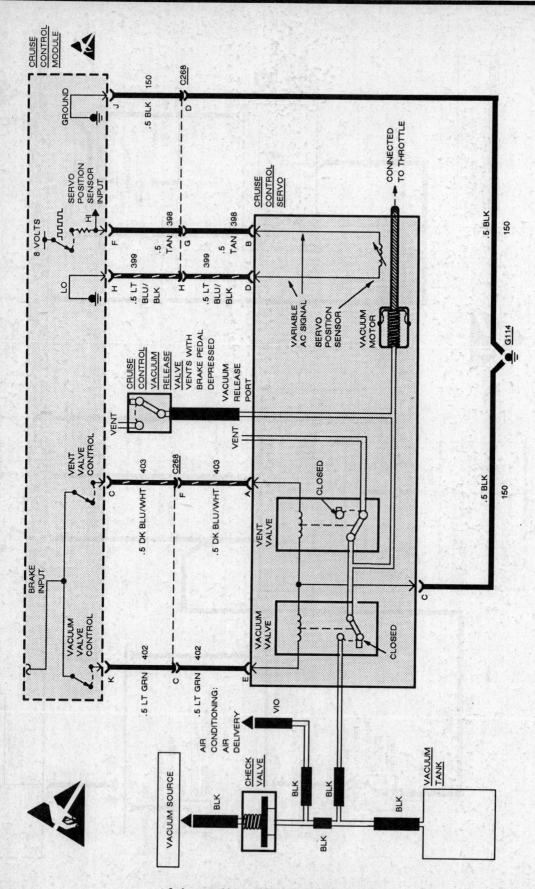

Cruise control L4 vin M 1982–89 All Models (con't).

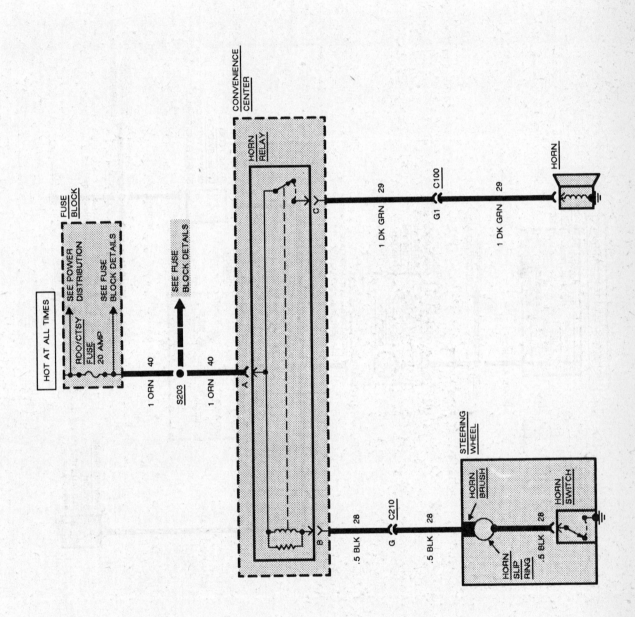

Horn 1982–89 All Models.

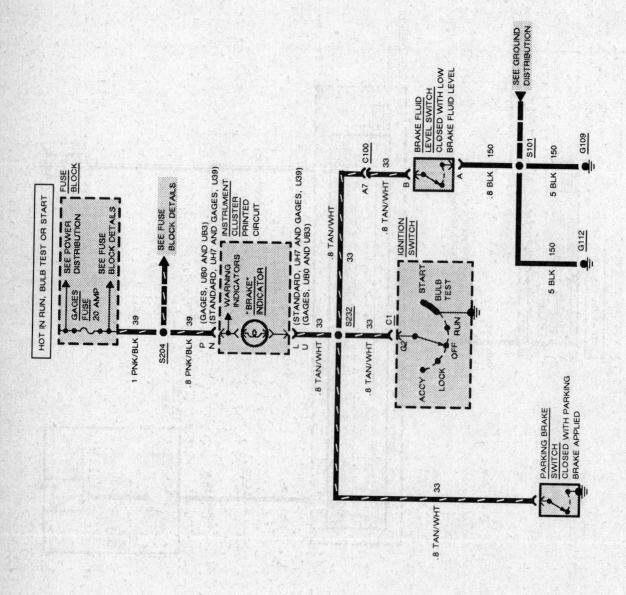

Brake warning system 1982–89 All Models.

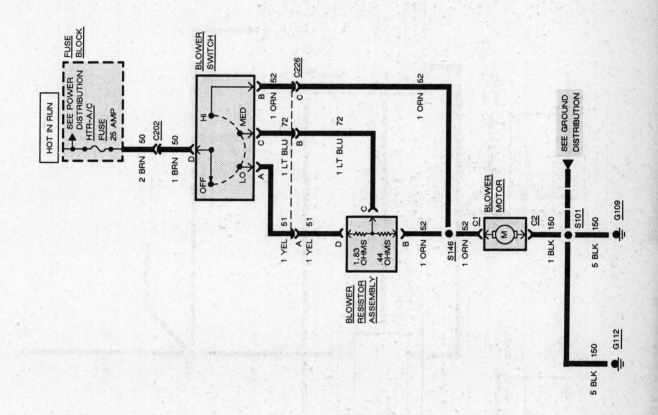

Heater 1982–89 All Models.

COUPE AND SEDAN

INTERIOR LIGHTS DIMMING

WIPER SWITCH ASSEMBLY

WIPER/WASHER

WIPER SWITCH ASSEMBLY LIGHT

ON INDICATOR

REAR DEFOGGER SWITCH (ON/OFF MOMENTARY SWITCH)

.5 GRY 8

HOT IN RUN, BULB TEST OR START

FUSE BLOCK

SEE GROUND DISTRIBUTION

GAGES FUSE 20 AMP

SEE FUSE BLOCK DETAILS

SEE FUSE BLOCK DETAILS

.8 PNK/BLK 39

.8 LT BLU 292

1 PPL/WHT 293

.8 BLK 150

SEE GROUND DISTRIBUTION

1 PNK/BLK

S204

REAR DEFOGGER TIMER RELAY

FUSE BLOCK

POWER DOOR LOCKS

HOT AT ALL TIMES

PWR/ACC CIRCUIT BREAKER 35 AMP

PWR ACC

(NOT USED)

(GRN)

2 ORN/BLK 60

.8 PNK/BLK 39

SOLID STATE TIMER

.8 BLK 150

S205

150

3 BLK

G200

3 ORN/BLK 60

PWR/ACC CIRCUIT BREAKER 35 AMP

3 PPL/WHT 293

S211

3 PPL/WHT 293

C201 .5 PPL 192

C327 PPL 192

REAR DEFOGGER

BLK

G314

Rear defogger 1982–89 All Models.

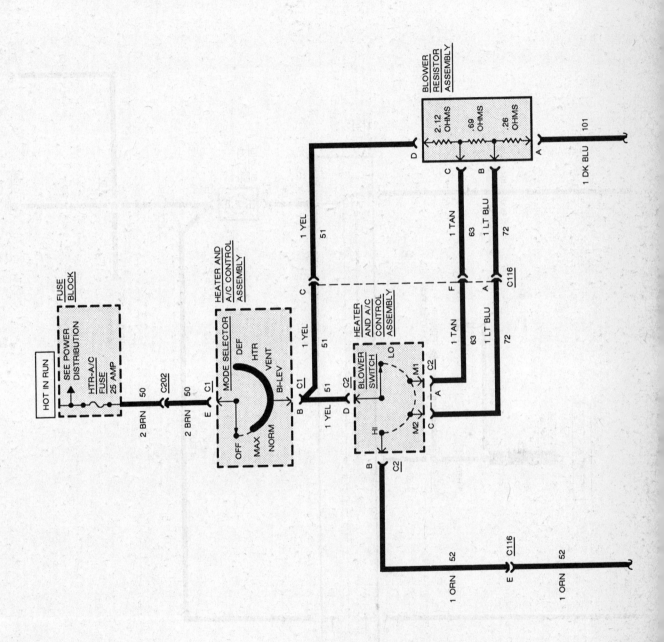

C60, MANUAL

A/C blower controls 1982–89 All Models.

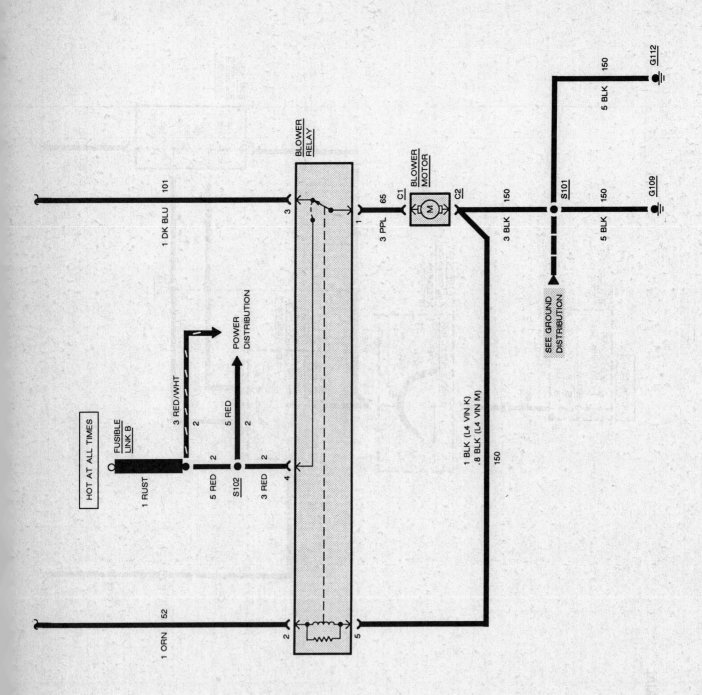

A/C blower controls 1982–89 All Models (con't).

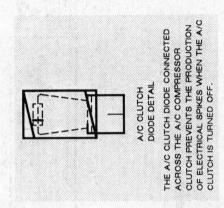

A/C CLUTCH DIODE DETAIL

THE A/C CLUTCH DIODE CONNECTED ACROSS THE A/C COMPRESSOR CLUTCH PREVENTS THE PRODUCTION OF ELECTRICAL SPIKES WHEN THE A/C CLUTCH IS TURNED OFF.

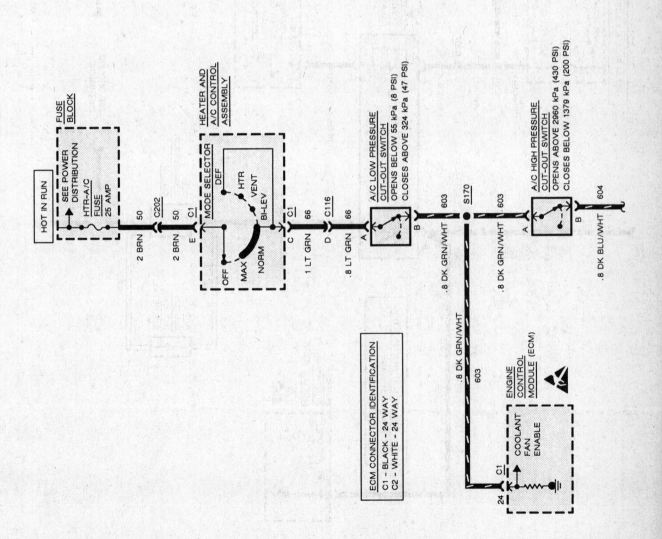

A/C compressor controls L4 vin K 1982–89 All Models.

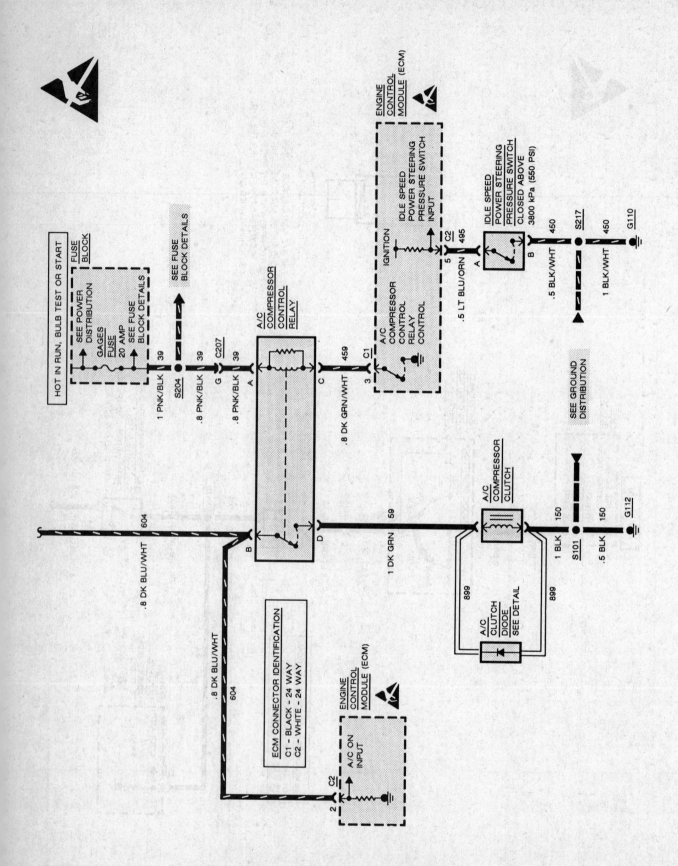

A/C compressor controls L4 vin K 1982–89 All Models (con't).

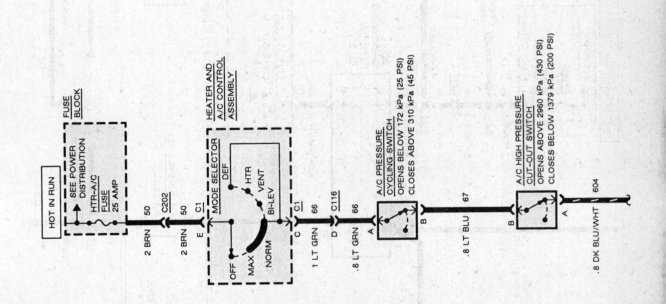

C60, MANUAL, L4 VIN M

A/C compressor controls L4 vin M 1982–89 All Models.

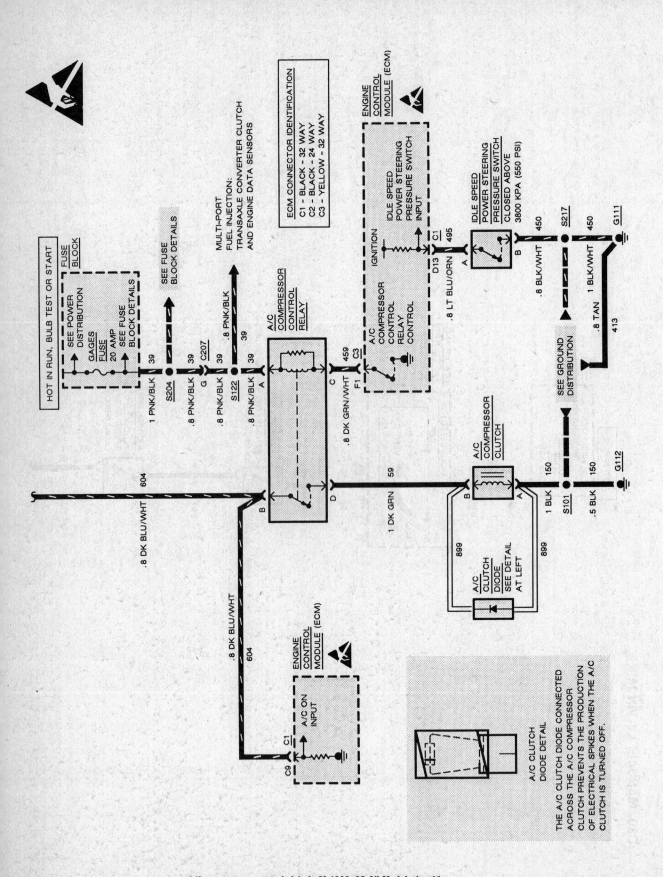

A/C compressor controls L4 vin M 1982–89 All Models (con't).

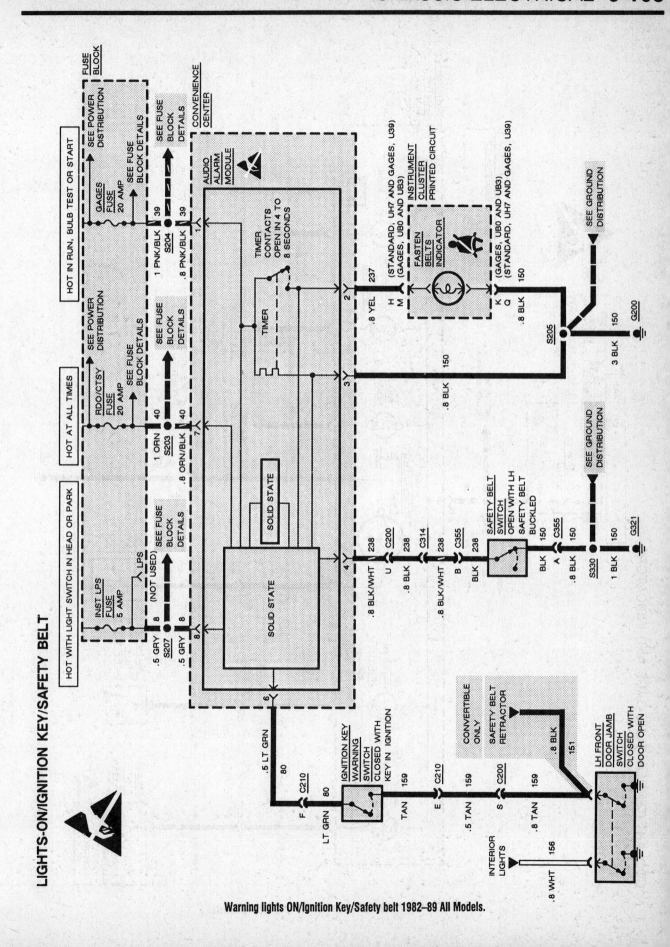

Warning lights ON/Ignition Key/Safety belt 1982–89 All Models.

COOLANT TEMPERATURE GAGE AND INDICATORS

INSTRUMENT CLUSTER PRINTED CIRCUIT

ECM CONNECTOR IDENTIFICATION
C1 - BLACK - 24 WAY
C2 - WHITE - 24 WAY

GAGES

VOLTS INDICATOR

"SERV. ENG. SOON" INDICATOR

"BRAKE" INDICATOR

S .8 BRN 25 STARTER AND CHARGING SYSTEM

O .5 BRN/WHT 419 THROTTLE BODY INJECTION AND MULTI-PORT FUEL INJECTION

L .8 TAN/WHT 33 BRAKE WARNING SYSTEM

SEE GROUND DISTRIBUTION

HOT IN RUN, BULB TEST OR START

FUSE BLOCK

SEE POWER DISTRIBUTION

GAGES FUSE 20 AMP

SEE FUSE BLOCK DETAILS

SEE FUSE BLOCK DETAILS

1 PNK/BLK 39

S204

.8 PNK/BLK 39

N

COOLANT TEMPERATURE GAGE

INDICATORS

Q .8 BLK 150 S205 3 BLK 150 G200

COOLANT TEMPERATURE SENDER
RESISTANCE:
1365 OHMS AT 38° C (100° F)
55 OHMS AT 127° C (260° F)

P .8 DK GRN 35 C100 .8 DK GRN 35 B

F5

OIL PRESSURE INDICATOR

T .5 TAN 31 E5 .8 TAN 31 A

FUEL PUMP SWITCH/ OIL PRESSURE SWITCH
OPENS AT 13.8 kPa (2 PSI)

UPSHIFT INDICATOR
(MANUAL TRANSAXLE ONLY)

I .8 TAN/BLK 456 C207 .8 TAN/BLK 456 C1 (L4 VIN K) 7

ENGINE CONTROL MODULE (ECM)

H

UPSHIFT INDICATOR CONTROL

MANUAL TRANSAXLE ONLY

Coolant temperature gauge and indicators 1982–89 All Models.

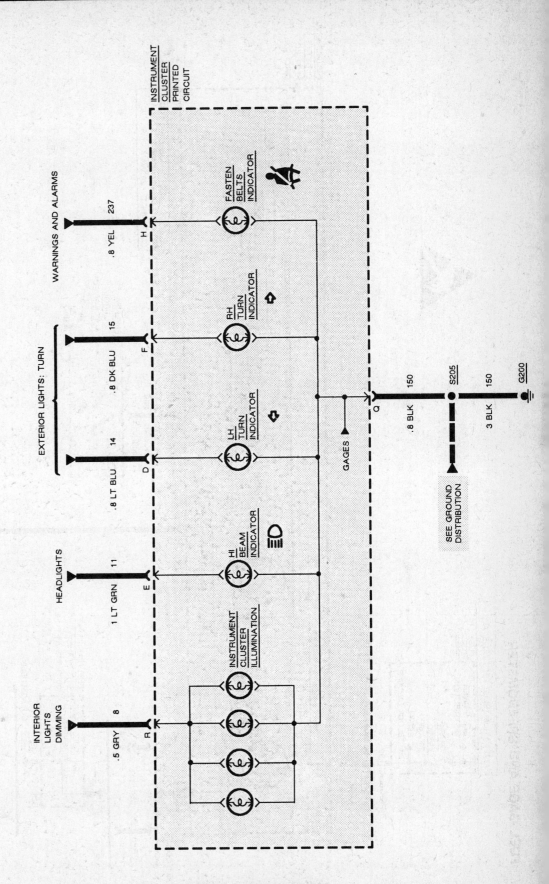

Indicators and illumination 1982–89 All Models.

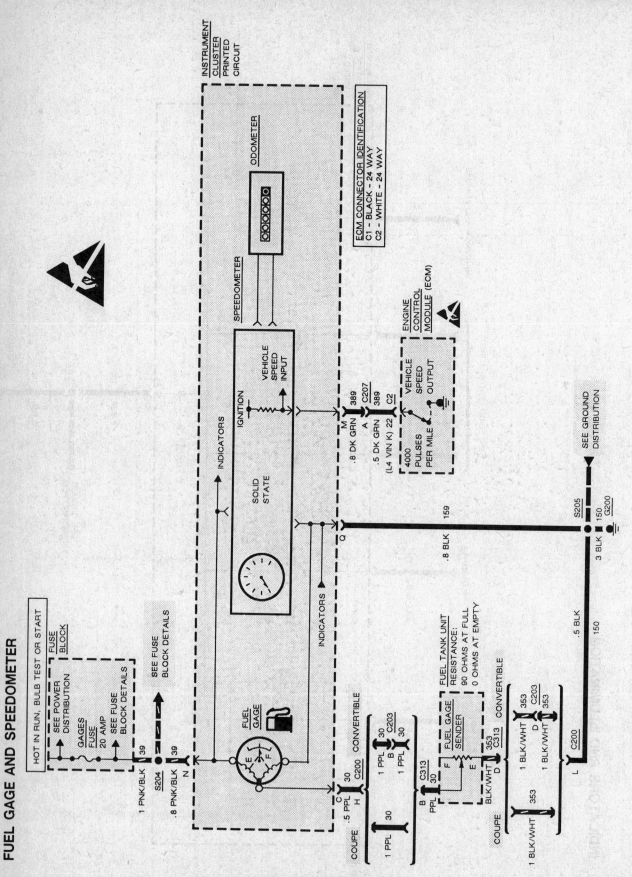

Fuel gauge and speedometer 1982–89 All Models.

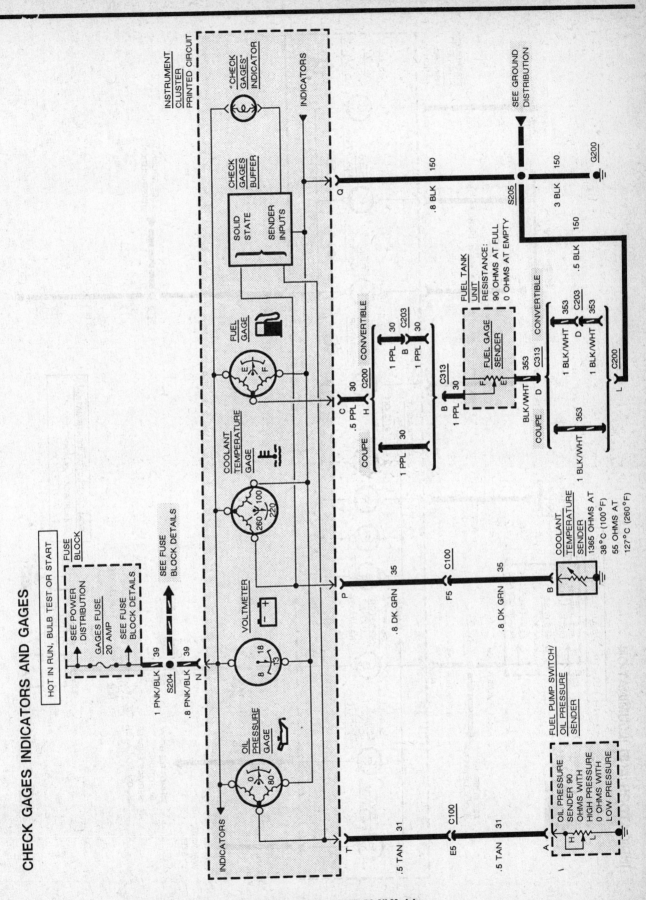

Check gauges indicators 1982–89 All Models.

INDICATORS AND ILLUMINATION

Indicators and illumination 1982–89 All Models.

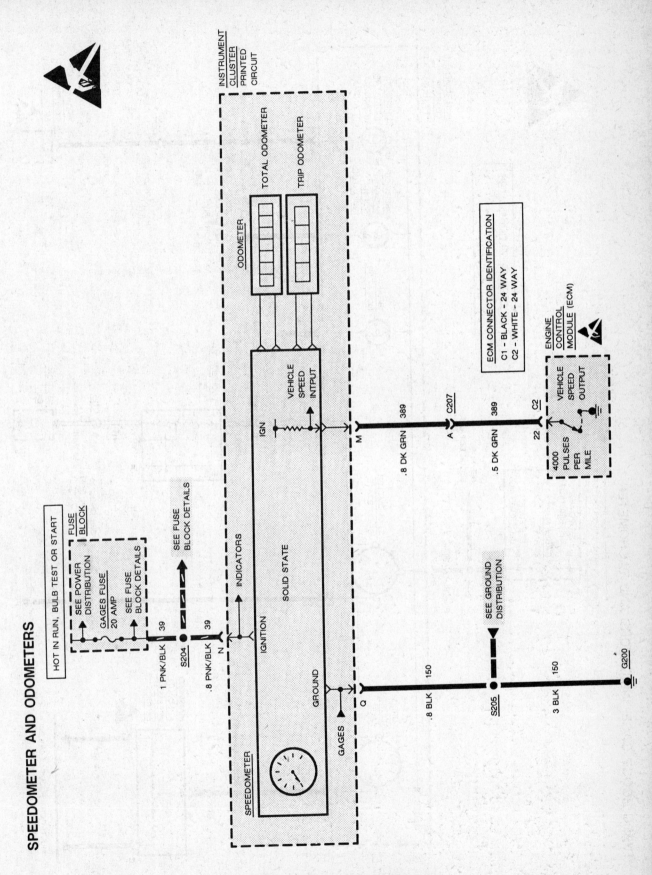

SPEEDOMETER AND ODOMETERS

Speedometer and odometers 1982–89 All Models.

TURBO BOOST GAGE, INDICATORS AND TACHOMETER

INSTRUMENT CLUSTER PRINTED CIRCUIT

UPSHIFT INDICATOR (MANUAL TRANSAXLE ONLY)

"SERVICE ENGINE SOON" INDICATOR

"BRAKE" INDICATOR

L4 VIN K

ECM CONNECTOR IDENTIFICATION

C1 - BLACK - 24 WAY
C2 - WHITE - 24 WAY

L4 VIN K WITH MANUAL TRANSAXLE ONLY

ENGINE CONTROL MODULE (ECM)

456   C207   456   C1
.8 TAN/BLK   H   .8 TAN/BLK   7

THROTTLE BODY INJECTION AND MULTI-PORT FUEL INJECTION

.5 BRN/WHT 419   V

BRAKE WARNING SYSTEM

.8 TAN/WHT 33   U

TACHOMETER FILTER

121 C100 121 C125 121   121 C125 121 C2 IGNITION COIL
.8 WHT D6 .8 WHT/BLK B WHT/BLK   WHT A .8 WHT A

HOT IN RUN, BULB TEST OR START

FUSE BLOCK

SEE POWER DISTRIBUTION

GAGES FUSE 20 AMP

SEE FUSE BLOCK DETAILS

SEE FUSE BLOCK DETAILS

39   39
1 PNK/BLK   S204   1 PNK/BLK   P

TACHOMETER SOLID STATE

SEE GROUND DISTRIBUTION

G200

150   150
.8 BLK   S205   3 BLK

K

INDICATORS

L4 VIN M ONLY

MULTI-PORT FUEL INJECTION ENGINE DATA SENSORS

MANIFOLD ABSOLUTE PRESSURE (MAP) SENSOR

452
A   .8 BLK

L4 VIN M ONLY

TURBO BOOST GAGE

GAGES

432 C207 432   .8 LT GRN 432   432
A   R   S218   B
.8 LT GRN   .8 LT GRN   .8 LT GRN

MULTI-PORT FUEL INJECTION ENGINE DATA SENSORS

474
C   .8 GRY/RED

Turbo boost gauge, indicators and tachometer 1982–89 All Models.

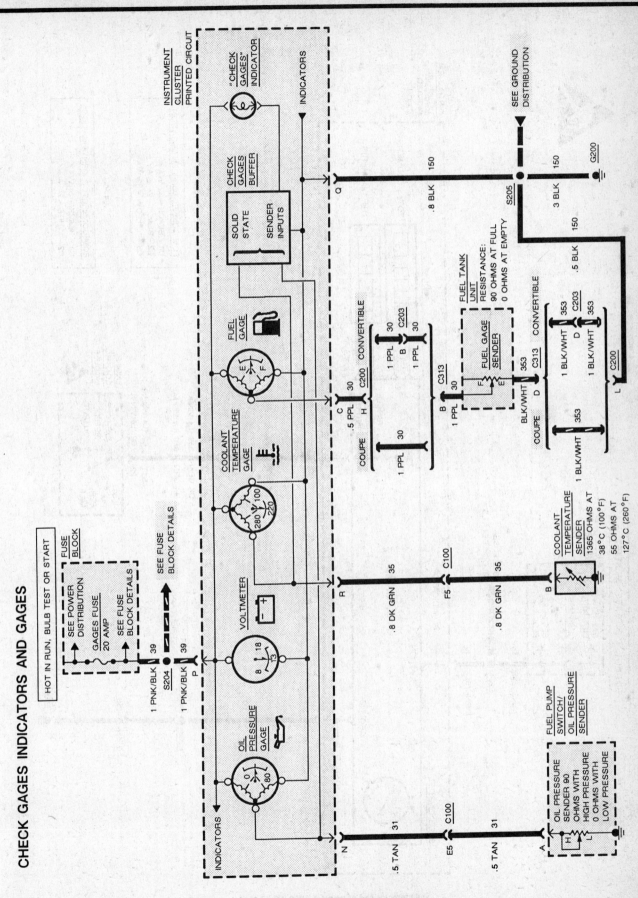

Check gauges indicators 1982–89 All Models.

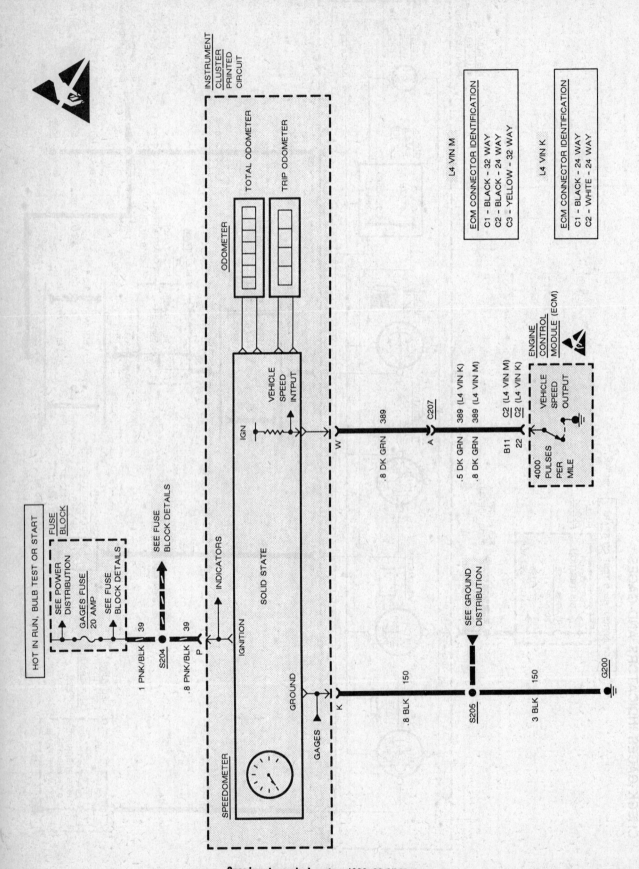

Speedometer and odometers 1982–89 All Models.

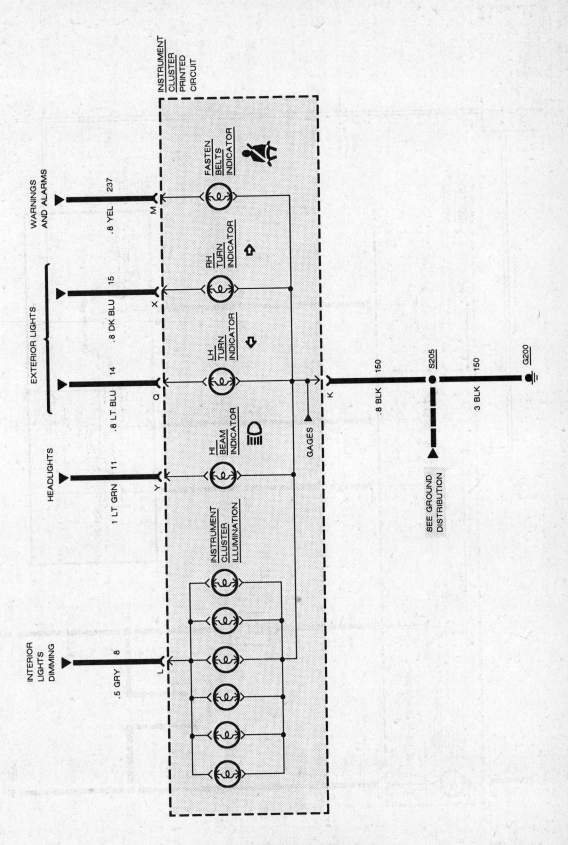

Indicators and illumination 1982–89 All Models.

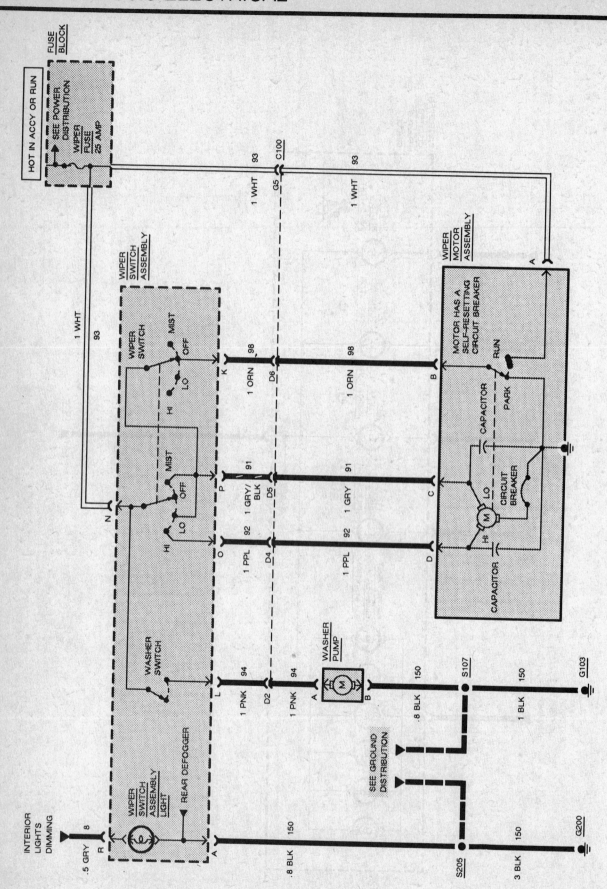

Standard Wiper/Washer 1982–89 All Models.

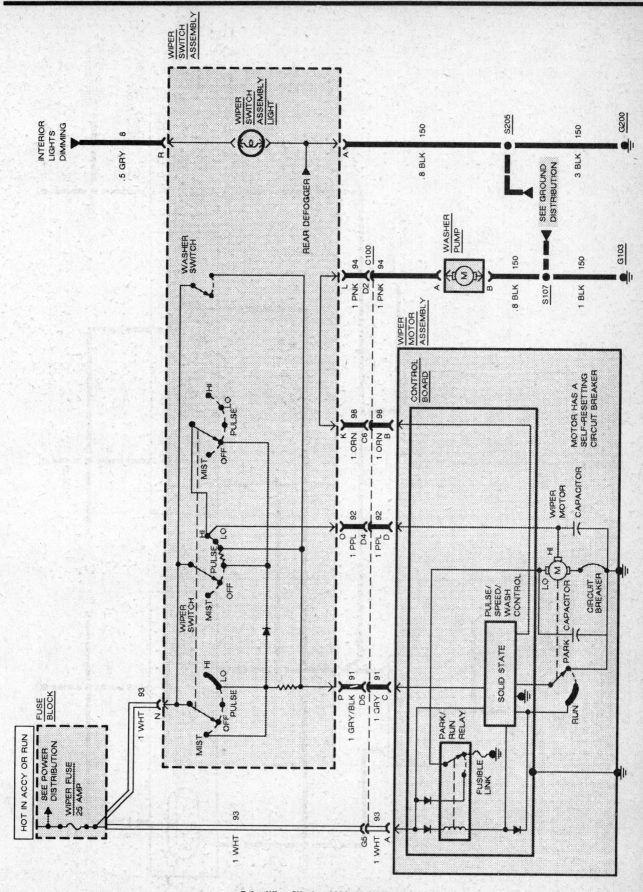

Pulse Wiper/Washer 1982–89 All Models.

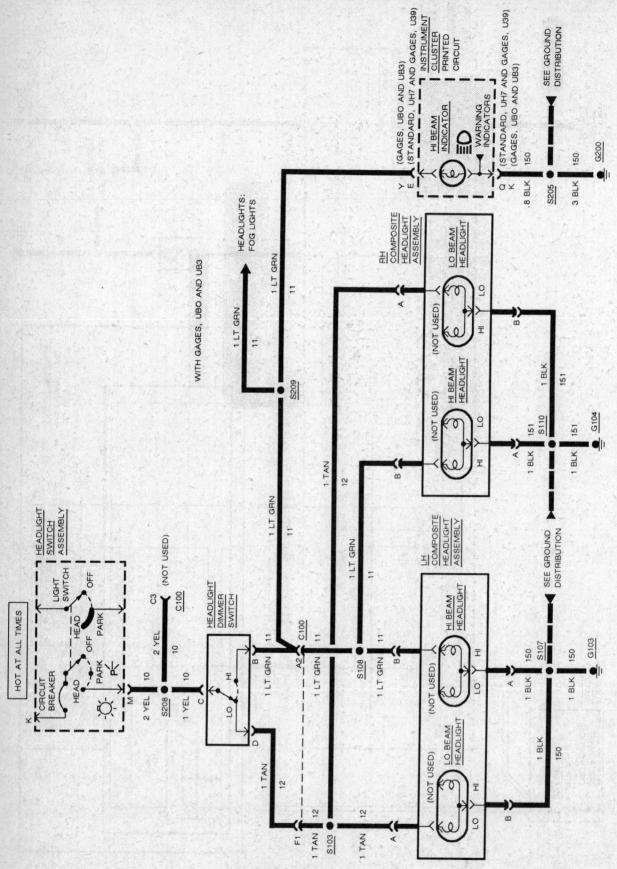

Headlights W/O doors 1982–89 All Models.

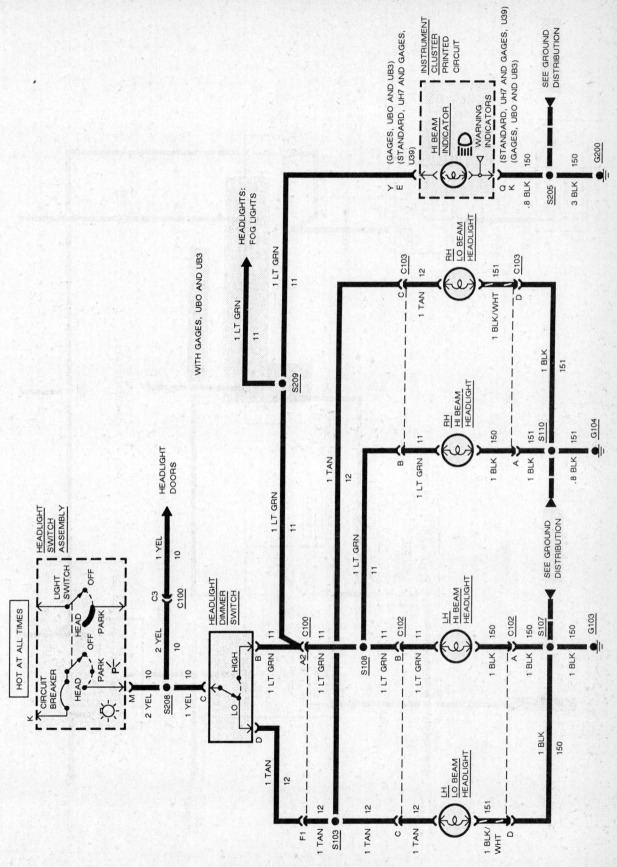

Headlights With doors 1982–89 All Models.

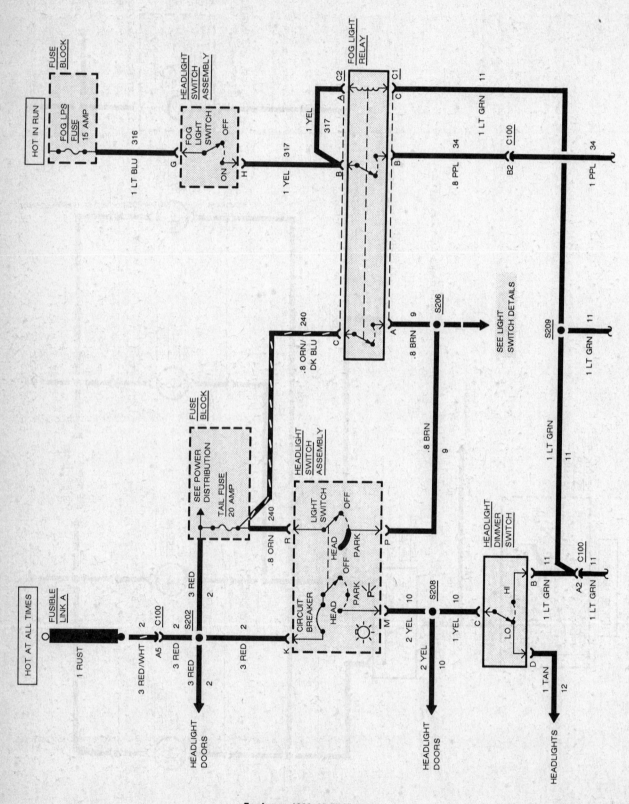

Fog Lamps 1982–89 All Models.

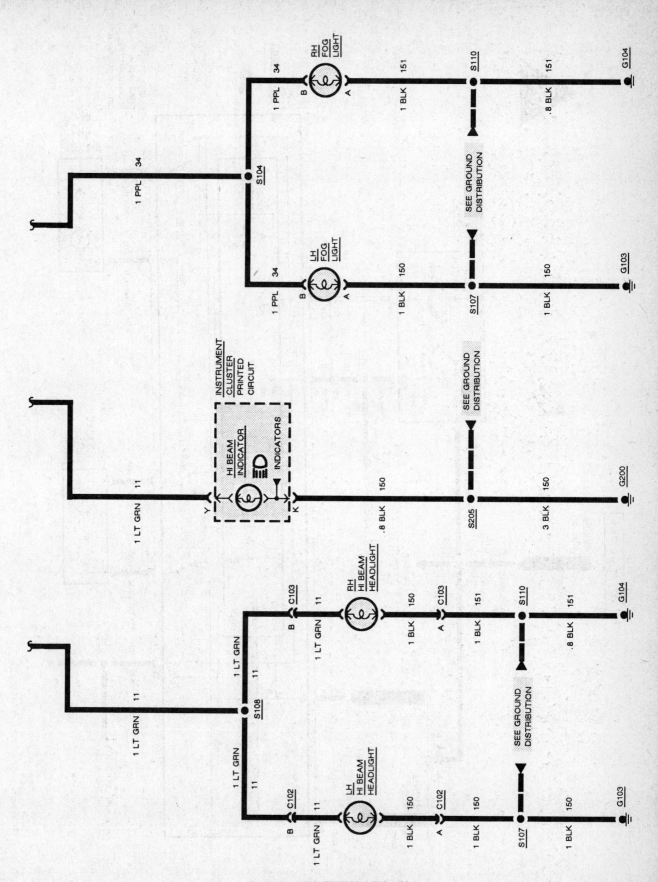

Fog Lamps 1982–89 All Models (con't).

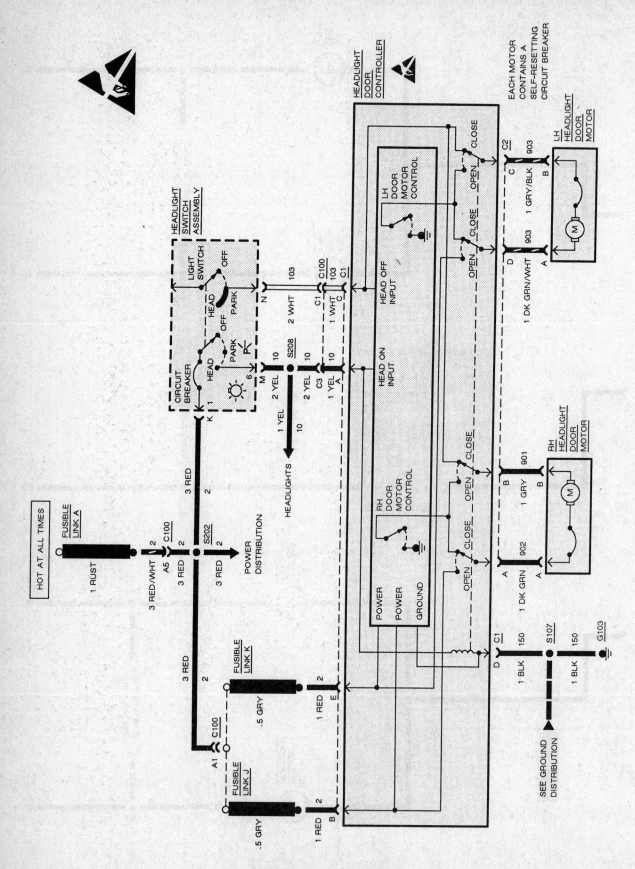

Headlight doors 1982–89 All Models.

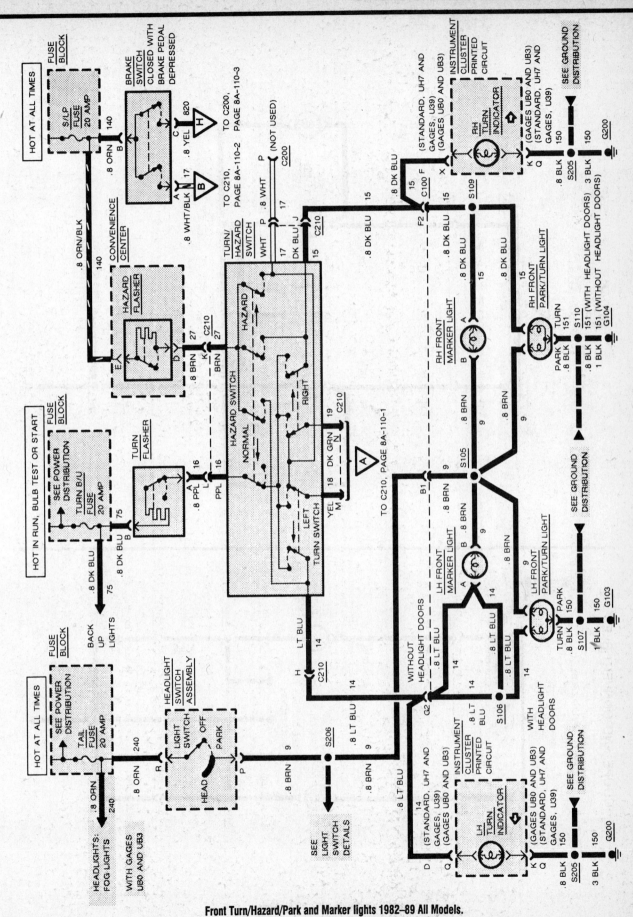

Front Turn/Hazard/Park and Marker lights 1982–89 All Models.

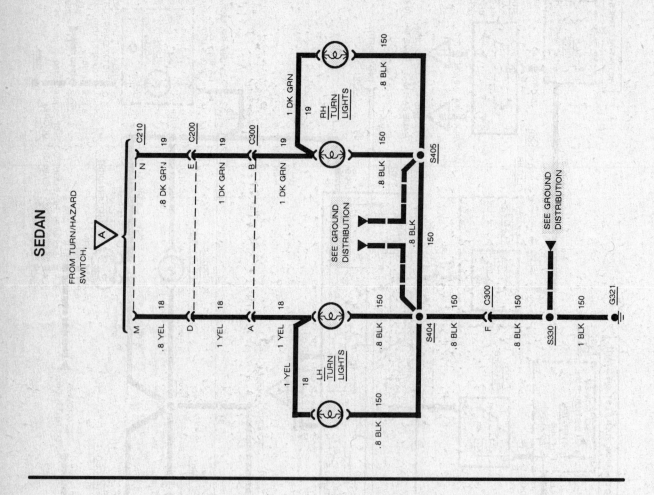

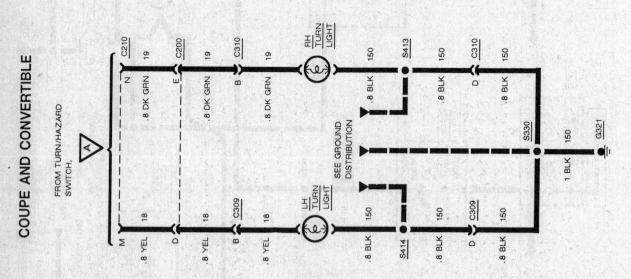

Turn/Hazard lights 1982–89 All Models.

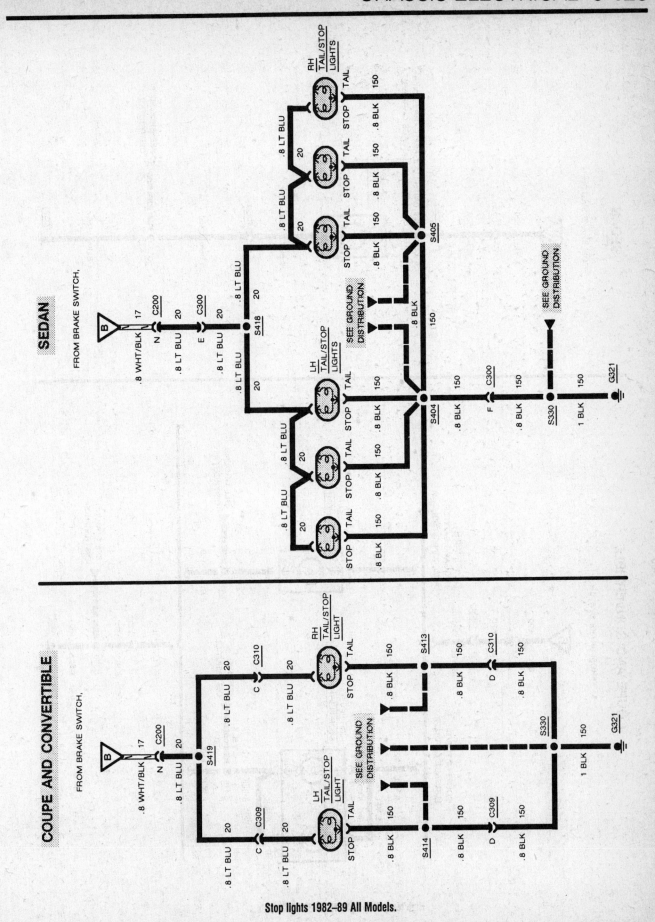

Stop lights 1982–89 All Models.

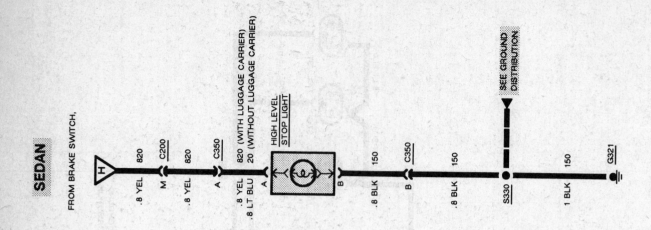

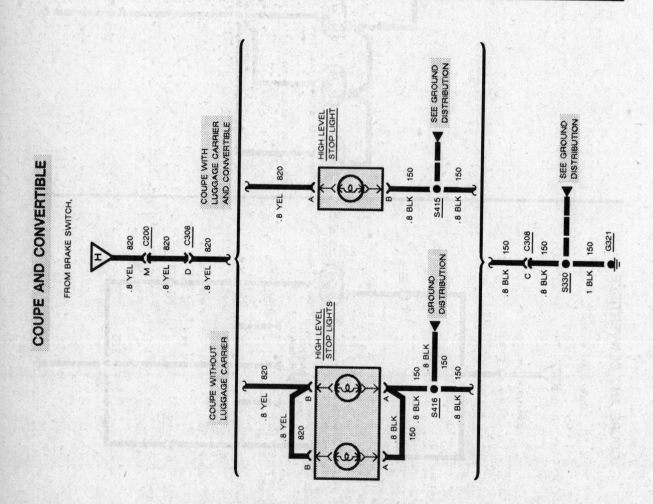

High level Stop light 1982–89 All Models.

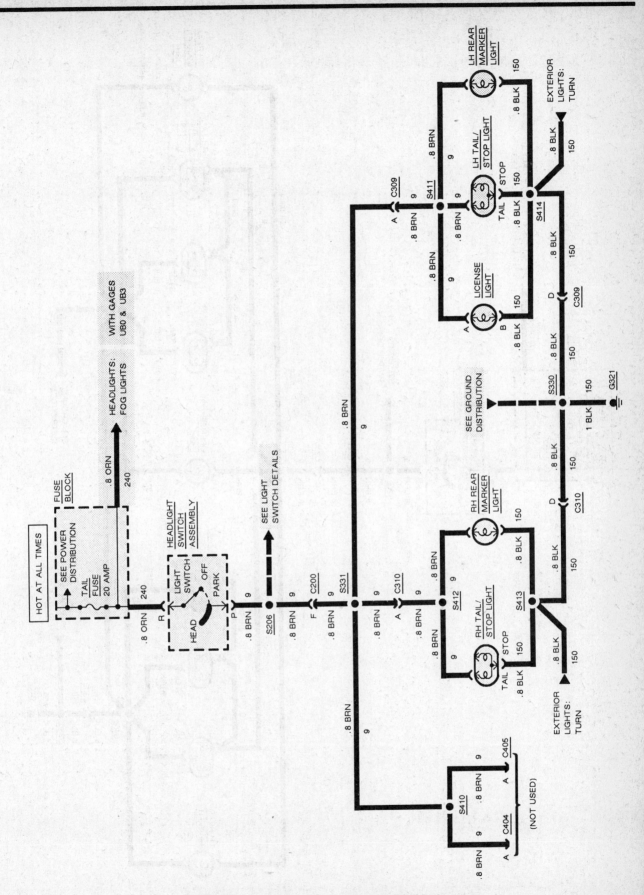

Rear Tail/Marker and license Coupe and convertible 1982–89 All Models.

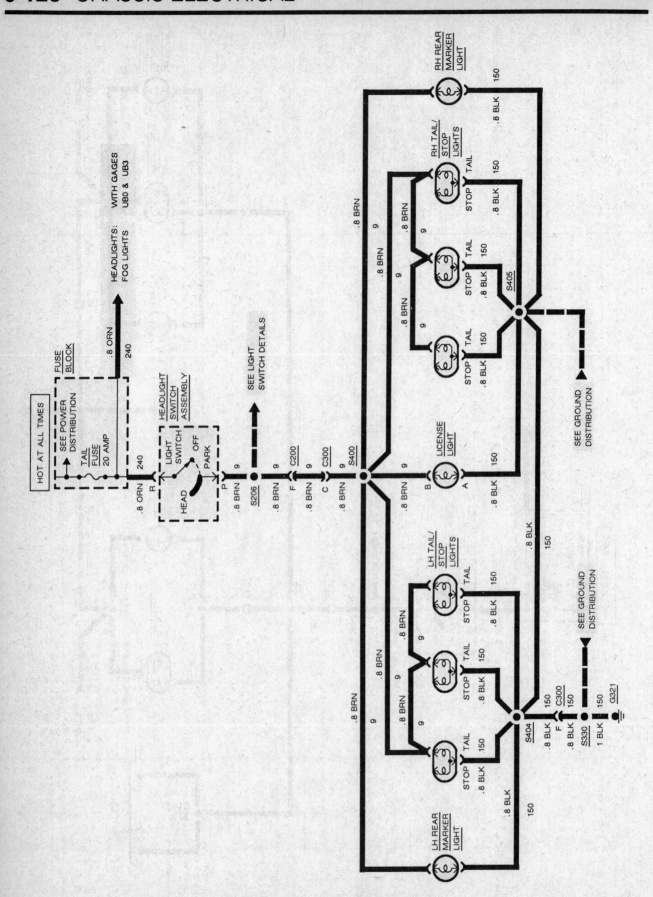

Rear Tail/Marker and license Sedan 1982–89 All Models.

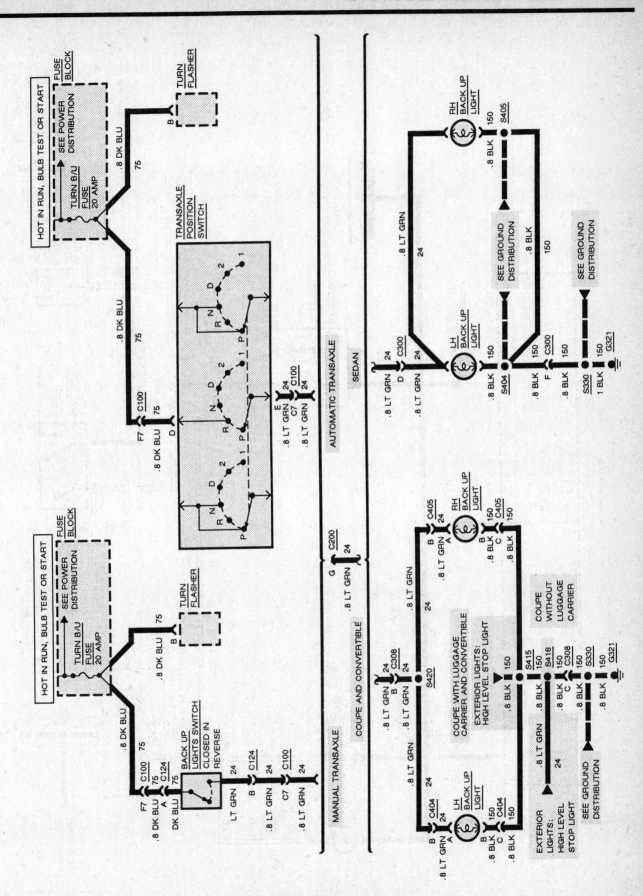

Back-up lights 1982-89 All Models.

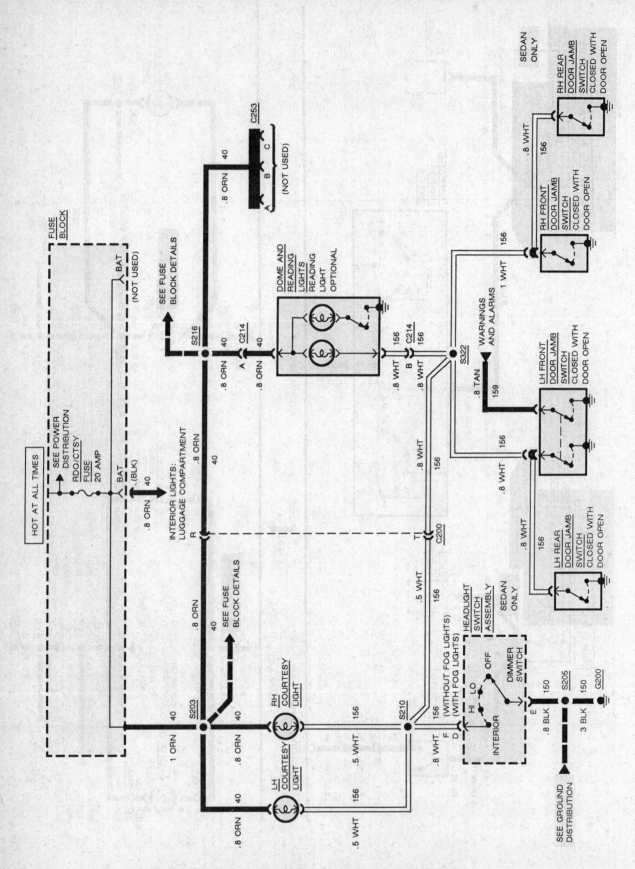

Courtesy, Dome, and Reading lights Sedan and Coupe 1982–89 All Models.

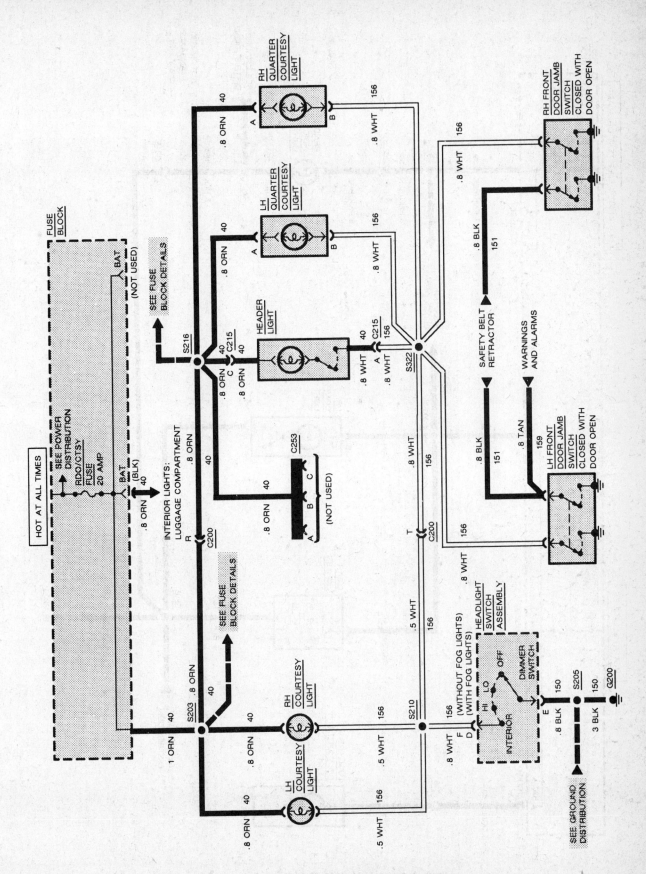

Courtesy, Quarter Courtesy and Header lights 1982–89 All Models.

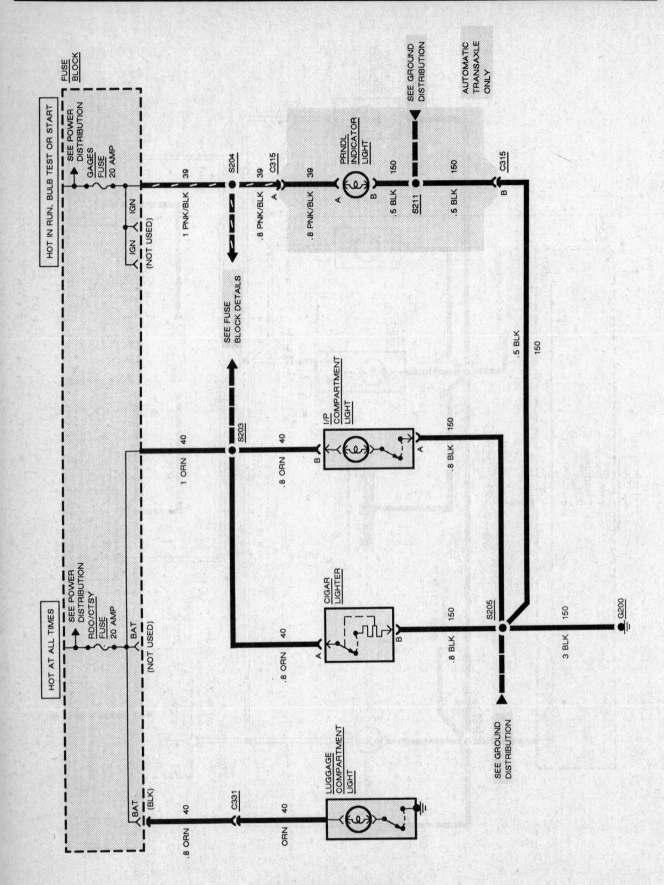

Accessory Lights 1982–89 All Models.

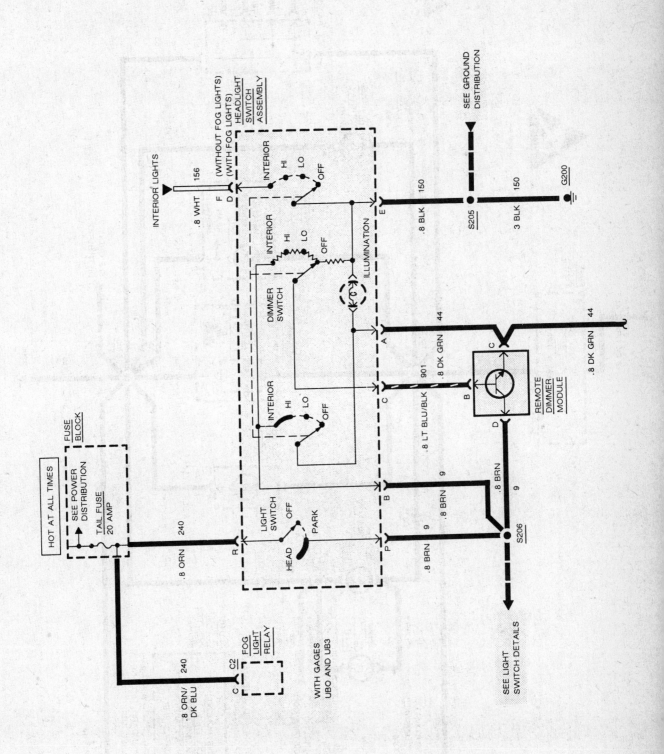

Dimming Interior Lights 1982–89 All Models.

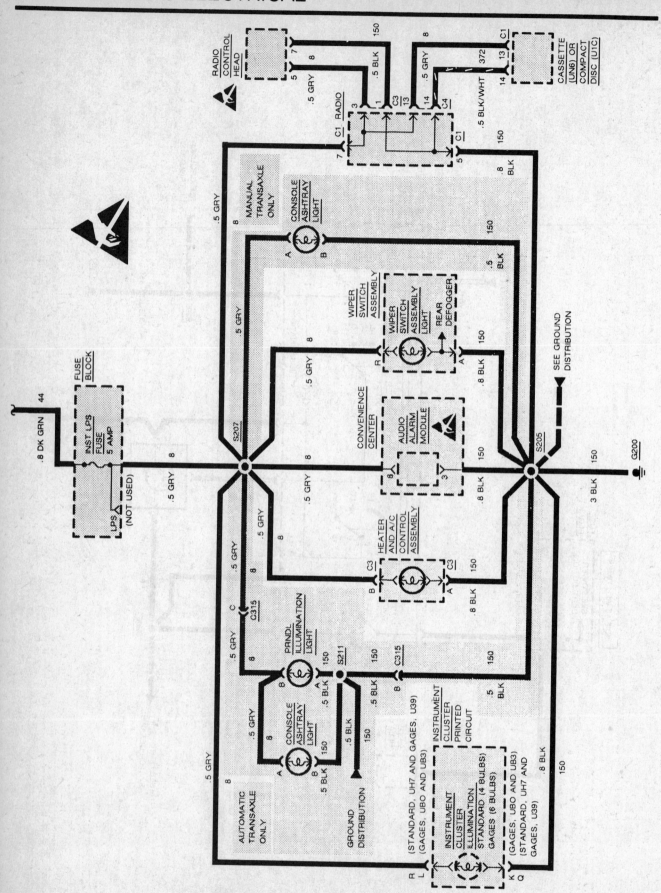

Dimming Interior Lights 1982–89 All Models (con't).

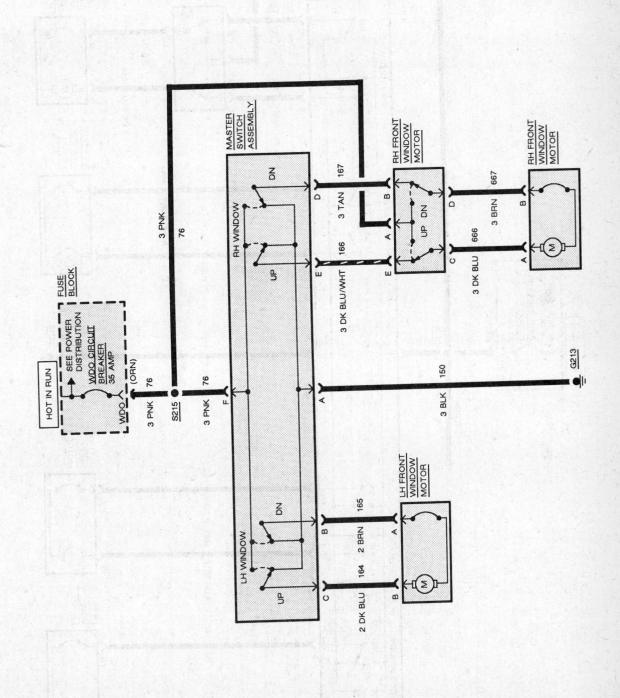

Power windows 2 door coupe 1982–89 All Models.

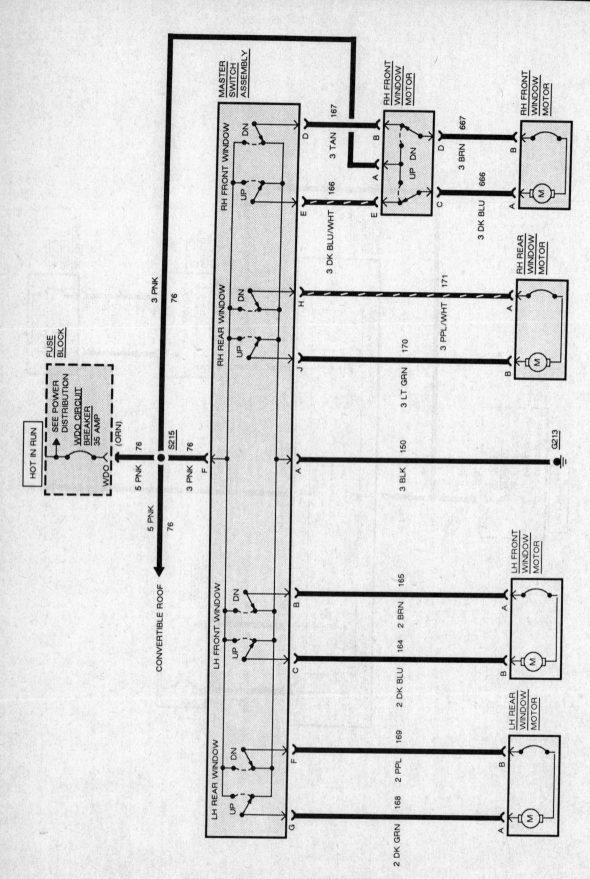

Power windows 2 door convertible 1982–89 All Models.

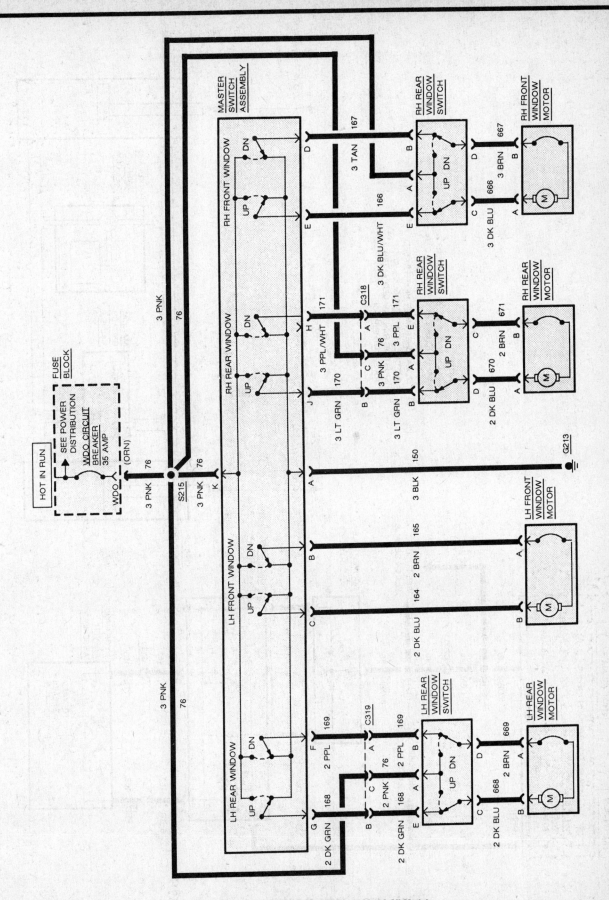

Power windows 4 door sedan 1982–89 All Models.

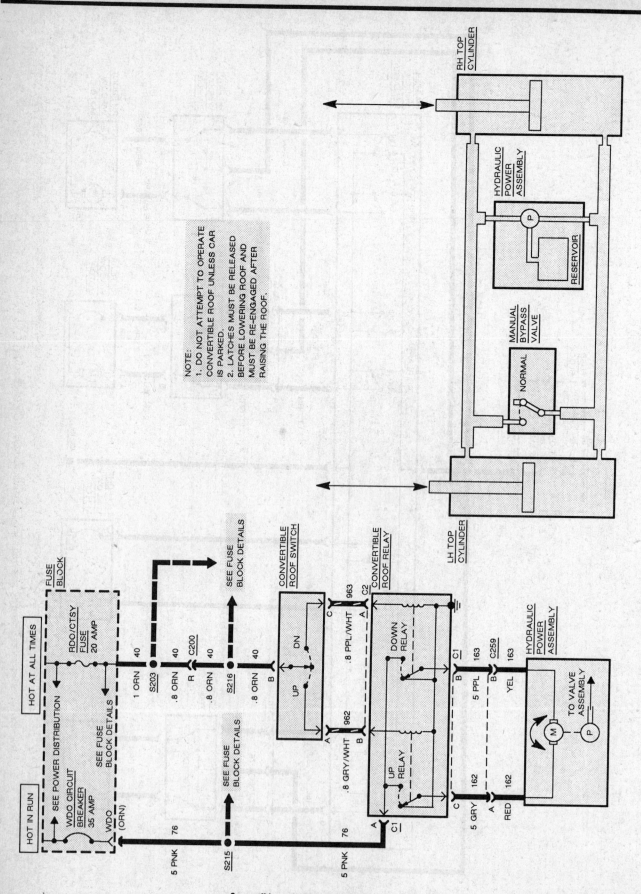

Convertible roof 1982–89 All Models.

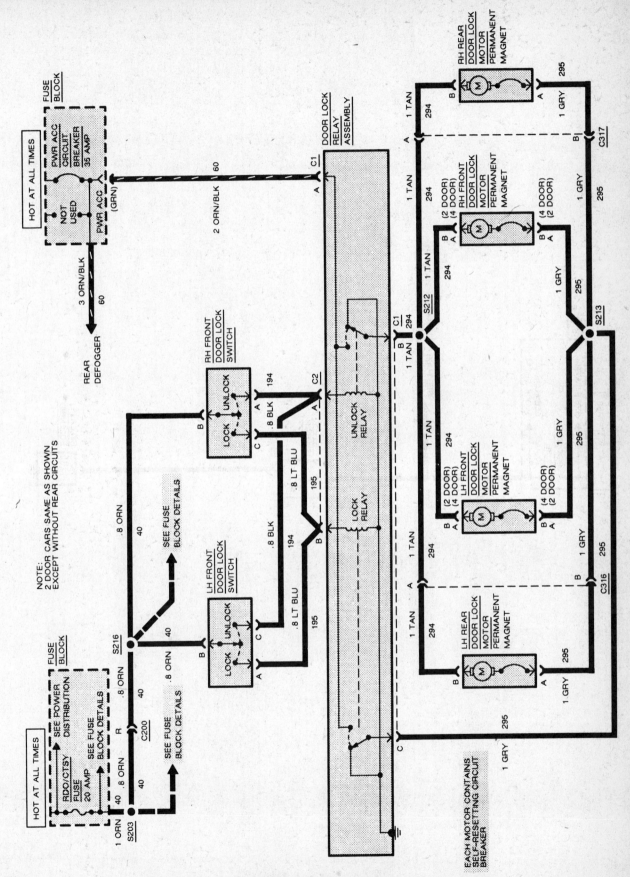

Power door locks 1982–89 All Models.

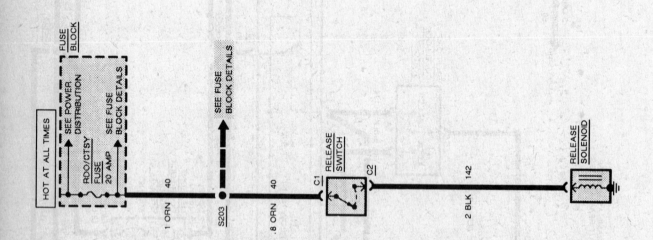

Luggage compartment lid release 1982–89 All Models.

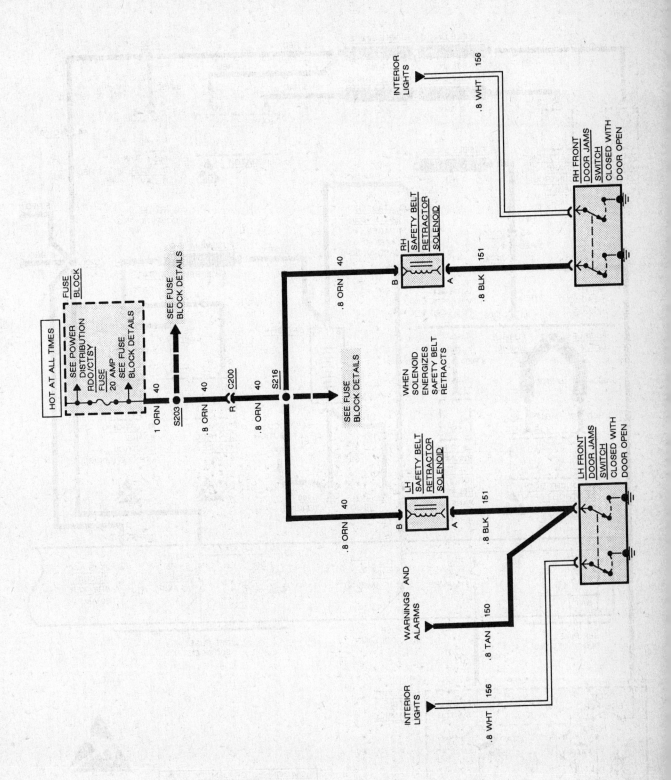

Safety belt retractors convertible 1982–89 All Models.

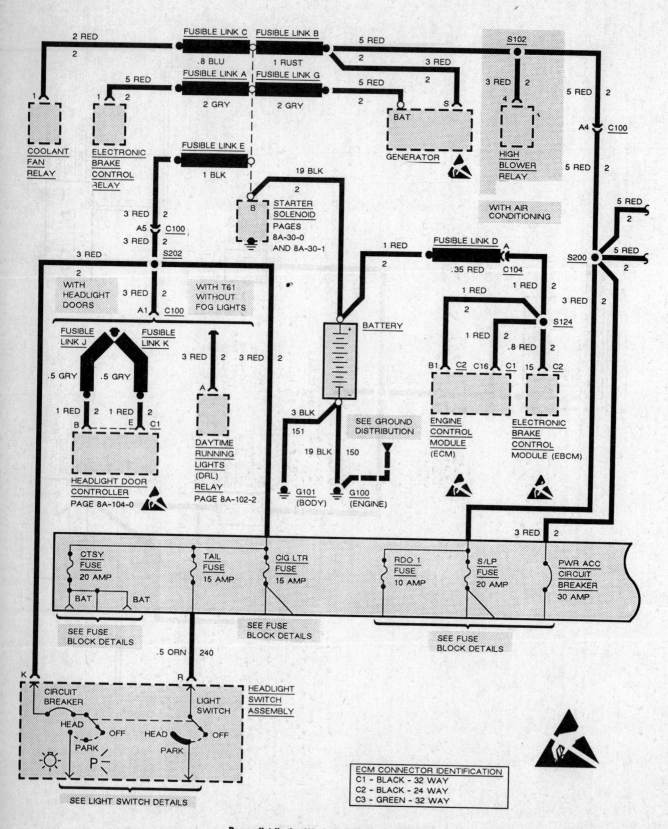

Power distribution V6 vin T 1990–92 All Models.

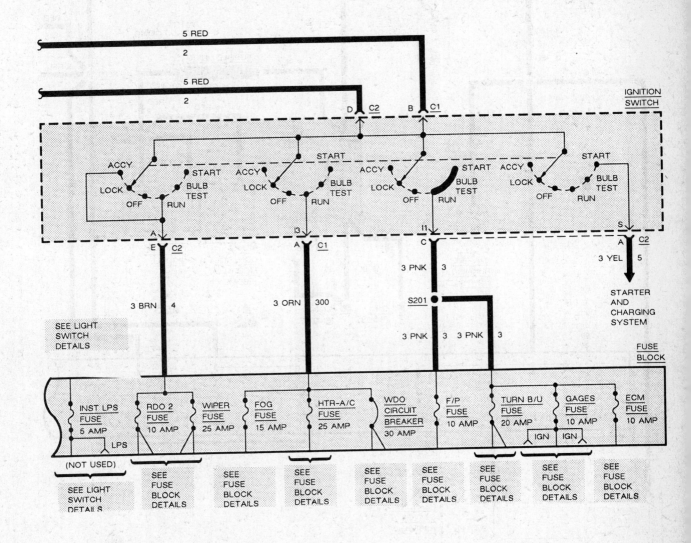

Power distribution V6 vin T 1990–92 All Models (con't).

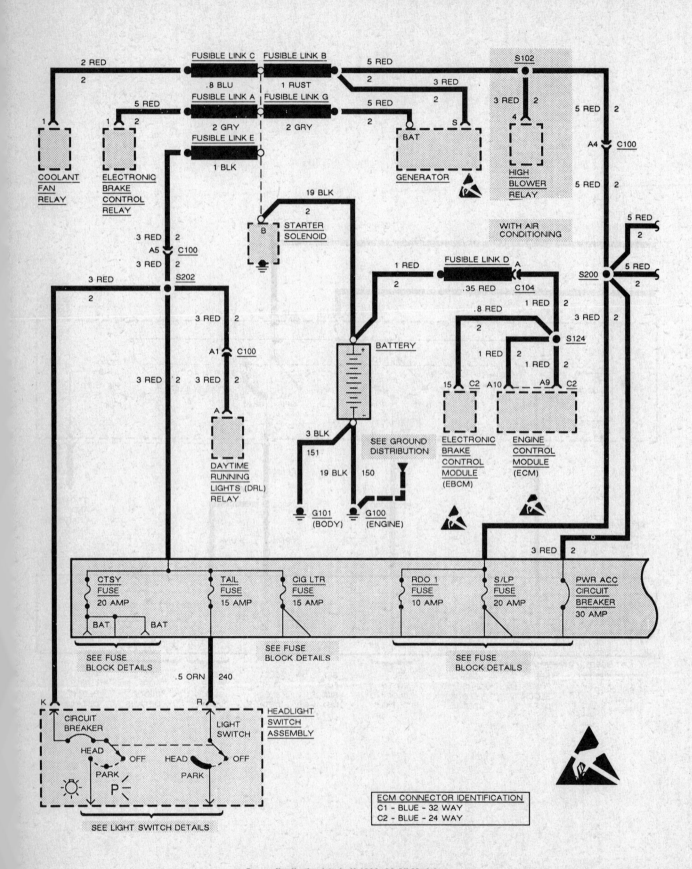

Power distribution L4 vin H 1990–92 All Models.

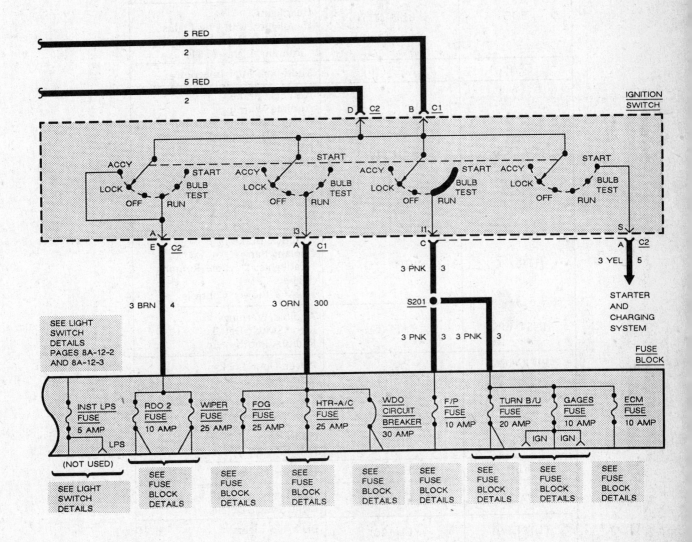

Power distribution L4 vin H 1990–92 All Models (con't).

FUSE	COLOR (AMPS)	SCHEMATICS
CIG LTR	BLU (15)	Interior Lights
CTSY	YEL (20)	Audible Warnings Automatic Door Locks Convertible Top Horn Interior Lights
ECM	RED (10)	Multi-port Fuel Injection
FOG	BLU (15)	Headlights Headlights: with Fog Lights Headlights: Daytime Running Lights (T61)
F/P	RED (10)	Multi-port Fuel Injection
GAGES	RED (10)	Antilock Brake Audible Warnings Brake Transaxle Shift Interlock (BTSI) Solenoid HVAC Instrument Panel Interior Lights Multi-port Fuel Injection Rear Defogger Wiper/Washer
HTR-A/C	WHT (25)	Antilock Brake Coolant Fan Headlights: Daytime Running Lights (T61) HVAC: Blower Controls
INST LPS	TAN (5)	Audible Warnings Light Switch Details Radio/Audio System
PWR ACC CIRCUIT BREAKER	(30)	Power Door Locks Rear Defogger
RDO 1	RED (10)	Radio/Audio System
RDO 2	RED (10)	Cruise Control Radio/Audio System
S/LP	YEL (20)	Exterior Lights
TAIL	BLU (15)	Headlights Light Switch Details
TURN B/U	YEL (20)	Back Up Lights Exterior Lights
WDO CIRCUIT BREAKER	(30)	Convertible Top Headlights: Daytime Running Lights (T61) Power Windows
WIPER	WHT (25)	Wiper/Washer: Standard Wiper/Washer: Pulse

Fuse block details 1990–92 All Models.

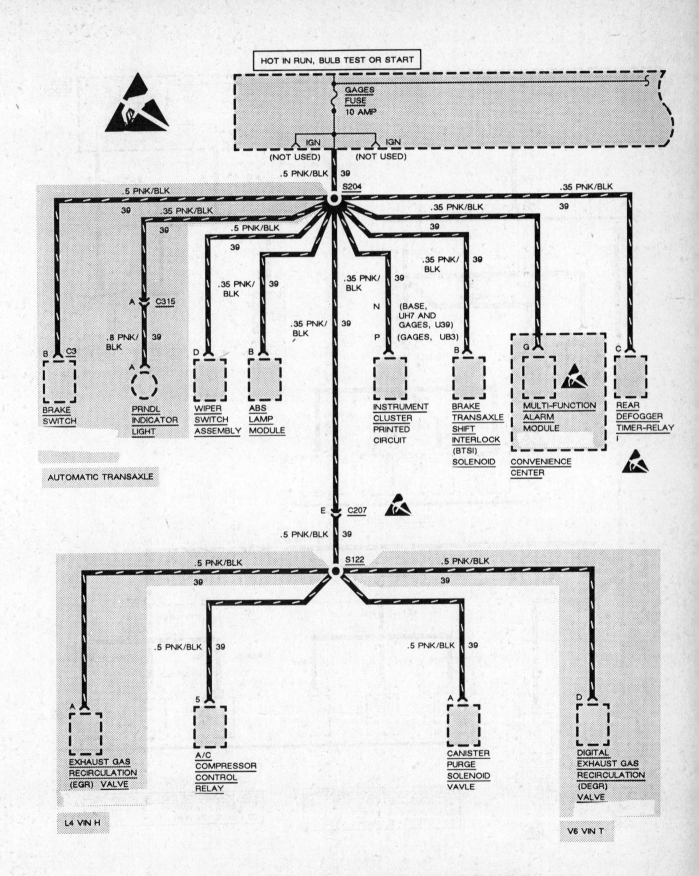

Fuse block details Gauges fuse, ECM fuse and Turn B/U fuse 1990–92 All Models.

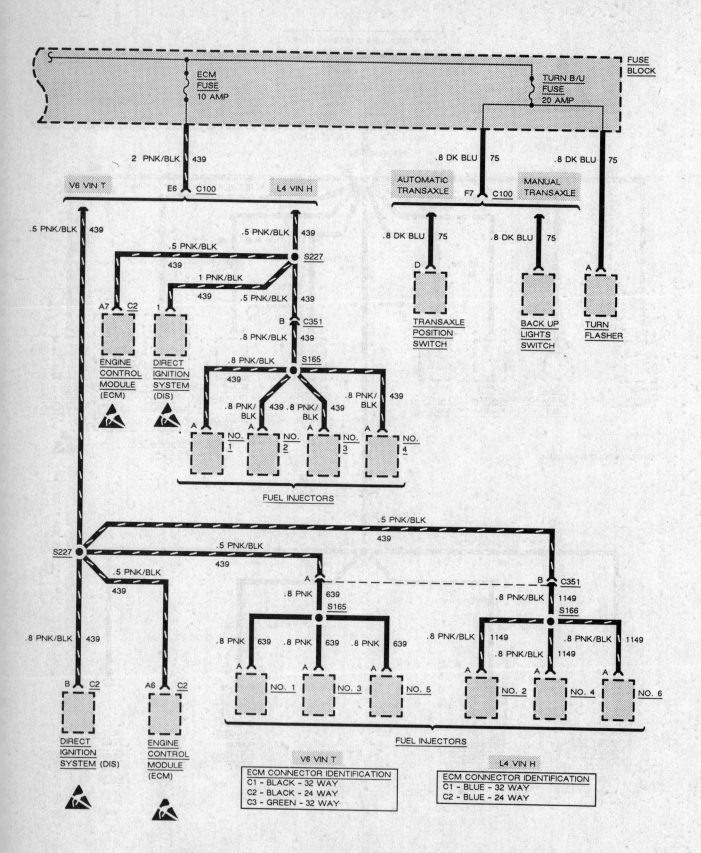

Fuse block details Gauges fuse, ECM fuse and Turn B/U fuse 1990–92 All Models (con't).

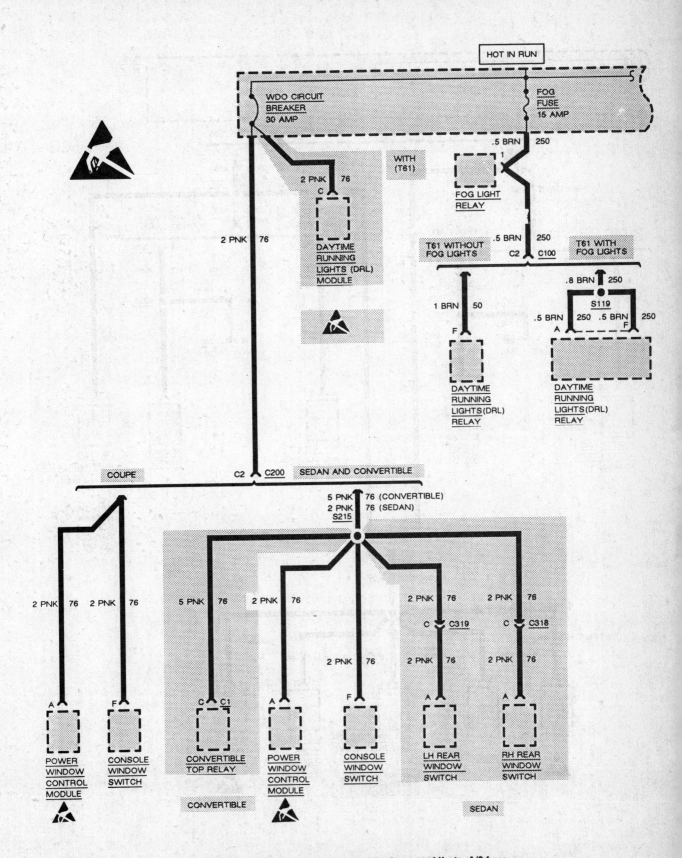

Fuse block details WDO circuit breaker, Fog Lamps and Heater A/C fuses.

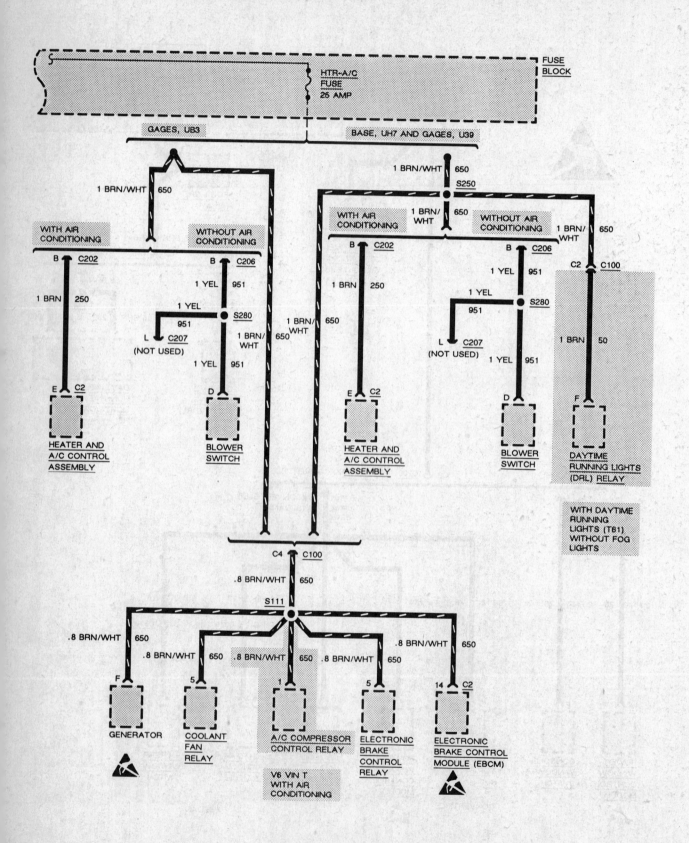

Fuse block details WDO circuit breaker, Fog Lamps and Heater A/C fuses (con't).

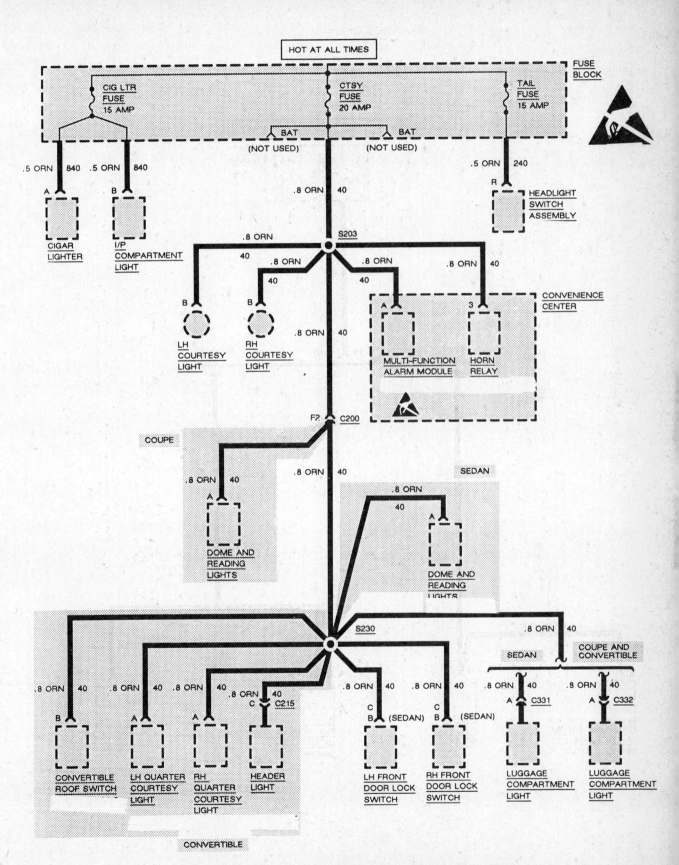

Fuse block details Cig Ltr fuse, Courtesy and Tail light fuse 1990-92 All Models.

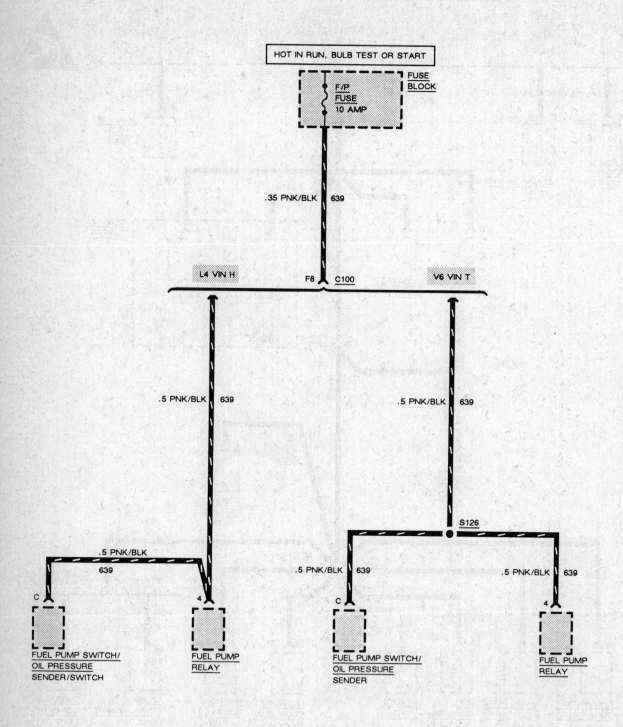

HOT IN RUN, BULB TEST OR START

F/P
FUSE
10 AMP

FUSE
BLOCK

.35 PNK/BLK   639

L4 VIN H   F8   C100   V6 VIN T

.5 PNK/BLK   639   .5 PNK/BLK   639

S126

.5 PNK/BLK
639

.5 PNK/BLK   639   .5 PNK/BLK   639

C   4   C   4

FUEL PUMP SWITCH/
OIL PRESSURE
SENDER/SWITCH

FUEL PUMP
RELAY

FUEL PUMP SWITCH/
OIL PRESSURE
SENDER

FUEL PUMP
RELAY

Fuse block details Fuel pump fuse 1990–92 All Models.

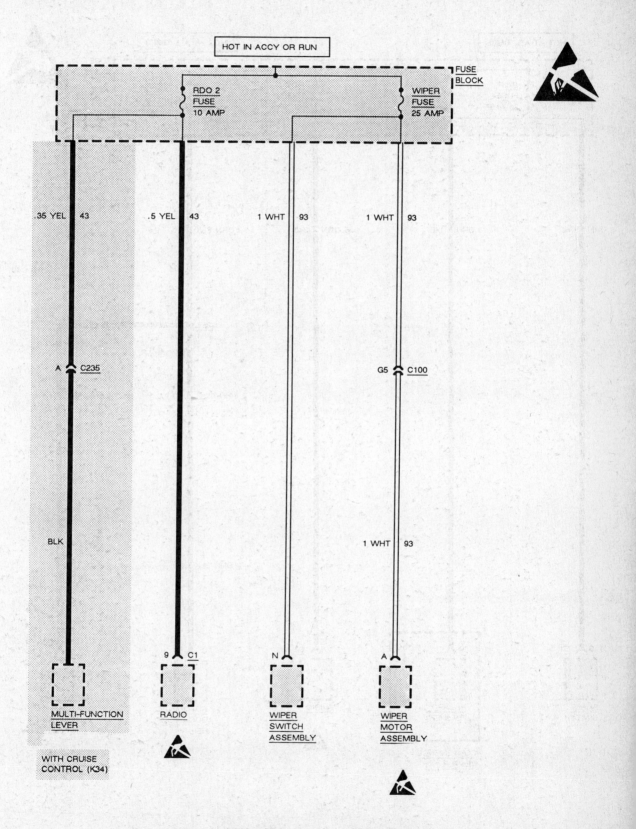

Fuse block details RDO 2 and Wiper fuse 1990–92 All Models.

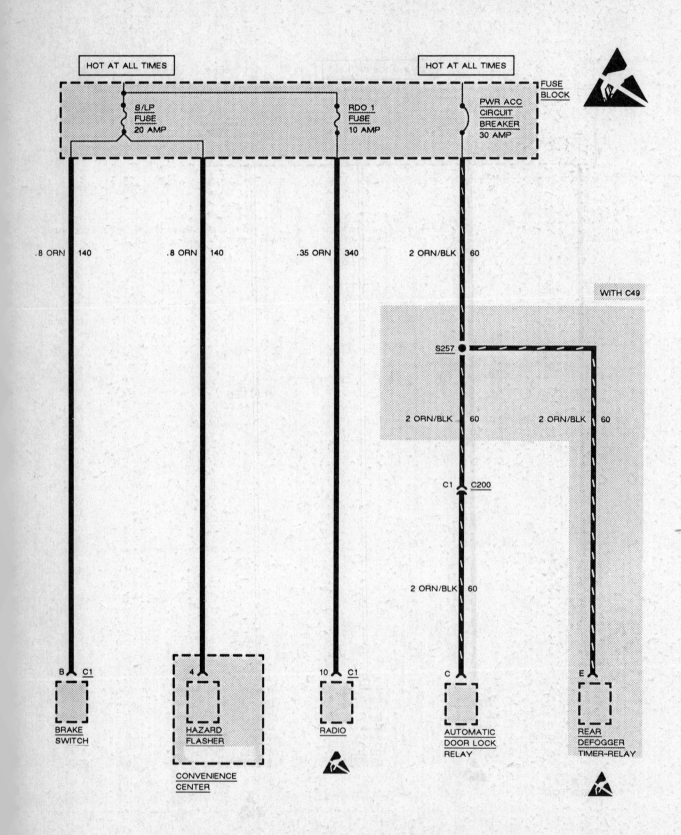

Fuse block details Power ACC circuit breaker, S/LP and RDO 1 fuse 1990–92 All Models.

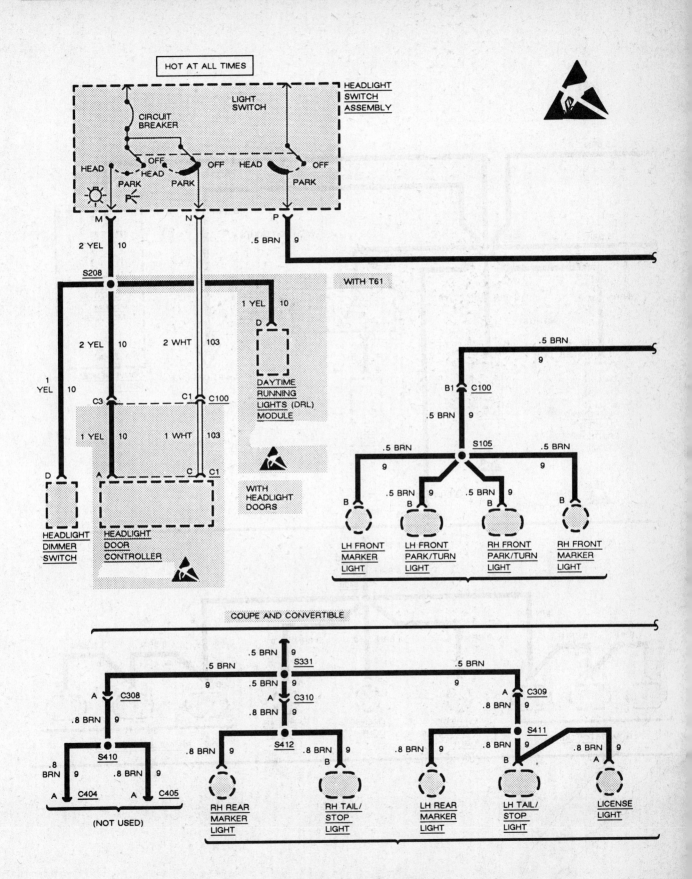

Light switch details 1990–92 All Models.

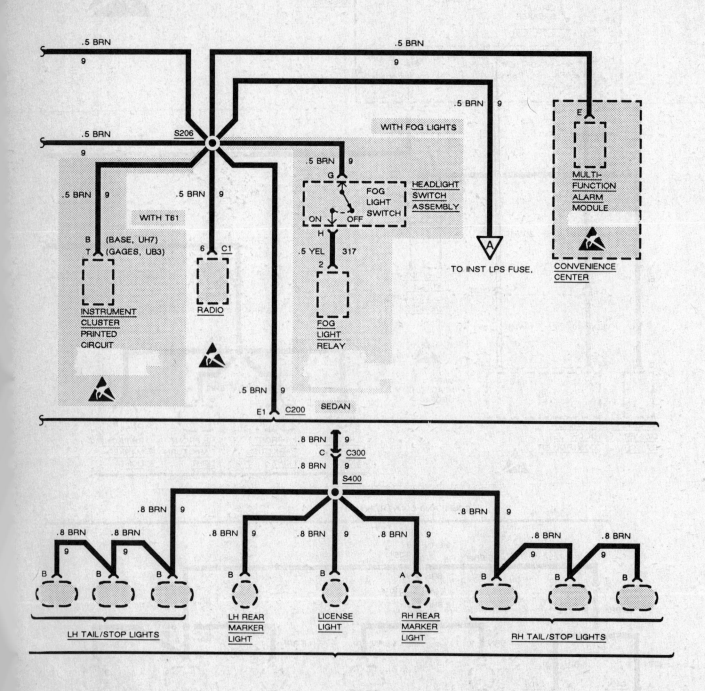

Light switch details 1990–92 All Models (con't).

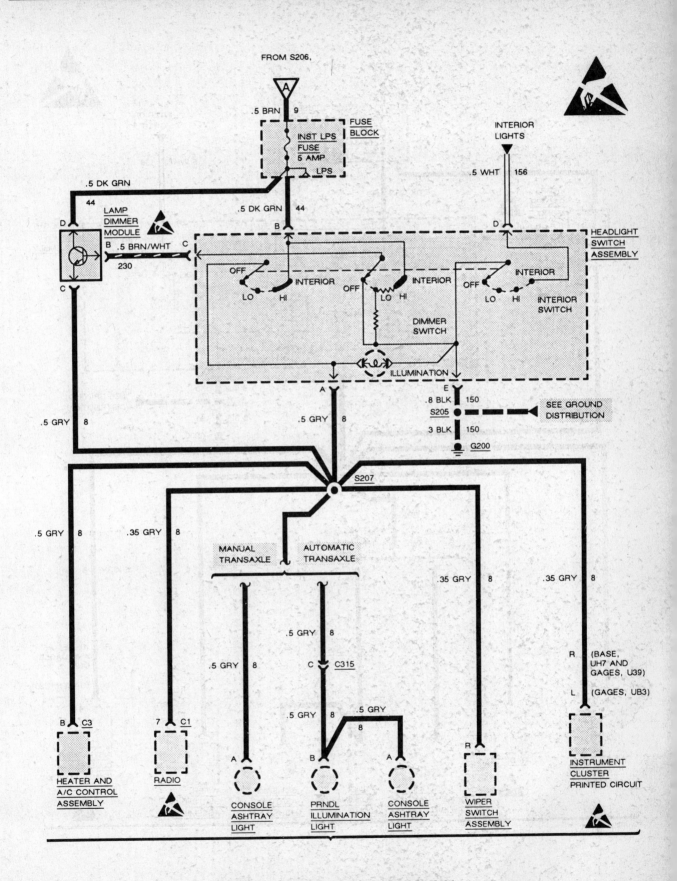

Light switch details with Fog lamps 1990–92 All Models.

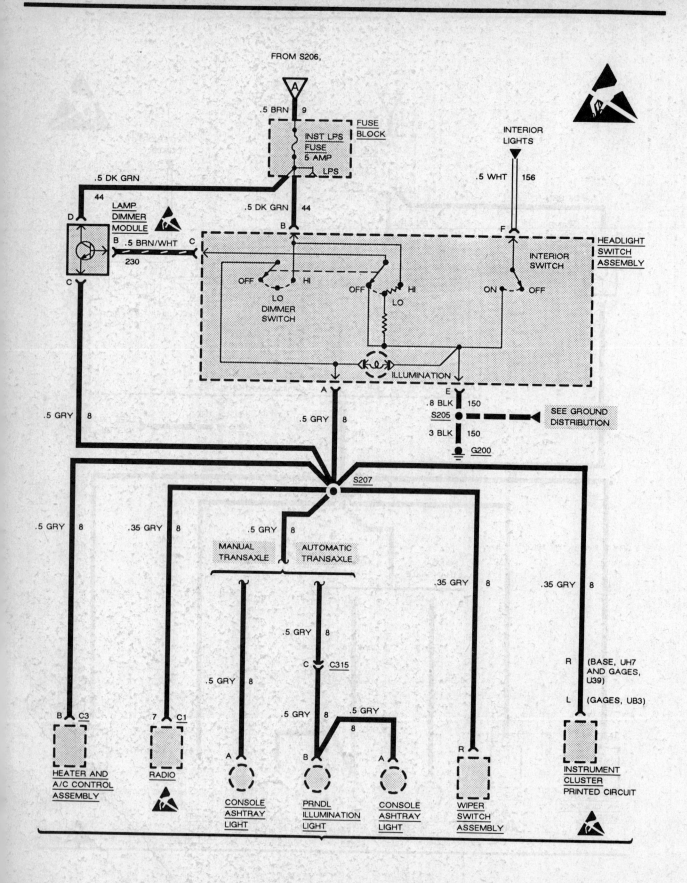

Light switch details without Fog lamps 1990–92 All Models.

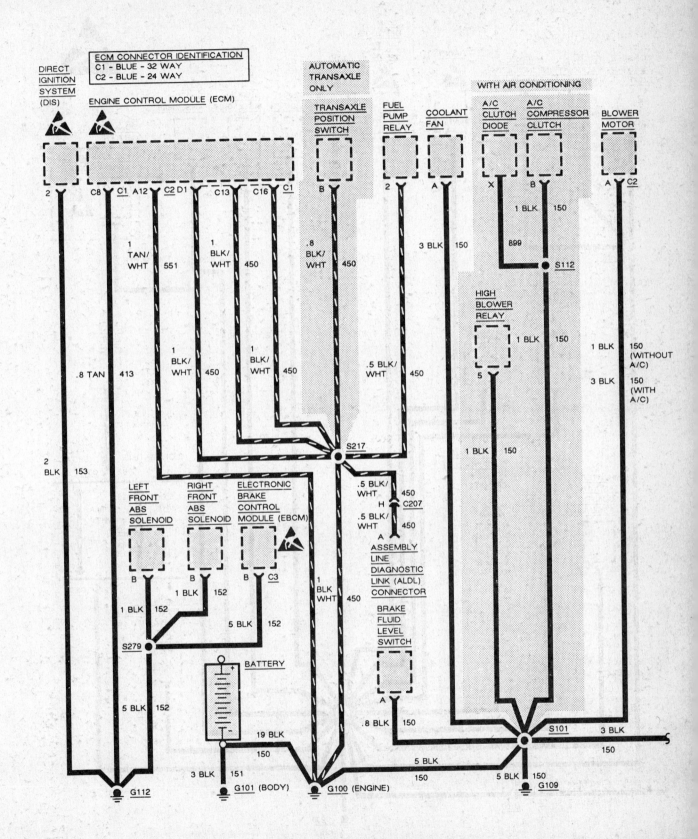

Engine Grounds L4 vin H 1990–92 All Models.

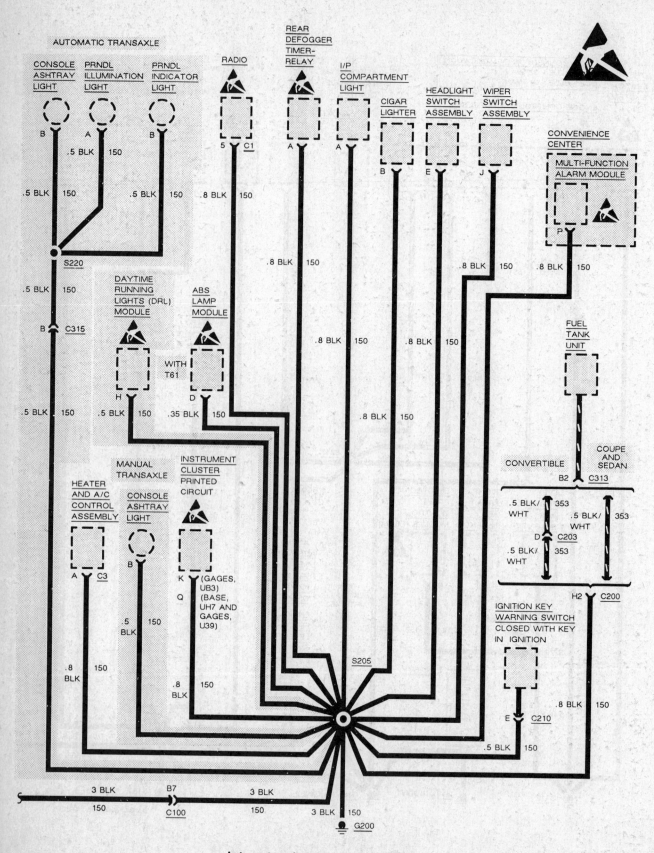

Instrument panel grounds 1990–92 All Models.

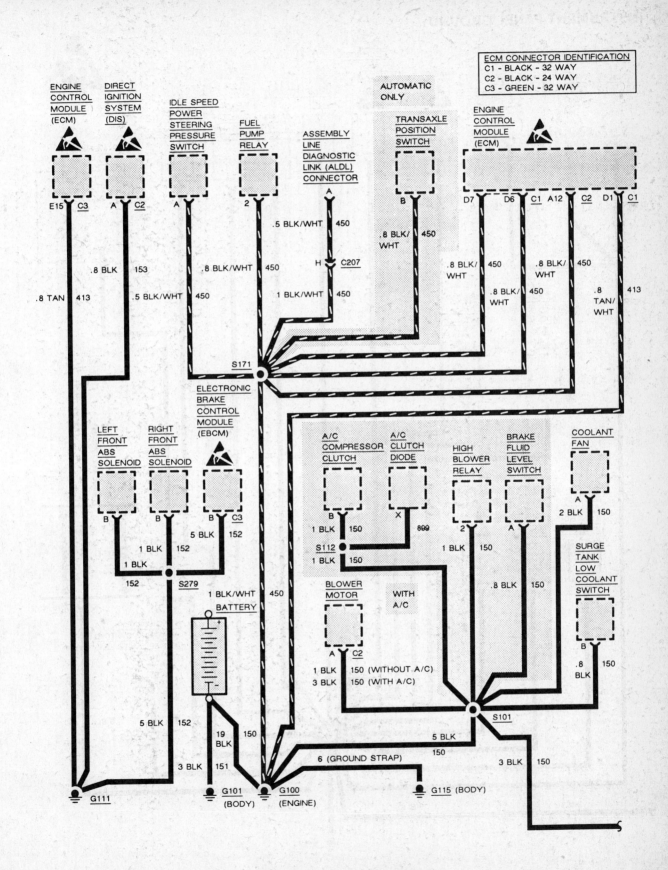

Engine Grounds V6 vin T 1990–92 All Models.

INSTRUMENT PANEL GROUND

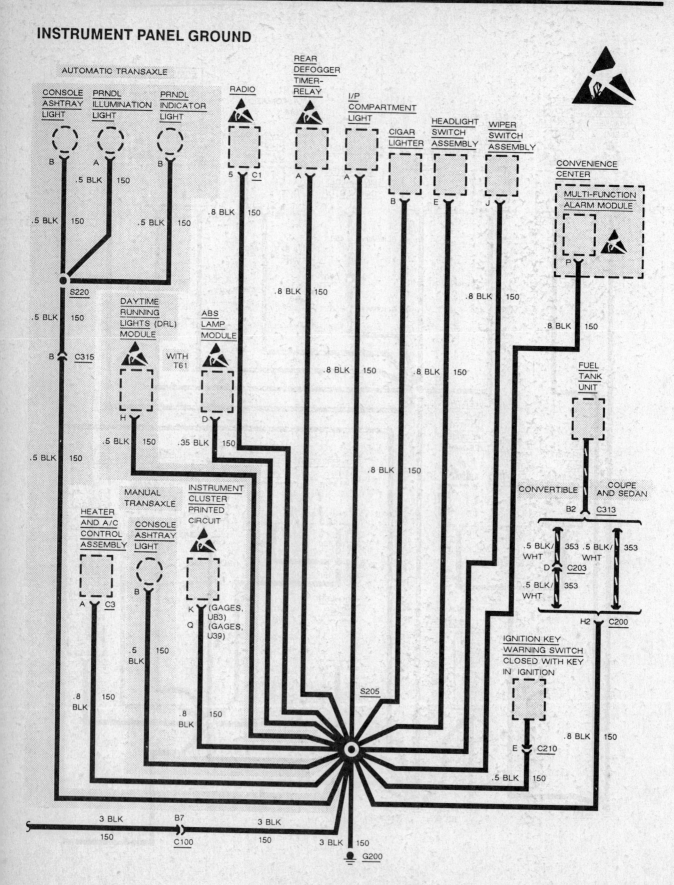

Instrument panel grounds 1990–92 All Models.

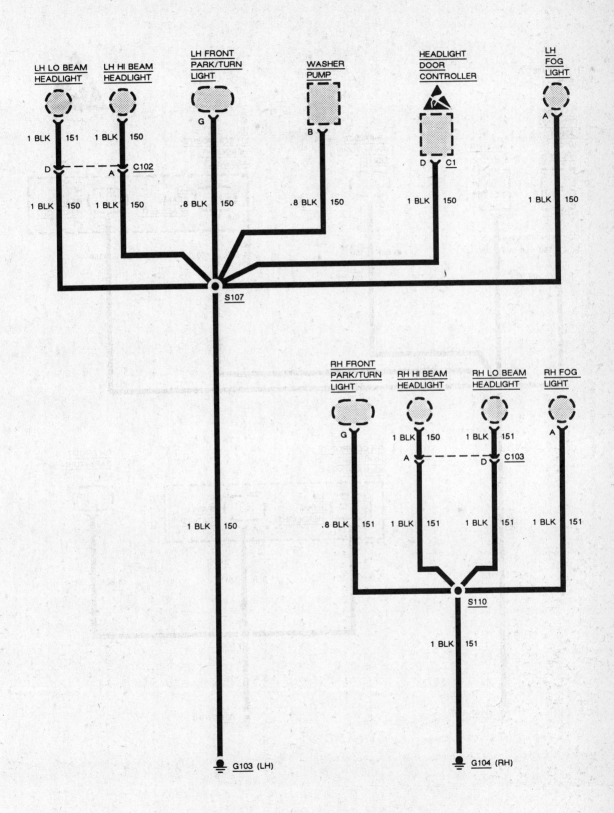

Front Lights grounds with Fog lamps 1990–92 All Models.

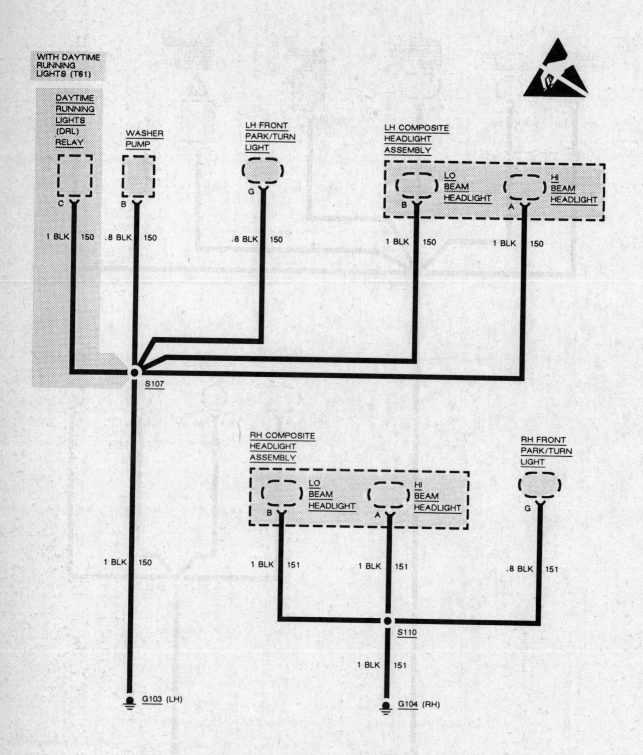

Front Lights grounds without Fog lamps 1990–92 All Models.

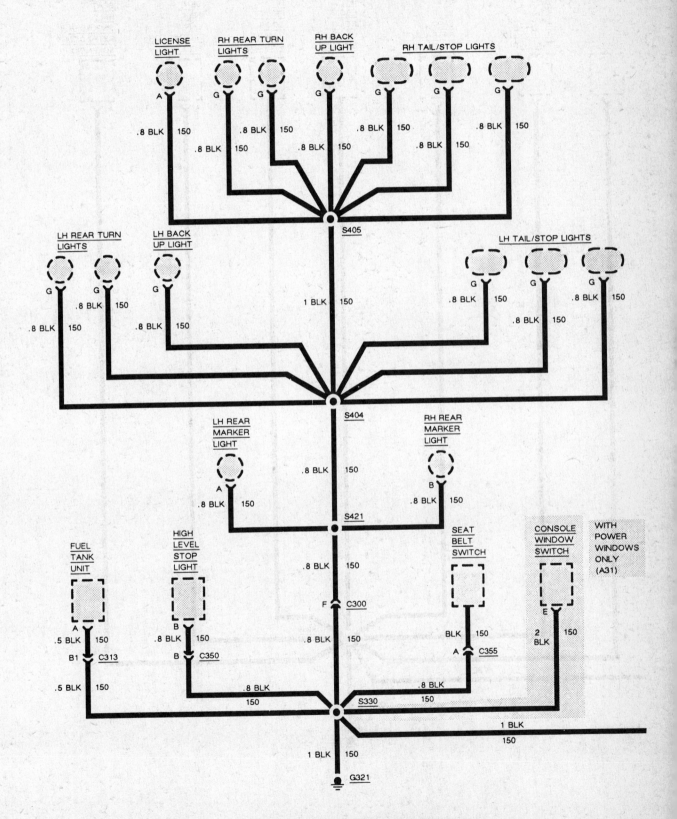

Ground distribution Sedan 1990–92 All Models.

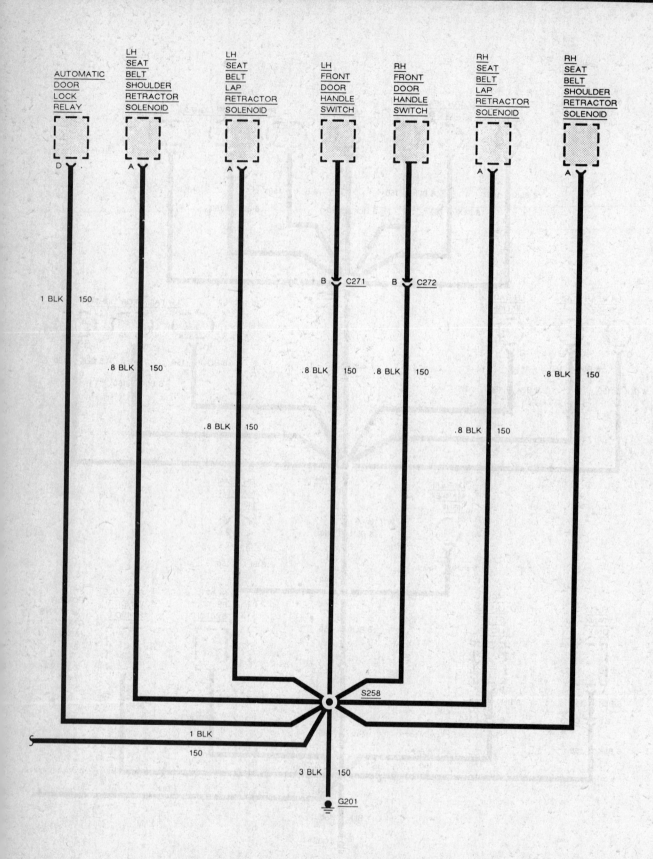

AUTOMATIC
DOOR
LOCK
RELAY

LH
SEAT
BELT
SHOULDER
RETRACTOR
SOLENOID

LH
SEAT
BELT
LAP
RETRACTOR
SOLENOID

LH
FRONT
DOOR
HANDLE
SWITCH

RH
FRONT
DOOR
HANDLE
SWITCH

RH
SEAT
BELT
LAP
RETRACTOR
SOLENOID

RH
SEAT
BELT
SHOULDER
RETRACTOR
SOLENOID

D

A

A

A

A

B   C271

B   C272

1 BLK   150

.8 BLK   150

.8 BLK   150   .8 BLK   150

.8 BLK   150

.8 BLK   150

.8 BLK   150

S258

1 BLK
150

3 BLK   150

G201

Door locks and automatic Seat belts Sedan 1990–92 All Models.

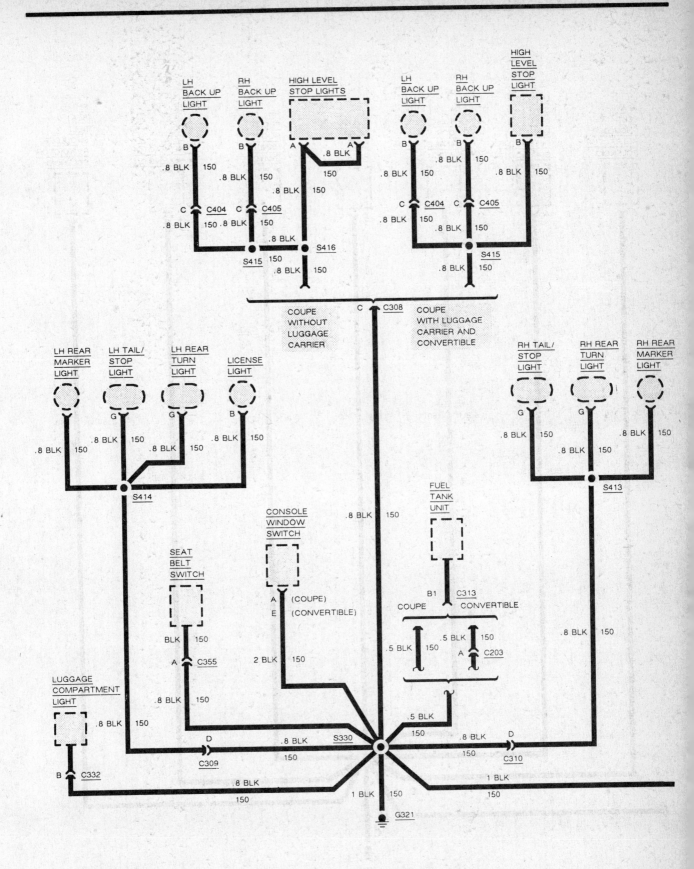

Ground distribution Coupe and Convertible 1990–92 All Models.

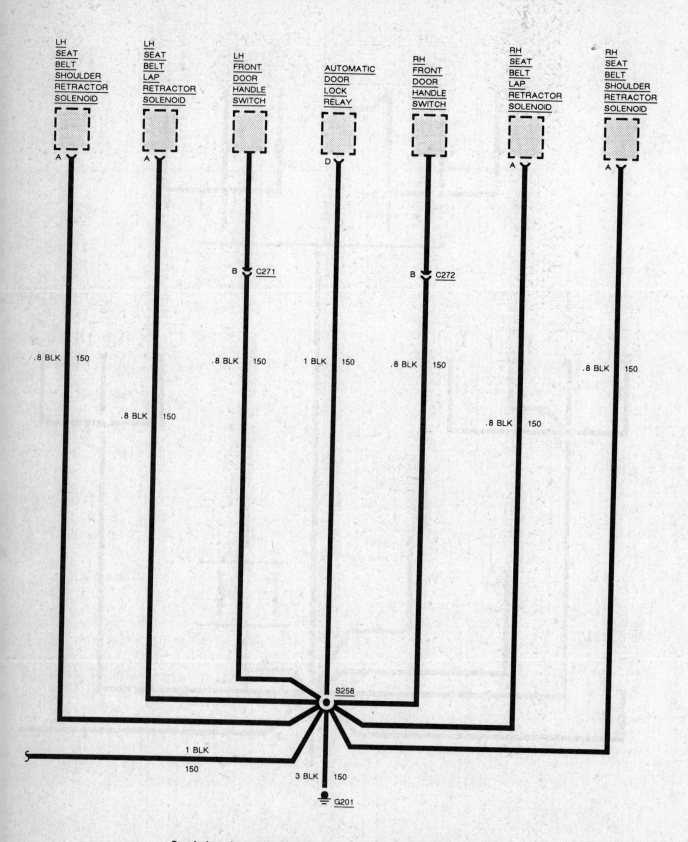

Door locks and automatic Seat belts Coupe and Convertible 1990–92 All Models.

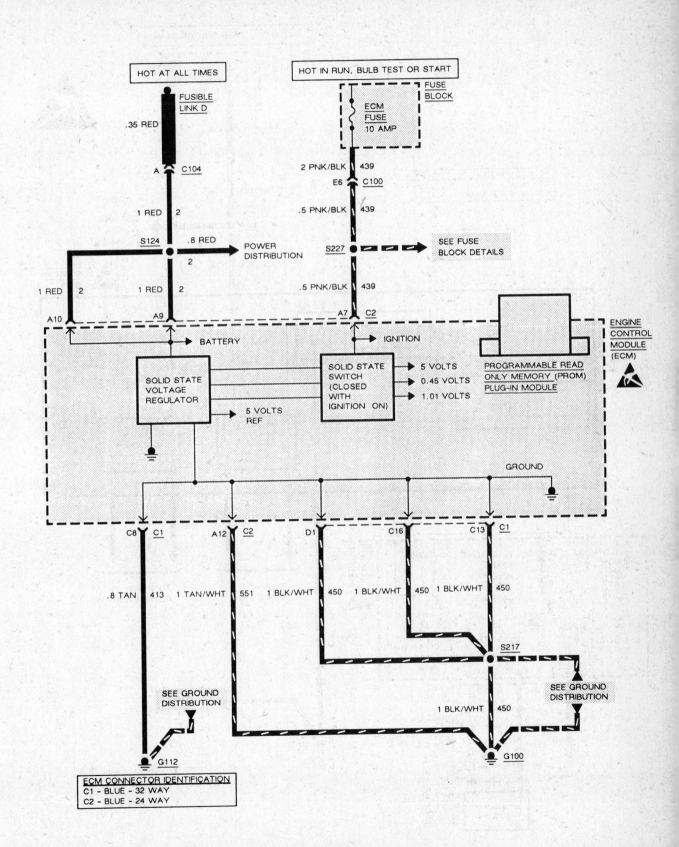

Power and Grounds MPI L4 vin H 1990–92 All Models.

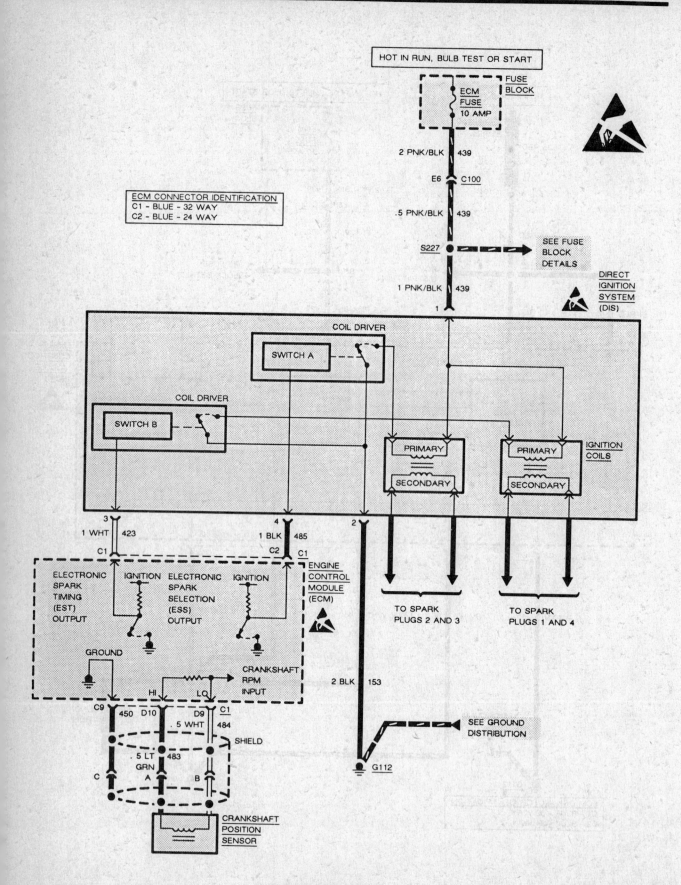

HOT IN RUN, BULB TEST OR START

FUSE BLOCK

ECM FUSE 10 AMP

2 PNK/BLK 439

E6 C100

.5 PNK/BLK 439

S227 — SEE FUSE BLOCK DETAILS

1 PNK/BLK 439

DIRECT IGNITION SYSTEM (DIS)

ECM CONNECTOR IDENTIFICATION
C1 - BLUE - 32 WAY
C2 - BLUE - 24 WAY

COIL DRIVER

SWITCH A

COIL DRIVER

SWITCH B

PRIMARY
SECONDARY

PRIMARY
SECONDARY

IGNITION COILS

3
1 WHT 423
C1

4
1 BLK 485
C2   C1

2

TO SPARK PLUGS 2 AND 3

TO SPARK PLUGS 1 AND 4

ELECTRONIC SPARK TIMING (EST) OUTPUT

IGNITION

ELECTRONIC SPARK SELECTION (ESS) OUTPUT

IGNITION

ENGINE CONTROL MODULE (ECM)

GROUND

CRANKSHAFT RPM INPUT

HI   LO

2 BLK 153

C9   450   D10   D9   C1
.5 WHT 484

SHIELD

.5 LT GRN 483

C   A   B

SEE GROUND DISTRIBUTION

G112

CRANKSHAFT POSITION SENSOR

Ignition L4 vin H 1990–92 All Models.

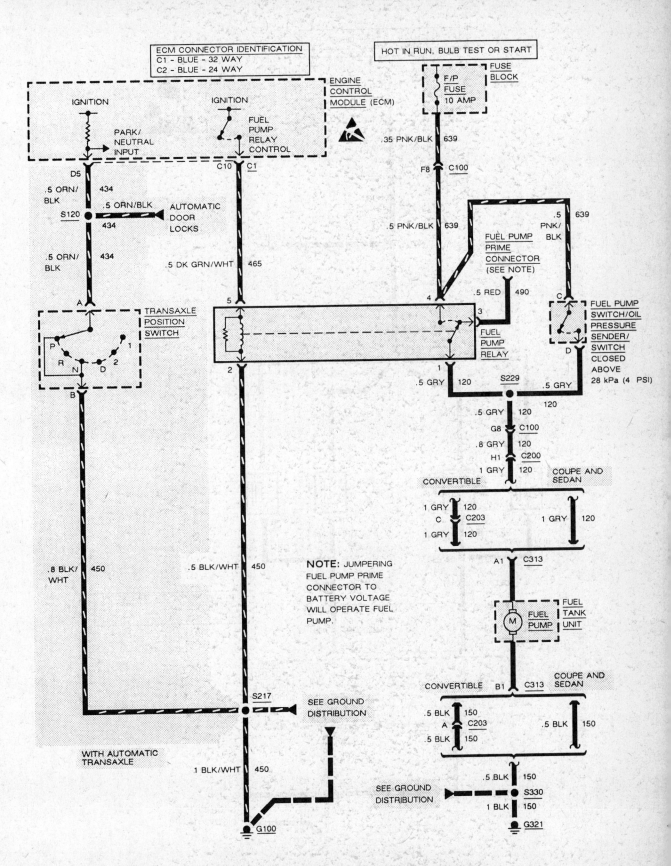

Fuel control and engine data sensors L4 vin H 1990-92 All Models.

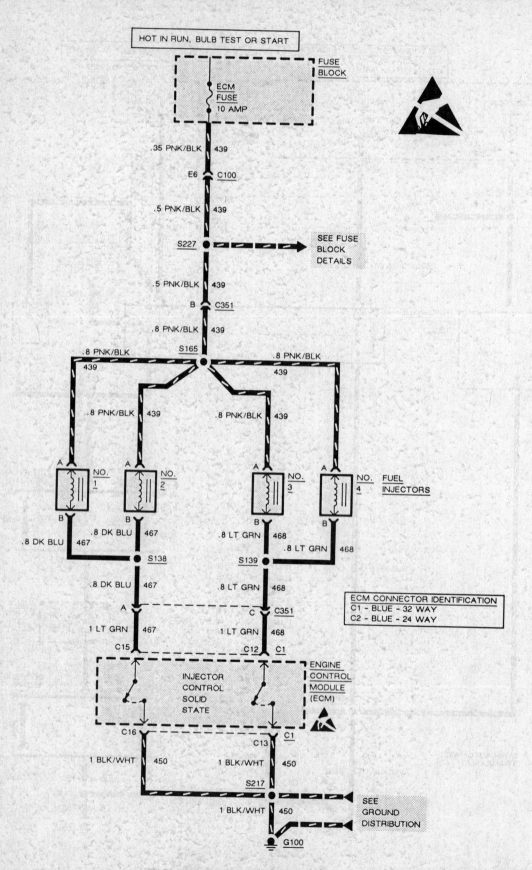

Fuel Injectors L4 vin H 1990–92 All Models.

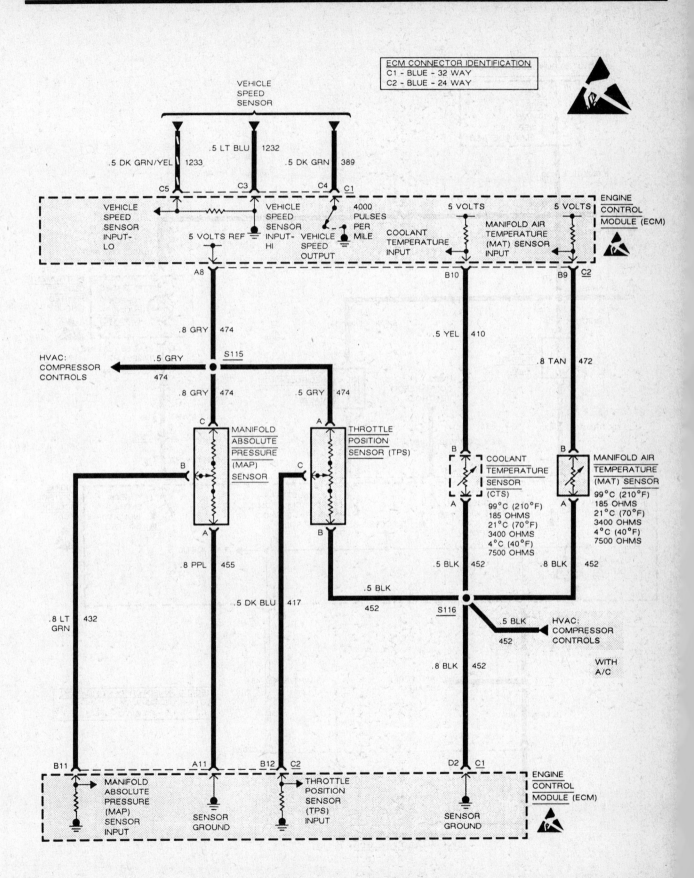

Engine Data Sensors 1990–92 All Models.

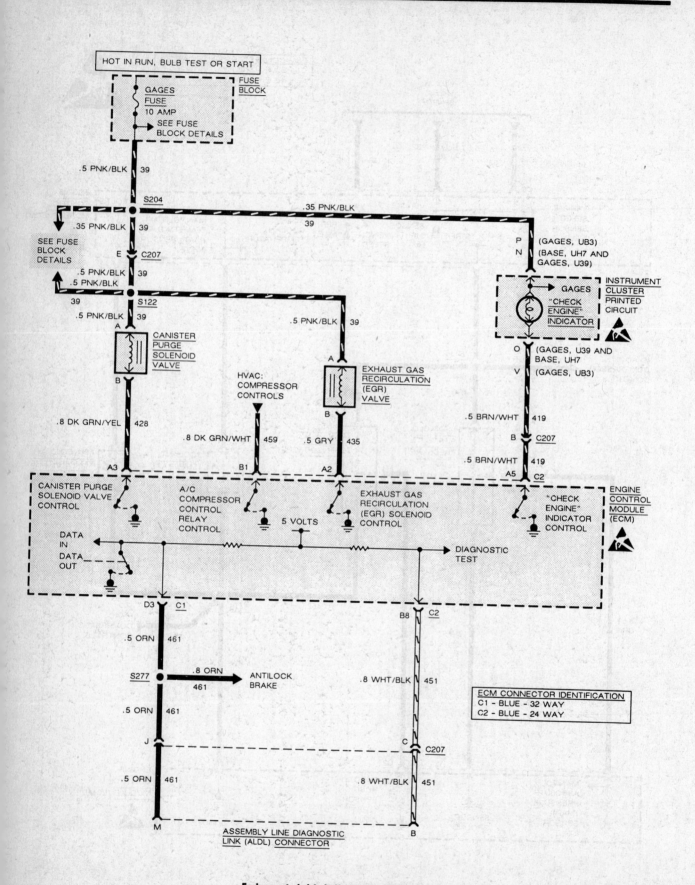

HOT IN RUN, BULB TEST OR START

FUSE BLOCK

GAGES FUSE 10 AMP

SEE FUSE BLOCK DETAILS

.5 PNK/BLK 39

S204

.35 PNK/BLK 39

SEE FUSE BLOCK DETAILS

E C207

.5 PNK/BLK 39

.5 PNK/BLK

39 S122

.5 PNK/BLK 39

A CANISTER PURGE SOLENOID VALVE

B

.8 DK GRN/YEL 428

HVAC: COMPRESSOR CONTROLS

.8 DK GRN/WHT 459

.35 PNK/BLK

.5 PNK/BLK 39

A EXHAUST GAS RECIRCULATION (EGR) VALVE

B

.5 GRY 435

P (GAGES, UB3)
N (BASE, UH7 AND GAGES, U39)

INSTRUMENT CLUSTER PRINTED CIRCUIT

GAGES "CHECK ENGINE" INDICATOR

O (GAGES, U39 AND BASE, UH7)
V (GAGES, UB3)

.5 BRN/WHT 419

B C207

.5 BRN/WHT 419

A3 B1 A2 A5 C2

CANISTER PURGE SOLENOID VALVE CONTROL

A/C COMPRESSOR CONTROL RELAY CONTROL

5 VOLTS

EXHAUST GAS RECIRCULATION (EGR) SOLENOID CONTROL

"CHECK ENGINE" INDICATOR CONTROL

ENGINE CONTROL MODULE (ECM)

DATA IN

DATA OUT

DIAGNOSTIC TEST

D3 C1

.5 ORN 461

S277 .8 ORN ANTILOCK BRAKE
461

.5 ORN 461

J

.5 ORN 461

M

B8 C2

.8 WHT/BLK 451

C C207

.8 WHT/BLK 451

B

ECM CONNECTOR IDENTIFICATION
C1 - BLUE - 32 WAY
C2 - BLUE - 24 WAY

ASSEMBLY LINE DIAGNOSTIC LINK (ALDL) CONNECTOR

Engine controls L4 vin H 1990–92 All Models.

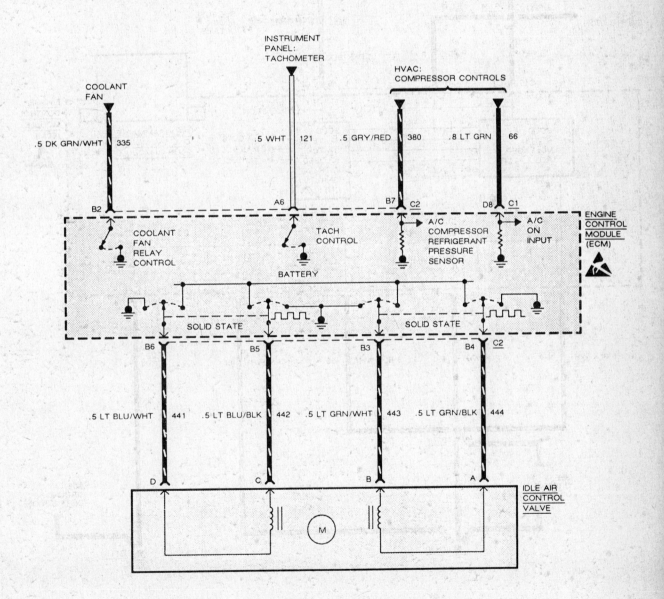

Engine controls L4 vin H 1990–92 All Models (con't).

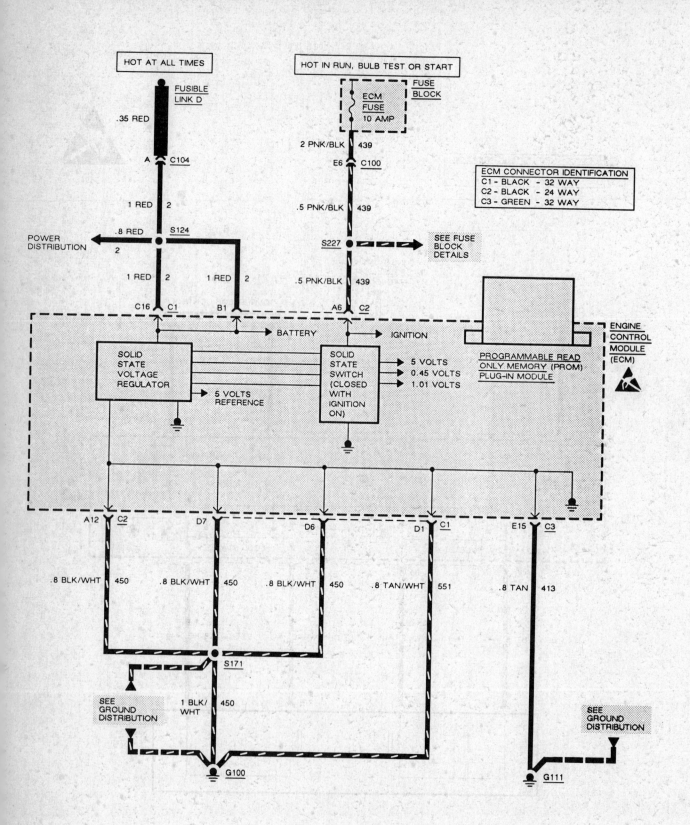

Power and Grounds MPI V6 vin T 1990-92 All Models.

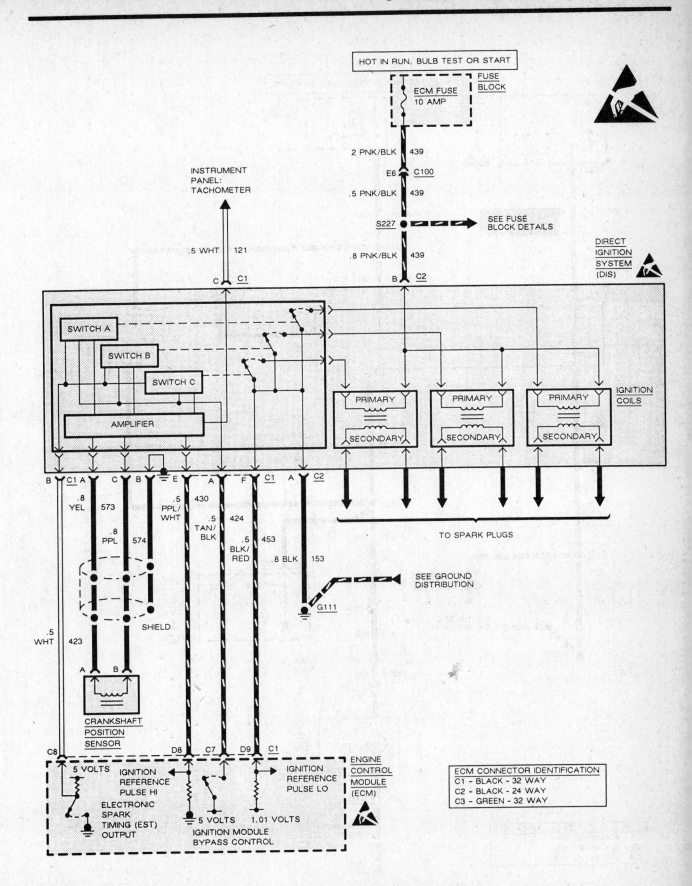

HOT IN RUN, BULB TEST OR START

FUSE BLOCK

ECM FUSE
10 AMP

2 PNK/BLK   439

E6   C100

.5 PNK/BLK   439

S227   SEE FUSE BLOCK DETAILS

.8 PNK/BLK   439

B   C2

DIRECT IGNITION SYSTEM (DIS)

INSTRUMENT PANEL: TACHOMETER

.5 WHT   121

C   C1

SWITCH A

SWITCH B

SWITCH C

AMPLIFIER

PRIMARY   SECONDARY

PRIMARY   SECONDARY

PRIMARY   SECONDARY

IGNITION COILS

B   C1 A   C   B   E   A   F   C1   A   C2

.8 YEL   573

.8 PPL   574

.5 PPL/WHT   430

.5 TAN/BLK   424

.5 BLK/RED   453

.8 BLK   153

G111

SEE GROUND DISTRIBUTION

TO SPARK PLUGS

SHIELD

.5 WHT   423

A   B

CRANKSHAFT POSITION SENSOR

C8   D8   C7   D9   C1

ENGINE CONTROL MODULE (ECM)

5 VOLTS

IGNITION REFERENCE PULSE HI

ELECTRONIC SPARK TIMING (EST) OUTPUT

5 VOLTS   1.01 VOLTS

IGNITION MODULE BYPASS CONTROL

IGNITION REFERENCE PULSE LO

ECM CONNECTOR IDENTIFICATION
C1 - BLACK - 32 WAY
C2 - BLACK - 24 WAY
C3 - GREEN - 32 WAY

Ignition V6 vin T 1990–92 All Models.

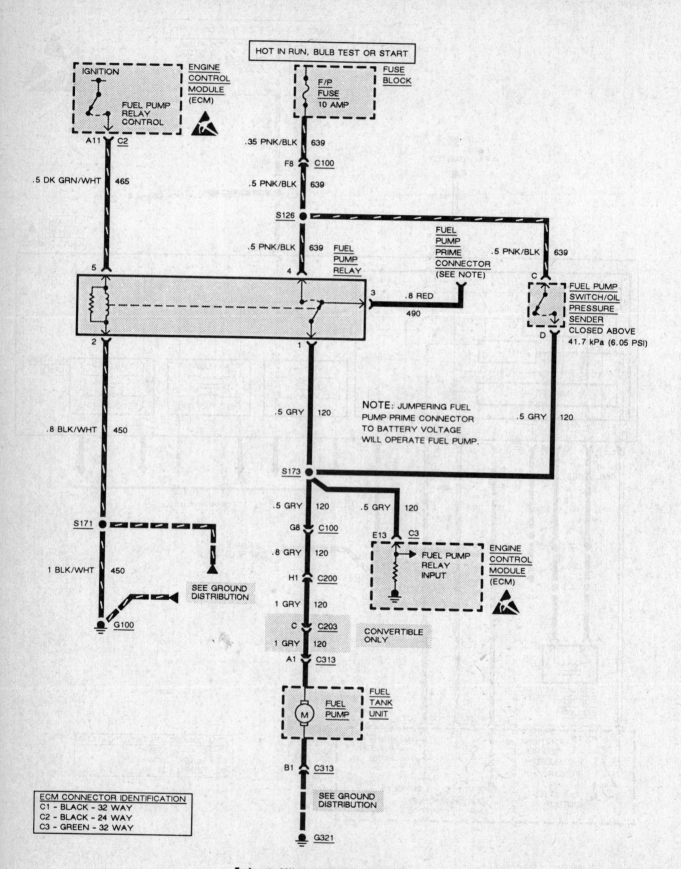

Fuel control V6 vin T 1990–92 All Models.

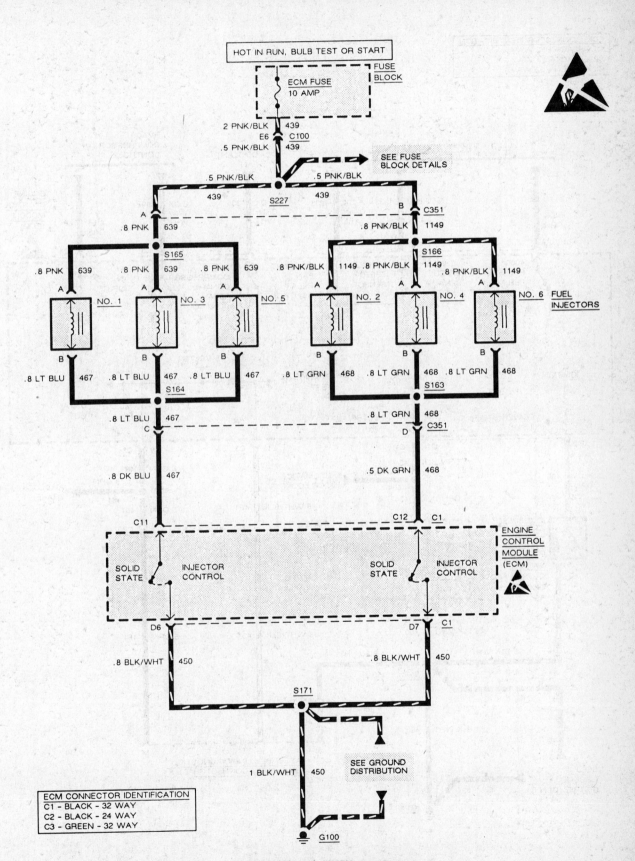

Fuel Injectors V6 vin T 1990–92 All Models.

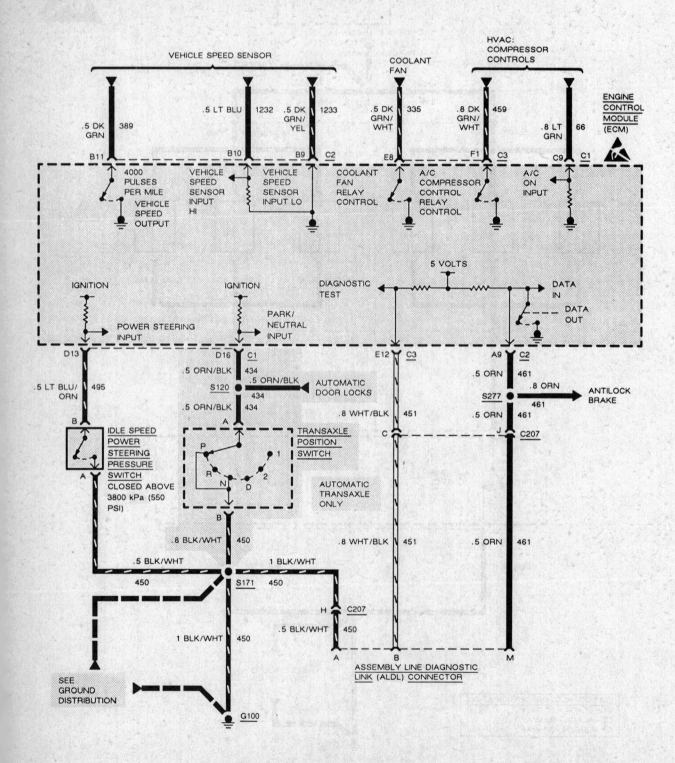

Power and Grounds MPI V6 vin T 1990–92 All Models.

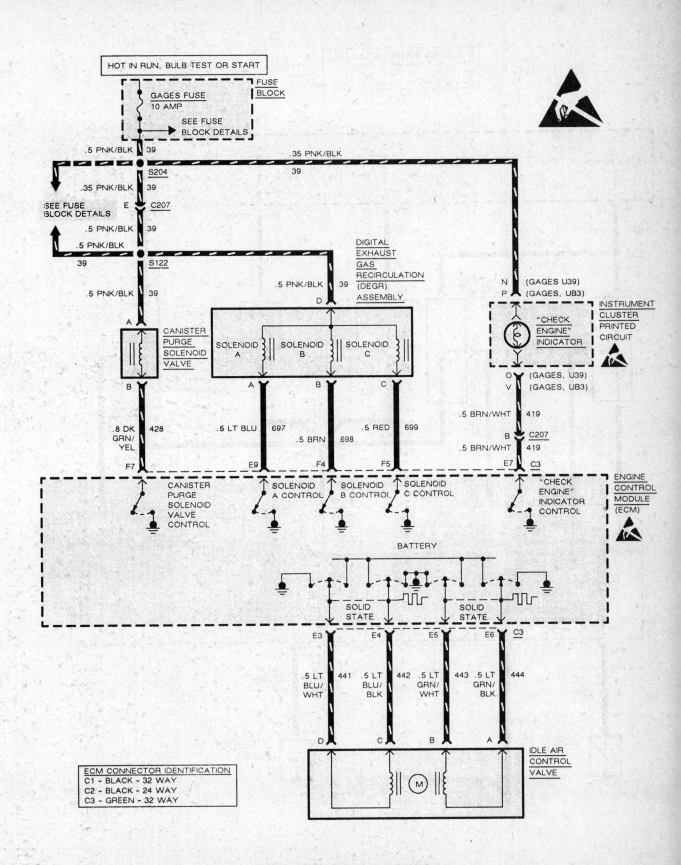

Engine controls V6 vin T 1990–92 All Models.

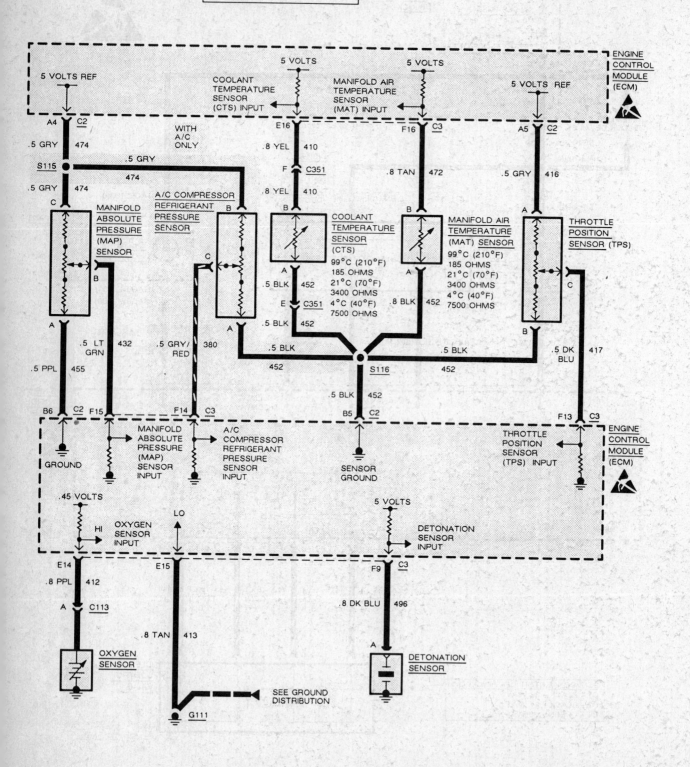

ECM CONNECTOR IDENTIFICATION
C1 – BLACK – 32 WAY
C2 – BLACK – 24 WAY
C3 – GREEN – 32 WAY

Engine Data Sensors V6 vin T 1990–92 All Models.

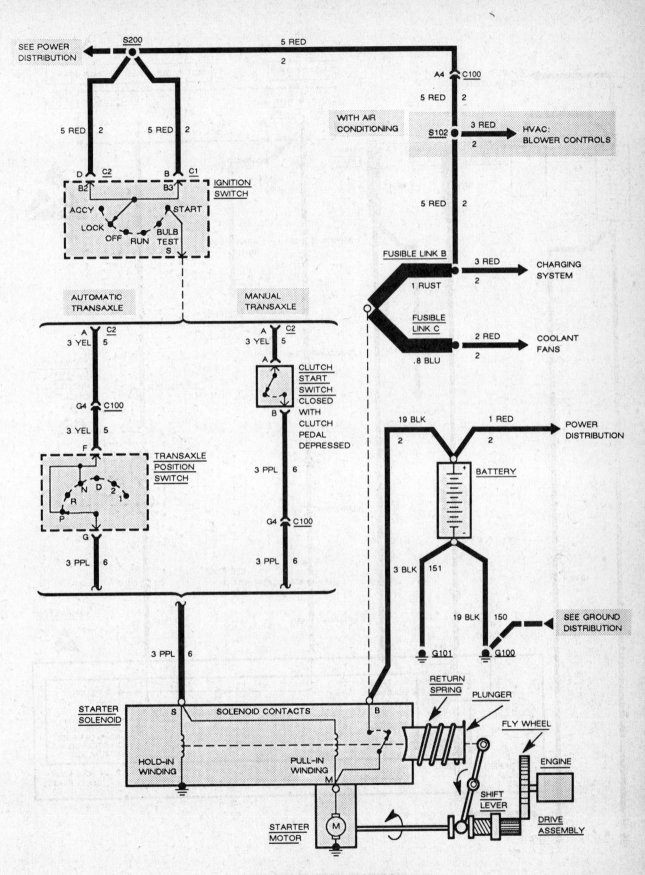

Starter system 1990–92 All Models.

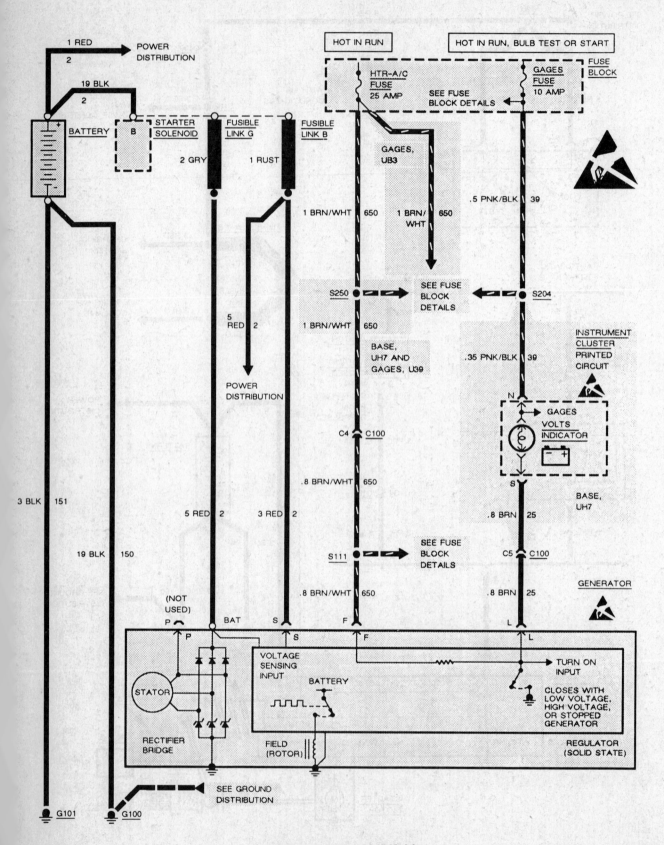

Charging system 1990–92 All Models.

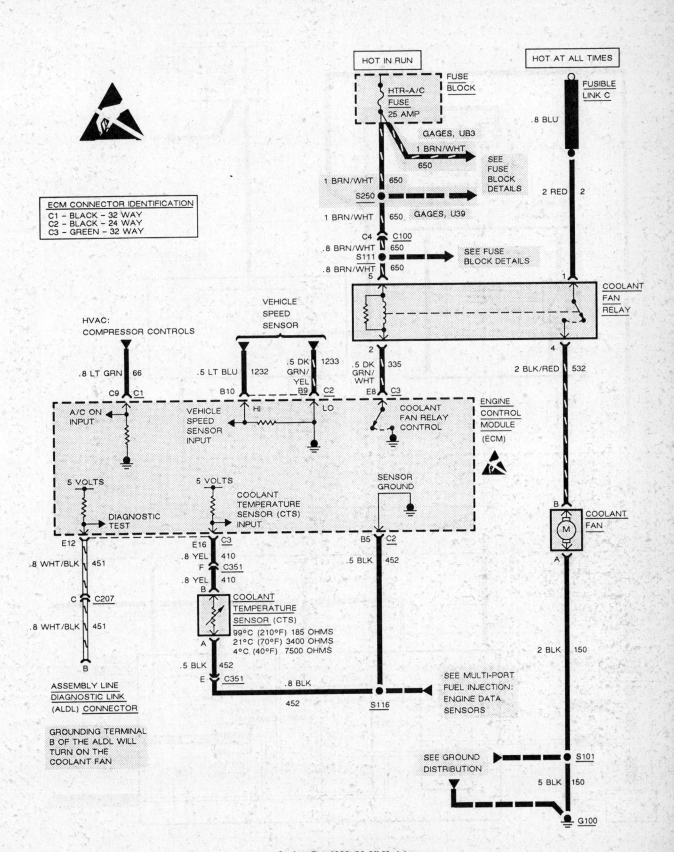

ECM CONNECTOR IDENTIFICATION
C1 – BLACK – 32 WAY
C2 – BLACK – 24 WAY
C3 – GREEN – 32 WAY

HOT IN RUN

HOT AT ALL TIMES

FUSE BLOCK

HTR-A/C FUSE 25 AMP

FUSIBLE LINK C

.8 BLU

GAGES, UB3

1 BRN/WHT 650

SEE FUSE BLOCK DETAILS

1 BRN/WHT 650

2 RED 2

S250

1 BRN/WHT 650 GAGES, U39

C4 C100

.8 BRN/WHT 650 SEE FUSE BLOCK DETAILS

S111

.8 BRN/WHT 650

5

1

COOLANT FAN RELAY

HVAC: COMPRESSOR CONTROLS

VEHICLE SPEED SENSOR

2

4

.8 LT GRN 66

.5 LT BLU 1232

.5 DK GRN/ YEL 1233

.5 DK GRN/ WHT 335

2 BLK/RED 532

C9 C1

B10 B9 C2

E8 C3

A/C ON INPUT

HI

LO

COOLANT FAN RELAY CONTROL

VEHICLE SPEED SENSOR INPUT

ENGINE CONTROL MODULE (ECM)

5 VOLTS

5 VOLTS

SENSOR GROUND

DIAGNOSTIC TEST

COOLANT TEMPERATURE SENSOR (CTS) INPUT

B

COOLANT FAN

E12

E16 C3

B5 C2

A

.8 WHT/BLK 451

.8 YEL 410

.5 BLK 452

F C351

.8 YEL 410

2 BLK 150

C C207

B

COOLANT TEMPERATURE SENSOR (CTS)

99°C (210°F) 185 OHMS
21°C (70°F) 3400 OHMS
4°C (40°F) 7500 OHMS

.8 WHT/BLK 451

B

A

.5 BLK 452

E C351

.8 BLK

SEE MULTI-PORT FUEL INJECTION: ENGINE DATA SENSORS

452

ASSEMBLY LINE DIAGNOSTIC LINK (ALDL) CONNECTOR

S116

SEE GROUND DISTRIBUTION

S101

GROUNDING TERMINAL B OF THE ALDL WILL TURN ON THE COOLANT FAN

5 BLK 150

G100

Coolant Fan 1990–92 All Models.

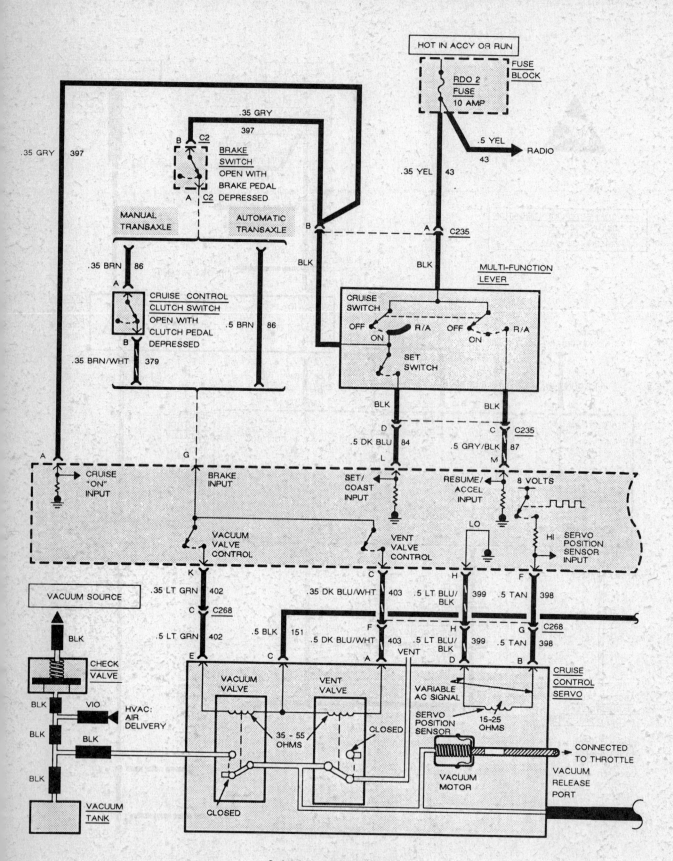

Cruise Control 1990–92 All Models.

V6 VIN T

ECM CONNECTOR IDENTIFICATION
C1 - BLACK - 32 WAY
C2 - BLACK- 24 WAY
C3 - GREEN - 32 WAY

L4 VIN H

ECM CONNECTOR IDENTIFICATION
C1 - BLUE - 32 WAY
C2 - BLUE- 24 WAY

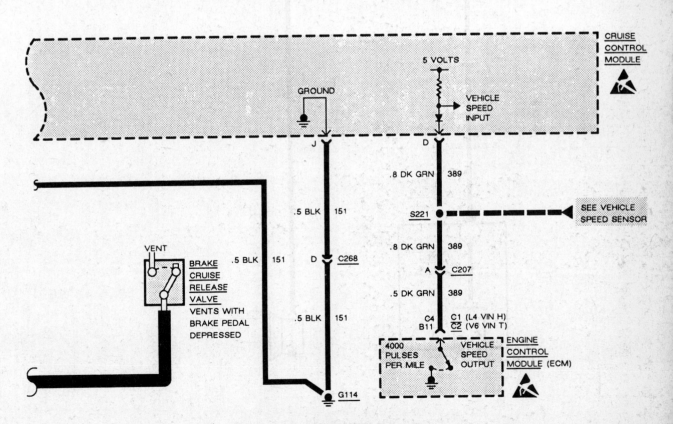

Cruise Control 1990–92 All Models (con't).

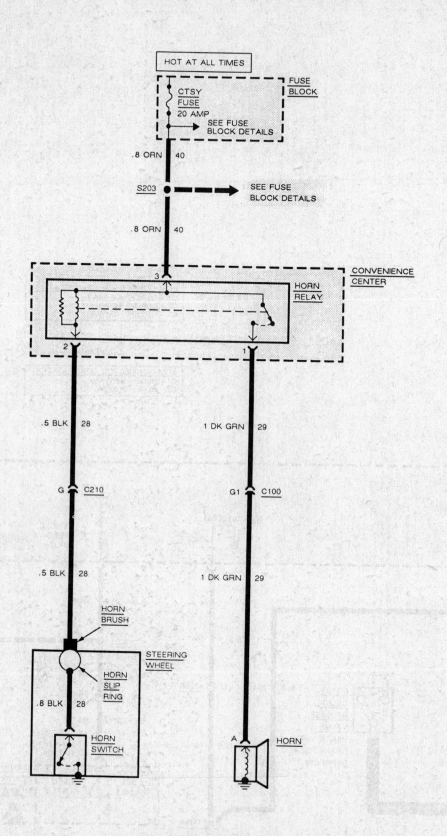

HOT AT ALL TIMES

FUSE BLOCK

CTSY FUSE 20 AMP

SEE FUSE BLOCK DETAILS

.8 ORN 40

S203

SEE FUSE BLOCK DETAILS

.8 ORN 40

CONVENIENCE CENTER

3

HORN RELAY

2 1

.5 BLK 28

1 DK GRN 29

G C210

G1 C100

.5 BLK 28

1 DK GRN 29

HORN BRUSH

STEERING WHEEL

HORN SLIP RING

.8 BLK 28

HORN SWITCH

A HORN

Horn 1990–92 All Models.

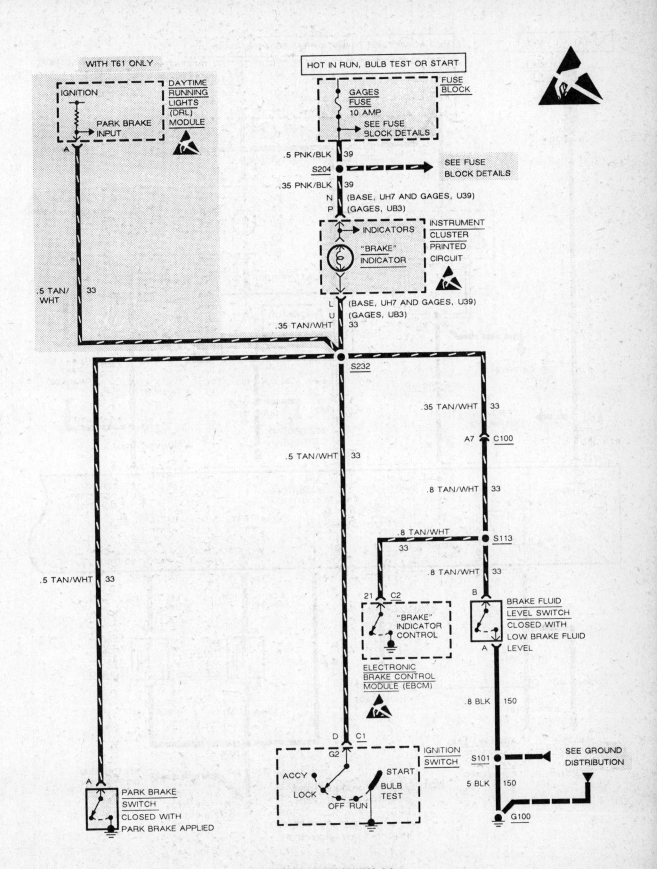

Brake Warning 1990–92 All Models.

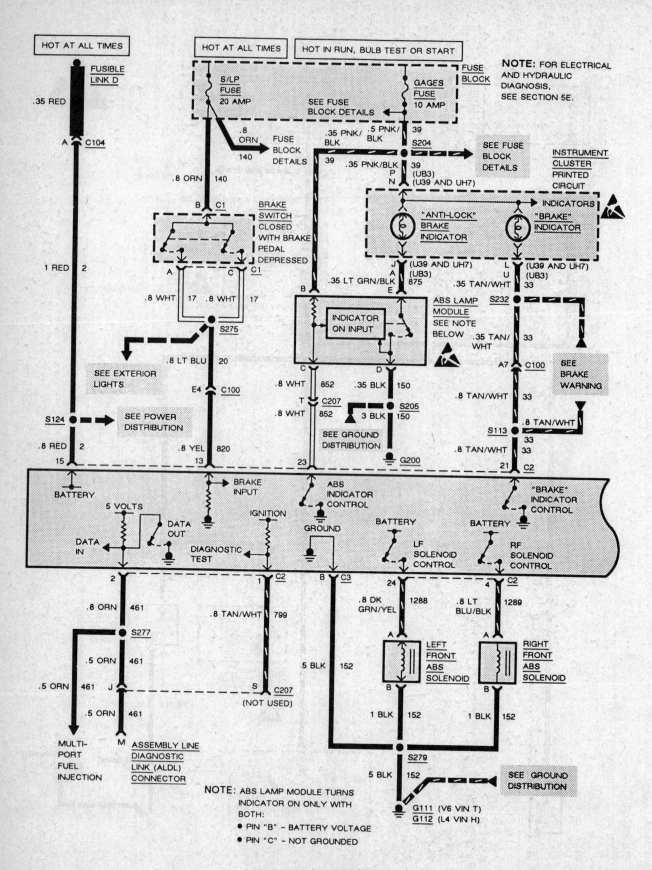

Antilock Brake 1990–92 All Models.

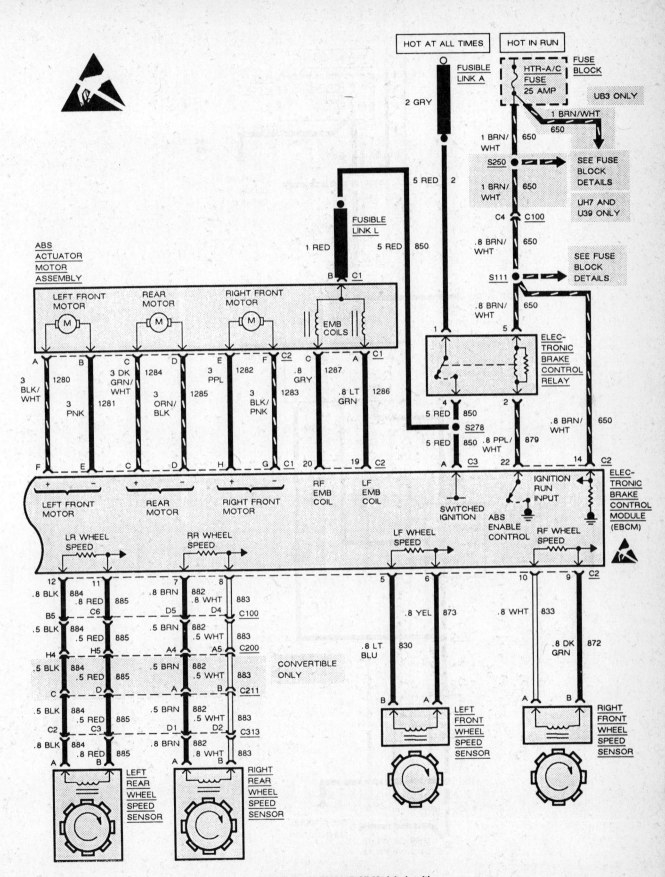

Antilock Brake 1990-92 All Models (con't).

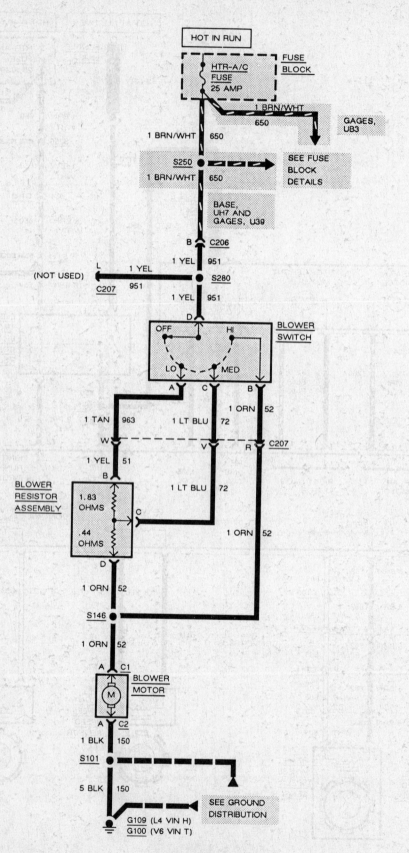

Heater 1990–92 All Models.

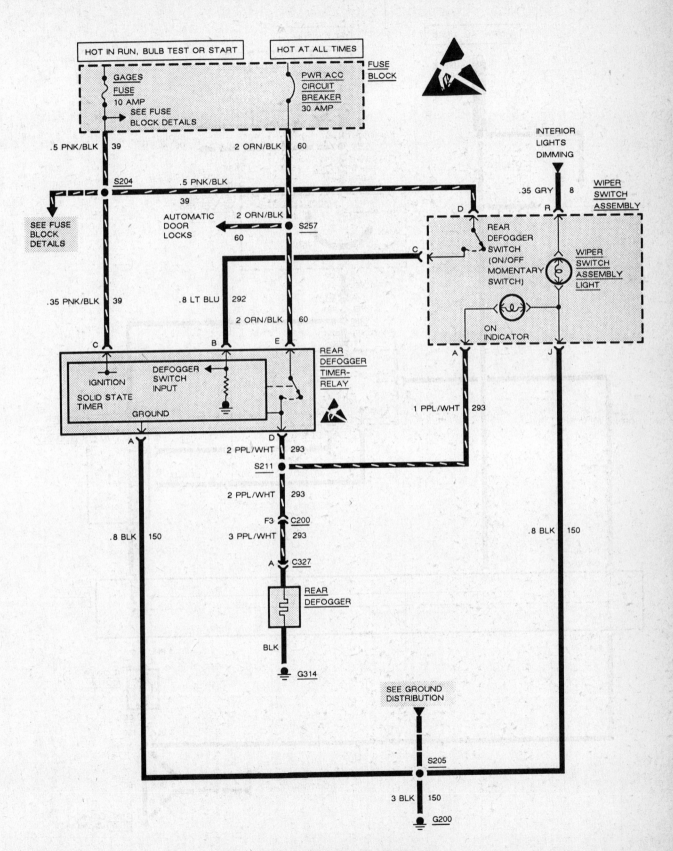

HOT IN RUN, BULB TEST OR START

HOT AT ALL TIMES

FUSE BLOCK

GAGES
FUSE
10 AMP
SEE FUSE
BLOCK DETAILS

PWR ACC
CIRCUIT
BREAKER
30 AMP

INTERIOR
LIGHTS
DIMMING

WIPER
SWITCH
ASSEMBLY

.5 PNK/BLK   39

2 ORN/BLK   60

.35 GRY   8

S204   .5 PNK/BLK
39

SEE FUSE
BLOCK
DETAILS

AUTOMATIC
DOOR
LOCKS

2 ORN/BLK
60   S257

D

C

REAR
DEFOGGER
SWITCH
(ON/OFF
MOMENTARY
SWITCH)

R

WIPER
SWITCH
ASSEMBLY
LIGHT

.35 PNK/BLK   39

.8 LT BLU   292

2 ORN/BLK   60

ON
INDICATOR

C

B

E

REAR
DEFOGGER
TIMER-
RELAY

A

J

IGNITION

DEFOGGER
SWITCH
INPUT

SOLID STATE
TIMER

GROUND

1 PPL/WHT   293

A

D

.8 BLK   150

2 PPL/WHT   293

S211

2 PPL/WHT   293

.8 BLK   150

F3   C200

3 PPL/WHT   293

A   C327

REAR
DEFOGGER

BLK

G314

SEE GROUND
DISTRIBUTION

S205

3 BLK   150

G200

Rear Defogger 1990–92 All Models.

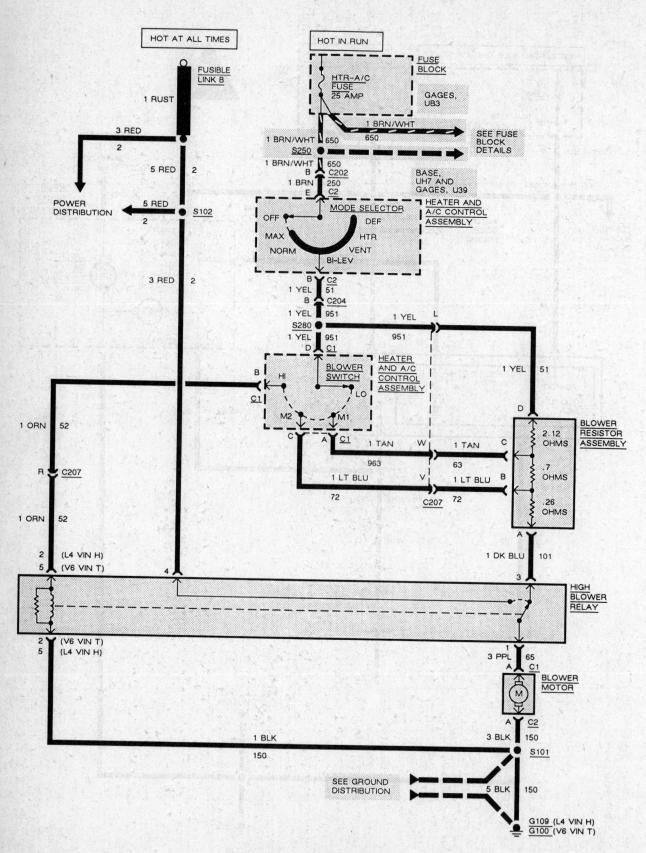

HVAC Blower Controls 1990–92 All Models.

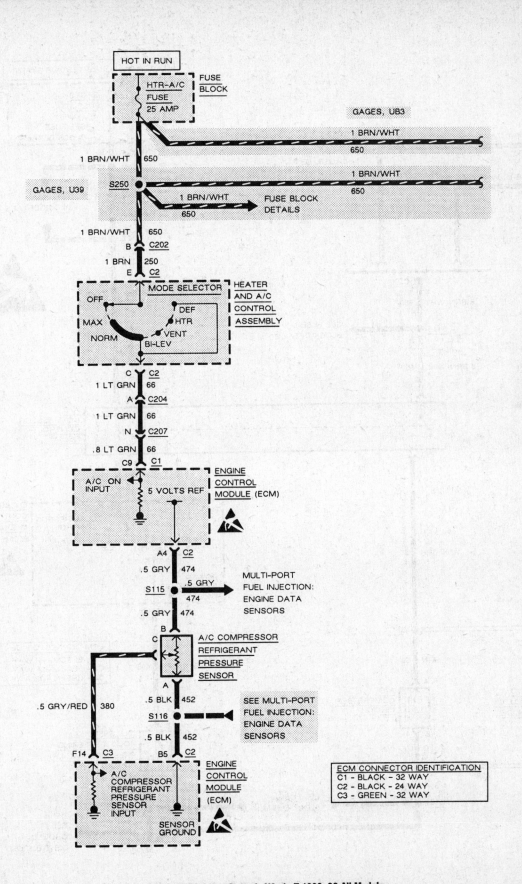

HVAC Compressor Controls V6 vin T 1990–92 All Models.

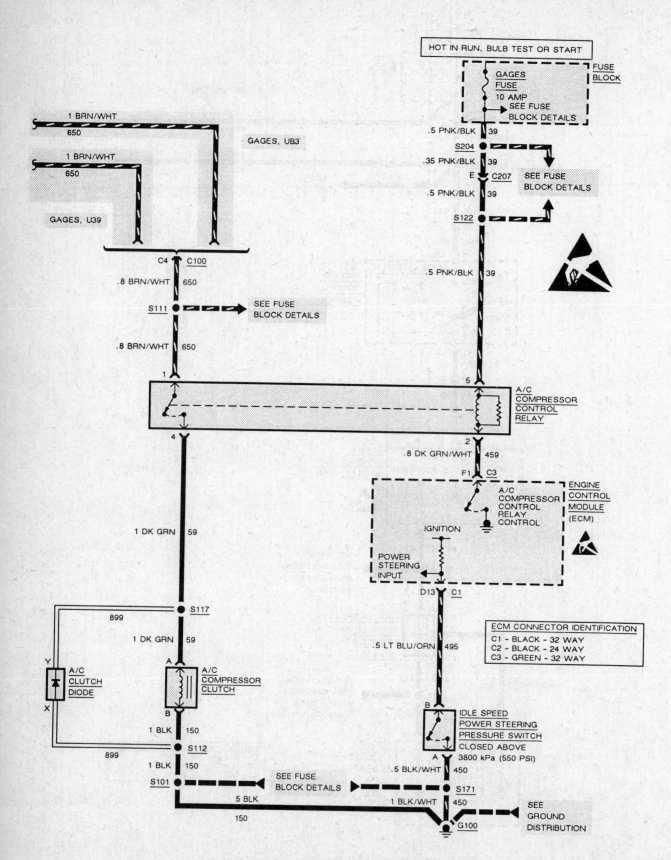

HVAC Compressor Controls V6 vin T 1990–92 All Models (con't).

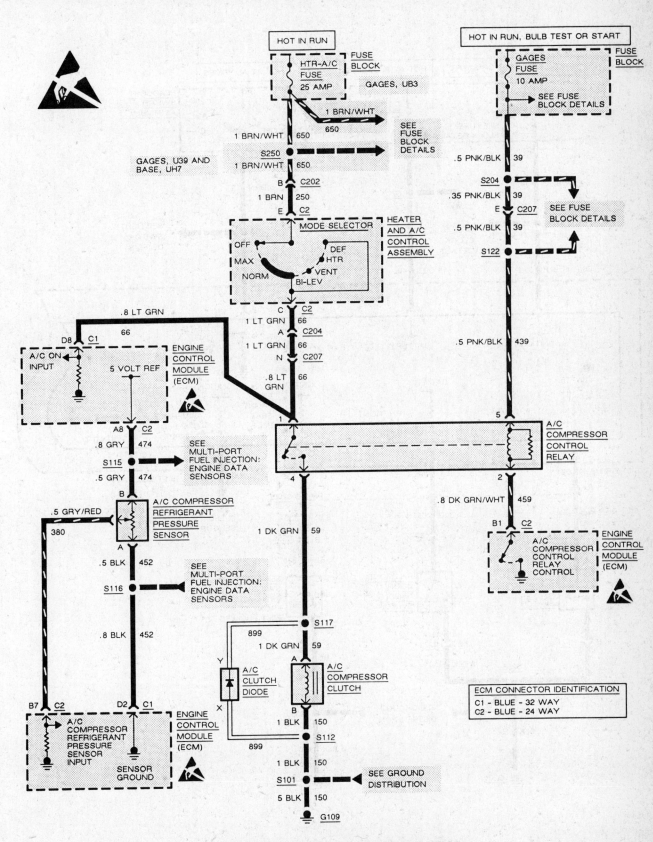

HVAC Compressor Controls L4 vin H 1990-92 All Models.

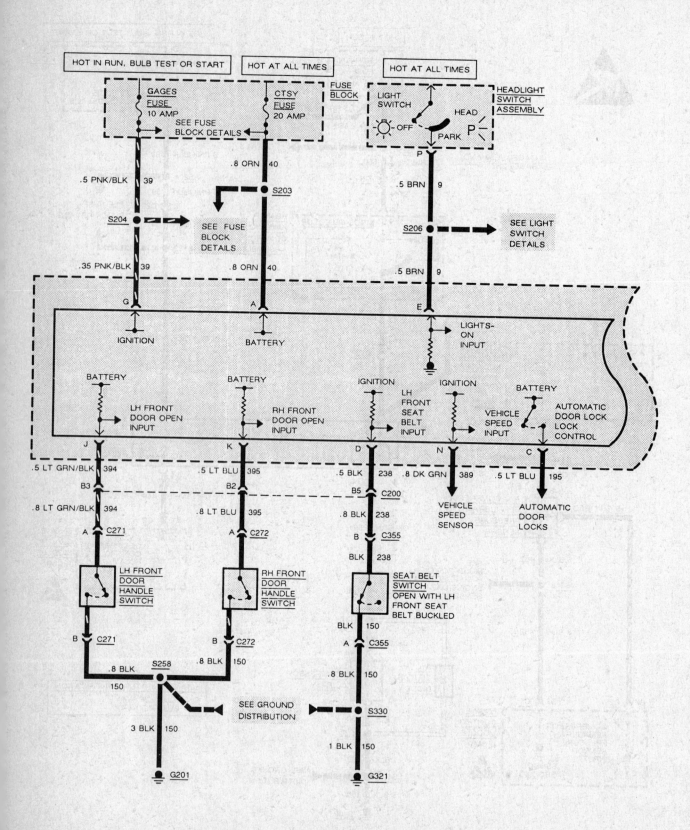

Audible Warnings Lights on/Ignition/Seatbelts 1990–92 All Models.

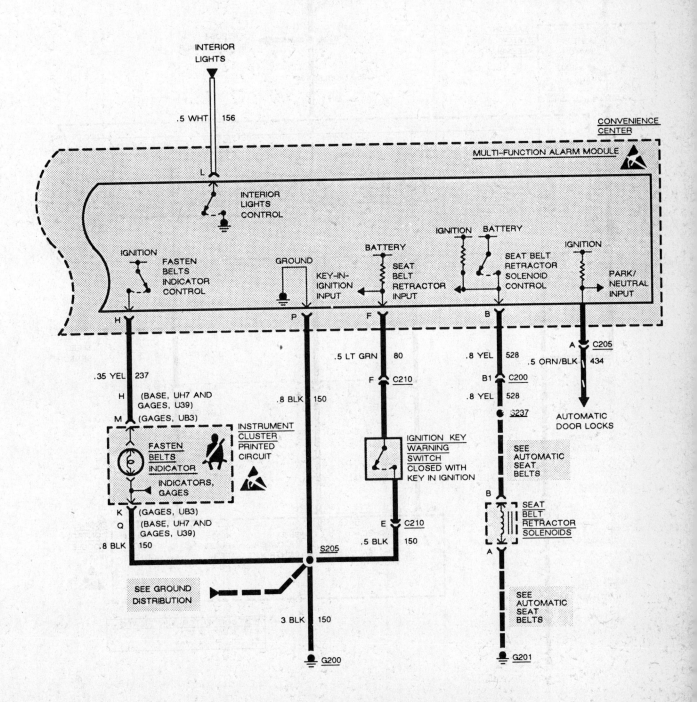

INTERIOR
LIGHTS

.5 WHT | 156

CONVENIENCE
CENTER

MULTI-FUNCTION ALARM MODULE

L

INTERIOR
LIGHTS
CONTROL

IGNITION
FASTEN
BELTS
INDICATOR
CONTROL

GROUND

KEY-IN-
IGNITION
INPUT

BATTERY
SEAT
BELT
RETRACTOR
INPUT

IGNITION   BATTERY

SEAT BELT
RETRACTOR
SOLENOID
CONTROL

IGNITION

PARK/
NEUTRAL
INPUT

H   P   F   B   A ⌁ C205

.35 YEL | 237   .8 BLK | 150   .5 LT GRN | 80   .8 YEL | 528   .5 ORN/BLK | 434

F ⌁ C210   B1 ⌁ C200

H | (BASE, UH7 AND
    GAGES, U39)
M | (GAGES, UB3)

.8 YEL | 528
S237

AUTOMATIC
DOOR LOCKS

INSTRUMENT
CLUSTER
PRINTED
CIRCUIT

FASTEN
BELTS
INDICATOR

INDICATORS,
GAGES

IGNITION KEY
WARNING
SWITCH
CLOSED WITH
KEY IN IGNITION

SEE
AUTOMATIC
SEAT
BELTS

K | (GAGES, UB3)
Q | (BASE, UH7 AND
    GAGES, U39)

E ⌁ C210

SEAT
BELT
RETRACTOR
SOLENOIDS

.8 BLK | 150   .5 BLK | 150

S205

SEE GROUND
DISTRIBUTION

SEE
AUTOMATIC
SEAT
BELTS

3 BLK | 150

⏚ G200   ⏚ G201

Audible Warnings Lights on/Ignition/Seatbelts 1990–92 All Models (con't).

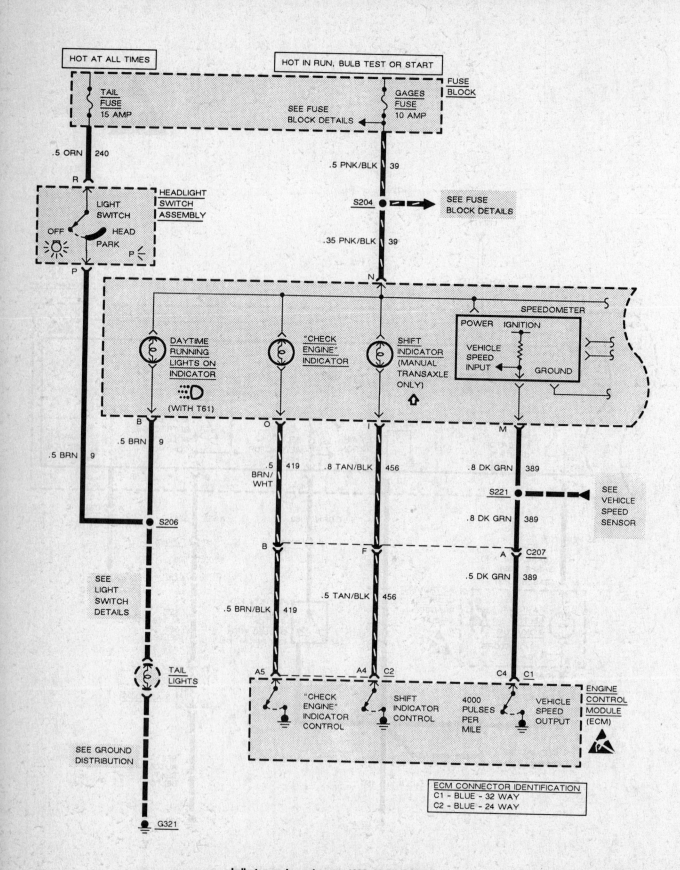

Indicators and speedometer 1990–92 All Models.

*   WITHOUT T61
** WITH T61

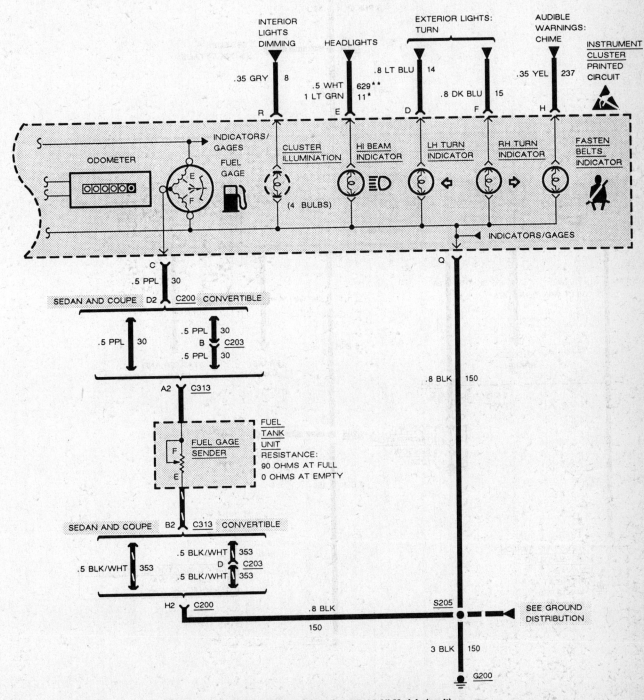

Indicators and speedometer 1990–92 All Models (con't).

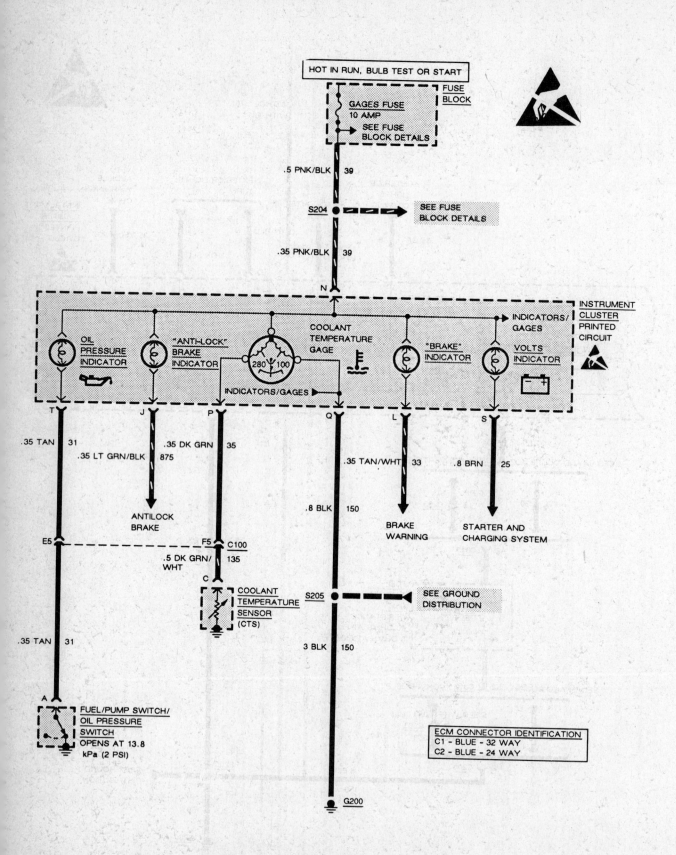

Coolant Temperature gauge and indicators 1990–92 All Models.

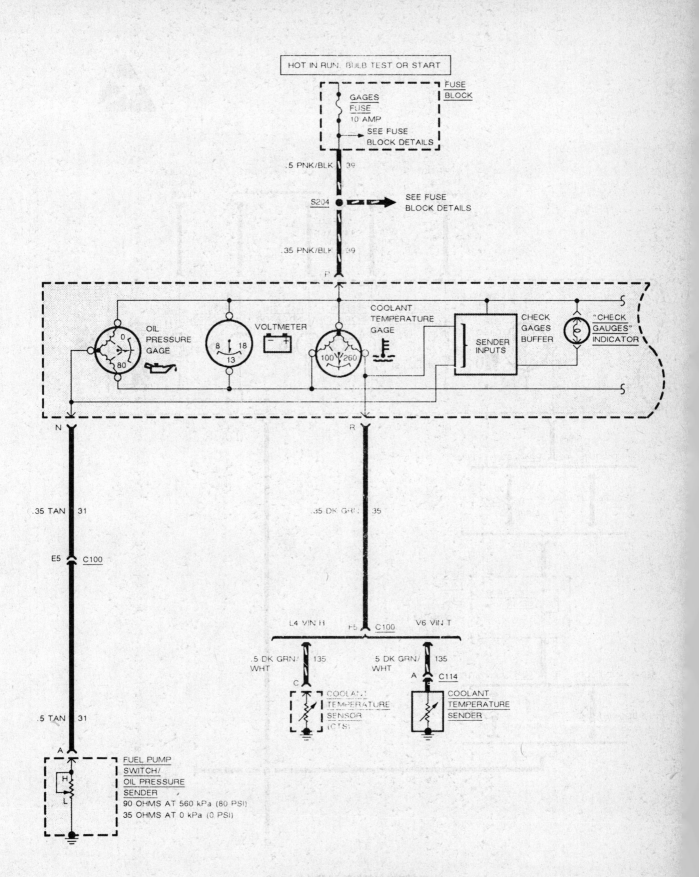

Cluster Gauges 1990–92 All Models.

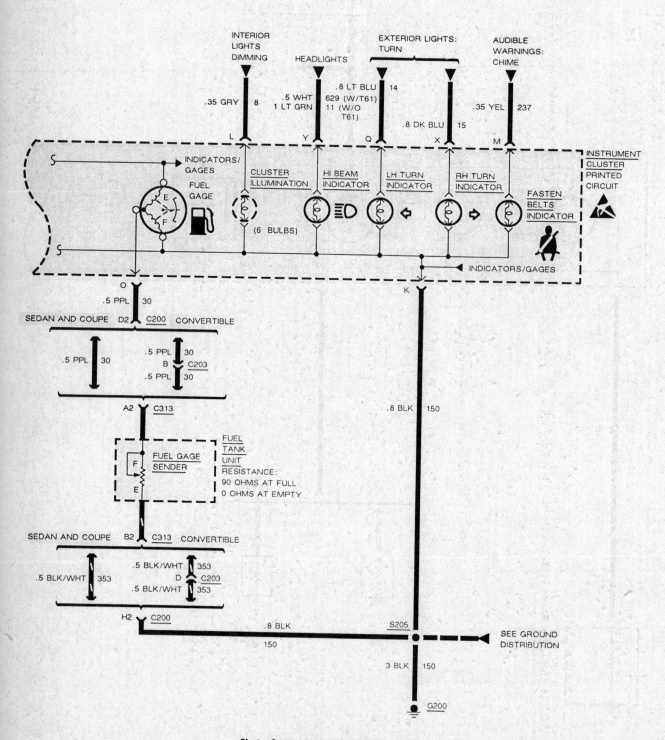

Cluster Gauges 1990–92 All Models (con't).

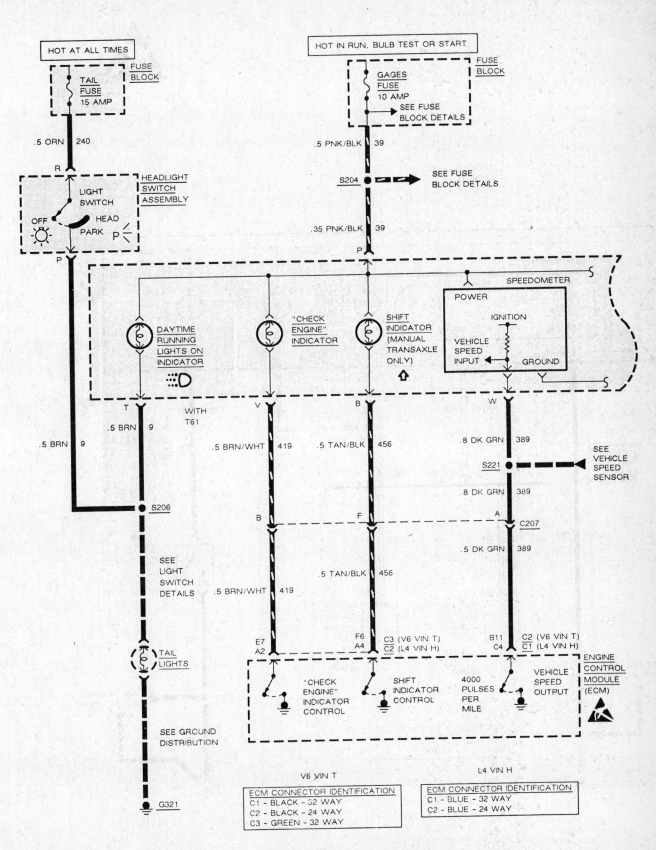

UB3 Cluster Gauges 1990–92 All Models.

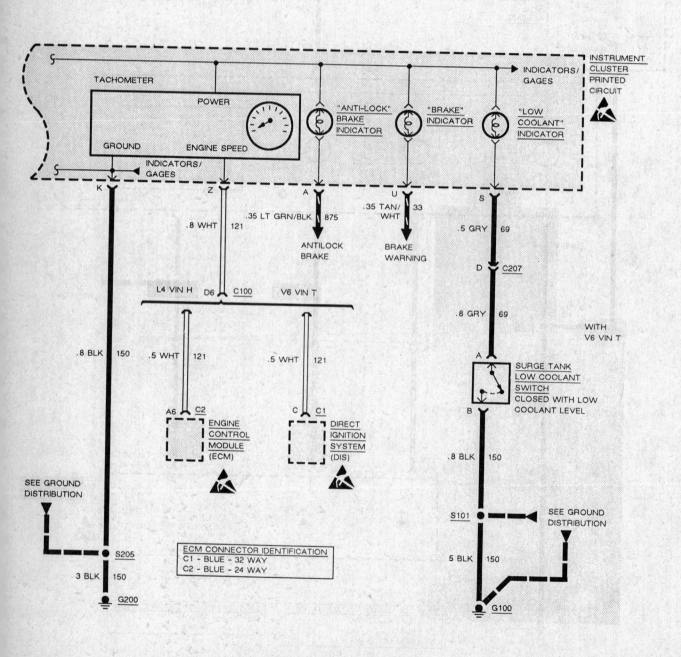

UB3 Cluster Gauges 1990–92 All Models (con't).

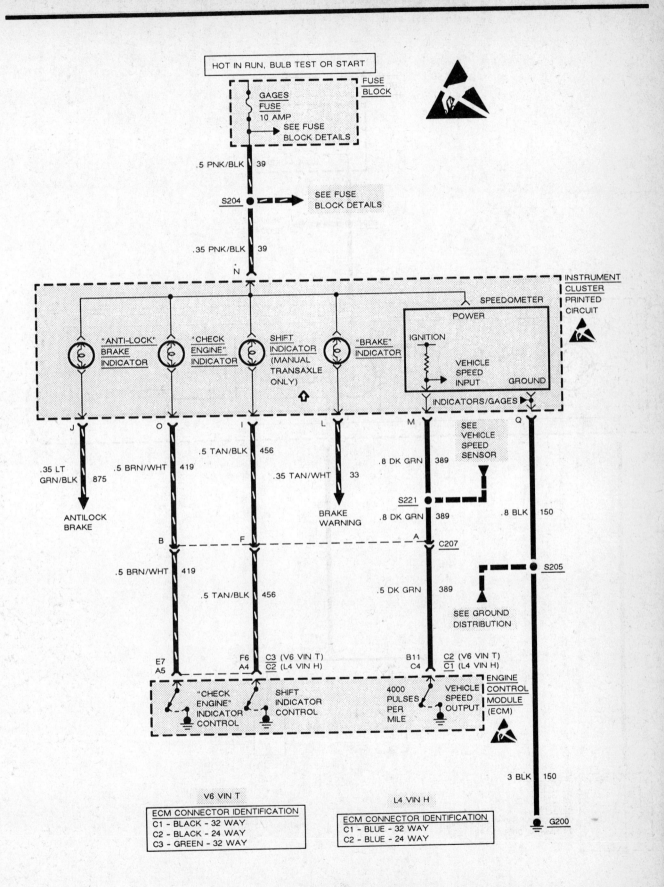

HOT IN RUN, BULB TEST OR START

GAGES FUSE 10 AMP — SEE FUSE BLOCK DETAILS

FUSE BLOCK

.5 PNK/BLK 39

S204 — SEE FUSE BLOCK DETAILS

.35 PNK/BLK 39

N

INSTRUMENT CLUSTER PRINTED CIRCUIT

SPEEDOMETER

POWER

"ANTI-LOCK" BRAKE INDICATOR

"CHECK ENGINE" INDICATOR

SHIFT INDICATOR (MANUAL TRANSAXLE ONLY)

"BRAKE" INDICATOR

IGNITION

VEHICLE SPEED INPUT

GROUND

INDICATORS/GAGES

J — O — I — L — M — Q

.35 LT GRN/BLK 875

.5 BRN/WHT 419

.5 TAN/BLK 456

.35 TAN/WHT 33

.8 DK GRN 389

SEE VEHICLE SPEED SENSOR

ANTILOCK BRAKE

BRAKE WARNING

S221

.8 DK GRN 389

.8 BLK 150

B — F — A — C207

.5 BRN/WHT 419

.5 TAN/BLK 456

.5 DK GRN 389

S205

SEE GROUND DISTRIBUTION

E7 A5 — F6 A4 — C3 (V6 VIN T) C2 (L4 VIN H) — B11 C4 — C2 (V6 VIN T) C1 (L4 VIN H)

ENGINE CONTROL MODULE (ECM)

"CHECK ENGINE" INDICATOR CONTROL

SHIFT INDICATOR CONTROL

4000 PULSES PER MILE

VEHICLE SPEED OUTPUT

3 BLK 150

G200

V6 VIN T

ECM CONNECTOR IDENTIFICATION
C1 - BLACK - 32 WAY
C2 - BLACK - 24 WAY
C3 - GREEN - 32 WAY

L4 VIN H

ECM CONNECTOR IDENTIFICATION
C1 - BLUE - 32 WAY
C2 - BLUE - 24 WAY

U39 Cluster Gauges 1990–92 All Models.

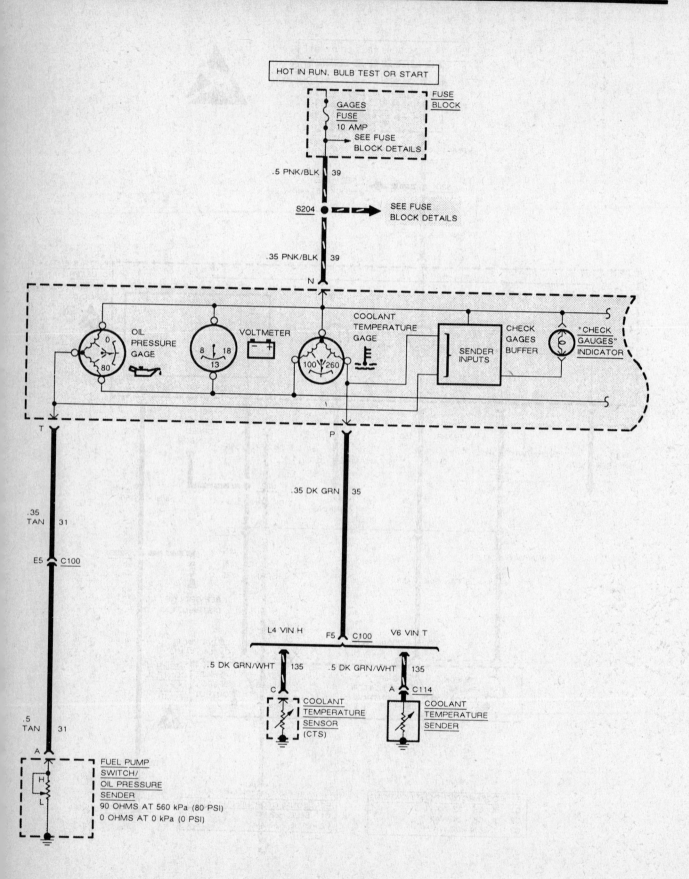

HOT IN RUN, BULB TEST OR START

FUSE BLOCK

GAGES FUSE 10 AMP

SEE FUSE BLOCK DETAILS

.5 PNK/BLK 39

S204

SEE FUSE BLOCK DETAILS

.35 PNK/BLK 39

N

OIL PRESSURE GAGE

VOLTMETER

8 13 18

0 80

COOLANT TEMPERATURE GAGE

100 260

SENDER INPUTS

CHECK GAGES BUFFER

"CHECK GAGES" INDICATOR

T

P

.35 DK GRN 35

.35 TAN 31

E5 C100

L4 VIN H

F5 C100

V6 VIN T

.5 DK GRN/WHT 135

.5 DK GRN/WHT 135

C

COOLANT TEMPERATURE SENSOR (CTS)

A C114

COOLANT TEMPERATURE SENDER

.5 TAN 31

A

FUEL PUMP SWITCH/ OIL PRESSURE SENDER
90 OHMS AT 560 kPa (80 PSI)
0 OHMS AT 0 kPa (0 PSI)

H
L

U39 Cluster Gauges 1990–92 All Models.

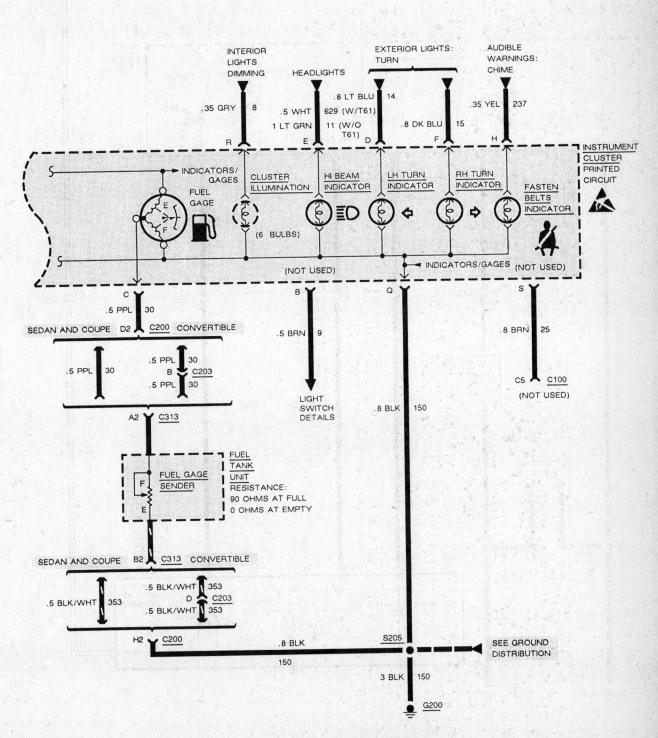

U39 Cluster Gauges 1990–92 All Models (con't).

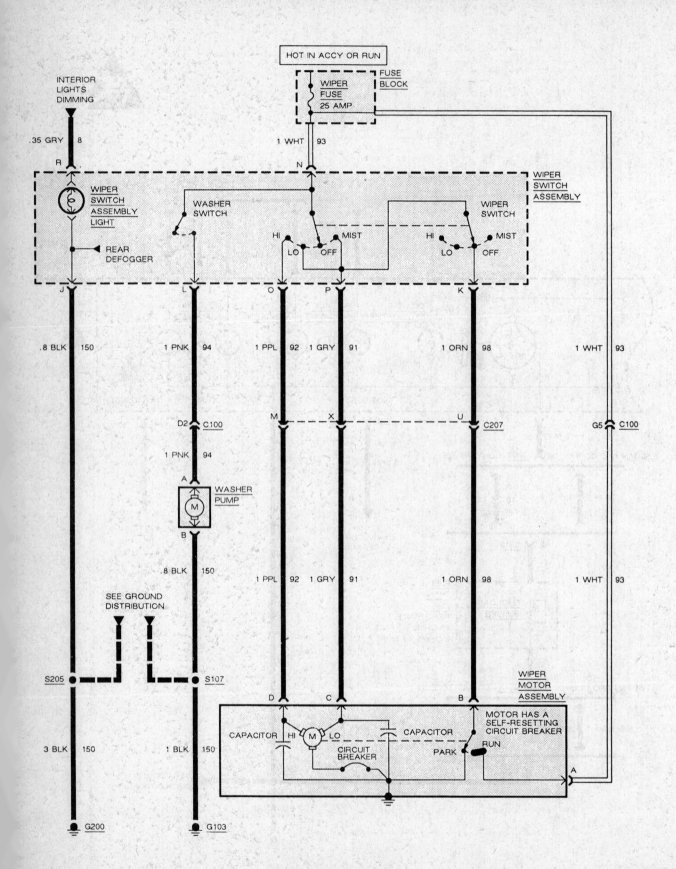

Wiper/Washer 1990–92 All Models.

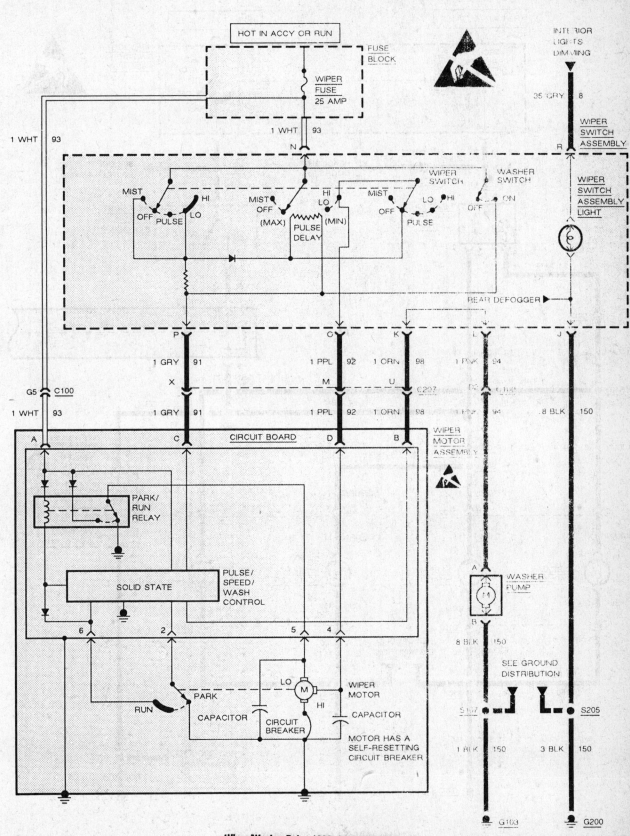

Wiper/Washer Pulse 1990–92 All Models.

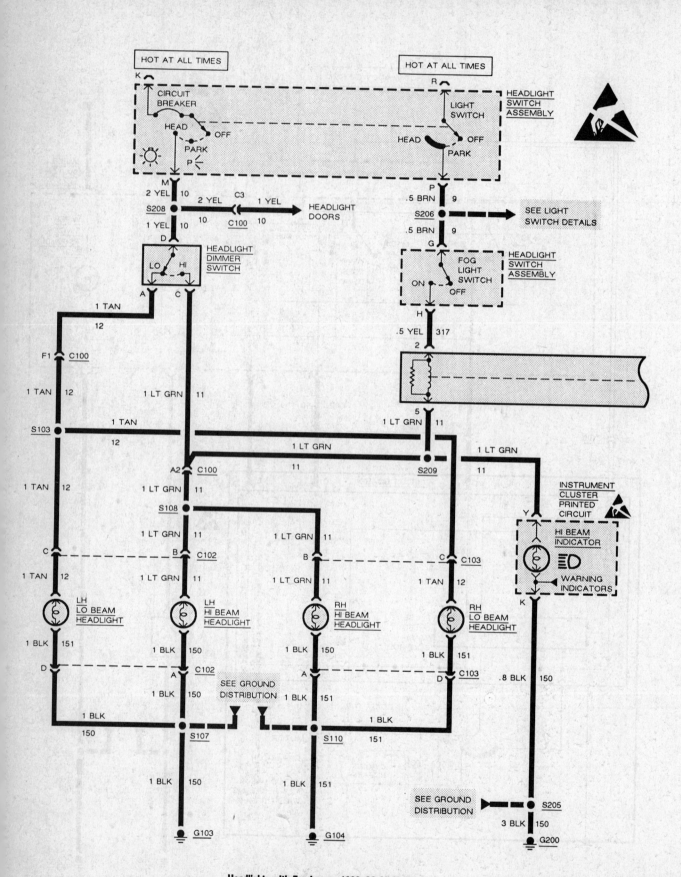

Headlights with Fog Lamps 1990–92 All Models.

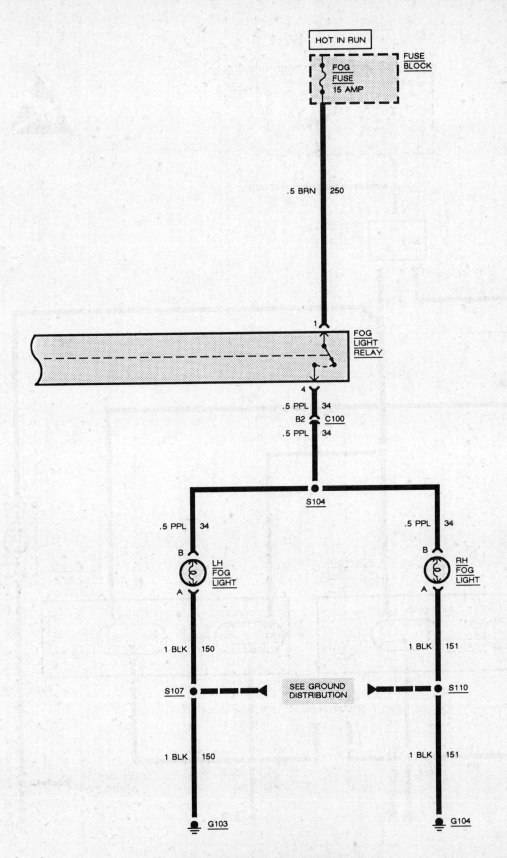

Headlights with Fog Lamps 1990–92 All Models (con't).

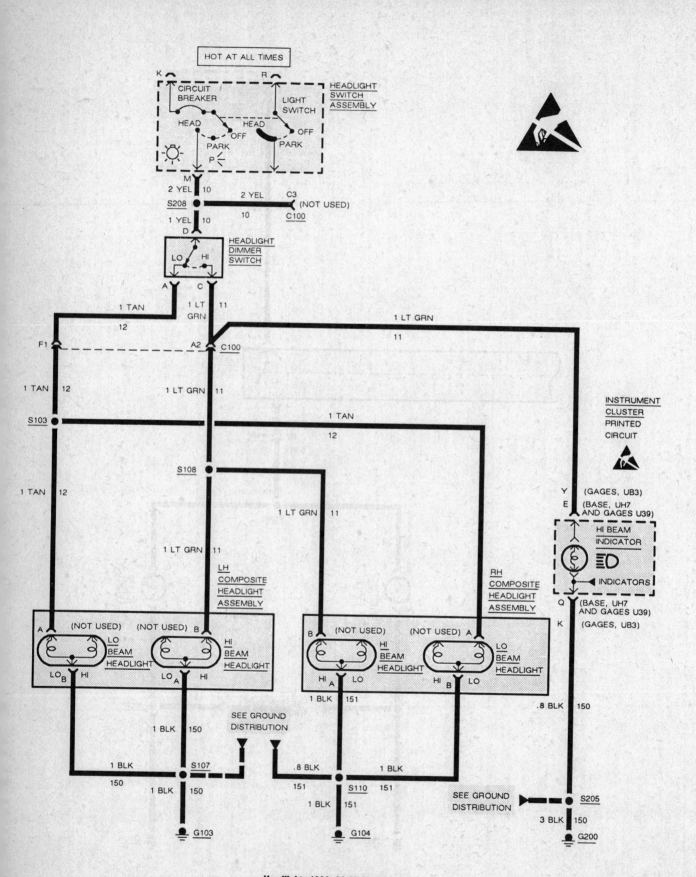

Headlights 1990–92 All Models.

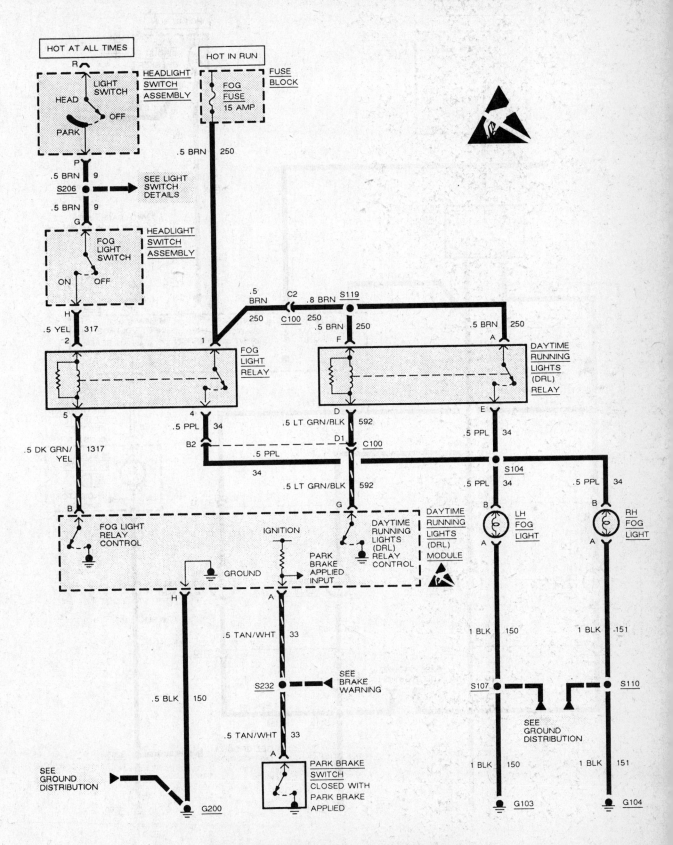

Daytime running Lights with Fog Lamps 1990–92 All Models.

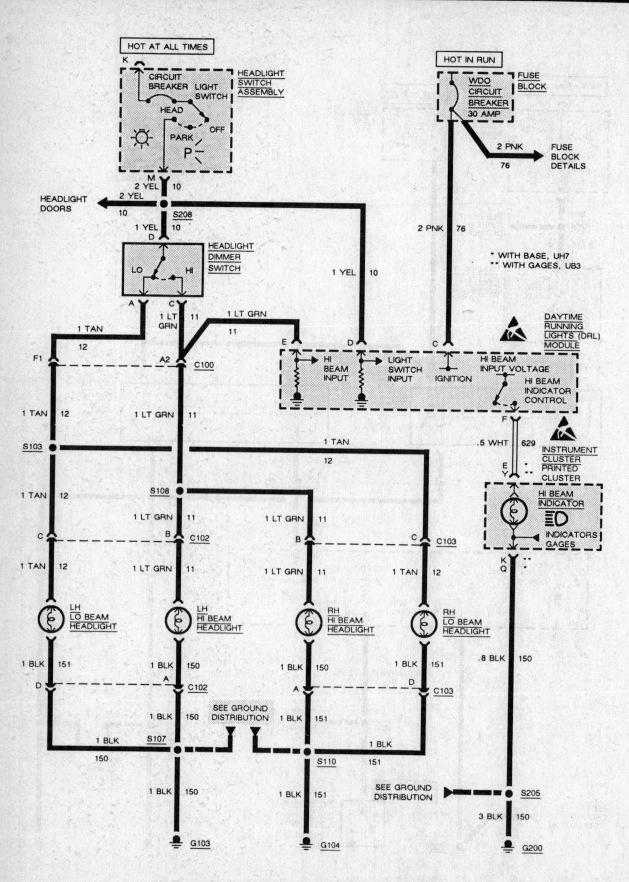

Daytime running Lights with Fog Lamps 1990–92 All Models (con't).

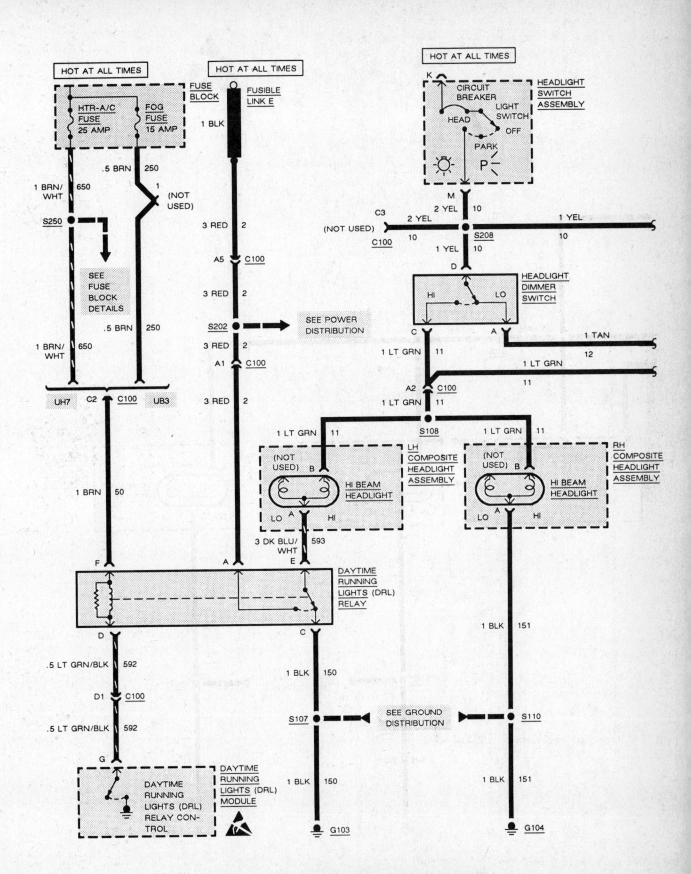

Daytime running Lights without Fog Lamps 1990–92 All Models.

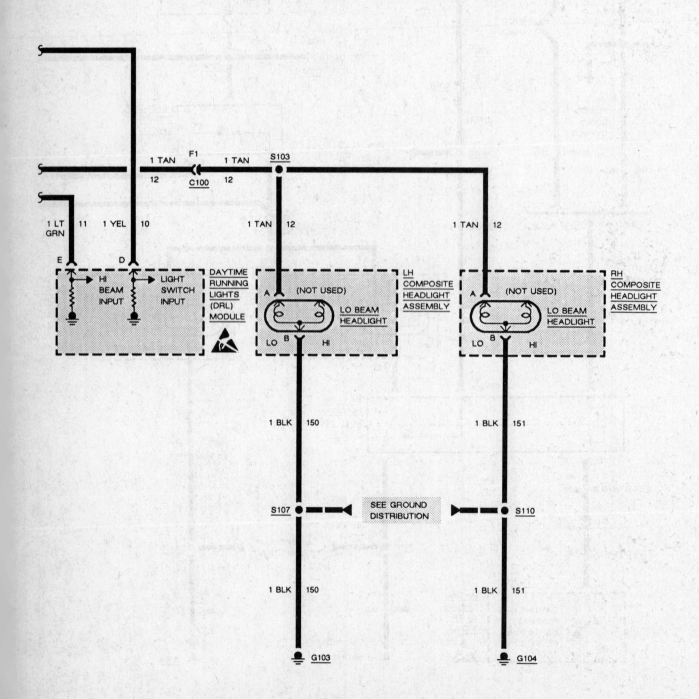

Daytime running Lights without Fog Lamps 1990–92 All Models (con't).

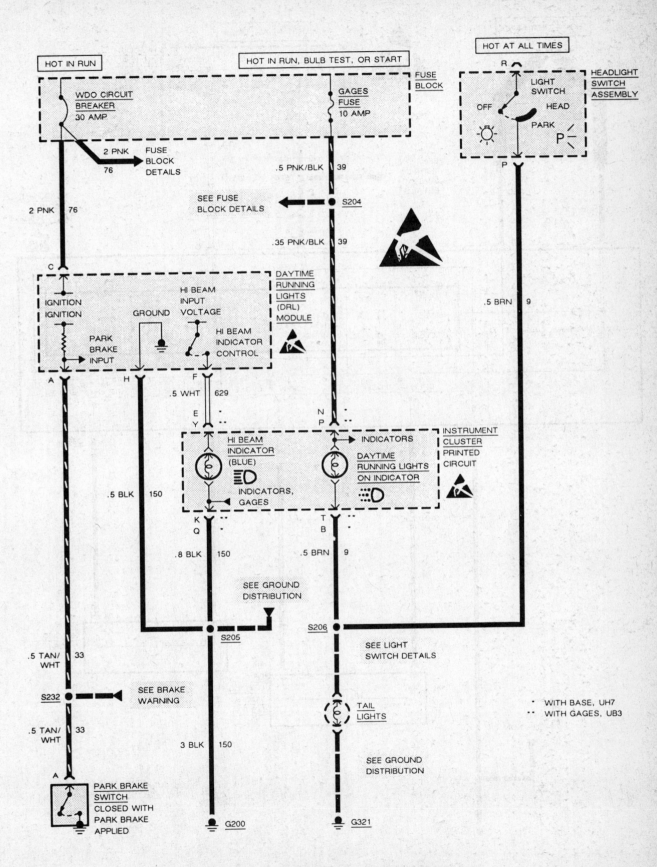

Daytime running Lights without Fog Lamps 1990–92 All Models.

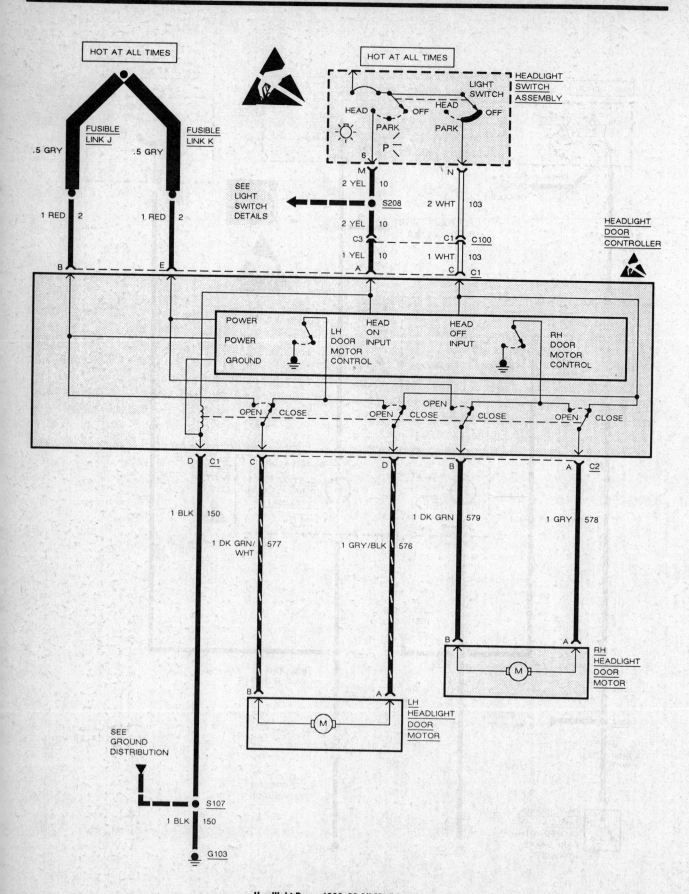

Headlight Doors 1990–92 All Models.

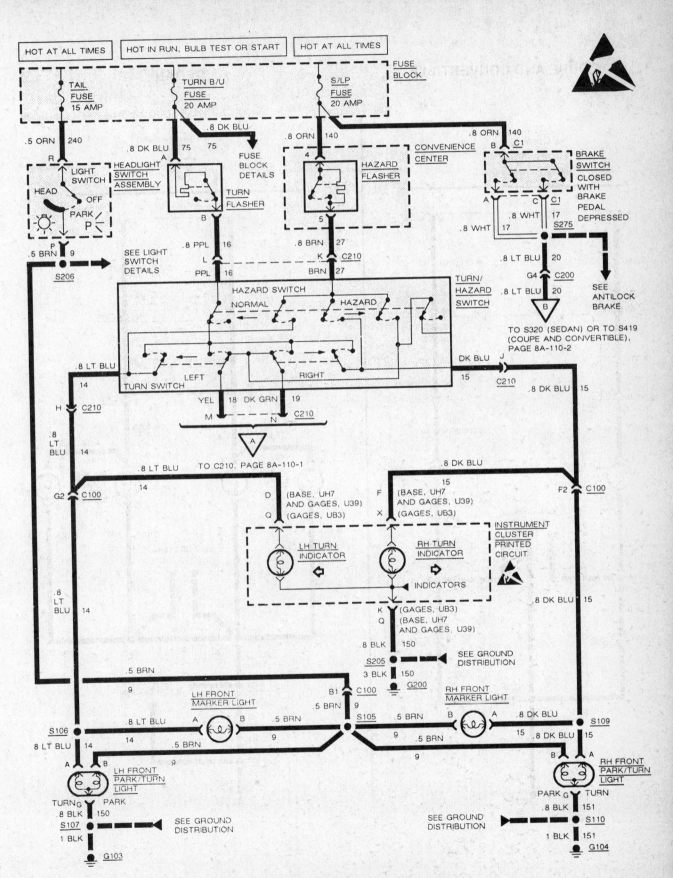

Front Turn/Hazard/Marker/Park Lights 1990–92 All Models.

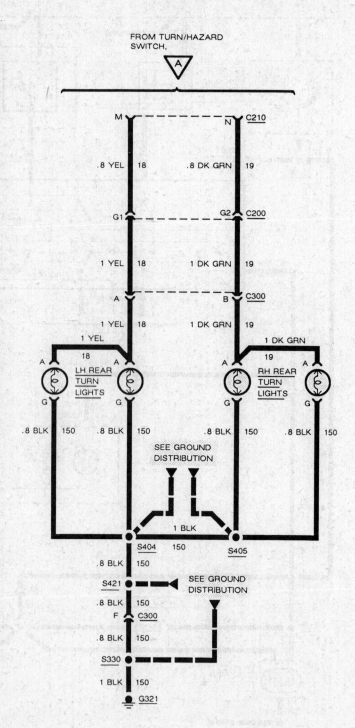

COUPE AND CONVERTIBLE

FROM TURN/HAZARD
SWITCH,
A

M   N   C210

.8 YEL   18   .8 DK GRN   19

G1   G2   C200

.8 YEL   18   .8 DK GRN   19

B   C309   B   C310

.8 YEL   18   .8 DK GRN   19

A   A
LH REAR TURN LIGHT   RH REAR TURN LIGHT
G   G

SEE GROUND DISTRIBUTION

.8 BLK   150   .8 BLK   150

S414   S413

8 BLK   150   .8 BLK   150

D   C309   D   C310

.8 BLK   150   .8 BLK   150

S330

1 BLK   150

G321

SEDAN

FROM TURN/HAZARD
SWITCH,
A

M   N   C210

.8 YEL   18   .8 DK GRN   19

G1   G2   C200

1 YEL   18   1 DK GRN   19

A   B   C300

1 YEL   18   1 DK GRN   19

1 YEL   1 DK GRN
18   19

A   A   A   A
LH REAR TURN LIGHTS   RH REAR TURN LIGHTS
G   G   G   G

.8 BLK   150   .8 BLK   150   .8 BLK   150   .8 BLK   150

SEE GROUND DISTRIBUTION

1 BLK

S404   150   S405

.8 BLK   150

S421   SEE GROUND DISTRIBUTION

.8 BLK   150
F   C300

.8 BLK   150

S330

1 BLK   150

G321

Rear Turn/Hazard Lights 1990–92 All Models.

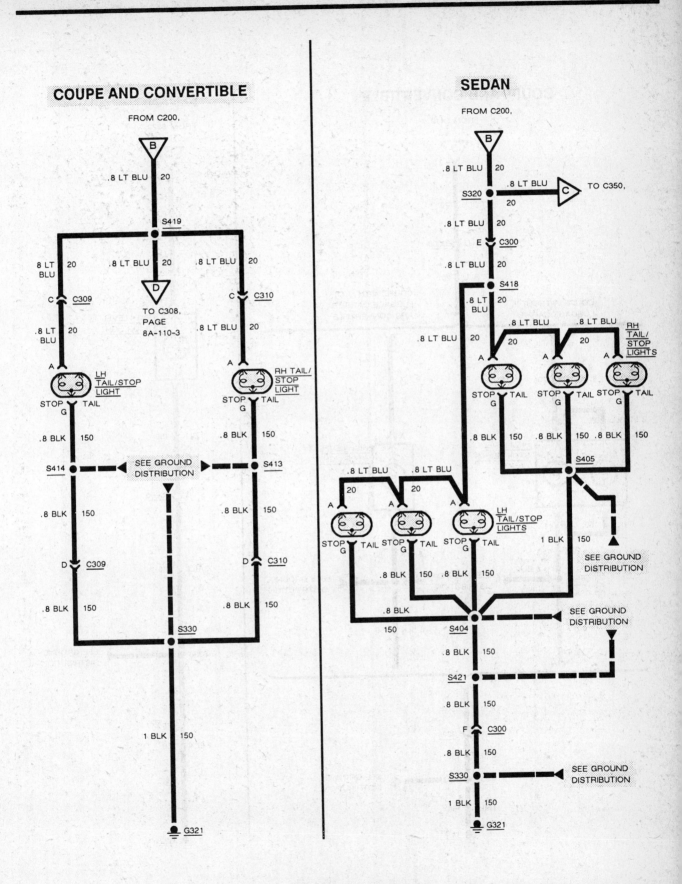

Rear Brake Lights 1990–92 All Models.

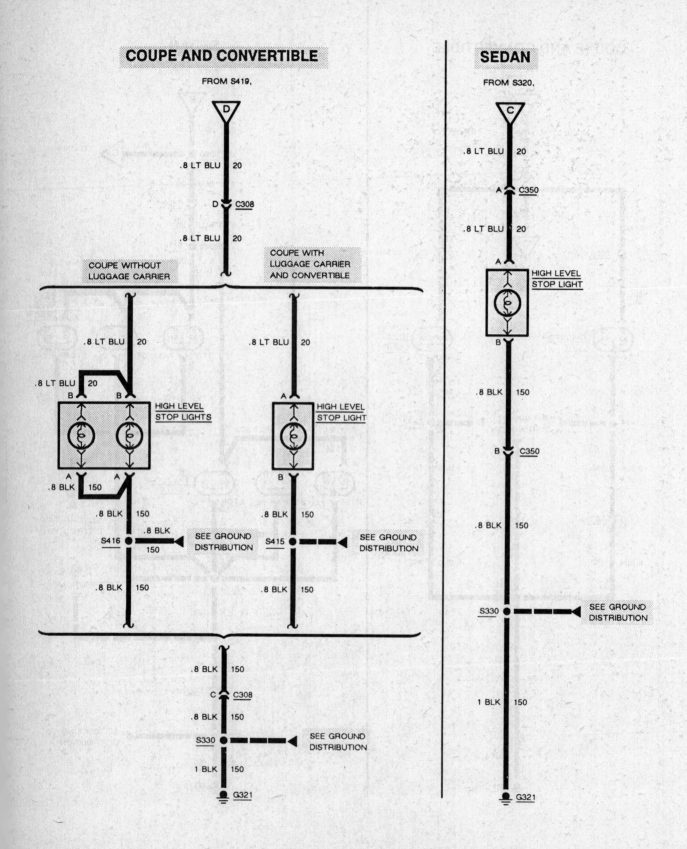

High Level Brake Light 1990–92 All Models.

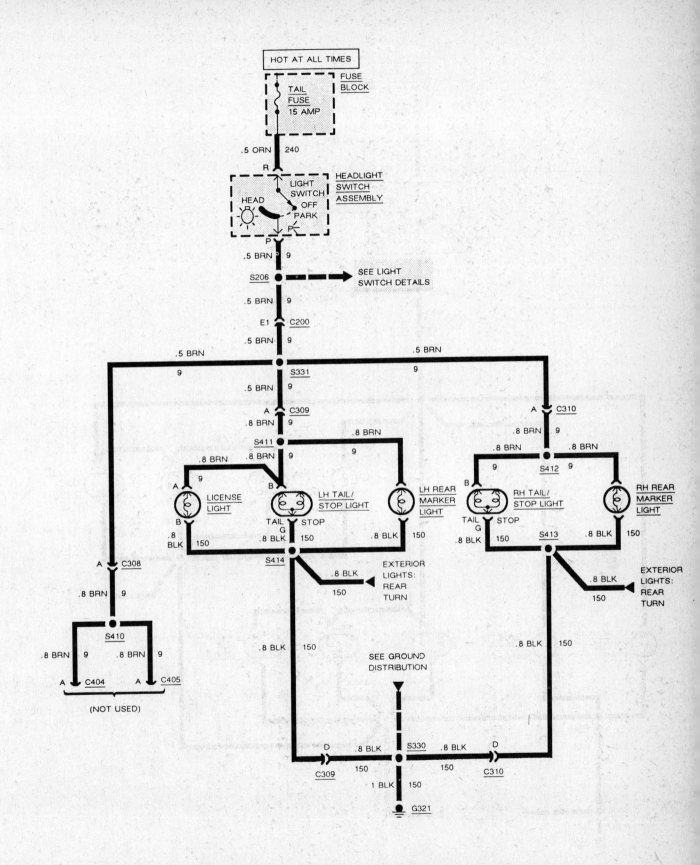

Rear Tail/marker/License Lights Coupe and Convertible 1990–92 All Models.

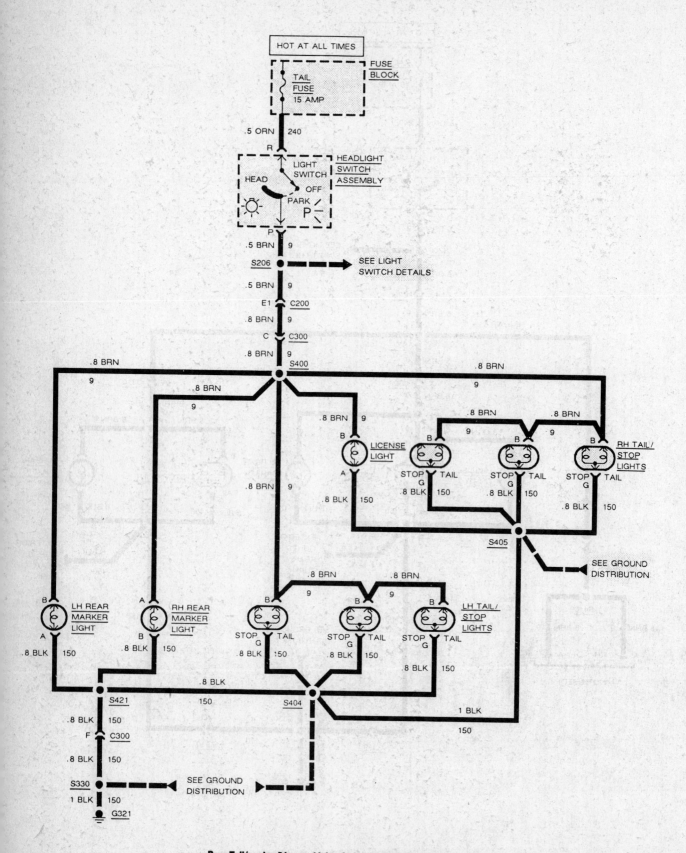

Rear Tail/marker/License Lights Sedan 1990–92 All Models.

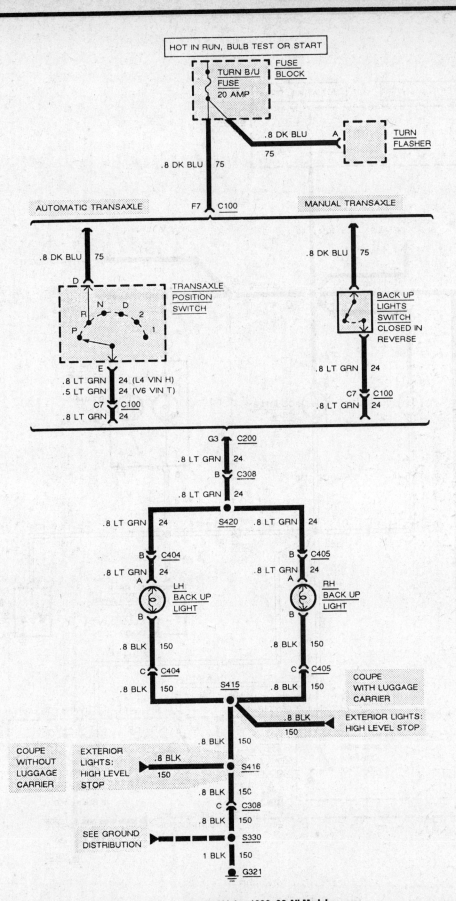

Backup Lights 1990–92 All Models.

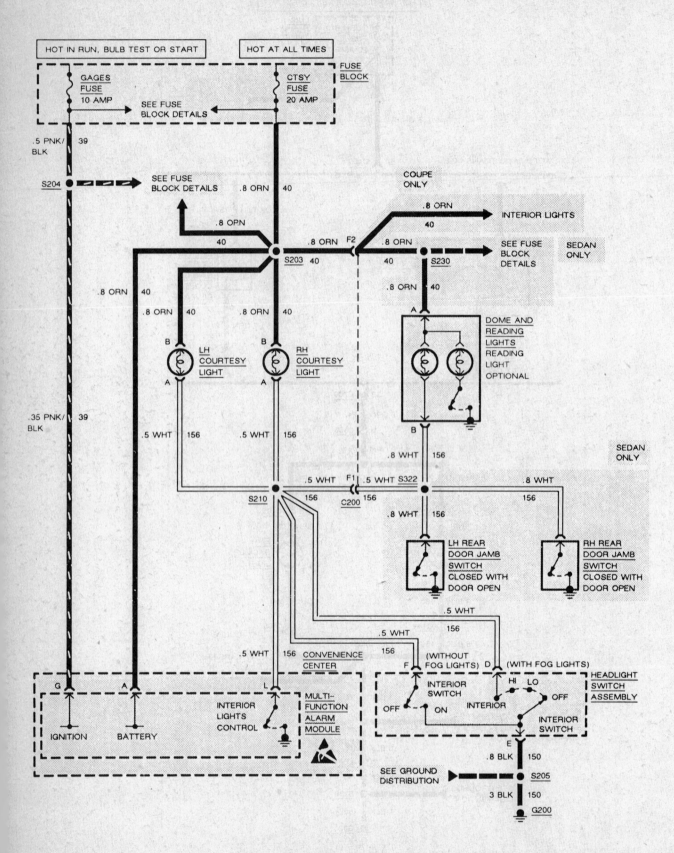

Interior Lights Sedan and Coupe 1990–92 All Models.

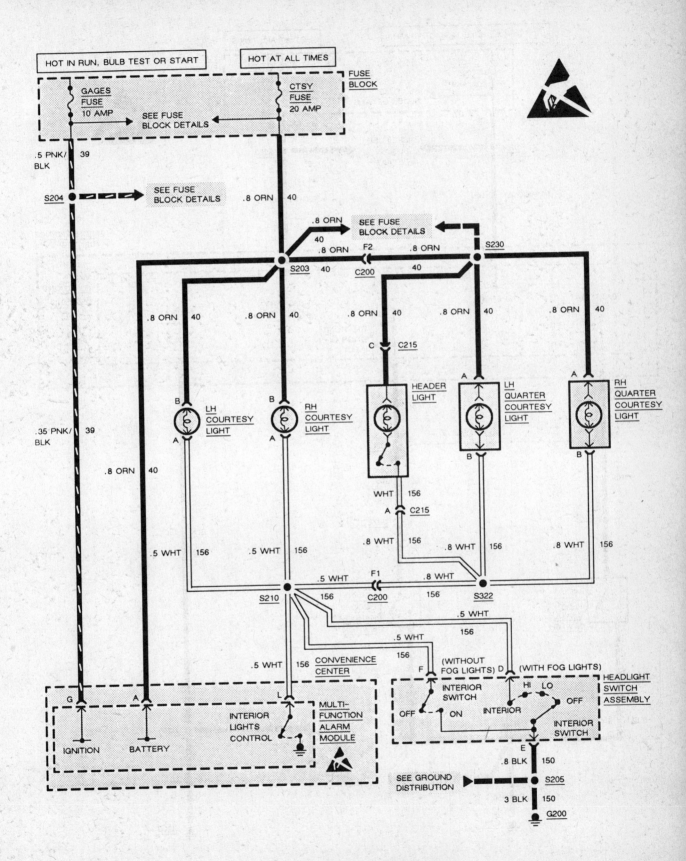

Interior Lights Convertible 1990–92 All Models.

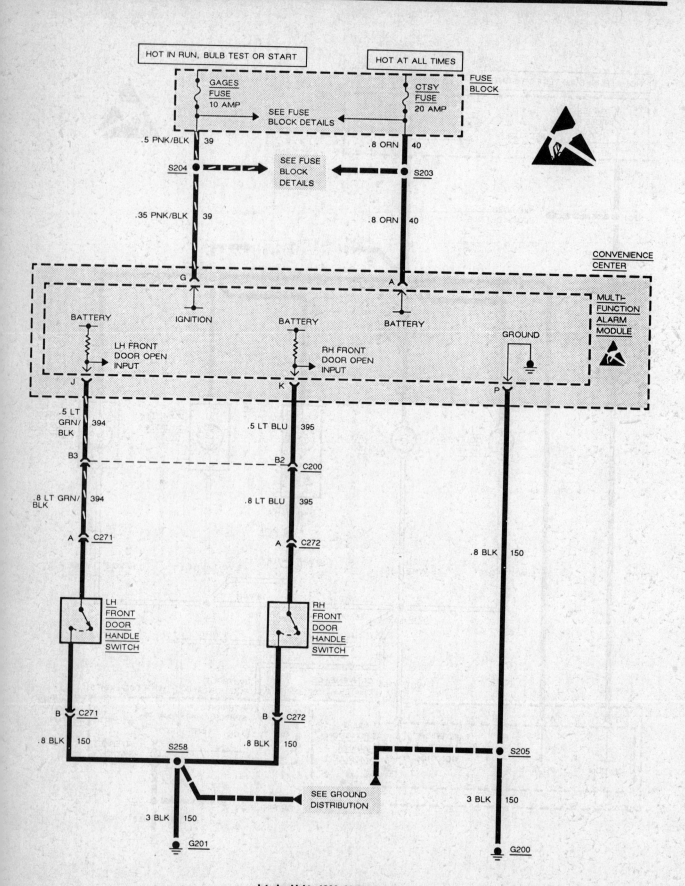

Interior Lights 1990–92 All Models.

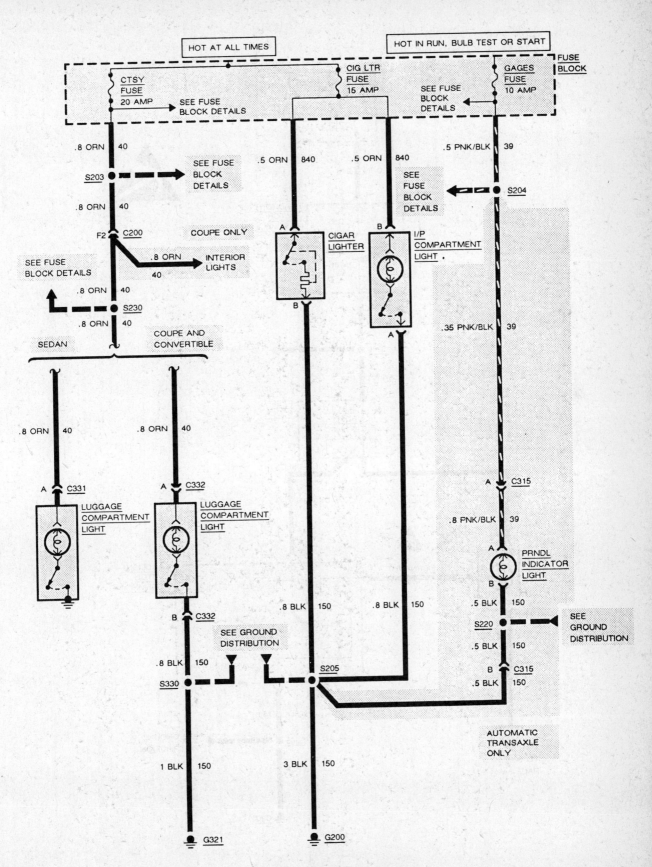

Interior Lights 1990–92 All Models.

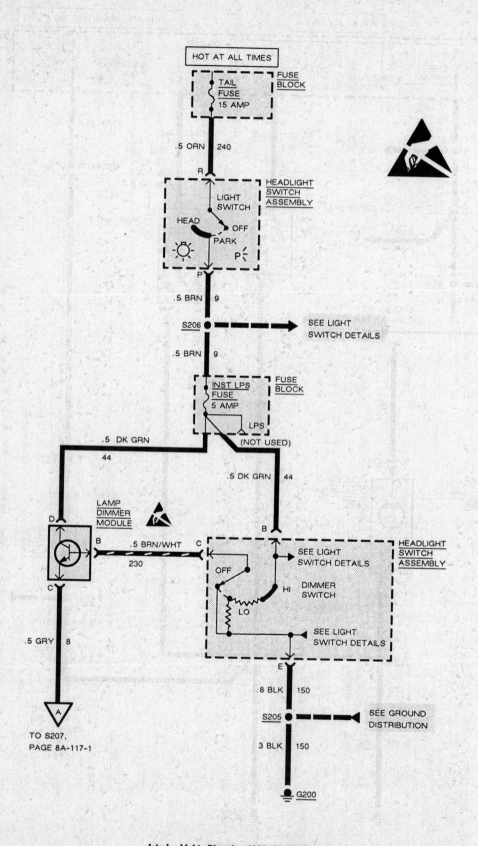

Interior Lights Dimming 1990–92 All Models.

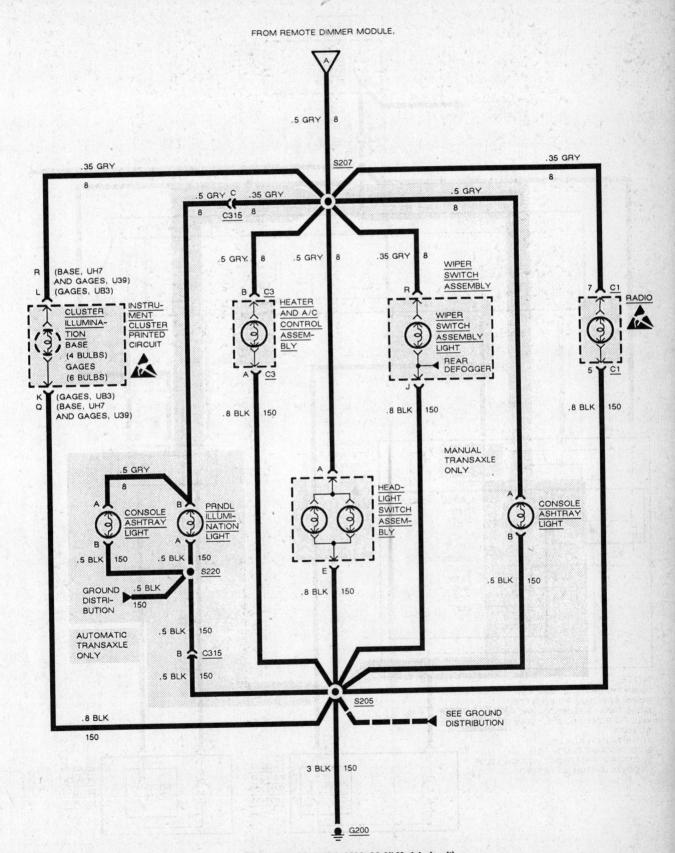

FROM REMOTE DIMMER MODULE,

A

.5 GRY   8

S207

.35 GRY
8

.35 GRY
8

.5 GRY C .35 GRY
8   8
C315

.5 GRY
8

.5 GRY   8   .5 GRY   8   .35 GRY   8

WIPER
SWITCH
ASSEMBLY

R (BASE, UH7
    AND GAGES, U39)
L (GAGES, UB3)

B C3   HEATER
          AND A/C
          CONTROL
          ASSEM-
A C3   BLY

R   WIPER
           SWITCH
           ASSEMBLY
           LIGHT

           REAR
           DEFOGGER

7 C1   RADIO

CLUSTER
ILLUMINA-
TION
BASE
(4 BULBS)
GAGES
(6 BULBS)

INSTRU-
MENT
CLUSTER
PRINTED
CIRCUIT

5 C1

K (GAGES, UB3)
Q (BASE, UH7
    AND GAGES, U39)

.8 BLK   150

.8 BLK   150

J

.8 BLK   150

.8 BLK   150

MANUAL
TRANSAXLE
ONLY

.5 GRY
8

A   A

A C315   B PRNDL
             ILLUMI-
             NATION
             LIGHT
B   A

CONSOLE
ASHTRAY
LIGHT

HEAD-
LIGHT
SWITCH
ASSEM-
BLY

A   CONSOLE
           ASHTRAY
B   LIGHT

.5 BLK   150   .5 BLK   150

GROUND
DISTRI-
BUTION

.5 BLK
150

E

.5 BLK   150

AUTOMATIC
TRANSAXLE
ONLY

.5 BLK   150

B C315

.8 BLK   150

.5 BLK   150

S205   SEE GROUND
          DISTRIBUTION

.8 BLK

150

3 BLK   150

G200

Interior Lights Dimming 1990–92 All Models (con't).

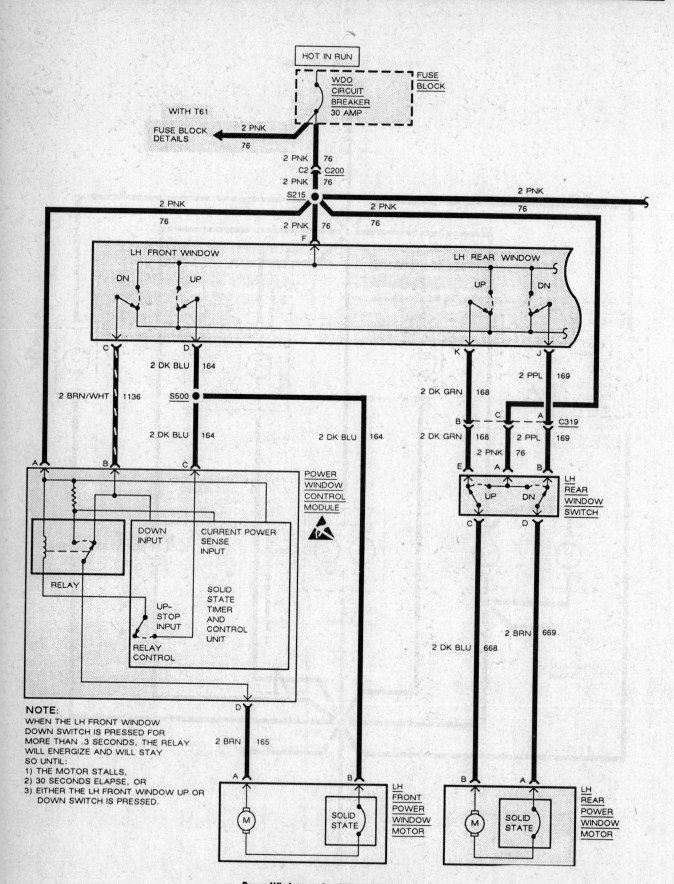

Power Windows sedan 1990–92 All Models.

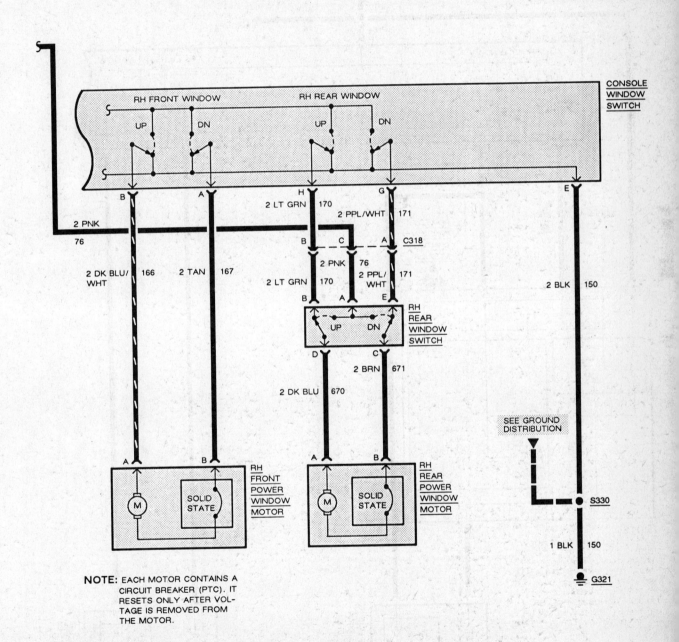

NOTE: EACH MOTOR CONTAINS A CIRCUIT BREAKER (PTC). IT RESETS ONLY AFTER VOLTAGE IS REMOVED FROM THE MOTOR.

Power Windows sedan 1990–92 All Models (con't).

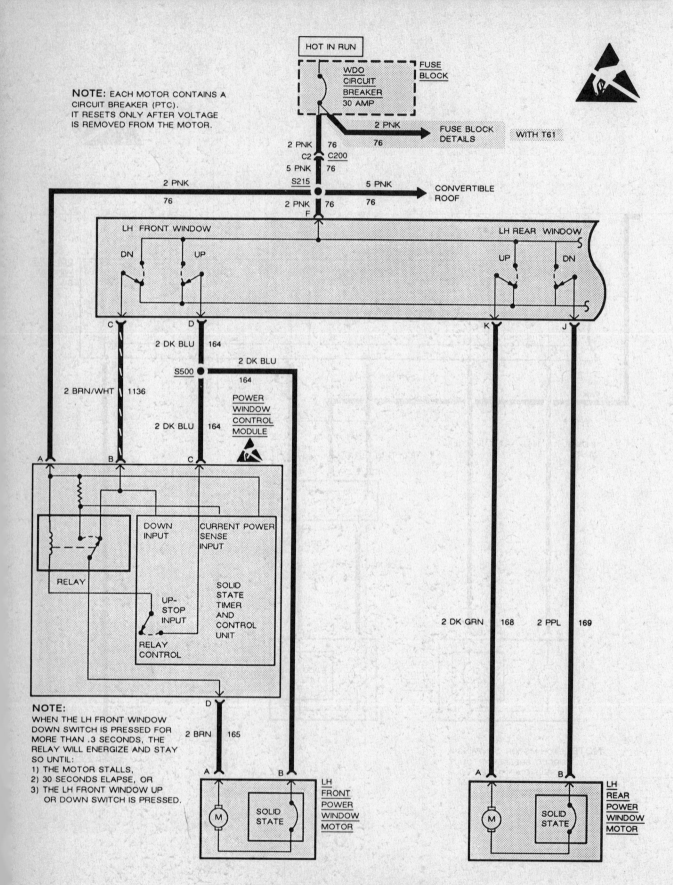

NOTE: EACH MOTOR CONTAINS A
CIRCUIT BREAKER (PTC).
IT RESETS ONLY AFTER VOLTAGE
IS REMOVED FROM THE MOTOR.

HOT IN RUN

WDO
CIRCUIT
BREAKER
30 AMP

FUSE
BLOCK

2 PNK
76

FUSE BLOCK
DETAILS

WITH T61

2 PNK 76
C2 C200
5 PNK 76

S215

2 PNK
76

5 PNK
76

CONVERTIBLE
ROOF

2 PNK 76
F

LH FRONT WINDOW

LH REAR WINDOW

DN   UP

UP   DN

C   D

K   J

2 DK BLU 164

2 DK BLU

S500

164

2 BRN/WHT 1136

POWER
WINDOW
CONTROL
MODULE

2 DK BLU 164

A   B   C

DOWN
INPUT

CURRENT POWER
SENSE
INPUT

RELAY

SOLID
STATE
TIMER
AND
CONTROL
UNIT

UP-
STOP
INPUT

2 DK GRN 168   2 PPL 169

RELAY
CONTROL

D

NOTE:
WHEN THE LH FRONT WINDOW
DOWN SWITCH IS PRESSED FOR
MORE THAN .3 SECONDS, THE
RELAY WILL ENERGIZE AND STAY
SO UNTIL:
1) THE MOTOR STALLS,
2) 30 SECONDS ELAPSE, OR
3) THE LH FRONT WINDOW UP
   OR DOWN SWITCH IS PRESSED.

2 BRN 165

A   B

M

SOLID
STATE

LH
FRONT
POWER
WINDOW
MOTOR

A   B

M

SOLID
STATE

LH
REAR
POWER
WINDOW
MOTOR

Power Windows Convertible 1990–92 All Models.

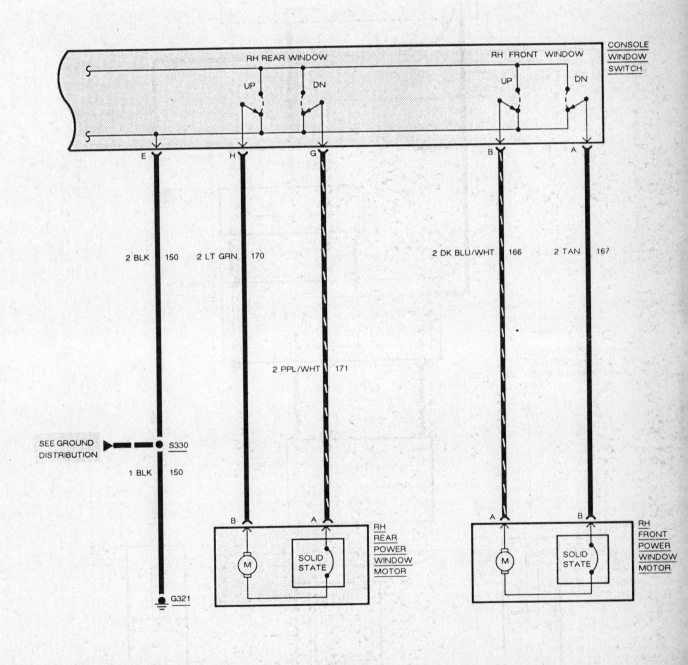

Power Windows Convertible 1990–92 All Models (con't).

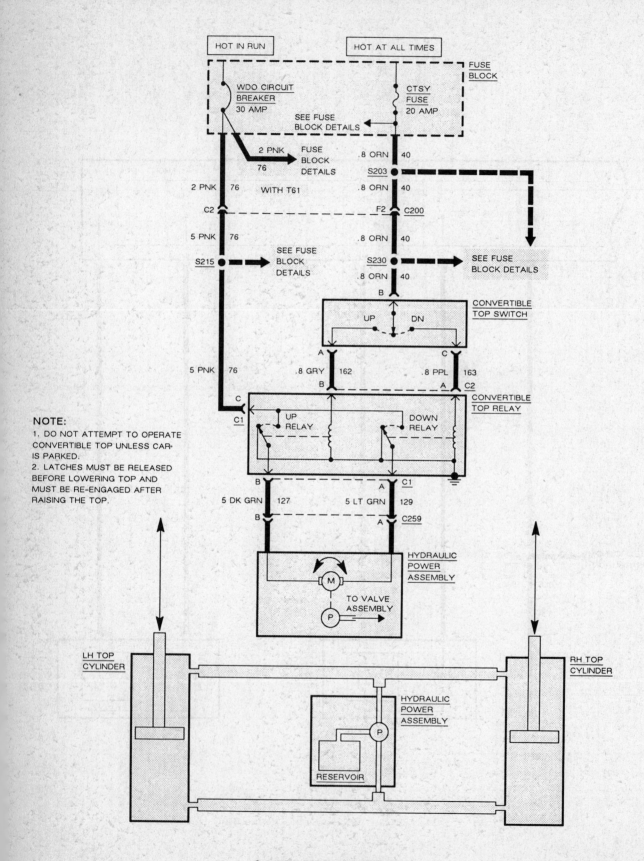

NOTE:
1. DO NOT ATTEMPT TO OPERATE CONVERTIBLE TOP UNLESS CAR IS PARKED.
2. LATCHES MUST BE RELEASED BEFORE LOWERING TOP AND MUST BE RE-ENGAGED AFTER RAISING THE TOP.

Convertible Top 1990–92 All Models.

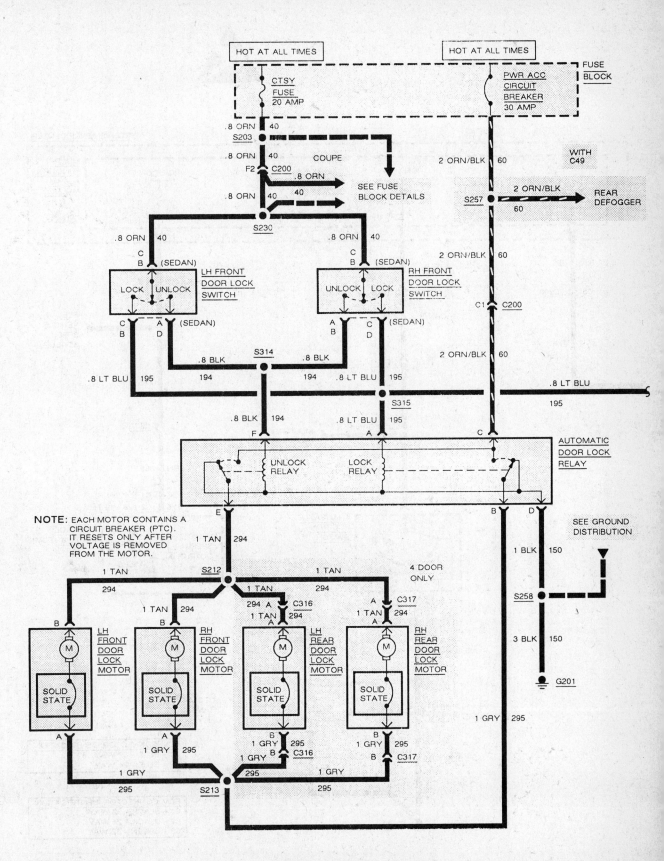

Automatic Door Locks 1990–92 All Models.

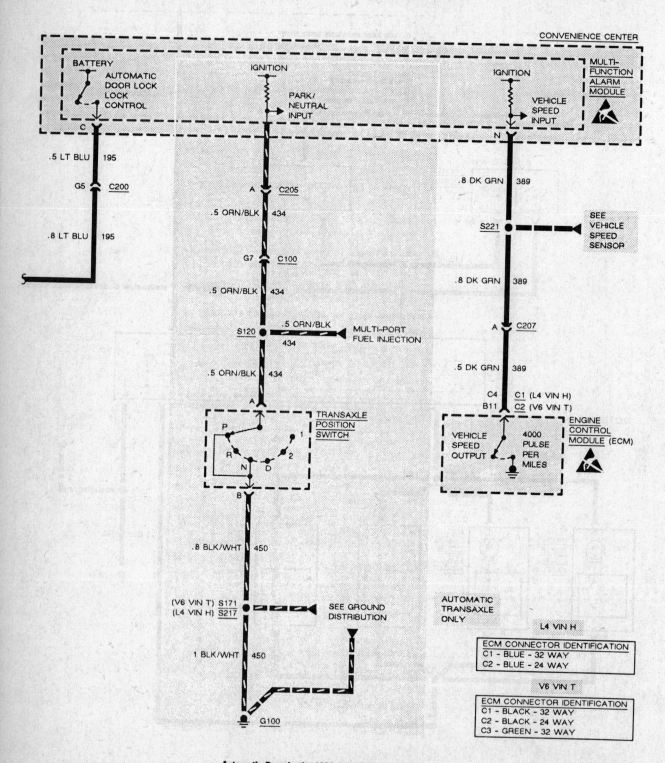

CONVENIENCE CENTER

BATTERY
AUTOMATIC
DOOR LOCK
LOCK
CONTROL

IGNITION

PARK/
NEUTRAL
INPUT

IGNITION

VEHICLE
SPEED
INPUT

MULTI-
FUNCTION
ALARM
MODULE

C

.5 LT BLU 195

G5 C200

.8 LT BLU 195

A C205

.5 ORN/BLK 434

G7 C100

.5 ORN/BLK 434

S120 .5 ORN/BLK
434

MULTI-PORT
FUEL INJECTION

.5 ORN/BLK 434

A

TRANSAXLE
POSITION
SWITCH

P   1
R   2
N   D

B

.8 BLK/WHT 450

(V6 VIN T) S171
(L4 VIN H) S217

SEE GROUND
DISTRIBUTION

1 BLK/WHT 450

G100

N

.8 DK GRN 389

S221

SEE
VEHICLE
SPEED
SENSOR

.8 DK GRN 389

A C207

.5 DK GRN 389

C4 C1 (L4 VIN H)
B11 C2 (V6 VIN T)

VEHICLE
SPEED
OUTPUT

4000
PULSE
PER
MILES

ENGINE
CONTROL
MODULE (ECM)

AUTOMATIC
TRANSAXLE
ONLY

L4 VIN H

ECM CONNECTOR IDENTIFICATION	
C1 – BLUE – 32 WAY	
C2 – BLUE – 24 WAY	

V6 VIN T

ECM CONNECTOR IDENTIFICATION	
C1 – BLACK – 32 WAY	
C2 – BLACK – 24 WAY	
C3 – GREEN – 32 WAY	

Automatic Door Locks 1990–92 All Models (con't).

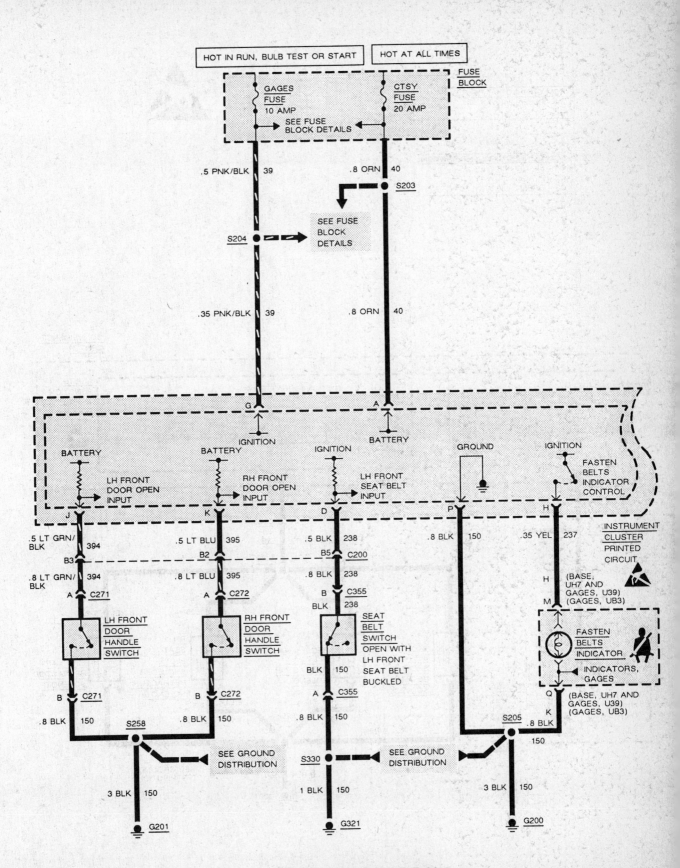

Automatic Seat Belts 1990–92 All Models.

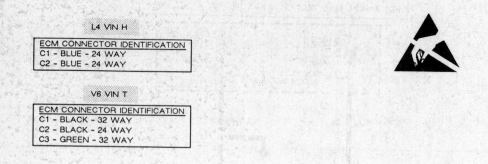

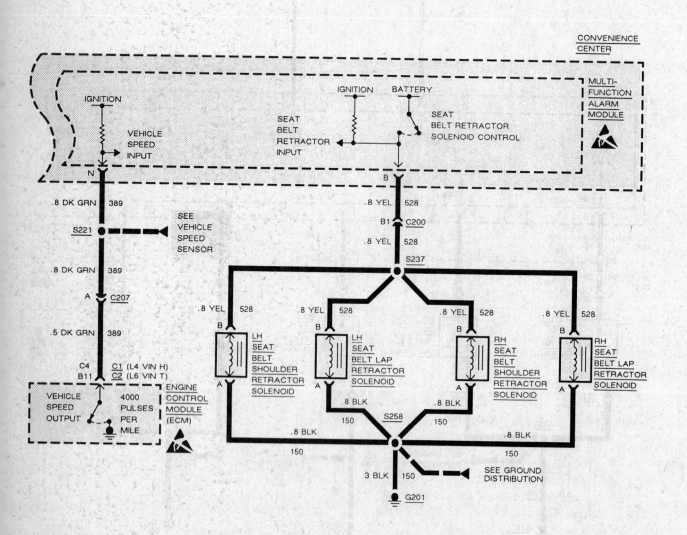

Automatic Seat Belts 1990–92 All Models (con't).

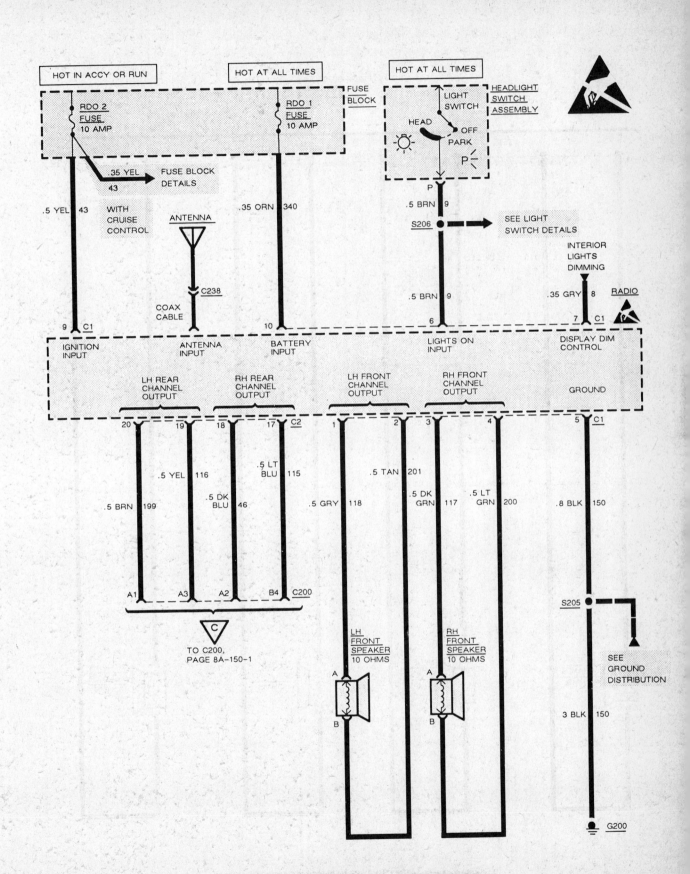

Radio/Audio systems UM7, UN6 and U1C 1982–92 All Models.

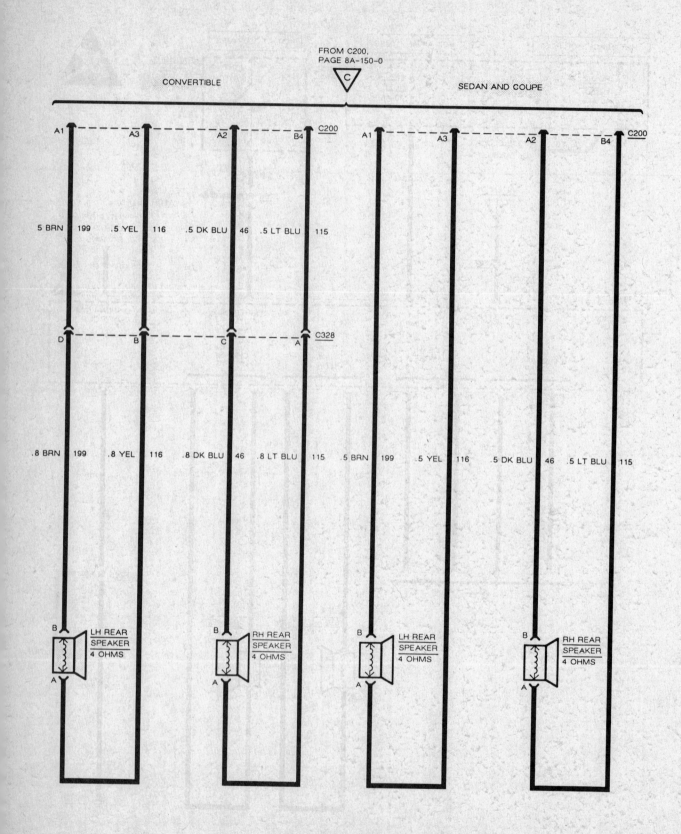

Radio/Audio systems UM7, UN6 and U1C 1982–92 All Models (con't).

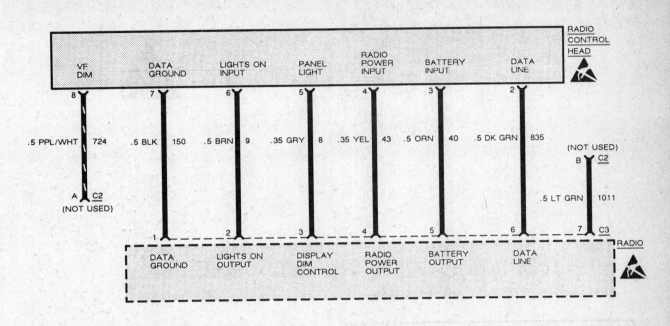

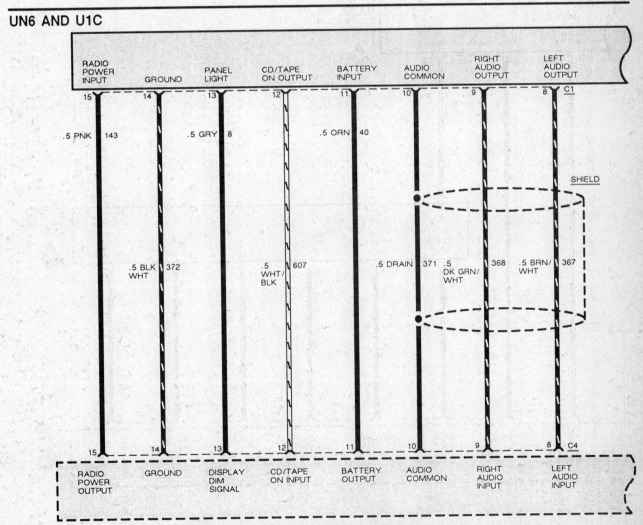

Radio/Audio systems UM7, UN6 and U1C 1982–92 All Models (con't).

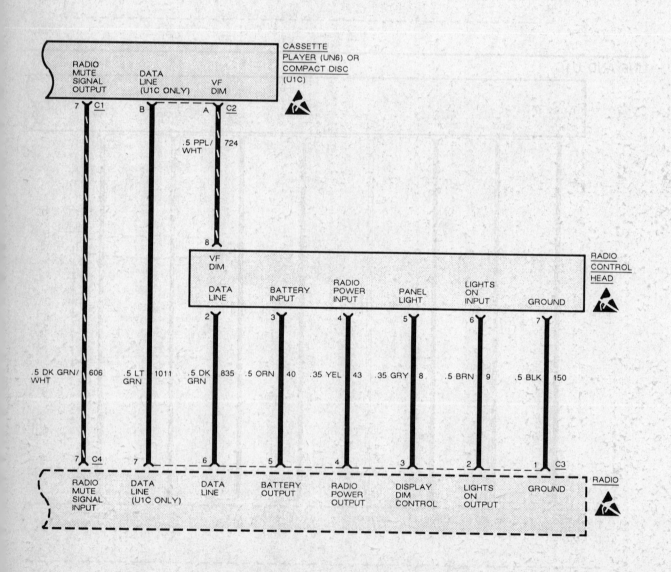

Radio/Audio systems UM7, UN6 and U1C 1982–92 All Models (con't).

Troubleshooting Basic Turn Signal and Flasher Problems

Most problems in the turn signals or flasher system can be reduced to defective flashers or bulbs, which are easily replaced. Occasionally, problems in the turn signals are traced to the switch in the steering column, which will require professional service.

F = Front   R = Rear   ● = Lights off   o = Lights on

Problem		Solution
Turn signals light, but do not flash		• Replace the flasher
No turn signals light on either side		• Check the fuse. Replace if defective. • Check the flasher by substitution • Check for open circuit, short circuit or poor ground
Both turn signals on one side don't work		• Check for bad bulbs • Check for bad ground in both housings
One turn signal light on one side doesn't work		• Check and/or replace bulb • Check for corrosion in socket. Clean contacts. • Check for poor ground at socket
Turn signal flashes too fast or too slow		• Check any bulb on the side flashing too fast. A heavy-duty bulb is probably installed in place of a regular bulb. • Check the bulb flashing too slow. A standard bulb was probably installed in place of a heavy-duty bulb. • Check for loose connections or corrosion at the bulb socket
Indicator lights don't work in either direction		• Check if the turn signals are working • Check the dash indicator lights • Check the flasher by substitution

Troubleshooting Basic Turn Signal and Flasher Problems

Most problems in the turn signals or flasher system can be reduced to defective flashers or bulbs, which are easily replaced. Occasionally, problems in the turn signals are traced to the switch in the steering column, which will require professional service.

F = Front   R = Rear   ● = Lights off   o = Lights on

Problem		Solution
One indicator light doesn't light		• On systems with 1 dash indicator: See if the lights work on the same side. Often the filaments have been reversed in systems combining stoplights with taillights and turn signals. Check the flasher by substitution • On systems with 2 indicators: Check the bulbs on the same side Check the indicator light bulb Check the flasher by substitution

Troubleshooting Basic Lighting Problems

Problem	Cause	Solution
Lights		
One or more lights don't work, but others do	• Defective bulb(s) • Blown fuse(s) • Dirty fuse clips or light sockets • Poor ground circuit	• Replace bulb(s) • Replace fuse(s) • Clean connections • Run ground wire from light socket housing to car frame
Lights burn out quickly	• Incorrect voltage regulator setting or defective regulator • Poor battery/alternator connections	• Replace voltage regulator • Check battery/alternator connections
Lights go dim	• Low/discharged battery • Alternator not charging • Corroded sockets or connections • Low voltage output	• Check battery • Check drive belt tension; repair or replace alternator • Clean bulb and socket contacts and connections • Replace voltage regulator

Troubleshooting Basic Lighting Problems

Problem	Cause	Solution
Lights		
Lights flicker	• Loose connection • Poor ground • Circuit breaker operating (short circuit)	• Tighten all connections • Run ground wire from light housing to car frame • Check connections and look for bare wires
Lights "flare"—Some flare is normal on acceleration—if excessive, see "Lights Burn Out Quickly"	• High voltage setting	• Replace voltage regulator
Lights glare—approaching drivers are blinded	• Lights adjusted too high • Rear springs or shocks sagging • Rear tires soft	• Have headlights aimed • Check rear springs/shocks • Check/correct rear tire pressure
Turn Signals		
Turn signals don't work in either direction	• Blown fuse • Defective flasher • Loose connection	• Replace fuse • Replace flasher • Check/tighten all connections
Right (or left) turn signal only won't work	• Bulb burned out • Right (or left) indicator bulb burned out • Short circuit	• Replace bulb • Check/replace indicator bulb • Check/repair wiring
Flasher rate too slow or too fast	• Incorrect wattage bulb • Incorrect flasher	• Flasher bulb • Replace flasher (use a variable load flasher if you pull a trailer)
Indicator lights do not flash (burn steadily)	• Burned out bulb • Defective flasher	• Replace bulb • Replace flasher
Indicator lights do not light at all	• Burned out indicator bulb • Defective flasher	• Replace indicator bulb • Replace flasher

Troubleshooting Basic Dash Gauge Problems

Problem	Cause	Solution
Coolant Temperature Gauge		
Gauge reads erratically or not at all	• Loose or dirty connections • Defective sending unit	• Clean/tighten connections • Bi-metal gauge: remove the wire from the sending unit. Ground the wire for an instant. If the gauge registers, replace the sending unit.
	• Defective gauge	• Magnetic gauge: disconnect the wire at the sending unit. With ignition ON gauge should register COLD. Ground the wire; gauge should register HOT.
Ammeter Gauge—Turn Headlights ON (do not start engine). Note reaction		
Ammeter shows charge Ammeter shows discharge Ammeter does not move	• Connections reversed on gauge • Ammeter is OK • Loose connections or faulty wiring • Defective gauge	• Reinstall connections • Nothing • Check/correct wiring • Replace gauge
Oil Pressure Gauge		
Gauge does not register or is inaccurate	• On mechanical gauge, Bourdon tube may be bent or kinked	• Check tube for kinks or bends preventing oil from reaching the gauge
	• Low oil pressure	• Remove sending unit. Idle the engine briefly. If no oil flows from sending unit hole, problem is in engine.
	• Defective gauge	• Remove the wire from the sending unit and ground it for an instant with the ignition ON. A good gauge will go to the top of the scale.
	• Defective wiring	• Check the wiring to the gauge. If it's OK and the gauge doesn't register when grounded, replace the gauge.
	• Defective sending unit	• If the wiring is OK and the gauge functions when grounded, replace the sending unit
All Gauges		
All gauges do not operate	• Blown fuse • Defective instrument regulator	• Replace fuse • Replace instrument voltage regulator
All gauges read low or erratically	• Defective or dirty instrument voltage regulator	• Clean contacts or replace
All gauges pegged	• Loss of ground between instrument voltage regulator and car • Defective instrument regulator	• Check ground • Replace regulator

Troubleshooting Basic Dash Gauge Problems

Problem	Cause	Solution
Warning Lights		
Light(s) do not come on when ignition is ON, but engine is not started	• Defective bulb • Defective wire • Defective sending unit	• Replace bulb • Check wire from light to sending unit • Disconnect the wire from the sending unit and ground it. Replace the sending unit if the light comes on with the ignition ON.
Light comes on with engine running	• Problem in individual system • Defective sending unit	• Check system • Check sending unit (see above)

Troubleshooting the Heater

Problem	Cause	Solution
Blower motor will not turn at any speed	• Blown fuse • Loose connection • Defective ground • Faulty switch • Faulty motor • Faulty resistor	• Replace fuse • Inspect and tighten • Clean and tighten • Replace switch • Replace motor • Replace resistor
Blower motor turns at one speed only	• Faulty switch • Faulty resistor	• Replace switch • Replace resistor
Blower motor turns but does not circulate air	• Intake blocked • Fan not secured to the motor shaft	• Clean intake • Tighten security
Heater will not heat	• Coolant does not reach proper temperature • Heater core blocked internally • Heater core air-bound • Blend-air door not in proper position	• Check and replace thermostat if necessary • Flush or replace core if necessary • Purge air from core • Adjust cable
Heater will not defrost	• Control cable adjustment incorrect • Defroster hose damaged	• Adjust control cable • Replace defroster hose

Troubleshooting Basic Windshield Wiper Problems

Problem	Cause	Solution
Electric Wipers		
Wipers do not operate— Wiper motor heats up or hums	• Internal motor defect • Bent or damaged linkage • Arms improperly installed on linking pivots	• Replace motor • Repair or replace linkage • Position linkage in park and reinstall wiper arms
Electric Wipers		
Wipers do not operate— No current to motor	• Fuse or circuit breaker blown • Loose, open or broken wiring • Defective switch • Defective or corroded terminals • No ground circuit for motor or switch	• Replace fuse or circuit breaker • Repair wiring and connections • Replace switch • Replace or clean terminals • Repair ground circuits
Wipers do not operate— Motor runs	• Linkage disconnected or broken	• Connect wiper linkage or replace broken linkage
Vacuum Wipers		
Wipers do not operate	• Control switch or cable inoperative • Loss of engine vacuum to wiper motor (broken hoses, low engine vacuum, defective vacuum/fuel pump) • Linkage broken or disconnected • Defective wiper motor	• Repair or replace switch or cable • Check vacuum lines, engine vacuum and fuel pump • Repair linkage • Replace wiper motor
Wipers stop on engine acceleration	• Leaking vacuum hoses • Dry windshield • Oversize wiper blades • Defective vacuum/fuel pump	• Repair or replace hoses • Wet windshield with washers • Replace with proper size wiper blades • Replace pump

TORQUE SPECIFICATIONS

Component	English	Metric
COMPRESSOR ATTACHMENT		
2.2L (VIN 4)		
Compressor Bracket to Engine	67 ft. lbs.	93 Nm
Compressor to Bracket—Front	67 ft. lbs.	93 Nm
Compressor to Bracket—Rear	23 ft. lbs.	31 Nm
3.1L (VIN T)		
Compressor Bracket to Engine	67 ft. lbs.	93 Nm
Compressor to Bracket—Front	35 ft. lbs.	47 Nm
Compressor to Bracket—Rear	23 ft. lbs.	31 Nm
A/C FITTINGS		
Accumulator	31 ft. lbs.	42 Nm
Compressor	25 ft. lbs.	34 Nm
Condenser	19 ft. lbs.	25 Nm
Evaporator	13 ft. lbs.	17 Nm
Inline Filter (When Installed)	11 ft. lbs.	15 Nm

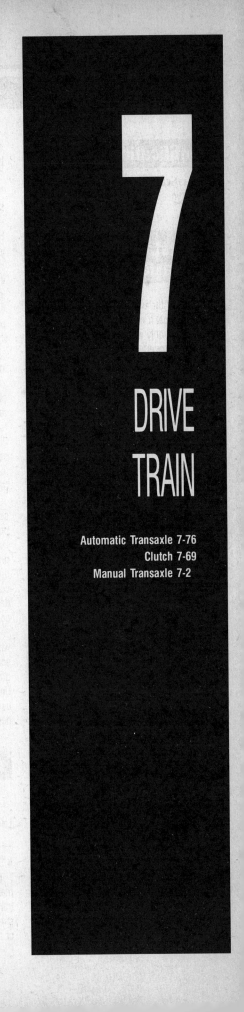

7

DRIVE TRAIN

MANUAL TRANSAXLE

Identification

Refer to Section 1 for a complete identification of all the types of transaxles used.

Understanding the Transaxle

Because of the way an internal combustion engine breathes, it can produce torque, or twisting force, only within a narrow speed range. Most modern, overhead valve engines must turn at about 2,500 rpm to produce their peak torque. By 4,500 rpm they are producing so little torque that continued increases in engine speed produce no power increases.

The torque peak on overhead camshaft engines is, generally, much higher, but much narrower.

The manual transaxle and clutch are employed to vary the relationship between engine speed and the speed of the wheels so that adequate engine power can be produced under all circumstances. The clutch allows engine torque to be applied to the transaxle input shaft gradually, due to mechanical slippage. The car can, consequently, be started smoothly from a full stop.

The transaxle changes the ratio between the rotating speeds of the engine and the wheels by the use of gears. 4-speed or 5-speed transaxles are most common. The lower gears allow full engine power to be applied to the wheels during acceleration at low speeds.

The transaxle contains a mainshaft which passes all the way through the transaxle, from the clutch to the halfshafts. This shaft is separated at 1 point, so that front and rear portions can turn at different speeds.

Power is transmitted by a countershaft in the lower gears and reverse. The gears of the countershaft mesh with gears on the mainshaft, allowing power to be carried from one to the other. All the countershaft gears are integral with that shaft, while several of the mainshaft gears can either rotate independently of the shaft or be locked to it. Shifting from one gear to the next causes one of the gears to be freed from rotating with the shaft and locks another to it. Gears are locked and unlocked by internal dog clutches which slide between the center of the gear and the shaft. The forward gears usually employ synchronizers; friction members which

smoothly bring gear and shaft to the same speed before the toothed dog clutches are engaged.

The clutch is operating properly if:

1. It will stall the engine when released with the vehicle held stationary.

2. The shift lever can be moved freely between 1st and reverse gears when the vehicle is stationary and the clutch disengaged.

A clutch pedal free-play adjustment is incorporated in the linkage. If there is about 1–2 in. (25–50mm) of motion before the pedal begins to release the clutch, it is adjusted properly. Inadequate free-play wears all parts of the clutch releasing mechanisms and may cause slippage. Excessive free-play may cause inadequate release and hard shifting of gears.

Some clutches use a hydraulic system in place of mechanical linkage. If the clutch fails to release, fill the clutch master cylinder with fluid to the proper level and pump the clutch pedal to fill the system with fluid. Bleed the system in the same way as a brake system. If leaks are located, tighten loose connections or overhaul the master or slave cylinder as necessary.

Front wheel drive cars do not have conventional rear axles or driveshafts. Instead, power is transmitted from the engine to a transaxle, or a combination of transmission and drive axle, in one unit. Both the transmission and drive axle accomplish the same function as their counterparts in a front engine/rear drive axle design. The difference is in the location of the components.

In place of a conventional driveshaft, a front wheel drive design uses 2 driveshafts, sometimes called halfshafts, which couple the drive axle portion of the transaxle to the wheels. Universal joints or constant velocity joints are used just as they would in a rear wheel drive design.

Adjustments

LINKAGE

◆ SEE FIGS. 1 and 2

No adjustments are possible on the 1988–92 manual transaxle shifting cables or linkage. If the transaxle is not engaging completely, check for stretched cables or broken shifter components or a faulty transaxle.

4-Speed

1982–87

1. Disconnect the negative battery cable.

2. Place the transaxle in 1st gear, then loosen the shift cable attaching nuts **E** at the transaxle lever **D** and **F**.

3. Remove the console trim plate and remove the shifter boot and retainer.

4. With the shift lever in the 1st gear position (pulled to the left and held against the stop) insert a yoke clip to hold the lever hard against the reverse lockout stop as shown in view **D**. Install a No. 22 ($5/32$ in.) drill bit into the alignment hole at the side of the shifter assembly as shown in view **C**.

5. Remove the lash from the transaxle by rotating the upright select lever (lever D) while tightening the cable attaching pin nut **E**.

6. Tighten nut **E** on letter **F**.

7. Remove the drill bit and yoke at the shifter assembly, install the shifter boot and retainer and connect the negative battery cable.

8. Connect the negative batery cable.

9. Install the shifter boot and trim plate.

10. Road test the vehicle to check for good gate feel during shifting. Fine tune the adjustment as necessary.

5-Speed

1983–85

1. Disconnect the negative battery cable.

2. Place the transaxle in 3rd gear. Remove the lock pin **H** and reinstall with the tapered end down. This will lock the transaxle in 3rd gear.

3. Loosen the shift cable attaching nuts **E** at the transaxle lever **G** and **F**.

4. Remove the console trim plate and remove the shifter boot. Remove the console.

5. Install a No. 22 ($²f5/32$ in.) drill bit into the alignment hole at the side of the shifter assembly as shown in view **A**.

6. Align the hole in select lever (view B) with the slot in the shifter plate and install a $3/16$ in. drill bit.

7. Tighten nut **E** at levers **G** and **F**.

8. Remove the drill bits from the alignment holes at the shifter. Remove lockpin **H**.

9. Install the console, shifter boot and retainer and connect the negative battery cable.

10. Road test the vehicle to check for good gate feel during shifting. Fine tune the adjustment as necessary.

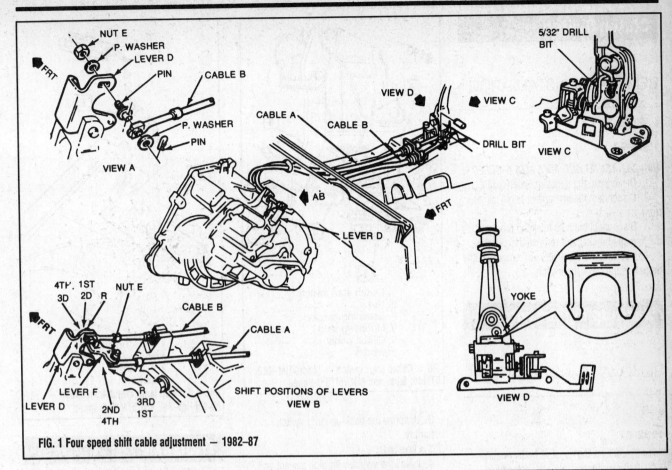

FIG. 1 Four speed shift cable adjustment — 1982–87

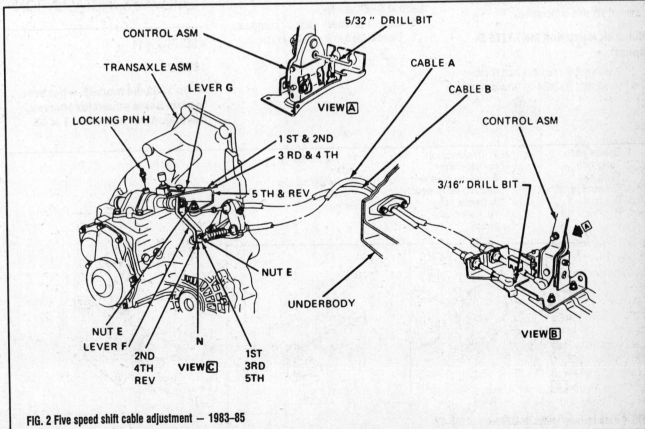

FIG. 2 Five speed shift cable adjustment — 1983–85

Clutch Switch

REMOVAL & INSTALLATION

♦ SEE FIG. 3

1988–92

HM–282, ISUZU AND MK7/MT5 5-SPEED

1. Disconnect the negative battery cable.
2. Disconnect the instrument panel harness from the switch.
3. Disconnect the nuts retaining the switch to the harness bracket and remove the switch.
4. Installation is the reverse of removal. Verify proper operation of the switch.

Back-up Light Switch

REMOVAL & INSTALLATION

♦ SEE FIGS. 4-7

1982–87

1. Disconnect the negative battery cable.
2. Remove the console and replace the switch at the side of the shifter.

HM–282, Isuzu and MK7/MT5 5-Speed

1. Disconnect the negative battery cable.
2. Disconnect the back-up lamp connector.

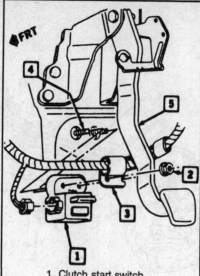

1. Clutch start switch
2. Nut
3. Retaining bracket
4. Mounting stud
5. Clutch pedal assembly

FIG. 3 Clutch start switch — Model HM–282, 5TM40, Isuzu and MK7/MT5 5-Speed

3. Unscrew the back-up lamp switch assembly.

To install:

4. Install the switch with pipe sealant and tighten to 80–84 inch lbs.
5. Connect the switch electrical connector.
6. Connect the negative battery cable.

1. Back-up switch assembly
2. Transaxle assembly

FIG. 5 Back-up lamp switch installation — Model HM–282 and 5TM40 5-speed

Transaxle

REMOVAL & INSTALLATION

♦ SEE FIGS. 8-14

1982–88

➡ On 1982–84 models, whenever the transaxle mount is removed, the alignment bolt M6 × 1 × 65

1. Detent plate
2. Tang hole
3. Tang slot
4. "Neutral" notch
5. R
6. P
7. Transmission control shifter
8. Neutral start and back-up lamp switch
9. Carrier tang
10. Park brake switch
11. Transmission shifter
12. Retaining clip
13. Back-up lamp switch

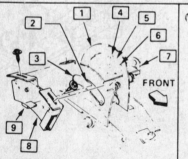
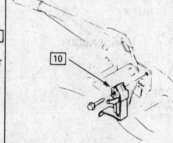
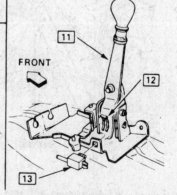

FIG. 4 Back-up lamp switch installation — 1982–87

must be installed in the right front engine mount to prevent power train misalignment

1. Disconnect the negative battery cable.

2. Install an engine holding bar so that one end is supported on the cowl tray over the wiper motor and the other end rests on the radiator support. Use padding and be careful not to damage the paint or body work with the bar. Attach a lifting hook to the engine lift ring and to the bar and raise the engine enough to take the pressure off the motor mounts.

➡ **If a lifting bar and hook is not available, a chain hoist can be used, however, during the procedure the vehicle must be raised, at which time the chain hoist must be adjusted to keep tension on the engine/transaxle assembly.**

3. Remove the heater hose clamp at the transaxle mount bracket. Disconnect the electrical connector and remove the horn assembly on 4 cyl. models.

4. Remove the transaxle mount attaching bolts. Discard the bolts attaching the mount to the side frame: New bolts must be used at installation.

5. On 1982–84 models, disconnect the clutch cable from the clutch release lever. On 1985–87 models, disconnect the clutch slave cylinder from the transaxle support bracket and lay aside. Remove the transaxle mount bracket attaching bolts and nuts.

6. On V6 engines remove the following:

   a. Remove the air intake duct from the air cleaner.

   b. Remove the left fender brace.

   c. Disconnect the M.A.T. sensor lead at the air cleaner.

   d. Disconnect the mass air flow sensor lead.

   e. Remove the PCV pipe retaining clamp from the air intake duct.

   f. Remove the clamp retaining the air intake duct to the throttle body.

   g. Remove the Mass Air Flow Sensor mounting boltRemove the air cleaner bracket mounting bolts at the battery tray.

   h. Remove the air cleaner, mass air flow sensor and air intake duct as an assembly.

   i. Remove the heat shield at the crossover pipe and remove the crossover pipe.

6. Disconnect the shift cables and retaining clips at the transaxle. Disconnect the ground cables at the transaxle mounting stud.

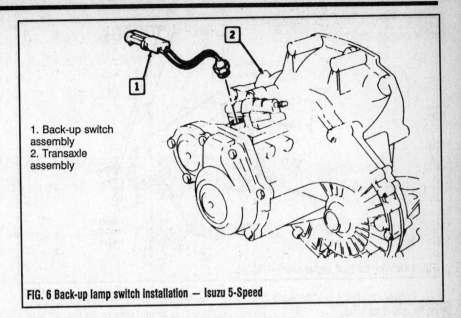

1. Back-up switch assembly
2. Transaxle assembly

FIG. 6 Back-up lamp switch installation — Isuzu 5-Speed

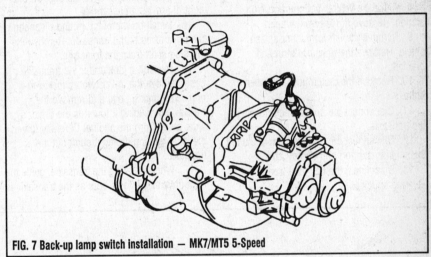

FIG. 7 Back-up lamp switch installation — MK7/MT5 5-Speed

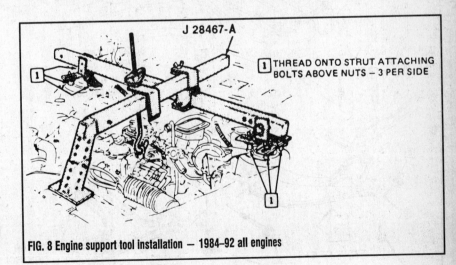

J 28467-A

1 THREAD ONTO STRUT ATTACHING BOLTS ABOVE NUTS – 3 PER SIDE

FIG. 8 Engine support tool installation — 1984–92 all engines

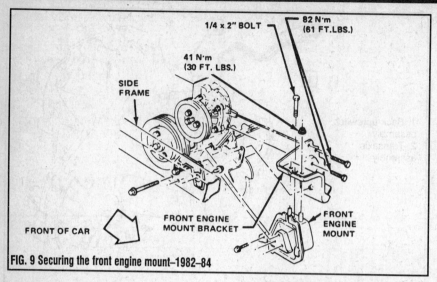

FIG. 9 Securing the front engine mount–1982–84

7. Remove the four upper transaxle-to-engine mounting bolts.

8. Raise the vehicle and support it on stands. Remove the left front wheel.

9. Remove the left front inner splash shield. Remove the transaxle strut and bracket.

10. Remove the clutch housing cover bolts.

11. Disconnect the speedometer cable at the transaxle.

12. Disconnect the stabilizer bar at the left suspension support and control arm.

13. Disconnect the ball joint from the steering knuckle.

14. Remove the left suspension support attaching bolts and remove the support and control arm as an assembly.

15. Install boot protectors and disengage the drive axles at the transaxle. Remove the left side shaft from the transaxle.

16. Position a jack under the transaxle case, remove the lower two transaxle-to-engine mounting bolts and remove the transaxle by sliding it towards the driver's side, away from the engine. Carefully lower the jack, guiding the right shaft out the transaxle.

17. When installing the transaxle, guide the right drive axle into its bore as the transaxle is

being raised. The right drive axle CANNOT be readily installed after the transaxle is connected to the engine. Tighten the transaxle-to-engine mounting bolts to 55 ft. lbs. Tighten the suspension support-to-body attaching bolts to 59 ft. Lbs. on 1985–87 models and 65–67 ft. lbs. on all other years. Tighten the clutch housing cover bolts to 10 ft. lbs. Using new bolts, install and tighten the transaxle mount-to-side frame to 40 ft. lbs. When installing the bolts attaching the mount-to-transaxle bracket on the 1982–84 models, check the alignment bolt at the engine mount. If excessive effort is required to remove the alignment bolt, realign the powertrain components and tighten the bolts to 40 ft. lbs., and then remove the alignment bolt.

1989–92

EXCEPT ISUZU TRANSAXLE

1. Disconnect the negative battery cable.

2. Install an engine holding support fixture (bar), J–28467–A or equivalent.

➡ **If a lifting bar and hook is not available, a chain hoist can be used, however, during the procedure the vehicle must be raised, at which time the chain hoist must be adjusted to keep tension on the engine/transaxle assembly.**

3. Remove the left sound insulator.

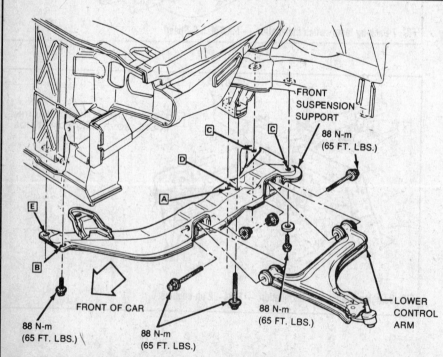

FIG. 11 The front suspension support must be attached in this sequence

FRONT SUSPENSION SUPPORT ATTACHING BOLT/SCREW SEQUENCE

1. INSTALL LOOSELY, THE CENTER SCREW INTO HOLE A.

2. INSTALL LOOSELY, THE TIE BAR SCREW INTO THE SMALL SLOTTED OUTBOARD HOLE.

3. INSTALL AND TORQUE BOTH BOLTS IN THE REAR HOLES.

4. INSTALL AND TORQUE 2ND CENTER HOLE D BOLT/SCREW.

5. TORQUE CENTER HOLE A BOLT.

6. INSTALL OTHER TIE BAR BOLT (FRONT HOLE E) AND TORQUE.

7. TORQUE 2ND BOLT/SCREW IN THE (FRONT HOLE B).

4. Disconnect the clutch master cylinder pushrod from the clutch pedal.

5. Remove the air cleaner and air intake duct assembly.

6. Remove the clutch actuator cylinder from the transaxle support bracket and lay it aside.

7. Remove the transaxle mount through bolt.

8. Raise and support the vehicle safely.

9. Remove the exhaust crossover bolts at the right hand manifold.

10. Lower the vehicle.

11. Disconnect the transaxle mount bracket.

12. Disconnect the shift cables and linkage.

13. Remove the transaxle mount tube.

14. Remove the upper transaxle to engine bolts.

15. Raise and support the vehicle safely.

16. Remove the left front tire and wheel.

17. Remove the left front inner splash shield.

18. Disconnect the transaxle strut and bracket.

19. Drain the transaxle.

20. Remove the clutch housing cover bolts.

21. Disconnect the speedometer cable.

22. Disconnect the stabilizer shaft at the left suspension support and control arm.

23. Remove the left suspension support attaching bolts and swing the suspension support aside.

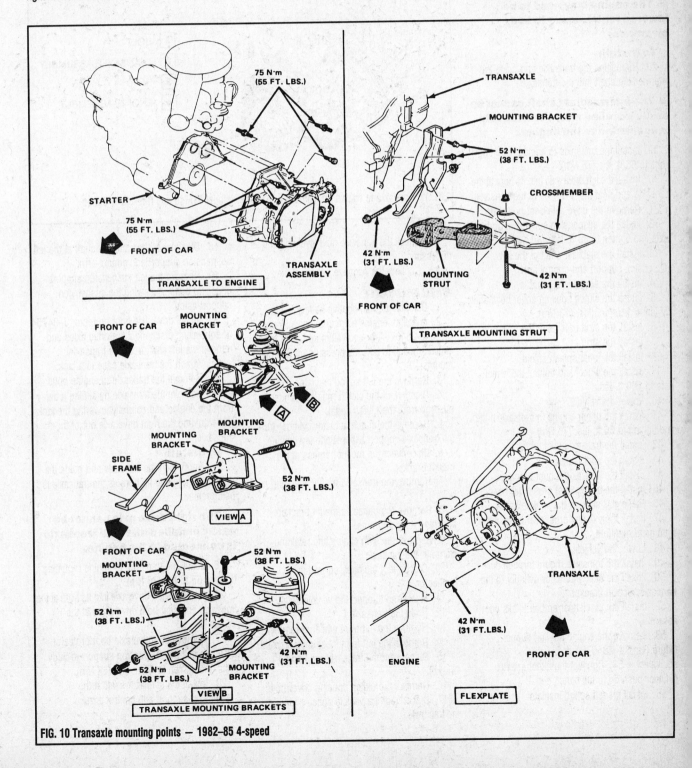

FIG. 10 Transaxle mounting points — 1982–85 4-speed

24. Install drive axle boot protector J–34754 or equivalent and remove the left drive axle from the transaxle.

25. Attach the transaxle case to a jack.

26. Remove the ramaining transaxle to engine bolts.

27. Remove the transaxle by sliding it away from the engine and carefully lowering the jack while guiding the intermediate shaft out of the transaxle.

➡ **The engine may need to be lowered for transaxle to body clearance.**

To Install:

28. Reposition the transaxle and guide the intermediate shaft into the transaxle.

➡ **The Intermediate shaft cannot be easily Installed after the transaxle Is connected to the engine.**

29. Install the transaxle to engine mounting bolts to 55 ft. lbs (75 Nm).

30. Install the left drive axle into its bore at the transaxle and seat the driveaxle at the transaxle.

31. Remove the drive axle boot protector.

32. Install the suspension support to body bolts and tighten to 65 ft. lbs. (88 Nm).

33. Install the stabiizer shaft at the left suspension support and control arm.

34. Install the speedometer cable.

35. Install the clutch housing cover bolts and tighten to 115 inch lbs. (13 Nm).

36. Install the strut bracket to the transaxle.

37. Install the strut.

38. Install the inner splash shield.

39. Install the wheel and tighten the wheel nuts to 100 ft. lbs.

40. Lower the vehicle.

41. Install the upper engine to transaxle bolts and tighten to 55 ft. lbs. (75 Nm).

42. Install the transaxle vent tube.

43. Install the shift cables.

44. Install the transaxle mount bracket.

45. Install the left exhaust crossover bolts.

46. Raise and support the vehicle safely.

47. Install the exhaust crossover bolts at the right hand manifold.

48. Lower the vehicle.

49. Install the transaxle mount through bolt.

50. Install the clutch actuator cylinder to the transaxle support bracket.

52. Install the air cleaner and air intake duct assembly.

53. Remove the engine holding support fixture (bar), J–28467–A or equivalent. ◆54. Connect the clutch master cylinder pushrod to the clutch pedal.

55. Install the left sound insulator.

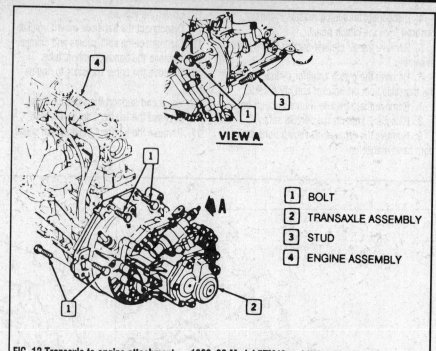

VIEW A

1	BOLT
2	TRANSAXLE ASSEMBLY
3	STUD
4	ENGINE ASSEMBLY

FIG. 12 Transaxle to engine attachment — 1989–92 Model 5TM40 and HM–282 5-Speed

56. Check the transaxle fluid level and add as necessary.

55. Connect the negative battery cable.

ISUZU TRANSAXLE

1. Disconnect the negative battery cable.

2. Install an engine holding support fixture (bar), J–28467–A or equivalent and raise the engine enough to take the pressure off the motor mounts.

3. Remove the left sound insulator.

4. Disconnect the clutch master cylinder pushrod from the clutch pedal.

5. Remove the clutch actuator cylinder from the transaxle support bracket and lay it aside.

6. Disconnect the mount harness at the mount bracket.

7. Remove the transaxle mount attaching bolts.

8. Remove the transaxle mount bracket attaching bolts and nuts.

9. Remove the shift cables and retaining clamp at the transaxle.

10. Disconnect the back-up switch connector.

11. Raise and support the vehicle safely.

12. Drain the transaxle.

13. Remove the left front wheel assembly.

14. Remove the left front inner splash shield.

15. Disconnect the transaxle strut and bracket.

16. Remove the clutch housing cover bolts.

17. Disconnect the vehicle speed sensor at the transaxle.

18. Disconnect the stabilizer shaft at the left suspension support and control arm.

19. Remove the left suspension support attaching bolts and swing the suspension support aside.

20. Install drive axle boot protector J–34754 or equivalent, disconnect the drive axles and remove the left shaft from the transaxle.

21. Attach the transaxle case to a jack.

22. Remove the transaxle to engine bolts.

23. Remove the transaxle by sliding it away from the engine and carefully lowering the jack while guiding the right drive axle out of the transaxle.

To Install:

24. Reposition the transaxle and guide the right drive axle into its bore as the transaxle is being raised.

➡ **The right drive axle cannot be easily Installed after the transaxle Is connected to the engine.**

25. Install the transaxle to engine mounting bolts to 55 ft. lbs (75 Nm).

26. Install the left drive axle into its bore at the transaxle and seat both drive axles at the transaxle.

27. Remove the drive axle boot protector.

28. Install the suspension support to body bolts and tighten to 65 ft. lbs. (88 Nm).

29. Install the stabilizer shaft at the suspension support and control arm.

30. Install the vehicle speed sensor at the transaxle.

31. Install the clutch housing cover bolts and tighten to 115 inch lbs. (13 Nm).

32. Install the strut bracket to the transaxle.

33. Install the strut.

34. Install the inner splash shield.

35. Install the wheel and tighten the wheel nuts to 100 ft. lbs.

36. Lower the vehicle.

37. Install the ground cables at the transaxle mounting studs.

38. Install the back-up switch connector.

39. Install the actuator cylinder to the transaxle bracket aligning the pushrod into the pocket of the clutch release lever and install the retaining nuts and tighten evenly to prevent damage to the cylinder.

40. Install the transaxle mount bracket.

41. Install the transaxle mount to side frame and install the bolts.

42. Install the wiring harness at the transaxle mount bracket.

43. Install the bolt attaching the mount to the transaxle bracket and tigten to 88 ft. lbs. (120 Nm).

44. Remove the engine holding support fixture (bar), J–28467–A or equivalent.

45. Install the shift cables.

46. Check the transaxle fluid level and add as necessary.

47. Connect the negative battery cable.

OVERHAUL

All Except Isuzu

AXLE SHAFT SEAL REPLACEMENT
◆ SEE FIGS. 15-53

➡ **To perform this procedure, you will need a seal installer backed up by a driver handle. Use GM Part Nos. J–26938 and J–8092 or the equivalent.**

1. Disconnect the negative battery cable. Remove the axle from the car as described in the appropriate car section.

2. Carefully pry the old axle seal out of the transaxle.

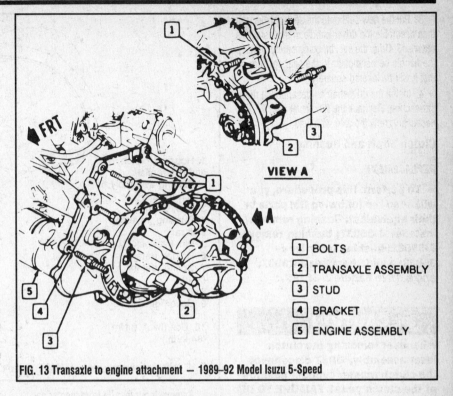

VIEW A

1	BOLTS
2	TRANSAXLE ASSEMBLY
3	STUD
4	BRACKET
5	ENGINE ASSEMBLY

FIG. 13 Transaxle to engine attachment — 1989–92 Model Isuzu 5-Speed

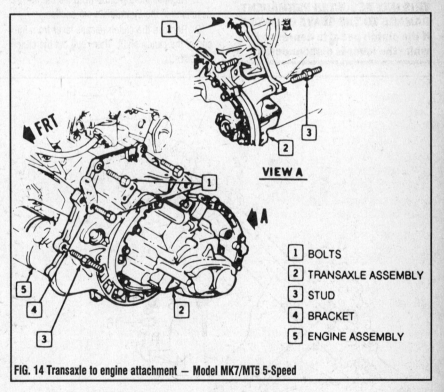

VIEW A

1	BOLTS
2	TRANSAXLE ASSEMBLY
3	STUD
4	BRACKET
5	ENGINE ASSEMBLY

FIG. 14 Transaxle to engine attachment — Model MK7/MT5 5-Speed

3. Put the new seal onto the seal installer and then assemble the driver handle to the installer's outer end. Drive the seal in, being careful to keep the handle perpendicular to the seal aperture so that it will be located squarely.

4. Install the driveshaft as described in the car section. Recheck the fluid level and, if necessary, refill the axle with fluid.

Clutch Shaft and Bushing

REPLACEMENT

➡ **To perform this procedure, you will need the following GM parts or their equivalent: Bushing remover/installer J–36037; bushing remover J–36032; bushing installer J–36033; a slide hammer J–23907; and a drive handle J–36190.**

✳✳ **CAUTION**

Whenever removing the clutch lever assembly, FIRST disconnect the clutch master cylinder pushrod at the clutch pedal. FAILURE TO DO THIS MAY RESULT IN PERMANENT DAMAGE TO THE SLAVE CYLINDER, if the clutch pedal is depressed while the lever is disconnected.

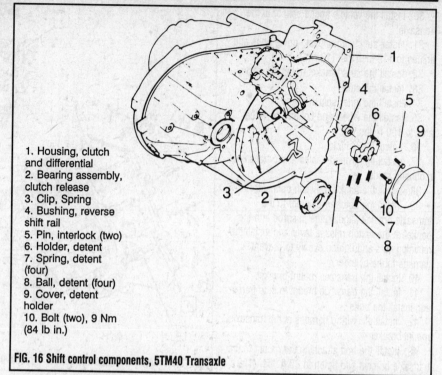

1. Housing, clutch and differential
2. Bearing assembly, clutch release
3. Clip, Spring
4. Bushing, reverse shift rail
5. Pin, interlock (two)
6. Holder, detent
7. Spring, detent (four)
8. Ball, detent (four)
9. Cover, detent holder
10. Bolt (two), 9 Nm (84 lb in.)

FIG. 16 Shift control components, 5TM40 Transaxle

1. Remove the transaxle from the car as described in the appropriate car section.

2. Remove the clutch release lever from the end of the clutch shaft. Then, pull out the clutch shaft seal.

3. Drive the upper clutch shaft bushing into the transaxle housing with a hammer and the bushing remover/installer. Then, turn the clutch shaft slightly for clearance and remove it from the clutch housing.

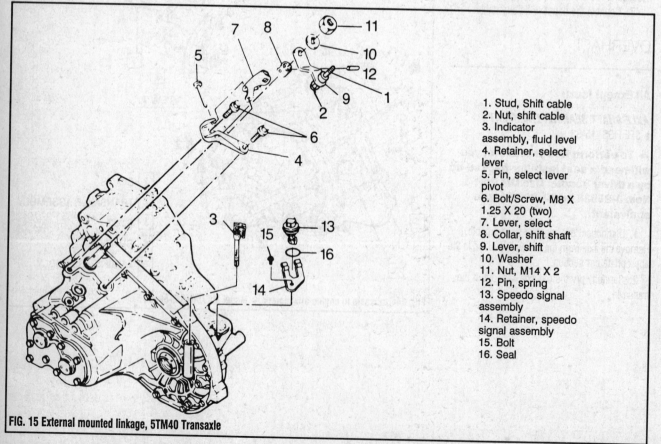

1. Stud, Shift cable
2. Nut, shift cable
3. Indicator assembly, fluid level
4. Retainer, select lever
5. Pin, select lever pivot
6. Bolt/Screw, M8 X 1.25 X 20 (two)
7. Lever, select
8. Collar, shift shaft
9. Lever, shift
10. Washer
11. Nut, M14 X 2
12. Pin, spring
13. Speedo signal assembly
14. Retainer, speedo signal assembly
15. Bolt
16. Seal

FIG. 15 External mounted linkage, 5TM40 Transaxle

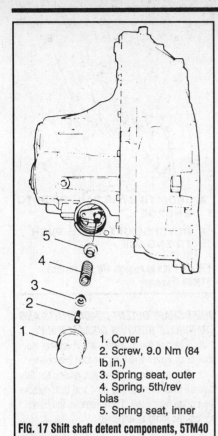

1. Cover
2. Screw, 9.0 Nm (84 lb in.)
3. Spring seat, outer
4. Spring, 5th/rev bias
5. Spring seat, inner

FIG. 17 Shift shaft detent components, 5TM40 Transaxle

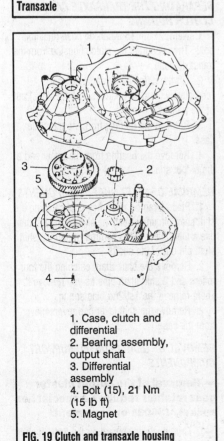

1. Case, clutch and differential
2. Bearing assembly, output shaft
3. Differential assembly
4. Bolt (15), 21 Nm (15 lb ft)
5. Magnet

FIG. 19 Clutch and transaxle housing components, 5TM40 Transaxle

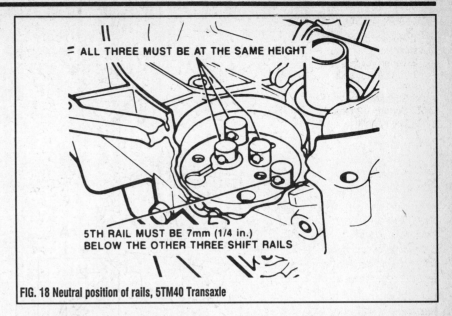

ALL THREE MUST BE AT THE SAME HEIGHT

5TH RAIL MUST BE 7mm (1/4 in.) BELOW THE OTHER THREE SHIFT RAILS

FIG. 18 Neutral position of rails, 5TM40 Transaxle

4. Install the bushing remover and slide hammer, engaging the second step on the bushing remover below the bushing and then tighten the screw to expand the legs and force the bushing out of its position in the housing. Then, remove the bushing and tools.

5. Install the lower bushing by slipping it onto the end of tool 36033 or equivalent. Slide the tool and new bushing through the upper bushing bore and down into the lower bore, and then use the slide hammer to force the bushing fully into the bore.

6. Install the clutch shaft.

7. Install the upper bushing with J–36037 or equivalent. Tap the busing into the bore until the line on the tool is flush with the housing surface.

8. Install the dust seal. Then, install the clutch release lever, torquing the through bolt to 37 ft. lbs.

9. Reinstall the transaxle. Check the fluid level and, if necessary, add fluid.

Shift Shaft Seal

REPLACEMENT

➡ **To perform this procedure, you will need a seal installer GM tool No. J–35823 or equivalent.**

1. Loosen the pinch bolt on the shift shaft lever. Then, remove the lever from the shaft.

2. Slide the cylindrical seal off the shaft.

3. Use the seal installer to install the seal onto the shaft. Then, install the pinch bolts and torque the through bolt/nut to 20 ft. lbs.

A. LOCATION OF PIN (158)

FIG. 20 Shift lever pin removal, 5TM40 Transaxle

Disassembly of Transaxle

EXTERNAL LINKAGE REMOVAL

✳✳ CAUTION

The shift shaft must NOT turn during the next step, or the transaxle may be damaged.

1. Fit a large wrench onto the shift lever to keep it from turning; then, unscrew the nut located at the top of the shift shaft.

2. Remove the washer, lever, pivot pin, and pivot.

3. Remove the pin and then the collar located just below the shift lever.

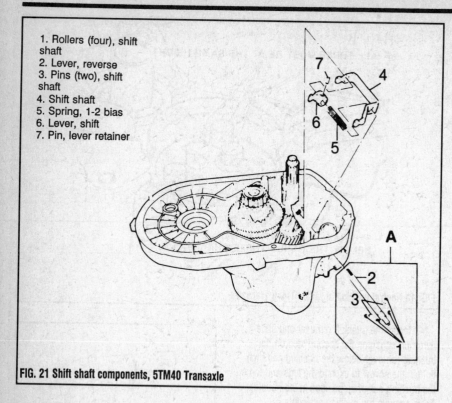

1. Rollers (four), shift shaft
2. Lever, reverse
3. Pins (two), shift shaft
4. Shift shaft
5. Spring, 1-2 bias
6. Lever, shift
7. Pin, lever retainer

FIG. 21 Shift shaft components, 5TM40 Transaxle

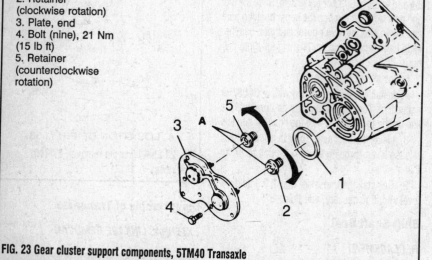

1. Shim (selective)
2. Retainer (clockwise rotation)
3. Plate, end
4. Bolt (nine), 21 Nm (15 lb ft)
5. Retainer (counterclockwise rotation)

FIG. 23 Gear cluster support components, 5TM40 Transaxle

4. Remove the bolts that hold the shift lever bracket to the transaxle case and then remove the bracket.

5. Unscrew and remove the fluid level indicator and then the washer underneath it.

6. Remove the electronic speedometer signal unit, the retainer mounting bolt, and the retainer.

SHIFT RAIL DETENT AND CLUTCH AND DIFFERENTIAL HOUSING DISASSEMBLY

1. Remove the clutch throwout bearing. Puncture the detent holder cover near its center and then use an awl or similar tool to pry it off.

2. Earlier models only have an interlock plate. If the transaxle has this piece, remove the 2 interlock plate mounting bolts and then remove the interlock plate.

3. Remove the detent holder, springs (4), and interlock pins (2).

4. Remove the four detent balls.

5. Remove the reverse shift rail bushing by prying it loose via the 2 slots using small prying instruments.

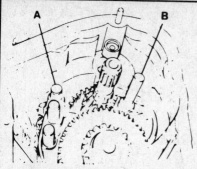

A. 3RD/4TH GEAR RAIL, PUSH TO ENGAGE

B. REVERSE GEAR RAIL, PUSH TO ENGAGE

FIG. 22 Push to engage 4th and reverse, 5TM40 Transaxle

SHIFT SHAFT DETENT COMPONENTS AND TRANSAXLE HOUSING DISASSEMBLY

1. Remove the snapring which retains the shift shaft cover and then remove the cover.

2. Remove the screw which retains the 5th/reverse bias outer spring seat and then remove the spring seat itself. Then, remove the bias spring and inner spring seat.

SEPARATING THE TRANSAXLE CASE AND CLUTCH HOUSING

1. Remove the 15 transaxle case retaining bolts. Then separate the clutch housing from the transaxle case.

2. Lift the differential gear assembly (complete with roller bearings on both sides) out of the transaxle case.

3. Remove the magnet from the transaxle case.

4. Remove the bearing from the upper end of the output shaft.

REMOVAL OF SHIFT SHAFT COMPONENTS

1. Place a rag or other means of catching the shift shaft pin underneath he shift shaft, and then use a thin object and a hammer to tap the shift shaft pin out of the shaft.

2. Remove the shift shaft, catching the four rollers and 2 shift shaft pins as you remove it. Then, remove the 1st/2nd bias spring.

2. Remove the shift lever and reverse lever from the case.

REMOVAL OF GEAR CLUSTER SUPPORT COMPONENTS

➡ **Removal of the output cluster gear retainer requires a special hex socket, J36031 or equivalent.**

1. First, push downward on the 3rd/4th shift rail to engage 4th gear. Then, do the same for the reverse shift rail to engage reverse.

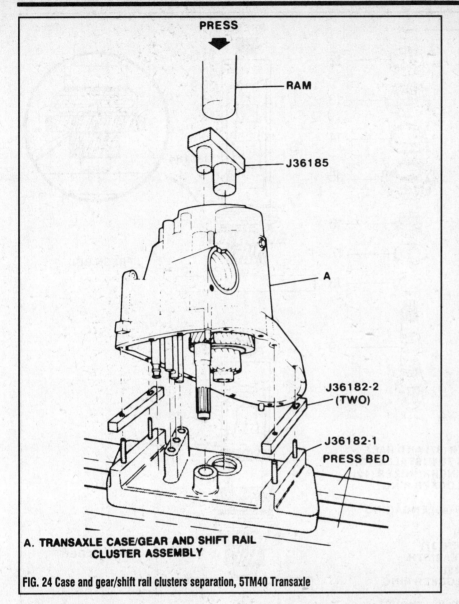

A. TRANSAXLE CASE/GEAR AND SHIFT RAIL CLUSTER ASSEMBLY

FIG. 24 Case and gear/shift rail clusters separation, 5TM40 Transaxle

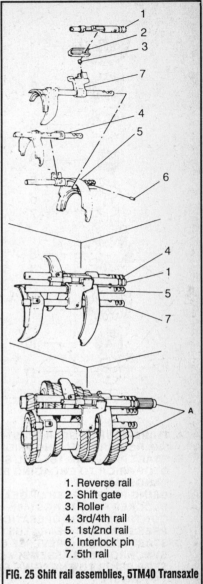

1. Reverse rail
2. Shift gate
3. Roller
4. 3rd/4th rail
5. 1st/2nd rail
6. Interlock pin
7. 5th rail

FIG. 25 Shift rail assemblies, 5TM40 Transaxle

2. Remove the nine retaining bolts from the transaxle end plate. Then remove the end plate.

3. Remove and retain the selective shim from the groove in the housing on the output shaft side.

4. Remove the oil shield located in the center of the same area of the housing; then unscrew and remove the output gear cluster retainer, turning it **clockwise** in order to do so.

5. Remove the input gear cluster retainer using the same tool (rotation is normal). Then, shift both shift rails back to neutral.

REMOVAL OF GEAR CLUSTERS

➡ **To perform this procedure, you'll need: a hydraulic press, a gear cluster and transaxle case assembly and disassembly pallet,** Tool No. J–36182–1 or equivalent; 2 **disassembly adapters J–36282–2 or equivalent, and a J–36185 gear cluster remover.**

1. Slide the adapters onto the 2 pegs on either side of the press. Position the pallet and adapters in the press. Then, position the transaxle case and gear cluster assembly onto the pallet and adapters. Make sure the pilots at the ends of the shift rails and input and output shafts align with the corresponding holes in the fixture.

2. Position the gear cluster remover on top of the shaft support bearings and pilot surfaces.

3. Locate the ram of the press squarely on top of the gear cluster remover. Then, press the shafts and gear clusters out of the transaxle case.

REMOVAL OF SHIFT RAILS

4. Remove the transaxle case from the press. Remove the 1–2 shift rail assembly. Then, remove the lock pin from the assembly.

5. Remove the 3–4 rail assembly. Remove the 5th gear rail assembly. Finally, remove the reverse rail assembly.

6. Remove the shift gate. Disengage and then remove the shift gate roller.

DISASSEMBLY AND INSPECTION

➡ **You'll need an oven that will produce 250°F (121°C) and hold gear assemblies or the gear cluster and other small parts to reassemble the unit. You'll also need hot tap water to heat the speedometer gear prior to**

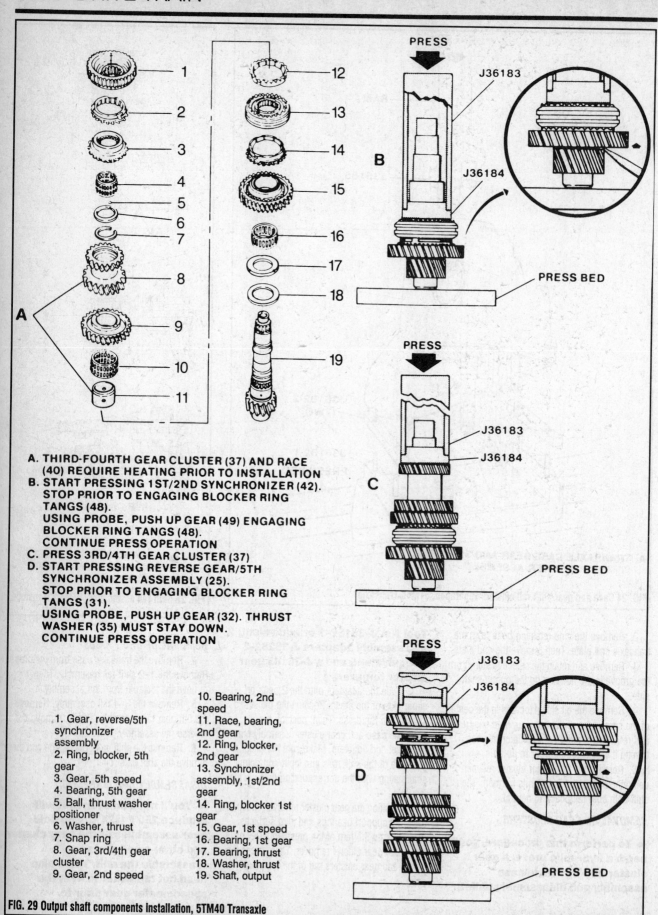

A. THIRD-FOURTH GEAR CLUSTER (37) AND RACE
(40) REQUIRE HEATING PRIOR TO INSTALLATION
B. START PRESSING 1ST/2ND SYNCHRONIZER (42).
STOP PRIOR TO ENGAGING BLOCKER RING
TANGS (48).
USING PROBE, PUSH UP GEAR (49) ENGAGING
BLOCKER RING TANGS (48).
CONTINUE PRESS OPERATION
C. PRESS 3RD/4TH GEAR CLUSTER (37)
D. START PRESSING REVERSE GEAR/5TH
SYNCHRONIZER ASSEMBLY (25).
STOP PRIOR TO ENGAGING BLOCKER RING
TANGS (31).
USING PROBE, PUSH UP GEAR (32). THRUST
WASHER (35) MUST STAY DOWN.
CONTINUE PRESS OPERATION

1. Gear, reverse/5th
synchronizer
assembly
2. Ring, blocker, 5th
gear
3. Gear, 5th speed
4. Bearing, 5th gear
5. Ball, thrust washer
positioner
6. Washer, thrust
7. Snap ring
8. Gear, 3rd/4th gear
cluster
9. Gear, 2nd speed

10. Bearing, 2nd
speed
11. Race, bearing,
2nd gear
12. Ring, blocker,
2nd gear
13. Synchronizer
assembly, 1st/2nd
gear
14. Ring, blocker 1st
gear
15. Gear, 1st speed
16. Bearing, 1st gear
17. Bearing, thrust
18. Washer, thrust
19. Shaft, output

FIG. 29 Output shaft components Installation, 5TM40 Transaxle

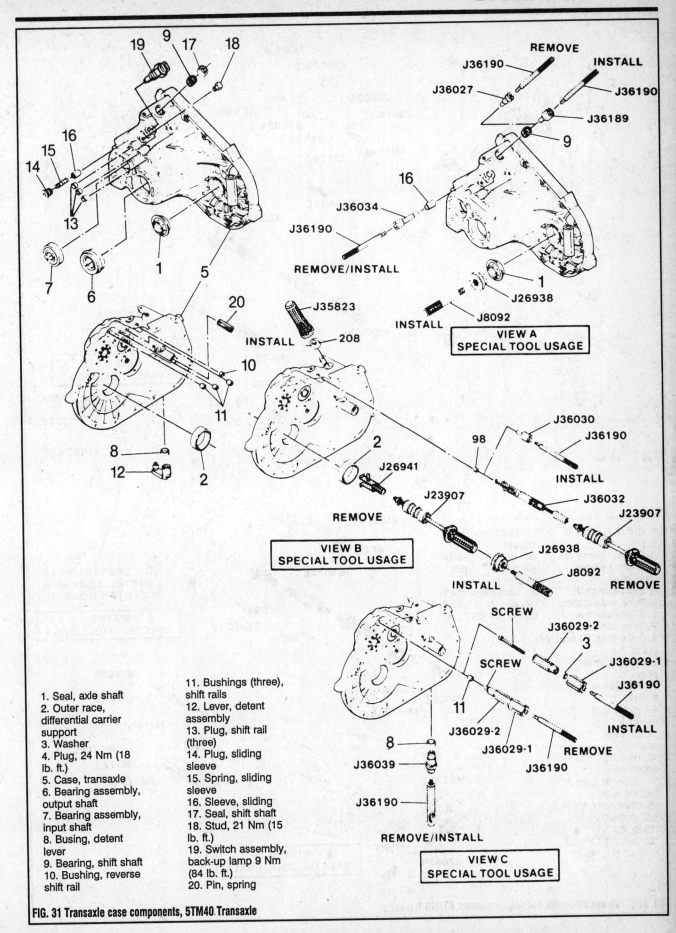

1. Seal, axle shaft
2. Outer race, differential carrier support
3. Washer
4. Plug, 24 Nm (18 lb. ft.)
5. Case, transaxle
6. Bearing assembly, output shaft
7. Bearing assembly, input shaft
8. Busing, detent lever
9. Bearing, shift shaft
10. Bushing, reverse shift rail

11. Bushings (three), shift rails
12. Lever, detent assembly
13. Plug, shift rail (three)
14. Plug, sliding sleeve
15. Spring, sliding sleeve
16. Sleeve, sliding
17. Seal, shift shaft
18. Stud, 21 Nm (15 lb. ft.)
19. Switch assembly, back-up lamp 9 Nm (84 lb. ft.)
20. Pin, spring

FIG. 31 Transaxle case components, 5TM40 Transaxle

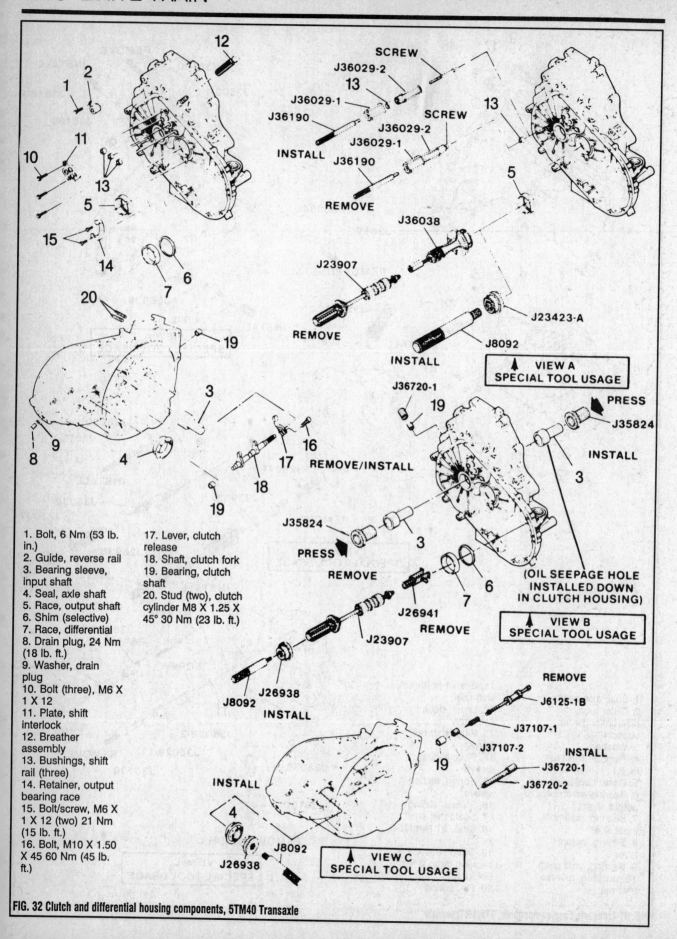

1. Bolt, 6 Nm (53 lb. in.)
2. Guide, reverse rail
3. Bearing sleeve, input shaft
4. Seal, axle shaft
5. Race, output shaft
6. Shim (selective)
7. Race, differential
8. Drain plug, 24 Nm (18 lb. ft.)
9. Washer, drain plug
10. Bolt (three), M6 X 1 X 12
11. Plate, shift interlock
12. Breather assembly
13. Bushings, shift rail (three)
14. Retainer, output bearing race
15. Bolt/screw, M6 X 1 X 12 (two) 21 Nm (15 lb. ft.)
16. Bolt, M10 X 1.50 X 45 60 Nm (45 lb. ft.)
17. Lever, clutch release
18. Shaft, clutch fork
19. Bearing, clutch shaft
20. Stud (two), clutch cylinder M8 X 1.25 X 45° 30 Nm (23 lb. ft.)

FIG. 32 Clutch and differential housing components, 5TM40 Transaxle

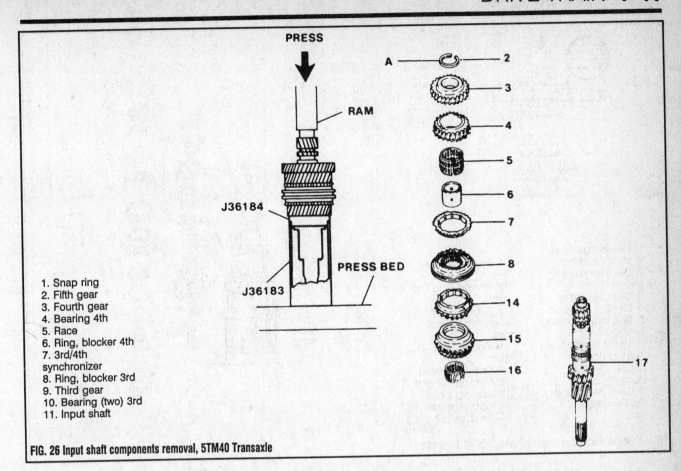

PRESS

RAM

J36184

J36183

PRESS BED

A — 2

3

4

5

6

7

8

14

15

16

17

1. Snap ring
2. Fifth gear
3. Fourth gear
4. Bearing 4th
5. Race
6. Ring, blocker 4th
7. 3rd/4th synchronizer
8. Ring, blocker 3rd
9. Third gear
10. Bearing (two) 3rd
11. Input shaft

FIG. 26 Input shaft components removal, 5TM40 Transaxle

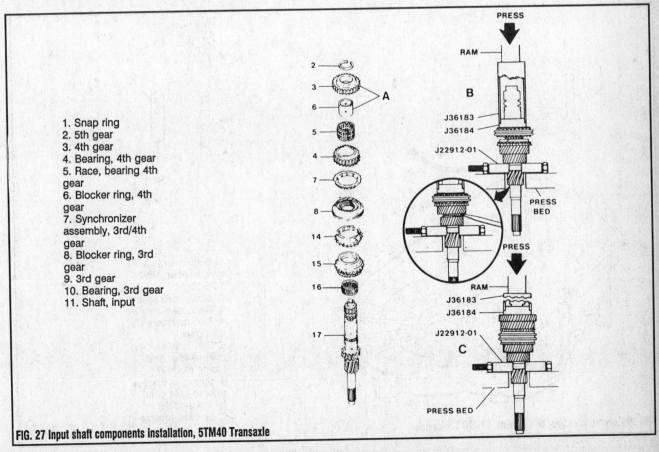

PRESS

RAM

B

J36183
J36184

J22912-01

PRESS BED

PRESS

RAM

J36183
J36184

J22912-01

C

PRESS BED

2
3
6 — A
5
4
7
8
14
15
16
17

1. Snap ring
2. 5th gear
3. 4th gear
4. Bearing, 4th gear
5. Race, bearing 4th gear
6. Blocker ring, 4th gear
7. Synchronizer assembly, 3rd/4th gear
8. Blocker ring, 3rd gear
9. 3rd gear
10. Bearing, 3rd gear
11. Shaft, input

FIG. 27 Input shaft components installation, 5TM40 Transaxle

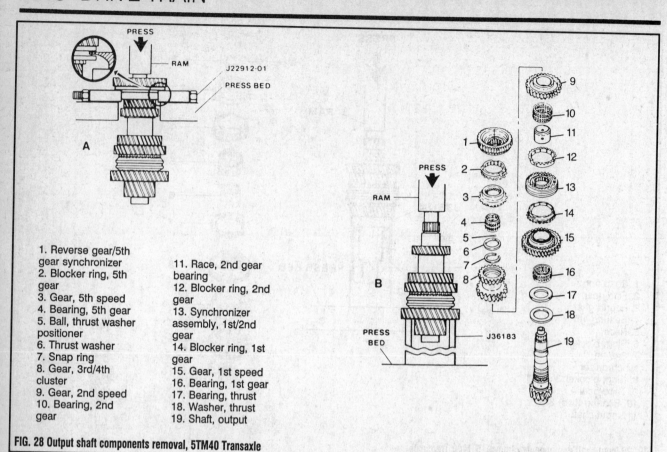

1. Reverse gear/5th gear synchronizer
2. Blocker ring, 5th gear
3. Gear, 5th speed
4. Bearing, 5th gear
5. Ball, thrust washer positioner
6. Thrust washer
7. Snap ring
8. Gear, 3rd/4th cluster
9. Gear, 2nd speed
10. Bearing, 2nd gear
11. Race, 2nd gear bearing
12. Blocker ring, 2nd gear
13. Synchronizer assembly, 1st/2nd gear
14. Blocker ring, 1st gear
15. Gear, 1st speed
16. Bearing, 1st gear
17. Bearing, thrust
18. Washer, thrust
19. Shaft, output

FIG. 28 Output shaft components removal, 5TM40 Transaxle

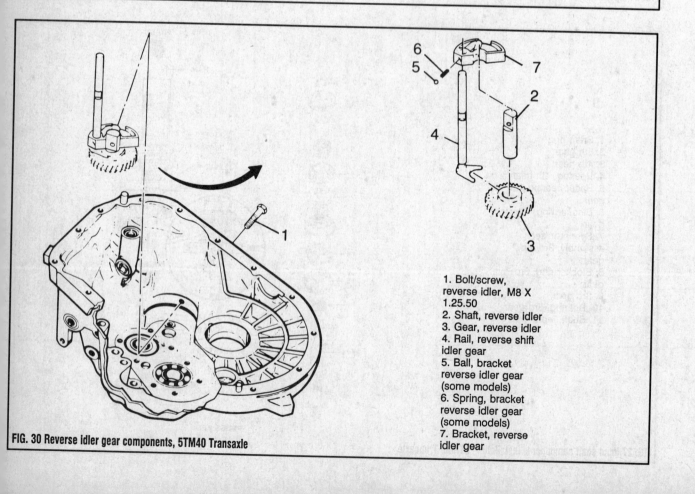

1. Bolt/screw, reverse idler, M8 X 1.25.50
2. Shaft, reverse idler
3. Gear, reverse idler
4. Rail, reverse shift idler gear
5. Ball, bracket reverse idler gear (some models)
6. Spring, bracket reverse idler gear (some models)
7. Bracket, reverse idler gear

FIG. 30 Reverse idler gear components, 5TM40 Transaxle

assembly. To disassemble and reassemble the input shaft, you'll need a hydraulic press, a J–22912–01 gear remover/installer, a press tube J–36183 or equivalent and a reducer J–36184 for the input/output shaft gears. Use a heavy assembly lubricant, part No. 1052931 or equivalent to pre-lube parts during assembly for protection until the gearbox lubricates itself and is broken in.

INPUT SHAFT DISASSEMBLY AND ASSEMBLY

➡ **Before disassembly, carefully identify and label the blocker rings for 3rd and 4th gears, as they are easily confused during assembly.**

1. Remove the snapring from the top of the shaft. Position the shaft with the snapring groove upward and the lower end inserted into the press tube and reducer. Center the top of the shaft under the press ram. Press the shaft downward and out of the gears and associated parts. Remove the gear, bearing, race, 2 blocking rings, and the synchronizer assembly and associated gear.

2. Remove the 3rd gear bearing.

3. Clean all parts in a safe solvent and air dry them. Then inspect as follows:

   a. Inspect the shaft for spline wear or cracks and replace it if any are visible.

   b. Inspect the gear teeth for scuffing, nicks, burrs, or breaks and replace gears that show such defects.

   c. Inspect the bearings by rotating them slowly and checking for roughness in rotation, burrs or pits, and replace as necessary.

   d. Inspect the bearing races and shaft bearing surfaces for scoring, wear, or overheating and replace parts as necessary.

   e. Inspect the snapring for nicks, distortion, or wear and replace if any of these conditions exist.

   f. See the head below referring to "Synchronizer Disassembly and Inspection". Inspect the synchronizer as described there, and replace defective parts.

   g. Very slight defects in all parts except bearings can sometimes be removed with a soft stone or crocus cloth. It is permissible to clean up and re-use parts in this manner if only a small amount of metal must be removed.

4. Heat the 5th gear assembly and bearing race for 10 minutes in an oven preheated to 250°F (121°C).

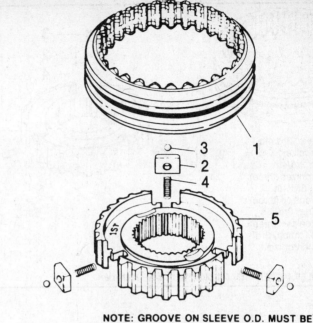

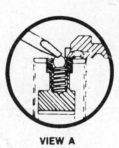
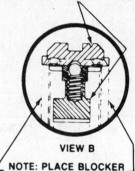

NOTE: GROOVE ON SLEEVE O.D. MUST BE POSITIONED OVER THINNER SIDE OF HUB

VIEW A

VIEW B

NOTE: PLACE BLOCKER RINGS (41) & (48) HERE

1. SLEEVE, 1ST/2ND SYNCHRONIZER
2. KEY, 1ST/2ND SYNCHRONIZER (THREE)
3. BALL, 1ST/2ND SYNCHRONIZER (THREE)
4. SPRING, 1ST/2ND SYNCHRONIZER (THREE)
5'. HUB, 1ST/2ND SYNCHRONIZER

1ST/2ND ASSEMBLY PROCEDURES

 Install

1. Sleeve, 1st/2nd synchronizer
2. Key, 1st/2nd synchronizer (three)
3. Ball, 1st/2nd synchronizer (three)
4. Spring, 1st/2nd synchronizer (three)
5. Hub, 1st/2nd synchronizer

FIG. 33 1st/2nd gear synchronizer components, 5TM40 Transaxle

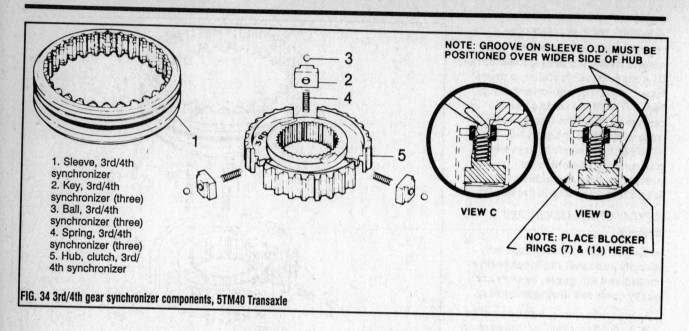

NOTE: GROOVE ON SLEEVE O.D. MUST BE POSITIONED OVER WIDER SIDE OF HUB

VIEW C

VIEW D

NOTE: PLACE BLOCKER RINGS (7) & (14) HERE

1. Sleeve, 3rd/4th synchronizer
2. Key, 3rd/4th synchronizer (three)
3. Ball, 3rd/4th synchronizer (three)
4. Spring, 3rd/4th synchronizer (three)
5. Hub, clutch, 3rd/4th synchronizer

FIG. 34 3rd/4th gear synchronizer components, 5TM40 Transaxle

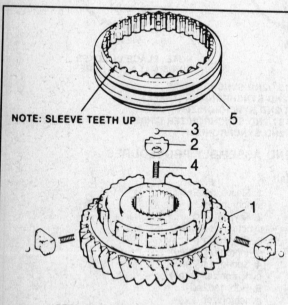

NOTE: SLEEVE TEETH UP

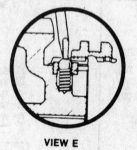

VIEW E

VIEW F

NOTE: PLACE BLOCKER RING (31) HERE

1. Gear, reverse
2. Key, 5th synchronizer (three)
3. Ball, 5th synchronizer (three)
4. Spring, 5th synchronizer (three)
5. Sleeve, 5th synchronizer

5TH ASSEMBLY PROCEDURES

Install

1. Spring (29) into key (27)
2. Spring and key assemblies, teeth on keys out into slots on gear (26).
3. Sleeve (30), teeth up. Align the ball and spring pockets.
4. Position assembly as in View E.
5. Balls (28):
   - push the ball into the sleeve using a screwdriver
   - push the sleeve (30) down just enough to retain the ball
   - "cock" the sleeve just enough to allow installation of the remaining balls (one at a time).
6. Blocker ring (31) on the synchronizer assembly:
   - make sure blocker ring tangs line up with the keys.
7. Center the hub, keys and balls by pushing on the blocker ring, View F. Balls will "click" into position.

FIG. 35 5th gear synchronizer components, 5TM40 Transaxle

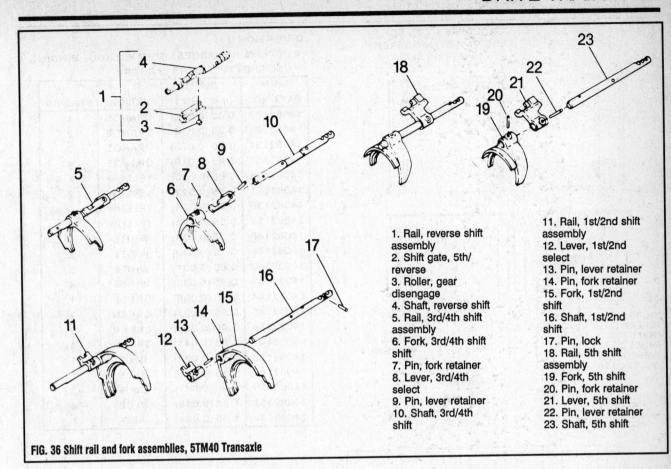

1. Rail, reverse shift assembly
2. Shift gate, 5th/reverse
3. Roller, gear disengage
4. Shaft, reverse shift
5. Rail, 3rd/4th shift assembly
6. Fork, 3rd/4th shift shift
7. Pin, fork retainer
8. Lever, 3rd/4th select
9. Pin, lever retainer
10. Shaft, 3rd/4th shift

11. Rail, 1st/2nd shift assembly
12. Lever, 1st/2nd select
13. Pin, lever retainer
14. Pin, fork retainer
15. Fork, 1st/2nd shift
16. Shaft, 1st/2nd shift
17. Pin, lock
18. Rail, 5th shift assembly
19. Fork, 5th shift
20. Pin, fork retainer
21. Lever, 5th shift
22. Pin, lever retainer
23. Shaft, 5th shift

FIG. 36 Shift rail and fork assemblies, 5TM40 Transaxle

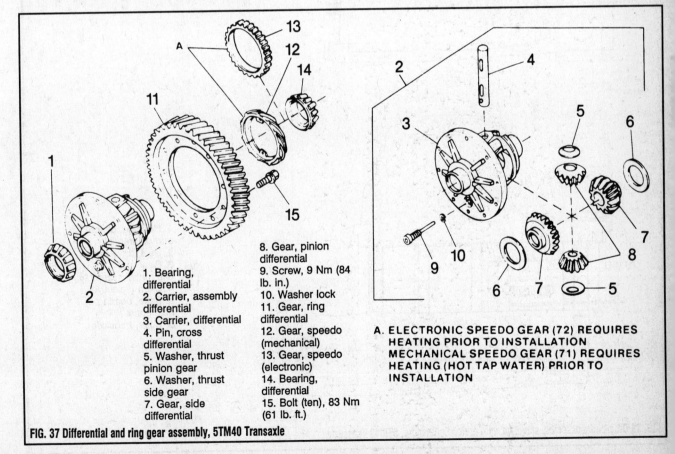

1. Bearing, differential
2. Carrier, assembly differential
3. Carrier, differential
4. Pin, cross differential
5. Washer, thrust pinion gear
6. Washer, thrust side gear
7. Gear, side differential

8. Gear, pinion differential
9. Screw, 9 Nm (84 lb. in.)
10. Washer lock
11. Gear, ring differential
12. Gear, speedo (mechanical)
13. Gear, speedo (electronic)
14. Bearing, differential
15. Bolt (ten), 83 Nm (61 lb. ft.)

A. ELECTRONIC SPEEDO GEAR (72) REQUIRES HEATING PRIOR TO INSTALLATION MECHANICAL SPEEDO GEAR (71) REQUIRES HEATING (HOT TAP WATER) PRIOR TO INSTALLATION

FIG. 37 Differential and ring gear assembly, 5TM40 Transaxle

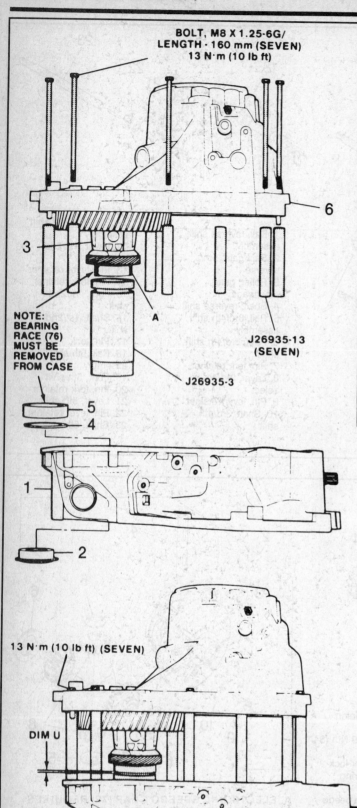

BOLT, M8 X 1.25-6G/
LENGTH - 160 mm (SEVEN)
13 N·m (10 lb ft)

NOTE:
BEARING
RACE (76)
MUST BE
REMOVED
FROM CASE

A

J26935-3

J26935-13
(SEVEN)

3

5

4

1

2

13 N·m (10 lb ft) (SEVEN)

DIM U

DIMENSION U
— DETERMINE LARGEST SHIM WITHOUT BINDING
— USE SHIM TWO SIZES LARGER

SHIM PART NO.	DIM U mm	(IN.)	COLOR	STRIPES
14082132	0.30	(0.012)	ORANGE	1
14082133	0.35	(0.014)	ORANGE	2
14082134	0.40	(0.016)	ORANGE	3
14082135	0.45	(0.018)	ORANGE	4
14082136	0.50	(0.020)	YELLOW	1
14082137	0.55	(0.022)	YELLOW	2
14082138	0.60	(0.024)	YELLOW	3
14082139	0.65	(0.026)	YELLOW	4
14082140	0.70	(0.028)	WHITE	1
14082141	0.75	(0.030)	WHITE	2
14082142	0.80	(0.031)	WHITE	3
14082143	0.85	(0.033)	WHITE	4
14082144	0.90	(0.035)	GREEN	1
14082145	0.95	(0.037)	GREEN	2
14082146	1.00	(0.039)	GREEN	3
14082147	1.05	(0.041)	GREEN	4
14082148	1.10	(0.043)	BLUE	1
14082149	1.15	(0.045)	BLUE	2
14082150	1.20	(0.047)	BLUE	3
14082151	1.25	(0.049)	BLUE	4
14082152	1.30	(0.051)	RED	1

1. Housing, clutch and differential
2. Seal, drive axle
3. Gear and differential assembly
4. Shim (selective)
5. Race, bearing differential
6. Case, transaxle

FIG. 38 Differential assembly selective shim preload procedure, 5TM40 Transaxle

5. Prelube all parts on wear surfaces as the assembly proceeds. While the gear is heating, assemble the two 3rd gear bearings and then the 3rd gear to the shaft. Install the 3rd gear with the cone upward. Then, install blocking ring.

6. Assemble the shaft into the press tube and reducer and position the remover/installer so that the two, small diameter permanent gears near the bottom of the shaft straddle the installer. Position the assembly onto the press so that the shaft protrudes down through the hole in the press bed.

7. Install the two 3rd gear bearings, 3rd gear (with the cone upward) and synchronizer blocking ring onto the shaft. Position the synchronizer onto the top of the shaft with the side marked "3rd gear" and the small outside diameter groove of the sleeve toward the 3rd gear. Position the gear installer on top of the synchronizer unit. Start the press operation cautiously and watch the position of the synchronizer. Stop the press before the synchronizer unit tangs touch those on the gears. Then, lift the 3rd gear blocking ring and 3rd gear so that their tangs fit into the tangs on the synchronizer. Then, press the synchronizer on until it is seated. Carefully remove any shavings that may have been created during the pressing operation.

8. Install the bearing race (preheated) and the bearing. Install the 4th gear blocking ring.

9. Install the 4th gear, cone downward.

10. Install the shaft assembly into the press tube and reducer and position the assembly squarely on the press. Install the 5th gear (preheated) on top, flat side down. Press the gear into position and install the snapring.

OUTPUT SHAFT DISASSEMBLY AND ASSEMBLY

➡ **To perform this procedure, you will need: a press of at least 15 tons capacity; an input/output shaft gear remover/installer J–22912–01 or equivalent; a J–36183 or equivalent input/output shaft gears press tube; a J–36184 input/output shaft press tube installer; and an oven that will produce 250°F (121°C) and hold gear assemblies or the gear cluster and other small parts. Before proceeding with disassembly, identify and label the blocking rings for 5th, 2nd, and 1st gears. They must be reinstalled in the correct positions. Use a heavy assembly lubricant, part No. 1052931 or equivalent to pre-lube**

parts during assembly for protection until the gearbox lubricates itself and is broken in.

1. Install the gear remover/installer and shaft assembly into the press. The remover/installer has a tang which must locate in the shifting fork groove of the reverse/5th gear synchronizer assembly. The remover/installer rests on the press bed.

2. Press the shaft downward so the reverse/5th gear synchronizer assembly is pressed off the top. Then, remove the shaft from the press and remove: the blocker ring, 5th speed gear, 5th gear bearing, thrust washer, and thrust washer positioner ball.

3. Using snapring pliers, open and then work the snapring off the shaft.

4. Install the shaft in the press, supported via the lower side of the 1st speed gear by the input/output shaft gears press tube, resting on the press bed. Use the press ram, resting against the top of the shaft, to force the shaft downward (this will require at least 15 tons pressure) and force the 1st gear and parts above it off the shaft. Separate the following parts from the shaft: 2nd gear, bearing, bearing race, 1–2 synchronizer, blocking rings, 3–4 gear cluster, 1st gear, bearing, caged thrust bearing, and thrust washer.

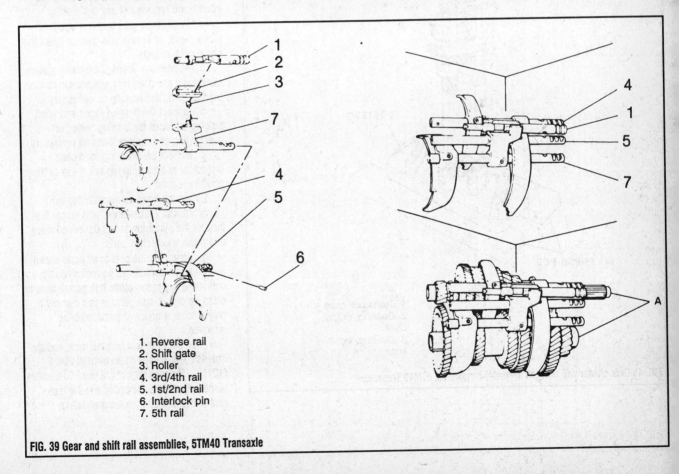

1. Reverse rail
2. Shift gate
3. Roller
4. 3rd/4th rail
5. 1st/2nd rail
6. Interlock pin
7. 5th rail

FIG. 39 Gear and shift rail assemblies, 5TM40 Transaxle

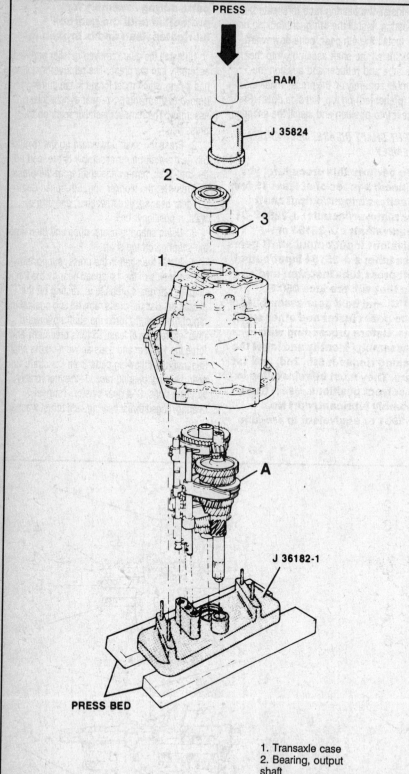

PRESS

RAM

J 35824

2

3

1

A

J 36182-1

PRESS BED

1. Transaxle case
2. Bearing, output shaft
3. Bearing, input shaft

FIG. 40 Gear cluster and shift rail assembly installation, 5TM40 Transaxle

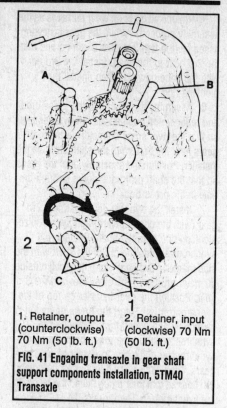

A

B

2

C

1

| 1. Retainer, output (counterclockwise) 70 Nm (50 lb. ft.) | 2. Retainer, input (clockwise) 70 Nm (50 lb. ft.) |

FIG. 41 Engaging transaxle in gear shaft support components installation, 5TM40 Transaxle

5. Clean all parts in a safe solvent and air dry them. Then inspect as follows:

a. Inspect the shaft for spline wear or cracks and replace it if any are visible.

b. Inspect the gear teeth for scuffing, nicks, burrs, or breaks and replace gears that show such defects.

c. Inspect the bearings by rotating them slowly and checking for roughness in rotation, burrs or pits, and replace as necessary.

d. Inspect the bearing races and shaft bearing surfaces for scoring, wear, or overheating and replace parts as necessary.

e. Inspect the snapring for nicks, distortion, or wear and replace if any of these conditions exist.

f. See the head below referring to "Synchronizer Disassembly and Inspection". Inspect the synchronizer as described there, and replace defective parts.

g. Very slight defects in all parts except bearings can sometimes be removed with a soft stone or crocus cloth. It is permissible to clean up and re-use parts in this manner if only a small amount of metal must be removed.

6. Put the 2nd gear bearing race, and the 3rd–4th gear cluster in an oven at 250°F (121°C). The race requires at least 10 minutes preheating before assembly and the gear cluster at least 20 minutes preheating.

7. Install the thrust washer onto the shaft, **chamfer downward**. Then, install the caged thrust bearing, **needles downward**.

8. Install the 1st gear bearing. Then, install the 1st gear, cone upward. Install the 1st gear blocking ring.

9. Position the shaft into the press with the bottom protruding through the press bed. Locate the 1–2 synchronizer assembly on top of the shaft, with the side marked "1st" and the smaller outside diameter groove on the sleeve facing 1st gear. Use the J–36183 or equivalent input/output shaft gears press tube and the J–36184 input/output shaft press tube installer. Start pressing the synchronizer assembly onto the shaft, but stop before the tangs of the gear and synchronizer touch. Lift and rotate the blocking ring and gear **making sure the thrust washer stays downward in position** in order to engage the tangs. Then, continue the pressing operation until the synchronizer assembly is seated. Carefully remove all metal shavings.

10. Install the 2nd gear bearing race (preheated), 2nd gear bearing, and 2nd gear with the cone downward .

11. **Position the preheated 3rd–4th gear cluster onto the shaft. Make sure the larger outside diameter gear is below the smaller one. Use the press and press tube reducer to press the cluster into position.**

12. **Install the snapring with snapring pliers. Then, install the thrust washer positioning ball, holding it in position with petroleum jelly. Install the thrust washer, aligning the slot in it with the ball.**

13. **Install the 5th gear bearing and then install the 5th gear, with the cone upward. Install the 5th gear blocking ring.**

14. **Position the shaft in the press. Position the reverse gear/5th synchronizer assembly onto the shaft. Position the input/output shaft gear press tube and press tube reducer on top of the synchronizer assembly. Start pressing the synchronizer assembly onto the shaft, but stop before the tangs of the gear and synchronizer touch. Lift and rotate the blocking ring and gear making sure the thrust washer stays downward in position** in order to engage the tangs. Then, continue the pressing operation until the synchronizer assembly is seated. Carefully remove all metal shavings.

DISASSEMBLY AND ASSEMBLY OF THE REVERSE IDLER GEAR

1. Remove the bolt which runs through the transaxle case and into the reverse idler gear sliding spindle shaft. Then, remove the shift rail, gear, shaft, and bracket.

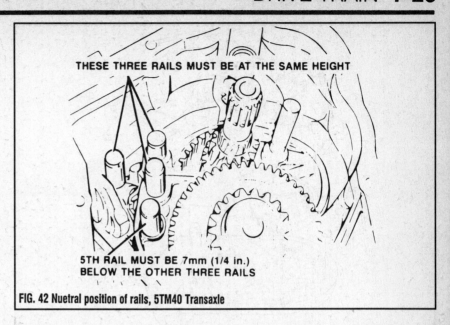

THESE THREE RAILS MUST BE AT THE SAME HEIGHT

5TH RAIL MUST BE .7mm (1/4 in.) BELOW THE OTHER THREE RAILS

FIG. 42 Nuetral position of rails, 5TM40 Transaxle

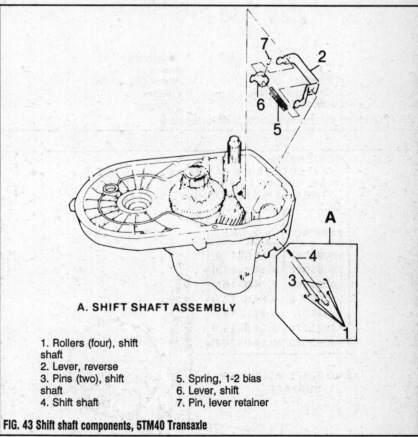

A. SHIFT SHAFT ASSEMBLY

1. Rollers (four), shift shaft
2. Lever, reverse
3. Pins (two), shift shaft
4. Shift shaft
5. Spring, 1-2 bias
6. Lever, shift
7. Pin, lever retainer

FIG. 43 Shift shaft components, 5TM40 Transaxle

2. Remove the reverse idler gear shift rail, detent ball and spring.

3. Clean all parts in a safe solvent and air dry them. Then inspect as follows:

a. Inspect the shaft for scoring, wear or cracks or signs of overheating and replace it if any are visible.

b. Inspect the gear teeth for scuffing, nicks, burrs, or breaks and replace gears that show such defects.

c. Inspect the bushing inside the gear, checking for scores, burrs, out-of-roundness, or overheating, and replace as necessary.

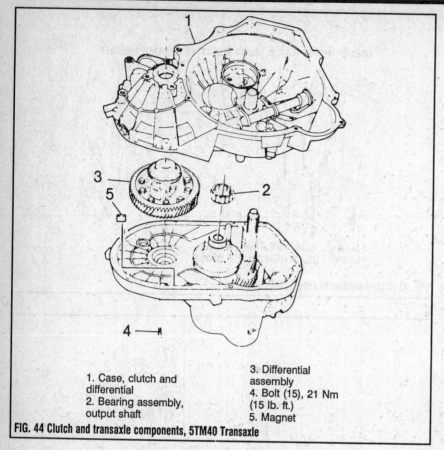

1. Case, clutch and differential
2. Bearing assembly, output shaft
3. Differential assembly
4. Bolt (15), 21 Nm (15 lb. ft.)
5. Magnet

FIG. 44 Clutch and transaxle components, 5TM40 Transaxle

DIMENSION A
- SELECTED SHIM CAN BE 0.03 mm (0.001 IN.) ABOVE OR 0.12 mm (0.004 IN.) BELOW THE END PLATE MOUNTING SURFACE

PART NO.	DIM. A mm (IN.)
14092067	4.54 (0.179)
14092068	4.64 (0.183)
14092069	4.74 (0.187)
14092070	4.84 (0.191)
14092071	4.94 (0.194)
14092072	5.04 (0.198)
14092073	5.14 (0.202)

END PLATE MOUNTING SURFACE

DIM. A

1. Bearing, output shaft support
2. Retainer, bearing 70 Nm (50 lb. ft.)

FIG. 45 Output shaft support bearing selective shim procedure, 5TM40 Transaxle

d. Very slight defects in all parts except bearings can sometimes be removed with a soft stone or crocus cloth. It is permissible to clean up and re-use parts in this manner if only a small amount of metal must be removed.

4. Assemble all parts as described in the following steps, lubricating wear surfaces with a lubricant designed to protect the parts till they become lubricated by normal gearbox operation such as GM part No. 1052931.

5. Install the detent spring and ball into the reverse idler bracket.

6. Install the shift rail into the reverse idler gear bracket. Then, install the reverse idler gear onto the shaft with the slot in the gear facing the threaded hole in the shaft.

7. Install the entire assembly into the transaxle. Then, install the fastening bolt and torque it to 16 ft. lbs.

DISASSEMBLY AND ASSEMBLY OF THE TRANSAXLE CASE

➡ **To perform this procedure, you will need the following special tools or equivalent: J–8092 universal driver handle; J–23907 slide hammer and adapter set; J–36027 shift shaft bearing remover; J–36029 shift rail bushing remover and installer; J–36032 clutch shaft inner bushing and reverse shift rail remover; J–36034 sliding sleeve bushing remover and installer; J–36039 shift detent lever bushing remover and installer; J–36181 differential bearing cup remover; J–36190 universal driver handle. Throughout this disassembly procedure, note that it is not necessary to remove bushings or bearings as a matter of routine. Inspect the bearing or bushing and the mating surface of the corresponding shaft. Inspect bushings for scores, burrs, out-of-round wear, or bluing (from overheating). Remove the bearing or bushing and replace it and the corresponding part only if there is evidence of damage or it is clear that the part is worn out.**

1. Remove the snapring and plug from the rear of the sliding sleeve bore. Then, remove the screw-in spring retainer, the spring, and the sliding sleeve. Remove (if necessary) the sliding sleeve bushing with J–36034 and J–36190 or equivalent.

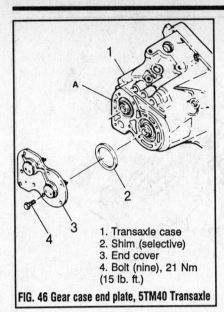

1. Transaxle case
2. Shim (selective)
3. End cover
4. Bolt (nine), 21 Nm (15 lb. ft.)

FIG. 46 Gear case end plate, 5TM40 Transaxle

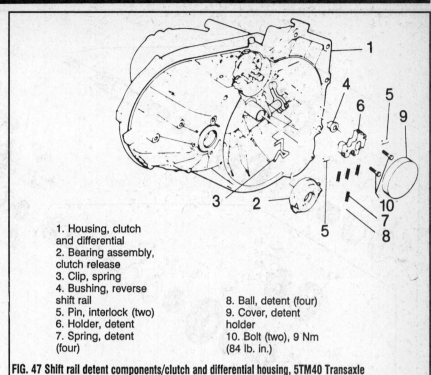

1. Housing, clutch and differential
2. Bearing assembly, clutch release
3. Clip, spring
4. Bushing, reverse shift rail
5. Pin, interlock (two)
6. Holder, detent
7. Spring, detent (four)

8. Ball, detent (four)
9. Cover, detent holder
10. Bolt (two), 9 Nm (84 lb. in.)

FIG. 47 Shift rail detent components/clutch and differential housing, 5TM40 Transaxle

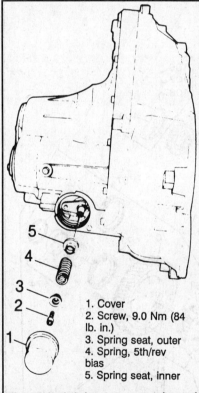

1. Cover
2. Screw, 9.0 Nm (84 lb. in.)
3. Spring seat, outer
4. Spring, 5th/rev bias
5. Spring seat, inner

FIG. 49 Shift shaft detent components/transaxle housing, 5TM40 Transaxle

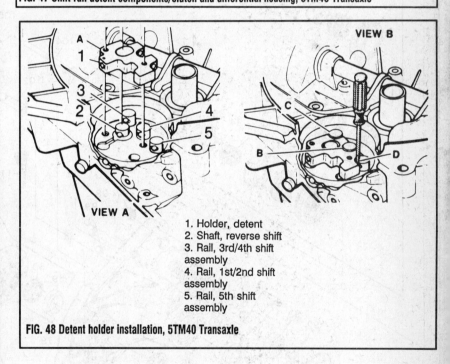

1. Holder, detent
2. Shaft, reverse shift
3. Rail, 3rd/4th shift assembly
4. Rail, 1st/2nd shift assembly
5. Rail, 5th shift assembly

FIG. 48 Detent holder installation, 5TM40 Transaxle

2. Remove the detent lever. If its wear surface is scored or worn, also remove the bushing it rides in with J–36039 and J–36190 or equivalent.

3. Pry out the shift shaft seal with a small, flat-bladed screwdriver.

4. If necessary, remove the shift shaft bearing with J–36027 and J–36190 or equivalent.

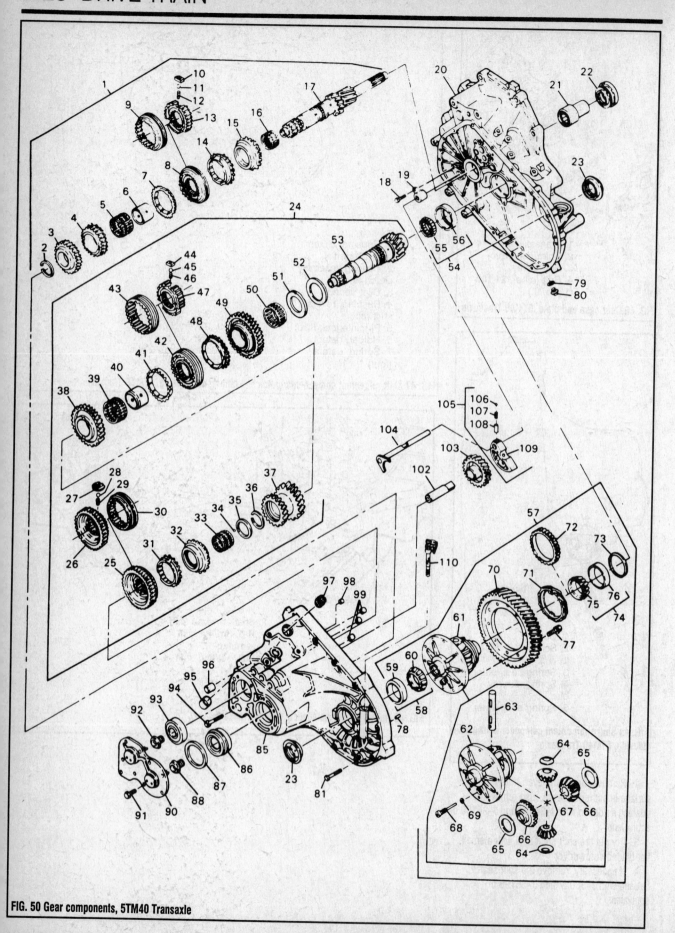

FIG. 50 Gear components, 5TM40 Transaxle

1. SHAFT & GEAR ASSEMBLY, INPUT CLUSTER
2. SNAP RING
3. GEAR, FIFTH INPUT
4. GEAR, FOURTH INPUT
5. BEARING, CAGE
6. RACE, NEEDLE
7. RING, BLOCKER 4TH
8. SYNCHRONIZER ASSEMBLY, 3RD/4TH
9. SLEEVE, 3RD/4TH SYNCHRONIZER
10. KEY, 3RD/4TH SYNCHRONIZER (THREE)
11. BALL, 3RD/4TH SYNCHRONIZER (THREE)
12. SPRING, 3RD/4TH SYNCHRONIZER (THREE)
13. HUB, CLUTCH, 3RD/4TH SYNCHRONIZER
14. RING, BLOCKER 3RD
15. GEAR, THIRD INPUT
16. BEARING, CAGE (TWO)
17. SHAFT, INPUT
18. BOLT/SCREW, M6 X 1 X 12
19. GUIDE, REVERSE SHIFT RAIL
20. HOUSING, CLUTCH AND DIFFERENTIAL
21. BEARING/SLEEVE ASSEMBLY, INPUT SHAFT
22. BEARING ASSEMBLY, CLUTCH RELEASE
23. SEAL, OIL DRIVE AXLE
24. SHAFT & GEAR ASSEMBLY, OUTPUT CLUSTER
25. GEAR, REVERSE OUTPUT/5TH SYNCHRONIZER ASSEMBLY
26. GEAR, REVERSE
27. KEY, 5TH SYNCHRONIZER (THREE)
28. BALL, 5TH SYNCHRONIZER (THREE)
29. SPRING, 5TH SYNCHRONIZER (THREE)
30. SLEEVE, 5TH SYNCHRONIZER
31. RING, BLOCKER 5TH GEAR
32. GEAR, 5TH SPEED OUTPUT
33. BEARING, 5TH SPEED OUTPUT
34. BALL, THRUST WASHER POSITIONER
35. WASHER, THRUST
36. SNAP RING

37. GEAR, 3RD/4TH CLUSTER
38. GEAR, 2ND OUTPUT
39. BEARING, 2ND OUTPUT
40. RACE, BEARING 2ND OUTPUT
41. RING, BLOCKER 2ND GEAR
42. SYNCHRONIZER ASSEMBLY, 1ST/2ND GEAR
43. SLEEVE, 1ST/2ND SYNCHRONIZER
44. KEY, 1ST/2ND SYNCHRONIZER (THREE)
45. BALL, 1ST/2ND SYNCHRONIZER (THREE)
46. SPRING, 1ST/2ND SYNCHRONIZER (THREE)
47. HUB, 1ST/2ND SYNCHRONIZER
48. RING, BLOCKER 1ST GEAR
49. GEAR, 1ST OUTPUT
50. BEARING, 1ST OUTPUT
51. BEARING, THRUST
52. WASHER, THRUST
53. SHAFT, OUTPUT
54. BEARING, OUTPUT SHAFT SUPPORT
55. BEARING, OUTPUT
56. RACE, BEARING OUTPUT
57. GEAR AND DIFFERENTIAL ASSEMBLY
58. BEARING ASSEMBLY, DIFFERENTIAL
59. RACE, BEARING DIFFERENTIAL
60. BEARING, DIFFERENTIAL
61. CASE, DIFFERENTIAL ASSEMBLY
62. CASE, DIFFERENTIAL
63. PIN, CROSS DIFFERENTIAL
64. WASHER, THRUST PINION GEAR
65. WASHER, THRUST SIDE GEAR
66. GEAR, SIDE DIFFERENTIAL
67. GEAR, PINION DIFFERENTIAL
68. BOLT/SCREW, PINION GEAR SHAFT
69. WASHER, LOCK
70. GEAR, RING DIFFERENTIAL
71. GEAR, SPEEDO OUTPUT (MECHANICAL)
72. GEAR, SPEEDO OUTPUT (ELECTRONIC)
73. SHIM, DIFFERENTIAL (SELECTIVE)
74. BEARING ASSEMBLY, DIFFERENTIAL
75. BEARING, DIFFERENTIAL

76. RACE, BEARING DIFFERENTIAL
77. BOLT/SCREW, DIFFERENTIAL RING (10)
78. PIN (TWO)
79. PLUG, OIL DRAIN
80. WASHER
81. BOLT/SCREW, TRANSAXLE CASE, M8 X 1.25.50 (15)
85. CASE, TRANSAXLE
86. BEARING ASSEMBLY, OUTPUT SHAFT
87. SHIM, OUTPUT GEAR (SELECTIVE)
88. RETAINER, OUTPUT GEAR BEARING
90. END PLATE, TRANSAXLE CASE
91. BOLT/SCREW, M8 X 1 X 18 (9)
92. RETAINER, INPUT GEAR BEARING
93. BEARING ASSEMBLY, INPUT SHAFT
94. BOLT/SCREW, REVERSE IDLER, M8 X 1.25.50
95. BUSHING, DETENT LEVER
96. BUSHING, SLIDING SLEEVE
97. BEARING, NEEDLE SHIFT SHAFT
98. BUSHING, REVERSE RAIL
99. BUSHING, SHIFT RAIL (THREE)
102. SHAFT, REVERSE IDLER
103. GEAR, REVERSE IDLER
104. RAIL, REVERSE SHIFT IDLER GEAR
105. BRACKET ASSEMBLY, REVERSE IDLER GEAR
106. BALL, BRACKET REVERSE IDLER GEAR
107. SPRING, BRACKET REVERSE IDLER GEAR
108. SLEEVE, DETENT BRACKET REVERSE IDLER GEAR
109. BRACKET, REVERSE IDLER GEAR
110. INDICATOR ASSEMBLY, TRANSAXLE FLUID LEVEL

FIG. 51 Index Gear components, 5TM40 Transaxle

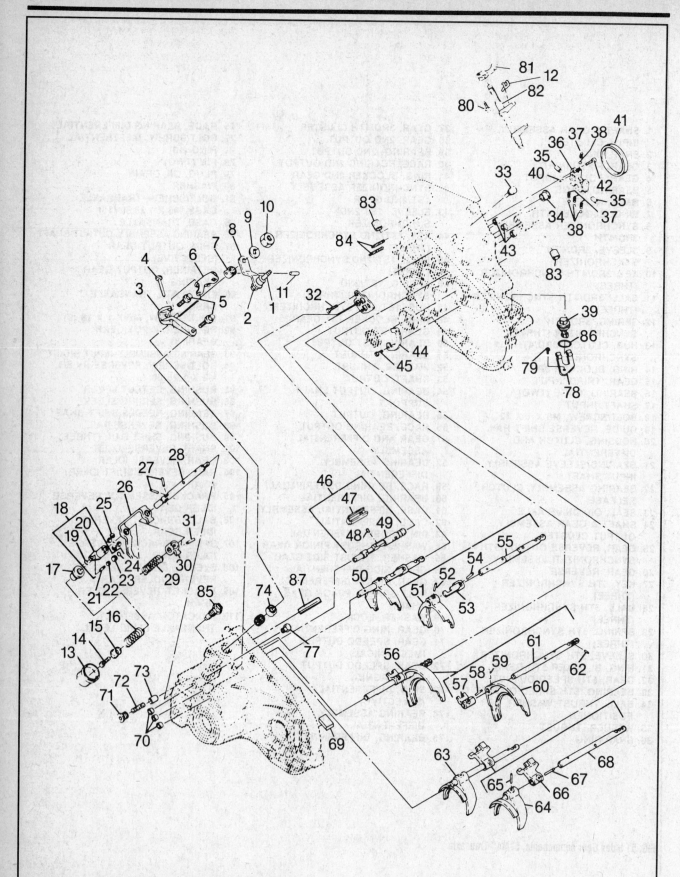

FIG. 52 Shift mechanism and case components, 5TM40 Transaxle

100. STUD, SHIFT CABLE	157. LEVER, SHIFT	192. PIN, LEVER RETAINER
101. NUT, SHIFT CABLE STUD	158. PIN, ROLL	193. PIN, FORK RETAINER
130. RETAINER, SELECTOR LEVER	159. BOLT/SCREW, M6 X 1 X 12	194. FORK, 1ST/2ND SHIFT
131. PIN, SELECTOR LEVER PIVOT	(THREE)	195. SHAFT, 1ST/2ND SHIFT
132. BOLT (TWO), M8 X 1.25 X 20	166. BREATHER ASSEMBLY	196. PIN, LOCK
(TWO)	167. BUSHING, REVERSE SHIFT RAIL	197. RAIL, 5TH SHIFT ASSEMBLY
133. LEVER, SELECTOR	168. PIN, INTERLOCK (TWO)	198. FORK, 5TH SHIFT
134. COLLAR, SHIFT SHAFT	169. HOLDER, DETENT	199. PIN, FORK RETAINER
135. LEVER, SHIFT	170. SPRING, DETENT (FOUR)	200. LEVER, 5TH SHIFT
136. WASHER	171. BALL, DETENT (FOUR)	201. PIN, LEVER RETAINER
137. NUT, M14 X 2	172. SPEEDO SIGNAL ASSEMBLY	202. SHAFT, 5TH SHIFT
138. PIN, SPRING	173. PIN, SPRING	203. MAGNET, CHIP COLLECTOR
139. CLIP, SPRING	174. COVER, DETENT HOLDER	204. PLUG, SHIFT RAIL (THREE)
140. COVER, SHIFT SHAFT	175. BOLT/SCREW, M6 X 1 X 30	205. PLUG
141. BOLT/SCREW, M20 X 1.5	(TWO)	206. SPRING, SLIDING SLEEVE
142. SEAT, SPRING 5TH DETENT	176. BUSHINGS, SHIFT RAIL (THREE)	207. SLEEVE, SLIDING
OUTER	178. RETAINER, OUTPUT BEARING	208. SEAL, SHIFT SHAFT
143. SPRING	RACE	209. PLUG
144. SEAT, SPRING 5TH DETENT	179. BOLT/SCREW, M6 X 1 X 12	210. SNAP RING
INNER	(TWO)	211. STUD
145. LEVER, DETENT ASSEMBLY	180. RAIL, REVERSE SHIFT	212. SPEEDO SIGNAL ASSEMBLY,
146. RETAINER, PIN DETENT	ASSEMBLY	RETAINER
147. LEVER, DETENT	181. SHIFT GATE, 5TH/REVERSE	213. BOLT, M6 X 16
148. PIN, DETENT LEVER	182. ROLLER, GEAR DISENGAGE	214. BOLT, M10 X 1.50 X 40
149. SPACER, DETENT LEVER	183. SHAFT, REVERSE SHIFT	215. LEVER, CLUTCH RELEASE
150. ROLLER, DETENT LEVER	184. RAIL, 3RD/4TH SHIFT ASSEMBLY	216. SHAFT, CLUTCH FORK
151. RETAINER, PIN DETENT	185. FORK, 3RD/4TH SHIFT SHAFT	217. BEARING ASSEMBLY, CLUTCH SHAFT
152. ROLLER, DETENT (FOUR)	186. PIN, FORK RETAINER	218. STUD, CLUTCH CYLINDER
153. LEVER, REVERSE	187. LEVER, 3RD/4TH SELECT	(TWO) M8 X 1.25 X 45°
154. PIN, DETENT LEVER ROLLERS	188. PIN, LEVER RETAINER	219. SWITCH ASSEMBLY,
(TWO)	189. SHAFT, 3RD/4TH SHIFT	BACK-UP LAMP
155. SHAFT, SHIFT	190. RAIL, 1ST/2ND SHIFT ASSEMBLY	220. SEAL
156. SPRING, 3RD/4TH BIAS	191. LEVER, 1ST/2ND SELECT	221. PIN, SPRING (SOME MODELS)

FIG. 53 Index Shift mechanism and case components, 5TM40 Transaxle

5. Remove the axle shaft seal. As necessary, remove the outer race for the differential carrier support bearing with J–36181 and J–8092. Then, remove the three shift rail plugs from the transaxle case.

6. (As necessary) remove the input shaft support bearing. Remove the output shaft support bearing.

7. Remove (as necessary) the three shift rail bushings with J–36029 and J–31690. Use the small end of the J–36029–2 adapter in the bushing.

8. As necessary, remove the reverse shift rail bushing with J–36032 and J–23907. Remove the stud that screws into the top of one of the shift rail bushing bores.

9. Inspect the case as follows:

a. Inspect the bearing race bores for wear, scratches, or grooves.

b. Inspect the gear teeth for scuffing, nicks, burrs, or breaks and replace gears that show such defects.

c. Inspect the bushings for scoring, burrs or pits, out-of-round or evidence of overheating (bluing) and replace as necessary.

d. Inspect the case for cracks, the threaded openings in the case for damaged threads, and the mounting faces for nicks, burrs, or scratches. Replace the case if it is cracked. Clean up damaged threads with a used tap of the correct size (a brand-new tap will cut oversize threads).

e. Very slight defects in all parts except bearings can sometimes be removed with a soft stone or crocus cloth. It is permissible to clean up and re-use parts in this manner if only a small amount of metal must be removed.

➡ **The following special tools or equivalent designs from other sources are required to reassemble the case:**
J–26938 differential seal and race installer; J–35823 shift shaft seal installer; J–36209 shift rail bushing remover/installer; J–36034 sliding sleeve bushing remover/installer; J–36039 shift detent lever remover/installer; J–36189 shift shaft bearing installer; J–26190 universal driver handle.

1. If it has been removed, install the shift shaft bearing with J–36189 and J–36190. Install the shift shaft seal with J–35823.

2. If it they been removed, install the three shift rail bushings. In doing this, install the bearings on the J–36029–2 adapter and retain them with the J–36029–1.

3. If it has been removed, install the reverse rail bushing with J–36030 and J–36190.

4. Install the differential carrier support outer bearing race with J–26938.

5. Install the axle seals with J–26938.

6. Install the three shift rail plugs into the case, screwing them in just until they are even with the surface of the case.

7. If it has been removed, install the detent lever bushing with J–36039 and J–36190. Then, install the detent lever.

8. If it has been removed, install the sliding sleeve bushing with J–36034 and J–36190.

9. Install the sliding sleeve bushing with J–36034 and J–36190. Then, install the sliding sleeve, spring, and retaining screw, torquing the retaining screw to 32 ft. lbs.

10. Install the plug into the sliding sleeve bore, and then install the snapring, flat side up.

11. Install the stud with the chamfer outward, torquing to 15 ft. lbs.

➡ To perform this procedure you will need the following special tools or equivalent designs from other sources: a hydraulic press; a J–8092 universal driver handle; J–23907 slide hammer and adapter set; J–35824 input bearing assembly remover and installer; J–36029 shift rail bushing remover/installer; J–36032 clutch shaft inner bushing/reverse shift rail remover; J–36037 clutch shaft upper bushing remover/installer; J–36038 output shaft race bearing remover; J–36181 differential; bearing cup remover. Throughout this disassembly procedure, note that it is not necessary to remove bushings or bearings as a matter of routine. Inspect the bearing or bushing and the mating surface of the corresponding shaft. Inspect bushings for scores, burrs, out-of-round wear, or bluing (from overheating). Remove the bearing or bushing and replace it and the corresponding part only if there is evidence of damage or it is clear that the part is worn out.

1. Remove the 2 axle bearing race retainer bolts and the retainer. Remove the race with J–36038 and J–23907.

2. Remove the bolts, washers, spacer, and interlock plate.

3. Remove its mounting bolt and the reverse rail guide.

4. Remove the rear axle seal.

5. Remove the differential bearing race and selective shim pack with J–36181 and J–8092.

6. With a small screwdriver, pry out the clutch shaft seal.

7. Remove the upper bushing for the outer end of the clutch shaft with J–36037. Then, remove the clutch shaft itself. Remove the inner clutch shaft bushing with the J–36032 and J–23907.

8. Place the assembly in a hydraulic press. Fit the J–35824 into the end of the bearing sleeve assembly. Then, press the sleeve out of the case via the outer end of the special tool.

9. Remove the shift rail bushings by inserting the small end of the J–36029–2 adapter into each bushing.

10. Remove the drain plug and washer. Remove the breather assembly.

11. Inspect the assembly as follows:

   a. Clean all parts in solvent and allow them to dry.

   b. Inspect the housing bearing race bore for wear, scratches or grooves.

c. Inspect the case for cracks, damaged threads, or nicks, burrs, or scratches in the mounting faces.

d. Replace the case if there are any cracks. Very slight defects can sometimes be removed with a soft stone or crocus cloth. It is permissible to clean up and re-use the case in this manner if only a small amount of metal must be removed.

➡ The following tools are required to reassemble the case: a hydraulic press; a J–8092 universal drive handle; a J–23423–A differential/output shaft bearing cup installer; a J–35824 input bearing assembly remover/installer; a J–36029 shift rail bushing installer; a J–36033 clutch shaft inner bushing installer; a J–36037 clutch shaft upper bushing remover/installer; a J–36190 universal driver handle; and Loctite 242® or equivalent. Do not install the differential bearing race and axle seal until later, when the bearing is shimmed for proper preload.

1. Install the drain plug with a new washer, and torque it to 18 ft. lbs.

2. As necessary, install new shift rail bushings. Use tools J–36029 and J–36190, placing the bushing on the J–36029–2 adapter and retaining them between the –1 and –2 sections of the tool. **Make sure the bushings do not protrude into the transaxle case side of the clutch housing** .

3. Coat the outside diameter with a small amount of Loctite 242® or equivalent. **Make sure the Oil seepage hole faces DOWNWARD inside the clutch housing**. Then, install a new bearing sleeve assembly with a hydraulic press and J–35842.

4. As necessary, install a new inner clutch shaft bushing with J–36033 and J–36190. Then, install the clutch shaft.

5. As necessary, install a new outer clutch shaft bushing with J–36037. Make sure the bushing is positioned so that the outer end is flush with the bottom of the seal bore.

6. Install a new clutch shaft seal.

7. Install a new reverse rail guide with the short side going into its bore, and then install the retaining bolt, torquing to 15 ft. lbs.

8. Install a new output shaft bearing race, with J–23423–A and J–8092, **aligning cutouts in the race with the slots in the case** .

9. Install the output shaft retainer and bolts, torquing to 15 ft. lbs.

10. Coat the retaining bolts with Loctite 242® or equivalent and install the interlock plate, spacers, washers, and retaining bolts, torquing to 15 ft. lbs. Install the breather assembly.

SYNCHRONIZER DISASSEMBLY, INSPECTION, AND ASSEMBLY

1. Wrap each unit tightly in a shop rag to retain parts. Press the center hub of each unit through the sleeve to disassemble.

2. Clean all parts with solvent and then allow them to air dry. Inspect each unit as follows:

   a. Inspect all hub and ring teeth for excess wear, scuffing, nicks, burrs, or actual breakage and replace defective parts.

   b. Check synchronizer keys for either wear or distortion and replace those which are found to be defective.

   c. Check the detent balls and retaining springs for distortion, cracks or wear. Replace defective parts.

   d. Very slight defects in all parts except bearings can sometimes be removed with a soft stone or crocus cloth. It is permissible to clean up and re-use parts in this manner if only a small amount of metal must be removed.

3. Assemble the 1st/2nd and 3rd/4th synchronizer assemblies as follows:

   a. Position the synchronizer sleeve with the smaller outside diameter groove upward. Position the hub with the side marked "1st" upward on the 1st/2nd synchronizer and the side marked "3rd" upward on the 3rd/4th synchronizer. Turn the sleeve so that the ball detents in the sleeve will correspond with the ball and spring pockets in the hub. Then, slide the sleeve onto the hub.

   b. Insert each spring into its corresponding key. Lift the sleeve just enough to provide clearance and then install each of these assemblies into the sleeve/hub assembly with the bevel cut on the key facing the sleeve. Slip each ball into the hole in the end of the key, depress it with a flat bladed screwdriver and rock the sleeve downward and over the ball to retain it. When all three spring, key, and ball assemblies are installed, slide the sleeve downward until the balls click into position in the detents inside the sleeve.

4. Assemble the 5th synchronizer assembly as follows:

   a. Position the gear with the integral synchronizer hub upward. Insert each detent spring into the indentation in the rear of one of the semi-circular keys. Position each key with the semi-circle downward and the teeth outward. Insert each key/spring assembly into one of the slots in the integral hub.

b. Position the synchronizer sleeve with the teeth upward and oriented to align the spring pockets in the hub with the ball detents in the sleeve.

c. Slide the sleeve far enough onto the hub to retain the keys. Position each ball into the indentation in the end of one of the keys, depress it with the blade of a conventional screwdriver, and then rock that area of the sleeve down just far enough to retain the ball. When all the balls are retained by the sleeve, slide it downward until the balls click into position in the detents.

INSPECTION OF SHIFT RAIL AND FORK ASSEMBLIES

Clean all parts in solvent and allow them to air dry. Inspect the shafts for wear or scoring. Inspect the forks for wear, scoring or distortion (bends). Inspect the levers for wear or distortion such as bending. Replace parts as necessary. Note that the major rail/fork assemblies are replaceable only as complete units. Individual parts are not serviced.

DIFFERENTIAL AND RING GEAR DISASSEMBLY AND ASSEMBLY

➡ **To perform this procedure, you will need the following GM special tools or equivalent designs from other sources: J–2241–11 or J–23598 side bearing puller adapter; J–22888 bearing remover; (2) J–22888–35 bearing remover leg.**

1. Remove the ten ring gear bolts and then separate the ring gear from the differential carrier assembly.

2. Remove the differential bearings with the bearing remover and the side bearing puller adapter.

3. Remove the speedometer cable or sending unit drive gear (it cannot be removed without breaking it).

4. Remove the bolt and washer that retain the cross-differential pin. Slide the pin out and then remove the 2 side differential gears and the 2 differential pinion gears, each with its own washer.

5. Inspect the differential components as follows:

a. Clean all parts in solvent and allow them to air dry.

b. Inspect gears for scuffed, nicked, burred, or broken teeth.

c. Inspect the carrier for distortion, out-of-round bores, and scoring and replace it if any of these conditions is present.

d. Inspect the differential bearings for roughness of rotation, burrs, or pits.

e. Inspect the 2 sets of 2 thrust washers for wear, scuffing, nicks, or burrs.

f. Very slight defects can sometimes be removed with a soft stone or crocus cloth. It is permissible to clean up and re-use parts in this manner if only a small amount of metal must be removed. Clean up or, if necessary, replace defective parts.

➡ **To assemble the differential and ring gear, you will need the following special tools or equivalent designs from other than GM sources: a hydraulic press; a J–22919 differential inner bearing installer; hot tap water to heat the mechanical speedometer drive gear; a 250°F (121°C) oven to heat the electronic type of speedometer drive gear. Supply both new bolts (10) for attaching the ring gear to the differential carrier and a new speedometer drive gear before beginning work. Note also that if the transaxle or clutch and differential case, differential carrier, or differential bearing assemblies have been replaced, new selective shims must be installed to provide proper bearing preload, according to "Selecting and Installing New Differential Selective Shims" below.**

6. If the transaxle uses a mechanical speedometer drive gear (which is made of nylon), preheat it in hot tap water for five minutes. If it uses an electronic speedometer drive gear (made of steel), preheat it in an oven at 250°F (121°C) for 120 minutes before installing it. Install the drive gear. Allow it to cool before proceeding.

7. Install the 2 differential bearings, using the press and the Inner Bearing Installer so the bearings will not be damaged.

8. Install the side differential gears and their 2 thrust washers. Install the pinion gears and their 2 washers onto the cross-differential pin. Install the pin and its retaining capscrew with its lockwasher. Torque the capscrew to 84 inch lbs.

9. Install the ring gear onto the differential carrier with the chamfer on the inside diameter facing the carrier. Install the 10 new mounting bolts, and torque them to 61 ft. lbs. If the parts mentioned in the note above have been replaced, perform "Selecting and Installing New Differential Selective Shims" below.

SELECTING AND INSTALLING NEW DIFFERENTIAL SELECTIVE SHIMS

➡ **To perform this procedure, you will need the following GM special tools or equivalent designs from other sources: J–8092 universal drive handle; J–26935 shim selection set; J–26938 and J–8092 axle seal and bearing race installer.**

1. Install the seven spacers (J–26935–13) into the inner side of the transaxle case and slide the long attaching bolts through from the outside.

2. Install the bearing race directly over the differential bearing on the clutch and differential housing side even though it will eventually be mounted in the clutch and differential housing. Then, install the J–26935–3 spacer over the bearing cup.

3. Bolt the clutch and differential housing over the spacers and torque the long through-bolts to 10 ft. lbs. Then, measure the width of the slot in the spacer (dimension **U**) with a feeler gauge. Use gauges of the dimensions for **U** shown in the chart. Use the largest gauge that does not bind in the slot. When you have determined the proper dimension, read down the list of dimensions and pick the one 2 sizes larger.

4. Remove the through bolts, separate the case halves, and remove the spacers. Install the selected shim of the proper size into the bore in the clutch and differential housing case.

5. Install the bearing race with the bearing race and axle seal installer. Install the axle seal with the same special tools.

Assembly of The Transaxle

ASSEMBLY OF THE GEARSHIFT RAILS AND SUPPORT COMPONENTS

➡ **To perform this procedure, you will need a hydraulic press, a J–35824 or equivalent output/input shaft support bearing installer, a J–36031 or equivalent retainer bolt hex socket, and a J–36182–1 or equivalent gear cluster a transaxle case assembly/disassembly pallet, and petroleum jelly.**

1. Position the input and output shafts next to each other with corresponding gears in normal mesh. Then install the following parts:

a. The 1-2 shift rail

b. Install the lock pin in the end of the 1–2 shift rail, using petroleum jelly to retain it.

c. The 3–4 shift rail.

d. The 5th shift rail.

e. The Reverse shift rail.

f. The shift gate and disengage roller.

2. Position the entire gear cluster and shift rail assembly onto the assembly/disassembly pallet, aligning the shift rail and shaft pilots with the corresponding holes in the fixture.

3. Install the transaxle case over the shafts, aligning the bearing bores with the shaft pilots. Install a new output shaft bearing, using the output shaft support bearing installer and the press. Install a new input shaft bearing in the same way.

4. Slide the shift rails so as to engage both 4th and reverse gears. Then, check that the output and input shaft bearings are still fully seated in the case.

5. Install new output and input shaft bearing retainers with the retainer bolt hex socket, torquing both to 50 ft. lbs. Then, shift both forks back to Neutral position. Turn the transaxle case over and support it.

ASSEMBLY OF THE SHIFT SHAFT

1. Install the reverse shift lever. Install the forward shift lever and bias spring.

2. Assemble the four shift shaft rollers and 2 shift shaft pins into the shift shaft, using petroleum jelly to retain them in place. Then, slide the shift shaft assembly into the gearbox by gently tapping it with a light hammer, aligning the hole in the shaft with the hole in the shift lever. Install the shift lever retaining pin so its ends are even with the surface of the shift lever.

ASSEMBLY OF THE CLUTCH AND DIFFERENTIAL HOUSING

➡ You will need a sealant equivalent to GM Part No. 1052942 to perform this procedure.

1. Apply the sealant mentioned above to the outside of the bolt hole pattern in the flange of the gear case.

2. Position the differential assembly into the case. Then, install the output shaft bearing to the upper end of the output shaft, turning it so the small inside diameter of the bearing cage faces the clutch housing.

3. Install the magnet into the case.

4. Install the clutch housing onto the transaxle case, and install the attaching bolts, torquing them to 15 ft. lbs.

SELECTING AND INSTALLING NEW OUTPUT SHAFT SUPPORT BEARING SELECTIVE SHIMS

➡ To perform this procedure, you will need a J-2600-19 metric dial depth gauge or equivalent, an ordinary michrometer, and a sealer such as 1052942.

1. First, inspect the output bearing to be sure the it is fully seated in its bore. Make sure the associated bearing retainer is properly torqued, breaking loose the bolts and retorquing, if necessary.

2. Use the depth dial gauge to measure the distance between the end plate mounting surface and outer race of the output shaft bearing. The arms of the gauge rest on the mounting surface and the actuating pin of the dial gauge rests on the race. Consult the chart and select the shim dimension ("A") closest to the gauge reading. Slip the shim into position.

3. Subtract the thickness of the shim (as shown in the chart) from the gauge reading found in the step above. Make sure the result does not exceed 0.03mm or, if shim thickness exceeds the measurement (so you get a minus value), the difference is not greater than 0.03mm. In other words, the upper surface of the shim can be as much as 0.03mm above or 0.03mm below the end plate mounting surface. If necessary, change the shim to the next thinner one to correct a dimension more than 0.03mm above the mounting surface; change it to the next thicker one to correct a dimension more than 0.03mm below the mounting surface.

INSTALLING THE TRANSAXLE CASE END PLATE

4. Install the oil slinger onto the upper surface of the bearing. Apply the sealer mentioned in the note above to the bolt hole pattern for the outside end plate. Then, install the end plate and the nine bolts, and torque the bolts to 15 ft. lbs.

INSTALLING THE SHIFT RAIL DETENT INTO THE CLUTCH AND DIFFERENTIAL HOUSING

1. Fill the breather hole in the case with petroleum jelly. Position the shift rails in neutral position in order to expose all the interlock notches. Position the reverse shift rail so that the detent ball sits in the notch on the rail and, at the same time, on the reverse bushing.

2. Install the reverse shift rail bushing. Then, install the four detent balls into the notches in the shift rails and retain them with petroleum jelly.

3. Install the 2 interlock pins and four springs into the bores of the detent holder.

4. Install the assembled detent holder. Work the balls into the spring pockets, using a small screwdriver. Pry the reverse rail upward to permit its detent ball to enter the spring pocket.

5. Now, use the screwdriver to gently pry the holder into a position which will cause the bolt holes to align with the threads in the detent holder assembly. On earlier models install the interlock plate.

6. If the transaxle uses the interlock plate, make sure the 3–4 shift rail protrudes fully through the center of the lock plate and that the 1–2 shift rail protrudes fully through the aperture in the outer edge. If the 1–2 rail does not protrude fully, the entire shift mechanism will be locked up when the unit is assembled. Then, install the interlock plate or holder mounting bolts and torque them to 84 inch lbs.

7. Install the protective cover by tapping it until it is seated in its bore in the transaxle case.

8. Apply a high temperature grease to its inside bore, and then install the clutch throwout bearing.

INSTALLING THE SHIFT SHAFT DETENT COMPONENTS INTO THE TRANSAXLE HOUSING

1. Install the inner spring seat followed by the 5th/Reverse bias spring. Hold this spring in position while installing the outer spring seat and then starting the fastening screw. Torque the screw to 84 inch lbs.

2. Install the protective cover so that its retaining ring is past the snapring groove and then install the snapring.

INSTALLING THE TRANSAXLE EXTERNALLY MOUNTED LINKAGE

Install the external linkage in reverse order of removal. Observe the following torques: bracket bolts 17 ft. lbs.; lever attaching nut 61 ft. lbs. (hold the lever against tightening torque); electronic speedometer sensor assembly retaining bolt 84 inch lbs. Replace the fluid level indicator washer.

Isuzu 5-Speed

Transaxle Case
◆ SEE FIGS. 54-104

DISASSEMBLY

1. Remove the clutch release bearing. Attach the transaxle to the transaxle holding fixture tool No. J-33366.

2. Remove the 7 rear cover bolts and the cover.

3. Remove the control box assembly together with the four bolts from the case.

4. Shift the transaxle into gear, then remove the 5th speed drive and the driven gear retaining nuts from the input and the output shaft. Shift the transaxle back into Neutral and aligning the detents on the shift rails.

5. Remove the detent spring retaining bolts for the 1st–2nd, the 3rd–4th and the Reverse–5th speeds. Remove the detent springs and the detent balls. Remove the Reverse detent spring retaining bolts, the spring and the detent.

6. Place the 5th speed synchronizer in Neutral, then remove the roll pin from the 5th gear shift fork and the 5th gear synchronizer hub, the sleeve, the roller bearing and the gear. Remove the shift fork as an assembly from the output shaft. Remove the 5th speed gear from the input shaft.

7. Remove the Torx® bolts from the bearing retainer, then the bearing retainer and the shims from the input and the output shafts.

8. Remove the Reverse idler shaft–to–case bolt.

9. Using tools No. J–22888 and J–22888–30, remove the output shaft collar and the thrust washer.

10. Remove the transaxle case-to-clutch housing bolts and separate the cases.

11. Remove the Reverse idler gear and the Reverse idler shaft.

12. Lift the 5th gear shaft. With the detent aligned facing the same way, remove the 5th and the Reverse shafts at the same time.

13. Using a punch and a hammer, remove the roll pin from the 1–2 shift fork. Slide the shaft upward to clear the housing, then remove the fork and the shaft from the case.

14. Remove the cotter pin, then remove the pin and the Reverse shift lever.

15. Remove the input and the output shafts with the 3–4 shift fork and the shaft as an assembly.

16. Remove the differential case assembly.

17. Remove the Reverse shift bracket together with the four bolts and the three interlock pins.

18. Remove the rear bearing outer race from the transaxle case, then the input shaft race.

19. Remove the outer races from the input shaft front bearing, the output shaft front and the differential side bearings.

20. Remove the input shaft seal from the housing, then the clutch shaft seal only when replacement is required.

21. Drive the bushing toward the inside of the housing, then remove the fork assembly only when replacing the clutch fork assembly.

ASSEMBLY

Before reassembly, attach the clutch housing to the transaxle holding fixture (if removed).

1. Install the input shaft seal.

2. Install the front outer bearing races for the input shaft, the output shaft and the differential into the clutch housing. Press the input, the output and the differential races into the housing.

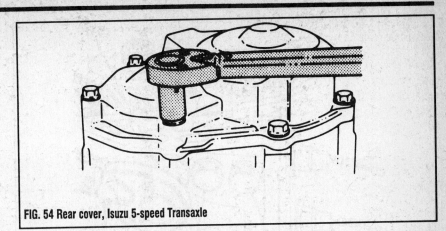

FIG. 54 Rear cover, Isuzu 5-speed Transaxle

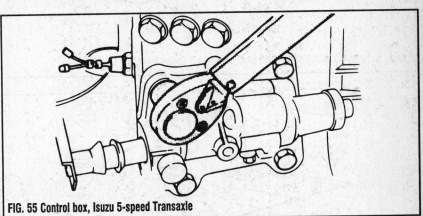

FIG. 55 Control box, Isuzu 5-speed Transaxle

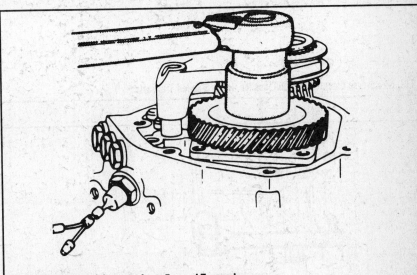

FIG. 56 5th gear retaining nuts, Isuzu 5-speed Transaxle

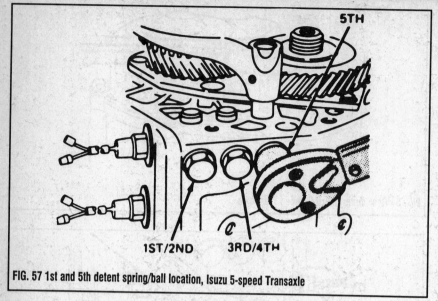

FIG. 57 1st and 5th detent spring/ball location, Isuzu 5-speed Transaxle

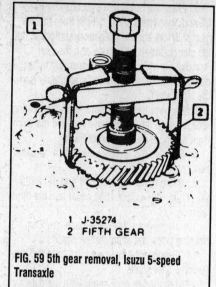

1 J-35274
2 FIFTH GEAR

FIG. 59 5th gear removal, Isuzu 5-speed Transaxle

FIG. 58 Reverse detent spring/ball location, Isuzu 5-speed Transaxle

J25359-6

FIG. 60 Bearing and shim retainer, Isuzu 5-speed Transaxle

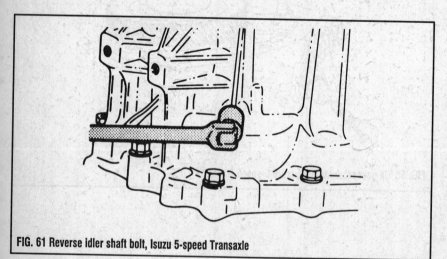

FIG. 61 Reverse idler shaft bolt, Isuzu 5-speed Transaxle

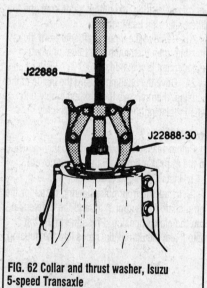

FIG. 62 Collar and thrust washer, Isuzu 5-speed Transaxle

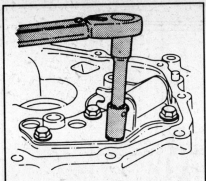

FIG. 66 Reverse shift lever and bracket, Isuzu 5-speed Transaxle

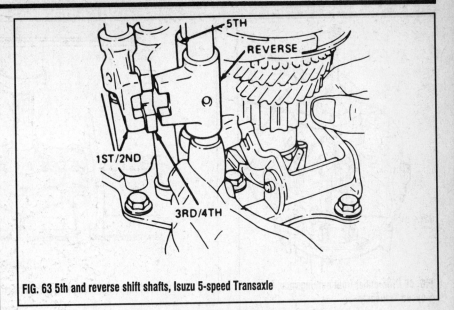

FIG. 63 5th and reverse shift shafts, Isuzu 5-speed Transaxle

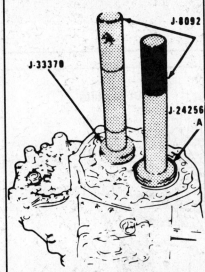

FIG. 67 Input/output rear bearing races, Isuzu 5-speed Transaxle

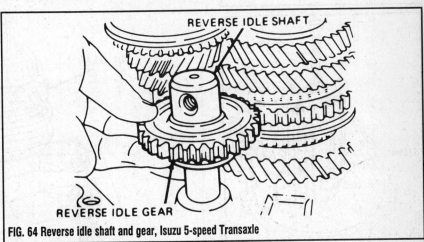

FIG. 64 Reverse idle shaft and gear, Isuzu 5-speed Transaxle

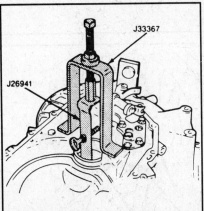

FIG. 68 Input/output front bearing races, Isuzu 5-speed Transaxle

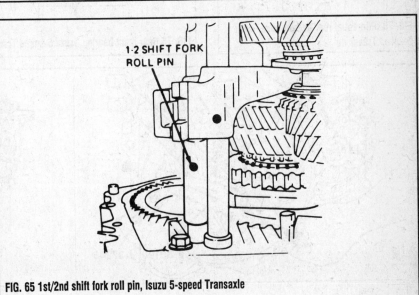

FIG. 65 1st/2nd shift fork roll pin, Isuzu 5-speed Transaxle

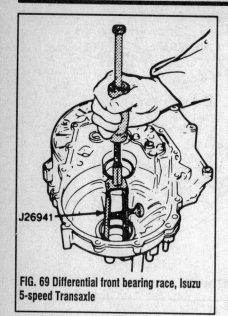

FIG. 69 Differential front bearing race, Isuzu 5-speed Transaxle

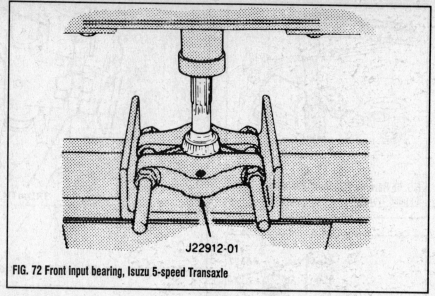

FIG. 72 Front input bearing, Isuzu 5-speed Transaxle

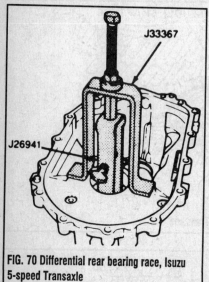

FIG. 70 Differential rear bearing race, Isuzu 5-speed Transaxle

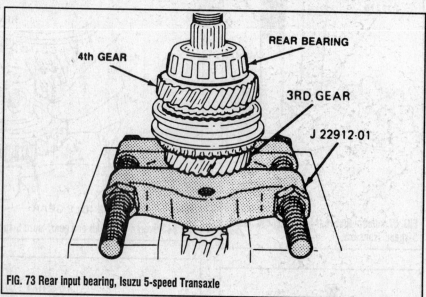

FIG. 73 Rear input bearing, Isuzu 5-speed Transaxle

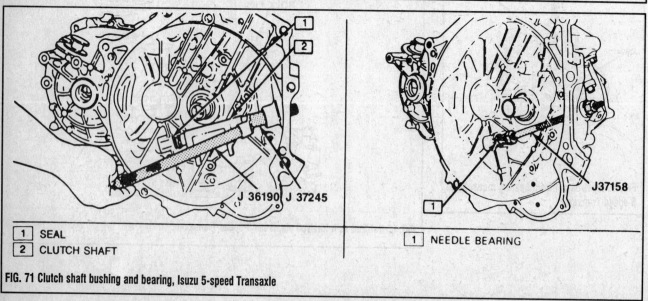

1	SEAL
2	CLUTCH SHAFT

1	NEEDLE BEARING

FIG. 71 Clutch shaft bushing and bearing, Isuzu 5-speed Transaxle

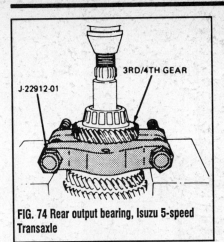

FIG. 74 Rear output bearing, Isuzu 5-speed Transaxle

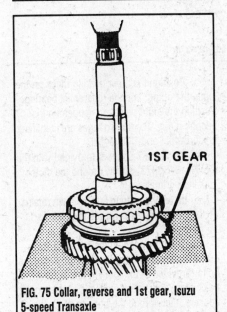

FIG. 75 Collar, reverse and 1st gear, Isuzu 5-speed Transaxle

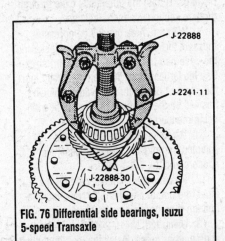

FIG. 76 Differential side bearings, Isuzu 5-speed Transaxle

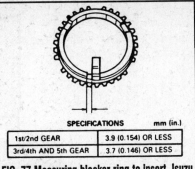

SPECIFICATIONS	mm (in.)
1st/2nd GEAR	3.9 (0.154) OR LESS
3rd/4th AND 5th GEAR	3.7 (0.146) OR LESS

FIG. 77 Measuring blocker ring to insert, Isuzu 5-speed Transaxle

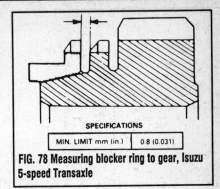

SPECIFICATIONS	
MIN. LIMIT mm (in.)	0.8 (0.031)

FIG. 78 Measuring blocker ring to gear, Isuzu 5-speed Transaxle

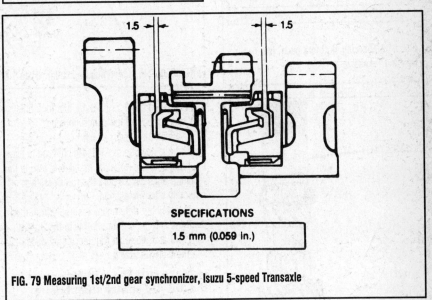

SPECIFICATIONS

1.5 mm (0.059 in.)

FIG. 79 Measuring 1st/2nd gear synchronizer, Isuzu 5-speed Transaxle

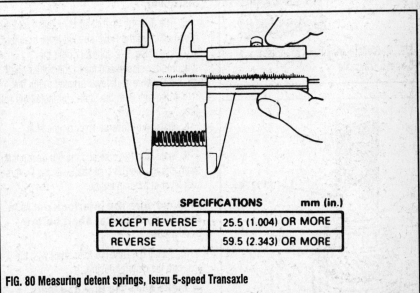

SPECIFICATIONS	mm (in.)
EXCEPT REVERSE	25.5 (1.004) OR MORE
REVERSE	59.5 (2.343) OR MORE

FIG. 80 Measuring detent springs, Isuzu 5-speed Transaxle

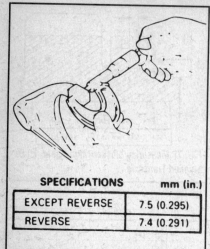

SPECIFICATIONS	mm (in.)
EXCEPT REVERSE	7.5 (0.295)
REVERSE	7.4 (0.291)

FIG. 81 Measuring shift fork pads, Isuzu 5-speed Transaxle

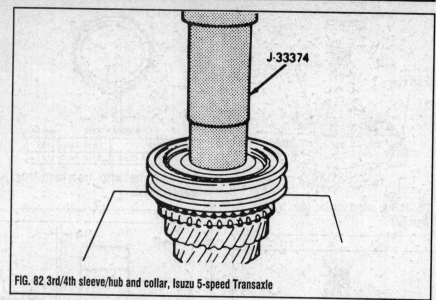

FIG. 82 3rd/4th sleeve/hub and collar, Isuzu 5-speed Transaxle

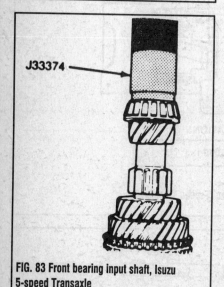

FIG. 83 Front bearing input shaft, Isuzu 5-speed Transaxle

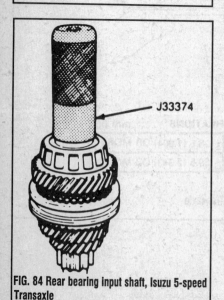

FIG. 84 Rear bearing input shaft, Isuzu 5-speed Transaxle

3. Apply grease to the three interlock pins and install them on the clutch housing.

4. Install the Reverse shift bracket on the clutch housing. Use the 3rd–4th shift rod to align the bracket to the housing. Install and torque the retaining bolts. Make sure the rod operates smoothly after installation.

5. Install the differential assembly first, then the input and the output shaft with the 3rd–4th shift fork and the shaft together as an assembly into the clutch housing.

➡ **Make sure the interlock pin is in the 3rd–4th shifter shaft before installing.**

6. The 3rd–4th shift shaft is installed into the raised collar of the Reverse shift lever bracket.

7. Install the 1–2 shift fork onto the synchronizer sleeve and insert the shifter shaft into the Reverse shift lever bracket. Align the hole in the fork with the shaft and install the roll pin.

8. Install the Reverse lever on the shift bracket.

9. Install the Reverse and the 5th gear shifter shaft; engage the Reverse shaft with the Reverse shift lever at the same time.

➡ **Make sure the interlock pin is in the 5th gear shifter shaft before installing.**

10. Install the Reverse idler shaft with the gear into the clutch housing.

➡ **Make sure the Reverse lever is engaged in the gear collar.**

11. Using tool No. J–33373, measure and determine the shim size.

a. Position the outer bearing races on the input, the output and the differential bearings. Position the shim selection gauges on the bearing races. The three gauges are identified: Input, Output and Differential.

b. Place the 7 spacers (provided with the tool No. J–33373) evenly around the clutch housing perimeter.

c. Install the bearing and the shim retainer on the transaxle case. Torque the bolts to 11–16 ft. lbs.

d. Carefully position the transaxle case over the gauges and on the spacers. Install the bolts (provided in the tool kit) and tighten the bolts alternately until the case is seated on the spacers, then torque the bolts to 10 ft. lbs.

e. Rotate each gauge to seat the bearings. Rotate the differential case through three revolutions in each direction.

f. With the three gauges compressed, measure the gap between the outer sleeve and the base pad using the available shim sizes. Use the largest shim that can be placed into the gap and drawn through without binding; this will be the correct shim for the bearing being measured.

g. When each of the three shims selected, remove the transaxle case, the spacers and the three gauges.

12. Position the shim selected for the input, the output and the differential into the bearing race bores in the transaxle case.

13. Using tool No. J–24256–A, J–8092 and an arbor press, install the rear input shaft bearing race; press the bearing until it is seated in its bore.

14. Using tool No. J–33370, J–8092 and an arbor press, install the rear output shaft bearing; press the bearing until it is seated in its bore.

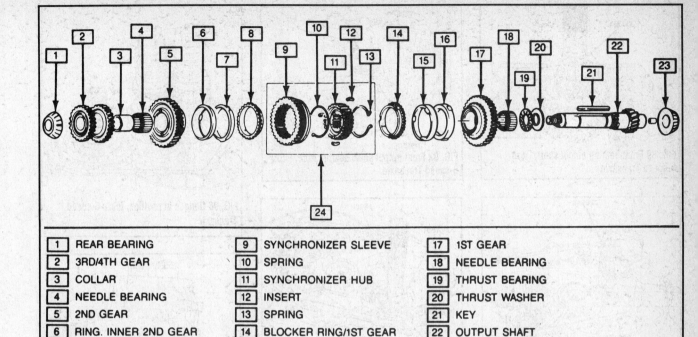

1 REAR BEARING	**9** SYNCHRONIZER SLEEVE	**17** 1ST GEAR
2 3RD/4TH GEAR	**10** SPRING	**18** NEEDLE BEARING
3 COLLAR	**11** SYNCHRONIZER HUB	**19** THRUST BEARING
4 NEEDLE BEARING	**12** INSERT	**20** THRUST WASHER
5 2ND GEAR	**13** SPRING	**21** KEY
6 RING. INNER 2ND GEAR	**14** BLOCKER RING/1ST GEAR	**22** OUTPUT SHAFT
7 RING. OUTER 2ND GEAR	**15** RING. OUTER/1ST GEAR	**23** FRONT BEARING
8 BLOCKER RING 2ND GEAR	**16** RING. INNER/1ST GEAR	**24** 1ST/2ND GEAR SYNCHRONIZER ASSEMBLY

FIG. 85 Exploded view of output shaft components, Isuzu 5-speed Transaxle

15. Using tool No. J–8611–01, J–8092 and an arbor press, install the rear differential case bearing race; press the bearing until it is seated in its bore.

16. Apply a 1/8 in. (3mm) bead of Loctite® 514 to the mating surfaces of the clutch housing and the transaxle case.

17. Be sure the magnet is installed in the transaxle case.

18. Install the case on the clutch housing and the Reverse idle shaft bolt into the case, then torque the bolt to 22–33 ft. lbs.

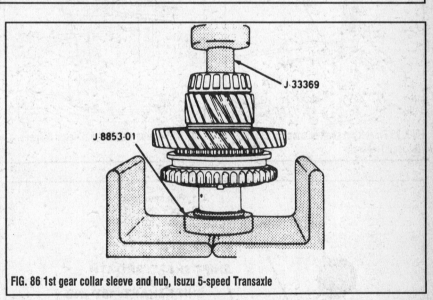

FIG. 86 1st gear collar sleeve and hub, Isuzu 5-speed Transaxle

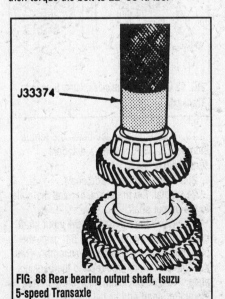

FIG. 88 Rear bearing output shaft, Isuzu 5-speed Transaxle

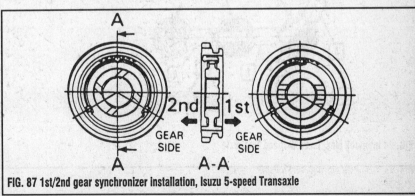

FIG. 87 1st/2nd gear synchronizer installation, Isuzu 5-speed Transaxle

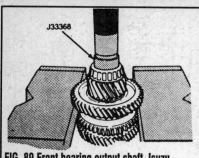

FIG. 89 Front bearing output shaft, Isuzu 5-speed Transaxle

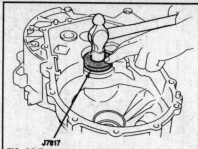

FIG. 92 Front output shaft bearing race, Isuzu 5-speed Transaxle

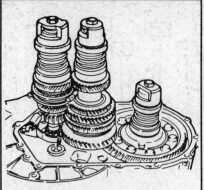

FIG. 96 Gauges in position, Isuzu 5-speed Transaxle

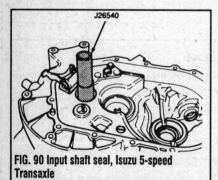

FIG. 90 Input shaft seal, Isuzu 5-speed Transaxle

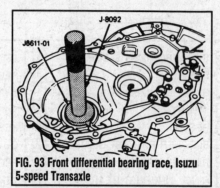

FIG. 93 Front differential bearing race, Isuzu 5-speed Transaxle

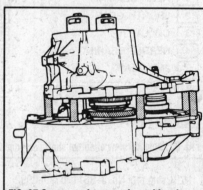

FIG. 97 Gauges and spacers in position, Isuzu 5-speed Transaxle

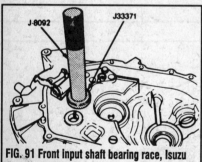

FIG. 91 Front input shaft bearing race, Isuzu 5-speed Transaxle

FIG. 95 Reverse shift bracket, Isuzu 5-speed Transaxle

FIG. 98 Checking shim sizes, Isuzu 5-speed Transaxle

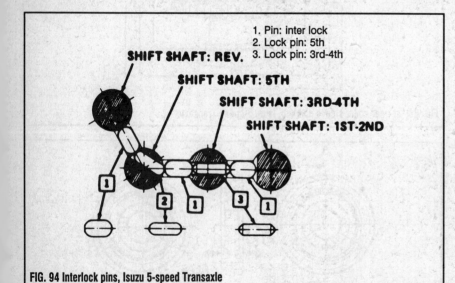

1. Pin: inter lock
2. Lock pin: 5th
3. Lock pin: 3rd-4th

SHIFT SHAFT: REV.

SHIFT SHAFT: 5TH

SHIFT SHAFT: 3RD-4TH

SHIFT SHAFT: 1ST-2ND

FIG. 94 Interlock pins, Isuzu 5-speed Transaxle

19. Install the 14 case bolts and torque them to 22–33 ft. lbs. (in a diagonal sequence).

20. Install the drive axle seals.

21. Install the thrust washer and the collar to the output shaft.

22. Install the 5th gear to the input shaft. Install the needle bearing, the 5th gear, the blocking ring, the hub/sleeve assembly (with the shift fork in its groove) and the backing plate on the output shaft. Align the shift fork on the shifter shaft and install the roll pin.

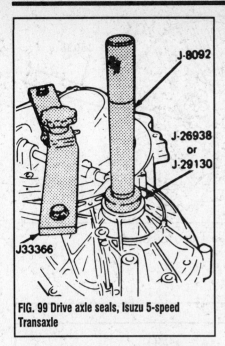

FIG. 99 Drive axle seals, Isuzu 5-speed Transaxle

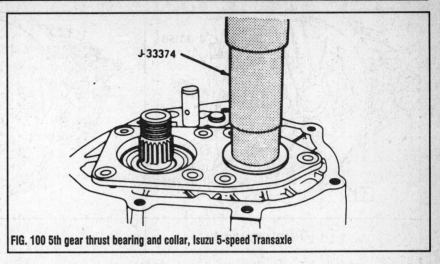

FIG. 100 5th gear thrust bearing and collar, Isuzu 5-speed Transaxle

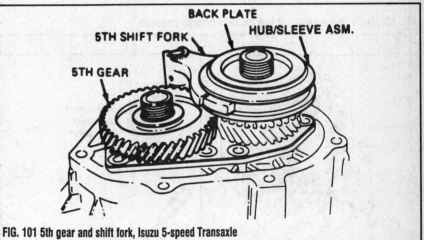

FIG. 101 5th gear and shift fork, Isuzu 5-speed Transaxle

23. Install the Reverse detent balls and the springs, then the 1st–2nd, the 3rd–4th and the 5th speed gears. Install the bolts and torque to 15–21 ft. lbs.

24. Apply Loctite® 262 to the input and the output shaft threads. Install new retaining nuts and torque to 87–101 ft. lbs.; stake the nuts after reaching the final torque.

25. Install the gasket and the control box assembly on the transaxle case, then torque the bolts to 11–16 ft. lbs.

➡ **Make sure the transaxle shifts properly before installing the rear cover.**

26. Install the gasket and the rear cover with the 7 bolts, then torque the bolts to 11–16 ft. lbs.

27. Install the clutch fork assembly (if removed). Using tool No. J–28412, install the bushing into the upper hole. Install the oil seal. Before installing the bushing, apply grease to both the interior and the exterior.

28. Install the clutch release bearing.

Input Shaft

DISASSEMBLY

1. Using tool No. J–22912–01 and an arbor press, remove the front bearing.

2. Pull out the rear bearing 4th gear, the 3rd–4th synchronizer assembly and 3rd gear as an assembly.

➡ **This procedure requires a arbor press and tool No. J–22912–01.**

3. Remove the outer parts from, the input shaft.

Output Shaft

DISASSEMBLY

1. Using tool No. J–22227–A and an arbor press, remove the front bearing.

2. Using tool No. J–22912–01 and an arbor press, remove the rear bearing and the 3rd–4th gear as an assembly.

3. Remove the key, the 2nd gear, the needle bearing and the blocking ring.

4. Using an arbor press, remove the collar, the Reverse gear assembly and the 1st gear as an assembly.

Drive Axles (Halfshafts)

These vehicles use unequal-length halfshafts. All halfshafts incorporate a male spline; the shafts interlock with the transaxle gears through the use of barrel-type snaprings. Four constant velocity joints are used, two on each shaft. The inner joints are of the double offset design; the outer joints are Rzeppa-type.

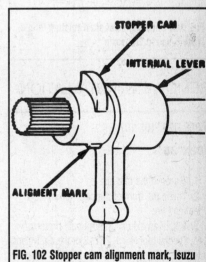

FIG. 102 Stopper cam alignment mark, Isuzu 5-speed Transaxle

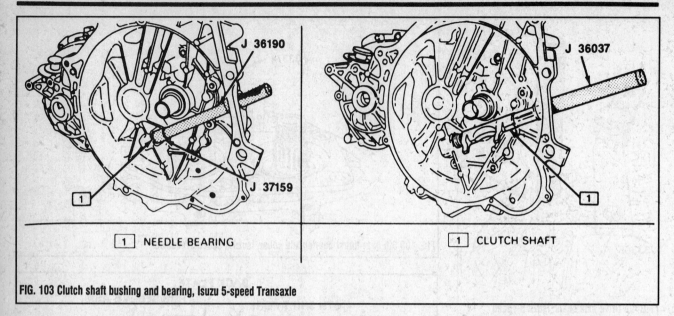

| 1 | NEEDLE BEARING |

| 1 | CLUTCH SHAFT |

FIG. 103 Clutch shaft bushing and bearing, Isuzu 5-speed Transaxle

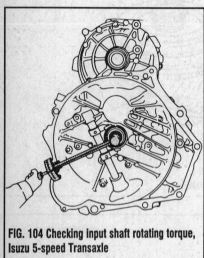

FIG. 104 Checking input shaft rotating torque, Isuzu 5-speed Transaxle

REMOVAL & INSTALLATION

◆ SEE FIGS. 105-107

1982-86

1. Remove the hub nut.
2. Raise the front of the car. Remove the wheel and tire.
3. Install an axle shaft boot seal protector, G.M. special tool No. J–28712 or the equivalent, onto the seal.
4. Disconnect the brake hose clip from the MacPherson strut, but do not disconnect the hose from the caliper. Remove the brake caliper from the spindle, and hang the caliper out of the way by a length of wire. Do not allow the caliper to hang by the brake hose.

1. Hub nut
2. Washer
3. Knuckle & hub assembly
4. Drive axle—outer joint
5. Drive axle—inner joint

FIG. 105 Drive axle removal — 1987–88

5. Mark the camber alignment cam bolt for reassembly. Remove the cam bolt and the upper attaching bolt from the strut and spindle.
6. Pull the steering knuckle assembly from the strut bracket.
7. Using G.M. special tool J–28468 or the equivalent, remove the axle shaft from the transaxle.

8. Using G.M. special tool J–28733 or the equivalent spindle remover, remove the axle shaft from the hub and bearing assembly.
9. If a new drive axle is to be installed, a new knuckle seal should be installed first.
10. Loosely install the drive axle into the transaxle and steering knuckle.
11. Loosely attach the steering knuckle to the suspension strut.

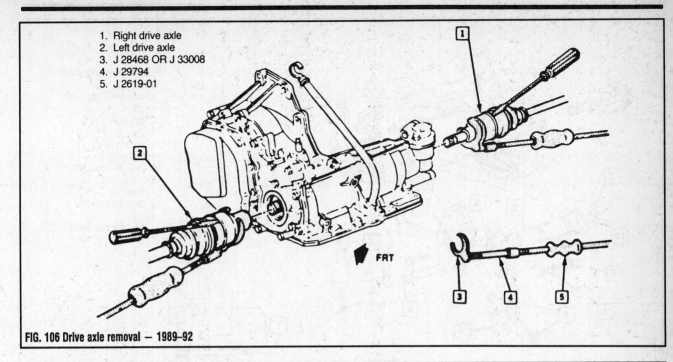

1. Right drive axle
2. Left drive axle
3. J 28468 OR J 33008
4. J 29794
5. J 2619-01

FRT

FIG. 106 Drive axle removal — 1989–92

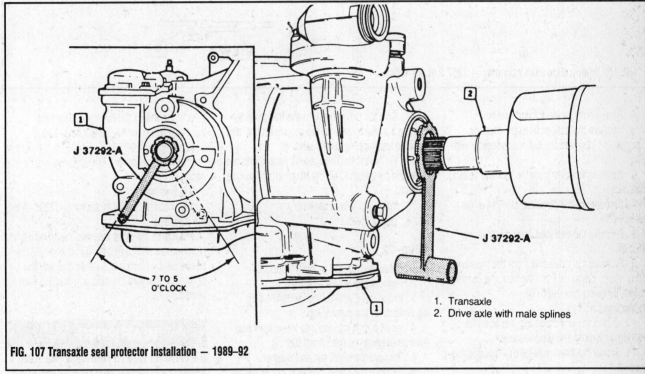

J 37292-A

J 37292-A

7 TO 5
O'CLOCK

1. Transaxle
2. Drive axle with male splines

FIG. 107 Transaxle seal protector installation — 1989–92

12. Install the brake caliper. Tighten the bolts to 30 ft. lbs. (40Nm.).

13. The drive axle is an interference fit in the steering knuckle. Press the axle into place, then install the hub nut. When the shaft begins to turn with the hub, insert a drift through the caliper into one of the cooling slots in the rotor to keep it from turning. Tighten the hub nut to 70 ft. lbs. (100Nm.). to completely seat the shaft.

14. Load the hub assembly by lowering it onto a jackstand. Align the camber cam bolt marks made during removal, install the bolt and tighten to 140 ft. lbs. (190 Nm.). Tighten the upper nut to the same value.

15. Install the axle shaft all the way into the transaxle using a screwdriver inserted into the groove provided on the inner retainer. Tap the screwdriver until the shaft seats in the transaxle.

16. Connect the brake hose clip to the strut. Install the tire and wheel, lower the car, and tighten the hub nut to 185 ft. lbs. (260 Nm.).

1987–88

1. Raise the car and suitably support.
2. Remove the wheel assembly.
3. Insert a drift into the into the caliper and rotor to prevent the rotor from turning.

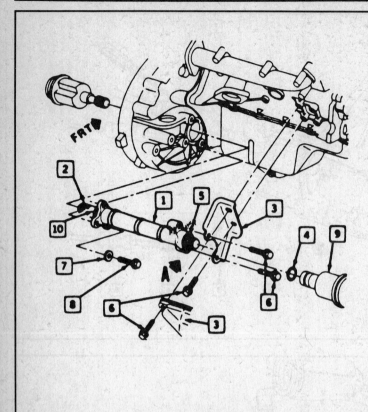

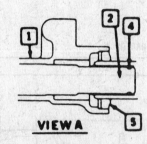

1. Intermediate shaft assembly
2. Intermediate axle shaft
3. Bracket
4. Axle shaft retaining ring
5. Lip seal
6. Bolt 50 Nm (37 lbs. ft.)
7. Washer
8. Bolt 25 Nm (18 lbs. ft.)
9. Right drive axle
10. "O" ring seal

FIG. 108 Intermediate shaft assembly — 1987 2.8L V6 engine

4. Remove the shaft nut and washer.

5. Remove the caliper from the steering knuckle and suspend the caliper assembly with a wire.

6. Remove the rotor from the hub and bearing assembly.

7. Disconnect the stabilizer shaft from the control arm.

8. Remove the ball joint from the steering knuckle.

9. Remove the drive axle from the transaxle. Remove the driveaxle from the hub and bearing assembly using tool J–28733.

To Install:

10. Install the drive axle into the hub and bearing assembly and the transaxle.

11. Install the lower ball joint to the steering knuckle.

12. Install the stabilizer shaft to the control arm.

13. Install the rotor to the hub and bearing assembly.

14. Install the caliper to the steering knuckle.

15. Install a washer and a new shaft nut.

16. Insert a drift into the into the caliper and rotor to prevent the rotor from turning and torque drive axle nut to 185 ft. lbs. (260 Nm).

17. Seat the drive axle into the transaxle by placing a screwdriver into the groove on the joint housing and tapping until seated.

18. Verify that the drive axle is seated into the transaxle by grasping on the housing and pulling outward.

19. Install the wheel assembly.

20. Lower the car

1989–92

1. Raise the car and suitably support.

2. Remove the wheel assembly.

3. Install drive seal protector J34754 or equivalent, on the outer joint.

4. Insert a drift into the into the caliper and rotor to prevent the rotor from turning.

4. Remove the shaft nut and washer.

5. Remove the lower ball joint cotter pin and nut and loosen the joint using tool J 38892 or equivqlent. If removing the right axle, turn the wheel to the left, if removing the left axle, turn the wheel to the right.

6. Separate the joint, with a pry bar between the suspension support.

7. Disengage the axle from the hub and bearing using J 28733–A or equivalent.

8. Separate the hub and bearing assembly from the drive axle and move the strut and knuckkle assembly rearward.

9. Disconnect the inner joint from the transaxle using tool J–28468 or J–33008 attached to J–29794 and J–2619–01 or from the intermediate shaft (V6 and Turbo engines), if equipped.

To install:

10. Install axle seal protector J–37292–A into the transaxle.

11. Insert the drive axle into the transaxle or intermediate shaft (V6 and Turbo engines), if equipped, by placing a suitable tool into the groove on the joint housing and tapping until seated.

✳✳ WARNING

Be careful not to damage the axle seal or dislodge the transaxle seal garter spring when installing the axle.

12. Verify that the drive axle is seated into the transaxle by grasping on the housing and pulling outward.

13. Install the drive axle into the hub and bearing assembly.

14. Install the lower ball joint to the knuckle.

Tighten the ball joint to steering knuckle nut to 41 ft. lbs. (55 Nm) and install the cotter pin.

15. Install the washer and new drive shaft nut.

16. Insert a drift into the caliper and rotor to prevent the rotor from turning and tighten the drive shaft nut to 185 ft. lbs. (260 Nm).

17. Remove both J–37292–B and J–34754 seal protectors.

18. Install the tire and wheel assembly.

19. Lower the vehicle and connect the negative battery cable.

Intermediate shaft

REMOVAL & INSTALLATION

♦ SEE FIGS. 108-111

2.8L and 3.1L V6 engine

1987

1. Install engine support bar J–28467.
2. Raise the car and suitably support.
3. Remove the wheel assembly.
4. Drain the transaxle.
5. Install the modified outer seal protector J–34754.
6. Remove the stabilizer shaft from the right control arm.
7. Remove the right ball joint from the knuckle.
8. Disconnect the drive axle from the intermediate axle shaft.
9. Remove the two housing to bracket bolts.
10. Remove the bottom bracket to engine bolt and loosen the top bolt, rotate the bracket out of the way.
11. Remove the 3 bolts holding the housing to the transaxle.
12. Carefully disengage the intermediate axle shaft from the transaxle and remove the intermediate shaft assembly.

To Install:

13. Place the intermediate shaft into position and lock the intermediate axle shaft into the transaxle.
14. Install the 3 bolts holding the housing to the transaxle and tighten to 18 ft. lbs.
15. Rotate the bracket into position and install the bottom bolt, tighten both bolts to 37 ft. lbs.
16. Install the two housing to bracket bolts and tighten to 37 ft. lbs.
17. Coat the splines with chassis grease.

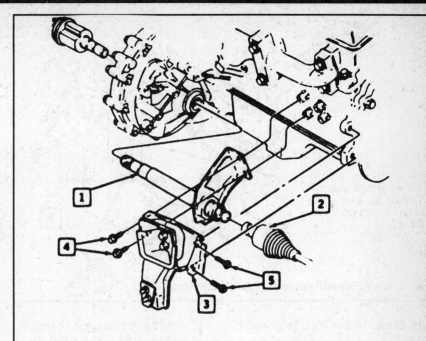

1. Intermediate shaft
2. Right axle shaft
3. Engine mount bracket
4. Bolt 52 Nm (38 lbs. ft.)
5. Bolt 62 Nm (46 lbs. ft.)

FIG. 109 Intermediate shaft assembly — 1988–90 2.8L and 3.1L V6 engine

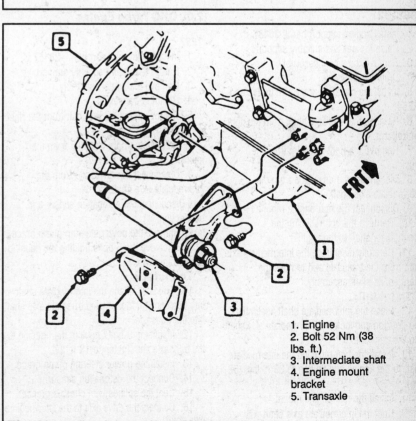

1. Engine
2. Bolt 52 Nm (38 lbs. ft.)
3. Intermediate shaft
4. Engine mount bracket
5. Transaxle

FIG. 110 Intermediate shaft assembly — 1991–92 3.1L V6 engine

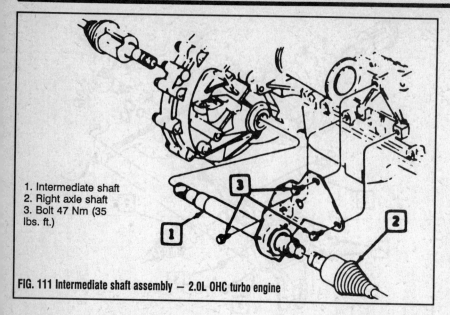

1. Intermediate shaft
2. Right axle shaft
3. Bolt 47 Nm (35 lbs. ft.)

FIG. 111 Intermediate shaft assembly — 2.0L OHC turbo engine

18. Connect the drive axle to the intermediate axle shaft.

19. Connect the right ball joint to the knuckle.

20. Install the stabilizer shaft to the right control arm.

21. Install the wheel.

22. Lower the car and fill the transaxle with the proper fluid.

1988–92

1. Install engine support bar J–28467.

2. Raise the car and suitably support.

3. Remove the wheel assembly.

4. Drain the transaxle.

5. Install the modified outer seal protector J–34754.

6. Remove the stabilizer shaft from the right control arm.

7. Remove the right ball joint from the knuckle.

8. Disconnect the drive axle from the intermediate axle shaft.

9. Disconnect the rear engine mount.

10. Remove the bolt retaining the intermediate shaft to the engine.

11. Carefully disengage the intermediate axle shaft from the transaxle and remove the intermediate shaft assembly.

To Install:

12. Place the intermediate shaft assembly into position and lock the intermediate axle shaft into the transaxle.

13. Install the bolt retaining the intermediate shaft to the engine and tighten to 38 ft. lbs. (52 Nm).

14. Install the rear engine mount.

15. Coat the intermediate axle shaft with chassis grease and install the intermediate axle shaft to the drive axle.

16. Install the right ball joint to the knuckle.

17. Install the stabilizer shaft to the right control arm.

18. Remove the seal protector tool.

19. Install the wheel and lower the vehicle.

20. Remove the engine support bar holding fixture.

21. Fill the transaxle with the proper fluid.

2.0L OHC Turbo Engine

1987

1. Install engine support bar J–28467.

2. Raise the car and suitably support.

3. Remove the wheel assembly.

4. Drain the transaxle.

5. Remove the stabilizer shaft from the right control arm.

6. Remove the right ball joint from the knuckle.

7. Disconnect the drive axle from the intermediate axle shaft.

8. Disconnect the detonation sensor and connection.

9. Remove the power steering pump brace.

10. Remove the 3 bolts holding the housing to the transaxle.

To Install:

11. To install, place the intermediate shaft into position and lock the intermediate axle shaft into the transaxle.

12. Install the 3 bolts holding the housing to the transaxle and tighten to 18 ft. lbs.

13. Install the power steering pump brace.

14. Connect the detonation sensor.

15. Coat the splines with chassis grease.

16. Connect the drive axle to the intermediate axle shaft.

17. Connect the right ball joint to the knuckle.

18. Install the stabilizer shaft to the right control arm.

19. Install the wheel.

20. Lower the car and fill the transaxle with the proper fluid.

1988–90

1. Install engine support bar J–28467 or equivalent.

2. Raise the car and suitably support.

3. Remove the right wheel assembly.

4. Drain the transaxle.

5. Install the modified outer seal protector J–34754.

6. Remove the stabilizer shaft from the right control arm.

7. Remove the right ball joint from the knuckle.

8. Disconnect the drive axle from the intermediate axle shaft.

9. Remove the bracket to engine bolts and one stud and carefully disengage the intermediate axle shaft from the transaxle and remove the intermediate shaft assembly.

To Install:

10. Place the intermediate shaft into position and lock the intermediate axle shaft into the transaxle.

11. Install the bracket to engine bolts and one stud and tighten to 35 ft. lbs. (47 Nm).

12. Coat the splines with chassis grease.

13. Connect the drive axle to the intermediate axle shaft.

14. Connect the right ball joint to the knuckle.

15. Install the stabilizer shaft to the right control arm.

16. Install the wheel.

17. Lower the car and fill the transaxle with the proper fluid.

CONSTANT VELOCITY JOINT (DRIVE AXLE) OVERHAUL

1982–85 Double Off-Set and 1982–90 Tri-Pot Design

▶ SEE FIGS. 112-133

For all overhaul procedures for the 1982–85 Double Off-Set type and 1982–90 Tri-Pot type drive axles, please refer to the illustrated procedures.

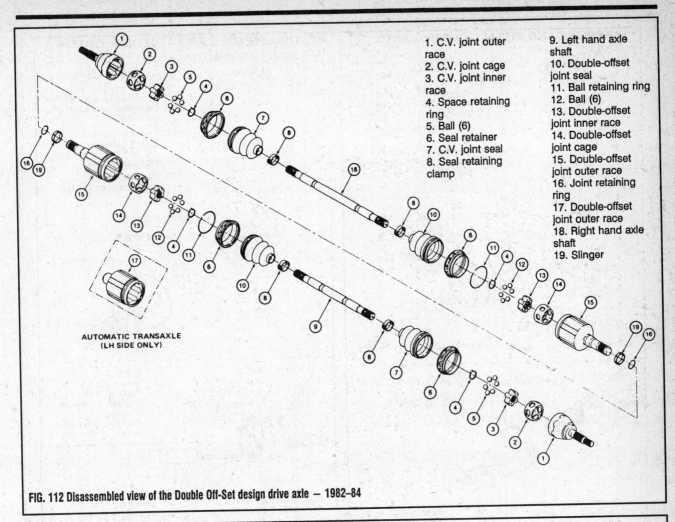

1. C.V. joint outer race
2. C.V. joint cage
3. C.V. joint inner race
4. Space retaining ring
5. Ball (6)
6. Seal retainer
7. C.V. joint seal
8. Seal retaining clamp
9. Left hand axle shaft
10. Double-offset joint seal
11. Ball retaining ring
12. Ball (6)
13. Double-offset joint inner race
14. Double-offset joint cage
15. Double-offset joint outer race
16. Joint retaining ring
17. Double-offset joint outer race
18. Right hand axle shaft
19. Slinger

AUTOMATIC TRANSAXLE
(LH SIDE ONLY)

FIG. 112 Disassembled view of the Double Off-Set design drive axle — 1982–84

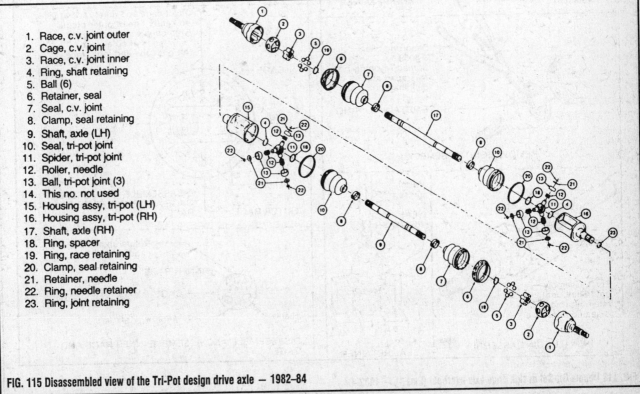

1. Race, c.v. joint outer
2. Cage, c.v. joint
3. Race, c.v. joint inner
4. Ring, shaft retaining
5. Ball (6)
6. Retainer, seal
7. Seal, c.v. joint
8. Clamp, seal retaining
9. Shaft, axle (LH)
10. Seal, tri-pot joint
11. Spider, tri-pot joint
12. Roller, needle
13. Ball, tri-pot joint (3)
14. This no. not used
15. Housing assy, tri-pot (LH)
16. Housing assy, tri-pot (RH)
17. Shaft, axle (RH)
18. Ring, spacer
19. Ring, race retaining
20. Clamp, seal retaining
21. Retainer, needle
22. Ring, needle retainer
23. Ring, joint retaining

FIG. 115 Disassembled view of the Tri-Pot design drive axle — 1982–84

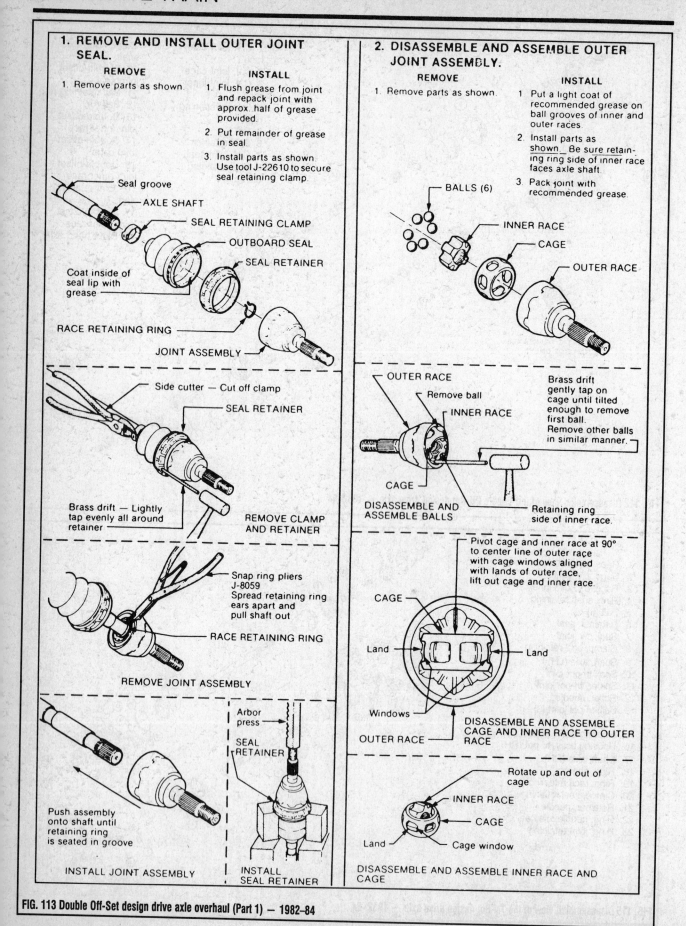

1. REMOVE AND INSTALL OUTER JOINT SEAL.

REMOVE

1. Remove parts as shown.

INSTALL

1. Flush grease from joint and repack joint with approx. half of grease provided.

2. Put remainder of grease in seal.

3. Install parts as shown. Use tool J-22610 to secure seal retaining clamp.

- Seal groove
- AXLE SHAFT
- SEAL RETAINING CLAMP
- OUTBOARD SEAL
- SEAL RETAINER
- Coat inside of seal lip with grease
- RACE RETAINING RING
- JOINT ASSEMBLY

- Side cutter — Cut off clamp
- SEAL RETAINER
- Brass drift — Lightly tap evenly all around retainer
- REMOVE CLAMP AND RETAINER

- Snap ring pliers J-8059 Spread retaining ring ears apart and pull shaft out
- RACE RETAINING RING
- REMOVE JOINT ASSEMBLY

- Push assembly onto shaft until retaining ring is seated in groove
- INSTALL JOINT ASSEMBLY

- Arbor press
- SEAL RETAINER
- INSTALL SEAL RETAINER

2. DISASSEMBLE AND ASSEMBLE OUTER JOINT ASSEMBLY.

REMOVE

1. Remove parts as shown.

INSTALL

1. Put a light coat of recommended grease on ball grooves of inner and outer races.

2. Install parts as shown. Be sure retaining ring side of inner race faces axle shaft.

3. Pack joint with recommended grease.

- BALLS (6)
- INNER RACE
- CAGE
- OUTER RACE

- OUTER RACE
- Remove ball
- INNER RACE
- CAGE
- DISASSEMBLE AND ASSEMBLE BALLS
- Brass drift gently tap on cage until tilted enough to remove first ball. Remove other balls in similar manner.
- Retaining ring side of inner race.

- Pivot cage and inner race at 90° to center line of outer race with cage windows aligned with lands of outer race, lift out cage and inner race.
- CAGE
- Land
- Land
- Windows
- OUTER RACE
- DISASSEMBLE AND ASSEMBLE CAGE AND INNER RACE TO OUTER RACE

- Rotate up and out of cage
- INNER RACE
- CAGE
- Land
- Cage window
- DISASSEMBLE AND ASSEMBLE INNER RACE AND CAGE

FIG. 113 Double Off-Set design drive traxle overhaul (Part 1) — 1982–84

3. REMOVE AND INSTALL INNER JOINT SEAL

REMOVE

1. Remove parts as shown.

INSTALL

1. Flush grease from joint. Repack joint with approx. half of grease provided.
2. Put remainder of grease in seal.
3. Install parts as shown. Use tool J-22610 to secure seal retaining clamp.

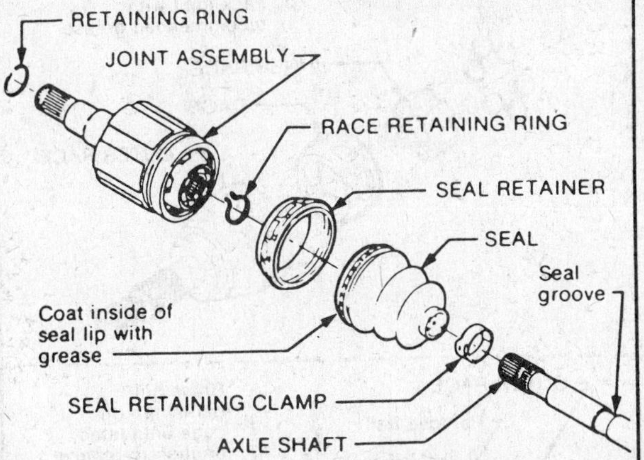

- RETAINING RING
- JOINT ASSEMBLY
- RACE RETAINING RING
- SEAL RETAINER
- SEAL
- Seal groove
- Coat inside of seal lip with grease
- SEAL RETAINING CLAMP
- AXLE SHAFT

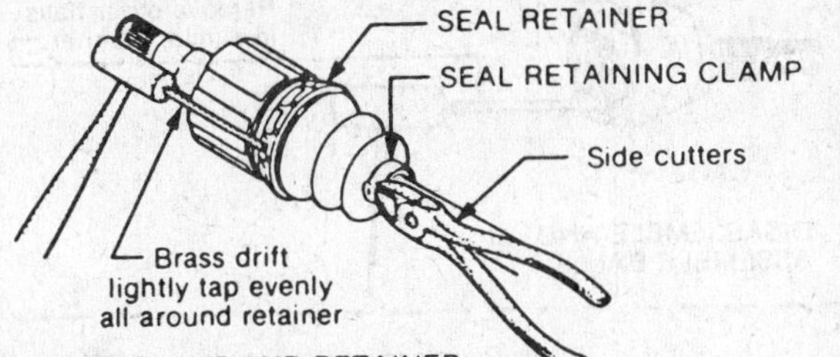

- SEAL RETAINER
- SEAL RETAINING CLAMP
- Side cutters
- Brass drift lightly tap evenly all around retainer

REMOVE CLAMP AND RETAINER

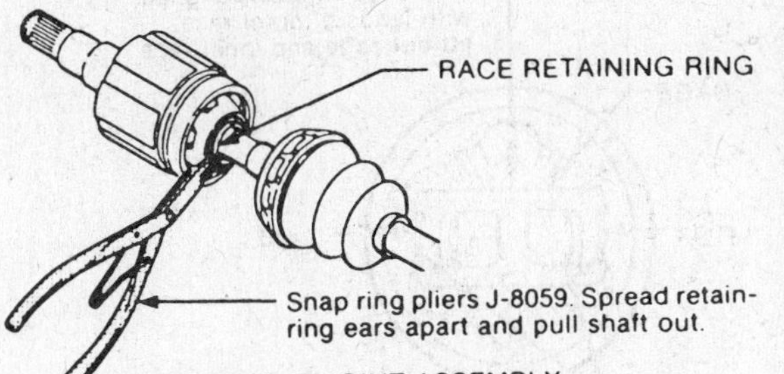

- RACE RETAINING RING
- Snap ring pliers J-8059. Spread retaining-ring ears apart and pull shaft out.

REMOVE JOINT ASSEMBLY

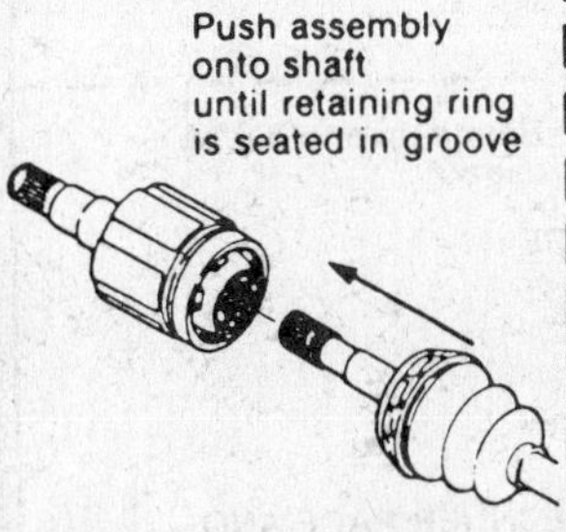

Push assembly onto shaft until retaining ring is seated in groove

Arbor press

SEAL RETAINER

INSTALL JOINT ASSEMBLY 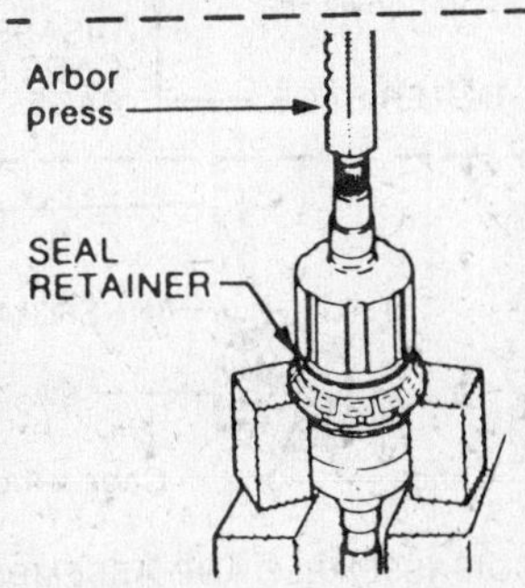 | **INSTALL SEAL RETAINER**

4. DISASSEMBLE AND ASSEMBLE INNER JOINT

REMOVE

1. Remove parts as shown.

INSTALL

1. Install parts as shown. Retaining ring side of inner race and small end of cage face axle shaft.
2. Pack joint with recommended grease.

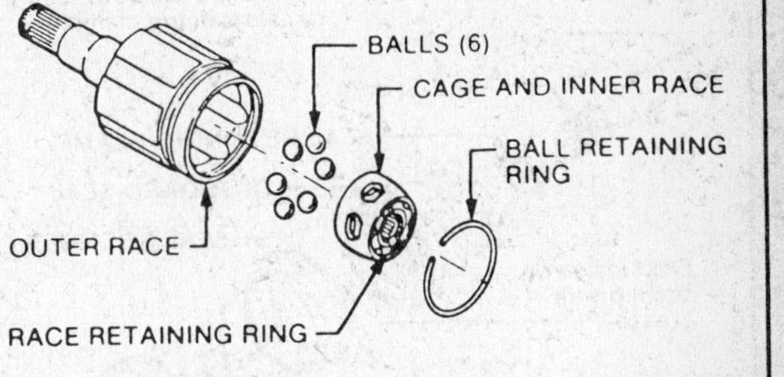

- BALLS (6)
- CAGE AND INNER RACE
- BALL RETAINING RING
- OUTER RACE
- RACE RETAINING RING

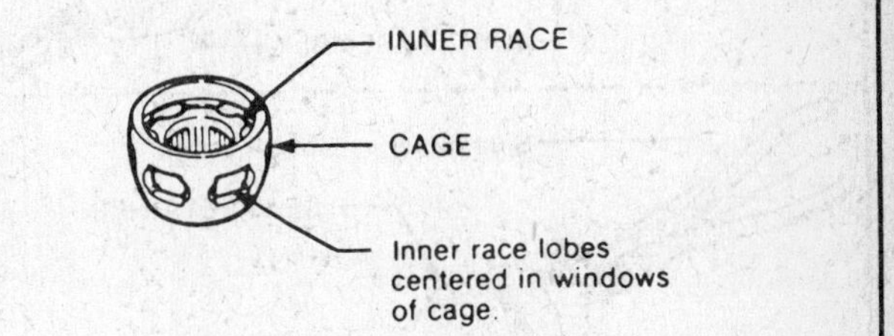

- INNER RACE
- CAGE
- Inner race lobes centered in windows of cage.

POSITION INNER RACE IN CAGE

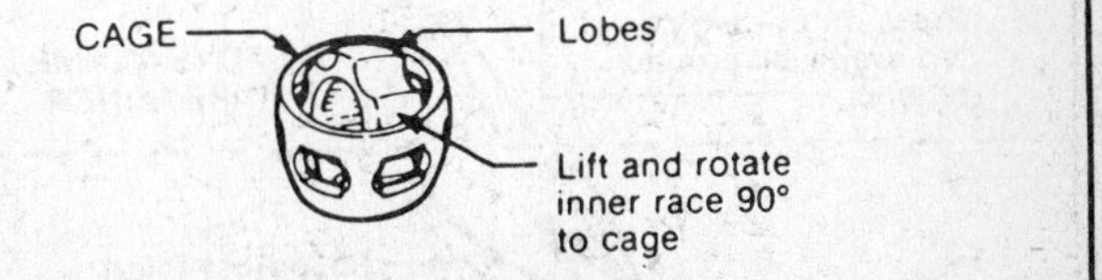

- CAGE
- Lobes
- Lift and rotate inner race 90° to cage

ROTATE INNER RACE

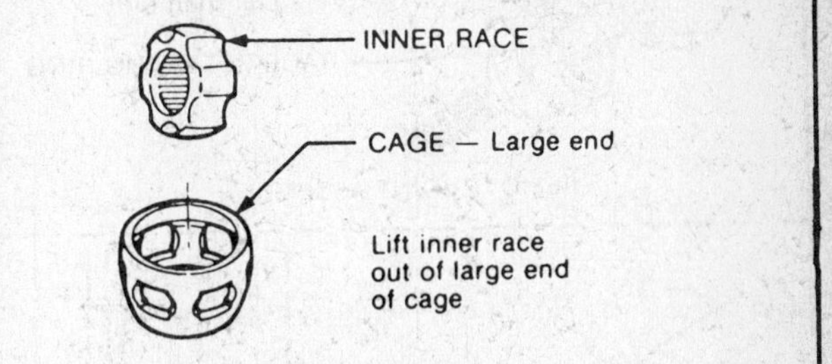

- INNER RACE
- CAGE — Large end
- Lift inner race out of large end of cage

REMOVE INNER RACE FROM CAGE

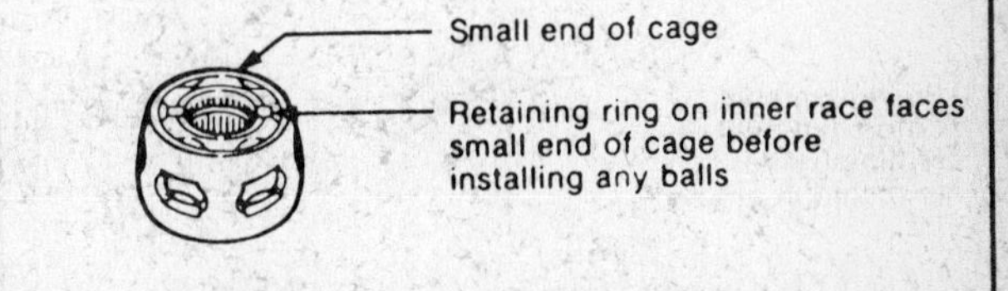

- Small end of cage
- Retaining ring on inner race faces small end of cage before installing any balls

INSTALL INNER RACE IN CAGE

FIG. 114 Double Off-Set design drive axle overhaul (Part 2) — 1982–84

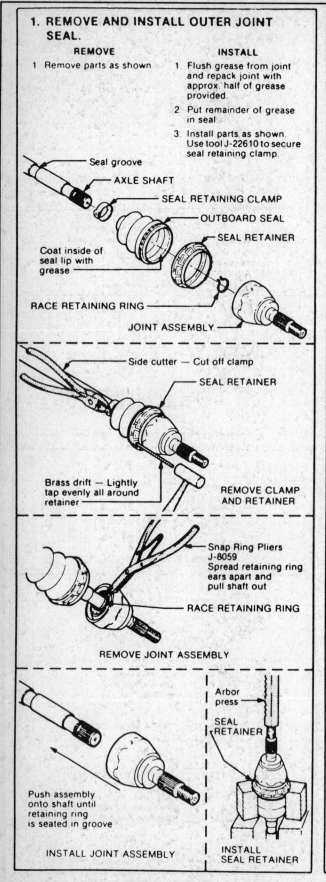

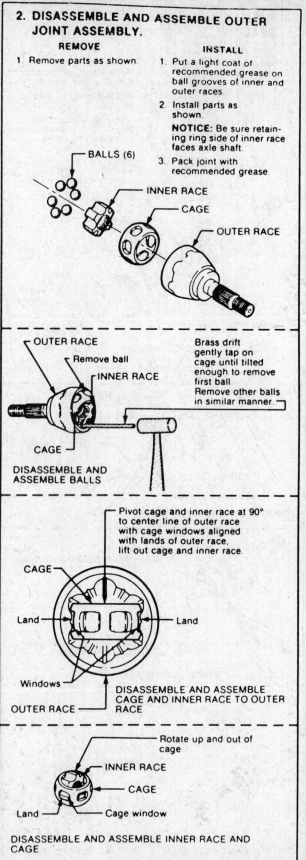

1. REMOVE AND INSTALL OUTER JOINT SEAL.

REMOVE

1 Remove parts as shown

INSTALL

1. Flush grease from joint and repack joint with approx. half of grease provided.
2. Put remainder of grease in seal.
3. Install parts as shown. Use tool J-22610 to secure seal retaining clamp.

- Seal groove
- AXLE SHAFT
- SEAL RETAINING CLAMP
- OUTBOARD SEAL
- SEAL RETAINER
- Coat inside of seal lip with grease
- RACE RETAINING RING
- JOINT ASSEMBLY

- Side cutter — Cut off clamp
- SEAL RETAINER
- Brass drift — Lightly tap evenly all around retainer
- REMOVE CLAMP AND RETAINER

- Snap Ring Pliers J-8059 Spread retaining ring ears apart and pull shaft out
- RACE RETAINING RING

REMOVE JOINT ASSEMBLY

- Push assembly onto shaft until retaining ring is seated in groove
- INSTALL JOINT ASSEMBLY

- Arbor press
- SEAL RETAINER
- INSTALL SEAL RETAINER

2. DISASSEMBLE AND ASSEMBLE OUTER JOINT ASSEMBLY.

REMOVE

1. Remove parts as shown.

INSTALL

1. Put a light coat of recommended grease on ball grooves of inner and outer races.
2. Install parts as shown.
   NOTICE: Be sure retaining ring side of inner race faces axle shaft.
3. Pack joint with recommended grease.

- BALLS (6)
- INNER RACE
- CAGE
- OUTER RACE

- OUTER RACE
- Remove ball
- INNER RACE
- CAGE
- Brass drift gently tap on cage until tilted enough to remove first ball Remove other balls in similar manner.

DISASSEMBLE AND ASSEMBLE BALLS

- Pivot cage and inner race at 90° to center line of outer race with cage windows aligned with lands of outer race, lift out cage and inner race.
- CAGE
- Land
- Land
- Windows
- OUTER RACE
- DISASSEMBLE AND ASSEMBLE CAGE AND INNER RACE TO OUTER RACE

- Rotate up and out of cage
- INNER RACE
- CAGE
- Land
- Cage window

DISASSEMBLE AND ASSEMBLE INNER RACE AND CAGE

FIG. 116 Tri-Pot design drive axle overhaul (Part 1) — 1982–84

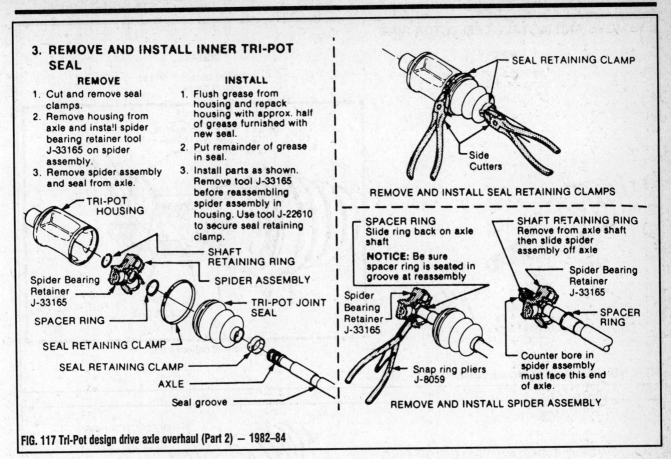

3. REMOVE AND INSTALL INNER TRI-POT SEAL

REMOVE

1. Cut and remove seal clamps.
2. Remove housing from axle and install spider bearing retainer tool J-33165 on spider assembly.
3. Remove spider assembly and seal from axle.

INSTALL

1. Flush grease from housing and repack housing with approx. half of grease furnished with new seal.
2. Put remainder of grease in seal.
3. Install parts as shown. Remove tool J-33165 before reassembling spider assembly in housing. Use tool J-22610 to secure seal retaining clamp.

TRI-POT HOUSING

SHAFT RETAINING RING

SPIDER ASSEMBLY

Spider Bearing Retainer J-33165

SPACER RING

TRI-POT JOINT SEAL

SEAL RETAINING CLAMP

SEAL RETAINING CLAMP

AXLE

Seal groove

SEAL RETAINING CLAMP

Side Cutters

REMOVE AND INSTALL SEAL RETAINING CLAMPS

SPACER RING
Slide ring back on axle shaft

NOTICE: Be sure spacer ring is seated in groove at reassembly

Spider Bearing Retainer J-33165

Snap ring pliers J-8059

SHAFT RETAINING RING
Remove from axle shaft then slide spider assembly off axle

Spider Bearing Retainer J-33165

SPACER RING

Counter bore in spider assembly must face this end of axle.

REMOVE AND INSTALL SPIDER ASSEMBLY

FIG. 117 Tri-Pot design drive axle overhaul (Part 2) — 1982–84

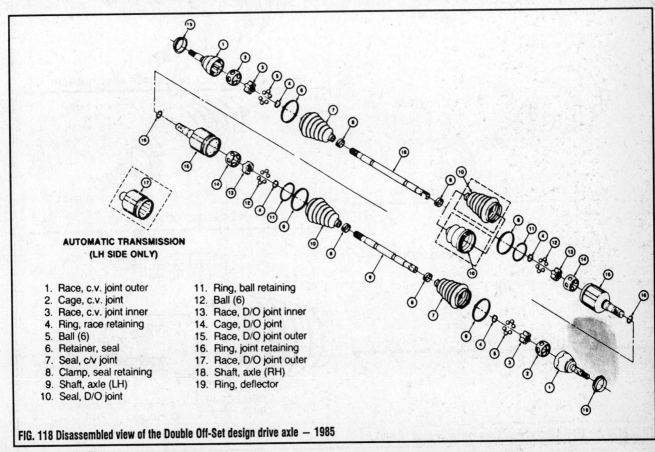

AUTOMATIC TRANSMISSION (LH SIDE ONLY)

1. Race, c.v. joint outer
2. Cage, c.v. joint
3. Race, c.v. joint inner
4. Ring, race retaining
5. Ball (6)
6. Retainer, seal
7. Seal, c/v joint
8. Clamp, seal retaining
9. Shaft, axle (LH)
10. Seal, D/O joint
11. Ring, ball retaining
12. Ball (6)
13. Race, D/O joint inner
14. Cage, D/O joint
15. Race, D/O joint outer
16. Ring, joint retaining
17. Race, D/O joint outer
18. Shaft, axle (RH)
19. Ring, deflector

FIG. 118 Disassembled view of the Double Off-Set design drive axle — 1985

1. REMOVE AND INSTALL DEFLECTOR RING

REMOVE

1. Use brass drift to remove damaged deflector ring.

INSTALL

1. Install deflector ring as shown below.

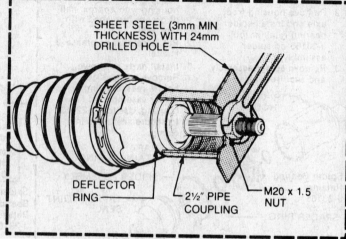

SHEET STEEL (3mm MIN THICKNESS) WITH 24mm DRILLED HOLE

DEFLECTOR RING

2½" PIPE COUPLING

M20 x 1.5 NUT

Install deflector ring

FIG. 119 Double Off-Set design drive axle overhaul (Part 1) — 1985

1. REMOVE AND INSTALL DEFLECTOR RING

REMOVE

1. For damaged deflector ring, remove parts as shown.

INSTALL

1. Install part as shown.

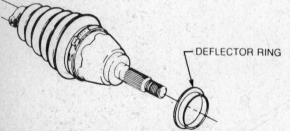

DEFLECTOR RING

AXLE ASSEMBLY WITH STEEL DEFLECTOR RING

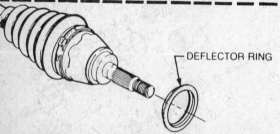

DEFLECTOR RING

AXLE ASSEMBLY WITH RUBBER DEFLECTOR RING

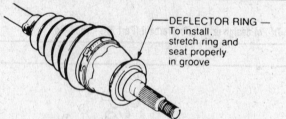

DEFLECTOR RING — To install, stretch ring and seat properly in groove

REMOVE AND INSTALL DEFLECTOR RING (RUBBER)

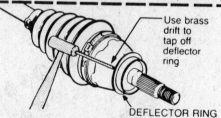

Use brass drift to tap off deflector ring

DEFLECTOR RING

REMOVE DEFLECTOR RING (STEEL)

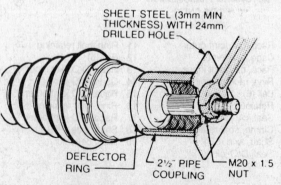

SHEET STEEL (3mm MIN THICKNESS) WITH 24mm DRILLED HOLE

DEFLECTOR RING

2½" PIPE COUPLING

M20 x 1.5 NUT

INSTALL DEFLECTOR RING (STEEL)

FIG. 120 Double Off-Set design drive axle overhaul (Part 2) — 1985

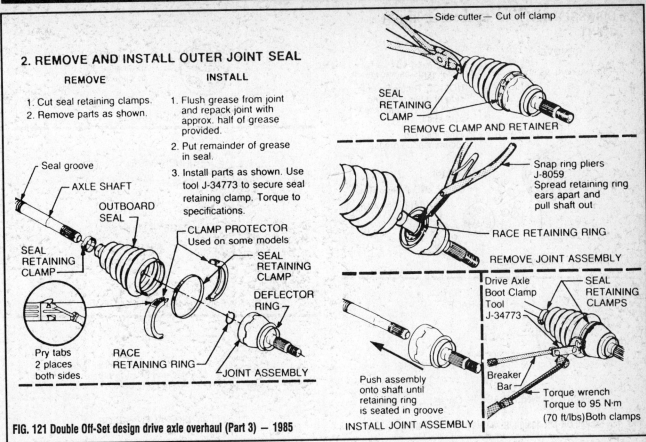

2. REMOVE AND INSTALL OUTER JOINT SEAL

REMOVE

1. Cut seal retaining clamps.
2. Remove parts as shown.

INSTALL

1. Flush grease from joint and repack joint with approx. half of grease provided.
2. Put remainder of grease in seal.
3. Install parts as shown. Use tool J-34773 to secure seal retaining clamp. Torque to specifications.

Seal groove

AXLE SHAFT

OUTBOARD SEAL

SEAL RETAINING CLAMP

CLAMP PROTECTOR Used on some models

SEAL RETAINING CLAMP

DEFLECTOR RING

Pry tabs 2 places both sides.

RACE RETAINING RING

JOINT ASSEMBLY

Side cutter — Cut off clamp

SEAL RETAINING CLAMP

REMOVE CLAMP AND RETAINER

Snap ring pliers J-8059 Spread retaining ring ears apart and pull shaft out

RACE RETAINING RING

REMOVE JOINT ASSEMBLY

Drive Axle Boot Clamp Tool J-34773

SEAL RETAINING CLAMPS

Push assembly onto shaft until retaining ring is seated in groove

Breaker Bar

Torque wrench Torque to 95 N·m (70 ft/lbs) Both clamps

INSTALL JOINT ASSEMBLY

FIG. 121 Double Off-Set design drive axle overhaul (Part 3) — 1985

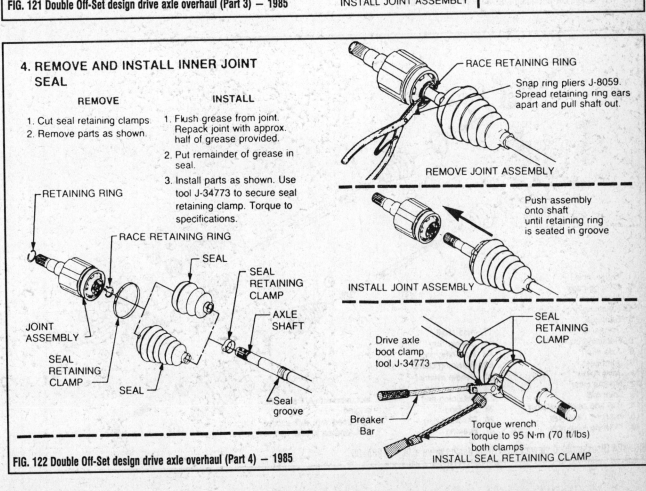

4. REMOVE AND INSTALL INNER JOINT SEAL

REMOVE

1. Cut seal retaining clamps.
2. Remove parts as shown.

INSTALL

1. Flush grease from joint. Repack joint with approx. half of grease provided.
2. Put remainder of grease in seal.
3. Install parts as shown. Use tool J-34773 to secure seal retaining clamp. Torque to specifications.

RETAINING RING

RACE RETAINING RING

SEAL

SEAL RETAINING CLAMP

AXLE SHAFT

JOINT ASSEMBLY

SEAL RETAINING CLAMP

SEAL

Seal groove

RACE RETAINING RING

Snap ring pliers J-8059 Spread retaining ring ears apart and pull shaft out.

REMOVE JOINT ASSEMBLY

Push assembly onto shaft until retaining ring is seated in groove

INSTALL JOINT ASSEMBLY

Drive axle boot clamp tool J-34773

SEAL RETAINING CLAMP

Breaker Bar

Torque wrench torque to 95 N·m (70 ft/lbs) both clamps

INSTALL SEAL RETAINING CLAMP

FIG. 122 Double Off-Set design drive axle overhaul (Part 4) — 1985

5. DISASSEMBLE AND ASSEMBLE INNER JOINT

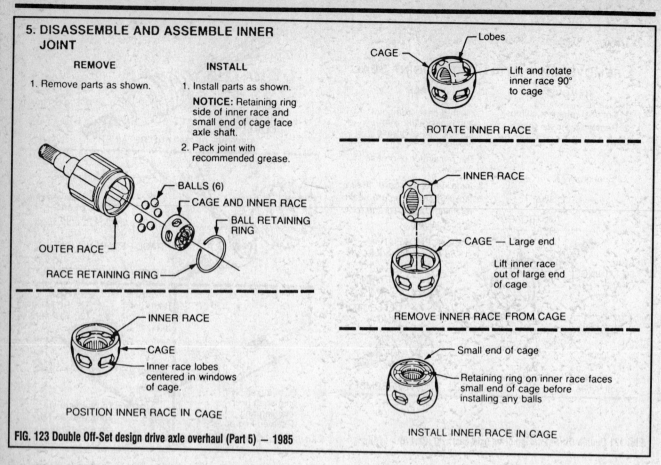

REMOVE

1. Remove parts as shown.

INSTALL

1. Install parts as shown.

   NOTICE: Retaining ring side of inner race and small end of cage face axle shaft.

2. Pack joint with recommended grease.

BALLS (6)

CAGE AND INNER RACE

BALL RETAINING RING

OUTER RACE

RACE RETAINING RING

CAGE — Lobes

Lift and rotate inner race 90° to cage

ROTATE INNER RACE

INNER RACE

CAGE — Large end

Lift inner race out of large end of cage

REMOVE INNER RACE FROM CAGE

INNER RACE

CAGE

Inner race lobes centered in windows of cage.

POSITION INNER RACE IN CAGE

Small end of cage

Retaining ring on inner race faces small end of cage before installing any balls

INSTALL INNER RACE IN CAGE

FIG. 123 Double Off-Set design drive axle overhaul (Part 5) — 1985

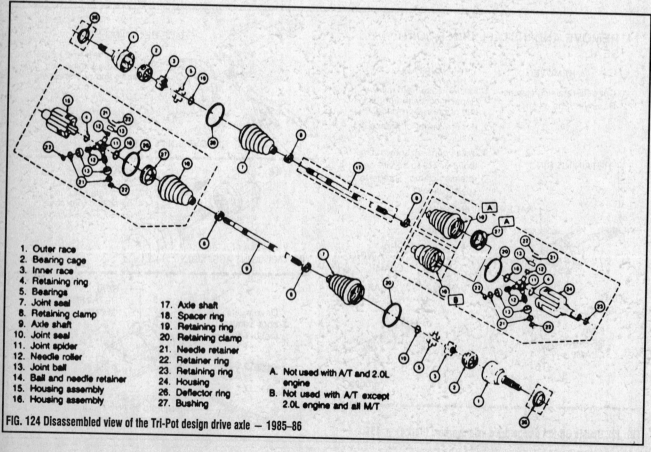

1. Outer race
2. Bearing cage
3. Inner race
4. Retaining ring
5. Bearings
7. Joint seal
8. Retaining clamp
9. Axle shaft
10. Joint seal
11. Joint spider
12. Needle roller
13. Joint ball
14. Ball and needle retainer
15. Housing assembly
16. Housing assembly
17. Axle shaft
18. Spacer ring
19. Retaining ring
20. Retaining clamp
21. Needle retainer
22. Retainer ring
23. Retaining ring
24. Housing
26. Deflector ring
27. Bushing

A. Not used with A/T and 2.0L engine
B. Not used with A/T except 2.0L engine and all M/T

FIG. 124 Disassembled view of the Tri-Pot design drive axle — 1985-86

1. REMOVE AND INSTALL DEFLECTOR RING

REMOVE

1. Use brass drift to remove damaged deflector ring.

INSTALL

1. Install deflector ring as shown below.

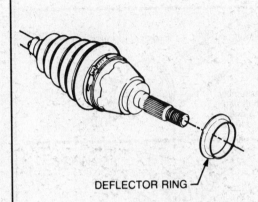

DEFLECTOR RING

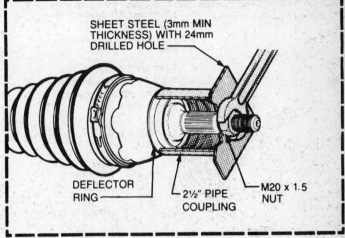

SHEET STEEL (3mm MIN THICKNESS) WITH 24mm DRILLED HOLE

DEFLECTOR RING

2½" PIPE COUPLING

M20 x 1.5 NUT

Install deflector ring

FIG. 125 Tri-Pot design drive axle overhaul (Part 1) — 1985–86

1. REMOVE AND INSTALL DEFLECTOR RING

REMOVE

1. For damaged deflector ring, remove parts as shown.

INSTALL

1. Install part as shown.

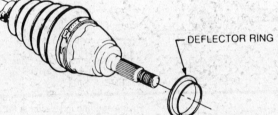

DEFLECTOR RING

AXLE ASSEMBLY WITH STEEL DEFLECTOR RING

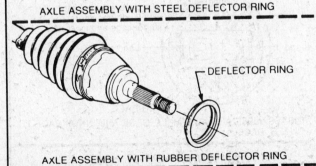

DEFLECTOR RING

AXLE ASSEMBLY WITH RUBBER DEFLECTOR RING

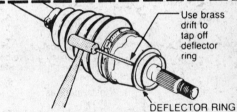

DEFLECTOR RING — To install, stretch ring and seat properly in groove

REMOVE AND INSTALL DEFLECTOR RING (RUBBER)

Use brass drift to tap off deflector ring

DEFLECTOR RING

REMOVE DEFLECTOR RING (STEEL)

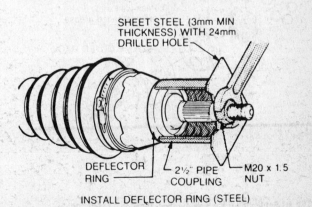

SHEET STEEL (3mm MIN THICKNESS) WITH 24mm DRILLED HOLE

DEFLECTOR RING

2½" PIPE COUPLING

M20 x 1.5 NUT

INSTALL DEFLECTOR RING (STEEL)

FIG. 126 Tri-Pot design drive axle overhaul (Part 2) — 1985–86

2. REMOVE AND INSTALL OUTER JOINT SEAL

REMOVE

1. Cut seal retaining clamps.
2. Remove parts as shown.

INSTALL

1. Flush grease from joint and repack joint with approx. half of grease provided.
2. Put remainder of grease in seal.
3. Install parts as shown. Use tool J-34773 to secure seal retaining clamp. Torque to specifications.

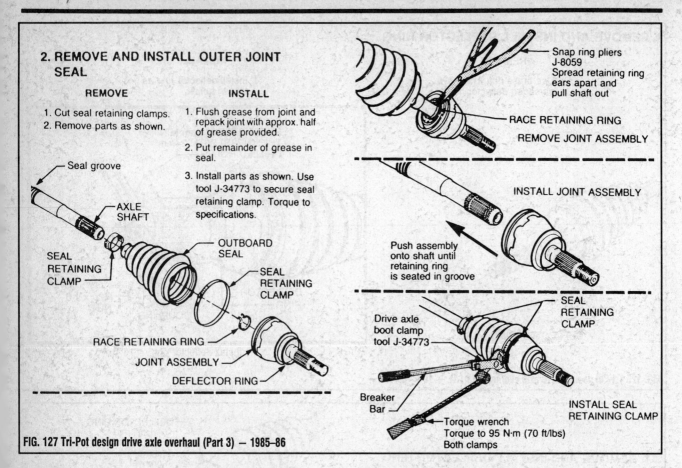

FIG. 127 Tri-Pot design drive axle overhaul (Part 3) — 1985–86

3. DISASSEMBLE AND ASSEMBLE OUTER JOINT ASSEMBLY

REMOVE

1. Remove parts as shown.

INSTALL

1. Put a light coat of recommended grease on ball grooves of inner and outer races.
2. Install parts as shown.

NOTICE: Be sure retaining ring side of inner race faces axle shaft.

3. Pack joint with recommended grease.

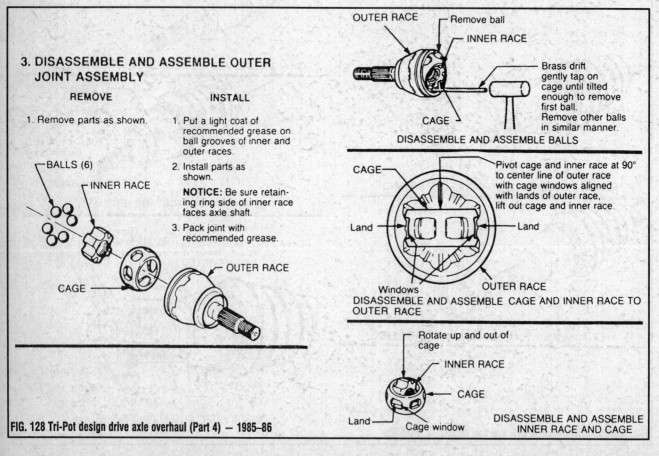

FIG. 128 Tri-Pot design drive axle overhaul (Part 4) — 1985–86

4. REMOVE AND INSTALL INNER TRI-POT SEAL

REMOVE

1. Cut seal retaining clamps.
2. Remove parts as shown.

INSTALL

1. Flush grease from housing and repack housing with approx. half of grease furnished with new seal.
2. Put remainder of grease in seal.
3. Install parts as shown. Use tool J-34773 to secure seal retaining clamp. Torque to specifications.

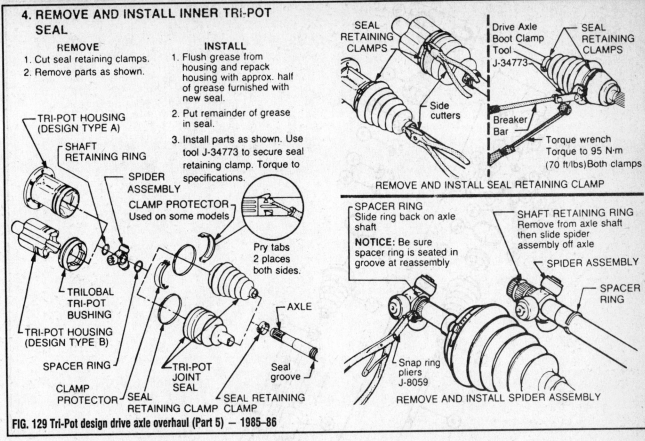

FIG. 129 Tri-Pot design drive axle overhaul (Part 5) — 1985–86

5. DISASSEMBLE AND ASSEMBLE INNER JOINT

REMOVE

1. Remove parts as shown.

INSTALL

1. Install parts as shown.

NOTICE: Retaining ring side of inner race and small end of cage face axle shaft.

2. Pack joint with recommended grease.

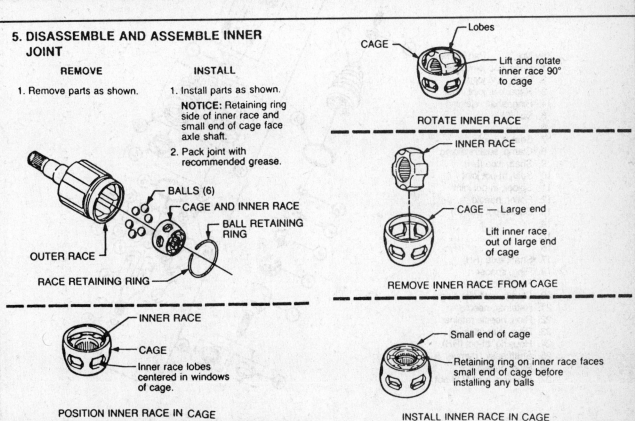

FIG. 130 Tri-Pot design drive axle overhaul (Part 6) — 1985–86

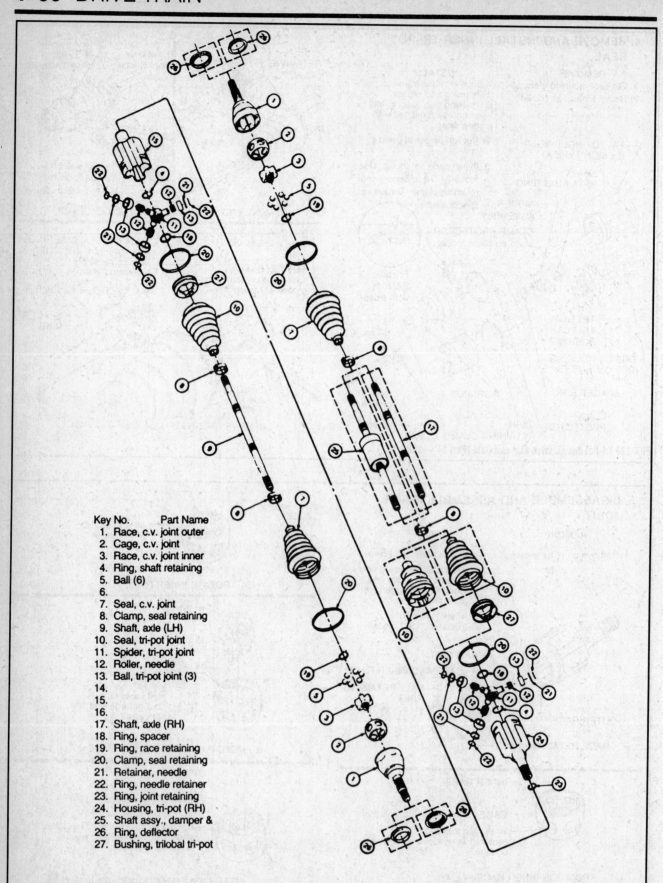

Key No.   Part Name
1. Race, c.v. joint outer
2. Cage, c.v. joint
3. Race, c.v. joint inner
4. Ring, shaft retaining
5. Ball (6)
6.
7. Seal, c.v. joint
8. Clamp, seal retaining
9. Shaft, axle (LH)
10. Seal, tri-pot joint
11. Spider, tri-pot joint
12. Roller, needle
13. Ball, tri-pot joint (3)
14.
15.
16.
17. Shaft, axle (RH)
18. Ring, spacer
19. Ring, race retaining
20. Clamp, seal retaining
21. Retainer, needle
22. Ring, needle retainer
23. Ring, joint retaining
24. Housing, tri-pot (RH)
25. Shaft assy., damper &
26. Ring, deflector
27. Bushing, trilobal tri-pot

FIG. 131 Disassembled view of the Tri-Pot design drive axle — 1987–90

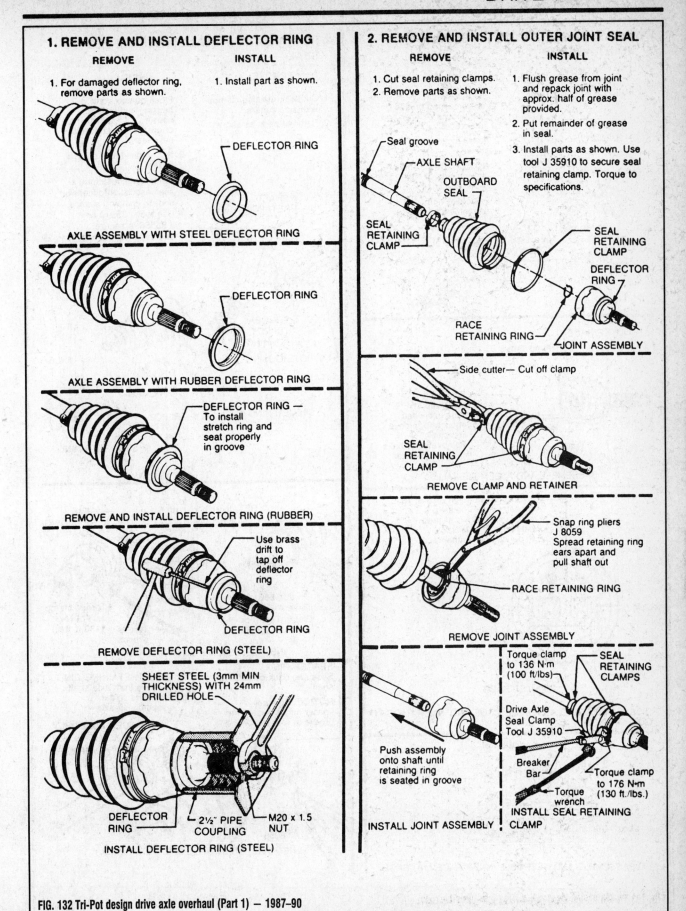

1. REMOVE AND INSTALL DEFLECTOR RING

REMOVE

1. For damaged deflector ring, remove parts as shown.

INSTALL

1. Install part as shown.

— DEFLECTOR RING

AXLE ASSEMBLY WITH STEEL DEFLECTOR RING

— DEFLECTOR RING

AXLE ASSEMBLY WITH RUBBER DEFLECTOR RING

— DEFLECTOR RING — To install stretch ring and seat properly in groove

REMOVE AND INSTALL DEFLECTOR RING (RUBBER)

Use brass drift to tap off deflector ring

DEFLECTOR RING

REMOVE DEFLECTOR RING (STEEL)

SHEET STEEL (3mm MIN THICKNESS) WITH 24mm DRILLED HOLE

DEFLECTOR RING — 2½" PIPE COUPLING — M20 x 1.5 NUT

INSTALL DEFLECTOR RING (STEEL)

2. REMOVE AND INSTALL OUTER JOINT SEAL

REMOVE

1. Cut seal retaining clamps.
2. Remove parts as shown.

INSTALL

1. Flush grease from joint and repack joint with approx. half of grease provided.
2. Put remainder of grease in seal.
3. Install parts as shown. Use tool J 35910 to secure seal retaining clamp. Torque to specifications.

Seal groove
AXLE SHAFT
OUTBOARD SEAL
SEAL RETAINING CLAMP
SEAL RETAINING CLAMP
DEFLECTOR RING
RACE RETAINING RING
JOINT ASSEMBLY

Side cutter — Cut off clamp

SEAL RETAINING CLAMP

REMOVE CLAMP AND RETAINER

Snap ring pliers J 8059 Spread retaining ring ears apart and pull shaft out

RACE RETAINING RING

REMOVE JOINT ASSEMBLY

Push assembly onto shaft until retaining ring is seated in groove

INSTALL JOINT ASSEMBLY

Torque clamp to 136 N·m (100 ft/lbs)
SEAL RETAINING CLAMPS
Drive Axle Seal Clamp Tool J 35910
Breaker Bar
Torque wrench
Torque clamp to 176 N·m (130 ft./lbs.)

INSTALL SEAL RETAINING CLAMP

FIG. 132 Tri-Pot design drive axle overhaul (Part 1) — 1987–90

3. DISASSEMBLE AND ASSEMBLE OUTER JOINT ASSEMBLY

REMOVE

1. Remove parts as shown.

INSTALL

1. Put a light coat of recommended grease on ball grooves of inner and outer races.

2. Install parts as shown.

   NOTICE: Be sure retaining ring side of inner race faces axle shaft.

3. Pack joint with recommended grease.

BALLS (6)
INNER RACE
CAGE
OUTER RACE

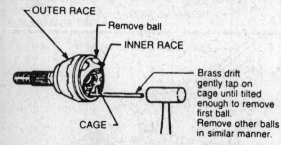

OUTER RACE
Remove ball
INNER RACE
Brass drift gently tap on cage until tilted enough to remove first ball. Remove other balls in similar manner.
CAGE

DISASSEMBLE AND ASSEMBLE BALLS

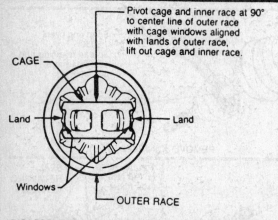

Pivot cage and inner race at 90° to center line of outer race with cage windows aligned with lands of outer race, lift out cage and inner race.

CAGE
Land
Land
Windows
OUTER RACE

DISASSEMBLE AND ASSEMBLE CAGE AND INNER RACE TO OUTER RACE

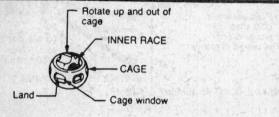

Rotate up and out of cage
INNER RACE
CAGE
Land
Cage window

DISASSEMBLE AND ASSEMBLE INNER RACE AND CAGE

4. REMOVE AND INSTALL INNER TRI-POT SEAL

REMOVE

1. Cut seal retaining clamps with side cutters.

2. Remove parts as shown.

INSTALL

1. Flush grease from housing and repack housing with approx. half of grease furnished with new seal.

2. Put remainder of grease in seal.

3. Refer to manufacturer's seal installation dimension prior to crimping clamps. Use tool J 35910 or J 35566 to secure seal retaining clamps.

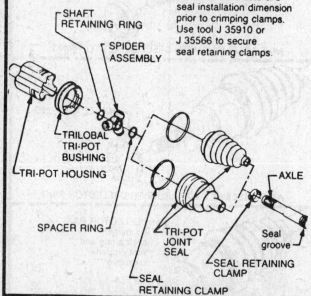

SHAFT RETAINING RING
SPIDER ASSEMBLY
TRILOBAL TRI-POT BUSHING
TRI-POT HOUSING
SPACER RING
SEAL RETAINING CLAMP
TRI-POT JOINT SEAL
AXLE
Seal groove
SEAL RETAINING CLAMP

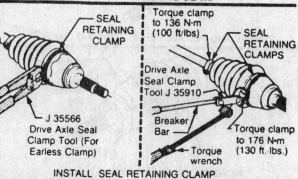

SEAL RETAINING CLAMP
J 35566 Drive Axle Seal Clamp Tool (For Earless Clamp)

Torque clamp to 136 N·m (100 ft/lbs)
SEAL RETAINING CLAMPS
Drive Axle Seal Clamp Tool J 35910
Breaker Bar
Torque wrench
Torque clamp to 176 N·m (130 ft. lbs.)

INSTALL SEAL RETAINING CLAMP

SPACER RING
Slide ring back on axle shaft

NOTICE: Be sure spacer ring is seated in groove at reassembly

SHAFT RETAINING RING
Remove from axle shaft then slide spider assembly off axle

SPIDER ASSEMBLY
SPACER RING
Snap ring pliers J 8059

REMOVE AND INSTALL SPIDER ASSEMBLY

FIG. 133 Tri-Pot design drive axle overhaul (Part 2) — 1987–90

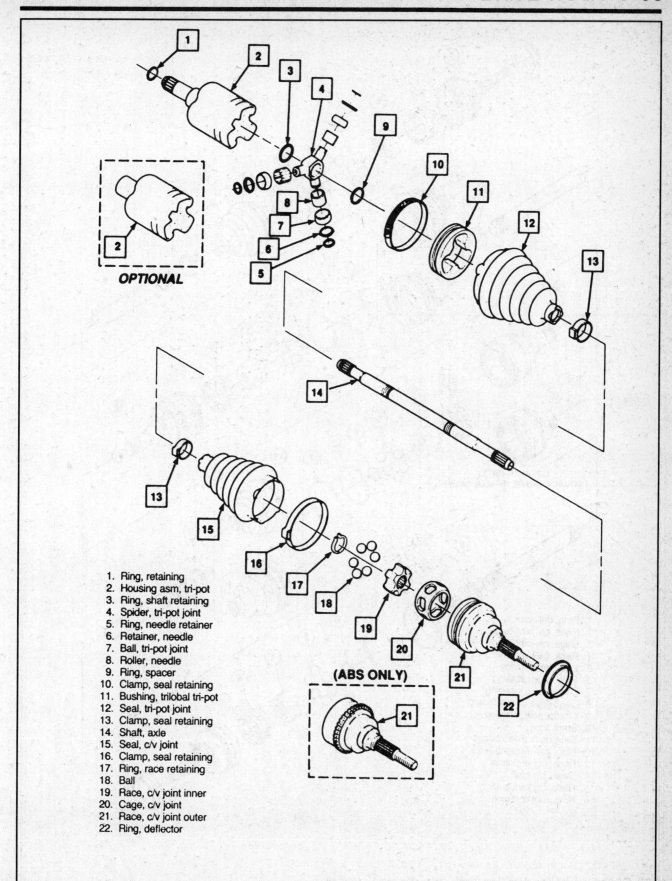

OPTIONAL

(ABS ONLY)

1. Ring, retaining
2. Housing asm, tri-pot
3. Ring, shaft retaining
4. Spider, tri-pot joint
5. Ring, needle retainer
6. Retainer, needle
7. Ball, tri-pot joint
8. Roller, needle
9. Ring, spacer
10. Clamp, seal retaining
11. Bushing, trilobal tri-pot
12. Seal, tri-pot joint
13. Clamp, seal retaining
14. Shaft, axle
15. Seal, c/v joint
16. Clamp, seal retaining
17. Ring, race retaining
18. Ball
19. Race, c/v joint inner
20. Cage, c/v joint
21. Race, c/v joint outer
22. Ring, deflector

FIG. 134 Disassembled view of the Tri-Pot design drive axle — 1991–92

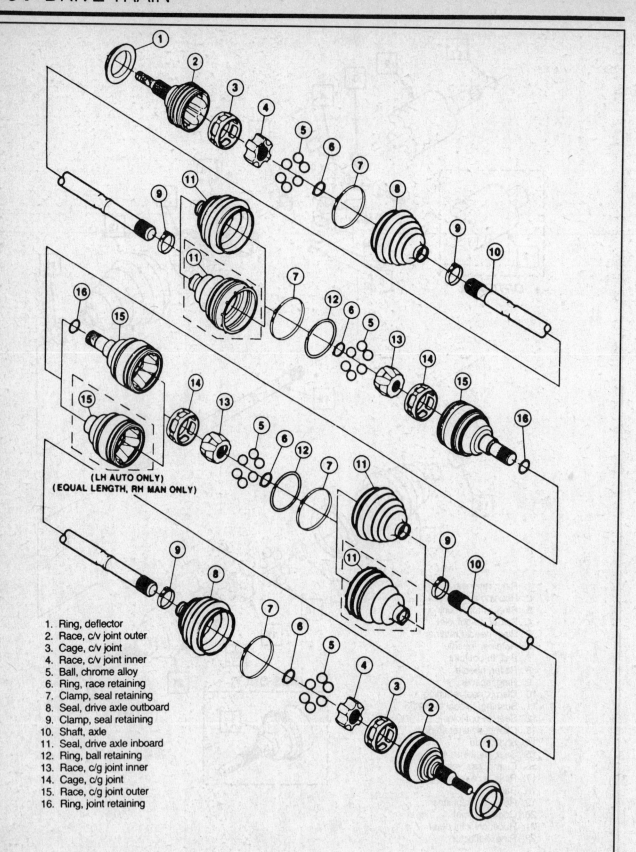

1. Ring, deflector
2. Race, c/v joint outer
3. Cage, c/v joint
4. Race, c/v joint inner
5. Ball, chrome alloy
6. Ring, race retaining
7. Clamp, seal retaining
8. Seal, drive axle outboard
9. Clamp, seal retaining
10. Shaft, axle
11. Seal, drive axle inboard
12. Ring, ball retaining
13. Race, c/g joint inner
14. Cage, c/g joint
15. Race, c/g joint outer
16. Ring, joint retaining

(LH AUTO ONLY)
(EQUAL LENGTH, RH MAN ONLY)

FIG. 135 Disassembled view of the Cross-Groove design drive axle — 1990–92

1990–92 Cross Groove and 1991–92 Tri-Pot Design

▶ SEE FIGS. 134 and 135

All 1990–92 models equipped with the Hydra-Matic® 5TM40 5-speed manual transaxle use the Cross-Groove type drive axle. All other models use the Tri-Pot type drive axle. The following overhaul procedures incorporate both designs, unless otherwise noted.

Outer Deflector Ring

REMOVAL & INSTALLATION

▶ SEE FIGS. 136 and 137

1. Remove the axle shaft.
2. Clamp the axle shaft in a soft jawed vise.
3. Using a brass drift and a hammer, remove the deflecting ring from the CV outer race.

To install:

4. Position and square up the deflecting ring at press diameter of CV outer race.
5. Using a 3 in. pipe coupling, M24 × 1.5 nut, and a fabricated sheet metal sleeve, tighten the nut until the deflector bottoms against the shoulder of the CV outer joint.

Outer Joint Seal

REMOVAL & INSTALLATION

▶ SEE FIGS. 138-140

1. Remove the large seal retaining clamp from the CV joint with a side cutter and discard.
2. Remove the small seal retaining clamp on the axle shaft with a side cutter and discard.
3. Separate the joint seal from the CV join race at large diameter and slide the seal away from the joint along the axle shaft.
4. Wipe the excess grease from the face of the CV joint inner race.
5. Spread the ears on the race retaining ring with snap ring pliers and remove the CV joint from the axle shaft.
6. Remove the seal from the axle shaft.
7. Disassemble the joint and flush the grease prior to installing a new seal.

To install:

8. Install the small retaining clamp on the neck of the new seal, but do not crimp.

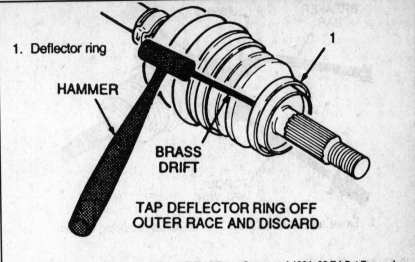

1. Deflector ring

HAMMER

BRASS DRIFT

TAP DEFLECTOR RING OFF OUTER RACE AND DISCARD

FIG. 136 Outer deflector ring removal — 1990–92 Cross Groove and 1991–92 Tri-Pot Type axle

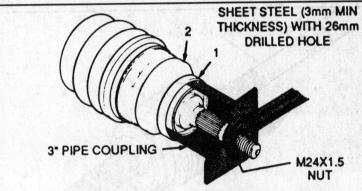

SHEET STEEL (3mm MIN THICKNESS) WITH 26mm DRILLED HOLE

3" PIPE COUPLING

M24X1.5 NUT

SQUARE UP DEFLECTOR RING AND TIGHTEN NUT UNTIL RING BOTTOMS AGAINST SHOULDER OF OUTER RACE

1. Deflector ring   2. CV joint outer race

FIG. 137 Outer deflector ring installation — 1990–92 Cross Groove and 1991–92 Tri-Pot Type axle

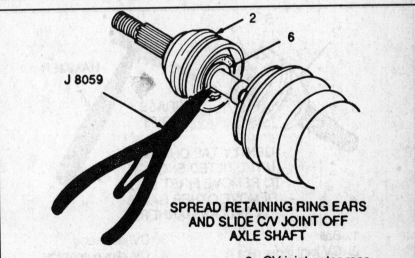

J 8059

SPREAD RETAINING RING EARS AND SLIDE C/V JOINT OFF AXLE SHAFT

1. Race retaining ring   2. CV joint outer race

FIG. 138 CV joint and axle separation — 1990–92 Cross Groove and 1991–92 Tri-Pot Type axle

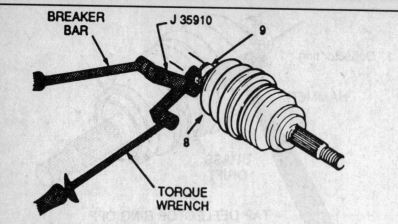

1. Drive axle outboard seal   2. Seal retaining clamp

FIG. 139 Seal retaining clamp installation — 1990–92 Cross Groove and 1991–92 Tri-Pot Type axle

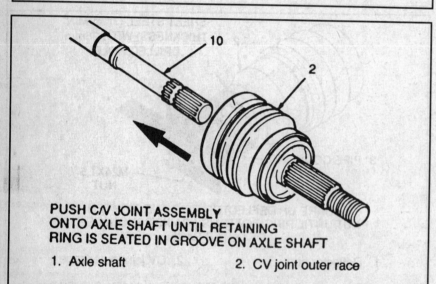

PUSH C/V JOINT ASSEMBLY
ONTO AXLE SHAFT UNTIL RETAINING
RING IS SEATED IN GROOVE ON AXLE SHAFT

1. Axle shaft   2. CV joint outer race

FIG. 140 CV-joint to axle installation — 1990–92 Cross Groove and 1991–92 Tri-Pot Type axle

GENTLY TAP ON CAGE
UNTIL TILTED ENOUGH
TO REMOVE FIRST BALL.
REMOVE OTHER BALLS
IN SIMILAR MANNER.

1. Ball   3. CV joint cage
2. CV joint inner race   4. CV joint outer race

FIG. 141 CV-joint ball removal — 1990–92 Cross Groove and 1991–92 Tri-Pot Type axle

9. Slide the seal onto the axle shaft and position the neck of the seal in the seal groove on the axle shaft.

10. Crimp the seal retaining clamp with J 35910 seal clamp tool or equivalent, to 100 ft. lbs. (136 Nm).

11. Place approximately half of the grease provided in the seal kit, inside the seal and repack the CV joint with the remaining grease.

12. Push the CV joint onto the axle shaft until the retaining ring is seated in the groove on the axle shaft.

13. Slide the large diameter of the seal with the large seal retaining clamp in place over the outside of the CV joint race and locate the lip of the seal in the groove on the race.

✳✳ WARNING

The seal must not be dimpled or out of shape in any way. If it is not shaped correctly, equalize pressure in the seal and reshape properly by hand.

14. Crimp the seal retaining clamp with J 35910 seal clamp tool or equivalent, to 130 ft. lbs. (176 Nm).

Outer Joint Assembly

REMOVAL & INSTALLATION

◆ SEE FIGS. 141-143

1. Remove the outer joint seal as outlined earlier.

2. Using a brass drift and a hammer, lightly tap on the inner race cage until it has tilted sufficiently to remove one of the balls. Remove the other balls in the same manner.

3. Pivot the cage 90 degrees and, with the cage ball windows aligned with the outer joint windows, lift out the cage and the inner race.

4. The inner race can be removed from the cage by pivoting it 90° and lifting out. Clean all parts thoroughly and inspect for wear.

To install:

5. To install, put a light coat of the grease provided in the rebuilding kit onto the ball grooves of the inner race and outer joint.

6. Install the parts in the reverse order of removal.

FIG. 142 Outer race and cage separation — 1990–92 Cross Groove and 1991–92 Tri-Pot Type axle

➡ **Make sure that the retaining ring side of the inner race faces the axle shaft.**

7. Install the outer seal as outlined earlier.

Cross Groove Joint Seal

REMOVAL & INSTALLATION

◆ SEE FIGS. 144-147

1. Cut the seal retaining clamps with a side cutter.

2. Separate the seal from the C/G joint race at the large diameter and slide the seal away from the joint along the axle shaft.

3. Wipe the excess grease from the C/G joint inner race.

4. Spread the ears on the retaining ring with snap ring pliers and remove the C/G joint from the axle shaft.

6. Remove the seal from the axle shaft.

7. Remove the seal from the shaft.

➡ **The cross-groove joint design uses precision grinding and selected dimensional component fits for proper assembly and operation. Due to its complexity, disassembly is not recommended.**

8. Flush the grease from the joint prior to installing a new seal.

To Install:

9. Install the small retaining clamp on the neck of the new seal, but do not crimp.

10. Slide the seal onto the axle shaft and position the neck of the seal in the seal groove on the axle shaft.

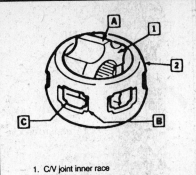

1. C/V joint inner race
2. C/V joint cage
3. Rotate inner race up and out of cage
4. Cage window
5. Inner race land

FIG. 143 Inner race and cage separation — 1990–92 Cross Groove and 1991–92 Tri-Pot Type axle

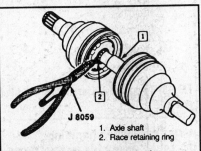

J 8059

1. Axle shaft
2. Race retaining ring

FIG. 144 C/G-joint and axle separation — 1990–92 Cross Groove axle

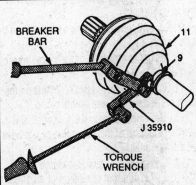

BREAKER BAR

J 35910

TORQUE WRENCH

1. Seal retaining clamp   2. Drive axle inboard seal

FIG. 145 Seal retaining clamp installation — 1990–92 Cross Groove axle

11. Crimp the seal retaining clamp with J 35910 seal clamp tool or equivalent, to 100 ft. lbs. (136 Nm).

12. Place approximately half of the grease provided in the seal kit, inside the seal and repack the C/G joint with the remaining grease.

13. Push the C/G joint onto the axle shaft until the retaining ring is seated in the groove on the axle shaft.

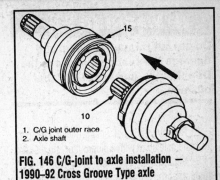

1. C/G joint outer race
2. Axle shaft

FIG. 146 C/G-joint to axle installation — 1990–92 Cross Groove Type axle

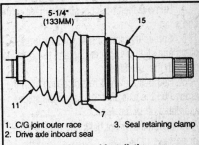

5-1/4" (133MM)

1. C/G joint outer race   3. Seal retaining clamp
2. Drive axle inboard seal

FIG. 147 C/G-joint seal installation measure 1990–92 Cross Groove Type axle

14. Slide the large diameter of the seal over the outside of the C/G joint and locate the lip of the seal in the groove on ball retainer.

❋❋ WARNING

The seal must not be dimpled or out of shape in any way. If it is not shaped correctly, equalize pressure in the seal and reshape properly by hand.

15. Crimp the seal retaining clamp with J 35910 seal clamp tool or equivalent, to 130 ft. lbs. (176 Nm).

Inner Tri-Pot Seal

REMOVAL & INSTALLATION

◆ SEE FIGS. 148-153

1. Remove the larger seal retaining clamp from the tri-pot joint with a side cutter and discard.

✳✳ WARNING

Do not cut through the seal and damage the sealing surface of the tri-pot outer housing and triobal bushing.

2. Remove the small seal retaining clamp from the axle shaft with a side cutter and discard.

3. Separate the seal from the trilobal tri-pot bushing at the large diameter and slide the seal away from the joint along the axle shaft.

4. Remove the tri-pot housing from the spider and shaft.

5. Spread the spacer ring with snap ring pliers and slide the spacer ring and tri-pot spider back on the axle shaft.

6. Remove the shaft retaining ring from the groove on the axle shaft and slide the spider assembly off of the shaft.

7. Check the tri-pot balls and needle rollers for damage or wear.

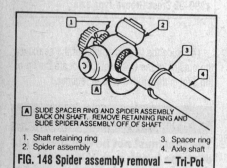

A SLIDE SPACER RING AND SPIDER ASSEMBLY
BACK ON SHAFT. REMOVE RETAINING RING AND
SLIDE SPIDER ASSEMBLY OFF OF SHAFT

1. Shaft retaining ring   3. Spacer ring
2. Spider assembly   4. Axle shaft

FIG. 148 Spider assembly removal — Tri-Pot type axle

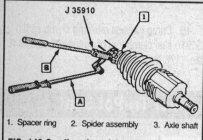

J 35910

1. Spacer ring   2. Spider assembly   3. Axle shaft

FIG. 149 Small seal retaining clamp installation — Tri-Pot type axle

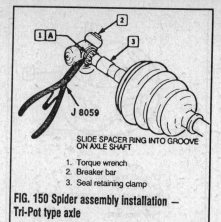

J 8059

SLIDE SPACER RING INTO GROOVE
ON AXLE SHAFT

1. Torque wrench
2. Breaker bar
3. Seal retaining clamp

FIG. 150 Spider assembly installation — Tri-Pot type axle

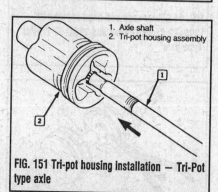

1. Axle shaft
2. Tri-pot housing assembly

FIG. 151 Tri-pot housing installation — Tri-Pot type axle

➡ **Use care when handling the spider assembly as the tri-pot balls and rollers may separate from the spider trunnions.**

8. Remove the trilobal tri-pot bushing from the tri-pot housing.

9. Remove the spacer ring and seal from the axle shaft.

10. Flush the grease from the tri-pot housing.

To Install:

11. Install the small retaining clamp on the neck of the new seal, but do not crimp.

12. Slide the seal onto the axle shaft and position the neck of the seal in the seal groove on the axle shaft.

13. Crimp the seal retaining clamp with J 35910 seal clamp tool or equivalent, to 100 ft. lbs. (136 Nm).

14. Install the spacer ring on the axle shaft and beyond the 2nd groove.

15. Slide the tri-pot spider asembly against the spacer ring on the shaft.

➡ **Make sure the counterbored face of the tri-pot spider faces the end of the shaft.**

16. Install the shaft retaining ring in the groove of the axle shaft with the snap ring pliers.

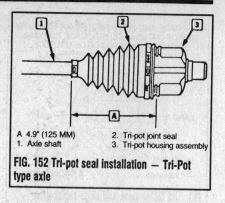

A 4.9" (125 MM)   2. Tri-pot joint seal
1. Axle shaft   3. Tri-pot housing assembly

FIG. 152 Tri-pot seal installation — Tri-Pot type axle

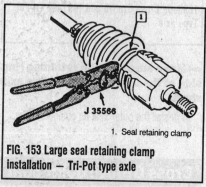

J 35566

1. Seal retaining clamp

FIG. 153 Large seal retaining clamp installation — Tri-Pot type axle

17. Slide the tri-pot spider towards the end of the shaft and reseat the spacer ring in the groove on the shaft.

18. Place approximately half of the grease provided in the seal kit, inside the seal and repack the tri-pot housing with the remaining grease.

19. Install the trilobal tri-pot bushing to the tri-pot housing.

20. Position the larger clamp on the seal.

21. Slide the tri-pot housing over the tri-pot spider.

22. Slide the large diameter of the seal, with the larger clamp in place, over the outside of the trilobal bushing and loacet the lip of the seal in the bushing groove.

23. Position the tri-pot assembly at the proper vehicle dimension as shown.

✳✳ WARNING

The seal must not be dimpled or out of shape in any way. If it is not shaped correctly, equalize pressure by carefully inserting a thin flat blunt tool (no sharp edges) between the large seal opening and the bushing and reshape properly by hand.

24. Crimp the seal retaining clamp with J 35566 seal clamp tool or equivalent.

CLUTCH

❋❋ CAUTION

The clutch driven disc contains asbestos, which has been determined to be a cancer causing agent. Never clean clutch surfaces with compressed air! Avoid inhaling any dust from any clutch surface! When cleaning clutch surfaces, use a commercially available brake cleaning fluid.

ADJUSTMENT

♦ SEE FIG. 154

All 1982–84 models have a self-adjusting clutch mechanism located on the clutch pedal, eliminating the need for periodic free play adjustments. The self-adjusting mechanism should be inspected periodically as follows:

1. Depress the clutch pedal and look for the pawl on the self-adjusting mechanism to firmly engage the teeth on the ratchet.

2. Release the clutch. The pawl should be lifted off of the teeth by the metal stop on the bracket.

On 1985 and later models, the hydraulic clutch system provides automatic clutch adjustment. No adjustment of clutch linkage or pedal position is required.

Neutral Start Switch

♦ SEE FIG. 155

1982–84

A neutral start switch is located on the clutch pedal assembly; the switch prevents the engine from starting unless the clutch is depressed. If the switch is faulty, it can be unbolted and replaced without removing the pedal assembly from the car. No adjustments for the switch are provided.

Neutral Start/Back-Up Light Switch

REPLACEMENT

1985–87

1. Disconnect the negative battery cable.
2. Remove the console.
3. Disconnect the wiring, then replace the switch at the side of the shifter.
4. Installation is the reverse of removal. (See Back-up Switch removal and installation earlier in this Section.

Clutch Pedal

♦ SEE FIGS. 157-162

The clutch pedal and bracket are serviced as an assembly.

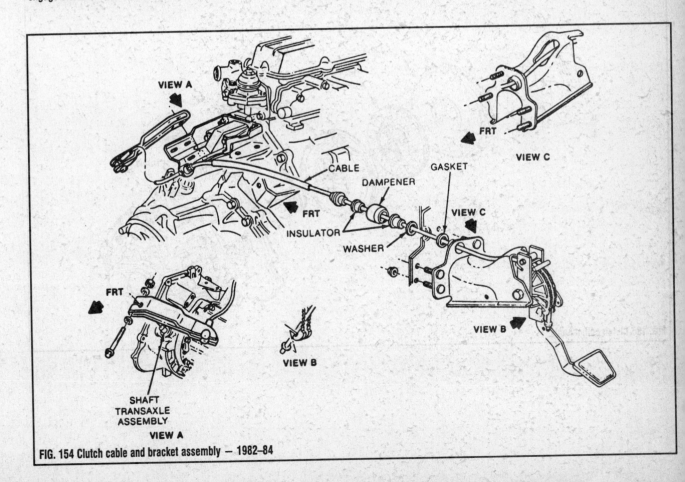

FIG. 154 Clutch cable and bracket assembly — 1982–84

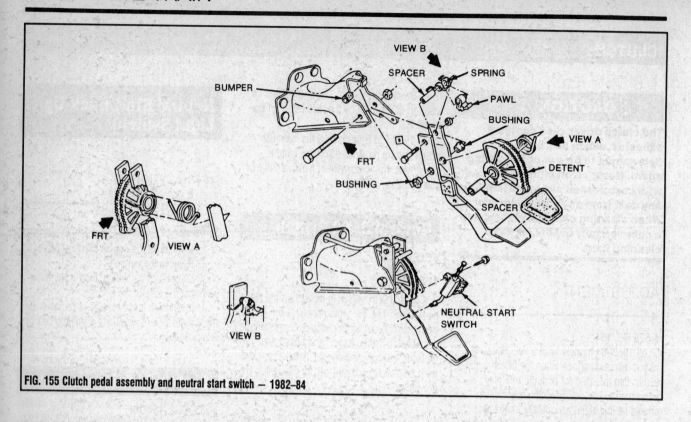

FIG. 155 Clutch pedal assembly and neutral start switch — 1982–84

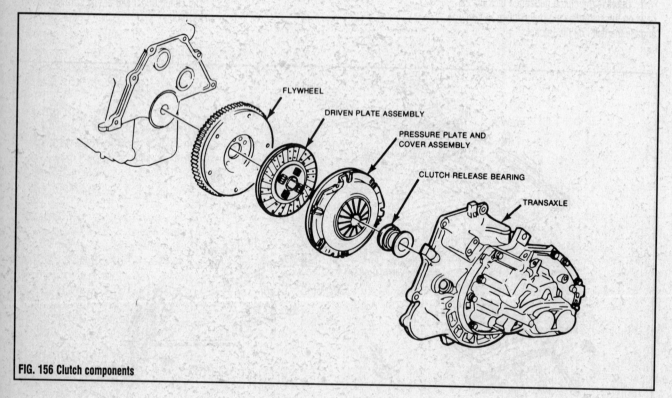

FIG. 156 Clutch components

REMOVAL & INSTALLATION

1. Disconnect the battery ground cable.
2. Remove the sound insulator from inside the vehicle.
3. Disconnect the master cylinder pushrod from the clutch pedal.
4. Remove the clutch pedal and bracket mounting nuts.
5. Remove the clutch pedal and bracket assembly.

To Install:

6. Position the clutch pedal and bracket assembly into vehicle.
7. Install the retaining nuts. Starting with the upper left side nut and moving clockwise, tighten the nuts to 16 ft.lbs.
8. Lubricate and install the master cylinder pushrod bushing onto the clutch pedal.
9. Connect the clutch master cylinder pushrod to the clutch pedal. If equipped with cruise control check the switch adjustment at the clutch pedal bracket.
10. Install the sound insulator.
11. Connect the battery ground cable.

Driven Disc and Pressure Plate

♦ SEE FIG. 156

REMOVAL & INSTALLATION

1. Remove the transaxle.
2. Mark the pressure plate assembly and the flywheel so that they can be assembled in the same position. They were balanced as an assembly at the factory.
3. Loosen the attaching bolts one turn at a time until spring tension is relieved.
4. Support the pressure plate and remove the bolts. Remove the pressure plate and clutch disc. Do not disassemble the pressure plate assembly; replace it if defective.
5. Inspect the flywheel, clutch disc, pressure plate, throwout bearing and the clutch fork and pivot shaft assembly for wear. Replace the parts as required. If the flywheel shows any signs of overheating, or if it is badly grooved or scored, it should be refaced or replaced.

6. Clean the pressure plate and flywheel mating surfaces thoroughly. Position the clutch disc and pressure plate into the installed position, and support with a dummy shaft or clutch aligning tool. The clutch plate is assembled with the damper springs offset toward the transaxle. One side of the factory supplied clutch disc is stamped "Flywheel Side".
7. Install the pressure plate-to-flywheel bolts. Tighten them gradually in a criss-cross pattern.
8. Lubricate the outside groove and the inside recess of the release bearing with high temperature grease. Wipe off any excess. Install the release bearing.
9. Install the transaxle.

Clutch Cable

REPLACEMENT

1982–84

1. Press the clutch pedal up against the bumper stop so as to release the pawl from the detent. Disconnect the clutch cable from the release lever at the transaxle assembly. Be careful that the cable does not snap back toward the rear of the car as this could damage the detent in the adjusting mechanism.
2. Remove the hush panel from inside the car.
3. Disconnect the clutch cable from the detent end tangs. Lift the locking pawl away from the detent and then pull the cable forward between the detent and the pawl.
4. Remove the windshield washer bottle.
5. From the engine side of the cowl, pull the clutch cable out to disengage it from the clutch pedal mounting bracket. The insulators, dampener and washers may separate from the cable in the process.
6. Disconnect the cable from the transaxle mounting bracket and remove it.
7. Install the cable into both insulators, damper and washer. Lubricate the rear insulator with tire mounting lube or the like to ease installation into the pedal mounting bracket.

8. From inside the car, attach the end of the cable to the detent. Be sure to route the cable underneath the pawl and into the detent cable groove.
9. Press the clutch pedal up against the bumper stop to release the pawl from the detent. Install the other end of the cable at the release lever and the transaxle mount bracket.
10. Install the hush panel and the windshield washer bottle.
11. Check the clutch operation and adjust as detailed earlier in this Section.

Clutch Hydraulic System

♦ SEE FIGS. 157-162

REMOVAL & INSTALLATION

➡ **The clutch hydraulic system is used on 1985 and later models and is serviced as a complete unit. It has been bled of air and filled with fluid. Individual components of the system are not available separately.**

2.0L Engine

1. Disconnect the negative battery cable.
2. Remove the hush panel from inside the vehicle.
3. Disconnect the clutch master cylinder push rod from the clutch pedal.
4. Remove the clutch master cylinder retaining nuts at the front of the dash.
5. Remove the slave cylinder (1985–87) or actuator (1988–90) retaining nuts at the transaxle.
6. Remove the hydraulic system as a unit from the vehicle.

To Install:

7. Install the new slave cylinder or actuator to the transaxle support bracket aligning the push rod into the pocket on the clutch fork outer lever. Tighten the retaining nuts evenly to prevent damage to the slave cylinder. Tighten to 14–20 ft. lbs.

➡ **Do not remove the plastic push rod retainer from the slave or actuator cylinder. The straps will break on the first clutch pedal application.**

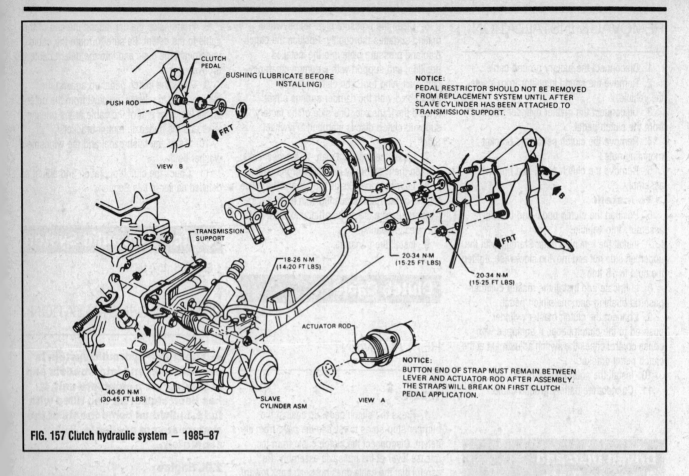

CLUTCH PEDAL

BUSHING (LUBRICATE BEFORE INSTALLING)

PUSH ROD

FRT

VIEW B

NOTICE:
PEDAL RESTRICTOR SHOULD NOT BE REMOVED FROM REPLACEMENT SYSTEM UNTIL AFTER SLAVE CYLINDER HAS BEEN ATTACHED TO TRANSMISSION SUPPORT.

TRANSMISSION SUPPORT

18-26 N·M (14-20 FT LBS)

20-34 N·M (15-25 FT LBS)

20-34 N·M (15-25 FT LBS)

FRT

ACTUATOR ROD

40-60 N·M (30-45 FT LBS)

SLAVE CYLINDER ASM

VIEW A

NOTICE:
BUTTON END OF STRAP MUST REMAIN BETWEEN LEVER AND ACTUATOR ROD AFTER ASSEMBLY. THE STRAPS WILL BREAK ON FIRST CLUTCH PEDAL APPLICATION.

FIG. 157 Clutch hydraulic system — 1985–87

8. Position the clutch master cylinder to the front of the dash. Install the retaining nuts and tighten the nuts evenly to prevent damage to the master cylinder. Tighten to 15–25 ft. lbs.

9. Remove the pedal restrictor from the push rod. Lube the push rod bushing on the clutch pedal. Connect the push rod to the clutch pedal and install the retaining clip.

10. If equipped with cruise control, check the switch adjustment at the pedal bracket.

☀ WARNING

When adjusting the cruise control switch, do not exert an upward force on the clutch pedal pad of more than 20 lbs. or damage to the master cylinder push rod retaining ring can result.

11. Install the hush panel.

12. Press the clutch pedal down several times. This will break the plastic retaining straps on the slave or actuator cylinder push rod. Do not remove the plastic button on the end of the push rod.

13. Connect the negative battery cable.

2.8L and 3.1L V6 Engine

1. Disconnect the negative battery cable.

2. Remove the air cleaner, mass air flow sensor and the air intake duct as an assembly.

3. Disconnect the electrical lead at the washer bottle. Remove the attaching bolts and washer bottle from the vehicle.

4. If equipped with cruise control, remove the mounting bracket retaining nuts from the strut tower.

5. Remove the hush panel from inside the vehicle.

6. Disconnect the clutch master cylinder push rod from the clutch pedal.

7. Remove the clutch master cylinder retaining nuts at the front of the dash.

8. Remove the slave or actuator cylinder retaining nuts at the transaxle.

9. Remove the hydraulic system as a unit from the vehicle.

To install:

10. Install the new slave or actuator cylinder to the transaxle support bracket aligning the push rod into the pocket on the clutch fork outer lever. Tighten the retaining nuts evenly to prevent damage to the slave cylinder. Tighten to 14–20 ft. lbs.

➡ **Do not remove the plastic push rod retainer from the slave or actuator cylinder. The straps will break on the first clutch pedal application.**

11. Position the clutch master cylinder to the front of the dash. Install the retaining nuts and tighten the nuts evenly to prevent damage to the master cylinder. Tighten to 15–25 ft. lbs.

12. Remove the pedal restrictor from the push rod. Lube the push rod bushing on the clutch pedal. Connect the push rod to the clutch pedal and install the retaining clip.

13. If equipped with cruise control, check the switch adjustment at the pedal bracket.

☀ WARNING

When adjusting the cruise control switch, do not exert an upward force on the clutch pedal pad of more than 20 lbs. or damage to the master cylinder push rod retaining ring can result.

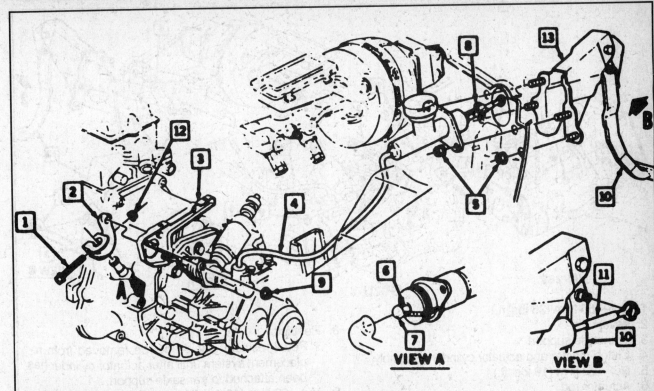

1. Bolt—50 N·m (36 lbs. ft.)
2. Lever
3. Transaxle support
4. Clutch master and actuator cylinder assembly
5. Nut—23 N·m (17 lbs. ft.)
6. Actuator rod
7. Button
    Button end of strap must remain between lever
    and actuator rod after assembly. The straps will
    break on first clutch pedal application.
8. Restrictor
    Pedal restrictor should not be removed from re-
    placement system until after slave cylinder has
    been attached to transaxle support.
9. Nut—22 N·m (16 lbs. ft.)
10. Clutch pedal
11. Master cylinder pushrod—lubricate before installing
12. Nut
13. Bracket

FIG. 158 Clutch hydraulic system — 1988–89

14. Install the hush panel.
15. Press the clutch pedal down several times. This will break the plastic retaining straps on the slave or actutator cylinder push rod. Do not remove the plastic button on the end of the push rod.
16. Install the air cleaner, mass air flow sensor and the air intake duct as an assembly.
17. Connect the negative battery cable.

Slave (Actuator) Cylinder

REMOVAL & INSTALLATION

1990–92 With 2.3 and 3.1L Engines

1. Disconnect the negative terminal from the battery.
2. Remove the air cleaner assembly.
3. Disconnect the slave cylinder nuts at the transaxle.
4. Disconnect the quick connect fitting on the hydraulic line and remove the slave cylinder from the vehicle.
   To install:
5. Connect the quick connect fitting on the hydraulic line and install the master cylinder to the vehicle.
6. Install the slave cylinder to the transaxle support bracket, aligning the pushrod into the pocket on the clutch fork lever. Tighten the retaining nuts evenly to 19 ft. lbs. (25 Nm).

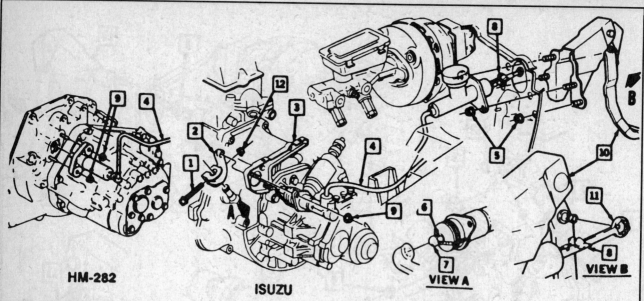

HM-282

ISUZU

VIEW A

VIEW B

1. Bolt—50 N·m (36 lbs. ft.)
2. Lever
3. Transaxle support
4. Clutch master and actuator cylinder assembly
5. Nut—22 N·m (16 lbs. ft.)
6. Actuator rod
7. Button
   Button end of strap must remain between lever and actuator rod after assembly. The straps will break on first clutch pedal application.

8. Restrictor
   Pedal restrictor should not be removed from replacement system until after actuator cylinder has been attached to transaxle support.
9. Nut—22 N·m (16 lbs. ft.).
10. Clutch pedal and bracket
11. Master cylinder pushrod—lubricate before installing
12. Nut

FIG. 159 Clutch hydraulic system — 1990

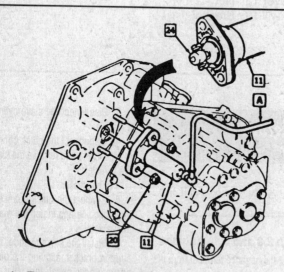

1. To clutch master cylinder
2. Clutch master and actuator cylinder assembly
3. Nut
4. Pushrod retainer (do not remove)

FIG. 160 Clutch hydraulic actuator — 1991–92 Model 5TM40 transaxle

7. Depress the clutch pedal several times to break the plastic retaining straps; DO NOT remove the plastic button from the end of the push rod.
8. Install the air cleaner assembly.
9. Connect the negative battery cable.

SYSTEM BLEEDING

1988–89

1. Remove any dirt or grease around the reservoir cap so that dirt cannot enter the system.
2. Fill the reservoir with an approved DOT 3 brake fluid.
3. Loosen, but do not remove, the bleeder screw on the slave cylinder.
4. Fluid will now flow from the master cylinder to the slave cylinder.

➡ **It is important that the reservoir remain filled throughout the procedure.**

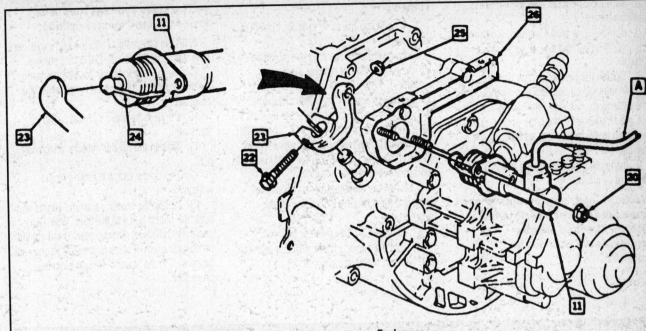

1. To clutch master cylinder
2. Clutch master and actuator cylinder assembly
3. Nut
4. Bolt—50 N•m (36 lbs. ft.)
5. Lever
6. Pushrod retainer (do not remove)
7. Nut
8. Transaxle support

FIG. 161 Clutch hydraulic actuator — 1991–92 Isuzu transaxle

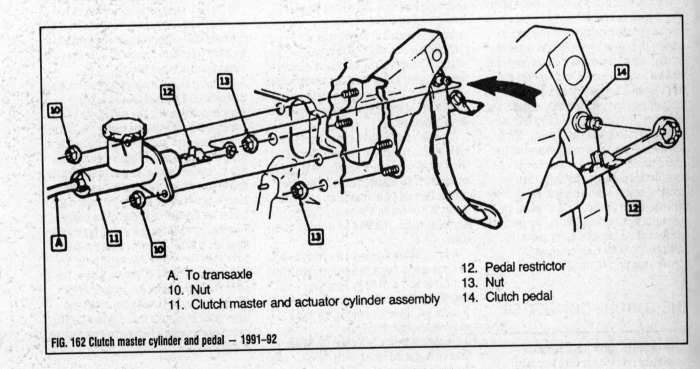

A. To transaxle
10. Nut
11. Clutch master and actuator cylinder assembly
12. Pedal restrictor
13. Nut
14. Clutch pedal

FIG. 162 Clutch master cylinder and pedal — 1991–92

5. Air bubbles should now appear at the bleeder screw.

6. Continue this procedure until a steady stream of fluid without any air bubbles is present.

7. Tighten the bleeder screw. Check the fluid level in the reservoir and refill to the proper mark.

8. The system is now fully bled. Check the clutch operation by starting the engine, pushing the clutch pedal to the floor and placing the transaxle in reverse.

9. If any grinding of the gears is noted, repeat the entire procedure.

➡ **Never under any circumstances reuse fluid that has been in the system. The fluid may be contaminated with dirt and moisture.**

1990–92

1. Disconnect the slave cylinder from the transaxle.

2. Loosen the master cylinder mounting attaching nuts. Do not remove the master cylinder.

3. Remove any dirt or grease around the reservoir cap so dirt cannot enter the system. Fill the reservoir with an approved DOT 3 brake fluid.

4. Depress the hydraulic actuator cylinder pushrod approximately 0.787 in. (20.0mm) into the slave cylinder bore and hold.

5. Install the diaphragm and cap on the reservoir while holding the slave cylinder pushrod.

6. Release the slave cylinder pushrod.

7. Hold the slave cylinder vertically with the pushrod end facing the ground.

➡ **The slave cylinder should be lower than the master cylinder.**

8. Press the pushrod into the slave cylinder bore with short 0.390 in. (10.0mm) strokes.

9. Observe the reservoir for air bubbles. Continue until air bubbles no longer enter the reservoir.

10. Connect the slave cylinder to the transaxle.

11. Tighten the master cylinder attaching nuts.

12. Top-up the clutch master cylinder reservoir.

13. To test the system, start the engine and push the clutch pedal to the floor. Wait 10 seconds and select reverse gear. There should be no gear clash. If clash is present, air may still be present in the system. Repeat bleeding procedure.

AUTOMATIC TRANSAXLE

Understanding Automatic Transaxles

The automatic transaxle allows engine torque and power to be transmitted to the drive wheels within a narrow range of engine operating speeds. The transaxle will allow the engine to turn fast enough to produce plenty of power and torque at very low speeds, while keeping it at a sensible rpm at high vehicle speeds. The transaxle performs this job entirely without driver assistance. The transaxle uses a light fluid as the medium for the transmission of power. This fluid also works in the operation of various hydraulic control circuits and as a lubricant. Because the transaxle fluid performs all of these three functions, trouble within the unit can easily travel from one part to another. For this reason, and because of the complexity and unusual operating principles of the transaxle, a very sound understanding of the basic principles of operation will simplify troubleshooting.

THE TORQUE CONVERTER

The torque converter replaces the conventional clutch. It has three functions:

1. It allows the engine to idle with the vehicle at a standstill, even with the transaxle in gear.

2. It allows the transaxle to shift from range to range smoothly, without requiring that the driver close the throttle during the shift.

3. It multiplies engine torque to an increasing extent as vehicle speed drops and throttle opening is increased. This has the effect of making the transaxle more responsive and reduces the amount of shifting required.

The torque converter is a metal case which is shaped like a sphere that has been flattened on opposite sides. It is bolted to the rear end of the engine's crankshaft. Generally, the entire metal case rotates at engine speed and serves as the engine's flywheel.

The case contains three sets of blades. One set is attached directly to the case. This set forms the torus or pump. Another set is directly connected to the output shaft, and forms the turbine. The third set is mounted on a hub which, in turn, is mounted on a stationary shaft through a one-way clutch. This third set is known as the stator.

A pump, which is driven by the converter hub at engine speed, keeps the torque converter full of transaxle fluid at all times. Fluid flows continuously through the unit to provide cooling.

Under low speed acceleration, the torque converter functions as follows:

The torus is turning faster than the turbine. It picks up fluid at the center of the converter and, through centrifugal force, slings it outward. Since the outer edge of the converter moves faster than the portions at the center, the fluid picks up speed.

The fluid then enters the outer edge of the turbine blades. It then travels back toward the center of the converter case along the turbine blades. In impinging upon the turbine blades, the fluid loses the energy picked up in the torus.

If the fluid were now to immediately be returned directly into the torus, both halves of the converter would have to turn at approximately the same speed at all times, and torque input and output would both be the same.

In flowing through the torus and turbine, the fluid picks up 2 types of flow, or flow in 2 separate directions. It flows through the turbine blades, and it spins with the engine. The stator, whose blades are stationary when the vehicle is being accelerated at low speeds, converts one type of flow into another. Instead of allowing the fluid to flow straight back into the torus, the stator's curved blades turn the fluid almost 90° toward the direction of rotation of the engine. Thus the fluid does not flow as fast toward the torus, but is already spinning when the torus picks it up. This has the effect of allowing the torus to turn much faster than the turbine. This difference in speed may be compared to the difference in speed between the smaller and larger gears in any gear train. The result is that engine power output is higher, and engine torque is multiplied.

As the speed of the turbine increases, the fluid spins faster and faster in the direction of engine rotation. As a result, the ability of the stator to redirect the fluid flow is reduced. Under cruising conditions, the stator is eventually forced to rotate on its one-way clutch in the direction of engine rotation. Under these conditions, the torque converter begins to behave almost like a solid shaft, with the torus and turbine speeds being almost equal.

THE PLANETARY GEARBOX

The ability of the torque converter to multiply engine torque is limited. Also, the unit tends to be more efficient when the turbine is rotating at relatively high speeds. Therefore, a planetary gearbox is used to carry the power output of the turbine to the halfshafts.

Planetary gears function very similarly to conventional transaxle gears. However, their construction is different in that three elements make up one gear system, and, in that all three elements are different from one another. The three elements are: an outer gear that is shaped like a hoop, with teeth cut into the inner surface; a sun gear, mounted on a shaft and located at the very center of the outer gear; and a set of three planet gears, held by pins in a ring-like planet carrier, meshing with both the sun gear and the outer gear. Either the outer gear or the sun gear may be held stationary, providing more than one possible torque multiplication factor for each set of gears. Also, if all three gears are forced to rotate at the same speed, the gearset forms, in effect, a solid shaft.

Most modern automatics use the planetary gears to provide either a single reduction ratio of about 1.8:1, or 2 reduction gears: a low of about 2.5:1, and an intermediate of about 1.5:1. Bands and clutches are used to hold various portions of the gearsets to the transaxle case or to the shaft on which they are mounted. Shifting is accomplished, then, by changing the portion of each planetary gearset which is held to the transaxle case or to the shaft.

THE SERVOS AND ACCUMULATORS

The servos are hydraulic pistons and cylinders. They resemble the hydraulic actuators used on many familiar machines, such as bulldozers. Hydraulic fluid enters the cylinder, under pressure, and forces the piston to move to engage the band or clutches.

The accumulators are used to cushion the engagement of the servos. The transaxle fluid must pass through the accumulator on the way to the servo. The accumulator housing contains a thin piston which is sprung away from the discharge passage of the accumulator. When fluid passes through the accumulator on the way to the servo, it must move the piston against spring pressure, and this action smooths out the action of the servo.

THE HYDRAULIC CONTROL SYSTEM

The hydraulic pressure used to operate the servos comes from the main transaxle oil pump. This fluid is channeled to the various servos through the shift valves. There is generally a manual shift valve which is operated by the transaxle selector lever and an automatic shift valve for each automatic upshift the transaxle provides: i.e., 2-speed automatics have a low/high shift valve, while 3-speeds have a 1-2 valve, and a 2-3 valve.

There are 2 pressures which effect the operation of these valves. One is the governor pressure which is affected by vehicle speed. The other is the modulator pressure which is affected by intake manifold vacuum or throttle position. Governor pressure rises with an increase in vehicle speed, and modulator pressure rises as the throttle is opened wider. By responding to these 2 pressures, the shift valves cause the upshift points to be delayed with increased throttle opening to make the best use of the engine's power output.

Most transaxles also make use of an auxiliary circuit for downshifting. This circuit may be actuated by the throttle linkage or the vacuum line which actuates the modulator, or by a cable or solenoid. It applies pressure to a special downshift surface on the shift valve or valves.

The transaxle modulator also governs the line pressure, used to actuate the servos. In this way, the clutches and bands will be actuated with a force matching the torque output of the engine.

Identification

All of the J-cars use the Turbo Hydra-Matic 125C automatic transaxle as optional equipment. This is a fully automatic unit of conventional design, incorporating a four element hydraulic torque converter, a compound planetary gear set, and a dual sprocket and drive link assembly.

The sprockets and drive link (Hy-Vo chain) connect the torque converter assembly to the transaxle gears. The transaxle also incorporates the differential assembly, which is of conventional design. Power is transmitted from the transaxle to the final drive and differential assembly through helical cut gears.

No overhaul procedures are given in this book because of the complexity of the transaxle. Transaxle removal and installation, adjustment, and halfshaft removal, installation, and overhaul procedures are covered.

By September 1, 1991, Hydra-Matic will have changed the name designation of the THM 125C automatic transaxle. The new name designation for this transaxle will be Hydra-Matic 3T40. Transaxles built between 1989 and 1990 will serve as transitional years in which a dual system, made up of the old designation and the new designation will be in effect.

Fluid Pan and Filter Pan removal

Fluid and filter changes are covered in Section 1.

Adjustments

SHIFT CONTROL CABLE ADJUSTMENT

▸ SEE FIGS. 163 and 164
1. Place the shift lever in the **N**.

➡ **Neutral can be found by rotating the transaxle selector shaft counterclockwise from P through R to N.**

2. Loosely attach the cable to the transaxle shift lever with a nut. Assemble the cable to the cable bracket and to shift lever. Tighten the cable to transaxle shift lever nut.

➡ **The lever must be held out of P when torquing the nut.**

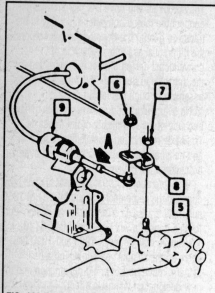
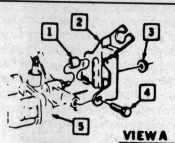

VIEW A

1. Spacer
2. Bracket
3. Nut—27 N·m (20 lbs. ft.)
4. Bolt—27 N·m (20 lbs. ft.)
5. Transaxle asm.
6. Nut—20 N·m (15 lbs. ft.)
7. Nut—27 N·m (20 lbs. ft.)
8. Lever
9. Cable

FIG. 163 Engine compartment shift control

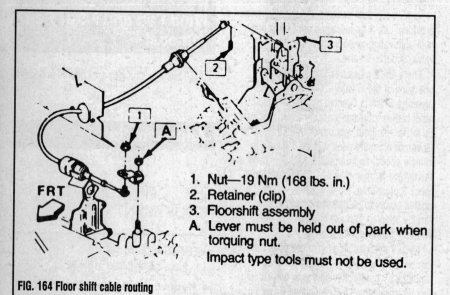

1. Nut—19 Nm (168 lbs. in.)
2. Retainer (clip)
3. Floorshift assembly
A. Lever must be held out of park when torquing nut.
   Impact type tools must not be used.

FIG. 164 Floor shift cable routing

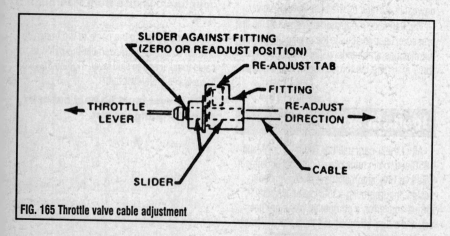

FIG. 165 Throttle valve cable adjustment

THROTTLE VALVE (TV) CABLE ADJUSTMENT

◆ SEE FIG. 165

Setting of the TV cable must be done by rotating the throttle lever at the carburetor or throttle body. Do not use the accelerator pedal to rotate the throttle lever.

1. With the engine off, depress and hold the reset tab at the engine end of the TV cable.
2. Move the slider until it stops against the fitting.
3. Release the rest tab.
4. Rotate the throttle lever to its full travel.
5. The slider must move (racthet) toward the lever when the lever is rotated to its full travel position.
6. Recheck after the engine is hot and road test the vehicle.

Neutral Start Switch

◆ SEE FIG. 166-168

The automatic transaxle utilizes the neutral safety switch and back-up light switch as a combined unit. This switch is located under the console, next to the shifter on 1982–86 models and on top of the of the transaxle on 1987–91 models.

REMOVAL & INSTALLATION

1982–86

1. Disconnect the negative battery cable.
2. Remove the console and replace the switch at the side of the shifter.

1987–92

1. Disconnect the negative battery cable and the electrical connector from the switch.
2. Remove the switch-to-transaxle screws and the switch.

To Install:

3. Place the transaxle's shift control lever in the **N** notch in the detent plate.
4. Position the switch onto the transaxle and install the screws loosely.
5. Perform a switch adjustment which follows.
6. Connect the negative battery cable.
7. Start the engine and check the switch operation.

ADJUSTMENT

1. Disconnect the negative battery cable.
2. Loosen the switch attaching screws.
3. Rotate the switch on the shifter assembly to align the service adjustment hole with the carrier tang hole.
4. Using a 3/8 in. drill bit or gauge pin, insert it into the service adjustment hole to a depth of 5/8 in. (15mm).
5. Tighten the switch-to-transaxle screws and remove the drill bit or gauge pin.
6. Connect the negative battery cable and test the switch operation.

Transaxle

REMOVAL & INSTALLATION

1982–86

1. Disconnect the negative battery cable where it attaches to the transaxle.
2. On the 1982–84 models, insert a 1/4 in. × 2 in. bolt into the hole in the right front motor mount to prevent any mislocation during the transaxle removal.
3. On 4-cylinder engines, remove the air cleaner.
4. On V6 engines remove the following:
   a. Remove the air intake duct from the air cleaner.
   b. Remove the left fender brace.

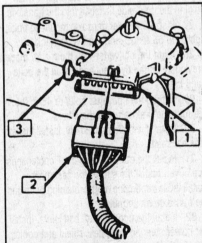

1. Neutral start and back-up lamp switch
2. Switch conn.
3. "T" latch

FIG. 168 "T" latch wiring connector used on the neutral start/back-up switch — 1987–92

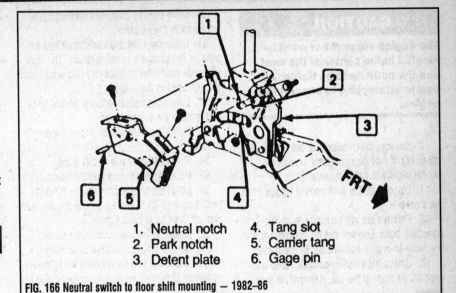

1. Neutral notch
2. Park notch
3. Detent plate
4. Tang slot
5. Carrier tang
6. Gage pin

FIG. 166 Neutral switch to floor shift mounting — 1982–86

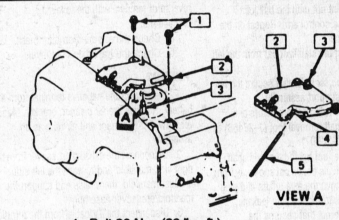

VIEW A

1. Bolt 30 N·m (22 lbs. ft.)
2. Switch asm.
3. Trans. shaft
4. Service adjustment hole
5. 3/32 inch drill bit or 2.34 dia. gage pin

FIG. 167 Neutral/back-up switch adjustment — 1987–92

c. Disconnect the M.A.T. sensor lead at the air cleaner.
d. Disconnect the mass air flow sensor lead.
e. Remove the PCV pipe retaining clamp from the air intake duct.
f. Remove the clamp retaining the air intake duct to the throttle body.
g. Remove the Mass Air Flow Sensor mounting bolt. Remove the air cleaner bracket mounting bolts at the battery tray.
h. Remove the air cleaner, mass air flow sensor and air intake duct as an assembly.
i. Remove the heat shield at the crossover pipe and remove the crossover pipe.

5. Disconnect the T.V. cable at the throttle body.
6. Unscrew the bolt securing the T.V. cable to the transaxle. Pull up on the cable cover at the transaxle until the cable can be seen. Disconnect the cable from the transaxle rod.
7. Remove the wiring harness retaining bolt at the top of the transaxle.
8. Remove the hose from the air management valve and then pull the wiring harness up and out of the way.
9. Install an engine support bar as shown in the illustration. Raise the engine just enough to take the pressure off the motor mounts.

✺ CAUTION

The engine support bar must be located in the center of the cowl and the bolts must be tightened before attempting to support the engine.

10. Remove the transaxle mount and bracket assembly. It may be necessary to raise the engine slightly to aid in removal.

11. Disconnect the shift control linkage from the transaxle.

12. Remove the top transaxle-to-engine mounting bolts. Loosen, but do not remove, the transaxle-to-engine bolt nearest to the starter.

13. Unlock the steering column. Raise and support the front of the car. Remove the front wheels.

14. Pull out the cotter pin and loosen the castellated ball joint nut until the ball joint separates from the control arm. Repeat on the other side of the car.

15. Disconnect the stabilizer bar from the left lower control arm.

16. Remove the six bolts that secure the left front suspension support assembly.

17. Install drive axle seal protectors and connect an axle shaft removal tool (J–28468) to a slide hammer (J–23907).

18. Position the tool behind the axle shaft cones and then pull the cones out and away from the transaxle. Remove the axle shafts and plug the transaxle bores to reduce fluid leakage.

19. Remove the nut that secures the transaxle control cable bracket to the transaxle, then remove the engine-to-transaxle stud.

20. Disconnect the speedometer cable at the transaxle.

21. Disconnect the transaxle strut (stabilizer) at the transaxle.

22. Remove the four retaining screws and remove the torque converter shield.

23. Scribe a mark for on the flywheel for reassembly and remove the three bolts securing the torque converter to the flex plate.

24. Disconnect and plug the oil cooler lines at the transaxle. Remove the starter.

25. Remove the screws that hold the brake and fuel line brackets to the left side of the underbody. This will allow the lines to be moved slightly for clearance during transaxle removal.

26. Remove the bolt that was loosened in Step 12.

27. Remove the transaxle to the left.

To install:

28. Position the transaxle in the car.

29. Place a small amount of light grease on the torque converter pilot hub.

30. Make sure to properly seat the torque convertor in the oil pump.

31. Guide the right drive axle shaft into its bore as the transaxle is being raised. The right transaxle cannot be installed AFTER the transaxle is connected to the engine.

32. Lower the transaxle to the engine bolts and remove the transaxle jack.

33. Install the transaxle to engine support bracket.

34. Install the transaxle cooler lines.

35. Position the LH axle into the transaxle.

36. Install the torque converter to flywheel bolts torque to 46 ft. lbs. Re-torque the first bolt afetr all three have been tightened.

37. Install the transaxle converter shield.

38. When installing the front suspension support assembly you must follow the tightening sequence shown in the illustration at the end of Section 7.

39. The remainder of the installation is the reverse of removal with the following precautions.
  a. Check the suspension alignment.
  b. Check the transaxle fluid level.

1987–92

1. Disconnect the negative terminal from the battery. Remove the air cleaner, bracket, Mass Air Flow (MAF) sensor and air tube as an assembly.

2. Disconnect the exhaust crossover from the right side manifold and remove the left side exhaust manifold, then, raise and support the manifold/crossover assembly.

3. Disconnect the TV cable from the throttle lever and the transaxle.

4. Remove the vent hose and the shift cable from the transaxle.

5. Remove the fluid level indicator and the filler tube.

6. Using the engine support fixture tool J–28467 or equivalent and the adapter tool J–35953 or equivalent, install them on the engine.

7. Remove the wiring harness-to-transaxle nut.

8. Label and disconnect the wires for the speed sensor, TCC connector and the neutral safety/back up light switch.

9. Remove the upper transaxle-to-engine bolts.

10. Remove the transaxle-to-mount through bolt, the transaxle mount bracket and the mount.

11. Raise and safely support the vehicle.

12. Remove the front wheel assemblies.

13. Disconnect the shift cable bracket from the transaxle.

14. Remove the left side splash shield.

15. Using a modified halfshaft seal protector tool J–34754 or equivalent, install one on each halfshaft to protect the seal from damage and the joint from possible failure.

16. Using care not to damage the halfshaft boots, disconnect the halfshafts from the transaxle.

17. Remove the torsional and lateral strut from the transaxle. Remove the left side stabilizer link pin bolt.

18. Remove the left frame support bolts and move it out of the way.

19. Disconnect the speedometer wire from the transaxle.

20. Remove the transaxle converter cover and matchmark the converter to the flywheel for assembly.

21. Disconnect and plug the transaxle cooler pipes.

22. Remove the transaxle-to-engine support.

23. Using a transaxle jack, position and secure it to the transaxle and remove the remaining transaxle-to-engine bolts.

24. Make sure the torque converter does not fall out and remove the transaxle from the vehicle.

➡ **The transaxle cooler and lines should be flushed any time the transaxle is removed for overhaul or to replace the pump, case or converter.**

To install:

25. Put a small amount of grease on the pilot hub of the converter and make sure the converter is properly engaged with the pump.

26. Raise the transaxle to the engine while guiding the right-side halfshaft into the transaxle.

27. Install the lower transaxle mounting bolts, tighten to 55 ft. lbs. and remove the jack.

28. Align the converter with the marks made previously on the flywheel and install the bolts hand tight.

29. Torque the converter bolts to 46 ft. lbs.; retorque the first bolt after the others.

30. Install the starter assembly. Install the left side halfshaft.

31. Install the converter cover, oil cooler lines and cover. Install the sub-frame assembly. Install the lower engine mount retaining bolts and the transaxle mount nuts.

32. Install the right and left ball joints. Install the power steering rack, heat shield and cooler lines to the frame.

33. Install the right and left inner fender splash shields. Install the tire assemblies.

34. Lower the vehicle. Connect all electrical leads. Install the upper transaxle mount bolts, tighten to 55 ft. lbs.

35. Attach the crossover pipe to the exhaust manifold. Connect the EGR tube to the crossover.

36. Connect the TV cable and the shift cable. Install the air cleaner and inlet tube.

37. Remove the engine support tool. Connect the negative battery cable.

Halfshafts

REMOVAL, INSTALLATION AND OVERHAUL

These vehicles use unequal-length halfshafts. All halfshafts except the left-hand inboard joint incorporate a male spline; the shafts interlock with the transaxle gears through the use of barrel-type snaprings. The left-hand inboard shaft uses a female spline which installs over a stub shaft protruding from the transaxle. Four constant velocity joints are used, two on each shaft. The inner joints are of the double offset design; the outer joints are Rzeppa-type.

REMOVAL & INSTALLATION

♦ SEE FIGS. 105-107

1982-86

1. Remove the hub nut.
2. Raise the front of the car. Remove the wheel and tire.
3. Install an axle shaft boot seal protector, G.M. special tool No. J–28712 or the equivalent, onto the seal.
4. Disconnect the brake hose clip from the MacPherson strut, but do not disconnect the hose from the caliper. Remove the brake caliper from the spindle, and hang the caliper out of the way by a length of wire. Do not allow the caliper to hang by the brake hose.
5. Mark the camber alignment cam bolt for reassembly. Remove the cam bolt and the upper attaching bolt from the strut and spindle.
6. Pull the steering knuckle assembly from the strut bracket.
7. Using G.M. special tool J–28468 or the equivalent, remove the axle shaft from the transaxle.
8. Using G.M. special tool J–28733 or the equivalent spindle remover, remove the axle shaft from the hub and bearing assembly.
9. If a new drive axle is to be installed, a new knuckle seal should be installed first.
10. Loosely install the drive axle into the transaxle and steering knuckle.

11. Loosely attach the steering knuckle to the suspension strut.

12. Install the brake caliper. Tighten the bolts to 30 ft. lbs. (40Nm.).

13. The drive axle is an interference fit in the steering knuckle. Press the axle into place, then install the hub nut. When the shaft begins to turn with the hub, insert a drift through the caliper into one of the cooling slots in the rotor to keep it from turning. Tighten the hub nut to 70 ft. lbs. (100Nm.). to completely seat the shaft.

14. Load the hub assembly by lowering it onto a jackstand. Align the camber cam bolt marks made during removal, install the bolt and tighten to 140 ft. lbs. (190 Nm.). Tighten the upper nut to the same value.

15. Install the axle shaft all the way into the transaxle using a screwdriver inserted into the groove provided on the inner retainer. Tap the screwdriver until the shaft seats in the transaxle.

16. Connect the brake hose clip to the strut. Install the tire and wheel, lower the car, and tighten the hub nut to 185 ft. lbs. (260 Nm.).

1987-88

1. Raise the car and suitably support.
2. Remove the wheel assembly.
3. Insert a drift into the into the caliper and rotor to prevent the rotor from turning.
4. Remove the shaft nut and washer.
5. Remove the caliper from the steering knuckle and suspend the caliper assembly with a wire.
6. Remove the rotor from the hub and bearing assembly.
7. Disconnect the stabilizer shaft from the control arm.
8. Remove the ball joint from the steering knuckle.
9. Remove the drive axle from the transaxle. Remove the driveaxle from the hub and bearing assembly using tool J–28733.

To install:

10. Install the drive axle into the hub and bearing assembly and the transaxle.
11. Install the lower ball joint to the steering knuckle.
12. Install the stabilizer shaft to the control arm.
13. Install the rotor to the hub and bearing assembly.
14. Install the caliper to the steering knuckle.
15. Install a washer and a new shaft nut.
16. Insert a drift into the into the caliper and rotor to prevent the rotor from turning and torque drive axle nut to 185 ft. lbs. (260 Nm.).
17. Seat the drive axle into the transaxle by placing a screwdriver into the groove on the joint housing and tapping until seated.
18. Verify that the drive axle is seated into the transaxle by grasping on the housing and pulling outward.

19. Install the wheel assembly.
20. Lower the car

1989-92

1. Raise the car and suitably support.
2. Remove the wheel assembly.
3. Install drive seal protector J34754 or equivalent, on the outer joint.
4. Insert a drift into the into the caliper and rotor to prevent the rotor from turning.
5. Remove the shaft nut and washer.
6. Remove the lower ball joint cotter pin and nut and loosen the joint using tool J 38892 or equivqlent. If removing the right axle, turn the wheel to the left, if removing the left axle, turn the wheel to the right.
7. Separate the joint, with a pry bar between the suspension support.
8. Disengage the axle from the hub and bearing using J 28733–A or equivalent.
9. Separate the hub and bearing assembly from the drive axle and move the strut and knuckkle assembly rearward.
10. Disconnect the inner joint from the transaxle using tool J–28468 or J–33008 attached to J–29794 and J–2619–01 or from the intermediate shaft (V6 and Turbo engines), if equipped.

To install:

11. Install axle seal protector J–37292–A into the transaxle.
12. Insert the drive axle into the transaxle or intermediate shaft (V6 and Turbo engines), if equipped, by placing a suitable tool into the groove on the joint housing and tapping until seated.

❊❊❊ WARNING

Do not damage the axle seal or dislodge the transaxle seal garter spring when installing the axle.

13. Verify that the drive axle is seated into the transaxle by grasping on the housing and pulling outward.
14. Install the drive axle into the hub and bearing assembly.
15. Install the lower ball joint to the knuckle. Tighten the ball joint to steering knuckle nut to 41 ft. lbs. (55 Nm) and install the cotter pin.
16. Install the washer and new drive shaft nut.
17. Insert a drift into the caliper and rotor to prevent the rotor from turning and tighten the drive shaft nut to 185 ft. lbs. (260 Nm.).
18. Remove both J–37292–B and J–34754 seal protectors.
19. Install the tire and wheel assembly.
20. Lower the vehicle and connect the negative battery cable.

TORQUE SPECIFICATIONS – ISUZU

Actuator Cylinder Support to Transaxle .... 54 N·m (37 Lbs. Ft.)
Back-Up Switch Assembly to Transaxle .... 33 N·m (24 Lbs. Ft.)
Clutch Housing Cover to Transaxle .... 13 N·m (115 Lbs. In.)
Front Transaxle Strut to Body Bolt... 54 N·m (40 Lbs. Ft.)
Front Transaxle Strut to Transaxle .... 68 N·m (50 Lbs. Ft.)
Rear Transaxle Mount to Body .... 30 N·m (23 Lbs. Ft.)
Rear Mount Bracket to Mount .... 120 N·m (88 Lbs. Ft.)
Rear Mount Bracket to Transaxle .... 54 N·m (40 Lbs. Ft.)
Shift Cable Grommet to Shroud .... 2 N·m (18 Lbs. In.)
Shift Control to Floor... 24 N·m (18 Lbs. Ft.)
Shift Control Box to Transaxle .... 17 N·m (13 Lbs. Ft.)
Shift Linkage Retainer to Transaxle Case .... 23 N·m (17 Lbs. Ft.)
Shift Retainer to Transaxle Case .... 10 N·m (90 Lbs. In.)
Speedometer/Vehicle Speed Sensor Housing to Transaxle .... 9 N·m (84 Lbs. In.)
Transaxle Shift Cable Bracket to Cables .... 27 N·m (19 Lbs. Ft.)
Transaxle Shift Lever to Cable Stud .... 25 N·m (18 Lbs. Ft.)
Transaxle to Engine Bolts and Studs.. 75 N·m (55 Lbs. Ft.)

TORQUE SPECIFICATIONS – MODEL 5TM40

Back-Up Switch Assembly to Transaxle .... 33 N·m (24 Lbs. Ft.)
Clutch Housing Cover to Transaxle .... 13 N·m (115 Lbs. In.)
Front Transaxle Strut to Body Bolt... 54 N·m (40 Lbs. Ft.)
Front Transaxle Strut to Transaxle .... 68 N·m (50 Lbs. Ft.)
Rear Transaxle Mount to Body .... 30 N·m (23 Lbs. FT.)
Rear Mount Bracket to Mount .... 120 N·m (88 Lbs. Ft.)
Rear Mount Bracket to Transaxle .... 54 N·m (40 Lbs. Ft.)
Shift Cable Grommet to Shroud .... 2 N·m (18 Lbs. In.)
Shift Control to Floor... 24 N·m (18 Lbs. Ft.)
Shift Linkage Retainer to Transaxle Case .... 23 N·m (17 Lbs.Ft.)
Shift Shaft to Lever Nut... 83 N·m (61 Lbs. Ft.)
Speedometer/Vehicle Speed Sensor Housing To Transaxle .... 9 N·m (84 Lbs. In.)

Description of Usage	Torque
Reverse shift rail guide	6 N.m (53 lb. in.)
Differential pin	9 N·m (80 lb. in.)
Differential gear	83 N·m (61 lb. ft.)
Fluid drain plug	24 N·m (18 lb. ft.)
Clutch housing to gear housing	21 N·m (15 lb. ft.)
Output shaft bearing support	70 N·m (50 lb. ft.)
End plate to gear housing	21 N·m (15 lb. ft.)
Input shaft bearing support	70 N·m (50 lb. ft.)
Reverse idler gear bracket	21 N·m (15 lb. ft.)
Shift pivot bracket	23 N·m (17 lb. ft.)
Shift lever nut	83 N·m (61 lb. ft.)
Shift shaft detent	9 N·m (80 lb. in.)
Interlock plate	21 N·m (15 lb. ft.)
Shift rail detent holder	9 N·m (80 lb. in.)
Output bearing race	21 N·m (15 lb. ft.)
Sliding sleeve detent	44 N·m (32 lb. ft.)
Stud	21 N·m (15 lb. ft.)
Electronic speed sensor retainer	9 N·m (80 lb. in.)
Stud	30 N·m (23 lb. ft.)
Back-up lamp switch assembly	9 N·m (80 lb. in.)

5TM40 Transaxle Torque Specifications

Reverse Shift Bracket Retaining Bolts	17 N·m	13 lb.ft.
Transaxle Case to Clutch Housing Bolts	38 N·m	28 lb.ft.
Reverse Idle Shaft Bolt	38 N·m	28 lb.ft.
Detent Spring Retaining Bolts	25 N·m	18 lb.ft.
Input/Output Shaft Retaining Nuts	128 N·m	94 lb.ft.
Control Box to Case Bolts	17 N·m	13 lb.ft.
Rear Cover Bolts	17 N·m	13 lb.ft.
Bearing and Shim Retainer Screws	17 N·m	13 lb.ft.

LUBE CAPACITY — 1.9 LITERS (2.01 QT.)

LUBE RECOMMENDED — MANUAL TRANSAXLE OIL NO. 12345349 OR EQUIVALENT

Isuzu 5-speed Transaxle Torque Specifications

Troubleshooting the Manual Transmission

Problem	Cause	Solution
Transmission shifts hard	• Clutch adjustment incorrect • Clutch linkage or cable binding • Shift rail binding	• Adjust clutch • Lubricate or repair as necessary • Check for mispositioned selector arm roll pin, loose cover bolts, worn shift rail bores, worn shift rail, distorted oil seal, or extension housing not aligned with case. Repair as necessary.
	• Internal bind in transmission caused by shift forks, selector plates, or synchronizer assemblies • Clutch housing misalignment • Incorrect lubricant • Block rings and/or cone seats worn	• Remove, dissemble and inspect transmission. Replace worn or damaged components as necessary. • Check runout at rear face of clutch housing • Drain and refill transmission • Blocking ring to gear clutch tooth face clearance must be 0.030 inch or greater. If clearance is correct it may still be necessary to inspect blocking rings and cone seats for excessive wear. Repair as necessary.
Gear clash when shifting from one gear to another	• Clutch adjustment incorrect • Clutch linkage or cable binding • Clutch housing misalignment • Lubricant level low or incorrect lubricant • Gearshift components, or synchronizer assemblies worn or damaged	• Adjust clutch • Lubricate or repair as necessary • Check runout at rear of clutch housing • Drain and refill transmission and check for lubricant leaks if level was low. Repair as necessary. • Remove, disassemble and inspect transmission. Replace worn or damaged components as necessary.
Transmission noisy	• Lubricant level low or incorrect lubricant • Clutch housing-to-engine, or transmission-to-clutch housing bolts loose • Dirt, chips, foreign material in transmission • Gearshift mechanism, transmission gears, or bearing components worn or damaged • Clutch housing misalignment	• Drain and refill transmission. If lubricant level was low, check for leaks and repair as necessary. • Check and correct bolt torque as necessary • Drain, flush, and refill transmission • Remove, disassemble and inspect transmission. Replace worn or damaged components as necessary. • Check runout at rear face of clutch housing

8

SUSPENSION
AND
STEERING

WHEELS

Wheels Front and Rear

REMOVAL & INSTALLATION

▶ SEE FIGS. 1 and 2

1. Remove the hub cap, if so equipped.
2. Loosen the lug nuts on the wheel to be removed.
3. Raise and safely support vehicle on jack stands.

➡ **Always use a suitable floor jack for raising the vehicle to be serviced. Never use the jacking device supplied with the vehicle for vehicle service, that jacking device is designed for emergency use only to change a flat tire.**

4. Remove the wheel lug nuts and remove the wheel assembly.
5. Installation is the reverse of the removal procedure. Tighten the wheel lug nuts to 100 ft. lbs.

INSPECTION

Inspect the tread for abnormal wear, check for nails or other foreign material embedded into the tire. To check for leaks, submerse the wheel assembly into a tub of water and watch for air bubbles.

Wheels must be replaced if they are bent, dented, leak air through welds, have enlongated bolt holes, if wheel nuts won't stay tight, or if the wheels are heavily rusted. Replacement wheels must be equivalent to the original equipment wheels in load capacity, diameter, rim width, offset, and mounting configuration.

A wheel of improper size may affect wheel bearing life, brake cooling, speedometer/odometer calibration, vehicle ground clearance and tire clearance to the body and/or chassis.

➡ **Replacement with used wheels is not recommended as their service history may have included severe treatment or very high mileage and they could fail without warning.**

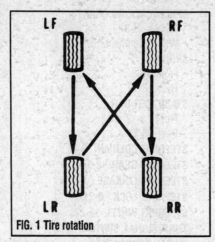
FIG. 1 Tire rotation

Wheel Lug Studs

All models use metric wheel nuts and studs. The nut will have the word "metric" stamped on the face and the stud will have the letter "M" into the threaded end.

The thread size of the metric wheel nuts and wheel studs are M12X1.5, this signifies:

- M = Metric
- 12 = Diameter in millimeters
- 1.5 = Millimeters per thread

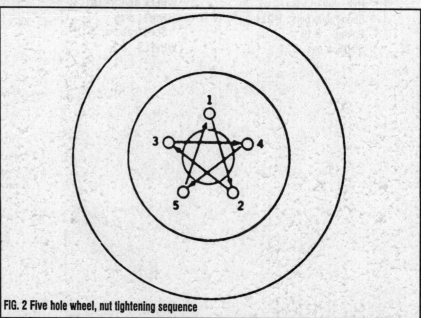
FIG. 2 Five hole wheel, nut tightening sequence

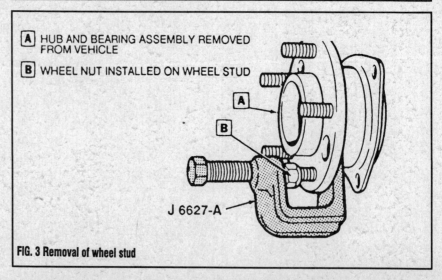

[A] HUB AND BEARING ASSEMBLY REMOVED FROM VEHICLE

[B] WHEEL NUT INSTALLED ON WHEEL STUD

J 6627-A

FIG. 3 Removal of wheel stud

REPLACEMENT

♦ SEE FIGS. 3 and 4

The hub and bearing assembly must be removed from the vehicle to perform this procedure.

1. Using special tool J6627–A or equivalent, remove the stud to be replaced.

➡ **Never try to reuse a wheel stud. Once a wheel stud has been removed, discard it and replace it with a new one.**

2. Install the wheel stud into flange.
3. Place a couple of washers onto the threaded side of wheel stud.

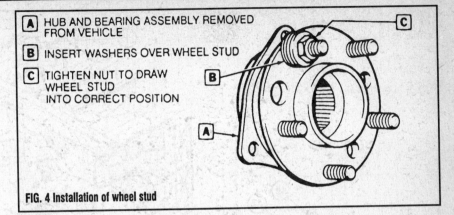

A. HUB AND BEARING ASSEMBLY REMOVED FROM VEHICLE

B. INSERT WASHERS OVER WHEEL STUD

C. TIGHTEN NUT TO DRAW WHEEL STUD INTO CORRECT POSITION

FIG. 4 Installation of wheel stud

4. Install the wheel stud nut and tighten until the stud is fully seated against the flange.

5. Remove the wheel nut and washers.
6. Install the hub/bearing, and other related parts onto vehicle.

FRONT SUSPENSION

The J-cars use MacPherson strut front suspension designs. A MacPherson strut combines the functions of a shock absorber and an upper suspension member (upper arm) into one unit. The strut is surrounded by a coil spring, which provides normal front suspension functions.

The strut bolts to the body shell at its upper end, and to the steering knuckle at the lower end. The strut pivots with the steering knuckle by means of a sealed mounting assembly at the upper end which contains a preloaded, non-adjustable bearing.

The steering knuckle is connected to the chassis at the lower end by a conventional lower control arm, and pivots in the arm in a preloaded ball joint of standard design. The knuckle is fastened to the ball joint stud by means of a castellated nut and cotter pin.

Advantages of the MacPherson strut design, aside from its relative simplicity, include reduced weight and friction, minimal intrusion into the engine and passenger compartments, and ease of service.

Springs and Shock Absorbers

TESTING

The function of the shock absorber is to dampen harsh spring movement and provide a means of dissipating the motion of the wheels so

FIG. 5 Front suspension assembly

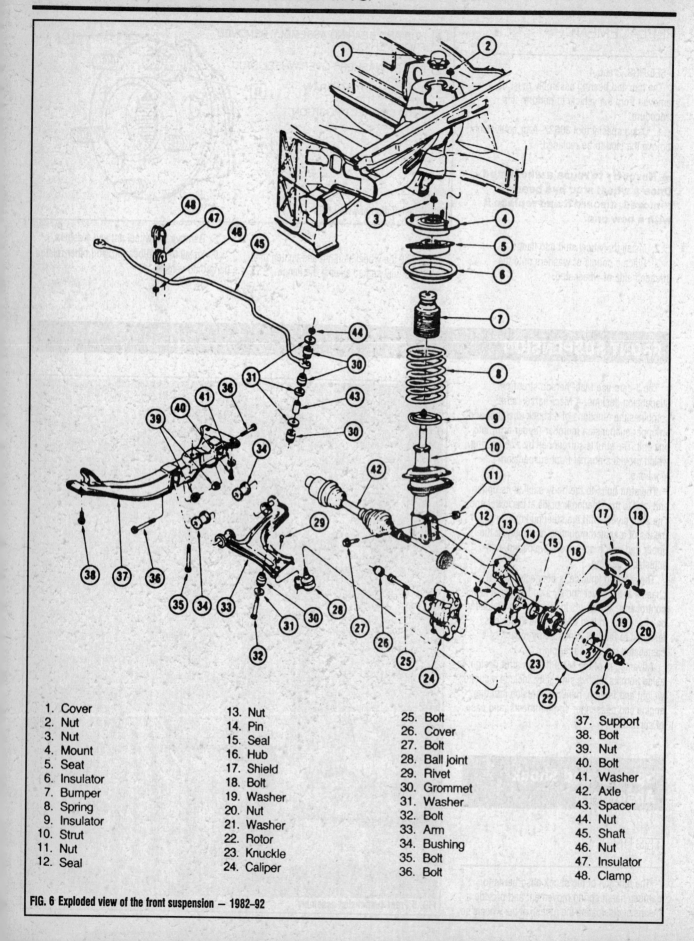

1. Cover
2. Nut
3. Nut
4. Mount
5. Seat
6. Insulator
7. Bumper
8. Spring
9. Insulator
10. Strut
11. Nut
12. Seal
13. Nut
14. Pin
15. Seal
16. Hub
17. Shield
18. Bolt
19. Washer
20. Nut
21. Washer
22. Rotor
23. Knuckle
24. Caliper
25. Bolt
26. Cover
27. Bolt
28. Ball joint
29. Rivet
30. Grommet
31. Washer
32. Bolt
33. Arm
34. Bushing
35. Bolt
36. Bolt
37. Support
38. Bolt
39. Nut
40. Bolt
41. Washer
42. Axle
43. Spacer
44. Nut
45. Shaft
46. Nut
47. Insulator
48. Clamp

FIG. 6 Exploded view of the front suspension — 1982–92

FIG. 7 Front lower strut mounting location

1. Working under the hood, pry off the shock cover and then unscrew the upper strut-to-body nuts.

2. Loosen the wheel nuts, raise and support the car and allow the suspension to hang free, then remove the wheel and tire.

❖ WARNING

Use care to prevent damage from over extension of the drive shaft joints. When either end of the shaft is disconnected, over extension of the joint could result in separation of the internal components and possible joint failure. The steering knuckle should be supported and drive axle joint protectors should be used.

3. Install a drive axle joint protective cover (modified), such as J–34754 or equivalent.

4. Use a two-armed puller and press the tie rod out of the strut bracket.

5. Remove both strut-to-steering knuckle bolts and carefully lift out the strut.

6. Installation is in the reverse order of removal. Observe the following torques:

- Upper strut-to-body nuts: 18–20 ft. lbs.
On 1982–87 models, be sure that the flat sides of the strut-to-knuckle bolt heads are horizontal (see illustration) before tightening.
- Tighten the strut-to-knuckle bolts to 140 ft. lbs. (1982) and 133 ft. lbs. (1983–92).

STRUT MODIFICATION

▶ SEE FIG. 10

This modification is made only if a camber adjustment is anticipated.

1. Place the strut in a vise. This step is not absolutely necessary; filing can be accomplished by disconnecting the strut from the steering knuckle.

2. File the holes in the outer flanges so as to enlarge the bottom holes until they match the slots already in the inner flanges.

3. Camber adjustment procedures are detailed later in this Section.

that the shocks encountered by the wheels are not totally transmitted to the body and, therefore, to you and your passengers. As the wheel moves up and down, the shock absorber shortens and lengthens, thereby imposing a restraint on movement by its hydraulic action.

A good way to see if your shock absorbers are functioning correctly is to push one corner of the car until it is moving up and down for almost the full suspension travel, then release it and watch its recovery. If the car bounces slightly about one more time and then comes to a rest, the shock is alright. If the car continues to bounce excessively, the shocks will probably require replacement.

MacPherson Struts

REMOVAL & INSTALLATION

▶ SEE FIGS. 5–9

The struts retain the springs under tremendous pressure even when removed from the car. For these reasons, several expensive special tools and substantial specialized knowledge are required to safely and effectively work on these parts. We recommend that if spring or shock absorber repair work is required, you remove the strut or struts involved and take them to a repair facility which is fully equipped and familiar with the car.

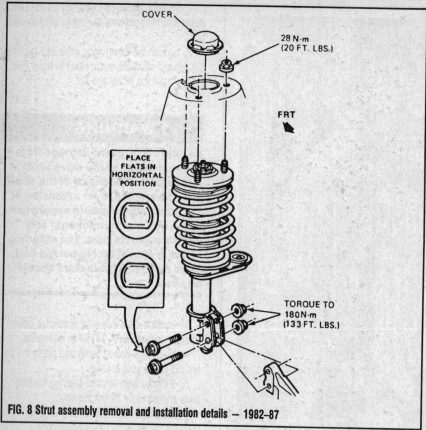

FIG. 8 Strut assembly removal and installation details — 1982-87

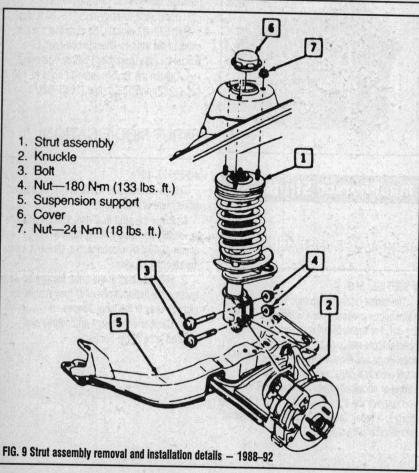

1. Strut assembly
2. Knuckle
3. Bolt
4. Nut—180 N·m (133 lbs. ft.)
5. Suspension support
6. Cover
7. Nut—24 N·m (18 lbs. ft.)

FIG. 9 Strut assembly removal and installation details — 1988-92

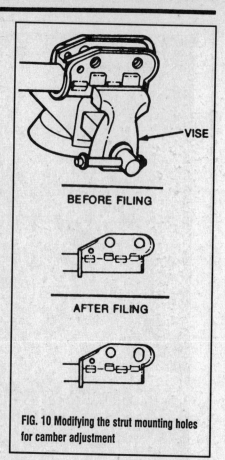

FIG. 10 Modifying the strut mounting holes for camber adjustment

REMOVAL & INSTALLATION

♦ SEE FIGS. 11–15

❋❋ CAUTION

The coil springs are retained under considerable pressure. They can exert enough force to cause serious injury. Exercise extreme caution when disassembling the strut for coil spring removal.

This procedure requires the use of a spring compressor and several other special tools. It cannot be performed without them. If you do not have access to these tools, DO NOT attempt to disassemble the strut!

1982–84

1. Remove the strut assembly.
2. Clamp the spring compressor J26584 in a vise. Position the strut assembly in the bottom adapter of the compresser and install the special tool J26584–86 (see illustration). Be sure that the adapter captures the strut and that the locating pins are engaged.

3. Rotate the strut assembly so that the top mounting assembly lip aligns with the compressor support notch. Insert two top adapters (J26584–88) between the top mounting assembly and the top spring seat. Position the adapters so that the split lines are in the 3 o'clock and 9 o'clock positions.

4. Using a 1 in. socket, turn the screw on top of the compressor clockwise until the top support flange contacts the adapters. Continue turning the screw until the coil spring is compressed approximately 1/2 in. (13mm) or 4 complete turns. Never bottom the spring or the strut damper rod.

5. Unscrew the nut from the strut damper shaft and then lift off the top mounting assembly.

6. Turn the compressor adjusting screw counterclockwise until the spring tension has been relieved. Remove the adapters and then remove the coil spring.

To Install:

7. Clamp the strut compressor body J 26584 in a vise.

8. Position the strut assembly in the bottom adapter of the compresser and install the special tool J26584–86 (see illustration). Be sure that the adapter captures the strut and that the locating pins are engaged.

9. Position the spring on the strut. Make sure the spring is properly seated on the bottom of the spring plate.

10. Install the spring strut seat assembly on top of the spring.

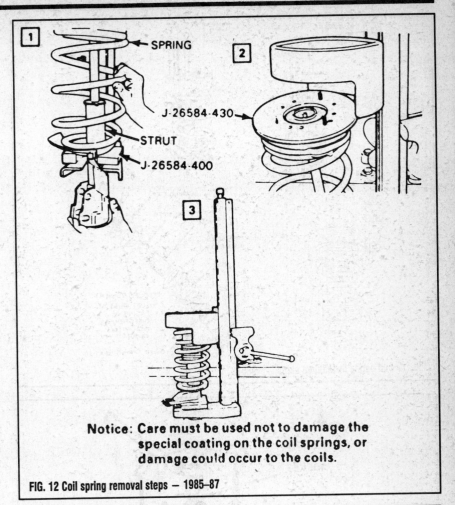

Notice: Care must be used not to damage the special coating on the coil springs, or damage could occur to the coils.

FIG. 12 Coil spring removal steps — 1985–87

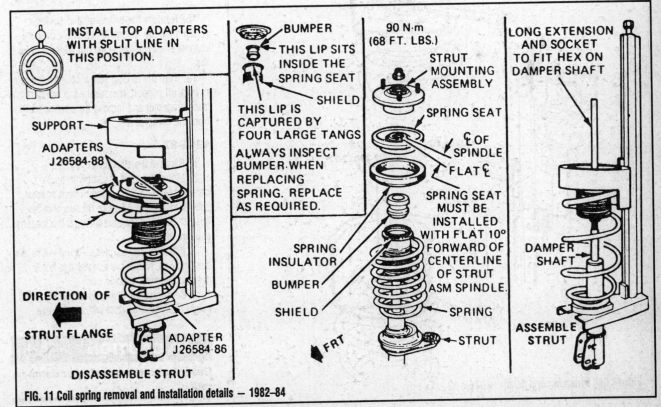

FIG. 11 Coil spring removal and installation details — 1982–84

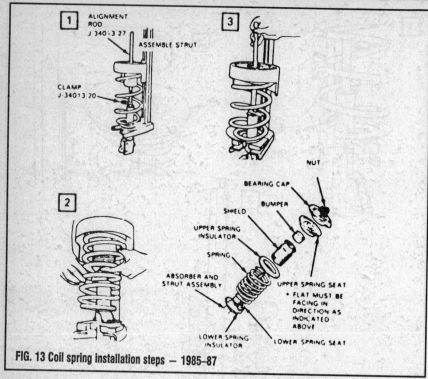

FIG. 13 Coil spring installation steps — 1985–87

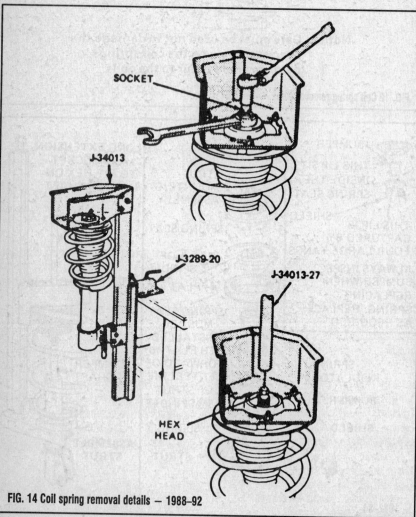

FIG. 14 Coil spring removal details — 1988–92

11. Place BOTH J 26584–88 top adapters over the spring seat assemblies.

12. Turn the compressor forcing the screw until the compressor top support just contacts the top adapters (do not compress the spring at this time).

13. Install long extension with a socket to fit the hex on the damper shaft through the top of the spring seat. Use the extension to guide the components during reassembly.

✸✸ WARNING

NEVER place a hard tool such as pliers or screwdriver against the polished surface of the damper shaft. The shaft can be held up with your fingers or an extension in order to prevent it from receding into the strut assembly while the spring is being compressed.

14. Compress the screw by turning the screw clockwise until approximately 1½ in. (38mm) of damper shaft extends through the top spring plate.

✸✸ WARNING

Do not compress the spring until it bottoms.

15. Remove the extension and socket, position the top mounting assembly over the damper shaft and install the nut. Tighten to 68 ft. lbs.

16. Turn the forcing screw counterclockwise to back off support, remove the top adapters and bottom adapter and remove the strut assembly from the compressor.

1985–87

1. Remove the strut assembly.

2. Mount the strut assembly in spring compressor J–26584, using bottom adapter, special tool J–26584–400. Be sure that the adapter captures the strut and that the locating pins are engaged.

3. Place the top adapter, J–26584–430, on the strut cap. Notice the adapter has holes designating each specific car.

4. Compress the strut approximately ½ its height after initial contact with the top cap.

✸✸ CAUTION

Never bottom the spring or damper rod!

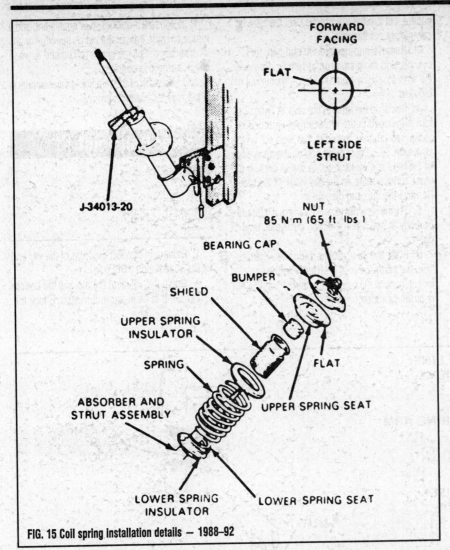

FIG. 15 Coil spring installation details — 1988–92

12. Compress the spring until approximately 1 in. (25mm) of the damper rod protrudes through the bearing cap and not any further. Install and tighten the nut to 59 ft. lbs. (80 Nm).

13. Remove the damper rod clamp J–34013–20.

14. Back off the spring compressor and remove the strut assembly.

1988–92

1. Remove the strut assembly.

2. Mount the strut compressor J–34013 in holding fixture J–3289–20.

3. Mount the strut assembly into strut compressor. Note that the strut compressor has strut mounting holes drilled for specific car lines.

4. Compress the strut approximately ½ its height after initial contact with the top cap.

❈❈ CAUTION

Never bottom the spring or dampener rod!

5. Remove the nut from the strut dampener shaft and place alignment rod J–34013–27 on top of the dampener shaft. Use the rod to guide the dampener shaft straight down through the spring cap while decompressing the spring. Remove the components.

To Install:

6. Install the bearing cap into the strut compressor if previously removed.

7. Mount the strut assembly in strut compressor, using bottom locking pin only. Extend the dampener shaft and install clamp J–34013–20 on the dampener shaft.

8. Install the spring over the dampener and swing the assembly up so the upper locking pin can be installed.

9. Install all shields, bumpers and insulators on the spring seat. Install the spring seat on top of the spring. Be sure the flat on the upper spring seat is facing in the proper direction. The spring seat flat should be facing the same direction as the centerline of the strut assembly spindle.

10. Install the guiding rod and turn the forcing screw while the guiding rod centers the assembly. When the threads on the dampener shaft are visable, remove the guiding rod and install the nut. Tighten the nut to 65 ft. lbs. (85 Nm). Use a crowsfoot line wrench while holding the dampener shaft with a socket.

11. Remove the clamp.

5. Remove the nut from the strut damper shaft and place alignment rod J–34013–27 on top of the damper shaft. Use the rod to guide the damper shaft straight down through the spring cap while decompressing the spring. Remove the components.

To Install:

6. Mount the strut assembly in spring compressor J–26584, using bottom adapter, special tool J–26584–400. Be sure that the adapter captures the strut and that the locating pins are engaged.

7. Position the spring on the strut and make sure the spring is properly seated on the spring plate.

8. Install all shields, bumpers and insulators on the spring seat. Install the spring seat on top of the spring.

9. Install the bearing cap on spring seat and make sure they are centered together and aligned properly.

➡ **The upper spring seat flat must be aligned ± 10 degrees with the lower strut to knuckle attachment.**

10. Place the top adapter, J–26584–430, on the strut cap. Lower the compressor to capture the cap. Pull up the damper rod to full extension and clamp in place with J–34013–20.

11. Insert alignment rod J–34013–27 throught the bearing and spring caps and position on top of the damper rod. Compress the spring and guide the damper rod through the bearing cap using the alignment rod during compression.

➡ **During compression of the spring be sure to use the guide rod to guide the shaft through the exact center of the bearing. If the threads of the damper rod catch on the bearing cap and prevent the rod from passing cleanly through the bearing, stop compressing immediately. Decompress the spring and begin again.**

Strut Cartridge

REMOVAL & INSTALLATION

◆ SEE FIG. 16

On 1982–87 models only, the internal piston rod, cylinder assembly and fluid can be replaced utilizing a service cartridge and nut. Internal threads are located inside the tube immediately below a cut line groove.

1. Remove the strut and the coil springs. Clamp the strut in a vise. Do not overtighten it as this will cause damage to the strut tube.

2. Locate the cut line groove just below the top edge of the strut tube. It is imperative that the groove be accurately located as any mislocation will cause inner thread damage. Using pipe cutters, cut around the groove until the tube is completely cut through.

3. Remove and discard the end cap, the cylinder and the piston rod assembly. Remove the strut assembly from the vise and pour out the old fluid.

4. Reclamp the strut in the vise. A flaring cup tool is included in the replacement cartridge kit to flare and deburr the edge that was cut on the strut tube. Place the flaring cup on the open edge of the tube and strike it with a mallet until its flat outer surface rests on the top edge of the tube. Remove the cup and discard it.

5. Try the new nut to make sure that it threads properly. If not, use the flaring cup again until it does.

6. Place the new strut cartridge into the tube. Turn the cartridge until it settles into the indentations at the base of the tube. Place the nut over the cartridge.

7. Using tool J–29778–A or equivalent, and a torque wrench, tighten the nut as specified in the kit drirections. Pull the piston rod up and down to check for proper operation.

8. Installation of the remaining components is in the reverse order of removal.

Lower Ball Joint

◆ SEE FIGS. 17–20

INSPECTION

1. Raise and support the front of the car and let the suspension hang free.

2. Grasp the wheel at the top and the bottom and shake it in an in-and-out motion. Check for

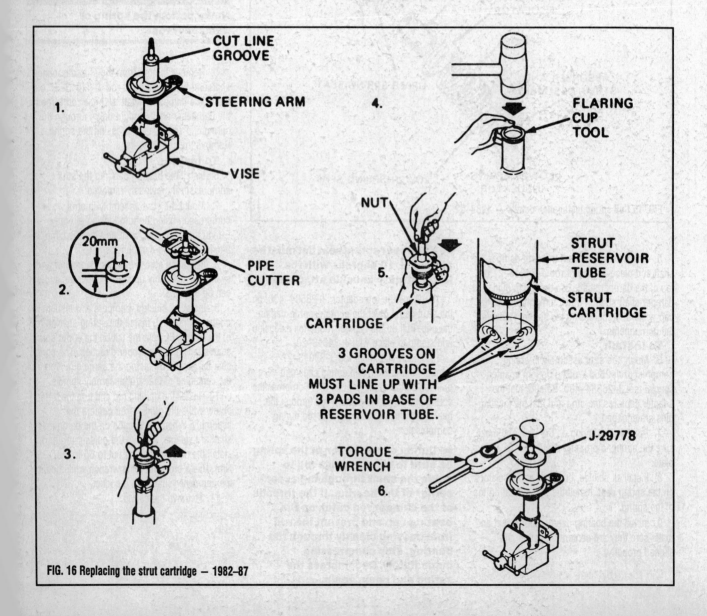

FIG. 16 Replacing the strut cartridge — 1982–87

any horizontal movement of the steering knuckle relative to the lower control arm. Replace the ball joint if such movement is noted.

3. If the ball stud is disconnected from the steering knuckle and any looseness is detected, or if the ball stud can be twisted in its socket using finger pressure, replace the ball joint.

REMOVAL & INSTALLATION

Only one ball joint is used in each lower arm. The MacPherson strut design does not use an upper ball joint.

1982–87

1. Loosen the wheel nuts, raise the car, and remove the wheel.

2. Use a $1/8$ in. (3mm) drill bit to drill a hole through the center of each of the three ball joint rivets.

3. Use a $1/2$ in. (13mm) drill bit to drill completely through the rivet.

4. Use a hammer and punch to remove the rivets. Drive them out from the bottom.

5. Use the special tool J29330 or a ball joint removal tool to separate the ball joint from the steering knuckle (see illustration). Don't forget to remove the cotter pin.

6. Disconnect the stabilizer bar from the lower control arm. Remove the ball joint.

7. Install the new ball joint into the control arm with the three bolts supplied as shown and torque to 50 ft. lbs. Installation of the remaining components is in the reverse order of removal. Tighten the castellated nut on the ball joint to 55 ft. lbs. and use a new cotter pin. Check the toe setting and adjust as necessary.

1988–92

1. Raise and support the vehicle safely.

2. Place jack stands under the suspension support.

3. Lower the car slightly so the weight of the car rests on the suspension supports and not the control arms.

4. Remove the tire and wheel assembly.

✳✳✳ WARNING

Use care to prevent damage from over extension of the drive shaft joints. When either end of the shaft is disconnected, over extension of the joint could result in separation of the internal components and possible joint failure. The steering knuckle should be supported and drive axle joint protectors should be used.

---

5. Install a drive axle joint protective cover (modified), such as J–34754 or equivalent.

6. Remove the cotter pin from the ball joint.

7. Use the special ball joint removal tool, J–29330 or equivalent, to separate the ball joint from the steering knuckle.

8. Use a $1/8$ in. (3mm) drill bit to drill a hole through the center of each of the three ball joint rivets.

9. Use a $1/2$ in. (13mm) drill bit to drill completely through the rivet.

10. Loosen the stabilizer shaft bushing assembly nut.

11. Remove the ball joint from the steering knuckle and control arm.

To Install:

12. Install the new ball joint into the control arm with the three bolts supplied as shown and torque to specifications given in the kit.

13. Install the ball joint to the knuckle and tighten the not to a mimimum of 37 ft. lbs. (50 Nm) or a maximum of 55 ft. lbs. (75 Nm) torque to install the pin.

14. Tighten the stabilizer insulator clamp nuts to 16 ft. lbs. (22 Nm).

15. Remove the seal protector.

16. Install the tire and wheel assembly.

17. Raise the car slightly to allow removal of the jack stands and lower the car.

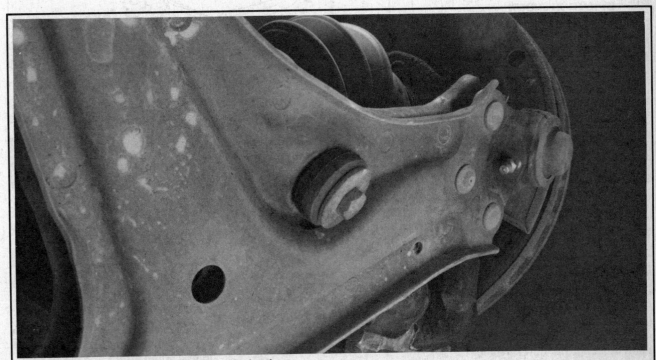

FIG. 17 Lower control arm showing ball joint mounting location

USING 1/8" DRILL, DRILL A PILOT HOLE COMPLETELY THROUGH THE RIVET.

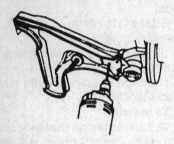

DRILL PILOT HOLE

USING A 1/2" OR 13mm DRILL, DRILL COMPLETELY THROUGH THE RIVET. REMOVE BALL JOINT. DO NOT USE EXCESSIVE FORCE TO REMOVE BALL JOINT.

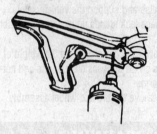

DRILL FINAL HOLE

PLACE J 29330 INTO POSITION AS SHOWN. LOOSEN NUT AND BACK OFF UNTIL . . .

. . . THE NUT CONTACTS THE TOOL. CONTINUE BACKING OFF THE NUT UNTIL THE NUT FORCES THE BALL STUD OUT OF THE KNUCKLE.

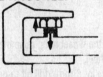

SEPARATING BALL JOINT FROM KNUCKLE USING J29330

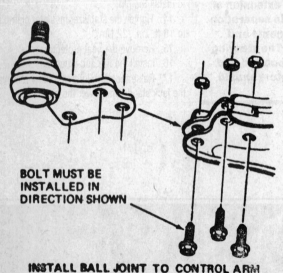

BOLT MUST BE INSTALLED IN DIRECTION SHOWN

INSTALL BALL JOINT TO CONTROL ARM

75 N·m (55 FT. LBS.)

FRT

FIG. 18 Ball joint removal and installation details — 1982–87

Stabilizer Bar (Sway Bar)

REMOVAL & INSTALLATION

♦ SEE FIGS. 21 and 22

➡ **On 1984-86 vehicles, a squawk noise from the front stabilizer bar insulator bushings may be corrected by installing a new Teflon lined bushing. The new bushings are being used on later models.**

1. Safely raise the car and allow the front lower control arms to hang free.
2. Remove the left front wheel and tire.
3. Disconnect the stabilizer shaft from the control arms.
4. Disconnect the stabilizer shaft from the support assemblies.
5. Loosen the front bolts and remove the bolts from the rear and center of the support assemblies.
6. When installing the stabilizer, loosely assemble all components while insuring that the stabilizer is centered, side to side.

Control Arm/Suspension Support

REMOVAL & INSTALLATION

♦ SEE FIGS. 23 and 24

1. Raise and support the front of the car. Remove the wheel.

➡ **Use care to prevent damage from over extension of the drive shaft joints. When either end of the shaft is disconnected, over extension of**

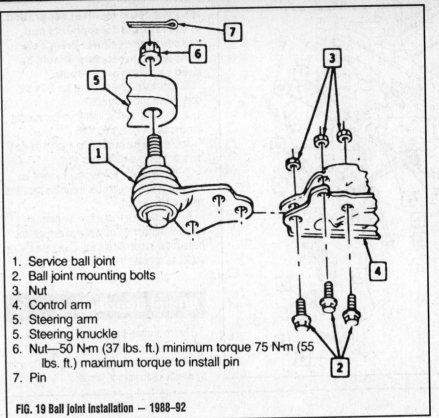

1. Service ball joint
2. Ball joint mounting bolts
3. Nut
4. Control arm
5. Steering arm
5. Steering knuckle
6. Nut—50 N·m (37 lbs. ft.) minimum torque 75 N·m (55 lbs. ft.) maximum torque to install pin
7. Pin

FIG. 19 Ball joint installation — 1988–92

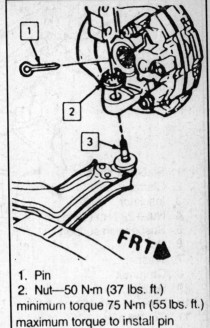

1. Pin
2. Nut—50 N·m (37 lbs. ft.) minimum torque 75 N·m (55 lbs. ft.) maximum torque to install pin
3. Ball joint

FIG. 20 Ball joint to knuckle installation — 1988–92

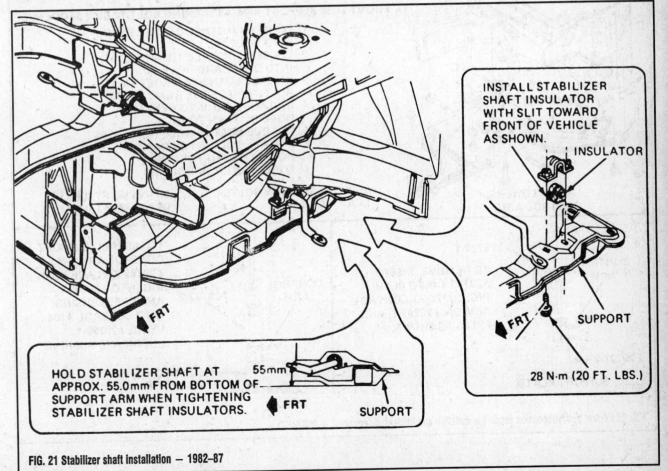

INSTALL STABILIZER SHAFT INSULATOR WITH SLIT TOWARD FRONT OF VEHICLE AS SHOWN.

INSULATOR

SUPPORT

28 N·m (20 FT. LBS.)

HOLD STABILIZER SHAFT AT APPROX. 55.0mm FROM BOTTOM OF SUPPORT ARM WHEN TIGHTENING STABILIZER SHAFT INSULATORS.

55mm

SUPPORT

FIG. 21 Stabilizer shaft installation — 1982–87

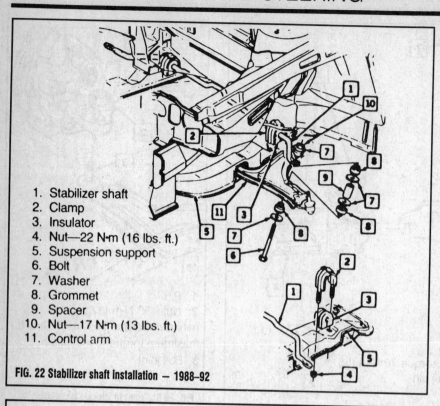

1. Stabilizer shaft
2. Clamp
3. Insulator
4. Nut—22 N·m (16 lbs. ft.)
5. Suspension support
6. Bolt
7. Washer
8. Grommet
9. Spacer
10. Nut—17 N·m (13 lbs. ft.)
11. Control arm

FIG. 22 Stabilizer shaft installation — 1988–92

the joint could result in separation of the internal components and possible joint failure. Drive axle joint (boot) protectors should be used on this type of repair.

2. Disconnect the stabilizer bar from the control arm and/or support.

3. Separate the ball joint from the steering knuckle as previously detailed.

4. Remove the two control arm-to-support bolts and remove the control arm.

5. If control arm support bar removal is necessary, unscrew the six mounting bolts and remove the support.

6. Installation is in the reverse order of removal. Tighten the control arm support rail bolts in the sequence shown. Check the toe and adjust as necessary.

Wheel Bearings

The front wheel bearings are sealed, non-adjustable units which require no periodic attention. They are bolted to the steering knuckle by means of an integral flange.

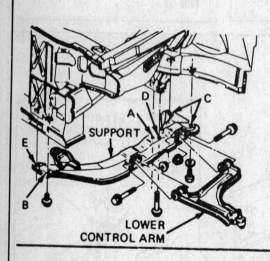

FRONT SUSP SUPPORT ASM ATTACHING BOLT/SCREW SEQUENCE

1. LOOSELY INSTALL CENTER BOLT INTO HOLE (A).
2. LOOSELY INSTALL TIE BAR BOLT INTO OUTBOARD HOLE (B).
3. INSTALL BOTH REAR BOLTS INTO HOLES (C) TORQUE REAR BOLTS.
4. INSTALL BOLT INTO CENTER HOLE(D), THEN TORQUE.
5. TORQUE BOLT IN HOLE (A).
6. INSTALL BOLT INTO FRONT HOLE (E), THEN TORQUE.
7. TORQUE BOLT IN HOLE (B).

SUPPORT-TO-BODY BOLTS . . . . 90 N·m (63 FT. LBS.)
LCA PIVOT BOLTS . . . . .95 N·m (67 FT. LBS.)

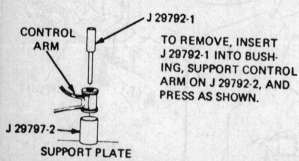

TO REMOVE, INSERT J 29792-1 INTO BUSHING, SUPPORT CONTROL ARM ON J 29792-2, AND PRESS AS SHOWN.

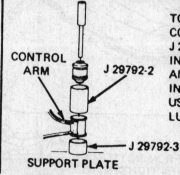

TO INSTALL, SUPPORT CONTROL ARM ON J 29792-3, PLACE BUSHING INTO J 29792-2, AND PRESS BUSING INTO CONTROL ARM USING J 29792-1. LUBRICATE BUSHING.

FIG. 23 Control arm/suspension support installation and tightening sequence — 1982–87

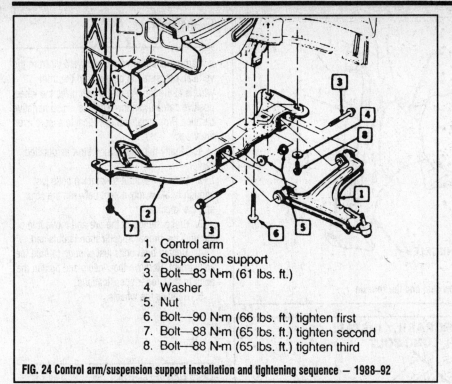

1. Control arm
2. Suspension support
3. Bolt—83 N·m (61 lbs. ft.)
4. Washer
5. Nut
6. Bolt—90 N·m (66 lbs. ft.) tighten first
7. Bolt—88 N·m (65 lbs. ft.) tighten second
8. Bolt—88 N·m (65 lbs. ft.) tighten third

FIG. 24 Control arm/suspension support installation and tightening sequence — 1988–92

Front Hub, Knuckle And Bearing

REMOVAL & INSTALLATION

♦ SEE FIGS. 25–27

✳ WARNING

You will need a special tool to pull the bearing free of the halfshaft (drive axle), G.M. tool no. J-28733 or the equivalent. You should also use a halfshaft boot protector, G.M. tool no. J-28712 or J-34754 or the equivalent, to protect the parts from damage.

1. Remove the wheel cover, loosen the hub nut, and raise and support the car. Remove the front wheel.
2. Install the drive axle boot cover.
3. Remove and discard the hub nut. Be sure to use a new one on assembly, not the old one.
4. Remove the brake caliper and rotor:
   a. Remove the caliper mounting bolts.
   b. Remove the caliper from the knuckle and suspend from a length of wire. Do not allow the caliper to hang from the brake hose. Pull the rotor from the knuckle.
5. Remove the three hub and bearing attaching bolts. If the old bearing is to be reused, match mark the bolts and holes for installation. The brake rotor splash shield will have to come off, too.
6. Attach a puller, G.M. part no. J-28733 or the equivalent, and remove the bearing. If corrosion is present, make sure the bearing is loose in the knuckle before using the puller.

To Install:

7. Clean the mating surfaces of all dirt and corrosion. Check the knuckle bore and knuckle seal for damage. If a new bearing is to be installed, remove the old knuckle seal and install a new one. Grease the lips of the new seal before installation; install with a seal driver made for the purpose, G.M. tool no. J-28671 or the equivalent.
8. Push the bearing onto the halfshaft. Install a new washer and hub nut.
9. Tighten the new hub nut on the halfshaft until the bearing is seated. If the rotor and hub start to rotate as the hub nut is tightened, insert a long bolt through the cut-out in the hub assembly to prevent rotation. Do not apply full torque to the hub nut at this time. Just seat the bearing.
10. Install the brake shield and the bearing retaining bolts. Tighten the bolts evenly to 63 ft. lbs. (85 Nm).
11. Install the caliper and rotor. Be sure that the caliper hose isn't twisted. Install the caliper bolts and tighten to 21–38 ft. lbs. (28–51 Nm.).
12. Install the wheel. Lower the car. Tighten the hub nut to 185 ft. lbs. (260 Nm.)

Front End Alignment

♦ SEE FIG. 28

The toe setting is the only adjustment normally required on a J-car. However, in special circumstances, such as damage due to road hazard, collision, etc., camber may be adjusted after modifying the strut as detailed earlier in this Section. Caster is not adjustable.

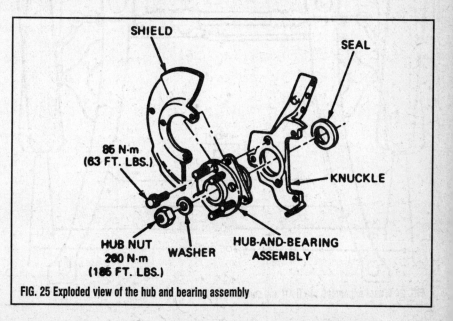

FIG. 25 Exploded view of the hub and bearing assembly

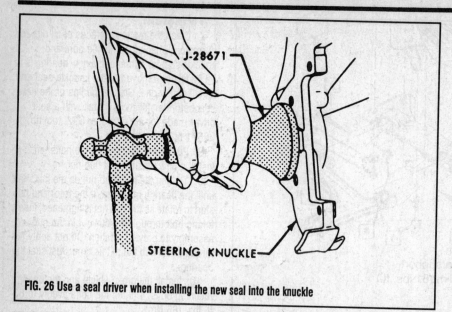

FIG. 26 Use a seal driver when installing the new seal into the knuckle

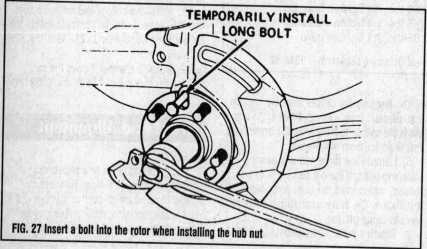

FIG. 27 Insert a bolt into the rotor when installing the hub nut

CAMBER

Camber is the inward or outward tilt from the vertical, measured in degrees, of the front wheels at the top. An onward tilt gives the wheel positive camber; an inward tilt is called negative camber. Proper camber is critical to assure even tire wear.

1. Modify the suspension strut as detailed earlier.
2. Loosen the strut-to-knuckle bolts just enough to allow movement between the strut and the knuckle.
3. Grasp the top of the tire and move it in or out until the proper specification is obtained.
4. Tighten both bolts just enough to hold the adjustment. Remove the wheels and tighten the bolts to the proper specifications.
5. Replace the wheels.

TOE

◆ SEE FIGS. 29 and 30

Toe is the amount, measured in a fraction of a millimeter, that the wheels are closer together at one end than the other. Toe-in means that the front wheels are closer together at the front than the rear; toe-out means the rear of the front wheels are closer together than the front. J-cars are designed to have a slight amount of toe-out.

Toe is adjusted by turning the tie rods. It must be checked after camber has been adjusted, but it can be adjusted without disturbing the camber setting. You can make this adjustment without

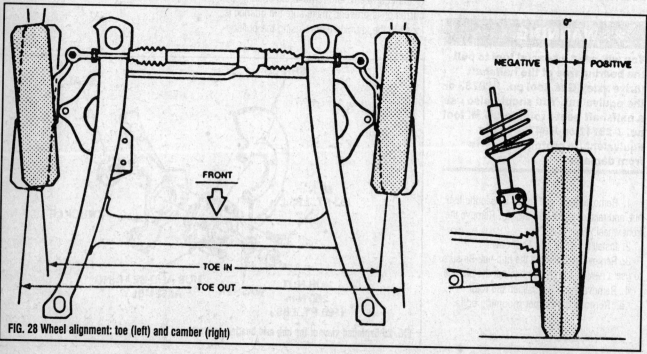

FIG. 28 Wheel alignment: toe (left) and camber (right)

FIG. 29 Tie rod attaching location

OUTER TIE ROD

STRUT DAMPER

ADJUST TOE SETTING HERE

LOOSEN CLAMP BOLTS TO ADJUST TOE. RE-TIGHTEN TO 20 N·m (14 LB. FT.)

FIG. 30 Toe adjustment is made at the tie rods

special equipment if you make very careful measurements. The wheels must be straight ahead.

1. Toe can be determined by measuring the distance between the centers of the tire treads, at the front of the tire and at the rear. If the tread pattern makes this impossible, you can measure between the edges of the wheel rims, but make sure to move the car forward and measure in a couple of places to avoid errors caused by bent rims or wheel runout.

2. If the measurement is not within specifications, loosen the nuts at the steering knuckle end of the tie rod, and remove the tie rod boot clamps. Rotate the tie rods to align the toe to specifications. Rotate the tie rods evenly, or the steering wheel will be crooked when you're done.

3. When the adjustment is correct, tighten the nuts to 14 ft. lbs. (20 Nm.). Adjust the boots and tighten the clamps.

WHEEL ALIGNMENT

Year	Model	Caster ① Range (deg.)	Caster ① Preferred Setting (deg.)	Camber Range (deg.)	Camber Preferred Setting (deg.)	Toe-in (in.)
1982	Cavalier	NA	NA	0.10P–1.10P	0.60P	0.125P
	Cimarron	NA	NA	0.10P–1.10P	0.60P	0.125P
	Firenza	NA	NA	0.10P–1.10P	0.60P	0.125P
	Skyhawk	NA	NA	0.10P–1.10P	0.60P	0.125P
	2000	NA	NA	0.10P–1.10P	0.60P	0.125P
1983	Cavalier	NA	NA	0.20P–1.20P	0.70P	0.13N
	Cimarron	NA	NA	0.20P–1.20P	0.70P	0.13N
	Firenza	NA	NA	0.20P–1.20P	0.70P	0.13N
	Skyhawk	NA	NA	0.20P–1.20P	0.70P	0.13N
	2000	NA	NA	0.20P–1.20P	0.70P	0.13N

WHEEL ALIGNMENT

| Year | Model | Caster [1] | | Camber | | Toe-in (in.) |
		Range (deg.)	Preferred Setting (deg.)	Range (deg.)	Preferred Setting (deg.)	
1984	Cavalier	NA	NA	0.20P–1.20P	0.70P	0.13N
	Cimarron	NA	NA	0.20P–1.20P	0.70P	0.13N
	Firenza	NA	NA	0.20P–1.20P	0.70P	0.13N
	Skyhawk	NA	NA	0.20P–1.20P	0.70P	0.13N
	2000 Sunbird	NA	NA	0.20P–1.20P	0.70P	0.13N
1985	Cavalier	0.70P–2.70P	1.70P	0.20P–1.50P	0.80P	0.13N
	Cimarron	0.70P–2.70P	1.70P	0.20P–1.50P	0.80P	0.13N
	Firenza	0.70P–2.70P	1.70P	0.20P–1.50P	0.80P	0.13N
	Skyhawk	0.70P–2.70P	1.70P	0.20P–1.50P	0.80P	0.13N
	Sunbird	0.70P–2.70P	1.70P	0.20P–1.50P	0.80P	0.13N
1986	Cavalier	0.70P–2.70P	1.70P	0.20P–1.50P	0.80P	0.06N
	Cimarron	0.70P–2.70P	1.70P	0.20P–1.50P	0.80P	0.06N
	Firenza	0.70P–2.70P	1.70P	0.20P–1.50P	0.80P	0.06N
	Skyhawk	0.70P–2.70P	1.70P	0.20P–1.50P	0.80P	0.06N
	Sunbird	0.70P–2.70P	1.70P	0.20P–1.50P	0.80P	0
1987	Cavalier	0.70P–2.70P	1.70P	0.20P–1.50P	0.80P	0 [2]
	Cimarron	0.70P–2.70P	1.70P	0.20P–1.50P	0.80P	0
	Firenza	0.70P–2.70P	1.70P	0.20P–1.50P	0.80P	0
	Skyhawk	0.70P–2.70P	1.70P	0.20P–1.50P	0.80P	0
	Sunbird	0.70P–2.70P	1.70P	0.20P–1.50P	0.80P	0
1988	Cavalier	1.70P–4.20P	1.70P	0.20N–1.80P	0.80P [3]	0
	Cimarron	1.70P–4.20P	1.70P	0.20N–1.80P	0.80P	0
	Firenza	1.70P–4.20P	1.70P	0.20N–1.80P	0.80P	0
	Skyhawk	1.70P–4.20P	1.70P	0.20N–1.80P	0.80P	0
	Sunbird	1.70P–4.20P	1.70P	0.20N–1.80P	0.80P	0
1989	Cavalier	0.70P–2.70P	1.70P	0.20N–1.80P	0.80P [3]	0
	Skyhawk	0.70P–2.70P	1.70P	0.20N–1.80P	0.80P	0
	Sunbird	0.70P–2.70P	1.70P	0.20N–1.80P	0.80P	0
1990	Cavalier	0.70P–2.70P	1.70P	0.20N–1.80P	0.80P [3]	0
	Sunbird	0.70P–2.70P	1.70P	0.20N–1.80P	0	0
1991	Cavalier	0.70P–2.70P	1.70P	0.70N–0.70P	0	0
	Sunbird	0.70P–2.70P	1.70P	0.70N–0.70P	0	0
1992	Cavalier	0.70P–2.70P	1.70P	0.70N–0.70P	0	0
	Sunbird	0.70P–2.70P	1.70P	0.70N–0.70P	0	0

[1] Caster is not adjustable on all models
[2] Z-24 with option S6 0.13N degrees
[3] Z-24 0 degrees

REAR SUSPENSION

The J-cars have a semi-independent rear suspension system which consists of an axle with trailing arms and two coil springs and two shock absorbers, two upper spring insulators and two spring compression bumpers. The axle assembly attaches to the body through a rubber bushing located at the front of each control arm. The brackets are integral with the underbody side rails. A stabilizer bar is available as an option.

Two coil springs are used, each being retained between a seat in the underbody and one on the control arm. A rubber cushion is used to isolate the coil spring upper end from the underbody seat, while the lower end sits on a combination bumper and spring insulator.

The double acting shock absorbers are filled with a calibrated amount of fluid and sealed during production. They are non-adjustable, non-refillable and cannot be disassembled.

A single unit hub and bearing assembly is bolted to both ends of the rear axle assembly; it is a sealed unit and must be replaced as one if found to be defective.

Springs

REMOVAL & INSTALLATION

◆ SEE FIGS. 31 and 32

❉❉ CAUTION

The coil springs are under a considerable amount of tension. Be very careful when removing or installing them; they can exert enough force to cause very serious injuries. Make sure vehicle is safely supported on the proper type equipment.

1. Raise and support the car on a hoist. Do not use a twin-post hoist. The swing arc of the axle may cause it to slip from the hoist when the bolts are removed. If a suitable hoist is not available, raise and support the car on jackstands, and use a jack under the axle.

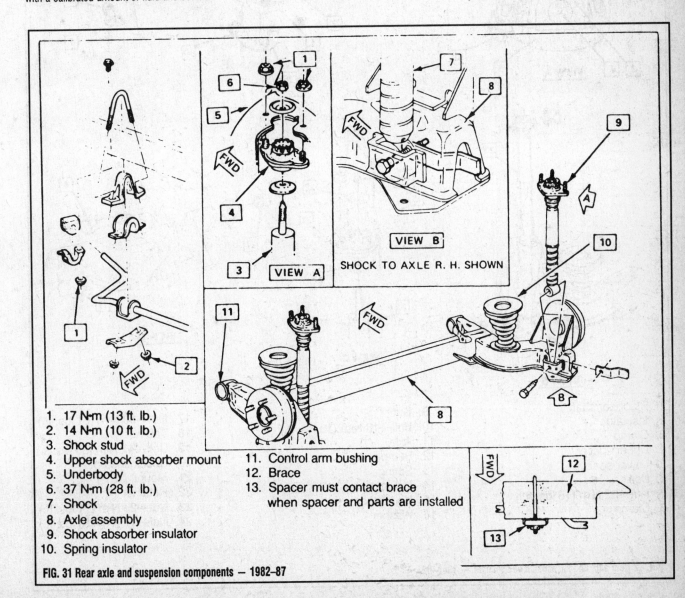

1. 17 N·m (13 ft. lb.)
2. 14 N·m (10 ft. lb.)
3. Shock stud
4. Upper shock absorber mount
5. Underbody
6. 37 N·m (28 ft. lb.)
7. Shock
8. Axle assembly
9. Shock absorber insulator
10. Spring insulator
11. Control arm bushing
12. Brace
13. Spacer must contact brace when spacer and parts are installed

FIG. 31 Rear axle and suspension components — 1982–87

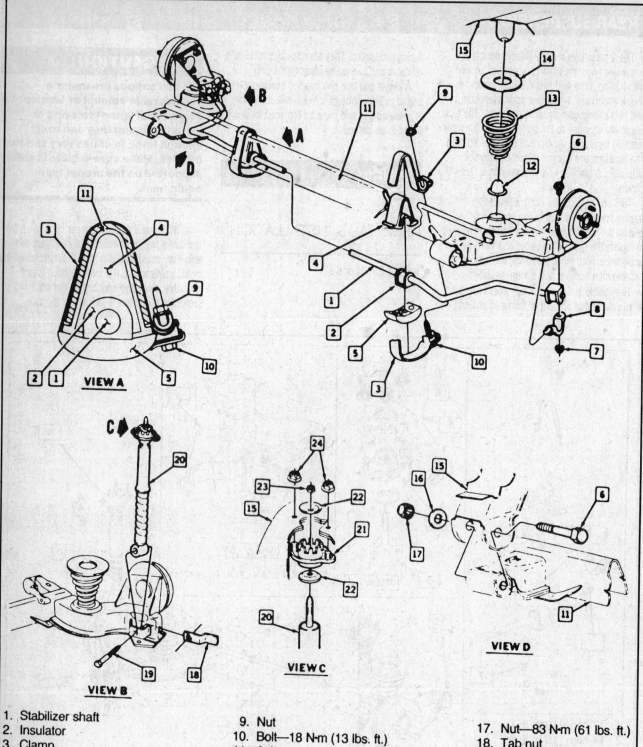

1. Stabilizer shaft
2. Insulator
3. Clamp
4. Upper spacer
5. Lower spacer
6. Bolt
7. Nut—22 N·m (16 lbs. ft.)
8. Clamp

9. Nut
10. Bolt—18 N·m (13 lbs. ft.)
11. Axle
12. Bumper
13. Spring
14. Insulator
15. Underbody
16. Washer

17. Nut—83 N·m (61 lbs. ft.)
18. Tab nut
19. Bolt—47 N·m (35 lbs. ft.)
20. Shock absorber
21. Mount
22. Retainer
23. Nut—29 N·m (21 lbs. ft.)
24. Nut—17 N·m (13 lbs. ft.)

FIG. 32 Rear axle and suspension components — 1988-92

2. Support the axle with a jack that can be raised and lowered.

3. Remove the brake hose attaching brackets (right and left), allowing the hoses to hang freely. Do not disconnect the hoses.

4. Remove both shock absorber lower attaching bolts from the axle.

5. Lower the axle. Remove the coil spring and insulator.

To Install:

6. Position the spring and insulator on the axle. The leg on the upper coil of the spring must be parallel to the axle.

➡ **Prior to installing springs, it may be necessary to install the upper insulators to the body with adhesive to keep them in position while raising the axle assembly. The ends of the upper coil in the spring must be positioned in the spring seat and within 15mm of the spring stop.**

7. Install the shock absorber bolts. Tighten to 41 ft. lbs. (55 Nm.). Install the brake line brackets. Tighten to 8 ft. lbs. (11 Nm.).

Shock Absorbers

TESTING

Visually inspect the shock absorber. If there is evidence of leakage and the shock absorber is covered with oil, the shock is defective and should be replaced.

If there is no sign of excessive leakage (a small amount of weeping is normal) bounce the car at one corner by pressing down on the fender or bumper and releasing. When you have the car bouncing as much as you can, release the fender or bumper. The car should stop bouncing after the first rebound. If the bouncing continues past the center point of the bounce more than once, the shock absorbers are worn and should be replaced.

REMOVAL & INSTALLATION

➡ **Do not remove both shock absorbers at one time as suspending rear axle at full length could result in damage to the brake lines/hoses.**

1. Open the hatch or trunk lid, remove the trim cover if present, and remove the upper shock absorber nut.

2. Raise and support the car at a convenient working height if you desire. It is not necessary to remove the weight of the car from the shock absorbers, however, so you can leave the car on the ground if you prefer.

3. Remove the lower attaching bolt and remove the shock.

To Install:

4. If new shock absorbers are being installed, repeatedly compress them while inverted and extend them in their normal upright position. This will purge them of air.

5. Install the shocks in the reverse order of removal. Tighten the lower mount nut and bolt to 55 ft. lbs. (41 Nm.), the upper to 13 ft. lbs. (17 Nm.).

Rear Axle/Control Arm

The control arms and axle are are one unit. The axle structure itself maintains the gometrical relationship of the wheels relative to the body. The axle assembly attaches to the underbody through a rubber bushing located at the front of each control arm. Each control arm bolts to underbody brackets.

REMOVAL & INSTALLATION

1. Raise the vehicle and support the with jackstands under the control arms.

2. Remove the stabilizer bar from the axle assembly.

3. Remove the wheel and tire assembly and brake drum.

❊❊❊ WARNING

Do not hammer on the brake drum as damage to the bearing could result!

4. Remove the shock absorber lower attaching bolts and paddle nuts at the axle and disconnect the shocks from the control arm.

5. Disconnect the parking brake cable (and rear ABS wiring connector and clip if so equipped) from the axle assembly.

6. Disconnect the brake line at the brackets from the axle assembly.

7. Lower the rear axle and remove the coil springs and insulators.

8. Remove the control arm bolts from the underbody bracket and lower the axle.

9. Remove the hub attaching bolts and remove the hub, bearing and backing plate assembly.

To Install:

10. Install the hub, bearing and backing plate assembly. Hold the nuts and tighten the attaching bolts to 39 ft. lbs.

11. Place the axle assembly on a transmission jack and raise into position. Attach the control arms to the underbody bracket with bolts and nuts. Do not torque the bolts at this time. It will be necessary to torque the bolts of the control arm at standing height.

12. Install the stabilizer bar to the axle assembly.

13. Install the brake line connections to the axle assembly.

14. Attach the brake cable to the rear axle assembly (and rear ABS wiring connector and clip if so equipped).

15. Position the coil springs and insulators in seats and raise the rear axle.

16. The end of the upper coil on the springs must be parallel to the axle assembly and seated in the pocket.

17. Install the shock absorber lower attachment bolts and paddle nuts to the rear axle and torque the bolts to 41 ft. lbs.

18. Install the parking brake cable to the guide hook and adjust as necessary.

19. Install the brake drums and wheel and tire assemblies. Tighten the lug nuts.

20. Bleed the brake system and lower the car.

Stabilizer Bar

REMOVAL & INSTALLATION

1. Raise the vehicle and support the body with jackstands.

2. Remove the nuts and bolts at both the axle and control arm attachments and remove the control arm and remove the bracket, insulator and stabilizer bar.

3. Install the U-bolts, upper clamp, spacer and insulators in the trailing axle. Position the stabilizer bar in the insulators and loosely install the lower clamp and nuts.

4. Attach the end of the stabilizer bar to the control arms and torque all nuts to 13. ft. lbs.

5. Torque the axle attaching nut to 10 ft. lbs.

6. Lower the vehicle.

Rear Hub and Bearing

REMOVAL & INSTALLATION

◆ SEE FIG. 33

1. Loosen the wheel lug nuts. Raise and support the car and remove the wheel.

2. Remove the brake drum. Removal procedures are covered in the next Section, if needed.

✳✳ WARNING

Do not hammer on the brake drum to remove; damage to the bearing will result.

3. Remove the four hub and bearing retaining bolts and remove the assembly from the axle.

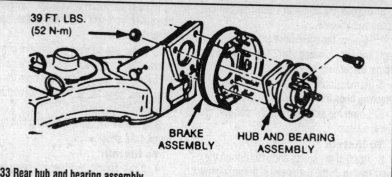

FIG. 33 Rear hub and bearing assembly

The top rear attaching bolt will not clear the brake shoe when removing the hub and bearing assembly. Partially remove the hub and bearing assembly prior to removing this bolt.

4. Disconnect the rear ABS wheel speed sensor wire connector.

5. Installation is the reverse. Hub and bearing bolt torque is 39 ft. lbs. (52 Nm.).

Rear End Alignment

The Rear end alignment is not adjustable. If the Rear wheels appear to be out of alignment, inspect the underbody and rear suspension for damaged and or broken parts.

STEERING

Most J-cars are equipped with, as standard equipment, (except Cimarron), a Saginaw manual rack and pinion steering gear. The pinion is supported by and turns in a sealed ball bearing at the top and a pressed-in roller bearing at the bottom. The rack moves in bushings pressed into each end of the rack housing.

Wear compensation occurs through the action of an adjuster spring which forces the rack against the pinion teeth. This adjuster eliminates the need for periodic pinion preload adjustments. Preload is adjustable only at overhaul.

The inner tie rod assemblies are bolted to the front of the rack. A special bushing is used, allowing both rocking and rotating motion of the tie rods. Any service other than replacement of the outer tie rods or the boots requires removal of the unit from the car.

The power steering gear is an integral unit and shares most features with the manual gear. A rotary control valve directs the hydraulic fluid to either side of the rack piston. The integral rack piston is attached to the rack and converts the hydraulic pressure into left or right lenear motion. A vane-type constant displacement pump with integral reservoir provides hydraulic pressure. No in-car adjustments are necessary or possible on the system, except for periodic belt tension checks and adjustments for the pump. See Section One for belt tension adjustments.

Steering Wheel

REMOVAL & INSTALLATION

◆ SEE FIGS. 34–38

Standard Wheel

1. Disconnect the negative cable at the battery.

2. Pull the pad from the wheel. The horn lead is attached to the pad at one end; the other end of the pad has a wire with a spade connector. The horn lead is disconnected by pushing and turning; the spade connector is simply unplugged.

3. Remove the retainer under the pad (if so equipped).

4. Remove the steering shaft nut.

5. There should be alignment marks already present on the wheel and shaft. If not, matchmark the parts.

6. Remove the wheel with a puller.

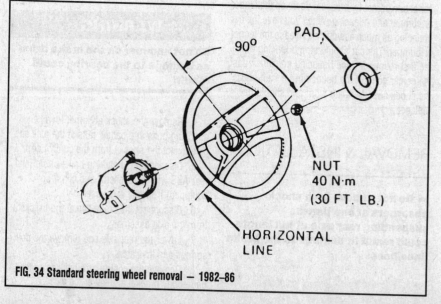

FIG. 34 Standard steering wheel removal — 1982–86

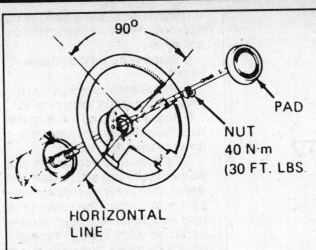

FIG. 35 Sport steering wheel removal — 1982–86

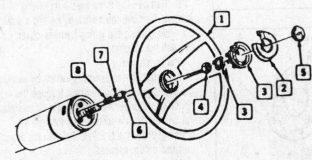

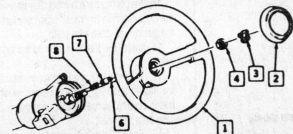

1. Steering wheel
2. Cap
3. Retainer
4. Nut—41 N·m (30 lbs. ft.)
5. Emblem
6. Insulator
7. Eyelet
8. Spring

FIG. 36 Steering wheel removal — 1988–90

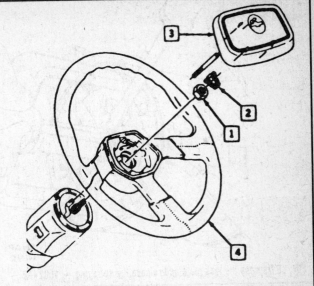

1. Nut 41 N·m (30 lbs. ft.) 3. Steering wheel pad
2. Retainer   4. Steering wheel

FIG. 37 Steering wheel removal — 1991–92

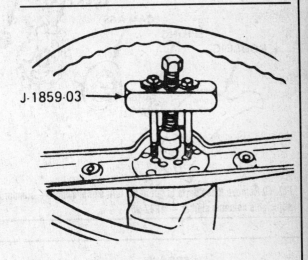

J-1859-03

FIG. 38 Remove the steering wheel with a puller

To Install:

7. Install the wheel on the shaft, aligning the matchmarks. Install the shaft nut and tighten to 30 ft. lbs. (40 Nm.).

8. Install the retainer.

9. Plug in the spade connector, and push and turn the horn lead to connect. Install the pad. Connect the negative battery cable.

Sport Wheel

1. Disconnect the negative cable at the battery.

2. Pry the center cap from the wheel.

3. Remove the retainer (if so equipped).

4. Remove the shaft nut.

5. If the wheel and shaft do not have factory installed alignment marks, matchmark the parts before removal of the wheel.

6. Install a puller and remove the wheel. A horn spring, eyelet and insulator are underneath; don't lose the parts.

To Install:

7. Install the spring, eyelet and insulator into the tower on the column.

8. Align the matchmarks and install the wheel onto the shaft. Install the retaining nut and tighten to 30 ft. lbs. (40 Nm.).

9. Install the retainer. Install the center cap. Connect the negative battery cable.

Turn Signal Switch

REMOVAL & INSTALLATION

♦ SEE FIGS. 39–41

1982–90

1. Remove the steering wheel. Remove the trim cover.

2. Pry the cover from the steering column.

3. Position a U-shaped lockplate compressing tool on the end of the steering shaft

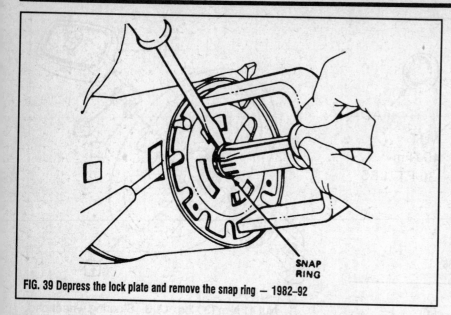

FIG. 39 Depress the lock plate and remove the snap ring — 1982–92

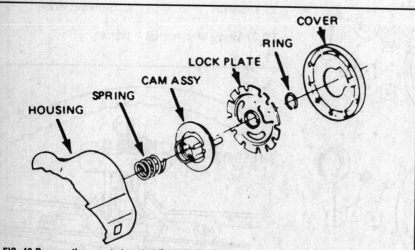

FIG. 40 Remove these parts to get at the turn signal switch — standard column shown, adjustable columns similar — 1982–90

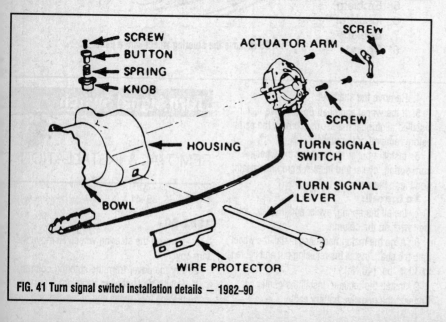

FIG. 41 Turn signal switch installation details — 1982–90

and compress the lock plate by turning the shaft nut clockwise. Pry the wire snapring out of the shaft groove.

4. Remove the tool and lift the lockplate off the shaft.

5. Slip the cancelling cam, upper bearing preload spring, and thrust washer off the shaft.

6. Remove the turn signal lever. Remove the hazard flasher button retaining screw and remove the button, spring and knob.

7. Pull the switch connector out of the mast jacket and tape the upper part to facilitate switch removal. Attach a long piece of wire to the turn signal switch connector. When installing the turn signal switch, feed this wire through the column first, and then use this wire to pull the switch connector into position. On tilt wheels, place the turn signal and shifter housing in low position and remove the harness cover.

8. Remove the three switch mounting screws. Remove the switch by pulling it straight up while guiding the wiring harness cover through the column.

To Install:

9. Install the replacement switch by working the connector and cover down through the housing and under the bracket. On tilt models, the connector is worked down through the housing, under the bracket, and then the cover is installed on the harness.

10. Install the switch mounting screws and the connector on the mast jacket bracket. Install the column-to-dash trim plate.

11. Install the flasher knob and the turn signal lever.

12. With the turn signal lever in neutral and the flasher knob out, slide the thrust washer, upper bearing preload spring, and cancelling cam onto the shaft.

13. Position the lock plate on the shaft and press it down until a new snapring can be inserted in the shaft groove. Always use a new snapring when assembling.

14. Install the cover and the steering wheel.

1991–92

1. Disconnect the negative battery cable.

2. Remove the pad and horn lead, retainer and nut and remove the steering wheel from the column, using a suitable puller.

3. Remove the 2 lower column cover retaining screws.

4. Remove the 3 bottom retaining screws from lower column cover.

5. Separate the rose bud fastener (integral to wire harness) from the jacket assembly.

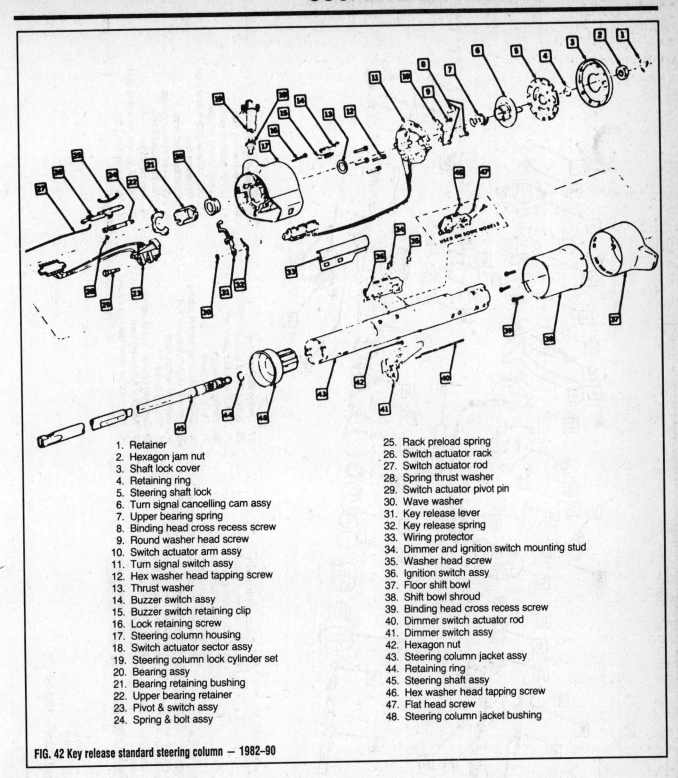

1. Retainer
2. Hexagon jam nut
3. Shaft lock cover
4. Retaining ring
5. Steering shaft lock
6. Turn signal cancelling cam assy
7. Upper bearing spring
8. Binding head cross recess screw
9. Round washer head screw
10. Switch actuator arm assy
11. Turn signal switch assy
12. Hex washer head tapping screw
13. Thrust washer
14. Buzzer switch assy
15. Buzzer switch retaining clip
16. Lock retaining screw
17. Steering column housing
18. Switch actuator sector assy
19. Steering column lock cylinder set
20. Bearing assy
21. Bearing retaining bushing
22. Upper bearing retainer
23. Pivot & switch assy
24. Spring & bolt assy
25. Rack preload spring
26. Switch actuator rack
27. Switch actuator rod
28. Spring thrust washer
29. Switch actuator pivot pin
30. Wave washer
31. Key release lever
32. Key release spring
33. Wiring protector
34. Dimmer and ignition switch mounting stud
35. Washer head screw
36. Ignition switch assy
37. Floor shift bowl
38. Shift bowl shroud
39. Binding head cross recess screw
40. Dimmer switch actuator rod
41. Dimmer switch assy
42. Hexagon nut
43. Steering column jacket assy
44. Retaining ring
45. Steering shaft assy
46. Hex washer head tapping screw
47. Flat head screw
48. Steering column jacket bushing

FIG. 42 Key release standard steering column — 1982–90

6. Remove the turn signal switch retaining screws.

7. Depress the locking tab and remove the 2 wire harness connector from the switch.

8. Depress the locking tab and remove the cruise connector from the wire harness, if so equipped.

9. Installation is the reverse of removal. Torque the cover and switch retaining screws to 49 inch lbs. (5.5 Nm) and the steering wheel retaining nut to 30 ft. lbs. (41 Nm).

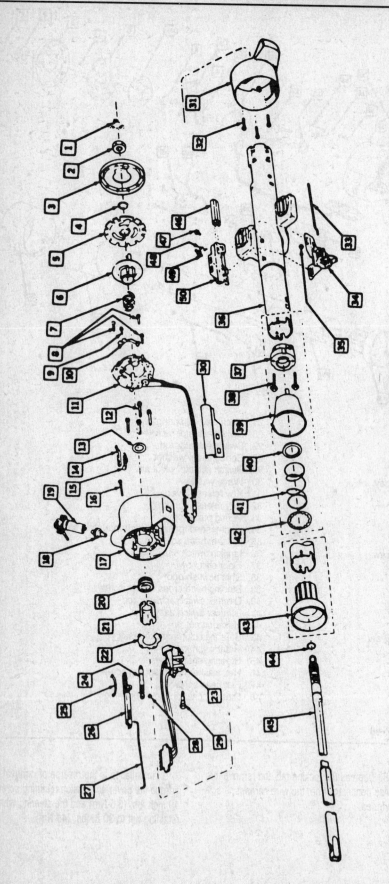

1. Retainer
2. Hexagon jam nut
3. Shaft lock cover
4. Retaining ring
5. Steering shaft lock
6. Turn signal cancelling cam asm
7. Upper bearing spring
8. Binding head cross recess screw
9. Round washer head screw
10. Switch actuator arm asm
11. Turn signal switch asm
12. Hex washer head tapping screw
13. Thrust washer

14. Buzzer switch asm
15. Buzzer switch retaining clip
16. Lock retaining screw
17. Steering column housing
18. Switch actuator sector
19. Steering column lock cylinder set
20. Bearing asm
21. Bearing retaining bushing
22. Upper bearing retainer
23. Pivot & switch asm
24. Lock bolt
25. Rack preload spring
26. Switch actuator rack

27. Switch actuator rod
28. Spring thrust washer
29. Switch actuator pivot pin
30. Wiring protector
31. Floor shift bowl
32. Binding hd cross recess screw
33. Dimmer switch actuator rod
34. Dimmer switch asm
35. Hexagon nut
36. Steering column jacket asm
37. Adapter & bearing asm
38. Hex washer head tapping screw

39. Bearing retainer
40. Lower bearing seat
41. Lower bearing spring
42. Lower spring retainer
43. Strg. column jacket bushing
44. Retaining ring
45. Steering shaft asm
46. Ign. switch housing asm
47. Washer head screw
48. Pan hd screw
49. Dimr & ign sw mounting stud
50. Ignition switch asm

FIG. 43 Park lock standard steering column — 1982–90

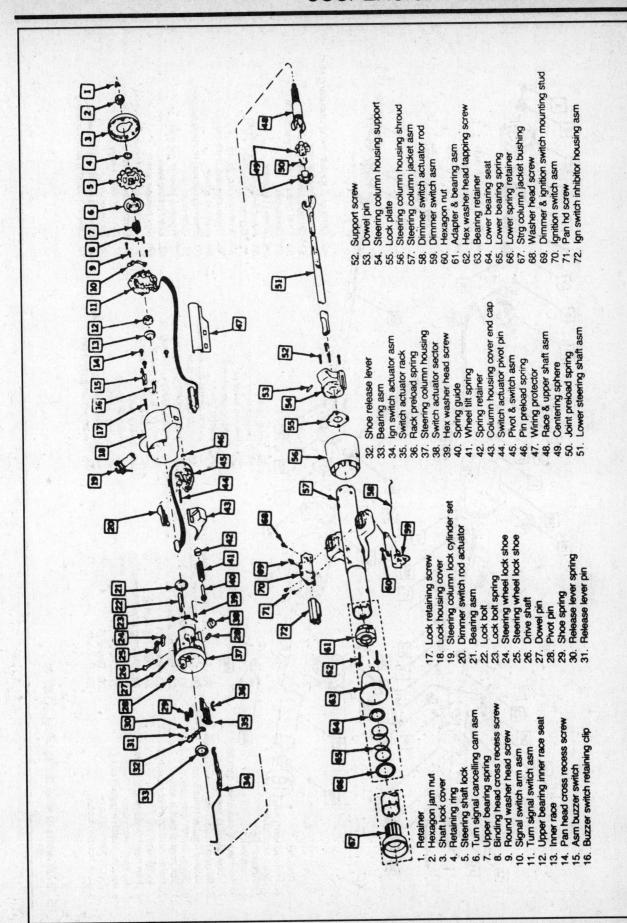

1. Retainer
2. Hexagon jam nut
3. Shaft lock cover
4. Retaining ring
5. Steering shaft lock
6. Turn signal cancelling cam asm
7. Upper bearing spring
8. Binding head cross recess screw
9. Round washer head screw
10. Signal switch arm asm
11. Turn signal switch asm
12. Upper bearing inner race seat
13. Inner race
14. Pan head cross recess screw
15. Asm buzzer switch
16. Buzzer switch retaining clip
17. Lock retaining screw
18. Lock housing cover
19. Steering column lock cylinder set
20. Dimmer switch rod actuator
21. Bearing asm
22. Lock bolt
23. Lock bolt spring
24. Steering wheel lock shoe
25. Steering wheel lock shoe
26. Drive shaft
27. Dowel pin
28. Pivot pin
29. Shoe spring
30. Release lever spring
31. Release lever pin
32. Shoe release lever
33. Bearing asm
34. Ign switch actuator asm
35. Switch actuator rack
36. Rack preload spring
37. Steering column housing
38. Switch actuator sector
39. Hex washer head screw
40. Spring guide
41. Wheel tilt spring
42. Spring retainer
43. Column housing cover end cap
44. Switch actuator pivot pin
45. Pivot & switch asm
46. Pin preload spring
47. Wiring protector
48. Race & upper shaft asm
49. Centering sphere
50. Joint preload spring
51. Lower steering shaft asm
52. Support screw
53. Dowel pin
54. Steering column housing support
55. Lock plate
56. Steering column housing shroud
57. Steering column jacket asm
58. Dimmer switch actuator rod
59. Dimmer switch asm
60. Hexagon nut
61. Adapter & bearing asm
62. Hex washer head tapping screw
63. Bearing retainer
64. Lower bearing seat
65. Lower bearing spring
66. Lower spring retainer
67. Strg column jacket bushing
68. Washer head screw
69. Dimmer & ignition switch mounting stud
70. Ignition switch asm
71. Pan hd screw
72. Ign switch inhibitor housing asm

FIG. 44 Park lock tilt wheel steering column — 1982–90

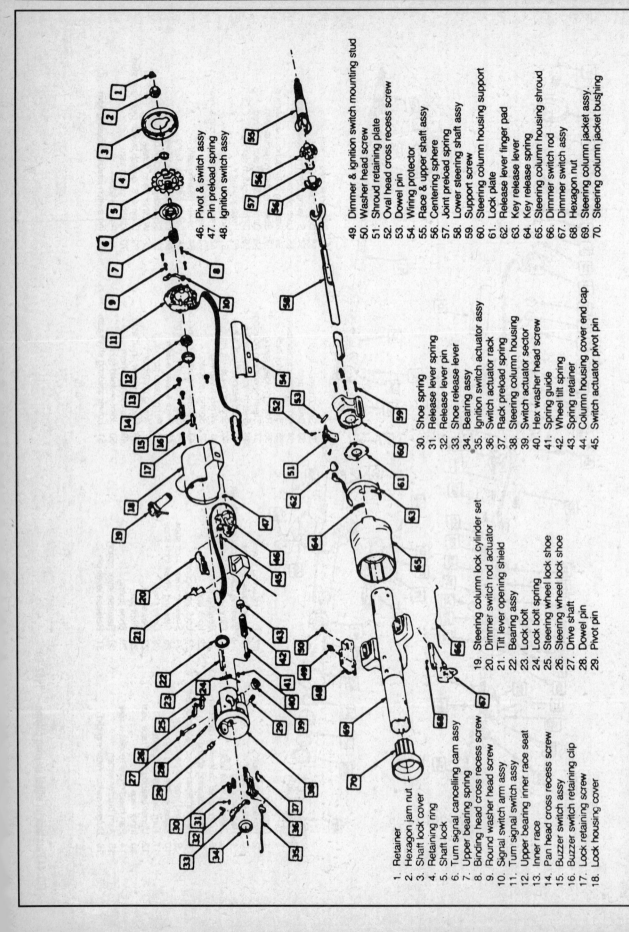

1. Retainer
2. Hexagon jam nut
3. Shaft lock cover
4. Retaining ring
5. Shaft lock
6. Turn signal cancelling cam assy
7. Upper bearing spring
8. Binding head cross recess screw
9. Round washer head washer
10. Signal switch arm assy
11. Turn signal switch assy
12. Upper bearing inner race seat
13. Inner race
14. Pan head cross recess screw
15. Buzzer switch assy
16. Buzzer switch retaining clip
17. Lock retaining screw
18. Lock housing cover

19. Steering column lock cylinder set
20. Dimmer switch rod actuator
21. Tilt lever opening shield
22. Bearing assy
23. Lock bolt
24. Lock bolt spring
25. Steering wheel lock shoe
26. Steering wheel lock shoe
27. Drive shaft
28. Dowel pin
29. Pivot pin

30. Shoe spring
31. Release lever spring
32. Release lever pin
33. Shoe release lever
34. Bearing assy
35. Ignition switch actuator assy
36. Switch actuator rack
37. Rack preload spring
38. Steering column housing
39. Switch actuator sector
40. Hex washer head screw
41. Wheel tilt spring
42. Wheel tilt spring
43. Spring retainer
44. Column housing cover end cap
45. Switch actuator pivot pin

46. Pivot & switch assy
47. Pin preload spring
48. Ignition switch assy

49. Dimmer & ignition switch mounting stud
50. Washer head screw
51. Shroud retaining plate
52. Oval head cross recess screw
53. Dowel pin
54. Wiring protector
55. Race & upper shaft assy
56. Centering sphere
57. Joint preload spring
58. Lower steering shaft assy
59. Support screw
60. Steering column housing support
61. Lock plate
62. Release lever finger pad
63. Key release lever
64. Key release spring
65. Steering column housing shroud
66. Dimmer switch rod
67. Dimmer switch lever
68. Hexagon nut
69. Steering column jacket assy.
70. Steering column jacket bushing

FIG. 45 Key release tilt wheel steering column — 1982-90

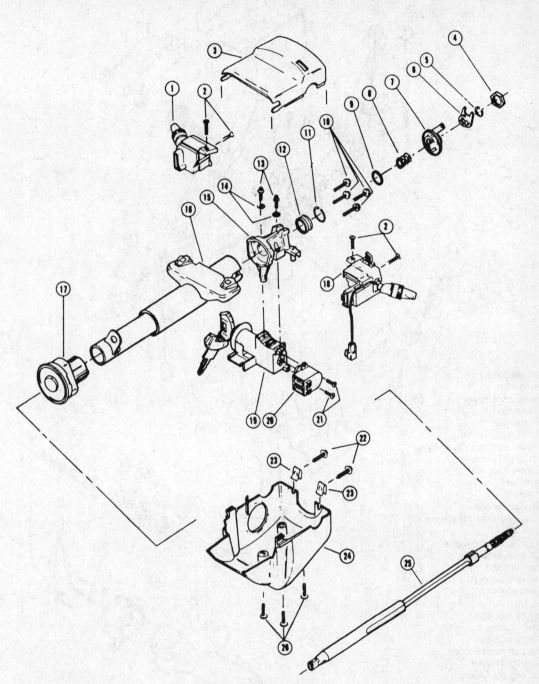

1. Switch, wash/wipe
2. Screw, switch
3. Cover, strg col, upper
4. Nut, hexagon
5. Ring, retaining
6. Cam, orientation plate
7. Cam asm, turn signal cancelling
8. Spring, upper strg shaft
9. Washer, thrust
10. Screw, hex hd tapping
11. Ring, retaining
12. Bearing asm
13. Bolt, shear
14. Washer, shear bolt
15. Housing, steering column
16. Jacket asm, steering column
17. Bushing asm, strg col jacket
18. Switch, turn signal
19. Lock cyl asm, ign switch &
20. Switch asm, ignition
21. Screw, ign switch
22. Screw, pan head 6-lobed
23. Nut, spring (U-type)
24. Cover, strg col, lower
25. Shaft asm, steering column
26. Screw, pan head 6-lobed

FIG. 46 Disassembled view of the standard steering column — 1991–92

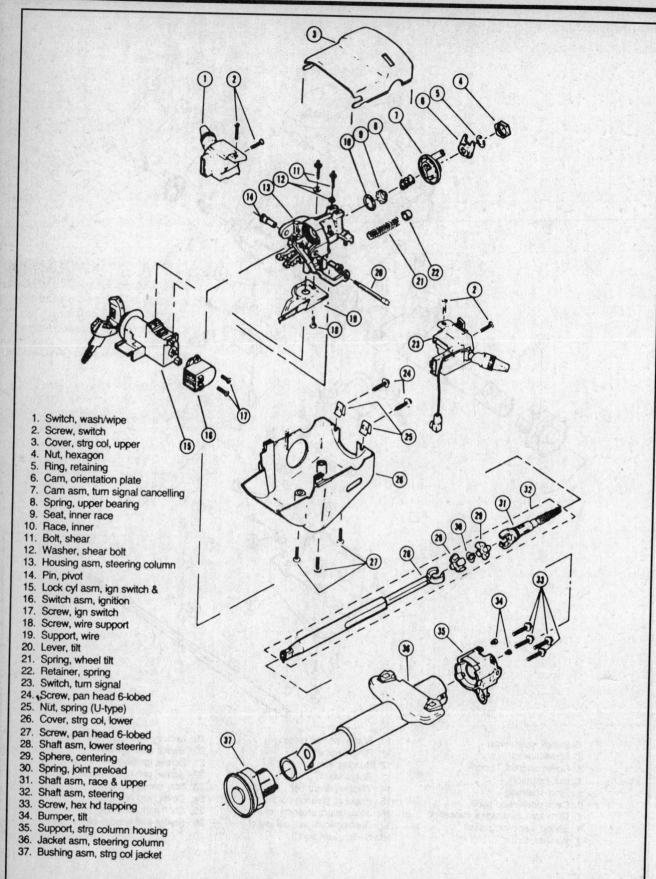

1. Switch, wash/wipe
2. Screw, switch
3. Cover, strg col, upper
4. Nut, hexagon
5. Ring, retaining
6. Cam, orientation plate
7. Cam asm, turn signal cancelling
8. Spring, upper bearing
9. Seat, inner race
10. Race, inner
11. Bolt, shear
12. Washer, shear bolt
13. Housing asm, steering column
14. Pin, pivot
15. Lock cyl asm, ign switch &
16. Switch asm, ignition
17. Screw, ign switch
18. Screw, wire support
19. Support, wire
20. Lever, tilt
21. Spring, wheel tilt
22. Retainer, spring
23. Switch, turn signal
24. Screw, pan head 6-lobed
25. Nut, spring (U-type)
26. Cover, strg col, lower
27. Screw, pan head 6-lobed
28. Shaft asm, lower steering
29. Sphere, centering
30. Spring, joint preload
31. Shaft asm, race & upper
32. Shaft asm, steering
33. Screw, hex hd tapping
34. Bumper, tilt
35. Support, strg column housing
36. Jacket asm, steering column
37. Bushing asm, strg col jacket

FIG. 47 Disassembled view of the tilt steering column – 1991–92

Ignition Switch

REMOVAL & INSTALLATION

♦ SEE FIGS. 42–48

1982–90

The switch is located on the steering column and is completely inaccessible without first lowering the steering column. The switch is actuated by a rod and rack assembly. A gear on the end of the lock cylinder engages the toothed upper end of the rod.

1. Lower the steering column; be sure to properly support it.

2. Put the switch in the **Off-Unlocked** position. With the cylinder removed, the rod is in **Off-Unlocked** position when it is in the next to the uppermost detent.

3. Remove the two switch screws and remove the switch assembly.

4. Before installing, move the new switch slider (standard columns with automatic transmission) to the extreme left position. Move the switch slider (stanadrd columns with manual transmission) to the extreme left position. Move the slider (adjustable columns with automatic transmission) to the extreme right position and then move the slider one detent to the left (off lock). Move the slider (adjustable columns with manual transmission) to the extreme right position.

5. Install the activating rod into the switch and assemble the switch on the column. Tighten the mounting screws. Use only the specified screws, since overlength screws could impair the collapsibility of the column.

6. Reinstall the steering column.

1991–92

1. Disconnect the negative battery cable.

2. Remove the pad and horn lead, retainer and nut and remove the steering wheel from the column, using a suitable puller.

3. Remove the tilt lever, if so equipped.

4. Remove the 2 lower column cover retaining screws.

5. Remove the 3 bottom retaining screws from lower column cover.

6. Depress the locking tabs and remove the 2 wire harness connectors from the ignition switch.

7. Remove the ignition switch screws and remove the ignition switch from the housing.

To install:

8. Connect the ignition switch to the lock cylinder housing. Make sure the tab on the lock cylinder shaft aligns with the slotted opening on the ignition switch. Tighten the ignition switch retaining screws to 21 inch lbs. (2.4 Nm).

9. The remainder of the installation is the reverse of removal. Torque the cover and switch retaining screws to 49 inch lbs. (5.5 Nm) and the steering wheel retaining nut to 30 ft. lbs. (41 Nm).

Ignition Lock Cylinder

REMOVAL & INSTALLATION

♦ SEE FIGS. 49 and 50

1982–90

1. Remove the steering wheel.

2. Turn the lock to the Run position.

3. Remove the lock plate, turn signal switch or combination switch, and the key warning buzzer switch. The warning buzzer switch can be fished out with a bent paper clip.

4. Remove the lock cylinder retaining screw and lock cylinder.

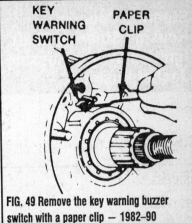

FIG. 49 Remove the key warning buzzer switch with a paper clip — 1982–90

✱✱ WARNING

If the screw is dropped on removal, it could fall into the column, requiring complete disassembly to retrieve the screw.

5. Rotate the cylinder clockwise to align the cylinder key with the keyway in the housing.

6. Push the lock all the way in.

7. Install the screw. Tighten to 15 inch lbs.

8. The rest of installation is the reverse of removal. Turn the lock to Run to install the key warning buzzer switch, which is simply pushed down into place.

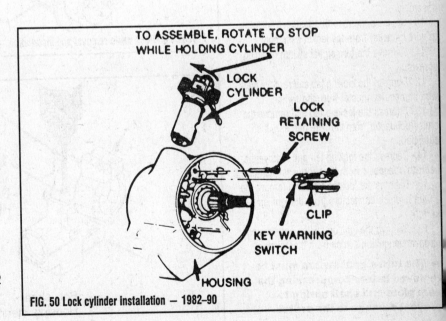

FIG. 50 Lock cylinder installation — 1982–90

Steering Column Housing Steering Shaft Ignition Switch Housing Jacket Bushing

DISASSEMBLY

♦ SEE FIGS. 51–53

1991–92

1. Disconnect the negative battery cable.
2. Remove the pad and horn lead, retainer and nut and remove the steering wheel from the column, using a suitable puller.
3. Remove the tilt lever, if so equipped.
4. Remove the 2 lower column cover retaining screws.
5. Remove the 3 bottom retaining screws from lower column cover.
6. Disconnect the park lock cable from the ignition switch and lock cylinder assembly by depressing the locking tab with a small screwdriver.
7. Disconnect the wire harness at the balkhead.
8. Remove the steering column from the vehicle as outlined in this section.
9. Remove the steering column jacket bushing from from the lower end of the jacket assembly.
10. Separate the rose bud fastener (integral to wire harness) from the jacket assembly.
11. Remove the turn signal switch retaining screws.
12. Depress the locking tab and remove the 2 wire harness connector from the switch.
13. Depress the locking tab and remove the cruise connector from the wire harness, if so equipped.
14. Depress the locking tab and remove the harness connector from the wipe/wash switch.
15. Depress the locking tabs and remove the 2 wire harness connectors from the ignition switch.
16. Remove the ignition switch screws and remove the ignition switch from the housing.

➡ **The turn signal switch must be removed before compressing the cam plate and shaft spring to prevent damage to the switch.**

17. Compress the cam plate and shaft spring with tools J 23653–91 and J 23653–C or equivalent, and remove the retaining ring,

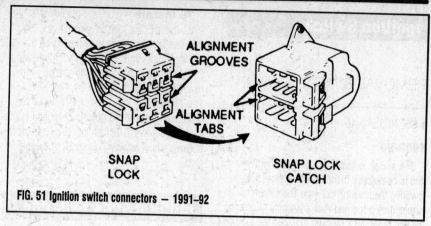
FIG. 51 Ignition switch connectors — 1991–92

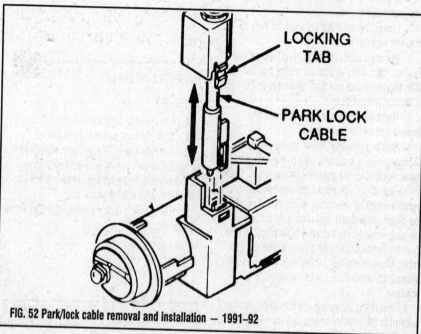
FIG. 52 Park/lock cable removal and installation — 1991–92

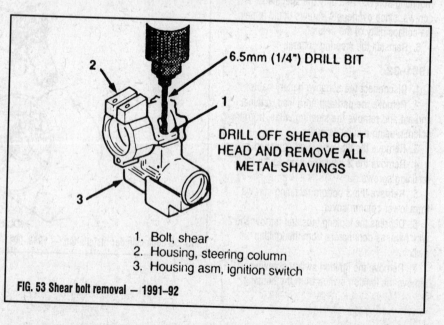

6.5mm (1/4") DRILL BIT

DRILL OFF SHEAR BOLT HEAD AND REMOVE ALL METAL SHAVINGS

1. Bolt, shear
2. Housing, steering column
3. Housing asm, ignition switch

FIG. 53 Shear bolt removal — 1991–92

orientation cam plate, cancelling cam assembly, upper steering shaft spring and thrust washer.

18. Place the lock cylinder in the **RUN** position.

19. Remove the steering shaft assembly from the lower end of the jacket assembly.

20. Remove the shear bolts, shear bolt washers and ignition switch housing as follows:

   a. Drill of the head of the shear bolts with a ¼ in. (6mm) drill bit.

   b. Separate the washers and switch housing from the column housing.

   c. Remove the threaded ends of the shear bolts from the ignition switch housing with pliers.

   d. Clean all metal shavings from the housing.

21. Remove the 4 hex head screws from the housing.

22. Separate the column housing from the jacket assembly.

To Install:

➡ **Firmly seat all the fasteners in the following steps before tightening them to the specified torque.**

23. Install the column housing to the jacket assembly and torque to 47 inch lbs. (5.3 Nm).

24. Install the ignition switch housing to the column housing with shear bolt washers and shear bolts. Torque the shear bolts until the bolt head separates from the body, approximately 11 Nm.

25. Place the lock cylinder in the **RUN** position.

26. Install the steering shaft assembly into the lower end of the jacket assembly until bottomed.

27. Place the lock cylinder in the **OFF** position and remove the key.

28. Rotate the steering shaft until the lock bolt engages and locks the steering shaft into position.

29. Install the thrust washer and upper steering shaft spring on the steering shaft.

30. Install the cancelling cam and orientation cam plate.

31. Install the retaining ring into the groove on the shaft.

32. Install the jacket bushing over the lower end of the steering shaft, into the lower end of the jacket assembly and snap into position.

33. Connect the 2 wire harness connectors to the ignition switch.

34. Install the wipe/wash switch retaining screws and tighten to 49 inch lbs. (5.5 Nm).

35. Install the turn siganl switch retaining screws and tighten to 49 inch lbs. (5.5 Nm).

36. Install the steering column in the vehicle as outlined later in this section.

37. Connect the wire harness at the balkhead.

38. Connect the park lock cable to the ignition switch and lock cylinder assembly.

39. Install the rose bud fastener (integral to wiring harness) to the jacket assembly.

40. Torque the upper and lower cover screws to 49 inch lbs. (5.5 Nm) and the steering wheel retaining nut to 30 ft. lbs. (41 Nm).

Steering Column

REMOVAL & INSTALLATION

♦ SEE FIGS. 54 and 55

✳✳✳ WARNING

Once the steering column is removed from the car, the column is extremely susceptible to damage. Dropping the column assembly on its end could collapse the steering shaft or loosen the plastic injections which maintain column rigidity. Leaning on the column assembly could cause the jacket to bend or deform. Under no conditions should the end of the shaft be hammered upon. Any of the above damage could impair the column's collapsible design.

1. Disconnect the battery ground cable.

2. Remove the left instrument panel sound insulator.

3. Remove the left instrument panel trim pad and steering column trim collar.

4. Remove the horn contact pad, (only if column is to be disassembled).

5. Remove the steering wheel, (only if column is to be disassembled).

6. Disconnect the steering shaft to intermediate shaft connection.

7. Remove the column bracket support bolts and column bracket support nut.

8. Disconnect any electrical connections.

9. Remove the steering column.

10. Insert the steering shaft into the flexible coupling and raise the coupling into position.

11. Loosely install the three steering column attaching bolts.

12. Center the steering shaft within the steering column jacket bushing and tighten the lower attaching bolt. This can be done by moving

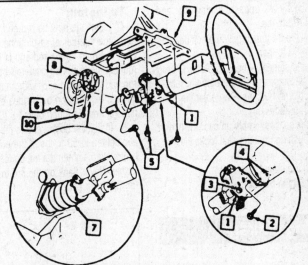

1. Upper support
2. Bolt—install first—27 N·m (20 lbs. ft.)
3. Bolt—install second—27 N·m (20 lbs. ft.)
4. Bolt—install these bolts last—27 N·m (20 lbs. ft.)
5. Bolt—27 N·m (20 lbs. ft.)
6. Upper pinch bolt—46 N·m (34 lbs. ft.)
7. Seal
8. Coupling
9. Instrument panel bracket
10. Lower pinch bolt—40 N·m (29 lbs. ft.)

FIG. 54 Steering column mounting — 1982–90

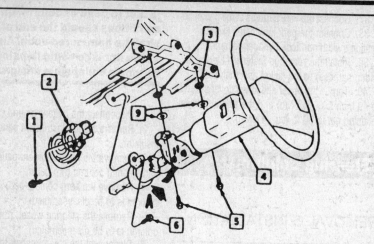

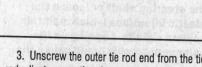

1. Upper pinch bolt—40 N·m (29 lbs. ft.)
2. Flange and steering coupling
3. Retainers
4. Steering column
5. Bolt—26 N·m (20 lbs. ft.)
6. Bolt—26 N·m (20 lbs. ft.)
7. Bolt 30 N·m (22 lbs. ft.)
8. Steering column upper support
9. Shims

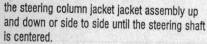

FIG. 55 Steering column mounting — 1991–92

the steering column jacket jacket assembly up and down or side to side until the steering shaft is centered.

13. Tighten the two upper attaching bolts and torque to 20–22 ft. lbs.

14. Install the flexible coupling pinch bolt and torque to 30–34 ft. lbs.

15. Turn the steering wheel from stop to stop and observe if the steering shaft binds or rubs against the column bushing. Re-center the steering shaft if necessary.

16. Pull the seal assembly up over the end of the column bushing until the seal locks into place.

17. Install the sound insulator.
18. Connect the battery cable.

Steering Linkage

REMOVAL & INSTALLATION

Tie Rod Ends

♦ SEE FIG. 56

1. Loosen both pinch bolts at the outer tie rod.

2. Remove the tie rod end from the strut assembly using a suitable removal tool.

3. Unscrew the outer tie rod end from the tie rod adjuster, counting the number of revolutions required before they are disconnected.

To Install:

4. Install the new tie rod end, screwing it on the same number of revolutions as counted in Step 3. When the tie rod end is installed, the tie rod adjuster must be centered between the tie rod and the tie rod end, with an equal number of threads exposed on both sides of the adjuster nut. Tighten the pinch bolts to 20 ft. lbs.

5. Install the tie rod end to the strut assembly and tighten to 50 ft. lbs. If the cotter pin cannot be installed, tighten the nut up to $\frac{1}{16}$ in. (1.6mm) further. Never back off the nut to align the holes for the cotter pin.

6. Have the front end alignment checked or adjusted.

Rack and Pinion Unit

REMOVAL & INSTALLATION

♦ SEE FIGS. 57 and 58

1. From the driver's side, remove the sound insulator.

2. From under the instrument panel, pull the seal assembly down from the steering column and remove the upper pinch bolt from the flexible coupling.

3. Remove the air cleaner and the windshield washer jar, if necessary for easier access.

4. On power steering models: disconnect the pressure line from the steering gear and remove the screw securing the pressure line bracket to the cowl. Move the pressure line aside.

5. Raise and support the car on jackstands.
6. Remove both front wheels.
7. Disconnect both tie rods from the struts.
8. Lower the car.
9. Remove the right side rack mounting clamp.

10. Remove the left side rack mounting clamp.

11. Move the gear forward slightly. On power steering models, disconnect the fluid return pipe from the gear.

12. Remove the lower pinch bolt from the flexible coupling and separate the rack from the coupling.

13. Remove the dash seal from the rack assembly.

14. Raise and support the car on jackstands.

15. On some models it may be necessary to remove the splash shield from the inner, left fender.

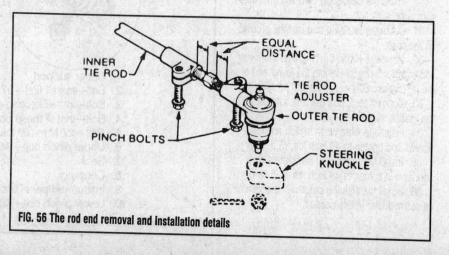

FIG. 56 The rod end removal and installation details

16. Turn the left knuckle and hub assembly to the full left turn position and remove the rack and pinion assembly through the access hole on the left fender.

17. Installation is the reverse of removal while noting the following points:

a. If the mounting studs backed out during removal, it will be necessary to re-position them prior to rack installation. Double-nut the stud so that it can be torqued to 15 ft. lbs.

b. It will be good to have a helper inside the car to guide the flexible coupling onto the stub shaft and onto the steering column.

c. Observe the following torques:
- Coupling-to-stub shaft:
  - 37 ft. lbs. (1982–86)
  - 29–30 ft. lbs. (1987–92)
- Coupling-to-column: 30 ft. lbs.
- Mounting clamps:
  - 28 ft. lb. (1982–86)
  - 22 ft. lbs. (1987–92)
- Tie rod nuts: 35–37 ft. lbs.

Power Steering Pump

REMOVAL & INSTALLATION

♦ SEE FIGS. 59–61

1. Disconnect the negative battery cable.

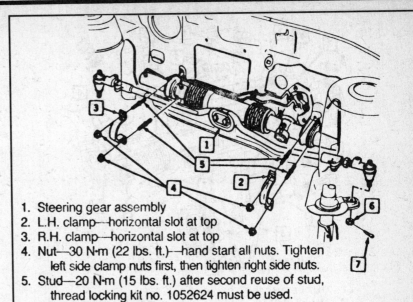

1. Steering gear assembly
2. L.H. clamp—horizontal slot at top
3. R.H. clamp—horizontal slot at top
4. Nut—30 N•m (22 lbs. ft.)—hand start all nuts. Tighten left side clamp nuts first, then tighten right side nuts.
5. Stud—20 N•m (15 lbs. ft.) after second reuse of stud, thread locking kit no. 1052624 must be used.
6. Nut—50 N•m (35 lbs. ft.)
   75 N•m (50 lbs. ft.) maximum to install cotter pin
7. Cotter pin

FIG. 57 Power rack and pinion mounting — 1988–92

2. Disconnect the vent hole at the carburetor if so equipped.

3. Loosen the adjusting bolt and pivot bolt on the pump or release tension on drive belt tensioner assembly; remove the pump's drive belt.

4. Remove the three pump-to-bracket or mounting bolts (through the access hole in the pulley as necessary) and remove the adjusting bolt if so equipped.

5. Remove the high pressure fitting from the pump.

6. Disconnect the reservoir-to-pump hose from the pump.

7. Remove the pump.

8. Installation is in the reverse order of removal. Adjust the belt tension and bleed the system.

STANDARD DRIVE BELT ADJUSTMENT

The belt tension on most components is adjusted by moving the component (power steering pump) within the range of the slotted bracket. Check the belt tension every 12 months or 10,000 miles. Push in on the drive belt about midway between the crankshaft pulley and the driven component. If the belt deflects more than $9/16$ in. (14mm) or less than $3/8$ in. (9.5mm), adjustment is required.

1. Loosen the adjustment nut and bolt in the slotted bracket. Slightly loosen the pivot bolt.

2. Pull (don't pry) the component outward to increase tension. Push inward to reduce tension. Tighten the adjusting nut and bolt and the pivot bolt.

3. Recheck the drive belt tension and readjust if necessary.

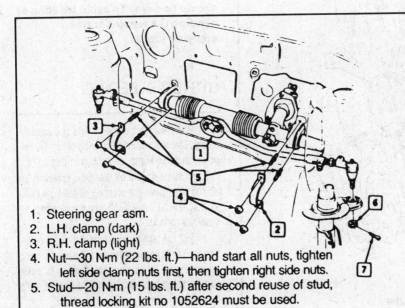

1. Steering gear asm.
2. L.H. clamp (dark)
3. R.H. clamp (light)
4. Nut—30 N•m (22 lbs. ft.)—hand start all nuts, tighten left side clamp nuts first, then tighten right side nuts.
5. Stud—20 N•m (15 lbs. ft.) after second reuse of stud, thread locking kit no 1052624 must be used.
6. Nut 50 N•m (35 lbs. ft.)
   75 N•m (50 lbs. ft.) maximum to install cotter pin
7. Cotter pin

FIG. 58 Manual rack and pinion mounting — 1988–92

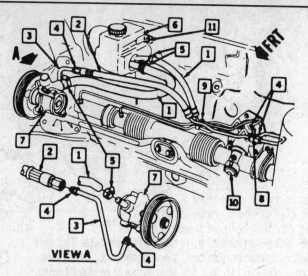

VIEW A

1. OUTLET HOSE
2. INLET HOSE
3. INLET PIPE
4. 27 N•m (20 LBS. FT.)
5. CLAMP 1.7 N•m (15 LBS. IN.)
6. RESERVOIR
7. POWER STEERING PUMP
8. IDLE SPEED POWER STEERING PRESSURE SWITCH
9. RETAINER
10. STEERING GEAR
11. SCREW — 8 N•m (71 LBS. IN.)

FIG. 59 Power steering line routing 1.8L and 2.0L L4 engines

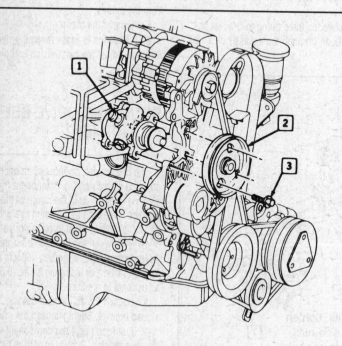

1. POWER STEERING PUMP
2. PULLEY
3. BOLT — 27 N•m (20 LBS. FT.)

FIG. 60 Power steering pump mounting 1.8L and 2.0L L4 engines

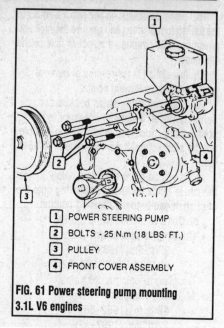

1. POWER STEERING PUMP
2. BOLTS - 25 N.m (18 LBS. FT.)
3. PULLEY
4. FRONT COVER ASSEMBLY

FIG. 61 Power steering pump mounting 3.1L V6 engines

SERPENTINE BELT BELT ADJUSTMENT

Serpentine belt is tensioned by loosening a bolt and rotating the belt tensioner. The correct belt tension is indicated on the indicator mark of the belt tensioner. If the indicator mark is not within specification, replace the belt or the tensioner.

➡ **To remove or install the belt, push and rotate the tensioner. Care should be taken to avoid twisting or bending the tensioner when applying torque.**

SYSTEM BLEEDING

1. Raise the front of the vehicle and support safely. This will minimize steering effort. Fill the power steering pump reservoir with Dexron®II.

2. With the engine off, keep the reservoir full as someone turns the steering wheel from lock to lock several times. Stop with the steering system at one lock.

3. Pull the high tension lead out of the coil. Continue to keep the reservoir full while cranking the engine for 30 seconds at a time (with a one minute rest in between), until fluid level remains constant.

4. Turn the steering wheel to the opposite lock and repeat Step 3.

5. Reconnect the high tension lead, start the engine and allow it to idle. Turn the wheel from lock to lock several times. Note the level of the fluid.

6. Lower the vehicle to the ground. Note the fluid level. Repeat Step 5, stopping with the wheel at the centered position.

7. The fluid level should not have risen more than 0.2 in. (5mm). If it has, repeat Step 6 until the level does not rise appreciably.

TORQUE SPECIFICATIONS

Component	English	Metric
All wheels	100 lbs. ft.	140 Nm
Suspension support center bolts	66 lbs. ft.	90 Nm
Suspension support front bolts	65 ft. lbs.	88 Nm
Suspension support rear bolts	65 ft. lbs.	88 Nm
Stabilizer shaft to suspension support nuts	16 ft. lbs.	22 Nm
Stabilizer shaft to control arm nuts	13 lbs. ft.	17 Nm
Strut assembly to body nuts	18 lbs. ft.	24 Nm
Steering knuckle to strut assembly nuts	133 lbs. ft.	180 Nm
Ball joint stud nut	41–50 lbs. ft.	55–65 Nm
Control arm to suspension support bolts	61 lbs. ft.	83 Nm
Drive shaft nut	185 lbs. ft.	260 Nm
Hub and bearing assembly to steering knuckle bolts	70 lbs. ft.	95 Nm
Caliper to knuckle bolts	38 lbs. ft.	51 Nm
Tie rod end to strut nut	37 lbs. ft.	50 Nm
Strut dampener shaft nut	65 lbs. ft.	85 Nm
Upper shock absorber mounting bolt to body	13 lbs. ft.	17 Nm
Upper shock absorber mounting nut	21 lbs. ft.	29 Nm
Lower shock absorber mounting bolt	35 lbs. ft.	47 Nm
Stabilizer shaft insulator to axle clamp nuts	13 lbs. ft.	18 Nm
Stabilizer shaft insulator to control arm clamp nuts	16 lbs. ft.	22 Nm
Axle to body bracket nut	68 lbs. ft.	93 Nm
Brake line bracket to body screw	8 lbs. ft.	11 Nm
Brake line bracket to axle screw	11 lbs. ft.	15 Nm
Hub and bearing to axle bolts	37 lbs. ft.	50 Nm
Dimmer and ignition switch mounting stud	35 in. ft.	4 Nm
Washer head screw	35 in. ft.	4 Nm
Dimmer switch screw	35 in. ft.	4 Nm
Adjuster plug locknut	50 lbs. ft.	70 Nm
Steering column lower pinch bolt	30 lbs. ft.	41 Nm
Steering column upper pinch bolt	30 lbs. ft.	41 Nm
Inner tie rod bolts	65 lbs. ft.	90 Nm
Pinion lockout	26 lbs. ft.	35 Nm
Pinion preload	16 lbs. in.	1.8 Nm
Power steering inlet line fittings	19 lbs. ft.	26 Nm
Rack & pinion mounting clamp nuts	22 lbs. ft.	30 Nm
Tie rod end to steering knuckle nut	37 lbs. ft.	50 Nm
Tie rod pinch bolts	41 lbs. ft.	55 Nm
Steering hose end clamps	15 lbs. in.	1.7 Nm
Rack and pinion cylinder line fittings at valve end	14 lbs. ft.	18 Nm
Rack and pinion cylinder line fittings at cylinder end	20 lbs. ft.	28 Nm
Idle speed pressure switch	116 in. ft.	13 Nm

Troubleshooting the Turn Signal Switch

Problem	Cause	Solution
Instrument panel turn indicator lights on but not flashing	• Burned out or damaged front or rear turn signal bulb	• Replace bulb
	• If vehicle lights do not operate, check light sockets for high resistance connections, the chassis wiring for opens, grounds, etc.	• Repair chassis wiring as required
	• Inoperative flasher	• Replace flasher
	• Loose chassis to column harness connection	• Connect securely
	• Inoperative turn signal switch	• Replace turn signal switch
	• To determine if turn signal switch is defective, substitute new switch into circuit and operate switch by hand. If the vehicle's lights operate normally, signal switch is inoperative.	• Replace turn signal switch
Stop light not on when turn indicated	• Loose column to chassis connection	• Connect securely
	• Disconnect column to chassis connector. Connect new switch into system without removing old.	• Replace signal switch
Stop light not on when turn indicated (cont.)	Operate switch by hand. If brake lights work with switch in the turn position, signal switch is defective.	
	• If brake lights do not work, check connector to stop light sockets for grounds, opens, etc.	• Repair connector to stop light circuits using service manual as guide
Turn indicator panel lights not flashing	• Burned out bulbs	• Replace bulbs
	• High resistance to ground at bulb socket	• Replace socket
	• Opens, ground in wiring harness from front turn signal bulb socket to indicator lights	• Locate and repair as required
Turn signal lights flash very slowly	• High resistance ground at light sockets	• Repair high resistance grounds at light sockets
	• Incorrect capacity turn signal flasher or bulb	• Replace turn signal flasher or bulb
	• If flashing rate is still extremely slow, check chassis wiring harness from the connector to light sockets for high resistance	• Locate and repair as required
	• Loose chassis to column harness connection	• Connect securely
	• Disconnect column to chassis connector. Connect new switch into system without removing old. Operate switch by hand. If flashing occurs at normal rate, the signal switch is defective.	• Replace turn signal switch

Troubleshooting the Turn Signal Switch (cont.)

Problem	Cause	Solution
Hazard signal lights will not flash—turn signal functions normally	• Blow fuse • Inoperative hazard warning flasher • Loose chassis-to-column harness connection • Disconnect column to chassis connector. Connect new switch into system without removing old. Depress the hazard warning lights. If they now work normally, turn signal switch is defective. • If lights do not flash, check wiring harness "K" lead for open between hazard flasher and connector. If open, fuse block is defective	• Replace fuse • Replace hazard warning flasher in fuse panel • Conect securely • Replace turn signal switch • Repair or replace brown wire or connector as required

Troubleshooting the Power Steering Pump

Problem	Cause	Solution
Chirp noise in steering pump	• Loose belt	• Adjust belt tension to specification
Belt squeal (particularly noticeable at full wheel travel and stand still parking)	• Loose belt	• Adjust belt tension to specification
Growl noise in steering pump	• Excessive back pressure in hoses or steering gear caused by restriction	• Locate restriction and correct. Replace part if necessary.
Growl noise in steering pump (particularly noticeable at stand still parking)	• Scored pressure plates, thrust plate or rotor • Extreme wear of cam ring	• Replace parts and flush system • Replace parts
Groan noise in steering pump	• Low oil level • Air in the oil. Poor pressure hose connection.	• Fill reservoir to proper level • Tighten connector to specified torque. Bleed system by operating steering from right to left—full turn.
Rattle noise in steering pump	• Vanes not installed properly • Vanes sticking in rotor slots	• Install properly • Free up by removing burrs, varnish, or dirt
Swish noise in steering pump	• Defective flow control valve	• Replace part
Whine noise in steering pump	• Pump shaft bearing scored	• Replace housing and shaft. Flush system.

Troubleshooting the Power Steering Pump (cont.)

Problem	Cause	Solution
Hard steering or lack of assist	· Loose pump belt · Low oil level in reservoir **NOTE:** Low oil level will also result in excessive pump noise · Steering gear to column misalignment · Lower coupling flange rubbing against steering gear adjuster plug · Tires not properly inflated	· Adjust belt tension to specification · Fill to proper level. If excessively low, check all lines and joints for evidence of external leakage. Tighten loose connectors. · Align steering column · Loosen pinch bolt and assemble properly · Inflate to recommended pressure
Foaming milky power steering fluid, low fluid level and possible low pressure	· Air in the fluid, and loss of fluid due to internal pump leakage causing overflow	· Check for leaks and correct. Bleed system. Extremely cold temperatures will cause system aeration should the oil level be low. If oil level is correct and pump still foams, remove pump from vehicle and separate reservoir from body. Check welsh plug and body for cracks. If plug is loose or body is cracked, replace body.
Low pump pressure	· Flow control valve stuck or inoperative · Pressure plate not flat against cam ring	· Remove burrs or dirt or replace. Flush system. · Correct
Momentary increase in effort when turning wheel fast to right or left	· Low oil level in pump · Pump belt slipping · High internal leakage	· Add power steering fluid as required · Tighten or replace belt · Check pump pressure. (See pressure test)
Steering wheel surges or jerks when turning with engine running especially during parking	· Low oil level · Loose pump belt · Steering linkage hitting engine oil pan at full turn · Insufficient pump pressure	· Fill as required · Adjust tension to specification · Correct clearance · Check pump pressure. (See pressure test). Replace flow control valve if defective.
Steering wheel surges or jerks when turning with engine running especially during parking (cont.)	· Sticking flow control valve	· Inspect for varnish or damage, replace if necessary
Excessive wheel kickback or loose steering	· Air in system	· Add oil to pump reservoir and bleed by operating steering. Check hose connectors for proper torque and adjust as required.
Low pump pressure	· Extreme wear of cam ring · Scored pressure plate, thrust plate, or rotor · Vanes not installed properly · Vanes sticking in rotor slots · Cracked or broken thrust or pressure plate	· Replace parts. Flush system. · Replace parts. Flush system. · Install properly · Freeup by removing burrs, varnish, or dirt · Replace part

9

BRAKES

BRAKE SYSTEM

♦ SEE FIGS. 1 and 2

These cars have a diagonally split hydraulic system. This differs from conventional practice in that the left front and right rear brakes are on one hydraulic circuit, and the right front and left rear are on the other.

A diagonally split system necessitates the use of a special master cylinder design. The master cylinder incorporates the functions of a standard tandem master cylinder, plus a warning light switch and proportioning valves. On 1985–86 V6 models the proportioning valve is located on the framne rail. Additionally, the master cylinder is designed with a quick take-up feature which provides a large volume of fluid to the brakes at low pressure when the brakes are initially applied. The low pressure fluid acts to quickly fill the large displacement requirements of the system.

The front disc brakes are single piston sliding caliper units. Fluid pressure acts equally against the piston and the bottom of the piston bore in the caliper. This forces the piston outward until the pad contacts the rotor. The force on the caliper bore forces the caliper to slide over, carrying the other pad into contact with the other side of the rotor. The disc brakes are self-adjusting.

Rear drum brakes are conventional duo-servo units. A dual piston wheel cylinder, mounted to the top of the backing plate, actuates both brake shoes. Wheel cylinder force to the shoes is supplemented by the tendency of the shoes to wrap into the drum (servo action). An actuating link, pivot and lever serve to automatically engage the adjuster as the brakes are applied when the car is moving in reverse. Provisions for manual adjustment are also provided. The rear brakes also serve as the parking brakes; linkage is mechanical.

Vacuum boost is a standard unit. The booster is a conventional tandem vacuum unit.

EXTERNAL CONDITIONS THAT AFFECT BRAKE PERFORMANCE

Tires

Tires having unequal contact and grip on road will cause unequal braking. Tires must be equally inflated, identical in size and the tread pattern of the right and left tires must be approximately equal.

FIG. 1 Front Disc brake assembly

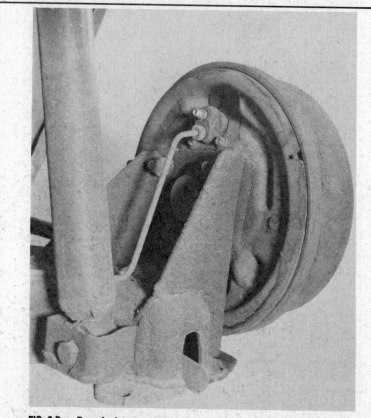

FIG. 2 Rear Drum brake assembly

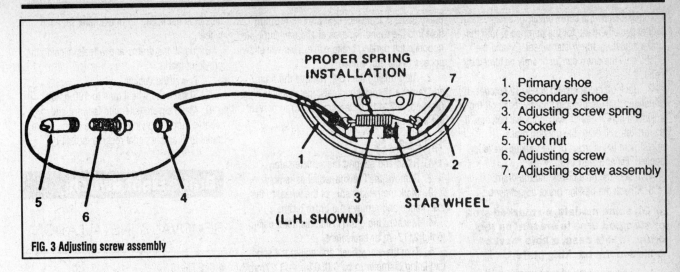

PROPER SPRING
INSTALLATION

(L.H. SHOWN)

STAR WHEEL

1. Primary shoe
2. Secondary shoe
3. Adjusting screw spring
4. Socket
5. Pivot nut
6. Adjusting screw
7. Adjusting screw assembly

FIG. 3 Adjusting screw assembly

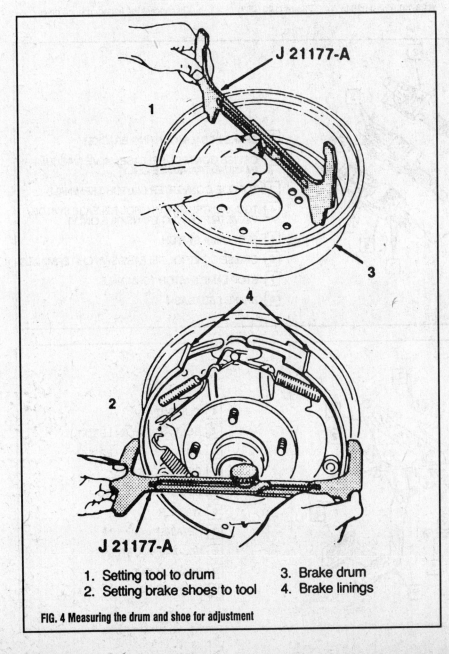

J 21177-A

J 21177-A

1. Setting tool to drum
2. Setting brake shoes to tool
3. Brake drum
4. Brake linings

FIG. 4 Measuring the drum and shoe for adjustment

Vehicle Loading

A heavily loaded vehicle requires more braking effort. When a vehicle has unequal loading, the most heavily loaded wheels require more braking power than others.

Wheel Alignment

Misalignment of the wheels, particularly in regard to excessive camber and caster, will cause the brakes to pull to one side.

Trailer Towing

Towing a trailer requires longer braking distances and tends to overheat the brakes sooner.

ADJUSTMENT

Disc Brakes

The front disc brakes are inherently self-adjusting. No adjustments are either necessary or possible.

Drum Brakes

▶ SEE FIGS. 3 and 4

The drum brakes are designed to self-adjust when applied with the car moving in reverse. However, they can also be adjusted manually. This manual adjustment should also be performed whenever the linings are replaced.

1982–86

1. Use a punch to knock out the stamped area on the brake drum. If this is done with the drum installed on the car, the drum must then be removed to clean out all metal pieces. After adjustments are complete, obtain a hole cover from your dealer (Part no. 4874119 or the equivalent) to prevent entry of dirt and water into the brakes.

2. Use an awl, a screwdriver, or an adjusting tool especially made for the purpose to turn the brake adjusting screw star wheel. Expand the shoes until the drum can just barely be turned by hand.

3. Back off the adjusting screw 12 notches. If the shoes still are dragging lightly, back off the adjusting screw one or two additional notches. If the brakes still drag, the parking brake adjustment is incorrect or the parking brake is applied. Fix and start over.

4. Install the hole cover into the drum.

5. Check the parking brake adjustment.

➡ **On some models, no marked area or stamped area is present on the drum. In this case, a hole must be drilled in the backing plate:**

1. All backing plates have two round flat areas in the lower half through which the parking brake cable is installed. Drill a ½ in. (13mm) hole into the round flat area on the backing plate opposite the parking brake cable. This will allow access to the star wheel.

2. After drilling the hole, remove the drum and remove all metal particles. Install a hole plug (Part no. 4874119 or the equivalent) to prevent the entry of water or dirt.

1987–92

1. Raise and support the vehicle safely.

2. Remove the tire and wheel assembly.

3. Mark the relationship of the wheel to the axle flange and remove the brake drum.

4. Measure the drum inside diameter using tool J 2177-A, or equivalent.

5. Turn the star wheel, and adjust the shoe and lining diameter to be 0.050 in. — 1.27mm (1987–90) or 0.030 in. — 0.76mm (1991–92)

less than the inside drum diameter for each wheel.

6. Install the drums and wheels aligning the previous marks.

7. Lower the vehicle.

8. Tighten the wheel nuts to 100 ft. lbs.

9. Make several alternate forward and reserve stops applying firm force to the brake pedal until ample pedal reserve is built up.

Brake Light Switch

REMOVAL & INSTALLATION

♦ SEE FIG. 5

1. Disconnect the battery ground cable.

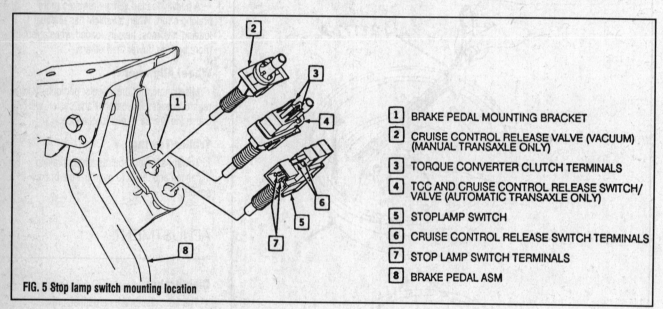

1	BRAKE PEDAL MOUNTING BRACKET
2	CRUISE CONTROL RELEASE VALVE (VACUUM) (MANUAL TRANSAXLE ONLY)
3	TORQUE CONVERTER CLUTCH TERMINALS
4	TCC AND CRUISE CONTROL RELEASE SWITCH/VALVE (AUTOMATIC TRANSAXLE ONLY)
5	STOPLAMP SWITCH
6	CRUISE CONTROL RELEASE SWITCH TERMINALS
7	STOP LAMP SWITCH TERMINALS
8	BRAKE PEDAL ASM

FIG. 5 Stop lamp switch mounting location

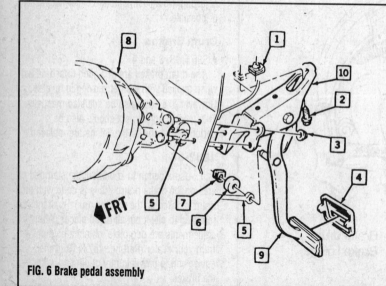

1	CLIP NUT
2	BOLT - 32 N.m (24 LBS. FT.)
3	NUT - 21 N.m (15 LBS. FT.)
4	PEDAL COVER
5	BOOSTER PUSH ROD
6	WASHER
7	RETAINER
8	VACUUM BOOSTER
9	BRAKE PEDAL
10	BRACKET

FIG. 6 Brake pedal assembly

2. Remove the drivers side hush panel.

3. Remove the retaining nut from switch.

4. Disconnect the electrical connector, and remove the switch.

5. Installation is the reverse of the removal procedure.

Brake Pedal

REMOVAL & INSTALLATION

♦ SEE FIG. 6

1. Disconnect the battery ground cable.

2. Remove the lower steering column panel.

3. Remove the brake pedal bracket.

4. Disconnect the pushrod from the brake pedal.

5. Remove the pivot bolt and bushing.

6. Remove the brake pedal.

To Install:

7. Positon the brake pedal.

8. Install the bushing and pivot bolt, tighten to 25 ft.lbs.

9. Connect the pushrod to the brake pedal.

10. Install the brake pedal bracket.

11. Install the lower steering column panel.

12. Connect the battery ground cable.

Master Cylinder

REMOVAL & INSTALLATION

♦ SEE FIGS. 7-9

1. Unplug the electrical connector from the master cylinder.

2. Place a number of cloths or a container under the master cylinder to catch the brake fluid. Disconnect the brake tubes from the master cylinder; use a flare nut wrench if one is available. Tape over open ends of the tubes.

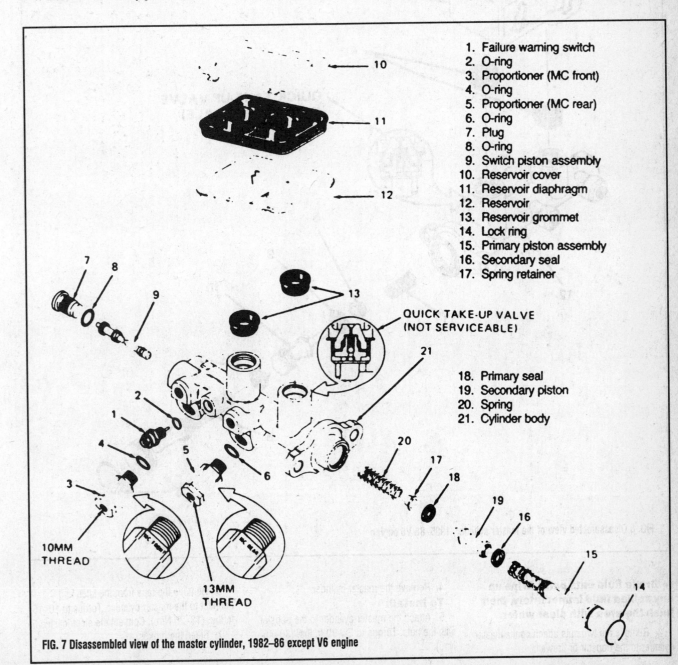

1. Failure warning switch
2. O-ring
3. Proportioner (MC front)
4. O-ring
5. Proportioner (MC rear)
6. O-ring
7. Plug
8. O-ring
9. Switch piston assembly
10. Reservoir cover
11. Reservoir diaphragm
12. Reservoir
13. Reservoir grommet
14. Lock ring
15. Primary piston assembly
16. Secondary seal
17. Spring retainer

18. Primary seal
19. Secondary piston
20. Spring
21. Cylinder body

QUICK TAKE-UP VALVE (NOT SERVICEABLE)

10MM THREAD

13MM THREAD

FIG. 7 Disassembled view of the master cylinder, 1982–86 except V6 engine

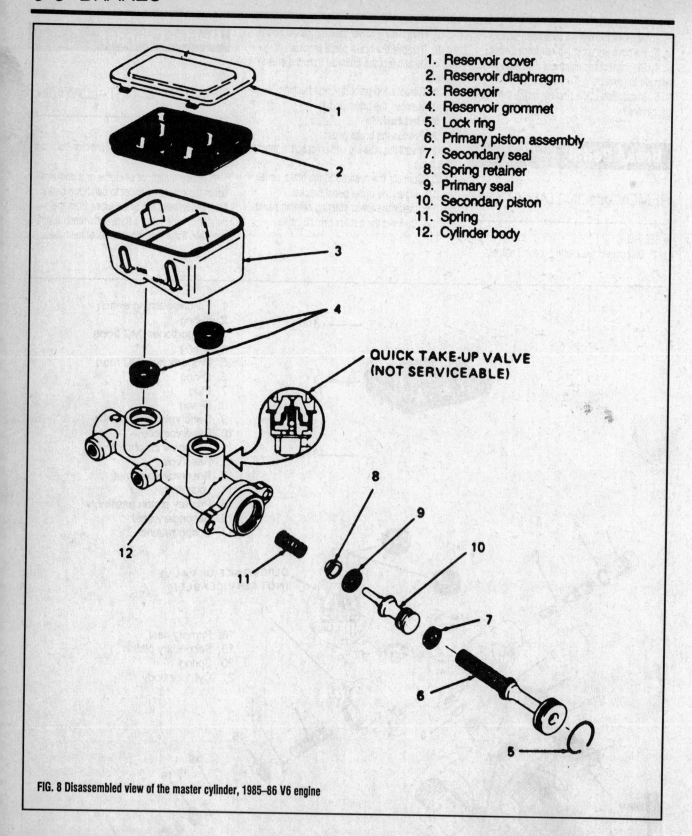

1. Reservoir cover
2. Reservoir diaphragm
3. Reservoir
4. Reservoir grommet
5. Lock ring
6. Primary piston assembly
7. Secondary seal
8. Spring retainer
9. Primary seal
10. Secondary piston
11. Spring
12. Cylinder body

QUICK TAKE-UP VALVE
(NOT SERVICEABLE)

FIG. 8 Disassembled view of the master cylinder, 1985–86 V6 engine

➡ **Brake fluid eats paint. Wipe up any spilled fluid immediately, then flush the area with clear water.**

3. Remove the two nuts attaching the master cylinder to the booster or firewall.

4. Remove the master cylinder.

To install:

5. Attach the master cylinder to the booster with the nuts. Torque to 22–30 ft. lbs. (30–45 Nm.).

6. Remove the tape from the lines and connect to the master cylinder. Torque to 10–15 ft. lbs. (13–20 Nm.). Connect the electrical lead.

7. Bleed the brakes.

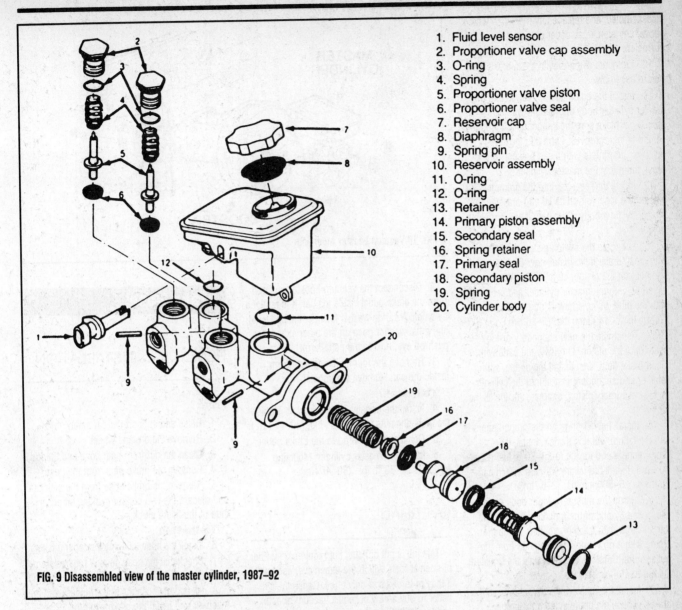

1. Fluid level sensor
2. Proportioner valve cap assembly
3. O-ring
4. Spring
5. Proportioner valve piston
6. Proportioner valve seal
7. Reservoir cap
8. Diaphragm
9. Spring pin
10. Reservoir assembly
11. O-ring
12. O-ring
13. Retainer
14. Primary piston assembly
15. Secondary seal
16. Spring retainer
17. Primary seal
18. Secondary piston
19. Spring
20. Cylinder body

FIG. 9 Disassembled view of the master cylinder, 1987–92

OVERHAUL

This is a tedious, time-consuming job. You can save yourself a lot of trouble by buying a new master cylinder from your dealer or parts supply house.

1. Remove the master cylinder.

2. Remove the reservoir cover and drain the fluid.

3. Unbolt the proportioners and failure warning switch from the side of the master cylinder body. Discard the O-rings found under the proportioners. Use new ones on installation. There may or may not be an O-ring under the original equipment failure warning switch. If there is, discard it. In either case, use an O-ring upon assembly.

4. Clamp the master cylinder body in a vise, taking care not to crush it. Depress the primary piston with a wooden dowel and remove the lock ring with a pair of snapring pliers.

5. The primary and secondary pistons can be removed by applying compressed air into one of the outlets at the end of the cylinder and plugging the other three outlets. The primary piston must be replaced as an assembly if the seals are bad. The secondary piston seals are replaceable. Install these new seals with the lips facing outwards.

6. Inspect the bore for corrosion. If any corrosion is evident, the master cylinder body must be replaced. Do not attempt to polish the bore with crocus cloth, sandpaper, or anything else. The body is aluminum; polishing the bore won't work.

7. To remove the failure warning switch piston assembly, remove the allen head plug from the end of the bore and withdraw the assembly with a pair of needlenose pliers. The switch piston assembly seals are replaceable.

8. The reservoir can be removed from the master cylinder body if necessary. Clamp the body in a vise by its mounting flange. Use a prey bar to remove the reservoir. If the reservoir is removed, remove the reservoir grommets and discard them. The quick takeup valves under the grommets are accessible after the retaining snaprings are removed. Use snapring pliers; no other tool will work.

9. Clean all parts in denatured alcohol and allow to air dry. Do not use anything else to clean, and do not wipe dry with a rag, which will leave bits of lint behind. Inspect all parts for corrosion or wear. Generally, it is best to replace all rubber parts whenever the master cylinder is

disassembled, and replace any metal part which shows any sign whatsoever of wear or corrosion.

10. Lubricate all parts with clean brake fluid before assembly.

11. Install the quick take-up valves into the master cylinder body and secure with the snaprings. Make sure the snaprings are properly seated in their grooves. Lubricate the new reservoir grommets with clean brake fluid and press them into the master cylinder.

12. Install the reservoir into the grommets by placing the reservoir on its lid and pressing the master cylinder body down onto it with a rocking motion.

13. Lubricate the switch piston assembly with clean brake fluid. Install new O-rings and retainers on the piston. Install the piston assembly into the master cylinder and secure with the plug, using a new O-ring on the plug. Torque is 40–140 inch lbs. (5–16 Nm.).

14. Assemble the new secondary piston seals onto the piston. Lubricate the parts with clean brake fluid, then install the spring, spring retainer and secondary piston into the cylinder. Install the primary piston, depress, and install the lock ring.

15. Install new O-rings on the proportioners and the failure warning switch. Install the proportioners and torque to 18–30 ft. lbs. (25–40 Nm.). Install the failure warning switch and torque to 15–50 inch lbs. (2–6 Nm.).

16. Clamp the master cylinder body upright into a vise by one of the mounting flanges. Fill the reservoir with fresh brake fluid. Pump the piston with a dowel until fluid squirts from the outlet ports. Continue pumping until the expelled fluid is free of air bubbles.

17. Install the master cylinder, and bleed the brakes. Check the brake system for proper operation. Do not move the car until a hard brake pedal is obtained and the brake system has been thoroughly checked for soundness.

Vacuum Booster

REMOVAL & INSTALLATION

◆ SEE FIG. 10

1. Remove the master cylinder from the booster. It is not necessary to disconnect the lines from the master cylinder. Just move the cylinder aside.

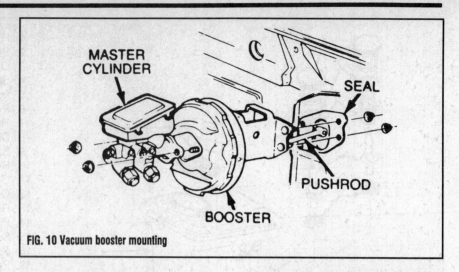

FIG. 10 Vacuum booster mounting

2. Disconnect the vacuum booster pushrod from the brake pedal inside the car. It is retained by a bolt. A spring washer is under the bolt head, and a flat washer goes on the other side of the pushrod eye, next to the pedal arm.

3. Remove the four attaching nuts from inside the car. Remove the booster.

To Install:

4. Install the booster on the firewall. Tighten the mounting nuts to 22–33 ft. lbs. (30–45 Nm.).

5. Connect the pushrod to the brake pedal.

6. Install the master cylinder. Mounting torque is 22–33 ft. lbs. (30–45 Nm.).

OVERHAUL

This job is not difficult, but requires a number of special tools which are expensive, especially if they're to be used only once. Generally, it's better to buy a new or rebuilt vacuum booster and install it yourself.

Proportioning Valves and Failure Warning Switch

These parts are installed in the master cylinder body on all models except the 1985–86 V6 engine. On these models the proportioning valve and the brake pressure differential warning switch is located to the left frame rail below the master cylinder. Refer to the master cylinder overhaul for replacement instructions for the four cylinder models.

Brake Hose

REMOVAL & INSTALLATION

Front

1. Raise and support the car safely.
2. Remove the tire and wheel .
3. Clean the dirt from both hose end fittings.
4. Remove the brake pipe from the hose.
5. Remove the brake hose from the caliper and discard the two copper gaskets on either side of the fitting block.

To Install:

6. Install the hose using new copper gaskets.
7. Check that the hose doesn't rub in extreme left and right turn conditions.
8. Fill and maintain the brake fluid level in the reservoir and bleed the brake system.

Rear

1. Raise and support the car safely.
2. Clean the dirt from both hose end fittings.
3. With the aid of a backup wrench, disconnect the brake pipe fitting on both ends of the brake hose.
4. Remove the retaining clips from both ends.
5. After installing the hose fill and maintain the brake fluid level in the reservoir and bleed the brake system.

Bleeding

◆ SEE FIGS. 11 and 12

➡ **For vehicles equipped with "Anti-Lock Brake System" refer to the service procedure in that section.**

The purpose of bleeding the brakes is to expel air trapped in the hydraulic system. The system must be bled whenever the pedal feels spongy, indicating that compressible air has entered the system. It must also be bled whenever the system has been opened or repaired. You will need a helper for this job.

Always maintain the brake fluid level in the reservoir during the bleeding procedure. Adjust the rear brakes before starting the brake bleeding procedure.

If the master cylinder is know or suspected to have air in the bore (this condition is present when master cylinder assembly is replaced it must be bleed first), then it must be bled BEFORE any wheel cylinder or caliper in the following manner. Connect 2 short pieces of brake line to the outlet fittings, bend them until the free end is below the fluid level in the master cylinder reservoir. Fill the reservoir with fresh brake fluid. Pump the piston slowly until no more air bubbles appear in the reservoirs. Disconnect the 2 short lines, refill the master cylinder and securely install the cylinder caps.

If the master cylinder is on the vehicle, it can still be bled, using a flare nut wrench. Open the brake lines slightly with the flare nut wrench while pressure is applied to the brake pedal by a helper inside the vehicle. Be sure to tighten the line before the brake pedal is released. Repeat the process with both lines until no air bubbles come out.

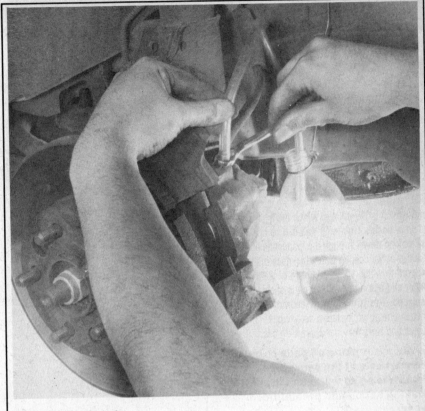

FIG. 11 Bleeding the brakes

1. The sequence for bleeding for 1982-91 vehicles is right rear, left front, left rear and right front. The sequence for bleeding 1992 vehicles is right rear, left rear, right front and left front. If the car has power brakes, remove the vacuum by applying the brakes several times. Do not run the engine while bleeding the brakes.

2. Clean all the bleeder screws. You may want to give each one a shot of penetrating solvent to loosen it up; seizure is a common problem with bleeder screws, which then break off, sometimes requiring replacement of the part to which they are attached.

3. Fill the master cylinder with DOT 3 brake fluid.

Check the level of the fluid often when bleeding, and refill the reservoirs as necessary. Don't let them run dry, or you will have to repeat the process.

4. Attach a length of clear vinyl tubing to the bleeder screw on the wheel cylinder. Insert the other end of the tube into a clear, clean jar half filled with brake fluid.

5. Have your assistant slowly depress the brake pedal (rapid pumping of the brake pedal pushes the master cylinder secondary piston down the bore in a way that makes it difficult to bleed the system). As this is done, open the bleeder screw $1/3$–$1/2$ of a turn, and allow the fluid to run through the tube. Then close the bleeder screw before the pedal reaches the end of its travel. Have your assistant slowly release

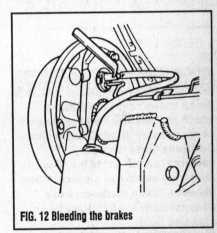

FIG. 12 Bleeding the brakes

the pedal. Repeat this process until no air bubbles appear in the expelled fluid.

6. Repeat the procedure on the other three brakes, checking the level of fluid in the master cylinder reservoir often.

After you're done, there should be no sponginess in the brake pedal feel. If there is, either there is still air in the line, in which case the process should be repeated, or there is a leak somewhere, which of course must be corrected before the car is moved.

FRONT DISC BRAKES

Pads

INSPECTION

The pad thickness should be inspected every time that the tires are removed for rotation. The outer pad an be checked by looking in at each end, which is the point at which the highest rate of wear occurs. The inner pad can be checked by looking down through the inspection hole in the top of the caliper. If the thickness of the pad is worn to within $\frac{1}{32}$ in. (0.8mm) of the rivet at either end of the pad, all the pads should be replaced. This is the factory recommended measurement; your state's automobile inspection laws may not agree with this.

➡ **Always replace all pads on both front wheels at the same time. Failure to do so will result in uneven braking action and premature wear.**

REMOVAL & INSTALLATION

♦ SEE FIGS. 13-26

❄ CAUTION

Brake shoes contain asbestos, which has been determined to be a cancer causing agent. Never clean the brake surfaces with compressed air! Avoid inhaling any dust from any brake surface! When cleaning brake surfaces, use a commercially available brake cleaning fluid.

1. Siphon $\frac{2}{3}$ of the brake fluid from the master cylinder reservoir. Loosen the wheel lug nuts and raise the car. Remove the wheel.

2. Position a C-clamp across the caliper so that it presses on the pads and tighten it until the caliper piston bottoms in its bore.

➡ **If you haven't removed some brake fluid from the master cylinder, it will overflow when the piston is retracted.**

FIG. 13 Use a brake cleaning solvent to clean the dust off of the brakes

FIG. 14 Bend tang straight to release the brake pad

FIG. 15 Use a ratchet with the appropriate size hex head tool to remove the attaching bolts

FIG. 16 Removal of the attaching bolt

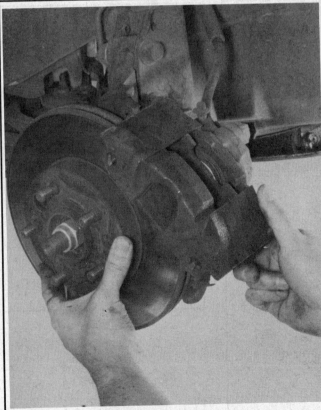

FIG. 17 Pull the caliper assembly up to remove from spindle and rotor

FIG. 18 Suspending the caliper with a wire hook from the suspension assembly

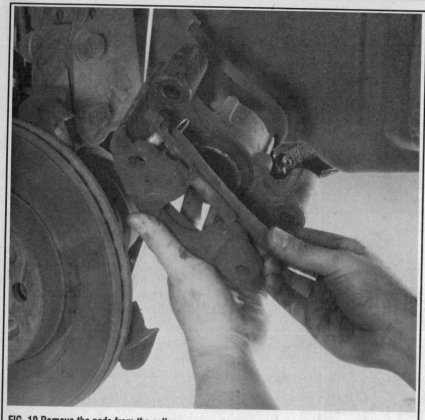

FIG. 19 Remove the pads from the caliper

FIG. 20 Disc brake pads and caliper retaining bolts

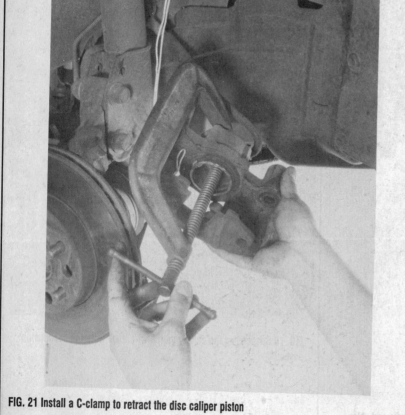

FIG. 21 Install a C-clamp to retract the disc caliper piston

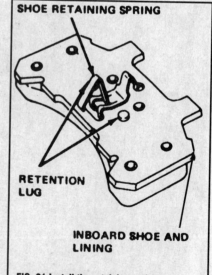

SHOE RETAINING SPRING

RETENTION LUG

INBOARD SHOE AND LINING

FIG. 21 Install the retaining spring on the inboard pad

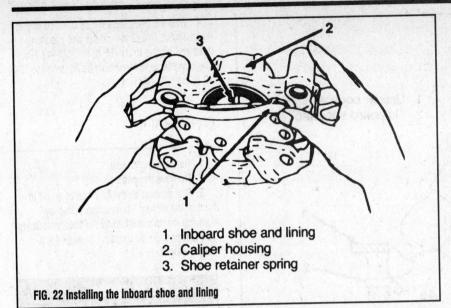

1. Inboard shoe and lining
2. Caliper housing
3. Shoe retainer spring

FIG. 22 Installing the inboard shoe and lining

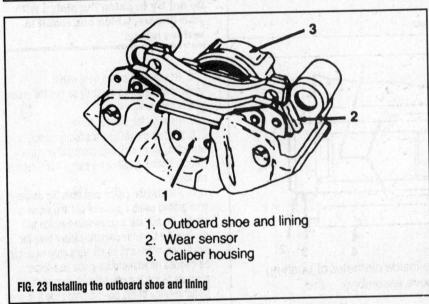

1. Outboard shoe and lining
2. Wear sensor
3. Caliper housing

FIG. 23 Installing the outboard shoe and lining

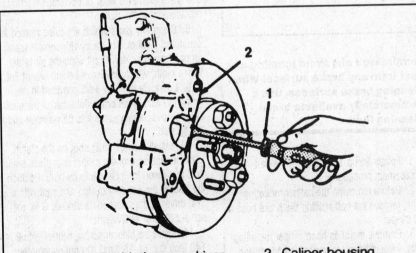

1. Large flat-blade screwdriver   2. Caliper housing

FIG. 24 First step of cinching the shoe to the caliper

3. Remove the C-clamp.

4. Remove the allen head caliper mounting bolts. Inspect the bolts for corrosion, and replace as necessary.

5. Remove the caliper from the steering knuckle and suspend it from the body of the car with a length of wire. Do not allow the caliper to hang by its hose.

6. Remove the pad retaining springs and remove the pads from the caliper.

7. Remove the plastic sleeves and the rubber bushings from the mounting bolt holes.

8. Install new sleeves and bushings. Lubricate the sleeves with a light coating of silicone grease before installation. These parts must always be replaced when the pads are replaced. The parts are usually included in the pad replacement kits.

➡ **On 1987–92 models the mounting bolt and sleeve comes as an assembly. Lubricate in the same manner.**

9. Install the outboard pad into the caliper.

10. Install the retainer spring on the inboard pad. A new spring should be included in the pad replacement.

11. Install the new inboard pad into the caliper. The retention lugs fit into the piston.

12. Install the caliper onto the steering knuckle. Tighten the mounting bolts to 21–35 ft. lbs. (28–47 Nm.).

13. Apply a firm force 3 times to the brake to seat linings.

14. Pry up on the outboard shoe with a LARGE flat blade screwdriver or similar tool, between the outboard shoe and the flange and hat section of the rotor. Keep the tool in place during the following step.

✳✳✳ CAUTION

Use a suitable size prying tool that will not break and cause physical injury.

15. Hold moderate force of 50 lbs. (222 N) on the brake pedal and cinch the outboard shoe tabs, using a plastic mallet and a ball peen hammer, as shown in the illustration.

16. Install the wheel and lower the car. Fill the master cylinder to its proper level with fresh brake fluid meeting DOT 3 specifications. Since the brake hose wasn't disconnected, it isn't really necessary to bleed the brakes, although most mechanics do this as a matter of course.

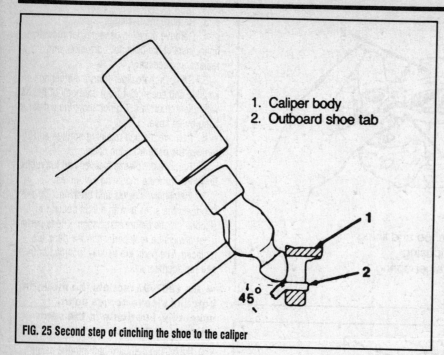

1. Caliper body
2. Outboard shoe tab

FIG. 25 Second step of cinching the shoe to the caliper

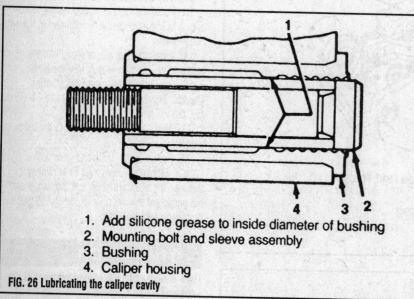

1. Add silicone grease to inside diameter of bushing
2. Mounting bolt and sleeve assembly
3. Bushing
4. Caliper housing

FIG. 26 Lubricating the caliper cavity

Brake Caliper

REMOVAL & INSTALLATION

◆ SEE FIGS. 27-32

1. Follow Steps 1, 2 and 3 of the pad replacement procedure.
2. Before removing the caliper mounting bolts, remove the bolt holding the brake hose to the caliper.
3. Remove the allen head caliper mounting bolts. Inspect them for corrosion and replace them if necessary.

4. With the pads installed as outlined in pad replacement, install the caliper and mounting bolts and torque to 21–35 ft. lbs. (28–47 Nm.). The brake hose fitting should be tightened to 18–30 ft. lbs. (24–40 Nm.).

OVERHAUL

1. Remove the caliper.
2. Remove the pads.
3. Place some cloths or a slat of wood in front of the piston. Remove the piston by applying compressed air to the fluid inlet fitting. Use just enough air pressure to ease the piston from the bore.

4. Remove the piston boot with a screwdriver, working carefully so that the piston bore is not scratched.
5. Remove the bleeder screw.
6. Inspect the piston for scoring, nicks, corrosion, wear, etc., and damaged or worn chrome plating. Replace the piston if any defects are found.
7. Remove the piston seal from the caliper bore groove using a piece of pointed wood or plastic. Do not use a screwdriver, which will damage the bore. Inspect the caliper bore for nicks, corrosion, and so on. Very light wear can be cleaned up with crocus cloth. Use finger pressure to rub the crocus cloth around the circumference of the bore; do not slide it in and out. More extensive wear or corrosion warrants replacement of the part.
8. Clean any parts which are to be reused in denatured alcohol. Dry them with compressed air or allow to air dry. Don't wipe the parts dry with a cloth, which will leave behind bits of lint.
9. Lubricate the new seal, provided in the repair kit, with clean brake fluid. Install the seal in its groove, making sure it is fully seated and not twisted.
10. Install the new dust boot on the piston. Lubricate the bore of the caliper with clean brake fluid and insert the piston into its bore. Position the boot in the caliper housing and seat with a seal driver of the appropriate size, or G.M. tool no. J-29077 or equivalent.
11. Install the bleeder screw, tightening to 80–140 inch lbs. (9–16 Nm.). Do not overtighten.
12. Install the pads, install the caliper, and bleed the brakes.

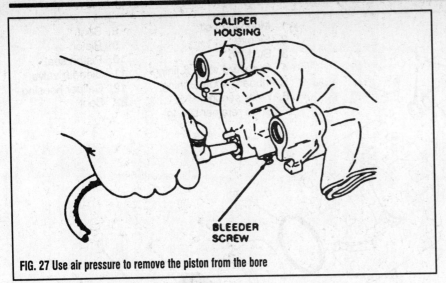

FIG. 27 Use air pressure to remove the piston from the bore

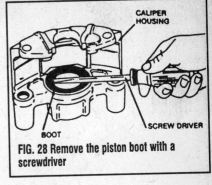

FIG. 28 Remove the piston boot with a screwdriver

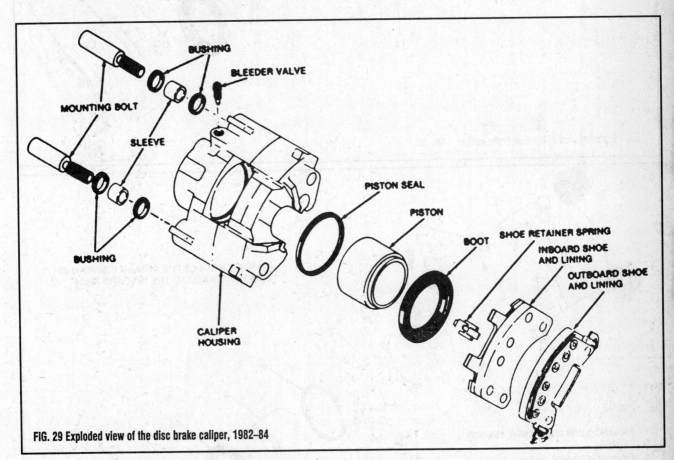

FIG. 29 Exploded view of the disc brake caliper, 1982–84

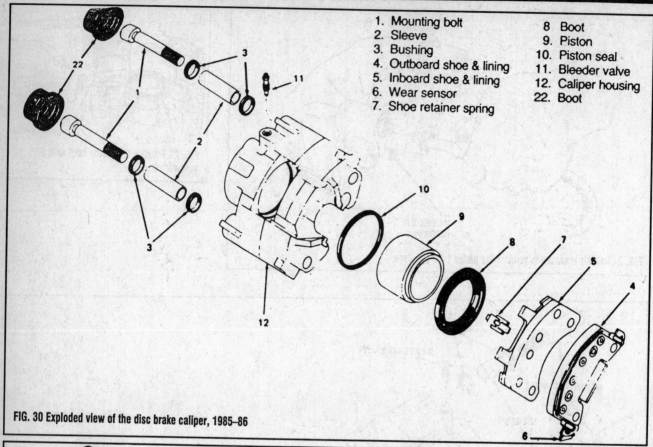

1. Mounting bolt
2. Sleeve
3. Bushing
4. Outboard shoe & lining
5. Inboard shoe & lining
6. Wear sensor
7. Shoe retainer spring
8. Boot
9. Piston
10. Piston seal
11. Bleeder valve
12. Caliper housing
22. Boot

FIG. 30 Exploded view of the disc brake caliper, 1985–86

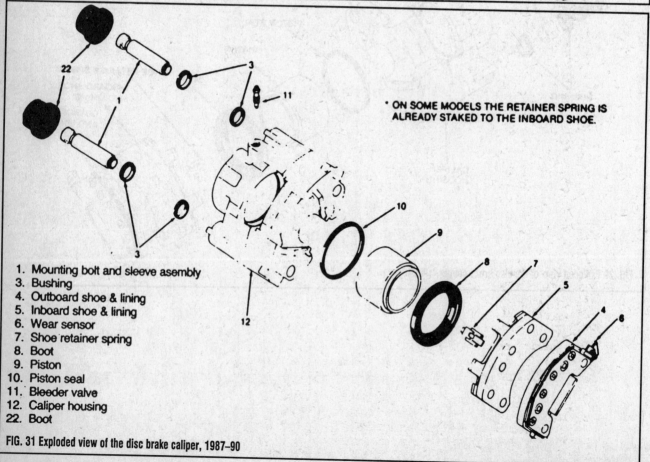

* ON SOME MODELS THE RETAINER SPRING IS ALREADY STAKED TO THE INBOARD SHOE.

1. Mounting bolt and sleeve asembly
3. Bushing
4. Outboard shoe & lining
5. Inboard shoe & lining
6. Wear sensor
7. Shoe retainer spring
8. Boot
9. Piston
10. Piston seal
11. Bleeder valve
12. Caliper housing
22. Boot

FIG. 31 Exploded view of the disc brake caliper, 1987–90

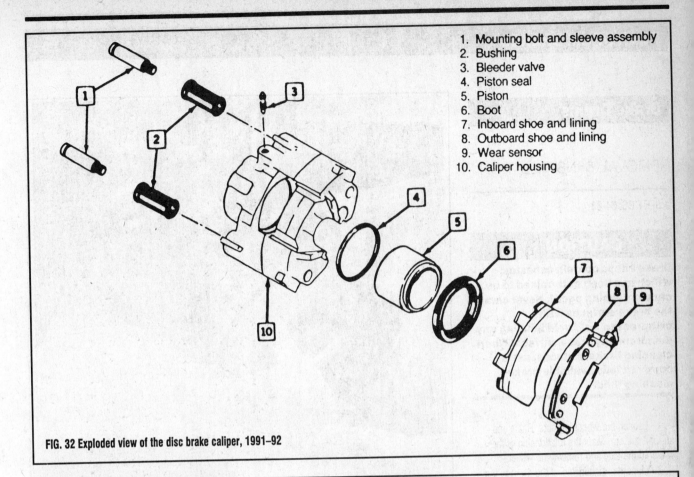

1. Mounting bolt and sleeve assembly
2. Bushing
3. Bleeder valve
4. Piston seal
5. Piston
6. Boot
7. Inboard shoe and lining
8. Outboard shoe and lining
9. Wear sensor
10. Caliper housing

FIG. 32 Exploded view of the disc brake caliper, 1991–92

Brake Disc (Rotor)

REMOVAL & INSTALLATION

1. Remove the caliper.
2. Remove the rotor.
3. To install, reposition the rotor and install the caliper and pads as outlined earlier.

INSPECTION

◆ SEE FIG. 33

1. Check the rotor surface for wear or scoring. Deep scoring, grooves or rust pitting can be removed by refacing, a job to be referred to your local machine shop or garage. Minimum thickness is stamped on the rotor (21.08 mm). If the rotor will be thinner than this after refinishing, it must be replaced.

2. Check the rotor parallelism; it must vary less thn 0.013 mm measured at four or more points around the circumference. Make all measurements at the same distance in from the edge of the rotor. Refinish the rotor if it fails to meet this specification.

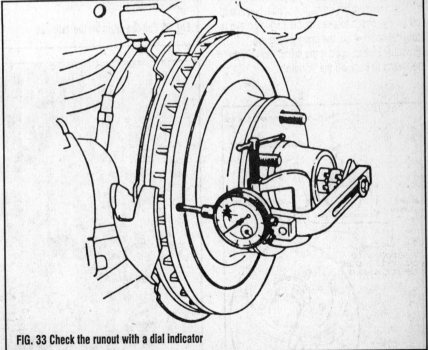

FIG. 33 Check the runout with a dial indicator

3. Measure the disc runout with a dial indicator. If runout exceeds 0.127 mm, and the wheel bearings are OK (if runout is being measured with the disc on the car), the rotor must be refaced or replaced as necessary.

REAR DRUM BRAKES

Brake Drums

REMOVAL & INSTALLATION

◆ SEE FIGS. 34-38

❊❊ CAUTION

Brake shoes contain asbestos, which has been determined to be a cancer causing agent. Never clean the brake surfaces with compressed air! Avoid inhaling any dust from any brake surface! When cleaning brake surfaces, use a commercially available brake cleaning fluid.

1. Loosen the wheel lug nuts. Raise and support the car. Mark the relationship of the wheel to the axle and remove the wheel.

2. Mark the relationship of the drum to the axle and remove the drum. If it cannot be slipped off easily, check to see that the parking brake is fully released. If so, the brake shoes are probably locked against the drum. Perform the following to back off the adjuster:

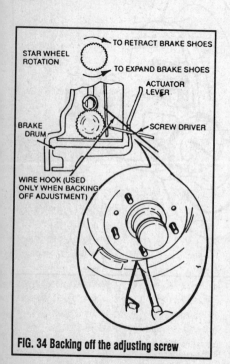

FIG. 34 Backing off the adjusting screw

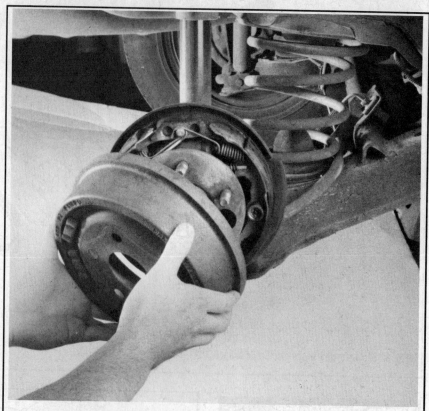

FIG. 35 Pull the drum off the axle hub

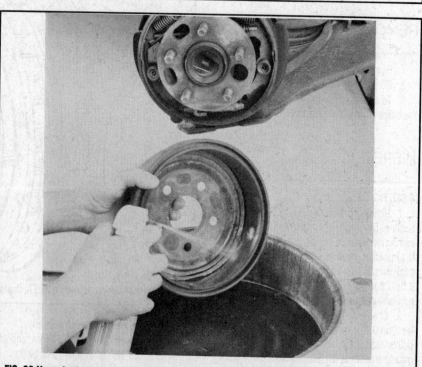

FIG. 36 Use a brake cleaning solvent to clean the dust off of the brake drum

a. Use a punch to knock out the stamped area on the brake drum. If this is done with the drum installed on the car, the drum must then be removed to clean out all metal pieces. After adjustments are complete, obtain a hole cover from your dealer (Part no. 4874119 or the equivalent) to prevent entry of dirt and water into the brakes.

b. Use an awl, a screwdriver, or an adjusting tool especially made for the purpose to turn the brake adjusting screw star wheel.

3. To install, reposition the drum making sure to align the matchmarks made during removal. Lug nut torque is 100 ft. lbs. (140 Nm.).

INSPECTION

1. After removing the brake drum, wipe out the accumulated dust with a damp cloth.

❄ CAUTION

Do not blow the brake dust out of the drums with compressed air or lungpower. Brake linings contain asbestos, a known cancer causing substance. Dispose of the cloth used to clean the parts after use.

2. Inspect the drums for cracks, deep grooves, roughness, scoring, or out-of-roundness. Replace any drum which is cracked; do not try to weld it up.

3. Smooth any slight scores by polishing the friction surface with fine emery cloth. Heavy or extensive scoring will cause excessive lining wear and should be removed from the drum through resurfacing, a job to be referred to your local machine shop or garage. The maximum finished diameter of the drums is 200.64mm. The drum must be replaced if the diameter is 201.40mm or greater.

Brake Shoes

❄ CAUTION

Brake shoes contain asbestos, which has been determined to be a cancer causing agent. Never clean the brake surfaces with compressed air! Avoid inhaling any dust from any brake surface! When cleaning brake surfaces, use a commercially available brake cleaning fluid.

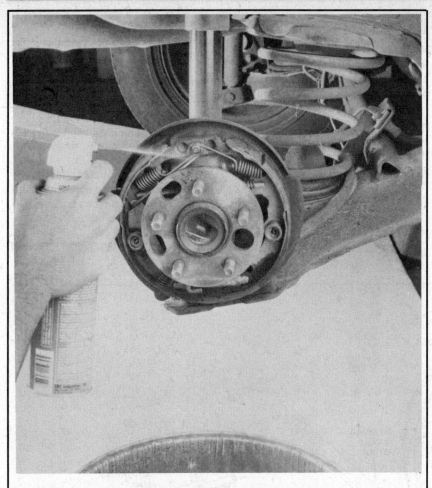

FIG. 37 Use a brake cleaning solvent to clean the dust off of the brakes

FIG. 38 Maximum brake drum diameter specifications are stamped on the outside of each drum

INSPECTION

After removing the brake drum, inspect the brake shoes. If the lining is worn down to within $\frac{1}{32}$ in. (0.8mm) of a rivet, the shoes must be replaced.

➡ **This figure may disagree with your state's automobile inspection laws.**

If the brake lining is soaked with brake fluid or grease, it must be replaced. If this is the case, the brake drum should be sanded with crocus cloth to remove all traces of brake fluid, and the wheel cylinders should be rebuilt. Clean all grit from the friction surface of the drum before replacing it.

If the lining is chipped, cracked, or otherwise damaged, it must be replaced with a new lining.

➡ **Always replace the brake linings in sets of two on both ends of the axle. Never replace just one shoe, or both shoes on one side.**

Check the condition of the shoes, retracting springs, and holddown springs for signs of overheating. If the shoes or springs have a slight blue color, this indicates overheating and replacement of the shoes and springs is recommended. The wheel cylinders should be rebuilt as a precaution against future problems.

REMOVAL & INSTALLATION

◆ SEE FIGS. 39-57

✳✳ CAUTION

Brake shoes contain asbestos, which has been determined to be a cancer causing agent. Never clean the brake surfaces with compressed air! Avoid inhaling any dust from any brake surface! When cleaning brake surfaces, use a commercially available brake cleaning fluid.

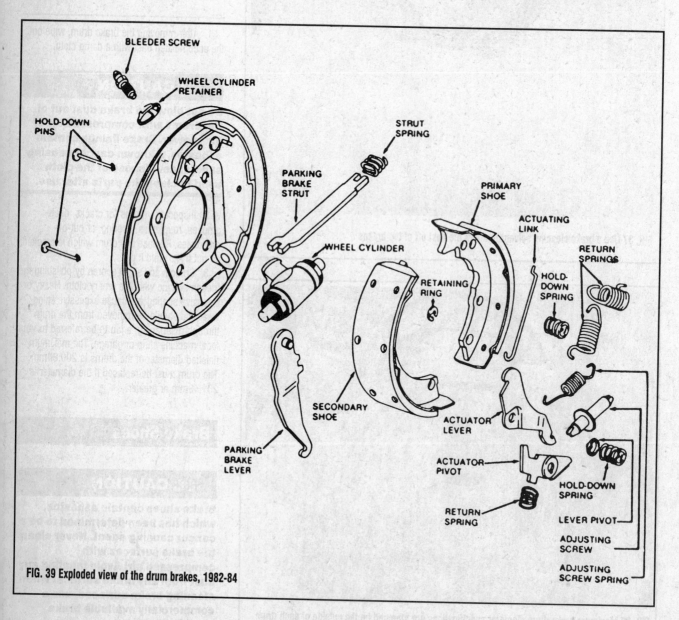

FIG. 39 Exploded view of the drum brakes, 1982-84

1. Loosen the lug nuts on the wheel to be serviced, raise and support the car, and remove the wheel and brake drum.

➡ **It is not really necessary to remove the hub and wheel bearing assembly from the axle, but it does make the job easier. If you can work with the hub and bearing assembly in place, skip down to Step 3.**

2. Remove the four hub and bearing assembly retaining bolts and remove the assembly from the axle.

3. Remove the return springs from the shoes with a pair of needle nose pliers. There are also special brake spring pliers for this job.

4. Remove the hold down springs by gripping them with a pair of pliers, then pressing down and turning 90 degrees. There are special tools to grab and turn these parts, but pliers work fairly well.

5. Remove the shoe holddown pins from behind the brake backing plate. They will simply slide out once the holddown spring tension is relieved.

6. Lift up the actuator lever for the self-adjusting mechanism and remove the actuating link. Remove the actuator lever, pivot, and the pivot return spring.

7. Spread the shoes apart to clear the wheel cylinder pistons and remove the parking brake strut and spring.

8. If the hub and bearing assembly is still in place, spread the shoes far enough apart to clear it.

9. Disconnect the parking brake cable from the lever. Remove the shoes, still connected by their adjusting screw spring, from the car.

10. With the shoes removed, note the position of the adjusting spring and remove the spring and adjusting screw.

11. Remove the C-clip from the parking brake lever and remove the lever from the secondary shoe.

12. Use a damp cloth to remove all dirt and dust from the backing plate and brake parts. See the warning about brake dust in the drum removal procedure.

13. Check the wheel cylinders by carefully pulling the lower edges of the wheel cylinder boots away from the cylinders. If there is excessive leakage, the inside of the cylinder will be moist with fluid. If leakage exists, a wheel cylinder overhaul is in order. Do not delay, because brake failure could result.

➡ **A small amount of fluid will be present to act as a lubricant for the wheel cylinder pistons. Fluid spilling from the boot center hole, after the piston is removed, indicates cup leakage and the necessity for cylinder overhaul.**

14. Check the backing plate attaching bolts to make sure that they are tight. Use fine emery cloth to clean all rust and dirt from the shoe contact surfaces on the plate.

15. Lubricate the fulcrum end of the parking brake lever with brake grease specially made for

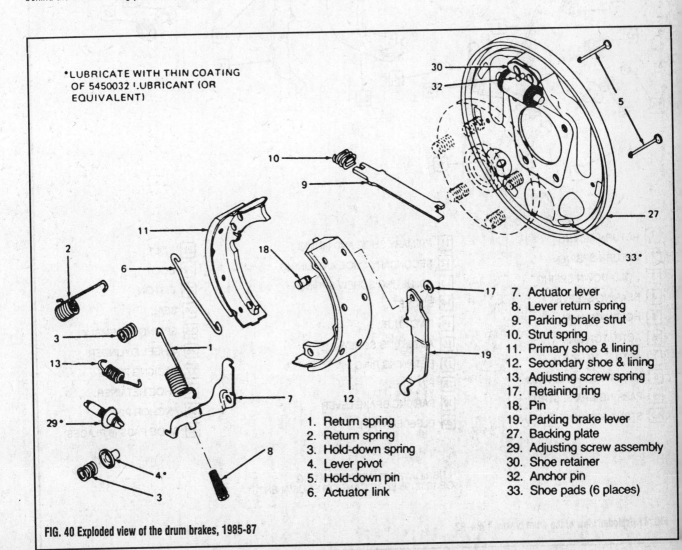

•LUBRICATE WITH THIN COATING OF 5450032 LUBRICANT (OR EQUIVALENT)

1. Return spring
2. Return spring
3. Hold-down spring
4. Lever pivot
5. Hold-down pin
6. Actuator link
7. Actuator lever
8. Lever return spring
9. Parking brake strut
10. Strut spring
11. Primary shoe & lining
12. Secondary shoe & lining
13. Adjusting screw spring
17. Retaining ring
18. Pin
19. Parking brake lever
27. Backing plate
29. Adjusting screw assembly
30. Shoe retainer
32. Anchor pin
33. Shoe pads (6 places)

FIG. 40 Exploded view of the drum brakes, 1985-87

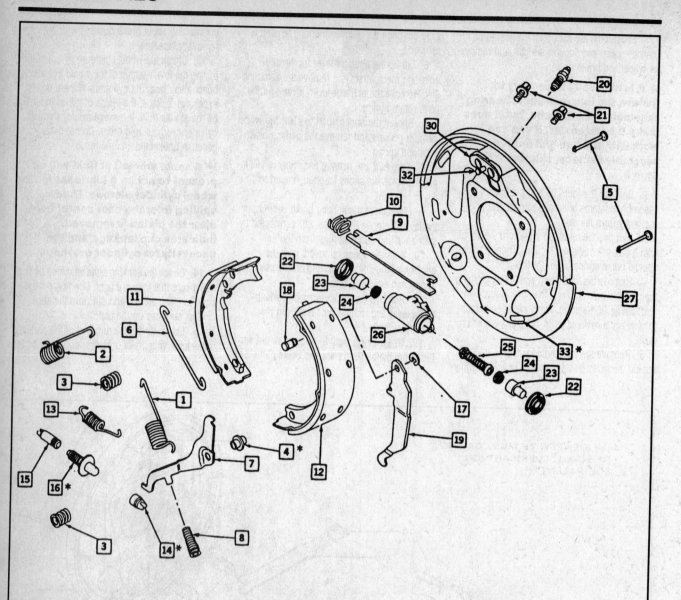

1. RETURN SPRING
2. RETURN SPRING
3. HOLD-DOWN SPRING
4. BEARING SLEEVE
5. HOLD-DOWN PIN
6. ACTUATOR LINK
7. ACTUATOR LEVER
8. LEVER RETURN SPRING
9. PARKING BRAKE STRUT
10. STRUT SPRING

11. PRIMARY SHOE AND LINING
12. SECONDARY SHOE AND LINING
13. ADJUSTING SCREW SPRING
14. SOCKET
15. PIVOT NUT
16. ADJUSTING SCREW
17. RETAINING RING
18. PIN
19. PARKING BRAKE LEVER
20. BLEEDER VALVE

21. BOLT
22. BOOT
23. PISTON
24. SEAL
25. SPRING ASSEMBLY
26. WHEEL CYLINDER
27. BACKING PLATE
30. SHOE RETAINER
32. ANCHOR PIN
33. SHOE PADS (6 PLACES)

*LUBRICATE WITH THIN COATING
OF 1052196 LUBRICANT OR EQUIVALENT

FIG. 41 Exploded view of the drum brakes, 1988–92

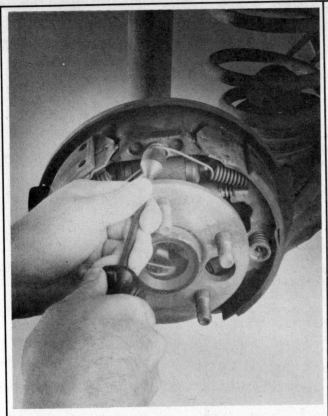

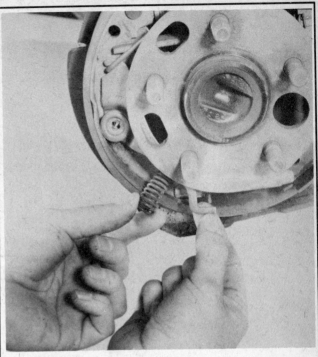

FIG. 43 Lift the actuator lever and remove the return spring

FIG. 42 Using a spring removal tool, remove the upper front side spring

FIG. 44 Remove the actuator link

FIG. 45 Using a hold down spring removal tool, remove the hold down spring (1 each side)

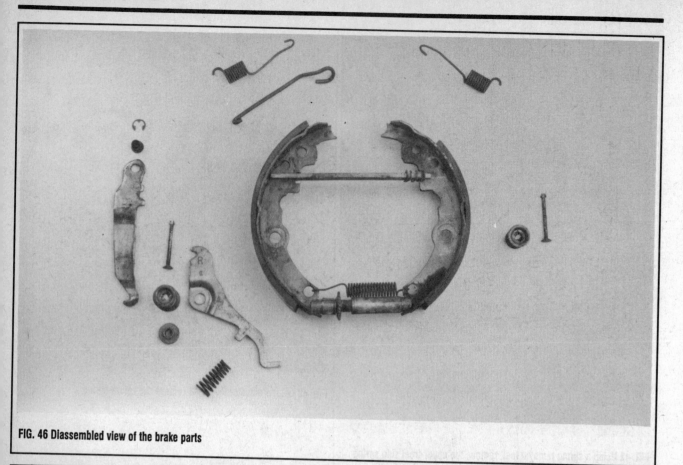

FIG. 46 Diassembled view of the brake parts

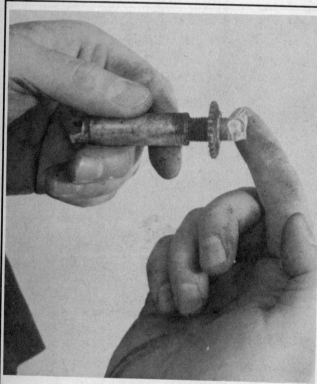

FIG. 47 Lubricate the star wheel on the adjusting screw

FIG. 48 Clean and lubricate the areas shown. Donot use an excessive ammount of lubricant in these areas

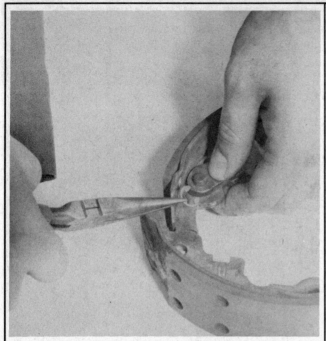

FIG. 49 Install the parking brake lever, adjusting screw, and adjusting screw spring onto the new brake shoes. Proper spring installation is with the coils over the adjuster, not the star wheel

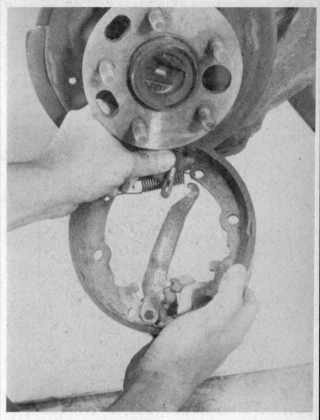

FIG. 50 Align the parking brake lever with the parking brake cable

FIG. 51 Install the cable end into the lever

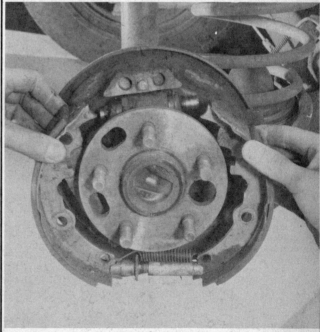

FIG. 52 Spread the shoes enough to clear the axle and seat them against the backing plate

FIG. 53 Install the hold down pins and position the lever pivot bushing

FIG. 54 Position the actuator pivot onto bushing and install the hold down spring

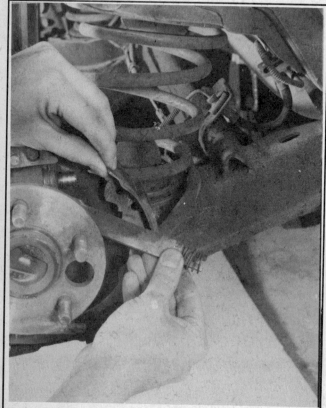

FIG. 55 Spread the other shoe out far enough to position the parking brake strut and spring between the brake shoes

FIG. 56 Install the hold down spring

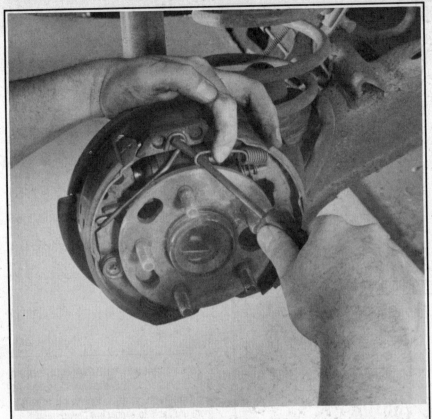

FIG. 57 Install the actuating link, and upper return springs

braking action and the parking brake. The brakes must not be applied severely immediately after installation. They should be used moderately for the first 200 miles of city driving or 1000 miles of highway driving, to allow the linings to conform to the shape of the drum.

Wheel Cylinders

REMOVAL & INSTALLATION

1982–87
◆ SEE FIGS. 58-60

❈❈ CAUTION

Brake shoes contain asbestos, which has been determined to be a cancer causing agent. Never clean the brake surfaces with compressed air! Avoid inhaling any dust from any brake surface! When cleaning brake surfaces, use a commercially available brake cleaning fluid.

the purpose. Install the lever on the secondary shoe and secure with C-clip.

16. Install the adjusting screw and spring on the shoes, connecting them together. The coils of the spring must not be over the star wheel on the adjuster. The left and right hand springs are not interchangeable. Do not mix them up.

17. Lubricate the shoe contact surfaces on the backing plate with the brake grease. Be certain when you are using this stuff that none of it actually gets on the linings or drums. Apply the same grease to the point where the parking brake cable contacts the plate. Use the grease sparingly.

18. Spread the shoe assemblies apart and connect the parking brake cable. Install the shoes on the backing plate, engaging the shoes at the top temporarily with the wheel cylinder pistons. Make sure that the star wheel on the adjuster is lined up with the adjusting hole in the backing plate, if the hole is back there.

19. Spread the shoes apart slightly and install the parking brake strut and spring. Make sure that the end of the strut without the spring engages the parking brake lever. The end with the spring engages the primary shoe (the one with the shorter lining).

20. Install the actuator pivot, lever and return spring. Install the actuating link in the shoe retainer. Lift up the actuator lever and hook the link into the lever.

21. Install the holddown pins through the back of the plate, install the lever pivots and holddown springs. Install the shoe return springs with a pair of pliers. Be very careful not to stretch or otherwise distort these springs.

22. Take a look at everything. Make sure the linings are in the right place, the self-adjusting mechanism is correctly installed, and the parking brake parts are all hooked up. If in doubt, remove the other wheel and take a look at that one for comparison.

23. Measure the width of the linings, then measure the inside width of the drum. Adjust the linings by means of the adjuster so that the drum will fit onto the linings.

24. Install the hub and bearing assembly onto the axle if removed. Tighten the retaining bolts to 35 ft. lbs. (55 Nm.).

25. Install the drum and wheel. Adjust the brakes using the procedure given earlier in this Section. Be sure to install a rubber hole cover in the knock-out hole after the adjustment is complete. Adjust the parking brake.

26. Lower the car and check the pedal for any sponginess or lack of a hard feel. Check the

1. Loosen the wheel lug nuts, raise and support the car, and remove the wheel. Remove the drum and brake shoes. Leave the hub and wheel bearing assembly in place.

2. Remove any dirt from around the brake line fitting. Disconnect the brake line.

3. Remove the wheel cylinder retainer by using two awls or punches with a tip diameter of 1/8 in. (3mm) or less. Insert the awls or punches into the access slots between the wheel cylinder pilot and retainer locking tabs. Bend both tabs away simultaneously. Remove the wheel cylinder from the backing plate.

To install:

4. Position the wheel cylinder against the backing plate and hold it in place with a wooden block between the wheel cylinder and the hub and bearing assembly.

5. Install a new retainer over the wheel cylinder abutment on the rear of the backing plate by pressing it into place with a 1 1/8 in. 12-point socket and an extension.

6. Install a new bleeder screw into the wheel cylinder. Install the brake line and tighten to 10–15 ft. lbs. (13–20 Nm.).

7. The rest of installation is the reverse of removal. After the drum is installed, bleed the brakes using the procedure outlined earlier in this Section.

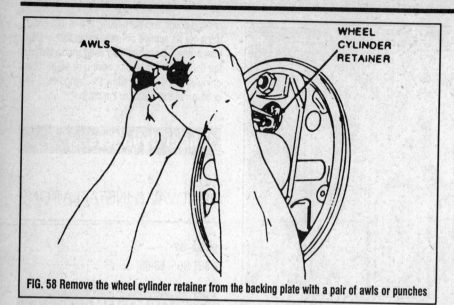

FIG. 58 Remove the wheel cylinder retainer from the backing plate with a pair of awls or punches

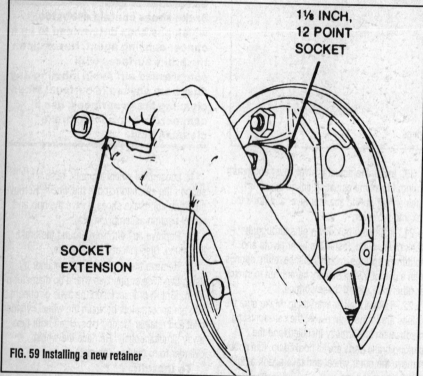

FIG. 59 Installing a new retainer

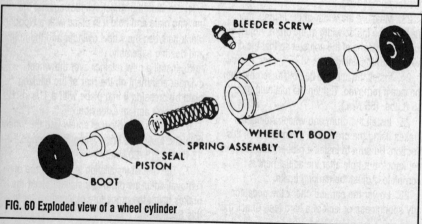

FIG. 60 Exploded view of a wheel cylinder

1988–92

1. Raise and support the rear of the vehicle on jackstands. Remove the tire and brake drum.
2. Clean any dirt from around the wheel cylinder.
3. Disconnect and plug the brake line from the wheel cylinder.
4. Remove the wheel cylinder bolts using a #6 Torx socket.
5. Remove the wheel cylinder.

To Install:

6. Position the wheel assembly and hold in place with a wooden block between the cylinder and axle flange.
7. Install the wheel cylinder bolts using a # 6 Torx socket and tighten to 15 ft. lbs. (20 Nm).
8. Install the inlet tube nut and torque to 13 ft. lbs. (17 Nm).
9. Bleed the brake system. Inspect the brake operation.

OVERHAUL

As is the case with master cylinders, overhaul kits are available for the wheel cylinders. And, as is the case with master cylinders, it is usually more profitable to simply buy new or rebuilt wheel cylinders rather than rebuilding them. When rebuilding wheel cylinders, avoid getting any contaminants in the system. Always install new high quality brake fluid; the use of improper fluid will swell and deteriorate the rubber parts.

1. Remove the wheel cylinders.
2. Remove the rubber boots from the cylinder ends. Discard the boots.
3. Remove and discard the pistons and cups.
4. Wash the cylinder and metal parts in denatured alcohol.

❈❈ WARNING

Never use mineral based solvents to clean the brake parts.

5. Allow the parts to air dry and inspect the cylinder bore for corrosion or wear. Light corrosion can be cleaned up with crocus cloth; use finger pressure and rotate the cloth around the circumference of the bore. Do not move the cloth in and out. Any deep corrosion or pitting or wear warrants replacement of the parts.
6. Rinse the parts and allow to dry. Do not dry with a rag, which will leave bits of lint behind.
7. Lubricate the cylinder bore with clean brake fluid. Insert the spring assembly.
8. Install new cups. Do not lubricate prior to assembly.
9. Install the new pistons.

10. Press the new boots onto the cylinders by hand. Do not lubricate prior to assembly.

11. Install the wheel cylinders. Bleed the brakes after installation of the drum.

Brake Backing Plate

REMOVAL & INSTALLATION

◆ SEE FIG. 61

1. Raise and safely support vehicle on jack stands.

2. Remove the wheel assembly and brake drum.

3. Remove the brake shoes, parking brake cable and wheel cylinder.

4. Spin the axle to align each of the four retaining bolts through the opening of the axle and remove the bolts.

5. Remove the axle hub and backing plate.

6. Installation is the reverse of the removal procedure. Tighten the axle hub bolts to 38 ft.lbs.

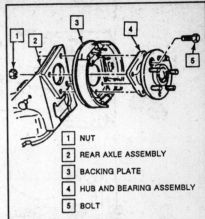

1	NUT
2	REAR AXLE ASSEMBLY
3	BACKING PLATE
4	HUB AND BEARING ASSEMBLY
5	BOLT

FIG. 61 Removal of the hub and bearing assembly to remove the backing plate

PARKING BRAKE

ADJUSTMENT

◆ SEE FIGS. 62 and 63

1. Raise and support the car with both rear wheels off the ground.

2. If the vehicle is equipped with a hand parking brake lever, pull the parking brake lever exactly 5 ratchet clicks. If the vehicle is equipped with a foot operated parking brake, pull the parking brake lever exactly 2 ratchet clicks.

3. Loosen the equalizer locknut, then tighten the adjusting nut until the left rear wheel can just be turned backward using two hands, but is locked in forward rotation.

4. Tighten the locknut.

5. Release the parking brake. Rotate the rear wheels; there should be no drag.

6. Lower the car.

Cable

REMOVAL & INSTALLATION

Front Cable

1. Place the gear selector in Neutral and apply the parking brake.

2. Remove the center console as detailed in Section 6.

3. Disconnect the parking brake cable from the lever.

4. Remove the cable retaining nut and the bracket securing the front cable to the floor panel.

5. Raise the car and loosen the equalizer nut.

6. Loosen the catalytic converter shield and then remove the parking brake cable from the body.

7. Disconnect the cable from the equalizer and then remove the cable from the guide and the underbody clips.

To Install:

8. Position the cable to the equalizer, guide and underbody clips.

9. Install the parking brake cable to the body and tighten the catalytic converter shield.

10. Tighten the equalizer nut.

11. Install the cable retaining nut and the bracket securing the front cable to the floor panel.

12. Connect the parking brake cable to the lever.

13. Install the center console as detailed in Section 6.

14. Adjust the cable.

Right and Left Rear Cables

1. Raise and support the rear of the car.

2. Back off the equalizer nut until the cable tension is eliminated.

3. Remove the tires, wheels and brake drums.

4. Insert a screwdriver between the brake shoe and the top part of the brake adjuster bracket. Push the bracket to the front and then release the top brake adjuster rod.

5. Remove the rear hold down spring. Remove the actuator lever and the lever return spring.

6. Remove the adjuster screw spring.

7. Remove the top rear brake shoe return spring.

8. Unhook the parking brake cable from the parking brake lever.

9. Depress the conduit fitting retaining tangs and then remove the conduit fitting from the backing plate.

10. Remove the cable end button from the connector.

11. Depress the conduit fitting retaining tangs and remove the conduit fitting from the axle bracket.

To Install:

12. Install the conduit fitting to the axle bracket.

13. Install the cable end button to the connector.

14. Install the conduit fitting to the backing plate.

15. Hook the parking brake cable to the parking brake lever.

16. Install the top rear brake shoe return spring.

17. Install the adjuster screw spring.

18. Install the rear hold down spring. Install the actuator lever and the lever return spring.

19. Install the top brake adjuster rod.

20. Install the tires, wheels and brake drums.

21. Adjust the cable.

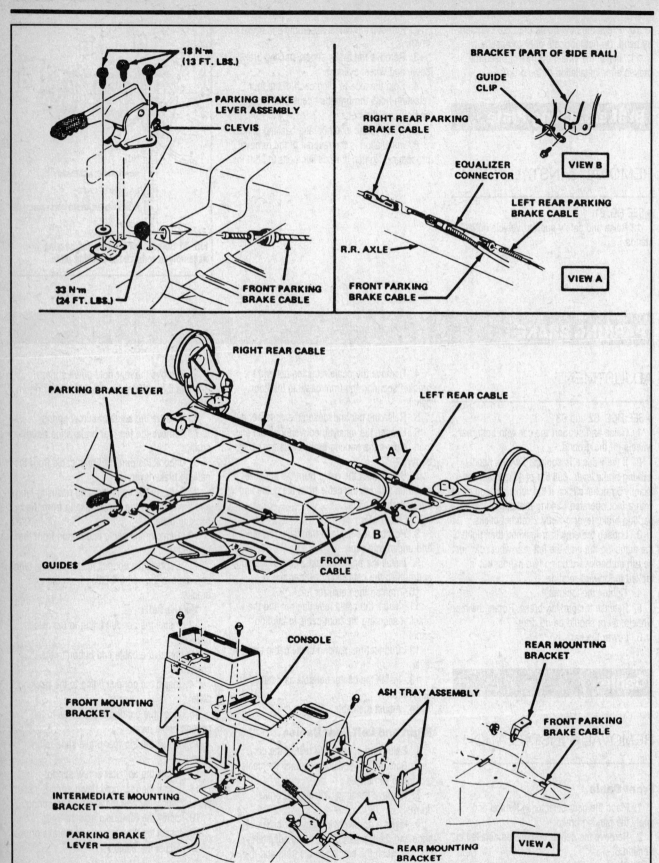

FIG. 62 Parking brake cable routing–1982–86

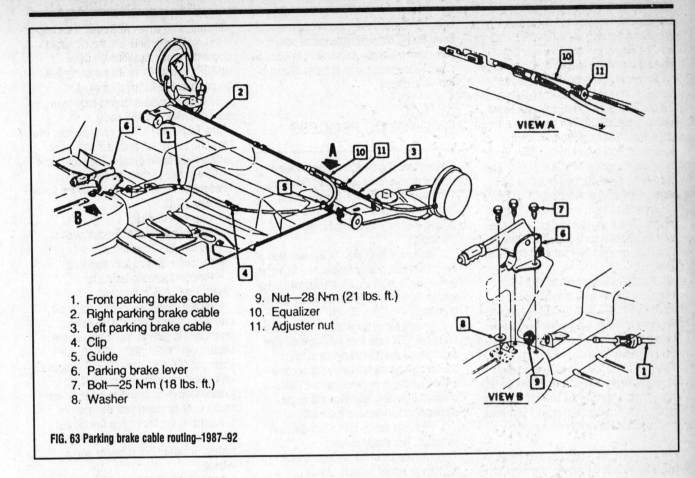

1. Front parking brake cable
2. Right parking brake cable
3. Left parking brake cable
4. Clip
5. Guide
6. Parking brake lever
7. Bolt—25 N·m (18 lbs. ft.)
8. Washer
9. Nut—28 N·m (21 lbs. ft.)
10. Equalizer
11. Adjuster nut

FIG. 63 Parking brake cable routing–1987–92

ANTI-LOCK BRAKE SYSTEM

Description and Operation

ABS-VI has been designed to improve the controllability and steerability of a vehicle during braking that would cause one or more wheels to lock. ABS-VI accomplishes this objective by controlling the hydraulic pressure applied to each wheel brake.

BASIC KNOWLEDGE REQUIRED

Before using this section, it is important that you have a basic knowledge of the following items. Without this basic knowledge, it will be difficult to use the diagnostic procedures contained in this section.

Basic Electrical Circuits — You should understand the basic theory of electricity and know the meaning of voltage, current (amps) and resistance (ohms). You should understand what happens in a circuit with an open or shorted wire. You should be able to read and understand a wiring diagram.

Use Of Circuit Testing Tools — You should know how to use a test light and how to use jumper wires to bypass components to test circuits. You should be familiar with the High Impedance Multimeter (DVM) J 34029–A. You should be able to measure voltage, resistance and current and be familiar with the meter controls and how to use them correctly.

ONBOARD DIAGNOSTICS

The ABS-VI contains sophisticated onboard diagnostics that, when accessed with a bidirectional "Scan" tool, are disigned to identify

the source of any system fault as specifically as possible, including whether or not the fault is intermittent. There are 58 diagnostic fault codes to assist the service technician with diagnosis. The last diagnostic fault code to occur is specifically identified, and specific ABS data is stored at the time of this fault, also, the first five codes set. Additionally, using a bidirectional "Scan" tool, each input and output can be monitored, thus enabling fault confirmation and repair verification. Manual control of components and automated functional tests are also available when using a GM approved "Scan" tool. Details of many of these functions are contained in the following sections.

ENHANCED DIAGNOSTICS

Enhanced Diagnostic Information, found in the CODE HISTORY function of the bidirectional "Scan" tool, is designed to provide the service technician with specific fault occurrence information. For each of the first five (5) and the very last diagnostic fault codes stored, data is stored to identify the specific fault code number, the number of failure occurrences, and the number of drive cycles since the failure first and last occurred (a drive cycle occurs when the ignition is turned "ON" and the vehicle is driven faster than 10 mph). However, if a fault is present, the drive cycle counter will increment by turning the ignition "ON" and "OFF". These first five (5) diagnostic fault codes are also stored in the order of occurrence. The order in which the first 5 faults occurred can be useful in determining if a previous fault is linked to the most recent faults, such as an intermittent wheel speed sensor which later becomes completely open.

During difficult diagnosis situations, this information can be used to identify fault occurrence trends. Does the fault occur more frequently now than it did during the last time when it only failed 1 out of 35 drive cycles? Did the fault only occur once over a large number of drive cycles, indication an unusual condition present when the fault occurred? Does the fault occur infrequently over a large number of drive cycles, indication special diagnosis techniques may be required to identify the source of the fault?

If a fault occurred 1 out of 20 drive cycles, the fault is intermittent and has not reoccurred for 19 drive cycles. This fault may be difficult or impossible to duplicate and may have been caused by a severe vehicle impact (large pot hole, speed bump at high speed, etc.) that momentarily opened an electrical connector or caused unusual vehicle suspension movement. Problem resolution is unlikely, and the problem may never reoccur (check diagnostic aids proved for that code). If the fault occurred 3 out of 15 drive cycles, the odds of finding the cause are still not good, but you know how often it occurs and you can determine whether or not the fault is becoming more frequent based on an additional or past occurances visit if the source of the problem can not or could not be found. If the fault occurred 10 out of 20 drive cycles, the odds of finding the cause are very good, as the fault may be easily reproduced.

By using the additional fault data, you can also determine if a failure is randomly intermittent or if it has not reoccurred for long periods of time due to weather changes or a repair prior to this visit. Say a diagnostic fault code occurred 10 of 20 drive cycles but has not reoccurred for 10 drive cycles. This means the failure occurred 10 of 10 drive cycles but has not reoccurred since. A significant environmental change or a repair

occurred 10 drive cycles ago. A repair may not be necessary if a recent repair can be confirmed. If no repair was made, the service can focus on diagnosis techniques used to locate difficult to recreate problems.

DIAGNOSTIC PROCESS

When servicing the ABS-VI, the following steps should be followed in order. Failure to follow thest steps may result in the loss of important diagnostic data and may lead to difficult and time consuming diagnosis procedures.

1. Using a bidirectional "Scan" tool, read all current and history diagnostic codes. Be certain to note which codes are current diagnostic code failures. DO NOT CLEAR CODES unless directed to do so.

2. Using a bidirectional "Scan" tool, read the CODE HISTORY data. Note the diagnostic fault codes stored and their frequency of failure. Specifically note the last failure that occurred and the conditions present when this failure occurred. This "last failure" should be the starting point for diagnosis and repair.

3. Perform a vehicle preliminary diagnosis inspection. This should include:

   a. Inspection of the compact master cylinder for proper brake fluid level.

   b. Inspection of the ABS hydraulic modulator for any leaks or wiring damage.

   c. Inspection of brake components at all four (4) wheels. Verify no drag exists. Also verify proper brake apply operation.

   d. Inspection for worn or damaged wheel bearings that allow a wheel to "wobble".

   e. Inspection of the wheel speed sensors and their wiring. Verify correct air gap range, solid sensor attachment, undamaged sensor toothed ring, and undamaged wiring, especially at vehicle attachment points.

   f. Verify proper outer CV joint alignment and operation.

   g. Verify tires meet legal tread depth requirements.

4. If no codes are present, or mechanical component failure codes are present, perform the automated modulator test using the Tech 1 or T-100 to isolate the cause of the problem. If the failure is intermittent and not reproducible, test drive the vehicle while using the automatic snapshot feature of the bidirectional "Scan" tool.

Perform normal acceleration, stopping, and turning maneuvers. If this does not reproduce the failure, perform an ABS stop, on a low coefficient surface such as gravel, from approximately 30–50 mph (48–80 km/h)

while triggering on any ABS code. If the failure is still not reproducible, use the enhanced diagnostic information found in CODE HISTORY to determine whether or not this failure should be further diagnosed.

5. Once all system failures have been corrected, clear the ABS codes.

The Tech 1 and T-100, when plugged into the ALDL connector, becomes part of the vehicle's electronic system. The Tech 1 and T-100 can also perform the following functions on components linked by the Serial Data Link (SDL):

- Display ABS data
- Display and clear ABS trouble codes
- Control ABS components
- Perform extensive ABS diagnosis
- Provide diagnostic testing for "Intermittent" ABS conditions.

Each test mode has specific diagnosis capabilities which depend upon various keystrokes. In general, five (5) keys control sequencing: "YES," "NO", "EXIT", "UP" arrow and "DOWN" arrow. The FO through F9 keys select operating modes, perform functions within an operating mode, or enter trouble code or model year designations.

In general, the Tech 1 has five (5) test modes for diagnosing the antilock brake system. The five (5) test modes are as follows:

MODE FO: DATA LIST — In this test mode, the Tech 1 continuously monitors wheel speed data, brake switch status and other inputs and outputs.

MODE F1: CODE HISTORY — In this mode, fault code history data is displayed. This data includes how many ignition cycles since the fault code occurred, along with other ABS information. The first five (5) and last fault codes set are included in the ABS history data.

MODE F2: TROUBLE CODES — In this test mode, trouble codes stored by the EBCM, both current ignition cycle and history, may be displayed or cleared.

MODE F3: ABS SNAPSHOT — In this test mode, the Tech 1 captures ABS data before and after a fault occurrence or a forced manual trigger.

MODE F4: ABS TESTS — In this test mode, the Tech 1 performs hydraulic modulator functional tests to assist in problem isolation during troubleshooting. Included here is manual control of the motors which is used prior to bleeding the brake system.

Press F7 to covert from English to metric.

DISPLAYING CODES

Diagnostic fault codes can only be read through the use of a bidirectional "Scan" tool. There are no provisions for "Flash Code" diagnostics.

CLEARING CODES

The trouble codes in EBCM memory are erased in one of two ways:
1. Tech 1 "Clear Codes" selection.
2. Ignition cycle default.

These two methods are detailed below. Be sure to verify proper system operation and absence of codes when clearing procedure is completed.

The EBCM will not permit code clearing until all of the codes have been displayed. Also, codes cannot be cleared by unplugging the EBCM, disconnecting the battery cables, or turning the ignition "OFF" (except on an ignition cycle default).

Tech 1 "Clear Codes" Method

Select F2 for trouble codes. After codes have been viewed completely, Tech 1 will ask, "CLEAR ABS CODES"; ANSWER "yes." Tech 1 will then read, "DISPLAY CODE HIST. DATA"? "LOST" IF CODES CLEARED. "NO" TO CLEAR CODES. Answer "NO" and codes will be cleared.

Ignition Cycle Default

If no diagnostic fault code occurs for 100 drive cycles (a drive cycle occurs when the ignition is turned "ON" and the vehicle is driven faster than 10 mph), any existing fault codes are cleared from the EBCM memory.

INTERMITTENT FAILURES

As with most electronic systems, intermittent failures may be difficult to accurately diagnose. The following is a method to try to isolate an intermittent failure especially wheel speed circuitry failures.

If an ABS fault occurs, the "ABS" warning light indicator will be "ON" during the ignition cycle in which the fault was detected. If it is an intermittent problem which seems to have corrected itself ("ABS" warning light "OFF"), a history trouble code will be stored. Also stored will be the history data of the code at the time the fault occurred. The Tech 1 must be used to read ABS history data.

INTERMITTENTS AND POOR CONNECTIONS

Most intermittents are caused by faulty electrical connections or wiring, although occassionally a sticking relay or solenoid can be a problem. Some items to check are:
1. Poor mating of connector halves, or terminals not fully seated in the connector body (backed out).
2. Dirt or corrosion on the terminals. The terminals must be clean and free of any foreign material which could impede proper terminal contact.
3. Damaged connector body, exposing the terminals to moisture and dirt, as well as not maintaining proper terminal orientation with the component or mating connector.
4. Improperly formed or damaged terminals. All connector terminals in problem circuits should be checked carefully to ensure good contact tension. Use a corresponding mating terminal to check for proper tension. Refer to "Checking Terminal Contact" in this section for the specific procedure.
5. The J 35616-A Connector Test Adapter Kit must be used whenever a diagnostic procedure requests checking or probing a terminal. Using the adapter will ensure that no damage to the terminal will occur, as well as giving an idea of whether contact tension is sufficient. If contact tension seems incorrect, refer to "Checking Terminal Contact" in this section for specifics.
6. Poor terminal-to-wire connection. Checking this requires removing the terminal from the connector body. Some conditions which fall under this description are poor crimps, poor solder joints, crimping over wire insulation rather than the wire itself, corrosion in the wire-to-terminal contact area, etc.
7. Wire insulation which is rubbed through, causing an intermittent short as the bare area touches other wiring or parts of the vehicle.
8. Wiring broken inside the insulation. This condition could cause a continuity check to show a good circuit, but if only 1 or 2 strands of a multi-strand type wire are intact, resistance could be far too high.

Checking Terminal Contact

When diagnosing an electrical system that uses Metri-Pack 150/280/480/630 series terminals (refer to Terminal Repair Kit J 38125-A instruction manual J 38125-4 for terminal identification), it is important to check terminal contact between a connector and component, or between inline connectors, before replacing a suspect component.

Frequently, a diagnostic chart leads to a step that reads "Check for poor connection". Mating terminals must be inspected to ensure good terminal contact. A poor connection between the male and female terminal at a connector may be the result of contamination or deformation.

Contamination is caused by the connector halves being improperly connected, a missing or damaged connector seal, or damage to the connector itself, exposing the terminals to moisture and dirt. Contamination, usually in underhood or underbody connectors, leads to terminal corrosion, causing an open circuit or an intermittently open circuit.

Deformation is caused by probing the mating side of a connector terminal without the proper adapter, improperly joining the connector halves or repeatedly separating and joining the connector halves. Deformation, usually to the female terminal contact tang, can result in poor terminal contact causing an open or intermittently open circuit.

Follow the procedure below to check terminal contact.
1. Separate the connector halves. Refer to Terminal Repair Kit J 38125-A instruction manual J 38125-4, if available.
2. Inspect the connector halves for contamination. Contamination will result in a white or green buildup within the connector body or between terminals, causing high terminal resistance, intermittent contact or an open circuit. An underhood or underbody connector that shows signs of contamination should be replaced in its entirety: terminals, seals, and connector body.
3. Using an equivalent male terminal from the Terminal Repair Kit J 38125-A, check the retention force of the female terminal in question by inserting and removing the male terminal to the female terminal in the connector body. Good terminal contact will require a certain amount of force to separate the terminals.
4. Using an equivalent female terminal from the Terminal Repair Kit J 38125-A, compare the retention force of this terminal to the female terminal in question by joining and separating the male terminal to the female terminal in question. If the retention force is significantly different between the two female terminals, replace the female terminal in question, using a terminal from Terminal Repair Kit J 38125-A.

Anti-Lock Brake System Service

♦ SEE FIGS. 64-76

Precaution

Failure to observe the following precautions may result in system damage.

• Before performing electric arc welding on the vehicle, disconnect the Electronic Brake Control Module (EBCM) and the hydraulic modulator connectors.

• When performing painting work on the vehicle, do not expose the Electronic Brake Control Module (EBCM) to temperatures in excess of 185°F (85°C) for longer than 2 hrs. The system may be exposed to temperatures up to 200°F (95°C) for less than 15 min.

• Never disconnect or connect the Electronic Brake Control Module (EBCM) or hydraulic modulator connectors with the ignition switch ON.

• Never disassemble any component of the Anti-Lock Brake System (ABS) which is designated non-serviceable; the component must be replaced as an assembly.

• When filling the master cylinder, always use Delco Supreme 11 brake fluid or equivalent, which meets DOT-3 specifications; petroleum base fluid will destroy the rubber parts.

Electrical Connectors

Some ABS-VI components are equipped with electrical connectors using a Connector Position Assurance (CPA) lock.

1. Remove the lock before separating the electrical connectors.

2. Be careful not to damage the locking pin during removal.

3. Make sure that the rubber connector seal is in place on the connector before and after connection.

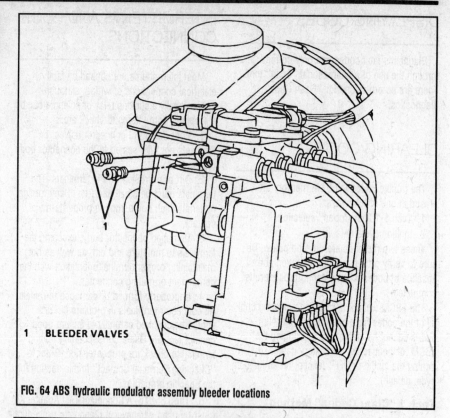

1   BLEEDER VALVES

FIG. 64 ABS hydraulic modulator assembly bleeder locations

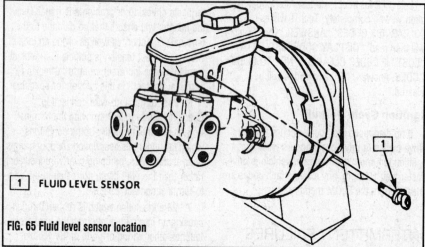

1   FLUID LEVEL SENSOR

FIG. 65 Fluid level sensor location

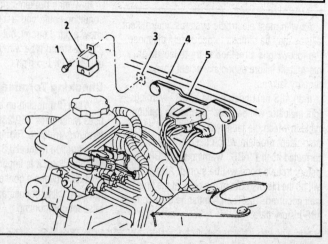

1	BOLT SCREW
2	ENABLE RELAY
3	CLENCH NUT
4	DASH PANEL
5	EBCM

FIG. 66 The Enable relay location

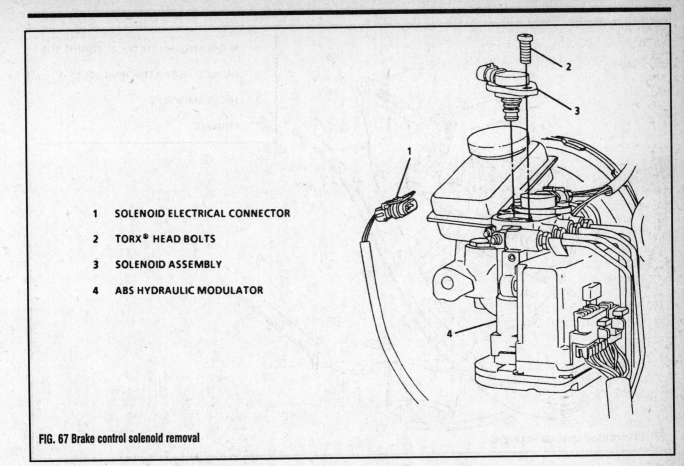

1   SOLENOID ELECTRICAL CONNECTOR

2   TORX® HEAD BOLTS

3   SOLENOID ASSEMBLY

4   ABS HYDRAULIC MODULATOR

FIG. 67 Brake control solenoid removal

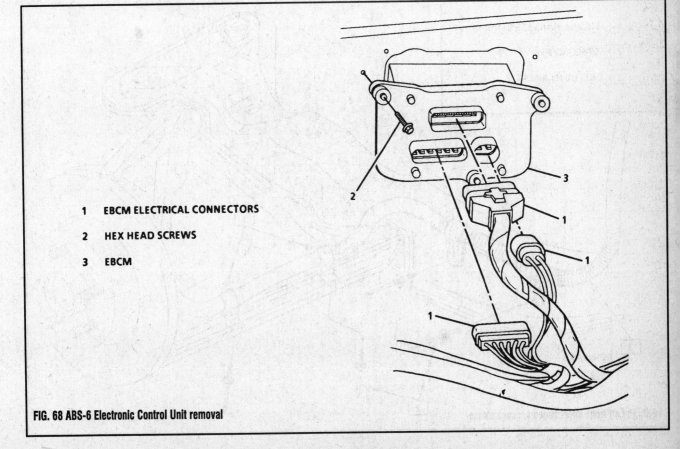

1   EBCM ELECTRICAL CONNECTORS

2   HEX HEAD SCREWS

3   EBCM

FIG. 68 ABS-6 Electronic Control Unit removal

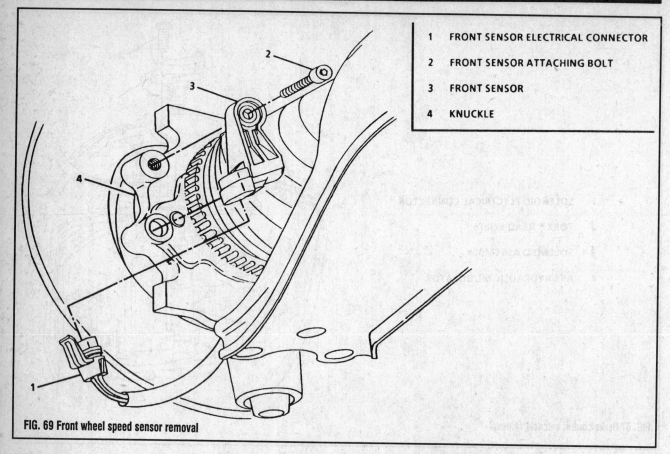

1   FRONT SENSOR ELECTRICAL CONNECTOR

2   FRONT SENSOR ATTACHING BOLT

3   FRONT SENSOR

4   KNUCKLE

FIG. 69 Front wheel speed sensor removal

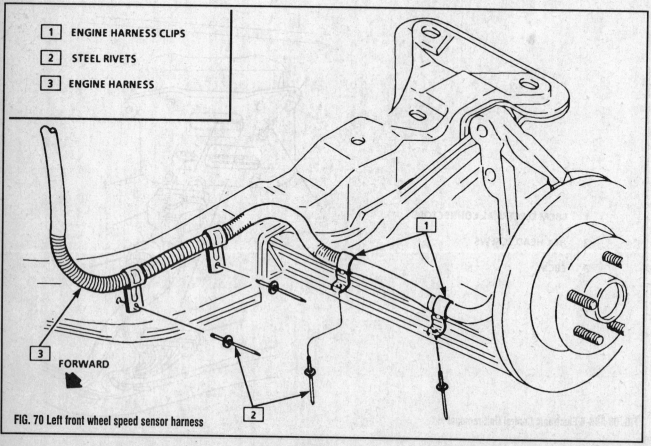

1   ENGINE HARNESS CLIPS

2   STEEL RIVETS

3   ENGINE HARNESS

FORWARD

FIG. 70 Left front wheel speed sensor harness

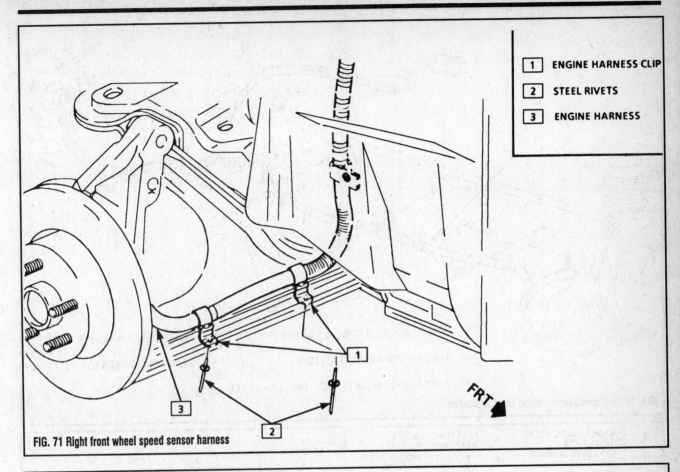

1	ENGINE HARNESS CLIP
2	STEEL RIVETS
3	ENGINE HARNESS

FRT

FIG. 71 Right front wheel speed sensor harness

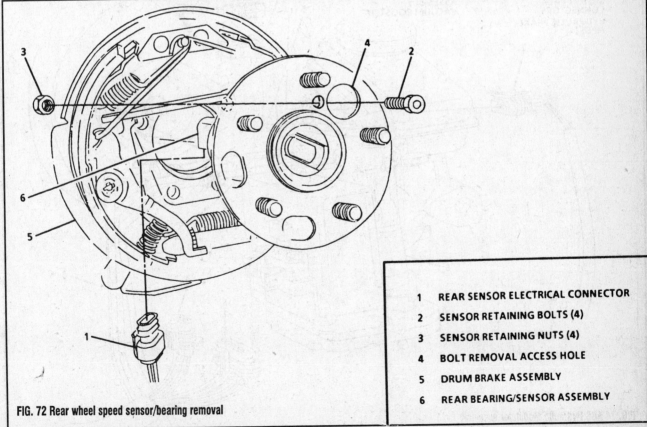

1	REAR SENSOR ELECTRICAL CONNECTOR
2	SENSOR RETAINING BOLTS (4)
3	SENSOR RETAINING NUTS (4)
4	BOLT REMOVAL ACCESS HOLE
5	DRUM BRAKE ASSEMBLY
6	REAR BEARING/SENSOR ASSEMBLY

FIG. 72 Rear wheel speed sensor/bearing removal

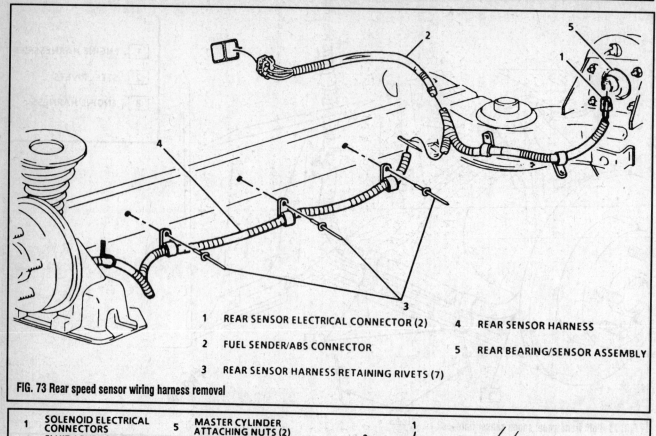

1	REAR SENSOR ELECTRICAL CONNECTOR (2)	4	REAR SENSOR HARNESS
2	FUEL SENDER/ABS CONNECTOR	5	REAR BEARING/SENSOR ASSEMBLY
3	REAR SENSOR HARNESS RETAINING RIVETS (7)		

FIG. 73 Rear speed sensor wiring harness removal

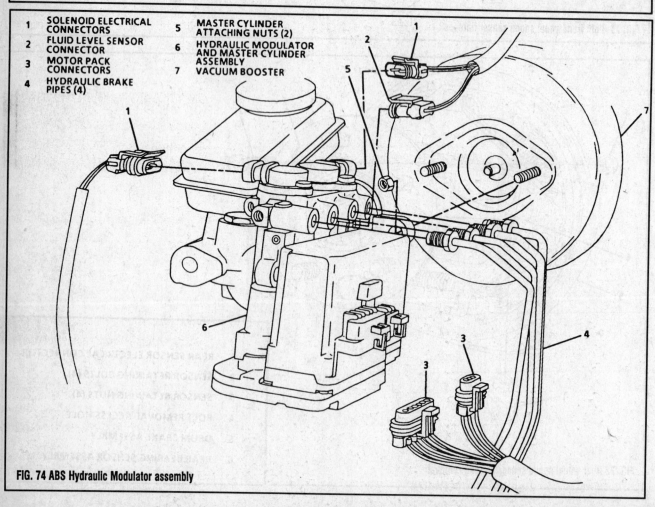

1	SOLENOID ELECTRICAL CONNECTORS	5	MASTER CYLINDER ATTACHING NUTS (2)
2	FLUID LEVEL SENSOR CONNECTOR	6	HYDRAULIC MODULATOR AND MASTER CYLINDER ASSEMBLY
3	MOTOR PACK CONNECTORS	7	VACUUM BOOSTER
4	HYDRAULIC BRAKE PIPES (4)		

FIG. 74 ABS Hydraulic Modulator assembly

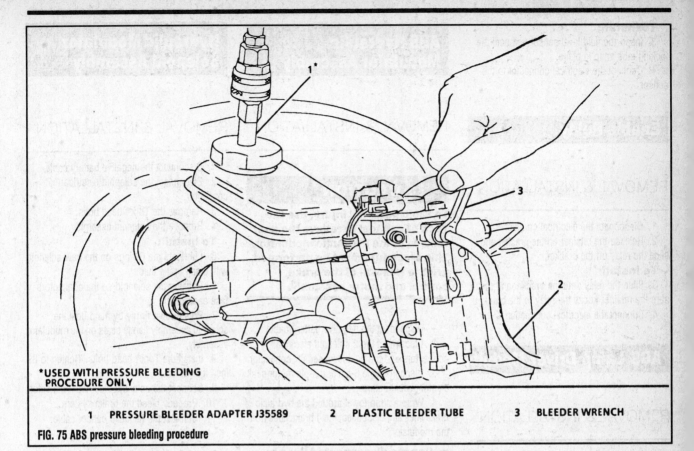

*USED WITH PRESSURE BLEEDING
PROCEDURE ONLY

| 1 | PRESSURE BLEEDER ADAPTER J35589 | 2 | PLASTIC BLEEDER TUBE | 3 | BLEEDER WRENCH |

FIG. 75 ABS pressure bleeding procedure

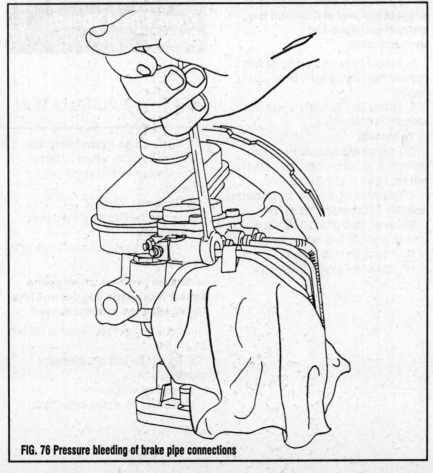

FIG. 76 Pressure bleeding of brake pipe connections

4. Always install the lock after ther
connection is made.

ABS Hydraulic Modulator Assembly Bleeder Valves

REMOVAL & INSTALLATION

1. Remove the bleeder valve or valves.
2. Install the bleeeder valve and tighten to 65
inch lbs. (7 Nm).

Fluid Level Sensor

REMOVAL & INSTALLATION

1. Disconnect the electrical connection from
the fluid level sensor.
2. Remove the fluid level sensor using needle
nose pliers to compress the switch locking tabs
at the inboard side of the master cylinder.

To Install:

3. Insert the fluid level sensor unit until the locking tabs snap in place.

4. Connect the electrical connector to the sensor.

Enable Relay

REMOVAL & INSTALLATION

1. Disconnect the electrical connection.

2. Release the retainer on the bracket and slide the relay off the bracket.

To Install:

3. Slide the relay onto the bracket and make sure the retainer kocks the relay to the bracket.

4. Connect the electrical connection.

ABS Lamp Driver Module

REMOVAL & INSTALLATION

1. Disconnect the negative battery cable.

2. Remove the right side lower sound insulator panel.

3. Slide the glove box all the way out or remove it completely.

4. The lamp driver module is above the cruise control module taped to the instrument panel harness and is light green in color.

5. Open the connector and slide the circuit board out of the connector.

To Install:

6. Install the circuit board to the connector.

7. Reposition the connector to the instrument panel harness and make sure it is retaped in place.

8. Slide the glove box back into the dash or reinstall the screws, if removed.

9. Install the right side lower sound insulator panel.

10. Connect the negative battery cable.

ABS Hydraulic Modulator Assembly

REMOVAL & INSTALLATION

❊❊ CAUTION

To avoid personal injury, use the Tech I Scan tool to relieve the gear tension in the hydraulic modulator. This procedure must be performed prior to removal of the brake control and motor assembly.

1. Disconnect the negative battery cable.

2. Disconnect the 2 solenoid electrical connectors and the fluid level sensor connector.

3. Disconnect the 6-pin and 3-pin motor pack electrical connectors.

4. Wrap a shop towel around the hydraulic brake lines and disconnect the 4 brake lines from the modulator.

➡ **Cap the disconnected lines to prevent the loss of fluid and the entry of moisture and contaminants.**

5. Remove the 2 nuts attaching the ABS hydraulic modulator assembly to the vacuum booster.

6. Remove the ABS hydraulic modulator assembly from the vehicle.

To Install:

7. Install the ABS hydraulic modulator assembly to the vehicle. Install the 2 attaching nuts and tighten to 20 ft. lbs. (27 Nm).

8. Connect the 4 brake pipes to the modulator assembly. Tighten to 13 ft. lbs. (17 Nm).

9. Connect the 6-pin and 3-pin electrical connectors and the fluid level sensor connector.

10. Properly bleed the system.

11. Connect the negative battery cable.

Hydraulic Modulator Solenoid Assembly

REMOVAL & INSTALLATION

1. Disconnect the negative battery cable.

2. Disconnect the solenoid electrical connector.

3. Remove the Torx® head bolts.

4. Remove the solenoid assembly.

To Install:

5. Lubricate the O-rings on the new solenoid with clean brake fluid.

6. Position the solenoid so the connectors face each other.

7. Press down firmly by hand until the solenoid assembly flange seats on the modulator assembly.

8. Install the Torx® head bolts. Tighten to 39 inch lbs. (5 Nm).

9. Connect the solenoid electrical connector.

10. Properly bleed the brake system.

11. Connect the negative battery cable.

Front Wheel Speed Sensor

REMOVAL & INSTALLATION

1. Disconnect the negative battery cable.

2. Raise and safely support the vehicle.

3. Disconnect the front sensor electrical connector.

4. Remove the Torx® bolt.

5. Remove the front wheel speed sensor.

To Install:

6. Install the front wheel speed sensor on the mounting bracket.

➡ **Ensure the front wheel speed sensor is properly aligned and lays flat against the bracket bosses.**

7. Install the Torx® bolt. Tighten to 106 inch lbs. (12 Nm).

8. Connect the front sensor electrical connector.

9. Lower the vehicle.

10. Connect the negative battery cable.

Rear Wheel Bearing And Speed Sensor Assembly

REMOVAL & INSTALLATION

➡ **The rear integral wheel bearing and sensor assembly must be replaced as a unit.**

1. Disconnect the negative battery cable.
2. Raise and safely support the vehicle.
3. Remove the rear wheel.
4. Remove the brake drum.
5. Disconnect the rear sensor electrical connector.
6. Remove the bolts and nuts attaching the rear wheel bearing and speed sensor assembly to the backing plate.

➡ **With the rear wheel bearing and speed sensor attaching bolts and nuts removed, the drum brake assembly is supported only by the brake line connection. To avoid bending or damage to the brake line, do not bump or exert force on the assembly.**

7. Remove the rear wheel bearing and speed sensor assembly.

To Install:

8. Install the rear wheel bearing and speed sensor assembly by aligning the bolt hoses in the wheel bearing and speed sensor assembly, drum brake assembly and rear suspension bracket. Install the attaching bolts and nuts. Tighten to 38 ft. lbs. (52 Nm).
9. Connect the rear speed sensor electrical connector.
10. Install the brake drum.
11. Install the rear wheel.
12. Lower the vehicle.
13. Connect the negative battery cable.

ABS Manual Bleeding Procedure

Brake Control Assembly

➡ **Only use brake fluid from a sealed container which meets DOT 3 specifications.**

1. Clean the area around the master cylinder cap.
2. Check fluid level in master cylinder reservoir and top-up, as necessary. Check fluid level frequently during bleeding procedure.
3. Attach a bleeder hose to the rear bleeder valve on the brake control assembly. Slowly open the bleeder valve.
4. Depress the brake pedal slowly until fluid begins to flow.
5. Close the valve and release the brake pedal.
6. Repeat for the front bleeder valve on the brake control assembly.

➡ **When fluid flows from both bleeder valves, the brake control assembly is sufficiently full of fluid. However, it may not be completely purged of air. Bleed the individual wheel calipers/cylinders and return to the control assembly to purge the remaining air.**

Wheel Calipers/Cylinders

➡ **Prior to bleeding the rear brakes, the rear displacement cylinder must be returned to the top-most position. This can be accomplished using the Tech I Scan tool or T-100 (CAMS), by entering the manual control function and applying the rear motor.**

If a Tech I or T-100 are unavailable, bleed the front brakes. Ensure the pedal is firm. Carefully drive the vehicle to a speed above 4 mph to cause the ABS system to initialize. This will return the rear displacement cylinder to the top-most position.

1. Clean the area around the master cylinder cap.
2. Check fluid level in master cylinder reservoir and top-up, as necessary. Check fluid level frequently during bleeding procedure.
3. Raise and safely support the vehicle.
4. Attach a bleeder hose to the bleeder valve of the right rear wheel and submerge the opposite hose in a clean container partially filled with brake fluid.
5. Open the bleeder valve.
6. Slowly depress the brake pedal.
7. Close the bleeder valve and release the brake pedal.
8. Wait 5 seconds.
9. Repeat Steps 5–8 until the pedal begins to feel firm and no air bubbles appear in the bleeder hose.
10. Repeat Steps 5–9, until the pedal is firm and no air bubbles appear in the brake hose, for the remaining wheels in the following order:
    a. left rear
    b. right front
    c. left front.
11. Lower the vehicle.

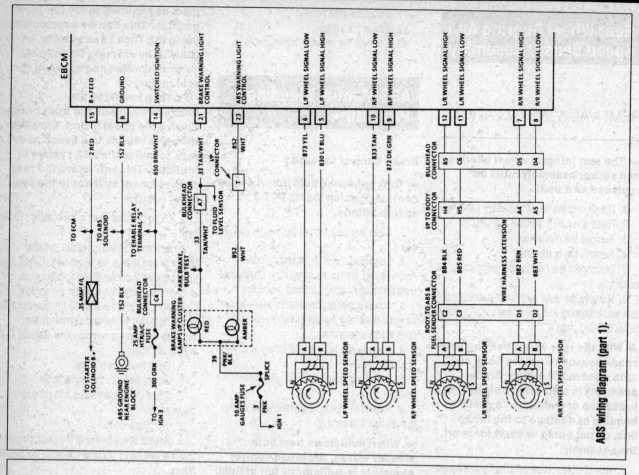

ABS wiring diagram (part 1).

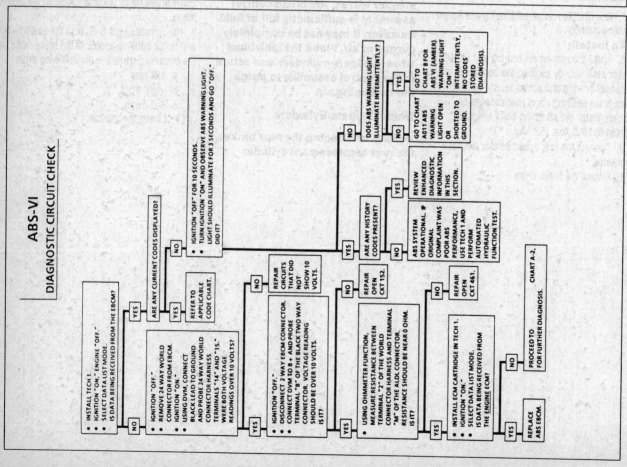

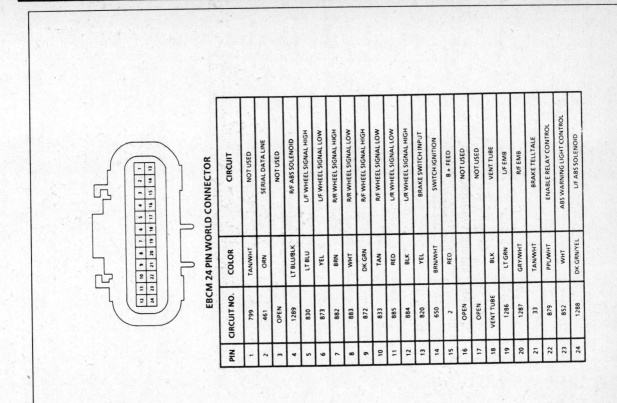

EBCM 24 PIN WORLD CONNECTOR

PIN	CIRCUIT NO.	COLOR	CIRCUIT
1	799	TAN/WHT	NOT USED
2	461	ORN	SERIAL DATA LINE
3	OPEN		NOT USED
4	1289	LT BLU/BLK	R/F ABS SOLENOID
5	830	LT BLU	L/F WHEEL SIGNAL HIGH
6	873	YEL	L/F WHEEL SIGNAL HIGH
7	882	BRN	R/R WHEEL SIGNAL HIGH
8	883	WHT	R/R WHEEL SIGNAL LOW
9	872	DK GRN	R/F WHEEL SIGNAL HIGH
10	833	TAN	R/F WHEEL SIGNAL LOW
11	885	RED	L/R WHEEL SIGNAL LOW
12	884	BLK	L/R WHEEL SIGNAL HIGH
13	820	YEL	BRAKE SWITCH INPUT
14	650	BRN/WHT	SWITCH IGNITION
15	2	RED	B + FEED
16	OPEN		NOT USED
17	OPEN		NOT USED
18	VENT TUBE	BLK	VENT TUBE
19	1286	LT GRN	L/F EMB
20	1287	GRY/WHT	R/F EMB
21	33	TAN/WHT	BRAKE TELLTALE
22	879	PPL/WHT	ENABLE RELAY CONTROL
23	852	WHT	ABS WARNING LIGHT CONTROL
24	1288	DK GRN/YEL	L/F ABS SOLENOID

EBCM connector view (part 1).

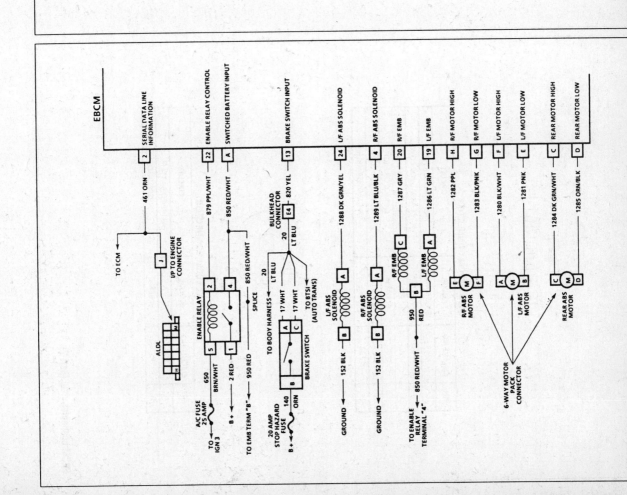

ABS wiring diagram (part 2).

CHART A

ABS (AMBER) WARNING LIGHT "ON" CONSTANTLY, NO CODES STORED

- USING TECH 1, COMMAND (AMBER) WARNING LIGHT "OFF."
- WARNING LIGHT SHOULD BE "OFF."
- IS IT?

NO → REFER TO SECTION 8C FOR FURTHER DIAGNOSIS.

YES → FAULT IS NOT PRESENT AT THIS TIME.

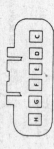

6 WAY EBCM CONNECTOR

PIN	CIRCUIT NO.	COLOR	CIRCUIT
C	1284	DK GRN/WHT	REAR MOTOR HIGH
D	1285	ORN/BLK	REAR MOTOR LOW
E	1281	PNK	L/F MOTOR LOW
F	1280	BLK/WHT	L/F MOTOR HIGH
G	1283	BLK/PNK	R/F MOTOR LOW
H	1282	PPL	R/F MOTOR HIGH

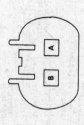

2 WAY EBCM CONNECTOR

PIN	CIRCUIT NO.	COLOR	CIRCUIT
A	850	RED/WHT	SWITCHED BATTERY INPUT
B	152	BLK	GROUND

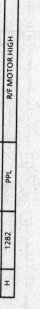

EBCM connector view (part 2).

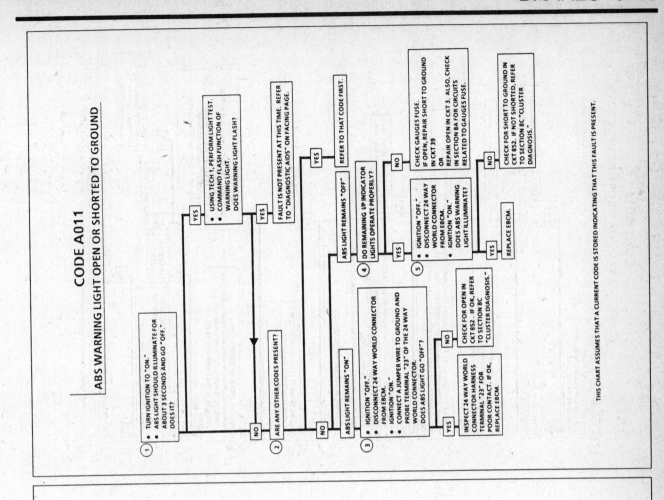

CODE A011
ABS WARNING LIGHT OPEN OR SHORTED TO GROUND

1
- TURN IGNITION TO "ON."
- ABS LIGHT SHOULD ILLUMINATE FOR ABOUT 3 SECONDS AND GO "OFF."
  DOES IT?

YES → USING TECH 1, PERFORM LIGHT TEST. COMMAND FLASH FUNCTION OF WARNING LIGHT.
DOES WARNING LIGHT FLASH?

YES → FAULT IS NOT PRESENT AT THIS TIME. REFER TO "DIAGNOSTIC AIDS" ON FACING PAGE.

NO

2 ARE ANY OTHER CODES PRESENT?

YES → REFER TO THAT CODE FIRST.

NO

ABS LIGHT REMAINS "ON"

ABS LIGHT REMAINS "OFF"

3
- IGNITION "OFF."
- DISCONNECT 24 WAY WORLD CONNECTOR FROM EBCM.
- IGNITION "ON."
- CONNECT A JUMPER WIRE TO GROUND AND PROBE TERMINAL "23" OF THE 24 WAY WORLD CONNECTOR.
  DOES ABS LIGHT GO "OFF"?

4 DO REMAINING I/P INDICATOR LIGHTS OPERATE PROPERLY?

YES

INSPECT 24 WAY WORLD CONNECTOR HARNESS TERMINAL "23" FOR POOR CONTACT. IF OK, REPLACE EBCM.

NO

CHECK FOR OPEN IN CKT 852. IF OK, REFER TO SECTION 8C "CLUSTER DIAGNOSIS."

NO → CHECK GAUGES FUSE. IF OPEN, REPAIR SHORT TO GROUND IN CKT 39 OR REPAIR OPEN IN CKT 3. ALSO, CHECK IN SECTION 8A FOR CIRCUITS RELATED TO GAUGES FUSE.

YES

5
- IGNITION "OFF."
- DISCONNECT 24 WAY WORLD CONNECTOR FROM EBCM.
- IGNITION "ON."
  DOES ABS WARNING LIGHT ILLUMINATE?

YES → REPLACE EBCM.

NO → CHECK FOR SHORT TO GROUND IN CKT 852. IF NOT SHORTED, REFER TO SECTION 8C "CLUSTER DIAGNOSIS."

THIS CHART ASSUMES THAT A CURRENT CODE IS STORED INDICATING THAT THIS FAULT IS PRESENT.

CHART B
ABS-VI (AMBER) WARNING LIGHT "ON" INTERMITTENTLY, NO CODES STORED

NOTICE: DIAGNOSTIC CIRCUIT CHECK MUST BE COMPLETED FIRST BEFORE USING THIS CHART.

- IGNITION "OFF."
- DISCONNECT 24 WAY WORLD CONNECTOR.
- CONNECT A TEST LIGHT TO GROUND AND PROBE TERMINAL "15" OF THE 24 WAY WORLD HARNESS CONNECTOR.
- OBSERVE TEST LIGHT WHEN MOVING WIRE HARNESS AND CONNECTORS.
  TEST LIGHT SHOULD STAY ON STEADY.
  DOES IT?

YES

- CONNECT TEST LIGHT BETWEEN GROUND AND 24 WAY WORLD CONNECTOR HARNESS TERMINAL "14."
- TURN IGNITION "ON" AND OBSERVE TEST LIGHT WHEN MOVING WIRE HARNESS AND CONNECTORS.
  TEST LIGHT SHOULD STAY ON STEADY.
  DOES IT?

NO → REPAIR INTERMITTENT CONNECTION IN CKT 2.

YES

PROBLEM IS NOT PRESENT AT THIS TIME. INTERMITTENTS COULD BE CAUSED BY INCORRECT WIRING HARNESS ROUTING OR LOOSE GROUND CONNECTIONS.

NO → REPAIR INTERMITTENT CONNECTION IN CKT 650.

THIS CHART ASSUMES THAT A CURRENT CODE IS STORED INDICATING THAT THIS FAULT IS PRESENT.

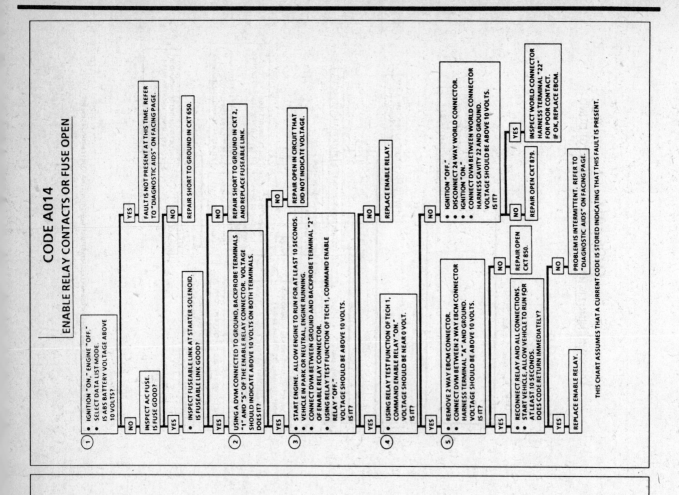

CODE A014

ENABLE RELAY CONTACTS OR FUSE OPEN

(1)
- IGNITION "ON," ENGINE "OFF."
- SELECT DATA LIST MODE.
- IS ABS BATTERY VOLTAGE ABOVE 10 VOLTS?

YES → FAULT IS NOT PRESENT AT THIS TIME. REFER TO "DIAGNOSTIC AIDS" ON FACING PAGE.

NO →
- INSPECT A/C FUSE.
- IS FUSE GOOD?

NO → REPAIR SHORT TO GROUND IN CKT 650.

YES →
- INSPECT FUSEABLE LINK AT STARTER SOLENOID.
- IS FUSEABLE LINK GOOD?

NO → REPAIR SHORT TO GROUND IN CKT 2, AND REPLACE FUSEABLE LINK.

YES →
(2)
- USING A DVM CONNECTED TO GROUND, BACKPROBE TERMINALS "1" AND "5" OF THE ENABLE RELAY CONNECTOR. VOLTAGE SHOULD INDICATE ABOVE 10 VOLTS ON BOTH TERMINALS. DOES IT?

NO → REPAIR OPEN IN CIRCUIT THAT DID NOT INDICATE VOLTAGE.

YES →
(3)
- START ENGINE. ALLOW ENGINE TO RUN FOR AT LEAST 10 SECONDS.
- VEHICLE IN PARK OR NEUTRAL, ENGINE RUNNING.
- CONNECT DVM BETWEEN GROUND AND BACKPROBE TERMINAL "2" OF ENABLE RELAY CONNECTOR.
- USING RELAY TEST FUNCTION OF TECH 1, COMMAND ENABLE RELAY "OFF."
- VOLTAGE SHOULD BE ABOVE 10 VOLTS. IS IT?

NO → REPLACE ENABLE RELAY.

YES →
(4)
- USING RELAY TEST FUNCTION OF TECH 1, COMMAND ENABLE RELAY "ON." VOLTAGE SHOULD BE NEAR 0 VOLT. IS IT?

YES →
(5)
- REMOVE 2 WAY EBCM CONNECTOR.
- CONNECT DVM BETWEEN 2 WAY EBCM CONNECTOR HARNESS TERMINAL "A" AND GROUND. VOLTAGE SHOULD BE ABOVE 10 VOLTS. IS IT?

NO →
- IGNITION "OFF."
- DISCONNECT 24 WAY WORLD CONNECTOR.
- IGNITION "ON."
- CONNECT DVM BETWEEN WORLD CONNECTOR HARNESS CAVITY 22 AND GROUND. VOLTAGE SHOULD BE ABOVE 10 VOLTS. IS IT?

YES → INSPECT WORLD CONNECTOR HARNESS TERMINAL "22" FOR POOR CONTACT. IF OK, REPLACE EBCM.

NO → REPAIR OPEN CKT 879.

YES →
- REPAIR OPEN CKT 850.

NO →
- RECONNECT RELAY AND ALL CONNECTIONS. START VEHICLE. ALLOW VEHICLE TO RUN FOR AT LEAST 10 SECONDS. DOES CODE RETURN IMMEDIATELY?

YES → REPLACE ENABLE RELAY.

NO → PROBLEM IS INTERMITTENT. REFER TO "DIAGNOSTIC AIDS" ON FACING PAGE.

THIS CHART ASSUMES THAT A CURRENT CODE IS STORED INDICATING THAT THIS FAULT IS PRESENT.

CODE A013

ABS WARNING LIGHT CIRCUIT SHORTED TO BATTERY

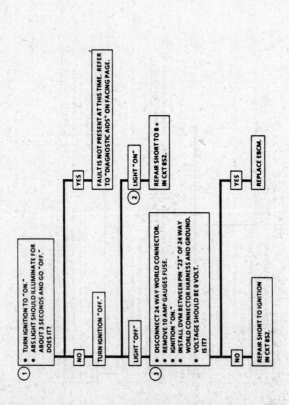

(1)
- TURN IGNITION TO "ON."
- ABS LIGHT SHOULD ILLUMINATE FOR ABOUT 3 SECONDS AND GO "OFF." DOES IT?

YES → FAULT IS NOT PRESENT AT THIS TIME. REFER TO "DIAGNOSTIC AIDS" ON FACING PAGE.

NO →
- TURN IGNITION "OFF."

LIGHT "OFF" →
(3)
- DISCONNECT 24 WAY WORLD CONNECTOR.
- REMOVE 10 AMP GAUGES FUSE.
- IGNITION "ON."
- INSTALL DVM BETWEEN PIN "23" OF 24 WAY WORLD CONNECTOR HARNESS AND GROUND. VOLTAGE SHOULD BE 0 VOLT. IS IT?

NO → REPAIR SHORT TO IGNITION IN CKT 852.

LIGHT "ON" →
(2)
- REPAIR SHORT TO B + IN CKT 852.

YES → REPLACE EBCM.

THIS CHART ASSUMES THAT A CURRENT CODE IS STORED INDICATING THAT THIS FAULT IS PRESENT.

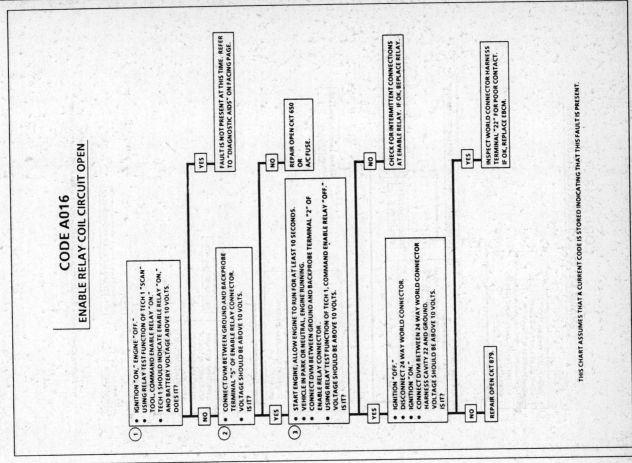

CODE A016
ENABLE RELAY COIL CIRCUIT OPEN

1.
- IGNITION "ON," ENGINE "OFF."
- USING RELAY TEST FUNCTION OF TECH 1 "SCAN" TOOL, COMMAND ENABLE RELAY "ON."
- TECH 1 SHOULD INDICATE ENABLE RELAY "ON," AND BATTERY VOLTAGE ABOVE 10 VOLTS. DOES IT?

YES → FAULT IS NOT PRESENT AT THIS TIME. REFER TO "DIAGNOSTIC AIDS" ON FACING PAGE.

NO →

2.
- CONNECT DVM BETWEEN GROUND AND BACKPROBE TERMINAL "5" OF ENABLE RELAY CONNECTOR. VOLTAGE SHOULD BE ABOVE 10 VOLTS. IS IT?

NO → REPAIR OPEN CKT 650 OR A/C FUSE.

YES →

3.
- START ENGINE, ALLOW ENGINE TO RUN FOR AT LEAST 10 SECONDS. VEHICLE IN PARK OR NEUTRAL, ENGINE RUNNING. CONNECT DVM BETWEEN GROUND AND BACKPROBE TERMINAL "2" OF ENABLE RELAY CONNECTOR.
- USING RELAY TEST FUNCTION OF TECH 1, COMMAND ENABLE RELAY "OFF." VOLTAGE SHOULD BE ABOVE 10 VOLTS. IS IT?

NO → CHECK FOR INTERMITTENT CONNECTIONS AT ENABLE RELAY. IF OK, REPLACE RELAY.

YES →

- IGNITION "OFF."
- DISCONNECT 24 WAY WORLD CONNECTOR.
- IGNITION "ON."
- CONNECT DVM BETWEEN 24 WAY WORLD CONNECTOR HARNESS CAVITY 22 AND GROUND. VOLTAGE SHOULD BE ABOVE 10 VOLTS. IS IT?

YES → INSPECT WORLD CONNECTOR HARNESS TERMINAL "22" FOR POOR CONTACT. IF OK, REPLACE EBCM.

NO → REPAIR OPEN CKT 879.

THIS CHART ASSUMES THAT A CURRENT CODE IS STORED INDICATING THAT THIS FAULT IS PRESENT.

CODE A015
ENABLE RELAY CONTACTS SHORTED TO BATTERY

ARE THERE ANY EMB CODES PRESENT?

YES → PROCEED TO THAT CODE FIRST.

NO →

1.
- START ENGINE, ALLOW ENGINE TO RUN FOR AT LEAST 10 SECONDS. VEHICLE IN PARK OR NEUTRAL, ENGINE RUNNING.
- USE RELAY TEST FUNCTION OF TECH 1 "SCAN" TOOL AND COMMAND ENABLE RELAY "OFF."
- TECH 1 SHOULD INDICATE ENABLE RELAY IS "OFF," AND BATTERY VOLTAGE LESS THAN 5 VOLTS. DOES IT?

YES → FAULT IS NOT PRESENT AT THIS TIME. REFER TO "DIAGNOSTIC AIDS" ON FACING PAGE.

NO →

2.
- IGNITION "OFF."
- DISCONNECT ENABLE RELAY.
- CONNECT DVM BETWEEN TERMINAL "4" OF ENABLE RELAY CONNECTOR AND GROUND. VOLTAGE SHOULD BE NEAR 0 VOLT. IS IT?

NO → REPAIR SHORT TO BATTERY IN CKT 850 ON CKT 950.

YES →

3.
- CONNECT DVM BETWEEN B + AND BACKPROBE TERMINAL "2" OF THE ENABLE RELAY CONNECTOR. VOLTAGE SHOULD BE NEAR 0 VOLT. IS IT?

YES → REPLACE ENABLE RELAY.

NO →

- DISCONNECT 24 WAY WORLD CONNECTOR.
- CONNECT DVM BETWEEN 24 WAY WORLD CONNECTOR HARNESS CAVITY 22 AND B +. VOLTAGE SHOULD BE 0 VOLT. IS IT?

YES → REPLACE EBCM.

NO → REPAIR SHORT TO GROUND IN CKT 879.

THIS CHART ASSUMES THAT A CURRENT CODE IS STORED INDICATING THAT THIS FAULT IS PRESENT.

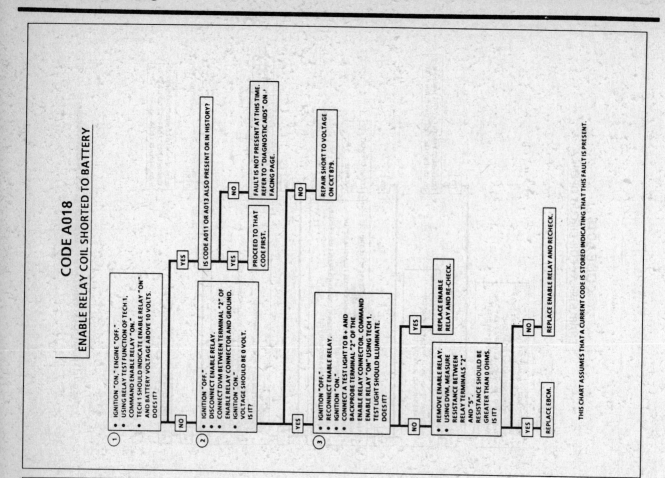

CODE A018

ENABLE RELAY COIL SHORTED TO BATTERY

① • IGNITION "ON." ENGINE "OFF."
  • USING RELAY TEST FUNCTION OF TECH 1, COMMAND ENABLE RELAY "ON."
  • TECH 1 SHOULD INDICATE ENABLE RELAY "ON" AND BATTERY VOLTAGE ABOVE 10 VOLTS.
  DOES IT?

NO → ② • IGNITION "OFF."
  • DISCONNECT ENABLE RELAY.
  • CONNECT DVM BETWEEN TERMINAL "2" OF ENABLE RELAY CONNECTOR AND GROUND.
  • IGNITION "ON."
  VOLTAGE SHOULD BE 0 VOLT.
  IS IT?

YES → IS CODE A011 OR A013 ALSO PRESENT OR IN HISTORY?

NO → FAULT IS NOT PRESENT AT THIS TIME. REFER TO "DIAGNOSTIC AIDS" ON FACING PAGE.

YES → PROCEED TO THAT CODE FIRST.

From ②:
NO → REPAIR SHORT TO VOLTAGE ON CKT 879.

YES → ③ • IGNITION "OFF."
  • RECONNECT ENABLE RELAY.
  • IGNITION "ON."
  • CONNECT A TEST LIGHT TO B+ AND BACKPROBE TERMINAL "2" OF THE ENABLE RELAY CONNECTOR. COMMAND ENABLE RELAY "ON" USING TECH 1. TEST LIGHT SHOULD ILLUMINATE.
  DOES IT?

YES → REPLACE ENABLE RELAY AND RE-CHECK.

NO → • REMOVE ENABLE RELAY.
  • USING DVM, MEASURE RESISTANCE BETWEEN RELAY TERMINALS "2" AND "5".
  RESISTANCE SHOULD BE GREATER THAN 0 OHMS.
  IS IT?

YES → REPLACE EBCM.

NO → REPLACE ENABLE RELAY AND RECHECK.

THIS CHART ASSUMES THAT A CURRENT CODE IS STORED INDICATING THAT THIS FAULT IS PRESENT.

CODE A017

ENABLE RELAY COIL SHORTED TO GROUND

① • START ENGINE. ALLOW ENGINE TO RUN FOR AT LEAST 10 SECONDS.
  • VEHICLE IN PARK OR NEUTRAL.
  • WITH ENGINE RUNNING USE RELAY TEST FUNCTION OF TECH 1 "SCAN" TOOL AND COMMAND ENABLE RELAY "OFF."
  • TECH 1 SHOULD INDICATE ENABLE RELAY IS "OFF," AND BATTERY VOLTAGE LESS THAN 5 VOLTS.
  DOES IT?

YES → FAULT IS NOT PRESENT AT THIS TIME. REFER TO "DIAGNOSTIC AIDS" ON FACING PAGE.

NO → ② • IGNITION "OFF."
  • DISCONNECT 24 WAY WORLD CONNECTOR.
  • IGNITION "ON."
  • CONNECT DVM BETWEEN B+ AND BACKPROBE TERMINAL "2" OF THE ENABLE RELAY CONNECTOR. VOLTAGE SHOULD BE 0 VOLT.
  IS IT?

From ②:
YES → ③ • IGNITION "OFF."
  • RECONNECT 24 WAY WORLD CONNECTOR.
  • CONNECT DVM BETWEEN B+ AND BACKPROBE TERMINAL "2" OF THE ENABLE RELAY CONNECTOR. VOLTAGE SHOULD BE 0 VOLT.
  IS IT?

NO → • DISCONNECT ENABLE RELAY AND REPEAT STEP 2. VOLTAGE SHOULD BE 0 VOLT.
  IS IT?

YES → REPLACE ENABLE RELAY.

NO → REPAIR SHORT TO GROUND IN CKT 879.

From ③:
NO → REPLACE EBCM.

YES → FAULT IS INTERMITTENT. CLEAR CODES AND RE-CHECK.

THIS CHART ASSUMES THAT A CURRENT CODE IS STORED INDICATING THAT THIS FAULT IS PRESENT.

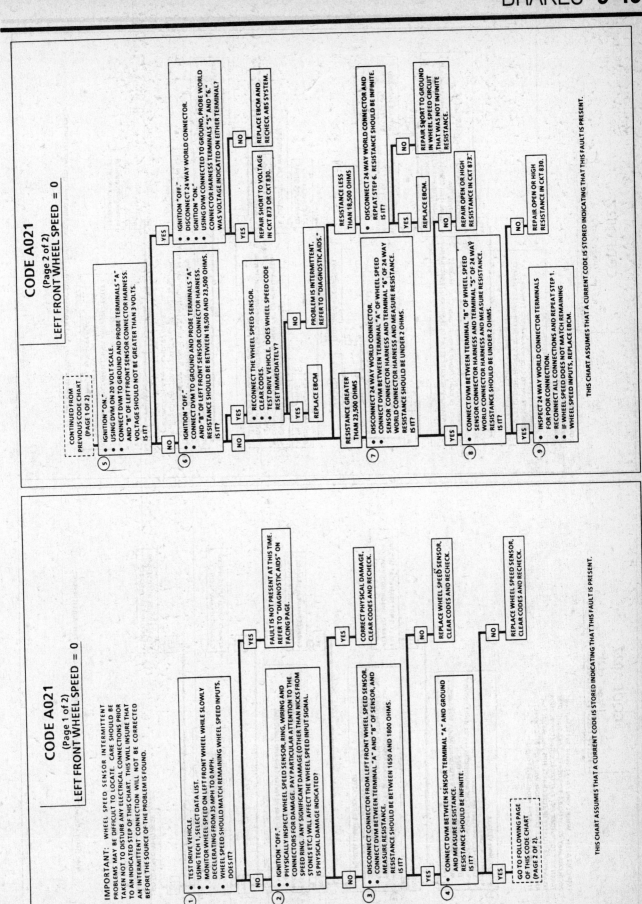

CODE A021
(Page 1 of 2)
LEFT FRONT WHEEL SPEED = 0

IMPORTANT: WHEEL SPEED SENSOR INTERMITTENT PROBLEMS MAY BE DIFFICULT TO LOCATE. CARE SHOULD BE TAKEN NOT TO DISTURB ANY ELECTRICAL CONNECTIONS PRIOR TO AN INDICATED STEP OF THIS CHART. THIS WILL INSURE THAT AN INTERMITTENT CONNECTION WILL NOT BE CORRECTED BEFORE THE SOURCE OF THE PROBLEM IS FOUND.

1. TEST DRIVE VEHICLE.
- USING TECH 1, SELECT DATA LIST.
- MONITOR WHEEL SPEED ON LEFT FRONT WHEEL WHILE SLOWLY DECELERATING FROM 35 MPH TO 0 MPH.
- WHEEL SPEED SHOULD MATCH REMAINING WHEEL SPEED INPUTS. DOES IT?

YES → FAULT IS NOT PRESENT AT THIS TIME. REFER TO "DIAGNOSTIC AIDS" ON FACING PAGE.

NO →

2. IGNITION "OFF."
- PHYSICALLY INSPECT WHEEL SPEED SENSOR, RING, WIRING AND CONNECTORS FOR DAMAGE. PAY PARTICULAR ATTENTION TO THE SPEED RING. ANY SIGNIFICANT DAMAGE (OTHER THAN NICKS FROM STONES ETC.) WILL AFFECT THE WHEEL SPEED INPUT SIGNAL. IS PHYSICAL DAMAGE INDICATED?

YES → CORRECT PHYSICAL DAMAGE, CLEAR CODES AND RECHECK.

NO →

3. DISCONNECT CONNECTOR FROM LEFT FRONT WHEEL SPEED SENSOR.
- CONNECT DVM BETWEEN TERMINAL "A" AND "B" OF SENSOR, AND MEASURE RESISTANCE.
- RESISTANCE SHOULD BE BETWEEN 1650 AND 1800 OHMS. IS IT?

NO → REPLACE WHEEL SPEED SENSOR, CLEAR CODES AND RECHECK.

YES →

4. CONNECT DVM BETWEEN SENSOR TERMINAL "A" AND GROUND AND MEASURE RESISTANCE.
- RESISTANCE SHOULD BE INFINITE. IS IT?

NO → REPLACE WHEEL SPEED SENSOR, CLEAR CODES AND RECHECK.

YES → GO TO FOLLOWING PAGE OF THIS CODE CHART (PAGE 2 OF 2).

THIS CHART ASSUMES THAT A CURRENT CODE IS STORED INDICATING THAT THIS FAULT IS PRESENT.

CODE A021
(Page 2 of 2)
LEFT FRONT WHEEL SPEED = 0

CONTINUED FROM PREVIOUS CODE CHART (PAGE 1 OF 2)

5. IGNITION "ON."
- USING DVM ON 20 VOLT SCALE.
- CONNECT DVM TO GROUND AND PROBE TERMINALS "A" AND "B" OF LEFT FRONT SENSOR CONNECTOR HARNESS. VOLTAGE SHOULD NOT BE GREATER THAN 3 VOLTS. IS IT?

YES → IGNITION "OFF."
- DISCONNECT 24 WAY WORLD CONNECTOR.
- IGNITION "ON."
- USING DVM CONNECTED TO GROUND, PROBE WORLD CONNECTOR HARNESS TERMINALS "5" AND "6." WAS VOLTAGE INDICATED ON EITHER TERMINAL?

   NO → REPLACE EBCM AND RECHECK ABS SYSTEM.
   YES → REPAIR SHORT TO VOLTAGE IN CKT 873 OR CKT 830.

NO →

6. IGNITION "OFF."
- CONNECT DVM TO GROUND AND PROBE TERMINALS "A" AND "B" OF LEFT FRONT SENSOR CONNECTOR HARNESS. RESISTANCE SHOULD BE BETWEEN 18,500 AND 23,500 OHMS. IS IT?

NO → RECONNECT THE WHEEL SPEED SENSOR.
- CLEAR CODES.
- TEST DRIVE VEHICLE. DOES WHEEL SPEED CODE RESET IMMEDIATELY?

   YES → REPLACE EBCM
   NO → PROBLEM IS INTERMITTENT. REFER TO "DIAGNOSTIC AIDS."

RESISTANCE GREATER THAN 23,500 OHMS

RESISTANCE LESS THAN 18,500 OHMS → DISCONNECT 24 WAY WORLD CONNECTOR AND REPEAT STEP 6. RESISTANCE SHOULD BE INFINITE. IS IT?

   YES → REPLACE EBCM.
   NO → REPAIR OPEN OR HIGH RESISTANCE IN CKT 873.

7. DISCONNECT 24 WAY WORLD CONNECTOR.
- CONNECT DVM BETWEEN TERMINAL "A" OF WHEEL SPEED SENSOR CONNECTOR HARNESS AND TERMINAL "6" OF 24 WAY WORLD CONNECTOR HARNESS AND MEASURE RESISTANCE. RESISTANCE SHOULD BE UNDER 2 OHMS. IS IT?

NO → REPAIR SHORT TO GROUND IN WHEEL SPEED CIRCUIT THAT WAS NOT INFINITE RESISTANCE.

YES →

8. CONNECT DVM BETWEEN TERMINAL "B" OF WHEEL SPEED SENSOR CONNECTOR HARNESS AND TERMINAL "S" OF 24 WAY WORLD CONNECTOR HARNESS AND MEASURE RESISTANCE. RESISTANCE SHOULD BE UNDER 2 OHMS. IS IT?

NO → REPAIR OPEN OR HIGH RESISTANCE IN CKT 830.

YES →

9. INSPECT 24 WAY WORLD CONNECTOR TERMINALS FOR POOR CONNECTION.
- RECONNECT ALL CONNECTIONS AND REPEAT STEP 1. IF WHEEL SPEED DOES NOT MATCH REMAINING WHEEL SPEED INPUTS, REPLACE EBCM.

THIS CHART ASSUMES THAT A CURRENT CODE IS STORED INDICATING THAT THIS FAULT IS PRESENT.

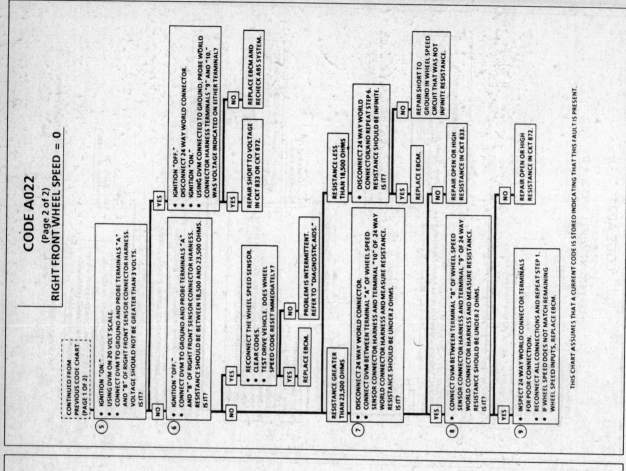

CODE A022
(Page 1 of 2)
RIGHT FRONT WHEEL SPEED = 0

IMPORTANT: WHEEL SPEED SENSOR INTERMITTENT PROBLEMS MAY BE DIFFICULT TO LOCATE. CARE SHOULD BE TAKEN NOT TO DISTURB ANY ELECTRICAL CONNECTIONS PRIOR TO AN INDICATED STEP OF THIS CHART. THIS WILL INSURE THAT AN INTERMITTENT CONNECTION WILL NOT BE CORRECTED BEFORE THE SOURCE OF THE PROBLEM IS FOUND.

1. • TEST DRIVE VEHICLE.
   • IGNITION "ON."
   • USING TECH 1, SELECT DATA LIST.
   • MONITOR WHEEL SPEED ON RIGHT FRONT WHEEL WHILE SLOWLY DECELERATING FROM 35 MPH TO 0 MPH. WHEEL SPEED SHOULD MATCH REMAINING WHEEL SPEED INPUTS. DOES IT?

   YES → FAULT IS NOT PRESENT AT THIS TIME, REFER TO "DIAGNOSTIC AIDS" ON FACING PAGE.

2. • IGNITION "OFF."
   • PHYSICALLY INSPECT WHEEL SPEED SENSOR, RING, WIRING AND CONNECTORS FOR DAMAGE. PAY PARTICULAR ATTENTION TO THE SPEED RING. ANY SIGNIFICANT DAMAGE (OTHER THAN NICKS FROM STONES ETC.) WILL AFFECT THE WHEEL SPEED INPUT SIGNAL. IS PHYSICAL DAMAGE INDICATED?

   YES → CORRECT PHYSICAL DAMAGE, CLEAR CODES AND RECHECK.

3. • DISCONNECT CONNECTOR FROM RIGHT FRONT WHEEL SPEED SENSOR.
   • CONNECT DVM BETWEEN TERMINALS "A" AND "B" OF SENSOR, AND MEASURE RESISTANCE. RESISTANCE SHOULD BE BETWEEN 1650 AND 1800 OHMS. IS IT?

   NO → REPLACE WHEEL SPEED SENSOR, CLEAR CODES AND RECHECK.

4. • CONNECT DVM BETWEEN SENSOR TERMINAL "A" AND GROUND AND MEASURE RESISTANCE. RESISTANCE SHOULD BE INFINITE. IS IT?

   NO → REPLACE WHEEL SPEED SENSOR, CLEAR CODES AND RECHECK.

   YES → GO TO FOLLOWING PAGE OF THIS CODE CHART (PAGE 2 OF 2).

THIS CHART ASSUMES THAT A CURRENT CODE IS STORED INDICATING THAT THIS FAULT IS PRESENT.

CODE A022
(Page 2 of 2)
RIGHT FRONT WHEEL SPEED = 0

CONTINUED FROM PREVIOUS CODE CHART (PAGE 1 OF 2)

5. • IGNITION "ON."
   • USING DVM ON 20 VOLT SCALE.
   • CONNECT DVM TO GROUND AND PROBE TERMINALS "A" AND "B" OF RIGHT FRONT SENSOR CONNECTOR HARNESS. VOLTAGE SHOULD NOT BE GREATER THAN 3 VOLTS. IS IT?

   YES → • IGNITION "OFF."
   • DISCONNECT 24 WAY WORLD CONNECTOR.
   • IGNITION "ON."
   • USING DVM CONNECTED TO GROUND, PROBE WORLD CONNECTOR HARNESS TERMINALS "9" AND "10." WAS VOLTAGE INDICATED ON EITHER TERMINAL?

   NO → REPLACE EBCM AND RECHECK ABS SYSTEM.

   YES → REPAIR SHORT TO VOLTAGE IN CKT 833 OR CKT 872.

6. • IGNITION "OFF."
   • CONNECT DVM TO GROUND AND PROBE TERMINALS "A" AND "B" OF RIGHT FRONT SENSOR CONNECTOR HARNESS. RESISTANCE SHOULD BE BETWEEN 18,500 AND 23,500 OHMS. IS IT?

   YES → • RECONNECT THE WHEEL SPEED SENSOR.
   • CLEAR CODES.
   • TEST DRIVE VEHICLE. DOES WHEEL SPEED CODE RESET IMMEDIATELY?

   NO → PROBLEM IS INTERMITTENT. REFER TO "DIAGNOSTIC AIDS."

   YES → REPLACE EBCM.

   (RESISTANCE GREATER THAN 23,500 OHMS)

7. • DISCONNECT 24 WAY WORLD CONNECTOR.
   • CONNECT DVM BETWEEN TERMINAL "A" OF WHEEL SPEED SENSOR CONNECTOR HARNESS AND TERMINAL "10" OF 24 WAY WORLD CONNECTOR HARNESS AND MEASURE RESISTANCE. RESISTANCE SHOULD BE UNDER 2 OHMS. IS IT?

   (RESISTANCE LESS THAN 18,500 OHMS)

   • DISCONNECT 24 WAY WORLD CONNECTOR AND REPEAT STEP 6. RESISTANCE SHOULD BE INFINITE. IS IT?

   YES → REPLACE EBCM.

   NO → REPAIR SHORT TO GROUND IN WHEEL SPEED CIRCUIT THAT WAS NOT INFINITE RESISTANCE.

8. **YES** → • CONNECT DVM BETWEEN TERMINAL "B" OF WHEEL SPEED SENSOR CONNECTOR HARNESS AND TERMINAL "9" OF 24 WAY WORLD CONNECTOR HARNESS AND MEASURE RESISTANCE. RESISTANCE SHOULD BE UNDER 2 OHMS. IS IT?

   NO → REPAIR OPEN OR HIGH RESISTANCE IN CKT 833.

9. **YES** → • INSPECT 24 WAY WORLD CONNECTOR TERMINALS FOR POOR CONNECTION.
   • RECONNECT ALL CONNECTIONS AND REPEAT STEP 1. IF WHEEL SPEED DOES NOT MATCH REMAINING WHEEL SPEED INPUTS, REPLACE EBCM.

   NO → REPAIR OPEN OR HIGH RESISTANCE IN CKT 872.

THIS CHART ASSUMES THAT A CURRENT CODE IS STORED INDICATING THAT THIS FAULT IS PRESENT.

CODE A023
(Page 2 of 2)
LEFT REAR WHEEL SPEED = 0

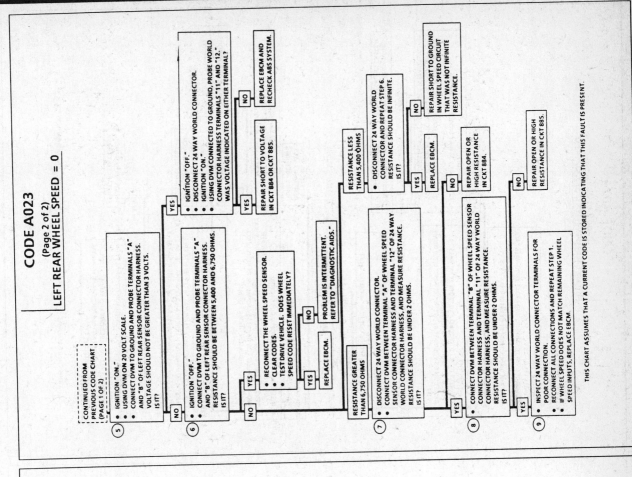

CODE A023
(Page 1 of 2)
LEFT REAR WHEEL SPEED = 0

IMPORTANT: WHEEL SPEED SENSOR INTERMITTENT PROBLEMS MAY BE DIFFICULT TO LOCATE. CARE SHOULD BE TAKEN NOT TO DISTURB ANY ELECTRICAL CONNECTIONS PRIOR TO AN INDICATED STEP OF THIS CHART. THIS WILL INSURE THAT AN INTERMITTENT CONNECTION WILL NOT BE CORRECTED BEFORE THE SOURCE OF THE PROBLEM IS FOUND.

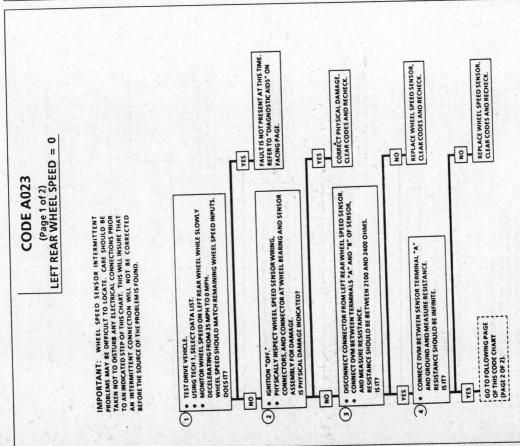

THIS CHART ASSUMES THAT A CURRENT CODE IS STORED INDICATING THAT THIS FAULT IS PRESENT.

CODE A024
(Page 2 of 2)
RIGHT REAR WHEEL SPEED = 0

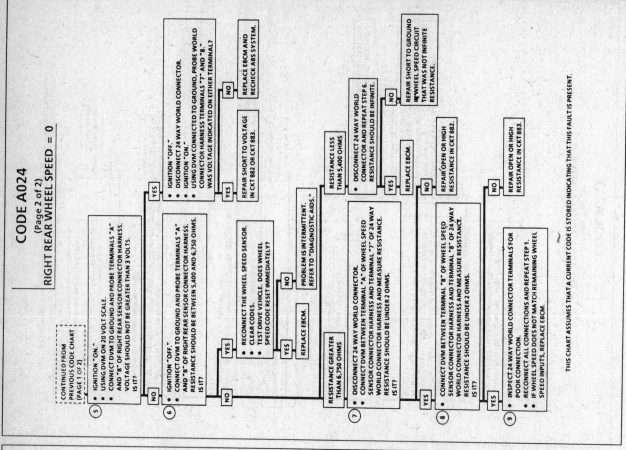

CONTINUED FROM PREVIOUS CODE CHART (PAGE 1 OF 2)

5
- IGNITION "ON."
- USING DVM ON 20 VOLT SCALE.
- CONNECT DVM TO GROUND AND PROBE TERMINALS "A" AND "B" OF RIGHT REAR SENSOR CONNECTOR HARNESS. VOLTAGE SHOULD NOT BE GREATER THAN 3 VOLTS. IS IT?

- IGNITION "OFF."
- DISCONNECT 24 WAY WORLD CONNECTOR.
- IGNITION "ON."
- USING DVM CONNECTED TO GROUND, PROBE WORLD CONNECTOR HARNESS TERMINALS "7" AND "8." WAS VOLTAGE INDICATED ON EITHER TERMINAL?

REPAIR SHORT TO VOLTAGE IN CKT 882 OR CKT 883.

REPLACE EBCM AND RECHECK ABS SYSTEM.

6
- IGNITION "OFF."
- CONNECT DVM TO GROUND AND PROBE TERMINALS "A" AND "B" OF RIGHT REAR SENSOR CONNECTOR HARNESS. RESISTANCE SHOULD BE BETWEEN 5,400 AND 6,750 OHMS. IS IT?

- RECONNECT THE WHEEL SPEED SENSOR.
- CLEAR CODES.
- TEST DRIVE VEHICLE. DOES WHEEL SPEED CODE RESET IMMEDIATELY?

PROBLEM IS INTERMITTENT. REFER TO "DIAGNOSTIC AIDS."

REPLACE EBCM.

RESISTANCE GREATER THAN 6,750 OHMS

RESISTANCE LESS THAN 5,400 OHMS

7
- DISCONNECT 24 WAY WORLD CONNECTOR.
- CONNECT DVM BETWEEN TERMINAL "A" OF WHEEL SPEED SENSOR CONNECTOR HARNESS AND TERMINAL "7" OF 24 WAY WORLD CONNECTOR HARNESS AND MEASURE RESISTANCE. RESISTANCE SHOULD BE UNDER 2 OHMS. IS IT?

- DISCONNECT 24 WAY WORLD CONNECTOR AND REPEAT STEP 6. RESISTANCE SHOULD BE INFINITE.

REPLACE EBCM.

REPAIR SHORT TO GROUND IN WHEEL SPEED CIRCUIT THAT WAS NOT INFINITE RESISTANCE.

8
- CONNECT DVM BETWEEN TERMINAL "B" OF WHEEL SPEED SENSOR CONNECTOR HARNESS AND TERMINAL "8" OF 24 WAY WORLD CONNECTOR HARNESS AND MEASURE RESISTANCE. RESISTANCE SHOULD BE UNDER 2 OHMS. IS IT?

REPAIR OPEN OR HIGH RESISTANCE IN CKT 882.

9
- INSPECT 24 WAY WORLD CONNECTOR TERMINALS FOR POOR CONNECTION.
- RECONNECT ALL CONNECTIONS AND REPEAT STEP 1.
- IF WHEEL SPEED DOES NOT MATCH REMAINING WHEEL SPEED INPUTS, REPLACE EBCM.

REPAIR OPEN OR HIGH RESISTANCE IN CKT 883.

THIS CHART ASSUMES THAT A CURRENT CODE IS STORED INDICATING THAT THIS FAULT IS PRESENT.

CODE A024
(Page 1 of 2)
RIGHT REAR WHEEL SPEED = 0

IMPORTANT: WHEEL SPEED SENSOR INTERMITTENT PROBLEMS MAY BE DIFFICULT TO LOCATE. CARE SHOULD BE TAKEN NOT TO DISTURB ANY ELECTRICAL CONNECTIONS PRIOR TO AN INDICATED STEP OF THIS CHART. THIS WILL INSURE THAT AN INTERMITTENT CONNECTION WILL NOT BE CORRECTED BEFORE THE SOURCE OF THE PROBLEM IS FOUND.

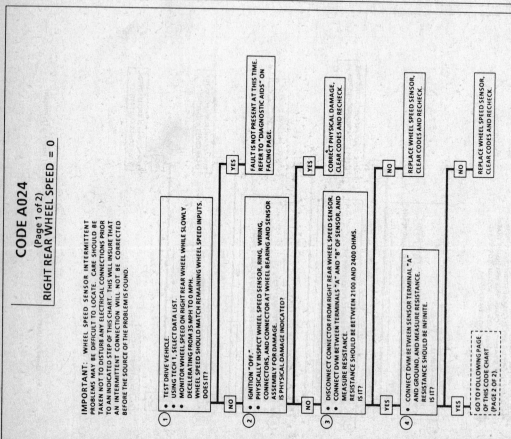

1
- TEST DRIVE VEHICLE.
- USING TECH 1, SELECT DATA LIST.
- MONITOR WHEEL SPEED ON RIGHT REAR WHEEL WHILE SLOWLY DECELERATING FROM 35 MPH TO 0 MPH. WHEEL SPEED SHOULD MATCH REMAINING WHEEL SPEED INPUTS. DOES IT?

FAULT IS NOT PRESENT AT THIS TIME. REFER TO "DIAGNOSTIC AIDS" ON FACING PAGE.

2
- IGNITION "OFF."
- PHYSICALLY INSPECT WHEEL SPEED SENSOR, RING, WIRING, CONNECTORS, AND CONNECTOR AT WHEEL BEARING AND SENSOR ASSEMBLY FOR DAMAGE. IS PHYSICAL DAMAGE INDICATED?

CORRECT PHYSICAL DAMAGE, CLEAR CODES AND RECHECK.

3
- DISCONNECT CONNECTOR FROM RIGHT REAR WHEEL SPEED SENSOR.
- CONNECT DVM BETWEEN TERMINALS "A" AND "B" OF SENSOR, AND MEASURE RESISTANCE. RESISTANCE SHOULD BE BETWEEN 2100 AND 2400 OHMS. IS IT?

REPLACE WHEEL SPEED SENSOR, CLEAR CODES AND RECHECK.

4
- CONNECT DVM BETWEEN SENSOR TERMINAL "A" AND GROUND, AND MEASURE RESISTANCE. RESISTANCE SHOULD BE INFINITE. IS IT?

REPLACE WHEEL SPEED SENSOR, CLEAR CODES AND RECHECK.

GO TO FOLLOWING PAGE OF THIS CODE CHART (PAGE 2 OF 2).

THIS CHART ASSUMES THAT A CURRENT CODE IS STORED INDICATING THAT THIS FAULT IS PRESENT.

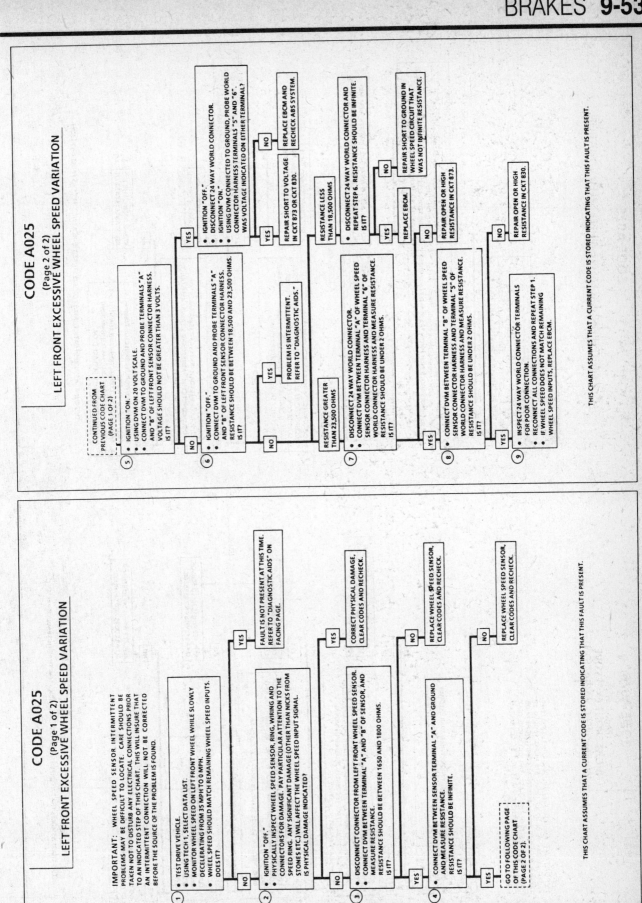

CODE A025
(Page 2 of 2)
LEFT FRONT EXCESSIVE WHEEL SPEED VARIATION

CONTINUED FROM PREVIOUS CODE CHART (PAGE 1 OF 2)

5
- IGNITION "ON."
- USING DVM ON 20 VOLT SCALE.
- CONNECT DVM TO GROUND AND PROBE TERMINALS "A" AND "B" OF LEFT FRONT SENSOR CONNECTOR HARNESS. VOLTAGE SHOULD NOT BE GREATER THAN 3 VOLTS. IS IT?

YES →
- IGNITION "OFF."
- DISCONNECT 24 WAY WORLD CONNECTOR.
- IGNITION "ON."
- USING DVM CONNECTED TO GROUND, PROBE WORLD CONNECTOR HARNESS TERMINALS "5" AND "6". WAS VOLTAGE INDICATED ON EITHER TERMINAL?

NO → REPLACE EBCM AND RECHECK ABS SYSTEM.

YES → REPAIR SHORT TO VOLTAGE IN CKT 873 OR CKT 830.

6
- IGNITION "OFF."
- CONNECT DVM TO GROUND AND PROBE TERMINALS "A" AND "B" OF LEFT FRONT SENSOR CONNECTOR HARNESS. RESISTANCE SHOULD BE BETWEEN 18,500 AND 23,500 OHMS. IS IT?

YES → PROBLEM IS INTERMITTENT. REFER TO "DIAGNOSTIC AIDS."

RESISTANCE LESS THAN 18,500 OHMS
- DISCONNECT 24 WAY WORLD CONNECTOR AND REPEAT STEP 6. RESISTANCE SHOULD BE INFINITE. IS IT?

NO → REPAIR SHORT TO GROUND IN WHEEL SPEED CIRCUIT THAT WAS NOT INFINITE RESISTANCE.

YES → REPLACE EBCM.

RESISTANCE GREATER THAN 23,500 OHMS

7
- DISCONNECT 24 WAY WORLD CONNECTOR.
- CONNECT DVM BETWEEN TERMINAL "A" OF WHEEL SPEED SENSOR CONNECTOR HARNESS AND TERMINAL "6" OF WORLD CONNECTOR HARNESS AND MEASURE RESISTANCE. RESISTANCE SHOULD BE UNDER 2 OHMS. IS IT?

NO → REPAIR OPEN OR HIGH RESISTANCE IN CKT 873.

YES

8
- CONNECT DVM BETWEEN TERMINAL "B" OF WHEEL SPEED SENSOR CONNECTOR HARNESS AND TERMINAL "5" OF WORLD CONNECTOR HARNESS AND MEASURE RESISTANCE. RESISTANCE SHOULD BE UNDER 2 OHMS. IS IT?

NO → REPAIR OPEN OR HIGH RESISTANCE IN CKT 830.

YES

9
- INSPECT 24 WAY WORLD CONNECTOR TERMINALS FOR POOR CONNECTION.
- RECONNECT ALL CONNECTIONS AND REPEAT STEP 1.
- IF WHEEL SPEED DOES NOT MATCH REMAINING WHEEL SPEED INPUTS, REPLACE EBCM.

THIS CHART ASSUMES THAT A CURRENT CODE IS STORED INDICATING THAT THIS FAULT IS PRESENT.

CODE A025
(Page 1 of 2)
LEFT FRONT EXCESSIVE WHEEL SPEED VARIATION

IMPORTANT: WHEEL SPEED SENSOR INTERMITTENT PROBLEMS MAY BE DIFFICULT TO LOCATE. CARE SHOULD BE TAKEN NOT TO DISTURB ANY ELECTRICAL CONNECTIONS PRIOR TO AN INDICATED STEP OF THIS CHART. THIS WILL INSURE THAT AN INTERMITTENT CONNECTION WILL NOT BE CORRECTED BEFORE THE SOURCE OF THE PROBLEM IS FOUND.

1
- TEST DRIVE VEHICLE.
- USING TECH 1, SELECT DATA LIST.
- MONITOR WHEEL SPEED ON LEFT FRONT WHEEL WHILE SLOWLY DECELERATING FROM 35 MPH TO 0 MPH.
- WHEEL SPEED SHOULD MATCH REMAINING WHEEL SPEED INPUTS. DOES IT?

YES → FAULT IS NOT PRESENT AT THIS TIME. REFER TO "DIAGNOSTIC AIDS" ON FACING PAGE.

NO

2
- IGNITION "OFF."
- PHYSICALLY INSPECT WHEEL SPEED SENSOR, RING, WIRING AND CONNECTORS FOR DAMAGE. PAY PARTICULAR ATTENTION TO THE SPEED RING. ANY SIGNIFICANT DAMAGE (OTHER THAN NICKS FROM STONES ETC.) WILL AFFECT THE WHEEL SPEED INPUT SIGNAL. IS PHYSICAL DAMAGE INDICATED?

YES → CORRECT PHYSICAL DAMAGE, CLEAR CODES AND RECHECK.

NO

3
- DISCONNECT CONNECTOR FROM LEFT FRONT WHEEL SPEED SENSOR.
- CONNECT DVM BETWEEN TERMINAL "A" AND "B" OF SENSOR, AND MEASURE RESISTANCE. RESISTANCE SHOULD BE BETWEEN 1650 AND 1800 OHMS. IS IT?

NO → REPLACE WHEEL SPEED SENSOR, CLEAR CODES AND RECHECK.

YES

4
- CONNECT DVM BETWEEN SENSOR TERMINAL "A" AND GROUND AND MEASURE RESISTANCE. RESISTANCE SHOULD BE INFINITE. IS IT?

NO → REPLACE WHEEL SPEED SENSOR, CLEAR CODES AND RECHECK.

YES → GO TO FOLLOWING PAGE OF THIS CODE CHART (PAGE 2 OF 2).

THIS CHART ASSUMES THAT A CURRENT CODE IS STORED INDICATING THAT THIS FAULT IS PRESENT.

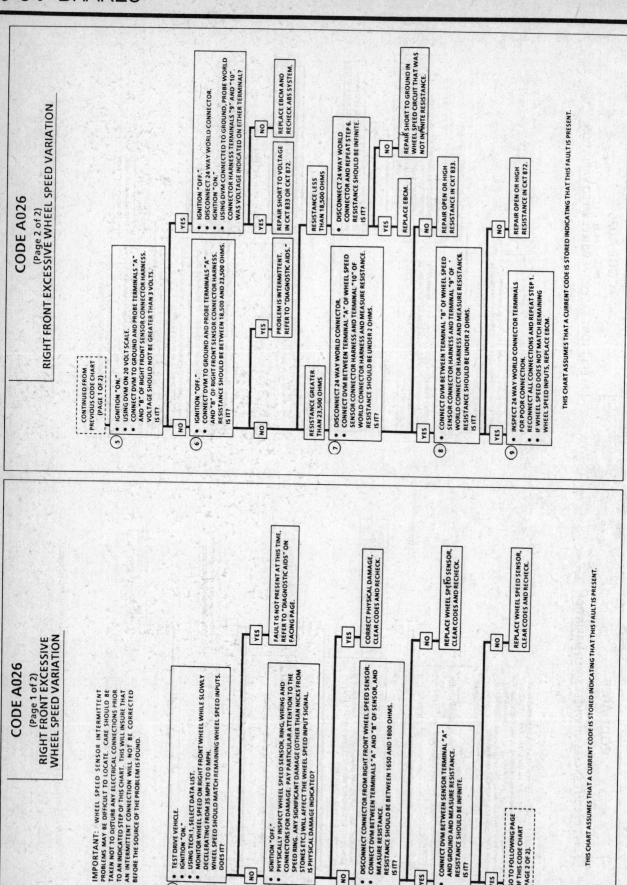

CODE A026
(Page 2 of 2)
RIGHT FRONT EXCESSIVE WHEEL SPEED VARIATION

CONTINUED FROM PREVIOUS CODE CHART (PAGE 1 OF 2)

(5)
• IGNITION "ON."
• USING DVM ON 20 VOLT SCALE.
• CONNECT DVM TO GROUND AND PROBE TERMINALS "A" AND "B" OF RIGHT FRONT SENSOR CONNECTOR HARNESS. VOLTAGE SHOULD NOT BE GREATER THAN 3 VOLTS. IS IT?

YES →
• IGNITION "OFF."
• DISCONNECT 24 WAY WORLD CONNECTOR.
• IGNITION "ON."
• USING DVM CONNECTED TO GROUND, PROBE WORLD CONNECTOR HARNESS TERMINALS "9" AND "10." WAS VOLTAGE INDICATED ON EITHER TERMINAL?

NO → REPLACE EBCM AND RECHECK ABS SYSTEM.

YES → REPAIR SHORT TO VOLTAGE IN CKT 833 OR CKT 872.

NO ↓

(6)
• IGNITION "OFF."
• CONNECT DVM TO GROUND AND PROBE TERMINALS "A" AND "B" OF RIGHT FRONT SENSOR CONNECTOR HARNESS. RESISTANCE SHOULD BE BETWEEN 18,500 AND 23,500 OHMS. IS IT?

YES → PROBLEM IS INTERMITTENT. REFER TO "DIAGNOSTIC AIDS."

NO ↓

RESISTANCE GREATER THAN 23,500 OHMS

RESISTANCE LESS THAN 18,500 OHMS

(7)
• DISCONNECT 24 WAY WORLD CONNECTOR.
• CONNECT DVM BETWEEN TERMINAL "A" OF WHEEL SPEED SENSOR CONNECTOR HARNESS AND TERMINAL "10" OF WORLD CONNECTOR HARNESS AND MEASURE RESISTANCE. RESISTANCE SHOULD BE UNDER 2 OHMS. IS IT?

• DISCONNECT 24 WAY WORLD CONNECTOR AND REPEAT STEP 6. RESISTANCE SHOULD BE INFINITE. IS IT?

YES → REPAIR SHORT TO GROUND IN WHEEL SPEED CIRCUIT THAT WAS NOT INFINITE RESISTANCE.

NO → REPLACE EBCM.

YES → REPAIR OPEN OR HIGH RESISTANCE IN CKT 833.

NO ↓

(8)
• CONNECT DVM BETWEEN TERMINAL "B" OF WHEEL SPEED SENSOR CONNECTOR HARNESS AND TERMINAL "9" OF WORLD CONNECTOR HARNESS AND MEASURE RESISTANCE. RESISTANCE SHOULD BE UNDER 2 OHMS. IS IT?

NO → REPAIR OPEN OR HIGH RESISTANCE IN CKT 872.

YES ↓

(9)
• INSPECT 24 WAY WORLD CONNECTOR TERMINALS FOR POOR CONNECTION.
• RECONNECT ALL CONNECTIONS AND REPEAT STEP 1. IF WHEEL SPEED DOES NOT MATCH REMAINING WHEEL SPEED INPUTS, REPLACE EBCM.

THIS CHART ASSUMES THAT A CURRENT CODE IS STORED INDICATING THAT A CURRENT CODE IS STORED INDICATING THAT THIS FAULT IS PRESENT.

CODE A026
(Page 1 of 2)
RIGHT FRONT EXCESSIVE WHEEL SPEED VARIATION

IMPORTANT: WHEEL SPEED SENSOR INTERMITTENT PROBLEMS MAY BE DIFFICULT TO LOCATE. CARE SHOULD BE TAKEN NOT TO DISTURB ANY ELECTRICAL CONNECTIONS PRIOR TO AN INDICATED STEP OF THIS CHART. THIS WILL INSURE THAT AN INTERMITTENT CONNECTION WILL NOT BE CORRECTED BEFORE THE SOURCE OF THE PROBLEM IS FOUND.

(1)
• TEST DRIVE VEHICLE.
• IGNITION "ON."
• USING TECH 1, SELECT DATA LIST.
• MONITOR WHEEL SPEED ON RIGHT FRONT WHILE SLOWLY DECELERATING FROM 35 MPH TO 0 MPH. WHEEL SPEED SHOULD MATCH REMAINING WHEEL SPEED INPUTS. DOES IT?

YES → FAULT IS NOT PRESENT AT THIS TIME, REFER TO "DIAGNOSTIC AIDS" ON FACING PAGE.

NO ↓

(2)
• IGNITION "OFF."
• PHYSICALLY INSPECT WHEEL SPEED SENSOR, RING, WIRING AND CONNECTORS FOR DAMAGE. PAY PARTICULAR ATTENTION TO THE SPEED RING. ANY SIGNIFICANT DAMAGE (OTHER THAN NICKS FROM STONES ETC.) WILL AFFECT THE WHEEL SPEED INPUT SIGNAL. IS PHYSICAL DAMAGE INDICATED?

YES → CORRECT PHYSICAL DAMAGE, CLEAR CODES AND RECHECK.

NO ↓

(3)
• DISCONNECT CONNECTOR FROM RIGHT FRONT WHEEL SPEED SENSOR.
• CONNECT DVM BETWEEN TERMINALS "A" AND "B" OF SENSOR, AND MEASURE RESISTANCE. RESISTANCE SHOULD BE BETWEEN 1650 AND 1800 OHMS. IS IT?

NO → REPLACE WHEEL SPEED SENSOR, CLEAR CODES AND RECHECK.

YES ↓

(4)
• CONNECT DVM BETWEEN SENSOR TERMINAL "A" AND GROUND AND MEASURE RESISTANCE. RESISTANCE SHOULD BE INFINITE. IS IT?

NO → REPLACE WHEEL SPEED SENSOR, CLEAR CODES AND RECHECK.

YES ↓

GO TO FOLLOWING PAGE OF THIS CODE CHART (PAGE 2 OF 2).

THIS CHART ASSUMES THAT A CURRENT CODE IS STORED INDICATING THAT THIS FAULT IS PRESENT.

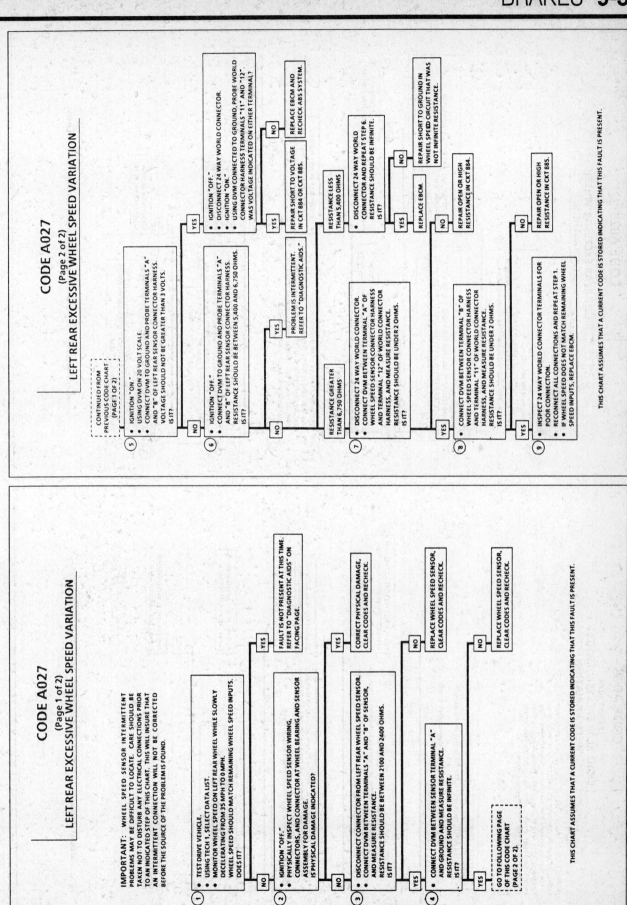

CODE A027
(Page 2 of 2)
LEFT REAR EXCESSIVE WHEEL SPEED VARIATION

CONTINUED FROM PREVIOUS CODE CHART (PAGE 1 OF 2)

5.
- IGNITION "ON."
- USING DVM ON 20 VOLT SCALE.
- CONNECT DVM TO GROUND AND PROBE TERMINALS "A" AND "B" OF LEFT REAR SENSOR CONNECTOR HARNESS. VOLTAGE SHOULD NOT BE GREATER THAN 3 VOLTS. IS IT?

NO → 6.
- IGNITION "OFF."
- CONNECT DVM TO GROUND AND PROBE TERMINALS "A" AND "B" OF LEFT REAR SENSOR CONNECTOR HARNESS. RESISTANCE SHOULD BE BETWEEN 5,400 AND 6,750 OHMS. IS IT?

YES →
- IGNITION "OFF."
- DISCONNECT 24 WAY WORLD CONNECTOR.
- IGNITION "ON."
- USING DVM CONNECTED TO GROUND, PROBE WORLD CONNECTOR HARNESS TERMINALS "11" AND "12". WAS VOLTAGE INDICATED ON EITHER TERMINAL?

NO → REPLACE EBCM AND RECHECK ABS SYSTEM.

YES → REPAIR SHORT TO VOLTAGE IN CKT 884 OR CKT 885.

NO (from 6) →
RESISTANCE GREATER THAN 6,750 OHMS

YES (from 6) → PROBLEM IS INTERMITTENT. REFER TO "DIAGNOSTIC AIDS."

7.
- DISCONNECT 24 WAY WORLD CONNECTOR.
- CONNECT DVM BETWEEN TERMINAL "A" OF WHEEL SPEED SENSOR CONNECTOR HARNESS AND TERMINAL "12" OF WORLD CONNECTOR HARNESS, AND MEASURE RESISTANCE. RESISTANCE SHOULD BE UNDER 2 OHMS. IS IT?

RESISTANCE LESS THAN 5,400 OHMS

- DISCONNECT 24 WAY WORLD CONNECTOR AND REPEAT STEP 6. RESISTANCE SHOULD BE INFINITE. IS IT?

NO → REPAIR SHORT TO GROUND IN WHEEL SPEED CIRCUIT THAT WAS NOT INFINITE RESISTANCE.

YES → REPLACE EBCM.

8.
- CONNECT DVM BETWEEN TERMINAL "B" OF WHEEL SPEED SENSOR CONNECTOR HARNESS AND TERMINAL "11" OF WORLD CONNECTOR HARNESS, AND MEASURE RESISTANCE. RESISTANCE SHOULD BE UNDER 2 OHMS. IS IT?

NO → REPAIR OPEN OR HIGH RESISTANCE IN CKT 884.

9.
- INSPECT 24 WAY WORLD CONNECTOR TERMINALS FOR POOR CONNECTION.
- RECONNECT ALL CONNECTIONS AND REPEAT STEP 1.
- IF WHEEL SPEED DOES NOT MATCH REMAINING WHEEL SPEED INPUTS, REPLACE EBCM.

NO → REPAIR OPEN OR HIGH RESISTANCE IN CKT 885.

THIS CHART ASSUMES THAT A CURRENT CODE IS STORED INDICATING THAT THIS FAULT IS PRESENT.

CODE A027
(Page 1 of 2)
LEFT REAR EXCESSIVE WHEEL SPEED VARIATION

IMPORTANT: WHEEL SPEED SENSOR INTERMITTENT PROBLEMS MAY BE DIFFICULT TO LOCATE. CARE SHOULD BE TAKEN NOT TO DISTURB ANY ELECTRICAL CONNECTIONS PRIOR TO AN INDICATED STEP OF THIS CHART. THIS WILL INSURE THAT AN INTERMITTENT CONNECTION WILL NOT BE CORRECTED BEFORE THE SOURCE OF THE PROBLEM IS FOUND.

1.
- TEST DRIVE VEHICLE.
- USING TECH 1, SELECT DATA LIST.
- MONITOR WHEEL SPEED ON LEFT REAR WHEEL WHILE SLOWLY DECELERATING FROM 35 MPH TO 0 MPH. WHEEL SPEED SHOULD MATCH REMAINING WHEEL SPEED INPUTS. DOES IT?

YES → FAULT IS NOT PRESENT AT THIS TIME. REFER TO "DIAGNOSTIC AIDS" ON FACING PAGE.

NO → 2.
- IGNITION "OFF."
- PHYSICALLY INSPECT WHEEL SPEED SENSOR WIRING, CONNECTORS, AND CONNECTOR AT WHEEL BEARING AND SENSOR ASSEMBLY FOR DAMAGE. IS PHYSICAL DAMAGE INDICATED?

YES → CORRECT PHYSICAL DAMAGE, CLEAR CODES AND RECHECK.

NO → 3.
- DISCONNECT CONNECTOR FROM LEFT REAR WHEEL SPEED SENSOR.
- CONNECT DVM BETWEEN TERMINALS "A" AND "B" OF SENSOR, AND MEASURE RESISTANCE. RESISTANCE SHOULD BE BETWEEN 2100 AND 2400 OHMS. IS IT?

NO → REPLACE WHEEL SPEED SENSOR, CLEAR CODES AND RECHECK.

YES → 4.
- CONNECT DVM BETWEEN SENSOR TERMINAL "A" AND GROUND AND MEASURE RESISTANCE. RESISTANCE SHOULD BE INFINITE. IS IT?

NO → REPLACE WHEEL SPEED SENSOR, CLEAR CODES AND RECHECK.

YES → GO TO FOLLOWING PAGE OF THIS CODE CHART (PAGE 2 OF 2).

THIS CHART ASSUMES THAT A CURRENT CODE IS STORED INDICATING THAT THIS FAULT IS PRESENT.

CODE A028
(Page 2 of 2)
RIGHT REAR EXCESSIVE WHEEL SPEED VARIATION

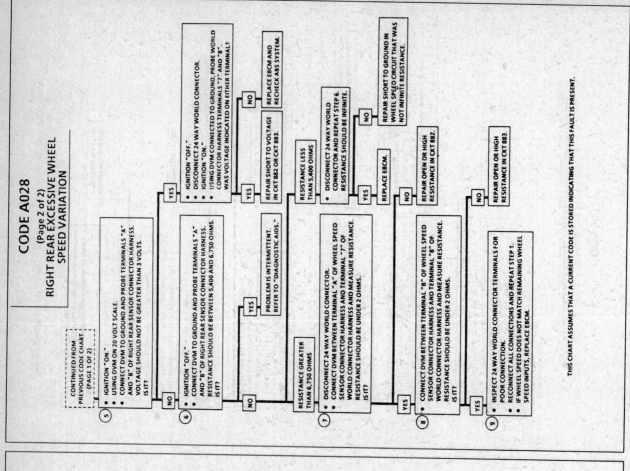

CONTINUED FROM PREVIOUS CODE CHART (PAGE 1 OF 2)

5.
- IGNITION "ON."
- USING DVM 20 VOLT SCALE.
- CONNECT DVM TO GROUND AND PROBE TERMINALS "A" AND "B" OF RIGHT REAR SENSOR CONNECTOR HARNESS.

VOLTAGE SHOULD NOT BE GREATER THAN 3 VOLTS. IS IT?

YES →
- IGNITION "OFF."
- DISCONNECT 24 WAY WORLD CONNECTOR.
- IGNITION "ON."
- USING DVM CONNECTED TO GROUND, PROBE WORLD CONNECTOR HARNESS TERMINALS "7" AND "8."

WAS VOLTAGE INDICATED ON EITHER TERMINAL?

NO → REPLACE EBCM AND RECHECK ABS SYSTEM.

YES → REPAIR SHORT TO VOLTAGE IN CKT 882 OR CKT 883.

NO →

6.
- IGNITION "OFF."
- CONNECT DVM TO GROUND AND PROBE TERMINALS "A" AND "B" OF RIGHT REAR SENSOR CONNECTOR HARNESS.

RESISTANCE SHOULD BE BETWEEN 5,400 AND 6,750 OHMS. IS IT?

YES → PROBLEM IS INTERMITTENT. REFER TO "DIAGNOSTIC AIDS."

NO →

RESISTANCE GREATER THAN 6,750 OHMS

RESISTANCE LESS THAN 5,400 OHMS

7.
- DISCONNECT 24 WAY WORLD CONNECTOR.
- CONNECT DVM BETWEEN TERMINAL "A" OF WHEEL SPEED SENSOR CONNECTOR HARNESS AND TERMINAL "7" OF WORLD CONNECTOR HARNESS AND MEASURE RESISTANCE.

RESISTANCE SHOULD BE UNDER 2 OHMS. IS IT?

- DISCONNECT 24 WAY WORLD CONNECTOR AND REPEAT STEP 6. RESISTANCE SHOULD BE INFINITE.

NO → REPAIR SHORT TO GROUND IN WHEEL SPEED CIRCUIT THAT WAS NOT INFINITE RESISTANCE.

YES → REPLACE EBCM.

YES →

8.
- CONNECT DVM BETWEEN TERMINAL "B" OF WHEEL SPEED SENSOR CONNECTOR HARNESS AND TERMINAL "8" OF WORLD CONNECTOR HARNESS AND MEASURE RESISTANCE.

RESISTANCE SHOULD BE UNDER 2 OHMS. IS IT?

NO → REPAIR OPEN OR HIGH RESISTANCE IN CKT 882.

YES →

9.
- INSPECT 24 WAY WORLD CONNECTOR TERMINALS FOR POOR CONNECTION.
- RECONNECT ALL CONNECTIONS AND REPEAT STEP 1. IF WHEEL SPEED DOES NOT MATCH REMAINING WHEEL SPEED INPUTS, REPLACE EBCM.

NO → REPAIR OPEN OR HIGH RESISTANCE IN CKT 883.

THIS CHART ASSUMES THAT A CURRENT CODE IS STORED INDICATING THAT THIS FAULT IS PRESENT.

CODE A028
(Page 1 of 2)
RIGHT REAR EXCESSIVE WHEEL SPEED VARIATION

IMPORTANT: WHEEL SPEED SENSOR INTERMITTENT PROBLEMS MAY BE DIFFICULT TO LOCATE. CARE SHOULD BE TAKEN NOT TO DISTURB ANY ELECTRICAL CONNECTIONS PRIOR TO AN INDICATED STEP OF THIS CHART. THIS WILL INSURE THAT AN INTERMITTENT CONNECTION WILL NOT BE CORRECTED BEFORE THE SOURCE OF THE PROBLEM IS FOUND.

1.
- TEST DRIVE VEHICLE.
- USING TECH 1, SELECT DATA LIST.
- MONITOR WHEEL SPEED ON RIGHT REAR WHEEL WHILE SLOWLY DECELERATING FROM 35 MPH TO 0 MPH.

WHEEL SPEED SHOULD MATCH REMAINING WHEEL SPEED INPUTS. DOES IT?

YES → FAULT IS NOT PRESENT AT THIS TIME. REFER TO "DIAGNOSTIC AIDS" ON FACING PAGE.

NO →

2.
- IGNITION "OFF."
- PHYSICALLY INSPECT WHEEL SPEED SENSOR WIRING, CONNECTORS, AND CONNECTOR AT WHEEL BEARING AND SENSOR ASSEMBLY FOR DAMAGE.

IS PHYSICAL DAMAGE INDICATED?

YES → CORRECT PHYSICAL DAMAGE, CLEAR CODES AND RECHECK.

NO →

3.
- DISCONNECT CONNECTOR FROM RIGHT REAR WHEEL SPEED SENSOR.
- CONNECT DVM BETWEEN TERMINALS "A" AND "B" OF SENSOR, AND MEASURE RESISTANCE.

RESISTANCE SHOULD BE BETWEEN 2100 AND 2400 OHMS. IS IT?

NO → REPLACE WHEEL SPEED SENSOR, CLEAR CODES AND RECHECK.

YES →

4.
- CONNECT DVM BETWEEN SENSOR TERMINAL "A" AND GROUND, AND MEASURE RESISTANCE.

RESISTANCE SHOULD BE INFINITE. IS IT?

NO → REPLACE WHEEL SPEED SENSOR, CLEAR CODES AND RECHECK.

YES → GO TO FOLLOWING PAGE OF THIS CODE CHART (PAGE 2 OF 2).

THIS CHART ASSUMES THAT A CURRENT CODE IS STORED INDICATING THAT THIS FAULT IS PRESENT.

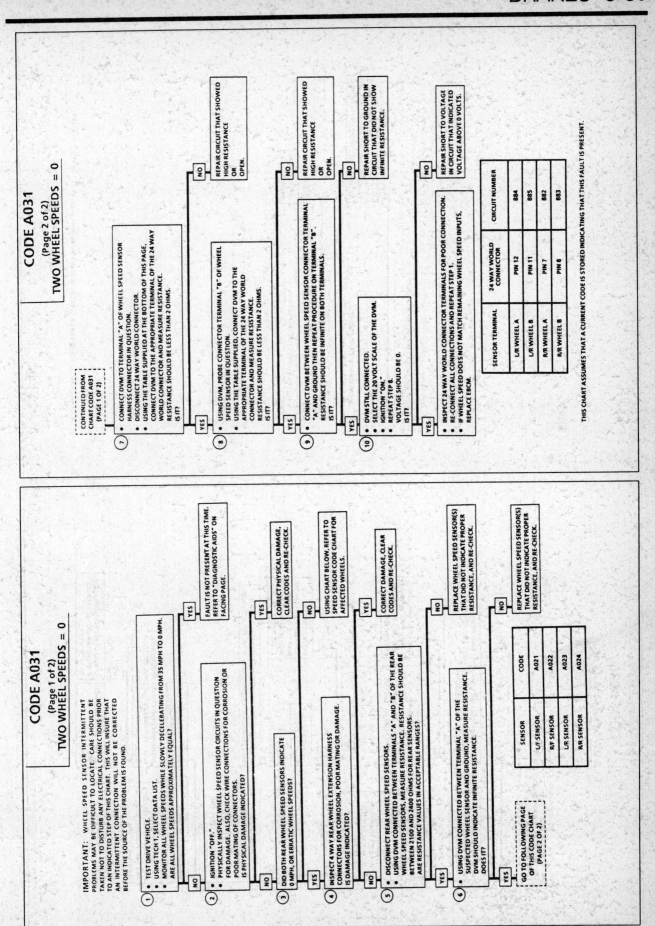

CODE A031
(Page 1 of 2)
TWO WHEEL SPEEDS = 0

IMPORTANT: WHEEL SPEED SENSOR INTERMITTENT PROBLEMS MAY BE DIFFICULT TO LOCATE. CARE SHOULD BE TAKEN NOT TO DISTURB ANY ELECTRICAL CONNECTIONS PRIOR TO AN INDICATED STEP OF THIS CHART. THIS WILL INSURE THAT AN INTERMITTENT CONNECTION WILL NOT BE CORRECTED BEFORE THE SOURCE OF THE PROBLEM IS FOUND.

① • TEST DRIVE VEHICLE.
• USING TECH 1, SELECT DATA LIST.
• MONITOR ALL WHEEL SPEEDS WHILE SLOWLY DECELERATING FROM 35 MPH TO 0 MPH.
• ARE ALL WHEEL SPEEDS APPROXIMATELY EQUAL?

YES → FAULT IS NOT PRESENT AT THIS TIME. REFER TO "DIAGNOSTIC AIDS" ON FACING PAGE.

NO

② • IGNITION "OFF."
• PHYSICALLY INSPECT WHEEL SPEED SENSOR CIRCUITS IN QUESTION FOR DAMAGE. ALSO, CHECK WIRE CONNECTIONS FOR CORROSION OR POOR MATING OF CONNECTORS.
• IS PHYSICAL DAMAGE INDICATED?

YES → CORRECT PHYSICAL DAMAGE, CLEAR CODES AND RE-CHECK.

NO

③ • DID BOTH REAR WHEEL SPEED SENSORS INDICATE 0 MPH, OR ERRATIC WHEEL SPEEDS?

NO → USING CHART BELOW, REFER TO SPEED SENSOR CODE CHART FOR AFFECTED WHEELS.

YES

④ • INSPECT 4 WAY REAR WHEEL EXTENSION HARNESS CONNECTORS FOR CORROSION, POOR MATING OR DAMAGE.
• IS DAMAGE INDICATED?

YES → CORRECT DAMAGE, CLEAR CODES AND RE-CHECK.

NO

⑤ • DISCONNECT REAR WHEEL SPEED SENSORS.
• USING DVM CONNECTED BETWEEN TERMINALS "A" AND "B" OF THE REAR WHEEL SPEED SENSORS, MEASURE RESISTANCE. RESISTANCE SHOULD BE BETWEEN 2100 AND 2400 OHMS FOR REAR SENSORS.
• ARE RESISTANCE VALUES IN ACCEPTABLE RANGES?

NO → REPLACE WHEEL SPEED SENSOR(S) THAT DID NOT INDICATE PROPER RESISTANCE, AND RE-CHECK.

YES

⑥ • USING DVM CONNECTED BETWEEN TERMINAL "A" OF THE SUSPECTED WHEEL SENSOR AND GROUND, MEASURE RESISTANCE. DVM SHOULD INDICATE INFINITE RESISTANCE.
• DOES IT?

NO → REPLACE WHEEL SPEED SENSOR(S) THAT DID NOT INDICATE PROPER RESISTANCE, AND RE-CHECK.

YES

GO TO FOLLOWING PAGE OF THIS CODE CHART (PAGE 2 OF 2)

SENSOR	CODE
L/F SENSOR	A021
R/F SENSOR	A022
L/R SENSOR	A023
R/R SENSOR	A024

CODE A031
(Page 2 of 2)
TWO WHEEL SPEEDS = 0

CONTINUED FROM CHART CODE A031 (PAGE 1 OF 2)

⑦ • CONNECT DVM TO TERMINAL "A" OF WHEEL SPEED SENSOR HARNESS CONNECTOR IN QUESTION.
• DISCONNECT 24 WAY WORLD CONNECTOR.
• USING THE TABLE SUPPLIED AT THE BOTTOM OF THIS PAGE, CONNECT DVM TO THE APPROPRIATE TERMINAL OF THE 24 WAY WORLD CONNECTOR AND MEASURE RESISTANCE. RESISTANCE SHOULD BE LESS THAN 2 OHMS.
• IS IT?

NO → REPAIR CIRCUIT THAT SHOWED HIGH RESISTANCE OR OPEN.

YES

⑧ • USING DVM, PROBE CONNECTOR TERMINAL "B" OF WHEEL SPEED SENSOR IN QUESTION.
• USING THE TABLE SUPPLIED, CONNECT DVM TO THE APPROPRIATE TERMINAL OF THE 24 WAY WORLD CONNECTOR AND MEASURE RESISTANCE. RESISTANCE SHOULD BE LESS THAN 2 OHMS.
• IS IT?

NO → REPAIR CIRCUIT THAT SHOWED HIGH RESISTANCE OR OPEN.

YES

⑨ • CONNECT DVM BETWEEN WHEEL SPEED SENSOR CONNECTOR TERMINAL "A" AND GROUND THEN REPEAT PROCEDURE ON TERMINAL "B". RESISTANCE SHOULD BE INFINITE ON BOTH TERMINALS.
• IS IT?

NO → REPAIR SHORT TO GROUND IN CIRCUIT THAT DID NOT SHOW INFINITE RESISTANCE.

YES

⑩ • DVM STILL CONNECTED.
• SELECT THE 20 VOLT SCALE OF THE DVM.
• IGNITION "ON."
• REPEAT STEP 8.
• VOLTAGE SHOULD BE 0.
• IS IT?

NO → REPAIR SHORT TO VOLTAGE IN CIRCUIT THAT INDICATED VOLTAGE ABOVE 0 VOLTS.

YES

• INSPECT 24 WAY WORLD CONNECTOR TERMINALS FOR POOR CONNECTION.
• RE-CONNECT ALL CONNECTIONS AND REPEAT STEP 1.
• IF WHEEL SPEED DOES NOT MATCH REMAINING WHEEL SPEED INPUTS, REPLACE EBCM.

SENSOR TERMINAL	24 WAY WORLD CONNECTOR	CIRCUIT NUMBER
L/R WHEEL A	PIN 12	884
L/R WHEEL B	PIN 11	885
R/R WHEEL A	PIN 7	882
R/R WHEEL B	PIN 8	883

THIS CHART ASSUMES THAT A CURRENT CODE IS STORED INDICATING THAT THIS FAULT IS PRESENT.

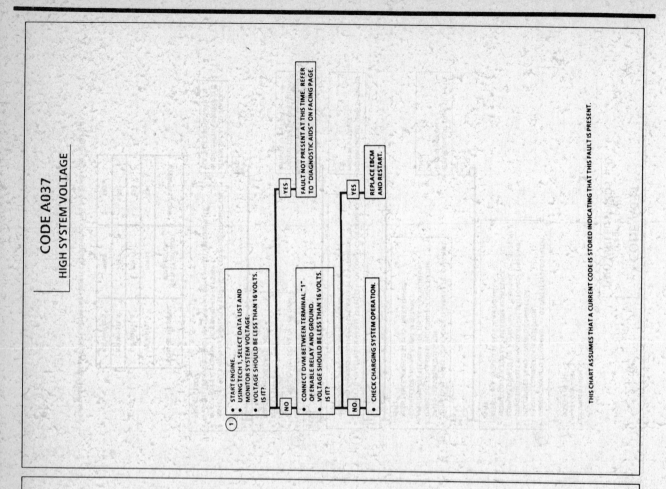

CODE A037
HIGH SYSTEM VOLTAGE

① START ENGINE.
- USING TECH 1, SELECT DATA LIST AND MONITOR SYSTEM VOLTAGE.
- VOLTAGE SHOULD BE LESS THAN 16 VOLTS. IS IT?

YES → FAULT NOT PRESENT AT THIS TIME. REFER TO "DIAGNOSTIC AIDS" ON FACING PAGE.

NO → CONNECT DVM BETWEEN TERMINAL "1" OF ENABLE RELAY AND GROUND.
- VOLTAGE SHOULD BE LESS THAN 16 VOLTS. IS IT?

YES → REPLACE EBCM AND RESTART.

NO → CHECK CHARGING SYSTEM OPERATION.

THIS CHART ASSUMES THAT A CURRENT CODE IS STORED INDICATING THAT THIS FAULT IS PRESENT.

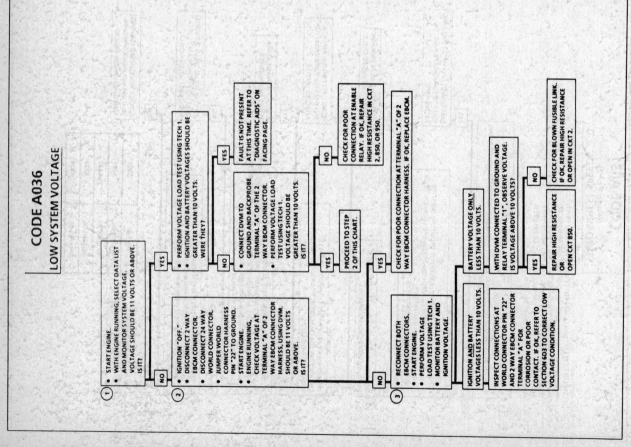

CODE A036
LOW SYSTEM VOLTAGE

① START ENGINE.
- WITH ENGINE RUNNING, SELECT DATA LIST AND MONITOR SYSTEM VOLTAGE.
- VOLTAGE SHOULD BE 11 VOLTS OR ABOVE. IS IT?

② IGNITION "OFF."
- DISCONNECT 2 WAY EBCM CONNECTOR.
- DISCONNECT 24 WAY WORLD CONNECTOR.
- JUMPER WORLD CONNECTOR HARNESS PIN "22" TO GROUND.
- START ENGINE.
- ENGINE RUNNING, CHECK VOLTAGE AT TERMINAL "A" OF 2 WAY EBCM CONNECTOR HARNESS, USING DVM. SHOULD BE 11 VOLTS OR ABOVE. IS IT?

YES → PERFORM VOLTAGE LOAD TEST USING TECH 1.
- IGNITION AND BATTERY VOLTAGES SHOULD BE GREATER THAN 10 VOLTS. WERE THEY?

YES → FAULT IS NOT PRESENT AT THIS TIME. REFER TO "DIAGNOSTIC AIDS" ON FACING PAGE.

NO → CONNECT DVM TO GROUND AND BACKPROBE TERMINAL "A" OF THE 2 WAY EBCM CONNECTOR.
- PERFORM VOLTAGE LOAD TEST USING TECH 1.
- VOLTAGE SHOULD BE GREATER THAN 10 VOLTS. IS IT?

YES → PROCEED TO STEP 2 OF THIS CHART.

NO → CHECK FOR POOR CONNECTION AT ENABLE RELAY. IF OK, REPAIR HIGH RESISTANCE IN CKT 2, 850, OR 950.

③ RECONNECT BOTH EBCM CONNECTORS.
- START ENGINE.
- PERFORM VOLTAGE LOAD TEST USING TECH 1.
- MONITOR BATTERY AND IGNITION VOLTAGE.

YES → CHECK FOR POOR CONNECTION AT TERMINAL "A" OF 2 WAY EBCM CONNECTOR HARNESS. IF OK, REPLACE EBCM.

NO → IGNITION AND BATTERY VOLTAGES LESS THAN 10 VOLTS.

INSPECT CONNECTIONS AT WORLD CONNECTOR PIN "22" AND 2 WAY EBCM CONNECTOR TERMINAL "A" FOR CORROSION OR POOR CONTACT. IF OK, REFER TO SECTION 603 TO CORRECT LOW VOLTAGE CONDITION.

BATTERY VOLTAGE ONLY LESS THAN 10 VOLTS.

WITH DVM CONNECTED TO GROUND AND RELAY TERMINAL "1", OBSERVE VOLTAGE. IS VOLTAGE ABOVE 10 VOLTS?

YES → REPAIR HIGH RESISTANCE OR OPEN CKT 850.

NO → CHECK FOR BLOWN FUSIBLE LINK. IF OK, REPAIR HIGH RESISTANCE OR OPEN IN CKT 2.

CODE A038

LEFT FRONT EMB WILL NOT HOLD MOTOR

NOTICE: TESTING EMB WITH JUMPER WIRES TO VOLTAGE OR GROUND WILL DESTROY THE EMB.

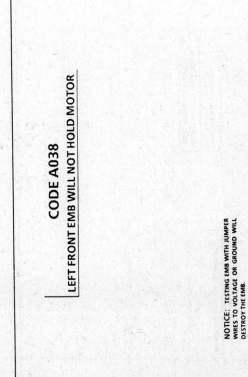

IS CODE A067 ALSO PRESENT?

NO → YES → PROCEED TO THAT CODE FIRST.

1. • IGNITION "ON," ENGINE "OFF."
   • USING TECH 1, SELECT EMB FUNCTIONAL TEST.
   • APPLY FIRM PRESSURE ON BRAKE PEDAL.
   • PERFORM EMB FUNCTIONAL TEST.
   • BRAKE PEDAL SHOULD NOT FALL OR RISE DURING THIS TEST.
   DID IT?

YES → 2. USING TECH 1, PERFORM GEAR TENSION RELIEF FUNCTION.
   REPLACE MOTOR PACK ASSEMBLY.

NO → FAULT IS NOT PRESENT AT THIS TIME. REFER TO "DIAGNOSTIC AIDS" ON FACING PAGE.

CODE A041

RIGHT FRONT EMB WILL NOT HOLD MOTOR

NOTICE: TESTING EMB WITH JUMPER WIRES TO VOLTAGE OR GROUND WILL DESTROY THE EMB.

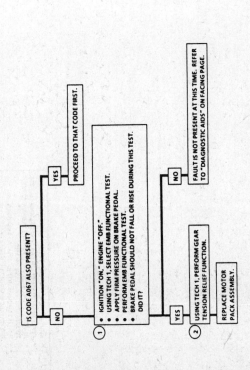

IS CODE A071 ALSO PRESENT?

NO → YES → PROCEED TO THAT CODE FIRST.

1. • IGNITION "ON," ENGINE "OFF."
   • USING TECH 1, SELECT EMB FUNCTIONAL TEST.
   • APPLY FIRM PRESSURE ON BRAKE PEDAL.
   • PERFORM EMB FUNCTIONAL TEST.
   • BRAKE PEDAL SHOULD NOT FALL OR RISE DURING THIS TEST.
   DID IT?

YES → 2. USING TECH 1, PERFORM GEAR TENSION RELIEF FUNCTION.
   REPLACE MOTOR PACK ASSEMBLY.

NO → FAULT IS NOT PRESENT AT THIS TIME. REFER TO "DIAGNOSTIC AIDS" ON FACING PAGE.

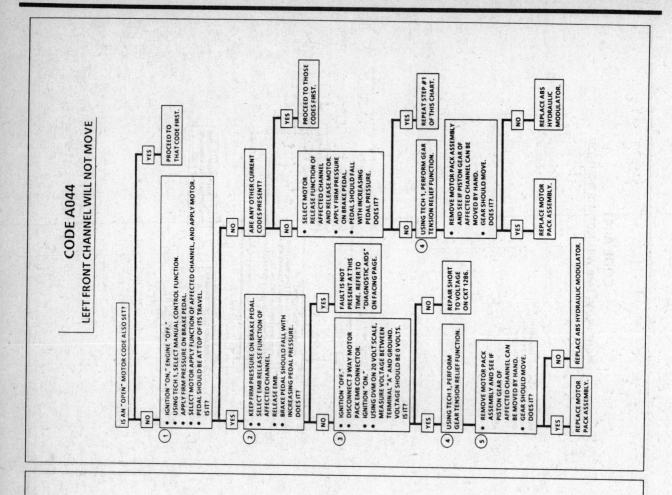

CODE A044

LEFT FRONT CHANNEL WILL NOT MOVE

IS AN "OPEN" MOTOR CODE ALSO SET?

NO → ① IGNITION "ON," ENGINE "OFF."
- USING TECH 1, SELECT MANUAL CONTROL FUNCTION.
- APPLY FIRM PRESSURE ON BRAKE PEDAL.
- SELECT MOTOR APPLY FUNCTION OF AFFECTED CHANNEL, AND APPLY MOTOR.
- PEDAL SHOULD BE AT TOP OF ITS TRAVEL. IS IT?

YES → PROCEED TO THAT CODE FIRST.

NO → ARE ANY OTHER CURRENT CODES PRESENT?

YES → PROCEED TO THOSE CODES FIRST.

NO → SELECT MOTOR RELEASE FUNCTION OF AFFECTED CHANNEL AND RELEASE MOTOR.
- APPLY FIRM PRESSURE ON BRAKE PEDAL.
- PEDAL SHOULD FALL WITH INCREASING PEDAL PRESSURE. DOES IT?

YES → ④ USING TECH 1, PERFORM GEAR TENSION RELIEF FUNCTION.

YES → REPEAT STEP #1 OF THIS CHART.

② KEEP FIRM PRESSURE ON BRAKE PEDAL.
- SELECT EMB RELEASE FUNCTION OF AFFECTED CHANNEL.
- RELEASE EMB.
- BRAKE PEDAL SHOULD FALL WITH INCREASING PEDAL PRESSURE. DOES IT?

YES → FAULT IS NOT PRESENT AT THIS TIME. REFER TO "DIAGNOSTIC AIDS" ON FACING PAGE.

NO → ③ IGNITION "OFF."
- DISCONNECT 3 WAY MOTOR PACK EMB CONNECTOR.
- IGNITION "ON."
- USING DVM ON 20 VOLT SCALE, MEASURE VOLTAGE BETWEEN TERMINAL "A" AND GROUND. VOLTAGE SHOULD BE 0 VOLTS. IS IT?

NO → REPAIR SHORT TO VOLTAGE ON CKT 1286.

YES → ④ USING TECH 1, PERFORM GEAR TENSION RELIEF FUNCTION.

⑤ REMOVE MOTOR PACK ASSEMBLY AND SEE IF PISTON GEAR OF AFFECTED CHANNEL CAN BE MOVED BY HAND. GEAR SHOULD MOVE. DOES IT?

YES → REPLACE MOTOR PACK ASSEMBLY.

NO → REPLACE ABS HYDRAULIC MODULATOR.

REMOVE MOTOR PACK ASSEMBLY AND SEE IF PISTON GEAR OF AFFECTED CHANNEL CAN BE MOVED BY HAND. GEAR SHOULD MOVE. DOES IT?

YES → REPLACE MOTOR PACK ASSEMBLY.

NO → REPLACE ABS HYDRAULIC MODULATOR.

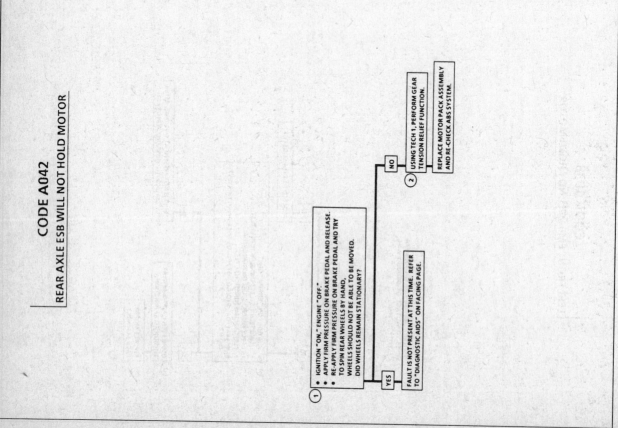

CODE A042

REAR AXLE ESB WILL NOT HOLD MOTOR

① IGNITION "ON," ENGINE "OFF."
- APPLY FIRM PRESSURE ON BRAKE PEDAL AND RELEASE.
- RE-APPLY FIRM PRESSURE ON BRAKE PEDAL AND TRY TO SPIN REAR WHEELS BY HAND,
WHEELS SHOULD NOT BE ABLE TO BE MOVED. DID WHEELS REMAIN STATIONARY?

YES → FAULT IS NOT PRESENT AT THIS TIME. REFER TO "DIAGNOSTIC AIDS" ON FACING PAGE.

NO → ② USING TECH 1, PERFORM GEAR TENSION RELIEF FUNCTION.

REPLACE MOTOR PACK ASSEMBLY AND RE-CHECK ABS SYSTEM.

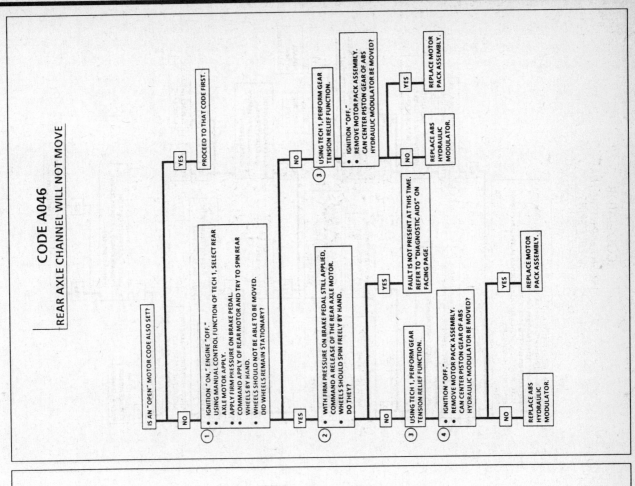

CODE A046

REAR AXLE CHANNEL WILL NOT MOVE

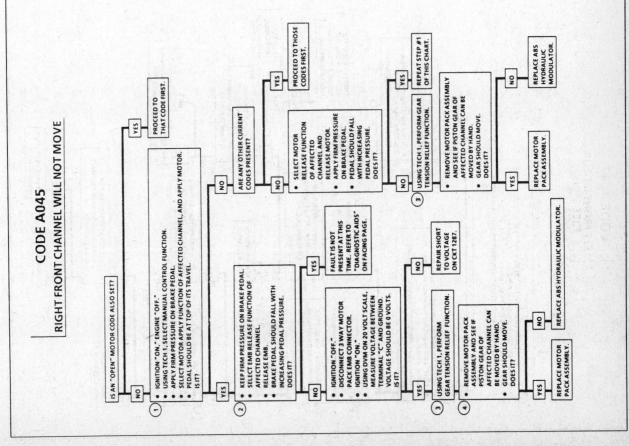

CODE A045

RIGHT FRONT CHANNEL WILL NOT MOVE

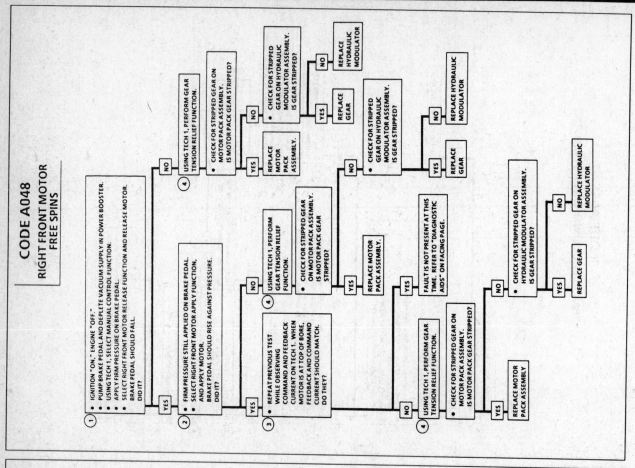

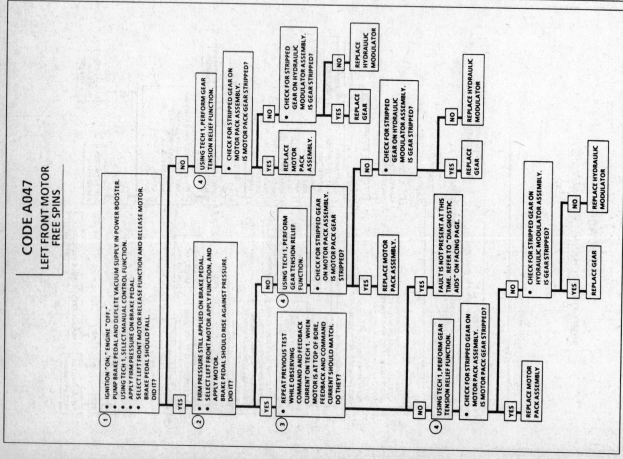

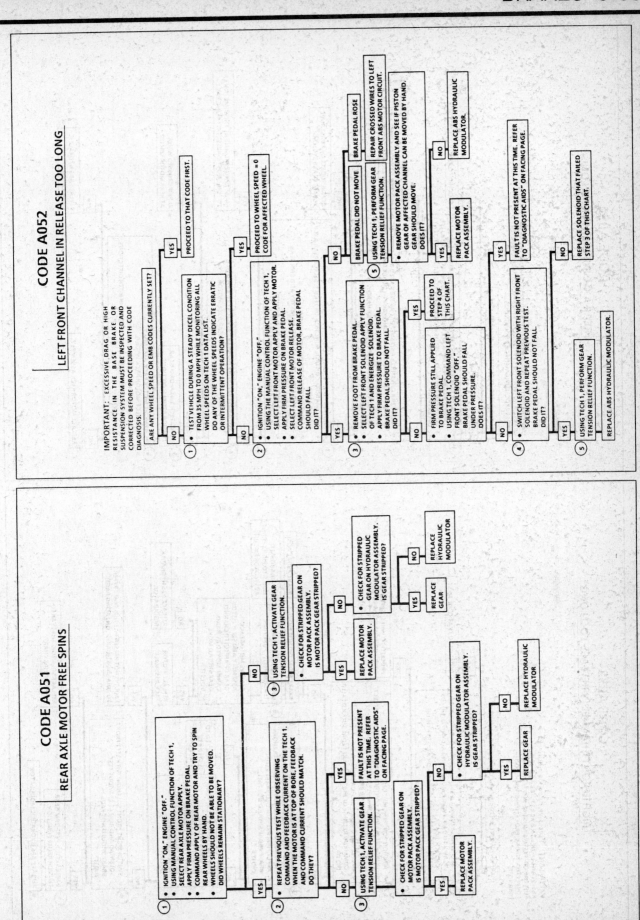

CODE A054
REAR AXLE IN RELEASE TOO LONG

IMPORTANT: EXCESSIVE DRAG OR HIGH RESISTANCE IN THE BASE BRAKE OR SUSPENSION SYSTEM MUST BE INSPECTED AND CORRECTED BEFORE PROCEEDING WITH CODE DIAGNOSIS.

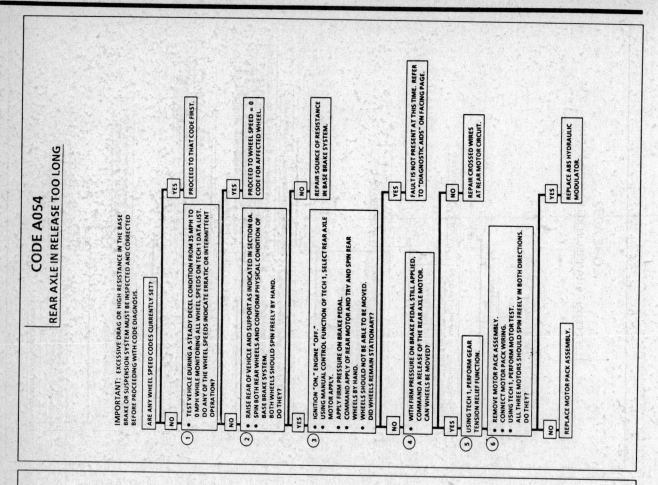

CODE A053
RIGHT FRONT CHANNEL IN RELEASE TOO LONG

IMPORTANT: EXCESSIVE DRAG OR HIGH RESISTANCE IN THE BASE BRAKE OR SUSPENSION SYSTEM MUST BE INSPECTED AND CORRECTED BEFORE PROCEEDING WITH CODE DIAGNOSIS.

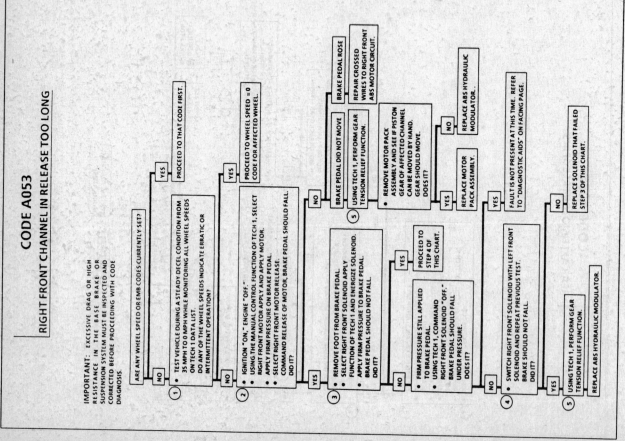

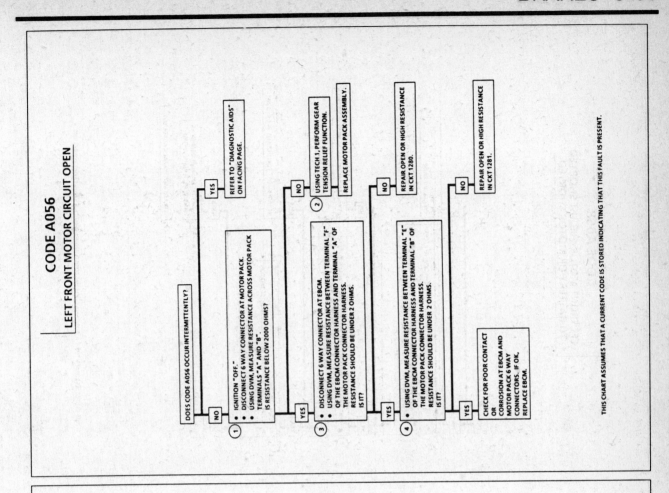

CODE A056
LEFT FRONT MOTOR CIRCUIT OPEN

1.
- IGNITION "OFF."
- DISCONNECT 6 WAY CONNECTOR AT MOTOR PACK.
- USING DVM, MEASURE RESISTANCE ACROSS MOTOR PACK TERMINALS "A" AND "B".
- IS RESISTANCE BELOW 2000 OHMS?

DOES CODE A056 OCCUR INTERMITTENTLY?

YES → REFER TO "DIAGNOSTIC AIDS" ON FACING PAGE.

NO →

2. USING TECH 1, PERFORM GEAR TENSION RELIEF FUNCTION. REPLACE MOTOR PACK ASSEMBLY.

NO →

3.
- DISCONNECT 6 WAY CONNECTOR AT EBCM.
- USING DVM, MEASURE RESISTANCE BETWEEN TERMINAL "F" OF THE EBCM CONNECTOR HARNESS AND TERMINAL "A" OF THE MOTOR PACK CONNECTOR HARNESS. RESISTANCE SHOULD BE UNDER 2 OHMS. IS IT?

NO → REPAIR OPEN OR HIGH RESISTANCE IN CKT 1280.

YES →

4.
- USING DVM, MEASURE RESISTANCE BETWEEN TERMINAL "E" OF THE EBCM CONNECTOR HARNESS AND TERMINAL "B" OF THE MOTOR PACK CONNECTOR HARNESS. RESISTANCE SHOULD BE UNDER 2 OHMS. IS IT?

NO → REPAIR OPEN OR HIGH RESISTANCE IN CKT 1281.

YES →

CHECK FOR POOR CONTACT OR CORROSION AT EBCM AND MOTOR PACK 6 WAY CONNECTORS. IF OK, REPLACE EBCM.

THIS CHART ASSUMES THAT A CURRENT CODE IS STORED INDICATING THAT THIS FAULT IS PRESENT.

CODE A055
MOTOR DRIVER FAULT DETECTED

1.
- IGNITION "ON," ENGINE "OFF."
- USING TECH 1, "SCAN" CODES.
- ARE ANY MOTOR OR EMB CODES CURRENTLY SET?

YES → PROCEED TO THAT CODE FIRST.

NO →

2. CLEAR CODES. DOES CODE A055 RE-SET?

NO → FAULT IS NOT PRESENT AT THIS TIME. REFER TO "DIAGNOSTIC AIDS" ON FACING PAGE.

YES →

ARE ANY MOTOR OR EMB CODES SET WITH CODE A055?

YES → PROCEED TO THE MOTOR OR EMB CODE(S) THAT SET.

NO →

3. CHECK FOR CORROSION OR POOR CONTACT AT 3 WAY AND 6 WAY MOTOR PACK CONNECTORS. IF OK, REPLACE EBCM.

THIS CHART ASSUMES THAT A CURRENT CODE IS STORED INDICATING THAT THIS FAULT IS PRESENT.

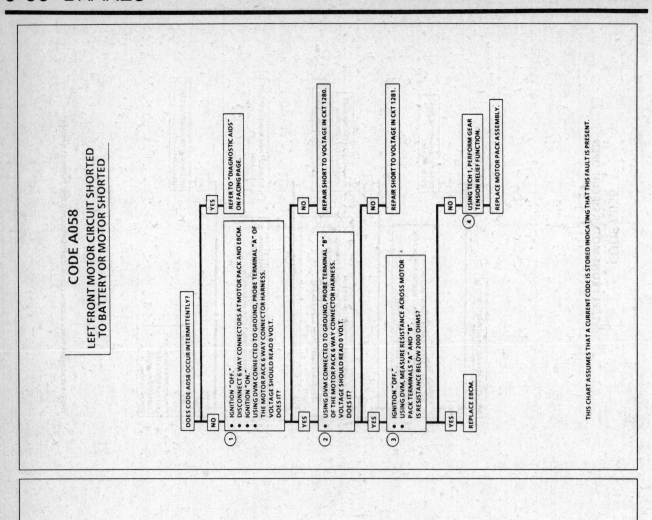

CODE A058

LEFT FRONT MOTOR CIRCUIT SHORTED
TO BATTERY OR MOTOR SHORTED

DOES CODE A058 OCCUR INTERMITTENTLY?

YES — REFER TO "DIAGNOSTIC AIDS" ON FACING PAGE.

NO

1.
- IGNITION "OFF."
- DISCONNECT 6 WAY CONNECTORS AT MOTOR PACK AND EBCM.
- IGNITION "ON."
- USING DVM CONNECTED TO GROUND, PROBE TERMINAL "A" OF THE MOTOR PACK 6 WAY CONNECTOR HARNESS. VOLTAGE SHOULD READ 0 VOLT.
DOES IT?

NO — REPAIR SHORT TO VOLTAGE IN CKT 1280.

YES

2.
- USING DVM CONNECTED TO GROUND, PROBE TERMINAL "B" OF THE MOTOR PACK 6 WAY CONNECTOR HARNESS. VOLTAGE SHOULD READ 0 VOLT.
DOES IT?

NO — REPAIR SHORT TO VOLTAGE IN CKT 1281.

YES

3.
- IGNITION "OFF."
- USING DVM, MEASURE RESISTANCE ACROSS MOTOR PACK TERMINALS "A" AND "B". IS RESISTANCE BELOW 2000 OHMS?

NO — 4. USING TECH 1, PERFORM GEAR TENSION RELIEF FUNCTION.
REPLACE MOTOR PACK ASSEMBLY.

YES — REPLACE EBCM.

THIS CHART ASSUMES THAT A CURRENT CODE IS STORED INDICATING THAT THIS FAULT IS PRESENT.

CODE A057

LEFT FRONT MOTOR CIRCUIT SHORTED TO GROUND

DOES CODE A057 OCCUR INTERMITTENTLY?

YES — REFER TO "DIAGNOSTIC AIDS" ON FACING PAGE.

NO

1.
- IGNITION "OFF."
- DISCONNECT 6 WAY CONNECTORS AT MOTOR PACK AND EBCM.
- USING DVM CONNECTED TO GROUND, PROBE TERMINAL "A" OF THE MOTOR PACK 6 WAY CONNECTOR HARNESS. RESISTANCE SHOULD BE INFINITE.
IS IT?

NO — REPAIR SHORT TO GROUND IN CKT 1280.

YES

2.
- USING DVM CONNECTED TO GROUND, PROBE TERMINAL "B" OF THE MOTOR PACK 6 WAY CONNECTOR HARNESS. RESISTANCE SHOULD BE INFINITE.
IS IT?

NO — REPAIR SHORT TO GROUND IN CKT 1281.

YES

3.
- USING DVM CONNECTED TO GROUND, PROBE TERMINAL "A" OF THE MOTOR PACK. RESISTANCE SHOULD BE INFINITE.
IS IT?

NO — 4. USING TECH 1, PERFORM GEAR TENSION RELIEF FUNCTION.
REPLACE MOTOR PACK ASSEMBLY.

YES — REPLACE EBCM AND RECHECK ABS SYSTEM.

THIS CHART ASSUMES THAT A CURRENT CODE IS STORED INDICATING THAT THIS FAULT IS PRESENT.

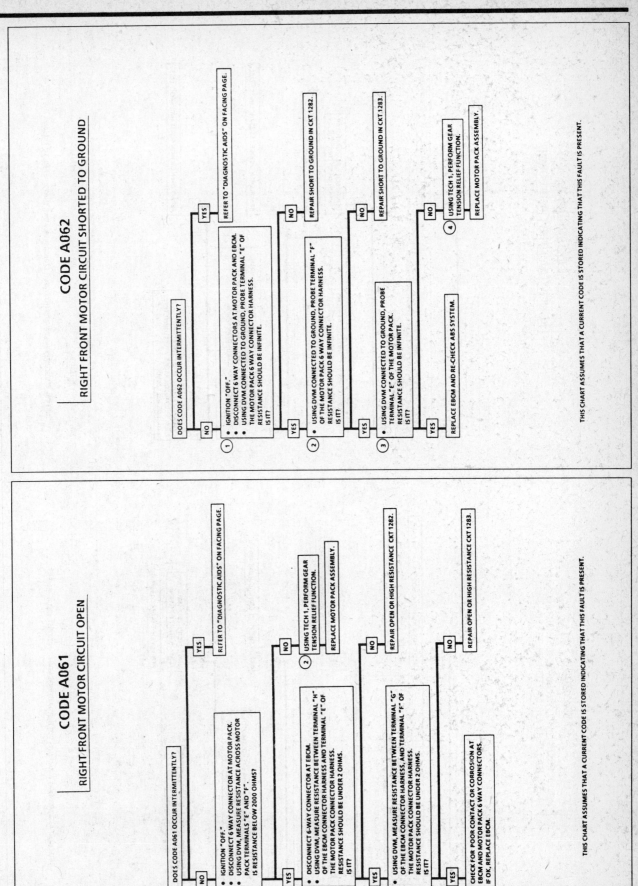

CODE A062

RIGHT FRONT MOTOR CIRCUIT SHORTED TO GROUND

DOES CODE A062 OCCUR INTERMITTENTLY?

YES → REFER TO "DIAGNOSTIC AIDS" ON FACING PAGE.

NO

① IGNITION "OFF."
- DISCONNECT 6 WAY CONNECTORS AT MOTOR PACK AND EBCM.
- USING DVM CONNECTED TO GROUND, PROBE TERMINAL "E" OF THE MOTOR PACK 6 WAY CONNECTOR HARNESS. RESISTANCE SHOULD BE INFINITE.
IS IT?

NO → REPAIR SHORT TO GROUND IN CKT 1282.

YES

② USING DVM CONNECTED TO GROUND, PROBE TERMINAL "F" OF THE MOTOR PACK 6 WAY CONNECTOR HARNESS. RESISTANCE SHOULD BE INFINITE.
IS IT?

NO → REPAIR SHORT TO GROUND IN CKT 1283.

YES

③ USING DVM CONNECTED TO GROUND, PROBE TERMINAL "E" OF THE MOTOR PACK. RESISTANCE SHOULD BE INFINITE.
IS IT?

YES → REPLACE EBCM AND RE-CHECK ABS SYSTEM.

NO

④ USING TECH 1, PERFORM GEAR TENSION RELIEF FUNCTION.

REPLACE MOTOR PACK ASSEMBLY.

THIS CHART ASSUMES THAT A CURRENT CODE IS STORED INDICATING THAT THIS FAULT IS PRESENT.

CODE A061

RIGHT FRONT MOTOR CIRCUIT OPEN

DOES CODE A061 OCCUR INTERMITTENTLY?

YES → REFER TO "DIAGNOSTIC AIDS" ON FACING PAGE.

NO

① IGNITION "OFF."
- DISCONNECT 6 WAY CONNECTOR AT MOTOR PACK.
- USING DVM, MEASURE RESISTANCE ACROSS MOTOR PACK TERMINALS "E" AND "F".
IS RESISTANCE BELOW 2000 OHMS?

YES

③ DISCONNECT 6-WAY CONNECTOR AT EBCM.
- USING DVM, MEASURE RESISTANCE BETWEEN TERMINAL "H" OF THE EBCM CONNECTOR HARNESS AND TERMINAL "E" OF THE MOTOR PACK CONNECTOR HARNESS. RESISTANCE SHOULD BE UNDER 2 OHMS.
IS IT?

NO → USING TECH 1, PERFORM GEAR TENSION RELIEF FUNCTION. ②

REPLACE MOTOR PACK ASSEMBLY.

YES

④ USING DVM, MEASURE RESISTANCE BETWEEN TERMINAL "G" OF THE EBCM CONNECTOR HARNESS, AND TERMINAL "F" OF THE MOTOR PACK CONNECTOR HARNESS. RESISTANCE SHOULD BE UNDER 2 OHMS.
IS IT?

NO → REPAIR OPEN OR HIGH RESISTANCE CKT 1282.

YES

CHECK FOR POOR CONTACT OR CORROSION AT EBCM AND MOTOR PACK 6 WAY CONNECTORS. IF OK, REPLACE EBCM.

NO → REPAIR OPEN OR HIGH RESISTANCE CKT 1283.

THIS CHART ASSUMES THAT A CURRENT CODE IS STORED INDICATING THAT THIS FAULT IS PRESENT.

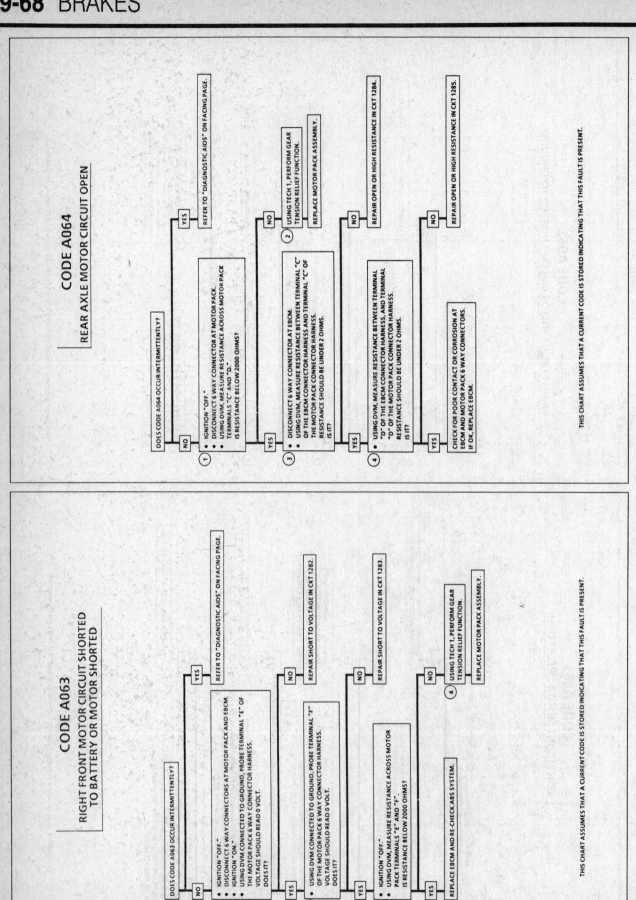

CODE A064

REAR AXLE MOTOR CIRCUIT OPEN

DOES CODE A064 OCCUR INTERMITTENTLY?

YES → REFER TO "DIAGNOSTIC AIDS" ON FACING PAGE.

NO

① • IGNITION "OFF."
• DISCONNECT 6 WAY CONNECTOR AT MOTOR PACK.
• USING DVM, MEASURE RESISTANCE ACROSS MOTOR PACK TERMINALS "C" AND "D."
IS RESISTANCE BELOW 2000 OHMS?

NO → ② USING TECH 1, PERFORM GEAR TENSION RELIEF FUNCTION.
REPLACE MOTOR PACK ASSEMBLY.

YES

③ • DISCONNECT 6 WAY CONNECTOR AT EBCM.
• USING DVM, MEASURE RESISTANCE BETWEEN TERMINAL "C" OF THE EBCM CONNECTOR HARNESS AND TERMINAL "C" OF THE MOTOR PACK CONNECTOR HARNESS.
RESISTANCE SHOULD BE UNDER 2 OHMS.
IS IT?

NO → REPAIR OPEN OR HIGH RESISTANCE IN CKT 1284.

YES

④ • USING DVM, MEASURE RESISTANCE BETWEEN TERMINAL "D" OF THE EBCM CONNECTOR HARNESS, AND TERMINAL "D" OF THE MOTOR PACK CONNECTOR HARNESS.
RESISTANCE SHOULD BE UNDER 2 OHMS.
IS IT?

NO → REPAIR OPEN OR HIGH RESISTANCE IN CKT 1285.

YES → CHECK FOR POOR CONTACT OR CORROSION AT EBCM AND MOTOR PACK 6 WAY CONNECTORS.
IF OK, REPLACE EBCM.

THIS CHART ASSUMES THAT A CURRENT CODE IS STORED INDICATING THAT THIS FAULT IS PRESENT.

CODE A063

RIGHT FRONT MOTOR CIRCUIT SHORTED TO BATTERY OR MOTOR SHORTED

DOES CODE A063 OCCUR INTERMITTENTLY?

YES → REFER TO "DIAGNOSTIC AIDS" ON FACING PAGE.

NO

① • IGNITION "OFF."
• DISCONNECT 6 WAY CONNECTORS AT MOTOR PACK AND EBCM.
• IGNITION "ON."
• USING DVM CONNECTED TO GROUND, PROBE TERMINAL "E" OF THE MOTOR PACK 6 WAY CONNECTOR HARNESS.
VOLTAGE SHOULD READ 0 VOLT.
DOES IT?

NO → REPAIR SHORT TO VOLTAGE IN CKT 1282.

YES

② • USING DVM CONNECTED TO GROUND, PROBE TERMINAL "F" OF THE MOTOR PACK 6 WAY CONNECTOR HARNESS.
VOLTAGE SHOULD READ 0 VOLT.
DOES IT?

NO → REPAIR SHORT TO VOLTAGE IN CKT 1283.

YES

③ • IGNITION "OFF."
• USING DVM, MEASURE RESISTANCE ACROSS MOTOR PACK TERMINALS "E" AND "F."
IS RESISTANCE BELOW 2000 OHMS?

NO → ④ USING TECH 1, PERFORM GEAR TENSION RELIEF FUNCTION.
REPLACE MOTOR PACK ASSEMBLY.

YES → REPLACE EBCM AND RE-CHECK ABS SYSTEM.

THIS CHART ASSUMES THAT A CURRENT CODE IS STORED INDICATING THAT THIS FAULT IS PRESENT.

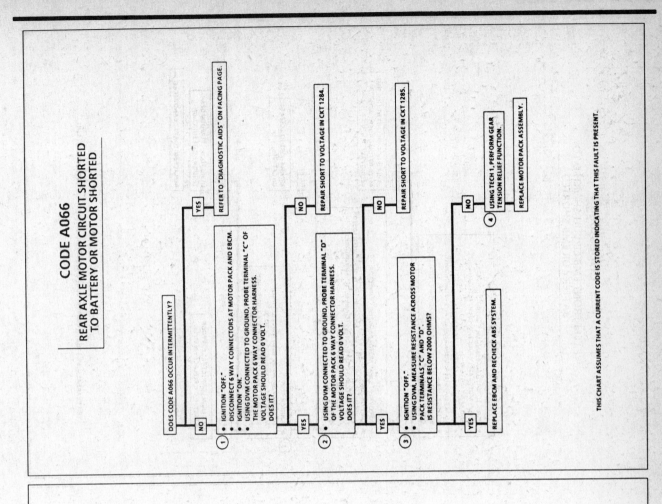

CODE A066

REAR AXLE MOTOR CIRCUIT SHORTED TO BATTERY OR MOTOR SHORTED

DOES CODE A066 OCCUR INTERMITTENTLY?

YES → REFER TO "DIAGNOSTIC AIDS" ON FACING PAGE.

NO

① • IGNITION "OFF."
• DISCONNECT 6 WAY CONNECTORS AT MOTOR PACK AND EBCM.
• IGNITION "ON."
• USING DVM CONNECTED TO GROUND, PROBE TERMINAL "C" OF THE MOTOR PACK 6 WAY CONNECTOR HARNESS. VOLTAGE SHOULD READ 0 VOLT.
DOES IT?

NO → REPAIR SHORT TO VOLTAGE IN CKT 1284.

YES

② • USING DVM CONNECTED TO GROUND, PROBE TERMINAL "D" OF THE MOTOR PACK 6 WAY CONNECTOR HARNESS. VOLTAGE SHOULD READ 0 VOLT.
DOES IT?

NO → REPAIR SHORT TO VOLTAGE IN CKT 1285.

YES

③ • IGNITION "OFF."
• USING DVM, MEASURE RESISTANCE ACROSS MOTOR PACK TERMINALS "C" AND "D". IS RESISTANCE BELOW 2000 OHMS?

NO → USING TECH 1, PERFORM GEAR TENSION RELIEF FUNCTION.
④ → REPLACE MOTOR PACK ASSEMBLY.

YES → REPLACE EBCM AND RECHECK ABS SYSTEM.

THIS CHART ASSUMES THAT A CURRENT CODE IS STORED INDICATING THAT THIS FAULT IS PRESENT.

CODE A065

REAR AXLE MOTOR CIRCUIT SHORTED TO GROUND

DOES CODE A065 OCCUR INTERMITTENTLY?

YES → REFER TO "DIAGNOSTIC AIDS" ON FACING PAGE.

NO

① • IGNITION "OFF."
• DISCONNECT 6 WAY CONNECTORS AT MOTOR PACK AND EBCM.
• USING DVM CONNECTED TO GROUND, PROBE TERMINAL "C" OF THE MOTOR PACK 6 WAY CONNECTOR HARNESS. RESISTANCE SHOULD BE INFINITE.
IS IT?

NO → REPAIR SHORT TO GROUND IN CKT 1284 AND REPEAT TEST #1 OF THIS CHART.

YES

② • USING DVM CONNECTED TO GROUND, PROBE TERMINAL "D" OF THE MOTOR PACK 6 WAY CONNECTOR HARNESS. RESISTANCE SHOULD BE INFINITE.
IS IT?

NO → REPAIR SHORT TO GROUND IN CKT 1285 AND REPEAT TEST #1 OF THIS CHART.

YES

③ • USING DVM CONNECTED TO GROUND, PROBE TERMINAL "C" OF THE MOTOR PACK. RESISTANCE SHOULD BE INFINITE.
IS IT?

NO → USING TECH 1, GEAR TENSION RELIEF FUNCTION.
④ → REPLACE MOTOR PACK ASSEMBLY.

YES → REPLACE EBCM AND RE-CHECK ABS SYSTEM.

THIS CHART ASSUMES THAT A CURRENT CODE IS STORED INDICATING THAT THIS FAULT IS PRESENT.

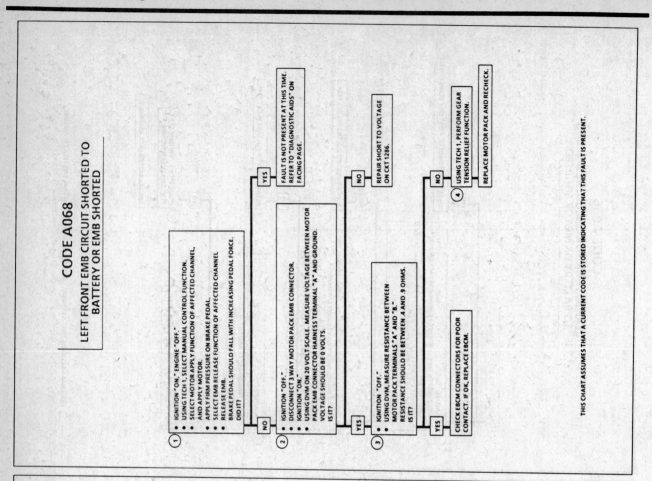

CODE A068

LEFT FRONT EMB CIRCUIT SHORTED TO BATTERY OR EMB SHORTED

1.
- IGNITION "ON," ENGINE "OFF."
- USING TECH 1, SELECT MANUAL CONTROL FUNCTION.
- SELECT MOTOR APPLY FUNCTION OF AFFECTED CHANNEL, AND APPLY MOTOR.
- APPLY FIRM PRESSURE ON BRAKE PEDAL.
- SELECT EMB RELEASE FUNCTION OF AFFECTED CHANNEL
- RELEASE EMB.
- BRAKE PEDAL SHOULD FALL WITH INCREASING PEDAL FORCE.

DID IT?

YES → FAULT IS NOT PRESENT AT THIS TIME. REFER TO "DIAGNOSTIC AIDS" ON FACING PAGE.

NO →

2.
- IGNITION "OFF."
- DISCONNECT 3 WAY MOTOR PACK EMB CONNECTOR.
- IGNITION "ON."
- USING DVM ON 20 VOLT SCALE. MEASURE VOLTAGE BETWEEN MOTOR PACK EMB CONNECTOR HARNESS TERMINAL "A" AND GROUND. VOLTAGE SHOULD BE 0 VOLTS.

IS IT?

NO → REPAIR SHORT TO VOLTAGE ON CKT 1286.

YES →

3.
- IGNITION "OFF."
- USING DVM, MEASURE RESISTANCE BETWEEN MOTOR PACK TERMINALS "A" AND "B." RESISTANCE SHOULD BE BETWEEN .4 AND .9 OHMS.

IS IT?

NO → (4) USING TECH 1, PERFORM GEAR TENSION RELIEF FUNCTION. REPLACE MOTOR PACK AND RECHECK.

YES → CHECK EBCM CONNECTORS FOR POOR CONTACT. IF OK, REPLACE EBCM.

THIS CHART ASSUMES THAT A CURRENT CODE IS STORED INDICATING THAT THIS FAULT IS PRESENT.

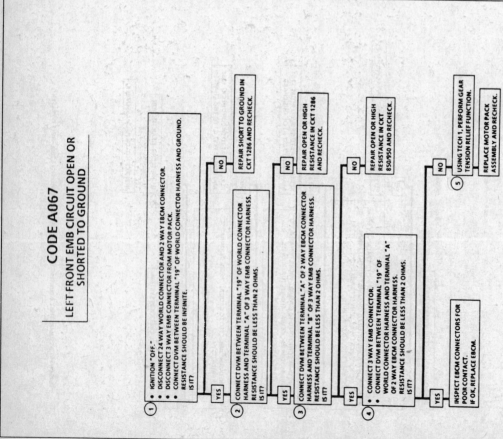

CODE A067

LEFT FRONT EMB CIRCUIT OPEN OR SHORTED TO GROUND

1.
- IGNITION "OFF."
- DISCONNECT 24 WAY WORLD CONNECTOR AND 2 WAY EBCM CONNECTOR.
- DISCONNECT 3 WAY EMB CONNECTOR FROM MOTOR PACK.
- CONNECT DVM BETWEEN TERMINAL "19" OF WORLD CONNECTOR HARNESS AND GROUND. RESISTANCE SHOULD BE INFINITE.

IS IT?

NO → REPAIR SHORT TO GROUND IN CKT 1286 AND RECHECK.

YES →

2.
- CONNECT DVM BETWEEN TERMINAL "A" OF 3 WAY EMB CONNECTOR HARNESS AND TERMINAL "19" OF WORLD CONNECTOR HARNESS. RESISTANCE SHOULD BE LESS THAN 2 OHMS.

IS IT?

NO → REPAIR OPEN OR HIGH RESISTANCE IN CKT 1286 AND RECHECK.

YES →

3.
- CONNECT DVM BETWEEN TERMINAL "A" OF 2 WAY EBCM CONNECTOR HARNESS AND TERMINAL "B" OF 3 WAY EMB CONNECTOR HARNESS. RESISTANCE SHOULD BE LESS THAN 2 OHMS.

IS IT?

NO → REPAIR OPEN OR HIGH RESISTANCE IN CKT 850/950 AND RECHECK.

YES →

4.
- CONNECT 3 WAY EMB CONNECTOR.
- CONNECT DVM BETWEEN TERMINAL "19" OF WORLD CONNECTOR HARNESS AND TERMINAL "A" OF 2 WAY EBCM CONNECTOR HARNESS. RESISTANCE SHOULD BE LESS THAN 2 OHMS.

IS IT?

NO → (5) USING TECH 1, PERFORM GEAR TENSION RELIEF FUNCTION. REPLACE MOTOR PACK ASSEMBLY AND RECHECK.

YES → INSPECT EBCM CONNECTORS FOR POOR CONTACT. IF OK, REPLACE EBCM.

THIS CHART ASSUMES THAT A CURRENT CODE IS STORED INDICATING THAT THIS FAULT IS PRESENT.

CODE A072

RIGHT FRONT EMB CIRCUIT SHORTED TO
BATTERY OR EMB SHORTED

1
- IGNITION "ON," ENGINE "OFF."
- USING TECH 1, SELECT MANUAL CONTROL FUNCTION.
- APPLY FIRM PRESSURE ON BRAKE PEDAL.
- SELECT MOTOR APPLY FUNCTION OF AFFECTED CHANNEL, AND APPLY MOTOR.
- SELECT EMB RELEASE FUNCTION OF AFFECTED CHANNEL.
- RELEASE EMB.
- BRAKE PEDAL SHOULD FALL.
  DID IT?

YES → FAULT IS NOT PRESENT AT THIS TIME. REFER TO "DIAGNOSTIC AIDS" ON FACING PAGE.

NO

2
- IGNITION "OFF."
- DISCONNECT 3 WAY MOTOR PACK EMB CONNECTOR.
- IGNITION "ON."
- USING DVM ON 20 VOLT SCALE, MEASURE VOLTAGE BETWEEN MOTOR PACK EMB CONNECTOR TERMINAL "C" OF EMB CONNECTOR HARNESS AND GROUND.
  VOLTAGE SHOULD BE 0 VOLT.
  IS IT?

NO → REPAIR SHORT TO VOLTAGE ON CKT 1287.

YES

3
- IGNITION "OFF."
- USING DVM, MEASURE RESISTANCE BETWEEN MOTOR PACK TERMINALS "B" AND "C".
  RESISTANCE SHOULD BE BETWEEN .4 AND .9 OHMS.
  IS IT?

NO
4
- USING TECH 1, PERFORM GEAR TENSION RELIEF FUNCTION.

REPLACE MOTOR PACK AND RECHECK.

YES → CHECK EBCM CONNECTORS FOR POOR CONTACT. IF OK, REPLACE EBCM.

THIS CHART ASSUMES THAT A CURRENT CODE IS STORED INDICATING THAT THIS FAULT IS PRESENT.

CODE A071

RIGHT FRONT EMB CIRCUIT OPEN
OR SHORTED TO GROUND

1
- IGNITION "OFF."
- DISCONNECT 24 WAY WORLD CONNECTOR AND 2 WAY EBCM CONNECTOR.
- DISCONNECT 3 WAY EMB CONNECTOR FROM MOTOR PACK.
- CONNECT DVM BETWEEN TERMINAL "20" OF WORLD CONNECTOR HARNESS AND GROUND.
  RESISTANCE SHOULD BE INFINITE.
  IS IT?

NO → REPAIR SHORT TO GROUND IN CKT 1287 AND RECHECK.

YES

2
- CONNECT DVM BETWEEN TERMINAL "20" OF WORLD CONNECTOR HARNESS AND TERMINAL "C" OF 3 WAY EMB CONNECTOR HARNESS.
  RESISTANCE SHOULD BE LESS THAN 2 OHMS.
  IS IT?

NO → REPAIR OPEN OR HIGH RESISTANCE IN CKT 1287 AND RECHECK.

YES

3
- CONNECT DVM BETWEEN TERMINAL "A" OF 2 WAY EBCM CONNECTOR HARNESS AND TERMINAL "B" OF 3 WAY EMB CONNECTOR HARNESS.
  RESISTANCE SHOULD BE LESS THAN 2 OHMS.
  IS IT?

NO → REPAIR OPEN OR HIGH RESISTANCE IN CKT 850/950 AND RECHECK.

YES

4
- CONNECT 3 WAY EMB CONNECTOR.
- CONNECT DVM BETWEEN TERMINAL "20" OF WORLD CONNECTOR HARNESS AND TERMINAL "A" OF 2 WAY EBCM CONNECTOR HARNESS.
  RESISTANCE SHOULD BE LESS THAN 2 OHMS.
  IS IT?

NO
5
- USING TECH 1, PERFORM GEAR TENSION RELIEF FUNCTION.

REPLACE MOTOR PACK ASSEMBLY AND RECHECK.

YES → INSPECT EBCM CONNECTORS FOR POOR CONTACT. IF OK, REPLACE EBCM.

THIS CHART ASSUMES THAT A CURRENT CODE IS STORED INDICATING THAT THIS FAULT IS PRESENT.

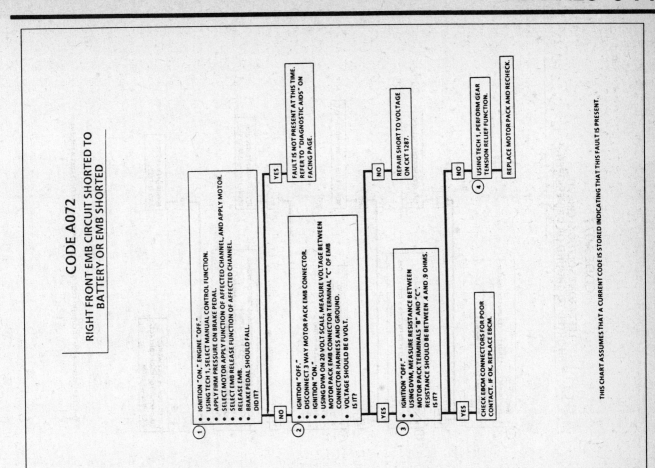

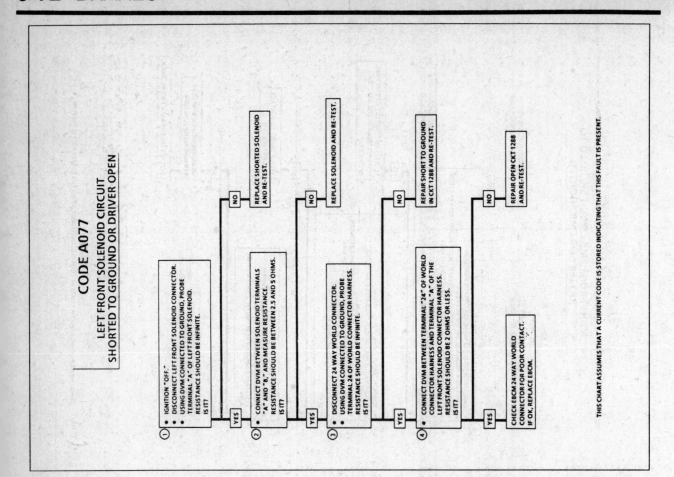

CODE A077

LEFT FRONT SOLENOID CIRCUIT
SHORTED TO GROUND OR DRIVER OPEN

1. • IGNITION "OFF."
   • DISCONNECT LEFT FRONT SOLENOID CONNECTOR.
   • USING DVM CONNECTED TO GROUND, PROBE TERMINAL "A" OF LEFT FRONT SOLENOID.
   RESISTANCE SHOULD BE INFINITE.
   IS IT?

   NO → REPLACE SHORTED SOLENOID AND RE-TEST.

   YES ↓

2. • CONNECT DVM BETWEEN SOLENOID TERMINALS "A" AND "B," AND MEASURE RESISTANCE.
   RESISTANCE SHOULD BE BETWEEN 2.5 AND 5 OHMS.
   IS IT?

   NO → REPLACE SOLENOID AND RE-TEST.

   YES ↓

3. • DISCONNECT 24 WAY WORLD CONNECTOR.
   • USING DVM CONNECTED TO GROUND, PROBE TERMINAL 24 OF WORLD CONNECTOR HARNESS.
   RESISTANCE SHOULD BE INFINITE.
   IS IT?

   NO → REPAIR SHORT TO GROUND IN CKT 1288 AND RE-TEST.

   YES ↓

4. • CONNECT DVM BETWEEN TERMINAL "24" OF WORLD CONNECTOR HARNESS AND TERMINAL "A" OF THE LEFT FRONT SOLENOID CONNECTOR HARNESS.
   RESISTANCE SHOULD BE 2 OHMS OR LESS.
   IS IT?

   NO → REPAIR OPEN CKT 1288 AND RE-TEST.

   YES ↓

   CHECK EBCM 24 WAY WORLD CONNECTOR FOR POOR CONTACT. IF OK, REPLACE EBCM.

THIS CHART ASSUMES THAT A CURRENT CODE IS STORED INDICATING THAT THIS FAULT IS PRESENT.

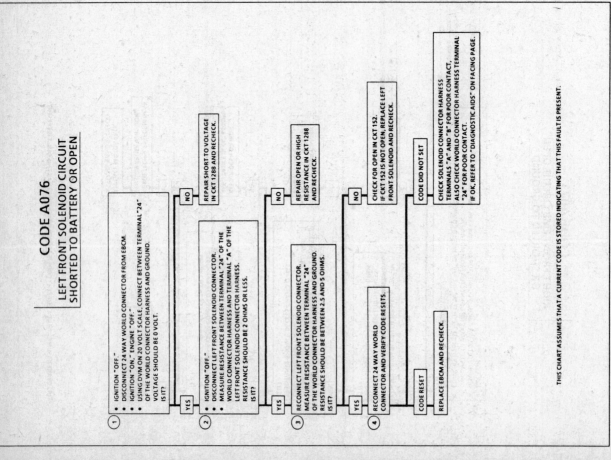

CODE A076

LEFT FRONT SOLENOID CIRCUIT
SHORTED TO BATTERY OR OPEN

1. • IGNITION "OFF."
   • DISCONNECT 24 WAY WORLD CONNECTOR FROM EBCM.
   • IGNITION "ON." ENGINE "OFF."
   • USING DVM ON 20 VOLT SCALE, CONNECT BETWEEN TERMINAL "24" OF THE WORLD CONNECTOR HARNESS AND GROUND.
   VOLTAGE SHOULD BE 0 VOLT.
   IS IT?

   NO → REPAIR SHORT TO VOLTAGE IN CKT 1288 AND RECHECK.

   YES ↓

2. • IGNITION "OFF."
   • DISCONNECT LEFT FRONT SOLENOID CONNECTOR.
   • MEASURE RESISTANCE BETWEEN TERMINAL "24" OF THE WORLD CONNECTOR HARNESS AND TERMINAL "A" OF THE LEFT FRONT SOLENOID CONNECTOR HARNESS.
   RESISTANCE SHOULD BE 2 OHMS OR LESS.
   IS IT?

   NO → REPAIR OPEN OR HIGH RESISTANCE IN CKT 1288 AND RECHECK.

   YES ↓

3. • RECONNECT LEFT FRONT SOLENOID CONNECTOR.
   • MEASURE RESISTANCE BETWEEN TERMINAL "24" OF THE WORLD CONNECTOR HARNESS AND GROUND.
   RESISTANCE SHOULD BE BETWEEN 2.5 AND 5 OHMS.
   IS IT?

   NO → CHECK FOR OPEN IN CKT 152. IF CKT 152 IS NOT OPEN, REPLACE LEFT FRONT SOLENOID AND RECHECK.

   YES ↓

4. • RECONNECT 24 WAY WORLD CONNECTOR AND VERIFY CODE RESETS.

   CODE RESET → REPLACE EBCM AND RECHECK.

   CODE DID NOT SET ↓

   CHECK SOLENOID CONNECTOR HARNESS TERMINALS "A" AND "B" FOR POOR CONTACT. ALSO CHECK WORLD CONNECTOR HARNESS TERMINAL "24" FOR POOR CONTACT. IF OK, REFER TO "DIAGNOSTIC AIDS" ON FACING PAGE.

THIS CHART ASSUMES THAT A CURRENT CODE IS STORED INDICATING THAT THIS FAULT IS PRESENT.

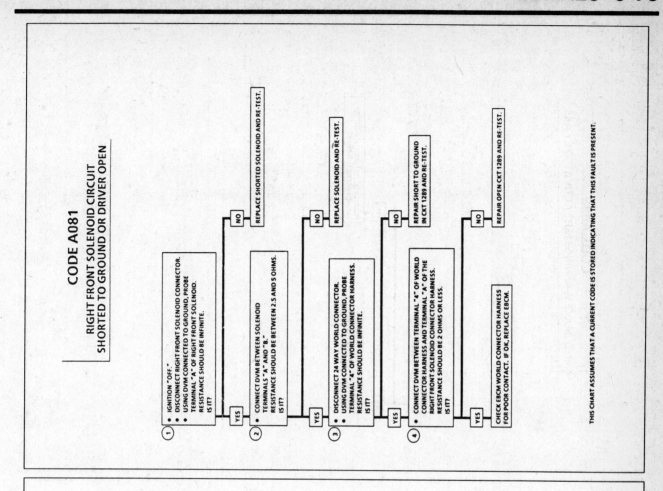

CODE A081

RIGHT FRONT SOLENOID CIRCUIT
SHORTED TO GROUND OR DRIVER OPEN

(1)
- IGNITION "OFF."
- DISCONNECT RIGHT FRONT SOLENOID CONNECTOR.
- USING DVM CONNECTED TO GROUND, PROBE TERMINAL "A" OF RIGHT FRONT SOLENOID. RESISTANCE SHOULD BE INFINITE.
IS IT?

NO → REPLACE SHORTED SOLENOID AND RE-TEST.

YES

(2)
- CONNECT DVM BETWEEN SOLENOID TERMINALS "A" AND "B." RESISTANCE SHOULD BE BETWEEN 2.5 AND 5 OHMS. IS IT?

NO → REPLACE SOLENOID AND RE-TEST.

YES

(3)
- DISCONNECT 24 WAY WORLD CONNECTOR.
- USING DVM CONNECTED TO GROUND, PROBE TERMINAL "4" OF WORLD CONNECTOR HARNESS. RESISTANCE SHOULD BE INFINITE. IS IT?

NO → REPAIR SHORT TO GROUND IN CKT 1289 AND RE-TEST.

YES

(4)
- CONNECT DVM BETWEEN TERMINAL "4" OF WORLD CONNECTOR HARNESS AND TERMINAL "A" OF THE RIGHT FRONT SOLENOID CONNECTOR HARNESS. RESISTANCE SHOULD BE 2 OHMS OR LESS. IS IT?

NO → REPAIR OPEN CKT 1289 AND RE-TEST.

YES

CHECK EBCM WORLD CONNECTOR HARNESS FOR POOR CONTACT. IF OK, REPLACE EBCM.

THIS CHART ASSUMES THAT A CURRENT CODE IS STORED INDICATING THAT THIS FAULT IS PRESENT.

CODE A078

RIGHT FRONT SOLENOID CIRCUIT
SHORTED TO BATTERY OR OPEN

(1)
- IGNITION "OFF."
- DISCONNECT 24 WAY WORLD CONNECTOR FROM EBCM.
- IGNITION "ON," ENGINE "OFF."
- USING DVM ON 20 VOLT SCALE, CONNECT BETWEEN TERMINAL "4" OF WORLD CONNECTOR AND GROUND. VOLTAGE SHOULD BE 0 VOLTS. IS IT?

NO → REPAIR SHORT TO VOLTAGE IN CKT 1289 AND RECHECK.

YES

(2)
- IGNITION "OFF."
- DISCONNECT RIGHT FRONT SOLENOID CONNECTOR.
- MEASURE RESISTANCE BETWEEN TERMINAL "4" OF THE WORLD CONNECTOR HARNESS AND TERMINAL "A" OF THE RIGHT FRONT SOLENOID CONNECTOR HARNESS. RESISTANCE SHOULD BE 2 OHMS OR LESS. IS IT?

NO → REPAIR OPEN CKT 1289 AND RECHECK.

YES

(3)
- RECONNECT RIGHT FRONT SOLENOID CONNECTOR.
- MEASURE RESISTANCE BETWEEN TERMINAL "4" OF THE WORLD CONNECTOR HARNESS AND GROUND. RESISTANCE SHOULD BE BETWEEN 2.5 AND 5 OHMS. IS IT?

NO → IF CKT 152 IS NOT OPEN, REPLACE RIGHT FRONT SOLENOID, AND RECHECK.

YES

(4)
- RECONNECT 24 WAY WORLD CONNECTOR AND VERIFY CODE RESETS.

CODE RESET. → REPLACE EBCM AND RECHECK.

CODE DID NOT SET. → CHECK SOLENOID CONNECTOR HARNESS TERMINALS "A" AND "B" FOR POOR CONTACT, ALSO CHECK WORLD CONNECTOR HARNESS TERMINAL "4" FOR POOR CONTACT. IF OK, REFER TO "DIAGNOSTIC AIDS" ON FACING PAGE.

THIS CHART ASSUMES THAT A CURRENT CODE IS STORED INDICATING THAT THIS FAULT IS PRESENT.

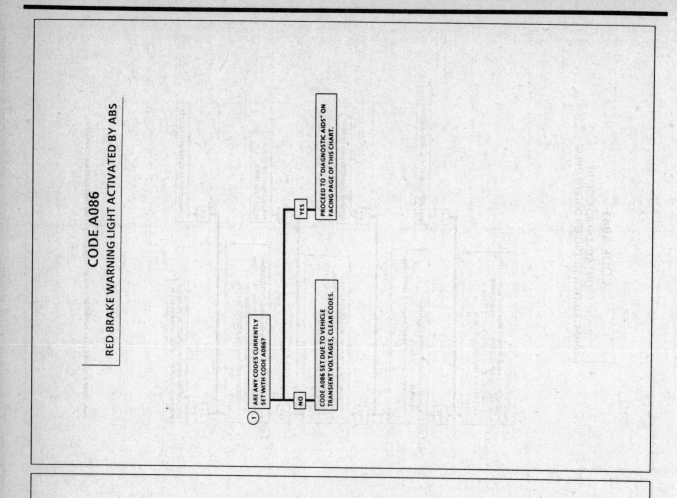

CODE A086
RED BRAKE WARNING LIGHT ACTIVATED BY ABS

① ARE ANY CODES CURRENTLY SET WITH CODE A086?

NO — CODE A086 SET DUE TO VEHICLE TRANSIENT VOLTAGES, CLEAR CODES.

YES — PROCEED TO "DIAGNOSTIC AIDS" ON FACING PAGE OF THIS CHART.

CODE A082
CALIBRATION MEMORY FAILURE

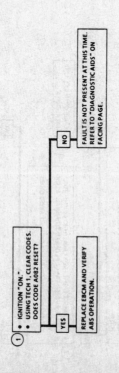

① • IGNITION "ON."
• USING TECH 1, CLEAR CODES.
DOES CODE A082 RESET?

YES — REPLACE EBCM AND VERIFY ABS OPERATION.

NO — FAULT IS NOT PRESENT AT THIS TIME. REFER TO "DIAGNOSTIC AIDS" ON FACING PAGE.

THIS CHART ASSUMES THAT A CURRENT CODE IS STORED INDICATING THAT THIS FAULT IS PRESENT.

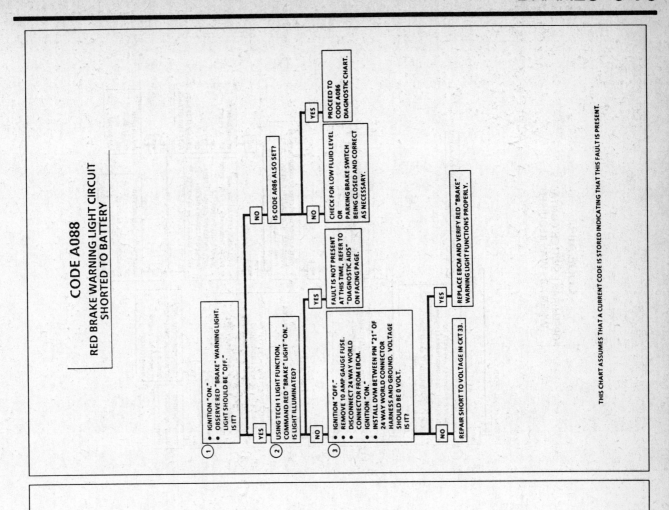

CODE A088
RED BRAKE WARNING LIGHT CIRCUIT SHORTED TO BATTERY

1.
- IGNITION "ON."
- OBSERVE RED "BRAKE" WARNING LIGHT. LIGHT SHOULD BE "OFF." IS IT?

YES →
2.
- USING TECH 1 LIGHT FUNCTION, COMMAND RED "BRAKE" LIGHT "ON." IS LIGHT ILLUMINATED?

NO → IS CODE A086 ALSO SET?

YES → PROCEED TO CODE A086 DIAGNOSTIC CHART.

NO → CHECK FOR LOW FLUID LEVEL OR PARKING BRAKE SWITCH BEING CLOSED AND CORRECT AS NECESSARY.

YES → FAULT IS NOT PRESENT AT THIS TIME. REFER TO "DIAGNOSTIC AIDS" ON FACING PAGE.

NO →
3.
- IGNITION "OFF."
- REMOVE 10 AMP GAUGE FUSE.
- DISCONNECT 24 WAY WORLD CONNECTOR FROM EBCM.
- IGNITION "ON."
- INSTALL DVM BETWEEN PIN "21" OF 24 WAY WORLD CONNECTOR HARNESS AND GROUND. VOLTAGE SHOULD BE 0 VOLT. IS IT?

YES → REPLACE EBCM AND VERIFY RED "BRAKE" WARNING LIGHT FUNCTIONS PROPERLY.

NO → REPAIR SHORT TO VOLTAGE IN CKT 33.

THIS CHART ASSUMES THAT A CURRENT CODE IS STORED INDICATING THAT THIS FAULT IS PRESENT.

CODE A087
RED BRAKE WARNING LIGHT CIRCUIT OPEN

1.
- IGNITION "ON."
- SELECT DATA LIST FUNCTION OF TECH 1.
- MONITOR BRAKE WARNING LIGHT STATUS.
- DOES BRAKE WARNING LIGHT INDICATE "CIRCUIT OPEN"?

NO → FAULT IS NOT PRESENT AT THIS TIME. REFER TO "DIAGNOSTIC AIDS" ON FACING PAGE.

YES →
2.
- SELECT LIGHT TEST FUNCTION OF TECH 1.
- COMMAND RED "BRAKE" LIGHT "ON."
- RED "BRAKE" WARNING LIGHT SHOULD BE "ON." IS IT?

YES → REPAIR POOR TERMINAL CONTACT OR HIGH RESISTANCE IN CKT 33.

NO →
3.
ARE INSTRUMENT PANEL INDICATOR LIGHTS WORKING PROPERLY?

NO → CHECK 10 AMP GAUGE FUSE. IS FUSE OPEN?

NO → REPAIR OPEN IN CKT 39.

YES → CHECK FOR OPEN OR SHORT IN CKT 3 OR CKT 39. IF OK, REPLACE FUSE.

YES →
4.
- IGNITION "OFF."
- DISCONNECT 24 WAY WORLD CONNECTOR FROM EBCM.
- IGNITION "ON."
- WITH JUMPER CONNECTED TO GROUND, PROBE PIN "21" OF 24 WAY WORLD CONNECTOR HARNESS. DOES RED "BRAKE" WARNING LIGHT ILLUMINATE?

NO → REPAIR OPEN CKT 33 OR OPEN "BRAKE" INDICATOR BULB. OR OPEN INSTRUMENT PANEL CIRCUITRY. REFER TO SECTION 8C FOR FURTHER DIAGNOSIS.

YES → CHECK FOR POOR TERMINAL CONTACT OF PIN "21" OF THE 24 WAY WORLD CONNECTOR. IF OK, REPLACE EBCM AND VERIFY RED "BRAKE" WARNING LIGHT FUNCTIONS PROPERLY.

THIS CHART ASSUMES THAT A CURRENT CODE IS STORED INDICATING THAT THIS FAULT IS PRESENT.

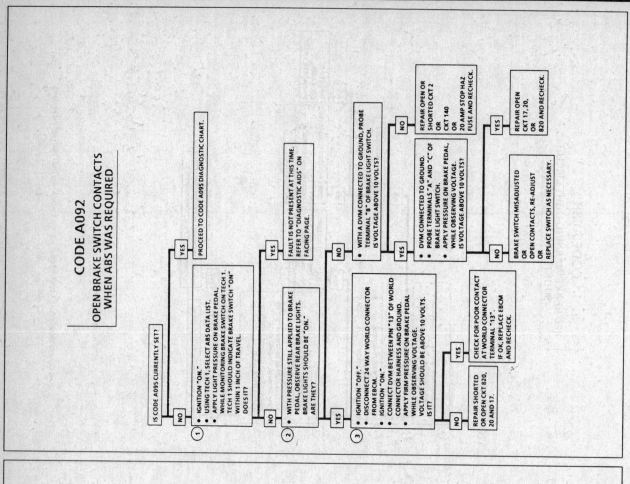

CODE A092

OPEN BRAKE SWITCH CONTACTS
WHEN ABS WAS REQUIRED

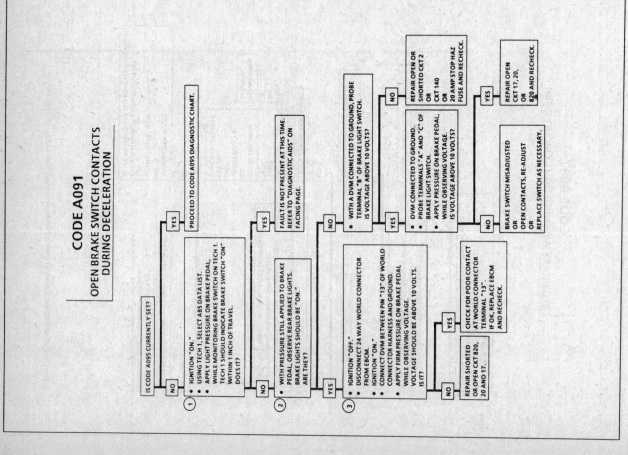

CODE A091

OPEN BRAKE SWITCH CONTACTS
DURING DECELERATION

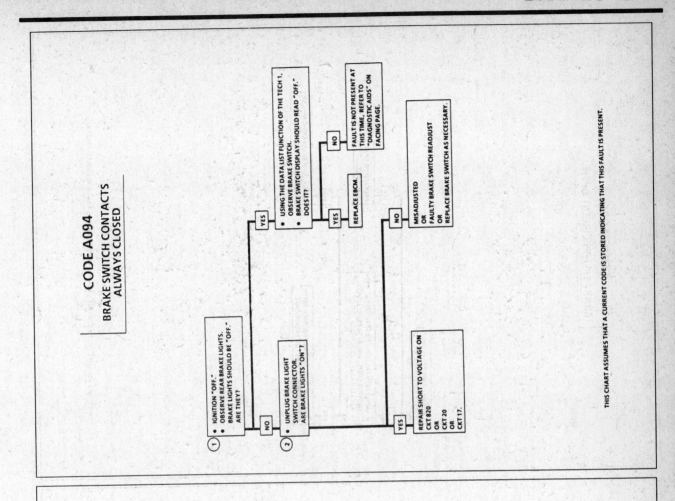

CODE A094

BRAKE SWITCH CONTACTS
ALWAYS CLOSED

① • IGNITION "OFF."
• OBSERVE REAR BRAKE LIGHTS.
BRAKE LIGHTS SHOULD BE "OFF."
ARE THEY?

NO

② • UNPLUG BRAKE LIGHT
SWITCH CONNECTOR.
ARE BRAKE LIGHTS "ON"?

YES

• USING THE DATA LIST FUNCTION OF THE TECH 1,
OBSERVE BRAKE SWITCH.
BRAKE SWITCH DISPLAY SHOULD READ "OFF."
DOES IT?

NO

FAULT IS NOT PRESENT AT
THIS TIME. REFER TO
"DIAGNOSTIC AIDS" ON
FACING PAGE.

YES

REPLACE EBCM.

NO

MISADJUSTED
OR
FAULTY BRAKE SWITCH
OR
REPLACE BRAKE SWITCH AS NECESSARY.

YES

REPAIR SHORT TO VOLTAGE ON
CKT 820
OR
CKT 20
OR
CKT 17.

THIS CHART ASSUMES THAT A CURRENT CODE IS STORED INDICATING THAT THIS FAULT IS PRESENT.

CODE A093

CODES A091 OR A092 SET IN CURRENT OR
PREVIOUS IGNITION CYCLE

① • IGNITION "ON."
• USING TECH 1, READ TROUBLE CODES.
IS CODE A091 OR A092 SET IN HISTORY
OR
CURRENT CODES?

YES

② • PROCEED TO CODE THAT SET
AND REPAIR AS NECESSARY.

NO

USING ENHANCED DIAGNOSTIC FUNCTION
OF TECH 1, VERIFY FAILURE FREQUENCY
WAS LOW AND CLEAR CODES.

THIS CHART ASSUMES THAT A CURRENT CODE IS STORED INDICATING THAT THIS FAULT IS PRESENT.

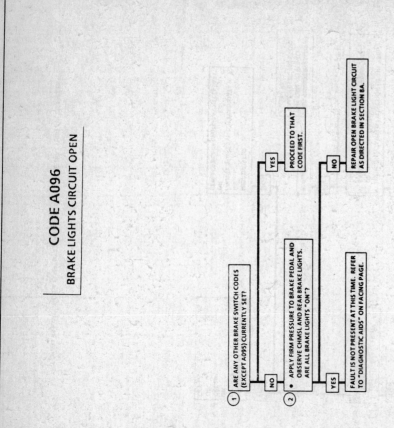

CODE A096
BRAKE LIGHTS CIRCUIT OPEN

1. ARE ANY OTHER BRAKE SWITCH CODES (EXCEPT A095) CURRENTLY SET?
   - YES → PROCEED TO THAT CODE FIRST.
   - NO →
2.
   - APPLY FIRM PRESSURE TO BRAKE PEDAL AND OBSERVE CHMSL AND REAR BRAKE LIGHTS. ARE ALL BRAKE LIGHTS "ON"?
   - YES → FAULT IS NOT PRESENT AT THIS TIME. REFER TO "DIAGNOSTIC AIDS" ON FACING PAGE.
   - NO → REPAIR OPEN BRAKE LIGHT CIRCUIT AS DIRECTED IN SECTION 8A.

THIS CHART ASSUMES THAT A CURRENT CODE IS STORED INDICATING THAT THIS FAULT IS PRESENT.

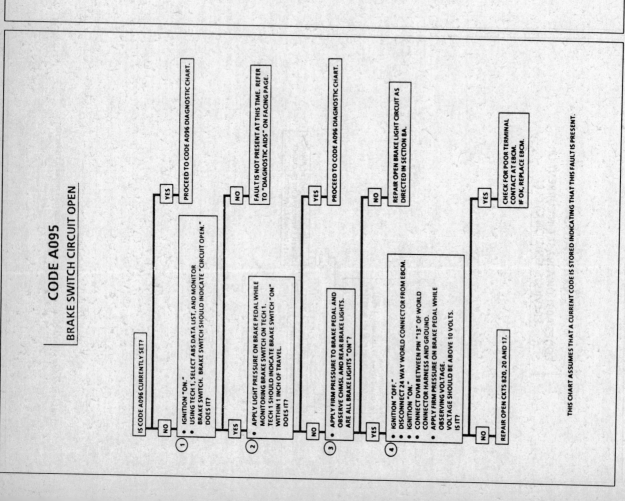

CODE A095
BRAKE SWITCH CIRCUIT OPEN

IS CODE A096 CURRENTLY SET?
- YES → PROCEED TO CODE A096 DIAGNOSTIC CHART.
- NO →
1.
   - IGNITION "ON."
   - USING TECH 1, SELECT ABS DATA LIST, AND MONITOR BRAKE SWITCH. BRAKE SWITCH SHOULD INDICATE "CIRCUIT OPEN." DOES IT?
   - YES →
2.
   - APPLY LIGHT PRESSURE ON BRAKE PEDAL WHILE MONITORING BRAKE SWITCH ON TECH 1. TECH 1 SHOULD INDICATE BRAKE SWITCH "ON" WITHIN 1 INCH OF TRAVEL. DOES IT?
   - NO → FAULT IS NOT PRESENT AT THIS TIME. REFER TO "DIAGNOSTIC AIDS" ON FACING PAGE.
   - YES →
3.
   - APPLY FIRM PRESSURE TO BRAKE PEDAL AND OBSERVE CHMSL AND REAR BRAKE LIGHTS. ARE ALL BRAKE LIGHTS "ON"?
   - YES → PROCEED TO CODE A096 DIAGNOSTIC CHART.
   - NO → REPAIR OPEN BRAKE LIGHT CIRCUIT AS DIRECTED IN SECTION 8A.
4.
   - IGNITION "OFF."
   - DISCONNECT 24 WAY WORLD CONNECTOR FROM EBCM.
   - IGNITION "ON."
   - CONNECT DVM BETWEEN PIN "13" OF WORLD CONNECTOR HARNESS AND GROUND.
   - APPLY FIRM PRESSURE ON BRAKE PEDAL WHILE OBSERVING VOLTAGE.
   - VOLTAGE SHOULD BE ABOVE 10 VOLTS. IS IT?
   - YES → CHECK FOR POOR TERMINAL CONTACT AT EBCM. IF OK, REPLACE EBCM.
   - NO → REPAIR OPEN CKTS 820, 20 AND 17.

THIS CHART ASSUMES THAT A CURRENT CODE IS STORED INDICATING THAT THIS FAULT IS PRESENT.

BRAKE SPECIFICATIONS

All measurements in inches unless noted

Year	Model	Master Cylinder Bore	Brake Disc Original Thickness	Brake Disc Minimum Thickness	Brake Disc Maximum Runout	Brake Drum Diameter Original Inside Diameter	Brake Drum Diameter Max. Wear Limit	Brake Drum Diameter Maximum Machine Diameter	Minimum Lining Thickness Front	Minimum Lining Thickness Rear
1982	All	0.94	0.885	0.830 ⑦	0.004	7.879	7.929	7.899	①	①
1983	All	0.94	0.885	0.830 ⑦	0.004	7.879	7.929	7.899	①	①
1984	All	0.94	0.885	0.830 ⑦	0.004	7.879	7.929	7.899	①	①
1985	All	0.94	0.885	0.830 ⑦	0.004	7.879	7.929	7.899	①	①
1986	All	0.94	0.885	0.830 ⑦	0.004	7.879	7.929	7.899	①	①
1987	All	0.94	0.885	0.830 ⑦	0.004	7.879	7.929	7.899	①	①
1988	Cavalier	②	0.885	0.830 ⑦	0.004	7.879	7.929	7.899	①	①
	Sunbird	③	0.885	0.830 ⑦	0.004	7.879	7.929	7.899	①	①
	Firenza	④	0.885	0.830 ⑦	0.004	7.879	7.929	7.899	①	①
	Skyhawk	⑤	0.885	0.830 ⑦	0.004	7.879	7.929	7.899	①	①
	Cimarron	⑥	0.885	0.830 ⑦	0.004	7.879	7.929	7.899	①	①
1989	All	0.874	0.885	0.830 ⑦	0.004	7.879	7.929	7.899	①	①
1990	All ⑧	0.874	0.885	0.830 ⑦	0.004	7.879	7.929	7.899	①	①
1991	All ⑧	0.874	0.885	0.830 ⑦	0.004	7.879	7.929	7.899	①	①
1992	All ⑧	0.874	0.885	0.830 ⑦	0.004	7.879	7.929	7.899	①	①

① Worn to within 0.030 inches of rivet at either end of the shoe.
② Prior to VIN 1G1F11W0J7109958—0.937 inches
Prior to VIN 1G1JE1114JJ136414—0.937 inches
After VIN 1G1JF11W0J7109957—0.874 inches
After VIN 1G1JE1114JJ136413—0.874 inches

③ Prior to VIN 1G2JB51K4J7506603—0.937 inches
After VIN 1G2JB51K4J7506602—0.874 inches
④ Prior to VIN 1G3JC51K7JK304666—0.937 inches
After VIN 1G3JC51K7JK304665—0.874 inches
⑤ Prior to VIN 1G4JS11KXJK409094—0.937 inches
After VIN 1G4JS11KXJK409093—0.874 inches

⑥ Prior to VIN 1G6JG51W1JJ502420—0.937 inches
After VIN 1G6JG51W1JJ502419—0.874 inches
⑦ Discard thickness 0.815 inches
⑧ Cavalier and Sunbird only

Troubleshooting the Brake System

Problem	Cause	Solution
Low brake pedal (excessive pedal travel required for braking action.)	• Excessive clearance between rear linings and drums caused by inoperative automatic adjusters	• Make 10 to 15 alternate forward and reverse brake stops to adjust brakes. If brake pedal does not come up, repair or replace adjuster parts as necessary.
	• Worn rear brakelining	• Inspect and replace lining if worn beyond minimum thickness specification
	• Bent, distorted brakeshoes, front or rear	• Replace brakeshoes in axle sets
	• Air in hydraulic system	• Remove air from system. Refer to Brake Bleeding.
Low brake pedal (pedal may go to floor with steady pressure applied.)	• Fluid leak in hydraulic system	• Fill master cylinder to fill line; have helper apply brakes and check calipers, wheel cylinders, differential valve tubes, hoses and fittings for leaks. Repair or replace as necessary.
	• Air in hydraulic system	• Remove air from system. Refer to Brake Bleeding.
	• Incorrect or non-recommended brake fluid (fluid evaporates at below normal temp).	• Flush hydraulic system with clean brake fluid. Refill with correct-type fluid.
	• Master cylinder piston seals worn, or master cylinder bore is scored, worn or corroded	• Repair or replace master cylinder
Low brake pedal (pedal goes to floor on first application—o.k. on subsequent applications.)	• Disc brake pads sticking on abutment surfaces of anchor plate. Caused by a build-up of dirt, rust, or corrosion on abutment surfaces	• Clean abutment surfaces
Fading brake pedal (pedal height decreases with steady pressure applied.)	• Fluid leak in hydraulic system	• Fill master cylinder reservoirs to fill mark, have helper apply brakes, check calipers, wheel cylinders, differential valve, tubes, hoses, and fittings for fluid leaks. Repair or replace parts as necessary.
	• Master cylinder piston seals worn, or master cylinder bore is scored, worn or corroded	• Repair or replace master cylinder
Spongy brake pedal (pedal has abnormally soft, springy, spongy feel when depressed.)	• Air in hydraulic system	• Remove air from system. Refer to Brake Bleeding.
	• Brakeshoes bent or distorted	• Replace brakeshoes
	• Brakelining not yet seated with drums and rotors	• Burnish brakes
	• Rear drum brakes not properly adjusted	• Adjust brakes

Troubleshooting the Brake System (cont.)

Problem	Cause	Solution
Decreasing brake pedal travel (pedal travel required for braking action decreases and may be accompanied by a hard pedal.)	• Caliper or wheel cylinder pistons sticking or seized • Master cylinder compensator ports blocked (preventing fluid return to reservoirs) or pistons sticking or seized in master cylinder bore • Power brake unit binding internally	• Repair or replace the calipers, or wheel cylinders • Repair or replace the master cylinder • Test unit according to the following procedure: (a) Shift transmission into neutral and start engine (b) Increase engine speed to 1500 rpm, close throttle and fully depress brake pedal (c) Slow release brake pedal and stop engine (d) Have helper remove vacuum check valve and hose from power unit. Observe for backward movement of brake pedal. (e) If the pedal moves backward, the power unit has an internal bind—replace power unit
Grabbing brakes (severe reaction to brake pedal pressure.)	• Brakelining(s) contaminated by grease or brake fluid • Parking brake cables incorrectly adjusted or seized • Incorrect brakelining or lining loose on brakeshoes • Caliper anchor plate bolts loose • Rear brakeshoes binding on support plate ledges • Incorrect or missing power brake reaction disc • Rear brake support plates loose	• Determine and correct cause of contamination and replace brakeshoes in axle sets • Adjust cables. Replace seized cables. • Replace brakeshoes in axle sets • Tighten bolts • Clean and lubricate ledges. Replace support plate(s) if ledges are deeply grooved. Do not attempt to smooth ledges by grinding. • Install correct disc • Tighten mounting bolts
Chatter or shudder when brakes are applied (pedal pulsation and roughness may also occur.)	• Brakeshoes distorted, bent, contaminated, or worn • Caliper anchor plate or support plate loose • Excessive thickness variation of rotor(s)	• Replace brakeshoes in axle sets • Tighten mounting bolts • Refinish or replace rotors in axle sets
Noisy brakes (squealing, clicking, scraping sound when brakes are applied.)	• Bent, broken, distorted brakeshoes • Excessive rust on outer edge of rotor braking surface	• Replace brakeshoes in axle sets • Remove rust

Troubleshooting the Brake System (cont.)

Problem	Cause	Solution
Hard brake pedal (excessive pedal pressure required to stop vehicle. May be accompanied by brake fade.)	• Loose or leaking power brake unit vacuum hose • Incorrect or poor quality brake-lining • Bent, broken, distorted brakeshoes • Calipers binding or dragging on mounting pins. Rear brakeshoes dragging on support plate.	• Tighten connections or replace leaking hose • Replace with lining in axle sets • Replace brakeshoes • Replace mounting pins and bushings. Clean rust or burrs from rear brake support plate ledges and lubricate ledges with molydisulfide grease. **NOTE:** If ledges are deeply grooved or scored, do not attempt to sand or grind them smooth—replace support plate.
	• Caliper, wheel cylinder, or master cylinder pistons sticking or seized • Power brake unit vacuum check valve malfunction	• Repair or replace parts as necessary • Test valve according to the following procedure: (a) Start engine, increase engine speed to 1500 rpm, close throttle and immediately stop engine (b) Wait at least 90 seconds then depress brake pedal (c) If brakes are not vacuum assisted for 2 or more applications, check valve is faulty
	• Power brake unit has internal bind	• Test unit according to the following procedure: (a) With engine stopped, apply brakes several times to exhaust all vacuum in system (b) Shift transmission into neutral, depress brake pedal and start engine (c) If pedal height decreases with foot pressure and less pressure is required to hold pedal in applied position, power unit vacuum system is operating normally. Test power unit. If power unit exhibits a bind condition, replace the power unit.

Troubleshooting the Brake System (cont.)

Problem	Cause	Solution
Hard brake pedal (excessive pedal pressure required to stop vehicle. May be accompanied by brake fade.)	• Master cylinder compensator ports (at bottom of reservoirs) blocked by dirt, scale, rust, or have small burrs (blocked ports prevent fluid return to reservoirs). • Brake hoses, tubes, fittings clogged or restricted • Brake fluid contaminated with improper fluids (motor oil, transmission fluid, causing rubber components to swell and stick in bores • Low engine vacuum	• Repair or replace master cylinder **CAUTION:** Do not attempt to clean blocked ports with wire, pencils, or similar implements. Use compressed air only. • Use compressed air to check or unclog parts. Replace any damaged parts. • Replace all rubber components, combination valve and hoses. Flush entire brake system with DOT 3 brake fluid or equivalent. • Adjust or repair engine
Dragging brakes (slow or incomplete release of brakes)	• Brake pedal binding at pivot • Power brake unit has internal bind • Parking brake cables incorrrectly adjusted or seized • Rear brakeshoe return springs weak or broken • Automatic adjusters malfunctioning • Caliper, wheel cylinder or master cylinder pistons sticking or seized • Master cylinder compensating ports blocked (fluid does not return to reservoirs).	• Loosen and lubricate • Inspect for internal bind. Replace unit if internal bind exists. • Adjust cables. Replace seized cables. • Replace return springs. Replace brakeshoe if necessary in axle sets. • Repair or replace adjuster parts as required • Repair or replace parts as necessary • Use compressed air to clear ports. Do not use wire, pencils, or similar objects to open blocked ports.
Vehicle moves to one side when brakes are applied	• Incorrect front tire pressure • Worn or damaged wheel bearings • Brakelining on one side contaminated • Brakeshoes on one side bent, distorted, or lining loose on shoe • Support plate bent or loose on one side • Brakelining not yet seated with drums or rotors • Caliper anchor plate loose on one side • Caliper piston sticking or seized • Brakelinings water soaked • Loose suspension component attaching or mounting bolts • Brake combination valve failure	• Inflate to recommended cold (reduced load) inflation pressure • Replace worn or damaged bearings • Determine and correct cause of contamination and replace brakelining in axle sets • Replace brakeshoes in axle sets • Tighten or replace support plate • Burnish brakelining • Tighten anchor plate bolts • Repair or replace caliper • Drive vehicle with brakes lightly applied to dry linings • Tighten suspension bolts. Replace worn suspension components. • Replace combination valve

Troubleshooting the Brake System (cont.)

Problem	Cause	Solution
Noisy brakes (squealing, clicking, scraping sound when brakes are applied.) (cont.)	• Brakelining worn out—shoes contacting drum of rotor	• Replace brakeshoes and lining in axle sets. Refinish or replace drums or rotors.
	• Broken or loose holdown or return springs	• Replace parts as necessary
	• Rough or dry drum brake support plate ledges	• Lubricate support plate ledges
	• Cracked, grooved, or scored rotor(s) or drum(s)	• Replace rotor(s) or drum(s). Replace brakeshoes and lining in axle sets if necessary.
	• Incorrect brakelining and/or shoes (front or rear).	• Install specified shoe and lining assemblies
Pulsating brake pedal	• Out of round drums or excessive lateral runout in disc brake rotor(s)	• Refinish or replace drums, re-index rotors or replace

TORQUE SPECIFICATIONS

Component	Metric	English
Proportioner Valve Caps	27 N•m	(20 lbs. ft.)
Brake Pipe Tube Nuts	17 N•m	(13 lbs. ft.)
Master Cylinder Assembly to Power Booster	27 N•m	(20 lbs. ft.)
Caliper Mounting Bolt and Sleeve Assembly	51 N•m	(38 lbs. ft.)
Caliper Inlet Fitting	45 N•m	(33 lbs. ft.)
Caliper Bleeder Valve	13 N•m	(115 lbs. in.)
Wheel Cylinder to Backing Plate Bolts	20 N•m	(15 lbs. ft.)
Bleeder Valve	7 N•m	(65 lbs. in.)
Inlet Tube Nut	17 N•m	(12 lbs. ft.)
Booster to Master Cylinder Attaching Nuts	27 N•m	(20 lbs. ft.)
Booster to Brake Pedal Attaching Nuts	21 N•m	(15 lbs. ft.)
ABS Hydraulic Modulator Bleeder Valves	7 N•m	(65 lbs. in.)
ABS Hydraulic Modulator Solenoid Assembly Torx® Head Bolt	5 N•m	(44 lbs. in.)
Electronic Brake Control Module (EBCM) Hex Head Screws	2 N•m	(14 lbs. in.)
Front Wheel Speed Sensor Bolt	12 N•m	(106 lbs. in.)
Bolts and Nuts Rear Wheel Bearing and Speed Sensor Assembly	50 N•m	(37 lbs. ft.)
Vacuum Booster Retaining Nuts	27 N•m	(20 lbs. ft.)
Four Brake Pipe Tube Nuts	37 N•m	(27 lbs. ft.)
Six Torx® Head Screws Attaching Gear Cover	4 N•m	(35 lbs. in.)
Four Torx© Head Screws Attaching Motor Pack Assembly	5 N•m	(44 lbs. in.)
Two Thru Bolts Attaching ABS Hydraulic Modulator To Master Cylinder Assembly	16 N•m	(12 lbs. ft.)

10

BODY

EXTERIOR

Doors

REMOVAL & INSTALLATION

▶ SEE FIG. 1

1. On doors equipped with power operated components proceed as folllows:

   a. Remove the door trim panel, insulator pad (if so equipped), and the inner panel water deflector.

   b. Disconnect the wiring components inside the door.

   c. Remove the rubber conduit from the door, then remove the wiring harness from the door through the conduit access hole.

2. Tape the area (on the door pillar and body pillar) above the lower hinge with fabric tape.

✳✳ CAUTION

Before performing the following step, cover the spring with a towel to prevent the spring from flying out and possibly causing personal injury!

3. Insert a suitable, long, flat bladed tool under the pivot point of the hold-open link and over top of the spring. The tool should be positioned so as not to apply pressure to the hold-open link. Cover the spring with a shop cloth and lift the tool to disengage the spring. The spring can also be removed by using tool J-28625, or equivalent, door hinge spring compressor tool. The tool is stamped right side and left side. For all the J-cars the tool stamped, "left side" is used to service the right side hinge spring. The tool stamped, "right side" is used to service the left hand hinge spring.

   a. Install the two jaws of the tool over the spring. The jaw with the slots slides over spring at the hold-open link. The jaw with the hole fits over the spring at the bubble on the door hinge pillar.

   b. Install the bolt to the jaws of the tool and tighten to compress the spring.

   c. Remove the tool and spring from the door hinge assembly. Do not remove the spring from the tool.

4. When removing the hinge pin, save the "barrel" clips as follows:

   a. Using two, suitable, flat bladed tools,

spread the clip enough to move the clip above the recess toward the pointed end of the pin.

   b. As the pin is removed, the clip will ride the shank of the pin and fall free.

   c. Reinstall the clips onto the pins before installing the door.

5. With the aid of a helper to support the door, remove the lower hinge pin, using a soft headed hammer and locking type pliers. The helper can aid in removing the hinge pin by raising and lowering the rear of the door.

6. Insert the bolt into the hole of the lower hinge to maintain door attachment during upper hinge pin removal.

7. Remove the upper hinge pin in the same manner as the lower. Remove the bolt from the lower hinge and remove the door from the body.

To install:

➡ **Before installing the door, replace the hinge pin clips or reuse the old clips as explained in the removal procedure.**

8. With the aid of a helper, position the door and insert a bolt in the lower hinge hole.

9. The upper hinge pin is inserted with the pointed end up. The lower hinge pin is inserted with the pointed end down. With the door in the full open position, install the upper hinge pin

using locking-type pliers and a soft headed hammer. Use a drift punch and hammer to complete pin installation.

10. Remove the screw from the lower hinge and install the lower hinge pin. The use of the special tool J-28625 or equivalent is the recommended method for installing the hinge spring.

✳✳ WARNING

If the spring is installed before installing the upper hinge pin, damage to the hinge bushings may result!

11. If the spring was removed using a long, flat bladed tool, install the spring as follows:

   a. Place the spring in tool J-28625 or equivalent.

   b. Place the tool and spring in a bench vise.

   c. Compress the tool in a vise and install the bolt until the spring is fully compressed.

   d. Remove the tool with the compressed spring from the vise and install in the proper position in the door lower hinge. The slot in the jaw of the tool fits over the hold-open link. The hole in the other jaw fits over the bubble.

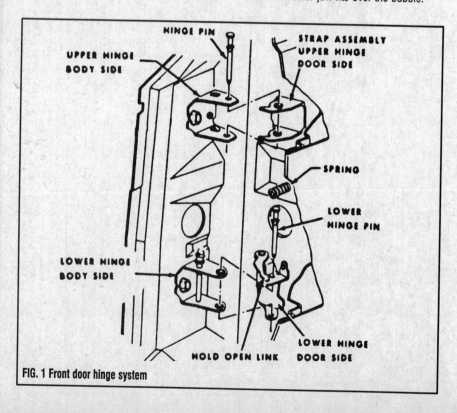

FIG. 1 Front door hinge system

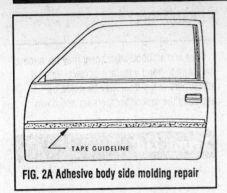

FIG. 2A Adhesive body side molding repair

e. Remove the bolt from the tool to install the spring.

f. Remove the tool from the door hinge. (The tool will fall out in three pieces). Cycle the door to check spring operation.

12. If tool J-28625 or equivalent was used to remove the spring, follow Steps d, e, and f above to install the spring.

13. Remove the tape from the door and body pillars.

14. On the doors with power operated components, install all previously removed parts.

ADJUSTMENTS

The front door hinges are made of steel and are welded to the door and bolted to the body hinge pillars. No adjustment provisions are used in this type of door system.

Molding, Emblem and Name Plate

REPLACEMENT

1. Wash affected panel area with soap and water and wipe dry. Remove all traces of adhesive from the body panel and back of molding using 3M General Purpose Adhesive Cleaner (part number 08984). Do not use this cleaner on air dry enamel.

2. Mark proper position of molding with a length of masking tape (see illustration). Use adjacent moldings as a guide if necessary.

3. If the body panel is below 70° degrees, warm body panel with heat lamp or heat gun before going to the next service step.

4. Apply a double-coated acrylic foam tape such as 3M Super Automotive Attachment Tape to the molding.

5. Align molding to tape guideline and press firmly in place.

Hood

REMOVAL & INSTALLATION

◆ SEE FIGS. 2-6

1. Raise the hood and install protective coverings over the fender areas to prevent damage to the painted surfaces and mouldings.

2. Mark the position of the hinge on the hood to aid alignment during installation.

3. While supporting the hood, preferably with the aid of an assistant, remove the hinge to hood screws on each side of the hood and remove the hood assembly.

4. Install the hood using the alignment marks made when removed.

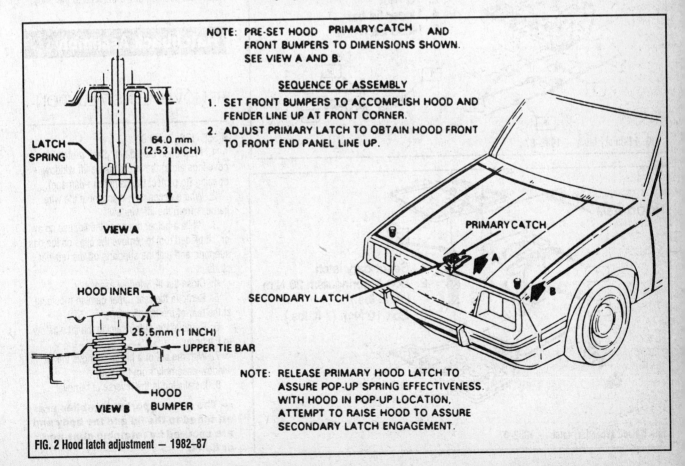

NOTE: PRE-SET HOOD PRIMARY CATCH AND FRONT BUMPERS TO DIMENSIONS SHOWN. SEE VIEW A AND B.

SEQUENCE OF ASSEMBLY

1. SET FRONT BUMPERS TO ACCOMPLISH HOOD AND FENDER LINE UP AT FRONT CORNER.
2. ADJUST PRIMARY LATCH TO OBTAIN HOOD FRONT TO FRONT END PANEL LINE UP.

NOTE: RELEASE PRIMARY HOOD LATCH TO ASSURE POP-UP SPRING EFFECTIVENESS. WITH HOOD IN POP-UP LOCATION, ATTEMPT TO RAISE HOOD TO ASSURE SECONDARY LATCH ENGAGEMENT.

FIG. 2 Hood latch adjustment — 1982–87

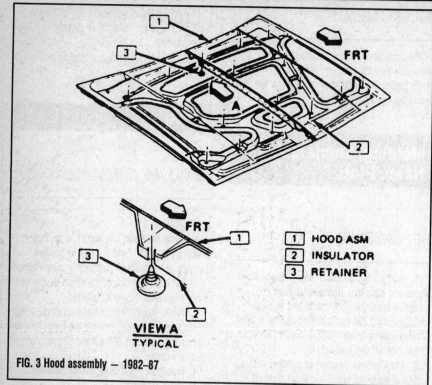

FIG. 3 Hood assembly — 1982–87

1. HOOD ASM
2. INSULATOR
3. RETAINER

VIEW A
TYPICAL

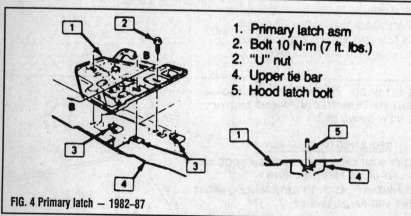

FIG. 4 Primary latch — 1982–87

1. Primary latch asm
2. Bolt 10 N·m (7 ft. lbs.)
2. "U" nut
4. Upper tie bar
5. Hood latch bolt

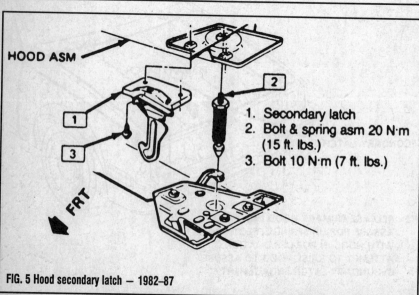

FIG. 5 Hood secondary latch — 1982–87

HOOD ASM

1. Secondary latch
2. Bolt & spring asm 20 N·m (15 ft. lbs.)
3. Bolt 10 N·m (7 ft. lbs.)

ALIGMENT

Fore and aft hood adjustment may be made at the hinge to hood attaching screws. Vertical adjustment at the front may be made by adjusting the rubber bumpers up and down.

Trunk Lid

REMOVAL & INSTALLATION

2- and 4-Door Sedans

The trunk lid hinge is welded to the body and bolts to the lid.

1. Open the trunk lid and place protective coverings over the rear compartment (to protect the paint from damage).

2. Mark the location of the hinge-to-trunk lid bolts and disconnect the electrical connections and wiring from the lid (if equipped).

3. Using an assistant (to support the lid), remove the hinge-to-lid bolts and the lid from the vehicle.

4. To install, reverse the removal procedures. Adjust the position of the trunk lid to the body.

Hatchback Assembly

REMOVAL & INSTALLATION

♦ SEE FIGS. 7 and 8

1. Prop open the lid and place protective coverings along the edges of the lift window opening (to protect the paint from damage).

2. Where necessary, disconnect the wire harness from the lift window.

3. While a helper supports the lid, use an awl or flat bladed tool to remove the clips on the gas supports and pull the supports off the retainer studs.

4. Close the lift window assembly.

5. Remove the rear upper garnish moulding at the rear of the headlining.

6. Remove the nuts retaining the lift window to the body.

7. With the aid of a helper, remove the lift window assembly from the body.

8. Installation is the reverse of removal.

➡ **The gas support assemblies are attached to the lid and the body and are secured by retaining clips and/ or bolts.**

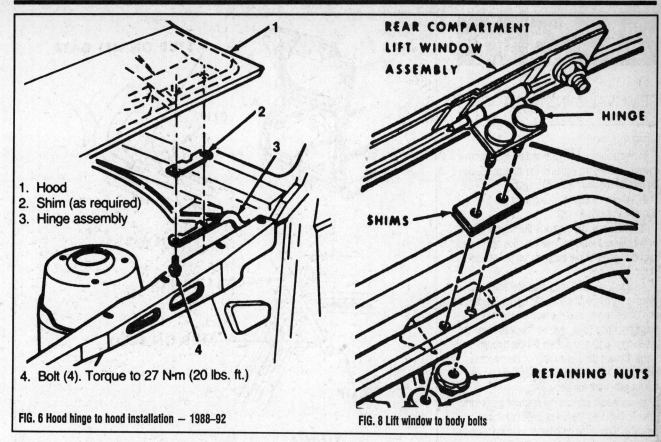

1. Hood
2. Shim (as required)
3. Hinge assembly

4. Bolt (4). Torque to 27 N·m (20 lbs. ft.)

FIG. 6 Hood hinge to hood installation — 1988–92

REAR COMPARTMENT LIFT WINDOW ASSEMBLY

HINGE

SHIMS

RETAINING NUTS

FIG. 8 Lift window to body bolts

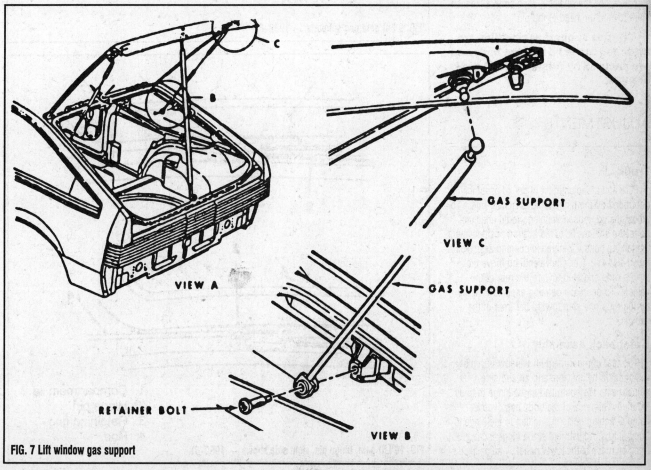

C

B

VIEW A

GAS SUPPORT

VIEW C

GAS SUPPORT

RETAINER BOLT

VIEW B

FIG. 7 Lift window gas support

Lift Gate (Station Wagon)

REMOVAL & INSTALLATION

▶ SEE FIGS. 9-12

1. Prop open the lift gate and place protective coverings along the edges of the lift gate opening (to protect the paint from damage).

2. Where necessary, disconnect the wire harness from the lift gate.

3. While a helper supports the lid, use an awl or flat bladed tool to remove the clips on the gas supports and pull the supports off the retainer studs.

4. Use a 3/16 in. (5mm) diameter rod to remove the hinge pins from the hinges. Place the end of the rod against the pointed end of the hinge pin; then strike the rod firmly to shear the retaining clip tabs and drive the pin through the hinge. Repeat the same thing on the opposite side hinge and with the aid of a helper remove the lift gate from the body.

5. To install, reverse the removal procedure. Prior to installing the hinge pins, install new retaining clips in the notches provide in the hinge pins. Position the retaining clips so that the tabs point toward the head of the pin.

➡ **The gas support assemblies are attached to the lid and the body and are secured by retaining clips and/ or bolts.**

ADJUSTMENTS

Trunk Lid

Fore and aft adjustment of the lid assembly is controlled by the hinge to lid attaching bolts. To adjust the lid, loosen the hinge to lid attaching bolts and shift the lid to the desired position, then tighten the bolts. To increase opening assist, use tool J-211412-1 or equivalent and move the torque rods one step toward the rear of the vehicle. To decrease opening assist, move the torque rods one step toward the front of the vehicle.

Hatchback Assembly

The rear compartment lift window assembly (hatchback) height, fore and aft and side adjustments are controlled at the hinge to body location. This area of the body has oversize hinge attaching holes in addition to the hinge to body shims. Adjustment at the hinge location must be made at the lower panel by adjusting the

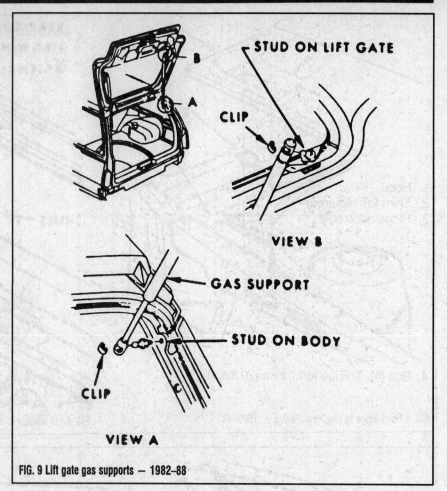

FIG. 9 Lift gate gas supports — 1982–88

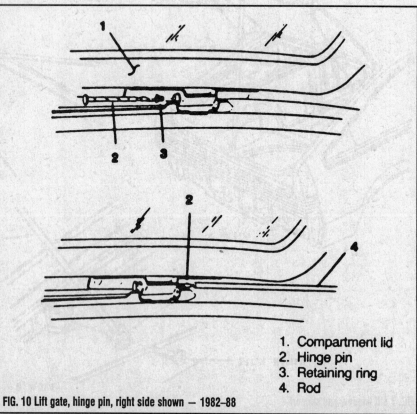

1. Compartment lid
2. Hinge pin
3. Retaining ring
4. Rod

FIG. 10 Lift gate, hinge pin, right side shown — 1982–88

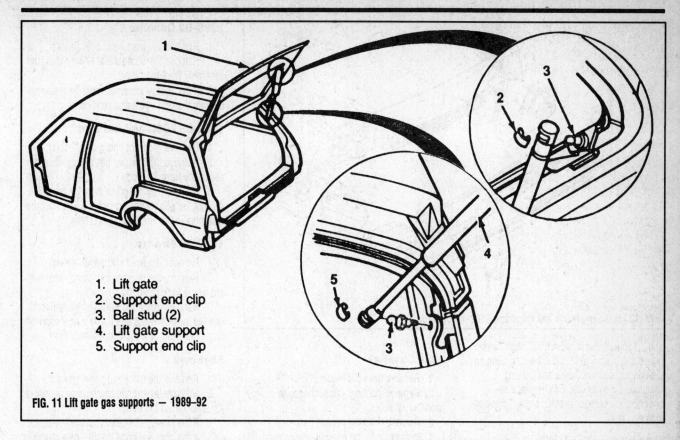

1. Lift gate
2. Support end clip
3. Ball stud (2)
4. Lift gate support
5. Support end clip

FIG. 11 Lift gate gas supports — 1989–92

rubber bumpers. The retaining bolts holding the hinge to body should be tightened to 15-20 ft. lbs.

Front Bumpers

REMOVAL & INSTALLATION

◆ SEE FIGS. 13-29

1982-83 Cavalier

1. Place a jack under the front bumper before removing the bolts to prevent it from dropping down when the bumper bolts are removed.

➡ **Do not rotate the energy absorber any more than needed to align the mounting holes.**

2. Remove the (1) bolt end cap to header panel right and left side. Remove the (2) end cap to fender nuts on the right and left side. Push the end cap off the bumper (plastic protrusions through holes in bumper bar).

3. Remove the bumper bolts on the right and left side at the energy absorbers and remove the bumper.

4. If the energy absorbers are to be replaced, remove the bolts and nuts from the unit, then remove the unit and the shims.

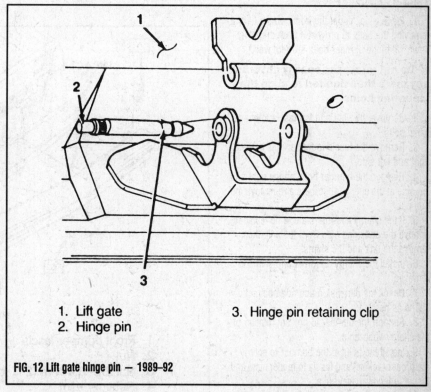

1. Lift gate
2. Hinge pin
3. Hinge pin retaining clip

FIG. 12 Lift gate hinge pin — 1989–92

5. Install the energy and absorber and shims if removed.

6. Check the dimension and add/subtract shims as needed.

7. Support the bumper to prevent rotation of the energy absorbers.

8. Install the bolts at the bumper to energy absorber brackets, and end cap to fender and front end panel nuts.

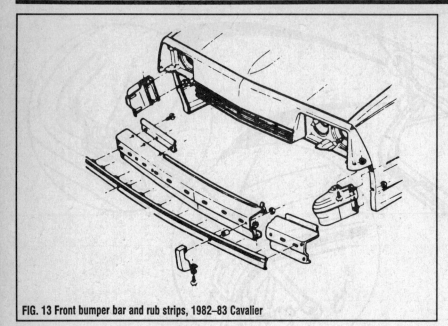

FIG. 13 Front bumper bar and rub strips, 1982–83 Cavalier

9. If adjustment is required to align bumper, loosen the energy absorber mounting bolts and position as required (holes are slotted). Adjustment side to side can be made by loosening the bumper bracket bolts. Torque all bolts and nuts.

1984-87 Cavalier

1. Place a jack under the front bumper before removing the bolts to prevent it from dropping down when the bumper bolts are removed.

➡ **Do not rotate the energy absorber any more than needed to align the mounting holes.**

2. Remove the right and left fascia to header panel bolts.

3. Remove the fascia to fender nuts in the right and left side.

4. Remove the bumper bolts on the right and left side at the energy absorbers and remove the bumper.

5. If the energy absorbers are to be replaced, remove the bolts and nuts from the unit, then remove the unit and the shims.

6. Install the energy absorber and shims if removed.

7. Check the dimension and add/subtract shims as needed.

8. Support the bumper to prevent rotation of the energy absorbers.

9. Install the bolts at the bumper to energy absorber brackets, and fascia to fender nuts, and fascia to fender panel bolts.

10. If adjustment is required to align bumper, loosen the energy absorber mounting bolts and position as required (holes are slotted). Adjustment side to side can be made by loosening the bumper bracket bolts. Torque all bolts and nuts.

1988 Cavalier

1. Remove the front fascia.
2. Remove the front impact bar to to energy absorber retainers.
3. Remove the front impact bar.
4. Installation is the reverse of removal.

1989–92 Cavalier

1. Remove the front end panel (fascia).
2. Remove the bumper bar/energy absorber assembly from the body.
3. If the energy absorber must be replaced, drill out the pop rivets and replace.

1982-89 2000 and Sunbird

1. Remove the front end panel (fascia).
2. Remove the bumper bar/energy absorber assembly from the body.
3. If the energy absorber must be replaced, drill out the pop rivets and install a new absorber with nuts, bolts and locking washers.

1982-88 Firenza

1. Remove the front end panel (fascia).
2. Remove the bumper bar/energy absorber assembly from the body.
3. If the energy absorber must be replaced, drill out the pop rivets and install a new absorber with nuts, bolts and locking washers.

Skyhawk

1. Remove the front end panel (fascia).
2. Remove the bumper bar/energy absorber assembly from the body.
3. If the energy absorber must be replaced, drill out the pop rivets and install a new absorber with nuts, bolts and locking washers.

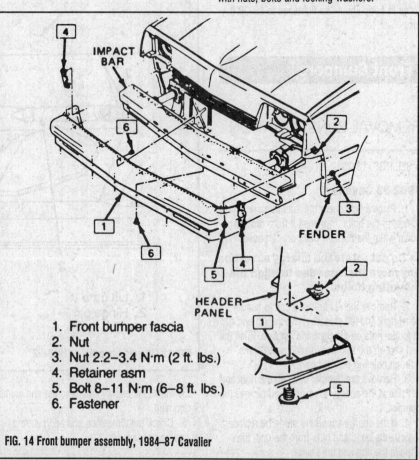

1. Front bumper fascia
2. Nut
3. Nut 2.2–3.4 N·m (2 ft. lbs.)
4. Retainer asm
5. Bolt 8–11 N·m (6–8 ft. lbs.)
6. Fastener

FIG. 14 Front bumper assembly, 1984–87 Cavalier

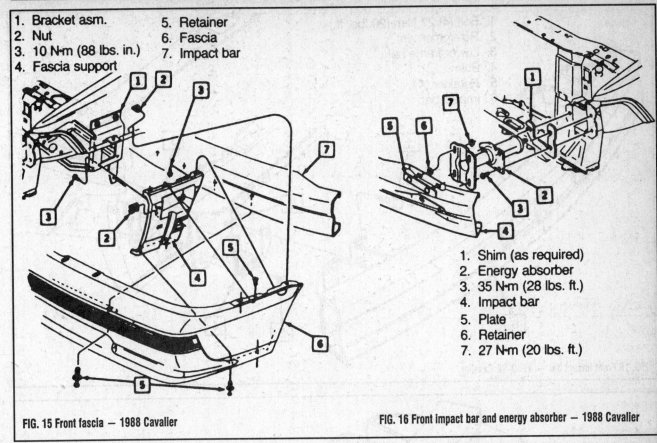

1. Bracket asm.
2. Nut
3. 10 N·m (88 lbs. in.)
4. Fascia support
5. Retainer
6. Fascia
7. Impact bar

1. Shim (as required)
2. Energy absorber
3. 35 N·m (28 lbs. ft.)
4. Impact bar
5. Plate
6. Retainer
7. 27 N·m (20 lbs. ft.)

FIG. 15 Front fascia — 1988 Cavalier

FIG. 16 Front impact bar and energy absorber — 1988 Cavalier

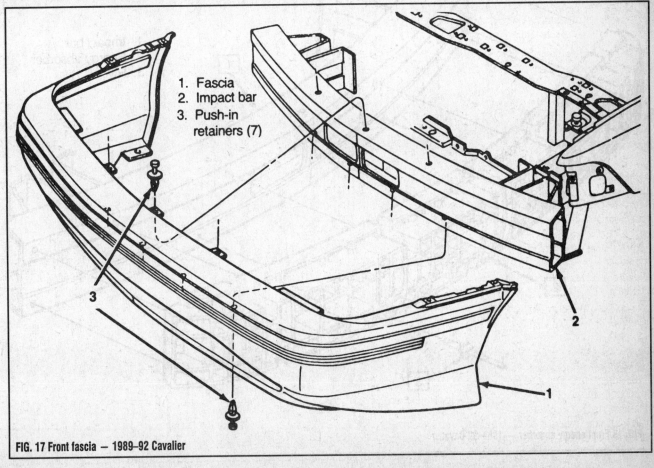

1. Fascia
2. Impact bar
3. Push-in retainers (7)

FIG. 17 Front fascia — 1989–92 Cavalier

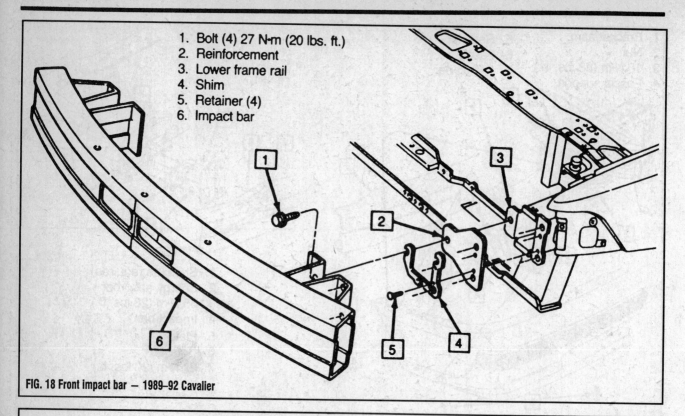

1. Bolt (4) 27 N·m (20 lbs. ft.)
2. Reinforcement
3. Lower frame rail
4. Shim
5. Retainer (4)
6. Impact bar

FIG. 18 Front impact bar — 1989–92 Cavalier

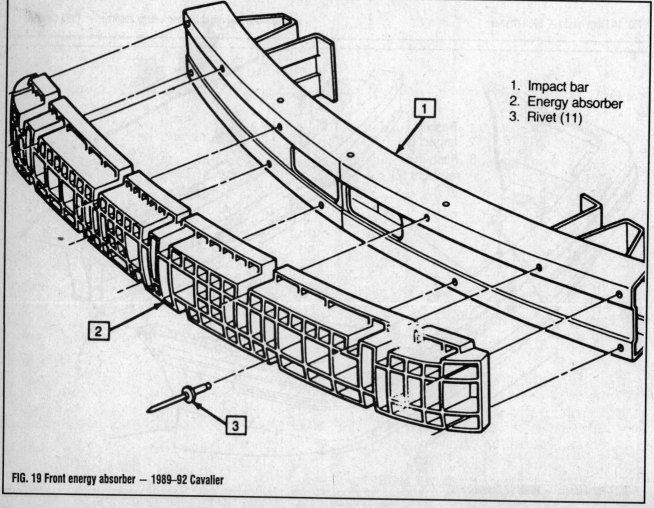

1. Impact bar
2. Energy absorber
3. Rivet (11)

FIG. 19 Front energy absorber — 1989–92 Cavalier

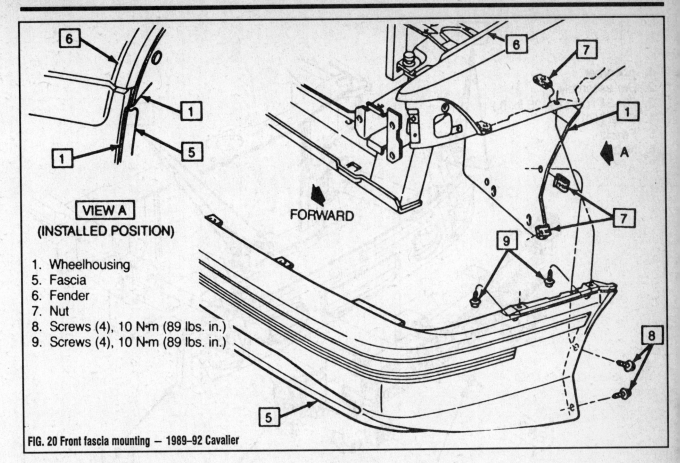

VIEW A
(INSTALLED POSITION)

1. Wheelhousing
5. Fascia
6. Fender
7. Nut
8. Screws (4), 10 N·m (89 lbs. in.)
9. Screws (4), 10 N·m (89 lbs. in.)

FORWARD

FIG. 20 Front fascia mounting — 1989–92 Cavalier

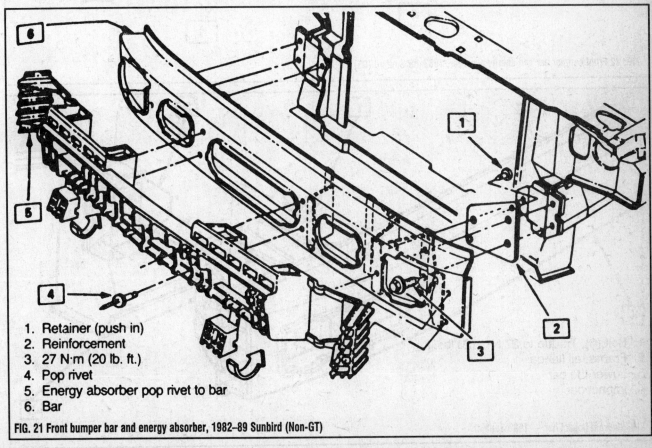

1. Retainer (push in)
2. Reinforcement
3. 27 N·m (20 lb. ft.)
4. Pop rivet
5. Energy absorber pop rivet to bar
6. Bar

FIG. 21 Front bumper bar and energy absorber, 1982–89 Sunbird (Non-GT)

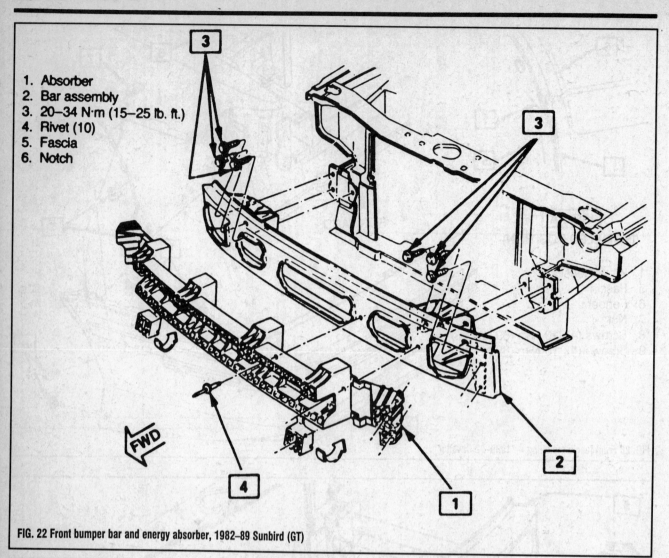

1. Absorber
2. Bar assembly
3. 20–34 N·m (15–25 lb. ft.)
4. Rivet (10)
5. Fascia
6. Notch

FWD

FIG. 22 Front bumper bar and energy absorber, 1982–89 Sunbird (GT)

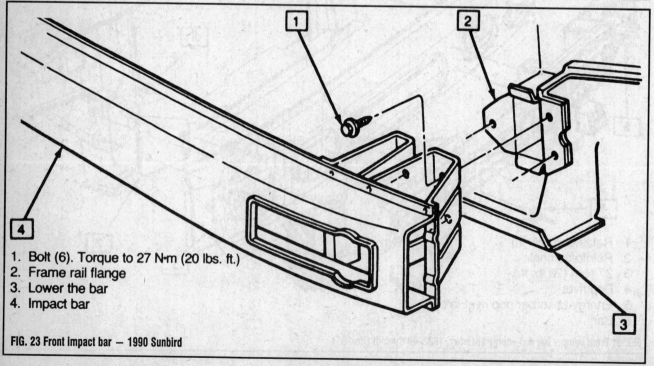

1. Bolt (6). Torque to 27 N·m (20 lbs. ft.)
2. Frame rail flange
3. Lower the bar
4. Impact bar

FIG. 23 Front impact bar — 1990 Sunbird

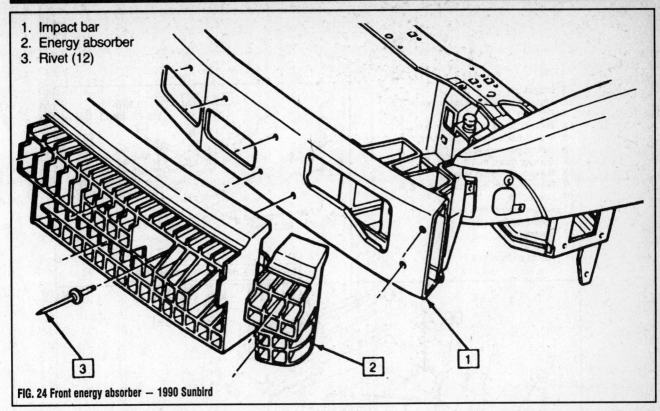

1. Impact bar
2. Energy absorber
3. Rivet (12)

FIG. 24 Front energy absorber — 1990 Sunbird

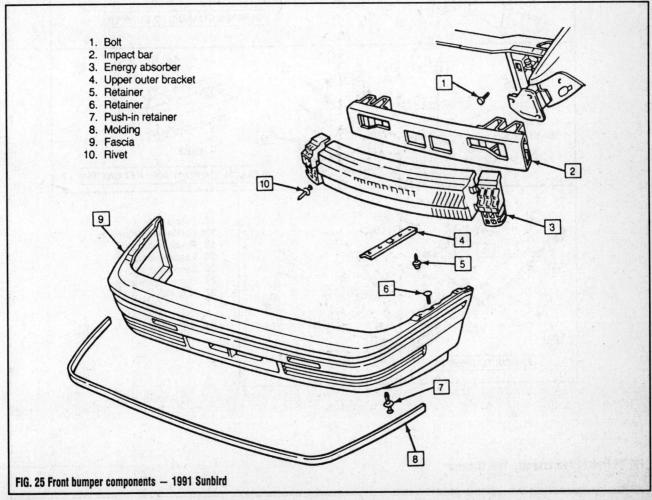

1. Bolt
2. Impact bar
3. Energy absorber
4. Upper outer bracket
5. Retainer
6. Retainer
7. Push-in retainer
8. Molding
9. Fascia
10. Rivet

FIG. 25 Front bumper components — 1991 Sunbird

1. Impact bar
2. Impact bar outer reinforcement rh & lh
3. Bolt (12)
4. Impact bar upper reinforcement
5. Impact bar lower reinforcement
6. Self-tapping screw (2)
7. Bumper guard rh & lh
8. Bumper guard rub strip (2)
9. Bumper guard reinforcement rh & lh
10. Spacer (2)
11. Fascia retainer rh & lh
12. Fascia retainer (2)
13. Retainer (8)
14. Retainer (4)
15. Fascia support rh & lh

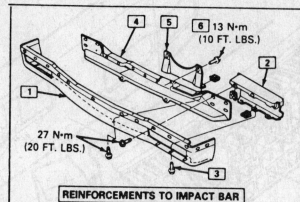

REINFORCEMENTS TO IMPACT BAR

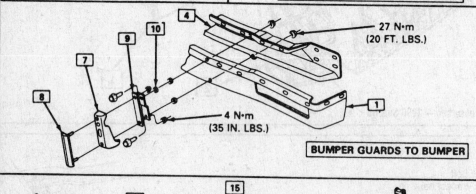

BUMPER GUARDS TO BUMPER

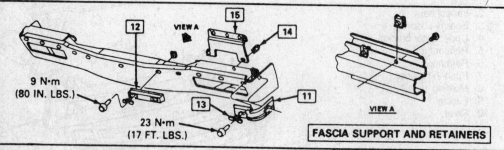

FASCIA SUPPORT AND RETAINERS

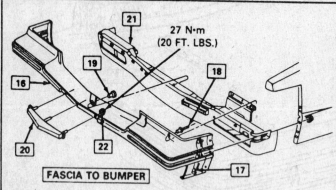

FASCIA TO BUMPER

16. Fascia
17. Fascia retainer rh & lh
18. Plastic retainer (6)
19. Fascia retainer
20. Fascia rub strip
21. Bumper assembly
22. Nuts (3)

FIG. 26 Front bumper assembly, 1985 Cimarron

1. Impact bar
2. Impact bar outer reinforcement rh & lh
3. Bolt (12)
4. Impact bar upper reinforcement
5. Impact bar lower reinforcement
6. Self-tapping screw (2)
7. Bumper guard rh & lh
8. Bumper guard rub strip (2)
9. Bumper guard reinforcement rh & lh
10. Spacer (2)
11. Fascia retainer rh & lh
12. Fascia retainer (2)
13. Retainer (8)
14. Retainer (4)
15. Fascia support rh & lh

16. Fascia
17. Fascia retainer rh & lh
18. Plastic retainer (6)
19. Fascia retainer
20. Fascia rub strip
21. Bumper assembly
22. Nuts (3)

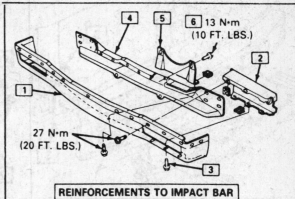
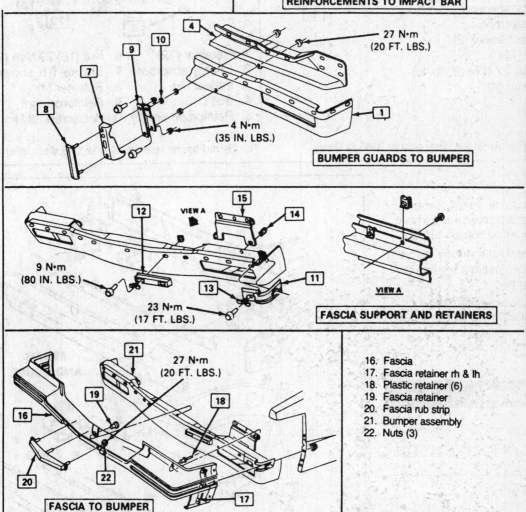

REINFORCEMENTS TO IMPACT BAR

BUMPER GUARDS TO BUMPER

FASCIA SUPPORT AND RETAINERS

FASCIA TO BUMPER

FIG. 27 Front bumper assembly, 1987–88 Cimarron

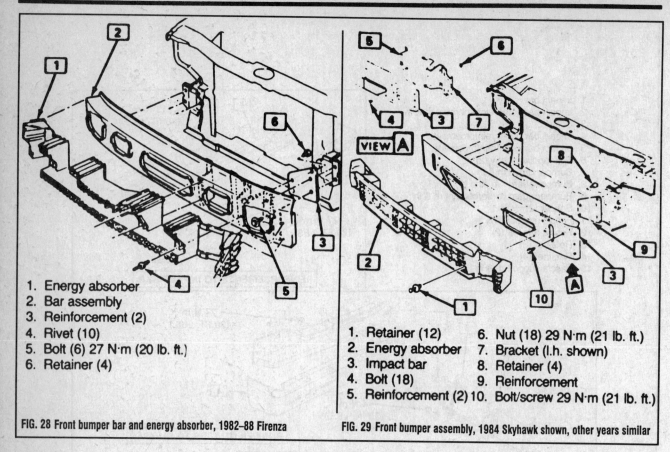

1. Energy absorber
2. Bar assembly
3. Reinforcement (2)
4. Rivet (10)
5. Bolt (6) 27 N·m (20 lb. ft.)
6. Retainer (4)

FIG. 28 Front bumper bar and energy absorber, 1982–88 Firenza

1. Retainer (12)	6. Nut (18) 29 N·m (21 lb. ft.)
2. Energy absorber	7. Bracket (l.h. shown)
3. Impact bar	8. Retainer (4)
4. Bolt (18)	9. Reinforcement
5. Reinforcement (2)	10. Bolt/screw 29 N·m (21 lb. ft.)

FIG. 29 Front bumper assembly, 1984 Skyhawk shown, other years similar

Cimarron

1. Place a jack under the front bumper before removing the bolts to prevent it from dropping down when the bumper bolts are removed.

➡ **Do not rotate the energy absorber any more than needed to align the mounting holes.**

2. Remove the bumper extensions.
3. Remove the four nuts each side securing the bumper to the energy absorber unit.
4. Installation is the reverse of removal.

Rear Bumpers

REMOVAL & INSTALLATION

▶ SEE FIGS. 30-54

1982-83

1. Place a jack under the rear bumper before removing the bolts to prevent it from dropping down when the bumper bolts are removed.

➡ **Do not rotate the energy absorber any more than needed to align the mounting holes.**

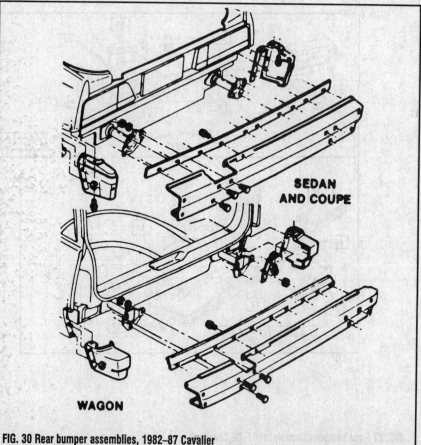

SEDAN AND COUPE

WAGON

FIG. 30 Rear bumper assemblies, 1982–87 Cavalier

2. Remove the end cap to fender (2) nuts and (1) bolt on the right and left side. Push the end cap off the bumper (plastic protrusions through holes in bumper bar).

3. Remove the bumper bolts on the right and left side at the energy absorbers and remove the bumper.

4. If the energy absorbers are to be replaced, remove the bolts and nuts from the unit, then remove the unit and the shims.

5. Install the energy and absorber and shims if removed.

6. Check the dimension and add/subtract shims as needed.

7. Support the bumper to prevent rotation of the energy absorbers.

8. Install the bolts at the bumper to energy absorber brackets, and end cap to fender nuts and bolts.

9. If adjustment is required to align bumper, loosen the energy absorber mounting bolts and position as required (holes are slotted). Adjustment side to side can be made by loosening the bumper bracket bolts. Torque all bolts and nuts.

1984-87

1. Place a jack under the rear bumper before removing the bolts to prevent it from dropping down when the bumper bolts are removed.

➡ **Do not rotate the energy absorber any more than needed to align the mounting holes.**

2. Remove the bumper bolts on the right and left side and remove the bumper.

3. If the energy absorbers are to be replaced, remove the bolts and nuts from the unit, then remove the unit and the shims.

4. Install the energy absorber and shims if removed.

5. Check the dimension and add/subtract shims as needed.

6. Support the bumper to prevent rotation of the energy absorbers.

7. Install the bolts at the bumper to energy absorber brackets, and end cap to fender nuts and bolts.

8. If adjustment is required to align bumper, loosen the energy absorber mounting bolts and position as required (holes are slotted). Adjustment side to side can be made by loosening the bumper bracket bolts. Torque all bolts and nuts.

1988-92

1. Remove side marker lamp assemblies.

2. Remove the lower push-in retainers and upper push-in retainers.

3. Remove fascia seal (except 4 door).

4. Remove the retainers and fascia with supports from vehicle.

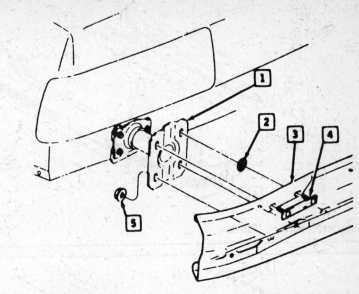

1. Retainer
2. Upper fascia support
3. Impact bar
4. Seal (JC models)
5. Impact bar

FIG. 31 Rear impact bar installation — 1988-89

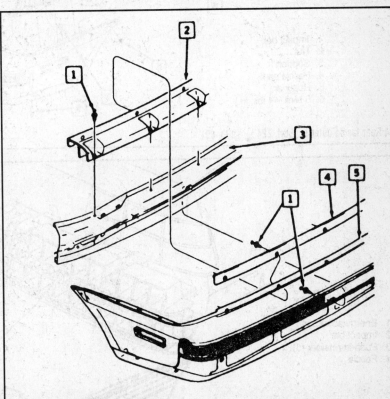

1. Energy absorber
2. Retainer
3. Impact bar
4. Plate asm.
5. 27 N•m (20 lbs. ft.)

FIG. 32 Rear fascia (Z24 similar) — 1988-89

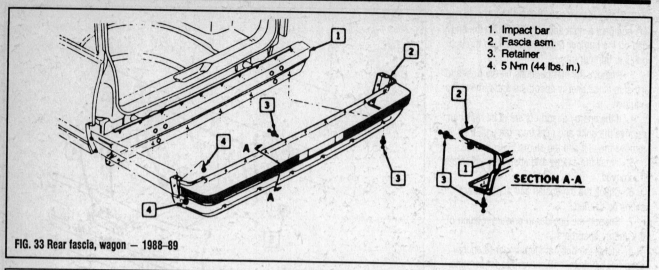

1. Impact bar
2. Fascia asm.
3. Retainer
4. 5 N·m (44 lbs. in.)

SECTION A-A

FIG. 33 Rear fascia, wagon — 1988–89

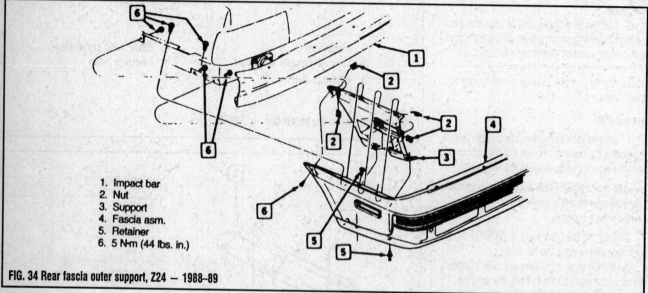

1. Impact bar
2. Nut
3. Support
4. Fascia asm.
5. Retainer
6. 5 N·m (44 lbs. in.)

FIG. 34 Rear fascia outer support, Z24 — 1988–89

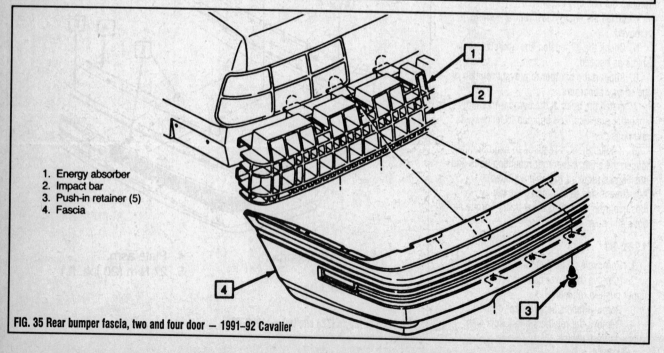

1. Energy absorber
2. Impact bar
3. Push-in retainer (5)
4. Fascia

FIG. 35 Rear bumper fascia, two and four door — 1991–92 Cavalier

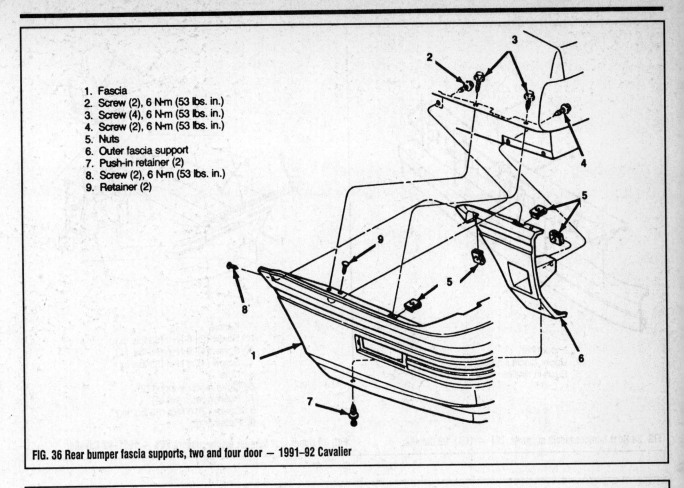

1. Fascia
2. Screw (2), 6 N·m (53 lbs. in.)
3. Screw (4), 6 N·m (53 lbs. in.)
4. Screw (2), 6 N·m (53 lbs. in.)
5. Nuts
6. Outer fascia support
7. Push-in retainer (2)
8. Screw (2), 6 N·m (53 lbs. in.)
9. Retainer (2)

FIG. 36 Rear bumper fascia supports, two and four door — 1991–92 Cavalier

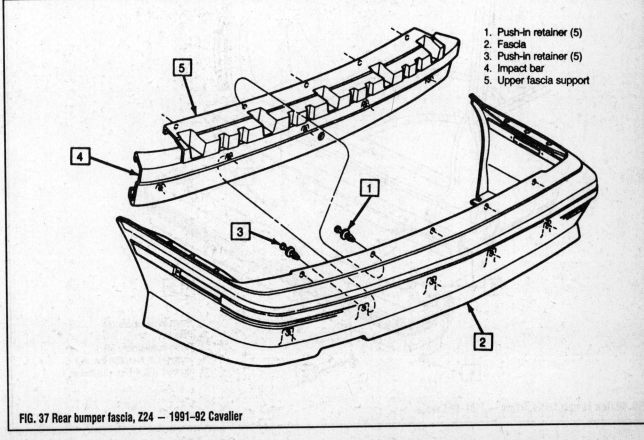

1. Push-in retainer (5)
2. Fascia
3. Push-in retainer (5)
4. Impact bar
5. Upper fascia support

FIG. 37 Rear bumper fascia, Z24 — 1991–92 Cavalier

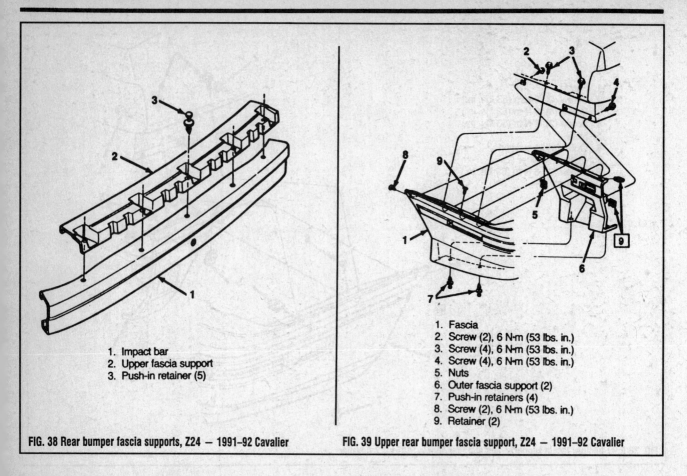

1. Impact bar
2. Upper fascia support
3. Push-in retainer (5)

FIG. 38 Rear bumper fascia supports, Z24 — 1991–92 Cavalier

1. Fascia
2. Screw (2), 6 N·m (53 lbs. in.)
3. Screw (4), 6 N·m (53 lbs. in.)
4. Screw (4), 6 N·m (53 lbs. in.)
5. Nuts
6. Outer fascia support (2)
7. Push-in retainers (4)
8. Screw (2), 6 N·m (53 lbs. in.)
9. Retainer (2)

FIG. 39 Upper rear bumper fascia support, Z24 — 1991–92 Cavalier

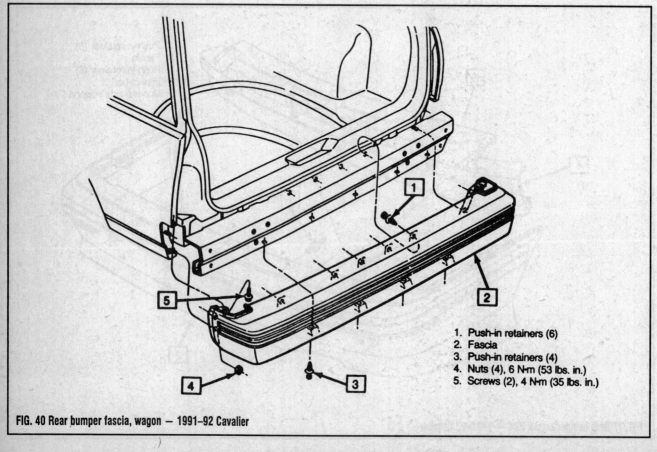

1. Push-in retainers (6)
2. Fascia
3. Push-in retainers (4)
4. Nuts (4), 6 N·m (53 lbs. in.)
5. Screws (2), 4 N·m (35 lbs. in.)

FIG. 40 Rear bumper fascia, wagon — 1991–92 Cavalier

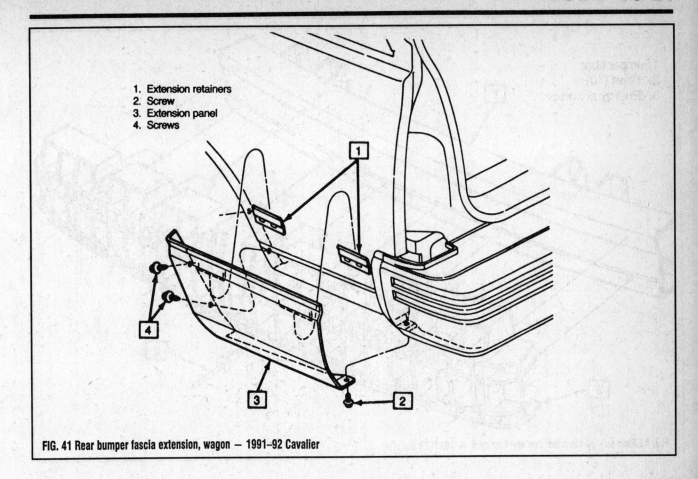

1. Extension retainers
2. Screw
3. Extension panel
4. Screws

FIG. 41 Rear bumper fascia extension, wagon — 1991–92 Cavalier

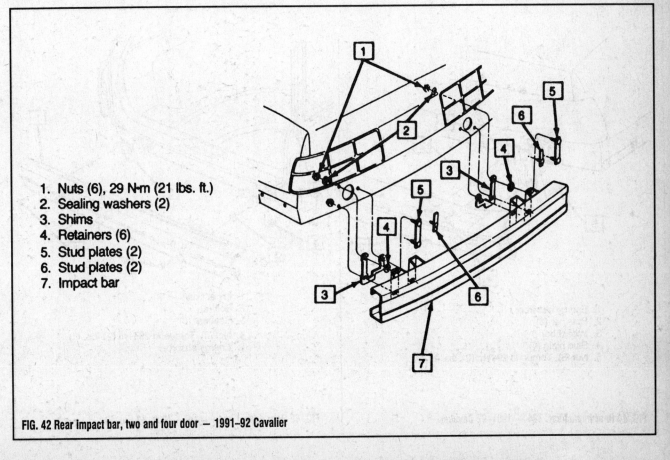

1. Nuts (6), 29 N·m (21 lbs. ft.)
2. Sealing washers (2)
3. Shims
4. Retainers (6)
5. Stud plates (2)
6. Stud plates (2)
7. Impact bar

FIG. 42 Rear impact bar, two and four door — 1991–92 Cavalier

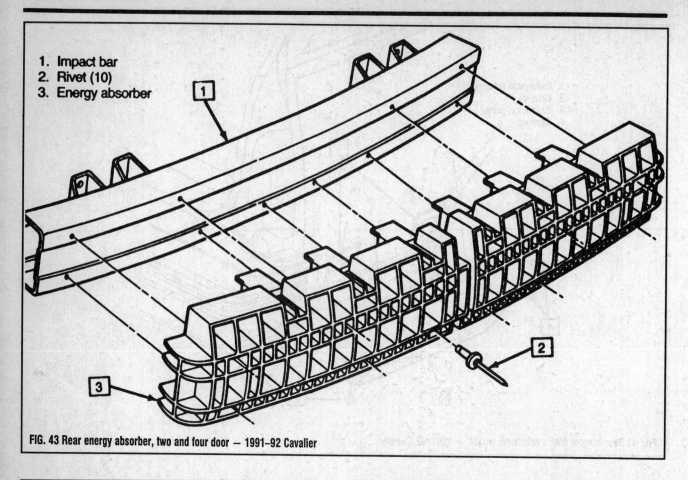

1. Impact bar
2. Rivet (10)
3. Energy absorber

FIG. 43 Rear energy absorber, two and four door — 1991–92 Cavalier

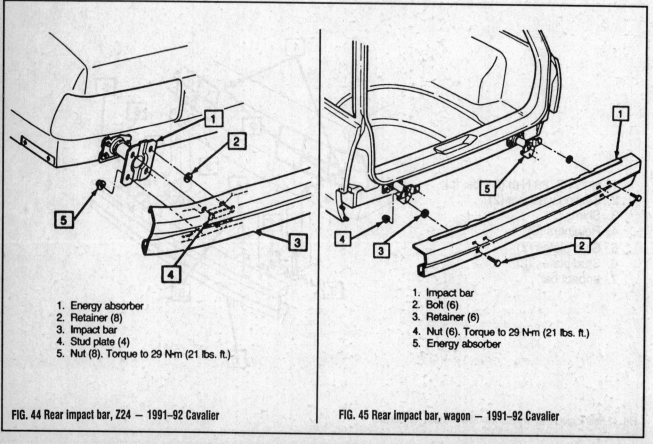

1. Energy absorber
2. Retainer (8)
3. Impact bar
4. Stud plate (4)
5. Nut (8). Torque to 29 N·m (21 lbs. ft.)

FIG. 44 Rear impact bar, Z24 — 1991–92 Cavalier

1. Impact bar
2. Bolt (6)
3. Retainer (6)
4. Nut (6). Torque to 29 N·m (21 lbs. ft.)
5. Energy absorber

FIG. 45 Rear impact bar, wagon — 1991–92 Cavalier

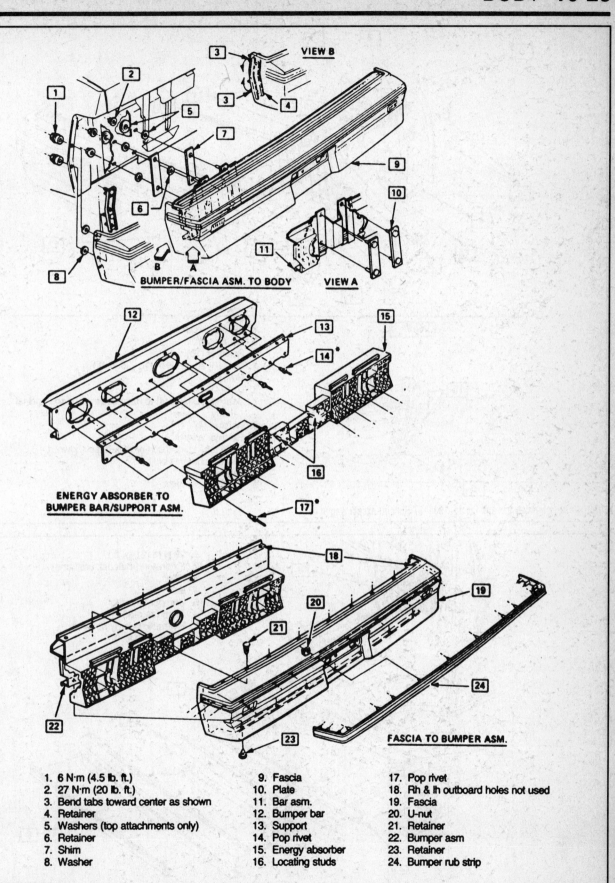

VIEW B

BUMPER/FASCIA ASM. TO BODY

VIEW A

ENERGY ABSORBER TO BUMPER BAR/SUPPORT ASM.

FASCIA TO BUMPER ASM.

1. 6 N·m (4.5 lb. ft.)
2. 27 N·m (20 lb. ft.)
3. Bend tabs toward center as shown
4. Retainer
5. Washers (top attachments only)
6. Retainer
7. Shim
8. Washer
9. Fascia
10. Plate
11. Bar asm.
12. Bumper bar
13. Support
14. Pop rivet
15. Energy absorber
16. Locating studs
17. Pop rivet
18. Rh & lh outboard holes not used
19. Fascia
20. U-nut
21. Retainer
22. Bumper asm
23. Retainer
24. Bumper rub strip

FIG. 46 Rear bumper bar assemblies, 1982–83 2000 and Sunbird except wagon

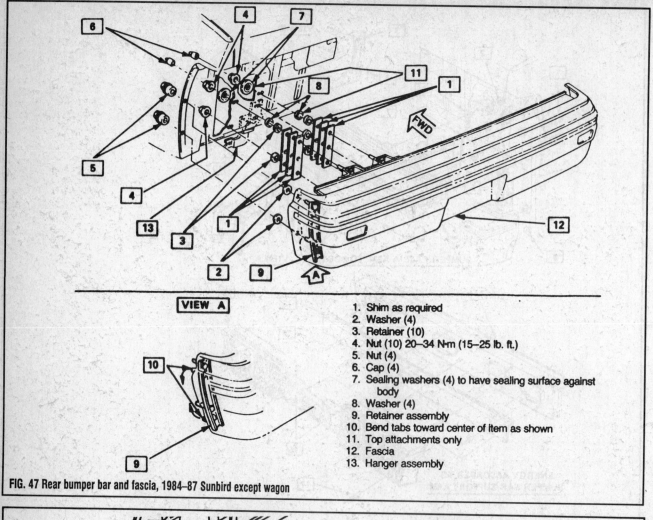

1. Shim as required
2. Washer (4)
3. Retainer (10)
4. Nut (10) 20—34 N·m (15—25 lb. ft.)
5. Nut (4)
6. Cap (4)
7. Sealing washers (4) to have sealing surface against body
8. Washer (4)
9. Retainer assembly
10. Bend tabs toward center of item as shown
11. Top attachments only
12. Fascia
13. Hanger assembly

FIG. 47 Rear bumper bar and fascia, 1984–87 Sunbird except wagon

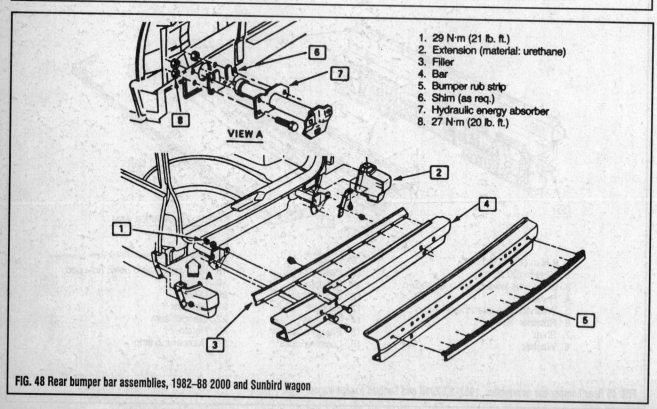

1. 29 N·m (21 lb. ft.)
2. Extension (material: urethane)
3. Filler
4. Bar
5. Bumper rub strip
6. Shim (as req.)
7. Hydraulic energy absorber
8. 27 N·m (20 lb. ft.)

FIG. 48 Rear bumper bar assemblies, 1982–88 2000 and Sunbird wagon

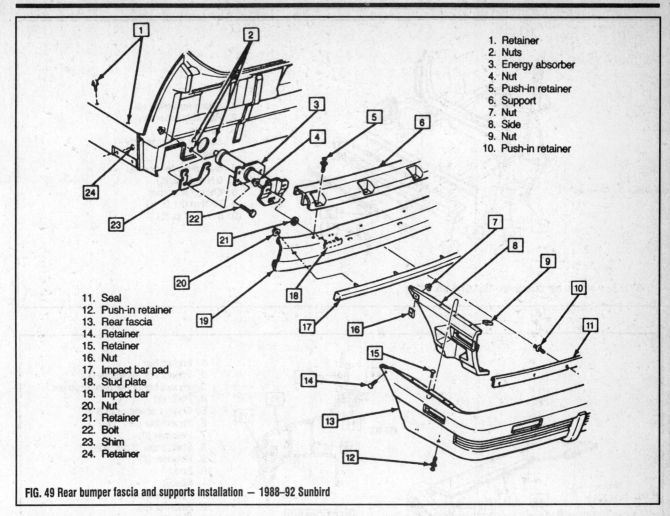

1. Retainer
2. Nuts
3. Energy absorber
4. Nut
5. Push-in retainer
6. Support
7. Nut
8. Side
9. Nut
10. Push-in retainer

11. Seal
12. Push-in retainer
13. Rear fascia
14. Retainer
15. Retainer
16. Nut
17. Impact bar pad
18. Stud plate
19. Impact bar
20. Nut
21. Retainer
22. Bolt
23. Shim
24. Retainer

FIG. 49 Rear bumper fascia and supports installation — 1988–92 Sunbird

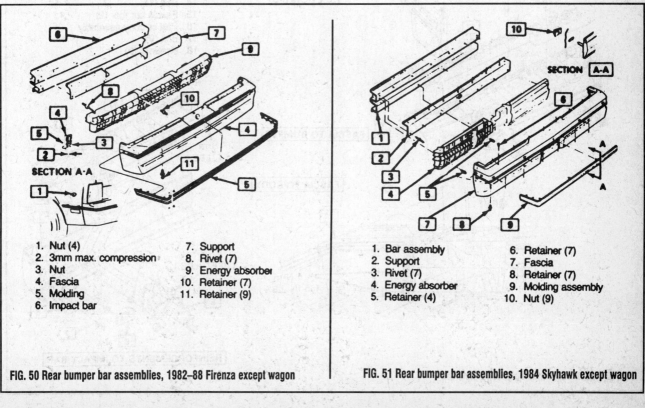

1. Nut (4)	7. Support	
2. 3mm max. compression	8. Rivet (7)	
3. Nut	9. Energy absorber	
4. Fascia	10. Retainer (7)	
5. Molding	11. Retainer (9)	
6. Impact bar		

FIG. 50 Rear bumper bar assemblies, 1982–88 Firenza except wagon

1. Bar assembly	6. Retainer (7)	
2. Support	7. Fascia	
3. Rivet (7)	8. Retainer (7)	
4. Energy absorber	9. Molding assembly	
5. Retainer (4)	10. Nut (9)	

FIG. 51 Rear bumper bar assemblies, 1984 Skyhawk except wagon

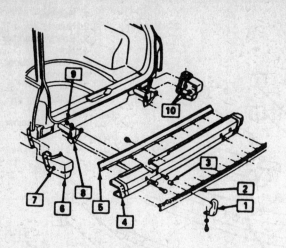

1. Guard assembly r&l
2. Rub strip assembly
3. Spacer
4. Bumper bar assembly
5. Filler
6. Bumper extension r&l
7. 6 N·m (4 lb. ft.)
8. Energy absorber
9. 29 N·m (21 lb. ft.)
10. 6 N·m (4 lb. ft.)

FIG. 52 Rear bumper bar assemblies, 1984 Skyhawk wagon

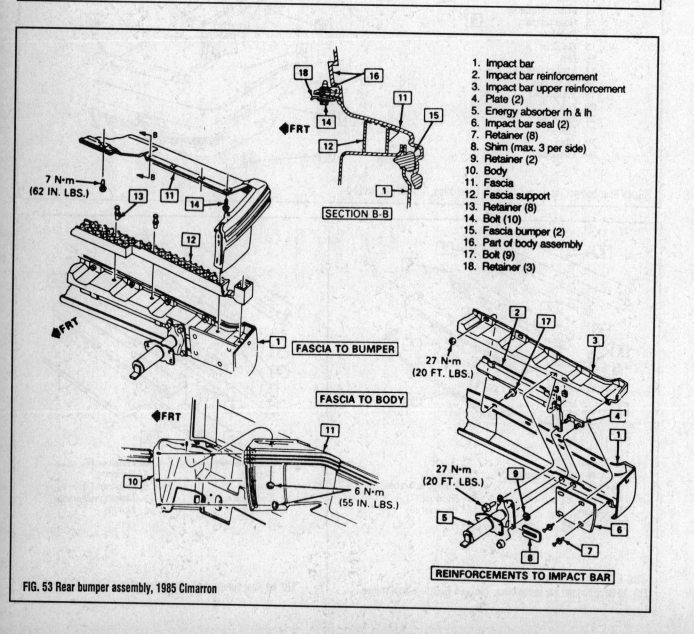

1. Impact bar
2. Impact bar reinforcement
3. Impact bar upper reinforcement
4. Plate (2)
5. Energy absorber rh & lh
6. Impact bar seal (2)
7. Retainer (8)
8. Shim (max. 3 per side)
9. Retainer (2)
10. Body
11. Fascia
12. Fascia support
13. Retainer (8)
14. Bolt (10)
15. Fascia bumper (2)
16. Part of body assembly
17. Bolt (9)
18. Retainer (3)

SECTION B-B

FASCIA TO BUMPER

FASCIA TO BODY

REINFORCEMENTS TO IMPACT BAR

FIG. 53 Rear bumper assembly, 1985 Cimarron

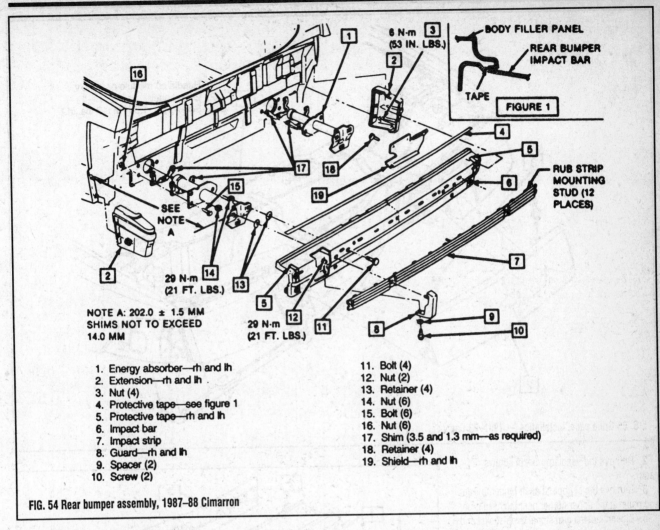

6 N·m
(53 IN. LBS.)

BODY FILLER PANEL

REAR BUMPER
IMPACT BAR

TAPE

FIGURE 1

RUB STRIP
MOUNTING
STUD (12
PLACES)

SEE
NOTE
A

29 N·m
(21 FT. LBS.)

NOTE A: 202.0 ± 1.5 MM
SHIMS NOT TO EXCEED
14.0 MM

29 N·m
(21 FT. LBS.)

1. Energy absorber—rh and lh
2. Extension—rh and lh
3. Nut (4)
4. Protective tape—see figure 1
5. Protective tape—rh and lh
6. Impact bar
7. Impact strip
8. Guard—rh and lh
9. Spacer (2)
10. Screw (2)

11. Bolt (4)
12. Nut (2)
13. Retainer (4)
14. Nut (6)
15. Bolt (6)
16. Nut (6)
17. Shim (3.5 and 1.3 mm—as required)
18. Retainer (4)
19. Shield—rh and lh

FIG. 54 Rear bumper assembly, 1987–88 Cimarron

5. Remove fascia support from impact bar.

6. Remove impact bar retaining nuts and remove the impact bar from energy absorbers.

7. Remove the energy absorber retaining nuts and remove the energy absorbers.

8. Installation is the reverse of the removal procedure. Transfer all supports, shims, brackets, retainers and moldings as necessary if replacing with new parts.

Grille

REMOVAL & INSTALLATION

SEE FIGS. 55-61

➡ **The following procedure includes removal of the front end panel.**

1982-87 Cavalier

1. Open the hood.

1. Headlamp & grille mounting panel
2. Grille
3. Push-in retainer (5)

FIG. 55 Grille panel installation — 1988–90 Cavalier

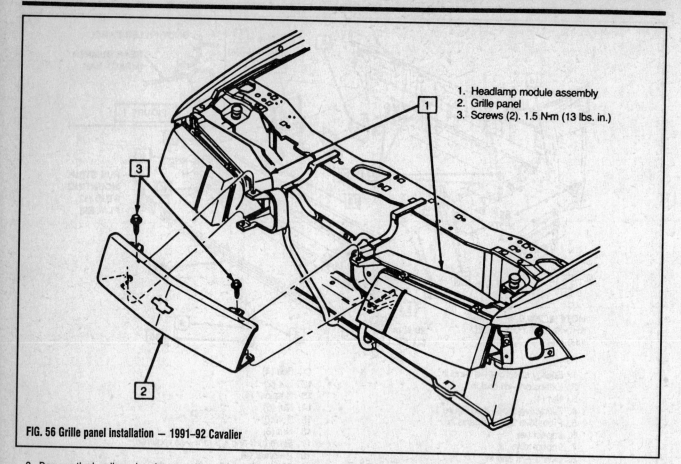

1. Headlamp module assembly
2. Grille panel
3. Screws (2). 1.5 N·m (13 lbs. in.)

FIG. 56 Grille panel installation — 1991–92 Cavalier

2. Remove the headlamp bezel screws (2 each).

3. Remove the (1) bolt at each fender to front end panel at the upper corner near the headlamp.

4. Disconnect the turn signal lamp socket and head lamp wiring.

5. Remove the (1) screw at each turn signal housing and remove the housings.

6. Remove the (1) bolt from the panel to radiator support located below the turn signal housing area.

7. Remove the (1) nut at the panel to the inner fender.

8. Remove the (2) nuts attaching the bumper end cap to the panel at each side.

9. Remove the (3) bolts at the baffles located at the radiator support.

10. Transfer the headlamps and grille.

11. Installation is the reverse of removal.

1988-90 Cavalier

1. Remove the grille push-in retainers.
2. Remove the grille panel.

To Install:

3. Install the grille panel to the headlamp and grille mounting panel.

4. Install the push-in retainers in the following sequence:

  a. Top center retainer
  b. Both upper outer retainers
  c. Both bottom retainers

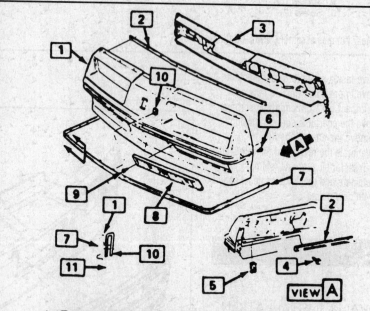

1. Front end panel (fascia)
2. Retainer
3. Reinforcement assembly
4. Screw (9)
5. Nut (16)
6. Screw (6)
7. Moulding
8. Grille (l.h. shown)
9. Screw (16)
10. Nut (15)
11. 3mm max compression

FIG. 57 Front end panel and grille assembly, 1982–88 Firenza

1991-92 Cavalier

1. Remove the grille retaining screws.
2. Remove the grille panel.

To Install:

3. Install the grille panel to the headlamp module assembly.
4. Install the retaining screws and tighten to 13 inch lbs.

Sunbird, Cimarron, Skyhawk, Firenza

On these models please refer to the illustrations. Begining 1990 the Sunbird has a seperate grille similar to that of the Cavalier, refer to those procedures for removal and installation.

Outside Remote Mirrors

♦ SEE FIGS. 62 and 63

With the remote control door outside mirror, the remote control mirror cable must be

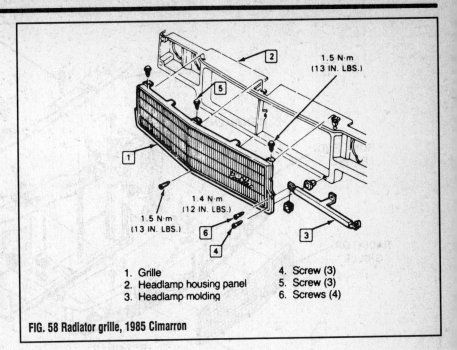

1. Grille
2. Headlamp housing panel
3. Headlamp molding
4. Screw (3)
5. Screw (3)
6. Screws (4)

FIG. 58 Radiator grille, 1985 Cimarron

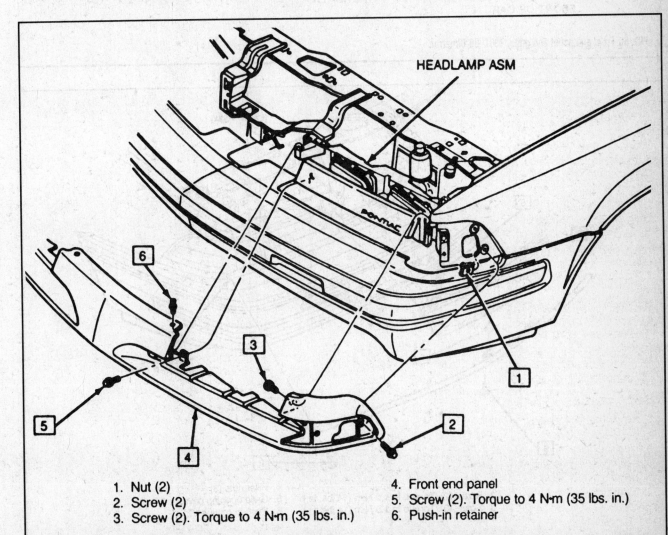

1. Nut (2)
2. Screw (2)
3. Screw (2). Torque to 4 N·m (35 lbs. in.)
4. Front end panel
5. Screw (2). Torque to 4 N·m (35 lbs. in.)
6. Push-in retainer

FIG. 59 Front grille opening panel, except LE model — 1990-92 Sunbird

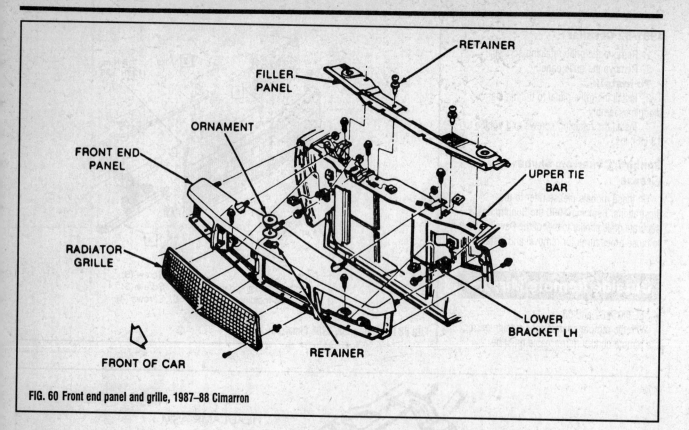

FIG. 60 Front end panel and grille, 1987–88 Cimarron

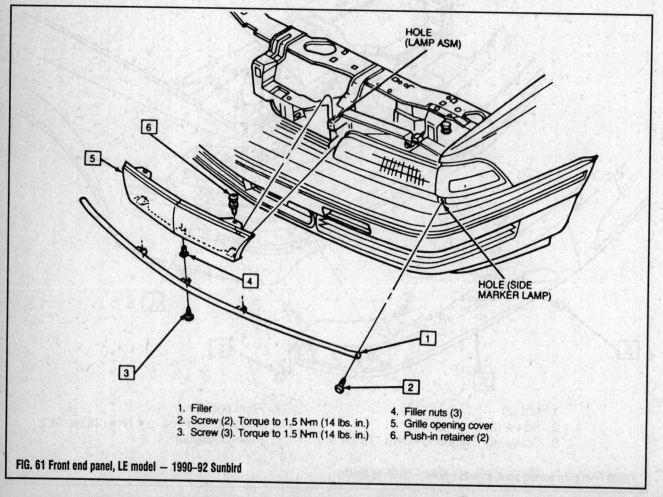

1. Filler
2. Screw (2). Torque to 1.5 N·m (14 lbs. in.)
3. Screw (3). Torque to 1.5 N·m (14 lbs. in.)
4. Filler nuts (3)
5. Grille opening cover
6. Push-in retainer (2)

FIG. 61 Front end panel, LE model — 1990–92 Sunbird

disengaged from the door trim assembly on the standard trim styles to permit trim panel removal.

On custom trim styles the remote control mirror cable must be disengaged from the upper trim panel and the upper trim panel must be removed to permit lower trim panel removal.

Refer to the illustrations for both custom trim and standard trim.

➡ **The mirror glass face may be replaced by placing a piece of tape over the glass then breaking the mirror face. Adhesive back mirror faces are available.**

REMOVAL & INSTALLATION

1. Remove the door trim panel as described in this Section. On standard trim styles, peel back the insulator and water deflector to gain access to the mirror cable.

2. Detach the cable from any retaining tabs in the door.

3. Remove the attaching nuts and remove the mirror and cable assembly from the door.

4. Install the base gasket and reverse the above to install the mirror.

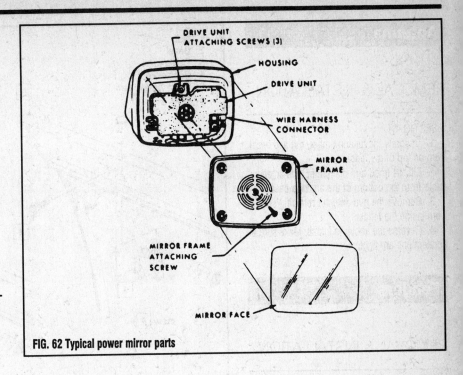

FIG. 62 Typical power mirror parts

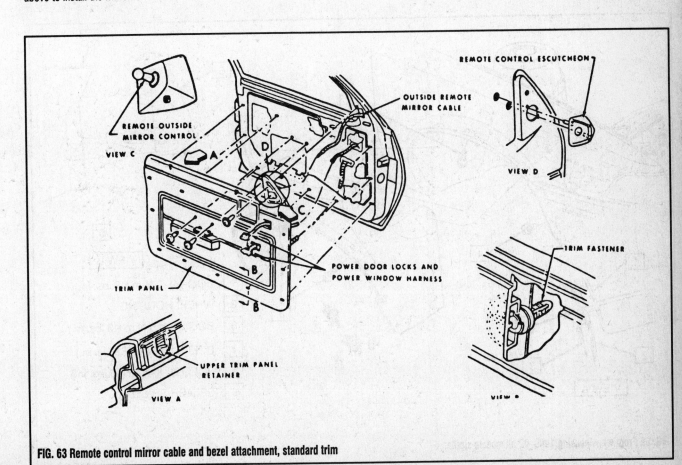

FIG. 63 Remote control mirror cable and bezel attachment, standard trim

Antenna

REMOVAL & INSTALLATION

♦ SEE FIG. 64

1. Unscrew the antenna mast, nut and bezel from on top of the fender.

2. Lift the hood and disconnect the antenna cable from the bottom of the antenna base.

3. Remove the two antenna retaining screws from inside the fender.

4. Reverse the above to install. Make sure all connections are tight.

Fenders

REMOVAL & INSTALLATION

♦ SEE FIGS. 65-69

1982–88

1. Remove the lower air deflector.

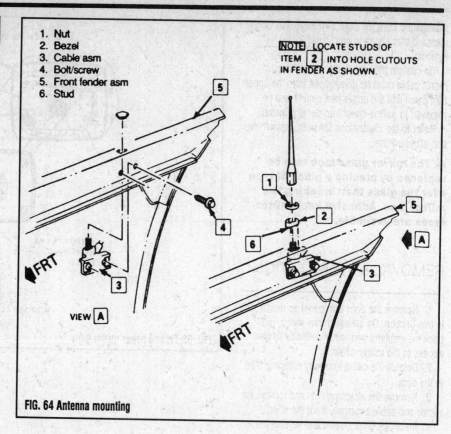

1. Nut
2. Bezel
3. Cable asm
4. Bolt/screw
5. Front fender asm
6. Stud

NOTE: LOCATE STUDS OF ITEM 2 INTO HOLE CUTOUTS IN FENDER AS SHOWN.

FIG. 64 Antenna mounting

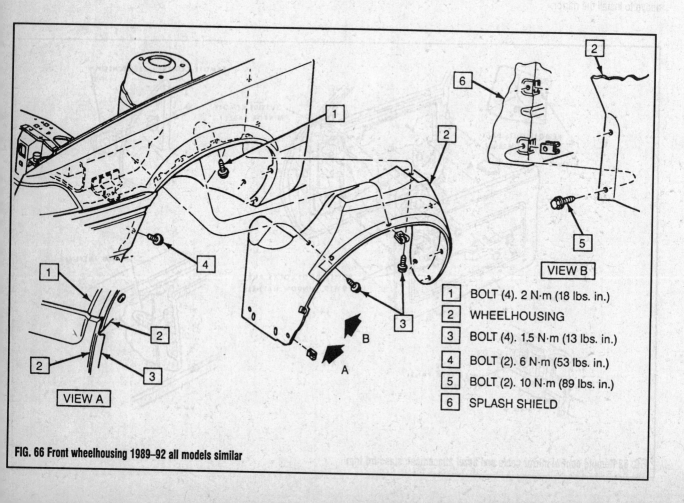

1	BOLT (4). 2 N·m (18 lbs. in.)
2	WHEELHOUSING
3	BOLT (4). 1.5 N·m (13 lbs. in.)
4	BOLT (2). 6 N·m (53 lbs. in.)
5	BOLT (2). 10 N·m (89 lbs. in.)
6	SPLASH SHIELD

VIEW A

VIEW B

FIG. 66 Front wheelhousing 1989–92 all models similar

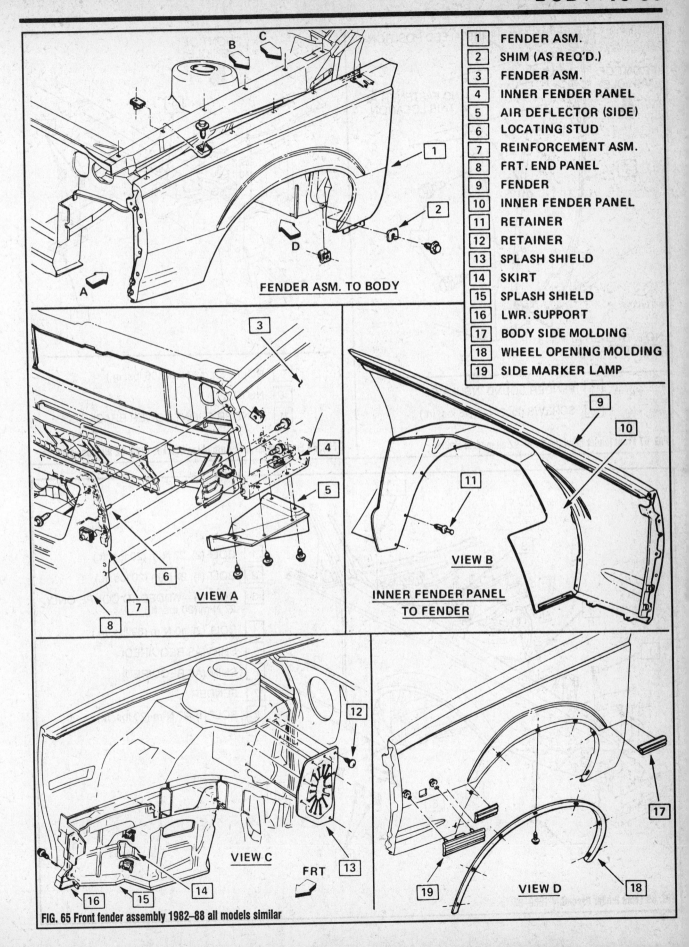

1	FENDER ASM.
2	SHIM (AS REQ'D.)
3	FENDER ASM.
4	INNER FENDER PANEL
5	AIR DEFLECTOR (SIDE)
6	LOCATING STUD
7	REINFORCEMENT ASM.
8	FRT. END PANEL
9	FENDER
10	INNER FENDER PANEL
11	RETAINER
12	RETAINER
13	SPLASH SHIELD
14	SKIRT
15	SPLASH SHIELD
16	LWR. SUPPORT
17	BODY SIDE MOLDING
18	WHEEL OPENING MOLDING
19	SIDE MARKER LAMP

FENDER ASM. TO BODY

VIEW A

VIEW B

INNER FENDER PANEL TO FENDER

VIEW C

FRT

VIEW D

FIG. 65 Front fender assembly 1982–88 all models similar

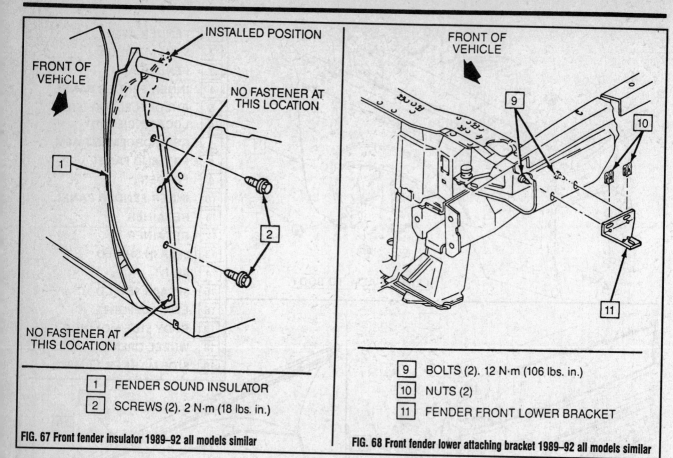

FRONT OF VEHICLE

INSTALLED POSITION

NO FASTENER AT THIS LOCATION

FRONT OF VEHICLE

NO FASTENER AT THIS LOCATION

| 1 | FENDER SOUND INSULATOR |
| 2 | SCREWS (2). 2 N·m (18 lbs. in.) |

FIG. 67 Front fender insulator 1989–92 all models similar

9	BOLTS (2). 12 N·m (106 lbs. in.)
10	NUTS (2)
11	FENDER FRONT LOWER BRACKET

FIG. 68 Front fender lower attaching bracket 1989–92 all models similar

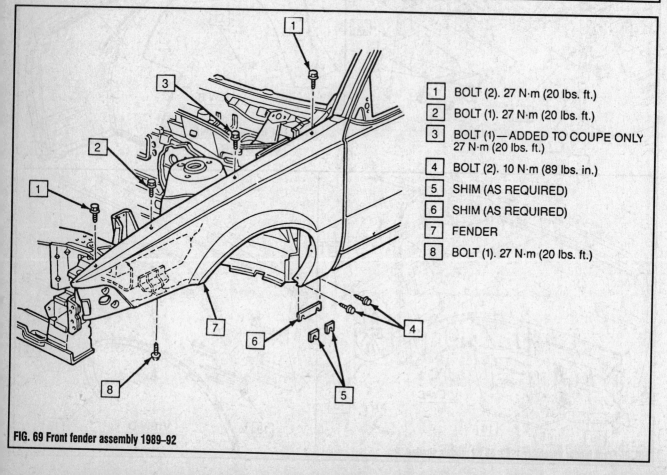

1	BOLT (2). 27 N·m (20 lbs. ft.)
2	BOLT (1). 27 N·m (20 lbs. ft.)
3	BOLT (1)—ADDED TO COUPE ONLY 27 N·m (20 lbs. ft.)
4	BOLT (2). 10 N·m (89 lbs. in.)
5	SHIM (AS REQUIRED)
6	SHIM (AS REQUIRED)
7	FENDER
8	BOLT (1). 27 N·m (20 lbs. ft.)

FIG. 69 Front fender assembly 1989–92

2. Remove the three front end attaching screws. Remove the grille for access to the top screw.

3. Remove the rocker panel molding if equipped, then remove the lower rear attaching screw. Note the number and location of shims for installation.

4. Remove the wiper arms and cowl vent assembly. The two screws at the inside edge of hinge at the cowl are hidden.

5. On fender with antenna, remove the antenna mast, nut and two retaining screws from fender. Allow the antenna housing to fall, the antenna will stay in the car.

6. Remove the top fender attaching screws, remove the fender assembly. Remove the inner fender panel and all attached parts and transfer onto new fender.

7. Installation is the reverse of the removal procedure.

1989–92

1. Remove the wiper arm assemblies, the shroud panel retaining screws, the washer nozzle hose and remove the shroud panel.

2. Remove the side marker lamp and rocker panel moulding if equipped.

3. Remove the front end panel.

4. Raise and safely support vehicle on jack stands. Remove the tire and wheel assembly, and remove the four attaching bolts from inner wheel housing and remove the wheel housing.

5. Remove the upper and lower fender attaching bolts and shims, note the number and location of shims for installation.

6. Remove the fender and transfer remaining parts onto the new fender.

7. Installation is the reverse of the removal procedure.

Convertible Top

TOP REPLACEMENT

◆ SEE FIGS. 70–82

1. Install a spacer stick between the no. 3 and no. 4 bow to keep the no. 4 bow in position.

2. Remove the rear belt mouldings by removing the attaching screws from rear compartment drain trough and then remove the quarter belt moldings by removing the screws and attaching nuts from rear compartment and underneath the right and left sides of folding top well.

3. Apply a protective cover on the rear deck surface and quarter panel painted areas.

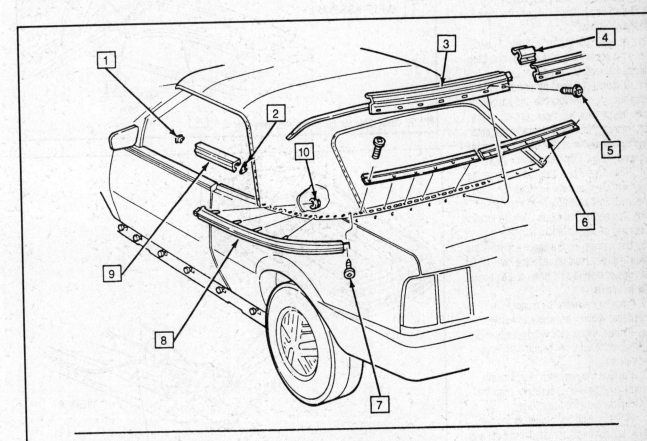

1	QUARTER PANEL BELT MOLDING CAP		6	RETAINER
2	ISOLATOR		7	SCREW
3	MOLDING ASSEMBLY BACK BELT		8	MOLDING QUARTER PANEL BELT
4	BACK BELT MOLDING CAP		9	MOLDING ASSEMBLY QUARTER BELT FRONT
5	SCREW		10	NUT

FIG. 70 Convertible quarter and back belt moldings

4. Using a sharp grease pencil, mark the location of the complete belt tacking strip (upper edge) on outer surface of top cover.

5. Raise the top to a suitable working height. Remove the front no. 1 bow seal and retainers. Detach welt assembly and top cover from the no. 1 bow.

6. Remove attaching screw from the rear of each side retention cable. Remove the cable forward end from the hole in front rail.

7. Remove the screws from the lower end of each rear retension cable and rear listing pocket. To ease the removal of rear retension cable screw, raise the top off windshield header. Pull the cables through listing pockets from the upper end.

8. Raise the top and remove rear rail seals and retainers.

9. Detach the top cover flaps from front rail and rear rail.

10. Remove the feature strip cap (end), feature strip and retainer. Remove the top cover from the no. 4 bow.

11. At underside of the no. 2 and 3 bows, remove the screws securing listing pocket top retainers and remove the retainers.

12. Disconnect the top cover from rear belt tacking strip. Note the location and spacing of staples before removing them.

13. Mark the location of rear window outer panels along balance of rear belt tacking strip, and the no. 4 bow (upper and lower edge).

14. Recheck the tack strip location markings on rear window assembly. Remove stay pads and rear window assembly from the rear belt tacking strip and the no. 4 bow. Note the location and spacing of staples before removal.

15. Use a sharp grease pencil and mark the location of all belt molding attaching holes on the lower edge of tacking strip or on quarter panels.

To install:

16. Transfer the reference marks from removed rear window assembly as follows:

a. Place the new rear window assembly on a clean covered work bench with inner surface down.

b. Position the removed rear window assembly over new one, carefully align the upper window with the lower one.

c. While holding both together securely, carefully lay out the trim material of both and transfer the rear window assembly reference marks along bottom portion of tacking strip.

d. Reverse the rear window assemblies by placing the new rear window assembly over the original as described above.

e. Reck the location of reverence marks. If any difference is noted, the average between the two is the correct reference to use. Mark the corrected references clearly. Trim off the excess material beyond the 1/2 in. (13mm)

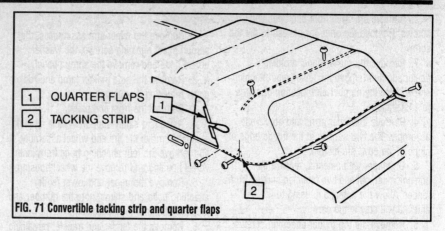

| 1 | QUARTER FLAPS |
| 2 | TACKING STRIP |

FIG. 71 Convertible tacking strip and quarter flaps

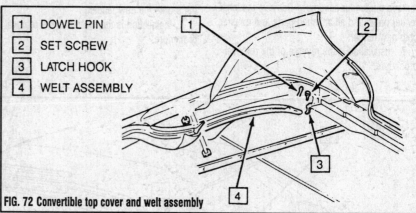

1	DOWEL PIN
2	SET SCREW
3	LATCH HOOK
4	WELT ASSEMBLY

FIG. 72 Convertible top cover and welt assembly

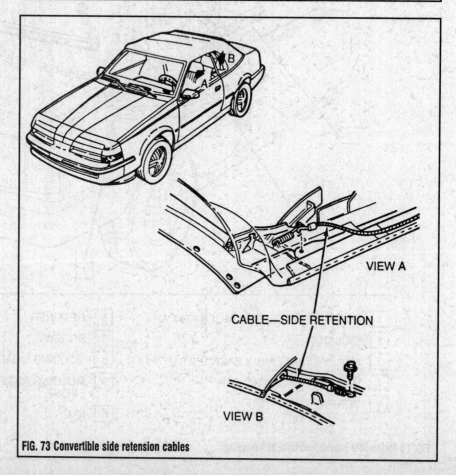

VIEW A

CABLE—SIDE RETENTION

VIEW B

FIG. 73 Convertible side retension cables

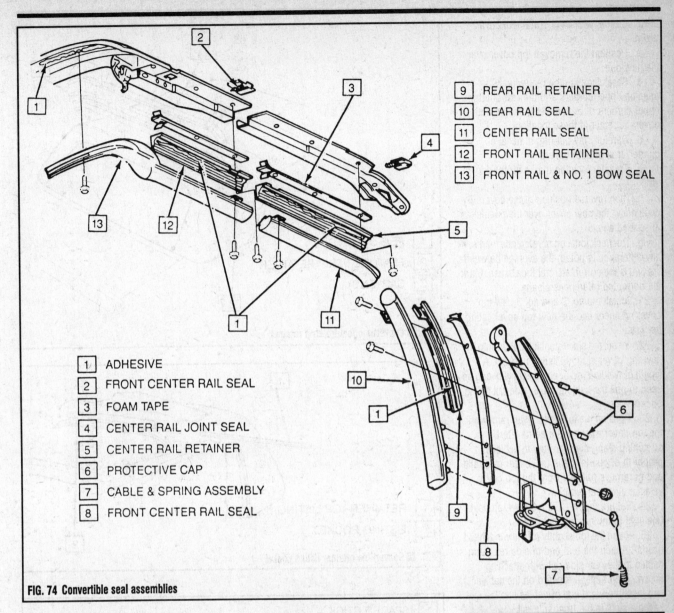

9	REAR RAIL RETAINER
10	REAR RAIL SEAL
11	CENTER RAIL SEAL
12	FRONT RAIL RETAINER
13	FRONT RAIL & NO. 1 BOW SEAL

1	ADHESIVE
2	FRONT CENTER RAIL SEAL
3	FOAM TAPE
4	CENTER RAIL JOINT SEAL
5	CENTER RAIL RETAINER
6	PROTECTIVE CAP
7	CABLE & SPRING ASSEMBLY
8	FRONT CENTER RAIL SEAL

FIG. 74 Convertible seal assemblies

allowance along the bottom and transfer the center mark from bottom center of removed rear window assembly to new one. Transfer of the reference marks must be done correctly for best results and minimum rework.

17. Lock the top to windshield header and install spacer sticks between the no.4 bow and and rear rail. Spacer stick should be installed between no.4 bow and rear rail back face. The purpose of the spacer sticks is to hold the no. 4 bow in its most rearward position, keeping tension on the top stay pads during the rear window assembly and top cover installation to belt tacking strips.

18. Position and center the new rear window assembly to the no. 4 bow according to reference marks and center notch. Using heavy duty 3/8 in. (9.5mm) stainless steel staples, staple the rear window assembly to the no. 4 bow. Staple from center to ends.

Avoid stretching, but keep the material flat during stapling.

19. Position and center the new rear window assembly to the rear tacking strip according to reference marks and center notch. Staple the rear window assembly to tacking strip as follows:

a. Pull rear window assembly down over the tacking strip to remove all fullness and staple the rear window assembly to the tacking strip. Staple from center to each end of the rear window assembly.

b. Apply downward tension to the rear window assembly at each point of staple installation.

⁂ CAUTION

Excessive heat may cause damage to the rear window. Extreme care should be exercised when following this procedure.

c. After rear window has been properly secured, trim off all excess material at the rear tacking strip. Staple stay pads to the no.4 bow and belt tacking strip and remove the spacer sticks. If wrinkles are present following installation, apply heat to the rear window surface using a hot air gun. The hot air gun should be held about 2 in. (51mm) from the rear window and moved in a circular motion.

20. Transfer the reference marks from the removed top cover to the new one as follows:

a. Place the new top cover on a suitable

clean surface, with inner surface of cover down.

b. Position the removed top cover over the new one.

c. Carefully align the rear window opening upper corners and the rear quarter upper corners of both covers. Secure both covers together at these locations.

d. Carefully lay out trim material of quarter area of both covers.

e. Transfer location marks for tacking strip.

f. Then reverse position of the covers by positioning the new cover over the original as described above.

g. Recheck location of reference marks. If any difference is noted, the average between the two is the corrected reference to use. Mark the corrected references clearly.

21. Install the no. 2 and no. 3 bow top cover retainers into the new top cover listing pockets.

22. Install the side retension cables into the new top cover side rail listing pockets. A length of welding rod or equivalent wire can be used to pull the cable through side rail listing pocket.

23. Position the top cover over framework, the top cover may require some lateral stretching along the rear bow to achieve proper fit of quarter flaps to the rear side rails and to remove fullness from the top cover valance over rear window.

24. Secure the no. 2 and 3 bow top cover retainers to the no. 2 and 3 bows.

25. Raise the top slightly off the windshield header. Attach the rear end of side retension cables to the rear side rail with attaching screw. Then apply a forward on the cables and install forward end of cables into the keyhole slots in the front side rail.

26. Install the rear retension cables into the rear listing pockets. Secure the lower ends of the cables and listing pockets to the quarter inner reinforcement with screws.

27. Install the center top cover rear valance over the no. 4 bow. Pull the top cover rear valance over no. 4 bow to remove all fullness from the rear valance. Staple the top cover to the no. 4 bow, starting at center and working towards each end. Avoid excessive stretching, but keep the material flat during stapling. Staples must be installed in a straight line in the center of no. 4 bow. Staples outboard of the seams should not be more than 2 in. (51mm) apart.

28. Apply adhesive to cementing surfaces of the rear side rail and to quarter flaps. Align the quarter flap seam with the edge of rear rail

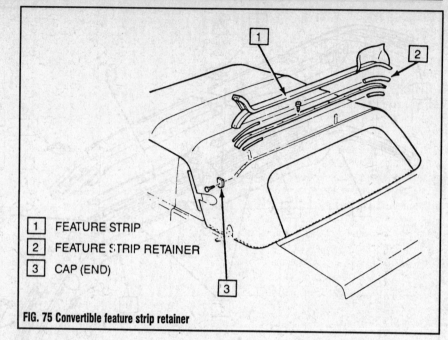

1	FEATURE STRIP
2	FEATURE STRIP RETAINER
3	CAP (END)

FIG. 75 Convertible feature strip retainer

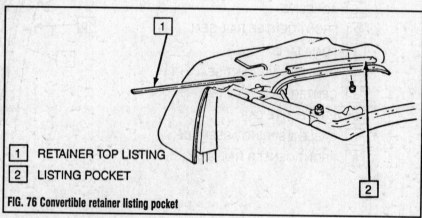

| 1 | RETAINER TOP LISTING |
| 2 | LISTING POCKET |

FIG. 76 Convertible retainer listing pocket

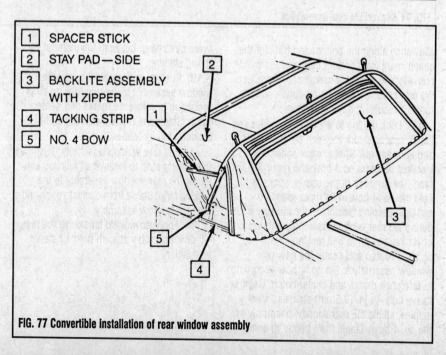

1	SPACER STICK
2	STAY PAD—SIDE
3	BACKLITE ASSEMBLY WITH ZIPPER
4	TACKING STRIP
5	NO. 4 BOW

FIG. 77 Convertible installation of rear window assembly

to remove all fullness from the rear top cover. With the quarter flap seam aligned with each rear rail, install a screw at belt tacking strip. Then cement the quarter flaps securely in place.

29. Install the side rail seal assembly to help maintain position of the quarter flaps.

30. Lock the top to the windshield header. Pull top cover straight forward at the seams to desired top fullness and align the top cover seams with the notches in no. 1 bow. While maintaining tension on cover over the top of no. 1 bow, make pencil mark on the cover outer surface along the forward edge of top no. 1 bow.

31. Raise the top off header to a suitable working height. Apply adhesive such as 3M 0864 or equivalent, to cementing area of the top no. 1 bow, surface of top cover and to front corner flaps. Pull top cover 1/4 in. (6mm) past the reference point over the no. 1 bow and secure.

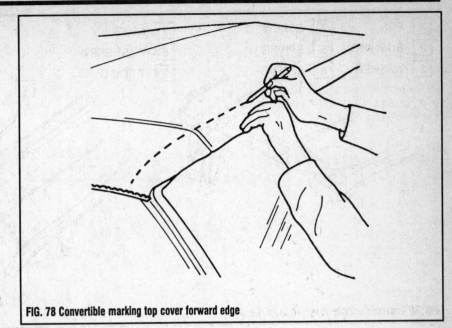

FIG. 78 Convertible marking top cover forward edge

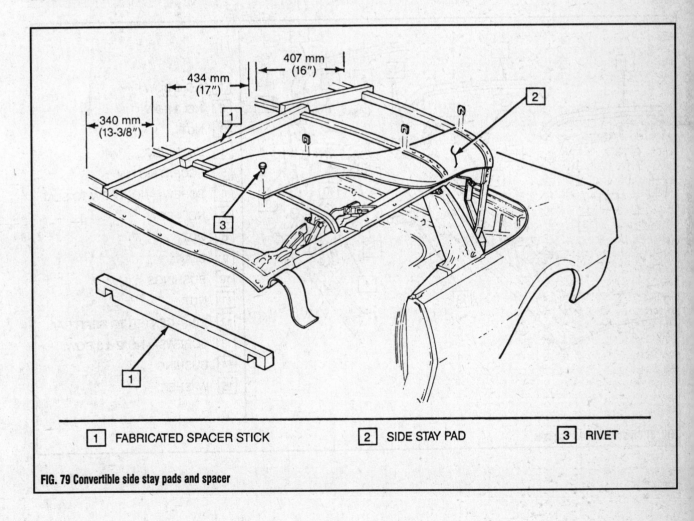

| 1 | FABRICATED SPACER STICK | 2 | SIDE STAY PAD | 3 | RIVET |

FIG. 79 Convertible side stay pads and spacer

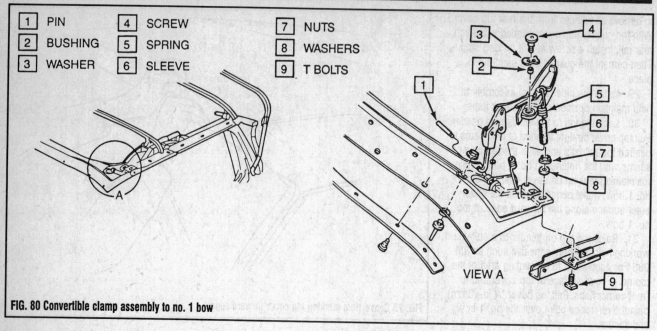

1 PIN	4 SCREW	7 NUTS
2 BUSHING	5 SPRING	8 WASHERS
3 WASHER	6 SLEEVE	9 T BOLTS

VIEW A

FIG. 80 Convertible clamp assembly to no. 1 bow

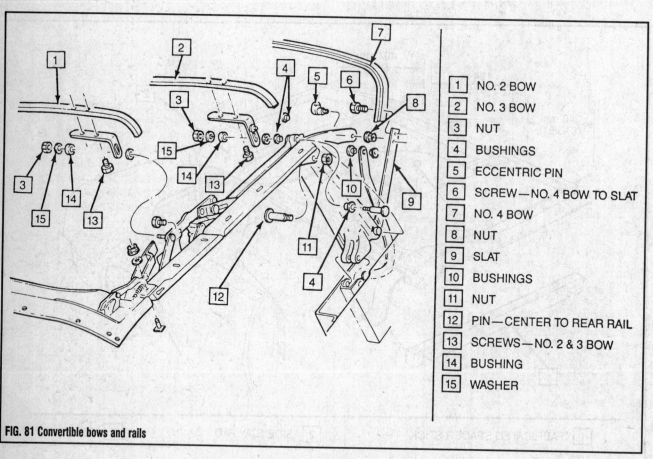

1	NO. 2 BOW
2	NO. 3 BOW
3	NUT
4	BUSHINGS
5	ECCENTRIC PIN
6	SCREW—NO. 4 BOW TO SLAT
7	NO. 4 BOW
8	NUT
9	SLAT
10	BUSHINGS
11	NUT
12	PIN—CENTER TO REAR RAIL
13	SCREWS—NO. 2 & 3 BOW
14	BUSHING
15	WASHER

FIG. 81 Convertible bows and rails

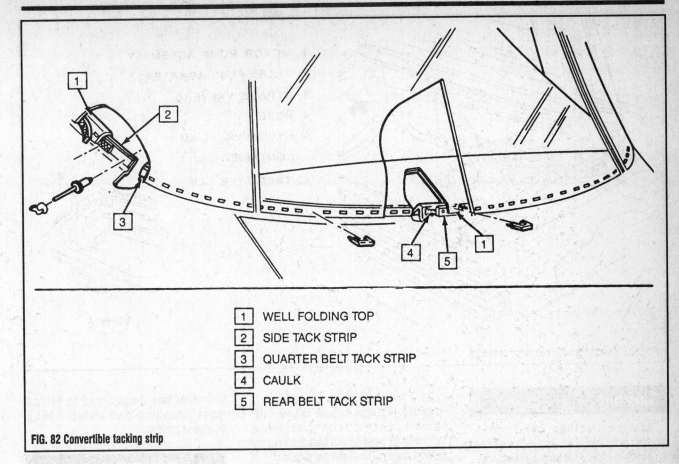

1	WELL FOLDING TOP
2	SIDE TACK STRIP
3	QUARTER BELT TACK STRIP
4	CAULK
5	REAR BELT TACK STRIP

FIG. 82 Convertible tacking strip

32. Trim the excess material to retaining screw holes for front rail and no. 1 bow seal.

33. Lower the top and lock to windshield header. Check appearance of the top trim, top operation and locking action of the top. If additional tension is needed in the top cover, repeat step 30 and pull the top cover farther forward. Staple and recheck the top for proper appearance and operation.

34. Align the welt assembly to no. 1 bow. Fold the vinyl flap back over the welt bulb and staple into position.

35. Apply adhesive to the stapled edge of the welt assembly and fold the vinyl flap over stapled surface of welt assembly.

36. Carefully align the front rail retainers. Secure in position with attaching screws.

37. Apply weatherstrip adhesive to the retainer inner surface. Attach the front rail and no. 1 bow seal assembly to the front rail retainer and accross the no. 1 bow. Secure the seal to the no. 1 bow with attaching screws.

38. Lock the top to the windshield header. Staple the top cover to the belt tacking strip starting at the rear rail and working rearward. Apply downward pressure to top cover at each point of staple installation. Avoid excessive stretching, but keep the material flat during stapling.

39. Install a pierce hole in the top material and tacking strip at each out board end of the no. 4 bow for feature strip and cap.

40. Install the rear bow feature strip retainer, feature strip and end caps using a clear silicone sealer.

41. Cut or pierce holes in the top cover and rear window assembly along the tacking strip for belt molding attaching studs and install belt moldings.

42. When complete, the folding top cover should be free from wrinkles and draws. Clean up top material and car as necessary.

MOTOR REPLACEMENT

◆ SEE FIG. 83

If any parts of the motor and pump assembly are found to be inoperable, it is recommended that the entire unit be replaced with a new motor and pump assembly.

1. Operate the top to the full up position.
2. Disconnect the battery ground cable.
3. Remove the partition in the rear compartment to expose the motor/pump unit.

4. Disconnect the wiring harness, then remove the ground wire attaching screw and ground wire.

5. Place absorbent rags below hose connections and end of reservoir.

6. Vent the reservoir by removing the filler plug then installing it.

7. Disconnect the hydraulic lines and cap open fittings to prevent leakage of fluid. Use a cloth to absorb any leaking fluid. Remove the motor/pump unit.

To Install:

8. Fill the reservoir unit with DEXRON IIE® transmission fluid. Position the motor/pump unit in place.

9. Connect the hydraulic hoses, ensuring that each hose assembly has a seal ring in place. Connect the wiring harness, ground wire and attaching screw.

10. Connect the battery ground cable and operate the top through its up and down cycles until all the air has been bled from the hydraulic circut.

11. Check connections for leaks and recheck the fluid in the reservoir. Level should be even with fill hole, install plug.

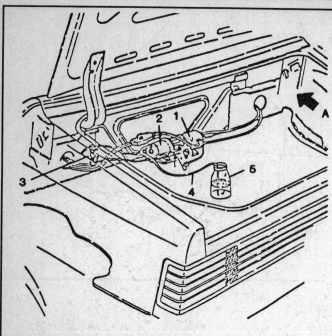

1. MOTOR PUMP ASSEMBLY
2. FILLER PLUG ADAPTER
3. BYPASS VALVE
4. HOSE
5. HYDRAULIC FLUID
   CONTAINER
6. TREE TYPE CLIP

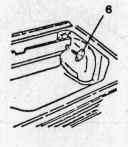

VIEW A

FIG. 83 Convertible motor and pump assembly

Sunroof

The vista vent is a hinged window panel mounted to the roof of the vehicle. The vista vent is opened by moving the latch release handle forward and up to lock it in this position. When open, the rear of the window is raised about 1½ in. (38mm).

The vista vent can also be removed completely. First open the panel as previously described. Then press the latch handle release tab and lift the panel up and back to disengage the front hinges. To reinstall the vista vent, position the forward edge of the opening. Line up the hinge blades with the hinge slots and engage completely. If hinge binds in slot, reposition the panel in opening, DO NOT FORCE! Depress the latch release tab and engage striker bar into latch recess. Rotate handle down and back to lock in the closed position.

✳ CAUTION

Never attempt to remove the roof panel while the vehicle is being driven! The panel may either fly off or fall inside which may cause damage or personal injury.

INTERIOR

Instrument Panel

REMOVAL & INSTALLATION

◆ SEE FIGS. 84-88

1982-88

1. Disconnect the battery ground cable.
2. Remove the left side I. P. (instrument panel) hush panel.
3. Remove the lower steering column trim cover and A/C outlet.
4. Remove center A/C duct and right close out panel (2 clips hold the A/C duct in the center). Disconnect the courtesy light.
5. Remove 3 steering column to I.P. bolts and lower steering column.
6. Remove the glove box door and trunk release switch, if so equipped.
7. Remove 2 radio to I.P. screws, disconnect electrical connectors and antenna lead from radio.
8. Remove 4 cluster to I.P. screws, disconnect the speedometer cable and remove 1 screw from speed sensor.
9. Remove 3 heater A/C control to I.P. screws. Remove clip and screw securing bowden cable to heater door.
10. Remove trim plate at right of steering column (spring clip attachment).
11. Disconnect the lighter connector. Remove headlamp switch knob and trimplate at left of steering column. Remove plastic nut at headlamp switch and remove the switch.

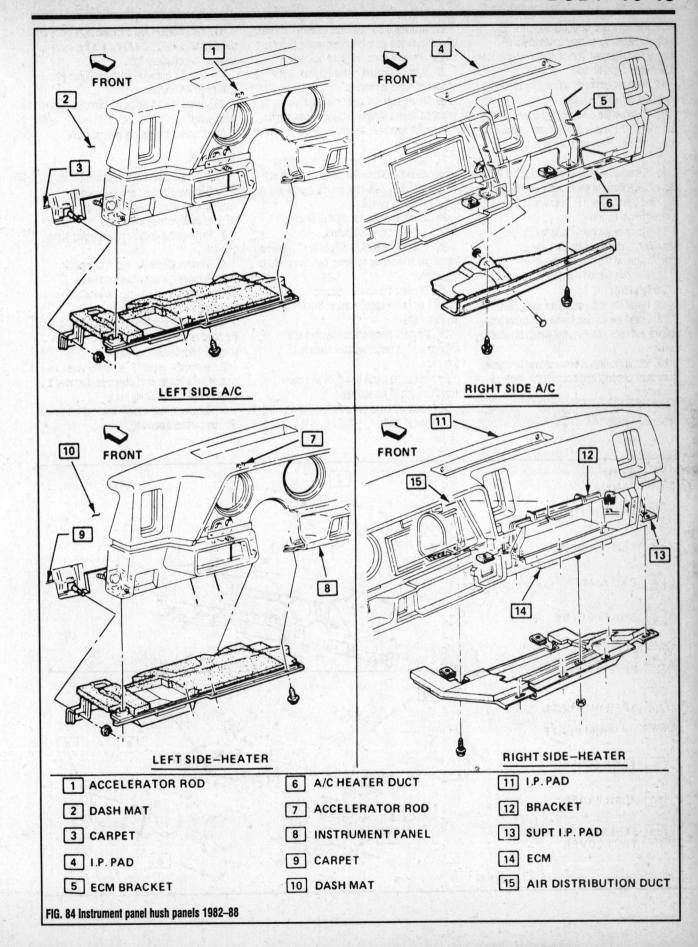

LEFT SIDE A/C

RIGHT SIDE A/C

LEFT SIDE—HEATER

RIGHT SIDE—HEATER

1 ACCELERATOR ROD	6 A/C HEATER DUCT	11 I.P. PAD
2 DASH MAT	7 ACCELERATOR ROD	12 BRACKET
3 CARPET	8 INSTRUMENT PANEL	13 SUPT I.P. PAD
4 I.P. PAD	9 CARPET	14 ECM
5 ECM BRACKET	10 DASH MAT	15 AIR DISTRIBUTION DUCT

FIG. 84 Instrument panel hush panels 1982–88

12. Remove rear defogger switch, if so equipped. Remove ashtray assembly and ashtray light. Remove hood release cable handle (1 screw and plastic nut).

13. Remove defroster grilles (pry up) and 4 screws at defroster outlets.

14. Remove the conveniece center (1 screw), I.P. harness and bulk head connector (2 nuts, 1 screw). Remove 1 brace to glove box screw.

15. Remove the nuts at either side of I.P. carrier lower back of panel and disconnect the electrical connectors (I.P. duct work must be removed from harness).

16. Remove the carrier and lay on seat. Remove A/C ductwork, screws and clips attaching the wiring harness to carrier.

17. Remove the radio speakers and grilles.

To Install:

18. Install the radio speakers and grilles.

19. Install the carrier. Install A/C ductwork, screws and clips attaching the wiring harness to carrier.

20. Install the nuts at either side of I.P. carrier lower back of panel and connect the electrical connectors.

21. Install the convenience center (1 screw), I.P. harness and bulk head connector (2 nuts, 1 screw). Install 1 brace to glove box screw.

22. Install defroster grilles (pry up) and 4 screws at defroster outlets.

23. Install rear defogger switch, if so equipped. Install ashtray assembly and ashtray light. Install hood release cable handle (1 screw and plastic nut).

24. Connect the lighter connector. Install headlamp switch knob and trimplate at left of steering column. Install the switch, Install plastic nut at headlamp switch.

25. Install trim plate at right of steering column (spring clip attachment).

26. Install 3 heater A/C control to I.P. screws. Install clip and screw securing bowden cable to heater door.

27. Connect the speedometer cable and Install 1 screw in speed sensor. Install 4 cluster to I.P. screws.

28. Connect electrical connectors and antenna lead to radio. Install 2 radio to I.P. screws.

29. Install the glove box door and trunk release switch, if so equipped.

30. Raise steering column. Install 3 steering column to I.P. bolts.

31. Install center A/C duct and right close out panel (2 clips hold the A/C duct in the center). Connect the courtesy light.

32. Install the lower steering column trim cover and A/C outlet.

33. Install the left side I. P. (instrument panel) hush panel.

34. Connect the battery ground cable.

1989–92

1. Disconnect the battery ground cable.

2. Remove The right and left sound insulators, steering column filler, right and left I.P.(instrument panel) trim plates.

3. Remove the console housing and glove box door.

4. Remove the heater and A/C control.

5. Remove the convenience center. Disconnect the forward lamp harness and engine harness from bulkhead.

6. Remove the bulkhead from cowl. Remove the hood release handle (retained by two set screws), and defroster grilles.

7. Remove 4 upper I.P. retaining screws located in defroster duct openings. Remove 2 lower corner I.P. retaining nuts.

8. Remove 1 screw to I.P. brace at left side of I.P. compartment opening.

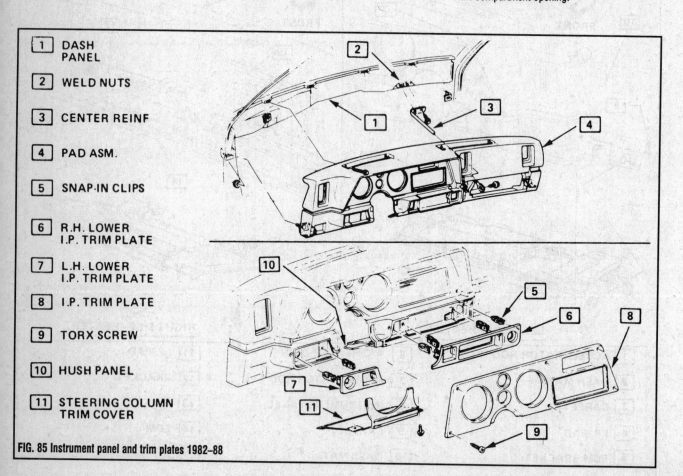

1	DASH PANEL
2	WELD NUTS
3	CENTER REINF
4	PAD ASM.
5	SNAP-IN CLIPS
6	R.H. LOWER I.P. TRIM PLATE
7	L.H. LOWER I.P. TRIM PLATE
8	I.P. TRIM PLATE
9	TORX SCREW
10	HUSH PANEL
11	STEERING COLUMN TRIM COVER

FIG. 85 Instrument panel and trim plates 1982–88

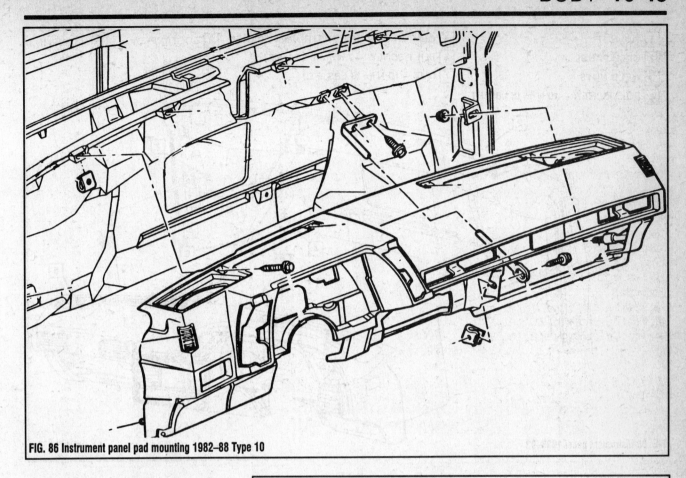

FIG. 86 Instrument panel pad mounting 1982–88 Type 10

9. Remove 2 nuts securing wire harness to neutral start switch (manual transmissions only).

10. Remove 3 steering column rertaining bolts, 2 at I.P. pad and 1 at cowl and lower steering column.

11. Pull I.P. assembly out far enough to disconnect ignition switch, headlamp dimmer switch and turn signal switch. Disconnect all other electrical wiring connectors, vacuum lines and radio antenna lead to remove the I.P. assembly.

12. Remove the instrument panel (I.P.) with wiring harness attached.

To Install:

13. Position the I.P to cowl and connect all electrical connectors and vacuum hoses.

14. Install 3 steering column retaining bolt. Install screw into I.P. brace at left side of I.P. compartment, tighten to 57 inch lbs.

15. Install 2 lower corner I.P. retaining nuts, tighten to 12 inch lbs. Install 4 screws through defroster ducts into cowl, tighten to 12 inch lbs.

16. Install 2 lower nuts securing wire harness to neutral start switch (manual transmission only).

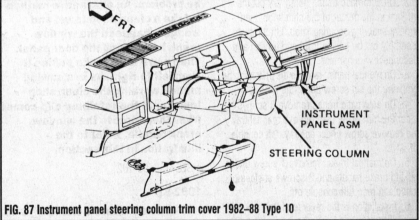

FIG. 87 Instrument panel steering column trim cover 1982–88 Type 10

17. Install defroster grilles, hood release handle, bulkhead and forward lamp and engine harness into bulkhead.

18. Install convenience center, heater A/C control assembly and glove box door.

19. Install console housing, right and left trim plates and steering column filler.

20. Install the left and right sound insulators.

21. Connect the battery ground cable.

Console

REMOVAL & INSTALLATION

▶ SEE FIGS. 89-97

1. Place gear selector in the neutral position and apply the parking brake. Remove front ashtray, then remove 2 screws (some models use Torx®) under ash tray.

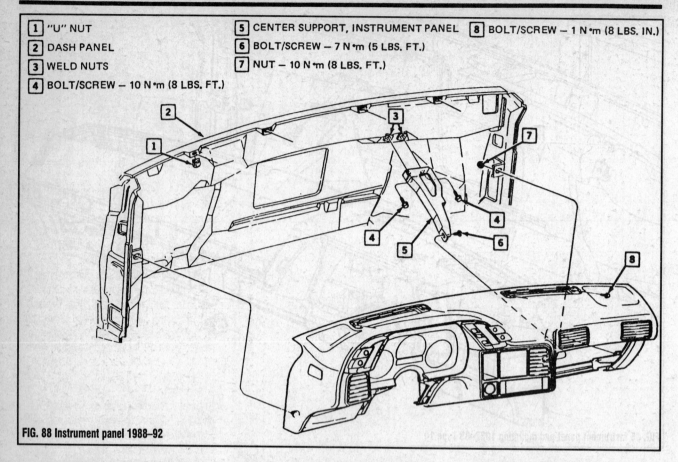

1. "U" NUT
2. DASH PANEL
3. WELD NUTS
4. BOLT/SCREW — 10 N•m (8 LBS. FT.)
5. CENTER SUPPORT, INSTRUMENT PANEL
6. BOLT/SCREW — 7 N•m (5 LBS. FT.)
7. NUT — 10 N•m (8 LBS. FT.)
8. BOLT/SCREW — 1 N•m (8 LBS. IN.)

FIG. 88 Instrument panel 1988–92

2. On automatic trans., gently pry out the emblem in the center of the shift knob, then remove snapring securing knob. Lift trimplate assembly out by pulling front end up first and disconnect wire harness.

3. On manual trans., remove the shift knob by removing the set screw under the knob.

4. On automatic trans., remove 3 screws under the trim plate, then remove rear ashtray and remove screw under ashtray. Lift console off.

5. On manual trans., remove 1 screw under parking brake handle and 2 screws at sides of console in rear. Lift console off.

6. Installation is the reverse of the removal procedure.

Door Panel

REMOVAL & INSTALLATION

➡ **Removing a window crank handle (with a retaining clip inside the handle) without the special tool can** be problem. **An alternative method is take a clean shop towel and wedge it between the window crank handle and the door panel. Then move it up, while pulling it from left to right, as in a sawing motion working the clean shop towel until the retaining clip comes free. Then remove the window crank handle. Refer to the illustration in this section.**

➧ SEE FIGS. 98-102

1982-87

A one piece trim panel is used on styles with standard trim. The custom trim has an upper metal trim panel. The one piece trim hangs over the door inner panel across the top and is secured by clips down the sides and across the bottom. It is retained by screws located in the areas of the top front of the
panel assembly.

1. Remove all door inside handles.
2. Remove the door inside locking rod knob.
3. Remove the screws inserted through the door armrest and pull the handle assembly into the door inner panel or armrest hanger support bracket.

4. On styles with remote control mirrors assemblies, disengage the end of the mirror control cable from the bezel on the standard trim, or from the upper trim panel on the custom trim. On custom trim, remove the upper trim panel.

5. On styles with power window or door lock controls located in the door trim panel, disconnect the wire harnesses at the switch assemblies. On the four door sedan and the two door hatchback, remove the switch cover by pushing down at the switch area and pulling down at the bottom of the cover. The switch and base may be removed from the trim with the cover removed.

6. Remove the remote control handle bezel screws.

7. Remove the screws used to hold the armrest to the inner panel.

8. Remove the screws and plastic retainers from the perimeter of the door trim using tool BT-7323A or equivalent and a screwdriver. To remove the trim panel, push the trim panel upward and outboard to disengage from the door inner panel at the beltline.

9. On styles with an insulator pad fastened to the door inner panel, use tool J-21104 or equivalent to remove the fasteners and the insulator pad.

10. On styles with the water defector held in place by fasteners, use tool BT-7323A or

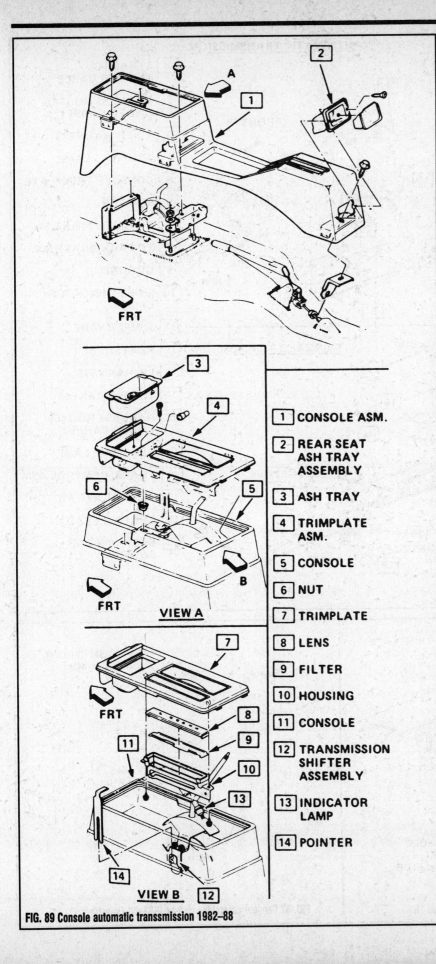

FIG. 100A Removing the window crank handle with a clean shop towel

equivalent to remove the fasteners and the water deflector.

11. On styles with the armrest bracket riveted to the inner panel and installed over the water deflector, drill out the armrest bracket rivets using a $\frac{3}{16}$ in. (5mm) drill bit.

12. To install the insulator pad or water deflector, locate the fasteners in the holes in the door inner panel and press in place. Replace all tape which may have been applied to assist in holding insulator pad or water deflector in place. Where necessary, install the armrest support bracket over the water deflector and onto the door inner panel using $\frac{3}{16}$ in. × $\frac{11}{32}$ in. (5mm × 9mm) rivets.

13. Before installing the door trim panel, check that all trim retainers are securely installed to the assembly and are not damaged. Replace retainers where required.

14. Connect all electrical components.

15. To install the door trim panel, locate the top of the assembly over the upper flange of the door inner panel, inserting the door handle through the handle slot in the panel and press down on the trim panel to engage the upper retaining clips.

16. Position the trim panel to the door inner panel so the trim retainers are align with the attaching holes in the panel and tap the retainers into the holes with the palm of your hand or a clean rubber mallet.

17. Install all previously removed items.

Front Door Lock

REMOVAL & INSTALLATION

◆ SEE FIGS. 103 and 104

1. Raise the door window and remove the door trim panel and water deflector.

2. Disengage the following rods at the lock assembly:

   a. Inside locking rod.

   b. Inside handle to locking rod.

   c. Lock cylinder to locking rod.

Parts legend

1	CONSOLE ASM.
2	REAR SEAT ASH TRAY ASSEMBLY
3	ASH TRAY
4	TRIMPLATE ASM.
5	CONSOLE
6	NUT
7	TRIMPLATE
8	LENS
9	FILTER
10	HOUSING
11	CONSOLE
12	TRANSMISSION SHIFTER ASSEMBLY
13	INDICATOR LAMP
14	POINTER

VIEW A

VIEW B

FIG. 89 Console automatic transsmission 1982–88

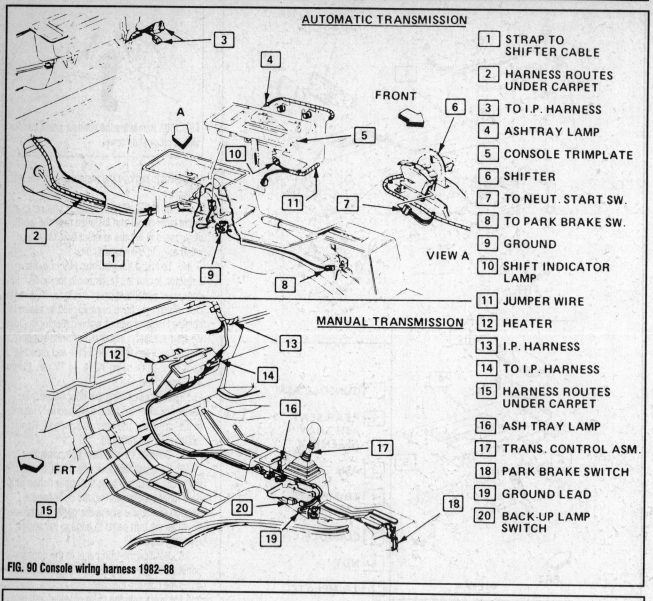

AUTOMATIC TRANSMISSION

1	STRAP TO SHIFTER CABLE
2	HARNESS ROUTES UNDER CARPET
3	TO I.P. HARNESS
4	ASHTRAY LAMP
5	CONSOLE TRIMPLATE
6	SHIFTER
7	TO NEUT. START SW.
8	TO PARK BRAKE SW.
9	GROUND
10	SHIFT INDICATOR LAMP
11	JUMPER WIRE
12	HEATER
13	I.P. HARNESS
14	TO I.P. HARNESS
15	HARNESS ROUTES UNDER CARPET
16	ASH TRAY LAMP
17	TRANS. CONTROL ASM.
18	PARK BRAKE SWITCH
19	GROUND LEAD
20	BACK-UP LAMP SWITCH

FRONT

VIEW A

MANUAL TRANSMISSION

FRT

FIG. 90 Console wiring harness 1982–88

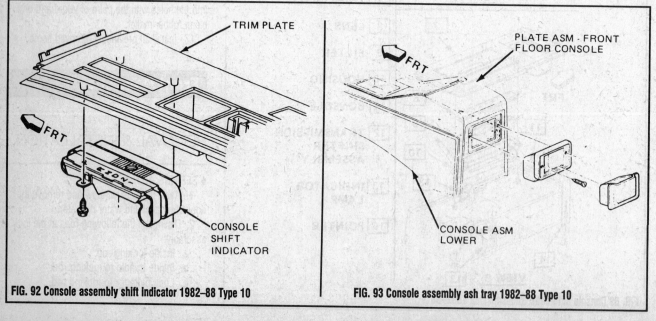

TRIM PLATE

FRT

CONSOLE SHIFT INDICATOR

PLATE ASM - FRONT FLOOR CONSOLE

FRT

CONSOLE ASM LOWER

FIG. 92 Console assembly shift indicator 1982–88 Type 10

FIG. 93 Console assembly ash tray 1982–88 Type 10

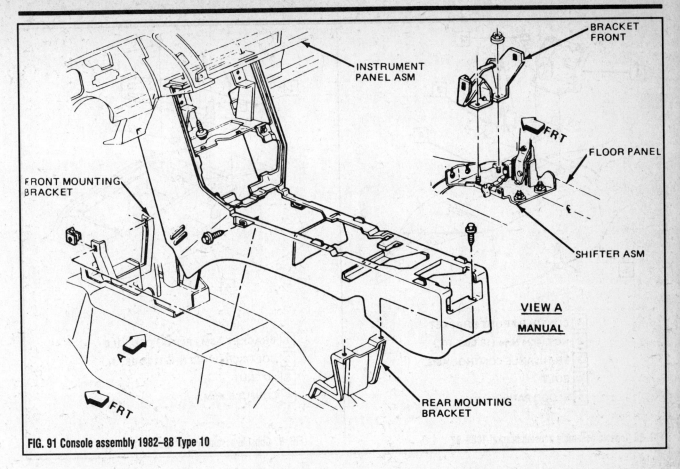

FIG. 91 Console assembly 1982–88 Type 10

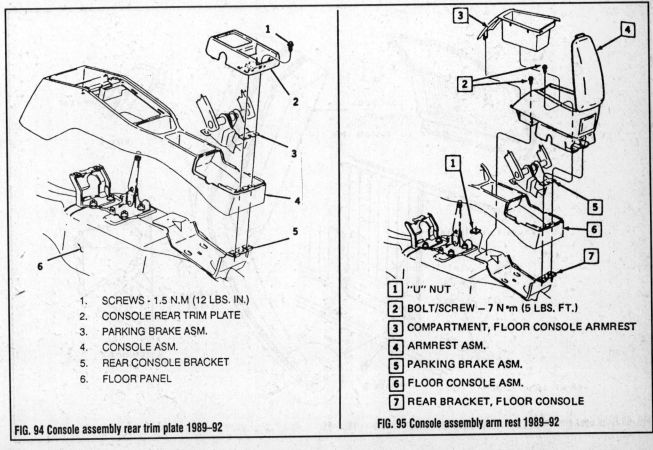

1. SCREWS - 1.5 N.M (12 LBS. IN.)
2. CONSOLE REAR TRIM PLATE
3. PARKING BRAKE ASM.
4. CONSOLE ASM.
5. REAR CONSOLE BRACKET
6. FLOOR PANEL

FIG. 94 Console assembly rear trim plate 1989–92

1 "U" NUT
2 BOLT/SCREW – 7 N•m (5 LBS. FT.)
3 COMPARTMENT, FLOOR CONSOLE ARMREST
4 ARMREST ASM.
5 PARKING BRAKE ASM.
6 FLOOR CONSOLE ASM.
7 REAR BRACKET, FLOOR CONSOLE

FIG. 95 Console assembly arm rest 1989–92

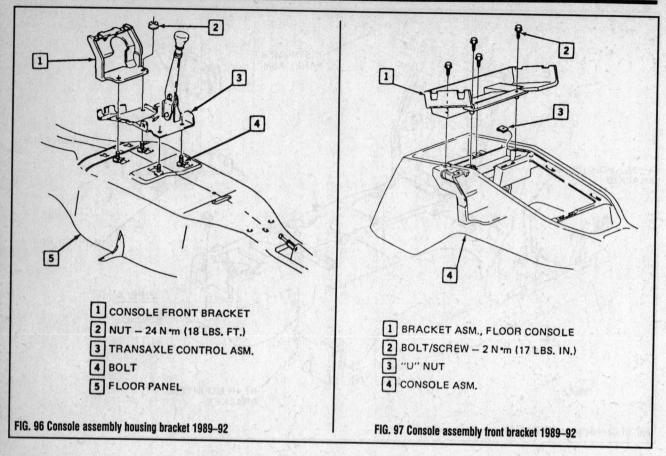

1 CONSOLE FRONT BRACKET
2 NUT — 24 N·m (18 LBS. FT.)
3 TRANSAXLE CONTROL ASM.
4 BOLT
5 FLOOR PANEL

FIG. 96 Console assembly housing bracket 1989–92

1 BRACKET ASM., FLOOR CONSOLE
2 BOLT/SCREW — 2 N·m (17 LBS. IN.)
3 "U" NUT
4 CONSOLE ASM.

FIG. 97 Console assembly front bracket 1989–92

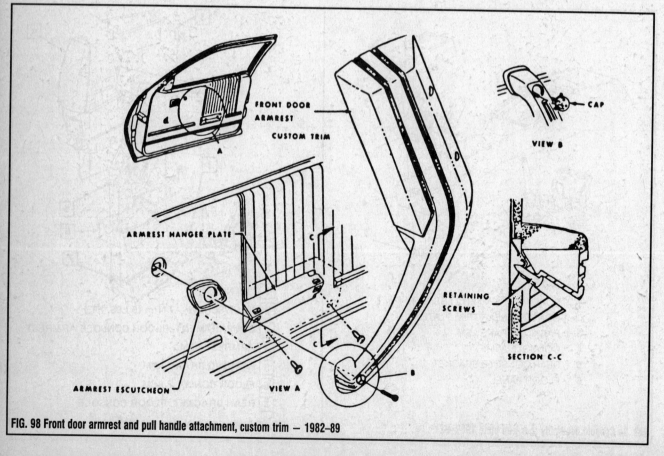

FRONT DOOR ARMREST
CUSTOM TRIM

A

CAP

VIEW B

ARMREST HANGER PLATE

C

C

RETAINING SCREWS

SECTION C-C

ARMREST ESCUTCHEON

VIEW A

B

FIG. 98 Front door armrest and pull handle attachment, custom trim — 1982–89

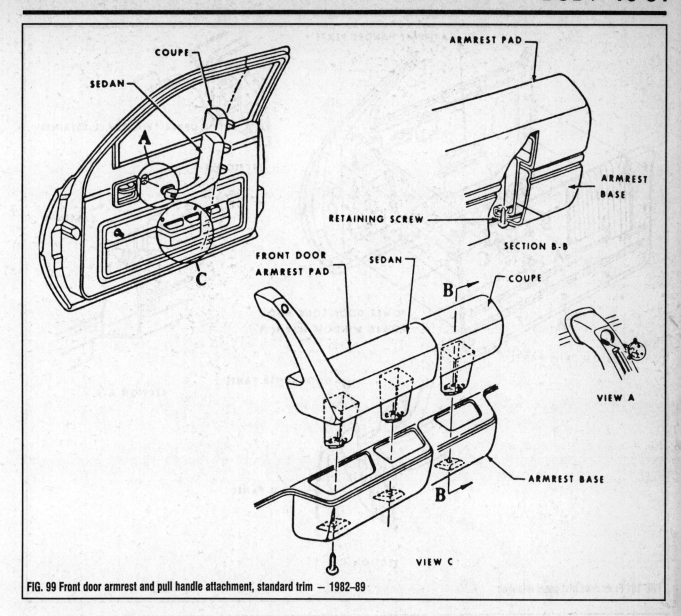

FIG. 99 Front door armrest and pull handle attachment, standard trim — 1982-89

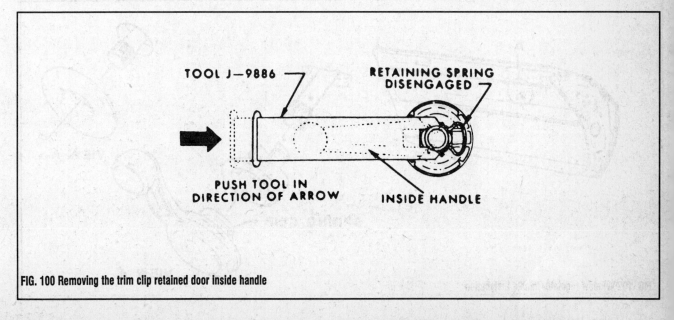

FIG. 100 Removing the trim clip retained door inside handle

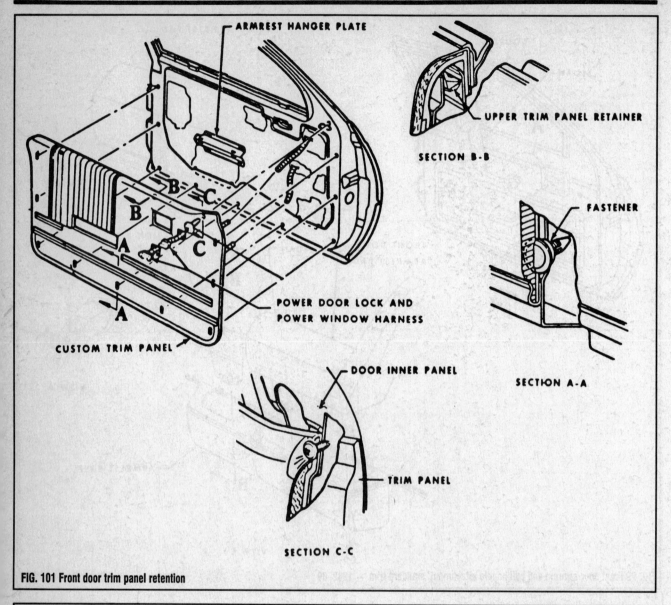

ARMREST HANGER PLATE

UPPER TRIM PANEL RETAINER

SECTION B-B

FASTENER

POWER DOOR LOCK AND
POWER WINDOW HARNESS

CUSTOM TRIM PANEL

SECTION A-A

DOOR INNER PANEL

TRIM PANEL

SECTION C-C

FIG. 101 Front door trim panel retention

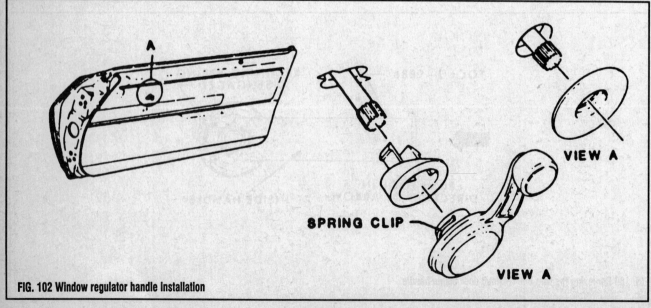

VIEW A

SPRING CLIP

VIEW A

FIG. 102 Window regulator handle installation

3. Remove the lock screws and lower the lock to disengage the outside handle to the lock rod. Remove the lock from the door.

4. To install, first install the the spring clips to the lock assembly, then reverse the removal procedure. Tighten the lock retaining screws to 80-100 inch lbs.

Rear Door Lock

REMOVAL & INSTALLATION

◆ SEE FIG. 105
1. Remove the door trim and water deflector.
2. Remove the door glass assembly and the stationary vent glass assembly.

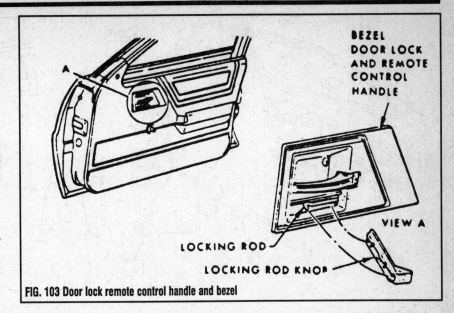

FIG. 103 Door lock remote control handle and bezel

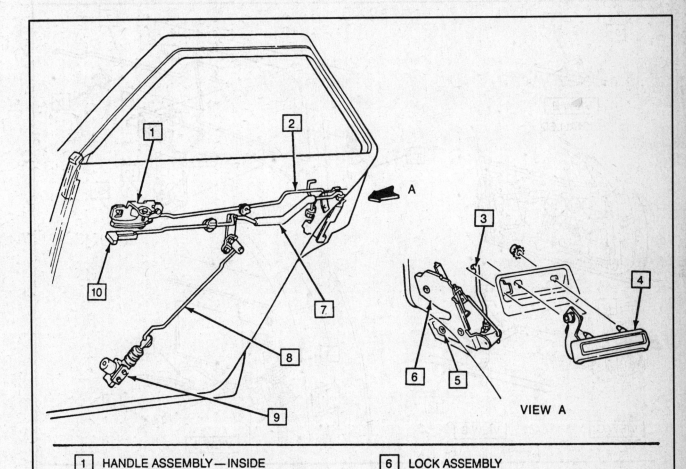

1	HANDLE ASSEMBLY—INSIDE		6	LOCK ASSEMBLY
2	ROD—LOCK REMOTE CONTROL TO LOCK		7	ROD—INSIDE LOCKING TO LOCK
3	ROD—OUTSIDE HANDLE TO LOCK		8	ROD—INSIDE LOCKING TO ACTUATOR
4	HANDLE ASSEMBLY—OUTSIDE		9	ACTUATOR ASSEMBLY—ELECTRIC LOCK
5	LOCK SCREWS (3)		10	KNOB—INSIDE LOCKING

FIG. 105 Rear door lock system

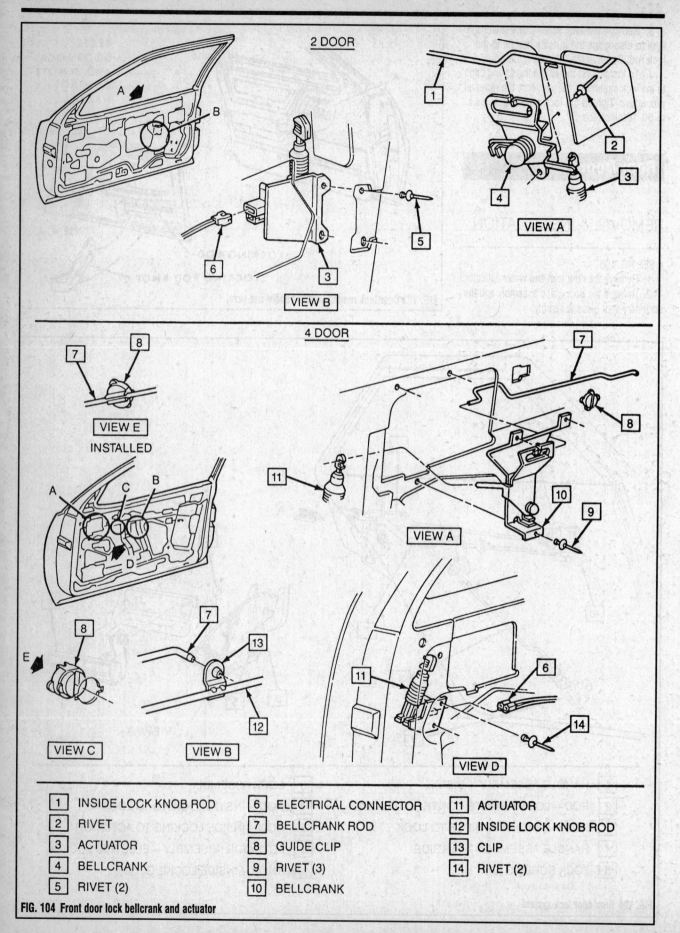

FIG. 104 Front door lock bellcrank and actuator

1	INSIDE LOCK KNOB ROD	6	ELECTRICAL CONNECTOR
2	RIVET	7	BELLCRANK ROD
3	ACTUATOR	8	GUIDE CLIP
4	BELLCRANK	9	RIVET (3)
5	RIVET (2)	10	BELLCRANK
11	ACTUATOR
12	INSIDE LOCK KNOB ROD
13	CLIP
14	RIVET (2)

3. Disconnect the inside handle to lock rod and inside locking knob to lock rod.

4. Disconnect the outside handle to lock rod.

5. Remove the lock screws and remove the lock through the access hole.

6. To install, reverse the removal procedure and tighten the lock retaining screws to 80-100 inch lbs.

Front Door Glass

REMOVAL & INSTALLATION

▶ SEE FIGS. 106 and 107

Except Convertible

1. Raise the door window to the full up position and remove the door trim panel and water deflector.

2. Remove the bolts holding the front glass retainer to the door inner panel and remove the retainer through the rear access hole. Lower the glass to approximately 3 in. (76mm) above the beltline.

4. Rotate the glass forward to disengage the window regulator roller from the sash channel.

5. Lower the glass into the door to disengage the rear guide (on the glass) from the rear run channel.

6. Using care, raise the glass while tilting forward and remove the glass inboard of the upper frame.

7. To install, tilt the front edge of the glass downward to locate the glass in the door.

8. Apply pressure rearward and snap the glass rear guide into the rear run channel.

9. Lower the glass to about 3 in. (76mm) above the beltline and install the widow regulator roller to sash channel.

10. Run the glass to the full up position.

11. Place the front glass retainer in position and install the bolts.

12. Check the window to make sure it operates correctly, then install the remaining trim parts.

Convertible

1. Remove the door trim panel, sound absorber, armrest bracket and water deflector.

2. Position the glass so that the up stop spanner nut on the glass is visible through the access hole.

3. Using tool J-22055 or equivalent, remove the spanner nut, bushing and stop from the glass.

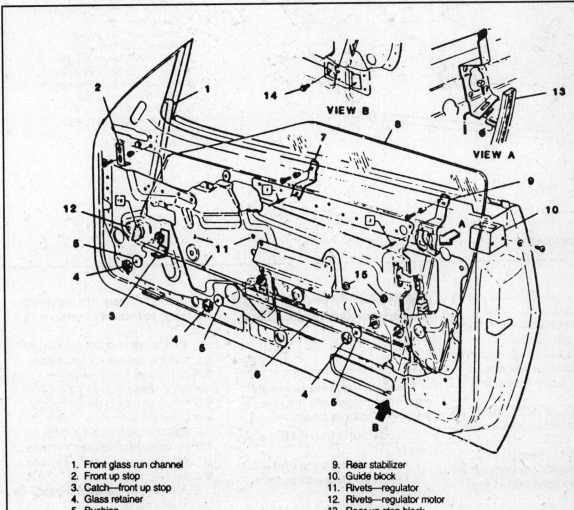

1. Front glass run channel
2. Front up stop
3. Catch—front up stop
4. Glass retainer
5. Bushing
6. Cam assembly door glass
7. Front stabilizer
8. Glass assembly
9. Rear stabilizer
10. Guide block
11. Rivets—regulator
12. Rivets—regulator motor
13. Rear up stop block
14. Rivets—rear cam assembly lower
15. Attaching nuts inner panel cam door reinforcement

FIG. 106 Front door hardware, convertible

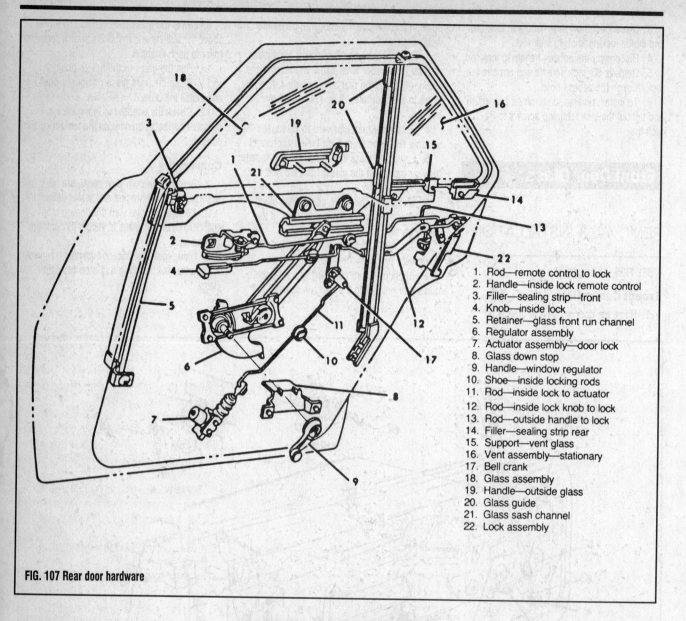

1. Rod—remote control to lock
2. Handle—inside lock remote control
3. Filler—sealing strip—front
4. Knob—inside lock
5. Retainer—glass front run channel
6. Regulator assembly
7. Actuator assembly—door lock
8. Glass down stop
9. Handle—window regulator
10. Shoe—inside locking rods
11. Rod—inside lock to actuator
12. Rod—inside lock knob to lock
13. Rod—outside handle to lock
14. Filler—sealing strip rear
15. Support—vent glass
16. Vent assembly—stationary
17. Bell crank
18. Glass assembly
19. Handle—outside glass
20. Glass guide
21. Glass sash channel
22. Lock assembly

FIG. 107 Rear door hardware

4. Position the glass so the spanner nuts are visible through the access hole.

5. Remove the spanner nuts and bushings.

6. Loosen the upper stabilizers.

7. Disengage the glass from the studs on the sash where the spanner nuts were removed.

8. Lower the regulator to the full-down position.

9. Grasp the glass and pull the glass up, with the front of the glass tilted down and remove the glass.

10. Installation is the reverse of removal. Before installing trim parts, check the window operation for proper alignment and adjust as needed.

Rear Door Glass

REMOVAL & INSTALLATION

➡ **The stationary vent assembly must be removed with the rear glass assembly as a unit.**

1. Remove the door trim panel and the water deflector.

2. Lower the glass to the full down position.

3. Remove the screws at the top of the division channel.

4. Remove the bolt holding the vent glass support at the belt.

5. Remove the screws at the rear of the door face holding the bottom of the division to the door.

6. Push the stationary vent assembly down and forward to disengage the vent assembly from the run channel. Now that the vent assembly is inboard of the door frame, lift up until the vent assembly is stopped against the door glass.

7. Raise the door glass 6-8 in. (152–203mm) and tilt the whole assembly rearward and disengage the roller from the glass sash channel.

8. To install, place the rear door glass in the vent division channel.

9. Load the rear window and vent assembly by lowering the assemblies through the door belt opening. Rotate the glass forward to engage the regulator roller in the glass sash channel. Reposition the vent glass into the door frame.

10. Replace the screws at the top of the division channel.

11. Replace the screws at the rear face of the door holding division and lower support in place.

12. Replace the bolt securing the division channel support at the belt.

13. Replace all previously removed trim.

Front Window Regulator And Motor

➡ **The following procedure includes both manual and power window regulator removal and installation. Besides the regulators, window motors and rollers including the washer and pin are serviced separately.**

REMOVAL & INSTALLATION

Except Convertible

1. Remove the door trim panel and the water deflector.

2. Raise the glass to the full up position and tape the glass to the door frame using fabric tape.

3. Punch out the center pins of the regulator rivets using a $1/4$ in. (6mm) drill bit. On electric regulators, drill out the rivets supporting the motor to the door inner panel.

4. Move the regulator rearward and disconnect the wiring harness from the motor, if so equipped. Disengage the roller on the regulator lift arm from the glass sash channel.

5. Remove the regulator through the rear access hole.

6. Using a $3/16$ in. (5mm) drill bit, drill out the motor attaching rivets and remove the motor from the regulator, if so equipped.

To install:

7. If so equipped, attach the motor to the regulator using a rivet tool and $3/16$ in. (5mm) rivets or $3/16$ in. (5mm) nuts and bolts.

8. Place the regulator through the rear access hole into the door inner panel. If an electric regulator is being installed, connect the wire connector to the motor prior to installing the regulator in the panel.

9. Locate the lift arm roller into the glass sash channel.

10. Using rivet tool J-29022 or equivalent, rivet the regulator to the inner panel of the door using $1/4$ in. × $1/2$ in. (6mm × 13mm) aluminum peel type rivets (part no. 9436175 or equivalent). If a rivet tool is not available, use the following nut and bolt method:

a. Install U-clips on the regulator and motor (if so equipped), at the attaching locations. Be sure to install clips with clinch nuts on the outboard side of the regulator.

b. Place the regulator through the rear access hole into the door inner panel. If an electric regulator is being installed, connect the wire connector to the motor prior to installing the regulator in the panel.

c. Locate the lift arm roller into the glass sash channel.

d. Align the regulator with the clinch nuts to the holes in the inner panel.

e. Attach the regulator and motor to the door inner panel with $1/4$ in.–20 × $1/2$ in. screws into $1/4$ in. nuts with integral washers. Tighten the screws to 90-125 inch lbs.

11. If an electrical window regulator is being installed use a rivet mentioned in step 10 to rivet the regulator motor to the door inner panel.

12. Replace all previously removed parts.

Cavalier Convertible

1. Remove the door trim panel, sound absorber, armrest bracket and water deflector.

2. Using a $1/4$ in. (6mm) drill bit, drill out the rivets supporting the motor to the door inner panel.

3. Disconnect the electrical connector from the regulator motor.

4. Support the door glass in the full-up position, using rubber wedge door stops.

5. Remove the nuts holding the cam assembly door reinforcement to the inner panel and remove the cam assembly.

6. Remove the bolt holding the upper portion of the rear cam assembly to the inner panel.

7. Using a $3/16$ in. (5mm) drill bit, drill out the rivets, holding the lower section of the rear cam assembly to the inner panel.

8. Remove the up stop from the rear cam assembly.

9. Remove the rear cam assembly through the access hole.

10. Disengage the regulator from the glass sash channel and remove the regulator through the access hole.

11. If equipped with an electric window regulator and you wish to remove the motor from the regulator proceed as follows:

❄ CAUTION

When removing the electric motor from the regulator, the sector gear must be locked in position. The regulator lift arm is under tension from the counterbalence spring and could cause personal injury if the sector gear is not locked in position.

a. Drill a hole through the regulator sector gear and backplate and install a bolt and nut to lock the sector gear in position.

b. Using a $3/16$ in. (5mm) drill bit, drill out the motor attaching rivets and remove the motor from the regulator.

c. To install the motor to the regulator use a rivet tool J-29022 or equivalent and install $3/16$ in. (5mm) rivets or $3/16$ in. (5mm) nuts and bolts. Remove the bolt and nut used to secure the sector gear in position.

To install:

12. Make sure the regulator is in the full up position.

13. Install the regulator arm rollers to the glass sash channel.

14. Install the rear cam assembly using $3/16$ in. (5mm) aluminum peel-type rivets making sure to install the up stop in the cam assembly.

15. Connect the electrical connector to the motor on the regulator.

16. Engage the roller on the regulator lift arm in the cam assembly door reinforcement.

17. Install the cam assembly door reinforcement to the inner panel.

18. Align the attaching holes in the regulator with the holes in the inner panel.

19. Install the regulator to the inner panel, using a rivet gun and $1/4$ in. × $1/2$ in. (6mm × 13mm) aluminum peel type rivets.

Rear Window Regulator

➡ **The following procedure includes both manual and power window regulator removal and installation. Besides the regulators, window motors and rollers including the washer and pin are serviced separately.**

REMOVAL & INSTALLATION

1. Remove the door trim panel and the water deflector.

2. Raise the glass to the full up position and tape the glass to the door frame using fabric tape.

3. Punch out the center pins of the regulator rivets using a 1/4 in. (6mm) drill bit. On electric regulators, drill out the rivets supporting the motor to the door inner panel.

4. Disconnect the wiring harness from the motor, if so equipped. Disengage the roller on the regulator lift arm from the glass sash channel.

5. Remove the regulator through the rear access hole.

6. Using a 3/16 in. (5mm) drill bit, drill out motor attaching rivets and remove the motor from the regulator, if so equipped.

7. To install, if so equipped, attach the motor to the regulator using a rivet tool and 3/16 in. (5mm) rivets or 3/16 in. (5mm) nuts and bolts.

8. Place the regulator through the rear access hole into the door inner panel. If an electric regulator is being installed, connect the wire connector to the motor prior to installing the regulator in the panel.

9. Locate the lift arm roller into the glass sash channel.

10. Using rivet tool J-29022 or equivalent, rivet the regulator to the inner panel of the door using 1/4 in. × 1/2 in. (6mm × 13mm) aluminum peel type rivets (part no. 9436175 or equivalent). If a rivet tool is not available, use the following nut and bolt method:

a. Install U-clips on the regulator and motor (if so equipped), at the attaching locations. Be sure to install clips with clinch nuts on the outboard side of the regulator.

b. Place the regulator through the rear access hole into the door inner panel. If an electric regulator is being installed, connect the wire connector to the motor prior to installing the regulator in the panel.

c. Locate the lift arm roller into the glass sash channel.

d. Align the regulator with the clinch nuts to the holes in the inner panel.

e. Attach the regulator and motor to the door inner panel with 1/4 in.–20 × 1/2 in. screws into 1/4 in. nuts with integral washers. Tighten the screws to 90-125 inch lbs.

11. If an electrical window regulator is being installed use a rivet mentioned in step 10 to rivet the regulator motor to the door inner panel.

12. Replace all previously removed parts.

Windshield Glass

REMOVAL & INSTALLATION

◆ SEE FIGS. 108-122

1. Remove the wiper arms and blades, if applicable.

2. Remove the lower winshield glass support. 1989–92 models remove the top vent grille panel if applicable.

3. Remove reveal moldings and/or retainers from around the glass.

4. If rear glass is to be removed, remove the quarter upper trim panels to access rear defogger if so equipped. Disconnect the rear defogger feed wire and ground wire.

5. Mask off area around the window to protect the painted surfaces.

6. Using a cold knife no. J24402-A and/or a power tool with a reciprocating blade, cut around the entire perimeter of the window. The blade of the tool must be kept as close as possible to the window edge during the cutout procedure. Remove the window glass.

To Install:

7. If reusing the same window glass, clean all residue from glass completely. Trim the old urethane evenly around the window frame. Touch up all knicks and scratches with the correct color paint around frame donot let the paint contaminate the urethane.

8. Install the acoustic sealing strip, if replacing the windshield. Peel the protective backing from sealing strip and install onto window glass 1/2" inboard of bottom edge.

9. Install the reveal molding. Position the window in opening, be sure the window sits flush with the body, if it doesnot sit flush remove the window glass and trim the urethane around the entire perimeter to bring the window flush with body. Apply tape from window to the body then slit the tape along window edge this will

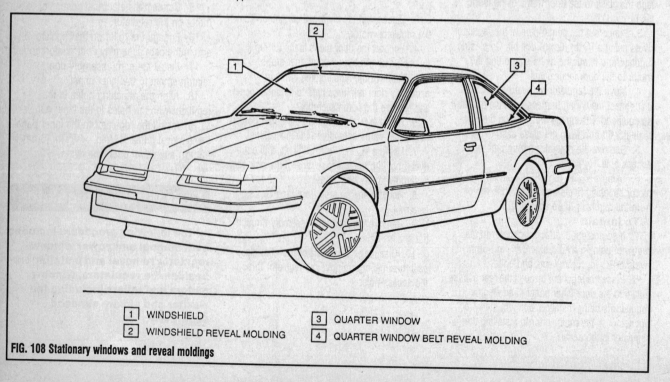

| 1 | WINDSHIELD | 3 | QUARTER WINDOW |
| 2 | WINDSHIELD REVEAL MOLDING | 4 | QUARTER WINDOW BELT REVEAL MOLDING |

FIG. 108 Stationary windows and reveal moldings

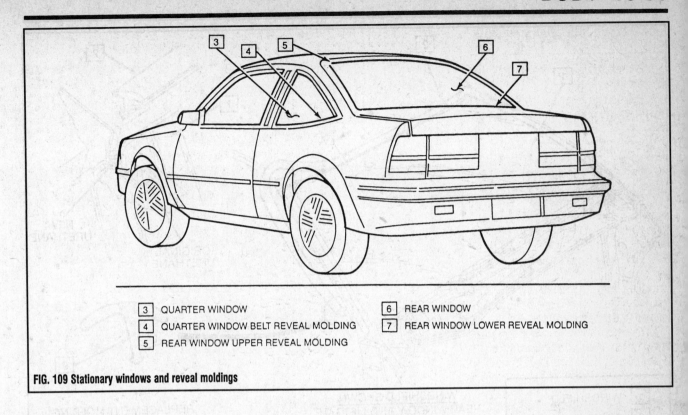

3 QUARTER WINDOW	6 REAR WINDOW
4 QUARTER WINDOW BELT REVEAL MOLDING	7 REAR WINDOW LOWER REVEAL MOLDING
5 REAR WINDOW UPPER REVEAL MOLDING	

FIG. 109 Stationary windows and reveal moldings

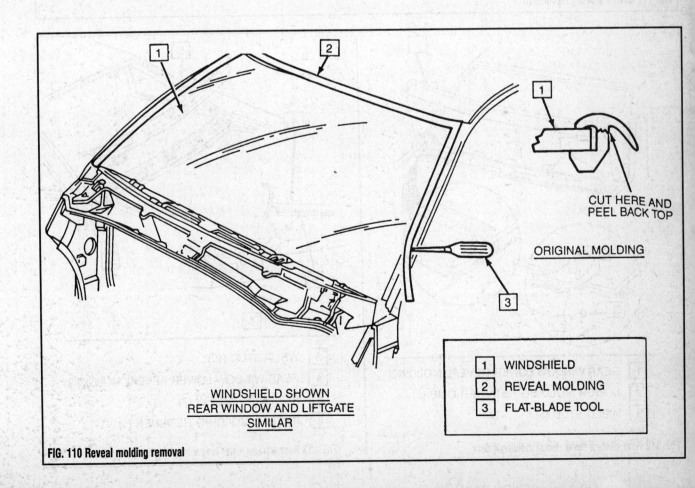

CUT HERE AND
PEEL BACK TOP

ORIGINAL MOLDING

WINDSHIELD SHOWN
REAR WINDOW AND LIFTGATE
SIMILAR

1	WINDSHIELD
2	REVEAL MOLDING
3	FLAT-BLADE TOOL

FIG. 110 Reveal molding removal

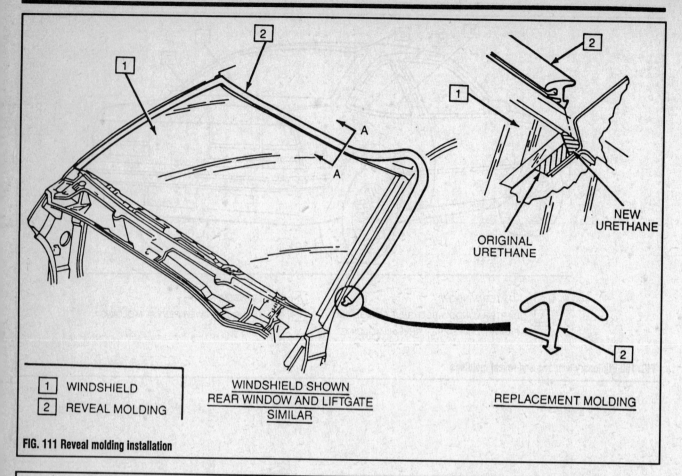

1	WINDSHIELD
2	REVEAL MOLDING

WINDSHIELD SHOWN
REAR WINDOW AND LIFTGATE
SIMILAR

NEW URETHANE

ORIGINAL URETHANE

REPLACEMENT MOLDING

FIG. 111 Reveal molding installation

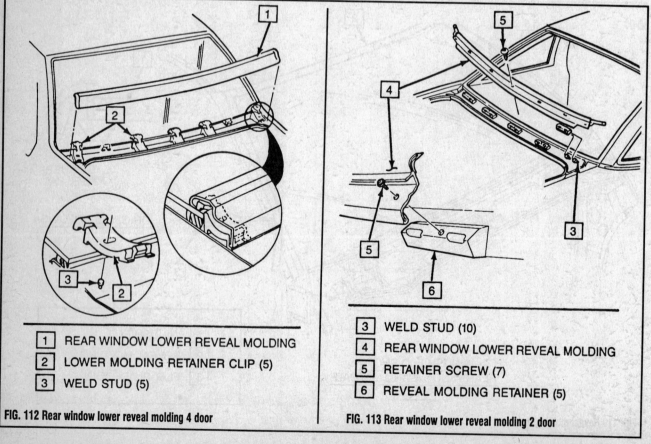

1	REAR WINDOW LOWER REVEAL MOLDING
2	LOWER MOLDING RETAINER CLIP (5)
3	WELD STUD (5)

FIG. 112 Rear window lower reveal molding 4 door

3	WELD STUD (10)
4	REAR WINDOW LOWER REVEAL MOLDING
5	RETAINER SCREW (7)
6	REVEAL MOLDING RETAINER (5)

FIG. 113 Rear window lower reveal molding 2 door

help align the window upon installation, remove the window.

10. Apply The clear primer around the edge of the window (supplied in window installation kit no.12345633 or equivalent). Apply the black primer to frame edge only if the urethane had to be removed from the body. If black primer was used wait five minutes before apply the necessary urethane.

11. With the aide of a helper lift the windshield into opening. On rear window installations it will be necessary to use suction cups to position the window into opening. With window in opening align the tape marks.

12. Press window firmly to wetout and set adhesive. Use care to avoid excessive squeezeout which would cause an appearance problem. Using a disposible brush or flat blade tool, paddle the material around the edge of window to ensure a water tight seal. If necessary paddle in addition material around the edge to fill voids in seal.

13. Apply tape from top of window glass to roof and also the sides. Water test the vehicle at once with a garden hose donot spray a hard stream directly onto the urethane sealer. If any leaks are found paddle in extra sealer to stop leak.

14. Install the upper trim panels if removed. Connect the rear defogger connectors, if so equipped.

15. Install the shroud top vent grille panel, if removed. Install the wipers, if removed. Allow 6 hours for the urethane to cure.

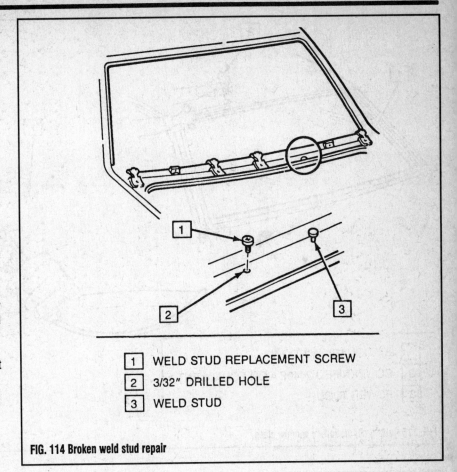

1	WELD STUD REPLACEMENT SCREW
2	3/32" DRILLED HOLE
3	WELD STUD

FIG. 114 Broken weld stud repair

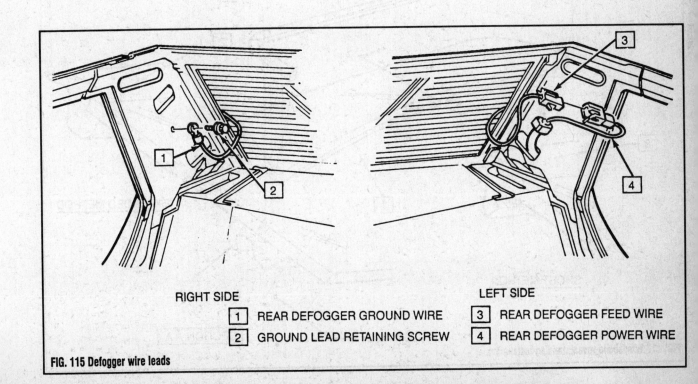

RIGHT SIDE

| 1 | REAR DEFOGGER GROUND WIRE |
| 2 | GROUND LEAD RETAINING SCREW |

LEFT SIDE

| 3 | REAR DEFOGGER FEED WIRE |
| 4 | REAR DEFOGGER POWER WIRE |

FIG. 115 Defogger wire leads

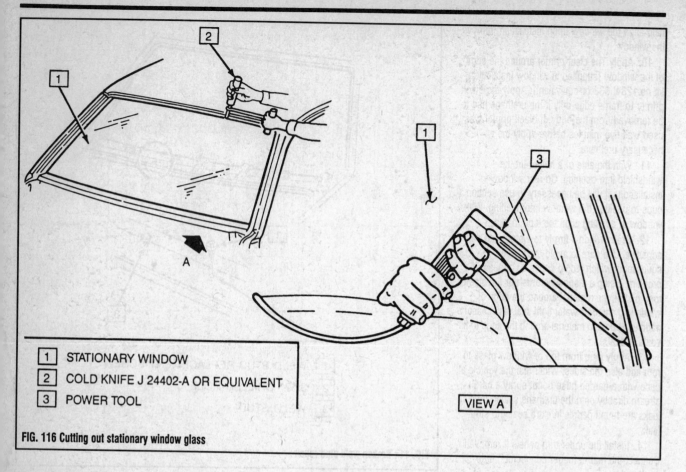

1. STATIONARY WINDOW
2. COLD KNIFE J 24402-A OR EQUIVALENT
3. POWER TOOL

VIEW A

FIG. 116 Cutting out stationary window glass

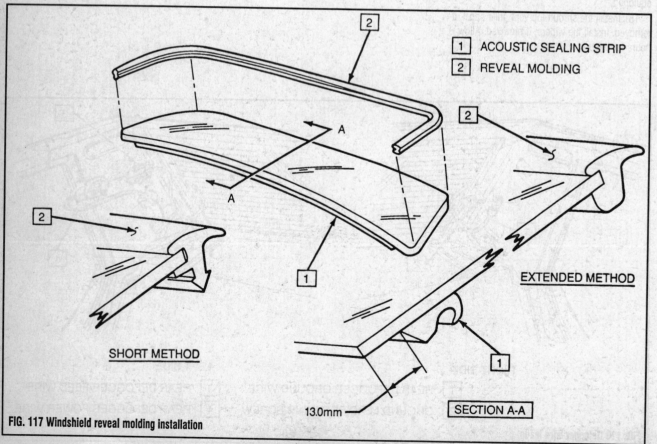

1. ACOUSTIC SEALING STRIP
2. REVEAL MOLDING

A

A

EXTENDED METHOD

SHORT METHOD

13.0mm

SECTION A-A

FIG. 117 Windshield reveal molding installation

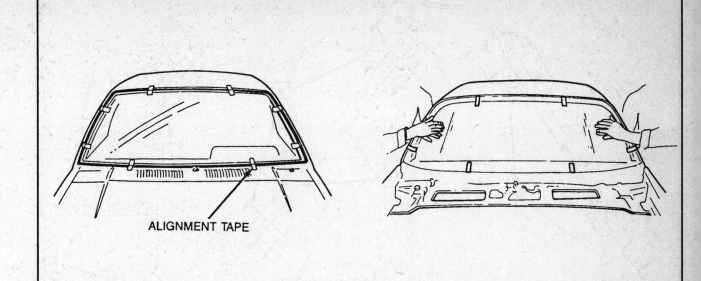

FIG. 118 Alignment tape installed

FIG. 119 Installation of winshield and/or rear window

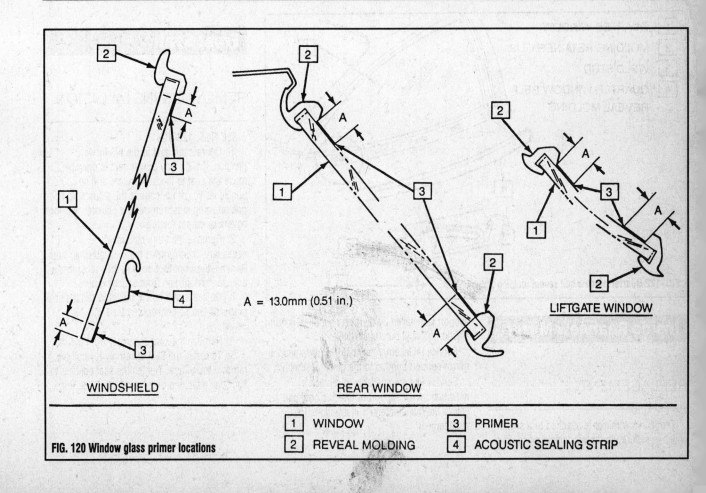

A = 13.0mm (0.51 in.)

WINDSHIELD

REAR WINDOW

LIFTGATE WINDOW

FIG. 120 Window glass primer locations

| 1 | WINDOW | 3 | PRIMER |
| 2 | REVEAL MOLDING | 4 | ACOUSTIC SEALING STRIP |

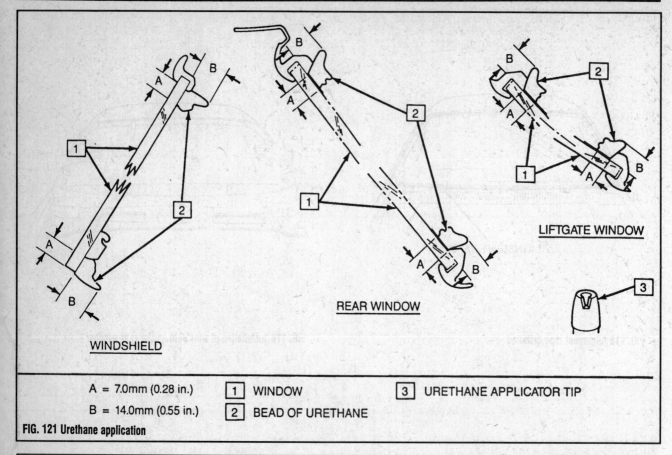

A = 7.0mm (0.28 in.)
B = 14.0mm (0.55 in.)

1	WINDOW
2	BEAD OF URETHANE
3	URETHANE APPLICATOR TIP

FIG. 121 Urethane application

WINDSHIELD

REAR WINDOW

LIFTGATE WINDOW

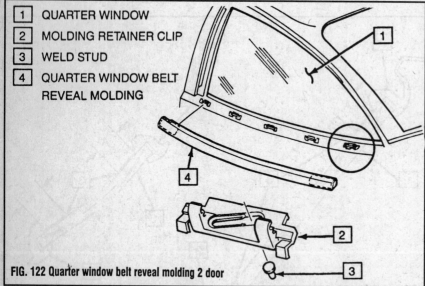

1	QUARTER WINDOW
2	MOLDING RETAINER CLIP
3	WELD STUD
4	QUARTER WINDOW BELT REVEAL MOLDING

FIG. 122 Quarter window belt reveal molding 2 door

Inside Rearview Mirror

REPLACEMENT

The rearview mirror is attached to a support which is secured to the windshield glass. This support is installed by the glass supplier using a plastic-polyvinyl butyl adhesive.

Service replacement windshield glass has the mirror support bonded to the glass assembly.

Service kits are available to replace a detached mirror support or install a new part. Follow the manufacturer's instructions for replacement.

Front Seat

REMOVAL & INSTALLATION

♦ SEE FIGS. 123-125

1. Operate the seat to the full-forward position. If a six way power seat is operable, move the seat to the full-forward and up positions. To gain access to the adjuster to floor pan retaining nuts, remove the adjuster rear foot covers or carpet retainers.

2. Remove the track covers where necessary, then remove the rear attaching nuts. Remove the front foot covers, then remove the adjuster to floor pan front attaching nuts.

3. On seats with power adjusters, tilt the seat rearward and disconnect the feed wire connector.

4. Remove the seat assembly from the car.

5. To install the seat assembly reverse the removal procedure. Tighten the seat adjuster to floor pan attaching bolts or nuts to 21 ft. lbs.

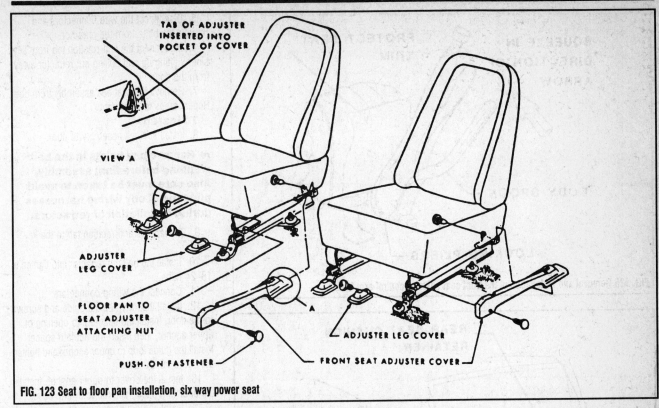

TAB OF ADJUSTER
INSERTED INTO
POCKET OF COVER

VIEW A

ADJUSTER
LEG COVER

FLOOR PAN TO
SEAT ADJUSTER
ATTACHING NUT

PUSH-ON FASTENER

ADJUSTER LEG COVER

FRONT SEAT ADJUSTER COVER

FIG. 123 Seat to floor pan installation, six way power seat

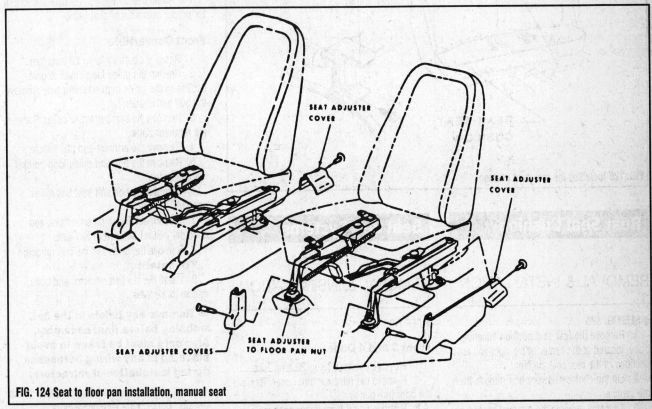

SEAT ADJUSTER
COVER

SEAT ADJUSTER
COVER

SEAT ADJUSTER COVERS

SEAT ADJUSTER
TO FLOOR PAN NUT

FIG. 124 Seat to floor pan installation, manual seat

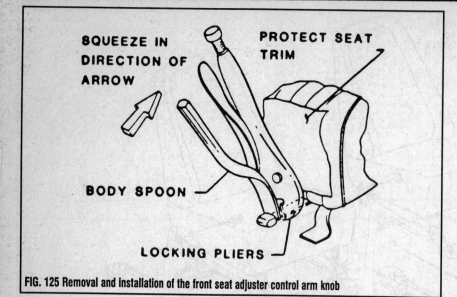

FIG. 125 Removal and installation of the front seat adjuster control arm knob

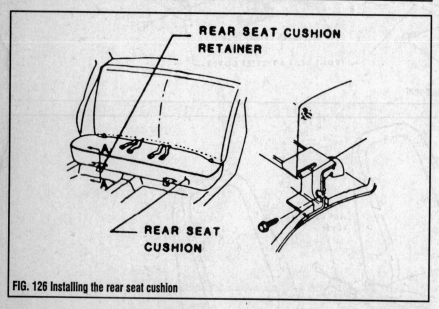

FIG. 126 Installing the rear seat cushion

Rear Seat Cushion

REMOVAL & INSTALLATION

◆ SEE FIG. 126

1. Remove the rear seat cushion attaching bolts, located at the center of the right and left sections of the rear seat cushion.
2. Lift the cushion upward and remove from the vehicle.
3. To install, reverse the removal procedure. Torque the seat cushion attaching bolts to 14-20 ft. lbs.

Seat Belt Systems

REMOVAL & INSTALLATION

◆ SEE FIGS. 127-134

Front 2 and 4 Door

1. Remove courtesy lamp 20 amp fuse.
2. Remove the retractor trim cover. Remove the door trim panel.
3. Remove cover from upper anchor. Remove the nut and spacer from guide loop and detach the guide loop.
4. Remove the screws and intermediate guide from the door.

5. Disconnect the wire connectors and remove the bolts from the retractor.
6. Disconnect the anti-rotation tab from key slot by lifting up and pulling out retractor away from the door.
7. Remove the seat belt assembly from door. Repeat steps for other door.
   To install:
8. Install seatbelt assembly to door.

➡ **Remove any twists in the belt webbing before final assembly. Also care must be taken to avoid pinching of any wiring harnesses during installation of retractors.**

9. Connect the anti-rotation tab to the key slot.
10. Install the bolts to retractor and tighten to 18–24 ft.lbs.
11. Connect the wiring connectors.
12. Install the intermediate guide and screws to the door. Install the spacer into opening of upper anchor, then insert the nut into spacer. Install the guide loop to upper anchor and tighten the nut to 16–22 ft.lbs.
13. Install the cover to upper anchor. Install the door trim panel, and retractor trim cover.
14. Install the courtesy lamp fuse and check for proper operation of seat belts.

Front Convertible

1. Remove courtesy lamp 20 amp fuse.
2. Unsnap the guide loop cover to gain access to the guide loop retaining bolt. Remove the bolt and spacer.
3. Remove the seat belt tower cover. Remove the retractor cover.
4. Remove the armrest and pull handle.
5. Remove the bolt and guide loop bracket, nut and screw.
6. Remove the bolt and seat belt tower support.
7. Disconnect the wire connectors, and shoulder belt retractor from key slot.
8. Remove the bolts and lap belt retractor.
   To install:
9. Install the lap belt retractor and bolts, tighten to 22 ft.lbs.

➡ **Remove any twists in the belt webbing before final assembly. Also care must be taken to avoid pinching of any wiring harnesses during installation of retractors.**

10. Connect the shoulder belt retractor to the key slot. Connect the wire connectors.
11. Install the seat belt tower support and tighten the bolt to 22 ft.lbs, tighten the screw to 22 ft.lbs, and the nut to 12 ft.lbs.

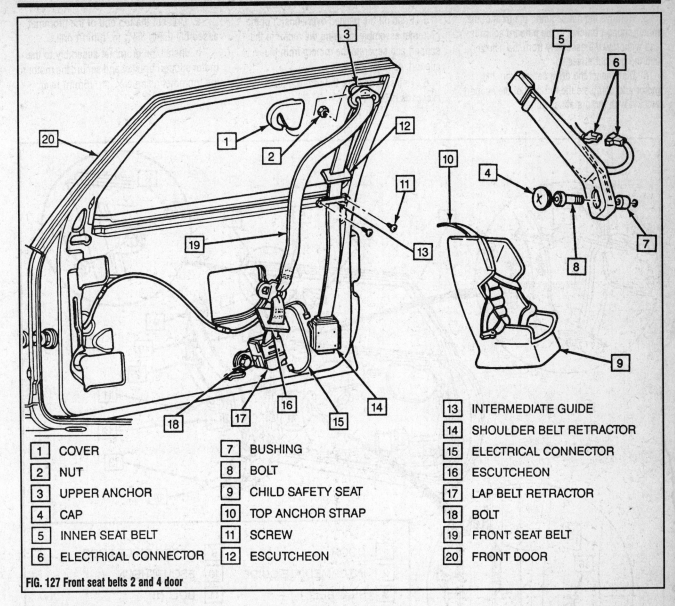

1	COVER	7	BUSHING	
2	NUT	8	BOLT	
3	UPPER ANCHOR	9	CHILD SAFETY SEAT	
4	CAP	10	TOP ANCHOR STRAP	
5	INNER SEAT BELT	11	SCREW	
6	ELECTRICAL CONNECTOR	12	ESCUTCHEON	

13	INTERMEDIATE GUIDE
14	SHOULDER BELT RETRACTOR
15	ELECTRICAL CONNECTOR
16	ESCUTCHEON
17	LAP BELT RETRACTOR
18	BOLT
19	FRONT SEAT BELT
20	FRONT DOOR

FIG. 127 Front seat belts 2 and 4 door

12. Install the guide loop bracket and bolt, tighten to 12 ft.lbs.

13. Install the armrest and pull handle, and seat belt tower cover.

14. Insert the bolt through the guide loop cover and guide loop, then install the spacer onto bolt. Position the guide loop onto tower cover and thread the bolt into tower support, tighten to 22 ft.lbs. Close the guide loop cover.

15. Install the courtesy lamp fuse and check for proper operation of seat belts.

Rear Seat Belts

1. Remove the rear seat cushion, seatback, lower quarter trim panel and anchor bolt.

2. Remove the retractor bolt and escutcheon. On convertible model, lift the escutcheon to expose the guide loop bolt then remove the escutcheon bolt and spacer.

3. Remove the belt anchor end through shelf opening into trunk area. On convertible model, pull the seat belt assembly through the brace, remove the bolt and seat belt assembly from vehicle.

To Install:

➡ **Remove any twists in the belt webbing before final assembly.**

4. Install the belt anchor end through shelf opening. On convertible model position the retractor assembly onto brace, install bolt and tighten to 22 ft.lbs.

5. Install the escutcheon and retractor bolt, tighten to 22 ft.lbs. Install the anchor bolt and tighten to 26–35 ft.lbs. On convertible model, feed the seat belt assembly through brace, position the spacer, guide loop and escutcheon. Install the bolt and tighten to 22 ft.lbs.

6. On convertible model, thread seat belt webbing through escutcheon, position anchor end of seat belt install bolt and tighten to 26–35 ft.lbs.

7. Install the lower quarter trim panel, rear seatback and cushion.

Power Seat Motors

REMOVAL & INSTALLATION

1. Remove the front seat assembly and place upside down on a clean surface.

2. Disconnect the motor feed wires from the motor.

3. Remove the nut securing the front of the motor support bracket to the inboard adjuster and withdraw the assembly from the adjuster and the gearnut drives.

4. Disconnect the drive cables from the motor and complete the removal of the support bracket with motors attached.

5. Grind off the peened over ends(s) of the grommet assembly securing the motor to the support and separate the motors from the support, as required.

6. To install, reverse the removal procedure except as noted:

a. Drill out the top end of the grommet assembly using a 3/16 in. (5mm) drill.

b. Install the grommet assembly to the motor support bracket and secure the motor to the grommet using a 3/16 in. (5mm) rivet.

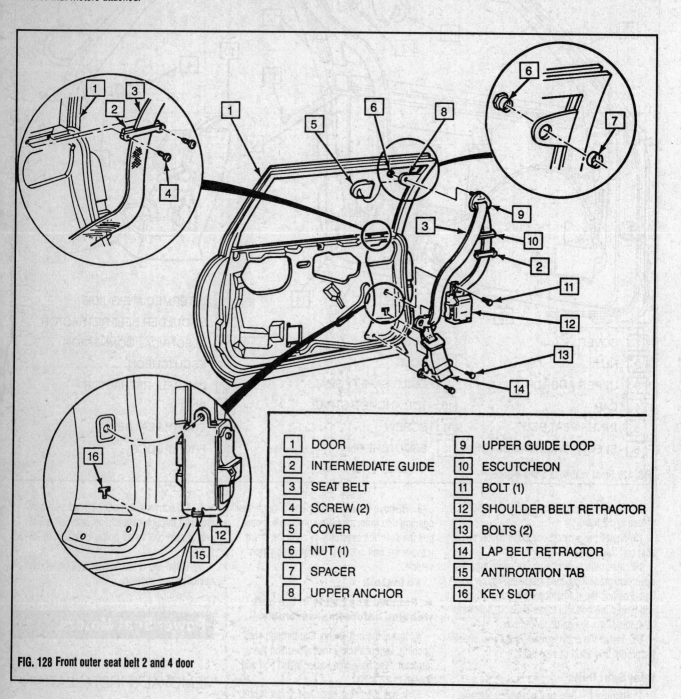

1	DOOR		9	UPPER GUIDE LOOP
2	INTERMEDIATE GUIDE		10	ESCUTCHEON
3	SEAT BELT		11	BOLT (1)
4	SCREW (2)		12	SHOULDER BELT RETRACTOR
5	COVER		13	BOLTS (2)
6	NUT (1)		14	LAP BELT RETRACTOR
7	SPACER		15	ANTIROTATION TAB
8	UPPER ANCHOR		16	KEY SLOT

FIG. 128 Front outer seat belt 2 and 4 door

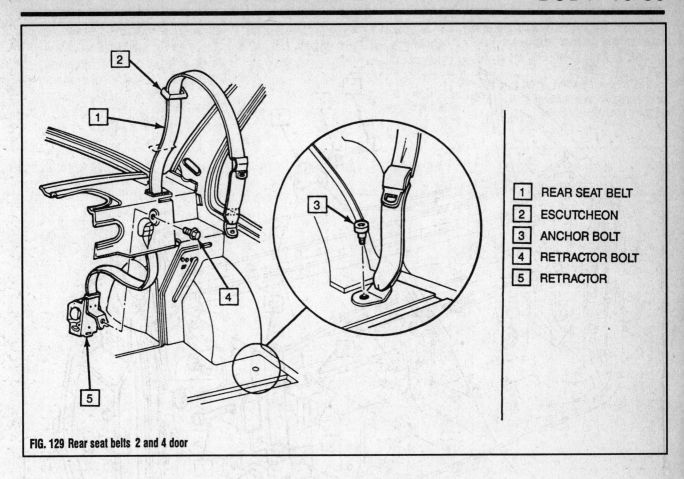

1	REAR SEAT BELT
2	ESCUTCHEON
3	ANCHOR BOLT
4	RETRACTOR BOLT
5	RETRACTOR

FIG. 129 Rear seat belts 2 and 4 door

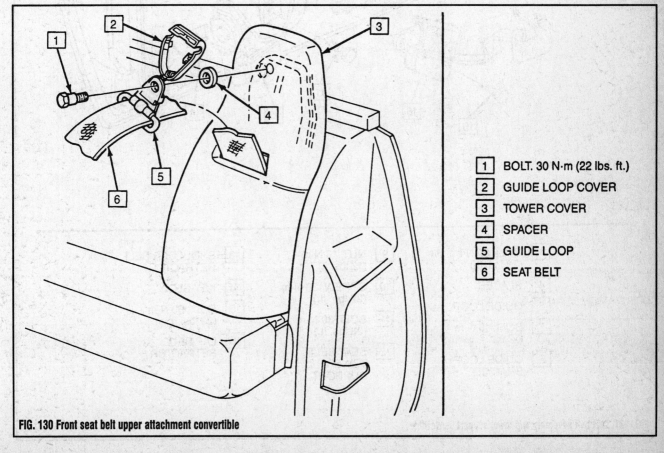

1	BOLT. 30 N·m (22 lbs. ft.)
2	GUIDE LOOP COVER
3	TOWER COVER
4	SPACER
5	GUIDE LOOP
6	SEAT BELT

FIG. 130 Front seat belt upper attachment convertible

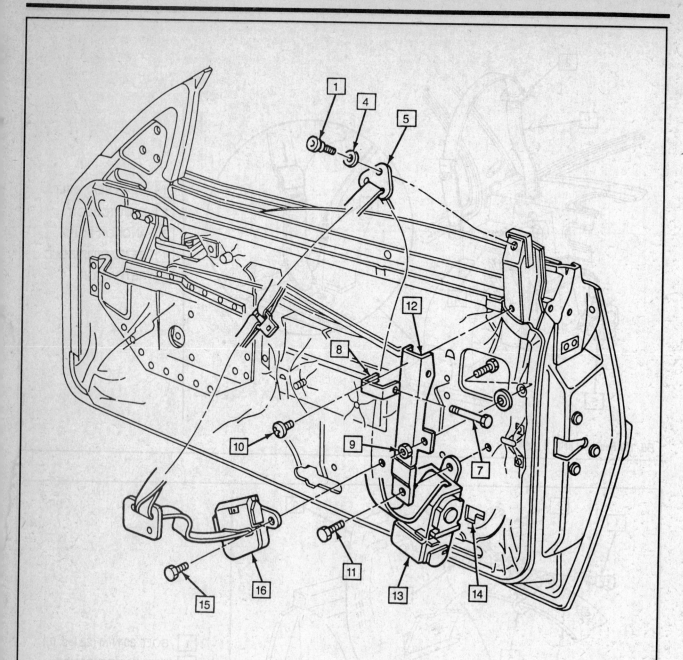

1	BOLT, 30 N·m (22 lbs. ft.)	9	NUT, 16 N·m (12 lbs. ft)	13	SHOULDER BELT RETRACTOR
4	SPACER	10	SCREW, 30 N·m (22 lbs. ft.)	14	KEY SLOT
5	GUIDE LOOP	11	BOLT, 30 N·m (22 lbs. ft.)	15	BOLT, 30 N·m (22 lbs. ft.)
7	BOLT, 16 N·m (12 lbs. ft.)	12	SEAT BELT TOWER SUPPORT	16	LAP BELT RETRACTOR
8	GUIDE LOOP BRACKET				

FIG. 131 Seat belt assembly and tower support convertible

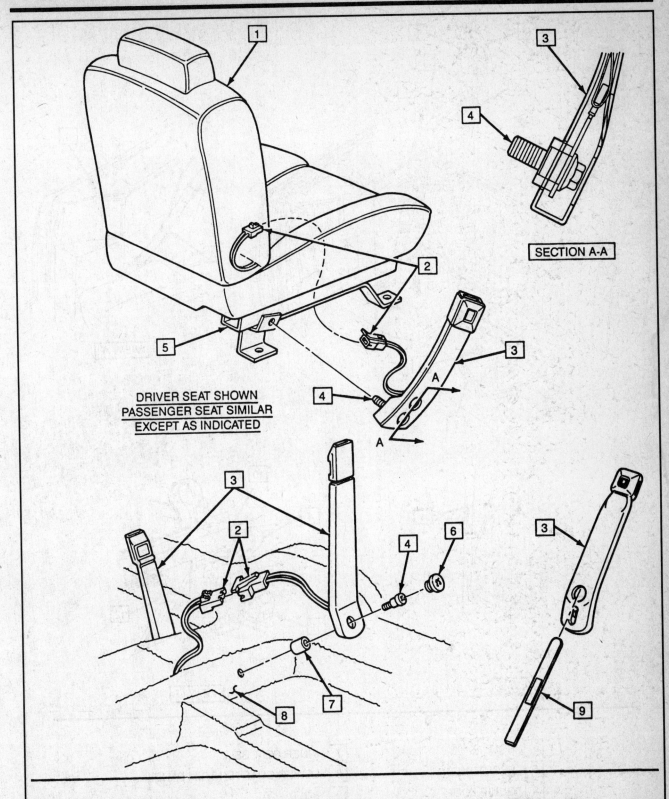

SECTION A-A

DRIVER SEAT SHOWN
PASSENGER SEAT SIMILAR
EXCEPT AS INDICATED

1	FRONT SEAT ASSEMBLY	4	BOLT (2)	7	SPACER
2	ELECTRICAL CONNECTORS (DRIVER'S SEAT ONLY)	5	SEAT ADJUSTER ASSEMBLY	8	FLOOR PAN CARPET
3	FRONT SEAT INNER SEAT BELT	6	BELT SLEEVE PLUG	9	STIFFENER

FIG. 132 Front seat inner seat belt

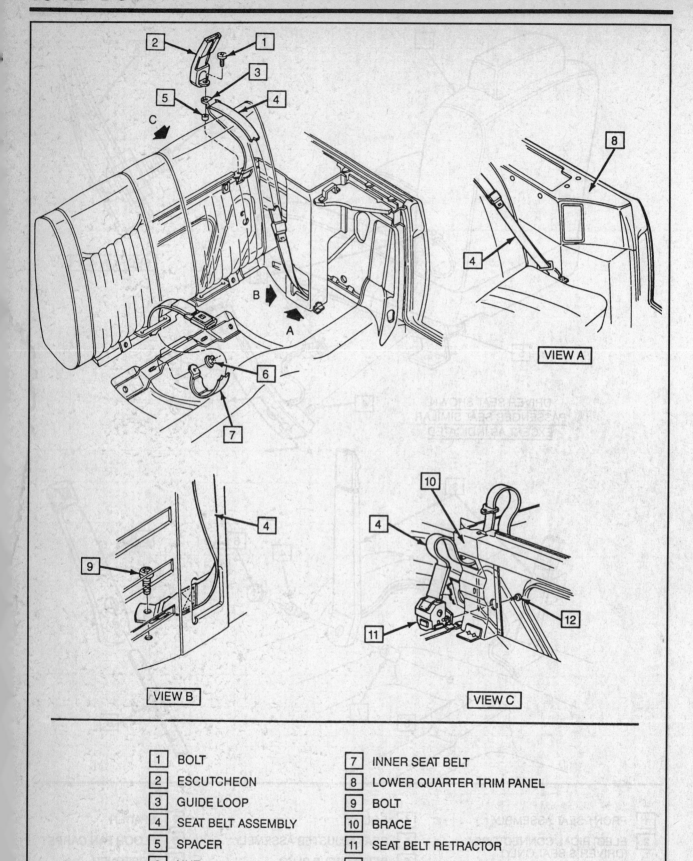

1	BOLT	7	INNER SEAT BELT
2	ESCUTCHEON	8	LOWER QUARTER TRIM PANEL
3	GUIDE LOOP	9	BOLT
4	SEAT BELT ASSEMBLY	10	BRACE
5	SPACER	11	SEAT BELT RETRACTOR
6	NUT	12	BOLT

FIG. 134 Rear seat belts convertible

BODY ALIGNMENT SPECIFICATIONS

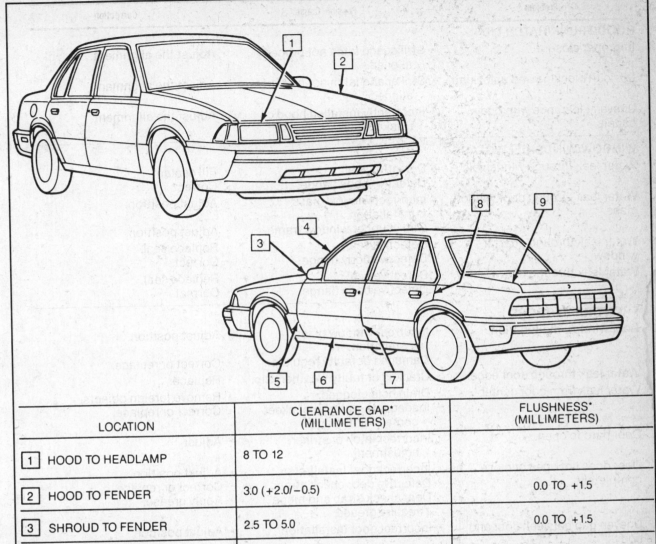

LOCATION	CLEARANCE GAP* (MILLIMETERS)		FLUSHNESS* (MILLIMETERS)
1 HOOD TO HEADLAMP	8 TO 12		
2 HOOD TO FENDER	3.0 (+2.0/−0.5)		0.0 TO +1.5
3 SHROUD TO FENDER	2.5 TO 5.0		0.0 TO +1.5
4 SIDE WINDOW TO WINDSHIELD	2 DR. 6.5 4 DR. 5.5	(+1.5/−1.0) (+1.5/−1.0)	4.0 (±1.5)
5 DOOR TO FENDER	4.0 TO 7.0	• TO BE PARALLEL WITHIN 1.5 mm	0.0 TO +1.5
6 DOOR TO ROCKER PANEL	6.0 (±1.5)		0.0 TO −1.5
7 FRONT DOOR TO REAR DOOR	WITH MOLDING 4.4 (+1.5/−1.0) WITHOUT MOLDING 5.0 (+1.5/−1.0)		0.0 TO −1.5
8 DOOR TO QUARTER PANEL	WITH MOLDING 4.4 (+1.5/−1.0) WITHOUT MOLDING 5.0 (+1.5/−1.0)		0.0 TO +1.5
9 DECK LID TO QUARTER PANEL	5.0 (±1.5)		−1.0 TO +0.5
	*OPENINGS MUST BE PARALLEL WITHIN 1.0 mm EXCEPT AS NOTED		

Hood, Trunk Lid, Hatch Lid, Glass and Doors

Problem	Possible Cause	Correction
HOOD/TRUNK/HATCH LID		
Improper closure.	• Striker and latch not properly aligned.	• Adjust the alignment.
Difficulty locking and unlocking.	• Striker and latch not properly aligned.	• Adjust the alignment.
Uneven clearance with body panels.	• Incorrectly installed hood or trunk lid.	• Adjust the alignment.
WINDOW/WINDSHIELD GLASS		
Water leak through windshield	• Defective seal. • Defective body flange.	• Fill sealant • Correct.
Water leak through door window glass.	• Incorrect window glass installation. • Gap at upper window frame.	• Adjust position. • Adjust position.
Water leak through quarter window.	• Defective seal. • Defective body flange.	• Replace seal. • Correct.
Water leak through rear window.	• Defective seal. • Defective body flange.	• Replace seal. • Correct.
FRONT/REAR DOORS		
Door window malfunction.	• Incorrect window glass installation. • Damaged or faulty regulator.	• Adjust position. • Correct or replace.
Water leak through door edge. Water leak from door center.	• Cracked or faulty weatherstrip. • Drain hole clogged. • Inadequate waterproof skeet contact or damage.	• Replace. • Remove foreign objects. • Correct or replace.
Door hard to open.	• Incorrect latch or striker adjustment.	• Adjust.
Door does not open or close completely.	• Incorrect door installation. • Defective door check strap. • Door check strap and hinge require grease.	• Adjust position. • Correct or replace. • Apply grease.
Uneven gap between door and body.	• Incorrect door installation.	• Adjust position.
Wind noise around door.	• Improperly installed weatherstrip. • Improper clearance between door glass and door weatherstrip. • Deformed door.	• Repair or replace. • Adjust. • Repair or replace.

MASTER

INDEX